	1943	1944	1945	1946	1947	1948	1949	1950	1951	1952	1953	1954
1	$100.5	$109.8	$121.7	$147.1	$165.4	$178.3	$181.2	$195.0	$209.8	$219.8	$232.6	$238.0
2	5.6	7.1	10.4	28.1	31.5	43.1	33.0	50.0	56.3	49.9	50.0	48.9
3	88.6	96.5	82.9	30.5	28.4	34.5	40.2	39.0	60.5	76.0	82.8	75.3
4	−2.2	−2.1	−1.4	5.0	9.0	3.5	3.8	.6	2.4	1.3	−.4	.9
5	192.5	211.4	213.6	210.7	234.3	259.4	258.1	284.6	327.0	347.0	365.4	363.1
6	10.9	12.0	12.5	10.7	13.0	15.5	17.3	19.1	22.0	24.0	26.5	28.8
7	181.6	199.4	201.0	200.0	221.3	244.0	240.8	265.5	307.0	323.0	338.9	334.3
8	11.3	16.8	19.8	19.1	23.1	20.5	24.1	23.6	27.7	30.8	33.3	32.5
9	170.3	182.6	181.2	180.9	198.2	223.5	216.7	241.9	279.3	292.2	305.6	301.8
10	4.6	5.2	6.1	6.0	5.7	5.2	5.7	6.9	8.2	8.6	8.7	9.9
11	14.1	12.9	10.7	9.1	11.3	12.5	10.4	17.9	22.4	19.5	20.2	17.2
12	5.4	5.2	3.0	2.4	5.8	11.0	10.4	8.6	9.5	9.3	7.9	6.7
13	5.1	6.4	9.8	15.6	16.2	15.8	17.0	19.9	17.5	18.2	10.4	21.6
14	151.4	165.7	171.2	179.3	191.6	210.4	208.3	228.5	256.7	273.1	288.3	289.8
15	17.8	18.9	20.9	18.7	21.5	21.1	18.6	20.8	29.2	34.4	35.8	32.9
16	133.6	146.8	150.3	160.6	170.1	189.3	189.7	207.7	227.5	238.7	252.5	256.9
17	100.5	109.8	121.7	147.1	165.4	178.3	181.2	195.0	209.8	219.8	332.6	238.0
18	33.0	36.9	28.7	13.5	4.7	11.0	8.5	12.6	17.7	18.9	19.8	18.9
19	374.1	401.7	392.9	337.9	336.8	350.4	351.8	380.4	412.2	429.0	448.9	439.8

	1943	1944	1945	1946	1947	1948	1949	1950	1951	1952	1953	1954
20	60.3	61.3	62.7	68.0	77.8	83.8	83.0	83.8	90.5	92.5	93.2	93.6
21	82.9	81.7	70.5	59.5	65.7	68.4	64.7	74.9	81.3	84.3	91.3	85.8
22	79.6	90.4	102.4	110.0	113.6	111.6	111.2	117.7	124.5	129.0	130.6	134.5
23	1.0	0.7	1.0	2.3	2.3	2.3	3.7	3.4	2.1	1.9	1.9	3.6
24	1.9	1.2	1.9	3.9	3.9	3.8	5.9	5.3	3.3	3.1	2.9	5.6
25	4.9	5.1	5.7	8.4	11.6	14.4	17.4	21.5	22.7	27.5	31.4	32.5

(Continued on back cover)

ECONOMICS

ECONOMICS

Principles, Problems, and Policies

Third Edition

CAMPBELL R. McCONNELL

Professor of Economics
University of Nebraska

McGRAW-HILL BOOK COMPANY

New York, St. Louis
San Francisco, Toronto
London, Sydney

To Lauren, Curt, and Beth

This third edition of *Economics* represents a very thorough revision of the second edition. Few chapters have escaped substantial rewriting, revisions of content, or organizational changes. Reasons for revision are both general—the innumerable changes in the economic milieu of the past several years—and specific—the solicited and voluntary criticisms of users of the second edition.

The purpose of all editions of this book has been and still is to introduce the beginning economics student to the principles essential to an understanding of fundamental economic problems and the policy alternatives society may utilize to contend with these problems. It is hoped that the ability to reason accurately and objectively about economic matters and the development of a lasting interest in economics will be two valuable by-products of this basic objective.

The present revision embodies a number of notable changes. A new summary chapter (Chapter 19) has been added to draw together and integrate the various aspects of employment theory and stabilization policy. Chapter 37 on income inequality has been almost entirely rewritten and reoriented toward the poverty issue. Chapter 42 on the Soviet economy has been completely rewritten and now focuses upon planning problems and growth prospects. The largely descriptive chapters (Chapters 7–9 and 35–38) have been tightened through the elimination of what proved to be superfluous material. The material of Part Two has been more rationally organized and distributed over six chapters as opposed to the five of the previous edition. The equation of exchange has replaced the discussion of

monetary aspects of fiscal policy, providing a more meaningful analysis of monetary policy. The discussion of elasticity in Chapter 23 has been rewritten and expanded for greater clarity. A short section on the economics of regulation has been added to the discussion of monopoly in Chapter 27. The general equilibrium analysis of Chapter 33 has been strengthened by the introduction of an elementary input-output table. Users of the second edition will discover innumerable other changes too numerous to detail.

The adoption of a multicolor format in this third edition is, in my judgment, an innovation of considerable esthetic merit and, more importantly, permits greater flexibility in the functional use of color.

In terms of content I feel this text embraces a number of departures in content and organization which distinguish it from other books in the field.

1. The principles course usually fails to provide students with a comprehensive and meaningful definition of economics. To remedy this shortcoming one complete chapter (Chapter 2) is devoted to a careful statement and development of the economizing problem and an exploration of its implications. The foundation thereby provided should be helpful in putting the many particular subject areas of economics into proper perspective.

2. There is a rather apparent intellectual lag among economists in their discussions of the economic functions of government. Government is an integral and increasingly important component of modern capitalism. Its economic role, therefore, should not be treated piecemeal or as an afterthought. This text attempts to overcome these diffi-

culties by introducing the economic functions of government early and according them systematic treatment in philosophical (Chapter 6), factual (Chapter 9), and controversial (Chapter 38) terms. A special effort is made to explode a number of popular myths which surround the operation of government in the economic sphere.

3. This volume puts considerable emphasis upon the crucial topic of economic growth. Chapter 20 develops a conceptual framework for analyzing economic growth and applies this framework in explaining the growth record of the American economy. Chapter 21 deals with a number of problems associated with the growth of our economy and suggests appropriate policies. Chapter 41 employs the conceptual framework of Chapter 20 in treating the obstacles to economic growth that plague the underdeveloped countries. An important segment of Chapter 42 concerns the growth record and prospects of Soviet Russia's command economy. Beyond this it will be found that the chapters on price theory pay special attention to the implications that the various market structures have for technological progress.

4. It is understandable that the elusiveness of general equilibrium analysis eminently qualifies this topic for omission at the principles level. The result, however, is a grievous shortcoming of most introductory courses. A sincere effort is made in this book to remedy this deficiency. Specifically, an entire chapter (Chapter 5) is devoted to the notion of the price system, and the nature and significance of general equilibrium analysis is explicitly outlined (Chapter 33).

5. This volume forgoes the presentation of necessarily sketchy descriptions of a number of alternative economic systems in favor of a detailed discussion of the Soviet economy and the challenge it poses for the Free World. I feel this emphasis upon the Soviet system is more vital, more timely, and decidedly more interesting to students.

6. I have purposely given considerable attention to microeconomics in general and to the theory of the firm in particular. There are several reasons for this emphasis. In the first place, the concepts of microeconomics are difficult for most beginning students. Short expositions usually compound these difficulties by raising more questions than they answer. Second, a majority of economists now agree that we possess the fiscal and monetary tools necessary for the maintenance of full employment. This tends to shift the economic spotlight back to the question of resource allocation and ultimately to the operation of the price system. Finally, I have coupled analysis of the various market structures with a discussion of the social implications of each. The impact of each market arrangement upon price and output levels, resource allocation, and the rate of technological advance is carefully assessed.

7. Chapter 33 is rather unique, I believe, in that it provides a concise statement of both the accomplishments and the shortcomings of American capitalism.

8. Another differentiating feature of this text is the treatment of the social imbalance question in Chapter 38. The objective here is to offer a balanced treatment of what may be the most important domestic economic issue of our times.

9. In the over-all selection of topics, considerable care has been exercised to include only those which have significant bearing upon the twin problems of full employment and allocative efficiency.

In terms of organization, this book has been written with the conviction that the basic prerequisite of an understandable economics text is the logical arrangement and clear exposition of subject matter. This concern with organization is most evident in Part One, which centers upon the step-by-step development of a comprehensive and realistic picture of American capitalism. This coherent group of introductory chapters is substituted for the traditional smattering of more-or-less unrelated background topics that ordinarily introduce the student to the study of economics.

Throughout this volume the exposition of each particular topic and concept is directly related to the level of difficulty which in my experience the average student is likely to encounter. It is for this reason that national income accounting, microeconomics, and to a lesser degree, employment theory are purposely accorded comprehensive and careful treatments. Simplicity in these instances is correlated with comprehensiveness, not brevity. Furthermore, my experience suggests that in the treatment of each basic topic—employment theory, money and banking, international economics, and so forth—it is highly desirable to couple analysis and policy. A three-step development of basic analytical tools is employed: (1) verbal description and illustration, (2) numerical examples, and (3) graphic presentation based upon these numerical illustrations.

The material is organized around seven basic topics: (1) an introduction to American capitalism; (2) national income, employment, and fiscal policy; (3) money and monetary policy; (4) American economic growth; (5) economics of the firm and resource allocation; (6) current domestic economic problems; and (7) international economics, the underdeveloped countries, and the Soviet economic challenge.

Part One is designed to introduce the method and subject matter of economics and to develop the ideological framework and the factual characteristics of American capitalism. This group of chapters develops in an orderly fashion the overall picture of how our economy operates. After an introduction to the methodology of economics in Chapter 1, an entire chapter is devoted to defining and explaining the economizing problem. Chapters 3 to 5 develop the capitalistic ideology and the notion of the most fundamental institution of capitalism—the price system. Early emphasis upon the price system is designed to provide the necessary orientation for the detailed treatment of pricing found in Part Five and to contribute to an understanding of the national income analysis of Part Two and, more specifically,

the topics of inflation and deflation. Chapter 6 introduces government as a basic economic component of modern capitalism; government's economic functions are systematically explained and evaluated. Upon this superstructure of a mixed public-private economy Chapters 7 to 9 add the factual information concerning the household, business, and government aggregates of the economy, thereby making our mixed capitalism model much more realistic.

Part Two treats national income analysis and fiscal policy. Chapter 10 on national income accounting reflects my conviction that this difficult topic merits detailed treatment. Chapter 11 employs the national income measures in describing the last four decades of American business cycle experience. This I feel is an important undertaking for college sophomores who, fortunately, have grown up amidst the virtually unabated prosperity of the last twenty-five years. The next four chapters are devoted to neo-Keynesian employment theory, fiscal policy, and the public debt.

Part Three emphasizes the balance sheet approach to money and banking. This approach seems most in accord with the goal of providing the student with an analytical tool needed in reasoning through, as opposed to memorizing, the economic impact of the various basic banking transactions. Just as fiscal policy is linked directly to income theory in Part Two, monetary policy immediately follows the discussion of money and banking. The first half of the book is completed with Part Four on American economic growth and problems related thereto.

For reasons already noted the treatment of pricing and resource allocation in Part Five is purposely detailed. Throughout Chapters 26 to 29 emphasis is placed upon the social implications of the various market structures. What is the significance of each market structure for price and output levels, resource allocation, and technological progress? Emphasis in the discussion of distribution—Chapters 30 to 32—is generally in accord with the relative quantitative importance of the various market shares in our economy. I have not belabored the analysis of interest, rent, and profits where, it seems to me, economic analysis leaves much to be desired. Chapter 33 provides a very simple verbal discussion of general equilibrium, an introduction to input-output analysis, and a summary evaluation of the operation of American capitalism.

Part Six deals with the domestic economic problems of monopoly, the farm problem, labor relations and collective bargaining, the economics of inequality and poverty, and social balance. In each of these chapters an attempt has been made to (1) describe the historical and factual background of the problem, (2) analyze its causes and effects, (3) explore government policy, and (4) offer a thought-provoking discussion of public policy alternatives.

The first two chapters of Part Seven survey international trade and finance. Chapter 41 explores the very crucial problems surrounding the efforts of the underdeveloped countries to achieve economic growth. Finally, Chapter 42 offers a relatively comprehensive discussion of the Soviet economy, emphasizing its planning processes and its growth prospects.

End-of-chapter summaries provide a concise, pointed recapitulation of each chapter. Much thought has gone into the end-of-chapter questions. Though purposely intermixed, these questions are of three general types. Some are designed to highlight the main points of each chapter. Others are "open-end" discussion or thought questions. Wherever pertinent, numerical problems which require the student to derive and manipulate key concepts and relationships are employed. Numerical problems are stressed in those chapters dealing with national income accounting and analysis, money and banking, and price theory. The bibliographical references at the end of each chapter are designed to provide both breadth and depth for the ambitious student. Yet care has been taken to see that these references are not beyond the grasp of the average college sophomore.

Students will find the *Study Guide to accompany McConnell: Economics* by Prof. Robert C. Bingham an invaluable supplement to the text.

This third edition of *Economics* is accompanied by the second, and greatly expanded, edition of a book of supplementary materials, *Economic Issues: Readings and Cases* which I have prepared. I am sufficiently immodest to feel that it embodies some distinctive features which make it a highly usable supplement for this or any other standard principles of economics textbook.

Though economics instructors are in general agreement as to the basic content of a principles of economics course, there are considerable differences of opinion as to what particular arrangement of material is best. The structure of this book is designed to provide considerable organizational flexibility. And I am happy to report that users of the first two editions have informed me that they accomplished substantial rearrangements of chapters with little sacrifice of continuity. Though I have chosen to move from macro- to microeconomics, there is no reason why the introductory material of Part One cannot be followed immediately by the microanalysis of Part Five. Similarly, in my judgment money and banking can best be taught after, rather than before, national income analysis. Those who disagree will encounter no problems by preceding Chapter 10 with Chapters 16, 17, and 18. Furthermore, some instructors will prefer to intersperse the microeconomics of Part Five with the problems chapters of Part Six. This is easily accomplished. Chapter 35 on the farm problem may follow Chapter 26 on pure competition; Chapter 34 on the social control of monopoly may follow Chapters 27 to 29 on imperfect competition. Chapter 36 on labor unions and collective bargaining may either precede or follow Chapter 31 on wages, and Chapter 37 on income inequality may follow Chapters 31 and 32 on the distributive shares of national income.

Finally, those interested in the one-semester course will be able to discern several possible groups of chapters that will be appropriate to such a course. A tentative outline for a one-semester course introducing both macro- and microeconomics is provided.

This endeavor has benefited greatly from the advice and counsel of many teachers and students. Let me first restate my debt to the reviewers of the original manuscript: L. S. Van Scoyoc of Bowling Green State University, John Auten of Rice Institute, J. J. Kaufman of Pennsylvania State University, Raymond W. Ritland of Auburn University, and Howell E. Jones of Bethany College. I owe a special debt to Prof. Arthur M. Okun of Yale University who contributed much to both the content and organization of this text. Also, I have unashamedly exploited the brainpower of a number of present and former University of Nebraska colleagues: Robert C. Bingham, Wallace C. Peterson, Clemens B. Thoman, and Harry M. Trebing. Many users of the first edition were kind enough to offer me their counsel and criticism: in particular I must mention Professors Clayton Hall and Fred Picard of Ohio University, David G. Brown of the University of North Carolina, and Carl Stern of Randolph-Macon. This third edition has benefited from comprehensive reviews provided by Kenneth O. Alexander of Michigan Technical University, James M. Cahill of Manhattan College, Ira Castles of Delta State College, Edward Coen of the University of Minnesota, Kalman Goldberg of Bradley University, Keith D. Evans of San Fernando Valley State College, Will Lyons of Franklin and Marshall College, Ray Marshall of the University of Texas, Glenn L. Simpson of Colorado State University, Janet L. Weston of the University of Illinois, and Simon N. Whitney of Rutgers University. Welcome and very helpful comments of a more specific character were received from Florence Jaffy of the College of San Mateo, Jan Kmenta of the University of Wisconsin, L. Emil Kreider of Southern Illinois University, and Eugene A. Mattis of West Virginia University. As tradition demands, I accept sole responsibility for all errors of omission and commission.

Campbell R. McConnell

CONTENTS

Chapter 15: Fiscal Policy and the Public Debt   268

PART THREE: MONEY, MONETARY POLICY, AND ECONOMIC STABILITY

Chapter 16: Money and Banking in American Capitalism   281

Chapter 17: How Banks Create Money   299

Chapter 18: The Federal Reserve Banks and Monetary Policy   321

SUGGESTED OUTLINE FOR A ONE-SEMESTER COURSE

ECONOMICS

PART ONE: AN INTRODUCTION TO AMERICAN CAPITALISM

CHAPTER 1

THE NATURE AND
METHOD OF ECONOMICS

Man, unfortunate creature, is plagued with wants. He wants, among other things, love, social recognition, and the material necessities and comforts of life. Man's striving to improve his material well-being, to "make a living," is the concern of economics. More specifically, economics is the study of man's behavior in producing, exchanging, and consuming the material goods and services he wants. Most of us think of economics in terms of specific problems—balancing the household budget, labor disputes, farm surpluses, taxes, debt, inflation, unemployment. Although limited, this thinking is not incorrect. These specific problems are fragments or signs of the larger problem of man's attempt to satisfy his material wants.

It is tempting to seek out immediately answers and solutions to specific problems of current interest. But this would be precipitate; certain preliminary matters must be discussed first. In particular, we must know the answers to these questions:

1. *Why* should we study economics?
2. *How* should we study economics—what are the proper procedures?
3. What specific problems, limitations, and pitfalls might we encounter in studying economics?

These topics will occupy our attention in this introductory chapter.

WHY STUDY ECONOMICS?

The answer to this question is threefold:
1. There is the matter of seeking knowledge for the sake of knowledge. We live in a complex physical and social environment—we ought to be curious about the nature of it. Economics helps us to comprehend that environment.

2. A basic understanding of economics is essential if we are to be well-informed citizens. Many of the specific problems of the day have important economic aspects, and we, in a democracy, who comprise that society make the ultimate decisions in meeting those problems. Intelligence at the polls therefore requires that we have a working knowledge of economics.

3. Economics is of practical value in business. An understanding of the overall operation of the economic system puts the businessman in a better position to formulate his policies. For example, if he understands the causes and consequences of inflation, he is better equipped during inflationary periods to make intelligent decisions concerning his enterprise than he might be otherwise. Indeed, more and more economists are appearing on the payrolls of large corporations. Their job? To gather and interpret economic information upon which rational business decisions can be made.

This last reason for studying economics must be interpreted with care. Economics is an academic, not a vocational, subject. Unlike accounting, advertising, corporation finance, and salesmanship, economics is not a how-to-make-money area of study.[1] A

[1] An economist has been defined as an individual with a Phi Beta Kappa key on one end of his watch chain and with no watch on the other.

knowledge of economics may be helpful in running a business, but this is not its primary objective. In economics, problems are examined from the social, not from the individual, point of view. The production, exchange, and consumption of goods and services are discussed from the viewpoint of society as a whole, not from the standpoint of one businessman's bankbook. Thus economics will prove of little direct value in helping us to sell used cars or insurance.

HOW SHOULD WE GO ABOUT IT?

What do economists do? What are their goals? What procedures do they employ? The title of this volume—*Economics: Principles, Problems, and Policies*—contains a thumbnail answer to the first two questions. Economists are concerned with the derivation of economic *principles* which are useful in the formulation of *policies* designed to solve economic *problems*. The procedure employed by the economist is that summarized in Figure 1–1. The economist must first ascertain and gather the facts which are relevant to consideration of a specific economic problem. This aspect of his job is sometimes called "descriptive economics." The economist then puts his collection of facts in order and summarizes them by "distilling out" a principle, that is, by generalizing about the way individuals and institutions actually behave. Deriving principles from facts is called "economic theory," or "economic analysis." Finally, the general knowledge of economic behavior which economic principles provide can then be used in formulating policies, that is, remedies or solutions, for correcting or avoiding the problem under scrutiny. This final aspect of the field is sometimes called "applied economics" or "policy economics."

Still using Figure 1–1 as a point of reference, let us now examine this three-step procedure in more detail.

Descriptive Economics

All sciences are empirical. All sciences are based upon facts, that is, upon observable and verifiable behavior of certain data or subject matter. In the physical sciences the factual data are inorganic. As a social science, economics is concerned with the behavior of individuals and institutions engaged in the production, exchange, and consumption of goods and services.

The first major step, then, in investigating a given problem or a specific segment of the economy is to gather the facts. This can be an infinitely complex task. The world of reality is cluttered with a myriad of interrelated facts. The economist therefore must use discretion in fact gathering. He must distinguish economic from noneconomic facts and then determine which economic facts are relevant and which are irrelevant for the specific problem under consideration. But even when this sorting process has been completed, the relevant economic facts may appear diverse and unrelated.

Economic Theory

A conglomeration of facts is relatively useless; mere description is not enough. To be meaningful, facts must be systematically arranged, interpreted, and generalized upon. This is the task of economic theory or analysis. Principles and theories—the end result of economic analysis—bring order and meaning to a number of facts by tying these facts together, putting them in correct relationship to one another, and generalizing upon them. "Theories without facts may be barren, but facts without theories are meaningless."[2]

The interplay between the levels of fact and theory is more complex than Figure 1–1 indicates. Principles and theories are meaningful statements drawn from facts, but

[2] Kenneth E. Boulding, *Economic Analysis,* 3d ed. (New York: Harper & Row, Publishers, Incorporated, 1955), p. 5.

facts, in turn, serve as a constant check on the validity of principles already established. Facts—how individuals and institutions actually behave in producing, exchanging, and consuming goods and services—change with time. This makes it essential that economists continuously check existing principles and theories against the changing economic environment. The history of economic ideas is strewn with once-valid generalizations about economic behavior which were rendered obsolete by the changing course of events.

Terminology. A word on terminology is essential at this juncture. Economists talk about "laws," "principles," "theories," and "models." These terms all mean essentially the same thing: generalizations, or statements of regularity, concerning the economic behavior of individuals and institutions. The term "economic law" is a bit misleading because it implies a high degree of exactness, universal application, and even moral rightness. So to a lesser degree does the term "principle." And some people incorrectly associate the term "theory" with idle pipe dreams and ivory-tower hallucinations, divorced from the facts and realities of the world. The term "model" has much to commend it. A model is a simplified picture of reality, an abstract generalization of how the relevant data actually behave. In this book these four terms will be used synonymously. The choice of terms in labeling any particular generalization will be governed by custom or convenience here. Hence, the relationship between the price of a product and the quantity consumers purchase will be called the "law" of demand, rather than the theory or principle of demand, because it is customary to so designate it.

These comments on terminology raise two points which merit further consideration: first, economic principles (laws, theories, or models) are *generalizations,* and second, they are *abstractions.*

Policies
Policy economics is concerned with controlling or influencing economic behavior or its consequences.

↑

Principles or theories
Theoretical economics involves generalizing about economic behavior.

↑

Facts
Descriptive economics is concerned with gathering the facts relevant to a specific problem or aspect of the economy.

FIGURE 1–1. THE RELATIONSHIP BETWEEN FACTS, PRINCIPLES, AND POLICIES IN ECONOMICS. In studying any problem or segment of the economy the economist must first gather the relevant facts. These facts must then be systematically arranged, interpreted, and generalized upon. These generalizations are useful, not only in explaining economic behavior but also in predicting and therefore controlling future events.

Generalizations. Economic principles are generalizations and, as such, subject to exceptions and to quantitatively imprecise statement. Economic facts are usually diverse; some individuals and institutions act one way and some another. Hence, economic principles are frequently stated in terms of averages or statistical probabilities. For example, when economists say that the average household earns an income of $6,140 per year, they are making a generalization. It is recognized that some households earn much more and a good many others much less. Yet this generalization, properly handled and interpreted, can be very meaningful and useful. Or an economist may conclude that 95 per cent of the time—95 chances out of 100—consumers will increase their purchases of a product when its price falls. Five per cent of the consumers constitute an exception to the general rule.

The main reason for the inexactness of economic principles is the fact that the economist cannot conduct controlled experiments—he does not have a laboratory in which he can create simplified and controlled conditions. The laboratory of the social sciences is the real world, where the specific aspects of human behavior we wish to examine cannot be readily isolated from the social and cultural milieu. The chemist can "make other things equal" in his controlled experiments; the economist cannot.

Unable to make other things equal in their analysis, economists do the next best thing: they *assume* other things are equal in isolating certain data for analysis. To illustrate: In analyzing the relationship between the price of product X and the amount of X purchased, economists assume that of all the factors influencing the amount of X purchased, only its price varies. To cut the problem down to size, they must assume that all other factors which might influence the amount of X purchased are unchanged or "equal." In this way economists can isolate the relationship between price and quantity demanded from all sorts of real-world complications. However, in applying the resulting generalization—consumers buy more of X at a low price than they do at a high price—to a real-world situation, exceptions may be encountered. Why? Because other things are not often equal in the real world. For example, an increase in incomes—another consideration which, in addition to a price

change, will cause the amount of X purchased to alter—may complicate the application of the general conclusion about the relationship between the price of X and the amount of X purchased. The economist may find that, although the price of X has risen, the quantity demanded has *increased* contrary to his generalization. This does not mean that the generalization is invalid, but rather that peculiar circumstances—higher incomes—have entered this particular application of the principle to upset its accuracy. This is merely an exception to the rule, and in economics such exceptions may be rather frequent. Economics is admittedly an inexact science.

Abstractions. Economic principles, or theories, are necessarily abstractions. They do not embody the full bloom of reality. The very process of sorting out noneconomic and irrelevant facts in the fact-gathering process involves abstracting from reality. Unfortunately, the abstractness of economic theory prompts the uninformed to identify theory as something which is impractical and unrealistic. This is nonsense! As a matter of fact, economic theories are practical for the simple reason that they are abstractions. The level of reality is too complex to be very meaningful. Economists theorize in order to give meaning to a maze of facts which would otherwise be confusing and useless and to put facts into a more usable, practical form. Thus to generalize is to abstract; generalization for this purpose is practical, and therefore so is abstraction. An economic theory is a model—a simplified picture or map—of some segment of the economy. This enables us to better understand reality because it avoids the details of reality. Finally, theories—*good* theories—are grounded on facts and therefore are realistic. Theories which do not fit the facts are simply not good theories.

Graphic expression. Theories, or models, can be expressed in many ways. For example, the physicist and chemist illustrate their theories by building Tinker-Toy arrangements of multicolored wooden balls that represent protons, neutrons, and so forth, held in proper relationship to one another by wires or sticks. Economists are not so lucky as to have theories that lend themselves to such tangible demonstrations. Economic models must take the form of verbal description, numerical tables, mathematical equations, or graphs. The last are particularly helpful and will be used with some frequency throughout this book. Most of the principles we shall encounter will explain the relationship between just two sets of economic facts, for example, the relationship between the price of a specific product

and the quantity of it which consumers buy. Simple two-dimensional graphs are a convenient and clear way of summarizing and manipulating these relationships.

As shown in Figure 1–2, graphs are drawn on squared paper divided into four quarters, or quadrants, by a horizontal axis and a vertical axis, which intersect at right angles. The point of intersection is called the *origin*. Each axis has a scale of numerical values. On the vertical axis, all values above the origin are positive, and all values below are negative. On the horizontal axis, values to the right of the origin are positive; those to the left are negative. The point of intersection, that is, the origin,

FIGURE 1–2. ECONOMIC PRINCIPLES CAN BE EXPRESSED GRAPHICALLY.
Two-dimensional graphs are a convenient way of presenting and manipulating relationships between data. The relationship between two sets of economic data whose numerical values are positive is shown in the upper right quadrant of the chart.

designates zero. Though the vertical and horizontal scales in Figure 1–2 measure the same numerical values, this need not be the case. Each unit on the vertical axis may measure $1, while the same distance on the horizontal axis denotes 1,000 bushels of corn.

In elementary economics we are virtually always concerned with the relationship between two sets of economic facts the values of which are positive. Hence, we are concerned with the upper right-hand quarter of the chart where both scales measure positive values.

Now let us explore an example or two to illustrate the construction and interpretation

TABLE 1–1. THE QUANTITIES OF CORN FARMERS WILL SUPPLY AT VARIOUS PRICES (hypothetical data)

Price per bushel	Bushels supplied per year
$5	12,000
4	10,000
3	7,000
2	4,000
1	1,000

of graphs. Suppose detailed factual investigation reveals that the relationship between the price of corn per bushel and the amount

FIGURE 1–3. RELATIONSHIP BETWEEN PRICE AND QUANTITY SUPPLIED.
Two sets of economic data which are directly related, such as price and quantity supplied, graph as an upsloping curve (SS).

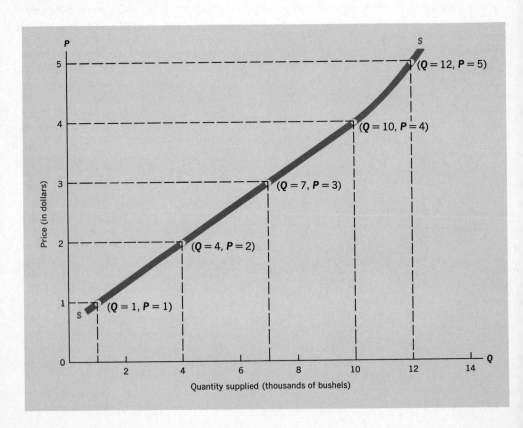

farmers are willing to produce and offer for sale per year is as shown in Table 1–1.

How can this be shown graphically? Simply by putting the two sets of facts—product price and quantity supplied—on the two axes of the chart and locating the five price–quantity supplied combinations shown in Table 1–1. Convention or convenience dictates which set of facts goes on the vertical axis and which on the horizontal axis. By convention, economists put "price" on the vertical and "quantity" on the horizontal axis, as indicated in Figure 1–3. The five price-quantity combinations are plotted on the chart by drawing perpendiculars from the appropriate points on the two axes. For example, in plotting the $5-12,000-bushel combination, perpendiculars must be drawn across from the vertical (price) axis at $5 and up from the horizontal (quantity-supplied) axis at 12,000 bushels. Their point of intersection locates the $5–12,000-bushel combination on the graph. The same procedure locates the other four price–quantity combinations. If it is assumed that the same general relationship between price and quantity supplied will prevail at all points between the five graphed, a line or curve can be drawn to connect these points. In this instance the two sets of data are *directly related;* that is, price and quantity supplied move in the same direction. As price increases, the quantity supplied increases. As price declines, so does the quantity supplied. When two sets of data are directly related, they will always graph as an upsloping line or curve, such as *SS* in Figure 1–3.

Now suppose that fact gathering reveals that the price of corn and the quantity which consumers will buy per year are related in the manner shown in Table 1–2. These data indicate that consumers will demand more corn when its price is low than they will when the price is high; that is, price and quantity are *inversely related.* If price increases, the amount purchased will decline. If price declines, the quantity purchased will increase. An inverse relation-

TABLE 1–2. THE QUANTITIES OF CORN CONSUMERS WILL PURCHASE AT VARIOUS PRICES (hypothetical data)

Price per bushel	Bushels demanded per year
$5	2,000
4	4,000
3	7,000
2	11,000
1	16,000

ship will always graph as a downsloping line or curve, such as *DD* in Figure 1–4.

Dangers of models. When properly constructed and interpreted, economic models are invaluable tools. But we must be aware of certain potential dangers in deriving and applying these models.

1. The fundamental danger in constructing an economic model or principle is that the economist might fail to distinguish correctly between relevant and irrelevant facts. If the economist "boils out" some relevant facts, the resulting principle may be a disjointed, misleading, and, at best, incomplete analytical tool. A related difficulty stems from the possibility that an overzealous economist might abstract from too many facts and construct a model which is hyperabstract and truly out of touch with reality.

2. In applying economic models, we must always recognize them for what they are— useful first approximations. It is easy, but dangerous, to slip into the practice of becoming so enthusiastic about logical clarity that we forget such models are simply rough outlines of reality. There may be many omissions between a simplified economic model and reality.

3. We must be on guard in applying economic models so as not to impute any ethical or moral qualities to them. Economic models are the analytical tools of the economist, and, as such, they are ethically neutral. Because they are constructed of facts, economic models afford general statements

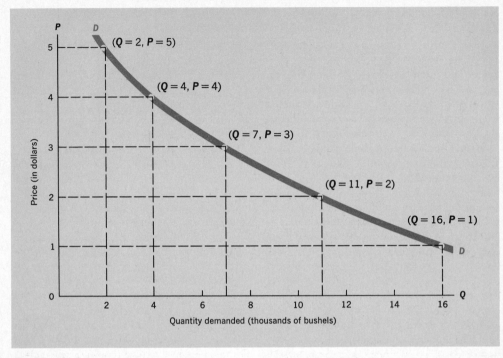

FIGURE 1–4. RELATIONSHIP BETWEEN PRICE AND QUANTITY DEMANDED.
Two sets of economic data which are inversely related, such as price and quantity
demanded, graph as a downsloping curve (*DD*).

about "what is," not indications of what "ought to be." Figure 1–3 does not tell us that farmers *should* supply more corn at higher prices than at lower prices, but rather that they *actually do*. Economic models are not tin gods to be worshiped as an end in themselves, or as a compendium of ethically desirable results. Instead, they should be recognized for what they are—a means to an end, a summary of factual data.

Policy Economics

Of what value are economic principles? The answer is twofold. There is first the matter of explanation for explanation's sake—economic principles help to explain to us why certain events occur the way they do. Through economic principles we can comprehend why prices change, how surpluses

and shortages of products arise, what causes depression and unemployment, and so forth. Our curiosity concerning these and similar phenomena can be satisfied through the development of economic principles to serve as tools for the understanding of reality.

Apart from pure explanation, economic principles can also be extremely valuable as predictive devices, and prediction is the prerequisite of control. If an undesirable event can be predicted by the application of an economic principle, that event can be influenced or controlled.

If we cannot control an event, we gain from prediction invaluable time to prepare for adjusting to its consequences. Ability to predict a rainstorm does not give us control over the weather, but it does permit us to prepare for it by carrying a raincoat and umbrella.

Values. It is evident that value judgments —opinions as to what is desirable or undesirable—come into the picture at this juncture. Descriptive economics and economic theory are both concerned with facts; the former immediately and the latter once removed. Policy economics necessarily entails value judgments as to the desirability of certain events. When operating at this level, economists are no longer functioning as scientists, but rather as policy makers. They are dealing not only with facts, but also with values.

An example or two will help at this point. Our previously noted principle of consumer behavior is the basis for one illustration: "Consumers generally buy more of a product at a low price than they do at a high price." Suppose a clothing merchant finds that he is greatly overstocked with summer clothing at a time when shipments of fall and winter clothing are due. The merchant has the problem of ridding himself of his undesired surplus stock of summer wear. Our principle of consumer behavior helps the merchant to solve this problem by predicting for him how consumers will react to price changes. In particular, the principle predicts that the merchant will be able to increase his sales and "move" the surplus by lowering prices. The merchant, formulating his price policies accordingly, "runs a sale." The surplus disappears.

A second example, of greater consequence to the economy as a whole, involves the fundamental principle that, within certain limits, there is a direct relationship between total spending and the level of employment in the economy. "If total spending increases (decreases), the volume of employment will rise (fall)." This principle can be invaluable to government in determining its economic policies. For example, if government economists note that available statistics indicate an actual slackening of total expenditures, the principle will permit them to predict the undesirable consequence of unemployment. Aware of this anticipated result, public officials are now in a position to set in motion certain government policies designed to bolster total spending and head off expected unemployment. In short, we must be able to predict in order to strengthen control. Economic principles help make prediction possible.

Economic goals of American capitalism. It is important at this point that we note and reflect upon a number of economic goals or values which are widely, though not universally, accepted in our society. These goals may be briefly listed as follows:

1. Economic growth. The production of more and better goods and services, or more simply stated, a higher standard of living, is desired.

2. Full employment. Suitable jobs should be available for all who are willing and able to work.

3. Price stability. Sizable upswings or downswings in the general price level, that is, inflation and deflation, should be avoided.

4. Economic freedom. Businessmen, workers, and consumers should enjoy a high degree of freedom in their economic activities.

5. An equitable distribution of income. No groups of citizens should face stark poverty while others wallow in luxury.

6. Economic security. Provision should be made for those who are chronically ill, disabled, handicapped, aged, or otherwise dependent.

Now this list of widely accepted goals provides the basis for several significant points. First, note that this or any other statement of basic economic goals inevitably entails problems of interpretation. What are "sizable" changes in the price level? What is a "high degree" of economic freedom? What is an "equitable" distribution of income? Although most of us might accept the above goals as generally stated, we might also disagree very substantially as to their specific meanings and hence as to the types of policies needed to attain these goals. It is noteworthy that, although goals

1 to 3 are subject to reasonably accurate measurement, the inability to quantify goals 4 to 6 undoubtedly contributes to any controversy over their specific meaning.

Second, certain of these goals are complementary in that to the extent one goal is achieved, some other goal or goals will also tend to be realized. For example, the achieving of full employment (goal 2) obviously means the elimination of unemployment, a basic cause of low incomes (goal 5) and economic insecurity (goal 6). Furthermore, considering goals 1 and 5, it is generally agreed that the sociopolitical tensions which may accompany a highly unequal distribution of income are tempered to the extent that all incomes are rising absolutely as a result of economic growth.

Third, some goals may be conflicting or mutually exclusive. Currently a number of highly regarded economists argue that those forces which further the attainment of economic growth and full employment may be the very same forces which cause inflation. That is, to some degree goals 1 and 2 may conflict with goal 3. Other economists are reluctantly concluding that to some extent economic growth and full employment (goals 1 and 2) may conflict with economic freedom (goal 4). It is felt that the expanding role of government which rapid growth and continuous full employment require will inevitably impinge upon the free choices of businessmen, workers, and consumers.

This leads us to a fourth point: When basic goals do conflict, society is forced to develop a system of priorities for the objectives it seeks. To illustrate: If full employment and price stability are to some extent mutually exclusive, that is, full employment entails some inflation and price stability entails some unemployment, society must decide upon the relative importance of these two goals. Suppose the relevant choice is between, say, a 3 per cent annual increase in the price level accompanied by full employment on the one hand, and a perfectly stable price level with 5 per cent of the labor force unemployed on the other. Which is the better choice? Or how about a compromise goal in the form of, say, a 1 per cent increase in the price level each year with 3 per cent of the labor force out of work? There is obviously ample room for disagreement here.

There would admittedly be disagreement among individuals in our society as to the priorities to be assigned these six goals, or, for that matter, as to whether this is a "correct" list in the first place. Now, finally, we must keep in mind that other societies can, and do, have substantially different goals. Soviet society—or perhaps more accurately the Soviet state—puts relatively greater emphasis upon goals 1 and 2 and, our experts tell us, may do a better job of achieving these goals than we do (Chapter 42). A good part of the explanation of the success of the Soviet Union in achieving rapid growth and full employment is that they attach a much lower priority than we do to other goals. In particular, Soviet disregard for economic freedom allows the use of policies for achieving full employment and rapid growth which would be completely unacceptable in our society. In short, other societies assign different weights or priorities to various goals, and these differing priorities may permit these other societies to do a better job in achieving certain of these objectives.

Formulating economic policy. The creation of specific policies designed to achieve the broad economic goals of our society is no simple matter. A brief examination of the basic steps in policy formulation is in order.

1. The first step is to make a clear statement of goals. If we seek "full employment," do we mean that everyone between, say, eighteen and sixty-five years of age has a job? Or do we mean that everyone who wants to work has a job? Should we allow for some "normal" unemployment caused by workers' voluntarily changing jobs?

2. Next we must state and recognize the possible effects of alternative policies designed to achieve the goal. This entails a clear-cut understanding of economic impact, costs, and political feasibility of alternative programs. Thus, for example, economists currently debate the relative merits and demerits of fiscal policy (changing government spending and taxes), monetary policy (altering the supply of money), or direct controls (public control of wages and prices) as alternative means of achieving and maintaining full employment.

3. We are obligated to both ourselves and future generations to look back upon our experiences with chosen policies and evaluate their effectiveness; it is only through this type of evaluation that we can hope to improve policy applications. Did a given change in taxes or the supply of money alter the level of employment to the extent originally predicted? If not, why not?

One final point: The formulation of economic policy is greatly complicated by the fact that our economy is a dynamic, changing organism. We must therefore not expect once-and-for-all answers to basic economic problems, but rather short-run adjustments which may rapidly become obsolete. What is correct policy today may be rendered inappropriate tomorrow by a rapidly changing economic milieu.

PITFALLS TO STRAIGHT THINKING

Our discussion of the economist's procedure has, up to this point, skirted some of the problems and pitfalls frequently encountered in deriving and applying economic principles. Some of these difficulties—for example, problems of terminology and bias —are almost self-evident. Indeed, they are so obvious that we tend to overlook them, which makes explicit comment imperative. Other difficulties, particularly those which take the form of logical pitfalls, are rather complex and most conducive to faulty economic reasoning.

Terminology

It is extremely important in studying any science to understand its terminology, but this is particularly so in the social sciences. There are three specific reasons why a clear, objective grasp of relevant terms will prove to be half the battle in understanding many aspects of economics:

1. The economic terminology to which we are exposed in newspapers and popular magazines is sometimes emotionally loaded. The writer—or more frequently the particular interest group he represents—may have a cause to further or an ax to grind, and his terms will be slanted to solicit the support of the reader. Hence, we may find a governmental irrigation project in the Great Plains region called "creeping socialism" by its opponents and "intelligent democratic planning" by its proponents. We must be prepared, therefore, to discount such terminology in achieving objectivity in the understanding of important economic issues.

2. It is embarrassing to admit that economists are often guilty of dual terminology— the unfortunate practice of using two or more labels to designate the same thing. In part, this is a matter of historical accident. It is also the result of economic inquirers discovering that two different theories or explanations are actually the same. The dual labels persist after the theories have been merged. For example, the terms "economic resources," "productive services," and "factors of production" have identical meanings. Similarly, in probing the causes of depression, we hear some authorities laying the blame at the door of "underconsumption," while others cite "oversaving" as the villain. The beginner who is not familiar with the definitions of these terms may envision a basic conflict of views. Actually, "oversaving" and "underconsumption," properly defined, refer essentially to the same phenomena.

3. It is important to keep in mind that no scientist is obligated to use common-sense

or man-in-the-street definitions of his terms. He may find it convenient and essential to define his terms in such a way that they are clearly at odds with the definitions held by laymen in everyday speech. So long as the economist is explicit and consistent in his definitions, he is on safe ground. A typical example: The term "investment" to John Q. Citizen is associated with the buying of bonds and stocks in the securities market. How often have we heard someone talking of investing in General Motors stock or government bonds? But to the economist, "investment" means the purchase of real capital assets such as machinery and equipment, or the construction of a new wing on a factory building, not the purely financial transaction of swapping cash or part of a bank balance for a neatly engraved piece of paper. As a matter of fact, we shall discover in Chapter 10 that what the layman calls "investment" is a swapping of assets or a form of saving, as the economist sees it.

Bias and Preconceptions

The beginning student in chemistry or physics traditionally knows little or nothing about the subject matter of these fields at the outset. He starts from scratch with a blank but, supposedly, clear mind. Not so in the social sciences in general or in economics in particular. For a variety of reasons the budding economist ordinarily launches into his field of study with a bundle of preconceptions about the operation of our economy and its component parts. Such issues as the farm problem, the public debt, the legitimate functions of labor unions, big business versus competition, the nature and operation of our tax system, and the like, are everyday topics of conversation. Unless we live in a void, most of us have some *preconceived notions* on these issues. Unfortunately, all too often these preconceptions are flatly wrong or, at best, partially true; in other cases they are hopelessly biased. Thus as neophyte economists—in contrast to physicists or chemists—

we start at a disadvantage in our search for truth, and our task in learning economics is doubled: we must recognize and "unlearn" misguided preconceptions, and we must supplant these inaccuracies with valid concepts and generalizations.

These observations contain an urgent plea for objectivity in studying economics. Economic principles can become a vice rather than a valuable analytical tool if, in using them, we are obsessed with a point of view. By approaching them from the angle or viewpoint of, say, management or labor, we jeopardize much of the value these principles hold for us. Dissociating ourselves from any particular viewpoint— whether that of the workingman, the businessman, or the farmer—will pay us dividends, because such associations can imperceptibly undermine our reason and hopelessly color our conclusions. Objectivity is an obvious prerequisite to the successful pursuit of scientific truth. This objectivity is most likely to be achieved when a *social point of view* is embraced. "How does this policy or action affect the economy (society) as a whole and *all* its relevant parts?" is a question much superior to "How does this policy or action affect me as a businessman or laborer?" We must keep an open mind in pursuing economic knowledge.

Fallacy of Composition: Micro and Macro

Many of the false preconceptions people have about economics are attributable to the fallacy of composition. This is the fallacy of contending that "what is true for the individual or part is necessarily also true for the group or whole." This is a logical fallacy; it is not correct. The validity of a particular generalization for an individual or part does not necessarily ensure its accuracy for the group or whole.

A noneconomic example may help: You are watching a football game on a sunny autumn afternoon. The home team executes an outstanding play. In the general excitement, you leap to your feet to get a better view. *Generalization:* "If you, *an individual,* stand, then your view of the game is improved." But does this also hold true for the group—for everyone watching the game? Certainly not! If everyone stands to watch the play, everyone—including you—is likely to have the same or even a worse view than he had when seated!

Now an illustration from economics: An *individual* farmer who is fortunate enough to realize a bumper crop is likely to find that his resulting income is larger than usual. This is a correct generalization. Does it apply to farmers as a *group?* Possibly not, for the simple reason that to the individual farmer, crop prices will not be influenced (reduced) by this bumper crop, because each farmer is producing a negligible fraction of the total farm output. But to farmers as a group, prices vary inversely with total output.[3] Thus, as all farmers realize bumper crops, the total supply of farm products rises, thereby depressing prices. If price declines overbalance the unusually large output, farm incomes *fall.*

In a sense, these comments on the fallacy of composition boil down to this: There are two essentially different levels of analysis at which the economist may derive laws concerning economic behavior. The level of macroeconomics is concerned either with the economy as a whole or with the basic subdivisions or aggregates—such as government, households, and businesses—which make up the economy. An aggregate is a collection of specific economic units which are treated *as if* they were one unit. Thus, we might find it convenient to lump together the 59 million households in our economy and treat them as if they were one huge unit. In dealing with aggregates, macroeconomics is concerned with obtaining an overview, or general outline, of the structure of the economy and the relationships between the major aggregates which constitute the economy. No attention is given

[3] This assumes there is no government price fixing.

to the specific units which make up the various aggregates. It is not surprising, then, to find that macroeconomics entails discussions of such magnitudes as *total* output, the *total* level of employment, *total* income, *total* expenditures, the *general* level of prices, and so forth, in analyzing various economic problems. The problems of unemployment and inflation, by the way, are the primary topics of macroeconomics. In short, macroeconomics examines the forest, not the trees. It gives us a bird's-eye view of the economy.

On the other hand, *microeconomics* is concerned with *specific* economic units and a *detailed* consideration of the behavior of these individual units. When operating at this level of analysis, the economist figuratively puts an economic unit, or very small segment of the economy, under the microscope to observe the details of its operation. Here we talk in terms of an individual industry, firm, or household and concentrate upon such magnitudes as the output of a *specific* product, the number of workers employed by a single firm, the revenue or income of a particular firm or household, the expenditures of a given firm or family, the price of a particular product, and so forth. In microeconomics we examine the trees, not the forest. Microeconomics is useful in achieving a worm's-eye view of some very specific component of our economic system.

The basic point is this: The fallacy of composition reminds us that *generalizations which are valid at one of these levels of analysis may or may not be valid at the other.*

Prosperity and Depression

Closely related to the fallacy of composition is the fact that notions or ideas which are valid during prosperity may be invalid during depression, or vice versa. Some economic principles rest upon a specific presupposition concerning the phase of the business cycle; the validity of a given principle may depend upon the existence of good times or bad times. For example, the economist deems thrift or saving as economically beneficial and therefore desirable during periods of prosperity involving sharp inflation. Why? Because, as we shall discover, a high level of saving will tend to reduce inflationary pressure. Yet during periods of depression, the economist is equally correct in generalizing to the effect that saving is an economic vice, the reason being that too much saving is the immediate cause of unemployment or depression.

Cause and Effect

The discovery of cause-and-effect relationships is an important and difficult part of any science. The absence of controlled experimentation adds significantly to the woes of the social scientist in isolating such cause-effect relationships. It is therefore exceedingly important to warn against grasping at straws in constructing cause-effect sequences. In particular, beware of the "after this, therefore, because of this" fallacy—the incorrect notion that simply because one event precedes another, the first is necessarily the cause of the second.

A classic example clearly indicates the fallacy inherent in such reasoning. Suppose that early each spring the medicine man of a native tribe performs his ritual by cavorting around the village in a green costume. A week or so later the trees and grass turn green. Can we safely conclude that event A, the medicine man's gyrations, has caused event B, the landscape's turning green? Most certainly not. "One who had many times seen a rabbit pursued by a dog, and had never seen rabbits and dogs otherwise, would think the rabbit the cause of the dog."

Assume that a sizable tax increase is put into effect by the government. Suppose, too, that employment increases noticeably a short time thereafter. Can we generalize that the tax boost caused the increase in employment? As Chapter 13 will reveal, a tax increase, as such, is usually conducive

to a drop in employment. Hence any cause-effect conclusion in this case would be premature indeed. In this case, unemployment would fall *despite*—not because of—the tax increase. Another example: Many people believe that the stock market crash of 1929 caused the Great Depression of the 1930s. Although there is an element of accuracy in this statement, it is basically incorrect. The stock market crash itself was a *result* of certain more fundamental forces within the economy which precipitated the Depression.

In short, cause-and-effect relationships are typically not self-evident in economics; the economist must look carefully before he leaps to the conclusion that event A caused event B. Certainly the simple fact that A preceded B is not sufficient to warrant any such conclusion.

Effect of Expectations

The anticipations, or expectations, of consumers and businesses are frequently of great importance in economics. This is so because the widespread anticipation of an event can prompt behavior which may cause the expected event to become a reality. For example, if consumers are suspicious that inflation lies on the economic horizon, they may increase their current levels of spending to "beat" expected higher prices. But increased consumer outlays are likely to cause the anticipated inflation to materialize. Such was the case at the start of the Korean conflict. Conversely, if the economy expects a siege of unemployment, its natural reaction is to retrench on spending. Building a nest egg of savings seems to be a logical means of financing ourselves through an anticipated economic slump. But increasing savings means less spending, and this is likely to cause expected unemployment to become a reality. Similarly, if speculators expect the price of a stock to dip, they will attempt to sell that stock before the decline occurs. The resulting increased offerings of that stock relative to the demand for it will then cause the value of that stock to nose-dive.

In short, what people think will happen has a vital influence upon what actually does occur in the economy.

Intentions versus Realizations

It is also important to recognize that what consumers or business firms attempt or intend to do may be considerably at odds with what they are actually able to accomplish or realize. In our own experience we may plan to wage a campaign of hard work and frugality each summer vacation in order to provide adequate finances for school expenses, but at summer's end we find we have managed to save considerably less than we had originally planned. Events can drastically alter plans. As a matter of fact, the very attempt to achieve a given goal may create certain circumstances which prevent the attainment of that objective. For example, we shall find in Chapter 13 that if the economy attempts to achieve too high a rate of saving, unemployment will result. Unemployment means lower incomes, and this in turn undermines the ability to save. The attempt to save too much may create a situation in which the economy can actually save little or nothing at all. Plans on the one hand and accomplishments on the other may be very different things.

Logical Explanations and Social Practice

Economics is concerned with both describing and explaining human behavior. Explanations in economics, however, occasionally fall short of logical standards. Thus, some explanations in the following chapters will not be "logical" but will, nevertheless, expound the actual operation of our economic units in terms of current social or business practice. For example, we might construct a more logical system of practices and regulations under which our monetary and banking system could operate than those

currently employed. It would be misleading, however, to devote our efforts to an understanding of such a logical masterpiece, since it is out of touch with reality. Of course, our system might be of great value as a guide to reform. Or we might later question the logic of classifying the construction of private residential housing as investment goods rather than as consumer goods. After all, housing is generally bought by individual consumers just as automobiles, bread, and shoes are purchased. Yet, for good reasons of their own, government statisticians classify private housing as an investment good. For us to learn it otherwise—despite the apparent logic of the situation—would be flatly incorrect. In short, we will occasionally find ourselves relying upon that's-the-way-it-is explanations in which logic is subservient to business or social practice.

Economic Quackery

A final general warning. The field of economics is, and always has been, a fertile ground for quacks and charlatans. While few feel capable of offering aid and advice to the nuclear physicist or research chemist, a great many people envision themselves as unrecognized geniuses in economics and politics. The world abounds with self-styled economists who stand ready to cure the world's ills with seemingly simple changes in the structure, legal framework, or ideology of our economy. Some half-baked schemes are frequently appealing in their directness and simplicity, and the task of undermining such schemes is not easy. The ideas of the quack chemist or physicist can be taken to the laboratory and quickly tested for validity. But no clear-cut testing ground is available for rapidly exposing the remedies of economic quacks. (However, one quite obvious earmark of a quack is his eagerness to engage in the highly unscientific practice of generalizing from a single, isolated case rather than from a carefully gathered broad base of empirical evidence.)

The economist's job is made even more difficult by the fact that hard scraping and manipulating will uncover statistics that "prove" just about any point desired![4] Thus, quack schemes often achieve considerable popular support before they are exposed and relegated to the scrap heap as nonsense or half-truths.

We should be foolish to accept medical advice for the treatment of cancer from our milkman or corner grocer. We should be silly if we let an automobile mechanic advise us on dental work. We ought to be equally hesitant to accept the economic analyses and remedies offered by untrained but highly vocal amateurs. Let us remember that answers to major economic problems are rarely self-evident or clear-cut. If they were, the given problem would in all likelihood have been solved and forgotten long ago. The best answers to complex economic problems rarely present themselves in terms of blacks and whites, but rather as varying shades of gray. Easy answers do not often go hand in hand with complex questions.

SUMMARY

1. Economics is studied for several reasons: **a.** It provides valuable knowledge concerning man's social environment and his behavior; **b.** it equips a democratic citizenry to render fundamental decisions intelligently; **c.** although not a vocational discipline, economics may provide the businessman with valuable information.

2. Economics is based upon facts concerning the activities of individuals and institutions in producing, exchanging, and consuming goods and services. The task of descriptive economics is the gathering of those economic facts which are relevant to a particular problem or specific segment of the economy.

[4] One can spend a profitable and highly entertaining evening with Darrell Huff's *How to Lie with Statistics* (New York: W. W. Norton & Company, Inc., 1954).

3. These facts are then studied, arranged, and generalized upon. The resulting generalizations are called "principles," "theories," or "models." The derivation of these principles is the task of economic theory.

4. Economic principles have several noteworthy characteristics. First, they are generalizations and, as such, are subject to exceptions and elude quantitatively precise statement. Further, economic principles are models of reality and are hence abstract; their usefulness depends upon this abstraction. Finally, economic principles often can be conveniently expressed on two-dimensional graphs.

5. In deriving and applying principles, the economist must **a.** not omit any relevant facts, **b.** recognize that principles are simplified models of reality, and **c.** take care not to impute any moral qualities to these principles.

6. Economic principles are particularly valuable as predictive devices; they are the bases for the formulation of economic policy designed to solve problems and control undesirable events.

7. Economic growth, full employment, price stability, economic freedom, equity in the distribution of income, and economic security are all widely accepted economic goals in our society. Some of these goals are complementary; others are mutually exclusive.

8. There are numerous pitfalls in studying economics which the beginner may encounter. Some of the more important chuckholes strewn along the road to economic understanding are **a.** terminological difficulties, **b.** biases and erroneous preconceptions, **c.** the fallacy of composition, **d.** the fact that the validity of some economic ideas may depend upon the stage of the business cycle, **e.** the difficulty of establishing clear cause-effect relationships, **f.** the fact that expectations may influence actual events, **g.** the fact that intentions and accomplishments may be at odds, **h.** possible discrepancies between logic and social practice, and finally, **i.** the ever-present threat of economic quackery.

QUESTIONS AND STUDY SUGGESTIONS

1. "The trouble with economics is that it is not practical. It has too much to say about theory and not enough to say about facts." Critically evaluate.
2. Define descriptive economics, economic theory, and policy economics, and explain the relationships between the three.
3. Analyze and explain the following quotation:[5]

   Facts are seldom simple and usually complicated; theoretical analysis is needed to unravel the complications and interpret the facts before we can understand them . . . the opposition of facts and theory is a false one; the true relationship is complementary. We cannot in practice consider a fact without relating it to other facts, and the relation is a theory. Facts by themselves are dumb; before they will tell us anything we have to arrange them, and the arrangement is a theory. Theory is simply the unavoidable arrangement and interpretation of facts, which gives us generalizations on which we can argue and act, in the place of a mass of disjointed particulars.

4. "As is the case with other sciences, economics is not content with merely descriptive knowledge. Economics tries to discern general patterns of uniformity in human behavior." Explain.
5. Of what significance is the fact that economics is not a laboratory science? What problems may be involved in deriving and applying economic principles?
6. "Like all scientific laws, economic laws are established in order to make successful prediction of the outcome of human actions."[6] Explain.
7. "Abstraction . . . is the inevitable price of generality . . . indeed abstraction and generality are virtually synonyms."[7] Explain.
8. To what extent would you accept the six economic goals stated and described in this chapter? What priorities would you assign to them? It has been said that we seek simply four goals: progress, stability, justice, and freedom. Is this list of goals compatible with that given in the chapter?
9. Interpret and explain the following quotation.[8] Do you agree with this view?

   In comparison with the free economy, the Russian system shows elements of decided strength. Its power to . . . carry out plans without opposition gives it an advantage that may overcome grave handicaps in other respects. If we reject this system, as we most decidedly do, we must found our rejection on our attachment to freedom, not on economic grounds. . . . We want freedom, and we are willing to pay an economic price for it, by sacrificing the larger output that we might have in a forced draft economy.

[5] Henry Clay, *Economics for the General Reader* (New York: The Macmillan Company, 1925), pp. 10–11.
[6] Oskar Lange, "The Scope and Method of Economics," *Review of Economic Studies*, vol. 13, 1945–1946, p. 20.
[7] George J. Stigler, *The Theory of Price* (New York: The Macmillan Company, 1947), p. 10.
[8] Henry C. Wallich, *The Cost of Freedom* (New York: Harper & Row, Publishers, Incorporated, 1960), p. 48.

10. Explain and give an illustration of (*a*) the fallacy of composition and (*b*) the "after this, therefore, because of this" fallacy. Why are cause-and-effect relationships difficult to isolate in the social sciences? Distinguish clearly between macroeconomics and microeconomics.

11. "Economists should never be popular; men who afflict the comfortable serve equally those who comfort the afflicted and one cannot suppose that American capitalism would long prosper without the critics its leaders find such a profound source of annoyance."[9] Interpret and evaluate.

12. Briefly explain the use of graphs as a means of presenting economic principles. What is an inverse relationship? How does it graph? What is a direct relationship? How does it graph? Graph and explain the relationships one would expect to find between (*a*) the number of inches of rainfall per month and the sale of umbrellas, (*b*) the amount of tuition and the level of enrollment at a university, and (*c*) the size of a university's athletic scholarships and the number of games won by its football team. In each case cite and explain how considerations other than those specifically mentioned might upset the expected relationship.

SELECTED REFERENCES

Boulding, Kenneth E.: *Economic Analysis,* 3d ed. (New York: Harper & Row, Publishers, Incorporated, 1955), chap. 1.

Keynes, J. N.: *The Scope and Method of Political Economy,* 4th ed. (New York: The Macmillan Company, 1930).

Lange, Oskar: "The Scope and Method of Economics," *Review of Economic Studies,* vol. 13, 1945–1946, pp. 19–32.

Lipsey, Richard G.: *An Introduction to Positive Economics* (London: Weidenfeld and Nicolson, 1963), chaps. 1 and 2.

Stigler, George J.: *The Theory of Price* (New York: The Macmillan Company, 1947), chap. 1.

Warner, Aaron W., and Victor R. Fuchs: *Concepts and Cases in Economic Analysis* (New York: Harcourt, Brace & World, Inc., 1958), chap. 1.

[9] John Kenneth Galbraith, *American Capitalism,* rev. ed. (Boston: Houghton Mifflin Company, 1956), p. 49.

CHAPTER 2

AN INTRODUCTION TO THE ECONOMIZING PROBLEM

The primary objective of this chapter is to introduce and explore certain fundamental considerations which constitute the foundation of economic science.

But we must be more specific. We shall first seek to introduce a more sophisticated definition of economics. No longer can we content ourselves with the mere statement that economics is concerned with man's behavior in making a living, or that economics has to do with the production, exchange, and consumption of goods and services. These accurate, but not particularly revealing, facts concerning the nature of economics must give way to a comprehensive understanding of the economizing problem. To this end, the sophisticated definition of economics will be illustrated, extended, and modified by the use of so-called production possibilities tables. We shall then restate and discuss the economizing problem in terms of certain practical questions. Finally, we shall survey briefly the different ways in which institutionally and ideologically diverse economies go about solving the economizing problem.

THE FOUNDATION OF ECONOMICS

Two fundamental facts provide a foundation for the field of economics. It is imperative that we carefully state and fully understand these two facts, since everything that follows in our study of economics depends directly or indirectly upon them. The first fact is this: *Society's material wants, that is, the material wants of its citizens and institutions, are virtually unlimited or insatiable.* Secondly: *Economic resources are limited or scarce.*

Unlimited Wants

Let us systematically examine and explain these two facts in the order stated. In the first statement, precisely what do we mean by "material wants"? We mean, first, the desires consumers have to obtain and use various *goods* and *services* which give pleasure or satisfaction.[1] An amazingly wide range of products fills the bill in this respect: houses, automobiles, toothpaste, pencils, onions, sweaters, and the like. In short, innumerable products which we sometimes classify as *necessities* (food, shelter, clothing) and *luxuries* (perfumes, yachts, mink coats) are all capable of satisfying human wants. Needless to say, that which is a luxury to Smith may be a necessity to Jones, and what is a commonplace necessity today may have been a luxury a few short years ago.

But services may satisfy our wants as much as tangible products. A repair job on our car, the removal of our appendix, a haircut, and even legal advice have in common with goods the fact that they satisfy human wants. As a matter of fact, on reflecting, we realize that we buy many goods, for example, automobiles and wash-

[1] This leaves a variety of wants—recognition, status, love, and so forth—for the other social sciences to worry about.

ing machines, for the services they render. The differences between goods and services are often less than they seem to be at first.

Material wants also include the desires which businesses and units of government seek to satisfy. Businesses want factory buildings, machinery, trucks, warehouses, and so forth. Government, reflecting the collective wants of its citizenry or goals of its own, seeks highways, schools, hospitals, and military hardware.

As a group, these material wants are, for practical purposes, *insatiable*, or *unlimited*.[2] This means simply that material wants for goods and services are incapable of being completely satisfied. A simple experiment will help to verify this point: Suppose we are asked to list those goods and services we want but do not now possess. If we take time to ponder our unfilled material wants, chances are our list will be impressive. And over a period of time, our wants seem to multiply so that, as we fill some of the wants on the list, at the same time we add new ones. Material wants, like rabbits, have a high reproduction rate. This is particularly so in the United States where the relatively rapid introduction of new products whets our appetites, and extensive advertising tries to persuade us that we need countless items we might not otherwise consider buying. Not too many years ago, the desire for television, air conditioners, stereophonic phonographs, and tubeless tires was nonexistent. Furthermore, we cannot stop with simple satisfaction: upon acquiring a

[2] It should be mentioned in passing that the fallacy of composition is relevant here. Our wants for a *particular* good or service can obviously be satisfied; that is, over a short period of time we can get sufficient amounts of toothpaste or beer. Certainly one appendicitis operation is par for the course. But goods *in general* are another story. Here we do not, and cannot, get enough. We shall have more to say about the satisfying of wants for specific goods in a later chapter.

lowly Ford or Chevrolet, we become interested in owning a Cadillac or a Lincoln.

In short, we may say that at any point in time the individuals and institutions which constitute society have innumerable unfulfilled material wants. Some of these wants—food, clothing, shelter—have biological roots. But some are also influenced by the conventions and customs of society: the specific kinds of food, clothing, and shelter we seek are frequently determined by the general social and cultural environment in which we live. Over time, wants change and multiply, abetted by the development of new products and by extensive advertising and sales promotion.

Finally—although we may be getting ahead of ourselves—let us emphatically add that the overall end or objective of all economic activity is the attempt to satisfy these diverse material wants.

Scarce Resources

Consider now the second fundamental fact: *Economic resources are limited or scarce.* What do we mean by "economic resources"? In general, we are referring to all the natural, human, and man-made resources that go into the production of goods and services. This obviously covers a lot of ground: factory and farm buildings and all sorts of equipment, tools, and machinery used in the production of manufactured goods and agricultural products; a variety of transportation and communication facilities; innumerable types of labor; and, last but not least, land and mineral resources of all kinds. There is an apparent need for a simplified classification of such resources, which we shall meet with the following categories: (1) *property* resources—land or raw materials and capital; (2) *human* resources—labor and entrepreneurial ability.

What does the economist mean by *land?* Much more than the layman. Land refers to all natural resources—all "free gifts of nature" which are usable in the productive process. Such resources as arable land, forests, mineral and oil deposits, and water resources come under this general classification. What about *capital?* Capital, or investment goods, has a variety of meanings attached to it. The one that is correct for our purposes refers to all man-made aids to production, that is, all tools, machinery, equipment, and factory, storage, transportation, and distribution facilities used in producing goods and services and getting them to the ultimate consumer. Capital goods ("tools") differ from consumer goods in that the latter satisfy wants directly, whereas the former do so indirectly by facilitating the production of consumable goods. We should note especially that the term "capital" as here defined does not refer to money. True, businessmen and economists often talk of "money capital," referring to money which is available for use in the purchase of machinery, equipment, and other productive facilities. But money, as such, produces nothing; hence, it is not to be considered as an economic resource.

Labor is a broad term which the economist uses in referring to all man's physical and mental talents usable in producing goods and services (with the exception of a special set of human talents—entrepreneurial ability—which, because of their special significance in a capitalistic economy, we choose to consider separately). Thus the services of both the lowly ditchdigger or gandy dancer and the skilled chemical engineer or nuclear physicist fall under the general heading of labor.

Finally, what can be said about this special human resource which we label *entrepreneurial ability* or, more simply, *enterprise?* We shall give the term a specific meaning by assigning four related functions to the entrepreneur.

1. The entrepreneur takes the initiative in combining the resources of land, capital, and labor in the production of a good or service. Both a sparkplug and a catalyst, the entrepreneur is at once the driving force behind production and the agent that combines the other resources in what he hopes will be a profitable venture.

2. He has the chore of making basic business-policy decisions, that is, those nonroutine decisions which set the course of a business enterprise.

3. The entrepreneur is an innovator—he is the one who attempts to introduce on a commercial basis new products, new productive techniques, or even new forms of business organization.

4. The entrepreneur is obviously a risk bearer. This is apparent from a close examination of his other three functions. The entrepreneur in a capitalistic system has no guarantee that he will make a profit. The reward for his time, efforts, and abilities may be attractive profits or immediate losses and eventual bankruptcy. In short, the entrepreneur risks not only his time, effort, and business reputation, but his invested funds and those of his associates or stockholders.

We shall see shortly how these resources are provided for business institutions in exchange for money income. The income received from supplying property resources—raw materials and capital equipment—is called *rental* and *interest income.* The income accruing to those who supply labor is called simply *wages* and includes salaries and various wage and salary supplements in the form of bonuses, commissions, royalties, and so forth. Entrepreneurial income is called *profits*, which, of course, may be a negative figure, that is, losses.

These four broad categories of economic resources, or *factors of production* as they are often called, leave room for debate when it comes to classifying specific resources. For example, suppose you receive a dividend on some General Motors stock which you may be fortunate enough to own. Is this an interest return for the capital equipment which the company was able to buy with the money you provided in buying GM stock? Or is this return a profit which compensates you for the risks involved in purchasing corporate stock? What about the earnings of a one-man general store where the owner is both the entrepreneur and the labor force? Are his earnings to be considered as wages or profit income? The answer to both queries is, "Some of each." The important point is this: Although we might quibble about classifying a given flow of income as wages, rent, interest, or profits, all income can be listed without too much arbitrariness under one of these general headings.

All economic resources, or factors of production, have one fundamental characteristic in common: *Economic resources are scarce or limited in supply.* Without a doubt, our economy possesses extremely large amounts of arable land, mineral deposits, capital equipment, and labor. These are, however, not infinitely large supplies; they have limits. A civilian labor force of 74 million workers may seem extremely large, but it is not an infinite amount. World War II, for example, reminded us of just how scarce labor actually is. Critical shortages of semiskilled and skilled labor constituted a formidable obstacle in the production of vitally needed armaments. Much the same can be said for the other factors of production.

One additional point: These economic resources—land, labor, capital, and entrepreneurial ability—are obviously the *means* by which we produce goods and services in trying to satisfy material wants. Consumption in the broadest sense of the term—that is, fulfilling the material wants of the institutions and individuals which make up society—is the objective of economic activity. We are now pointing out that the means of attaining the goal of consumption are our available supplies of various economic resources. And these resources, though perhaps abundant in the absolute sense, are scarce in relation to the demand for them in the production of goods and services.

ECONOMICS DEFINED

Recalling that wants are unlimited and resources are scarce, economics can be defined as *the social science concerned with the problem of using or administering scarce resources (the means of producing) so as to attain the greatest or maximum fulfillment of society's unlimited wants (the goal of producing).* Economics is concerned with "doing the best with what we have." If our wants are virtually unlimited and our resources are scarce, we cannot conceivably satisfy all of society's material wants. The next best thing is to achieve the greatest possible satisfaction of these wants. Economics is without a doubt a science of efficiency—efficiency in the use of scarce resources.

Precisely what is meant by *efficiency* as economists use the term? It means something akin to, but not identical with, the term "efficiency" as used in engineering. The mechanical engineer tells us that a steam locomotive is only "60 per cent efficient" because a large part—some 40 per cent—of the energy in its fuel is not transformed into useful power but is wasted through friction and heat loss. The maximum output of usable power is not derived from the inputs of fuel.

Economic efficiency is also concerned with *inputs* and *outputs*. Specifically, it is concerned with the relationship between the units of scarce resources which are put into the process of production and the resulting output of some wanted product; economic efficiency has to do with inputs of scarce resources and outputs of useful products.

We must recognize that the emphasis or priority placed upon various material wants differs as between societies. Capitalist-type systems, for example, the United States, tend to put great stress upon the satisfaction of the wants of households; the ultimate objective of production is generally regarded as consumption by individuals. Communist-type economies put greater stress upon the production of capital and military goods, which presumably enhance the power and prestige of the national state.

Full Employment and Full Production

Economic efficiency is achieved when full employment and full production are realized or, stated negatively, when unemployment and underemployment are avoided. A worker is clearly unemployed when he is involuntarily out of work. This is the man who is standing in a relief line or a bread line or waiting to pick up his unemployment compensation check. This is a case of *apparent unemployment* or simply *unemployment;* the worker obviously has no job connection. On the other hand, a worker may have a job but still be in a sense "unemployed." For example, a worker who is harvesting wheat by hand or cutting a lawn with a pair of scissors is "partially unemployed." In this case, however, it is a matter of *disguised unemployment* or, more simply, *underemployment.* The worker has a job but simply is not being employed efficiently. The *un*employed worker who has no job and the *under*employed worker who has a job but is producing in a highly inefficient manner differ more in degree than in kind. Both entail the relatively inefficient use of resources. The point is this: There are two major aspects of economic efficiency. On the one hand, there is the *full-employment* problem—the problem of providing jobs for all who are able and willing to work. On the other hand, there is the closely related *full-production* or resource-allocation problem—the problem of using employed resources in the most efficient manner. These two facets of economic efficiency are of such importance as to merit further comment.

Eliminating unemployment. Economic efficiency requires, first, that available resources be actually utilized in the production of goods and services rather than allowed to

lie idle. An unused locomotive is of zero efficiency. The same can be said for unemployed resources. Unutilized resources—both human and property—obviously mean waste and inefficiency. Unemployment is the height of economic inefficiency; when society fails to put its available resources into the productive process, it obviously realizes no output at all.

Note that we specify that all *available* resources should be employed. Each society has certain established customs and practices which determine what particular resources are available for employment. For example, legislation and custom provide that children and the very aged should not be employed. Also, we should not employ all our farmland every year; it is desirable for productivity to allow land to lie fallow periodically. Furthermore, society wants to avoid complete utilization and rapid exhaustion of particularly scarce resources in order to conserve them as long as possible. In short, society wants to employ only those resources that are available for employment and whose current employment is desirable.

In Part Two we shall discover that in a capitalistic economy it is the volume of total spending which determines the level at which resources are employed. If buyers are willing and able to spend in large amounts in satisfying their wants, entrepreneurs will respond by employing large amounts of resources in producing goods and services to fulfill these wants. Conversely, a meager volume of spending will mean unemployment.

Eliminating underemployment. But the full employment of all available resources is not sufficient for the attainment of economic efficiency. Society also seeks full production; that is, the production of goods must be carried out with a proper assignment or allocation of available resources and with use of the best available production techniques. In other words, society wants to get the maximum amount of goods and services produced with its limited inputs of employed resources. For example, if society's wants include both wheat and space probes, it would obviously entail an inefficient or uneconomical allocation of resources to assign astrophysicists and mathematicians to farming and experienced farmers to space research centers. Nor should we want Iowa's farmland planted to cotton and Alabama's to corn when experience indicates the opposite assignment would provide the nation substantially more of both products from the same amount of land. We also want to use the best production methods: for example, other things being equal, a given volume of resources will produce more corn when crop rotation is employed as a technique of production. To plant the same acres to corn year after year will wear out the soil and eventually result in a relatively small output. By employing the same amounts of land, capital, labor, and entrepreneurial resources and by practicing the technique of crop rotation, a larger output of corn can be realized.

Production Possibilities Table

The nature of the economizing problem can be brought into even clearer focus by the use of a production possibilities table.[3] This ingenious device reveals the core of the economizing problem: A full-employment, full-production economy cannot have an unlimited output of goods and services.

We make several specific assumptions to set the stage for our illustration.

1. Let us assume that the economy is operating at full employment and achieving full production. Neither *un*employment nor *under*employment exists.

2. Let us assume that the available supplies of the factors of production are fixed. But, of course, they can be shifted or reallocated, within limits, between different

[3] Paul A. Samuelson, *Economics*, 6th ed. (New York: McGraw-Hill Book Company, 1964), pp. 17–24.

uses; for example, an unskilled laborer can work on a farm, on an automobile assembly line, or in a munitions factory.

3. Let us assume that the technological state of the arts is constant; that is, technology does not change during the course of our analysis.

The second and third assumptions are another way of saying that we are looking at our economy at some specific point in time, or over a very short period of time. Over a relatively long period it would clearly be unrealistic to rule out technological advances and the possibility that resource supplies might vary. In short, we assume full employment and full production, fixed resources, and a fixed technology.

To simplify our illustration further, let us suppose that our economy is producing just two products—for example, drill presses and bread—instead of the innumerable goods and services actually produced. Bread is symbolic of *consumer goods,* that is, those goods and services which directly satisfy our wants; drill presses are symbolic of *capital goods,* that is, those goods which satisfy our wants *indirectly* by permitting more efficient production of consumer goods. Now is it not evident from the assumptions we have made that our economy is faced with a very fundamental choice? Our total supplies of resources are limited. Thus the total amounts of drill presses and bread that our economy is capable of producing are limited. Limited resources mean a limited output. A choice must be made as to what quantities of each product society wants produced. Since resources are limited in supply and fully employed, any increase in the production of drill presses will necessitate the shifting of resources away from the production of bread. And the reverse holds true: if we choose to step up the production of bread, needed resources must come at the expense of drill press production. Society cannot have its cake and eat it, too. This is the essence of the economizing problem.

Let us generalize by noting in Table 2–1 some of the alternative combinations of drill presses and bread which our economy might conceivably choose. Though the data in this and ensuing tables are hypothetical, the points illustrated are of tremendous practical significance. At alternative *A* our economy would be devoting all its resources to the production of drill presses, that is, capital goods. At alternative *E*, all our resources would be devoted to the production of bread, that is, consumer goods. Both these alternatives are clearly unrealistic extremes: Any economy typically strikes a balance in dividing its total output between capital and consumer goods. As we move from alternative *A* to *E*, we step up the production of consumer goods (bread). How? By shifting resources away from capital goods production. Remembering that consumer goods directly satisfy our wants, any movement toward alternative *E* looks tempting. In making this move, society increases the current satisfaction of its wants. But there is a cost involved. This shift of resources catches up with society over time as its stock of capital goods dwindles—or at least ceases to expand at the current rate—with the result that the efficiency of future production is impaired. In short, in moving from alternative *A* toward *E*, society is in effect choosing "more now" at the expense of "much more later." In moving from *E* toward *A*, society is choosing to forgo current consumption. This sacrifice of current consumption frees resources which can now be used in stepping up the production of capital goods. By building up its stock of capital in this way, society can anticipate more efficient production and, therefore, greater consumption in the future. The important point is this: *At any point in time, a full-employment, full-production economy must sacrifice some of product X to obtain more of product Y.* The basic fact that economic resources are scarce prohibits such an economy from having more of both X and Y.

TABLE 2–1. PRODUCTION POSSIBILITIES OF BREAD AND DRILL PRESSES WITH FULL EMPLOYMENT, 1966
(hypothetical data)

Type of product	Production alternatives				
	A	B	C	D	E
Bread (in hundred thousands)	0	1	2	3	4
Drill presses (in thousands)	10	9	7	4	0

Production Possibilities Curve

To ensure our understanding the production possibilities table, let us view these data graphically. We employ a simple two-dimensional graph, putting the output of drill presses on the vertical axis and the output of bread on the horizontal axis, as in Figure 2–1. Following the plotting procedure discussed in Chapter 1, we can locate the "production possibilities" or "transformation"[4] curve, as shown in Figure 2–1.

Optimum Product-mix

We know that each point on the production possibilities curve represents some maximum output of the two products. To realize the various combinations of bread and drill presses which fall on the production possibilities curve, society must achieve full employment and full production. All combinations of bread and drill presses on the curve represent maximum quantities attainable only as the result of the most efficient use of all available resources.

But now a final question arises: If all out-

---

[4] Why "transformation"? Because in moving from one alternative to another, say from *B* to *C*, we are in effect transforming drill presses into bread by shifting resources from the production of the former to the production of the latter.

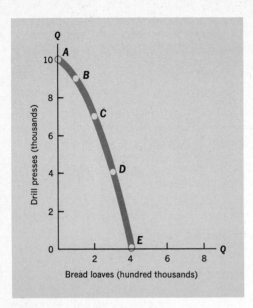

Q

A

10

B

8

C

6

4

D

2

0

E

Q

2   4   6   8

Bread loaves (hundred thousands)

Drill presses (thousands)

FIGURE 2–1. THE PRODUCTION POSSIBILITIES CURVE.
The production possibilities curve is concave in relation to the origin because of the law of increasing costs; economic resources are not completely adaptable as between alternative uses.

puts on the production possibilities curve reflect full employment and full production, which combination will society prefer? This is a subjective question—a moral issue—and the economist as a social scientist possesses no superior judgment or insight on this matter. For example, the Soviet Union has put great emphasis upon the rapid industrialization of its society. The United States, on the other hand, puts a relatively high priority upon satisfying the material wants of consumers. In terms of our production possibilities curve, the government of the Soviet Union has purposely chosen a "many drill presses–few loaves of bread" product-mix as its goal and has implemented its achievement through central planning. In comparison the individuals and institutions of the United States have selected a "few drill presses–many loaves of bread" product-mix, an output objective which has been

implemented largely through a system of markets and prices. Which of these goals is "best"? Is point B or point D superior in Figure 2–1? This, to repeat, is a nonscientific matter; it reflects the values of society as expressed by its control group—the dictatorship, the party, the electorate, the citizenry, the individual institutions, or some combination thereof. What the economist can say is that if a society's production possibilities are as in Table 2–1 *and* if that society seeks the product-mix indicated by, say, alternative B, it is using its resources inefficiently if it only realizes a total output comprised of 87⁄8 units of drill presses and 9⁄10 unit of loaves of bread. And he can also say that the society cannot hope to achieve a national output of 91⁄2 units of drill presses and 13⁄8 units of loaves of bread with its available resources. These are quantitative matters. But the economist cannot say that combination B is "better" or "worse" than combination D, for this is purely a qualitative matter.

Law of Increasing Costs

Implicit in Table 2–1 and Figure 2–1 is an important economic principle which must not escape us. The alert reader has probably noted that, in moving from alternative A to alternative E, the sacrifice of drill presses involved in getting each additional 100,000 units of bread increases. Hence, in moving from A to B, just 1 unit of drill presses is sacrificed for 1 more unit of bread; but going from B to C involves the sacrifice of 2 units of drill presses for 1 more of bread; then 3 of drill presses for 1 of bread; and finally 4 for 1. Why does the sacrifice of drill presses increase as we get more bread? The answer to this query is rather complex. But, simply stated, it amounts to this: *Economic resources are not completely adaptable to alternative uses.* As we attempt to step up bread production, resources which are less and less adaptable to agriculture must be induced, or "pushed," into that line of production. If we start at

A and move to *B*, we can first pick resources whose productivity of bread is greatest in relation to their productivity of drill presses. But as we move from *B* to *C*, *C* to *D*, and so forth, those resources which are highly productive of bread become increasingly scarce. To get more bread, resources whose productivity in drill presses is great in relation to their productivity in bread will be needed. It will obviously take more and more of such resources—and hence an increasingly great sacrifice of drill presses—to achieve a given increase of 1 unit in the production of bread. This lack of flexibility, or adaptability, on the part of resources and the resulting increase in the sacrifice of one good that must be made in the acquisition of more and more units of another good are sometimes termed the *law of increasing costs*, costs in this case being stated as sacrifices of goods and not in terms of dollars and cents. The reader should (1) verify that the law of increasing costs also holds true in moving from alternative *E* to alternative *A* and (2) explain how the shape (concave in relation to the origin) of the production possibilities curve in Figure 2–1 reflects this law.

SOME MODIFICATIONS

It is of signal importance to understand what happens when the three assumptions underlying the preceding explanation are released.

Unemployment and Underemployment

The first assumption was that our economy is characterized by full employment and full production. How would our analysis and conclusions be altered if idle resources were available or if employed resources were used inefficiently? With full employment and full production, our five alternatives represent a series of maximum outputs; that is, they illustrate what combinations of drill presses and bread might be produced when the economy is operating at its full capacity.

With *un*employment or *under*employment, the economy would obviously be producing less at each alternative.

Graphically, a situation of unemployment or underemployment can be illustrated by a point *inside* the original production possibilities curve, which has been reproduced in Figure 2–2. Point *U* is such a point. Here the economy is obviously falling short of the various maximum combinations of bread and drill presses reflected by all the points *on* the production possibilities curve. The dotted arrows in Figure 2–2 indicate three of the possible paths back to full employment and full production. A movement toward full employment and full production will obviously entail a greater output of one or both products. And there are points *outside* the production possibilities curve which

FIGURE 2–2. UNEMPLOYMENT AND THE PRODUCTION POSSIBILITIES CURVE.
Any point inside the production possibilities curve, such as *U*, indicates unemployment or underemployment. By moving toward full employment and full production, the economy can produce more of either or both of the two products, as the arrows indicate.

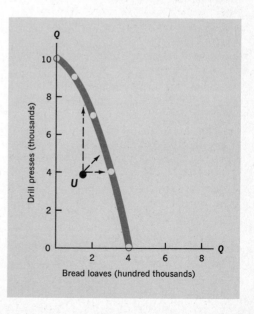

Drill presses (thousands) / Bread loaves (hundred thousands)

will be superior to any point on the curve, but such points are unobtainable, given the current supplies of resources and technology. The production barrier of full employment prohibits the production of any combination of capital and consumer goods lying outside the production possibilities curve.

It is interesting to note that in beginning to produce war goods for World War II the United States found itself with considerable unemployment. Hence, our economy was able to accomplish the production of an almost unbelievably large quantity of war goods and at the same time increase the volume of consumer goods output.[5] The Russians, on the other hand, entered World War II at almost capacity production; that is, they were operating close to full employment. Therefore, their military preparations entailed a considerable shifting of resources from the production of civilian goods and a concomitant drop in the standard of living.[6]

A Growing Economy

What happens to the production possibilities curve when we drop the remaining assumptions that the quantity and quality of resources and technology are fixed? The answer is: The production possibilities curve will shift to the right; that is, the total output of the economy will expand or grow.

Expanding resource supplies. Now let us drop the simplifying assumption that our total supplies of land, labor, capital, and entrepreneurial ability are fixed. Common sense tells us that over a period of time the rapidly growing population which we have in the United States will bring about significant increases in the supplies of labor

---

[5] There did occur, however, rather acute shortages of specific types of consumer goods.
[6] Needless to say, it is sheer folly to leap to the conclusion that this contrast illustrates the desirability of unemployment at the outbreak of hostilities!

TABLE 2–2. PRODUCTION POSSIBILITIES OF BREAD AND DRILL PRESSES WITH FULL EMPLOYMENT, 1986
(hypothetical data)

Type of product	Production alternatives				
	A′	B′	C′	D′	E′
Bread (in hundred thousands)	0	2	4	6	8
Drill presses (in thousands)	14	12	9	5	0

and entrepreneurial ability.[7] Historically, our stock of capital has increased at a remarkable, though unsteady, rate. And although we are depleting some of our oil and mineral deposits, new sources are constantly being discovered. The drainage of swamps and the development of irrigation programs add to our supply of arable land. Assuming continuous full employment and full production, the net result of these increased supplies of the factors of production will be the ability to produce more of both drill presses and bread. Thus in, say, 1986, the production possibilities of Table 2–1 may be obsolete, having given way to those shown in Table 2–2. Note that the greater abundance of resources results in a greater output of one or both products at each alternative; economic growth has occurred.

Technological advance. Our final simplifying assumption was that technology was constant. Simple observation tells us that technology has progressed with amazing rapidity over a long period of time. What does an advancing technology entail? New and better goods and improved ways of producing these goods. For the moment, let us think of technological advance as entailing

---

[7] This is not to say that population growth as such is always desirable. In Chapter 41 we shall discover that overpopulation is a constant drag upon the living standards of many underdeveloped countries.

simply improvements in capital facilities—more efficient machinery and equipment. How does such technological advance alter our earlier discussion of the economizing problem? In this way: Technological advance, by improving productive efficiency, allows society to produce more goods with a fixed amount of resources. As with increases in resource supplies, technological advance permits the production of more drill presses and more bread.

What happens to the production possibility curve of Figure 2–2 when the supplies of resources increase or an improvement in technology occurs? The curve shifts outward and to the right, as illustrated by the thin curve in Figure 2–3. Increases in resource supplies and technological advances permit us to enjoy a greater output of both bread and drill presses; the economy's productive potential has grown. But note this important point: Such a favorable shift in the production possibilities curve does not guarantee that the economy will operate at a point on that new curve. The economy might fail to realize its new potentialities. Some 74 million jobs will give us full employment at the present time, but ten years from now our labor force, because of a growing population, will be much larger, and 74 million jobs will not be sufficient to give us full employment. In short, the production possibilities curve may shift, but the economy may fail to produce at a point on that curve. On Figure 2–2 the student should pencil in two new production possibility curves: one to show the situation where a better technique for producing drill presses has been developed, the technology for producing bread being unchanged, and the other to illustrate an improved technology for bread, the technology for producing drill presses being constant.

Present choices and future curve location.
You may have anticipated this important point in the foregoing paragraphs: An economy's current choice of position on its production possibilities curve is a basic

FIGURE 2–3. ECONOMIC GROWTH AND THE PRODUCTION POSSIBILITIES CURVE.
The expanding resource supplies and technological advances which characterize a growing economy move the production possibilities curve outward and to the right. This permits the economy to enjoy larger quantities of both types of goods.

determinant of the future location of that curve. To illustrate this notion, let us designate the two axes of the production possibilities curve as "goods for the future" and "goods for the present," as in Figure 2–4a and b. By "goods for the future" we refer to such things as capital goods, research and education, preventive medicine, and so forth, which obviously tend to increase the quantity and quality of property resources, enlarge the stock of technological information, and improve the quality of human resources. By "goods for the present" we mean pure consumer goods in the form of foodstuffs, clothing, transistor radios, automobiles, power mowers, and so forth.

Now suppose there are two economies, Alphania and Betania, which at the moment are identical in every respect, except that Alphania's current (1966) choice of position on its production possibilities curve strongly favors "present goods" as opposed to "future goods." The dot in Figure 2–4a indicates this choice. Betania, on the other hand, renders a current (1966) choice which stresses large amounts of "future goods" and lesser amounts of "present goods" (Figure 2–4b). Now, all other things being the same, we can expect the future (1986) production possibilities curve of Betania to be further to the right than

that of Alphania. That is, by currently choosing an output which is more conducive to technological advance and to increases in the quantity and quality of property and human resources, Betania will tend to achieve greater economic growth than will Alphania, whose current choice of output puts less emphasis upon those goods and services which cause the production possibilities curve to shift rightward.

It is this sort of analysis, incidentally, which helps explain why the total output of the Soviet Union is expanding each year at a rate which is about twice as great as that of the United States (6 per cent for the U.S.S.R. as compared to about 3 per cent for the U.S.A.). The Soviet economy

FIGURE 2–4. AN ECONOMY'S PRESENT CHOICE OF POSITION ON ITS PRODUCTION POSSIBILITIES CURVE HELPS DETERMINE THE CURVE'S FUTURE LOCATION.
A current choice favoring "present goods," as rendered by Alphania in (a), will cause a modest rightward shift of the curve. A current choice favoring "future goods," as rendered by Betania in (b), will result in a greater rightward shift of the curve.

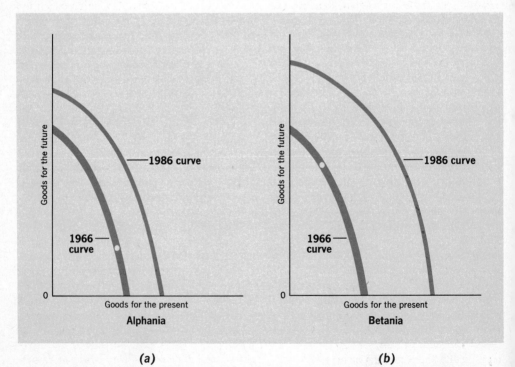

(a)   (b)

has been "plowing back" a larger proportion of its current output as goods for the future than has the United States. Relatively greater Soviet emphasis upon goods for the future also helps explain why the Soviet standard of living is currently so very low relative to that of the United States and, in particular, why automobiles are so scarce and housing so remarkably poor.

ECONOMIZING: FIVE FUNDAMENTAL QUESTIONS

In order to provide a broad understanding of the essence of the economizing problem, the preceding discussion is pitched at a fairly abstract level. Let us now be more practical and examine some of the specific questions or problems that any economic system must answer in attempting to use its scarce resources to achieve the maximum satisfaction of society's material wants. Basically, there are Five Fundamental Questions which must be answered in attempting to achieve and maintain efficiency in the use of scarce resources.

What Is to Be Produced

Society must somehow decide what collection of goods and services will most fully satisfy its wants. This decision concerning the composition of total output must be consistent with the production possibilities currently facing the economy. Choosing a combination of capital and consumer goods lying *inside* the production possibilities curve entails economic inefficiency in the form of unemployment. Seeking a combination *outside* the current production possibilities curve is unrealistic; society is obviously setting its sights on an unattainable target.

Actually, the basic question of determining what is to be produced can be divided into two closely related subquestions: First, what goods and services are to be produced? Second, in what quantities does society wants these goods produced?

Consider the first subquestion: What goods and services should be produced? Answering this entails, in effect, the setting up of a list of goods and services which society deems important enough to produce. How should society apportion its scarce resources among those products which it is capable of producing? Should our list include bread? Drill presses? Fords? Cadillacs? Color television? Mink coats? Buggy whips? Football stadiums? ICBMs? Society must somehow decide what items to include in—and what items to exclude from—the list of goods that are to be produced.

But this decision is only half the battle. Once society has decided what to produce, somehow it must then assign proper weights to each of the items on the list. Without asking how this decision has been reached, suppose society has decided that bread, drill presses, Fords, and football stadiums are the items from the above list which it actually wants to produce. The fact that resources are scarce tells us that society cannot produce unlimited amounts of the goods on this list. Must society now decide *how many* loaves of bread, *how many* drill presses, *how many* Fords, and *how many* football stadiums it wants in its total output? Society must not only decide the relative amounts of capital and consumer goods to be produced—the question posed in our production possibilities illustrations—but it must also determine the specific quantities of each type of capital goods and each type of consumer goods that will best fulfill society's material wants. Even in relatively primitive economies these decisions can become complex.

Remember, too, that in deciding the relative amounts of capital and consumer goods to be produced, society is of necessity weighing the relative merits of future, as opposed to current, want fulfillment. More resources devoted to technological research and to the expansion of the economy's capital facilities means fewer available for the production of goods for current consumption. The choice here is between more now or much more later. By cutting back on research and on the expansion of our productive facilities, society can produce a greater current output. But sacrificing some current consumption in order to free resources for research and capital expansion will mean an expanded output in the future.

These two subquestions—what goods shall we produce? in what quantities?—have been considered in a very simplified way in our analysis of the production possibilities tables. We solved—or dodged!—the first by assuming the economy had somehow decided to produce only bread and drill presses.

The answer to the second question entails society's choosing which one of the five alternatives—A, B, C, D, or E—yields the highest level of satisfaction. Thus the perennial question of consumer goods versus capital goods is part of the larger question of deciding the specific composition of the total output. In a wartime or mobilization situation, the question of civilian versus war goods falls under the same general heading.

Organizing Production

Hand in glove with our decision as to the composition of total output is another query: *How should this total output be produced?* This major question can also be broken into parts.

1. How does society steer resources into industries producing goods that we want produced and, conversely, keep resources away from industries producing goods wanted in very small amounts or not at all?

2. What firms in the various industries are to do the producing, and how are they to obtain the needed resources?

3. What is the most efficient combination of resources for each firm to use in producing a given level of output? More subtly, what is the best technology to use in production?

All these questions center upon the goal of achieving full production from society's available resources. A reminder: Although the question of organizing production is spelled out here in terms of an industrially advanced economy, similar questions would be pertinent for a primitive or underdeveloped economy.

Distributing Output

The third basic decision comes close to home: *How is society to divide or ration the total output among the various economic units which comprise our economic system?* How should the total output of consumer goods be shared by the various households in our economy? Similarly, how should any additions to our stock of capital equipment included in our total output be apportioned to the various industries and the individual firms in those industries? What part of total output should be given over to government? In short, the question of how the total output is to be distributed among households, businesses, and government must somehow be answered by society. Obviously, these questions involve not only economics but also politics and ethics.

Level of Resource Use

Society is obligated to determine the degree to which its economic resources are to be utilized. This decision is more complex than it first appears. Two related subquestions are involved:

1. To what degree is society *willing* to utilize its human and property resources?

2. To what extent is society actually *able* to employ its resources? Let us briefly explore these subquestions in the order stated.

A society which seeks to maximize the immediate fulfillment of its material wants must be willing to utilize its human and property resources to a very high degree. For human resources this means that both men and women must enter the labor force at an early age, retire at a very old age, and work long hours with few holidays and vacations in the intervening span of years. This obviously means little leisure. And leisure, after all, is a source of satisfaction— a part of our standard of living. What good is a stereo set or golf clubs if one has no time to use them? In all economies the decision as to how the time at the disposal of human resources is to be divided between production and leisure is influenced by sociocultural factors. The mores and customs of society are important in determining what percentage of the population is to work, the number of work hours, and, as a matter of fact, the intensity of labor.

The problem of resource conservation is primary in discussing the willingness of society to utilize its property resources currently. The nature of this decision can best be envisioned in terms of nonrenewable natural resources such as petroleum, natural gas, and a host of mineral deposits. The current rapid exploitation of these resources makes for a high output now but at the same time lessens the ability of the economy to produce in the future. A lower current rate of utilization would spread more evenly over time the output of goods and services whose production is dependent upon these resources.

Having determined the level of resource utilization which it desires, society must then achieve that level of resource use. Society must avoid the involuntary idleness of its human and property resources. Involuntary idleness is the height of economic inefficiency. To be efficient, any economic system must somehow provide for high and stable levels of employment. We shall discover in Part Two of this book that one of the basic defects of modern capitalism lies in the fact that it does not guarantee economic stability—full employment accompanied by a stable level of prices. Unemployment—actual or potential—is generally recognized as the greatest domestic problem which American capitalism currently faces. Inflation can be an equally potent adversary.

In a primitive Robinson Crusoe economy there is no problem of achieving full employment. The consumer and the producer are one and the same. Thus the producer, if he so desires, can spend all his waking hours in an effort to fulfill his material wants. Though we cannot pause at this point for lengthy explanations, it must be emphasized that the problem of achieving full employment is not so simple a task in such modern industrial societies as American capitalism. Here producers and consumers—sellers and buyers—have different identities, and their decision making is linked only imperfectly by the use of money in buying and selling both goods and resources. Hence, although consumers on the one hand and producers on the other both desire full employment, their nonidentity raises the possibility that inconsistencies in their spending and producing decisions may lead to unemployment. If the spending of buyers is deficient in amount, producers will not find it advantageous to employ all the economy's available resources. Why hire resources to produce goods that no one will buy? Conversely, too much spending may result in price inflation. In between lies some specific level of spending that will give the economy full employment with relatively stable prices. The point is this: Nothing guarantees that an industrially advanced economy—particularly a capitalistic economy—will operate at a point on its production possibilities curve. Finally, it is also worth noting that an economy with an expanding population and labor force must provide more and more jobs each year to sustain full employment; the *status quo* with respect to the level of employment is not enough in a growing economy.

Flexibility

To achieve the maximum fulfillment of society's material wants over time, the economy must be flexible and adaptable to change. Modern economies are far from static, unchanging things. Indeed, their basic feature is *change*. What changes? Several things: consumer tastes, the supplies of resources, and technology. Why does our basic objective of efficiency in the use of scarce resources demand that the economy be adaptable to such changes. Because a changing technology, changes in consumer tastes, and variations in resource supplies imply significant reallocations of our resources in order to preserve efficiency in their use. The collection of goods and services which maximizes consumer satisfactions today will fail to do so tomorrow if consumer wants have changed in the meantime. The collection of goods and services which pleased our parents in the 1920s will simply not be acceptable to us in the 1960s. Put more bluntly, we should not be particularly happy if today's output provided for large quantities of buggy whips and mustache cups at the expense of stereophonic phonographs, transistor radios, and ballpoint pens. Similarly, changing resource supplies and the development of improved techniques of production will call for changes in the combinations of resources used in the production of given products if efficiency is to be maintained.

And, needless to say, flexibility is a basic prerequisite of such sudden economic transformations as those entailed by the shift from peace to war and, for that matter, from war to peace. Gigantic and sudden reallocations of our resources are necessary in such emergency situations.

We should keep constantly in mind that scarcity of economic resources lurks behind all five of these Fundamental Questions and their component parts; the Five Questions are merely a breakdown of the basic economizing problem of scarce resources and unlimited wants. Also the apparent interrelatedness of these questions is almost self-evident, as we shall see in the following chapters, where we shall attempt to describe in detail how a capitalistic economy answers these questions. Indeed, it is difficult to treat the Five Questions independently of one another—they demand simultaneous treatment.

THE "ISMS"

If we lived in an isolated, one-man economy—a Robinson Crusoe economy—the answers we would provide to our list of questions would be relatively simple. But when millions of diverse and interdependent economic units exist, no simple answers to these queries present themselves. How is our society, for example, to strike a mutually acceptable balance between the business tycoon's demand for a Cadillac, the Negro's demand for improved housing, the school child's demand for bubble gum and roller skates, and the housewife's demand for an automatic washer? Certainly no simple answer can be expected. And, to complicate matters, we know that answers which are acceptable today may not be acceptable tomorrow. The preferences of economic units change over time, and so do productive techniques, supplies of resources, and standards of equity in distributing output. In short, there are no final, once-and-for-all answers of a universal nature to the questions which constitute the economizing problem.

Furthermore, we must recognize that *various societies have established different output goals and utilize different institutions and methods of organizing their resources in trying to fulfill these goals.* Generally speaking, a survey of modern, industrially advanced economies suggest there are two fundamentally different philosophies concerning the means of achieving the best answers to the Five Fundamental Questions. At one extreme, emphasis is put upon the freedom of individual economic units to make those choices which they feel are most appropriate in terms of their own specific objectives. The other extreme philosophizes that the sum of free economic choices by individual economic units is unlikely to result in efficiency in the use of scarce resources; hence, some omnipotent authoritarian power—presumably the state—is needed to answer the Five Questions. The former philosophy crudely describes the core of *pure,* or *laissez-faire, capitalism;* the latter, the basic tenet of authoritarian socialism, or *communism.* Between these two hypothetical extremes can be arrayed an infinite number of variations and compromises. There is, strictly speaking, an unlimited number of production goals and ways of attempting to achieve maximum fulfillment of any society's particular goals from its scarce resources.

Table 2–3 summarizes the fundamental assumptions, institutional characteristics, and basic methods employed in achieving efficiency in the use of resources which are associated with pure capitalism, communism, and an intermediate hybrid—liberal socialism. While students of comparative economic systems might quibble a bit about these descriptions, all would agree with the basic point emphasized by the table. And that point is: There are no unique or uni-versally accepted answers to the Five Fundamental Questions. Various societies, having different cultural and historical backgrounds, different mores and customs, and contrasting ideological frameworks—not to mention resources which differ both quantitatively and qualitatively—supply significantly different answers to the Five Questions. Russia, the United States, and Great Britain, for example, are all—in terms of their accepted goals, ideology, technologies, resources, and culture—attempting to achieve efficiency in the use of their respective resources. The best method for answering the Five Questions in one economy may be completely inappropriate for another economic system.

Table 2–3 is couched in terms of industrially advanced or "mature" economies. We shall discover in Chapter 41 that many nations of the world have highly under-

TABLE 2–3. THE "ISMS" AND THE ECONOMIZING PROBLEM

Economic system	Underlying assumption	Institutional characteristics	Method of solving economizing problem
Pure, or laissez-faire, capitalism	Each economic unit decides what choices and policies are best for it; such choices will prove to be in the social interest.	Private ownership of resources and business institutions; freedom of choice for consumers, resource suppliers, and enterprisers.	Emphasis upon a system of free, competitive markets—virtually no governmental planning or control.
Liberal, or democratic, socialism	Some governmental intervention is needed to improve upon the choices and policies of individual economic units.	Mixture of public and private ownership and public and private decision making.	Mixture of loose governmental planning and regulation of basic industry; reliance on system of markets and prices in other segments of economy.
Communism, or authoritarian socialism	The state is in the best position to know what choices and policies are beneficial for the economy as a whole and for its component parts.	Public ownership and control of the bulk of industry and agriculture; severe restriction of individual choices when in conflict with state-determined objectives	Governmental plans as established by central planning authority; heavy reliance on government directives some reliance on a price system to implement the plans.

developed economies. These *traditional* economies are characterized by feudalistic remnants of the Middle Ages. In these systems answers to the Five Fundamental Questions are shrouded in custom, habit, and tradition, all of which tend to perpetuate the *status quo.*

The ensuing four chapters undertake to explain how in the so-called *mixed capitalism* of the United States, which stands at some intermediate position between pure capitalism and liberal socialism in Table 2–3, decisions are made about the objectives of the economy, how production is to be organized, and how output is to be distributed. Chapter 3 discusses the institutional framework of capitalism and provides a very general picture of the operation of pure, or laissez-faire, capitalism. Chapter 4 explains the mechanics of supply and demand as price- and output-determining forces. The role of markets and prices in answering the Five Fundamental Questions is the topic of Chapter 5. Government is brought into the picture in Chapter 6, enlarging our picture of pure capitalism to one of mixed capitalism.

SUMMARY

1. The science of economics centers upon two basic facts: First, human material wants are virtually unlimited; second, economic resources are scarce.

2. Economic resources may be classified as property resources—materials and capital—or as human resources—labor and entrepreneurial ability.

3. Economics is concerned with the problem of administering scarce resources in the production of goods and services for the fulfillment of the material wants of society. Both the full employment and the full production of available resources are essential if this administration is to be efficient.

4. At any point in time a full-employment, full-production economy must sacrifice the output of some types of goods and services to achieve increased production of others.

5. Over time, technological advance and increases in the quantity and quality of human and property resources permit the economy to produce more of all goods and services. Society's choice as to the composition of current output is a determinant of the future location of the production possibilities curve.

6. Any economy faces Five Fundamental Questions in attempting to use its scarce resources to achieve the maximum fulfillment of its material wants. They are: **a.** What goods and services do we want to produce and in what specific amounts? **b.** How is production to be organized in getting these goods and services produced? **c.** How will this output of goods and services be distributed among the various economic units which make up the economic system? **d.** What must an economy do to obtain and maintain the full employment of its available resources? **e.** How does an economy provide the internal flexibility or adaptability required to maintain efficiency in the use of its resources?

7. The various economic systems of the world differ in their ideologies and their approaches in answering the Five Fundamental Questions.

QUESTIONS AND STUDY SUGGESTIONS

1. "Economics is the study of the principles governing the allocation of scarce means among competing ends when the objective of the allocation is to maximize the attainment of the ends."[8] Explain. Why is the problem of unemployment a part of the subject matter of economics?

[8] George J. Stigler, *The Theory of Price* (New York: The Macmillan Company, 1947), p. 12.

2. "Wants aren't insatiable. I can prove it. I get all the coffee I want to drink every morning at breakfast." Critically analyze. Explain: "Goods and services are scarce because resources are scarce."

3. What are economic resources? What are the major functions of the entrepreneur?

4. "Economics is concerned with two problems. One has to do with achieving full employment of the economy's available resources. The other has to do with allocating employed resources among various possible uses. Both aspects emphasize efficiency in the use of resources." Explain.

5. The following is a production possibilities table for war goods and civilian goods:

Type of product	Production alternatives				
	A	B	C	D	E
Automobiles (in millions)	0	2	4	6	8
Guided missiles (in thousands)	30	27	21	12	0

a. Show these production possibilities data graphically. What do the points on the curve indicate? How does the curve reflect the law of increasing costs? Explain.

b. Label point *G* inside the curve. What does it indicate? Label point *H* outside the curve. What does this point indicate? What must occur before the economy can attain the level of production indicated by point *H*?

c. Upon what assumptions is the production possibilities curve based? Be specific. What happens when each of these assumptions is released?

d. Suppose improvement occurs in the technology of producing guided missiles but not in the production of automobiles. Draw the new production possibilities curve. Now assume that a technological advance occurs in producing automobiles but not in producing guided missiles. Draw the new production possibilities curve. Finally, draw a production possibilities curve which reflects technological improvements in the production of both products.

6. "The present choice of position on the production possibilities curve is a major factor in economic growth." Explain.

7. State and thoroughly discuss the Five Fundamental Questions which all economies face. Why must an economy be adaptable to change in order to maintain efficiency in the use of scarce resources? Contrast the means by which pure capitalism, democratic socialism, and communism attempt to answer the Five Questions.

8. "Economics is . . . neither capitalist nor socialist: it applies to every society. Economics would disappear only in a world so rich that no wants were unfulfilled for lack of resources. Such a world is not imminent and may be impossible, for time is always limited."[9] Carefully evaluate and explain these statements. Do you agree that conceptually time is an economic resource?

[9] Joseph P. McKenna, *Intermediate Economic Theory* (New York: Holt, Rinehart and Winston, Inc., 1958), p. 2.

SELECTED REFERENCES

Due, John F., and Robert W. Clower: *Intermediate Economic Analysis,* 4th ed. (Homewood, Ill.: Richard D. Irwin, Inc., 1961), chap. 1.

Galbraith, John K.: *American Capitalism,* rev. ed. (Boston: Houghton Mifflin Company, 1956), chap. 2.

Heilbroner, Robert L.: *The Making of Economic Society* (Englewood Cliffs, N.J.: Prentice-Hall, Inc., 1962), chap. 1.

Heilbroner, Robert L.: *The Worldly Philosophers,* rev. ed. (New York: Simon and Schuster, Inc., 1961), chap. 2.

Knight, Frank H.: "Social Economic Organization," in Ralph C. Epstein and Arthur D. Butler (eds.): *Selections in Economics* (Buffalo, N.Y.: Economica Books, 1958), chap. 2.

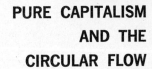

CHAPTER 3

PURE CAPITALISM
AND THE
CIRCULAR FLOW

The task of the present chapter is to describe the capitalist ideology and to explain how pure, or laissez-faire, capitalism operates. Strictly speaking, pure capitalism has never existed and probably never will. Why, then, do we bother to consider the operation of such an economy? Because it gives us a workable *first approximation* of how modern American capitalism functions, and approximations, when properly handled, can be very useful. In other words, pure capitalism constitutes a simplified point of reference which we shall then modify and adjust to correspond more closely to the reality of American capitalism.

In explaining the operation of pure capitalism, we shall discuss:

1. The institutional framework and basic assumptions which make up the capitalist ideology.

2. Certain institutions and practices common to all modern economies.

3. Capitalism and the circular flow of income.

4. How product and resource prices are determined.

5. The market system and the allocating of economic resources.

The first three topics constitute the present chapter; the latter two, Chapters 4 and 5.

CAPITALIST IDEOLOGY

Unfortunately, there is no neat and universally accepted definition of capitalism to aid us in our present task. We are therefore required to examine in some detail the basic tenets of capitalism to acquire a comprehensive understanding of what pure capitalism entails. In short, the framework of capitalism embodies the following institutions and assumptions: (1) private property, (2) freedom of enterprise and choice, (3) self-interest as the dominant motive, (4) competition, (5) reliance upon the price system, and (6) a limited role for government. Let us explore these characteristics to ensure our understanding them.

Private Property

Under a capitalistic system, the means of production—that is, scarce resources—are owned by private individuals and private institutions as opposed to government. Private property, coupled with the freedom to negotiate binding legal contracts, permits private persons or businesses to obtain, control, employ, and dispose of economic resources as they see fit. The institution of private property is sustained over time by the *right to bequeath,* that is, by the right of a property owner to designate the recipient of his property at the time of death.

Needless to say, there are broad legal limits to this right of private ownership. For example, the use of one's resources for the production of narcotics is prohibited by legislation. Nor is public ownership nonexistent. Even in pure capitalism, recognition is given to the fact that public ownership of certain "natural monopolies" may be essential to the achievement of efficiency in the use of resources of the economy.

Freedom of Enterprise and Choice

Closely related to private ownership of property is freedom of enterprise and choice. Capitalism charges its component parts with the responsibility of making certain choices, which are registered and made effective through the free markets of the economy. *Freedom of enterprise* means that under pure capitalism private business enterprises are free to obtain economic resources, to organize these resources in the production of a product of the firm's own choosing, and to sell this product in the markets of their choice. No artificial obstacles or restrictions imposed by government or other producers block an entrepreneur's choice to enter or leave a particular industry. *Freedom of choice* means that owners of property resources and money capital can employ or dispose of these resources as they see fit. It also means that laborers are free to enter any of those lines of work for which they are mentally and physically qualified. Finally, it means that consumers are at liberty, within the limits of their money incomes, to buy that collection of goods and services which they feel is most appropriate in satisfying their wants. Freedom of consumer choice may well be the most profound of these freedoms. The consumer is in a particularly strategic position in a capitalistic economy; in a sense, the consumer is sovereign. The range of free choices for suppliers of human and property resources is circumscribed by the choices of consumers. The consumer ultimately decides what the capitalistic economy should produce, and resource suppliers must make their free choices within the boundaries thereby delineated. Resource suppliers and businesses are not really "free" to produce goods and services consumers do not desire.

Again, broad legal limitations prevail in the expression of all these free choices.

Role of Self-interest

Since capitalism is individualistic, it is not surprising to find that the primary driving force of such an economy is the promotion of one's self-interest; each economic unit attempts to do what is best for itself. Hence, entrepreneurs aim at the maximization of their firms' profits or, as the case might be, the minimization of losses. And, other things being equal, owners of property resources attempt to achieve the highest price obtainable from the rent or sale of these resources. Given the amount and irksomeness of the effort involved, those who supply human resources will also attempt to obtain the highest possible incomes from their employment. Consumers, in purchasing a given product, will seek to obtain it at the lowest price. In short, capitalism presumes self-interest as the fundamental *modus operandi* for the various economic units as they express their free choices. The motive of self-interest gives direction and consistency to what might otherwise be an extremely chaotic economy.

Although self-interest is the basic motive underlying the functioning of capitalism, there are exceptions to the rule: Businesses and individuals do not always act in their own self-interest. Altruistic motives are part of the makeup of economic units. Yet self-interest is the best single statement of how economic units actually behave.

Competition

Freedom of choice exercised in terms of promoting one's own monetary returns provides the basis for competition, or economic rivalry, as a fundamental feature of capitalism. Competition, as economists see it, entails:

1. The presence of large numbers of independently acting buyers and sellers operating in the market for any particular product or resource

2. The freedom of buyers and sellers to enter or leave particular markets.

Let us briefly explore these two related aspects of competition:

1. The essence of competition is the widespread diffusion of economic power among the individual units—businesses and households—which comprise the economy. In particular, when a large number of buyers and sellers are present in a market, no one buyer or seller will be able to demand or offer a quantity of the product sufficiently large to noticeably influence its price. Let us examine this statement in terms of the selling or supply side of the product market.

We have all observed that, when a product becomes unusually scarce, its price will skyrocket. For example, an unseasonable frost in Florida may seriously curtail the output of citrus crops and raise the price of orange juice. Thus, if a single producer, or small group of producers acting together, can somehow control or restrict the total supply of a product, he can raise its price to his own advantage. By controlling supply, the producer can "rig the market" on his own behalf. Now the essence of competition is that there are so many sellers that each, *because he is contributing an almost negligible fraction of the total supply,* has virtually no control over the supply or, therefore, over the product price.

For example, suppose there are 10,000 farmers, each of whom is supplying 100 bushels of corn in the Kansas City grain market at some particular time when the price of corn happens to be $2 per bushel. Could a single farmer, who happens to be dissatisfied with the existing price, cause an artificial scarcity of corn and thereby boost the price above $2? The answer is obviously "No." Farmer Jones, by restricting his output from 100 to 75 bushels, exerts virtually no effect upon the total supply of corn. In fact, he only reduces total supply from 1,000,000 to 999,975 bushels. This obviously is not much of a shortage! Supply is virtually unchanged, and, therefore, the $2 price persists. In brief, competition means that each seller is providing a drop in the bucket of total supply. The individual seller can make no noticeable dent in total supply; hence, he cannot *as an individual producer*[1] manipulate product price. This is what is meant when it is pointed out that an individual competitive seller is "at the mercy of the market."

The same rationale applies to the demand side of the market. Buyers are plentiful and act independently. Thus no single buyer can manipulate the market to his advantage.

The important point is this: The widespread diffusion of economic power which competition involves controls the use and limits the potential abuse of that power. Economic rivalry prevents economic units from wreaking havoc upon one another as they attempt to further their self-interests. Competition imposes limits upon expressions of self-interest by buyers and sellers. Competition is a basic regulatory force in capitalism.

2. Competition also assumes that it is a simple matter for producers to enter (or leave) a particular industry; there are no artificial legal or institutional obstacles to prohibit the expansion (or contraction) of specific industries. This aspect of competition is prerequisite to the flexibility which is essential if an economy is to remain efficient over time. Freedom of entry is necessary if the economy is to adjust appropriately to changes in consumer tastes, technology, or resource supplies. This matter will receive detailed treatment in Chapter 5.

Markets and Prices

Private property, freedom of choice, and self-interest—all subject to the regulatory force of competition—set the stage for what is perhaps the basic feature of the capital-

[1] Of course, if a number of farmers simultaneously restricted their production, the resulting change in total supply could no longer be ignored, and price would rise.

istic system. *Capitalism is a market economy.* The decisions rendered by the buyers and sellers of products and resources are made effective through a system of markets. The preferences of sellers and buyers are registered on the supply and demand sides of various markets, and the outcome of these choices is a system of product and resource prices. These prices are guideposts upon which resource owners, entrepreneurs, and consumers make and revise their free choices in furthering their self-interests. Just as competition is the controlling mechanism, so a system of markets and prices is a basic organizing force. The price system is an elaborate communications system through which innumerable individual free choices are recorded, summarized, and balanced against one another. Those who obey the dictates of the price system are rewarded; those who ignore it are penalized by the system. Through this communications system, society renders its decisions concerning what the economy should produce, how production can be efficiently organized, and how the fruits of productive endeavor are to be distributed among the individual economic units which make up capitalism.

Not only is the price system the mechanism through which society renders decisions concerning how it allocates its resources and distributes the resulting output, but it is through the price system that these decisions are implemented and carried out. However, a word of caution: Economic systems based upon the ideologies of socialism and communism also depend upon price systems, but not to the same degree or in the same way as does pure capitalism. The socialistic and communistic societies use markets and prices merely to implement the decisions rendered wholly or in part by a central planning authority. In capitalism, the price system functions both as a device for rendering innumerable choices of free individuals and businesses and as a mechanism for implementing or carrying out these decisions.

In Chapters 4 and 5 we shall analyze the mechanics and the operation of a capitalistic price system.

Limited Government

A competitive capitalist economy is thought to be conducive to a high degree of efficiency in the use or allocation of its resources. Hence, there is allegedly little real need for governmental intervention in the operation of such an economy beyond its aforementioned role of imposing broad legal limits upon the exercise of individual choices and the use of private property. The historical development of the concept of pure capitalism as a self-regulating and self-adjusting type of economy precludes any significant economic role for government. As we shall see shortly, capitalism in practice has not been self-regulating to the degree economists once supposed. But for the moment, at least, our analysis will exclude government. Chapter 6 will elaborate the functions of government in present-day mixed capitalism.

OTHER CHARACTERISTICS

Private property, freedom of enterprise and choice, self-interest as a motivating force, competition, and reliance on a price system are all institutions and assumptions which are more or less exclusively associated with pure capitalism. In addition, there are certain institutions and practices which are characteristic of all modern economies. They are (1) the use of an advanced technology and large amounts of capital goods, (2) specialization according to the principle of comparative advantage, and (3) the use of money. Specialization and the use of an advanced technology are prerequisites to the efficient employment of any economy's resources. The use of money is a permissive characteristic which allows society more easily to practice and reap the benefits of specialization and the employment of advanced productive techniques.

Extensive Use of Capital Goods

All modern economies—whether they approximate the capitalist, socialist, or communist ideology—are based upon an advanced technology and the extensive use of capital goods. Under pure capitalism it is competition, coupled with freedom of choice and the desire to further one's self-interest, which provides the means for achieving a rapid rate of technological advance. The capitalistic framework is felt to be highly effective in harnessing incentives to develop new products and improved techniques of production. Why? Because the monetary rewards derived therefrom accrue directly to the innovator. Pure capitalism therefore presupposes the extensive use and rapid development of complex capital goods: tools, machinery, large-scale factories, and storage, transportation, and marketing facilities.

Why are the existence of an advanced technology and the extensive use of capital goods important? Because the most direct method of producing a product is usually the least efficient.[2] Even Robinson Crusoe avoided the inefficiencies of direct production in favor of "roundabout production." It would be ridiculous for a farmer—even a backyard farmer—to go at production with his bare hands. Obviously, it pays huge dividends in terms of a more efficient and, therefore, a more abundant output to fashion tools of production, that is, capital equipment, to aid in the productive process. The best way of getting water out of a well is not to dive in after it!

But there is a catch involved. As we recall our discussion of the production possibilities curve and the basic nature of the economizing problem, it is evident that, with full employment and full production, resources must be diverted from the production of consumer goods in order to be

used in the production of capital goods. We must currently tighten our belts as consumers to free resources for the production of capital goods which will increase productive efficiency and permit us to have a greater output of consumer goods at some future date. The Russian citizenry, for example, has paid for an accelerated rate of industrialization in terms of a standard of living below that which might have otherwise prevailed.

Specialization

The extent to which society relies upon specialization is astounding. The vast majority of consumers produce virtually none of the goods and services they consume and, conversely, consume little or nothing of what they produce. The hammer-shop laborer who spends his life stamping out parts for jet engines may never "consume" an airplane trip. The assembly-line worker who devotes eight hours a day to the installation of windows in Chevrolets may not own a car, or if he does, it may be a Ford. Few households seriously consider any extensive production of their own food, shelter, and clothing. Many a farmer sells his milk to the local creamery and then buys oleomargarine at the Podunk general store. Society learned long ago that self-sufficiency breeds inefficiency. The Jack-of-all-trades may be a very colorful individual, but he is certainly lacking in efficiency.

In what specific ways might human specialization—the division of labor—enhance productive efficiency? First, specialization permits individuals to take advantage of existing differences in their abilities and skills. If caveman A is strong, swift afoot, and accurate with a spear, and caveman B is weak and slow, but patient, this distribution of talents can be most efficiently utilized by making A a hunter and B a fisherman. Second, even if the abilities of A and B are identical, specialization may prove to be advantageous. Why? Because by devoting all his time to a single task, the

---

[2] Remember that consumer goods satisfy wants directly, while capital goods do so indirectly through the more efficient production of consumer goods.

doer is more likely to develop the appropriate skills and to discover improved techniques than when apportioning his time between a number of diverse tasks. One learns to be a good hunter by hunting! Finally, specialization—devoting all one's time to, say, a single task—obviously avoids the loss of time which is entailed in shifting from one job to another. For all these reasons the division of labor results in greater productive efficiency in the use of human resources.

Specialization also is desirable on a regional basis. Oranges could be grown in Nebraska, but because of the unsuitability of the land, rainfall, and temperature, the costs involved would be exceedingly high. Florida could probably achieve some success in the production of wheat, but, for similar reasons, such production would be found to be a relatively costly business. As a result, Nebraskans produce those products—wheat in particular—for which their resources are best adapted, and Floridians do the same, producing oranges and other citrus fruits. In so doing, both produce surpluses of their specialties. Then, very sensibly, Nebraskans and Floridians swap some of their surpluses. Specialization permits each area to put its best foot forward, that is, to turn out those goods which its resources can most efficiently produce. In this way both Nebraska and Florida can enjoy a larger amount of both wheat and oranges than would otherwise be the case. In short, human and geographical specialization are both essential in achieving efficiency in the use of resources.

These simple illustrations make very plausible the contention that specialization is economically desirable because it results in more efficient production. Indeed, the point is almost self-explanatory. But, because the concept of specialization is so vital to an understanding of the production and exchange processes of modern economies, let us tackle a couple of more exacting illustrations of the gains which accrue from specialization. Our examples will be simplified to make the principles involved as clear as possible.

Absolute advantage. Suppose there are two equally skilled farmers, Anderson and Brooks. They each own, say, 6-acre farms, and each devotes the same total amount of time to farming. There is just one difference: Their farmland is not of equal quality and fertility. We shall assume, to start with, that if Anderson devoted one-third of his time and land to the production of wheat and two-thirds to corn, he could produce 30 bushels of wheat and 10 bushels of corn. If Brooks devoted one-third of his time and land to the production of wheat and two-thirds to corn, his output would be 20 bushels of each product. We summarize this hypothetical data in Table 3–1, noting in parentheses the fraction of land and total working time each farmer devotes to the production of each crop.

TABLE 3–1. NONSPECIALIZED PRODUCTION OF WHEAT AND CORN (hypothetical data)

	Wheat, bushels	Corn, bushels
Anderson	30 ($\frac{1}{3}$)	10 ($\frac{2}{3}$)
Brooks	20 ($\frac{1}{3}$)	20 ($\frac{2}{3}$)
Total	50	30

Anderson obviously has an *absolute advantage* in producing wheat; by devoting one-third of his time and land to wheat, Anderson can produce a larger absolute amount of wheat—30 as compared with 20 bushels—than Brooks can by using the same amount of time and land. But Brooks has an absolute advantage when it comes to producing corn. Since the two farmers are equally skilled and devote the same amounts of time and land to the production of each good, the different absolute outputs tell us that Anderson's land is better suited to the production of wheat than Brooks's and, conversely, Brooks's land is better suited to corn than is Anderson's.

Should the farmers specialize? Yes, they most certainly should, because both stand to benefit. Anderson should devote full time and all his land to wheat, the product which his land produces most efficiently. Similarly, Brooks should use all his time and land to produce corn. If they do this, the data in Table 3–1 change to the data given in Table 3–2. The 1s in parentheses show that Anderson devotes full time and all his land to wheat and that Brooks does the same with respect to corn.

TABLE 3–2. SPECIALIZED PRODUCTION OF WHEAT AND CORN ACCORDING TO ABSOLUTE ADVANTAGE (hypothetical data)

	Wheat, bushels	Corn, bushels
Anderson	90 (1)	0
Brooks	0	30 (1)
Total	90	30

Comparing the totals of Tables 3–1 and 3–2, it is immediately evident that the two farmers taken together have the same total amount of corn and 40 bushels more wheat than they realized when *not* specializing. Supposing Brooks exchanges 10 bushels of corn for 40 bushels of Anderson's wheat; Anderson will then have 50 bushels of wheat and 10 bushels of corn. Brooks will have 40 bushels of wheat and 20 of corn. This is shown in Table 3–3.

TABLE 3–3. THE DISTRIBUTION OF WHEAT AND CORN AFTER EXCHANGE (hypothetical data)

	Wheat, bushels	Corn, bushels
Anderson	50	10
Brooks	40	20
Total	90	30

Comparing Tables 3–3 and 3–1, we note that both Brooks and Anderson have the same amount of corn they could have pro-

duced by not specializing and 20 bushels more of wheat apiece. Clearly, both farmers have benefited by specializing according to absolute advantage and by trading some of their specialties. *Specialization is apparently an excellent method for allocating scarce resources so as to get the greatest total output from them.* This is obvious from our simple example: The same total inputs, or resources, result in a greater total output when used under conditions of specialization.

Comparative advantage. Strange as it may first seem, specialized production also results in the more efficient employment of resources and therefore in a greater output when one farmer, say Anderson, has an absolute advantage in the production of both corn and wheat. Table 3–4 illustrates such a situation. In this example, we assume that Anderson's land is better suited to the production of both crops than is Brooks's. Hence, as both farmers devote one-third of their time and land to wheat and two-thirds to corn, Anderson will outproduce Brooks in both cases. Yet Anderson's absolute advantage in corn exceeds that in wheat. Anderson can outproduce Brooks in corn 2 to 1, but only 3 to 2 when it comes to wheat.

TABLE 3–4. NONSPECIALIZED PRODUCTION OF WHEAT AND CORN (hypothetical data)

	Wheat, bushels	Corn, bushels
Anderson	30 ($\frac{1}{3}$)	20 ($\frac{2}{3}$)
Brooks	20 ($\frac{1}{3}$)	10 ($\frac{2}{3}$)
Total	50	30

Economists say that an individual has a *relative*, or *comparative*, *advantage* in that product in which (1) his absolute advantage is greater (in the case of Anderson) or (2) his absolute *dis*advantage is less (in the case of Brooks). Anderson has an absolute advantage in both products, but that absolute advantage is relatively, or comparatively, greater in corn than in wheat. Hence, Anderson may be said to have a comparative advantage in corn. Brooks, on the other hand, is at an absolute disadvantage in the production of both goods; however, that absolute disadvantage is relatively less in wheat than in corn. Hence, Brooks is said to have a comparative advantage—though absolute disadvantage!—in wheat.

Now common sense does not tell us that Anderson and Brooks will benefit from specialization; this conclusion must await the completion of our illustration. But common sense does suggest that if specialization is to occur, it should be based upon comparative advantage. That is, Anderson should devote full time and all his land to corn, where he has the greater absolute advantage, and Brooks to wheat, where he faces the lesser absolute disadvantage. Specialization in this way changes the data of Table 3–4 in the manner indicated in Table 3–5.

TABLE 3–5. SPECIALIZED PRODUCTION OF WHEAT AND CORN ACCORDING TO COMPARATIVE ADVANTAGE
(hypothetical data)

	Wheat, bushels	Corn, bushels
Anderson	0	30 (1)
Brooks	60 (1)	0
Total	60	30

By comparing Tables 3–5 and 3–4, we discover that specialization according to *comparative advantage* results in the same total output of corn and a greater output of wheat. In this case, the gain resulting from specialization is 10 bushels of wheat. Specialization according to comparative advantage has obviously improved the allocation of resources; more output has resulted from the same volume of resource inputs.

Terms of trade. Using our example of comparative advantage, let us now look at the

trade which is likely to result between the two farmers. What will be the *terms of trade* between Anderson and Brooks; that is, at what rate will they exchange corn and wheat? We can safely say that Anderson will accept nothing *less than* 30 bushels of wheat for giving up 10 bushels of his corn. Why? Because, as a comparison of Tables 3–4 and 3–5 indicates, by not specializing in wheat but by devoting one-third of his time to it, Anderson could produce 30 bushels of wheat himself. And this would cut his corn production by only 10 bushels. Brooks, on the other hand, will certainly not give *more than* 40 bushels of wheat for 10 bushels of corn. How do we know? Because Table 3–4 tells us that Brooks, by devoting two-thirds of his time to corn production, could produce by himself 10 bushels of corn at a sacrifice of 40 units of wheat. In brief, the terms of trade must be 1 bushel of corn equals 3 bushels or more of wheat, or Anderson will not trade; the terms of trade must be 1 bushel of corn equals 4 bushels or less of wheat, or Brooks will not trade. Having established the upper and lower limits of the terms of trade, let us suppose that the two agrarians, being equally shrewd bargainers, settle on a rate of 1 bushel of corn equals 3½ bushels of wheat. Now, if Brooks swaps 35 bushels of his wheat for 10 bushels of Anderson's corn, Brooks and Anderson will have on hand the amounts of the two products shown in Table 3–6.

TABLE 3–6. THE DISTRIBUTION OF WHEAT AND CORN AFTER EXCHANGE
(hypothetical data)

	Wheat, bushels	Corn, bushels
Anderson	35	20
Brooks	25	10
Total	60	30

Comparison with Table 3–4 clearly shows that specialization and trade based upon comparative advantage have netted Anderson and Brooks each an extra 5 bushels of wheat and the same amounts of corn they would have realized by not specializing. The total gain from specializing is obviously 10 bushels of wheat.

It should be emphasized that specialization and an advanced technology go hand in hand. Specialization and technological advance reinforce one another. Anderson and Brooks are more likely to discover better techniques for producing corn and wheat when specializing than they would if each divided his energies between the two products. Specialization encourages technological advance, and technological advance in turn stimulates greater specialization.

One final word: Serious reflection on this matter of geographical and human specialization reveals certain drawbacks. For example, the monotony and drudgery of specialized work are well known. Brooks, for example, might be reluctant to produce only wheat, because this is much more tedious than dividing his efforts between wheat and corn. And imagine the boredom of our previously mentioned assembly-line worker who is still putting windows in Chevrolets. Second, specialization and mutual interdependence vary directly with one another. The less each of us produces for himself, the more we are dependent upon the output of others. The less wheat produced in Florida, the greater is that state's dependence upon Nebraska wheat. Specialization obviously makes Brooks dependent upon Anderson for corn and Anderson dependent upon Brooks for wheat. For the economy as a whole, it is not surprising to discover what profoundly serious consequences may stem from a transportation strike or, on a more localized basis, from the breakdown of an assembly line. A third problem centers upon the exchanging of the surpluses which specialization entails. An examination of this problem leads us into a discussion of the use of money in the economy.

Use of Money

Virtually all economies, advanced or primitive, are money-using. Money performs a variety of functions (see Chapter 16), but first and foremost it is a medium of exchange.

In our Anderson-Brooks example it was necessary for Brooks to trade 35 bushels of wheat for 10 bushels of Anderson's corn if both farmers were to share in the fruits of specialization. If trade were prohibited for some reason, the benefits of specializing according to comparative advantage might be lost to society. Why? Because consumers want a wide variety of products and, in the absence of trade, would tend to devote their human and material resources to many diverse types of production. If exchange could not occur or were very inconvenient to transact, Anderson and Brooks would be forced to be more self-sufficient, and the advantages of specialization would not be realized. *In short, a convenient means of exchanging goods is a prerequisite of specialization.*

Now exchange can, and sometimes does, occur on the basis of bartering, that is, swapping goods for goods. But bartering as a means of exchange can pose serious problems for the economy. Specifically, exchange by barter requires a *coincidence of wants* between the two transactors. In our example, we assumed that Brooks had excess wheat to trade and that he wanted to obtain corn. And we assumed Anderson had excess corn to swap and that he wanted to acquire wheat. So exchange occurred. But if this coincidence of wants did not exist, trade would be stymied. Let us pose such a problem.

Suppose Brooks does not want any of Anderson's corn but is interested in buying vegetables from Johnson, a third farmer. Ironically enough, Johnson wants Anderson's corn but not Brooks's wheat. And, to complicate matters, we shall say that Anderson wants some of Brooks's wheat but none of Johnson's vegetables. The situation is summarized in the three squares in Figure 3–1.

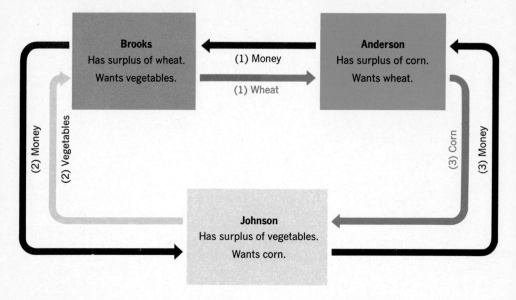

FIGURE 3–1. MONEY FACILITATES TRADE WHERE WANTS DO NOT COINCIDE.
By the use of money as a medium of exchange, trade can be accomplished, as
indicated by the arrows, despite a noncoincidence of wants. By facilitating exchange,
the use of money permits an economy to realize the efficiencies of specialization.

In no case do we find a coincidence of wants. Trade by barter would be difficult. To overcome such a stalemate, modern economies use *money,* which is simply a convenient social invention for facilitating the exchange of goods and services. Historically, cattle, cigarettes, shells, stones, pieces of metal, and many other diverse commodities have been used, with varying degrees of success, as a medium for facilitating exchange. But to be money, an item needs to pass only one test: *It must be generally acceptable by buyers and sellers in exchange.* Money is socially defined; whatever society accepts as a medium of exchange is money. Most modern economies, for reasons made clear in Chapter 16, find it convenient to use pieces of paper as money. We shall assume that this is the case with the Brooks-Anderson-Johnson economy; they use pieces of paper which they call "dollars" as money. Can the use of paper dollars as a medium of exchange overcome the stalemate we have posed?

Obviously it can, with trade occurring in this way:

1. Anderson can exchange money for some of Brooks's wheat.

2. Brooks can take the money realized from the sale of wheat and exchange it for some of Johnson's vegetables.

3. Johnson can then exchange the money received from his sale of vegetables for some of Anderson's surplus corn.

These transactions are shown by the arrows in Figure 3–1.

The willingness to accept paper money (or any other kind of money for that matter) as a medium of exchange has permitted a three-way trade which allows each farmer to specialize in one product and obtain the other product(s) he desires, despite a noncoincidence of wants. Barter, resting as it does upon a coincidence of wants, would have impeded this exchange and in so doing would have induced the three farmers to become nonspecialists. Of course, the efficiencies of specialization would then have been lost to the Brooks-Anderson-Johnson economy. Strange as it may first seem, two exchanges—surplus product for money and then money for a wanted product—are simpler than the product-for-product exchange which bartering entails! Indeed, in this example, product-for-product exchange would not be likely to occur at all.

A final example: Imagine a Detroit laborer producing crankshafts for Oldsmobiles. At the end of the week, instead of receiving a brightly colored piece of paper endorsed by the company comptroller, or a few pieces of paper neatly engraved in green and black, the laborer receives from the company paymaster four Oldsmobile crankshafts. Inconvenient as this is, and with no desire to hoard crankshafts, the laborer ventures into the Detroit business district, intent upon spending his hard-earned income on a basket of food, a suit of clothes, a baseball game, a haircut, and, in anticipation of a late return, a box of candy to pacify his wife. Needless to say, he is faced with some inconvenient and time-consuming trading, and he might not be able to negotiate any exchanges at all. Finding a clothing merchant who has a suit which meets his approval and who happens to be in the market for an Oldsmobile crankshaft is a formidable task. And, even if he locates a barber in need of a crankshaft, how is the barber going to make change for the laborer's haircut? Examples such as this make it evident that money is one of the great social inventions of man!

This, then, is the ideology of pure capitalism, the institutions peculiar to it, and the institutions it shares in common with alternative economic systems.

CIRCULAR FLOW OF INCOME

Our discussion has pointed out the role of markets and prices as a mechanism for the tabulation and communication of the decisions of individual economic units. In pure capitalism, the free decisions of businesses and households concerning what the econ-

omy should produce, how production should be organized, and how total output should be distributed are thus rendered effective through a system of markets and prices.

The next logical step in this discussion is to examine in some detail the nature of markets and prices. The remainder of this chapter is devoted to a general overview of the market system of pure capitalism for the purpose of pinpointing the two basic types of markets of pure capitalism and noting the character of the transactions which occur therein. In Chapter 4 a rather detailed examination of how specific prices are actually determined in pure capitalism is presented. Then Chapter 5 provides a more rigorous discussion of how pure capitalism goes about answering the Five Fundamental Questions through the workings of the price system.

Circular Flow Models

How does pure capitalism work? Several answers can be offered, depending upon the amount of detail one desires.

Real flows. In a barter economy households, which directly or indirectly (through their ownership of business corporations) own all economic resources, supply these resources to businesses as is shown in the upper loop of Figure 3–2. (Let us for the moment think of businesses simply as organizational charts, that is, institutions on paper apart from the capital, raw materials, labor, and entrepreneurial ability which breathe life into them and make them "going concerns.") Businesses, of course, will want resources, because these are the means by which goods and services are produced. In return for making their resources available for use by businesses, households will receive payments in kind; that is, they will be paid in terms of the goods and services they have helped produce. This flow of payments is shown in the lower loop of Figure 3–2. Of course, households, being paid in terms of crankshafts, shoes, doughnuts,

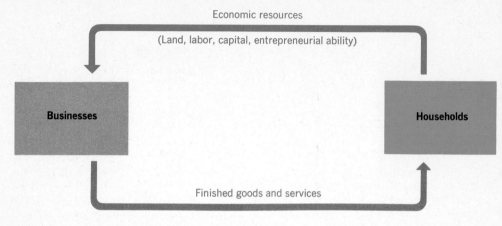

FIGURE 3–2. THE OPERATION OF A BARTER ECONOMY.
In a nonmonetary, or barter, economy households supply their economic resources
(upper loop) and receive finished goods and services (lower loop) in return.

and so forth, will face some difficult exchange problems in swapping goods for goods with one another in seeking to satisfy their various wants. In any event this simple picture of the economy does accurately locate the main *real* flows, that is, the flow of resources and the flow of goods and services which occur in a capitalistic economy.

Money flows. To circumvent problems of inconvenience in bartering, virtually all economies are money-using. How does our circular flow picture change as we progress from a barter to a monetary economy? The fact that money is a medium of exchange suggests that money is used as a go-between to facilitate the exchanges of resources and products which occur between businesses and households. In Figure 3–3, the upper loop shows a counterclockwise flow of resources accompanied by a clockwise flow of money payments of income in the form of wages, rent, interest, and profits. These income payments are made in the acquisition of resources and are looked upon as costs to the business firms making them. Note, incidentally, that in economics we treat profits—the expense involved in retaining the firm's supply of entrepreneurial ability—as a cost of production.

But money income received from the sale of resources does not, as such, have real value. Consumers cannot eat or wear coins and paper money. Households will want to obtain a share of the fruits of production by spending their money incomes. Indeed, money income received by a household for the resources it supplies constitutes dollar claims against the total output it helped produce. Households exercise these claims by spending their money incomes—all their incomes, let us assume—on the goods and services of their choice. The clockwise flow of consumption expenditures and the counterclockwise flow of goods and services shown in the lower loop of Figure 3–3 reflect the exchange of income for products. From the viewpoint of businesses, the flow of consumption expenditures coming from households is receipts or revenue.

In other words, in a monetary economy, households, as resource owners, sell their resources to businesses and, as consumers, spend the money income received therefrom in buying goods and services. Businesses must buy resources in order to produce goods and services; their finished products are then sold to households in exchange for consumption expenditures or, as businesses view it, receipts. The net result is a counterclockwise real flow of economic resources and finished goods and services and a clockwise money flow of income and consumption expenditures. These flows are simultaneous and repetitive.

Real flows, money flows, and markets. Figure 3–4 adds a final step to our circular flow picture. The cost-income and resource flows of the upper loop and the goods-expenditure flows of the lower loop of Figure 3–3 pass through markets where money is exchanged for resources and for goods and services. In the upper loop of Figure 3–4, income payments and resources flow through resource markets. Here households supply resources at certain existing market prices and receive money income in return from businesses that buy or demand these resources. Obviously, the amount of money income flowing through the resource markets and into the hands of households will depend upon the quantities of the various resources supplied by households and the prices at which they are sold. Similarly, in the lower loop, consumer expenditures and

goods and services pass through product markets. The size of these consumption flows will depend upon the quantities of the various goods and services purchased and the prices at which they sell. In other words, there are two basic types of markets in a capitalistic economy—resource markets and product markets. Businesses are on the buying or *demand* side of the resource markets, and households, as resource owners and suppliers, are on the selling or *supply* side. In the product market, these positions are reversed; households, as consumers, are on the buying or demand side, and businesses are on the selling or supply side. Each group of economic units both buys and sells.

Note that the specter of scarcity haunts these transactions. Because households have only limited amounts of resources to supply to businesses, the money incomes of consumers will be limited. This means that each consumer's income will go only so far. A limited number of dollars obviously will

FIGURE 3–3. THE OPERATION OF A MONETARY ECONOMY.
In a money-using economy households exchange their economic resources
for money income (upper loop), which can then be spent
on finished goods and services (lower loop).

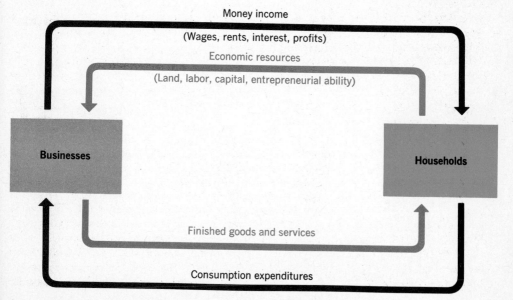

Money income

(Wages, rents, interest, profits)

Economic resources

(Land, labor, capital, entrepreneurial ability)

Businesses

Households

Finished goods and services

Consumption expenditures

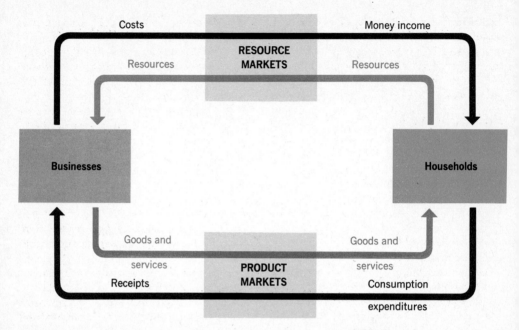

FIGURE 3–4. RESOURCE AND PRODUCT MARKETS IN A MONETARY ECONOMY.
The prices paid for the use of land, labor, capital, and entrepreneurial ability
are determined in the resource market shown in the upper loop. Businesses are on
the demand side and households on the supply side of this market. The prices
of finished goods and services are determined in the product market located in the
lower loop. Households are on the demand side and businesses on the supply
side of this market.

not permit the purchase of all the goods
and services which the consumer might like
to buy. The consumer is handicapped by
limited money income; he necessarily operates under a *budget restraint*. Similarly, because resources are scarce, the output of
finished goods and services is also necessarily limited. Scarcity permeates our entire
discussion.

Limitations

There are certain noteworthy shortcomings
and omissions inherent in the circular flow
overview of the workings of pure capitalism:
1. This simple model ignores the transactions which occur *within* the business and
household sectors of the economy. For example, the sales of processed materials to
manufacturers, parts to fabricators, and fin-

ished products to wholesalers and then to
retailers are all ignored. This is not a crucial
defect, however. At this stage of our discussion, these intrabusiness and intrahousehold
transactions are not vital to our understanding of how pure capitalism operates.
2. We must acknowledge that the circular flow model does not reflect the myriad
of facts and details about specific households, specific businesses, and specific resource and product markets. Indeed, the
main virtue of the circular flow model is
that it lays bare the fundamental operations
of pure capitalism without ensnaring the
viewer in a maze of details. We seek here
a view of the whole forest; the examination
of specific trees will come later.
3. The circular flow model makes no
mention of the economic role of government. The reason? The institutions of pure

capitalism would allegedly give rise to a self-contained, self-regulating economy in which government's role would be minor. In Chapter 6 the circular flow will be modified to reflect the economic functions of government in the mixed capitalism which now characterizes the American economy.

4. This model assumes that households spend exactly all their money income and that, therefore, the flows of income and expenditure are constant in volume. In real terms this means that the levels of output and employment are constant. Part Two of this book is concerned with the causes and effects of fluctuations in income and output flows.

5. Our discussion of the circular flow assumes the existence of certain resource and product prices, but it does not explain how resource and product prices are actually determined. This is the task to which we turn in the ensuing chapter: How are resource and product prices determined in a purely capitalistic economy?

SUMMARY

1. The capitalistic system is characterized by the private ownership of resources and the freedom of individuals to engage in the economic activities of their choice as a means for advancing their material well-being. Self-interest is the driving force of such an economy and competition functions as a regulatory or control mechanism. Capitalistic production is not organized in terms of a government plan but rather features the price system as a means of organizing and making effective the myriad of individual decisions which determine what is produced, the methods of production, and the sharing of output. Indeed, government plays a minor and relatively passive role.

2. Specialization according to the principle of comparative advantage and an advanced technology based on the extensive use of capital goods are features common to all modern economies. Functioning as a medium of exchange, money circumvents the problems entailed in bartering and thereby permits greater specialization.

3. An overview of the operation of the capitalistic system can be gained through the circular flow of income. This simplified model locates the product and resource markets and presents the major income-expenditure flows and resource-output flows which constitute the lifeblood of the capitalistic economy.

QUESTIONS AND STUDY SUGGESTIONS

1. "Capitalism may be characterized as an automatic self-regulating system motivated by the self-interest of individuals and regulated by competition."[3] Explain and evaluate.

2. Explain how the price system is a means of communicating and implementing decisions concerning the allocation of the economy's resources.

3. What advantages result from "roundabout" production? What problem is involved in increasing a full-employment, full-production economy's stock of capital goods? Illustrate this problem in terms of the production possibilities curve. Does an economy with unemployed resources face the same problem?

4. What are the advantages of specialization in the use of human and material resources? Be specific.

5. Dr. Johnson is an outstanding administrator. He is also an excellent teacher, better than anyone else on the staff. Yet the university employs

[3] Howard R. Bowen, *Toward Social Economy* (New York: Holt, Rinehart and Winston, Inc., 1948), p. 249.

Johnson as dean of his college rather than as a teacher. Explain in terms of the principle of comparative advantage how the university's choice might entail the most efficient use of its labor resources.

6. The following table shows the amounts of apples and oranges which Adams and Bingham, two equally skilled agrarians, can produce on their farms when each devotes one-third of his time and land to producing apples, and two-thirds to producing oranges.

	Apples, bushels	Oranges, bushels
Adams	40 ($\frac{1}{3}$)	30 ($\frac{2}{3}$)
Bingham	30 ($\frac{1}{3}$)	15 ($\frac{2}{3}$)
Total	70	45

a. According to the principle of comparative advantage, should these two farmers specialize? If so, what product should each produce?

b. What will be the total production of apples and oranges when the two farmers are specializing? What is the resulting gain in output?

c. What will be the limits of the terms of trade? At what rate would you estimate that Adams and Bingham would trade their surplus products?

d. Can you conclude from this illustration that specialization according to comparative advantage results in the more efficient use of the economy's resources? Explain.

7. What problems does barter entail? Be precise. Indicate the economic significance of money as a medium of exchange; explain and illustrate.

8. "Money is the only commodity that is good for nothing but to be gotten rid of. It will not feed you, clothe you, shelter you, or amuse you unless you spend or invest it. It imparts value only in parting."[4] Explain this statement.

9. Describe the operation of pure capitalism as portrayed by the circular flow of income. Emphasize the fact of scarcity throughout your discussion.

SELECTED REFERENCES

Bowen, Howard R.: *Toward Social Economy* (New York: Holt, Rinehart and Winston, Inc., 1948), chaps. 1–5.

Ebenstein, William: *Today's Isms,* 4th ed. (Englewood Cliffs, N.J.: Prentice-Hall, Inc., 1964), chap. 3.

Heilbroner, Robert L.: *The Making of Economic Society* (Englewood Cliffs, N.J.: Prentice-Hall, Inc., 1962), chaps. 2–4.

Loucks, William N.: *Comparative Economic Systems,* 7th ed. (New York: Harper & Row, Publishers, Incorporated, 1965), chap. 2.

Monsen, R. Joseph, Jr.: *Modern American Capitalism: Ideologies and Issues* (Boston: Houghton Mifflin Company, 1963).

[4] Federal Reserve Bank of Philadelphia, "Creeping Inflation," *Business Review,* August, 1957, p. 3.

CHAPTER 4

THE MECHANICS
OF INDIVIDUAL PRICES:
DEMAND AND SUPPLY

The much-simplified analysis of the operation of pure capitalism presented at the conclusion of Chapter 3 assumed that resources and goods and services sell for certain given prices. This permitted us to sidestep the fundamental question to which we now turn: How are prices "set," or determined, in pure capitalism? The answer is easy to state but a bit more difficult to understand. In short, prices are determined in the product market by the interaction of the supply decisions of competing businesses and the demand decisions of competing households. In the resource market, the demand decisions of competing businesses coupled with the supply decisions of competing households determine prices. Our immediate objective is to verify these answers. In doing so we shall concentrate on the product market, then shift our attention later in the chapter to the resource market. The immediate task is to explain the mechanics of prices. How does the interaction of demand and supply decisions set product and resource prices?

DEMAND

The term *demand* has a very definite meaning to the economist. Demand is defined as a schedule which shows the various amounts of a product which consumers are willing and able to purchase at each specific price in a set of possible prices during some specified period of time.[1] Demand simply portrays a series of alternative possibilities which can be set down in tabular form. As our definition of demand indicates, we usually view demand from the vantage point of price; that is, we read demand as showing the amounts consumers will buy at various possible prices. It is equally correct and sometimes more meaningful to view demand from the reference point of quantity. That is, instead of asking what quantities can be sold at various prices, we can ask what prices can be got from consumers for various quantities of a good. Table 4–1 is a hypothetical demand schedule for a single consumer who is purchasing bushels of corn.

This tabular portrayal of demand reflects the relationship between the price of corn and the quantity that our mythical consumer would be willing and able to purchase at each of these prices. Note that we say willing and *able,* because willingness alone is not effective in the market. I may be willing to buy a Cadillac, but if this willingness is not backed by the ability to buy, that is, by the necessary dollars, it will not be effective and, therefore, not reflected in the market. In Table 4–1, if the price of corn in the market happened to be $5 per

[1] In adjusting this definition to the resource market, simply substitute the word "resource" for "product" and "business" for "consumer."

TABLE 4–1. AN INDIVIDUAL BUYER'S DEMAND FOR CORN (hypothetical data)

Price per bushel	Quantity demanded per week
$5	10
4	20
3	35
2	55
1	80

bushel, our consumer would be willing and able to buy 10 bushels per week; if it were $4, 20 bushels per week; and so forth.

The demand schedule in and of itself does not tell us which of the five possible prices will actually exist in the corn market. As we have already said, this depends on demand *and* supply. Demand, then, is simply a tabular statement of a buyer's plans, or intentions, with respect to the purchase of a product.

Note that to be meaningful the quantities demanded at each price must relate to some specific time period—a day, a week, a month, and so forth. To say that "a consumer will buy 10 bushels of corn at $5 per bushel" is vague and meaningless. To say that "a consumer will buy 10 bushels of corn *per week* at $5 per bushel" is clear and very meaningful.

Law of Demand

A fundamental characteristic of demand is this: As price falls, the corresponding quantity demanded rises, or, alternatively, as price increases, the corresponding quantity demanded falls. In short, there is an *inverse* relationship between price and quantity demanded. Economists have labeled this inverse relationship the *law of demand*. Upon what foundation does this law rest? There are many levels on which the case can be argued, but it is sufficient for our purposes to rest the case on common sense and

simple observation.[2] People ordinarily *do* buy more of a given product at a low price than they do at a high price. To consumers price is an obstacle which deters them from buying. The higher this obstacle, the less of a product they will buy; the lower the price obstacle, the more they will buy. In other words, a high price discourages consumers from buying, and a low price encourages them to buy. The simple fact that businessmen have sales is concrete evidence of their belief in the law of demand. Bargain, or sales, days are based on the law of demand.

The law of demand can also be explained in terms of the substitutability of products for one another. There are usually (but not always) a number of reasonably good substitutes for any particular product. Hence, an increase in the price of this product will make consumers substitute other products for it. A decline in the price of the given product will induce consumers to substitute it for other products. To be more specific, if the price of butter goes up, consumers substitute oleomargarine and therefore purchase less butter at the higher price. If the price of butter declines, consumers substitute butter for oleomargarine, thereby purchasing more butter at the lower price.

The Demand Curve

This inverse relationship between product price and quantity demanded can be presented on a simple two-dimensional graph measuring quantity demanded on the horizontal axis and price on the vertical axis.[3] From Chapter 1, we recall that the process involved is simply that of locating on the

---

[2] Common sense and simple observation will give way to more sophisticated explanations in Chapter 24.

[3] Putting price on the vertical axis and quantity demanded on the horizontal axis is a matter of convention; we do it for the same reason the mathematician makes X the unknown quantity in his equations.

graph those five price-quantity possibilities shown in Table 4–1. We do this by drawing perpendiculars from the appropriate points on the two axes. Thus in plotting the "$5-price–10-quantity-demanded" possibility, we must draw a perpendicular from the horizontal (quantity) axis at 10 to meet a perpendicular drawn from the vertical (price) axis at $5. If this is done for all five possibilities, the result is a series of points as shown in Figure 4–1. Each of these points represents a specific price and the corresponding quantity which the consumer will choose to purchase at that price. Now, assuming the same inverse relationship between price and quantity demanded at all points between the ones graphed, we can

generalize on the inverse relationship between price and quantity demanded by drawing a curve to represent *all* price–quantity-demanded possibilities within the limits shown on the graph. The resulting curve is called a *demand curve* and is labeled *DD* in Figure 4–1. It slopes downward and to the right because the relationship it portrays between price and quantity demanded is inverse. The law of demand—people buy more at a low price than they do at a high price—is reflected in the downward slope of the demand curve.

What is the advantage of graphing our demand schedule? After all, Table 4–1 and Figure 4–1 contain exactly the same data and reflect the same relationship between

FIGURE 4–1. AN INDIVIDUAL BUYER'S DEMAND CURVE FOR CORN.
An individual's demand schedule graphs as a downsloping curve such as *DD*, because price and quantity demanded are inversely related. Specifically, the law of demand generalizes that consumers will buy more of a product as its price declines.

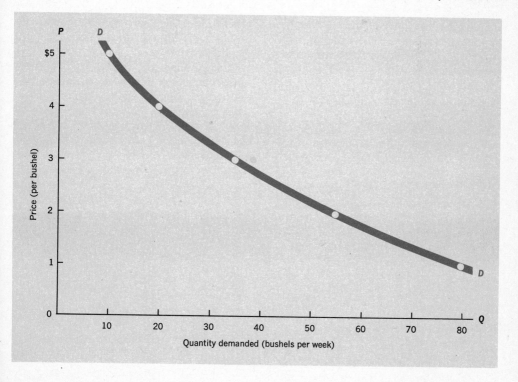

TABLE 4–2. MARKET DEMAND FOR CORN, THREE BUYERS (hypothetical data)

Price per bushel	Quantity demanded, first buyer		Quantity demanded, second buyer		Quantity demanded, third buyer		Total quantity demanded per week
$5	10	+	12	+	8	=	30
4	20	+	23	+	17	=	60
3	35	+	39	+	26	=	100
2	55	+	60	+	39	=	154
1	80	+	87	+	54	=	221

price and quantity demanded. The advantage of graphing is that it permits us to represent clearly a given relationship—in this case the law of demand—in a much simpler way than we could if we were forced to rely upon verbal and tabular presentation. A single curve on a graph, if understood, is simpler to state *and to manipulate* than tables and lengthy verbal presentations would be. Graphs are invaluable tools in economic analysis, as has been previously indicated. They permit simple expression and handling of ofttimes complex relationships.

Individual and Market Demand

Until now we have been dealing in terms of just one consumer. The assumption of competition makes us consider a situation in which a large number of buyers are in the market. The transition from an *individual* to a *market* demand schedule can be accomplished by the simple process of summing the quantities demanded by each consumer at the various possible prices. If there were just three buyers in the market, as is shown in Table 4–2, it would be a simple chore to determine the total quantities demanded at each price. Figure 4–2 shows the same summing procedure graphically, using only the $3 price to illustrate the adding-up process.

Competition, of course, entails many more than three buyers of a product. So—to avoid a lengthy addition process—let us suppose there are 200 buyers of corn in the market, each of whom chooses to buy the same amount at each of the various prices as our original consumer does. Thus, we can

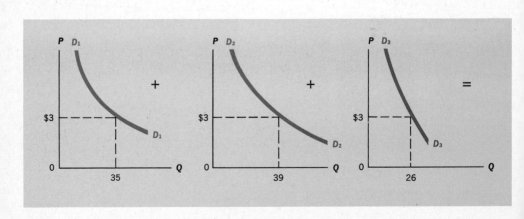

TABLE 4–3. MARKET DEMAND FOR CORN, 200 BUYERS (hypothetical data)

(1) Price per bushel	(2) Quantity demanded per week, single buyer		(3) Number of buyers in the market		(4) Total quantity demanded per week
$5	10	×	200	=	2,000
4	20	×	200	=	4,000
3	35	×	200	=	7,000
2	55	×	200	=	11,000
1	80	×	200	=	16,000

determine market demand by multiplying the quantity-demanded data of Table 4–1 by 200, as in Table 4–3.

Curve D_1 in Figure 4–3 indicates this market demand curve for the 200 buyers.

Determinants of Demand

What causes the demand schedule, for example, D_1 in Figure 4–3, to be in the exact position indicated? Why isn't the total demand curve for corn located at some position to the left or right of D_1? The answer is that in selecting any specific demand curve from the many demand curves that might exist, we are assuming that those factors which determine or "locate" consumer demand are of a given magnitude. In other words, the selection of a fixed demand schedule involves the assumption that the determinants of consumer demand are fixed or constant.

What are the determinants of market demand? The basic ones are: (1) the tastes or preferences of consumers, (2) the number of consumers in the market, (3) the money incomes of consumers, (4) the prices of related goods, and (5) consumer expectations with respect to future prices and incomes. The presentation of a given demand schedule, such as columns 1 and 4 of Table 4–3, or a single, stationary demand curve, such as D_1 in Figure 4–3, is based on the supposition that these determinants are fixed or constant.

Changes in Demand

What happens if one or more of the determinants of demand should change? The

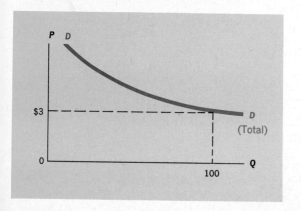

FIGURE 4–2. THE MARKET DEMAND CURVE IS THE SUM OF THE INDIVIDUAL DEMAND CURVES. Graphically the market demand curve (*D* total) is found by summing horizontally the individual demand curves (*D_1*, *D_2*, and *D_3*) of all consumers in the market.

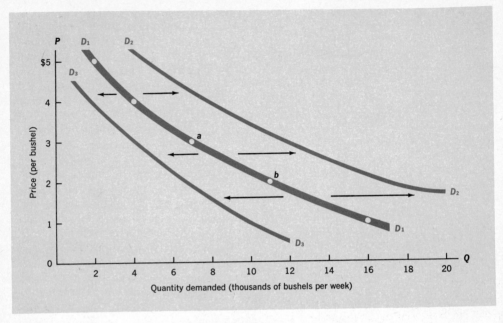

FIGURE 4–3. CHANGES IN THE DEMAND FOR CORN.
A change in one or more of the determinants of demand—consumer tastes, the
number of buyers in the market, money incomes, the prices of other goods, or
consumer expectations—will cause a change in demand. An increase in demand
shifts the demand curve to the right, as from D_1D_1 to D_2D_2. A decrease in demand
is shown graphically as a movement of the demand curve to the left, as from D_1D_1
to D_3D_3. A change in the quantity demanded involves a movement, caused by a
change in the price of the product under consideration, from one point to another—
as from a to b—on a fixed demand curve.

answer is obvious: A change in one or more
of the determinants will change the demand
schedule data in Table 4–3 and therefore
the location of the demand curve in Figure 4–3. Such a change in the demand
schedule data, or, graphically, a shift in the
location of the demand curve, is designated
as a *change in demand*.

More specifically, if consumers become
willing and able to buy more of this particular good at each possible price than is
reflected in column 4 of Table 4–3, an
increase in demand has occurred. In Figure 4–3 this increase in demand is reflected
in a shift of the demand curve to the right,
for example, from D_1 to D_2. Conversely, a

decrease in demand occurs when, because
of a change in one or more of the determinants, consumers buy less of the product
at each possible price than is indicated in
column 4 of Table 4–3. Graphically, a decrease in demand entails a shift of the demand curve to the left, for example, from
D_1 to D_3 in Figure 4–3.

Let us now examine the effect upon
demand of changes in each of the aforementioned determinants.

1. Tastes. A change in consumer tastes
favorable to this product—possibly prompted
by advertising or fashion changes—will
mean that more will be demanded at each
price, that is, demand will increase. An un-

favorable change in consumer preferences will cause demand to decrease, shifting the curve to the left.

2. Number of buyers. It is equally obvious that an increase in the number of consumers in a market—brought about perhaps by improvements in transportation or by population growth—will constitute an increase in demand. Fewer consumers will be reflected by a decrease in demand.

3. Income. The impact of changes in money income upon demand is a bit more complex. For most commodities a rise in income will cause an increase in demand. Consumers typically buy more shoes, steaks, stereos, and Scotch as their incomes increase. Conversely, the demand for such products will decline in response to a fall in incomes. Commodities the demand for which varies *directly* with money income are called superior, or *normal*, goods.

Although most products are normal goods, there are a few exceptions. Examples: As incomes increase beyond some point, the amounts of bread or potatoes or cabbages purchased at each price may be less because the higher incomes now allow consumers to buy more high-protein foods such as dairy products and meat. Similarly, rising incomes may cause the demands for hamburger and oleomargarine to decline as wealthier consumers switch to T-bones and butter. Goods whose demand varies *inversely* with a change in money income are called *inferior* or "poor man's" goods.

4. Prices of related goods. Whether a given change in the price of a related good will increase or decrease the demand for the product under consideration will depend upon whether the related good is a substitute for or a complement to it. For example, butter and oleomargarine are *substitute,* or competing, goods. When the price of butter rises, consumers will purchase a smaller amount of butter, and this will cause the demand for oleomargarine to increase. Conversely, as the price of butter falls, consumers will buy larger quantities of butter, causing the demand for oleomargarine to

decrease. To generalize: When the price of one good and the demand for another good are *directly* related, the two products are substitute goods. So it is with Lucky Strikes and Chesterfields, sugar and saccharin, Chevrolets and Fords, tea and coffee, and so forth.

But other pairs of products are *complementary* goods; they "go together." If the price of gasoline falls and, as a result, you drive your car more, this extra driving will increase your demand for motor oil. Conversely, an increase in the price of gasoline will diminish the demand for motor oil. Thus gas and oil are jointly demanded; they are complements. And so it is with ham and eggs, Scotch and soda, phonographs and records, golf clubs and golf balls, and so forth. Whenever the price of one good and the demand for another are *inversely* related, we can say that the two commodities are complements.

Many pairs of goods, of course, are not related at all—they are *independent* goods. For such pairs of commodities as, for example, butter and golf balls, potatoes and automobiles, bananas and wrist watches, we should expect that a change in the price of one would have little or no impact upon the demand for the other.

5. Expectations. Consumer expectations of higher future prices may prompt them to buy now in order to "beat" the anticipated price rises, and, similarly, the expectation of rising incomes may induce consumers to be less tightfisted in their current spending. Conversely, expectations of falling prices and income will tend to decrease the current demand for products.

We might summarize by saying that an increase in the demand for product X—the decision of consumers to buy more of X at each possible price—can be caused by (1) a favorable change in consumer tastes, (2) an increase in the number of buyers in the market, (3) a rise (fall) in income if X is a normal (inferior) good, (4) an increase (decrease) in the price of related good Y if Y is a substitute for (complement to) X, and (5) expectations of future increases in prices and incomes. Conversely, a decrease in the demand for X can be associated with (1) an unfavorable change in tastes, (2) a decrease in the number of buyers in the market, (3) a rise (fall) in income if X is an inferior (normal) good, (4) an increase (decrease) in the price of related good Y if Y is complementary to (a substitute for) X; and (5) expectations of future price and income declines.

Changes in the Quantity Demanded

A change in demand must not be confused with a change in the quantity demanded. We have noted that a *change in demand* refers to a shift in the entire demand curve either to the right (an increase in demand) or to the left (a decrease in demand). The consumer's state of mind concerning his purchases of this product has been altered. The cause: a change in one or more of the determinants of demand. As used by economists, the term "demand" refers to a schedule or curve; therefore, a change in demand must mean that the entire schedule has changed or that the curve has shifted its position.

In contrast, a *change in the quantity demanded* designates the movement from one point to another point—from one price-quantity combination to another—on a fixed demand curve. The cause of a change in the quantity demanded is a change in the price of the product under consideration. In Table 4–3 a decline in the price asked by suppliers of corn from $5 to $4 will increase the quantity of corn demanded from 2,000 to 4,000 bushels.

Figure 4–3 is helpful in making the distinction between a change in demand and a change in the quantity demanded. The shift of the demand curve D_1 to either D_2 or D_3 entails changes in demand. But the movement from point *a* to point *b* on curve D_1 is a change in the quantity demanded.

The reader should decide whether a change in demand or a change in the quan-tity demanded is involved in each of the following illustrations:

1. Consumer incomes rise, with the result that more jewelry is purchased.

2. A barber raises the price of haircuts and finds that his volume of business declines.

3. The price of Fords goes up, and, as a consequence, the sales of Chevrolets increase.

SUPPLY

Supply may be defined as *a schedule which shows the various amounts of a product which a producer is willing and able to produce and make available for sale in the market at each specific price in a set of possible prices during some specified time period.*[4] This schedule portrays a series of alternative possibilities, such as those shown in Table 4–4 for a single producer. Let us

TABLE 4–4. AN INDIVIDUAL PRODUCER'S SUPPLY OF CORN (hypothetical data)

Price per bushel	Quantity supplied per week
$5	60
4	50
3	35
2	20
1	5

just suppose that our producer, in this case, is a farmer producing corn, the demand for which we have just considered. Our defini-tion of supply indicates that supply is usu-ally viewed from the vantage point of price. That is, we read supply as showing the amounts producers will offer at various pos-sible prices. It is more useful and quite cor-rect in some instances to view supply from

---

[4] In talking of the resource market, our defini-tion of supply reads: a schedule which shows the various amounts of a resource which its owners are willing to supply in the market at each possible price in a series of prices during some period of time.

the reference point of quantity. Instead of asking what quantities will be offered at various prices, we can ask what prices will be required to induce producers to offer various quantities of a good.

Law of Supply

It will be immediately noted that Table 4–4 shows a *direct* relationship between price and quantity supplied. As price rises, the corresponding quantity supplied rises; as price falls, the quantity supplied also falls. This particular relationship is called the *law of supply*. It simply tells us that producers are willing to produce and offer for sale more of their product at a high price than they are at a low price. Why? This again is basically a common-sense matter.

Price, we recall, is a deterrent from the consumer's standpoint. The obstacle of a high price means that the consumer, being on the paying end of this price, will buy a relatively small amount of the product; the lower the price obstacle, the more the consumer will buy. The supplier, on the other hand, is on the receiving end of the product's price. To him, price is an inducement or incentive to produce and sell a product. The higher the price of the product, the greater the incentive to produce and offer it in the market.

It is important to note that the idea of a supply schedule or curve is based upon the assumption that individual sellers take product price as given, that is, they have no power to put price tags on their product. It does not make sense to ask how a seller will react to various prices if he is able to manipulate those prices himself. It does not make sense to ask someone how he will react to an event or set of data which he himself can control. It is like asking ourselves how we will respond to our own invitation to attend Saturday's football game.

You will also remember that the law of demand was explainable on the basis of product substitution. When the price of product X rises, consumers tend to substitute other goods for it, therefore buying less of X. When the price of X declines, consumers buy more of X, substituting it for other products. The direct relationship between price and quantity supplied can also be explained on the basis of substitutability. In many instances the resources and productive techniques used by a supplier are readily adaptable to a variety of products. A farmer's land and capital, for example, may be of about equal efficiency in producing corn, wheat, soy beans, milo, and so forth. As the market price of one of these products—say, wheat—rises, the farmer will shift his resources from the other commodities to wheat. Why? Because it pays him to produce more wheat when price goes up.

A simple example may help at this point. Suppose a farmer has just 2 acres of land. He finds from experience that these 2 acres are equally prolific in the production of both corn and wheat. Specifically, he has found that each acre is capable of producing *either* 20 bushels of wheat *or* 20 bushels of corn. Suppose, too, that no matter how our farmer decides to apportion his 2 acres between wheat and corn, his total costs of production are always the same—say $25. To begin, let us say that the price of wheat is $1 per bushel and that of corn is $2 per bushel. The farmer will obviously plant all his land to corn, producing 40 bushels. Total revenue will be $80 (= 40 × $2) and profits will be $55 (= $80 − $25). The output of wheat, the crop in which we are particularly interested, will be zero. To plant any wheat at a price of $1 per bushel will necessarily result in profits of less than $55. But what if the market price of wheat rises to $3, while the price of corn remains at $2? It would now be profitable for the farmer to shift all his resources to wheat, that is, to substitute wheat for corn production. By doing so, his total revenue will be increased to $120 (40 × $3) and his profits to $95 (= $120 − $25). Although this example is greatly simplified, the basic point is clear: It is profitable to substitute the production of relatively high-priced for the production of relatively low-priced goods by shifting resources accordingly. Given the $2 price of corn, no wheat will be produced when its price is $1 per bushel, but 40 bushels will be forthcoming when its price is $3. Product substitution explains this direct relationship between the price of wheat and the quantity supplied.

In practice, this substitution may be more complex and time-consuming than our illustration implies: very different products whose production requires radically different methods and resources may be involved.

The process may well necessitate the shifting of resources between different producers. The basic conclusion, however, still holds true.

The Supply Curve

As in the case of demand, it is convenient to present graphically the concept of supply. Our axes in Figure 4–4 are the same as those in Figure 4–3, except for the obvious change of "quantity demanded" to "quantity supplied." The graphing procedure is the same as that previously explained, but

FIGURE 4–4. CHANGES IN THE SUPPLY OF CORN.
A change in one or more of the determinants of supply—productive techniques, resource prices, the prices of other goods, price expectations, or the number of sellers in the market—will cause a change in supply. An increase in supply shifts the supply curve to the right, as from S_1S_1 to S_2S_2. A decrease in supply is shown graphically as a movement of the curve to the left, as from S_1S_1 to S_3S_3. A change in the quantity supplied involves a movement, caused by a change in the price of the product under consideration, from one point to another—as from *a* to *b*—on a fixed supply curve.

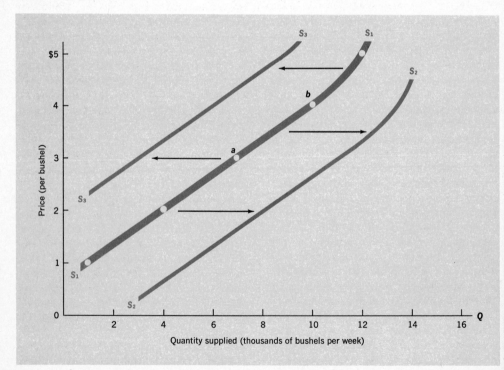

TABLE 4–5. MARKET SUPPLY OF CORN, 200 PRODUCERS (hypothetical data)

(1) Price per bushel	(2) Quantity supplied per week, single producer		(3) Number of sellers in the market		(4) Total quantity supplied per week
$5	60	×	200	=	12,000
4	50	×	200	=	10,000
3	35	×	200	=	7,000
2	20	×	200	=	4,000
1	5	×	200	=	1,000

of course the quantity data and relationship involved are different. The market supply data graphed in Figure 4–4 as S_1 are shown in Table 4–5, which assumes there are 200 suppliers in the market having the same supply schedules as the producer previously portrayed in Table 4–4.

Determinants of Supply

The determinants of demand have been noted and discussed. Changes in consumer tastes, the number of buyers, consumer incomes, the prices of related goods, and consumer expectations will all cause the demand for a particular product to shift.

A similar set of considerations determines the location of a supply curve. The basic determinants of supply are: (1) the technique of production, (2) resource prices, (3) prices of other goods, (4) price expectations, and (5) the number of sellers in the market. A change in any one or more of these determinants will cause the supply curve for a product to shift to either the right or the left. A shift to the right, from S_1 to S_2 in Figure 4–4, designates an *increase in supply:* producers are now offering more of the product at each possible price. A shift to the left, S_1 to S_3 in Figure 4–4, indicates a *decrease in supply:* suppliers are offering less at each price.

Changes in Supply

Let us consider the effect of changes in each of these determinants upon supply.

1 and 2. The first two determinants of supply—technology and resource prices—are the two components of production costs. And the relationship between production costs and supply is an intimate one. (As a matter of fact, in Chapter 26 we shall find that cost and supply data are synonymous.) For our present purposes, it is sufficient to note that anything which serves to lower production costs, that is, a technological improvement or a decline in resource prices, will increase supply. With lower costs, businessmen will find that it is profitable to offer a larger amount of the product at each possible price. An increase in the price of resources (a deterioration of technology being unlikely) will cause a decrease in supply; that is, the supply curve will shift to the left.

3. Changes in the prices of other goods can also shift the supply curve for a product. A decline in the price of corn may cause a farmer to produce and offer more wheat at each possible price. Conversely, a rise in the price of corn may make farmers less willing to produce and offer wheat in the market.

4. Expectations concerning the future

price of a product can also affect a producer's current willingness to supply that product. It is difficult, however, to generalize concerning the way the expectation of, say, higher prices will affect the present supply curve of a product. Farmers might withhold some of their current wheat harvest from the market, anticipating a higher wheat price in the future. This will cause a decrease in the current supply of wheat. On the other hand, in many types of manufacturing, expected price increases may induce firms to expand production immediately, causing supply to increase.

5. Finally, given the scale of operations of each firm, the larger the number of suppliers, the greater will be market supply. As more firms enter an industry, the supply curve will shift to the right. The smaller the number of firms in an industry, the less the market supply will be. This means that as firms leave an industry, the supply curve will shift to the left.

Changes in Quantity Supplied

The distinction between a change in supply and a change in the quantity supplied parallels that between a change in demand and a change in the quantity demanded. A *change in supply* is involved when the entire supply curve shifts. An increase in supply shifts the curve to the right; a decrease in supply shifts it to the left. The cause of a change in supply is a change in one or more of the determinants of supply. The term "supply" is used by economists to refer to a schedule or curve. A change in supply therefore must mean that the entire schedule has changed or that the curve has shifted.

A *change in the quantity supplied*, on the other hand, refers to the movement from one point to another point on a stable supply curve. The cause of such a movement is a change in the price of the specific product under consideration. In Table 4–5 a decline in the price of corn from $5 to $4

decreases the quantity of corn supplied from 12,000 to 10,000 bushels.

Shifting the supply curve from S_1 to S_2 or S_3 in Figure 4–4 obviously entails changes in supply. The movement from point a to point b on S_1, however, is merely a change in the quantity supplied.

The reader should determine which of the following involves a change in supply and which entails a change in the quantity supplied:

1. Because production costs decline, producers sell more automobiles.

2. The price of wheat declines, causing the number of bushels of corn sold per month to increase.

3. Fewer oranges are offered for sale because their price has decreased in retail markets.

SUPPLY AND DEMAND: MARKET EQUILIBRIUM

We may now put the concepts of supply and demand together to see how the interaction of the buying decisions of households and the selling decisions of producers will determine the price of a product and the quantity which is actually bought and sold in the market. In Table 4–6 columns 1 and 2 reproduce the market supply schedule for corn (from Table 4–5), and columns 2 and 3 the market demand schedule for corn (from Table 4–3). Note that in column 2 we are using a common set of prices. We assume competition—the presence of a large number of buyers and sellers.

Now the question to be faced is this: Of the five[5] possible prices at which corn might sell in this market, which will actually prevail as the market price for corn? Let us derive our answer through the simple process of trial and error. For no particular reason, we shall start with an examination of

[5] Of course, there are many possible prices; our simple example shows only five of them.

TABLE 4–6. MARKET SUPPLY AND DEMAND FOR CORN (hypothetical data)

(1) Total quantity supplied per week	(2) Price per bushel	(3) Total quantity demanded per week	(4) Surplus (+) or shortage (−) (arrows indicate effect on price)
12,000	$5	2,000	+10,000 ↓
10,000	4	4,000	+ 6,000 ↓
7,000	3	7,000	
4,000	2	11,000	− 7,000 ↑
1,000	1	16,000	−15,000 ↑

$5. Could this be the prevailing market price for corn? The answer is "No," for the simple reason that producers are willing to produce and supply to the market some 12,000 bushels of corn at this price while buyers, on the other hand, are only willing to take 2,000 bushels off the market at this price. In other words, the relatively high price of $5 encourages farmers to produce a great deal of corn, but that same high price discourages consumers from taking the product off the market. Other products appear as "better buys" when corn is high-priced. The result in this case is a 10,000-bushel *surplus* of corn in the market. This surplus, shown in column 4, is simply the excess of quantity supplied over quantity demanded at the price of $5.

Could a price of $5—even if it existed temporarily in the corn market—persist over a period of time? Certainly not. The very large surplus of corn would prompt competing sellers to bid down the price in order to encourage buyers to take this surplus off their hands. Suppose price gravitates down to $4. Now the situation has changed considerably. The lower price has encouraged buyers to take more of this product off the market and, at the same time, has induced farmers to use a smaller amount of resources in producing corn. The surplus, as a result, has diminished to 6,000 bushels. Because a surplus still exists, competition

among sellers will once again bid down the price of corn. We can conclude then that prices of $5 and $4 will be unstable, because they are "too high." The market price for corn must be something less than $4.

To avoid letting the cat out of the bag before we have a full appreciation of how supply and demand determine product price, let us now jump to the other end of our price column and examine $1 as the possible market price for corn. It is evident that at this price, quantity demanded is in excess of quantity supplied by 15,000 units. This relatively low price discourages farmers from devoting their resources to corn production; the same low price encourages consumers to attempt to buy more corn than would otherwise be the case. Corn is a "good buy" when its price is relatively low. In short, there is a 15,000-bushel *shortage* of corn. Can this price of $1 persist as the market price? No. Competition among buyers will bid up the price to something greater than $1. In other words, at a price of $1, many consumers who are willing and able to buy at this price will obviously be left out in the cold. Many potential consumers, in order to ensure that they will not have to do without, will express a willingness to pay some price in excess of $1 to ensure getting some of the available corn. Suppose this competitive bidding up of price by buyers boosts the price of corn to

$2. This higher price obviously has reduced, but not eliminated, the shortage of corn. For $2, farmers are willing to devote more resources to corn production, and some buyers who were willing to pay $1 for a bushel of corn will choose not to buy corn at a price of $2, deciding to use their incomes to buy other products or maybe to save more of their incomes. But a shortage of 7,000 bushels still exists at a price of $2. We can conclude that competitive bidding among buyers will push market price to some figure greater than $2.

By trial and error we have eliminated every price but $3. So let us now examine it. At a price of $3, *and only at this price,* the quantity which farmers are willing to produce and supply in the market is identical with the amount consumers are willing to buy. As a result, there is neither a shortage nor a surplus of corn at this price. We have already seen that a surplus causes price to decline and a shortage causes price to rise. With neither a shortage nor a surplus at $3, there is no reason for the actual price of corn to move away from this price. The economist calls this price the *equilibrium price,* equilibrium meaning "in balance" or "at rest." At $3, quantity supplied and quantity demanded are in balance; hence, $3 is the only stable price of corn under the supply and demand conditions shown in Table 4–6. Or, stated differently, the price of corn will be established where the supply decisions of producers and the demand decisions of buyers are mutually consistent. Such decisions are consistent with one another only at a price of $3. At any higher price, suppliers want to sell more than consumers want to buy; at any lower price, consumers want to buy more than producers are willing to offer for sale. Discrepancies between supply and demand intentions of sellers and buyers, respectively, will prompt price changes which subsequently will bring these two sets of plans into accord with one another.

A graphic analysis of supply and demand should yield the same conclusions. Figure 4–5 puts the market supply and market demand curves for corn on the same graph, the horizontal axis now reflecting both quantity demanded and quantity supplied. A close examination of this diagram clearly indicates that at any price above the equilibrium price of $3, quantity supplied will exceed quantity demanded. This surplus will cause a competitive bidding down of price by sellers eager to relieve themselves of their surplus. The falling price will cause less corn to be offered and will simultaneously encourage consumers to buy more. Any price below the equilibrium price will entail a shortage; that is, quantity demanded will exceed quantity supplied. Competitive bidding by buyers will push the price up toward the equilibrium level. And this rising price will simultaneously bring forth a greater supply from producers and ration buyers out of the market, thereby causing the shortage to vanish. Graphically, the intersection of the supply curve and the demand curve for the product will indicate the equilibrium point.

Rationing Function of Prices

The ability of the competitive forces of supply and demand to establish a price where supply and demand decisions are synchronized is sometimes called the *rationing function* of prices. In this case, the equilibrium price of $3 clears the market, leaving no burdensome surplus for the seller and no inconvenient shortage for the potential buyers. The composite of freely made individual buying and selling decisions sets this price which clears the market. In effect, the market mechanism of supply and demand says this: Any buyer who is willing and able to pay $3 for a bushel of corn will be able to acquire one; those who are not, will not. Similarly, any seller who is willing and able to produce bushels of corn and offer them for sale at a price of $3 will be able to do so successfully; those who are not, will not. Were it not that competitive prices automatically bring supply and de-

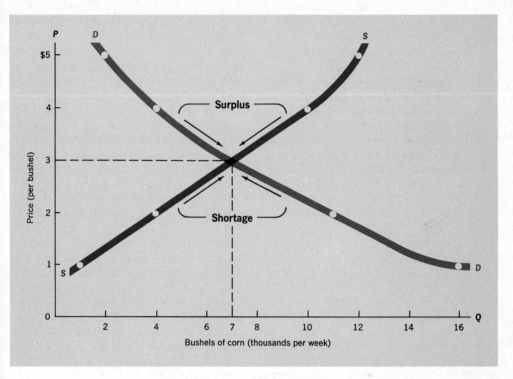

**FIGURE 4–5. THE EQUILIBRIUM PRICE AND QUANTITY FOR CORN AS
DETERMINED BY MARKET DEMAND AND SUPPLY.**
The intersection of the downsloping demand curve *D* and the upsloping supply curve
S indicates the equilibrium price and quantity, $3 and 7,000 bushels in this instance.
The shortages of corn which would exist at below-equilibrium prices drive price up and
in so doing increase the quantity supplied and reduce the quantity demanded until
equilibrium is achieved. The surpluses which above-equilibrium prices would entail
push price down and thereby increase the quantity demanded and reduce the quantity
supplied until equilibrium is achieved.

mand decisions into consistency with one another, some type of administrative control by government would be necessary to avoid or control the shortages or surpluses which might otherwise occur. We shall see in a later chapter some of the administrative problems involved when government steps into the picture and establishes a legal price higher or lower than the equilibrium price. Such *supported prices* and *ceiling prices* rob the price mechanism of its rationing ability, thereby making it necessary for government to assume responsibility for balancing quantity demanded and quantity

supplied. The important point is that free, competitive prices automatically synchronize buying and selling decisions and "clear the market"; this is the rationing function of prices.

Changes in Supply and Demand

It was noted earlier that demand might change because of fluctuations in consumer tastes or incomes, changes in consumer expectations, or variations in the prices of related goods. On the other hand, supply might vary in response to changes in technology or in resource prices. Our analysis would be incomplete if we did not stop to consider the effect of changes in supply and demand upon equilibrium price.

To keep our thinking on the straight and narrow, let us first analyze the effects of a change in demand, assuming that supply is conveniently constant. Suppose now that demand increases, as shown in Figure 4–6a. What is the effect upon price? Noting that the new intersection of the supply and demand curves is at a higher point on both the price and quantity axes, we can conclude that an increase in demand, other things (supply) being equal, will have a *price-increasing effect* and a *quantity-increasing effect*. (The value of graphic analysis now begins to become apparent; we need not fumble with figures in determining the effect on price and quantity but only compare the new with the old point of intersection on the graph.) A decrease in demand, as illustrated in Figure 4–6b, reveals *price-decreasing* and *quantity-decreasing effects*. Price falls, and quantity also declines. *In brief, we find a direct relationship between a change in demand and the resulting changes in equilibrium price and quantity.*

Let us reverse the procedure and analyze the effect of a change in supply on price, assuming that demand is constant. If supply increases, as in Figure 4–6c, the new intersection of supply and demand is obviously at a lower price. Equilibrium price falls; equilibrium quantity, however, increases. If supply decreases, on the other hand, this will tend to increase product price. Figure 4–6d illustrates this situation. Here price increases but quantity declines. In short, an increase in supply has a *price-decreasing* and a *quantity-increasing effect*. A decrease in supply has a *price-increasing* and a *quantity-decreasing effect*. *There is an inverse relationship between a change in supply and the resulting change in equilibrium price, but the relationship between a change in supply and the resulting change in equilibrium quantity is direct.*

Obviously, a host of more complex cases might arise, involving changes in both supply and demand. Two cases are possible when it is supposed that supply and demand change in *opposite directions*. Assume first that supply increases and demand decreases. What effect does this have upon equilibrium price? This example couples two price-decreasing effects, and the net result will be a price fall greater than that which would result from either change taken in isolation. How about equilibrium quantity? Here the effects of the changes in supply and demand are opposed: the increase in supply tends to increase equilibrium quantity, but the decrease in demand tends to reduce the equilibrium quantity. The direction of the change in quantity depends upon the relative sizes of the changes in supply and demand. The second possibility is for supply to decrease and demand to increase. Two price-increasing effects are involved here. We can predict an increase in equilibrium price greater than that caused by either change taken separately. The effect upon equilibrium quantity is again indeterminate, depending upon the relative size of the changes in supply and demand. If the decrease in supply is relatively larger than the increase in demand, the equilibrium quantity will be less than it was initially. But if the decrease in supply is relatively smaller than the increase in demand, the equilibrium quantity will increase as a result of these changes. The reader should trace through these two cases graphically to verify for himself the conclusions we have outlined.

What if supply and demand change in the *same direction*? Suppose first that supply and demand both increase. What is the effect upon equilibrium price? It depends. Here we must compare two conflicting effects upon price—the price-decreasing effect of the increase in supply and the price-increasing effect of the increase in demand. If the increase in supply is of greater magnitude than the increase in demand, the net effect will be for equilibrium price to de-

**FIGURE 4–6. CHANGES IN DEMAND AND SUPPLY
AND THE EFFECTS ON PRICE AND QUANTITY.**
The increase in demand of (*a*) and the decrease in demand of (*b*) indicate a direct
relationship between a change in demand and the resulting changes in equilibrium
price and quantity. The increase in supply of (*c*) and the decrease in supply of (*d*) show
an inverse relationship between a change in supply and the resulting change in
equilibrium price, but a direct relationship between a change in supply and the
accompanying change in equilibrium quantity.

(a)   (b)

(c)   (d)

crease. If the opposite holds true, equilibrium price will increase. The effect upon equilibrium quantity is certain: Increases in supply and in demand both have quantity-increasing effects. This means that equilibrium quantity will increase by an amount greater than that which either change would have entailed in isolation. In the second place, a decrease in both supply and demand can be subjected to similar analysis. If the decrease in supply is greater than the decrease in demand, equilibrium price will rise. If the reverse holds true, equilibrium price will fall. Because decreases in supply and demand both have quantity-decreasing effects, it can be predicted with certainty that equilibrium quantity will be less than that which prevailed initially.

Incidentally, the possibility that supply and demand will both change in a given period of time is not particularly unlikely. As a matter of fact, a single event might simultaneously affect both supply and demand. For example, a technological improvement in cheese production might lower both the supply of and the demand for fluid milk.

Needless to say, special cases might arise where a decrease in demand and a decrease in supply, on the one hand, and an increase in demand and an increase in supply, on the other, cancel out. In both these cases, the net effect upon equilibrium price will be zero; price will not change. The reader should again work out these more complex cases in terms of supply and demand curves to verify all these results.

The Resource Market

What about the shape of the supply and demand curves in the resource market? As in the product market, resource supply curves are typically upsloping, and resource demand curves are typically downsloping. Why?

Resource supply curves generally slope upward, that is, they reflect a *direct* relationship between resource price and quantity supplied, because it is in their own interests for resource owners to supply more of a particular resource at a high price than at a low price. High income payments in a particular occupation or industry encourage households to supply more of their human and property resources. Low income payments discourage resource owners from supplying resources in this particular occupation or industry and, as a matter of fact, encourage them to supply their resources elsewhere.

On the demand side, businesses, in trying to minimize production costs, shy away from the purchase of relatively high-priced resources and, conversely, prefer to use relatively low-priced resources when possible. Entrepreneurs will find it profitable to substitute low- for high-priced resources. More of a particular resource will be demanded at a low price than at a high price. The result? A downsloping demand curve for the various resources.

In short, just as the supply decisions of businesses and the demand decisions of consumers determine prices in the product market, so the supply decisions of households and demand decisions of businesses set prices in the resource market.

SUMMARY

1. Demand refers to a schedule which summarizes the willingness of buyers to purchase a given product during a specific time period at each of the various prices at which it might be sold. According to the law of demand, consumers will ordinarily buy more of a product at a low price than they will at a high price. Therefore, the relationship between price and quantity demanded is inverse; demand graphs as a downsloping curve.

2. Changes in one or more of the basic determinants of demand—consumer tastes, the number of buyers in the market, the money incomes of consumers, the prices of related goods, and consumer expectations—

will cause the market demand curve to shift. A shift to the right is an increase in demand; a shift to the left, a decrease in demand. A change in demand is to be distinguished from a change in the quantity demanded, the latter involving the movement from one point to another point on a fixed demand curve because of a change in the price of the product under consideration.

3. Supply is a schedule showing the amounts of a product which producers would be willing to offer in the market during a given time period at each possible price at which the commodity might be sold. The law of supply says that producers will offer more of a product at a higher price than they will at a low price. As a result, the relationship between price and quantity supplied is a direct one, and the supply curve is upsloping.

4. A change in productive techniques, resource prices, the prices of related goods, price expectations, or the number of sellers in the market will cause the supply curve of a product to shift. A shift to the right is an increase in supply; a shift to the left, a decrease in supply. In contrast, a change in the price of a given product will result in a change in the quantity supplied, that is, a movement from one point to another on a given supply curve.

5. Under competition, the interaction of market demand and market supply will adjust price to that point at which the quantity demanded and the quantity supplied are equal. This is the equilibrium price. The corresponding quantity is the equilibrium quantity. Equilibrium price and equilibrium quantity will change in response to a change in demand or supply.

6. The ability of market forces to synchronize selling and buying decisions so as to eliminate potential surpluses or shortages is sometimes termed the "rationing function of prices."

7. A change in either demand or supply will cause equilibrium price and quantity to change. There is a direct relationship between a change in demand and the resulting changes in equilibrium price and quantity. Though the relationship between a change in supply and the resulting change in equilibrium price is inverse, the relationship between a change in supply and equilibrium quantity is direct.

8. The concepts of supply and demand are also applicable to the resource market.

QUESTIONS AND STUDY SUGGESTIONS

1. Define demand. Explain the law of demand. Why does a demand curve slope downward? What are the determinants of demand? What happens to the demand curve when each of these determinants changes? Distinguish between a change in demand and a change in the quantity demanded, noting the cause(s) of each.

2. Define supply. Explain the law of supply. Why does the supply curve slope upward? What are the determinants of supply? What happens to the supply curve when each of these determinants changes? Distinguish between a change in supply and a change in the quantity supplied, noting the cause(s) of each.

3. Explain the following news dispatch from Hull, England: "The fish market here slumped today to what local commentators called 'a disastrous level'—all because of a shortage of potatoes. The potatoes are one of the main ingredients in a dish that figures on almost every café menu—fish and chips."

4. Suppose the total demand for wheat and the total supply of wheat per month in the Kansas City grain market are as follows:

Thousands of bushels demanded	Price per bushel	Thousands of bushels supplied	Surplus (+) or shortage (−)
90	$1.70	70	−20(-)
85	1.80	72	−13
80	1.90	73	−12
75	2.00	75	0
70	2.10	77	+7
65	2.20	79	+14
60	2.30	81	+21
55	2.40	83	+28

a. What will be the market or equilibrium price? What is the equilibrium quantity? Using the surplus-shortage column, explain why your answers are correct.

b. Using the above data, graph the demand for wheat and the supply of wheat. Be sure to label the axes of your graph correctly. Label equilibrium price "*P*" and equilibrium quantity "*Q*."

c. Why will $1.80 not be the equilibrium price in this market? Why not $2.30?

d. Now suppose that the government establishes a ceiling price of, say $1.90 for wheat. Explain carefully the effects of this ceiling price. Demonstrate your answer graphically. What might prompt government to establish a ceiling price?

e. Assume now that the government establishes a supported price of, say, $2.20 for wheat. Explain carefully the effects of this supported price. Demonstrate your answer graphically. What might prompt the government to establish this price support?

f. "Legally fixed prices strip the price mechanism of its rationing function." Explain this statement in terms of your answers to 4d and 4e.

5. What effect will each of the following have upon the demand for product B?
   a. Product B becomes more fashionable.
   b. The price of product C, a good substitute for B, goes down.
   c. Consumers anticipate declining prices and falling incomes.
   d. There is a rapid upsurge in population growth.

6. What effect will each of the following have upon the supply of product B?
   a. A technological advance in the methods of producing B.
   b. A decline in the number of firms in industry B.
   c. An increase in the prices of resources required in the production of B.
   d. The expectation that the equilibrium price of B will be lower in the future than it is currently.
   e. A decline in the price of product A, a good whose production

requires substantially the same techniques and resources as does the production of B.

7. Explain and illustrate graphically the effect of:
   a. An increase in income upon the demand curve of an inferior good.
   b. A drop in the price of product S upon the demand for substitute product T.
   c. A decline in income upon the demand curve of a normal good.
   d. An increase in the price of product J upon the demand for complementary good K.

8. "In the corn market, demand often exceeds supply and supply sometimes exceeds demand." "The price of corn rises and falls in response to changes in supply and demand." In which of these two statements are the terms "supply" and "demand" used correctly? Explain.

9. "Surpluses drive prices up; shortages drive them down." Do you agree?

10. How will each of the following changes in demand and/or supply affect equilibrium price and equilibrium quantity in a competitive market; that is, do price and quantity *rise, fall, remain unchanged,* or are the answers *indeterminate,* depending upon the magnitudes of the shifts in supply and demand? You should rely on a supply and demand diagram in verifying your answers.
    a. Supply decreases and demand remains constant.
    b. Demand decreases and supply remains constant.
    c. Supply increases and demand is constant.
    d. Demand increases and supply increases.
    e. Demand increases and supply is constant.
    f. Supply increases and demand decreases.
    g. Demand increases and supply decreases.
    h. Demand decreases and supply decreases.

11. "Prices are the automatic regulator that tend to keep production and consumption in line with each other." Explain.

SELECTED REFERENCES

Boulding, Kenneth E.: *Economic Analysis,* 3d ed. (New York: Harper & Row, Publishers, Incorporated, 1955), chaps. 4 and 5.

Henderson, Hubert: *Supply and Demand* (Chicago: The University of Chicago Press, 1958), chap. 2.

Warner, Aaron W., and Victor R. Fuchs: *Concepts and Cases in Economic Analysis* (New York: Harcourt, Brace & World, Inc., 1958), pp. 41–62, 79–82, and 94–115.

CHAPTER 5

THE FIVE FUNDAMENTAL
QUESTIONS AND
THE PRICE SYSTEM

We saw in Chapter 3 that the capitalist ideology makes clear the importance of freedom of enterprise and choice. Consumers are at liberty to buy what they choose; businesses, to produce and sell what they choose; and resource suppliers, to make their property and human resources available in whatever occupations they choose. Upon reflection, we might wonder why such an economy does not collapse in complete chaos. If consumers want bread, businesses choose to produce automobiles, and resource suppliers want to offer their services in manufacturing shoes, it would seem that production would be deadlocked because of the obvious inconsistency of these free choices.

Fortunately, two other features of capitalism—a system of markets and prices and the force of competition—provide the coordinating and organizing mechanisms which overcome the potential chaos posed by freedom of enterprise and choice. The competitive price system is a mechanism both for communicating the decisions of consumers, producers, and resource suppliers to one another and for synchronizing those decisions toward consistent production objectives.

Armed with an understanding of individual markets and prices gained from Chapter 4, we are now in a position to analyze the operation of the price system. More specifically, in this chapter we first want to understand how the price system operates as a mechanism for communicating and coordinating individual free choices.

Deferring the full-employment question until Part Two, we want to see how the price system answers the other four Fundamental Questions. How does the price system (1) determine what is to be produced, (2) organize production, (3) distribute total output, and (4) adapt itself to change? Then, secondly, we want to evaluate the operation of the market economy.

FRAMEWORK OF THE PRICE SYSTEM

If we could suddenly "freeze" a purely capitalist economy at some point in time, here is what we should find:

1. Households, as consumers, have a variety of material wants. For all practical purposes, these wants are unlimited. Possessing a limited money income derived from the sale of limited amounts of resources at their disposal, each household seeks to purchase that combination of goods and services which will give it the greatest satisfaction. These various consumer wants in effect are tallied on the demand side of the product market. The demand schedule or curve for each product communicates to producers how much competing consumers would purchase of that product at various prices. The demand curve for each product is downsloping, because consumers find it to their advantage to substitute low-priced for high-priced products. Because of the large number of consumers buying each product, no one significantly influences actual product prices.

2. Competing business institutions stand on the supply side of the product market. Their goal is to maximize profits. In so doing, they must decide what product will be most profitable to produce, in what quantity it will be most profitable to produce it, and what combination of resources will produce the desired output at the least cost. For the business sector as a whole, these decisions, which in effect indicate the willingness of businesses to produce and offer various products, are reflected in product supply curves. These supply curves are upsloping, indicating that, other things being equal, businesses will profit by substituting the production of high-priced for the production of low-priced goods. Together with the product demand curves which mirror consumer preferences, these supply curves will establish an equilibrium price for all those products which consumers might want and which businesses might be willing to supply.

3. Businesses require resources in accomplishing production. As we noted in Chapter 4, businesses will minimize their costs and, other things being equal, maximize their profits by substituting low-priced resources for high-priced resources; this means that resource demand curves will be downsloping. These resource demand curves will communicate to resource suppliers how much of each resource businesses will be willing to employ at various possible resource prices.

4. Finally, households as resource suppliers offer the land, labor, capital, and entrepreneurial talents which they own to businesses. The decisions of competing resource suppliers are reflected in resource supply curves. These curves are generally upsloping, reflecting the fact that households seek the greatest return from the sale of their resources. The upsloping nature of these curves implies that households not only want but within limits are able to shift resources from low-paying to high-paying lines of employment.

In brief, the product demand intentions of households and the product supply decisions of businesses will determine a series of product prices. Similarly, the resource demand decisions of businesses and the resource supply decisions of households will establish a series of resource prices.

ECONOMIC CHOICES, SCARCITY, AND SUBSTITUTABILITY

It is evident that our picture of the price system merely envisions a series of interrelated choices on the part of households as consumers and resource suppliers and businesses as producers and resource users. These choices are based upon the fact of scarcity and influenced by considerations of substitutability.

Society is faced with the problem of making economic choices because resources are scarce. If resources were infinitely abundant in relation to the demand for them, the economizing problem would dissolve in a sea of affluency. Consumers would not have to choose between various products; abundance would make it possible for every consumer to have any type and any amount of goods and services he desired. The same would be true for businesses in the using of resources to carry on production. But, unfortunately, this describes economic utopia, not economic reality; in real life, resources, and therefore products, are relatively scarce. Hence, consumers with money incomes limited by their sales of scarce resources are forced to choose between relatively scarce commodities. And businesses, possessing limited money receipts from the sale of relatively scarce products, must choose between scarce resources in carrying on their productive efforts. Indeed, the presence of the basic theme of scarcity in our picture of the price system is mirrored in the very fact that products and resources have price tags on them! Only when something is scarce in relation to the demand for it will it command a price in the market.

How does substitutability come into the picture? Within limits, both resources and products are versatile. Consumer wants can usually be satisfied with various goods. The want for a trip from New York to Chicago can be satisfied by purchasing a car, a train ticket, a plane ticket, or a bus ticket. Hunger can be satisfied by a wide variety of foods—a bowl of rice, a hamburger, or a sirloin steak. And so it is with producing specific products. Resources, within limits dictated by technology, are substitutable for one another. Various resource combinations can be employed in the production of most products. The nature of both the supply and demand choices in a market economy are strongly influenced by substitutability. The demand curve for a product is down-sloping because consumers will substitute other products for any particular product whose price happens to rise. And producers tend to substitute alternative resources for that resource whose price rises. Upsloping product and resource supply curves also imply substitutability. Producers tend to substitute high-priced for low-priced products in formulating their production intentions. And resource suppliers shift their human and property resources from low-paying to high-paying employments.

This, of course, is not to say that substitutability is perfect. It obviously is not. A bowl of rice is not a perfect substitute for a sirloin steak. Yet within limits the possibility of substitution exists in both the product and resource market. Indeed, if substitutability did not exist, businesses would have no choices to make in hiring resources to produce specific goods. And if resources were not versatile, households would have no choices to make in supplying them. Similarly, if various products were not substitutable, households would have no problem of choice in spending their incomes.

Thus we may say that economic choices must be rendered because resources, and therefore products, are scarce. The particular choices rendered by businesses and households depend upon:

1. The prices of resources and products as indicators of relative scarcities.

2. The possibilities of substituting be-tween resources, on the one hand, and products, on the other.

The interrelationship between scarcity and substitution is even more intimate than we have suggested. For example, if a product becomes particularly scarce, its price as an index of its relative scarcity will rise. This will signal buyers to substitute other products for the now higher-priced product. This substitution will rechannel consumer purchases away from this particularly scarce product toward others less scarce. Substitution eases this particularly acute scarcity by, in effect, transferring consumer purchases to other substitutable products. Through substitutability, society alters its choices so as to use less of particularly scarce products and resources and more of less scarce ones. By substituting, society conserves most on those products and resources which are most scarce.

OPERATION OF THE PRICE SYSTEM

Now with this point-in-time picture of the price system before us and with the significance of scarcity and substitutability in the making of economic choices clearly in mind, let us examine in some detail the manner in which the competitive price system would answer the Fundamental Questions.

Determining What Is to Be Produced

Given the product and resource prices established by competing buyers and sellers in both the product and resource markets, how would a purely capitalistic economy decide the types and quantities of goods to be produced? Remembering that businesses are motivated to seek profits and avoid losses, we can generalize that those goods and services which can be produced at a profit will be produced and those whose production entails a loss will not. And what determines profits or the lack of them? Two things:

1. The total receipts which a firm gets from selling a product.

2. The total costs of producing it.

Both total receipts and total costs are price-times-quantity figures. Total receipts are found by multiplying product price by the amount of the product sold. Total costs are found by multiplying the price of each resource used by the amount employed and summing the costs of each.

Economic profits. To say that those products which can be produced profitably will be produced and those which cannot will not is only an accurate generalization if the meaning of economic costs is clearly understood. In order to grasp the full meaning of costs, let us once again think of businesses as simply organizational charts, that is, businesses "on paper," distinct and apart from the capital, raw materials, labor, and entrepreneurial ability which make them going concerns. In order to become actual producing concerns, these "on paper" businesses must secure all four types of resources. The payments which must be made to secure and retain the needed amounts of these resources are *economic costs*. The per unit size of these costs will be determined by supply and demand conditions in the resource market. Now the point to note is that—as land, labor, and capital—entrepreneurial ability is a scarce resource and therefore has a price tag on it. Costs therefore must include not only wage and salary payments to labor and interest and rental payments for capital and land, but also payments to the entrepreneur for the functions he performs in organizing and combining the other resources in the production of some commodity. The cost payment for these contributions by the entrepreneur is called a *normal profit*. Hence, a product will be produced only when total receipts are large enough to pay wage, interest, rental, and normal profit costs. Now if total receipts from the sale of a product more than cover all production costs, including a normal profit, the remainder will accrue to the entrepreneur as the risk taker and organizing force in the going concern. This

return above costs is called a *pure,* or *economic, profit*. It is not an economic cost, because it need not be realized in order for the business to acquire and retain entrepreneurial ability.

Profits and expanding industries. A few hypothetical examples will explain more concretely how the price system determines what is to be produced. Suppose that the most favorable relationship between total revenue and total cost in producing product X occurs when the firm's output is 15 units. Assume, too, that the best combination of resources to use in producing 15 units of X entails 2 units of labor, 3 units of land, 1 of capital, and 1 of entrepreneurial ability, selling at prices of $2, $1, $3, and $3, respectively. Finally, suppose that the 15 units of X which these resources produce can be sold for $1 per unit. Will firms enter into the production of product X? Yes, they will. A firm producing product X under these conditions will be able to pay wage, rent, interest, and normal profit costs of $13 $[= (2 \times \$2) + (3 \times \$1) + (1 \times \$3) + (1 \times \$3)]$. The difference between total revenue of $15 and total costs of $13 will be an economic profit of $2.

This economic profit is evidence that industry X is a prosperous one. Such an industry will tend to expand as new firms, attracted by these above-normal profits, are created or shift from less profitable industries. But the entry of new firms will be a self-limiting process. As new firms enter industry X, the market supply of X will increase relative to the market demand. This will lower the market price of X to the end that economic profits will in time disappear. The market supply and demand situation prevailing when economic profits become zero will determine the total amount of X produced.

Losses and declining industries. But what if the initial market situation for product X were less favorable? Suppose conditions in the product market initially were such that the firm could sell the 15 units of X at a price of just 75 cents per unit. Total revenue would be $11.25 (= 15 × 75 cents). After paying wage, rental, and interest costs of $10, the firm would yield a below-normal profit of $1.25. In other words, losses of $1.75 (= $11.25 − $13) would be incurred. Certainly firms would not be attracted to this unprosperous industry. On the contrary, if these losses persisted, entrepreneurs would seek the normal or economic profits offered by more prosperous industries. This means that existing firms in industry X would in time go out of business entirely or migrate to other industries where normal or better profits prevail. However, as this happens, the market supply of X will fall relative to the market demand, thereby raising product price to the end that losses will in time disappear. Industry X will then stabilize itself in size. The market supply and demand situation that prevails at that point where economic profits are zero will determine the total output of product X.

"Dollar votes." The important role of consumer demand in determining the types and quantities of goods produced must be emphasized. Consumers, unrestrained by government and possessing money incomes from the sale of resources, spend their dollars upon those goods which they are most willing and able to buy. These expenditures are in effect "dollar votes" by which consumers register their wants through the demand side of the product market. If these votes are great enough to provide a normal profit, businesses will produce that product. An increase in consumer demand, that is, an increase in the dollar votes cast for a product, will mean economic profits for the industry producing it. These profits will signal the expansion of that industry and increases in the output of the product. A decrease in consumer demand, that is, fewer votes cast for the product, will result in losses and, in time, contraction of the adversely affected industry. As firms leave the industry, the output of the product declines. In short, the dollar votes of consumers play a key role in determining what products profit-seeking businesses will produce. As noted in Chapter 3, the capitalistic system is sometimes said to be characterized by *consumer sovereignty* because of the strategic role of consumers in determining the types and quantities of goods produced.

Market restraints on freedom. From the viewpoint of businesses, we now see that firms are not really "free" to produce what they wish. The demand decisions of consumers, by making the production of some products profitable and others not, restrict the choice of businesses in deciding what to produce. Business must synchronize their production choices with consumer choices or face the penalty of losses and eventual bankruptcy.

Much of the same holds true with respect to resource suppliers. In seeking to maximize the returns from the sale of their human and property resources, resource suppliers are prompted by the price system to make their choices in accord with consumer demands. If only those firms which produce goods wanted by consumers can operate profitably, only those firms will demand resources. Resource suppliers will not be "free" to allocate their resources to the production of goods consumers do not value very highly. The reason? There will be no firms producing such products, because consumer demand is not sufficient to make it profitable to do so. In short, consumers register their preferences on the demand side of the product market, and producers and resource suppliers respond appropriately in seeking to further their own self-interests. The price system communicates the wants of consumers to business and resource suppliers and elicits appropriate responses.

Organizing Production

How is production to be organized in a market economy? This fundamental ques-

tion, we recall, is composed of three subquestions:

1. How should resources be allocated
among specific industries?

2. What specific firms should do the producing in each industry?

3. What combination of resources—what
technology—should each firm employ?

The preceding section has answered the
first subquestion. The price system steers
resources to those industries whose products consumers want badly enough to make
their production profitable. It simultaneously deprives unprofitable industries of
scarce resources. If all firms had sufficient
time to enter prosperous industries and to
leave unprosperous industries, the output of
each industry would be large enough for
the firms to just make normal profits. If
total industry output at this point happens
to be 1,500 units and the most profitable
output for each firm is 15 units, as in our
previous example, the industry will obviously be made up of 100 competing firms.

The second and third subquestions are
closely intertwined. In a competitive market
economy, the firms which do the producing
are those which are willing and able to
employ the economically most efficient
technique of production. And what determines the most efficient technique?
Economic efficiency depends upon:

1. Available technology, that is, the alternative combinations of resources or inputs
which will produce the desired output.

2. The prices at which the needed resources can be obtained.

The combination of resources which is
most efficient economically depends not only
upon the physical or engineering data provided by available technology but also upon
the relative worth of the required resources
as measured by their market prices. Thus,
a technique which requires just a few physical inputs of resources to produce a given
output may be highly *inefficient* economically if the required resources are valued
very highly in the market. In other words,
economic efficiency entails getting a given
output of product with the smallest input
of scarce resources, when both output and
resource inputs are measured in dollars-and-
cents terms. In short, that combination of
resources which will produce, say, $15 worth
of product X at the lowest possible money
cost is the most efficient.

Table 5–1 will help illustrate these points.
Suppose there are three different techniques
by which the desired $15 worth of product
X can be produced. The quantity of each
resource required by each technique and
the prices of the required resources are
shown in Table 5–1. By multiplying the
quantities of the various resources required
by the resource prices in each of the three
techniques, the total cost of producing $15
worth of X by each technique can be determined. It can be concluded that technique
No. 2 is economically the most efficient of
the three, for the simple reason that it is
the least costly way of producing $15 worth
of X. Technique No. 2 permits society to
obtain $15 worth of output by using up a
smaller amount of resources—$13 worth—

TABLE 5–1. TECHNIQUES FOR PRODUCING $15 WORTH OF PRODUCT X (hypothetical data)

Resource	Technique No. 1	Technique No. 2	Technique No. 3	Price per unit of resource
Labor	4	2	1	$2
Land	1	3	4	1
Capital	1	1	2	3
Entrepreneurial ability	1	1	1	3
Total cost of $15 worth of X	$15	$13	$15	

than would be used up by the two alternative techniques. Technique No. 2 is the most efficient, because it gives society $15 worth of output for an input of $13 worth of resources; the alternative techniques entail an input of $15 worth of resources for the same amount of output.

But what guarantees that technique No. 2 will actually be used? After all, techniques No. 1 and No. 3 entail a normal profit and thereby will permit firms to survive at least for the moment by using either of these two techniques. The answer to this question is twofold.

1. Technique No. 2 allows the user an economic profit of $2. And firms seeking to further their own interests can be expected to employ techniques which permit them to realize the greatest profits. Firms will *want* to use the most efficient technique because it yields the greatest profit.

2. Competition will literally *force* firms to use the most efficient technique. The firm that fails to employ the least costly method of production will find that other existing firms or new firms coming into the industry will adopt the least costly technique. This leads to an increase in supply and hence to a reduction in the price of X. This will turn the normal profit of the inefficient firm into losses unless it switches to the most efficient technique. Thus, the competitive price system makes the adoption of the most efficient production techniques a condition of survival.

We must emphasize that a change in either technology or resource prices may cause the firm to shift from the technology now employed. For example, if the price of labor falls to 50 cents, technique No. 1 will be superior to technique No. 2. That is, businesses will find that they can lower their costs by shifting to a technology which involves the use of more of that resource whose price has fallen. This shift in techniques illustrates why resource demand curves are downsloping. In this case, a decline in the price of labor prompts businesses to shift to a technique employing more labor and less land. The reader should verify that a new technique involving 1 unit of labor, 4 of land, 1 of capital, and 1 of entrepreneurial ability will be preferable to all three techniques given in Table 5–1, assuming the resource prices given in the table.

Distributing Total Output

The price system enters the picture in two ways in solving the problem of distributing total output. Generally speaking, any given product will be distributed to consumers on the basis of their ability and willingness to pay the existing market price for it. If the price of X is $1 per unit, those buyers who are able and willing to pay that price will get a unit of this product; those who are not, will not. This, we recall, is the rationing function of equilibrium prices.

What determines a consumer's ability to pay the equilibrium price for X and other available products? The size of his money income. And money income in turn depends upon the types and quantities of the various property and human resources which the income receiver supplies and the prices which they command in the resource market. Thus, resource prices play a key role in determining the size of each household's claim against the total output of society. Within the limits of a consumer's money income, his willingness to pay the equilibrium price for X determines whether or not some of this product is distributed to him. And this willingness to buy X will depend upon his preference for X in comparison with available close substitutes for X and their relative prices. Thus, product prices play a key role in determining the expenditure patterns of consumers.

We should emphasize that there is nothing particularly ethical about the price system as a mechanism for distributing the output of pure capitalism. Those households which manage to accumulate large amounts of property resources by inheritance, through their business acumen, or by crook will receive large incomes and thus command large shares of the economy's total output. Others which offer only labor resources valued low by the price system will receive meager money incomes and small portions of total output. The price system is impersonal, and if money incomes are very unequally distributed, a very unequal distribution of the fruits of production will follow (see Chapter 37).

Providing for Flexibility

In order to ensure efficiency in the administration of its resources over a period of time, an economy must be flexible. That particular allocation of resources which is now the most efficient for a *given* pattern of consumer tastes, for a *given* range of technological alternatives, and for *given* supplies of resources can be expected to become obsolete and inefficient as consumer preferences change, new techniques of production are discovered, and resource supplies alter over time. Can the market economy negotiate adjustments in resource uses appropriate to such inevitable changes and thereby remain efficient? Furthermore, in addition to being permissive of, or adaptable to, such changes, is the market economy conducive to changes in technology and the stock of capital which are crucial to economic growth and a higher standard of living?

Is the price system adaptable to change?
Let us suppose a change occurs in consumer tastes. Specifically, let us say that consumers decide they want more shoes and fewer shirts than the economy is currently providing. Will the price system communicate this change to businesses and resource suppliers and prompt appropriate adjustments?

The assumed change in consumers' tastes will be communicated to producers through an increase in the demand for shoes and a decline in the demand for shirts. This means that shoe prices will rise and shirt prices will fall. Now, assuming firms in both

industries are enjoying precisely normal profits prior to these changes in consumer demand, higher shoe prices will mean economic profits for the shoe industry, and lower shirt prices will entail losses for the shirt industry. Self-interest guarantees that competitors will enter the prosperous shoe industry. Losses will in time force firms to leave the depressed shirt industry. As a matter of fact, some firms leaving the shirt industry might enter the shoe industry. But in all probability, most firms entering the shoe industry will be newly created and those leaving the shirt industry will become permanently defunct.

In any event, the prosperous shoe industry will expand, and the unprosperous shirt industry will contract. But these adjustments, we recall, are both self-limiting. The expansion of the shoe industry will continue only to the point at which the resulting increase in the market supply of shoes brings shoe prices back down to a level at which normal profits again prevail. Similarly, contraction in the shirt industry will persist until the accompanying decline in the market supply of shirts brings shirt prices up to a level at which the remaining firms can receive a normal profit. The crucial point to note is that these adjustments in the business sector are completely appropriate to the assumed changes in consumer tastes. Society, that is, consumers, wants more shoes and fewer shirts, and that is precisely what it is getting as the shoe industry expands and the shirt industry contracts.

But this analysis proceeds on the assumption that resource suppliers are agreeable to these adjustments. Will the price system prompt resource suppliers to reallocate their human and property resources from the shirt to the shoe industry, thereby permitting the output of shoes to expand at the expense of shirt production? The answer is "Yes."

The economic profits which initially follow the increase in demand for shoes will not only provide that industry with the inducement to expand but will also give it the added receipts with which to obtain the resources essential to its growth. Higher shoe prices will permit firms in that industry to pay higher prices for resources, thereby drawing resources from what are now less urgent, alternative employments. Willingness and ability to employ more resources in the shoe industry will be communicated back into the resource market through an increase in the demand for resources. Substantially the reverse occurs in the adversely affected shirt industry. The losses which the decline in consumer demand initially entails will cause a decline in the demand for resources in that industry. Workers and other resources released from the contracting shirt industry can now find employment in the expanding shoe industry. As a matter of fact, the increased demand for resources in the shoe industry will mean higher resource prices in that industry than those being paid in the shirt industry, where declines in resource demand have lowered resource prices. The resulting differential in resource prices will provide the incentive for resource owners to further their self-interests by reallocating their resources from the shirt to the shoe industry. And this, of course, is the precise shift needed to permit the shoe industry to expand and the shirt industry to contract.

The ability of the price system to communicate changes in such basic data as consumer tastes and to elicit appropriate responses from both businesses and resource suppliers is sometimes called the *directing* or *guiding function* of prices. By affecting product prices and profits, changes in consumer tastes direct the expansion of some industries and the contraction of others. These adjustments carry through to the resource market as expanding industries demand more resources and contracting industries demand fewer. The resulting changes in resource prices guide resources from the contracting to the expanding industries. In the absence of a price system, some administrative agency, presumably a governmental planning board, would have to undertake the task of directing business institutions and resources into specific lines of production.

Analysis similar to that outlined above would indicate that the price system would adjust appropriately to similar fundamental changes, for example, to changes in technology and changes in the relative supplies of various resources.

Is the price system conducive to change?

Adjusting to given changes is one thing; inducing changes, particularly desirable changes, is something else again. Is the competitive price system congenial to technological improvements and capital accumulation, the interrelated changes which lead to greater productivity and a higher level of material well-being for society? This is not an easy question to answer. We state our reply at this point without stopping for qualifications and modifications (see Chapter 29).

The ideology of pure capitalism, with its emphasis upon the competitive price system, is quite a fertile environment for technological advance. Competition provides the *opportunity* for entrepreneurs to introduce new techniques and new products, unimpeded by the artificial barriers which a noncompetitive environment might entail. The competitive price system also furnishes the *incentive* for technological advance. The introduction of cost-cutting techniques provides the innovating firm with a temporary advantage over its rivals. Lower production costs mean economic profits for the pioneering firm. By passing a part of its cost reduction on to the consumer through a lower product price, the innovating firm can achieve a sizable increase in sales and lucrative economic profits at the expense of rival firms. And, remember, because the monetary rewards of the successful introduction of a new technique will accrue to the innovating firm, the price system will be very effective in harnessing individual incentives in the cause of technological advance.

Looking at technological advance from the social point of view, we should note that the innovating firm's economic profits will be a temporary phenomenon. Other firms can also adopt the new cost-reducing technique. Indeed, as we have seen, they will be forced to do so. Why? Because by price cutting, the innovating firm will turn the once-normal profits of its competitors into losses. This is of considerable significance: It is in this fashion that the competitive price system communicates the technological improvements of one firm to all other firms in that industry. Rivals must follow the lead of the most progressive firm or suffer the immediate penalty of losses and the eventual pain of bankruptcy.

We should note that the lower product price which the technological advance permits will cause the innovating industry to expand. This expansion may be the result of existing firms expanding their rates of output or of new firms entering the industry under the lure of the economic profits initially created by a technological advance. This expansion, that is, the diversion of resources from nonprogressive to progressive industries, is as it should be. Sustained efficiency in the use of scarce resources demands that resources be continually reallocated from industries whose productive techniques are relatively less efficient to those whose techniques are relatively more efficient.

But technological advance typically entails the use of increased amounts of capital goods. Can the price system provide the capital goods upon which technological advance relies? More specifically, can the entrepreneur as an innovator command through the price system the resources necessary to produce the machinery and equipment upon which technological advance depends?

Obviously, he can. If society registers dollar votes for capital goods, the product market and resource market will adjust to these votes by producing capital goods. In other words, the price system acknowledges

dollar voting for both consumer and capital goods. Indeed, the relative sizes of these two types of dollar voting determine how a market economy will divide its total output between consumer goods, which satisfy wants directly, and capital goods, which satisfy wants indirectly through the more efficient production of consumer goods.

But who will register votes for capital goods? First, the entrepreneur as a receiver of profit income can be expected to apportion a part of his income to the accumulation of capital goods. By so doing he can achieve an even greater profit income in the future if his innovation proves successful. Furthermore, by paying a rate of interest, entrepreneurs can borrow portions of the incomes of other households and use these borrowed funds in casting dollar votes for the production of more capital goods.

In practice, the process of technological advance and capital accumulation is much more complex than envisioned here (see Chapter 12). The important point for present purposes is that the market economy provides the opportunity and incentive for technological advance and the means for providing the capital goods which such advance typically presumes.

Competition, Control, and the "Invisible Hand"

Though the price system is the organizing mechanism of pure capitalism, it is essential to recognize the role of competition as the mechanism of control in such an economy. The market mechanism of supply and demand communicates the wants of consumers (society) to businesses and through businesses to resource suppliers. It is competition, however, which forces businesses and resource suppliers to make appropriate responses. To illustrate: The impact of an increase in consumer demand for some product will raise that good's price above the wage, rent, interest, and normal profit costs of production. The resulting economic profits in effect are a signal to producers that society wants more of the product. It is competition—in particular, the ability of new firms to enter the industry—that simultaneously brings an expansion of output and a lowering of price back to a level just consistent with production costs. However, if the industry was not competitive, but dominated by, say, one huge firm which was able to prohibit the entry of potential competitors, that firm could enjoy economic profits by preventing the expansion of the industry.

But competition does more than guarantee responses appropriate to the wishes of society. It is competition which forces firms to adopt the most efficient productive techniques. In a competitive market, the failure of some firms to use the least costly production technique means eventual elimination by other competing firms who do employ the most efficient methods of production. Finally, we have seen that competition provides an environment conducive to technological advance.

A very remarkable aspect of the operation and the adjustments of a competitive price system is that a curious and important identity is involved—the identity of private and social interests. That is, firms and resource suppliers, seeking to further their own self-interest and operating within the framework of a highly competitive market system, will simultaneously, as though guided by an "invisible hand,"[1] promote the public or social interest. For example, we have seen that given a competitive environment, business firms use the least costly combination of resources in producing a given output because it is in their self-interest to do so. To act otherwise would be to forgo profits or even to risk bankruptcy over a period of time. But at the same time it is obviously also in the social interest to use scarce resources in the least costly, that is, most efficient, manner. To do

otherwise would be to produce a given output at a greater cost or sacrifice of alternative goods than is really necessary. Furthermore, in our more-shoes-fewer-shirts illustration, it is self-interest, awakened and guided by the competitive price system, which induces the very responses appropriate to the assumed change in society's wants. Businesses seeking to make higher profits and to avoid losses, on the one hand, and resource suppliers pursuing greater monetary rewards, on the other, negotiate the very changes in the allocation of resources and therefore the composition of output which society now demands. The force of competition, in other words, controls or guides the self-interest motive in such a way that it automatically, and quite unintentionally, furthers the best interests of society.

AN EVALUATION OF THE PRICE SYSTEM

Is the price system the best means of deciding how total output is to be determined, how production of that output should be organized, and how total output should be distributed? This is a complex question; any complete answer necessarily leaps the boundary of facts and enters the realm of values. This means there is no scientific answer to the query. The very fact that there exist many competing ways of allocating scarce resources is ample evidence of disagreement as to the effectiveness of the price system.

The Case for the Price System

1. The basic economic argument for the price system is that it leads to an efficient allocation of resources. The competitive price system, it is argued, guides resources into the production of those goods and services most wanted by society. It forces the use of the most efficient techniques in organizing resources for production, and it is conducive to the development and adoption of new and more efficient production

[1] Adam Smith, *The Wealth of Nations* (New York: Modern Library, Inc., originally published in 1776), p. 423.

techniques. In short, proponents of the price system argue that the "invisible hand" will in effect harness self-interest so as to provide society with the greatest output of wanted goods from its available resources. This, then, suggests the maximum economic efficiency.

2. The major noneconomic argument for the price system is its great emphasis upon personal freedom. The price system permits —indeed, it thrives upon—freedom of enterprise and choice. Entrepreneurs and workers are not herded from industry to industry to meet the production targets established by some omnipotent governmental agency. On the contrary, they are free to further their own self-interests, subject, of course, to the rewards and penalties imposed by the price system itself.

The Case against the Price System

The case against the price system is somewhat more complex. Critics of the market economy base their position on the following points:

1. They argue that capitalistic ideology is conducive to the demise of its main controlling mechanism—competition. The alleged weakening of competition as a control mechanism comes from two basic sources.

On the one hand, though desirable from the social point of view, competition is most irksome to the individual producer subject to its rigors. It is allegedly inherent in the free, individualistic environment of the capitalistic system that the profit-seeking entrepreneur will attempt to break free of the restraining force of competition in trying to better his position. Combination, conspiracy, cutthroat competition, and sheer productive efficiency are all means to the end of reducing competition and escaping its regulatory powers.

On the other hand, the very technological advance which the price system fosters has contributed to the decline of competition. Modern technology typically requires (1) the use of extremely large quantities of real capital, (2) large markets, (3) a complex, centralized, and closely integrated management, and (4) large and reliable sources of raw materials. Such an operation implies the need for producers who are large-scale not only in the absolute sense but also in relation to the size of the market. In other words, the achievement of maximum productive efficiency through the employment of the best available technology often requires the existence of a small number of large firms rather than a large number of small ones.

To the degree that competition declines, the price system will be weakened as a mechanism for efficiently allocating resources. Producers and resource suppliers will be less subject to the will of consumers; the sovereignty of producers and resource suppliers will then challenge and weaken the sovereignty of consumers. The "invisible hand" identity of private and social interest will begin to lose its grip.

2. Critics also challenge the assertion that the price system provides the goods most wanted by society. This criticism has several roots. First, to the extent that a weakening of competition, as discussed above, lessens consumer sovereignty, the price system becomes less proficient in allocating resources in precise accord with the wishes of consumers.

Second, critical socialists contend that the price system allows the more efficient, or more cunning, entrepreneurs to accumulate vast amounts of property resources, the accumulation process being extended through time by the right to bequeath. This, in addition to differences in the amount and quality of human resources supplied by various households, causes a highly unequal distribution of money incomes in a market economy. The result is that families differ greatly in their ability to express their wants in the market. The wealthy have more dollar votes than the poor. Hence, it is concluded that the price system allocates resources to the production of frivolous luxury goods for the rich at the expense of the output of necessities for the poor. A country that[2]

. . . spends money on champagne before it has provided milk for its babies is a badly managed, silly, vain, stupid, ignorant nation. . . . The only way in which such a nation can make itself wealthy and prosperous is by good housekeeping: that is by providing for its wants in order of their importance, and allowing no money to be wasted on whims and luxuries until the necessities have been thoroughly served.

In the third place, critics point out that the price system sometimes fails to register all the costs and benefits associated with the production of certain goods and services. That is, consumer demand only embodies the satisfactions which accrue to individual consumers who purchase goods and services; it does not reflect the fact that the purchase of such services as polio shots and chest X rays yields widespread benefits or satisfactions to the community (society) as a whole. Similarly, the supply decisions of producers hinge upon the costs which they must bear and do not reflect certain costs associated with production which might accrue to society as a whole. The smoke, smog, and pollution of rivers which have characterized the production of certain industries illustrate such costs. The point is this: Where demand and supply do not accurately reflect all the benefits and all the costs of production, the price system cannot be expected to bring about an allocation of resources which best satisfies the wants of society.

A final argument is this: The price system tabulates only individual wants. There are many wants involving goods and services which cannot be financed by individuals as such. For example, such goods and services as education, highways, and

[2] George Bernard Shaw, *The Intelligent Woman's Guide to Socialism and Capitalism* (New York: Brentano's, Inc., 1928), pp. 50–55. Used by permission of the Public Trustee and the Society of Authors.

national defense cannot be purchased in desired amounts by households on an individual basis. They can only be consumed economically on a social, or collective, basis. The price system, it is argued, is incapable of registering such social, or collective, wants.

3. The price system has also been criticized for its failure to adjust rapidly to drastic changes in society's production objectives. There is allegedly a persistent time lag between society's production targets and the actual pattern of resource allocation provided by the price system. Even in a highly competitive market economy, the occupational and geographic mobility of human resources will be far from perfect. Laborers are hesitant to sever social ties and move to a strange community to take a new job. Such a move may also be costly, particularly if the worker must equip himself with new skills. And property resources are usually reallocated through the price system with even less rapidity. In other words, the economy may be plagued with certain declining, or "sick," industries. This is the case with agriculture in the United States. For a variety of complex reasons (to be discussed in a later chapter), agriculture has declined significantly in its relative importance to the economy. This decline calls for an exodus of resources to expanding industries, an exodus which in practice has simply not been fast enough. The result? Too many resources engaged in the production of farm commodities whose relative importance to consumers has declined and not enough resources engaged in the production of antibiotics, synthetic fibers, and plastics.

In particular, critics contend that the price system is incapable of adjusting with rapidity and certainty to the dramatic alteration in production goals which war entails. The price system can make appropriate adjustments in time to modest shifts in the pattern of society's wants. It is not capable of rapidly reallocating its resources from civilian to war goods production in that critical situation in which time is the most important resource of all. The same general argument, of course, applies to somewhat less drastic changes in production goals caused by such considerations as the disruption of international trade due to, say, political considerations, or the sudden and unanticipated introduction of a particularly significant technological advance.

4. Finally, as we noted at the beginning of this chapter, the price system is widely recognized as an imperfect mechanism for providing the continuous, full employment of the economy's resources.

Which of these two positions is correct? To a degree both are. The several criticisms of the market economy are reasonably accurate and certainly too serious to ignore. On the other hand, we cannot judge an issue by the number of arguments pro and con. The basic economic argument for the price system—it tends to provide an efficient allocation of resources—is not easily undermined. In practice, the price system is—or at least can be—reasonably efficient.

Relevance, Realism, and the Price System

Does the price system of American capitalism function in the same fashion as the price system discussed in this chapter? In principle, yes; in detail, no. Our discussion of the price system provides us with a working model—a first approximation—of the actual price system of American capitalism. Our analysis presents a much-simplified, yet useful, picture of the real thing.

Specifically, the basic differences between the price system as pictured in this chapter and the actual price system of American capitalism are two in number:

1. In many product and resource markets, competition clearly has been supplanted by a few giant business corporations and huge labor unions. Competition is simply not as vigorous in practice as our discussion of the price system presumed. This means that the decisions of businesses and resource suppliers are less than per-

fectly synchronized with those of consumers and that changes in the production goals of society are less precisely communicated throughout the economy. Giant business and labor groups in American capitalism have the power to resist the dictates of consumer sovereignty and, as a matter of fact, will usually find it personally advantageous to do so.

2. Another major difference between our model price system and the market system of American capitalism lies in the economic role of government in the latter. In contrast with the passive, limited government envisioned in the ideology of pure capitalism, the government of American capitalism is an active and integral component of the economy. In particular, the economy of the United States has taken cognizance of the elements of truth which permeate the noted criticisms of the price system. Through government, society has taken steps to correct these shortcomings. Hence, government pursues policies designed, not only to preserve and bolster competition, but also to adjust certain inequities fostered by the price system, to speed on occasion the reallocation of resources, and to help maintain full employment. It is with these and related economic functions of government that the ensuing chapter is concerned.

Is our analysis of the price system realistic? Does it provide a workable description of the price system of American capitalism? One scholar has recently provided a meaningful reply to these questions:[3]

For all the new quality of twentieth-century industrial society, the great principles of self-interest and competition, however watered down or hedged about, still provide basic rules of behavior which no economic organization can afford to disregard entirely . . . the laws of the market can be discerned . . . if we look beneath the surface.

[3] Robert L. Heilbroner, *The Worldly Philosophers*, rev. ed. (New York: Simon and Schuster, Inc., 1961), p. 44.

SUMMARY

1. In a market economy, the interacting decisions of competing buyers and sellers will determine a system of product and resource prices at any given point in time.

2. The relative scarcity of economic resources makes the operation of any economy a matter of choosing between alternatives. At any point in time, these choices depend upon the relative scarcity of resources and products. Over time, the degree to which these choices are altered as product and resource prices change depends upon the willingness and ability of consumers to make substitutions among products and the willingness and ability of producers to make substitutions among resources. Substitutability tends to relieve particular scarcities of resources and products.

3. Those products whose production and sale yield total receipts sufficient to cover all costs, including a normal profit, will be produced. Those whose production will not yield a normal profit will not be produced.

4. Economic profits designate an industry as prosperous and signal its expansion. Losses mean an industry is unprosperous and result in a contraction of that industry. Industrial expansion and contraction are self-limiting processes. As expansion increases market supply relative to market demand, the price of a product falls to the point where all economic profits disappear. As contraction decreases market supply relative to market demand, the resulting increase in product price eliminates losses and makes the industry normally profitable once again.

5. Consumer sovereignty dominates a competitive market economy. The penalty of losses and lure of profits force both businesses and resource suppliers to channel their efforts in accordance with the wants of consumers.

6. Competition forces firms to use the least costly and therefore the most economically efficient productive techniques.

7. The price system plays a dual role in distributing total output among individual households. The prices commanded by the quantities and types of resources supplied by each household will determine the number of dollar claims against the economy's output each household receives. Given consumer tastes, product prices are of fundamental importance in determining consumer expenditure patterns. Within the limits of each household's money income, consumer preferences and the relative prices of products determine the distribution of total output.

8. The competitive price system can communicate changes in consumer tastes to resource suppliers and entrepreneurs, thereby prompting appropriate adjustments in the allocation of the economy's resources. The competitive price system also provides an environment conducive to technological advance and capital accumulation.

9. Competition, the primary mechanism of control in the market economy, will foster an identity of private and social interests; as though directed by an "invisible hand," competition harnesses the self-interest motives of business and resource suppliers so as to simultaneously further the social interest.

10. The basic virtue of the price system is its continuing emphasis upon efficiency. It produces what consumers want through the use of the most efficient techniques. Operation and adjustments of the price system are automatic in the sense that they are the result of individual, decentralized decisions, not the centralized decisions of government.

11. Criticisms of the price system are several: **a.** The controlling mechanism, competition, tends to weaken over time; **b.** inherent income inequalities, inability to register collective wants, and the exclusion of certain costs and satisfactions from supply and demand prevent the price system from producing that collection of goods most wanted by society; **c.** the price system reallocates resources too slowly during war and similar emergencies; **d.** the competitive price system does not guarantee continued full employment.

12. The price system of American capitalism differs from the competitive price system in that the former is characterized by **a.** giant corporations and unions in certain product and resource markets and **b.** government intervention in the economy to correct the major defects of the price system. Yet the competitive price system does provide a working model whereby we can understand the price system of American capitalism.

QUESTIONS AND STUDY SUGGESTIONS

1. Describe in detail how the price system answers the Five Fundamental Questions.
2. Why must economic choices be made? How do scarcity and substitutability influence the rendering of economic choices? Be specific.
3. "The capitalistic system is a profit and loss economy." Carefully analyze and explain the significance of this statement.
4. Define and explain the significance of "dollar voting," "consumer sovereignty," and the "invisible hand."
5. What is the directing or guiding function of the competitive price system? Contrast the guiding function with the rationing function discussed in Chapter 4.
6. "Production methods which are inferior in the engineering sense may be the most efficient methods in the economic sense." Explain.
7. Evaluate and explain the following statements:
   a. "The most important feature of capitalism is the absence of a central economic plan."
   b. "Competition is the indispensable disciplinarian of the market economy."
8. Explain fully the meaning and implications of the following quotation:[4]

   The beautiful consequence of the market is that it is its own guardian. If output prices or certain kinds of remuneration stray away from their socially ordained levels, forces are set into motion to bring them back to the fold. It is a curious paradox which thus ensues: the market, which is the acme of individual economic freedom, is the strictest taskmaster of all. One may appeal the ruling of a planning board or win the dispensation of a minister; but there is no appeal, no dispensation, from the anonymous pressures of the market mechanism. Economic freedom is thus more illusory than at first appears. One can do as one pleases in the market. But if one pleases to do what the market disapproves, the price of individual freedom is economic ruination.

9. Assume that a business firm finds that its profits will be at a maximum when it produces $40 worth of product A. Suppose also that each of

---

[4] *Ibid.*, p. 42.

the three techniques shown in the following table will produce the desired output.

Resource	Technique No. 1	Technique No. 2	Technique No. 3	Price per unit of resource
Labor	5	2	3	$3
Land	2	4	2	4
Capital	2	4	5	2
Entrepreneurial ability	4	2	4	2

a. Given the resource prices shown above, which technique will the firm choose? Why?

b. Assume now that a new technique, technique No. 4, is developed. It entails the use of 2 units of labor, 2 of land, 6 of capital, and 3 of entrepreneurial ability. Given the resource prices in the table, will the firm adopt the new technique? Explain your answer.

c. Suppose now that the price of labor falls to $1.50 per unit, all other resource prices being unchanged. What technique will the producer now choose? Explain.

d. "The price system causes the economy to conserve most in the use of those resources which are particularly scarce in supply. Resources which are scarcest relative to the demand for them have the highest prices. As a result, producers use these resources as sparingly as is possible." Evaluate this statement. Does your answer to question 9c bear out this contention? Explain.

10. Interpret and explain the following quotation in terms of Table 5–1:[5]

Soviet industrialization has taken place against the background of an abundance of manpower. . . . It was therefore economically sensible for them to use labor lavishly, substituting it whenever possible for capital goods, and bringing in more workers whenever it was possible by doing so to squeeze a bit more output out of existing enterprises. The result of such a policy was to make output per worker low, but it was still the correct thing to do in the light of the abundance of labor.

Output per Soviet worker is considerably lower than output per American worker. Does this necessarily mean that the Soviet economy is inefficient and wasteful as compared to the United States economy? Explain.

11. What are the major criticisms of the price system? Carefully evaluate these criticisms.

---

[5] Robert W. Campbell, "Problems of United States–Soviet Economic Comparisons," in Joint Economic Committee, *Comparisons of the United States and Soviet Economics* (Washington: Government Printing Office, 1960), p. 26.

SELECTED REFERENCES

Boulding, Kenneth E.: *Economic Analysis,* 3d ed. (New York: Harper & Row, Publishers, Incorporated, 1955), chap. 9.

Buckingham, Walter S., Jr.: *Theoretical Economic Systems* (New York: The Ronald Press Company, 1958), chaps. 2–4.

Heilbroner, Robert L.: *The Worldly Philosophers,* rev. ed. (New York: Simon and Schuster, Inc., 1961), chap. 3.

Kirzner, Israel M.: *Market Theory and the Price System* (Princeton, N.J.: D. Van Nostrand Company, Inc., 1963), chaps. 1–3.

Leeman, Wayne A. (ed.): *Capitalism, Market Socialism, and Central Planning* (Boston: Houghton Mifflin Company, 1963), chaps. 1, 2, 9–11.

Radford, R. A.: "The Economic Organization of a POW Camp," *Economica,* November, 1945, pp. 189–201.

Slichter, Sumner H.: "Free Private Enterprise," in Paul A. Samuelson, John R. Coleman, Robert L. Bishop, and Philip R. Saunders (eds.), *Readings in Economics,* 4th ed. (New York: McGraw-Hill Book Company, 1964), chap. 27.

CHAPTER 6

MIXED CAPITALISM AND THE ECONOMIC FUNCTIONS OF GOVERNMENT

We now begin the move from our abstract working model of pure capitalism to a discussion of American capitalism. In so doing we inject a significant dose of reality into our analysis.

All real-life economies are "mixed"; government and the price system share the function of answering the Five Fundamental Questions. Yet the various economies of the world differ drastically in the particular blend of government direction and market direction which they embody (see Table 2–3). The economy of Soviet Russia, the topic of the final chapter of this book, leans heavily toward the planned economy model. American capitalism, on the other hand, is predominantly a market economy. Yet the economic functions of government— Federal, state, and local—are of considerable significance. In American capitalism a number of strategic economic decisions are rendered, not by individuals as such, but collectively through government. A rough indicator of the relative importance of the market and government in American capitalism is the fact that in peacetime about four-fifths of the total output of the economy is provided by the market system, the remaining one-fifth being produced under the sponsorship of government. In short, the economy of the United States can be accurately described as *mixed capitalism.* Our economy holds *generally* to the capitalist ideology outlined in Chapter 3 and relies primarily upon the price system, the rudiments and functioning of which were outlined in Chapters 4 and 5. Government, however, in a variety of significant ways, assists and modifies the functioning of the price system.

ECONOMIC FUNCTIONS OF GOVERNMENT

The economic functions of government are many, and they are varied. As a matter of fact, the economic role of government is so broad in scope that it is virtually impossible to establish an all-inclusive list of its economic functions. We shall employ the following breakdown of government's economic activities as a pattern for our discussion, recognizing that some overlapping is unavoidable.

First, some of the economic functions of government are designed to strengthen and facilitate the operation of the price system. The two major activities of government in this area are:

1. Providing the legal foundation and a social environment conducive to the effective operation of the price system
2. Maintaining competition

Through a second group of functions, government supplements and modifies the operation of the price system. There are four major functions of government here. They involve:

3. Providing a minimum standard of living for all households in the economy
4. Adjusting the composition of total output to account for social costs and revenues
5. Providing society with social goods and services
6. Controlling unemployment and infla-

tion caused by the business cycle and promoting economic growth

Our immediate objective is simply that of seeing how government affects the character and operation of the economy. More specifically, we want to know how the economic functions of government affect

1. The level at which the economy is employing its available resources.

2. The efficiency with which the economy allocates its employed resources among alternative employments.

In short, we want to discover the role of government in the achievement of full employment and full production. We also seek a basic understanding of the methods or techniques by which government affects employment and resource allocation.

All six of government's economic functions—with rare exceptions—influence both the level of employment and the allocation of resources. But we can generalize that the first five functions have their basic impact upon resource allocation—they either draw resources from private to public uses or cause resources to be reallocated among alternative private uses. The sixth function is obviously aimed at the level of resource use. We defer discussion of this sixth function until Part Two.

Legal and Social Framework for the Price System

Government assumes the task of providing the legal framework and certain basic services prerequisite to the effective operation of a market economy. The necessary legal framework involves such things as providing for the legal status of business enterprises, defining the rights of private ownership, and providing for the enforcement of contracts. Government also establishes legal "rules of the game" to govern the relationships of businesses, resource suppliers, and consumers with one another. Through legislation, government is enabled to referee economic relationships, detect foul play, and exercise authority in imposing appropriate penalties. The basic services provided by government include the use of police powers to maintain internal order, provision of a system of standards for measuring the weight and quality of products, and establishment of a monetary system to facilitate the exchange of goods and services.

The Pure Food and Drug Act of 1906 and its various amendments provide an excellent example of how government has strengthened the operation of the price system. This act sets rules of conduct to govern producers in their relationships with consumers. It prohibits the sale of adulterated and misbranded foods and drugs, requires the net weights of products to be specified on their containers, establishes quality standards which must be stated on the labels of canned foods, and prohibits deceptive claims on patent-medicine labels. These measures all prevent fraudulent activities on the part of producers and, simultaneously, increase the public's confidence in the integrity of the price system. In later chapters we shall discuss similar legislation pertaining to labor-management relations and the relations of business firms to one another.

How is resource allocation affected by this type of government activity? Resource allocation will be altered and, in general, improved upon. Supplying a medium of exchange, ensuring the quality of products, defining ownership rights, and enforcing contracts tend to increase the volume of exchange. This widens markets and permits greater specialization in the use of both property and human resources. Such specialization, we saw in Chapter 3, means a more efficient allocation of resources.

Maintaining Competition

Competition is the basic regulatory mechanism in a capitalistic economy. It is the force which subjects producers and resource suppliers to the dictates of buyer or consumer sovereignty. With competition it is the supply and demand decisions of *many* sellers and buyers which determine market prices. This means that individual producers and resource suppliers can only adjust to the wishes of buyers as tabulated and communicated by the price system. Profits and survival await the competitive producers who obey the price system; losses and eventual bankruptcy are the lot of those who deviate from it. With competition, buyers are the boss, the market is their agent, and businesses their servant.

The growth of monopoly drastically alters this situation. What is monopoly? Broadly defined, it is the situation wherein the number of sellers becomes small enough for each seller to influence total supply and therefore the price of the commodity being sold. What is its significance? Simply this: When monopoly supplants competition, sellers can influence, or "rig," the market in terms of their own self-interests. Through their ability to influence total supply, monopolists can create artificial shortages of products and thereby enjoy higher prices and, very frequently, persistent economic profits. This is obviously in direct conflict with the interests of consumers. Monopolists are not regulated by the will of society as competitive sellers are. Producer sovereignty supplants consumer sovereignty to the degree that monopoly supplants competition. The result is that resources are allocated in terms of the profit-seeking interests of monopolistic sellers rather than in terms of the wants of society as a whole. In short, monopoly tends to cause a misallocation of economic resources. In later chapters we shall have more to say about the growth and characteristics of monopoly, and public policy toward business monopoly will be explored in considerable detail. The important points for present purposes are these:

1. Monopoly impairs the efficiency with which the price system allocates resources.

2. Government assumes responsibility for retarding monopoly or, where its growth is inevitable, for preventing undue abuse of monopoly power through some form of social regulation.

Even if the legal foundation of capitalistic institutions is assured and competition is maintained, there will still be a need for certain additional economic functions on the part of government. *The market economy at its best has certain biases and shortcomings which compel government to supplement and modify its operation.*

Minimum Standard of Living

The price system is an impersonal mechanism, and the distribution of income to which it gives rise may entail more inequality than society desires. Households owning resources which are very productive in turning out goods and services highly valued by society will realize large money incomes. But some households possess resources that are relatively unproductive or capable only of producing goods and services society does not value very highly. Worse yet, the aged, the physically and mentally handicapped, the widowed, and the unemployed are unable to earn any income at all through the price system. In short, the price system entails considerable inequality in the distribution of money income and therefore in the distribution of total output among individual households.

To remedy this situation, government has assumed the responsibility of providing a minimum standard of living for its citizenry. This responsibility is reflected in a variety of policies and programs. *Public assistance programs* provide emergency relief to the destitute, aid to the dependent and handicapped, unemployment compensation to the unemployed. These programs provide income for households which would otherwise have little or none. They achieve this goal by altering the income distribution which the price system provides. Other programs involve *direct market intervention*, in which the government alters income distribution by modifying the prices established by the forces of supply and demand. Price supports for farmers and minimum wage legislation both involve government price fixing designed to aid those whose incomes would otherwise be niggardly. Furthermore, the *taxation and expenditure* programs of government have a Robin Hood effect upon the economy: Federal taxes bear down relatively more on the rich than on the poor, and many government expenditures of these tax revenues are for goods and services the benefits of which accrue primarily to the poor. Free public medical and legal services are cases in point.

All these programs and policies will be discussed at some length in a later chapter. The question we now ask is this: How will these modifications in the distribution of income affect the structure of society's product demands and, therefore, the allocation of resources? The answer is most evident in the case of public assistance programs. These programs are financed through taxes levied upon households and businesses as a whole. These taxes cause consumers to pare the least essential items from their budgets and businesses to reduce the size of their dividend payments and their levels of investment spending. The receivers of the various public assistance payments, being on the lowest rung of the income ladder, will assumedly spend this income on bare necessities. The net result? The structure of consumer demand and ultimately the allocation of resources will be altered. Fewer resources will be allocated to the production of Buicks, fur coats, jewelry, entertainment, and the construction of capital facilities and more to the production of basic foodstuffs and clothing.

Adjusting Output for Social Costs and Revenues

The price system of pure capitalism operates in response to decisions made by *individual* consumers and *individual* business firms. In deciding what is to be produced and not produced, the price system reacts to the summation of individual wants or satisfactions. And the specific amounts of various goods produced will depend upon the costs which individual firms must bear in acquiring the resources necessary for production. The production of certain goods and services, however, may entail satisfactions and costs which accrue not to individual consumers and individual firms but rather to society as a whole. The price system contains a bias: It does not take into account certain social benefits and social costs which the production of specific goods may entail.

Social costs. Under competition, supply and demand will set product price at a level that will cover the costs of obtaining the economic resources needed in producing a particular commodity. These costs, which are determined in the resource market, are sometimes called *private costs*. They are costs which private business concerns *must* bear if they are to continue to obtain resources.

But the productive process may sometimes entail certain other costs which are not necessarily incorporated in the price system. These costs do not entail the direct depletion or using up of specific resources, but result rather in the overall debasement of the environment in which the production of a commodity occurs. Some examples will clarify this point. Occasionally a firm may avoid the expense of properly disposing of its waste materials by polluting near-by lakes or rivers with such wastes, thereby destroying the beauty and recreational value of these lakes and rivers. Or heavy industry may spew smoke and dust on an otherwise serene residential area rather than foot the cost of smoke- and dust-abatement equipment. Or production may entail unpleasant odors or the risk of explosions. In each case the guilty firms are shifting a portion of those costs which legitimately they should be expected to bear onto society as a whole. The costs which private industry shifts to society are called *social costs*.

How do social costs affect output and, therefore, the allocation of economic resources? By pushing some of their costs onto the community, firms find that their total costs of production are lower than would otherwise be the case. With lower costs, the producer will be in a position to produce a greater output of his product at each possible price (see Chapter 4). This greater supply, given consumer demand, means a lower price and a larger output of this product than would otherwise result. In other words, more of such goods are produced and sold than would be the case where *all* costs were borne directly by the producer. A greater output of these products occurs than a more accurate accounting of all costs—both private and social—would entail. In brief, a loophole in the price system—that is, the possibility of a firm's or industry's shifting some of its costs to society as a whole—creates a bias in favor of greater production of these products in which significant social costs are involved. Economic resources are misallocated accordingly; too many resources will be used in the production of those products which entail substantial social costs.

Recouping social costs. What can government do to correct this shortcoming of the price system? Two courses of action are plausible. Looking at our initial example, the first and most direct step is to legislate against the pollution of rivers and lakes, smoke and dust hazards, and so on. This forces the guilty firms to bear all costs connected with the production of the given product. Because costs are now higher, supply will fall. This means a rise in price, curtailed consumption of the product, and a reallocation of resources from the guilty firms or industries to alternative uses. A second and more indirect policy would be for government—specifically the local government of the community bearing the social costs—to levy special taxes on offending firms sufficient to cover the social costs. If the community must suffer the costs entailed in clearing its polluted rivers and lakes or suffer the inconvenience of having them polluted, the community is justified in recouping these costs from the guilty party. In effect, through a special tax, government

attempts to shove back onto those offending firms the costs which private industry has sought to avoid. With the added tax costs the producers will now have to demand a higher price at each possible level of output. This means a decline in supply relative to demand: price rises and sales decline. Resources will then be freed from these firms for other uses. The net result will be an improved allocation of resources—an allocation more consistent with the *total* costs of production. The tax will tend to correct the bias in the price system which arises when significant social costs are present. Similarly, smoke and dust hazards necessitate more frequent painting of houses, added medical costs, higher laundry bills, and so forth. Risks of explosion add to insurance premiums in the community. Once again special tax levies may help recoup these costs for the community.

Social revenues. But the reverse of this situation may also arise. In a competitive economy, goods are produced on the basis of *individual* wants. If the wants of many individual consumers are very intense for a particular product, producers will find it profitable to supply society with a large volume of that commodity. The number of individual consumers who want a product and the intensity with which they desire it depends upon the satisfactions, benefits, or "revenues"[1] which private consumers get from the particular product. The operation of the price system is thus geared to *private revenues*, or private benefits. This is so because goods and services in a purely capitalistic system are bought almost exclusively by private consumers acting as individuals. *As a result, the price system may overlook certain widespread benefits or revenues which accrue to the community as a whole*

---

[1] "Revenue" in this case is not a dollar-and-cents magnitude but rather a subjective concept. The revenue to which we refer in this case is the pleasure which consumers get from particular products.

when individuals consume certain goods and services. Such benefits are called *social revenues.* For example, chest X rays and polio immunization shots result in direct private benefits to the immediate consumer. But an early diagnosis of tuberculosis and the prevention of a contagious disease yield widespread benefits or revenues to the entire community. And these social revenues are significant. The price system of a purely capitalistic system has no way of responding to such social revenues. Why? Because pure capitalism is an individualistic economy which reacts only to the private revenues or satisfactions of individual consumers. Here, then, is another bias or shortcoming in the price system of pure capitalism—it does not take into account the total benefits or revenues accruing from the production of a product but only those benefits received directly and immediately by individual buyers.

Compensating for social revenues. How does this bias affect the allocation of resources in the economy? If our goal is to achieve the greatest satisfaction of wants, that is, the maximum amount of benefits or revenues *for the economy as a whole,* society should obviously allocate more resources to the production of those goods and services which entail significant social revenues than the price system provides.

Assuming that the social revenues involved are not inordinately large as compared with private revenues, government can encourage the production of such goods by subsidizing their output. This subsidy may assume a variety of forms—an outright bounty to the producer for each unit of output, favorable tax treatment, free use of government materials and facilities, and so forth. Regardless of its form, the subsidy will encourage firms to produce more of such products than would otherwise be the case, which, in turn, means a greater allocation of resources to their production. Government subsidization of the polio immunization program is a case in point. In

short, subsidies can be used to stimulate the output and consumption of those products from which the social revenues are too significant for society to ignore.

Social Goods and Services

There are certain types of goods and services which are produced in grossly insufficient amounts, or possibly not at all, in an economy that relies entirely upon the price system in answering the Five Fundamental Questions. Such products are called *social* or *collective goods.* If society is to obtain social goods in desired amounts, their production must be sponsored, or directly carried on, by government. It is important at the outset to contrast social goods with the *individual,* or *private,* goods which are produced by private enterprises through the price system.

Private goods and social goods. The bulk of the goods and services which we consume—for example, loaves of bread, shoes, Fords, transistor radios, suits, oranges, and so forth—are private goods. These goods have the following basic characteristics:

1. They are *divisible.* Private goods can be produced in units sufficiently small for individual households to purchase them out of their personal incomes.

2. The satisfactions, benefits, or "revenues" from the consumption of private goods are limited almost exclusively to the individual who purchases them.

3. It follows from these first two characteristics that private goods can be readily provided through the market system. Buyers reveal their preferences through market demand, and individual producers react accordingly. The specific amounts of private goods consumed depend upon such considerations as the preferences or tastes of households, the size of money incomes, production costs, and the relative prices of the various private goods. And in the case of private goods the so-called *exclusion principle* applies: Those who are not willing

and able to pay the market price for private goods are excluded from the benefits or enjoyment such goods confer.

Social goods and services—national defense, highways, education, police and fire protection, and so forth—differ from private goods in one or more of the following ways:

1. Social goods are *indivisible*. They come in such large units that they cannot be readily purchased by individual households or, therefore, profitably produced through the initiative of private industry.

2. Social goods, because of their bulk and nature, typically yield large and widespread benefits or satisfactions to the community and society as a whole. In other words, social goods entail very great and widely apportioned social revenues.

3. Social goods are *not* subject to the exclusion principle and therefore cannot be provided on the basis of buyer initiative through the market mechanism. The benefits from national defense, a flood-control or insect-abatement program, and the provision of police and fire protection or a judiciary system accrue to all who live in the nation or region where the service is rendered. These benefits cannot be effectively withheld; there is no mechanism, comparable to the market in the case of private goods, to exclude some particular individuals or groups from the benefits social goods provide. The inapplicability of the exclusion principle of the market makes it necessary that the production of social goods be sponsored, and sometimes directly undertaken, by government. This production is generally financed through taxes—compulsory levies—imposed upon society or regional beneficiaries as a whole. It is the inapplicability of the exclusion principle that makes tax finance necessary; consumers will ordinarily not make voluntary payments for goods and services whose benefits cannot be denied to them even if they do not help pay for them.

Social goods are thus purchased through the government on the basis of group, or collective, choices in contrast to private goods, which are purchased from private enterprises on the basis of individual choices. More specifically, the types and quantities of the various social goods produced are determined in a democracy by political means, that is, by voting. The quantities of the various social goods consumed are a matter of public policy.[2] These group decisions, made in the political arena, supplement the individual choices of households and businesses in answering the Five Fundamental Questions.

It should be very evident by now that the primary goal of government in supplying social goods and services is to reallocate resources. Social goods have characteristics which virtually preclude their production by private industry through the price system. Because social goods and services are recognized by society as being a desirable and essential segment of the economy's total output, it is safe to conclude that the price system, by virtue of its failure to provide sufficient resources for their production, misallocates economic resources. A basic economic function of government is the correction of this misallocation. Government must reflect and render effective the group wants of society which by their very nature are incapable of fulfillment through the price system as such.

Goods necessary for war and national defense are perhaps the most outstanding example of social goods. No one, short of a pacifist, would question the desirability of assigning a portion of the economy's resources for the production of those goods

[2] There are obvious differences between *dollar voting*, which dictates output in the private sector of the economy, and *political voting*, which determines output in the public sector. The rich man has many more votes to cast in the private sector than does the poor man. In the public sector, each—at least in theory—has an equal say. Furthermore, the children who cast their meager votes for bubble gum and comic books in the private sector are banned by virtue of their age from the registering of social choices.

and services necessary for its defense or the successful completion of a war. The goods and services involved come in tremendously large and extremely expensive units. Each modern aircraft, missile, and atomic submarine will bear a price tag involving millions of dollars. The benefits from the production of these goods are obviously widespread and not subject to the exclusion principle. Hence, if war goods are to be a part of the nation's total output, they must be provided through governmental action.

Allocating resources to social goods production. Precisely how are resources reallocated from the production of private goods to the production of social goods? In a full-employment economy, government is faced with the task of freeing resources from private employment to make them available for the production of social goods. During peacetime, the best means of releasing resources from private uses is to reduce private demand for them. This is accomplished by levying taxes on businesses and households, thereby diverting some of their incomes—some of their potential purchasing power—out of the income-expenditure streams. With lower incomes, businesses and households will be forced to curtail their investment and consumption spending. *In short, taxes tend to diminish private demand for goods and services, which in turn prompts a drop in the private demand for resources.* By diverting purchasing power from private spenders to government, taxes free resources from private uses. Government expenditure of the tax proceeds can then reabsorb these resources and provide social goods and services. For example, corporation and personal income taxes release resources from the production of investment goods—drill presses, boxcars, warehouses—and consumer goods—food, clothing, and television sets. Government expenditures tend to reabsorb these resources in the production of guided missiles, munitions, aircraft, and new schools and highways. Government purposely reallocates resources

to bring about significant changes in the composition of the economy's total output.

EVALUATING THE ECONOMIC ROLE OF GOVERNMENT

Thus far we have been content to state the major economic functions of government and to assess the overall impact of their successful performance upon the economy. There now arises a series of related questions which must be faced in any attempt to evaluate the economic role of government:

1. Is it desirable for government to perform the stated six functions?

2. How successful is government in performing its economic functions?

3. Is government playing too great a role in our economy?

Don't expect clear-cut answers to these queries. Indeed, there are none. Government's economic role is extremely difficult to evaluate. There are no simple quantitative standards by which the scope and quality of government's performance can be assessed. And, as a matter of fact, the above questions necessarily exceed the boundaries of economic science and plunge us into the larger realms of political theory and philosophy. Nevertheless, discussion of the issues involved may turn up some worthwhile insights and explode a few of the more popular misconceptions about the economic functions of government. In this way each of us may be in a more strategic position to formulate intelligent opinions on these questions.[3]

Desirability of Functions

Should government perform the six economic functions we have just discussed?

[3] The ambitious student will do well to compare the philosophies of government presented in Francis M. Bator, *The Question of Government Spending* (New York: Harper & Row, Publishers, Incorporated, 1960), and Henry C. Wallich, *The Cost of Freedom* (New York: Harper & Row, Publishers, Incorporated, 1960).

All things considered, there is rather startling agreement that these functions entail tasks which legitimately devolve on government. True, there is a small minority within the United States which espouses the philosophy that that government is best which governs least. At the other extreme, there are those who look upon an expansion of the functions of government as a panacea for any and all the ills of society. Though these groups are highly vocal, it must be emphasized that they are minorities. The vast majority of people are in fairly close agreement that government has an obligation in each of the six areas outlined and discussed in this chapter. This is not to deny that there is much controversy about specific actions of government. This controversy, however, is not so much concerned with whether or not government should perform the six functions as it is with how far these functions should be pursued. Few question the desirability of government's providing education, highways, and similar social goods. On the other hand, governmental action to provide electric power, medical care, and housing are very controversial borderline cases. Are these social goods? To what degree should government provide them? Furthermore, the nebulous nature of social revenues and social costs makes it very difficult to correct the resulting biases in the price system with any great degree of precision. This does not mean that the public disapproves of government action in this area; instead it only proves that the six functions are difficult to delineate and apply in specific cases. In short, the controversy surrounding the economic functions of government is more concerned with the application of these functions in specific instances than with the overall desirability of government's performing in these six areas. On the latter point there is general, though not unanimous, agreement.

Beyond these general comments, three more specific points are worth remembering:

1. The economic role of government in American capitalism is not a phenomenon of recent vintage. With the exception of the sixth function government has performed all the functions discussed to a greater or lesser degree throughout American economic history.

2. The actions of a democratic government mirror the will of society with considerable accuracy. This point is so obvious as to be frequently overlooked: A democratic government does essentially what the citizenry wants it to do.[4]

Government, in the United States, is not an independent entity; it does not possess a will of its own; it is not animated by purposes that are alien to the desires of its citizens. The American government is a creature of the American people; it responds to the pressures that they bring to bear upon it; its policies and its programs, wise or unwise, find their origin in organized demand and depend for their survival upon popular sufferance. . . . It [government] intervenes only when it is forced to intervene. It acts reluctantly, deliberately, and tardily, in response to overwhelming pressures. Criticism of public intervention is criticism, not of dictatorship, but of the results of the democratic process.

3. It must be emphasized that on economic grounds the sole test of the desirability of government's economic functions is the effect which their performance has upon the level of resource use and the efficiency with which resources are allocated. And we have seen that in each of the six functions discussed in this chapter government is aiming at a higher level of resource use or an improved allocation of employed resources by strengthening or modifying the operation of the price system. Now this is not to say that the standard of efficient resource use is the only criterion by which government activity is to be appraised. Nor is it to imply that the task of evaluation by any standard is an easy task. But it certainly does imply that each individual ac-

[4] Clair Wilcox, *Public Policies toward Business,* rev. ed. (Homewood, Ill.: Richard D. Irwin, Inc., 1960), pp. 8–9.

tion by government in the economic sphere should be evaluated separately for its effect upon the degree of efficiency in resource use in estimating its *economic* desirability. The actions of government must not be condoned or condemned per se, that is, adjudged good or bad simply because they are performed by government.

Effectiveness

Assuming some agreement as to the proper economic functions of government, a second question becomes relevant. How successful is government in performing these functions?

Again there is no simple answer. Though the overall goals of full employment and improved resource allocation may be commendable, it is of course possible that government has been relatively ineffective in attaining these goals. Whether or not government is actually successful in promoting these ends depends on

1. The ability of government to recognize resource misallocations and unemployment.

2. Government's ability to ascertain, and its willingness to legislate, effective remedial programs.

3. Government's capacity to administer such programs.

This is a tall order. There is ample room for errors in fact, judgment, and administration in the performance of government's economic functions. It is not too surprising that on occasion government has grossly misjudged the economic problems of society, failing to correct shortcomings of the price system as a result of inappropriate action or inaction. And government has sometimes failed to act decisively and rapidly in remedying well-recognized defects in the economy's operation. Then, too, there is persistent evidence that governmental agencies are bureaucratic, plagued by red tape and at times by wasteful administration. Worst of all, the interests of society have sometimes been neglected by government in promoting the ends of pressure groups or in the interest of political expediency.

But one must keep in mind that the private sector of the economy is by no means perfectly efficient; indeed, government's economic functions are largely attempts to correct the price system's shortcomings. "The relevant comparison is not between perfect markets and imperfect governments, nor between faulty markets and all-knowing, rational, benevolent governments, but between inevitably imperfect institutions."[5] Within this context the effectiveness of the public sector's performance is not without substantial defenses. At worst one can take the position that it is preferable to have government correct the defects of the price system in an imperfect or partial manner than not at all. Perhaps at best it can be argued that the historical record reveals that government on balance has clearly played a fundamental positive role in fostering the smooth operation and development of American capitalism.

Beyond these general observations each of us must establish his own opinion as to the effectiveness of government. Here are a few guideposts that may be of some assistance in reaching an intelligent opinion:

Noncomparable performance standards. *When attempting to gauge the efficiency of government's economic activities, it is usually not appropriate to use the performance standards of the private sector.* In particular, beware of dogmatic comparisons of governmentally operated or controlled enterprises and privately owned and operated businesses. Why? Because they are horses of different colors. They are different propositions and not subject to simple, clear-cut comparisons. Two considerations go far to explain the absence of a common standard for comparing the efficiency of the private and public sectors of American capitalism:

On the one hand, the objective of private businesses is profits, while that of government enterprise is "service to society," or

[5] Otto Eckstein, *Public Finance* (Englewood Cliffs, N.J.: Prentice-Hall, Inc., 1964), p. 19.

"promotion of the general welfare." Government and private enterprise are not seeking identical goals; therefore, they are not to be compared by the same standard of success. Now, admittedly, there is room for considerable overlapping in seeking profits and in serving society. As a group, business enterprises in producing innumerable goods and services undoubtedly perform a great service to the economy. Yet, in the final analysis, the immediate targets of government economic activities and private enterprise are essentially different. Businesses as a matter of necessity are seeking profits. And it is basically by their ability to do so that their success is judged. The economic activities of government, on the other hand, are judged by numerous standards, virtually all of which are somewhat subjective and therefore less precise quantitatively than a profit and loss statement. For example, there is no simple and accurate measure of the success of our national defense, public education, and highway construction programs. Rather there are many vague and diverse methods of evaluation. Unfortunately, it is ordinarily easy to find a standard to confirm one's bias or prejudgment of any given government program. In any event, the lack of a single, quantitatively precise measure of the success of governmental activities goes far to explain the endless debate over government spending and tax policies. The major point is obvious: It is hardly fair to take the standard of success for private industry, that is, net profits, and apply it as a criterion for judging the success or efficiency of government's economic activities. Put more concretely, let us not label our postal system as "inefficient" or "unsuccessful" simply because it fails to show a profit for the year's operations.

A second reason for avoiding the use of performance standards for the private sector of the economy in gauging the efficiency of government lies in the fact that the fallacy of composition may invalidate such comparisons. For example, it is tempting to take time-honored notions as to the propriety of private debt and apply them without qualification to public debt. The evils of the fallacy of composition must be kept clearly in mind to warn us that notions and principles which are accurate when applied to the debts of *individual* households or *individual* businesses may not be valid when applied to the aggregate of government. This point will be pursued at some length in Chapter 15.

Fallacy of limited decisions. In evaluating the economic performance of government, critics are prone to be guilty of what we shall call the *fallacy of limited decisions*. These critics implicitly assume that during any particular period of time there is a limited, or fixed, number of decisions to be made in connection with the operation of the economy. Hence, if government makes more of these decisions in performing its stated functions, the private sector of the economy will necessarily have fewer "free" decisions or choices to make. For example, critics argue that by making decisions to provide electric power, government will frighten off private businesses and private investors in this area of production. The net effectiveness of government in providing electric power, it is concluded, is very low when this discouragement of private production is taken into account.

Some serious reflection will reveal the fallacy which may plague such reasoning. The vast majority of the social goods and services provided by government are of such a nature that private businesses would simply not consider their production without government sponsorship. Highway construction and the manufacture of war goods are simply not undertaken by private enterprises on their own initiative. As a matter of fact, it can be plausibly argued that the range of free choice is *extended* by government sponsorship of the production of such social goods as highways, national defense, and education; these goods and services would simply not be available for consumer choice in the absence of government provision.

One can cogently argue that it is in large measure through the economic functions of government that we have been able to free ourselves in some measure from ignorance, poverty, disease, crime, discrimination, and so forth. Note, too, that in providing most social goods, government does not typically undertake production itself but rather purchases these goods through private enterprise. When government makes the decision to build an interstate highway, private concerns are given the responsibility for making a myriad of specific decisions and choices in connection with the carrying out of this decision.

Finally, it should be noted that during a depression the number of choices made by private businesses and households is greatly restricted. Why? Because production has been slowed and incomes drastically curtailed. The businessman has fewer choices to make concerning, for example, the types of products and combinations of resources he may use. Indeed, some firms will be temporarily closed down and making no decisions at all. The consumer has fewer decisions to make in disposing of his income, because his income is now very small or conceivably nonexistent. Now if government, by increased participation and intervention in the economy, can correct or even alleviate a depression, the number of decisions and choices open to both businesses and consumers will increase. That is, government, by making more decisions concerning the operation of the economy, might restore prosperity, permitting the number of private decisions to increase also. Hence, the number of private and public decisions made in the operation of the economy may, *within limits,* vary in the same direction. A large number of governmental decisions may or may not mean a smaller number of private decisions.

Remoteness of government transactions. The economic services of government seem vague and remote to the individual, because he does not acquire these services through specific purchases. This becomes clear upon contrasting purchases from private enterprise and purchases of social goods and services through government.

When John Doe buys a pair of shoes, he is party to an immediate and clear-cut this-for-that transaction. He hands over a part of his purchasing power—say, $15—to a shoe retailer and receives directly a product of his choosing in return. The buyer obviously regards the benefits he will receive from the shoes as worth the $15 expenditure, or he would simply not choose to make this transaction. Purchasing from a private enterprise is a voluntary and clear-cut bit of economic behavior. The consumer knows how much he is spending and precisely what he gets in return for his money.

This is not generally true of purchases which consumers make through government. Even though goods and services provided by government are received and paid for by consumers in general, there is no explicit this-for-that exchange. Hence, government transactions typically appear nebulous and decidedly out of focus to the typical taxpayer. National defense provides an excellent example. There is no doubt that the benefits of our national defense program which accrue to individuals and businesses in our economy are very great. Yet it is impossible to judge *how much* benefit from our military strength is enjoyed by individual households and business firms. Public education is another good example. The benefits of a public school system are received directly by students, semidirectly by the students' parents and families, and indirectly by the community and nation as a whole. In this case, those who pay the tax costs of the education—that is, the adult population of the community—are clearly receiving no explicit, clear-cut good or service in return. No this-for-that transaction occurs.

This vagueness between consumer expenditures in the form of taxes paid to government and benefits received results in many an uninformed taxpayer's feeling perfectly justified in griping about high taxes while simultaneously demanding better highways, more adequate police and fire protection, and an ever-improving educational system for his sons and daughters! We want the benefits of government's economic activities but are typically reluctant to foot the bill.

The point we are driving at is this: We must be careful not to write off government spending on goods and services as unproductive or wasteful just because no clear-cut this-for-that transaction is involved. Indeed, if a this-for-that relationship between spending and benefits received were present, government might not have to assume responsibility for providing the particular good or service. If it were feasible for individuals to consume national defense and education economically, in sufficient amounts and on a this-for-that basis, government would not have the chore of providing these goods and services. In short, government transactions may be every bit as beneficial or productive as the more direct this-for-that transactions characteristic of the private sector of the economy. Don't let the indirect, remote nature of government purchases cause you to prejudge such purchases as wasteful or unproductive.

Government spending and "economy." Finally, in evaluating the economic role of government, one should be wary of the now-popular myth that "economy in government" and "reduced government spending" are synonymous. As we are well aware from reading Chapter 2, economy is concerned with the efficient allocation of resources. Indiscriminate cutbacks in government spending on high-priority social goods and services *may* free resources for less essential low-priority private goods and services. The most efficient allocation of resources between social and private goods is vague at best. But this does not excuse us from tripping on the fallacy that providing less social goods and more private goods necessarily entails a more efficient allocation of re-

sources. It may or it may not. Each economic action on the part of government should be weighed on its own merits. Will the particular action result in a more efficient use of society's resources than now prevails? Is government in a better position to carry out this activity effectively than private industry? Beware of catchall rules which flatly approve or condemn any and all economic functions of government.

A concluding point should be emphasized: This series of comments is not designed to stack the deck in favor of government intervention and participation in the functioning of the economy. On the contrary, its purpose is to caution us against the widespread preconception that, by definition, the economic activities of government are "bad" and those of the private sector "good." It is easy and often convenient to accept the popular prejudice that the economic activities of government are "operation rathole," that is, that government activities are inherently less efficient and less productive than private economic activities. Such is not the case. Each instance concerning the appropriateness of public or private responsibility must be carefully judged on its own merits.

Too Much Government?

Precisely how large is government's role in American capitalism? Unfortunately, there is no simple way of measuring quantitatively the many diverse functions of government. Probably the best single indicator of government's economic role is its expenditure on goods and services expressed as a percentage of the economy's total output. Columns 3 and 4 of Table 6–1 suggest that government's role has expanded not only in absolute but also in relative terms. Note, however, that this growth has been somewhat sporadic. Government—Federal, state, and local combined—now accounts for about one-fifth of the total output of American capitalism. How is this long-run expansion of government's economic activities to

TABLE 6–1. GOVERNMENT PURCHASES AS A PERCENTAGE OF TOTAL OUTPUT, SELECTED YEARS, 1929–1964

(1) Year	(2) Total output (in billions)	(3) Government purchases of goods and services (in billions)	(4) Government purchases as a percentage of total output, or (3) ÷ (2)	(5) Government nondefense purchases (in billions)	(6) Government nondefense purchases as a percentage of total output, or (5) ÷ (2)
1929	$104.4	$ 8.5	8.1%	$ 7.2	6.9%
1933	56.0	8.0	14.3	6.0	10.7
1936	82.7	11.8	14.3	7.0	8.5
1939	91.1	13.3	14.6	12.0	13.2
1941	125.8	24.8	19.7	11.0	8.7
1944	211.4	96.5	45.7	7.5	3.6
1947	234.3	28.4	12.1	17.0	7.3
1951	329.0	60.5	18.4	26.6	8.1
1954	363.1	75.3	20.7	34.1	9.4
1958	441.7	92.6	21.0	48.1	10.9
1962	556.2	116.3	20.9	62.7	11.5
1964	622.6	128.3	20.6	73.2	11.6

Source: U.S. Department of Commerce data.

be explained? Causal factors are undoubtedly many, but two seem to be of paramount importance. On the one hand, war shifts the production target of the economy drastically in the direction of more social goods and fewer civilian goods. Note the upsurge of government purchases during World War II: in 1944 almost one-half of total output was taken by government. A lesser expansion of government spending accompanied the Korean conflict. The current cold war necessitates unusually high levels of military spending, keeping government's share of total output considerably above that of four or five decades ago. Note in columns 5 and 6 that were it not for the high level of military spending imposed by the cold war, government's share of total output would be far below the 20 per cent of column 4. Furthermore, postwar growth in nonmilitary government spending has been modest percentagewise.

A second factor has also contributed to the relative growth of government in the economy: As the incomes of American consumers have risen historically, the pattern of consumer wants has altered in the direction of relatively more social goods and relatively fewer private goods. The members of a relatively poor economy must take their entire incomes in the form of the most urgently needed commodities: food, shelter, and clothing—all private goods provided by the private sector of the economy through the price system. But after these basic wants have been largely fulfilled, the growing wealth of society permits it to turn its attention more and more to the satisfaction of somewhat less urgent, but nevertheless important, wants. Many of the wants in this second category entail social goods and services: education, streets and highways, police and fire protection. These goods, produced in minimal amounts in a poor and essentially rural economy, are demanded and provided in increasing amounts as the wealth of the society increases. As a matter of fact, the increasing complexity of a growing economy necessitates, and, indeed, economic growth itself depends upon, the provision of these social goods and services. The result is a tendency for government to play an increasingly important role in the economy as a provider of these social commodities and services.

A word of warning: Although Table 6–1 correctly portrays American capitalism as becoming more and more a mixed public-private economy, we must emphasize that government's role as an owner and operator of business enterprises has not expanded to any significant degree. The job of producing government's increased purchases of social goods and services still lies primarily within the realm of private enterprise. Government sponsors and handles the financing of highways, schools, and war goods, but their actual production is carried on by private enterprises. Roughly one-half the government's purchases are for goods and services produced by private, profit-guided producers. Production actually undertaken by government itself is relatively small, and its relative growth has been very modest. Consumers now buy relatively fewer goods directly from private enterprises but more goods indirectly from private enterprises through government. Private enterprise has expanded more or less proportionately with the total output of the economy.

The tendency for a growing economy to want the production of social goods and services to increase in proportion to the output of private goods and services does not, of course, rule out the possibility that government's role has expanded at a rate faster than is justified by this generalization. Does government provide too many goods and services at the present time?

There are some who emphatically argue that government's economic role has been grossly overextended. Others support the opposite view that a "social imbalance" exists in that the production of private goods has seriously outstripped the production of social goods. Children, underequipped with such social goods and services as schools, parks, playgrounds, and

police protection, are said to be grossly overequipped with such private goods as toys, clothing, and television sets. The most eloquent critic of this social imbalance summarizes the problem thus: [6]

The family which takes its mauve and cerise, air-conditioned, power-steered, and power-braked automobile out for a tour passes through cities that are badly paved, made hideous by litter, blighted buildings, billboards, and posts for wires that should long since have been put underground. . . . They picnic on exquisitely packaged food from a portable icebox by a polluted stream and go on to spend the night at a park which is a menace to public health and morals. Just before dozing off on an air mattress, beneath a nylon tent, amid the stench of decaying refuse, they may reflect vaguely on the curious unevenness of their blessings. Is this, indeed, the American genius?

The social imbalance thesis is sufficiently important to merit detailed discussion—pro and con—in Chapter 38.

SUMMARY

1. The American economy can be described as mixed capitalism. It is primarily a market economy, yet government influences the operation of the price system in a variety of ways.

2. The basic economic functions of government entail **a.** providing a legal and social framework appropriate to the effective operation of the price system, **b.** maintaining competition, **c.** providing a minimum standard of living for all the citizenry, **d.** adjusting total output to allow for social costs and social revenues, **e.** providing for the production of social goods and services, and **f.** controlling the business cycle. These functions are designed to assist the private sector of the economy in achieving full employment and full production.

[6] John Kenneth Galbraith, *The Affluent Society* (Boston: Houghton Mifflin Company, 1958), p. 253. The final section of this chapter draws heavily upon chaps. 18, 19, and 22 of Professor Galbraith's brilliant but disturbing book.

3. The economic role of government is difficult to evaluate. Society generally condones government activity in the six areas outlined above. However, there is considerable disagreement concerning the extent to which government should pursue these functions and whether specific governmental actions fall within the scope of these six functions. In evaluating the economic role of government, we should remember that **a.** for the most part the current economic functions of government are not a recent development, **b.** a democratic government generally mirrors the will of society, and **c.** the sole economic test of the desirability of governmental action is its effect upon the employment and allocation of resources.

4. Several guideposts are helpful in attempting to gauge the effectiveness of government in carrying out its economic functions: **a.** There is no common standard for measuring the performances of the public and private sectors of the economy; **b.** the fallacy of limited decisions may prejudice one's thinking in evaluating the effectiveness of government in the economic sphere; **c.** the fact that the economic transactions of government lack the immediacy and clarity of their private counterparts may incorrectly suggest that government is unproductive and inefficient in fulfilling its economic functions; **d.** minimal government spending and "economy" are not to be identified.

5. As measured by its purchases, government's economic role has increased historically in both absolute and relative terms. War and the more than proportionate increase in the demand for social goods which rising incomes entail help explain this growth. Simple observation suggests that American capitalism is probably more abundantly supplied with private goods than it is with social goods.

QUESTIONS AND STUDY SUGGESTIONS

1. Why is the American economy called "mixed capitalism"? Enumerate and briefly discuss the main economic functions of government.
2. Distinguish clearly between (a) social goods and private goods; (b) private revenues (benefits) and costs and social revenues and costs. Give illustrations of each. How should government modify the operation of the price system to allow for social goods and to take into account the presence of social costs and revenues? Emphasize the impact of governmental action upon the allocation of resources.
3. Define and explain the significance of the exclusion principle.
4. What difficulties arise in attempting to assess the economic role of government? Be specific.
5. Carefully evaluate this statement: "The public, as a general rule . . . gets less production in return for a dollar spent by government than from a dollar spent by private enterprise."[7]
6. "The conclusion seems inescapable that pure capitalism . . . would be subject to grave deficiencies and inconsistencies. Such a system would have little chance of survival."[8] Do you agree? Why?
7. "It is conceivable that the Federal government can contribute materially to economic stability and greater efficiency in the use of resources

[7] National Association of Manufacturers, *The American Individual Enterprise System* (New York: McGraw-Hill Book Company, 1946), p. 952.
[8] Howard R. Bowen, *Toward Social Economy* (New York: Holt, Rinehart and Winston, Inc., 1948), p. 321.

without interfering in the details of business and personal life." Do you agree? Explain.

8. Carefully evaluate the following statement, and contrast its philosophy with that evidenced in question 5:[9]

The admitted functions of government embrace a much wider field than can be easily included within the ring fence of a restrictive definition . . . it is hardly possible to find any ground of justification common to them all, except the comprehensive one of general expediency; nor to limit the interference of government by any universal rule, save the simple and vague one that it should never be admitted but when the case of expediency is strong.

9. Interpret and evaluate the following quotation:[10]

Plan or no plan? Everyone believes in planning in the literal sense of the word: and, for that matter, everyone believes that national governments should execute some plans for economic life. No one favors bad planning. Plan or no plan is no choice at all; the pertinent questions turn on particular techniques: Who shall plan, for what purposes, in what conditions, and by what devices? Free market or regulation? Again, this issue is badly posed. Both institutions are indispensable.

What do you feel are the virtues, if any, of government planning? How does the price system "plan"? Explain.

SELECTED REFERENCES

Bator, Francis M.: *The Question of Government Spending* (New York: Harper & Row, Publishers, Incorporated, 1960).

Due, John F.: *Government Finance,* 3d ed. (Homewood, Ill.: Richard D. Irwin, Inc., 1963), chaps. 1 and 2.

Joint Economic Committee: *Federal Expenditure Policy for Economic Growth and Stability* (Washington, D.C., 1957), particularly the papers submitted by Arnold M. Soloway, Solomon Barkin, Walter W. Heller, and Procter Thomson.

Petit, Thomas A.: *Freedom in the American Economy* (Homewood, Ill.: Richard D. Irwin, Inc., 1964).

Phelps, Edmund S. (ed.): *Private Wants and Public Needs,* rev. ed. (New York: W. W. Norton & Company, Inc., 1965).

Reagan, Michael D.: *The Managed Economy* (Fair Lawn, N.J.: Oxford University Press, 1963), particularly chaps. 8–12.

Wallich, Henry C.: *The Cost of Freedom* (New York: Harper & Row, Publishers, Incorporated, 1960), particularly chap. 2.

Wilcox, Clair: *Public Policies toward Business,* rev. ed. (Homewood, Ill.: Richard D. Irwin, Inc., 1960), chaps. 1, 2, and 32.

[9] John Stuart Mill, *Principles of Political Economy* (New York: Appleton-Century-Crofts, Inc., 1878), vol. II, p. 392.

[10] Robert A. Dahl and Charles E. Lindblom, *Politics, Economics and Welfare* (New York: Harper & Row, Publishers, Incorporated, 1953), p. 5.

CHAPTER 7

THE FACTS OF AMERICAN CAPITALISM: HOUSEHOLDS

This chapter and the ensuing two are designed to put meat on our bareboned model of mixed capitalism. We have discussed the three major aggregates of mixed capitalism —business, households, and government—on a very general and somewhat abstract basis. We must now add color to our crude sketch by painting in the factual characteristics of these three major transactors as they function in our American brand of mixed capitalism. In short, we must breathe reality into our abstract model by adding "the facts" of American economic life. The present chapter contributes factual information pertinent to households. The following two chapters do the same for the business and government sectors of the economy. In each case the discussion will focus upon the source of the sector's income or receipts and the manner in which it disposes of that income.

The household sector of American capitalism is currently composed of some 59 million families. These households play a dual role: They are the ultimate suppliers of all economic resources and simultaneously the major spending group in the economy. Hence, we shall consider households, first, as income receivers and, second, as spenders.

HOUSEHOLDS AS INCOME RECEIVERS

There are two related approaches to studying the facts of income distribution. The *functional distribution* of income is con-

cerned with the manner in which society's money income is divided among wages, rents, interest, and profits. Here total income is distributed according to the function performed by the income receiver. Wages are paid to labor, rents and interest compensate property resources, and profits flow to the owners of corporations and unincorporated businesses. The *personal distribution* of income has to do with the way in which the total money income of society is apportioned among individual households. A basic understanding of both the functional and the personal distribution of income is essential to understanding the role of households in American capitalism.

Functional Distribution of Income

The distributive shares of the national income for 1964 were as follows:

	Billions of dollars	Per cent of total
Wages and salaries ..	$361.7	71
Proprietors' income ..	52.0	10
Corporate profits ...	57.4	11
Interest	26.7	5
Rents	12.3	3
National income ..	$510.1	100

Figure 7–1 illustrates the changes that have taken place in the *absolute size* of these shares since 1929. Changes in the

FIGURE 7–1. THE FUNCTIONAL DISTRIBUTION OF NATIONAL INCOME IN BILLIONS OF DOLLARS, 1929 TO 1964.
All national income shares decrease absolutely during depression and increase absolutely during periods of prosperity and growth. Wages and salaries constitute the largest component of the national income. (U.S. Department of Commerce.)

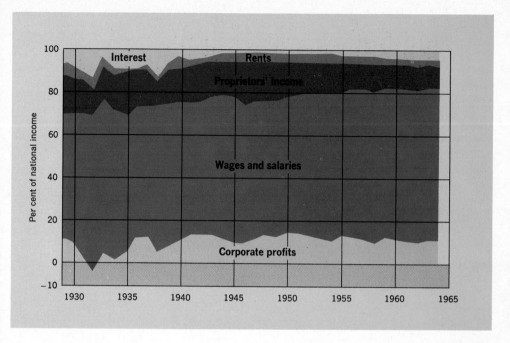

FIGURE 7–2. THE FUNCTIONAL DISTRIBUTION OF NATIONAL INCOME IN PERCENTAGES, 1929 TO 1964.
In relative terms the share of national income going to labor has been remarkably stable over time. Corporate profits have been very unstable, and interest and rental incomes have tended to decline. (U.S. Department of Commerce.)

relative shares of the national income since 1929 are shown in Figure 7–2. Certain generalizations are evident from an examination of these data:

1. It is clear from Figure 7–1 that all the shares of national income tend to expand during prosperity and to decline during depression. *In absolute terms,* none of the major income-receiving classes benefit from bad times. Thus the drastic decline in national income ushered in by the Great Depression of the 1930s affected all income groups adversely. On the other hand, the war-born prosperity of the early 1940s and the postwar boom significantly boosted the incomes of all groups.

2. In terms of the *relative* shares of national income, the outstanding fact shown in Figure 7–2 is the remarkable stability of

the share going to labor. With rare exceptions, labor's share of the national income over the last three decades has hovered two or three percentage points on either side of 67 per cent.

3. In contrast to the relative stability of labor's share, corporate profits have proved to be highly unstable over the years. In 1929 corporate profits accounted for about 12 per cent of the national income but became a negative figure (losses) during 1932 and 1933. Even since the beginning of World War II, corporate profits have fluctuated substantially in both absolute and percentage terms. Specifically, corporate profits have varied from 10 to 15 per cent of the national income in the last two decades.

4. Proprietors' incomes—that is, the in-

comes of doctors, lawyers, small business men, shopkeepers, farmers, and other unincorporated enterprises—have fluctuated between 10 and 20 per cent of the national income. As Figure 7–2 indicates, the percentage of national income going to this group has been declining somewhat since the close of World War II. No doubt depressed farm incomes have played a major role in this decline.

5. The relatively small shares of national income accruing to interest and rent receivers merit brief comment. Interest has varied considerably as a share of the national income. In 1929 interest receivers got about 7 per cent of the national income. Largely because of the drastic decline in national income, interest income rose as a share of the national income during the Great Depression of the 1930s. Then in the war years of the early 1940s a burgeoning national income and very low interest rates caused the interest share to fall to less than 2 per cent. In postwar years substantial increases in interest rates—partly the result of government policy—and very rapid growth in private debt have increased the interest share to a current figure of about 3 per cent. Since the mid-thirties rents have fluctuated generally between 3 and 5 per cent of the national income.

Personal Distribution of Income

Why is the personal distribution of money income important in understanding the operation of American capitalism? What impact does the distribution of money income among households have upon the operation of the economy? The manner in which income is distributed among families affects both the *size* and the *composition* of output.

1. The personal distribution of income is a major determinant of how society divides its money income between consumption and saving. We will discover in Chapters 12 and 13 that this division is of utmost significance in determining the levels of output and employment in the economy. Consumption,

being a form of spending, induces production and employment. Saving, defined by economists as that part of current income which is not spent on consumption, does not account for production and employment. It follows that a distribution of income which results in a large volume of saving in relation to consumption *may* be conducive to declining levels of production and employment. On the other hand, a distribution which entails a very small volume of saving in relation to consumption will promote high levels of production and employment.

2. The personal distribution of money income goes a long way toward determining the pattern of consumer spending in the economy. A highly unequal distribution of income among individual households results in an expenditure pattern much different from that which a more nearly equal distribution would entail. Generally speaking, the more unequal the distribution of a given total money income, the greater will be the demand for and the output of luxury goods. Businesses, as we have seen, usually find it to their advantage to adjust their outputs to consumer demands. As a consequence, the economy's product mix is largely geared to the composition of consumer expenditures. And in turn, the economy's product mix obviously determines the manner in which scarce resources are allocated.

To repeat, the personal distribution of income has direct and significant consequences for the two major aspects of economic science: (1) the level of resource use and (2) the allocation of resources among alternative uses.

What determines the amount of money income received by an individual household in, say, a year? Common sense tells us that (1) the quantities of the various human and property resources which a household is able and willing to supply to businesses, (2) the prices which these resources command in the resource market, and (3) the actual level of employment of these resources are the immediate determinants of a household's money income. For the majority of American households, labor service is the only resource supplied. Thus by taking, for example, 2,000 hours of labor service at a wage rate of $2 per hour, total money income for the year is found to be $4,000. But the third determinant poses a possible qualification: Though the household may be willing and able to supply 2,000 hours of labor service per year, there is no guarantee that businesses will purchase that amount. Money income depends on the extent to which businesses are willing to employ available supplies of resources. If businesses are only able to use profitably 1,500 of the hours offered, the workers' money income will obviously decline accordingly.

In capitalistic economies, money income is roughly based upon the contribution which a household's resources make to the total production of the economy. Households earn money incomes which are generally in accord with the value of their contributions to total output. If the resources in a household's possession are capable of efficiently producing goods which consumers want, the income earned will be high; if not, it will be low. The prices established by the forces of supply and demand in the resource market roughly gauge the relative worth or "productivity" of the various resources. If a business enterprise pays $2 an hour for unskilled labor and $4 per hour for highly skilled labor, it implies that the skilled labor is twice as productive as unskilled labor. If the market places a high value on the contributions of a resource to production, the supplying household receives a large income. If the market puts a low value on a resource's contribution, the supplying household's income tends to be low.

It is obvious that a distribution of income based upon productivity is likely to result in considerable inequality. The quantity and quality of resources owned by various households and the prices they can command in the resource market can and do vary quite widely. As a glance at Table 37–1 will verify, the lowest 29 per cent of all American consumer units in 1963 received only 9 per cent of total personal income. In Chapter 37 we shall discuss in considerable detail both factual and ethical aspects of income inequality and the various policies and institutional forces which have modified the productivity principle of income distribution.

HOUSEHOLDS AS SPENDERS

Having briefly discussed households as income receivers, let us now examine the other side of the coin by viewing households as disposers of income. How do households dispose of the income which they receive? In general terms the answer is simple: A part is given to government in the form of personal taxes, and the remainder is divided between personal consumption expenditures and personal saving. Specifically, here is the way in which households disposed of their personal income in 1964:[1]

	Billions of dollars	Per cent of total
Personal taxes	$ 59.6	12
Personal consumption expenditures	399.3	81
Personal saving	32.5	7
Personal income ..	$491.4	100

Figures 7–3 and 7–4 show the absolute and relative importance of personal taxes, consumption expenditures, and personal saving over the last three and a half decades. We note immediately that in absolute terms all three components move with personal

[1] The astute reader will note that the concept of national income, used in discussing households as income receivers, has been supplanted by the concept of personal income in analyzing households as disposers of income. The distinction between national income and personal income will be revealed in Chapter 10.

FIGURE 7–3. THE DISPOSITION OF PERSONAL INCOME
IN BILLIONS OF DOLLARS, 1929 TO 1964.
Consumption expenditures, personal tax payments, and personal saving have all
increased as personal income has expanded. Increases in personal saving during the
early 1940s reflect wartime scarcities of consumer goods and high money incomes.
(U.S. Department of Commerce.)

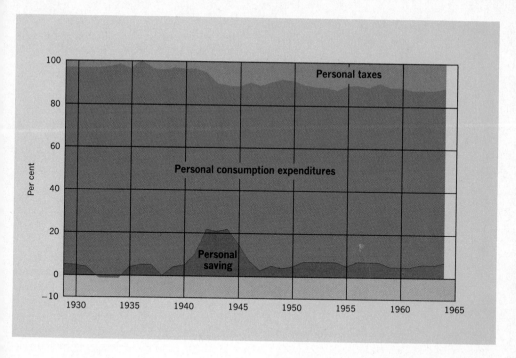

FIGURE 7–4. THE DISPOSITION OF PERSONAL INCOME IN PERCENTAGES, 1929 TO 1964.
Currently personal consumption expenditures account for about 81 per cent of personal income, personal taxes for 12 per cent, and personal saving for 7 per cent. (U.S. Department of Commerce.)

income. But let us examine each of these components separately.

Personal Taxes

Personal taxes, of which the Federal personal income tax is the major component, have risen sharply in both absolute and relative terms since 1941. In 1929, households paid $2.6 billion, or about 3 per cent of their $85.8 billion personal income, in personal taxes. In 1964, $59.6 billion, or about 12 per cent of that year's $491.4 billion personal income, flowed to government as personal taxes. World War II and the need to finance vast expenditures on war goods in the postwar era constitute the major explanatory factors.

The income received by households after personal taxes have been paid is called "disposable income." Remembering that economists define saving as "not spending," households have just two choices with their incomes after taxes—to spend or to save.

Personal Consumption Expenditures

Figures 7–3 and 7–4 clearly show that the bulk of personal income flows from income receivers back into the business sector of the economy as personal consumption expenditures. But note that although consumption has been increasing by large absolute amounts in recent years, it has declined in relative terms. The tendency for personal income to increase even more sharply than personal consumption expenditures has permitted this to be the case. As with personal taxes and personal saving, the amount of consumption which occurs depends upon the business cycle. The bad times of the thirties caused all three to contract. Yet, as Figure 7–4 shows, consumption actually increased in relative terms during the Depression. For example, during the Depression years of 1932 and 1933, households spent over 98 per cent of their personal income on consumer goods. Currently, households are spending over five times as much as they were during the depth of the Great Depression, but this still only amounts to about 81 per cent of personal income.

Since the size and composition of the economy's total output depend to a very considerable extent upon the size and composition of the flow of consumer spending, it is imperative that we examine how households divide their expenditures among the various goods and services competing for their dollars. Consumer expenditures may be classified in several ways. For example, classification is made on the basis of service or product and, in turn, by the durability of the products involved. Thus the U.S. Department of Commerce classifies consumer spending as (1) expenditures on nondurables, (2) expenditures on durables, and (3) expenditures on services. If a product generally has an expected life of three years or more, it is called a "durable good"; if its life is less than three years, it is labeled "nondurable." Automobiles, refrigerators, washing machines, television sets, and most furniture are good examples of consumer durables. Most food and clothing items are nondurables. Services, of course, refer to the services which lawyers, barbers, mechanics, and so forth provide to consumers.

Statistics show that of the $399.3 billion spent by consumers in 1964, $177.3 billion was for nondurables, $57.0 billion for durables, and $165.1 billion for services. This threefold breakdown is of considerable importance, because it reminds us that a good many consumer outlays are discretionary or postponable. During good times, durable, or "hard," goods are typically traded in or

scrapped before they become utterly useless. This is ordinarily the case with automobiles and most major household appliances. But if bad times threaten or begin to materialize, consumers may forgo expenditures on durables, choosing to put up with an old model car and outdated household appliances. When depression threatens, the desire to conserve dollars for the nondurable necessities of food and clothing may cause a radical shrinkage of expenditures on durables. Much the same is true of many services. True, one cannot postpone an operation for acute appendicitis. But education, dental work, and a wide variety of less pressing services can be deferred or, if necessary, forgone entirely. In brief, the durable goods and services segments of personal consumption expenditures are subject to considerably more variation over time than are expenditures on nondurables. As is true of saving, many types of spending on durables and services are expendable during an economic crisis. Table 7–1 provides us with a more detailed look at the composition of personal consumption expenditures.

Personal Saving: Flows versus Stocks

Those portions of current household incomes which are paid as taxes and consumed will remain within the income-expenditure streams of the economy, flowing in this case to government and businesses. However, saving—that part of the current income which is neither paid in taxes nor consumed —presents a different picture. In effect, households channel their current saving out of the income-expenditure streams and accumulate or stock this unspent income in various forms of financial assets. This means, of course, that "saving" is a slippery term. On one hand, it can refer to that portion of current (this year's) income which is not paid out in taxes or in the purchase of consumer goods but rather flows into bank accounts, insurance policies, bonds and stocks, and other financial assets which represent

TABLE 7–1. THE COMPOSITION OF PERSONAL CONSUMPTION EXPENDITURES, 1964

Types of consumption		Amount (billions of dollars)	Per cent of total
Durable goods		$ 57.0	14
Automobiles and parts	$24.2		6
Furniture and household equipment	24.0		6
All others	8.8		2
Nondurable goods		177.3	45
Clothing and shoes	33.4		8
Food and alcoholic beverages	41.7		23
Gasoline and oil	13.5		4
Tobacco, semidurable household furnishings, and others	38.7		10
Services		165.1	41
Household operations	24.4		6
Housing	51.5		13
Transportation	12.2		3
Personal services, recreation, and others	77.1		9
Personal consumption expenditures		$399.3	100

Source: U.S. Department of Commerce, *Survey of Current Business,* May, 1965, p. 6.

accumulated savings. On the other hand, the term "saving" is also used in referring to the present size of these financial assets which have been accumulated or stocked over a long period of years. Saving, in brief, can refer to a current flow of income into financial assets or to the accumulated size of such assets. In our discussion, we shall reserve the term "savings" (plural) for designating the accumulation or stock of financial assets held by households. The term "saving" (singular) will designate the portion of current income which flows into, or is added to, this accumulation. Occasionally we shall talk of "accumulated savings" or "the stock of savings," on the one hand, and "current saving" or "the flow of saving," on the other, to remind us of the savings-saving distinction.

Why do households want to save? After all, it is ultimately goods and services which satisfy consumer wants, not the pieces of paper which we call checkbooks, savings account books, and bonds. The reasons for saving are many and diverse, but they center around *security* and *speculation.* Households save to provide a nest egg for unforeseen contingencies—sickness, accident, unemployment—for retirement from the work force, or simply for the overall financial security of one's family. On the other hand, saving might well occur for speculation. One might channel a part of his income to the purchase of securities, speculating as to increases in their monetary value. Or, a household might accumulate funds in bank accounts or as idle dollars in a sugar bowl, speculating as to a change in the purchasing power of those dollars. Actually a good portion of the accumulated savings now in existence stems from World War II, which simultaneously brought prosperity and soaring money incomes, on the one hand, and rather severe shortages of many consumer durable goods, on the other.

The desire or willingness to save, however, is not enough. This willingness must be accompanied by the *ability* to save. And, as we shall discover later (Table 12–1), the ability to save depends basically upon the size of one's income. If income is very low, households may *dissave,* that is, they may consume in excess of their disposable incomes. They manage this by borrowing and by digging into savings which they may have accumulated in years when their incomes were higher. However, both saving and consumption vary directly with income; as households get more disposable income, they divide it between saving and consumption. Actually, the bulk of the personal saving that occurs in our economy is done by those households in the $50,000, $100,000, or higher income brackets. It is estimated that the top 5 per cent of the income receivers account for two-thirds of all personal saving in the United States. The top 10 per cent account for virtually all personal saving.[2]

SUMMARY

1. All three sectors of the economy—households, businesses, and government—receive and spend income. Much can be learned concerning the actual operation of American capitalism by analyzing the sources and uses of the income received by each sector.

2. In so far as the functional distribution of income is concerned, wages and salaries or labor income currently account for about 71 per cent of the national income. Corporate profits account for 11 per cent,

[2] Simon Kuznets, "Economic Growth and Income Inequality," *American Economic Review,* March, 1955, p. 7.

proprietors' income for 10 per cent, and interest and rental income for 5 per cent and 3 per cent of national income, respectively.

3. The manner in which personal income is distributed among individual households is a determinant of both the level and the composition of total output.

4. Households divide their personal incomes among personal taxes, personal consumption expenditures, and personal saving. Currently about 12 per cent of personal income is paid to government as personal taxes, 81 per cent is spent on consumer goods, and the remaining 7 per cent is saved.

5. Since World War II, personal taxes have risen sharply in both absolute and relative terms. The waging of World War II and the need for large armament expenditures in the postwar era have been the major causal factors underlying this upsurge.

6. In relative terms, personal consumption expenditures increase during bad times and decline during good times. However, in absolute terms consumption varies directly with the level of incomes. Expenditures on durables and the purchase of some services are more postponable than expenditures on nondurables. Since saving can be forgone entirely and indefinitely, personal consumption expenditures tend to be more stable over time than is personal saving.

7. Personal saving, defined as income which is not spent on consumer goods or in paying taxes, is directly related to the level of incomes. As income rises, both consumption and saving tend to increase absolutely.

QUESTIONS AND STUDY SUGGESTIONS

1. Distinguish between the personal distribution of income and the functional distribution of income.
2. What changes have taken place in the absolute and relative size of the major shares of national income? What accounts for these changes? How do you account for the relative stability of labor's share?
3. What implications does the personal distribution of income have for the size and composition of the economy's total output? For resource allocation? Explain.

4. "If we want capitalism, we must also accept inequality of income distribution." Evaluate and explain.
5. What happens to the volumes of consumption and saving as disposable income rises? What is "dissaving"? When is dissaving most likely to occur?
6. Distinguish between consumer durable goods and consumer nondurables. Give examples of each. Why is the demand for durables less stable than that for nondurables?
7. What changes have taken place in the absolute and relative size of personal taxes, personal consumption expenditures, and personal saving over the last three decades? Be specific.
8. Distinguish between saving as a "flow" and as a "stock." How did World War II increase the volume of personal savings?

SELECTED REFERENCES

Cochrane, Willard W., and Carolyn S. Bell: *The Economics of Consumption* (New York: McGraw-Hill Book Company, 1956), particularly chaps. 4 and 11–13.

Hicks, J. R., A. G. Hart, and J. W. Ford: *The Social Framework of the American Economy*, 2d ed. (Fair Lawn, N.J.: Oxford University Press, 1955), chap. 17.

Katona, George: *The Mass Consumption Society* (New York: McGraw-Hill Book Company, 1964).

Katona, George: *The Powerful Consumer* (New York: McGraw-Hill Book Company, 1960).

U.S. Department of Commerce: *Survey of Current Business*, April, 1964, pp. 3–30.

CHAPTER 8

THE FACTS OF
AMERICAN CAPITALISM:
BUSINESSES

Private businesses constitute the second major aggregate of American capitalism. This chapter is a factual description of the business segment of the economy. More specifically, the goals of our discussion are threefold:

1. The major characteristics of the business population will be explored. Emphasis here will be upon the diversity and fluidity of the business population, the various legal forms which private enterprises may assume, and the major industrial classifications.

2. The development of "big business" which has accompanied the development of the American economy will be explored in terms of the causes, the means, and the effects of this growth.

3. The dual role of businesses as producers and employers will be analyzed in terms of a single firm and then in terms of businesses as a group.

THE BUSINESS POPULATION

To avoid any possible confusion, we preface our discussion of the business population with some comments concerning terminology. In particular, one must distinguish between a plant, a firm, and an industry. A *plant* is a physical unit of production; it is a physical establishment in the form of a factory, farm, mine, retail or wholesale store, or warehouse which performs one or more specific functions in the fabrication and distribution of goods and services. A business

firm, on the other hand, is the business organization which owns and operates these plants. While most firms operate only one plant, many firms own and operate a number of plants. For example, without exception, each of the large steel firms of our economy—United States Steel, Bethlehem Steel, Republic Steel, and so forth—owns ore and coal mines, limestone quarries, coke ovens, blast furnaces, rolling mills, forge shops, foundries, and, in some cases, fabricating shops. The large chain stores in the retail grocery field are composed of hundreds or, in some instances, thousands of plants. In brief, a firm may be composed of many plants at the same stage of production or at many different stages of production. Economists call the former "horizontal" combinations and the latter "vertical" combinations.

An *industry* is a group of firms producing identical, or at least similar, products. Though an apparently simple concept, industries are usually difficult to identify in practice. For example, how are we to identify the automobile industry? The simplest answer is "All firms producing automobiles." But automobiles are heterogeneous products. While Cadillacs and Buicks are similar products, and Buicks and Fords are similar, and Fords and Ramblers are similar, and Ramblers and Volkswagens are similar, it is clear that Volkswagens and Cadillacs are very dissimilar. At least most buyers think so. And what about trucks? Certainly small come the shortcomings of the proprietorship than first appears and, indeed, raises some new potential problems which the sole proprietorship does not entail.

1. Whenever there are several people participating in management, this division of authority can lead to inconsistent, divided policies or to inaction when action is required. Worse yet, partners may flatly disagree on basic policy. For all these reasons, management in a partnership may be very unwieldy and cumbersome.

2. The finances of partnerships are still limited, although generally superior to those of a sole proprietorship. The financial resources of three or four partners may be such as to restrict severely the potential growth of an enterprise.

3. The continuity of a partnership is very precarious. The withdrawal or death of a partner generally entails the dissolution and complete reorganization of the firm. Needless to say, this may severely disrupt the firm's operations.

4. Finally, unlimited liability plagues a partnership, just as it does a proprietorship. As a matter of fact, each partner is now liable for all business debts incurred, not only as a result of his own management decisions, but also as a consequence of the actions of any other partner. A wealthy partner risks all his riches on the prudence of his partners.

Corporation. Corporations are legal entities, distinct and separate from the individuals who own them. As such, these governmentally created "legal persons" can acquire resources, own assets, produce and sell products, incur debts, extend credit, sue and be sued, and carry on all those functions which any other type of enterprise performs.

The advantages of the corporate form of business enterprise have catapulted this type of firm into a dominant position in modern American capitalism.

1. The corporation is by far the most effective form of business organization for raising money capital. The corporation features new methods of finance—the selling of stocks and bonds—which allow the firm to tap the savings of untold thousands of households. Through the securities market, corporations can pool the financial resources of extremely large numbers of people.[2] Furthermore, corporations ordinarily have easier access to bank credit than do other types of business organization. This is the case not only because corporations are better risks but also because they are more likely to provide banks with profitable accounts.

2. Corporations have the distinct advantage of *limited liability*. The owners (stockholders) of a corporation risk only what they paid for the stock purchased. Their personal assets are not at stake if the corporation founders on the rocks of bankruptcy. Creditors can sue the corporation as a legal person, but not the owners of that corporation as individuals. Once again, this eases the corporation's task in acquiring money capital.

3. As a legal entity, the corporation has a life independent of its owners and, for that matter, of its individual officials. Proprietorships are subject to sudden and unpredictable demise, but, legally at least, corporations are immortal. The transfer of corporate ownership through the sale of stock does not disrupt this continuity which the corporation boasts. In short, corporations have a certain permanence which is

[2] Financing by the sale of securities also has decided advantages from the viewpoint of the purchasers of these securities. First, households can now participate in enterprise and share the expected monetary reward therefrom without having to assume an active part in management. And, in addition, an individual can spread his risks by buying the securities of a variety of corporations. Finally, it is easy for the holder of corporate securities to dispose of his holdings. Organized stock exchanges facilitate the transfer of securities among buyers and sellers. Needless to say, this increases the willingness of savers to buy corporate securities.

lacking in other forms of business organization. This permanence is conducive to long-range planning and growth.

4. Corporations, because of their strategic position in acquiring money capital, typically have the ability to secure more specialized, and therefore more efficient, management than can proprietorships and partnerships.

5. Last but not least is the possible tax advantage which incorporation may give for an enterprise whose net profits are sizable. As we shall find in Chapter 9, the maximum 48 per cent marginal tax rate facing a corporation is preferable to the maximum 70 per cent marginal rate of the personal income tax.

These advantages are of tremendous significance and typically override any accompanying disadvantages. Yet the drawbacks of the corporate form of organization merit mentioning.

1. There is some red tape and legal expense in obtaining a corporate charter.

2. Corporate charters usually specify the corporation's field of operation, thus making the corporation seem less flexible than other forms in its business activities. In practice, however, these restrictions have tended to be very broad and, in some cases, are flatly ignored, rendering this particular shortcoming more apparent than real.

3. From the social point of view, it must be noted that the corporate form of enterprise lends itself to certain abuses. Because the corporation is a legal entity, unscrupulous businessmen sometimes can avoid personal responsibility for questionable business activities by adopting the corporate form of enterprise. And, despite legislation to the contrary, the corporate form of organization has been a cornerstone for the issue and sale of worthless securities. Note, however, that these are potential abuses of the corporate form, not inherent defects.

4. A further possible disadvantage of corporations has to do with the taxation of corporate income. Briefly, that part of corporate income which is paid out as dividends to stockholders is taxed twice—once as a part of corporate profits and again as a part of the stockholder's personal incomes. This disadvantage must be weighed against the previously noted fact that the maximum tax rates on corporate enterprises are less than those which may apply to unincorporated firms.

5. In the sole proprietorship and partnership forms, those who own the real and financial assets of the firm also manage or control those assets.[3] Most observers agree that this is as it should be. But in larger corporations, where the ownership of common stock is widely diffused over thousands or tens of thousands of stockholders, a fundamental cleavage between ownership and control will arise. This divorce of corporate ownership and control is intriguing, because, in theory at least, corporations are organized democratically. Each share of common stock has one vote in electing the firm's board of directors, which has ultimate authority for the operation of the enterprise. The more common stock you own, the more votes you have in selecting the corporation's officials.

How, then, do ownership and control come to be separated? The roots of the cleavage lie in the lethargy of the typical stockholder. Most stockholders simply do not exercise their voting rights or, if they do, merely sign these rights over by proxy to the corporation's present officers. And why not? The average stockholder knows nothing about the efficiency with which "his" corporation is being managed. So long as his dividends are regular and comparable in size to those received by the other members of his golf foursome who also hold common stock in various concerns, he is not troubled by the question of efficient management. And, after all, since the typical stockholder may own only 10 of 150,000 shares of common stock outstanding, his vote "really doesn't make a bit of differ-

[3] The silent-partner arrangement is the exception.

ence"! Not voting, or the automatic signing over of one's proxy to current corporate officials, typically has the effect of making those officials self-perpetuating.

The separation of ownership and control is of no fundamental consequence so long as the actions of the control (management) group and the wishes of the ownership (stockholder) group are in accord. The catch lies in the fact that the interests of the two groups are not always identical. For example, management, seeking the power and prestige which accompanies control over a *large* enterprise, may favor unprofitable expansion of the firm's operations, or a conflict of interest can easily develop with respect to current dividend policies. What portion of corporate earnings after taxes should be paid out as dividends, and what amount should be retained by the firm as undistributed profits? More obviously, corporation officials may vote themselves large salaries, pensions, bonuses, and so forth, out of corporate earnings which might otherwise be used for increased dividend payments.

But let us not go overboard. Most of the time, management and stockholder interests coincide. And, although abuses have occurred and undoubtedly will continue to occur, there can be little question that productive efficiency is greater under the present system than would be the case if large numbers of stockholders had an immediate hand in formulating basic corporate policy decisions. In short, the divorce of ownership and control which characterizes large corporations is permissive of certain abuses by the control group, but these abuses are not an inherent defect of the corporate form of enterprise.

To Incorporate or Not to Incorporate?

Which legal form of enterprise—proprietorship or corporation—is best? Probably the basic determinant of the legal form of enterprise is the amount of funds which a given line of production requires. For example, the corner magazine stand or the small curio or gift shop will have very modest money capital requirements. The only fixed assets which tie up some money capital are a few relatively inexpensive display counters. And the volume of business is so small that the need for "working capital" (funds which bridge the gap between costs and sales receipts) is also minimal. Why go to the cost and trouble of incorporating such a firm when the primary advantage of incorporating—the accessibility of large amounts of money capital through the sale of securities—is actually of little relevance? In contrast, modern technology and a much larger dollar volume of business make incorporation imperative in many lines of production. For example, in most branches of manufacturing—automobiles, steel, fabricated metal products, electrical equipment, household appliances, and so forth—very substantial money requirements for investment in fixed assets and for working capital are involved. The typical manufacturing concern in the United States may have $20,000 to $25,000 worth of capital equipment *per worker!* Given these circumstances, there is little choice. To exist is to incorporate. In brief, the best legal form of business enterprise varies from industry to industry, and the primary determinant of legal form is the money capital requirement of the particular industry.

TABLE 8–1. THE BUSINESS POPULATION BY FORM OF LEGAL ORGANIZATION

Form	Number of firms	Per cent of total
Sole proprietorships*	9,242,000	81
Partnerships	939,000	8
Corporations	1,190,000	11
Total	11,371,000	100

* Includes farmers and professional people in business for themselves.
Source: U.S. Department of Commerce data and author's estimates.

Actually the American business population is distributed among the three legal forms in the manner indicated in Table 8–1. It is strikingly clear that the proprietorship form is numerically dominant. Yet corporations, though small in number, are frequently large in size and scale of operations. In fact, corporations account for approximately 60 per cent of the output of all private business enterprises.

Industrial Distribution of the Business Population

What do the 11 million firms which compose the business sector of our economy produce? Table 8–2 measures in several different ways the significance of the various industry classifications. Column 2 indicates the numerical and percentage distribution of the business population among the various industries. Column 3 shows in both absolute and relative terms the portion of the national income originating in the various industries. Column 4 indicates the absolute and relative amounts of employment provided by each industry. Several points in Table 8–2 are noteworthy:

1. The relatively small number of firms in manufacturing account for about one-third of national income and total employment. These figures correctly suggest that the American capitalist economy is highly industrialized, characterized by gigantic business corporations in its manufacturing industries.

2. The wholesale and retail industries and the service industries (hotels, motels, personal services, and so forth) are heavily populated with firms and are simultaneously very important sources of employment and incomes in the economy.

TABLE 8–2. INDUSTRY CLASSES: NUMBER OF FIRMS, NATIONAL INCOME ORIGINATING, AND EMPLOYMENT PROVIDED*

(1) Industry	(2) Number of private businesses		(3) Contribution to national income		(4) Full-time workers employed	
	Thousands	Per cent	Billions	Per cent	Thousands	Per cent
Agriculture, forestry, and fisheries	4,700	50	$ 17.6	4	4,761	8
Mining	43	1	6.2	1	635	1
Construction	479	5	26.2	5	3,106	5
Manufacturing	324	4	154.7	30	17,303	27
Wholesale and retail trade	2,334	24	78.1	15	12,188	19
Finance, insurance, and real estate	405	4	57.0	11	2,944	5
Transportation, communications, and public utilities	210	2	42.3	8	3,976	6
Services	893	10	58.0	11	8,533	14
Government			70.0	14 }	9,502 }	15
Rest of world			4.1	1		
Total	9,338	100	$514.4	100	62,948	100

* Column 2 is for 1961, 3 for 1964, and 4 for 1964.
Source: U.S. Department of Commerce, U.S. Treasury Department, and *Economic Almanac, 1962.*

3. Note, too, the large number of firms engaged in agriculture but the relative insignificance of agriculture as a provider of incomes and jobs.

4. Table 8–2 reminds us that not all the economy's income and employment originate in private domestic enterprises. Government and foreign enterprises account for about 15 per cent of the economy's national income and employ about 15 per cent of the labor force.

BIG BUSINESS IN AMERICAN CAPITALISM

To a very significant extent, American capitalism is a "big-business" economy. A good many of our major industries are dominated by corporate giants which enjoy assets and annual sales revenues calculated in billions of dollars, employ hundreds of thousands of workers, have a hundred thousand or more stockholders, and earn annual profits after taxes running into hundreds of millions of dollars. The previously noted fact that corporations, although constituting only 11 per cent of the business population, produce 60 per cent of the economy's total output hints at the existence of large corporate producers. The major questions to be faced in connection with the existence of big businesses in American capitalism are these:

1. To what degree does big business prevail in the American economy?

2. Why and through what means have businesses sought "bigness"; that is, what are a firm's incentives for and means of growth?

3. What dangers, if any, are posed by the existence of giant business firms?

Extent of Bigness

To what degree does big business prevail in the American economy? Unfortunately, there exists no simple index to measure the economic power concentrated in the hands of big-business enterprises. Indeed, there is a host of conceptual and statistical problems

involved in deriving and interpreting statistics on big business.[4] Nevertheless, available statistics rather clearly portray the important role played by these corporate giants and the extent to which they dominate various industries.

It is notable that a recent study for the United States Senate's Antitrust and Monopoly Subcommittee concludes that whereas the 100 largest manufacturing corporations held 44 per cent of all net capital assets (property, plant, and equipment) of the nation's manufacturing corporations in 1929 and 48 per cent in 1947, these largest 100 corporations now hold almost 58 per cent of all net capital assets.[5] These data suggest that the concentration of economic power continues to increase in the United States. A glance at Table 29–1 reveals the degree of business concentration in certain major industries.

Incentives and Means for Bigness

What motivates businesses to grow? The incentives are complex and to some extent overlapping.

1. The desire to achieve greater *productive efficiency* has undoubtedly played a role in the growth of big business. Large firms are frequently in a better position to realize "mass-production economies" than are their small-scale brethren. Yet it seems that the production economies of many mergers are nil. Indeed, some consolidations have probably resulted in operating inefficiencies because of the complicated man-

---

[4] Because most large firms produce a variety of products, the already noted conceptual problem of clearly defining various industries arises. Statistical problems center around the question of choosing an appropriate measure of "bigness," or industrial concentration.

[5] See William N. Leonard, "Industrial Concentration and Growing Market Power," *Challenge,* December, 1964, pp. 28–32, for an excellent summary of recent data on economic concentration.

agement problems posed in attempting to coordinate a cumbersome industrial giant.[6]

2. The search for *power* and *prestige* by business leaders has been a factor in the growth of big business. Being the largest employer or controlling the largest quantity of real capital assets in a given industry carries a certain amount of prestige that is generally recognized and much sought for in the business world.

3. *Security* and *assurance of long-run survival* have been factors in the growth of big business. Combination is often effected to "diversify the product line" of a firm as a safeguard against seasonal and cyclical fluctuations in business activity. Diversification also affords some measure of protection against the risk of unfavorable changes in consumer tastes. A multiproduct firm, by not putting all its eggs in one basket, is in a better position to survive the fickleness of consumers. And, of course, the goal of a long-run survival prompts firms to branch out into newly developed industries where the prospects of future growth seem to be good. Similarly, combination may serve to ensure a firm of steady and continuing supplies of raw materials, semifinished goods, and product parts.

4. The seeking of *greater financial rewards* has been the dominant factor in the growth of big business. One aspect of this profit seeking has to do with the windfall gains, or promoter's profits, resulting from the immediate combination of several corporations. But of greater significance in the long pull is the enhancement of prospective profits through the demise of competition which combination typically entails.

The means by which once-small firms have evolved into huge industrial giants are essentially twofold. In a relatively few cases —for example, Ford Motor Company and

Alcoa (Aluminum Company of America)— gigantic business enterprises have developed primarily through *internal growth*, that is, through the reinvestment of the firm's earnings and the acquisition of additional funds for expansion by floating new issues of securities. However, the vast majority of firms now classified as "big businesses" have relied basically upon some form of business *combination*—mergers, consolidations, or the formation of trusts and holding companies— in achieving their present positions of dominance in their respective industries. The important point is that big business is a basic fact of American economic life. It is therefore highly relevant to probe briefly the implications of bigness in the business sector.

Should Big Business Be Feared?

This is a knotty question, permitting honest differences of opinion. Two basic schools of thought exist on this issue. We summarize these views here and defer a detailed analysis to subsequent chapters.

One school of thought holds that big business is a natural and necessary outgrowth of a progressive industrial economy. In particular, it is argued that modern technology requires (1) the use of extremely large quantities of real capital, (2) wide markets, (3) a complex, closely integrated management, and (4) large and reliable sources of raw materials. Such an operation implies the need for large-scale producers. In short, the achievement of maximum productive efficiency through the employment of the best available technology often presupposes the concentration of economic power. Efficient production is only attainable when business units are large.

Equally competent observers view the situation much differently. Though efficiency may require "bigness" up to a point, it is argued that many American businesses have grown far beyond the size necessary for the achievement of maximum productive efficiency. Indeed, it is pointed out that some

[6] See in particular Joe S. Bain, "Economies of Scale, Concentration, and the Condition of Entry in Twenty Manufacturing Industries," *American Economic Review*, March, 1954, pp. 15–39.

industrial giants are inefficient because they are too large; bureaucratic red tape has made them inflexible and unresponsive to fundamental changes in the economy. Furthermore, it is contended that bigness and monopoly power frequently go together. When this is the case, big businesses contain all the potential evils of monopoly power. This power may even be of a cumulative character: big-business employers prompt the growth of big labor unions, and the relations between the two may demand public control and therefore the growth of big government. All this implies fundamental changes in the capitalist ideology.

THE DUAL ROLE OF BUSINESSES

Businesses, as well as households, play a dual role in American capitalism. On the one hand, businesses are the main fountainhead of the economy's total output of goods and services; almost 85 per cent of total output is produced and sold by private enterprises (see Table 8–2). On the other hand, in accomplishing this production, businesses purchase or hire the bulk of the economy's available supplies of resources. In so doing, businesses provide employment and make wage, rent, interest, and profit payments to resource suppliers. In brief, businesses produce and sell goods and in so doing acquire money receipts. These money receipts in turn are used to pay the costs of employing the resources necessary in the productive process, not to mention tax revenues. As is true of the household sector, businesses receive and disburse money flows.

Income Statement: A Single Firm

The nature of these flows can best be visualized through the income or profit and loss statement of an individual firm. An income statement is simply an accounting statement which shows the sources of a firm's income or receipts and the manner in which these receipts are allocated or disbursed during any given year. More spe-

cifically, an income statement shows how much a firm gets in receipts from its sales of goods and services and how these receipts are apportioned among various production costs and profits. The statement balances because profits (or losses) are the difference between receipts and costs. Table 8–3 presents a simplified income statement for a manufacturing firm. We assume that this concern is a corporation which realizes all its receipts from the sale of a single product to wholesale firms A and B. Sales receipts (net of discounts and rebates) are $100,000.

How are these receipts apportioned between costs and profits? The left side of Table 8–3 provides the answer. Sizable payments for wages and salaries, materials provided by other firms, and interest and rental payments for the use of property resources are typical costs.

Item 5, depreciation, requires some explanation. Most resources—labor services and materials, for example—are used up in the accounting period in which they are purchased. Here the firm's monetary outlays coincide with the use of the particular resource. Capital equipment is a different story, however. A building or piece of machinery may last for many years, even though the actual payment for that machinery may occur entirely in the year of purchase. For example, suppose a $10,000 machine is purchased by a firm in 1966. Its estimated life is ten years. Now, if the entire $10,000 cost of this machine were figured in the income statement for 1966, that year's profits would be grossly understated. Indeed, sizable losses might be incurred. Then, in ensuing years, while the machine is actually being used up, profits would be overstated. The machinery would be contributing to output and therefore to receipts but would entail no cost to the firm. To avoid such arbitrary effects of durable machinery and building purchases upon annual profits and losses, accountants estimate that portion of the value of the machine which will be used up in each year of

TABLE 8–3. THE INCOME STATEMENT: A SINGLE FIRM (hypothetical data)

Allocations			Receipts		
(1) Wages and salaries		$ 35,000	(8) Sales of output		$100,000
(2) Materials		25,000	(a) To firm A ..	$40,000	
(3) Interest		8,000	(b) To firm B ..	60,000	
(4) Rents		4,000			
(5) Depreciation		1,000			
(6) Taxes		9,400			
(a) Payroll taxes	$ 3,000				
(b) Indirect business taxes (sales taxes, excises, etc.)	2,000				
(c) Corporate profits taxes	4,400				
(7) Corporate profits (after taxes)		17,600			
(a) Dividends	$10,000				
(b) Undistributed profits	7,600				
		$100,000			$100,000

its estimated ten-year life. This amount, called a "depreciation charge," is then apportioned more or less evenly over the ten-year period. In this way a more accurate picture of annual profits is achieved. Thus, although the actual disbursement for machinery may be made in one year, annual depreciation charges adjust the firm's profits as if the equipment costs occurred evenly over the lifetime of the machinery. In short, the depreciation charge is merely a bookkeeping entry which makes for a more accurate estimate of profits over a period of time.

Table 8–3 also indicates the importance of taxes as a cost of doing business. A corporation will be faced first with payroll taxes, which are contributions made in the financing of the social security programs. Sales and excise taxes are other important expenses. Such taxes are listed as "indirect business taxes" because they are not levied directly upon the firm as such but rather upon the product which the firm produces. Corporate income taxes are levied directly upon the net taxable profits of the corporation. What remains, corporate profits after

taxes, is typically divided among dividends paid out to stockholders and undistributed corporate profits or business saving.

Income Statement: The Business Sector

Table 8–4 is a consolidated income statement for the entire business sector of American capitalism for 1964. This is merely a gigantic income statement for all the business firms which make up the business sector of our economy. In most respects, it is similar to the income statement for a single firm.

The importance of the consolidated income statement for the business sector is that it provides us with a picture of the size and composition of the total output provided by the major producing sector of the economy.[7] The receipts side of this consolidated statement tells us that the business sector produced approximately

[7] For simplicity's sake, we assume that there is no change in inventories to cause a discrepancy between the volume of production and the volume of sales in any given year.

TABLE 8–4. THE INCOME STATEMENT: THE BUSINESS SECTOR, 1964 (billions of dollars)

Allocations		Receipts		
(1) Wages and salaries	$273	(8) Sales of output		$543
(2) Interest	14	(a) To consumers	$382	
(3) Rents	18	(b) To other		
(4) Depreciation	54	businesses	95*	
(5) Taxes	100	(c) To government	66	
(a) Payroll taxes ... $16				
(b) Indirect business taxes .. 58				
(c) Corporate income taxes . 26				
(6) Corporate profits (after taxes)	32			
(a) Dividends ... $20				
(b) Undistributed profits ... 12				
(7) Proprietors' income	52			
	$543			$543

* Includes foreign sales.
Source: Calculated from U.S. Department of Commerce data.

$543 billion worth of goods and services in 1964. The breakdown of these sales indicates in a general way the composition of this output. Some $382 billion, or 70 per cent of the business sector's production, was in the form of consumer goods; $95 billion, or 17 per cent, in the form of capital goods (machinery, equipment, and buildings) which firms produced and sold to one another; and $66 billion, or 13 per cent, took the form of social goods and services (mostly armaments) sold to government.

It should be emphasized that the consolidated income statement leaves out most interbusiness transactions. As a matter of fact, all transactions between businesses, except those where the buying firm is the actual user or consumer of the product, are concealed by the consolidated income statement. This is as it should be if we seek an accurate picture of the size and composition of the business sector's yearly output. The inclusion of "intermediate" transactions between businesses would lead to an exaggeration of the business sector's output. A simple illustration will make this evident. There are likely to be several stages of production in turning out a finished product. In producing a suit, the rancher sells wool to a mill for $10, the mill sells woolen

textiles to a manufacturer for $20, the manufacturer sells the finished suit to a wholesaler for $40, the wholesaler sells it to a retailer for $50, and the retailer sells it to you as a consumer for, say, $70. To include all these transactions would tell us that $190 (= $10 + $20 + $40 + $50 + $70) worth of production has occurred in making a suit. But this is nonsense! Only $70 worth of production has occurred. Why? Because the intermediate transactions leading up to the final sale of the product to the consumer are covered, or included in, the $70 selling price. The value of the raw wool, the value of the processing done at the mill, the value of the handling and distributional services performed by the wholesaler and retailer are all included in the $70. To count these intermediate transactions separately would be to exaggerate grossly the output of the business sector. However, we do include sales between businesses when the buying firm is the ultimate user of the product. The production of capital goods, that is, machinery and equipment, by some firms for use by other firms is as much a part of the year's production as is the production of shoes and soap flakes for consumers and of highways and schools for government. To omit these final sales of capital goods would be to understate the year's production.

On the disbursement side of the picture, we see how the businesses allocate their total receipts. In Table 8–4, items 1, 2, 3, 6a, and 7–item 7 added in acknowledging that the business sector is composed of both incorporated and nonincorporated businesses–are payments for resources supplied by households. These items, totaling $377 billion, are income payments from the viewpoint of households. Item 4, depreciation, is a bookkeeping adjustment to give us a more accurate picture of business profits. Tax items 5a, 5b, and 5c, totaling $101 billion, flow to government. Item 6b is that part of businesses profits which is retained in the business sector; it constitutes business saving. Percentagewise, about 70 per cent of business receipts flow as wage, rent, interest, and profit payments to households. Taxes account for about 18 per cent. The remaining 12 per cent is business saving and depreciation.

The reader will probably have noted that the allocation for materials has been dropped in moving from the single firm's income statement to the consolidated statement for the business sector. The reason again has to do with "intermediate" transactions. For the *individual* firm, relationships with other firms from which it buys materials are important, and such purchases must be listed as disbursements or allocations. But for businesses *as a group,* these transactions are self-canceling; payments from one firm to another in the purchase of materials offset one another. The allocation of $25,000 for materials by firm X is offset by $25,000 of receipts flowing to firm Y, the seller of the materials. In other words, the consolidated income statement eliminates or cancels the expenditures and receipts which occur between firms in the business sector and shows only the relationship of the business sector to the household and governmental sectors of the economy. Note that all the allocations shown in Table 8–4 flow to the household sector as income payments, to the

governmental sector as taxes, or simply stay in the business sector as undistributed receipts.

SUMMARY

1. The business population of American capitalism is both heterogeneous and fluid.

2. Sole proprietorships, partnerships, and corporations are the major legal forms which business enterprises may assume. Though proprietorships dominate numerically, the bulk of total output is produced by corporations. Corporations have grown to their position of dominance in the business sector primarily because they are **a.** characterized by limited liability and **b.** in a superior position to acquire money capital for expansion.

3. Manufacturing accounts for a larger percentage of national income and employment in American capitalism than does any other industrial classification. The wholesale, retail, and service industries are also major sources of income and employment.

4. Many basic industries in our economy are dominated by a small number of large corporations. Major incentives underlying the growth of these big businesses are: **a.** the desire to achieve greater productive efficiency, **b.** the search for power and prestige by business leaders, **c.** security and the assurance of a long-run survival, and **d.** the pursuit of greater financial rewards. Big businesses have developed by means of internal growth and by combination.

5. Economists disagree on the desirability of big businesses. One view holds that big businesses are essential for achieving efficient production. Others contend that many American businesses have grown far beyond the size essential for efficiency in production and have acquired considerable monopoly power as a result of size.

6. Income statements are useful analytical tools for the economist in that they reveal the sources of income and the disbursement thereof for an individual firm or the business sector as a whole.

QUESTIONS AND STUDY SUGGESTIONS

1. Distinguish clearly between a plant, a firm, and an industry. Why is an "industry" difficult to define in practice?
2. What are the major legal forms of business organization? Briefly state the advantages and disadvantages of each. How do you account for the dominant role of corporations in our economy?
3. Explain and evaluate the separation of ownership and control which characterizes the corporate form of business enterprise. Explain the following statement: [8]

   In the economic realm . . . [a] situation prevails that runs counter to the basic concept of democracy: corporation managers wield far-reaching power over stockholders and employees, and they constantly make decisions affecting the public interest, without any clearly defined responsibility to the public. Whereas in a capitalist democracy political policies are arrived at through processes of consent that begin at the bottom and end at the top, in corporate business economic policies are made from the top and passed on to the bottom.

4. What are the major industries in American capitalism in terms of (*a*) the number of firms in operation and (*b*) the amount of income and employment provided?
5. What factors have motivated the growth of big business in the United States? What are the pros and cons of big business?
6. Explain and evaluate the following statements:
   a. "It is the consumer, and the consumer alone, who casts the vote that determines how big any company should be."
   b. "The very nature of modern industrial society requires labor, government, and businesses to be 'big' and their bigness renders impossible the functioning of the older, small-scale, simpler, and more flexible capitalist system."[9]
   c. "The legal form which an enterprise assumes is dictated primarily by the financial requirements of its particular line of production."
7. What is an income statement? Of what value is a consolidated income statement for the business sector? Why does the consolidated income statement exclude all interbusiness transactions except the sale of capital goods to their ultimate users? Why is this desirable?

SELECTED REFERENCES

Bain, Joe S.: *Industrial Organization* (New York: John Wiley & Sons, Inc., 1959), chaps. 3 and 4.

Boulding, Kenneth E.: *Economic Analysis,* 3d ed. (New York: Harper & Row, Publishers, Incorporated, 1955), chaps. 23 and 24.

[8] William Ebenstein, *Today's Isms,* 3d ed. (Englewood Cliffs, N.J.: Prentice-Hall, Inc., 1961), p. 166.
[9] Eugene O. Golob, *The Isms* (New York: Harper & Row, Publishers, Incorporated, 1954), p. 53.

Buckingham, Walter S., Jr.: *Theoretical Economic Systems* (New York: The Ronald Press Company, 1958), chaps. 7 and 8.

Chandler, Alfred D., Jr. (ed.): *Giant Enterprise* (New York: Harcourt, Brace & World, Inc., 1964).

Cheit, Earl F. (ed.): *The Business Establishment* (New York: John Wiley & Sons, Inc., 1964).

Levin, Harvey J. (ed.): *Business Organization and Public Policy* (New York: Holt, Rinehart and Winston, Inc., 1958), chaps. 4–17.

McGuire, Joseph W.: *Business and Society* (New York: McGraw-Hill Book Company, 1963).

Robertson, Dennis, and Stanley Dennison: *The Control of Industry* (Welwyn, England: James Nisbet and Company, Ltd., 1960), chaps. 1–8.

CHAPTER 9

THE FACTS OF AMERICAN CAPITALISM: GOVERNMENT

Current facts characterizing the private sectors of the economy were discussed in Chapters 7 and 8. A factual look at the governmental or public sector of American capitalism is the basic task of the present chapter. The controversy surrounding the scope of government's economic role (see Chapter 6) makes it particularly important that the facts of government be clearly understood and placed in proper perspective.

DUAL ROLE OF GOVERNMENT

Although, as Chapter 6 revealed, there are many ways in which government affects economic life, it is through taxation and expenditures that the functions of government are most directly felt. Indeed, changes in the size and composition of government spending and the volume of tax revenues reflect with a fair degree of accuracy any changes in the size and character of government's role in the economy. It is with the public sector's role as a transactor, that is, as a receiver and disposer of "income," that this chapter is concerned.

One point must be emphasized at the outset. There is a significant difference between the transactions of the private and public sectors of the economy: the former are voluntary, and the latter compulsory. The receipts and expenditures of households and businesses are the result of voluntary decisions by those two aggregates in buying and selling goods and resources.

Government tax revenues are the result of compulsory levies: households and businesses have no choice but to pay taxes. To a lesser degree, this compulsion appears on the expenditure side of government's transactions. While no one is compelled to use governmentally provided highways, libraries, or health clinics, all physically and mentally capable children who are within stated age brackets must consume public education or its equivalent.

GROWTH OF GOVERNMENT TAX REVENUES AND EXPENDITURES

Our comments in this and the succeeding section are concerned with all units of Federal, state, and local government combined. Following this, we shall take a more detailed look at the taxation and expenditure features of each of the three levels of government.[1] Then, finally, we shall analyze the controversial problem of apportioning the tax burden in the economy.

Figures 9–1 and 9–2 make clear the growing importance of the public sector of the economy by summarizing the long-term *absolute* growth in government spending

[1] The statistics used in this chapter in discussing Federal, state, and local finance are not from the same sources; thus, the total government budget picture presented in Table 9–1 is not equal to the sum of the Federal, state, and local budgets shown in Tables 9–2 to 9–4.

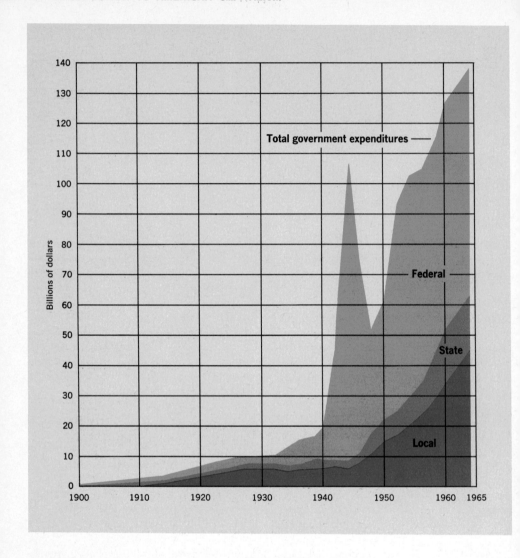

FIGURE 9–1. FEDERAL, STATE, AND LOCAL EXPENDITURES, 1902–1964.
Government expenditures have grown both absolutely and as a percentage of total
output. Hot and cold wars, population growth, more and better social goods, and
inflation are some of the more important factors underlying this growth. [U.S. Bureau
of the Census, *Governmental Finances in the United States, 1902–1957* (March,
1959) and census data.]

and taxation. But this is not all: Government's role as a transactor has also expanded
significantly in *relative* terms. In 1929 government expenditures claimed only about
8 per cent of total output. By 1939 this figure had expanded to 15 per cent. At the

peak of the war effort in 1943–1944, government expenditures had expanded to 45
per cent of total output. In the postwar era, government expenditures have been about
20 per cent of total output (see Table 6–1). The 20 per cent of total output purchased

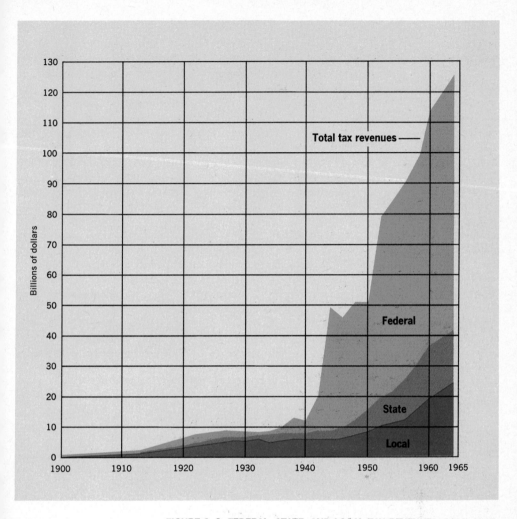

FIGURE 9–2. FEDERAL, STATE, AND LOCAL TAX REVENUES, 1902–1964.
Government tax collections have also increased significantly over time, roughly matching
the increases in government spending. [U.S. Bureau of the Census, *Governmental
Finances in the United States, 1902–1957* (March, 1959) and census data.]

by government in 1964 was largely financed
by an average tax bill of $723 presented to
every man, woman, and child in the United
States!

The spectacular growth in government
spending and, consequently, tax collections
has a multiplicity of causes. As noted in
Chapter 6, root causes center around the
desire of the citizenry to correct or alleviate
the instability, inefficiency, and inequities

which the price system of pure capitalism
may foster. But more immediate causes are
also abundant:

1. Hot and cold wars have sustained
Federal expenditures at peak levels since
1940. War and national defense are the
major causes of the phenomenal growth in
government spending and taxing over the
last two decades.

2. With population increases, more peo-

ple require services from the various levels of government.

3. The public has demanded more and better social goods and services to "match" the rising standard of living provided in the private sector of the economy. For example, we need better roads to accommodate more and better cars.

4. Inflation—generally rising prices—has forced government to spend larger and larger sums for given quantities of products.

And this list is by no means complete.

As with the business and household sectors of the economy, the receipt and expenditure of government income need not match in any particular year or period of years. Surpluses and deficits—the latter in particular—are not at all uncommon in so far as public finance is concerned. Figures 9–1 and 9–2 tell us, however, that tax collections have *generally* followed the trend of government spending. The major exception was the deficit financing which occurred during World War II.

CURRENT BUDGET OF THE PUBLIC SECTOR

In 1964 the total spending and taxing activities of all units of government—Federal, state, and local combined—stacked up as in Table 9–1.

Because tax receipts of $173.5 billion fell short of government expenditures of $179.1 billion, government units as a group incurred a deficit of about $5.6 billion in 1964.

Let us first discuss the major tax classifications listed in Table 9–1.

1. *Personal taxes* consist mainly of personal income taxes levied against the incomes of households and unincorporated businesses but also include inheritance (gift and death) taxes and taxes levied against the real and personal property of households.

2. *Indirect business taxes* consist primarily of sales and excise taxes, customs duties on imported goods, and business property taxes. These taxes are collected from corporations and unincorporated businesses.

3. *Corporate income taxes* are self-defining. They are taxes levied by government against the net earnings of incorporated businesses.

4. *Payroll taxes*, or social security contributions, represent the compulsory payments made by employees and employers in conjunction with the existing social security program.

On the expenditures side of the picture:

1. *Government purchases of goods and services* run the gamut from such ordinary

TABLE 9–1. TAX RECEIPTS AND EXPENDITURES OF THE GOVERNMENT SECTOR, 1964

Tax receipts	Billions of dollars	Per cent of total	Expenditures	Billions of dollars	Per cent of total
Personal taxes	$ 59.6	34	Purchases of goods and services	$128.6	72
Indirect business taxes	59.5	34	Transfer payments	50.5	28
Corporate income taxes	25.8	15	Total expenditures	$179.1	100
Payroll taxes	28.6	17			
Total tax receipts	$173.5	100			
Add deficit	5.6				
Total receipts	$179.1				

Source: U.S. Department of Commerce data. Because of rounding, figures may not add up to totals.

purchases as paper clips, typewriter ribbons, automobiles, and school buildings to such uniquely social goods as jet fighters, atomic submarines, superhighways, and space capsules. Purchases of services include the hiring of clerks, schoolteachers, judges, servicemen, and so forth.

2. *Transfer payments* are money expenditures for which government currently receives no products or services in return. Most government "welfare" expenditures fall in this classification, for example, social security payments to the aged, unemployment compensation, relief payments, and aid to the handicapped. A few transfer payments, called "subsidies," go to businesses, for example, certain payments to farmers under the current agricultural program. Because transfer payments rechannel tax revenues back to households and businesses, these payments in effect are "negative taxes."

There is a noteworthy difference between transfer payments and government purchases of goods and services. Through government spending on goods, society tends to reallocate resources from private to social goods consumption. Through transfers, government changes the composition of the output of private goods. If government taxes $10, we can expect purchases of private goods and services to decline by roughly that amount. In purchasing social goods and services with this $10 worth of tax revenue, government is in effect negotiating a substitution of social for private goods. Transfer payments are different: Instead of increasing social goods at the expense of private goods, transfers merely tend to "rearrange" private consumption. Though $10 in tax revenues will reduce the private goods consumption of taxpayers by about that amount, households to whom this $10 is transferred can be expected to increase their expenditures on private goods by about $10. But in all probability, the recipients will purchase somewhat different goods than the taxpayers. Hence, transfers alter the composition of private goods production.

FEDERAL, STATE, AND LOCAL FINANCE

Let us now examine taxation and expenditures at each level of government, noting first the relative economic significance of the three levels as revealed in Figures 9–1 and 9–2. Federal spending and taxing is significantly greater than the spending and taxing of state and local governments combined. It is also evident, however, that in the 1950s and 1960s spending and taxing have been increasing more rapidly at the state and local levels than at the Federal level.

Federal Finance

Now for a more detailed look at Federal tax revenues and expenditures. What types of goods and services does the Federal government purchase? And from what sources are taxes collected to finance these outlays? Table 9–2 tells the story for 1963.

Federal expenditures. Even a cursory glance at the Federal budget makes painfully clear the economic costs of mobilization and war. The first four categories of spending are the result of past wars, the present cold war, and the desire to head off future wars.

National security expenditures include outlays (1) to maintain and equip the armed services, (2) to provide military aid to our allies, (3) to support our atomic energy program, and (4) to finance armament and space research. National security outlays account for about 50 per cent of total Federal expenditures. But even this gigantic outlay belies the economic costs of wars and military preparedness. The next three types of spending are also closely associated with mobilization and war. *Veterans' services*—which include GI Bill payments, medical care, disability pay, and pensions to veterans and their dependents—obviously are expenditures resulting from the two World Wars and the Korean conflict. And, since the bulk of the Federal debt of some $319 billion was incurred in financing World War II, the annual payment of

TABLE 9–2. THE FEDERAL BUDGET, 1963

Tax receipts	Billions of dollars	Per cent of total	Expenditures	Billions of dollars	Per cent of total
Personal income taxes	$ 55.3	46	National security	$57.2	50
Corporate income			Veterans' services . . .	6.1	5
taxes	23.0	19	Interest on public debt	7.7	7
Payroll taxes	23.0	19	International affairs and		
Excise taxes	15.9	13	finance	2.5	2
Estate and gift taxes . .	2.3	2	Health, education, wel-		
Total	$119.5	100	fare	26.7	23
Less tax refunds . .	−6.0		Agriculture and agri-		
			cultural resources . .	3.5	3
Total tax receipts . .	$113.5		Natural resources	2.3	2
Add deficit	1.8		Commerce and housing	6.0	5
			General government . .	3.3	3
Total receipts	$115.3		Total expenditures .	$115.3	100

Source: U. S. Department of Commerce data. Because of rounding, figures may not add up to totals.

interest on the public debt also must be considered as a war-born outlay. Finally, *international affairs and finance* involve expenditures for the economic and technological development of foreign countries and the costs of administering our foreign affairs. In part, these outlays stem from altruistic motives. But a selfish reason dominates: these expenditures are designed to keep foreign ·countries from turning to communism. As a group, these four expenditure categories account for about $74 billion, or about 64 per cent, of total Federal outlays. War and military preparedness carry extremely high price tags. The remaining categories of spending listed in Table 9–2 are largely self-explanatory.

Federal receipts. The receipts side of Table 9–2 makes it clear that the Federal government relies on a variety of taxes for revenue. It is equally evident that the *personal income tax* and the *corporate income tax* are the basic revenue getters. About 46 cents of each dollar of gross tax revenue collected by the Federal government is in the form of personal income taxes. Another

19 cents of each dollar collected is accounted for by the corporate income tax. The remaining 35 cents comes primarily from payroll and excise taxes. What is the nature of these major sources of Federal revenue?

Personal income tax. The personal income tax is a tax levied on the incomes of households and unincorporated businesses after certain deductions and exemptions have been taken into account.[2] The basic characteristic of this tax is that progressive tax rates are applied to taxable income. The larger your taxable income, the higher the *rate* at which that income is taxed. As the personal income tax is applied in the United States, these higher and higher rates apply to the *increments* of income earned and not to total income. For example, a family of

[2] The major deductions and exemptions from gross income in determining taxable income are (1) business costs and expenses incurred in earning income, (2) gifts to charitable institutions, (3) interest payments, (4) most other tax payments, and (5) a $600 exemption for the taxpayer and each of his dependents.

four in 1966 would pay no income tax if its income was about $2,700[3] or less, because its taxable income would be zero. Assuming no additional deductions or exemptions, the next $1,000 of income earned would be taxed at a rate of 14 per cent. Thus, our family of four, earning a $3,700 income, would pay about $140 (14 per cent of $1,000) in personal income taxes. The next $1,000 chunk of income would be taxed at a slightly higher rate, 15 per cent. In other words, a family of four earning $4,700 would pay $290 in personal income taxes—nothing on the first $2,700, $140 on the next $1,000, and $150 on the next $1,000. Should you be fortunate enough to earn a taxable income of say, $40,000 per year, you would encounter a tax rate of 48 per cent on additional income falling in the next income bracket. And, at the extreme, those who pull down a taxable income in excess of $200,000 per year will find the Federal income tax claiming 70 per cent of each dollar earned in excess of $200,000. *Note:* You can never be worse off by making an extra dollar. At least 30 cents of it will be yours.

It is important to note that, although the *marginal tax rate*—the percentage of each *additional* chunk of income received which is paid in taxes—goes up sharply as income increases, the effective or *average tax rate*—the rate of tax paid on one's *total* income—is usually considerably less. Our mythical family, for example, encounters a marginal tax rate of 15 per cent on each dollar of income earned between $3,700 and $4,700, but the average rate of taxation is only 6.17 per cent ($290 divided by $4,700). However, as income rises, the marginal tax rates rise so sharply that even the average tax rate, though less than the marginal tax rate, comes to be large. Using the extreme example, a family receiving a taxable income of $200,000 per year will encounter the peak *marginal* tax rate of 70 per cent. The family's Federal income tax bill would be about $110,980, making the *average* tax rate about 56 per cent. In all fairness it must be noted that with the aid of a capable lawyer or tax accountant many wealthy taxpayers take advantage of legal loopholes in the personal income tax. It is doubtful, for example, that those few who fall in the higher tax brackets—where the average rate is, say, 55 or 60 per cent—actually pay at a rate in excess of, say, 35 or 40 per cent.

During World War II, the withholding system of collecting the Federal income tax was installed. Under this system, the employer deducts an employee's income taxes from his paycheck and forwards them to the Treasury. Although this method of payment puts the government in the position of a preferred creditor, there are distinct advantages in the withholding system for both the government and the taxpayer. From the government's point of view

1. Income tax evasion is reduced.

2. Tax receipts are most closely attuned to changes in tax rates and size of incomes.

3. The tax is generally easier to administer.

From the taxpayer's point of view, the system in effect puts his income tax bill on the installment plan and makes it somewhat less burdensome to pay.

Corporate income tax. The corporate income tax, the Federal government's second major source of revenue, has a relatively simple structure. Any corporation whose annual net earnings are under $25,000 is taxed at a rate of 22 per cent. For corporations earning in excess of $25,000, the rate on all dollars earned above the $25,000 mark is 48 per cent. For example, a corporation realizing a net annual income of $50,000 would pay $17,500 in corporate income taxes—$5,500 (22 per cent of the first $25,000) plus $12,000 (48 per cent of the remaining $25,000).

The corporate income tax, as mentioned earlier, entails a highly controversial problem—"double taxation." That particular part

---

[3] Four exemptions of $600 each plus a flat 10 per cent blanket deduction of $270 total just short of $2,700.

of the income stream which takes the form of dividends is taxed twice, while other forms of income are taxed but once. All corporate net income is first taxed under the corporate income tax as described above. In addition that portion of corporate earnings which flows to stockholders is taxed for a second time as personal income. This double taxation of dividends is felt by many economists to be a glaring inequity in the present structure of income taxes. The inequity, however, is at least partially offset by the fact that retained corporate earnings are not subject to tax rates higher than 48 per cent.

Sales and excise taxes. Commodity or consumption taxes may take the form of sales taxes or excise taxes. The difference between the two is basically one of degree. Sales taxes fall on a wide range of products while excises are taxes on a small, select list of commodities.

The Federal government does not levy a general sales tax; sales taxes are the bread and butter of most state governments. But as Table 9–2 indicates, the Federal government does collect excise taxes imposed upon such commodities as alcoholic beverages, tobacco, gasoline, trucks, and so forth.

Payroll and other taxes. Social security contributions, or payroll taxes, are the premiums paid on the compulsory insurance plans provided for by existing social security legislation. These taxes are paid by both employers and employees. For the most part, these funds flow into insurance trust funds held by the Federal government.

Table 9–2 also shows limited amounts of funds flowing to government as gift and estate taxes and as the result of the sales of various licenses and permits. Conspicuous by its absence is the property tax—the basic source of tax revenue for local units of government.

State and Local Finance

State and local governments employ essentially the same types of taxes as are imposed by the Federal government. However, the relative importance of the various taxes and tax rates differs greatly. In particular, while the Federal government finances itself largely through personal and corporate income taxation, state and local governments rely heavily upon sales and property taxes, respectively. And although there is considerable overlapping in the types of expenditures made by the three levels of government, national defense and related outlays account for the majority of Federal expenditures, whereas education, highways, and public welfare lead at state and local levels.

State expenditures and receipts. Note in Table 9–3 that the basic sources of tax revenue at the state level are sales and excise taxes, which account for about 58 per cent of all state tax revenues. State personal income taxes, which entail much more modest rates than those employed by the Federal government, run a poor second. Taxes on corporate income, property, inheritances, and a variety of licenses and permits constitute the remainder of state tax revenue. On the expenditure side of the picture, the major outlays of state governments are for (1) highway maintenance and construction and (2) education.

It is important to note that the budget statement shown in Table 9–3 contains aggregated data and therefore tells us little about the finances of individual states. States vary tremendously in the types of taxes employed. Thus, although sales and personal income taxes are the major sources of revenue for all state governments combined, thirteen states have no general sales tax and fourteen do not use the personal income tax. Furthermore, great variations in the size of tax receipts and disbursements exist among the states.

Local expenditures and receipts. The receipts and expenditures shown in Table 9–4 are for all units of local government. This

TABLE 9–3. CONSOLIDATED BUDGETS OF ALL STATE GOVERNMENTS, 1964

Tax receipts	Billions of dollars	Per cent of total	Expenditures	Billions of dollars	Per cent of total
Sales, excise, and			Highways	$ 7.9	32
gross receipts taxes	$14.0	58	Education	5.7	23
Personal income taxes	3.4	14	Public welfare	2.8	12
Corporate income			Health, hospitals	2.6	11
taxes	1.7	7	Police and general		
Property taxes	0.7	3	government	1.2	5
Death and gift taxes ..	0.6	2	Natural resources	1.2	5
Licenses, permits,			Interest on debt	0.8	3
and others	3.8	16	Others	2.1	9
Total tax receipts ..	$24.2	100	Total expenditures .	$24.3	100

Source: U.S. Bureau of the Census, *Compendium of State Finances in 1964.* Because of rounding, figures may not add up to totals.

includes counties, municipalities, townships, and school districts. One major source of revenue and a single basic use of revenue stand out: the bulk of the revenue received by local government comes from property taxation; the bulk of local revenue is spent for education. Other less important sources of funds and types of disbursements are self-explanatory.

Intergovernmental grants. The budget summaries shown in Tables 9–3 and 9–4 do not show intergovernmental grants which flow (1) from Federal to state and local governments and (2) from state to local governments. These grants have become increasingly large over the years and are currently of very considerable significance. For example, in 1964 the Federal government made grants of $10.1 billion to state and local governments—$8.9 billion to the states and $1.2 billion directly to local units of government. In the same year, state governments made grants of about $13.0 billion to local units of governments. Local governments were thus on the receiving end of $14.2 billion in grants from Federal and state governments.

The rationale underlying these grants is not too difficult to find. Federal grants to states are designed to help equalize income differentials between them. In effect, a portion of personal and corporate income tax revenues paid by citizens of wealthier states is paid out in grants which accrue primarily to the poorer states. Much the same holds true for state-to-local grants. The wealthier portions of a state may pay taxes which are apportioned out in favor of less fortunate areas in that state. Very often, though not always, this means that a state draws much of its tax revenues from the industrial metropolitan areas and favors depressed rural areas in its program of grants to local governments. Aside from equalizing tendencies, the existence of these grants also means that there is considerable financial dependency of state governments upon the Federal government and even greater dependence of local upon state governments.

A final important point: Table 9–4 suggests a very large deficit for local governments—specifically, a deficit of some $21.5 billion ($45.0 minus $23.5 billion). However, nontax revenues—$14.2 billion in Federal and state grants plus some $6.7 billion in sales receipts from municipally owned utilities, liquor stores, and a variety of other nontax sources—virtually eliminate this deficit.

TABLE 9–4. CONSOLIDATED BUDGET OF ALL LOCAL GOVERNMENTS, 1964

Tax receipts	Billions of dollars	Per cent of total	Expenditures	Billions of dollars	Per cent of total
Property taxes	$20.5	87	Education	$20.8	46
Sales and excises	1.8	8	Police, fire, and general		
Personal and corporate			government	4.4	10
income taxes	0.4	2	Highways	3.8	8
Licenses, permits,			Public welfare	3.0	7
and others	0.8	3	Health and hospitals ..	2.4	5
Total tax receipts ..	$23.5	100	Interest on debt	1.6	4
			Others	9.0	20
			Total expenditures	$45.0	100

Source: U.S. Bureau of the Census, *Governmental Finances in 1963–64.* Because of rounding, figures may not add up to totals. Data for fiscal year 1963–1964.

APPORTIONING THE TAX BURDEN

The very nature of social goods and services (see Chapter 6) makes it exceedingly difficult to measure precisely the manner in which their benefits are apportioned among individuals and institutions in the economy. It is virtually impossible to determine accurately the amount by which John Doe benefits from military installations, a network of highways, a public school system, and local police and fire protection.

The situation is a bit different on the taxation side of the picture. Statistical studies reveal rather clearly the manner in which the overall tax burden is apportioned. Needless to say, this is a question which affects each of us in a very vital way. Although the average citizen is concerned with the overall level of taxes, chances are he is even more interested in exactly how the tax burden is allocated among individual taxpayers.

Benefits Received versus Ability to Pay

Two basic philosophies as to how the economy's tax burden should be apportioned are evident in American capitalism:

The *benefits-received principle* of taxation asserts that households and businesses should purchase the goods and services of government in basically the same manner in which other commodities are bought. It is reasoned that those who benefit most from government-supplied goods or services should pay the taxes necessary for their financing. Some social goods are financed essentially on the basis of the benefits principle. For example, gasoline taxes are typically earmarked for the financing of highway construction and repairs. Those who benefit from good roads pay the cost of those roads. Difficulties immediately arise, however, when an accurate and widespread application of the benefits principle is considered:

1. How does one go about determining the benefits which individual households and businesses receive from national defense, education, and police and fire protection? The remoteness of government transactions (see Chapter 6) makes such a determination virtually impossible. Even in the case of highway finance, it is obvious, on second thought, that individual car owners benefit in different degrees from the existence of good roads. And those who do not own cars also benefit. Businesses certainly benefit greatly from any widening of their markets which good roads will encourage.

2. The shortcomings of the benefits principle become even more apparent when certain government welfare programs are considered. Relief payments and payments to the physically handicapped would be self-defeating if they were financed on the benefits principle. It would be ridiculous to think of taxing unemployed workers to finance the unemployment compensation payments which they receive. In short, government activities designed to redistribute income preclude the use of the benefits principle in their financing.

The *ability-to-pay principle* of taxation stands in sharp contrast to the benefits principle. Ability-to-pay taxation rests on the idea that the tax burden should be geared directly to one's financial position. As the ability-to-pay principle has come to be applied in the United States, it contends that individuals and businesses with larger incomes should pay more taxes—both absolutely and relatively—than those with more modest incomes.

What is the rationale of ability-to-pay taxation? Proponents argue that each additional dollar of income received by a household will yield smaller and smaller amounts of satisfaction. It is argued that, because consumers act rationally, the first dollars of income received in any period of time will be spent upon basic high-urgency goods. Successive dollars of income will go for less urgent goods and finally for trivial goods and services. This means that a dollar taken through taxes from a poor man who has few dollars constitutes a greater sacrifice on his part than does a dollar taken by taxes from the rich man who has many dollars. Hence, to balance the sacrifices which taxes impose on income receivers, it is contended that taxes should be apportioned according to the amount of income one receives.

This is appealing, but problems of application exist here, too. In particular, although we might agree that the household earning $10,000 per year has a greater ability to pay taxes than does the household receiving a paltry $3,000, exactly *how much more*

ability to pay does the first family have as compared with the second? There is no scientific way of measuring one's ability to pay taxes. Thus, in practice, the answer hinges upon guesswork, the tax views of the political party in power, expediency, and the urgency with which government needs revenue. As we shall discover in a few moments, the tax structure of our economy is somewhat more in tune with the ability-to-pay principle than with the benefits-received principle.

Progressive, Proportional, and Regressive Taxes

Any discussion of the ability-to-pay and the benefits-received principles of taxation leads ultimately to the question of tax rates and the manner in which tax rates change as the size of the tax base—that is, the value of that which is being taxed—increases. Taxes are ordinarily classified as being progressive, proportional, or regressive.

1. A tax is *progressive* if its rate *increases* as the tax base increases. Such a tax claims not only a large, absolute amount, but also a larger fraction or percentage of the tax base as the base increases.

2. A *regressive* tax is one whose rate *declines* as the tax base increases. Such a tax takes a smaller and smaller proportion of the tax base as the base increases. A regressive tax may or may not take a larger absolute amount of the tax base as the base expands.

3. A tax is *proportional* when its rate *remains the same*, regardless of the size of the tax base.

Let us illustrate in terms of an income tax. Here taxable income is obviously the tax base. Suppose the tax rates are such that everyone pays 10 per cent of his income in taxes, regardless of the size of his income. This would obviously be a proportional income tax. But suppose the rate structure is such that the household with an annual taxable income of less than $1,000 pays 5 per cent in income taxes, the household realizing an income of $1,000 to $2,000 pays 10 per cent, $2,000 to $3,000, pays 15 per cent, and so forth.[4] This, as we have already explained, would obviously be a *progressive* income tax. The final case is where the rates decline as taxable income rises: you pay 15 per cent if you earn less than $1,000, 10 per cent if you earn $1,000 to $2,000, 5 per cent if you earn $2,000 to $3,000, and so forth. This is a *regressive* income tax. Generally speaking, progressive taxes are those which bear down most heavily on the rich; regressive taxes are those which hit the poor hardest.

But there is a hidden difficulty in attempting to label taxes as progressive, regressive, or proportional. And that is the problem of choosing an appropriate tax base. As illustrated above, there is no real difficulty when you are dealing with the income tax: taxable income is your only choice. But with a sales tax, for example, it is a different story. *At first glance, it would seem that a sales tax of, say, 3 per cent is proportional. And it is, if you choose expenditures on taxable items as the tax base.* With this base you will pay 3 per cent, or 3 cents, on a $1 purchase and 3 per cent, or $30, on a $1,000 purchase.

Yet all taxes ultimately come out of someone's total income. So maybe income is a more appropriate base to use than the value of a consumer's purchases. For example, suppose that Smith has an income of $3,000 and spends all of it. Jones, on the other hand, earns an income of $6,000 and spends $4,000, or two-thirds of it. Now, assuming a 3 per cent sales tax applies to each dollar spent by these two individuals, Smith will obviously pay $90 (3 per cent of $3,000) worth of sales taxes and Jones will pay $120 (3 per cent of $4,000). Using expenditures as a base, the sales tax is obviously proportional; both Smith and Jones are paying 3 per cent of their total expenditures as sales taxes. But the picture changes

when income is substituted for expenditures as a tax base. Whereas *all* Smith's $3,000 income is subject to the sales tax, only two-thirds of Jones's $6,000 income is taxed. Jones in effect avoids sales taxation on $2,000 of his income by saving rather than spending that amount. As a result, Smith pays $90, or 3 per cent, of his $3,000 income as sales taxes, but Jones pays $120, or just 2 per cent, of his $6,000 income as sales taxes. *Using income rather than expenditures as a tax base, the sales tax turns out to be a regressive tax.* It is regressive because a larger portion of the poor man's income is exposed to the tax than is the case with a rich man. The latter avoids the tax on the part of his income that he saves.

Shifting and Incidence of Taxes

Suppose society has decided how it wants the current tax burden to be apportioned among specific households and businesses. Now a complicating factor arises. Taxes do not always stick where the government puts them. Some taxes can be *shifted* among various parties in the economy. It is therefore necessary to locate as best we can the final resting place or *incidence* of the major types of taxes.

Personal income tax. The incidence of the personal income tax generally falls on the individual upon whom the tax is levied; little chance exists for shifting. There is one possible exception worthy of note. Unions might regard personal income taxes as part of the cost of living and, as a result, bargain for higher wages. If they are successful, they may shift a portion of the tax from workers to employers. Generally, however, we can conclude that the individual upon whom the tax is initially levied bears the burden of the personal income tax. The same ordinarily holds true of inheritance taxes.

Corporate income tax. The incidence of the corporate income tax is much less certain.

---

[4] We refer here to average or effective tax rates, not to marginal tax rates.

The traditional view has it that a firm which is currently charging the profit-maximizing price and producing the profit-maximizing output will have no reason to change price or output when a corporate income tax is imposed. That price and output combination which yields the greatest profit before the tax will still be the most profitable after government takes a fixed percentage of the firm's profits in the form of income taxes. According to this view, the company's stockholders must bear the incidence of the tax in the form of lower dividends or a smaller amount of retained earnings. On the other hand, in recent years many economists have argued that the corporate income tax is shifted in part to consumers through higher prices and to resource suppliers through lower prices. In modern industry, where a small number of firms may control a market, producers may not be in the profit-maximizing position initially. The reason? By fully exploiting their market position currently, monopolistic firms might elicit adverse public opinion and governmental censure. Hence, they may await such events as the imposition of taxes, increases in tax rates, or wage increases by unions to provide adequate excuse for price increases with less fear of public criticism. When this actually occurs, a portion of the corporate income tax may be shifted to consumers through higher prices.

Both positions are plausible. Indeed, the incidence of the corporate income tax may well be shared by stockholders and the firm's customers and resource suppliers. The consensus seems to be that stockholders bear most of the tax.

Sales and excise taxes. Sales and excise taxes are the "hidden taxes" of our economy. They are hidden because such taxes are typically shifted by sellers to consumers through higher product prices. There may be some difference in the shiftability of sales taxes and excises, however. Because a sales tax covers a much wider range of products than an excise, there is little chance for consumers to resist the price boosts which sales taxes entail by reallocating their expenditures to untaxed products.

Excises, however, fall on a relatively short, select list of goods. This means that the possibility of consumers turning to substitute goods and services is greater. For example, an excise tax on theater tickets which does not apply to other types of entertainment might be difficult to pass on to consumers via price increases. Why? Because price boosts might result in considerable substituting of alternative types of entertainment by consumers. From the seller's point of view, the higher price will cause such a marked decline in sales that he will be better off to bear all, or a large portion of, the excise rather than the sharp decline in sales. With many excises, however, modest price increases have little or no effect on sales. Excises on gasoline, cigarettes, and alcoholic beverages are cases in point. Here there are few good substitute products to which consumers can turn as prices rise. For these commodities, the seller is in a better position to shift the tax.

In general, it is safe to say that the bulk, if not the entire amount, of a sales or excise tax will generally be shifted to the consumer through higher product prices.

Property taxes. Many property taxes are borne by the property owner for the simple reason that there is no other party to whom they can be shifted. This is typically true in the case of taxes on land, personal property, and owner-occupied residences. For example, even when land is sold, the property tax is not likely to be shifted. The buyer will tend to discount the value of the land to allow for the future taxes which he will be required to pay on it, and this will be reflected in the price he is willing to offer for the land.

Taxes on rented and business property are a different story. Taxes on rented property can be, and usually are, shifted wholly or in part from the owner to the tenant by

TABLE 9–5. THE PROBABLE INCIDENCE OF TAXES

Type of tax	Probable incidence
Personal income tax	The household or individual upon which it is levied.
Corporate income tax	Disagreement. Most economists feel the firm on which it is levied bears the incidence; others conclude the tax is passed, wholly or in part, to consumers.
Sales and excise taxes	With exceptions, consumers who buy the taxed products.
Property taxes	Owners in the case of land and owner-occupied residences; tenants in the case of rented property; consumers in the case of business property.

the simple process of boosting rents. Business property taxes are treated as a business cost and therefore are taken into account in establishing product price; thus such taxes are ordinarily shifted to the firm's customers.

Table 9–5 summarizes this discussion of the shifting and incidence of taxes.

The American Tax Structure

As we have seen, the Federal, state, and local governments of the United States employ a variety of taxes. Using income as the tax base, we have concluded that some of these taxes—the personal and corporate income taxes and inheritance taxes—are progressive, whereas others—sales taxes, excises, and property taxes—are for the most part regressive. What is the total picture? The most recent estimates—and these figures must be estimates because of the uncertainty of tax incidence—are shown in Table 9–6.

Employing family income as the tax base, column 2 of this table tells us the percentage of income taken by Federal taxes in each of the seven income classes. Column 3 presents the same information for all state

TABLE 9–6. ESTIMATED TAX RATES BY INCOME LEVELS, 1958
(taxes as a percentage of income)

(1) Family income level	(2) Federal taxes	(3) State and local taxes	(4) All taxes, or (2) + (3)
Under $2,000	15.7%	12.6%	28.3%
$2,000–$3,999	15.9	10.4	26.3
$4,000–$5,999	16.4	9.5	25.9
$6,000–$7,999	17.2	8.5	25.7
$8,000–$9,999	16.2	7.8	23.9
$10,000–$14,999	17.2	6.9	24.0
$15,000 and over	29.8	6.1	35.9
All income classes	19.2	8.2	27.4

Source: George A. Bishop, "The Tax Burden by Income Class, 1958," National Tax Journal, March, 1961, table 6, p. 54.

and local taxes. Finally, column 4 sums the two preceding columns and shows the percentage of income taken in Federal, state, and local taxes combined from each of the listed income groups. All taxes combined take over one-fourth of total personal income.

Column 4, of course, is the vital one. Note that slight regressivity is found in the "under $2,000" income class and that rather significant progressivity is evidenced in the very high "$15,000 and over" income class. But the basic conclusion is that *the tax burden is roughly proportional to income over the entire $2,000 to $14,999 income range*—a range which includes approximately 80 per cent of all families. The often heard lamentations as to the highly progressive character of our tax structure are simply not accurate in so far as the bulk of American income receivers are concerned. So far as most income receivers are affected, the progressivity which exists in Federal taxation (column 2), dominated by personal and corporate income taxation, is very substantially offset by the regressivity of state and local taxes (column 3), wherein sales and property taxes prevail.

SUMMARY

1. Historically, government tax receipts and expenditures have grown rapidly both in absolute amounts and relative to the size of the national income. This growth has been particularly marked over the last two decades.

2. Federal expenditures and tax revenues are much greater than those of state and local governments. The twin evils of mobilization and war have been the basic forces underlying the tremendous growth in Federal expenditures and tax collections.

3. About two-thirds of all Federal spending is for national defense and related programs. Personal and corporate income taxes combined account for two-thirds of the Federal government's tax revenue.

4. Approximately 58 per cent of all state revenue is derived from sales and excise taxes. The construction and maintenance of highways is the major state expenditure, accounting for 32 per cent of the total.

5. At the local level of government, property taxes provide about 87 per cent of total tax revenue. Education absorbs almost 46 per cent of local expenditures.

6. Intergovernmental grants generally contribute to income equality between states and between local units of government. But at the same time, these grants enhance the financial dependence of state and local governments.

7. The ability-to-pay principle of taxation is more evident in the American tax structure than is the benefits-received philosophy.

8. Taxes on personal and corporate incomes and inheritance taxes are progressive. General sales, excise, and property taxes tend to be regressive.

9. Sales and excise taxes are likely to be shifted; personal income taxes are not. There is disagreement as to whether or not corporate income taxes are shifted. The incidence of property taxes depends primarily upon whether or not the property is owner- or tenant-occupied.

10. Over the income range which includes the bulk of American households, the overall tax structure is roughly proportional.

QUESTIONS AND STUDY SUGGESTIONS

1. Describe the overall changes in government expenditures and taxes which have occurred during the last three decades. How do you account for these changes? Why might it be significant to distinguish between "transfer payments" and "government purchases of goods and services" in evaluating the growth of government expenditures and the impact of this spending upon resource allocation?

2. What is the most important source of revenue and the major type of expenditure at the Federal level? At the state level? At the local level?

3. Briefly describe the mechanics of the Federal personal income and corporate income taxes. Explain why the average or effective personal income tax rate is less than the marginal tax rate.

4. What are the effects of intergovernmental grants?

5. Distinguish clearly between the benefits-received and the ability-to-pay principles of taxation. Which philosophy is more evident in our present tax structure? Justify your answer. To which principle of taxation do you subscribe? Why?

6. Precisely what is meant by a progressive tax? A regressive tax? A proportional tax?

7. Comment upon the progressivity or regressivity of each of the following taxes:
   a. The Federal personal income tax
   b. A 3 per cent state general sales tax
   c. A Federal excise tax on playing cards
   d. A municipal property tax on real estate
   e. The Federal corporate income tax
   What is likely to be the incidence of each of these taxes?

8. "With expenditures as a base, the sales tax is proportional. But when income is substituted as the base, this tax is regressive." Explain. Which base do you feel is more appropriate?

9. Comment upon the overall progressivity of the American tax structure.

10. Explain and evaluate each of the following statements:
   a. "Any system of public finance should be conceived simply with a view to the maximum social advantage in the long run, and it follows that any tax system . . . should be conceived with the same object."
   b. "No tax on income can be a just tax unless it leaves individuals in the same relative condition in which it found them."
   c. "Because there is no sure definition of the limits to progression, no firm basis of its 'reasonable' use, no protection against its unconscionable abuse, those who uphold the system as a revenue device are playing into the hands of the group that would use progressive taxation as the means of destroying private capitalism and ushering in the collectivist state."
   d. "Even tho it be an open question whether all inequality in wealth and income be unjust, such great degrees of inequality as the modern world shows are regarded as not consonant with canons of justice. Very rich persons should be called to pay taxes not only in proportion to their incomes but more than in proportion."

SELECTED REFERENCES

Due, John F.: *Government Finance*, 3d ed. (Homewood, Ill.: Richard D. Irwin, Inc., 1963), particularly chaps. 3, 5, and 6.

Eckstein, Otto: *Public Finance* (Englewood Cliffs, N.J.: Prentice-Hall, Inc., 1964), chaps. 1, 3, and 6.

Groves, Harold M.: *Financing Government*, 6th ed. (New York: Holt, Rinehart and Winston, Inc., 1964), particularly chaps. 1, 2, 21, and 22.

Mosher, Frederick C., and Orville F. Poland: *The Costs of American Governments* (New York: Dodd, Mead & Company, Inc., 1964), particularly chaps. 1–4, 7, and 9.

Sharp, Ansel M., and Bernard F. Sliger: *Public Finance* (Homewood, Ill.: The Dorsey Press, 1964), chaps. 3, 5, and 13–20.

Smith, Dan Throop: *Federal Tax Reform* (New York: McGraw-Hill Book Company, 1961), particularly chap. 1.

PART TWO: NATIONAL INCOME,
EMPLOYMENT, AND FISCAL POLICY

CHAPTER 10

NATIONAL INCOME ACCOUNTING

Throughout Part One of this book there has reoccurred the flat statement that American capitalism does not consistently provide for the full employment of available resources. It has also been noted that the levels of employment and production depend upon the size of certain flows of expenditures and income. Part Two of this volume deals at length with the problem of measuring, explaining, and remedying, if need be, the volumes of employment, production, and income in the economy. Specifically, in the present chapter we seek an understanding of certain accounting techniques which assist us in gauging the level of production achieved by the economy. In Chapter 11 we shall take a look at the historical record of American capitalism as reflected in these accounts in order to appraise the past performance of our economy. Then in Chapters 12 and 13 we seek to explain those factors which determine the levels of employment and production in American capitalism. Finally, in Chapters 14 and 15 we explore the problems involved in deriving and applying public policies designed to improve the production performance of the economy.

MEASURING THE ECONOMY'S PERFORMANCE

The present task is that of defining and understanding a group of so-called social or national income accounting concepts which have been designed to measure the overall production performance of the economy. Why do we bother with such a project? Because social accounting does for the economy as a whole what private accounting does for the individual business enterprise or for that matter, for the household. The individual businessman is vitally interested in knowing how he is doing in his operations, but the answer is not always immediately discernible. Accurate measurement of the firm's flows of income and expenditures is needed to assess the firm's operations for the current year. With this information before him, the businessman can gauge the economic health of his firm. If things are going well, he can use his accounting data to explain his success. He might find that costs are down or that sales and product prices are up, resulting in large profits. If things are going badly, he can also look to his accounting measures to discover the immediate cause of his plight. And by examining his accounts over a period of time, the businessman can detect growth, stagnation, or decline for his firm and indications of the immediate causes. All this information is invaluable to the businessman in order for him to make intelligent policy decisions.

A system of national income accounting does much the same thing for the economy as a whole: it allows us to keep a finger on the economic pulse of the nation. The various measures which make up our social accounting system permit us to measure the level of production in the economy at some point in time and explain the immediate causes of that level of performance. Further, by comparing the national income accounts over a period of time it is possible to plot the long-run course which the economy has been following; the growth or decay of the economy will show up in the national income accounts. Finally, the information supplied by the national income accounts provides a basis for the formulation and application of public policies designed to improve the performance of the economy. In short, national income accounting allows us to keep tab on the economic health of society and to formulate intelligently policies which will improve that health.

GROSS NATIONAL PRODUCT

There are many conceivable measures of the economic well-being of society. It is generally agreed, however, that the best available indicator of an economy's health is its annual total output of goods and services or, as it is sometimes called, the economy's aggregate output. The basic social accounting measure of the total output of goods and services is called the *gross national product* or, simply, GNP. It is defined as *the total market value of all final goods and services produced*[1] *in the economy in one year*. Our definition of GNP is very explicit and merits considerable comment.

GNP Is a Monetary Measure

Note, first, that GNP measures the market value of annual output. GNP is a monetary measure. Indeed, it must be if we are

[1] We shall see that all the goods produced in a particular year may not be sold; some may be added to inventories. Any increase in inventories must be included in determining GNP, since GNP measures all current production regardless of whether or not it is sold.

to compare the heterogeneous collections of goods and services produced in different years and get a meaningful comparison of their relative worth. Put simply, if the economy produces three oranges and two apples in year 1 and two oranges and three apples in year 2, in which year is society better off? There is no answer to this question until price tags are attached to the various products as indicators of society's evaluation of their relative worth. The problem is resolved in Table 10–1, where it is assumed that the money price of the oranges is 2 cents and the price of apples is 3 cents. It can be concluded that year 2's output is superior to that of year 1. Why? Because society values year 2's output more highly; society is willing to pay more for the collection of goods produced in year 2 than that produced in year 1.

Adjusting GNP for Price Changes

But you might well object. You have read of inflation in the newspapers. Does this not mean that money prices and therefore the value of the dollar itself will change? You are quite right. The money value of different years' outputs can only be accurately compared if the value of money itself does not change because of inflation or deflation.

Stated differently, inflation or deflation complicates GNP because it is a price-times-quantity figure. The raw data from which the national income accountants estimate GNP are the total sales figures of business firms; these figures obviously embody changes in both the quantity of output and the level of prices. This means that a change in either quantity of total physical

TABLE 10–1. COMPARING HETEROGENEOUS OUTPUTS BY USING MONEY PRICES (hypothetical data)

Year	Annual outputs	Market value
1	3 oranges and 2 apples	3 at 2 cents + 2 at 3 cents = 12 cents
2	2 oranges and 3 apples	2 at 2 cents + 3 at 3 cents = 13 cents

output or the price level will affect the size of GNP. However, it is the quantity of goods produced and distributed to households which affects their standard of living and not the size of the price tags which these goods bear. The hamburger of 1956 which sold for 25 cents yielded the same satisfaction as does an identical hamburger selling for 35 cents in 1966. The problem then is one of adjusting a price-times-quantity figure so it will accurately reflect changes in physical output, not changes in prices.

Fortunately, national income accountants have been able to resolve this difficulty: they deflate GNP for rising prices and inflate it when prices are falling. These adjustments give us a picture of GNP for various years *as if* prices and the value of the dollar were constant.

Inflating and Deflating

Some examples will help us understand how GNP figures are adjusted for price changes. First, an exceedingly simple example: Assume our economy produces only one good, product X, and in the amounts indicated in Table 10–2 for years 1, 2, and 3. An examination of columns 1 and 2 tells us that the *money* GNPs for years 2 and 3, as shown in column 4, greatly overstate the increases in *real* output occurring in those two years. That is, the monetary measure of production (money GNP) does not accurately indicate the actual changes which have occurred in

physical output (real GNP). A considerable portion of the sharp increase in money GNP in years 2 and 3 is due to the drastic inflation shown in column 2, the remainder being due to the changes in physical output shown in column 1. Both increases in physical output and price increases are reflected in the money GNP.

Now the situation facing our social accountants is this: In gathering statistics from the financial reports of businesses and deriving GNP for years 1, 2, and 3, governmental accountants come up with the figures for money GNP shown in column 4. They will not know directly to what extent changes in price, on the one hand, and changes in quantity of output on the other, have accounted for the given increases in money GNP. Social accountants will not have before them the data of columns 1 and 2, but only the data of column 4. Being resourceful individuals, they attempt to adjust the money GNP figure for price changes. They do this by deriving a general price index which estimates overall changes in the price level. By expressing this index as a decimal and dividing it into money GNP, one can obtain real GNP. In our example, wherein we are dealing with only one product, a simple single price index number is all that is required. Such a price index is nothing more than *a percentage comparison from a fixed point of reference.* This point of reference, or bench mark, is called the *base year.* By comparing prices in previous and ensuing years with prices

TABLE 10–2. DEFLATING MONEY GNP (hypothetical data)

Year	(1) Units of output	(2) Price of X	(3) Price index, per cent	(4) Unadjusted, or money, GNP (1) × (2)	(5) Adjusted, or real, GNP (4) ÷ (3)
1	5	$10	100	$ 50	$50 (= $ 50 ÷ 1.00)
2	7	20	200	140	70 (= 140 ÷ 2.00)
3	8	25	250	200	80 (= 200 ÷ 2.50)
4	10	30			
5	11	28			

in the base year, we can tell how much prices have increased or decreased *relative to* what they were in the base year. Suppose product X sells for $10 in year 1, $20 in year 2, and $25 in year 3. Selecting year 1 as the base year, we can express the prices of product X in years 2 and 3 relative to X's price in year 1 through the the the formula

$$\text{Price index} = \frac{\text{price in any given year}}{\text{price in base year}} \times 100$$

We multiply the price comparison by 100 in order to express it as a percentage. Using year 2 as the given year, we find that

$$\text{Price index} = \frac{\$20}{\$10} \times 100 = 200 \text{ per cent}$$

and for year 3,

$$\text{Price index} = \frac{\$25}{\$10} \times 100 = 250 \text{ per cent}$$

For year 1 the index must be 100 per cent since the given year and the base year are identical. In this case,

$$\text{Price index} = \frac{\$10}{\$10} \times 100 = 100 \text{ per cent}$$

These index numbers simply tell us that the price of product X in the year 2 was 200 per cent of what it was in year 1 and in year 3 it was 250 per cent of year 1's price. The index numbers of column 3 can now be used to deflate the inflated money GNP figures of column 4. As already noted, *the simplest and most direct method of deflating is to express these index numbers as hundredths, that is, in decimal form, and divide them into the corresponding money GNP.*[2] Column 5 shows the results. These real GNP figures measure the value of total

[2] This yields the same result as the more complex procedure of dividing the money GNPs by the corresponding index number and multiplying the quotient by 100.

output in years 1, 2, and 3 as if the price of product X had been constant at $10 throughout the three-year period. Real GNP thus shows the market value of each year's output measured in terms of constant dollars, that is, dollars which have the same value, or purchasing power, as in the base year. Real GNP is clearly superior to money GNP as an indicator of the economy's productive performance over a period of time.

To ensure his understanding of the deflating process, the reader is urged to complete Table 10–2 for years 4 and 5. Second, it is recommended that you rework the entire deflating procedure using year 3 as the base year. You will find, by the way, that in this case you must inflate some of the money GNP data, just as we have deflated it in our examples.

Table 10–3 provides us with a much more realistic illustration of the inflating and deflating process. Here we are taking actual money GNP figures for selected years and adjusting them with an index of the general price level to obtain real GNP. Note that the base year is 1954. Because the long-run trend has been for the price level to rise, the problem is one of *inflating* the pre-1954 figures. This upward revision of money GNP acknowledges that prices were lower in years prior to 1954 and, as a result, money GNP figures understated the real output of those years. Column 4 indicates what GNP would have been in all these selected years if the 1954 price level had prevailed. However, the rising price level has caused the money GNP figures for the post-1954 years to overstate real output; hence, these figures must be *deflated* as in column 4 in order for us to gauge what GNP would have been in 1958, 1961, and 1964 if 1954 prices had actually prevailed. In short, while the money GNP figures reflect both output and price changes, the real GNP figures allow us to make a better estimate of changes in real output, because the real GNP figures, in effect, hold the price level constant. The reader should trace through the computations involved in deriving the real GNP figures given in

TABLE 10–3. ADJUSTING GNP FOR CHANGES IN THE PRICE LEVEL
(selected years, in billions of dollars)

(1) Year	(2) Money, or unadjusted, GNP	(3) Price level index,* per cent (1954 = 100)	(4) Real, or adjusted, GNP, 1954 dollars
1929	$104.4	57.4	$181.8
1933	56.0	44.2	126.6
1937	90.8	49.5	
1941	125.8	52.9	238.1
1945	213.6	68.0	314.1
1951	329.0	96.2	341.8
1954	363.1	100.0	363.1
1958	441.7	110.7	
1961	521.3	116.2	448.8
1964	622.6	120.7	516.0

* U.S. Department of Commerce implicit price deflators.
Source: U.S. Department of Commerce data.

Table 10–3 and also determine real GNP for years 1937 and 1958, for which the figures have been purposely omitted.

Double Counting

To measure total output accurately all goods and services produced in any given year must be counted once, but not more than once. Most products go through a series of production stages before reaching a market. As a result parts or components of most products are bought and sold many times. Hence, to avoid counting several times the parts of products that are sold and resold, GNP only includes the market value of final goods and ignores transactions involving intermediate goods.

By *final goods* we mean goods and services which are being purchased for final use and not for resale or further processing or manufacturing. Transactions involving *intermediate goods,* on the other hand, refer to purchases of goods and services for further processing and manufacturing or for resale. The sale of final goods is included and the sale of intermediate goods is excluded from GNP. Why? Because the value

of final goods includes all the intermediate transactions involved in their production. The inclusion of intermediate transactions would involve double counting and an exaggerated estimate of GNP.

An example will clarify this point. Suppose there are five stages of production in getting a Hart, Schaffner & Marx suit manufactured and into the hands of a consumer who, of course, is the ultimate or final user. As Table 10–4 indicates, firm A, a sheep ranch, provides $15 worth of wool to firm B, a wool processor. Firm A pays out the $15 it receives in wages, rents, interest, and profits. Firm B processes the wool and sells it to firm C, a suit manufacturer, for $25. What does firm B do with this $25? As noted, $15 goes to firm A, and the remaining $10 is used by B to pay wages, rents, interest, and profits for the resources needed in processing the wool. And so it goes. The manufacturer sells the suit to firm D, a clothing wholesaler, who in turn sells it to firm E, a retailer, and then, finally, it is bought for $70 by a consumer, the final user of the product. At each stage, the difference between what a firm has paid for the product and what it

TABLE 10–4. VALUE ADDED IN A FIVE-STAGE PRODUCTIVE PROCESS
(hypothetical data)

(1) Stage of production	(2) Sales value of materials or product	(3) Value added
		$15
Firm A, sheep ranch	$15	
		10
Firm B, wool processor	25	
		20
Firm C, suit manufacturer	45	
		10
Firm D, clothing wholesaler	55	
		15
Firm E, retail clothier	70	
		———
Consumer, the final user		$70

receives for its sale is paid out as wages, rent, interest, and profits for the resources used by that firm in helping to produce and distribute the suit.

The basic question is this: How much should we include in GNP in accounting for the production of this suit? Just $70, the value of the final product! Why? Because this figure includes all the intermediate transactions leading up to the product's final sale. It would be a gross exaggeration to sum all the intermediate sales figures and the final sales value of the product in column 2 and add the entire amount, $210, to GNP. This would be a serious case of double counting, that is, counting the final product and the sale and resale of its various parts in the multistage productive process.

There is an alternative means of determining the $70 figure which is to be included in GNP. And this is by the *value-added* method, that is, by summing the value added to the total worth of the product at each step in the productive process. Column 3 summarizes this procedure. Note that this measures the total income derived from the production and sale of the suit. As you might expect, it is easier for the national income accountants to count only final goods than to pursue the value-added method of deriving GNP.

GNP Excludes Nonproductive Transactions

GNP attempts to measure the annual production of the economy. In so doing, the many nonproductive transactions which occur each year must be carefully excluded. Nonproductive transactions are of two major types: (1) purely financial transactions and (2) secondhand sales.

Purely financial transactions in turn are of three general types: public transfer payments, private transfer payments, and the buying and selling of securities. We have already mentioned public transfer payments (Chapter 9). These are the social security payments, relief payments, and veterans' payments which government makes to particular households. These payments are in effect gifts; recipients make no contribution to current production in return for them. Thus, to include them in GNP would be to overstate this year's production. Private transfer payments, for example, a university student's monthly subsidy from home or an occasional gift from a wealthy relative, do not entail production but simply the transfer of funds from one private individual to another. Security transactions, that is, the buying and selling of stocks and bonds, are also excluded from GNP. Stock market transactions simply involve the swapping of paper assets. As such, these transactions do not directly involve current production. It should be noted, however, that by getting money from the hands of savers into the hands of spenders, some of these security transactions may indirectly give rise to spending which does account for output.

The reason for excluding secondhand sales from GNP is fairly obvious: Such sales either reflect no *current* production, or they involve double counting. For example, suppose you sell your 1963 Ford to a neighbor. This transaction would be excluded in determining GNP because no current production is involved. The inclusion of the sales of goods produced some years ago in this year's GNP would be an exaggeration of this year's output. Similarly, if you purchased a brand new Ford and resold it a week later to your neighbor, we should still want to exclude the resale transaction from the current GNP. Why? Because when you originally bought the new car, its value was included in GNP. To include its resale value would be to count it twice.

GNP Is Not an Ideal Measure

GNP is a reasonably accurate and extremely useful measure of national economic well-being. Nevertheless, despite adjustments for price level changes and the careful exclusion of intermediate and nonproductive transactions, it must be recognized that GNP is not an ideal measure of economic welfare. There are several reasons for this:

1. Nonmarket transactions. There are certain productive transactions which do not appear in the market. Hence, GNP as a measure of the market value of output fails to include these productive transactions. Standard examples include the productive services of the housewife, the efforts of the carpenter who repairs his own home, or the erudite professor who writes a scholarly but nonremunerative article. Such transactions are not reflected in the profit and loss statements of business firms and therefore escape the national income accountants. However, some very important nonmarket transactions, such as that portion of a farmer's output which the farmer consumes himself, are estimated by national income accountants.

2. Leisure. Over a long period of years leisure has increased very significantly. The current average work week is less than forty hours, whereas as late as the 1920s a sixty-five or seventy-hour work week was not uncommon in many industries. Increased leisure has added immeasurably to our well-being. Yet our system of social accounting does not directly take cognizance of this. Nor do the accounts reflect the satisfaction—the "psychic income"—which one might derive from his work.

3. Improved product quality. GNP is a quantitative rather than a qualitative measure. It does not accurately reflect improvements in the quality of products. This is a shortcoming: Quality improvement obviously affects economic well-being every bit as much as does the quantity of goods.

4. The composition and distribution of output. Changes in the composition and the allocation of total output among specific households may influence economic welfare. We have already encountered the view that the composition of total output is every bit as important as its magnitude. GNP reflects only the size of output and does not tell us anything about whether this collection of goods is "right" for society. And although there is anything but unanimity on this question, many economists feel that a more equal distribution of total output would increase national economic well-being. If these economists are correct, a future trend toward a more nearly equal distribution of

GNP would enhance the economic welfare of society. A less nearly equal future distribution will have the reverse effect. In short, GNP measures the size of total output but does not reflect changes in the composition and distribution of output which might also affect the economic well-being of society.

5. Per capita output. For many purposes the most meaningful measure of economic well-being is per capita output. Because GNP measures the size of total output but conceal or misrepresent changes in the standard of living of individual households in the economy. For example, GNP may rise significantly, but if population is also growing rapidly, the per capita standard of living may be relatively constant or may even be declining.

Two Sides to GNP

Recognizing the characteristics and the shortcomings of GNP as a measure of output, we now raise this question: How can the market value of any unit of output—or for that matter total output—be measured? How can we measure, for example, the market value of a cashmere sweater?

In two ways: First, we can simply look at how much a consumer, as the final user, spends in obtaining it. Second, we can add up all the wage, rental, interest, and profit incomes created in the production of the sweater. This is simply the value-added approach we spoke of above. These are, indeed, two ways of looking at the same thing. What is spent on a product is received as income by those who contributed to its production. Indeed, the circular flow model previously discussed is based upon this notion. If $20 is spent on the sweater, that is necessarily the total amount of income derived from its production. This equality of the expenditure for a product and the income derived from its production is guaranteed, because profit income serves as a balancing item. Profit—or loss—is the income which remains after wage, rent, and interest

incomes have been paid by the producer. If the wage, rent, and interest incomes which the firm must pay in getting the sweater produced are less than the $20 expenditure for the sweater, the difference will be the firm's profits.[3] Conversely, if wage, rent, and interest incomes exceed $20, then profits will be negative, that is, losses will be realized, to balance the expenditure on the product and the income derived from its production.

The same line of reasoning is also valid for the output of the economy as a whole. There are two different ways of looking at GNP: One is to look at GNP as the sum of all the expenditures involved in taking that total output off the market. This is called the *output,* or *expenditures, approach.* The other is to look at it in terms of the income derived or created from the production of the GNP. This is called the *earnings,* or *income,* or *allocations, approach* to the determination of GNP. A closer analysis of these two approaches will reveal that they amount to this: *GNP can be determined either by adding up all that is spent on this year's total output or by summing up all the incomes derived from the production of this year's output.* Putting this in the form of a simple equation we can say that

The amount spent on this year's total output $\left.\right\}$ = $\left\{\right.$ the money income derived from the production of this year's output

As a matter of fact, this is more than an equation: it is an identity. Buying—that is, spending money—and selling—that is, receiving money income—are actually two aspects of the same transaction. Buying and selling are two sides of the same shield. *What is spent on a product is income to those who*

[3] The term "profits" is used here in the accounting sense so as to include both normal profits and economic profits as defined in Part One.

*have contributed their human and prop-
erty resources in getting that product produced and to market.*

For the economy as a whole we can
expand the above identity to read as in
Table 10–5. This summary statement simply
tells us that all final goods produced in the
American economy are purchased either by
the three domestic sectors, households, government, and businesses, or by foreign
nations. It also shows us that the total
receipts which businesses acquire from the
sale of total output are allocated among the
various resource suppliers as wage, rent,
interest, and profit income. Later we shall
explain two additional nonincome allocations of total receipts. Using this summary
as a point of reference, let us point out in
some detail the meaning and significance
of the various types of expenditures and
the incomes derived therefrom.

THE EXPENDITURES APPROACH
TO GNP

To determine GNP through the expenditures approach, one must add up all types
of spending on finished or final goods and
services. But our national income accountants have much more sophisticated terms
for the different types of spending than the
ones we have employed in Table 10–5. We
must therefore familiarize ourselves with
these terms and their meanings.

Personal Consumption Expend

What we have simply called "
expenditures by households"
consumption expenditures" to the national
income accountants. It entails expenditures
by households on durable consumer goods
(automobiles, refrigerators, gas ranges, and
so forth), nondurable consumer goods
(bread, milk, beer, cigarettes, shirts, tooth
paste), and consumer expenditures for
services (of lawyers, doctors, mechanics,
barbers). We shall use the letter C to designate the total of these expenditures.

Government Purchases of Goods
and Services (G)

This classification of expenditures includes
all governmental spending, Federal, state,
and local, on the finished products of businesses and all direct purchases of resources
—labor, in particular—by government. It
excludes, however, all government transfer
payments, because such expenditures, as
previously noted, do not reflect any current
production but merely transfer governmental receipts to certain specific households.

Gross Private Domestic Investment (I_g)

This seemingly complicated term refers to
all investment spending by American busi-

TABLE 10–5. THE INCOME AND OUTPUT APPROACHES TO GNP

Output, or expenditures, approach		Income, or allocations, approach
Consumption expenditures by households plus Government purchases of goods and services plus Investment expenditures by businesses plus Expenditures by foreigners	= GNP =	Wages plus Rents plus Interest plus Profits plus Nonincome charges or allocations

ness firms. What is included as investment spending? Basically three things: (1) all final purchases of machinery, equipment, and tools by business enterprises; (2) all construction; and (3) changes in inventories. This obviously entails more than we have imputed to the term "investment" thus far. Hence, we must explain why each of these three items is included under the general heading of gross private domestic investment.

The reason for inclusion of the first group of items is apparent. This is simply a restatement of our original definition of investment spending as the purchase of tools, machinery, and equipment. The second item—all construction—merits some explanation. It is clear that the building of a new factory, warehouse, or grain elevator is a form of investment. But why include residential construction as investment rather than consumption? The reason is this: Apartment buildings are clearly investment goods because, like factories and grain elevators, they are income-earning assets. Other residential units which are rented are for the same reason investment goods. Finally, owner-occupied houses are classified as investment goods because they could be rented out to yield a money income return, even though the owner does not choose to do so. For these reasons all residential construction is considered as investment.

Inventory changes as investment. Remembering that GNP is designed to measure total current output, we must certainly make an effort to include in GNP any products which are produced *but not sold* this year. In short, if GNP is to be an accurate measure of total output, it must include the market value of any additions to inventories which accrue during the year. Were we to exclude an increase in inventories, GNP would understate the current year's total output. If businessmen have more goods on their shelves and in their warehouses at the end of the year than

they had at the start, the economy has produced more than it has consumed during this particular year. This increase in inventories obviously must be added to GNP as a measure of *current* production.

What about a decline in inventories? This must be subtracted in figuring GNP, because in such a situation the economy sells a total output which exceeds current production, the difference being reflected in an inventory reduction. Some of the GNP taken off the market this year reflects not current production but rather a drawing down of inventories which were on hand at the beginning of this year. And the inventories on hand at the start of any year's production represent the production of previous years. Consequently, a decline in inventories in any given year means that the economy has consumed more than it has produced in that year; that is, society has consumed all of this year's output plus some of the inventories inherited from previous years' production. Remembering that GNP is a measure of the current year's output, we must omit any consumption of past production, that is, any drawing down of inventories, in determining GNP.

Noninvestment transactions. We have discussed what investment is; it is equally important to emphasize what investment is not. Specifically, investment does not refer to the transfer of paper assets or secondhand tangible assets. The buying of stocks and bonds is excluded from the economist's definition of investment, because such purchases merely transfer the ownership of existing assets. The same holds true of the resale of existing assets. Investment is the construction or manufacture of *new* capital assets. It is the creation of such earning assets that gives rise to jobs and income, not the exchange of claims to existing capital goods.

We have broadened our concepts of investment and investment goods to include purchases of machinery and equipment, all construction, and changes in inventories.

Now let us focus our attention on the three modifiers, "gross," "private," and "domestic," which national income accountants see fit to use in describing investment. The second and third terms simply tell us, respectively, that we are talking about spending by private business enterprises as opposed to governmental (public) agencies and that the firms involved are American—as opposed to foreign—firms.

Gross versus net investment. The term "gross," however, cannot be disposed of so easily. *Gross private domestic investment* includes the production of all investment goods—those which are to replace the machinery and equipment used up in the current year's production plus any net additions to the economy's stock of capital. In short, gross investment includes both replacement and added investment. On the other hand, we reserve the term *net private domestic investment* to refer only to the added investment which has occurred in the current year. A simple example will make the distinction clear. In 1964 our economy produced about $88 billion worth of capital goods. However, in the process of producing the GNP in 1964 the economy used up some $54 billion worth of machinery and equipment. As a result, our economy added $34 (or $88 minus $54) billion to its stock of capital in 1964. Therefore, *gross* investment was $88 billion in 1964, but *net* investment was only $34 billion. The difference between the two is the value of the capital used up or depreciated in the production of 1964's GNP.

Net investment and economic growth. The relationship between gross investment and depreciation provides a good indicator of whether or not our economy is expanding, static, or declining. Figure 10–1 illustrates these three cases. When gross investment exceeds depreciation, as in Figure 10–1*a*, the economy is obviously expanding in the sense that its productive capacity—as measured by its stock of capital goods—is growing. More simply, net investment is a positive figure in an expanding economy. For example, as noted above, in 1964 gross investment was $88 billion, and $54 billion worth of capital goods were consumed in producing that year's GNP. This meant that our economy ended 1964 with $34 billion more capital goods than it had on hand at the start of the year. Increasing the supply of capital goods, you will recall, is a basic means of expanding the productive capacity of the economy (see Figures 2–3 and 2–4).

A stationary or static economy reflects the situation in which gross investment and depreciation are equal. This means the economy is just standing pat; it is producing just enough capital to replace what is consumed in producing the year's output—no more and no less. In 1942, as the United States attempted to push its production of military goods into high gear, our economy approximated this situation. Resources were purposely diverted from the production of capital goods for nonessential industries, and even in essential industries resources were used sparingly for the production of capital goods. Why? Because the wartime emergency demanded astonishing amounts of finished war goods, and the lion's share of our available resources was directed toward attaining that goal. Therefore, it is not surprising that in 1942 gross investment and depreciation were approximately equal —$10 billion. This meant that at the end of 1942 our stock of capital was about the same as at the start of that year. In other words, *net* investment was about zero. Our economy was a stationary one in the sense that its productive facilities failed to expand. Figure 10–1*b* represents the case of a static economy.

The unhappy case of a declining economy arises whenever gross investment is less than depreciation, that is, when the economy consumes more capital in a year than it manages to produce. Under such circumstances net investment will be a negative figure—the economy will be "disinvesting." Depressions foster such circumstances. Dur-

FIGURE 10–1. EXPANDING, STATIC, AND DECLINING ECONOMIES.
In an expanding economy (*a*), gross investment exceeds depreciation, which means
that the economy is making a net addition to its stock of capital facilities. In a static
economy (*b*), gross investment precisely replaces the capital facilities depreciated in
producing the year's output, leaving the stock of capital goods unchanged. In a
declining economy (*c*), gross investment is insufficient to replace the capital goods
depreciated by the year's production. As a result, the economy's stock of capital
declines.

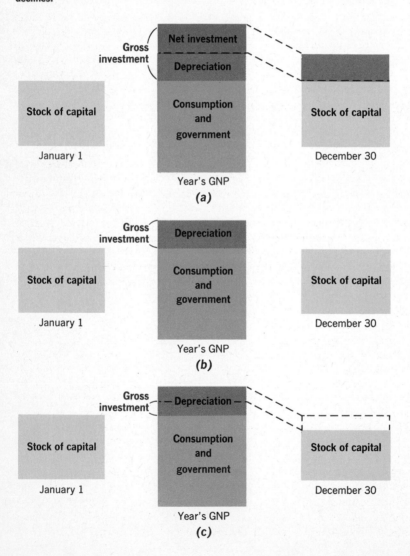

ing bad times, when production and employment are at a low ebb, the nation has a greater productive capacity than it is currently utilizing. Hence, there is little or no incentive to replace depreciated capital equipment, much less add to the existing stock. Depreciation is likely to outweigh gross investment, with the result that the nation's stock of capital is less at the end of the year than it was at the start. This was the case during the heart of the Great Depression. In 1933, for example, gross investment was only $1.4 billion, while the capital consumed during that year was $7.2 billion. Net disinvestment was therefore $5.8 billion. Figure 10–1c illustrates the case of a disinvesting, or declining, economy.

We shall use the symbol I to refer to domestic investment spending and attach the subscript g when referring to gross and n when referring to net investment.

Net Exports (X_n)

How do American international trade transactions enter into national income accounting? We can best explain it in this way: First, remember that we are trying to add up all spending in American markets which accounts for or induces the output of goods and services in the American economy. A bit of reflection will lead you to the conclusion that spending by foreigners on American goods will account for American output just as will spending by Americans. Hence, we want to add in what foreigners spend on American goods and services, that is, the value of American exports, in determining GNP by the expenditures approach. On the other hand, what about spending by Americans on goods and services brought into American markets by foreigners? Obviously this spending induces the output of foreign goods and services. Thus, in determining the GNP for the United States by the expenditures approach, we should want to subtract the value of American imports from total expenditures. Why? Because it

accounts for no domestic production. Rather than treat these two items—American exports and imports—separately, our national income accountants simply take the difference between the two. Hence, *net exports of goods and services* or, more simply, *net exports* is *the amount by which foreign spending on American goods and services exceeds American spending on foreign goods and services.* For example, should foreigners buy $9 billion worth of American exports and Americans buy $7 billion worth of foreign imports in a given year, net exports would be plus $2 billion. It must be emphasized that our definition of net exports might result in a negative figure. If foreigners spend $10 billion on American exports and Americans spend $12 billion on foreign imports, our "excess" of foreign spending over American spending is minus $2 billion.

The letter X_n will be used to designate net foreign investment.

The four categories of expenditures that we have discussed—personal consumption expenditures (C), government expenditures on goods and services (G), gross private domestic investment (I_g), and net foreign investment (X_n)—are comprehensive. They include all possible types of spending. Added together they measure the market value of the year's output; they measure GNP.

THE INCOME APPROACH TO GNP

During 1964 total expenditures (that is, $C + I_g + G + X_n$) were $622.6 billion. How was this $622.6 billion allocated or distributed as income? It would be most convenient if we could say that the total expenditures upon the economy's annual output flow to households as wage, rent, interest, and profit incomes. Unfortunately, the picture is complicated somewhat by two nonincome charges against the value of total output, that is, against GNP. These are (1) a capital consumption allowance and (2) indirect business taxes.

Depreciation: Capital Consumption Allowance

It was noted in Chapter 8 that the useful life of most capital equipment extends far beyond the year of purchase. Actual expenditures for capital goods and their productive life are not synchronized in the same accounting period. Hence, to avoid gross understatement of profit and therefore of total income in the year of purchase and overstatement of profit and of total income in succeeding years, individual businesses estimate the useful life of their capital goods and allocate the total cost of such goods more or less evenly over the life of the machinery. The annual charge which estimates the amount of capital equipment used up in each year's production is called "depreciation." Depreciation is essentially a bookkeeping entry designed to provide a more accurate statement of profit income and hence total income provided by a firm in each year.

If profits and total income for the economy as a whole are to be stated accurately, a gigantic depreciation charge for the economy as a whole must be made against the total receipts of the business sector. This depreciation charge is called a "capital consumption allowance." Why? Because that is exactly what it is—an allowance for capital goods which have been "consumed" in the process of producing this year's GNP. It is this huge depreciation charge which constitutes the previously noted difference between I_g and I_n. For present purposes, the significance of this charge lies in the fact that it claims a part of the business sector's receipts which is, therefore, not available for income payments to resource suppliers. In real terms, that is, in terms of physical goods and services, the capital consumption allowance tells us in effect that a portion of this year's GNP must be set aside to replace the machinery and equipment used up in accomplishing its production. In other words, all of GNP cannot be consumed as income by society without impairing the economy's stock of productive facilities.

Indirect Business Taxes

The second complicating nonincome charge arises from the presence of government. Government levies certain taxes—in particular, general sales taxes, excise and business property taxes, license fees, and customs duties—which business firms treat as costs of production and therefore add to the prices of the products they sell. These taxes, as a matter of fact, are called "indirect business taxes" because sales taxes and excises are not levied directly upon the corporation, partnership, or proprietorship as such but rather upon their products or services. Businessmen, knowing the sizes of such levies, pass them on to the consumer in the form of higher prices. We can think of it in this way: A firm produces a product designed to sell at, say, $1. As we have seen, the production of this item creates an equal amount of wages, rental, interest, and profit income. But now government, in need of revenue to finance its activities, imposes a 2 per cent sales tax on all products sold at retail. The retailer simply adds this 2 per cent to the price of the product, raising its price from $1 to $1.02 and thereby shifting the burden of the sales tax to consumers.

Obviously, this 2 per cent of total receipts which reflects the tax must be paid out to government before the remaining $1 can be paid to households as wage, rent, interest, and profit incomes. Government, in effect, is a preferred creditor. Furthermore, this flow of indirect business taxes to government is not earned income, because government contributes nothing directly to the production of the good in return for these sales tax receipts. As a matter of fact, in the case of sales and excise taxes the finished product is being handed to the consumer at the time the tax is levied. In short, we must be careful to exclude indirect business taxes when figuring the total income earned in each year by the factors of production.

Capital consumption allowances and indirect business taxes account for the nonincome allocations listed in Table 10–5. As just noted, what remains is wages, rents, interest, and profits. But for a variety of reasons national income statisticians need a more sophisticated breakdown of wages and profits than we have employed thus far in this discussion.

Wages

Specifically, wages are broken into two parts. The first we shall term *compensations to employees*. This high-sounding term includes all wages, salaries, bonuses, royalties, commissions, tips, and so forth, which flow back to labor suppliers as income. A second part of wages is *social security contributions*. This includes the required payments made by both employers and employees under our social security program.[4] We treat this part of wages separately because it flows not to households but rather to government. (We shall take payments out of our social security program into account later in this discussion.) To the businessman, social security contributions are a cost involved in obtaining labor; such payments constitute deferred wage income to be received later by the labor supplier. From the worker's viewpoint, his contributions to social security amount to wage income earned but withheld to be received in the future during his retirement or during a siege of unemployment. The important points are these: (1) Social security contributions constitute currently earned wage income but (2) are treated apart from other wage income because they flow to government instead of to households.

[4] As the social security program now stands, both employer and employee pay 4.2 per cent on each dollar earned up to $6,600 per year. Self-employed individuals pay 6.15 per cent on the first $6,600 earned each year. Social security legislation provides for future increases in these payroll tax rates. The American social security system is discussed in a later chapter.

Rents

Rents are almost self-explanatory. They consist of income payments received by households that supply property resources.

Interest

Interest refers to money income payments which flow from private businesses to the suppliers of money capital. For reasons to be noted later, government interest payments are excluded from interest income.

Proprietors' Income

What we have loosely termed "profits" is also broken into two basic accounts by national income accountants: One part is called proprietors' income or *income of unincorporated businesses* and the other *corporate profits*. The former account is largely self-defining. It refers to the profits of sole proprietorships, partnerships, and cooperatives. On the other hand, corporate profits cannot be dismissed so easily because corporate earnings may be distributed in several ways.

Corporate Profits

Generally speaking, three things can be done with corporate profits: First, a part will be claimed by, and therefore flow to, government as *corporate income taxes*. Second, a part of the remaining corporate profits will be paid out to stockholders as *dividends*. Such payments flow to households, which, of course, are the ultimate owners of all corporations. What remains of corporate profits after both corporate income taxes and dividends have been paid is called *undistributed corporate profits*. These retained corporate earnings, along with capital consumption allowances, are invested currently or in the future in new plants and equipment, thereby increasing the real assets of the investing businesses.

Table 10–6 summarizes our detailed dis-

TABLE 10–6. THE INCOME STATEMENT FOR THE ECONOMY, 1964 (in billions of dollars)

Receipts: expenditures approach		Allocations: income approach	
Personal consumption expenditures (C)	$399.3	Capital consumption allowance	$ 53.5
Government purchases of goods and services (G)	128.6	Indirect business taxes	59.0
		Compensations to employees	330.0
Gross private domestic investment (I_g)	87.7	Social security contributions	28.7
		Rents	12.3
Net exports (X_n)	7.0	Interest	26.7
		Proprietors' income	52.0
		Corporate income taxes	25.7
		Dividends	19.8
		Undistributed corporate profits	11.9
Gross national product	$622.6	Gross national product	$622.6

Source: U.S. Department of Commerce data. Details may not add up to totals because of rounding.

cussions of both the expenditure and income approaches to GNP. The reader will recognize that this is merely a gigantic income statement for the economy as a whole. The left-hand side tells us what the economy produced in 1964 and the total receipts derived from that production. The right-hand side indicates how the income derived from the production of 1964's GNP was allocated. One can determine GNP by either adding up the four types of expenditures on final goods and services or by adding up the ten categories of income which stem from that output's production. Because output and income are two sides of the same coin, the two sums will necessarily match.

OTHER SOCIAL ACCOUNTS

Our discussion thus far has centered upon GNP as a measure of the economy's annual output. However, there are certain related social accounting concepts of equal importance which can be derived from GNP. To round out our understanding of social accounting, it is imperative that we trace through the process of deriving these related concepts. This procedure will also enhance our understanding of how the

expenditure and income approaches to GNP dovetail one another. Our plan of attack will be to start with GNP and make a series of adjustments—additions and subtractions—necessary to the derivation of the related social accounts.

Net National Product (NNP)

GNP as a measure of total output has a basic defect: It tends to give us a somewhat exaggerated picture of this year's production. Why? *Because it fails to make allowance for that part of this year's output which is necessary to replace the capital goods consumed in the year's production.*

Two examples will help make this point clear: First, suppose a farmer starts the year by planting 20 bushels of wheat, realizing a total output of 400 bushels at the end of the year. Is it correct to represent his output for the year as 400 bushels? Certainly not. He would have had 20 bushels available if he had planted nothing at all. His net output for the year is 400 minus 20, or 380 bushels. This is a more accurate measure of the production that has actually occurred this year than is 400 bushels. Second, using hypothetical figures, suppose that on January 1, 1966, the economy had $100 billion worth of capital goods on hand. Assume also that during 1966 $40 billion worth of this equipment and machinery is used up in producing a GNP of $600 billion. Thus, on December 31, 1966, the stock of capital goods on hand stands at only $60 billion. Is it fair to say that the GNP figure of $600 billion accurately measures this year's output? No. It would be much more accurate to subtract from the year's GNP the $40 billion worth of capital goods which must be used to replace the machinery and equipment consumed in producing that GNP. This leaves a net output figure of $600 minus $40, or $560 billion.

In short, a figure for *net* output is a more accurate measure of a year's production than is *gross* output. In our system of social accounting we derive a figure for *net national product* (NNP) by subtracting the capital consumption allowance, which measures the value of the capital used up in a year's production, from GNP. Hence, in 1964:

	Billions
Gross national product	$622.6
Capital consumption allowance ...	−53.5
Net national product	$569.1

NNP then is simply GNP adjusted for depreciation charges. It measures the total annual output which the entire economy—households, businesses, and governments—might consume without impairing our capacity to produce in ensuing years.

It is a simple matter, by the way, to adjust Table 10–6 from GNP to NNP. On the income side we simply strike out capital consumption allowance. The other nine allocations should add up to an NNP of $569.1 billion. On the expenditure side, one must change gross private domestic investment to net private domestic investment by subtracting replacement investment as measured by the capital consumption allowance from the former figure. In 1964, a

gross investment figure of $87.7 billion less a depreciation charge of $53.5 billion results in a net private domestic investment figure of $34.2 billion and therefore an NNP of $569.1 billion.

National Income (NI)

In analyzing certain problems, we are vitally interested in how much income is *earned* by resource suppliers for their contributions of land, labor, capital, and entrepreneurial ability which go into the year's net production or, alternatively stated, how much it costs society in terms of economic resources to produce this net output. The only component of NNP which does not reflect the current productive contributions of economic resources is indirect business taxes. It will be recalled that government contributes nothing to production in return for the indirect business tax revenues which it receives; government is not considered to be a factor of production. Hence, to get a measure of total wage, rent, interest, and profit incomes earned from the production of the year's output, we must subtract indirect business taxes from NNP. The resulting figure is called the *national income*. From the viewpoint of resource suppliers it measures the incomes they have earned for their current contributions to production. From the viewpoint of businesses, national income measures factor or resource costs; national income reflects the market costs of the economic resources which have gone into the creation of this year's output. In 1964:

	Billions
Net national product	$569.1
Indirect business taxes	−59.0
National income	$510.1

A glance at Table 10–6 shows that national income can also be obtained through the income approach by simply adding up all the allocations with the exception of capital consumption allowances and indirect business taxes. That is, the eight allocations of GNP which remain after the two nonincome charges have been subtracted constitute the national income.

Personal Income (PI)

Income *earned* (national income) and income *received* (personal income) are likely to differ, for the simple reason that some income which is earned—social security contributions, corporate income taxes, and undistributed corporate profits—is not actually received by households, and, conversely, some income which is received—transfer payments—is not currently earned. Transfer payments, you may recall, are made up of such items as (1) old age and survivors' insurance payments and unemployment compensation, both of which stem from our social security program, (2) relief payments, (3) a variety of veterans' payments, for example, GI Bill of Rights and disability payments, and (4) interest payments on the public debt.[5] Obviously in moving from national income as a measure of income earned to personal income as an indicator of income actually received we must subtract from national income those three types of income which are earned but not received and add in

[5] Why include interest payments on government bonds as income *not* currently earned, particularly when interest on the bonds of private firms is included in national income as earned income? The rationale underlying the exclusion is this: War-bond sales financed the government's purchase of wartime assets, and, unlike the railroad equipment or factories purchased with the proceeds of private bond sales some ten or twenty years ago, wartime assets of 1940–1944 vintage no longer provide any current services for the economy.

Also included in transfer payments is a small amount of private transfers flowing from businesses to households in the form of pensions.

income received but not currently earned. This is done as follows:

	Billions
National income (income earned)	$510.1
Social security contributions	−28.7
Corporate income taxes	−25.7
Undistributed corporate profits	−11.9
Transfer payments	+47.6
Personal income (income received)	$491.4

It is possible that personal income may exceed national income. For example, in 1933 personal income exceeded national income by some $7 billion. This occurred because during the Great Depression the three subtracted items were small and the added item large. Can you explain why?

Disposable Income (DI)

In Chapter 7 we saw that households dispose of their personal income in three ways: First, a sizable portion flows to government in the form of *personal taxes*. Personal income taxes, personal property taxes, and inheritance taxes constitute personal taxes, the first of the three being by far the most important. What remains of personal income after personal taxes have been paid is *disposable income*. Households are free to dispose of disposable income as they see fit. Basically, the choices are two. Remembering that the economist conveniently defines personal saving as "not spending," or better, "that part of disposable income which is not spent on consumer goods," it is obvious that households divide their disposable income between personal consumption expenditures and personal saving. There are only two choices: to spend or to save. The difference between personal income and disposable income and the division of the latter are shown for 1964:

	Billions
Personal income (income received before personal taxes)	`$491.4
Personal taxes	−59.6
Disposable income (income received after personal taxes)	$431.8
Personal consumption expenditures	−399.3
Personal saving	$ 32.5

Personal saving is a residual, that is, the amount remaining after personal taxes and personal consumption expenditures have been taken out of personal income. Remember, too, that households might dissave; they may consume in excess of their disposable incomes by drawing upon past savings or by borrowing. Such was the case in 1933 when personal saving was minus $0.6 billion.

A final comment: It is worth noting that just as GNP, NNP, and NI can be derived by adding up their component parts, so can PI and DI. DI is obviously the sum of personal saving and personal consumption expenditures. PI is the sum of personal saving, personal consumption expenditures, and personal taxes. The reader should employ the figures used in the above calculation of personal saving to verify these points.

Relationships between Major Social Accounts

We have derived four new social accounting concepts from GNP: (1) net national product (NNP), the market value of the annual output net of capital consumption allowances, (2) national income (NI), income *earned* by the factors of production for their current contributions to production or the factor costs entailed in getting the year's total output produced, (3) personal income (PI), income *received* before personal taxes, and (4) disposable income (DI), income received less personal taxes. The

TABLE 10–7. THE RELATIONSHIPS BETWEEN GNP, NNP, NI, PI, AND DI IN 1964

	Billions
Gross national product (GNP) ...	$ 622.6
Capital consumption allowance .	−53.5
Net national product (NNP)	$ 569.1
Indirect business taxes	−59.0
National income (NI)	$ 510.1
Social security contributions ..	−28.7
Corporate income taxes	−25.7
Undistributed corporate profits .	−11.9
Transfer payments	+47.6
Personal income (PI)	$ 491.4
Personal taxes	−59.6
Disposable income (DI)	$ 431.8
Personal consumption expenditures (*C*)	−399.3
Personal saving	$ 32.5

relationships between these concepts are summarized in Table 10–7.

SUMMARY

Figure 10–2 embodies a comprehensive summary and synthesis of all the social accounting measures discussed in this chapter. As a more realistic and more complex expression of the circular flow model of the economy (discussed in Chapter 3), this figure merits careful study by the reader. Starting at the GNP rectangle in the upper left-hand corner, the expenditures side of GNP is shown to the left. For simplicity's sake, we have assumed net exports to be zero. Immediately to the right of the GNP rectangle are the ten income components of GNP and then the various additions and subtractions which are needed in the derivation of NNP, NI, and PI. In the household sector we see the flow of personal taxes out of PI and the division of DI between consumption and personal saving. In the government sector the flows of revenue in

FIGURE 10–2. NATIONAL OUTPUT AND THE FLOWS OF EXPENDITURE AND INCOME.
This figure is an elaborate circular flow diagram which fits the expenditures and allocations sides of GNP to one another. The reader should trace through the income and expenditures flows, relating them to the five basic national income accounting measures.

the form of four basic types of taxes are denoted on the right; on the left, government disbursements take the form of purchases of goods and services and transfers. To simplify, a balanced budget is assumed in the public sector. The position of the business sector is such as to emphasize, on the left, investment expenditures and, on the right, the three major sources of funds for business investment.

The major virtue of Figure 10–2 is that it simultaneously portrays the expenditure and income aspects of GNP, fitting the two approaches to one another. This figure correctly indicates that these flows of expenditure and income are part of a continuous, repetitive process. Cause and effect are intermingled: expenditures give rise to income, and out of this income arise expenditures which again flow to resource owners as income, and so forth.

Finally, the following concise definitions of the most important measures of the economy's performance should be thoroughly understood in studying Figure 10–2:

1. *Gross national product* (GNP) refers to the market value of all final goods and services produced in the economy in a given year.

2. *Net national product* (NNP) is gross national product minus capital consumption allowances (depreciation). NNP may also be found by summing personal consumption expenditures, *net* private domestic investment, government purchases of goods and services, and net exports.

3. *National income* (NI) is the total income *earned* by resource suppliers for their contributions to the production of GNP. National income also measures the costs of the resources used up in producing GNP. Its magnitude can be derived by subtracting indirect business taxes from NNP or by summing compensations to employees, social security contributions, rents, interest, proprietors' income, corporate income taxes, dividends, and undistributed corporate profits.

4. *Personal income* (PI) is the total income *received* by households during a given year. PI is determined by subtracting from national income that income which is earned but not received (social security contributions, corporate income taxes, and undistributed corporate profits) and adding that income which is received but not earned (transfer payments).

5. *Disposable income* (DI) is the portion of personal income which remains after the payment of personal taxes. Disposable income is divided between personal consumption expenditures and personal saving.

QUESTIONS AND STUDY SUGGESTIONS

1. "National income statistics are a powerful tool of economic understanding and analysis." Explain.
2. Why do national income accountants compare the market value of the total outputs in various years rather than actual physical volumes of production? Explain. What problem is posed by any comparison of the market values of various total outputs? How is this problem resolved?
3. Carefully and completely define (*a*) gross national product and (*b*) net national product. How do these measures differ?
4. What are final goods? Intermediate goods? What is double counting? Give an example. Why do national income accountants include only final goods in measuring total output?
5. "An economy's output is its income." Do you agree? Explain.
6. What is the difference between gross private domestic investment and net private domestic investment? If you were to determine net national

product through the expenditures approach, which of these two measures of investment spending would be appropriate? Explain.

7. Why are changes in inventories included as a part of investment spending? Suppose inventories declined by $1 billion during 1966. How would this affect the size of gross private domestic investment and gross national product in 1966? Explain.

8. Distinguish between an expanding, a static, and a declining economy.

9. "In 1933 net private domestic investment was minus $5.8 billion. This means in that particular year the economy produced no capital goods at all." Do you agree? Explain: "Though net investment can be positive, negative, or zero, it is quite impossible for gross investment to be less than zero."

10. Define net exports. Suppose foreigners spend $7 billion on American exports in a given year and Americans spend $5 billion on imports from abroad in the same year. What is the amount of America's net exports?

11. The following is a list of national income figures for a given year. All figures are in billions. The ensuing questions will ask you to determine the major national income measures by both the expenditure and income methods. The answers derived by each approach should be the same.

Personal consumption expenditures	$245
Government transfer payments	12
Rents	14
Capital consumption allowance (depreciation)	27
Social security contributions	9
Interest	13
Proprietors' income	31
Net exports	3
Dividends	16
Compensations to employees	212
Indirect business taxes	18
Undistributed corporate profits	21
Personal taxes	37
Corporate income taxes	19
Government purchases of goods and services	72
Net private domestic investment	33
Personal saving	16

a. Using the above data, determine GNP and NNP by both the expenditure and income methods.

b. Now determine NI (1) by making the required subtractions from GNP and (2) by adding up the types of income which comprise NI.

c. Make those adjustments for NI required in deriving PI. Now determine PI by adding up its various components.

d. Make the required adjustments from PI (as determined in 11c) to obtain DI. Also determine DI by adding up its component parts.

12. Given the following national income accounting data, compute (a) GNP, (b) NNP, and (c) NI. All figures are in billions.

Compensations to employees	$194.2
U.S. exports of goods and services	13.4
Capital consumption allowance	11.8
Government purchases of goods and services	59.4
Indirect business taxes	12.2
Net private domestic investment	52.1
Government transfer payments	13.9
U.S. imports of goods and services	16.5
Personal taxes	40.5
Personal consumption expenditures	219.1

13. The following table shows money GNP and an appropriate price index for a group of selected years. Compute real GNP.

Year	Money GNP, billions	Price level index, per cent (1954 = 100)	Real GNP, billions
1943	$192.5	64.9	$
1947	234.3	83.0	
1956	419.2	104.6	
1963	583.9	118.5	

Indicate in each calculation whether you are inflating or deflating the money GNP data.

14. Which of the following are actually included in deriving this year's GNP? Explain your answer in each case.
   a. Interest on an AT&T bond
   b. Social security payments received by a retired factory worker
   c. The services of a painter in painting his own home
   d. The income of a dentist
   e. The money received by Smith when he sells a 1960 Chevrolet to Jones
   f. The monthly allowance which a college student receives from home
   g. Rent received on a two-bedroom apartment
   h. The money received by Wilson when he resells this year's model Plymouth to Wilcox
   i. Interest received on government bonds
   j. A two-hour decline in the length of the work week
   k. The purchase of an AT&T bond
   l. A $2 billion increase in business inventories
   m. The purchase of ten shares of GM common stock
   n. The purchase of an insurance policy
   o. Wages paid to a domestic servant
   p. The market value of a housewife's services
   q. The purchase of a Renaissance painting by a public art museum
15. Explain: "A man diminishes the national income by marrying his cook."

SELECTED REFERENCES

Dernburg, Thomas F., and Duncan M. McDougall: *Macro-Economics,* 2d ed. (New York: McGraw-Hill Book Company, 1963), chaps. 1–4.

Edey, Harold C., and Alan T. Peacock: *National Income and Social Accounting* (London: Hutchinson and Company, Ltd., 1954).

Rosen, Sam: *National Income* (New York: Holt, Rinehart and Winston, Inc., 1963), chaps. 1–9.

Ruggles, Richard and Nancy D. Ruggles: *National Income Accounts and Income Analysis,* 2d ed. (New York: McGraw-Hill Book Company, 1956), particularly chaps. 1, 2, 6, and 7.

U.S. Department of Commerce: *Survey of Current Business.* July issues contain annual national income data.

CHAPTER 11

THE BUSINESS CYCLE:
UNEMPLOYMENT
AND INFLATION

Emphasis in Part One of this book was upon the essentially microeconomic problem of full production. To facilitate our discussion of how American capitalism allocates resources, we assumed that resources would be fully employed. But actual experience indicates that full employment cannot be taken for granted. Hence, in Parts Two and Three we seek to explore the problem of achieving and maintaining full employment in American capitalism.

The goals of the present chapter are fourfold. First, we introduce the "macroeconomic trilogy" of growth, full employment, and price stability. Next, we discuss total spending as the immediate determinant of the levels of employment and prices. Thirdly, the meanings and implications of unemployment and price instability are explored. Finally, the major characteristics of the American business cycle are discussed and its history sketched.

THE MACROECONOMIC TRILOGY

The broad spectrum of American economic history reflects quite remarkable economic expansion. Technological progress, rapid increases in productive capacity, and a standard of living which is the envy of the world are strategic facets of the dynamic character of our economy. But our long-run economic growth has not been steady. Rather, it has been interrupted by periods of economic instability. Periods of rapid

economic expansion have sometimes been marred by inflation, that is, price instability, and at other times have given way to recession and depression, that is, instability in employment and output. In short, secular economic growth has been interrupted and complicated by both unemployment and inflation.

Needless to say, what society seeks is economic growth *and* full employment *and* price stability along with other less quantifiable goals (see Chapter 1). The degree to which we have been successful in realizing this macroeconomic trilogy is depicted roughly by Figure 11–1 and in greater detail by the historical record embodied in the national income statistics (see tables inside covers). We defer any detailed treatment of economic growth until Part Four, allowing us to concentrate upon the problems involved in achieving full employment and price stability in Parts Two and Three.

SPENDING, EMPLOYMENT, AND THE PRICE LEVEL

Generally speaking, the levels of output and employment, on the one hand, and the level of prices, on the other, have a common determinant. And that determinant is the level of total spending. In a price-directed economy such as American capitalism, businesses produce only those goods which can be sold profitably. Now obviously, if total spending is large, that is, if the demand

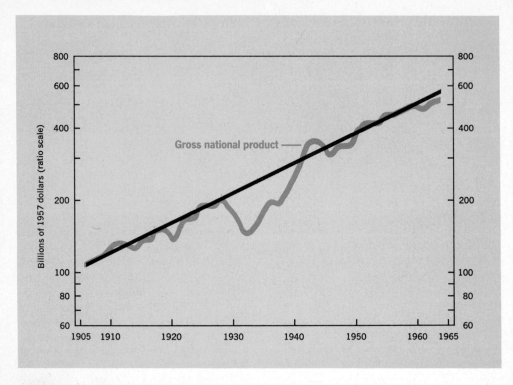

FIGURE 11–1. AMERICAN ECONOMIC GROWTH AND THE BUSINESS CYCLE.
The long-run, or secular, trend of GNP has been upward, but the level of economic activity has fluctuated around this trend. (U.S. Department of Commerce.)

for goods and services in general is great, businesses will be able to produce and profitably sell a large volume of goods and services. To accomplish a large volume of production, businesses will be required to employ a large volume of resources. And this means high incomes. In brief, a high level of spending will make profitable a large volume of output, and this entails a high level of employment. Conversely, a low level of total spending means that the demand for goods and services in general is depressed. This means, in turn, that the volume of output will be small; few goods and services can be sold profitably. And a small output can be produced with a small amount of resources. A low level of total spending means that resources will be involuntarily

unemployed. And, finally, unemployment means low incomes.

Although total spending, on the one hand, and output and employment, on the other, are directly related, this relationship is not completely rigid. When widespread unemployment prevails, a given increase in total spending will have a greater immediate impact[1] upon real output and employment than will that same increase in spending when the economy is operating near, or at, full employment. In particular, price changes loosen the link between changes in spending

[1] Our present discussion is concerned only with the initial impact of a change in spending upon output and employment. Secondary effects will be brought into account in ensuing chapters.

and the volumes of output and employment as the economy approaches full employment. Let us see exactly how this comes about.

Phase 1: Unemployment

Suppose initially that the economy has a large amount of unemployed resources at a time when total spending, for some reason or another, increases. In terms of specific goods, this will mean that demand has increased in relation to supply. As stated earlier, increases in the demand for specific products will have both a price-increasing and a quantity-increasing effect. During periods of substantial unemployment the price-increasing effect of an increase in demand will tend to be small and the output-increasing effect large. Why? Most obviously, there are large amounts of virtually all types of human and property resources which can be readily employed by firms *at current resource prices* to expand their outputs. Furthermore, the plants of many producers will be operating at less than their designed capacity during a period of unemployment. Hence, an expansion of output may result in a more efficient utilization of existing capital facilities. For both these reasons businesses will find that they can increase their output in response to an increase in consumer demand without any appreciable increase in their unit costs of production or, therefore, in the prices they need receive for their products. In short, during a period of widespread unemployment, an increase in demand will bring forth more or less proportionate increases in output and employment with little or no rise in prices.

Phase 2: Bottleneck Inflation

As total spending continues to rise, however, this picture will begin to change. As production expands, supplies of unemployed resources will not vanish simultaneously. Production bottlenecks appear in the form of shortages of certain specific resources, even though unemployment is still generally widespread. As they expand output, firms will find that there are no more idle supplies of, say, skilled labor or technicians or certain metal alloys. Therefore, the prices of these fully employed resources will begin to rise as firms, anxious to partake of returning prosperity, scramble to obtain them. These price increases will mean higher costs and, in turn, that producers must receive higher prices for their products. Labor unions will be quick to take advantage of the improved bargaining position which the decline in unemployment entails, pressing more fervently for wage increases. In addition to the developing scarcities of specific resources, costs will also rise as some firms tend to utilize their plants beyond their most efficient capacities, to man their plants with less productive workers, and to pay premium rates for overtime work. In other words, with moderate unemployment, increases in the demand for products in general will have both price-increasing and output-increasing effects. Prices rise because the unit costs of producers rise.

Phase 3: Pure Inflation

When the economy reaches full employment, prices will begin to rise very sharply as total spending continues to expand. At full employment the economy encounters the production barrier of scarce resources; the economy will be operating at capacity, at a point *on* its production possibilities curve. Businessmen as a group cannot respond to increases in spending by expanding real output. This is aptly termed *demand-pull inflation* by economists: Total demand in excess of society's productive capacity pulls the price level upward. Higher levels of total spending will simply bid up the prices of a fixed real output. At full employment, increases in spending will cause "pure" inflation to set in.

Figure 11–2 summarizes the relationship between the price level, on the one hand,

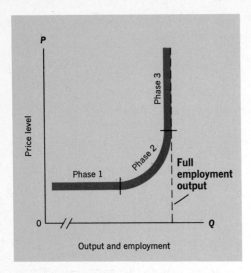

FIGURE 11–2. THE PRICE LEVEL AND THE LEVEL OF EMPLOYMENT.
The price level generally begins to rise before full employment is reached. At full employment additional spending tends to be purely inflationary.

and the levels of output and employment, on the other. The significance of the behavior of the price level as output and employment increase must be emphasized. When unemployment is great and widespread, the initial impact of an increase in total spending will be to bring forth more or less proportionate increases in output and employment (Phase 1). As the economy approaches full employment, however, the price level begins to rise. This means that a part of any increase in total expenditures will be dissipated in the form of higher prices, lessening its impact upon output and employment (Phase 2). If product X is selling at $1 per unit, a $10 increase in expenditures will induce a 10-unit increase in output. But, if the $10 increase in spending causes the price of X to rise to $2 per unit, the resulting increase in output will be just 5 units. As the economy approaches full employment, larger and larger increases in spending are required to increase real

output and employment by a given amount. Once at full employment, added spending will simply pull up the price level (Phase 3).

The relationship expressed in Figure 11–2 is only partially reversible. That is, many product and resource prices which are flexible upward as the economy approaches the full-employment output become relatively rigid and inflexible when declines in total spending result in reductions in output and employment. This is primarily the result of monopolistic power—the ability to influence prices—which many businesses and unions possess. Unions can usually resist wage cuts and sometimes secure modest wage boosts even though the total level of spending and therefore output and employment are falling. Monopolistic businesses are equally able to forestall reductions in product prices. Prices that go up during periods of full employment do not necessarily come down—at least all the way—when spending declines and unemployment ensues. It is not surprising that the long-run trend of the price level in American capitalism has been upward. The significance of the downward inflexibility of prices will become evident in Chapter 12.

Now our task is to assess more carefully the meaning and significance of both unemployment and price instability.

UNEMPLOYMENT

When the economist talks of "full employment," he does not mean that 100 per cent of the available labor force is working. In a dynamic, free economy a certain amount of unemployment is regarded as normal. At any point in time there will be some workers who are in the process of voluntarily changing jobs. Some others may be temporarily out of work because of some labor-saving technological improvement or a change in consumer tastes which has adversely affected employment in their industry. Others are temporarily laid off because of seasonality—

for example, bad weather in the construction industry—or model changeovers. And there will be some young workers who are looking for their first job. This largely unavoidable minimum of unemployment— often termed frictional unemployment—is estimated at 3 per cent of the labor force for the United States. Full employment therefore exists when 97 per cent of the labor force is employed, that is, when about 2.2 million of our 74 million civilian labor force is unemployed.

But in 1964, some 5.2 per cent of the civilian labor force or 3.9 million workers were out of work. And, for two reasons, these figures understate the unemployment problem. First, there are perhaps another one million workers who are working part time because full-time employment is not available to them. Second, there is another group of an estimated one million workers who have unsuccessfully sought employment and, discouraged by their efforts, have dropped out of the labor force. (One must be actively seeking work to be counted as unemployed in government figures.) Thus, actual unemployment may be closer to 5.9 million or 8 per cent of the labor force; stated differently, above-normal unemployment may be 3.7 million workers or 5 per cent of the labor force.

Regardless of the exact interpretation one gives to these statistics, above-normal or "true" unemployment entails great economic and social costs.

Economic Costs

The economic cost of unemployment is obviously forgone output, the goods and services which society could have produced but didn't. For example, the estimated 3.7 million of unemployment in 1964 probably cost the American economy $60 to $70 billion in forgone production. The cost of a prolonged depression can be astronomical.

One scholar has estimated the cost of the Great Depression of the 1930s in these terms:[2]

A full-employment output for the 1930s would have produced $650 billion additional goods and services in terms of the 1956 price level. Such a sum would have been higher than the material cost of World War II. It would have meant roughly $5,000 more in income for each individual in the United States in that decade, or $20,000 more for the average family. If all resources had been fully employed in this manner, every family could have had a new house, several new cars, and most of the other durable goods it desired.

Noneconomic Costs

But unemployment is much more than an economic catastrophe; it is a social catastrophe as well. Depression means idleness. And idleness means loss of skills, loss of self-respect, a plummeting of morale, and sociopolitical unrest. The following commentaries from the unemployed of the 1930s provide important insights into the noneconomic aspects of unemployment:[3]

The wife works while I look after the home. . . . Any long spell of unemployment leaves you with little to be proud of and much to be ashamed of. Our child is still too young to realize that it is her mother who works. We carefully keep her from knowing it.

These last few years since I've been out of the mills I don't seem able to take trouble, somehow; I've got no spirit for anything. But I didn't use to be like that.

[2] Sherman J. Maisel, *Fluctuations, Growth, and Forecasting* (New York: John Wiley & Sons, Inc., 1957), p. 18.

[3] Quotations cited in William H. Beveridge, *Full Employment in a Free Society* (New York: W. W. Norton & Company, Inc., 1945), pp. 243–244. The reader who wants to pursue the sociopolitical implications of prolonged unemployment will do well to consult David A. Shannon (ed.), *The Great Depression* (Englewood Cliffs, N.J.: Prentice-Hall, Inc., 1960).

My husband is a good man and he does a lot for me in the house. . . . But he is a changed man these last two years. He never complains, but I wish he would. It makes me unhappy to find him becoming quieter and quieter, when I know what he must be feeling. If I had someone to talk to about my troubles I should feel much better. . . . We quarrel far more now than we have ever done in our lives before. We would both rather be dead than go on like this.

It is no exaggeration to say that: [4]

A job gives hope for material and social advancement. It is a way of providing one's children a better start in life. It may mean the only honorable way of escape from the poverty of one's parents. It helps to overcome racial and other social barriers. In short . . . a job is the passport to freedom and to a better life. To deprive people of jobs is to read them out of our society.

History makes it all too clear that severe unemployment is conducive to rapid and sometimes violent social and political change. Witness the movement to the left of American political philosophy during the Depression of the 1930s. The Depression-inspired New Deal was a veritable revolution in American political and economic thinking. Witness also Hitler's ascent to power amidst a background of unemployment.

PRICE INSTABILITY: INFLATION AND DEFLATION

The problems and costs associated with a changing price level are more subtle than those of unemployment. Inflation is feared by all of us, criticized by most of us, and not clearly understood by many of us. What is inflation? Why is it to be feared? *Inflation is a rising general level of prices.* This does not mean, of course, that all prices are necessarily rising. Even during

[4] Henry R. Reuss, *The Critical Decade* (New York: McGraw-Hill Book Company, 1964), p. 133.

periods of acute inflation some specific prices may be relatively constant and others actually falling. Nor does inflation mean that prices rise evenly or proportionately. Indeed, one of the major sore spots of inflation lies in the fact that prices tend to rise very unevenly. Some spring upward; others rise at a more leisurely pace; others do not rise at all. The fundamental cause of inflation has already been explored. Generally speaking, inflation results when society attempts to spend beyond its capacity to produce.

Deflation is substantially the reverse of inflation—a falling general level of prices. Once again, deflation does not mean that all prices are falling evenly. Falling prices accompany declining levels of output and employment; the cause is a deficiency of total spending.

Redistributive Effects

In practice output and the level of prices typically move together. Inflation is usually associated with an expanding output (at least until full employment is achieved), and deflation is usually accompanied by a shrinking real output. But in order to isolate the effects of a changing price level upon the distribution of income, let us for the moment assume that real output is constant and at the full-employment level. Assuming the size of the pie is fixed, how does inflation affect the size of the slices going to different income receivers? At the close of our analysis we shall release this simplification and modify our conclusions accordingly.

Any analysis of the redistributive impact of inflation and deflation demands that we first distinguish carefully between real and money income. *Money income* is simply the number of dollars one receives in his pay envelope. *Real income,* on the other hand, is the amount of goods and services which a consumer can obtain with his money income. A moment's reflection will make clear that one's real income depends upon

(1) his money income and (2) the prices which he must pay for the goods and services he purchases.

Inflation penalizes fixed-money-income groups. With this distinction in mind it is easy to see why inflation arbitrarily penalizes people living on relatively fixed money incomes. Those households whose money incomes lag behind the rising level of product prices will find that their real incomes will deteriorate because of inflation. The purchasing power of each dollar's worth of income they receive will fall as prices rise. And, because they receive about the same number of dollars in their pay envelopes, their standard of living must decline accordingly.

Who are these people? The most obvious cases are pensioners, white-collar workers, schoolteachers, and those living on interest incomes. Some wage earners fall in this category. Those situated in declining industries or without the benefit of strong, aggressive unions may find that the price level skips ahead of their money incomes. Those employed in expanding industries and represented by vigorous unions may keep their wage incomes apace with, or ahead of, the rate of inflation.

Those living on flexible incomes will benefit from inflation. The money incomes of such households will spurt ahead of the price level, or cost of living, with the result that their real incomes are enhanced. Most businessmen and other profit receivers benefit from inflation. Product prices typically rise faster than do resource prices; that is, business receipts tend to grow at a faster rate than do costs. Thus profit incomes are likely to outdistance the rising tide of inflation.

Inflation benefits debtors at the expense of creditors. But this is not all. Inflation also redistributes income by altering the relationship between debtors and creditors. Specifically, inflation benefits debtors at the expense of creditors. Suppose you borrow

$1,000 from a bank, which you are to repay in two years. If in that period of time the general level of prices were to double, the $1,000 which you repay will have only half the purchasing power of the $1,000 originally borrowed. True, if we ignore interest charges, the same number of dollars are repaid as were borrowed. But each of these dollars will now, because of inflation, buy only half as much as it did when the loan was negotiated. As prices go up, the value of the dollar comes down. Thus, because of inflation, the borrower is given "dear" dollars but pays back "cheap" dollars.

Inflation lessens the value of savings. Inflation also casts its evil eye upon savers. As prices rise, the real value, or purchasing power, of a nest egg of liquid savings will deteriorate. Savings accounts, insurance policies, annuities, and other fixed-value paper assets which were once adequate to meet rainy-day contingencies or to provide for a comfortable retirement decline in real value during inflation. Mortgage holders and bondholders will be similarly affected. A household's accumulated claims upon the economy's output are worth less and less as prices rise. On the other hand, it should be noted that stock values are flexible and determined by current market conditions; hence, savings in this form will tend to increase in value with, or in some cases ahead of, the general level of prices.

Inflation arbitrarily "taxes" those who receive relatively fixed money incomes and "subsidizes" those who receive flexible money incomes. Inflation benefits debtors at the expense of creditors. Finally, inflation arbitrarily penalizes savers. It should come as no surprise that the effects of deflation are substantially the reverse. *Assuming no change in total output,* those with fixed money incomes will find their real incomes enhanced. Creditors will benefit at the expense of debtors. And savers will find that the purchasing power of their savings has grown as a result of falling prices.

Output Effects

We have assumed thus far that the economy's real output is fixed at the full-employment level. As a result, the redistributive effects of inflation and deflation have been in terms of some groups gaining absolutely at the expense of others. If the size of the pie is fixed and inflation causes some groups to get larger slices, other groups must necessarily get smaller slices. This is obviously modified somewhat when inflation is accompanied by an expanding real output, as would be the case when the economy is approaching, but has not yet attained, the full-employment output (Figure 11–2). When the pie is growing, the gains which inflation brings to some will exceed the losses which it imposes upon others. In brief, although the overall effects will be essentially the same, the redistributive impact of a given amount of inflation will tend to be less severe when inflation is accompanied by an expansion of real output.

Although mild inflation may be accompanied by an expanding real output, extreme inflation—"hyperinflation"—might well have adverse effects upon the level of production. There are two main reasons for this. In the first place, as we shall note shortly, hyperinflation may undermine the functioning of the monetary system, forcing the economy to rely upon exchange by barter. And barter, you recall (Chapter 3), inhibits specialization and thereby fosters inefficient production and a declining real output. Secondly, severe inflation encourages speculative, as opposed to productive, activity. Rather than invest in capital equipment, businessmen and savers find that the hoarding of goods and materials and the purchase of nonproductive wealth—jewels, precious metals, real estate, and so forth—are good hedges against inflation and hence more lucrative outlets for one's money.

What about deflation? Falling prices typically go along with depression and a declining total output. Hence, with a rapidly shrinking pie virtually all groups will get a smaller slice. In other words, those on relatively fixed incomes *who are able to hold their jobs* will find that their real incomes rise as a result of deflation. But these people may be few in number. Creditors *who are fortunate enough to collect from debtors* will gain. But these too may be few in number. And those *who are able to hold on to their savings* as the economy backslides into depression will find the purchasing power of their savings enhanced by lower prices. But these once again may be few in number. In short, during deflation fixed-money-income receivers, creditors, and savers are not likely to be better off in an absolute sense, because in all probability total output will be falling too. But they may be "less worse off" than flexible income receivers, debtors, and nonsavers.

Creeping Inflation

Virtually all economists condemn a sharply rising price level. Economists are divided, however, on the merits and demerits of mild or "creeping" inflation, that is, a 1, 2, or 3 per cent annual increase in the price level.

The case for creeping inflation. Despite the arbitrary redistributive effects of inflation, some competent economists[5] feel that creeping inflation may very well be desirable because of its expansionary effect upon the economy. Product prices, it is argued, tend to increase ahead of resource prices as the economy approaches full employment. This stimulates money profits and is conducive to additional investment spending, which, in turn, brings the economy closer to full employment. Furthermore, the larger stock of investment goods causes a favorable shift in the production possibilities

[5] See, for example, Alvin H. Hansen, *The American Economy* (New York: McGraw-Hill Book Company, 1957), pp. 45–47, and Sumner H. Slichter, "How Bad Is Inflation?" *Harper's Magazine*, August, 1952.

curve, and economic growth is the result. It is concluded that only under the pressure of a high, inflation-causing level of aggregate demand does American capitalism realize full employment, capacity production, and its maximum growth potential. Mild inflation is allegedly a small price to pay for the attainment of these objectives. It is recognized that mild inflation will tread on the toes of fixed-income receivers, creditors, and savers. But this redistributive impact should not be overemphasized: so long as the interest rate on savings exceeds the rate of inflation (and this has generally been the case since World War II), the purchasing power of savings will increase rather than diminish. For example, the purchasing power of a $1,000 savings account will increase if the annual interest rate is, say, 4 per cent and the annual increase in the price level only 2 or 3 per cent. In any event, any arbitrary redistributive effects will be more than offset by the benefits which inflation-born increases in output and employment will bring to the economy as a whole. More fixed-income employees will have jobs, creditors will be more certain of repayment, and prosperity will permit more households to enjoy the luxury of saving. The alternatives, as these economists see it, are full employment and growth accompanied by creeping inflation *or* price stability accompanied by unemployment and the failure of the economy to realize its growth potential. The former choice, they conclude, is far superior to the latter.

The case against creeping inflation. But other competent authorities[6] take a dim view of this position. They make two major arguments against creeping inflation. First, they contend that, when compounded over

[6] In recent years the monetary authorities in the United States have generally been opposed to creeping inflation. See, for example, Federal Reserve Bank of Philadelphia, "Creeping Inflation," *Business Review*, August, 1957.

the years, the redistributive impact of mild or creeping inflation can be very severe. A 3 per cent annual rise in prices will cause the price level to double in about twenty-three years! Second, it is argued that creeping inflation may readily snowball into hyper- or "galloping" inflation. And galloping inflation can precipitate depression. This second argument merits rather detailed consideration.

It is felt that as the economy draws close to the full-employment level, individual segments of the economy will exert pressure to keep their incomes rising ahead of the creeping inflation. But this pressure will cause creeping inflation to get up and run. It happens something like this: As prices persist in creeping upward, people come to expect them to rise further. So rather than let their idle savings and current incomes depreciate, people are induced to "spend now" to beat anticipated price rises. Businesses do the same in buying capital goods. Action on the basis of this "inflationary psychology" simply intensifies the pressure on prices, and inflation feeds upon itself. Furthermore, as the cost of living rises, labor demands and gets higher wages. Prosperity is not a good time for businessmen to risk strikes by resisting such demands. Businessmen recoup their rising labor costs by boosting the prices they charge consumers. And for good measure businesses are likely to jack prices up an extra notch or two to be sure that profit receivers keep abreast or ahead of the inflationary parade. As the cost of living skips merrily upward as a result of these price increases, labor once again has an excellent excuse to demand another round of wage increases. But this triggers another round of price increases. The net effect is a cumulative wage-price inflationary spiral. Wage and price rises feed upon each other, and this helps creeping inflation burst into galloping inflation. Thus, many economists feel that the trouble with a small dose of inflation is that it is not likely to remain small.

But, aside from capricious and disruptive effects upon the distribution of income, why is such hyperinflation to be feared? The answer is that hyperinflation can lead to a depression. As prices shoot up sharply and unevenly, normal economic relationships are disrupted. Businessmen do not know what to charge for their products. Consumers do not know what to pay. Money becomes "hot," because inflation is rapidly diminishing the purchasing power of the dollar. In the extreme case, inflation may become so severe as to render money virtually worthless. Resource suppliers will want to be paid in kind. Creditors will hide from debtors to escape the repayment of debts with cheap money. Money will cease to do its job as a medium of exchange and a standard of value. Nor will people want to store their wealth in the form of money. The economy will literally be thrown into a state of barter. As inflation increases in severity, businesses may find it more profitable to hoard both materials and finished products, awaiting further price increases. But by further restricting the availability of materials and products relative to the

demand for them, such action will merely tend to intensify inflationary pressures. Production and exchange grind toward a halt, and the net result is economic, social, and very possibly political chaos. Hyperinflation has precipitated monetary collapse, depression, and sociopolitical disorder. The conclusion? Mild inflation is a very risky foundation for achieving healthy economic progress.

Which view is correct? It is hard to say. Both have proved accurate in specific instances. American economic history reveals that many periods of healthy economic growth have entailed mild inflation. On the other hand, other nations of the world have had mild inflation that got out of control—particularly during wartime—and broke into galloping inflation with disastrous results:[7]

The inflation in Hungary exceeded all known records of the past. In August, 1946, 828 octillion (1 followed by 27 zeros) depreciated pengös equaled the value of 1 prewar pengö.

[7] Theodore Morgan, *Income and Employment*, 2d ed. (Englewood Cliffs, N.J.: Prentice-Hall, Inc., 1952), p. 361.

FIGURE 11–3. AMERICAN BUSINESS CYCLE EXPERIENCE.
The American economy has encountered periods of prosperity and depression. Only minor recessions have occurred since World War II. (Cleveland Trust Company.)

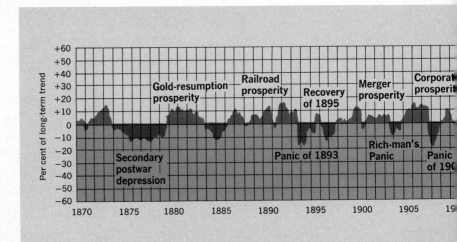

The price of the American dollar reached a value of 3×10^{22} (3 followed by 22 zeros) pengös. . . . In Germany of 1923 a larger box was needed to carry money to the grocery store than to bring back the groceries bought. . . . Prices rose some 116 times in Japan, 1939 to 1948.

We must settle for the conclusion that creeping inflation can be expansionary but that such inflation may expose the economy to the real risk of galloping inflation, particularly after full employment is achieved.[8]

THE BUSINESS CYCLE

What is the record of American capitalism in providing for stability in output, employment, and the price level? The record is a spotty one. At times the economy has suffered from prolonged periods of underspending, the consequences of such periods being widespread unemployment, low incomes, and a depressed GNP. At other times the economy has overspent; that is, it has spent in excess of its capacity to produce.

[8] See question 6 at the end of this chapter.

The result has been full employment and a high GNP, on the one hand, but inflation, that is, a rising level of prices, on the other. This is not to say United States history has been an uninterrupted series of economic ups and downs. On the contrary, the overall postwar record, for example, has been good—much better than economists had dared to hope for at the end of hostilities (see Figure 11–3). Yet even in this period there have been periods of inflation and recurring recessions. Thus the economy continues to be plagued by a business cycle.

Generally speaking, the term "business cycle" simply refers to the recurrent ups and downs in the level of economic activity which extend over a period of several years. Individual business cycles vary tremendously in detail. Yet all embody common phases which are variously labeled by different economists. Thus some economists talk of prosperity, recession, depression, and recovery as being the four phases of the business cycle. Others simply discern between the phases of expansion and contraction with upper and lower turning points to divide the two. Still other economists are content to talk merely in terms of the "upswing" and "downswing" of the business cycle.

Despite common phases, specific business cycles vary greatly. In particular, business cycles vary in duration and intensity. The Great Depression of the 1930s seriously undermined the level of business activity for an entire decade. By comparison, the business declines of 1924 and 1927 were minor in both intensity and duration, as have been our postwar recessions. Figure 11–3 provides ample historical evidence as to the existence of the business cycle and its irregularity as to duration and intensity.

Noncyclical Fluctuations

It must not be concluded that all changes in business activity are due to the business cycle. On the one hand, there are *seasonal variations* in business activity. For example, the pre-Christmas and pre-Easter buying rushes cause considerable fluctuations each year in the tempo of business activity, particularly in the retail industry. Agriculture, the automobile industry, construction—indeed, virtually all industries are subject to some degree of seasonality. These seasonal variations complicate the measurement of cyclical fluctuations in business activity. For example, an upswing in retail sales in December may or may not be evidence of a cyclical upswing in business activity. To speak with any degree of certainty, one would have to compare the increase in this December's retail sales with the increase in sales which statistical records for previous Decembers indicate as being normal. If retail sales normally double in December, a tripling of sales in December, 1966, would suggest a cyclical upswing in business activity. Conversely, if retail sales for the month fall short of doubling, a cyclical downswing is implied.

Business activity is also subject to a *secular trend*. The secular trend of an economy is its expansion or contraction over a long period of years, for example, fifty, one

hundred, or one hundred and fifty years. We simply note at this juncture that the long-run secular trend for American capitalism has been one of rather remarkable expansion, deferring detailed consideration of this growth until a later chapter. For present purposes the importance of this long-run expansion is that the business cycle involves fluctuations in business activity around a long-run growth trend. This is illustrated in Figure 11–1.

Note, too, that in Figure 11–3 cyclical fluctuations are measured as deviations from the long-run trend, a trend that has been persistently upwards. Needless to say, the long-run trend may influence the duration and intensity of particular phases of the business cycle.

Diverse Impact of Cycle

The business cycle is pervasive; it is felt in every nook and cranny of the economy. The interrelatedness of the economy allows few, if any, to escape the cold hand of depression or the fever of inflation. Yet we must keep in mind that various individuals and various segments of the economy are affected in different ways and in different degrees by the business cycle.

Durables versus nondurables. In so far as production and employment are concerned, those industries producing capital goods and consumer durables are typically hit hardest by depression. Output and employment in nondurable consumer goods industries are less sensitive to the cycle. Industries producing heavy capital goods, farm implements, automobiles, refrigerators, gas ranges, and similar products bear the brunt of bad times. Conversely, these "hard goods" industries seem to be stimulated most by expansion. Two facts go far to explain the vulnerability of hard goods industries to the cycle.

1. Within limits, the purchase of hard goods is postponable. Hence, as the economy slips into bad times, producers forestall the acquisition of more modern productive

facilities. The business outlook simply does not warrant increases in the stock of capital goods. In all probability the firm's present capital facilities will still be usable. Except in bad times capital goods are usually replaced before they are completely depreciated; when depression strikes, however, businessmen will patch up their outmoded equipment and make it do. As a result, investment in capital goods will decline sharply. Chances are that some firms, having excess plant capacity, will not even bother to replace all the capital which they are currently consuming. Net investment may be a negative figure.

Much the same holds true for consumer durables. When depression rolls around and the family budget must be trimmed, it is likely that plans for the purchases of durables will first feel the ax. You decide *not* to trade the old jalopy in on a new Belchfire Eight; the little woman is persuaded that she can survive the future without an electronic oven. The household retains its present television set, deferring the purchase of color. And so it goes. Food and clothing—consumer nondurables—are a different story. A family must eat and must clothe itself. These purchases are much less postponable. True, to some extent the quantity and most certainly the quality of these purchases will decline. But not so much as is the case with durables.

2. Most industries producing capital goods and consumer durables are industries of high concentration, wherein a relatively small number of firms dominate the market. As a result, these firms have sufficient monopoly power to resist lowering prices by restricting supply in the face of a declining demand. This means that the impact of a fall in demand centers primarily upon production and employment. The reverse holds true in nondurable, or soft, goods industries, which are for the most part highly competitive and characterized by low concentration. Price declines cannot be resisted in such industries, and the impact of a declining demand falls to a greater extent on prices than upon the levels of production. Figure 11–4 is informative on this point. It shows the percentage declines in price and quantity which occurred in ten selected industries as the economy fell from peak prosperity in 1929 to the depth of depression in 1933. Speaking very generally, high-concentration industries make up the top half of the table and low-concentration industries the bottom half. Note the drastic production declines and relatively modest price declines of the high-concentration industries, on the one hand, and the large price declines and relatively small output declines which took place in the low-concentration industries, on the other.

Incomes and income shares. What about incomes? On an industry basis our discussion of the employment and output effects of the cycle correctly implies that those whose livelihood is linked to the production of capital goods and consumer durables are likely to encounter the greatest variations in employment and incomes.[9] Unemployment will loom larger in such industries during bad times than it will elsewhere.

In terms of national income shares, we have seen previously (Figures 7–1 and 7–2) that rent and interest payments are fairly stable over the cycle. Corporate profits, on the other hand, are subject to considerably more dramatic fluctuations than are the other shares of national income. And, although wage incomes are subject to significant fluctuations in absolute size, labor's relative share of the national income is quite stable over the cycle. During periods of expansion increases in profit incomes usually run ahead of boosts in wage incomes. Similarly, during contraction wage incomes are relatively less flexible than profits. In other words, profit incomes rise and fall more sharply than wage incomes.

[9] Agriculture is a notable exception. The highly competitive nature of this industry makes agricultural incomes very sensitive to the business cycle, despite the fact that it produces nondurables.

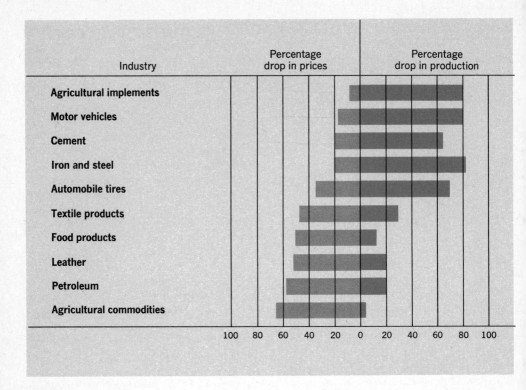

Industry	Percentage drop in prices	Percentage drop in production
Agricultural implements		
Motor vehicles		
Cement		
Iron and steel		
Automobile tires		
Textile products		
Food products		
Leather		
Petroleum		
Agricultural commodities		

100   80   60   40   20   0   20   40   60   80   100

FIGURE 11–4. RELATIVE PRICE AND PRODUCTION DECLINES IN TEN INDUSTRIES, 1929–1933.
The high concentration industries shown in the top half of this figure were characterized by relatively small price declines and large declines in output when the economy entered the Great Depression. In the low concentration industries of the bottom half, price declines were relatively large, and production fell by relatively small amounts.
[Gardiner C. Means, *Industrial Prices and Their Relative Flexibility* (Washington: Government Printing Office, 1935), p. 8.]

BUSINESS CYCLES SINCE 1920

Let us now apply our rudimentary understanding of the business cycle to survey the cyclical experiences of American capitalism since 1920. Such a summary gives us many valuable insights into both the causes and effects of economic fluctuations. The emphasis is upon variations in the different components of total spending.

We shall employ Table 11–1 to substantiate our description of the 1920s. Official U.S. Department of Commerce national income statistics are available

starting in 1929 and provide a factual backbone for our discussion of the ensuing three decades. These figures are presented in the inside covers of the book.

The Prosperity of the Twenties

Aside from a sharp but brief depression in 1921 and minor bouts with unemployment in 1924 and 1927, the 1920s were years of booming prosperity. This prosperity was reflected in an expanding GNP and in a level of unemployment which never exceeded 2 per cent of the labor force in the

TABLE 11–1. GNP, THE PRICE LEVEL, UNEMPLOYMENT, AND PRODUCTIVITY IN THE 1920s

(1) Year	(2) GNP, billions of current dollars	(3) Real GNP, billions of 1947 dollars	(4) Unemployment, millions	(5) Index of output per man-hour in manufacturing, per cent (1939 = 100)	(6) Consumers' price index, per cent (1947–1949 = 100)
1920	$ 91.6	$102.0	0.6	48.0	85.7
1921	70.0	93.0	4.8	55.2	76.4
1922	74.3	106.6	2.9	60.5	71.6
1923	85.5	119.5	0.7	59.5	72.9
1924	85.1	119.6	2.0	63.4	73.1
1925	93.6	130.3	0.8	67.6	75.0
1926	97.8	137.1	0.5	69.5	75.6
1927	95.8	137.6	1.6	71.3	74.2
1928	98.3	139.7	1.9	75.1	73.3
1929	104.4	149.3	0.4	78.1	73.3

Sources: Columns 2, 3, and 6 are from The National Industrial Conference Board, *The Economic Almanac, 1958* (New York: Thomas Y. Crowell Company, 1958), pp. 71, 394. Columns 4 and 5 are from U.S. Bureau of the Census, *Historical Statistics of the United States: 1789–1945* (1949), pp. 65, 70–71.

1923–1929 period. Furthermore, this growth was cloaked in general price stability (see columns 3, 4, and 6 of Table 11–1).

The major driving force underlying this period of prosperity was a high and prolonged level of investment spending on capital equipment and construction. The following interrelated causal factors contributed to this high rate of investment:

1. The strong demand for capital goods. World War I had created a backlog of demand for investment goods. Resources simply could not be spared from the production of armaments during the war for the production of investment goods to replace or expand the nation's stock of capital. As a result, the need for capital goods to replace those worn out and rendered obsolete during the war persisted into the 1920s.

2. The development of new products and industries. The spectacular rise of a group of new and important industries provided

both direct and indirect stimuli to investment spending during the twenties. The development of the automobile, electric power, radio, telephone, and electric refrigerator industries all called for tremendous amounts of investment spending in these and related industries. The most notable of these vigorous new industries was the automobile industry. Widespread acceptance of the automobile—annual production increased from 2.2 million in 1920 to 5.5 million by 1929—induced tremendous expansion in the industry. Of greater importance, however, were the secondary effects which the automobile industry had upon a host of related industries. The petroleum, rubber, steel, glass, and textile industries all expanded their facilities enormously to feed parts and materials into the booming auto industry. In addition, an estimated $10 billion was spent on roads and highways during the twenties.

Expansion was almost as impressive in other new industries. The annual production of refrigerators swelled from $13.3 million in 1921 to a thumping $111.7 million by 1929. In the radio industry production soared from $13.3 million in 1923 to $253.3 million in 1929.[10]

3. Declining labor costs and business optimism.
The development of mass-production techniques and simultaneous increases in specialization sharply boosted the productivity of labor during the 1920s (see Table 11–1, column 5). Teamed with the relative ineffectiveness of labor unions in boosting wage rates during this era, these productivity increases caused labor costs per unit of output to decline. The resulting expansion of profit margins created an environment of business optimism, and this in turn was also conducive to further investment spending.

4. The residential housing boom.
Construction expenditures expanded considerably during the early 1920s, reaching peak levels and a plateau late in the decade. This spending was not only the result of previously cited factors—the development of new industries and highway construction—but also stemmed to a great degree from a residential housing boom.

5. Other factors.
While the preceding factors are the major ones behind the booming twenties, a variety of other forces also played significant roles. Although monetary developments were not a prime mover in the prosperity of the 1920s, it can be said that monetary conditions were such as to permit prosperity to occur. Commercial banks were able to make money available in needed amounts and on reasonable terms. The stock market boom which accompanied the good times of the decade inflated stock prices, thereby creating conditions very favorable for business borrowing and investing.

[10] All production and investment data are from D. Hamburg, *Business Cycles* (New York: The Macmillan Company, 1951), pp. 411–412.

But the end of the decade brought an abrupt halt to this vigorous economic growth.

The Great Depression of the Thirties

In October of 1929 the stock market collapsed, ushering in the most severe and prolonged depression of modern times. GNP plummeted from $104.4 billion in 1929 to a low of $56 billion in 1933. Unemployment rose from 1.6 million to 12.8 million in the same period (lines 5 and 23 of the table on the inside covers).

Just as a high level of investment spending was the backbone of the booming twenties, so a low and sagging level of investment was the major weight that pulled American capitalism into the economic chaos of the thirties. Gross investment spending contracted from $16.2 billion in 1929 to $1.4 billion in 1933 (line 2 of the table)—a 90 per cent decline! To a considerable degree the reasons behind this decline in investment spending have their roots in those factors which underlay the high level of investment of the booming twenties.

1. Excess industrial capacity.
The new industries whose growth underscored the prosperity of the 1920s reached maturity late in that decade. The rapid expansion of these adolescent industries in the twenties occurred at a rate which could not be indefinitely maintained. The markets for these new consumer durables were becoming saturated. Hence, the rate of investment in the automobile and dependent industries began to level off and decline in the early 1930s. Much the same pattern applied to other industries whose growth had been so vigorous in the 1920s. Overexpansion in the previous decade came home to roost in the 1930s.

2. The decline in residential construction.
The 1920s was also an era of overbuilding. The high level of construction in the 1920s

was partially war-deferred construction; building occurred at a rapid rate in the 1920s to make up for the construction that was forgone during the emergency of World War I. And in part the decline in construction was due to a decline in the rate of population growth during the late twenties. In any event spending on construction began to level off as early as 1926, residential construction leading the decline. By the late twenties the construction industry had virtually collapsed.

3. The heavy hand of debt. Indebtedness expanded rapidly and became abnormally large as the economy burgeoned in the 1920s. This indebtedness assumed three basic forms: consumer credit, mortgage credit, and indebtedness for stock purchases. The growth of consumer credit—installment buying—had accompanied the development of the various new industries producing consumer durables in the 1920s. The building boom of the 1920s gave rise to heavy mortgage commitments on residential housing and commercial real estate.

The result of this tremendous growth in indebtedness was that by the late twenties much of the income of businesses and households was committed for the payment of interest and principal on past purchases, and hence not available for current expenditures. As expenditures declined, so did incomes and prices. And income declines prompted creditors to liquidate their debts as readily as possible. This was evidenced in a rising tide of business failures and mortgage foreclosures.

4. The stock market crash. The most dramatic facet of the Great Depression was the stock market crash of October, 1929. The optimism of the prosperous twenties had elevated stock market speculation to something of a national pastime. This speculation had bid up stock prices to the point where they were decidedly out of touch with reality; that is, the prices of stocks were far beyond the profit-making potentials of

the issuing firms. The necessary downward adjustment came with a vengeance in 1929. It was sudden, violent, cumulative.[11]

In that awful last week of October, 1929, the market collapsed. . . . The grim jokes of the period speak for themselves: it was said that with every share of Goldman Sachs you got a complimentary revolver, and that when you booked a hotel room the clerk inquired, 'For sleeping or jumping?'

As already noted, many stock purchases had been made on credit. Speculators found themselves hopelessly in debt with only pieces of now worthless paper as reward for their efforts.

The stock market crash had significant secondary effects. Most important was the accompanying unfavorable psychological repercussions; the buoyant optimism of the 1920s gave way to a wave of crippling pessimism. In particular the crashing of stock prices created most unfavorable conditions for acquiring additional money capital for investment or for any other purpose.

5. Shrinking of the money supply. Closely allied with the stock market crash and the rapid contraction of indebtedness was a very sharp reduction in the money supply in the early years of the Depression. The money supply of $26.4 billion of 1929 had shrunk to $19.8 billion by 1933 (line 22 of the table on the inside covers). This shrinkage was the result of certain complex forces operating both at home and abroad. In part the shrinkage was tied to the stock market crash and its effect upon the value of bank-held assets. In part it was the result of faulty policies invoked by the monetary authorities. In part it stemmed from the very structure of the banking system—a large number of small and relatively weak banks. The important point for our purposes

[11] Robert L. Heilbroner, *The Worldly Philosophers*, rev. ed. (New York: Simon and Schuster, Inc., 1961), pp. 215–216.

is that this drastic reduction in the supply of money contributed to the sharp decline in the volume of spending which characterized the early 1930s.

6. The declining price level. Once the contraction of the early 1930s was under way, deflation tended to reinforce that downswing in business activity. Falling product prices discouraged both consumption and investment spending. Consumers were prone to defer their purchases of durables in order to take advantage of anticipated price declines. Businessmen were discouraged from buying capital equipment for substantially the same reasons.

7. Other considerations. Though we have touched upon the major considerations underlying the Great Depression, many other factors also entered the picture. For example the enactment of restrictive tariffs, designed to shield domestic workers and their jobs from the rigors of international competition, backfired, dealing a death blow to the already declining volume of international trade. Rather than preserve jobs, higher tariffs only served to reduce trade and further intensify unemployment. Furthermore, drought conditions added materially to the woes of the agricultural segment of the economy in the mid-thirties. All these factors and more combined to turn the booming twenties into the stagnant thirties.

An outstanding feature of the Great Depression was its length. The economy made an abortive recovery in the mid-thirties (1933 to 1937), the "boom" of 1936 and early 1937 falling substantially short of the full-employment mark. This feeble upswing was caused by increases in both consumption and investment spending, but the very modest proportions of the latter caused the Depression to persist. The failure of investment spending to rally sufficiently has many roots. In part this was a backwash of the tremendous exploitation of investment opportunities in the residential and business construction industries during the 1920s. In part it was a carryover of the pessimistic repercussions of the stock market crash. In part investment lagged because of the failure of new investment-stimulating industries comparable to the automobile industry to appear in the thirties. In part investment may have remained depressed in the thirties because of the suspicion and hostility with which many businessmen viewed the controversial reform and recovery measures enacted by the New Deal; the economic intervention embodied in New Deal programs may well have frightened off some private investment outlays. Indeed, some economists came to believe in the late 1930s that the Great Depression was more than a cyclical downswing in business activity. They felt that it was the beginning of an era of persistent or "secular stagnation" in American capitalism. The dynamic, expansive forces of American capitalism were allegedly losing their force, to the end that persistent unemployment was to be the lot of the United States. With unemployment hovering close to 10 million in 1939 (line 23 of the table on the inside covers) the possibility of secular stagnation seemed to be an all-too-accurate viewpoint. But darkening war clouds in Europe were soon to resolve the persistent unemployment of the 1930s.

Prosperity and Inflation of the Forties

Prosperity and inflation were the economic bywords of the 1940–1949 decade. The mobilization of 1940 to 1941 and the all-out war effort of 1942 to 1945 paved the way for a vivid economic contrast with the depressed thirties. War has one great economic virtue—it creates jobs for the unemployed. But governmental expenditures in financing World War II did more than create jobs and boost output; they also gave rise to considerable inflationary pressure. Although this pressure was repressed by direct governmental controls during the war, it broke loose at the cessation of hostilities to boost the price level sharply in the postwar era. For convenience we divide this decade into the war years (1940 to 1945) and the postwar years (1946 to 1949). Although prosperity was a main feature of both periods, underlying causal factors differed.

The war years (1940 to 1945). The root causes of prosperity in the early forties contrast vividly with those which produced good times in the twenties:

1. The upsurge of military spending. Sharp increases in government military spending underlay the upsurge in output and employment which characterized the 1940–1945 period. As line 3 of the table on the inside covers clearly indicates, government spending boomed from a lowly $14.1 billion in 1940 to a peak of $96.5 billion by 1944. This tremendous expansion in armaments expenditures took many a worker out of the breadline and put him in the employment line of a defense plant.

2. Rising incomes and consumer spending. With employment and incomes rising as a result of increased government spending, we should not be surprised to find that consumption spending increased during the war years. It did: The $71.9 billion consumption level of 1940 rose steadily to $121.7 billion by 1945 and was destined to increase even more sharply in the postwar years (line 1 of the table on the inside covers).

3. The rise and forced decline of investment spending. The role of investment spending provides an interesting contrast. Investment spurted significantly in 1940 and 1941, basically in response to the increased demand for war goods. Armament production required the use of modern, specialized capital equipment. Furthermore, both defense and civilian industries correctly anticipated future scarcities of capital goods; hence, industry stepped up the level of investment spending accordingly.

But by the end of 1941 the economy was rapidly approaching the full-employment level of production. By 1943 "overfull" employment was achieved; that is, unemployment fell below the 3 per cent normal unemployment figure (lines 23 and 24 of the table on the inside covers). As a result, further expansion in the production of war and consumer goods had to come at the expense of the production of investment goods. This is precisely what happened. The nation "lived off its stock of capital" during the 1942–1945 period. Nonessential investment spending bore the brunt of this cutback. *Net* private domestic investment was negative throughout the height of the war effort in order to free as many resources as possible for the immediate production of war goods (lines 2 and 6 of the table).

4. Expansion of the money supply. Monetary factors played a significant role in the wartime boom. In the six years between 1939 and 1945 the nation's supply of money almost tripled! The 1939 money supply of about $36.2 billion rose to $102.4 billion by 1945 (line 22). This expansion made possible the tremendous increase in economic activity which the war necessitated.

5. Wartime inflationary pressures. By 1943 the American economy had clearly hit the production barrier of full employment. But the total level of spending continued to rise, government and consumption spending leading the way. The inevitable result of spending more and more dollars on a fixed amount of goods is inflation. And war is highly inflationary: it pours money into the pockets of civilians and military personnel but fails to turn out civilian goods at a matching rate.

During the war, however, this inflationary pressure was repressed with considerable success by a bevy of government controls. Price and wage controls were aimed directly at holding the lid on inflation. At the same time tax increases and intensive warbond campaigns tried to drain off excessive purchasing power to reduce spending and thereby relieve the pressure on prices. All things considered, these programs were successful in postponing inflation until the postwar era. After the war significant increases in the general price level did occur.

The postwar years (1946 to 1949). As the war drew to a successful close, forecasts of a severe postwar depression clouded the air. Drastic declines in government military spending were expected to precipitate such a crisis. But, aside from a very mild setback in 1945–1946, prosperity and economic growth persisted into the postwar era. The reasons once again lay in the components of total spending. The drastic $52.4 billion *decline* in government spending which occurred between 1945 and 1946 (line 3 of the table on the inside covers) was largely offset by a $49.5 billion *increase* in private (consumption, investment, and foreign) spending (lines 1, 2, and 4). Aside from a brief recession in 1949, the levels of consumption and investment spending increased in the postwar years to the extent that rather serious inflation resulted.

1. The investment backlog, reconversion, and the housing shortage. The desire to replace capital facilities used up during the war years created a large backlog of demand for capital goods. The need to modernize existing capital facilities plus the reconversion to civilian production added to this high level of demand for investment goods. Furthermore, the chronic problem of a housing shortage had reached acute proportions during the war, with the result that the postwar era unleashed a sharp increase in residential construction activity.

2. Government and the climate for investment. In 1946 the Federal government expressed a readiness to take positive steps to correct any serious deviations from full employment. This assurance undoubtedly provided a favorable psychological climate for the resulting high level of investment.

3. Net exports and postwar aid. Net exports also jumped sharply in the postwar era as foreign nations, flush with American loans and Marshall Plan dollars, eagerly sought American goods to aid in the reconstruction of their war-torn economies (line 4 of the table).

4. The postwar consumption boom. The lion's share of the drop in government military spending was filled by an abrupt increase in consumer spending. As line 1 of the table on the inside covers indicates, consumer spending jumped by over $25 billion between 1945 and 1946.

A host of factors contributed to the high level of consumption spending which persisted in the postwar years. First, the unavailability of consumer durables during the war meant that consumers emerged from the war with a backlog of demands for automobiles, washing machines, refrigerators, and so forth. Secondly, consumers had the means of financing a high volume of expenditures. Not only were current money incomes at record levels, but consumers had accumulated a huge volume of savings in the form of government bonds and other highly liquid assets during the war. This purchasing power was supplemented by (1) a hasty cut in personal taxes (line 15 of the table), (2) a significant increase in government transfer payments to veterans (line 13), and (3) rapid growth in the volume of consumer credit (line 25). Finally, on top of all this, prices were already rising and showed little sign of falling; it seemed sensible therefore to "spend now" before further price increases occurred. All the factors were present for a consumer spending orgy. And it came to pass.

5. Postwar inflation. High levels of spending not only maintained full employment in the postwar era; they also brought rather sharp inflation. Government was able to do a fair job of repressing inflationary pressure during the war. But it was politically impossible to hold the lid on the inflationary kettle once hostilities ended. The Office of Price Administration met a sudden death in 1946. With wartime controls out of the way the field was clear for open inflation to move into the economic spotlight. Successive rounds of wage and price increases were the order of the day, and the cost of living spiraled ever upward. As a result, the consumer price index, which stood at a relatively innocent 62.7 per cent in 1945, had soared to 83.8 per cent by 1948 (line 20 of the table). This spending spree leveled off in 1949, and the result was a mild recession. But the Korean conflict in 1950 quickly pushed the vision of depression to one side. Specifically, the Korean hostilities bolstered both government spending and consumer spending— the former because of the need for increased military outlays and the latter because households anticipated and wanted to "beat" war-born inflation and product shortages. As American capitalism entered the decade of the fifties, inflation was still the major economic problem of the day.

The Growth and Inflation of the Fifties

The decade of the 1950s is not easily assessed. The 1950s were characterized by overall prosperity, a rising price level, and significant economic growth, on the one hand, and two troublesome recessions and weakening of the growth rate late in the decade, on the other. Again, the general picture is explainable in terms of the major components of total spending.

The Korean conflict and the 1954 recession. We have already noted that the Communist invasion of South Korea in 1950 stimulated anticipatory buying by consumers and businessmen, both of whom expected shortages of goods and materials and inflated prices to result. This was followed in 1951 by a substantial increase in armament spending by the Federal government. The result was a buoyant, expanding economy in the 1950–1953 period. Total spending was high enough to induce substantial increases in real GNP and, in the 1951–1953 period, an unemployment rate of approximately 3 per cent of the labor force (lines 19 and 24 of the table). In fact, total spending was sufficiently strong to cause significant inflation; the consumer

price index rose from 83.8 in 1950 to 92.5 by 1952 (line 20).

But then came a readjustment. The war-born upsurge in consumer spending was too great to be sustainable, and in 1953 and 1954 consumption expenditures leveled off. Businessmen, having geared their production to the 1951–1952 high levels of consumption, found themselves with overlarge inventories of goods. The resulting cutback in production, coupled with a gradual cutback in Federal military spending as the Korean conflict drew to a close, paved the way for the relatively mild "inventory recession" in 1954.

The 1955–1957 durable goods boom. The 1954 recession might have been much more severe in duration and intensity were it not for the fact that long-term investment spending on machinery, equipment, and construction held up during this period. There were several factors at work which contributed to the stability of long-term investment:

1. Technological advances and continued long-term growth in population and incomes bolstered business investment in plant and equipment.

2. Population growth and governmental provision of favorable credit policies sustained the postwar demand for residential construction.

3. The expenditures of state and local governments on schools, highways, and similar social goods continued to expand steadily.

These investment-stimulating factors teamed with a rapidly expanding demand for consumer durables (particularly automobiles) to make 1955 a year of vigorous economic expansion. Substantial growth in consumer credit in 1954 and 1955 (line 25) and the increased demand for furniture and appliances which accompanied the high rate of residential construction were factors in this expansion of consumer spending on durables. Real GNP surged from $439.8 to $473.4 billion between 1954 and

1955. In 1956 and 1957 expenditures for residential housing and automobiles fell rather significantly, and, despite continued strong expenditures for plant and equipment and growing expenditures by state and local governments, the economy plateaued. As a result, although prosperity was sustained in 1956 and 1957, these were years of only modest economic growth. Note (line 24 of table) that unemployment hovered at the normal unemployment mark in the entire 1955–1957 period.

The 1958 recession and recovery. Though the 1958 recession was brief—lasting less than a year—it was also the most severe of the several post-World War II recessions. Note (line 19 of table) that real GNP fell by $7 billion between 1957 and 1958, more than in either the 1954 or 1949 recessions. Unemployment rose to 6.8 per cent of the labor force—clearly the highest figure in the post-World War II period (line 24). The basic cause of this recession was a substantial decline in business investment in machinery and equipment—a decline which was in part a reaction to the leveling of consumer spending in 1956 and 1957. In addition, the enactment of restrictive credit policies by the government in seeking to restrain the price level probably contributed to the downturn by also restraining purchases of housing and consumer durables. Furthermore, the automobile industry was simultaneously plagued by both market saturation and strong foreign competition.

Increased spending on consumer durables, an expansion of residential construction (aided by governmentally eased credit conditions), and increased government spending all underlay recovery in 1959. Increases in state and local government spending stemmed from continually expanding outlays on school and highway construction, whereas increases in Federal spending reflected an intensification of the cold war and, in no small measure, a reaction to Sputnik I.

The Sixties: Sluggish or Soaring?

Marred in 1959 by the longest steel strike in American history, the recovery from the 1958 recession was neither rapid nor complete. Each of the postwar recessions seemed to leave a larger and larger residue of unemployed workers. Newspaper headlines which lamented "creeping inflation" in the early 1950s were speaking of "creeping unemployment" as the 1960s began. Thus in 1960 the economy was marking time in another recession. While annual increases in real GNP had averaged 3.8 per cent in the 1947–1957 period, this rate had fallen to 2.5 per cent per year in the 1957–1960 period. Then in early 1961 the economy began an unusually long upturn which has lasted over four years. Real GNP rose from $531.2 billion in 1960 to $622.6 billion in 1964. As a result, earlier fears that the 1960s would be as sluggish as the late 1950s faded in favor of the much more optimistic view that the decade might indeed prove to be the "soaring sixties." Growth in all major components of total spending underlay this period of expansion. The exceptional performance of the economy in 1964 was due in part to a $11 billion tax cut, which boosted corporate profits and personal income, stimulating in turn investment and consumer spending. Expectations of further tax cuts have helped sustain an optimistic economic outlook.

Despite this prolonged period of economic expansion, serious problems still persist. In particular, unemployment remains at an above-normal level. There are several reasons for this. First, the baby boom of the immediate postwar years is now entering the labor force. While the labor force grew by about 0.8 million workers per year on the average in the 1950s, the prospects are for about 1.2 million new workers per year in the 1960s. At the same time, moreover, automation is imposing severe limits upon the number of job opportunities in manufacturing industries; manufacturing firms are using more and more labor-saving machinery and a slightly declining number of workers to meet production requirements. In recent years goods-producing industries have been offering fewer and fewer employment opportunities. Thirdly, as Western Europe and Japan have now realized full recovery from the devastation of World War II, the United States finds itself faced with sharp competition in holding world markets. Many industries which are substantially dependent upon foreign sales have cut production and laid off workers as West European and Japanese concerns gain larger shares of world markets (Chapter 40).

Concluding Observations

Our historical examination of the economic ups and downs of American capitalism yields several noteworthy conclusions:

1. The business cycle is clearly a complex phenomenon. In particular the factors which cause or contribute to prosperity and depression are most diverse. Though the immediate cause of the business cycle is changes in the volume of spending, we find that a host of different factors influence the course of total spending. Such diverse considerations as innovations, changes in the volume of indebtedness, productivity changes, business and consumer expectations, wars, droughts, population changes, and governmental policies at home and abroad all make for variations in total spending and, hence, in the level of economic activity.

2. The variability of investment spending as a component of total spending is also noteworthy. A surging level of investment was the backbone of the prosperous twenties. Similarly, a declining volume of investment ushered in the prolonged depression of the thirties. Sharp increases in investment helped fill the gap left by declining governmental spending at the close of World War II. Our review of recent business cycle experience strongly suggests that the forces which contribute most to economic in-

stability are those which bear upon the decisions of businessmen to invest.

3. Finally, our discussion suggests that within limits upswings and downswings in business activity tend to be cumulative. To illustrate: When the nation is at less than full employment, increases in, say, investment spending give rise to increases in output and employment. A higher level of employment means rising incomes, which prompt further increases in spending. Further increases in spending mean still further increases in output, employment, and incomes. The reverse interactions tend to occur as an initial decline in total spending causes the economy to backslide from a full-employment level of performance.

SUMMARY

1. The level of spending determines the levels of output, employment, and incomes in American capitalism. Inflation becomes increasingly severe as the economy approaches full employment; an increase in total spending at full employment only serves to boost the price level. The general price level is more flexible upward than downward.

2. It is considered normal for some 3 per cent of the labor force to be unemployed in our economy. The economic cost of unemployment consists of the goods and services which society forgoes when its resources are involuntarily idle. Unemployment is also conducive to a deterioration of national morale and to social and political unrest.

3. Inflation—a rising general level of prices—is caused by excessive spending. Deflation is caused by a deficiency of total spending. Inflation redistributes income at the expense of fixed-income receivers, creditors, and savers. Deflation has substantially the reverse effects.

4. Economists disagree as to the effect which inflation may have upon the level of performance achieved by the economy. Some argue that mild inflation is essential

in achieving full employment and maximum economic expansion. Another group feels that over time mild inflation has substantial and undesirable redistributive effects and that it is likely to precipitate hyperinflation and economic collapse by causing a breakdown in the monetary system and diverting otherwise productive energies to speculative activities.

5. Although characterized by common phases—recession, depression, recovery, and prosperity—business cycles vary greatly in duration and intensity.

6. All sectors of the economy are affected by the business cycle, but in varying ways and degrees. The cycle has greater output and employment ramifications in the capital goods and durable consumer goods industries than it does in nondurable goods industries. Over the cycle, price fluctuations are greater in competitive than in monopolistic industries. Profit incomes tend to fluctuate more than do other shares of the national income.

7. Historically, American capitalism has fostered both vigorous expansion and stagnation. An examination of our business cycle experience suggests that **a.** the factors which bear upon total spending and hence output, employment, and the price level are many and varied; **b.** variations in investment play a crucial role in cyclical fluctuations; and **c.** within limits prosperity and depression are cumulative.

QUESTIONS AND STUDY SUGGESTIONS

1. Carefully describe the relationship between total spending and the level of resource utilization. Explain the relationship between the price level and increases in total spending as the economy moves from substantial unemployment to moderate unemployment and, finally, to full employment. What is the significance of this relationship?

2. Carefully define "full employment." What is "normal unemployment"? Why is unemployment an economic problem? What are the noneconomic effects of unemployment?

3. Distinguish between money income and real income. Explain how an *increase* in one's money income and a *decrease* in his real income might occur simultaneously.

4. Evaluate as accurately as you can the manner in which each of the following individuals would be affected by fairly rapid inflation:
   a. A pensioned railroad worker; **b.** A department-store clerk; **c.** A UAW assembly-line worker; **d.** A heavily indebted farmer; **e.** A retired businessman whose current income is composed entirely of stock dividends; **f.** A widow whose income is derived entirely from interest on government bonds; **g.** The owner of an independent small-town department store.

5. "Inflation is a friend on the journey to full employment, but an enemy once the destination is reached." Evaluate and explain. Explain how severe inflation might lead to unemployment.

6. In August, 1957, William McChesney Martin, chairman of the Board of Governors of the Federal Reserve System, made the following statement before the Senate Finance Committee:

There is no validity whatever in the idea that any inflation, once accepted, can be confined to moderate proportions. Once the assumption is made that a gradual increase in prices is to be expected, and this assumption becomes a part of everybody's expectations, keeping a rising price level under control becomes incomparably more difficult than the problem of maintaining stability when that is the clearly expressed goal of public policy. Creeping inflation is neither a rational nor a realistic alternative to stability of the general price level.

Also in 1957, Alvin H. Hansen, noted Harvard economist, wrote the following comments:[12]

Periods of rapid growth have usually also been periods of moderate price increases. . . . It is not probable that we can achieve in the next twenty years anything like the growth of which we are capable, without some moderate increases in wholesale and consumer prices. . . . Thus I conclude that if in the pursuit of rigid price stability we permit, and even foster, a considerable amount of unemployment, we shall then fail to achieve the growth of which we are capable.

Contrast and evaluate carefully these two points of view. To which do you subscribe?

7. A noted television comedian once defined inflation as follows: "Inflation? That means your money today won't buy as much as it would have during the depression when you didn't have any." Is his definition accurate?

8. What are the major phases of the business cycle? How long do business cycles last? What are seasonal variations and secular trends in business activity? How do they complicate measurement of the business cycle?

9. Why does the business cycle affect durable goods industries more severely than industries producing nondurables? How are the various shares of the national income affected by prosperity and depression?

10. Briefly outline the major factors which contributed to the prosperity of the 1920s. Now explain the basic considerations underlying the Great Depression of the 1930s. What relationships, if any, can you cite between the causes of the booming twenties and the depressed thirties?

11. Explain the extended period of prosperity which has been with us for the last two decades. What importance would you attach to (a) business and consumer expectations, (b) consumer credit, (c) changes in the supply of money, and (d) government policies as causal factors in this prosperity? Use the statistics presented in this chapter where applicable to substantiate your answers. Now use these data to describe our economy's performance in the late 1950s and early 1960s.

SELECTED REFERENCES

Economic Report of the President (Washington: Government Printing Office, January, 1965).

---

[12] *The American Economy* (New York: McGraw-Hill Book Company, 1957), pp. 45–47.

Gordon, Robert A.: *Business Fluctuations*, 2d ed. (New York: Harper & Row, Publishers, Incorporated, 1961), particularly chaps. 8–11 and 14–16.

Haberler, Gottfried: *Prosperity and Depression* (Geneva: League of Nations, 1941), chap. 1.

Lee, Maurice W.: *Macroeconomics: Fluctuations, Growth and Stability*, 3d ed. (Homewood, Ill.: Richard D. Irwin, Inc., 1963), chaps. 1–10.

Myrdal, Gunnar: *Challenge to Affluence* (New York: Pantheon Books, a Division of Random House, Inc., 1962), particularly chaps. 1–4.

Ross, Arthur M. (ed.): *Unemployment and the American Economy* (New York: John Wiley & Sons, Inc., 1964).

U.S. Department of Commerce: *Survey of Current Business.* January issues survey the economy's performance in the preceding year.

CHAPTER 12

THE BACKGROUND
AND ANALYTICAL TOOLS
OF EMPLOYMENT THEORY

This and the following chapter are concerned with assessing the ability of a capitalistic economy to achieve the full employment of its resources. If the price system can provide for a reasonably efficient allocation of resources, what is to prevent it from providing for the full utilization of society's available resources?

More specifically, the objectives of the present chapter are threefold: In the first place, we want to understand why for many years economists thought capitalism was capable of providing for virtually uninterrupted full employment. Involved here is a discussion of the so-called classical theory of employment. Second, the shortcomings of the classical theory will be noted and analyzed. Then, finally, the tools of modern employment theory will be introduced and explained. In Chapters 13 and 14 we shall employ these tools to analyze the equilibrium levels of output and employment and extend our analysis to indicate the effects of government policies upon output and employment.

Three simplifying assumptions will greatly facilitate the achievement of these stated objectives:

1. A "closed economy" will be assumed. That is, our discussion will deal only with the domestic economy, deferring the complications arising from international trade transactions until later chapters.

2. Government will be ignored until Chapter 14, thereby permitting us in Chapters 12 and 13 to determine whether or not laissez-faire capitalism is capable of achieving full employment.

3. Although saving actually occurs in both the business and household sectors of the economy, we shall speak as if all saving were personal saving.[1]

One implication of the second and third assumptions is particularly noteworthy. These two assumptions permit us to treat NNP, NI, PI, and DI as being equal to one another for the simple reason that all the items which in practice distinguish them from one another are due to government (taxes and transfer payments) and business saving (see Table 10–7). This means that we can readily shift our discussion among these various output and income measures without encountering serious complications which would otherwise arise.

Now the ground is cleared to rephrase our basic question: Is capitalism able to achieve and maintain a full-employment noninflationary total output?

---

[1] When using NNP as our measure of total output, it is accurate to assume that the bulk of the economy's saving is done by households. Table 10–7 shows personal saving at $32.5 billion and undistributed corporate profits as $11.9 billion for 1964. If GNP were employed, however, capital consumption allowances of $53.5 billion would have to be included as a part of business saving, making business saving more than twice as great as personal saving.

THE CLASSICAL THEORY OF EMPLOYMENT

Answers to this question have varied historically. Until the Great Depression of the 1930s, many prominent economists—now called classical economists[2]—felt that the price system was capable of providing for the full employment of the economy's resources. It was acknowledged that now and then abnormal circumstances would arise in such forms as wars, political upheavals, droughts, speculative crises, gold rushes, and so forth, to push the economy from the path of full employment (see Figure 11–3). But it was contended that when these deviations occurred, automatic adjustments within the price system would soon restore the economy to the full-employment level of output. Though the classical theory of employment is now rejected by the vast majority of economists (including some who earlier were leaders in this school of thought), an analysis of classical thinking will lay a firm foundation for understanding modern employment theory.

The classical theory of employment was grounded on two basic notions. First, it was argued that underspending—that is, a level of spending insufficient to purchase a full-employment output—was most unlikely to occur. Second, even if a deficiency of total spending were to arise, price-wage adjustments would occur so as to ensure that the decline in total spending would not entail declines in real output, employment, and real incomes.

Say's Law

The classical economists' denial of the possibility of underspending was based upon their faith in Say's Law. Say's Law is the disarmingly simple notion that the very act of producing goods generates an amount of income exactly equal to the value of the goods produced. That is, the production of any output would automatically provide the wherewithal to take that output off the market. Supply creates its own demand.[3] As a matter of fact, the circular flow model of the economy and national income accounting both suggest something of this sort. The income generated from the production of any level of total output would, *when spent*, be just sufficient to provide a matching total demand. Assuming that the composition of output is in accord with consumer preferences, all markets would be cleared of their output. It would seem that all businessmen need do to sell a full-employment output is to produce that output; Say's Law guarantees sufficient purchasing power for its successful disposal.

Saving: a complicating factor. However, there is one obvious omission in this simple application of Say's Law. Although it is an accepted truism that output gives rise to an identical amount of money income (Chapter 10), there is no guarantee that the recipients of this income will spend it all. Some income might be saved (not spent) and therefore not reflected in product demand. Saving would constitute a break, or "leakage," in the income-expenditure flows and therefore undermine the effective operation of Say's Law. Saving is a withdrawal of funds from the income stream which will cause total expenditures to fall short of total output. If households saved a given portion of their incomes, supply would not create its own demand. Saving would cause a deficiency of total expenditures. The consequences? Unsold goods, cutbacks in production, unemployment, and falling incomes.

Saving, investment, and the interest rate. But the classical economists were reluctant to bow to those economists who suggested

---

[2] Most notable among the classical economists are John Stuart Mill, F. Y. Edgeworth, Alfred Marshall, and A. C. Pigou.

[3] Attributed to the nineteenth-century French economist J. B. Say.

that such a virtuous act as saving could give rise to underspending and the calamity of depression. Instead, they argued that saving would not really result in a deficiency of total demand, because each and every dollar saved would be invested by businesses. Businessmen, after all, do not plan to sell their entire output to consumers but rather produce a considerable portion of total output in the form of capital goods for sale to one another. In other words, investment spending by businesses is a supplement or addition to the income-expenditure stream. Thus, if businesses as a group intend to invest as much as households want to save, the levels of national output and employment will remain constant. Whether or not the economy could achieve and sustain a level of spending sufficient to provide a full-employment level of output and income therefore would depend upon whether businesses were willing to invest enough to offset the amount households want to save.

Now the classical economists argued that capitalism contained a very special price mechanism—the interest rate—which would guarantee an equality of saving and investment plans and therefore full employment. That is, the interest rate would see to it that dollars which leaked from the income-expenditure stream as saving would automatically reappear as dollars spent on investment goods. The rationale underlying the saving and investment equating adjustments of the interest rate was simple and, if not too carefully scrutinized, very plausible. The classical economists contended that, other things being equal, households normally prefer to consume rather than to save. The consumption of goods and services satisfies human wants; idle dollars do not. Hence, it was reasoned that consumers would save only if someone would pay them a rate of interest as a reward for their thriftiness. The greater the interest rate, the more dollars saved; that is, the saving (supply-of-dollars) curve of households would be upsloping as in Figure

12–1. And who would be inclined to pay for the use of saving? None other than investors—businessmen who seek money capital to replace and enlarge their plants and their stocks of capital equipment. Because the interest rate is a cost to borrowing businessmen, they will be willing to borrow and invest more at low than at high interest rates. This means that the investment (demand-for-dollars) curve of businesses is downsloping as in Figure 12–1. Classical economists concluded that the money market, wherein savers supply dollars and investors demand dollars, would establish an equilibrium price for the use of money—an equilibrium interest rate—at which the quantity of dollars saved (supplied) would equal the number of dollars invested (demanded). Saving, said the classicists, does not really constitute a break in the income-expenditure stream or a fatal flaw in Say's Law, because the money market or, more specifically, the interest rate will guarantee that each and every dollar saved will get into the hands of investors and be spent on capital equipment. Therefore, an increase in thriftiness is not a cause for social concern, because this simply shifts the supply-of-saving curve to the right. Although saving will for a time exceed investment and perhaps cause some temporary unemployment, the surplus of saving will drive the interest rate down to a new and lower equilibrium level. And this lower interest rate will expand the volume of investment spending until it again equals the amount of saving, thereby preserving full employment. In short, changes in the interest rate would guarantee the operation of Say's Law even in an economy in which substantial saving occurs. As the classical economists saw it, the economy was analogous to a gigantic bathtub wherein the watermark measured the level of output and employment. Any leakage down the drain of saving would be returned to the tub through the spigot of investment. This had to be the case, because the interest rate connected the drainpipe and the spigot!

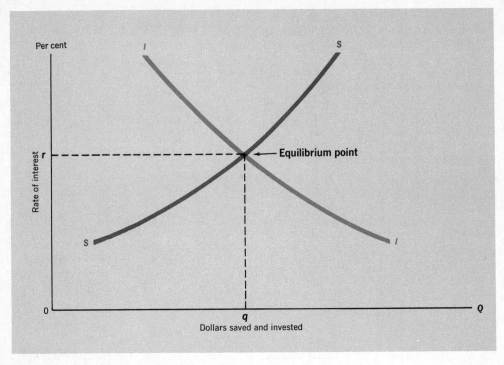

FIGURE 12–1. CLASSICAL VIEW OF THE INTEREST RATE.
The classical economists believed that the saving plans of households would be
reflected in a supply-of-dollars curve *S* and the investment plans of businesses in a
demand-for-dollars curve *I* in the money market. The equilibrium interest rate *r*, the
price paid for the use of money, would equate the amounts households and businesses
planned to save and invest, thereby guaranteeing a full-employment level of spending.

Price-Wage Flexibility

The classical economists bolstered their
conclusion that full employment is the norm
of capitalism with a second basic argument:
They argued that the level of output which
businessmen can sell depends not only upon
the level of total spending but also upon
the level of product prices. This meant that
even if the interest rate would somehow
temporarily fail to equate the amounts
which households wanted to save with the
investment intentions of businesses, any
resulting decline in total spending would
be offset by proportionate declines in the
price level. That is, $20 will buy four shirts
at $5, but $10 will buy the same number of

shirts if their price will only fall to $2.50.
Hence, if households somehow managed to
succeed in saving more than businesses
were willing to invest, the resulting decline
in total spending would not result in a
decline in real output, real income, and the
level of employment *if* product prices
declined in proportion to the decline in
expenditures.

And, according to the classical economists, this is precisely what would happen.
Competition among sellers would guarantee
it! As declines in product demand became
general, competing producers would lower
their prices to dispose of accumulating
surpluses. Hence, product prices would fall.
In other words, the result of saving would

be to lower prices; and lower prices, by increasing the value of the dollar would permit nonsavers to obtain more goods and services with their current money incomes. Saving would therefore simply lower prices, but not output and employment.

"But," ever-present skeptics asked, "doesn't this ignore the resource market? Although businesses can sustain their sales in the face of a declining demand by accepting lower product prices, won't they find it unprofitable to do so? As product prices decline, won't resource prices—particularly wage rates—have to decline significantly to permit businesses to produce *profitably* at the now lower prices?" The classical economists replied that wage rates must and would decline. General declines in product demand would be mirrored in declines in the demand for labor and other resources. The immediate result would be a surplus of labor, that is, unemployment, at the wage rate prevailing prior to these declines in the demand for labor. However, though not willing to employ all workers at the original wage rates, producers would find it profitable to employ additional workers at lower wage rates. The demand for labor, in other words, is downsloping; those workers unable to locate employment at the old higher wage rates could find jobs at the new lower wage rates.

Would workers be willing to accept lower wage rates? Competition among unemployed workers, according to the classical economists, would guarantee it. In competing for scarce jobs, idle workers would bid down wage rates until these rates (wage costs to employers) were so low that employers would once again find it profitable to hire all available workers. This would happen at the new lower equilibrium wage rate. The classical economists therefore concluded that *involuntary unemployment* was impossible. Anyone who was willing to work at the market-determined wage rate could readily find employment. Competition in the labor market ruled out involuntary idleness.

Classical Theory and Laissez Faire

Strictly speaking, each of these price system adjustments—fluctuations in the interest rate, on the one hand, and price-wage flexibility, on the other—seemed fully capable of maintaining full employment in a capitalistic economy. Working together, the classical economists felt, the two adjustment mechanisms made full employment a foregone conclusion. The classical economists came to embrace capitalism as a self-regulating economy wherein full employment was regarded as the norm. Capitalism was capable of "running itself." Government assistance in the operation of the economy was deemed unnecessary, nay, harmful. In an economy capable of achieving both full production and full employment, governmental interference could only be a detriment to its efficient operation.

KEYNES AND "THE NEW ECONOMICS"

One embarrassing fact persistently denied the validity of the classical theory of employment—recurring periods of prolonged unemployment and inflation. Now while one might explain a minor depression such as the brief downswings of 1924 and 1927 in terms of wars and similar external considerations, serious and prolonged downswings such as the Great Depression were not so easily rationalized. There is a remarkable inconsistency between a theory which concludes that unemployment is virtually impossible and a ten-year siege of very substantial unemployment.[4] And so various

---

[4] It is interesting to note that most of the classical economists stuck to their theoretical guns during the 1930s, arguing that (1) the reluctance of union and business monopolies to accept price and wage cuts, (2) misguided New Deal policies which sought to prevent price-wage declines, and (3) government policies in the area of money and banking which interfered with the operation of the interest rate prevented a quick recovery from the cyclical downswing of the early 1930s.

economists came to criticize both the rationale and the underlying assumptions of classical employment theory. They groped for a better, more realistic explanation of those forces which determine the level of employment.

Finally, in 1936 the renowned English economist, John Maynard Keynes, came forth with a new explanation of the level of employment in capitalistic economies. In his *General Theory of Employment, Interest, and Money*[5] Keynes virtually knocked the props out from under the classical view and, in doing so, touched off a major revolution in economic thinking on the question of unemployment. Though Keynes fathered "the new economics," many others have since refined and extended his work. In this and the following chapter we are concerned with modern employment theory as it stands today.

Modern employment theory contrasts sharply with the classical position. Its blunt conclusion is that capitalism simply does not contain any mechanisms capable of guaranteeing full employment. The economy, it is argued, might come to rest—that is, reach an aggregate output equilibrium—with either considerable unemployment or severe inflation. Full employment accompanied by a relatively stable level of prices is more of an accident than a norm. Capitalism is not a self-regulating system capable of perpetual prosperity; capitalism cannot be depended upon to "run itself." Furthermore, depressions should not be associated exclusively with external forces such as wars, droughts, and similar abnormalities. Rather the causes of unemployment and inflation lie to a very considerable degree in the failure of certain fundamental economic decisions—in particular, saving and investment decisions—to be completely synchronized in a capitalistic system. Internal in addition to external forces contribute to economic instability.

[5] New York: Harcourt, Brace & World, Inc., 1936.

Modern employment theorists back these sweeping contentions by rejecting the very mechanisms upon which the classical position is grounded—the interest rate and price-wage adjustments.

The Unlinking of Saving and Investment Plans

Modern employment theory rejects Say's Law by seriously questioning the ability of the interest rate to synchronize the saving and investment plans of households and businesses. The fact that modern capitalism is amply endowed with an elaborate money market involving innumerable banking and financial institutions does not diminish this skepticism of the interest rate as a mechanism capable of connecting the saving drain and the investment spigot. Most untenable was the classical contention that businessmen would invest more when households increased their rates of saving. After all, doesn't more saving mean less consumption? Can we really expect businessmen to expand their capital facilities as the markets for their products shrink? More generally, the modern view holds that savers and investors are essentially distinct groups that formulate their saving and investment plans for different reasons which, in each instance, are largely unrelated to the rate of interest.

1. Savers and investors are different groups. Who decides the amounts to be saved and invested in a capitalistic economy? (We continue to ignore government in our discussion.) Business organizations of all kinds and descriptions, and in particular corporations, make the vast majority of investment decisions. And who makes the saving decisions? Here the picture is a bit more cluttered. In a wealthy economy such as that of American capitalism, households save substantial amounts—at least when prosperity prevails (table on inside covers, line 18). It is true, of course, that business corporations also do a considerable amount of saving in the form of undistributed corporate profits. The important point is that to a significant degree saving and investment decisions are made by different groups of individuals (see footnote 1 of this chapter).

2. Savers and investors are differently motivated. Now the nonidentity of savers and investors would not necessarily be fatal to the classical theory if their decisions were motivated and synchronized by some common factor such as the interest rate. But this is simply not the case. Saving decisions are motivated by several considerations. Some save in order to make large purchases which exceed any single paycheck; households save to make down payments on automobiles or to buy television sets and automatic washers. Some saving is simply for the convenience of having a pool of liquid funds readily available to take advantage of any extraordinarily good buys which one may chance upon. Or saving may occur to provide for the future needs of an individual and his family: Households save to provide for the future retirement of the family breadwinner or to expose the offspring to the rigors of a college education. Or saving may be a precautionary, rainy-day measure—a means of protecting oneself against such unpredictable events as prolonged illness and unemployment. Or saving may simply be a deeply ingrained habit that is practiced on an almost automatic basis with no specific purposes in mind.

Regardless of specific motivation, the modern view emphasizes that the total amount which households desire to save is governed primarily by the level of national income, not by the rate of interest.[6] In particular, a higher level of income will mean a high volume of both saving and consumption for households individually and as a group. When income is low, households must spend their entire incomes to achieve an acceptable standard of living; indeed, low incomes may give rise to dissaving. Higher incomes, however, permit households to increase both consumption and the level of saving.

Why do businesses purchase capital goods? The motivation for investment spending, as we shall discover in a few pages, is complex. The interest rate—the cost of obtaining money capital with which to invest—undoubtedly is a consideration in formulating investment plans. But the interest rate is not the most important factor. The rate of profit which businessmen expect to realize on the investment is the really crucial determinant of the amounts businessmen desire to invest. As a matter of fact, the investment plans of businesses are generally rather insensitive to changes in the interest rate. In particular, during the downswing of the business cycle, profit expectations will be so bleak that the level of investment will be low and possibly declining despite substantial reductions in the interest rates. Interest rate reductions are not likely to stimulate investment spending when increases in saving (declines in consumption) make it most sorely needed. Furthermore, if interest rates are relatively low to start with, as they typically are in industrially advanced economies, it simply is not possible for further significant declines to occur.

It is also significant that investors are not entirely dependent upon the current supply of saving in obtaining money capital. We

[6] Even if the interest rate were to affect significantly the desire to save, there is no guarantee that households would want to save larger amounts at higher interest rates, as the classical economists presumed. To illustrate: If the interest rate is currently 3 per cent, a household will need to save $10,000 to provide a retirement income of $300 per year. If the interest rate rises to 6 per cent and the household decides that $300 is still a satisfactory retirement income, savings can be cut from $10,000 to only $5,000. A higher interest rate may result in less, not more, saving.

shall find in Chapter 17 that commercial banks do not merely transfer money capital from savers to investors but rather can actually create money by granting loans. This correctly implies that businesses may attempt to invest at a rate in excess of the amount households currently desire to save.

The modern position is that saving and investment plans can be at odds and thereby result in fluctuations in total output, total income, and the volume of employment. It is largely a matter of chance that households and businesses will desire to save and invest identical amounts. Modern economists have proved themselves better plumbers than their classical predecessors by recognizing that the saving drain and the investment spigot are not connected.

The Discrediting of Price-Wage Flexibility

But what of the second aspect of the classical position—the contention that downward price-wage adjustments will eliminate the unemployment effects of a decline in total spending?

1. Price-wage flexibility, modern theorists argue, simply does not exist to the degree necessary for ensuring the restoration of full employment in the face of a decline in total spending. The price system of modern capitalism is no longer a perfectly competitive one; rather it is riddled by market imperfections and circumscribed by practical and political obstacles which work against downward price-wage flexibility. To be specific, monopolistic producers, dominating many important product markets, will have both the ability and the desire to resist falling product prices as demand declines. And in the resource markets strong labor unions are equally persistent in holding the line against wage cuts. In this endeavor they are ably assisted by minimum-wage legislation, public opinion as to what are reasonable and "customary"

wage rates, and practical-minded politicians who are well aware of the power of labor at the polls. In short, as a practical matter downward price-wage flexibility cannot be expected to offset the unemployment effects of a decline in total spending.

2. Furthermore, even if price-wage declines accompanied a contraction of total spending, it is doubtful that these declines would help reduce unemployment. The reason? The volume of total money demand cannot remain constant as prices and wages decline. That is, lower prices and wages necessarily mean lower money incomes, and lower money incomes in turn entail further reductions in total spending. The net result is likely to be little or no change in the depressed levels of output and employment.

The modern view points out that the classicists were tripped up in their reasoning by the fallacy of composition. Because any particular group of workers typically buy only a small amount of what they produce, the product and therefore labor demand curves of a single firm can be regarded as independent of any wage (income) changes accorded its own workers. In other words it is correct to reason that a decline in its wage rate will move a *single firm* down its stable labor demand curve and result in more workers hired, that is, more employment. But the same reasoning, argue modern economists, is not applicable to the economy as a whole, to general wage cuts. Why? Because wages are the major source of income in the economy. Widespread wage declines will therefore result in declines in incomes and in the demand for both products and the labor used in producing them. The result is that employers will hire little additional labor (conceivably less labor) after the general wage cuts than they did before. What holds true for a single firm—a wage cut for its employees will not adversely affect labor demand—does not hold true for the economy as a whole—general wage cuts will lower money incomes and cause the demand for products and labor to decline generally.

To summarize: Modern theorists argue that, in the first place, prices and wages are in fact not flexible downward and, secondly, even if they were, it is doubtful that price-wage declines would alleviate widespread unemployment.

TOOLS OF MODERN EMPLOYMENT THEORY

By rejecting the analysis of the classical economists, we are in effect recognizing that there is no automatic mechanism with the capacity to make full employment the normal state of affairs in a capitalistic system. Yet the question remains: How are the levels of output and employment determined in modern capitalism?

The touchstone of any meaningful answer is that *the amount of goods and services produced and therefore the level of employment depend directly upon the level of total spending.* Subject to the economy's productive potential as determined by the scarce resources available to it, businessmen will produce that level of output which they can profitably sell. Men and machinery are idled when there are no markets for the goods and services they are capable of producing. Total spending, on the one hand, and total output and employment, on the other, vary directly. Therefore in explaining the economy's output-employment levels, we must obviously begin by examining the consumption and investment components of total spending.

CONSUMPTION AND SAVING

In terms of absolute size, consumption is the main component of total spending (see Figure 7–4). It is therefore of obvious importance to understand the major determinants of consumption spending. Because saving is "not spending," we simultaneously explore the determinants of saving.

Income-Consumption and Income-Saving Relationships

There are many considerations which influence the level of consumer spending. But common sense and available statistical data both suggest that the most important determinant of consumer spending is income—in particular, disposable income. And, of course, since saving is that part of disposable income which is not consumed, DI is also the basic determinant of personal saving.

As shown in Figure 12–2, national income statistics for the 1929–1964 period indicate that consumption and disposable income are directly related. As income rises, so does consumption; as income falls, so does consumption. We exclude here the war years, because the unavailability of certain consumer goods and the strong patriotic appeals to save made consumption abnormally low and saving unusually high. The straight line drawn through these points indicates the general nature of the relationship between consumption and disposable income. The blue 45-degree line is added to the diagram as a point of reference. Because this line bisects the 90-degree angle formed by the vertical and horizontal axes of the graph, each point on the 45-degree line must be equidistant from the two axes. Hence, all the dots falling on the 45-degree line indicate years in which households consumed all their disposable incomes. Points lying below the line indicate years in which disposable incomes exceeded consumption, that is, saving occurred. Those several points which are slightly above the 45-degree line indicate depression years in which households consumed slightly in excess of their disposable incomes, that is, dissaving occurred. The vertical distance of any dot below or above the 45-degree line measures the amount of saving or dissaving in that year.

Figure 12–2 does more than suggest a direct relationship between disposable income and consumption. The position of the

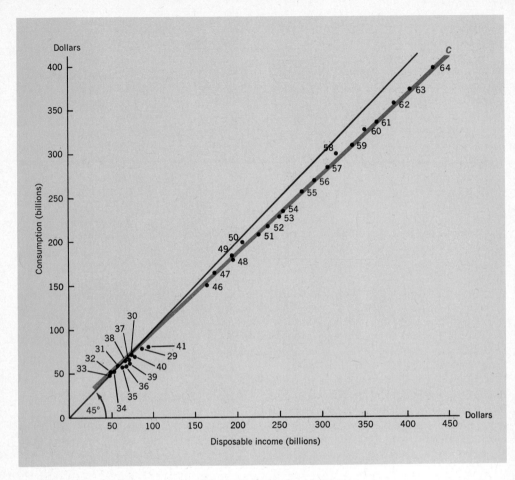

FIGURE 12–2. CONSUMPTION AND DISPOSABLE INCOME, 1929–1964.
Each dot in this figure shows disposable income and consumption expenditures in a
given year. All points on the 45-degree guideline indicate the situation in which
consumption and DI are equal. Thus dots falling below the 45-degree line indicate
that saving has occurred; dots above indicate dissaving. The C line generalizes on
the relationship between consumption and DI. It suggests that households spend
a larger portion of a small income than they do of a large income.
(U.S. Department of Commerce data.)

straight line C, which generalizes on the
income-consumption relationship, suggests
that households will spend a larger portion
of a small income than they will of a large
income. Or, in terms of saving, the data
suggest that households will save a smaller
portion of a small income than they will
of a large income.

Consumption Schedule and Saving Schedule

Figure 12–2 merely shows the amounts
households *actually did consume* (and
save) at the various levels of DI which
existed over an extended period of years.
Over this period of years changes in a good

many factors other than the level of DI itself undoubtedly occurred which affected the specific amounts consumed and saved at each of the DI levels. Because of the possible influence of nonincome determinants of consumption and saving, the income-consumption relationship of Figure 12–2 is not particularly useful as an analytic tool. What we need for analytical purposes is an income-consumption relationship—a consumption schedule—which shows the various amounts households will *plan* or *desire to consume* at various possible DI levels over some relatively short period of time wherein it is safe to assume other nonincome determinants are constant. The consumption schedule, you will note, is similar to the demand schedule discussed in Chapter 4, which shows how much of a particular product a group of buyers intend, or plan, to buy at each of the various possible prices at which the product might sell. The demand schedule was drawn up,

remember, on the supposition that nonprice determinants of the amount demanded were constant.

A hypothetical *consumption schedule* of the type we require is shown in columns 1 and 2 of Table 12–1. This schedule is plotted in Figure 12–3a. Now while this schedule is a theoretical relationship, it certainly makes sense in the absence of factual information to the contrary to draw it so it embodies the income-consumption relationships of Figure 12–2. The relationship between consumption and DI is direct, and, in addition, households will spend a *larger* proportion of a small DI than of a large DI.

It is a simple task to derive a *saving schedule*. Because disposable income equals consumption plus saving, we need only subtract consumption from disposable income to find the amount saved at each level of DI. Hence, columns 1 and 3 of Table 12–1 constitute the saving schedule. This sched-

TABLE 12–1. THE CONSUMPTION AND SAVING SCHEDULES (hypothetical data in billions)

(1) Level of output and income (NNP = DI)	(2) Consumption	(3) Saving, or (1) − (2)	(4) Average propensity to consume (APC) (2) ÷ (1)	(5) Average propensity to save (APS) (3) ÷ (1)	(6) Marginal propensity to consume (MPC) Δ (2)/Δ (1)	(7) Marginal propensity to save (MPS) Δ (3)/Δ (1)
$370	$375	$−5	1.01	−.01		
					.75	.25
390	390	0	1.00	0		
					.75	.25
410	405	5	.99	.01		
					.75	.25
430	420	10	.98	.02		
					.75	.25
450	435	15	.97	.03		
					.75	.25
470	450	20	.96	.04		
					.75	.25
490	465	25	.95	.05		
					.75	.25
510	480	30	.94	.06		
					.75	.25
530	495	35	.93	.07		

ule is plotted in Figure 12–3b. Note that there is a direct relationship between saving and DI but that saving constitutes a smaller proportion of a small DI than it does of a large DI. If households consume a smaller and smaller proportion of DI as DI goes up, they must save a larger and larger proportion.

Remembering that each point on the 45-degree line indicates an equality of DI and consumption, we see that dissaving would occur at the relatively low DI of $370 billion; that is, households will consume in excess of their current incomes by drawing down accumulated savings or by borrowing. Graphically, the vertical distance the consumption schedule lies *above* the 45-degree line is equal to the vertical distance the saving schedule lies *below* the horizontal axis at the $370 billion level of output and income (see Figure 12–3a and b). In this instance these two vertical distances each measure the $5 billion of *dissaving* which occurs at the $370 billion income level. At the $390 billion income level, households will "break even" by spending their entire incomes. Graphically, the consumption schedule cuts the 45-degree line, and the saving schedule cuts the horizontal axis at this income level. At all higher incomes households will plan to save a portion of their income. The vertical distance of the consumption schedule below the 45-degree line measures this saving, as does the vertical distance of the saving schedule above the horizontal axis. For example, at the $410 billion level of income both these distances indicate $5 billion worth of saving (see Figure 12–3a and b).

Average and Marginal Propensities

Columns 4 to 7 of Table 12–1 point up additional characteristics of the consumption and saving schedules.

That fraction, or percentage, of any given total income which is consumed is called the *average propensity to consume* (APC), and that fraction of any total income which is saved is called the *average propensity to save* (APS). For example, at the $470 billion level of income in Table 12–1 the APC is 45/47 or about 96 per cent, while the APS is obviously 2/47 or about 4 per cent. By calculating the APC and APS at each of the nine levels of DI shown in Table 12–1, we find that the APC falls and the APS rises as DI increases. The fraction of total DI which is consumed declines as DI rises, and this makes it essential that the fraction of DI which is saved rises as DI rises.

The fact that households consume a certain portion of some given total income—for example, 45/47 of a $470 billion disposable income—does not guarantee that they will consume the same proportion of any *change* in income which they might receive. The proportion, or fraction, of any change in income which is consumed is called the *marginal propensity to consume* (MPC), marginal meaning "extra." Or, alternatively stated, the MPC is the ratio of a change in consumption to the change in income which brought the consumption increase about; that is

$$\text{MPC} = \frac{\text{change in consumption}}{\text{change in income}}$$

FIGURE 12–3. CONSUMPTION AND SAVING SCHEDULES.
The two parts of this figure show the income-consumption and income-saving relationships graphically. Each point on the 45-degree line in (a) indicates an equality of DI and consumption. Therefore, because saving equals DI minus consumption, the saving schedule in (b) is found by subtracting the consumption schedule from the 45-degree guideline. Consumers "break even," that is, consumption equals DI (and saving therefore equals zero) at $390 billion for these hypothetical data.

(a)

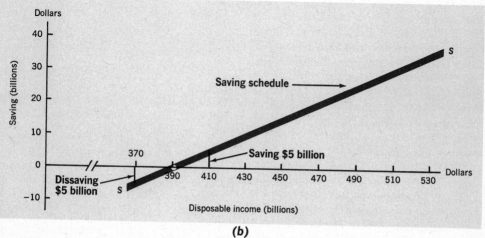

(b)

The fraction of any change in income which is saved is called the *marginal propensity to save* (MPS). That is, MPS is the ratio of a change in saving to the change in income which brought it about:

$$\text{MPS} = \frac{\text{change in saving}}{\text{change in income}}$$

Thus, if disposable income is currently $470 billion and households for some reason find that their incomes rise by $20 billion, we find that they will consume $^{15}\!/_{20}$ or $^3\!/_4$ and save $^5\!/_{20}$ or $^1\!/_4$ of that increase in income (see Table 12–1). In other words the MPC is $^3\!/_4$ or 75 per cent, and the MPS is $^1\!/_4$ or 25 per cent. The sum of the MPC and the MPS for any given change in disposable income must always be 1. That is, consuming and saving out of extra income is an either-or proposition; that fraction of any increase in income which is not spent is, by definition, saved. Therefore the fraction consumed (MPC) plus the fraction saved (MPS) must exhaust the whole increase in income. In our example 75 per cent plus 25 per cent equals 100 per cent, or 1.

Economists are not in complete agreement as to the behavior of the MPC and MPS as income increases. For many years it was presumed that the MPC declined and the MPS increased as income increased. That is, it was felt that a smaller and smaller fraction of increases in income would be consumed and a larger and larger fraction of these increases would be saved. Many economists now feel that the MPC and MPS for the economy as a whole are relatively constant. Statistical data such as those of Figure 12–2 support this position. We will assume the MPC and MPS to be constant not only because of this statistical evidence but also because a constant MPC and MPS will simplify our analysis considerably. You will note that for each of the eight $20 billion income increases shown in Table 12–1, consumption increases by $15 billion, that is by $^{15}\!/_{20}$ or $^3\!/_4$ of the increase in income, and saving increases by $5 bil-

lion, that is, by $^5\!/_{20}$ or $^1\!/_4$ of the increase in income. We assume the MPC and MPS to be constant at $^3\!/_4$ and $^1\!/_4$, respectively (see columns 6 and 7).[7]

Nonincome Determinants of Consumption and Saving

The level of disposable income is the basic determinant of the amounts households will consume and save, just as price is the basic determinant of the quantity demanded of

[7] The mathematically inclined reader will recognize that the MPC is the numerical value of the slope of the consumption schedule and the MPS is the numerical value of the slope of the saving schedule. The slope of any line can be measured by the ratio of the vertical change to the horizontal change involved in moving from one point to another point on that line. Thus, in the accompanying diagram, if the vertical change is 15 and the horizontal change is

20, between points A and B, the slope of the line is $^3\!/_4$. Now it is evident in the figure that the slope of the consumption schedule between any two points is measured by the change in consumption (the vertical change) relative to the change in income (the horizontal change). And this ratio, change in consumption/change in income, is the fraction of any change in income that is spent; that is, it measures the MPC. Similar reasoning tells us that the MPS measures the slope of the saving schedule.

any product. You will recall that changes in determinants other than price, such as consumer tastes, incomes, and so forth (Chapter 4), will cause the demand curve for a given product to shift location. Similarly, there are certain determinants other than income which might cause households to consume more or less at each possible level of DI and thereby change the locations of the consumption and saving schedules.

1. Stocks of liquid assets. Generally speaking, the greater the amounts of liquid assets —private and public bonds, stocks, insurance policies, bank accounts, and so forth— owned by consumers, the greater will be their willingness to consume at each possible level of DI. The ownership of liquid assets makes households feel more secure financially and hence more willing to spend out of current disposable income.

2. Stocks of durable goods on hand. If the economy has enjoyed an extended period of prosperity, consumers may find themselves well supplied with various durable goods. That is, the majority of families may own late-model cars, television sets, refrigerators, and other household appliances, all worthy of many years of future service. Hence, for a time many households will be "out of the market" for such products, with the result that consumers are willing to spend less and save more at each possible level of disposable income.

It is relevant to note that the "buying binge" that followed World War II can be largely explained in terms of the prolonged curtailment of durable consumer goods production and the spectacular increases in consumer incomes and liquid asset holdings which occurred during the war years of the early 1940s.

3. Expectations concerning incomes, prices, and product availability. Household expectations concerning future prices, money incomes, and the availability of goods may have a significant impact upon current spending and saving. Expectations of rising prices and product shortages tend to trigger more spending and less saving currently. Why? Because it is natural for consumers to seek to avoid paying higher prices or to be faced with the possibility of "doing without." Expected inflation and shortages induce people to "buy now" to escape higher future prices and bare shelves. Anticipated increases in money incomes bolster this tendency. The expectation of rising money incomes in the future tends to make consumers more footloose in their current spending.

Conversely, expected price declines, anticipations of shrinking incomes, and the feeling that goods will be abundantly available may induce consumers to retrench on their consumption and build up their savings.

4. Consumer indebtedness. The level of consumer credit can also be expected to affect the willingness of households to consume out of current income. If households are in debt to the degree that, say, 20 or 25 per cent of their current incomes are committed to installment payments on previous purchases, consumers may well be obliged to retrench on current consumption in order to reduce their indebtedness. Conversely, if consumer indebtedness is relatively low, households may consume at an unusually high rate by increasing this indebtedness.

5. Attitudes toward thrift. A final catchall item: An economy's general attitude toward frugality will help determine the amount of consumption and saving forthcoming at each possible level of DI. Attitudes toward thrift are governed as much by social and psychological considerations as they are by economic factors. If a society accepts the belief that saving is very virtuous and that "a dollar saved is a dollar earned," saving will tend to be greater and consumption less at each level of disposable income than would be the case where saving was held in lower esteem. There is some evidence to suggest that in the underdeveloped countries attitudes toward thrift are relatively weak, as most households are very anxious to consume in order to emulate the higher living standards of the more advanced nations.

Attitudes toward thrift can be influenced by government policies. During World War II the Federal government waged intensive propaganda campaigns to encourage households to save by buying war bonds. These campaigns—coupled with the hard fact that many consumer durables were unavailable or in scant supply—were fairly successful in boosting the saving schedule and therefore in lowering the consumption schedule. Peacetime government policies may also affect the consumption and saving schedules. By committing itself to policies designed to promote full employment, government may diminish the fear of unemployment and thereby weaken an important motive to save money.

6. Taxation. We shall find later in discussing fiscal policy that changes in taxes may shift the consumption and saving schedules through their impact upon disposable income.

Two final points are relevant to this discussion. First, the movement from one point to another on a given stable consumption schedule (for example, A to B on C_0 in Figure 12–4a) is called a *change in the amount consumed*. The sole cause of this change in the amount consumed is a change in the level of disposable income. On the other hand, a *change in the con-sumption schedule* refers to an upward or downward shift of the entire schedule, for example, from C_0 to C_1 or C_2 in Figure 12–4a. A relocation of the consumption schedule is obviously caused by changes in any one or more of the nonincome determinants just discussed. A similar terminological distinction applies to the saving schedule.

A second related point is that the consumption and saving schedules will necessarily shift in opposite directions. If households decide to consume *more* at each possible level of disposable income, this means that they want to save *less*, and vice versa. Graphically, if the consumption schedule shifts upward from C_0 to C_1 in Figure 12–4, the saving schedule will shift downward from S_0 to S_1. Similarly, a down-shift in the consumption schedule from C_0 to C_2 means an upshift in the saving schedule from S_0 to S_2.

Economists are in general agreement that the consumption and saving schedules are quite stable. This may be because consumption-saving decisions are strongly influenced by habit or because changes in the nonincome determinants frequently work in opposite directions and therefore tend to be self-canceling.

INVESTMENT

Now let us turn to the second component of private spending. What determines the rate of net investment spending? That is, what determines the amounts businesses want or plan to spend on additional machinery and equipment, new construction, and increases in inventories?

FIGURE 12–4. SHIFTS IN THE CONSUMPTION AND SAVING SCHEDULES. A change in any one or more of the nonincome determinants will cause the consumption and saving schedules to shift. If households consume more at each level of DI, they are necessarily saving less. Graphically this means that an upshift in the consumption schedule (C_0 to C_1) entails a downshift in saving schedule (S_0 to S_1). Conversely, if households consume less at each level of DI, they are saving more. A downshift in the consumption schedule (C_0 to C_2) is reflected in an upshift of the saving schedule (S_0 to S_2).

(a)

(b)

Determinants of Investment: Profit Expectations

The simplest answer to this query is that business investment is based upon the *expected net profits* which businesses hope to realize from such spending. But what are some of the more important factors which influence profit expectations?

1. Technological advance and innovation. Innovation—the development of new products and new techniques of production—is a major force underlying the level of investment. By putting innovating firms one jump ahead of competitors, new products frequently entail substantial profits. Realizing this, firms are anxious to invest in the capital equipment needed to produce these new products. Similarly, improved production methods mean lower costs and higher profits, and this too is conducive to a high rate of investment. In short, a rapid rate of innovation is conducive to a high level of investment, and vice versa.

2. Acquisition, maintenance, and operating costs. The initial costs of capital goods, along with the estimated costs of operating and maintaining those goods, are obviously important considerations in gauging the profitability of any particular investment. To the extent that these costs are high, expected *net* profits will be low and the level of investment will also be low. If these costs are relatively low, expected net profits and the level of investment will tend to be high. Note that the wage policies of unions affect profit expectations, because wage rates are clearly an operating cost.

3. The interest rate. The interest rate is a special type of cost involved in acquiring capital goods. Interest is a cost payment which investors must make in acquiring the money capital needed to negotiate the purchase of real capital. The higher this cost, the less the expected net profit on investment and hence the lower the level

of investment. The lower the interest cost, the greater the expected profits and thus the higher the level of investment spending.

4. Government policies. There is little doubt that taxes affect profit expectations and the level of investment. Businessmen look to estimated profits *after taxes* in making their investment decisions. Taxes, as an added cost of doing business, tend to dampen profit expectations and retard investment spending.

The impact of government expenditures upon the profit expectations of private firms is difficult to assess. In some cases government spending, by stimulating particular firms and industries and by alleviating depressed business conditions, improves profit expectations. On the other hand, certain types of government spending—for example, the development of public power— allegedly cause the profit expectations of private power producers to deteriorate, thereby retarding investment.

5. The stock of capital goods on hand. Just as the stock of consumer goods on hand affects household consumption-saving decisions, so the stock of capital goods on hand influences expected profits from additional investment in a given industry. To the extent that a given industry is well stocked with productive facilities and inventories of finished goods, investment will be retarded in that industry. The reason is obvious: Such an industry will be amply equipped to fulfill present and future market demand at prices which yield mediocre profits. If an industry has enough productive capacity or even excess productive capacity, profit expectations and further investment in that industry will not be appealing.

6. Expectations. We noted earlier that business investment is based upon *expected* profits. Capital goods are durable—they may have a life expectancy of ten or twenty years—and thus the profitability of any capital investment will depend upon businessmen's expectations of the *future* sales and *future* profitability of the product which the capital helps produce. To some significant degree the expectations of businessmen are a projection of current business conditions. If business is currently good, businessmen will tend to be optimistic about the future and will be quite willing to invest at a high level. Poor current business conditions will be conducive to dismal expectations with respect to future profits and therefore a low level of investment.

Investment and Income

In order to compare the investment decisions of businesses with the consumption-saving plans of households, we want to express investment plans in terms of the level of disposable income or NNP. That is, we want to construct an *investment schedule* which shows the amounts which businessmen as a group plan or intend to invest at each of the various possible levels of income or output. Such a schedule will mirror the investment plans or intentions of businessmen in the same way the consumption and saving schedules reflect the consumption and saving plans of households.

We shall assume in our analysis that business investment is geared to long-term profit expectations as influenced by such considerations as technological progress, population growth, and so forth, and therefore is autonomous or independent of the level of current income. In particular, our discussion will presume that the same amount of investment spending—say $20 billion—will be forthcoming at every level of income as reflected in columns 1 and 2 of Table 12–2 and I_n in Figure 12–5. This assumed independence of investment and the level of income is admittedly a simplification. A higher level of current income may well have a modest impact upon investment; a higher level of business activity may induce some investment spending on capital facilities as suggested by columns 1 and 3 of Table 12–2 and I'_n

TABLE 12–2. THE INVESTMENT SCHEDULE

(1) Level of output and income, billions	(2) Investment, billions, I_n	(3) Investment, billions, I'_n
$370	$20	$10
390	20	12
410	20	14
430	20	16
450	20	18
470	20	20
490	20	22
510	20	24
530	20	26

in Figure 12–5. Our simplification, however, is not too severely at odds with reality and will greatly facilitate later analysis.

Instability of Investment

In contrast to consumption, investment is unstable. Proportionately investment is the most volatile component of total spending (see Figure 12–6). Some of the more important factors which explain this variability are as follows:

1. Durability. Because of their durability, capital goods have a rather indefinite useful life. Within limits purchases of capital goods are discretionary and therefore postponable. Older equipment or buildings can be scrapped and entirely replaced, on the one hand, or patched up and used for a few more years, on the other. Optimism about the future may prompt businessmen to replace their older facilities, that is, to modernize their plants, and this obviously means a high level of investment. A slightly less optimistic view, however, may lead to very small amounts of investment as older facilities are repaired and kept in use.

2. Irregularity of innovation. We have noted that technological progress is a major determinant of investment. New products

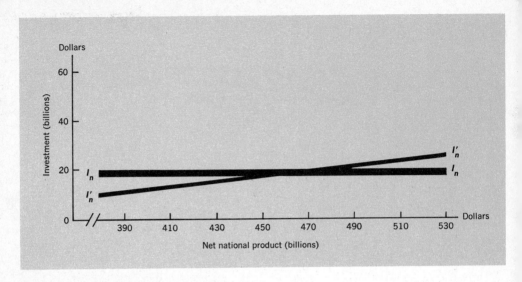

FIGURE 12–5. THE INVESTMENT SCHEDULE.
Our discussion will be facilitated by employing the investment schedule I_n, which assumes that the investment plans of businessmen are independent of the current level of income. Actually the investment schedule may be slightly upsloping, as suggested by I'_n.

and new processes provide a major stimulus to investment. However, history suggests that major innovations—railroads, electricity, automobiles, and so forth—occur quite irregularly, and when they do occur, these innovations induce a vast upsurge or "wave" of investment spending which in time recedes. To illustrate: The widespread acceptance of the automobile in the 1920s not only brought about substantial increases in investment in the automobile industry itself, but, as mentioned in our treatment of the prosperous twenties, also induced tremendous amounts of investment in such related industries as steel, petroleum, glass, and rubber, not to mention public investment in streets and highways. But when investment in these related industries was ultimately completed—that is, when they had created capital facilities sufficient to meet the needs of the automobile industry—total investment fell sharply.

3. Variability of profits. We know that businessmen invest only when they feel it

will be profitable to do so and that, to a significant degree, the expectation of future profitability is influenced by the size of current profits. Current profits, however, are themselves highly variable (Figures 7–1 and 7–2). Hence the variability of profits contributes to the volatile nature of the incentive to invest. Furthermore, the instability of profits may also cause investment fluctuations, because profits are a major source of funds for business investment. American businesses tend to prefer this internal source of financing to increases in external debt or stock issue. In short, expanding profits give businessmen both greater incentives and greater means to invest; declining profits have the reverse effects. The fact that actual profits are variable adds to the instability of investment.

4. Variability of expectations. We have already discussed how the durability of capital equipment results in the making of investment decisions upon the basis of *expected* net profits. Now, while there is a

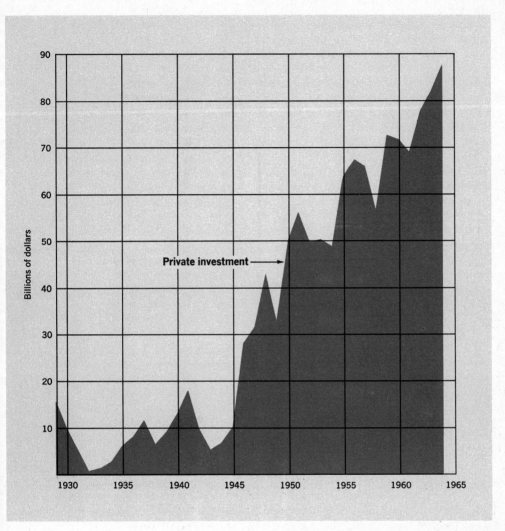

FIGURE 12–6. INSTABILITY OF INVESTMENT.
Private investment spending has varied sharply over time and therefore has been the
major cause of fluctuations in total spending, total output, employment,
and the price level.

tendency for businessmen to project current business conditions into the future, it is equally true that expectations are sometimes subject to radical revision when some event or combination of events suggests a significant change in future business conditions. What kinds of events make business confidence so capricious? Changes in the domestic political climate, cold-war de-velopments, changes in population growth and therefore anticipated market demand, court decisions in key labor or antitrust cases, legislative actions, strikes, changes in governmental economic policies, and a host of similar considerations may give rise to waves of business optimism or pes-simism.

The stock market merits specific comment in this regard. Businessmen frequently look to the stock market as an index or barometer of the overall confidence of society in future business conditions; a rising "bull" market signifies public confidence in the business future, whereas a falling "bear" market implies a lack of confidence. The stock market, however, is a highly speculative market, and initially modest changes in stock prices can be seriously intensified by less-informed participants who jump on the bandwagon by buying when prices begin to rise and by selling when stock prices start to fall. Recall our discussion in Chapter 11 of the important psychological repercussions of the 1929 stock market crash. Furthermore, by affecting the relative attractiveness of new capital as opposed to purchasing ownership claims (stock) to existing capital facilities, upsurges and slumps in stock values also affect the level of investment.

For these and similar reasons it is quite correct to associate most fluctuations in output and employment with changes in investment spending rather than changes in consumption. In terms of Figure 12–5 we can think of this volatility as being reflected in frequent and substantial upward and downward shifts in the investment schedule.

SUMMARY

1. Classical employment theory envisioned laissez-faire capitalism as being capable of providing virtually continuous full employment. This analysis was based on Say's Law and price-wage flexibility.

2. The classical economists argued that because supply creates its own demand, general overproduction was impossible. This conclusion was held to be valid even when saving occurred, because the interest rate would automatically synchronize the saving plans of households and the investment plans of businesses.

3. Classical employment theory also held that even if temporary declines in total spending were to occur, these declines

would be compensated for by downward price-wage adjustments to the end that real output, employment, and real income would not decline.

4. Modern employment theory rejects the notion that the interest rate would equate saving and investment by pointing out that savers and investors are substantially different groups who make their saving and investment decisions for different reasons—reasons which are largely unrelated to the interest rate.

5. Modern economists discredit price-wage flexibility on both practical and theoretical grounds. They argue that **a.** union and business monopolies, minimum wage legislation, and a host of related factors have virtually eliminated the possibility of substantial price-wage reductions and **b.** price-wage cuts will lower total income and therefore the demand for labor.

6. The basic tools of modern employment theory are the consumption, saving, and investment schedules, which show the various amounts households intend to consume and save and businesses plan to invest at the various possible income-output levels.

7. The locations of the consumption and saving schedules are determined by such factors as **a.** the amounts of liquid assets owned by households, **b.** the stocks of durables consumers have on hand, **c.** expectations of future income, future prices, and product availability, **d.** the relative size of consumer indebtedness, **e.** overall attitudes toward thrift and **f.** taxation. The consumption and saving schedules are relatively stable.

8. The *average* propensities to consume and save show the proportion or fraction of any level of *total* income that is consumed and saved. The *marginal* propensities to consume and save show the proportion or fraction of any *change* in total income that is consumed or saved.

9. The immediate determinant of investment spending is net profit expectation. This expectation is influenced by such objective factors as **a.** technological advance,

b. the acquisition, maintenance, and operating costs of real capital, **c.** the interest rate, **d.** government policies, **e.** the stocks of capital on hand, and **f.** expectations of future business conditions.

10. The durability of capital goods, the irregular occurrence of major innovations, profit volatility, and the variability of expectations all contribute to the high degree of instability of investment spending.

QUESTIONS AND STUDY SUGGESTIONS

1. What is Say's Law? Explain the classical economists' conclusion that Say's Law would prevail even in an economy where substantial saving occurred. What arguments have modern economists used to undermine the classical view that Say's Law would result in sustained full employment?
2. "Unemployment can be avoided so long as businesses are willing to accept lower product prices, and workers to accept lower wage rates." Critically evaluate.
3. Define (*a*) the average propensities to consume and save and (*b*) the marginal propensities to consume and save. How do these two sets of concepts differ? Why must the sum of the MPC and the MPS equal 1?
4. What are the basic determinants of the consumption-saving schedules? Of your own level of consumption? What are the basic determinants of investment? Why is the investment schedule less stable than the consumption-saving schedules?
5. Explain precisely what relationships are shown by (*a*) the consumption schedule, (*b*) the saving schedule, and (*c*) the investment schedule.
6. Complete the following table:

Level of output and income (NNP = DI)	Consumption	Saving
$240	$	$-4
260		0
280		4
300		8
320		12
340		16
360		20
380		24
400		28

a. Show the consumption and saving schedules graphically.
b. Determine the average propensity to consume and the average propensity to save for each level of income.
c. Now determine the MPC and MPS for each change in the income level.
d. Locate the break-even point. How is it possible for households to dissave at very low income levels?
e. If the proportion of total income which is consumed decreases and

the proportion which is saved increases as income rises, explain both verbally and graphically how the MPC and MPS can be relatively constant at various levels of income.

7. Explain how each of the following will affect the consumption and saving schedules or the investment schedule:
a. A decline in the amount of government bonds which consumers are holding; **b.** The threat of limited, nonnuclear war in Southeast Asia, leading the public to expect future shortages of consumer durables; **c.** A decline in the interest rate; **d.** A sharp decline in stock prices; **e.** An increase in the rate of population growth; **f.** The development of a significantly cheaper method of manufacturing pig iron from ore; **g.** The announcement that the social security program is to be expanded in terms of both coverage and size of benefits; **h.** The expectation that mild inflation will persist in the next decade.

8. Explain why an upshift in the consumption schedule necessarily involves an equal downshift in the saving schedule.

SELECTED REFERENCES

Chandler, Lester V.: *A Preface to Economics* (New York: Harper & Row, Publishers, Incorporated, 1947), chap. 7.

Dillard, Dudley: *The Economics of John Maynard Keynes* (Englewood Cliffs, N.J.: Prentice-Hall, Inc., 1948), chaps. 1, 2, and 12.

Galbraith, John Kenneth: *American Capitalism,* rev. ed. (Boston: Houghton Mifflin Company, 1956), chaps. 1–6.

Hague, Douglas C., and Alfred W. Stonier: *The Essentials of Economics* (New York: Longmans, Green & Co., Inc., 1955), chaps. 8 and 9.

Heilbroner, Robert L.: *The Worldly Philosophers,* rev. ed. (New York: Simon and Schuster, Inc., 1961), chap. 9.

Peterson, Wallace C.: *Income, Employment, and Economic Growth* (New York: W. W. Norton & Company, Inc., 1962), chap. 4.

Sirkin, Gerald: *Introduction to Macroeconomic Theory,* rev. ed. (Homewood, Ill.: Richard D. Irwin, Inc., 1965), chaps. 2–5.

CHAPTER 13

THE EQUILIBRIUM
LEVELS OF OUTPUT,
EMPLOYMENT, AND INCOME

This chapter is both a continuation and an expansion of Chapter 12. We seek, first, to use the consumption, saving, and investment schedules developed in Chapter 12 to explain the equilibrium levels of output, income, and employment. Next, changes in the equilibrium level of NNP are analyzed. We retain the simplifying assumptions of Chapter 12 which permitted us to equate NNP and DI until government is added to our discussion in Chapter 14.

We now have before us all the analytical tools necessary to explain the equilibrium levels of output, employment, and income. By *equilibrium output* we refer to that level of total output which, once achieved, will be sustained. It exists where the flow of income created by the production of the output gives rise to a level of total spending sufficient to clear the product market of that output. In pursuing the important task of determining and explaining the equilibrium level of output, two closely interrelated approaches—the *aggregate demand–aggregate supply* (or $C + I_n = NNP$) approach and the *saving-equals-investment* (or $S = I_n$) approach—will be employed. Both will be discussed tabularly and graphically.

AGGREGATE DEMAND–AGGREGATE SUPPLY APPROACH

Let us first analyze the aggregate demand–aggregate supply approach in terms of simple arithmetic data. Table 13–1 merely brings together the income-consumption and income-saving data of Table 12–1 and the simplified income-investment data of columns 1 and 2 in Table 12–2.

This table is in many respects similar to Table 4–6, the supply and demand table for a specific product. You will recall that the demand schedule shows the amount consumers plan to purchase, and the supply schedule the amount producers plan to offer, at various prices. The equilibrium price was located at the point where the quantity demanded and the quantity supplied were equal. Barring revisions in the buying plans of consumers or the selling plans of producers, price and the corresponding amount exchanged would not vary from their equilibrium levels. This same general type of reasoning can be applied to *aggregate* demand and *aggregate* supply with three notable differences. First, because total output is composed of heterogeneous goods, it is essential to state total supply in money terms rather than physical units. Second, the equilibrating factor is obviously the level of output and income rather than price. Third, and most important, it is quite accurate to regard the forces of supply and demand as playing equally important roles in determining the price of an individual product; changes in either supply or demand can alter equilibrium price. But in the case of aggregate equilibrium it is correct to envision aggregate demand as the crucial determining variable or force to

TABLE 13–1. DETERMINATION OF THE EQUILIBRIUM LEVELS OF EMPLOYMENT, OUTPUT, AND INCOME: THE PRIVATE SECTOR (hypothetical data)

(1) Possible levels of employment, millions	(2) Aggregate supply (output and income)* (NNP = DI), billions	(3) Consumption, billions	(4) Saving, billions	(5) Investment, billions	(6) Aggregate demand $(C + I_n)$, billions	(7) Tendency of employment, output, and incomes
40	$370	$375	$−5	$20	$395	Increase
45	390	390	0	20	410	Increase
50	410	405	5	20	425	Increase
55	430	420	10	20	440	Increase
60	450	435	15	20	455	Increase
65	470	450	20	20	470	Equilibrium
70	490	465	25	20	485	Decrease
75	510	480	30	20	500	Decrease
80	530	495	35	20	515	Decrease

* If government is ignored and it is assumed that all saving occurs in the household sector of the economy, NNP as a measure of aggregate supply is equal to NI, PI, and DI. This means that households receive a DI equal to the value of total output.

which the level of aggregate supply (NNP) adjusts. We should regard the aggregate supply schedule—the production intentions of businesses—as fixed and the actual amount produced by businessmen as responding to shifts in aggregate demand.

Column 2 of Table 13–1 is in effect the total, or aggregate, supply schedule for the economy. It indicates the various possible levels of total output—that is, the various possible NNPs—which the business sector of the economy might produce. *Producers are willing to offer each of these nine levels of output on the expectation that they will receive an identical amount of receipts of income from its sale.* That is, the business sector will produce $370 billion worth of output, thereby incurring $370 billion worth of wage, rent, interest, and profit costs, only if they expect that this output can be sold for $370 billion worth of receipts. Some $390 billion worth of output will be offered if businesses feel this output can be sold for $390 billion. And so it is for all the other possible levels of output.

The total, or aggregate, demand schedule is shown in column 6 of Table 13–1. It shows the total amount which will be spent at each possible output-income level. In dealing with the private sector of the economy the aggregate demand schedule simply shows the amount of consumption and net investment spending $(C + I_n)$ which will be forthcoming at each output-income level. We use net rather than gross investment because we are employing NNP rather than GNP as a measure of total output.

Now the question is this: Of the nine possible levels of NNP indicated in Table 13–1, which will be the equilibrium level? That is, which level of total output will the economy be capable of sustaining? The answer is: The equilibrium level of output is that output whose production will actually create total spending just sufficient to purchase that output. In other words, the equilibrium level of NNP is where the total quantity of goods supplied (NNP) is precisely equal to the total quantity of goods demanded $(C + I_n)$. Examination of the aggregate supply schedule of column 2 and the aggregate demand schedule of column 6 indicates that this equality exists only at the $470 billion level of NNP. This is the only level of output at which the economy is willing to spend precisely the amount necessary to take that output off the market. Here the annual rates of production and spending are in balance. There is no overproduction which results in a piling up of unsold goods and therefore cutbacks in the rate of production, nor is there an excess of total spending which draws down inventories and prompts increases in the rate of production. In short, there is no reason for businessmen to vary from this rate of production—this is therefore the equilibrium NNP.

To enhance our understanding of the meaning of the equilibrium level of NNP, let us examine other possible levels of NNP to see why they cannot be sustained. For example, at the $410 billion level of NNP businesses would find that if they produced this output, the income created by this production would give rise to $405 billion in consumer spending. Supplemented by $20 billion of investment, the total quantity demanded ($C + I_n$) would be $425 billion as shown in column 6. The economy obviously provides an annual rate of spending more than sufficient to purchase the current $410 billion rate of production. Because businessmen are producing at a lower rate than buyers are taking goods off the shelves, an unintended decline in business inventories will occur. Businessmen will adjust to this happy state of affairs by stepping up production. And a higher rate of output will mean more jobs and a higher level of total income. In short, if the total quantity of goods demanded exceeds the total quantity supplied, the latter will be driven upward. By making the same comparisons of NNP (column 2) and $C + I_n$ (column 6) at all other levels of NNP below the $470 billion equilibrium level, it will be found that the economy wants to spend in excess of the level at which businesses are willing to produce. The excess of total spending at all these levels of NNP will drive NNP upward to the $470 billion level.

The reverse holds true at all levels of NNP above the $470 billion equilibrium level. That is, businesses will find that the production of these total outputs fails to generate the levels of spending needed to take them off the market. Being unable to recover the costs involved in producing these outputs, businesses will cut back on their production. To illustrate: At the $510 billion level of output businessmen will be disappointed to find that their productive efforts have not generated enough spending to permit the sale of that output. Of the $510 billion worth of income which this output creates, $480 billion is received back by businesses as consumption spending. Though supplemented by $20 billion worth of investment spending, the total quantity demanded ($500 billion) falls $10 billion short of the $510 billion quantity supplied. Inventories of goods pile up, and businesses react to this unintended accumulation of unsold goods by cutting back on the rate of production. This decline in NNP will mean fewer jobs and a decline in total income. The reader should verify that deficiencies of total spending exist at all other levels of NNP in excess of the $470 billion level.

The equilibrium level of NNP exists where the total quantity supplied, measured by NNP, and the aggregate quantity demanded, $C + I_n$, are equal. Any excess of total spending over total output will drive the latter upward. Any deficiency of total spending will pull NNP downward.

The same analysis can be readily envisioned through a simple graph. In Figure 13–1 the 45-degree line indicates the aggregate supply schedule. Let us see why. Each point on the aggregate supply schedule will indicate the amounts which businessmen must expect to receive back as total spending in order to be induced to produce various possible outputs. As noted, businessmen will attempt to produce any total output only if they expect to receive back an equal amount of total spending. That is, businessmen will offer any level of NNP only if they expect $C + I_n$ to be just sufficient to clear that output off the market. For example, businessmen will offer a $390 billion NNP only when they expect $C + I_n$ to be $390 billion. If businesses expected total spending to be greater or less than $390 billion, they could be expected to offer

FIGURE 13-1. THE AGGREGATE DEMAND–AGGREGATE SUPPLY APPROACH TO THE EQUILIBRIUM NNP.
The aggregate supply schedule is the 45-degree line, because businesses will produce any given level of NNP only when they expect a level of total spending ($C + I_n$) just sufficient to dispose of that output. The equilibrium level of NNP is determined by the intersection of this aggregate supply schedule with the $C + I_n$, or aggregate demand, schedule. Only at this point are the production and purchasing plans of the economy consistent with one another.

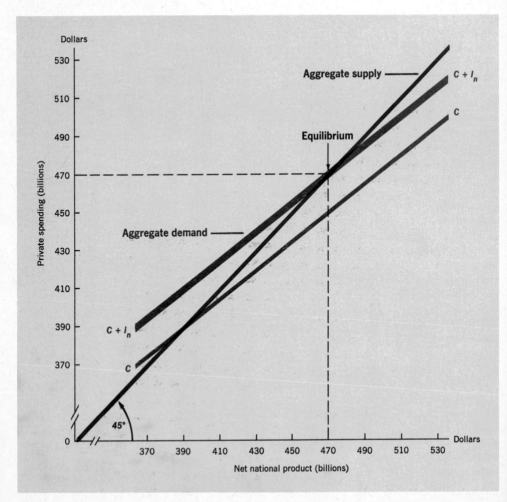

an equally larger or smaller total output. Thus, a series of points—a line—equidistant from the total output (NNP) axis and the total spending $(C + I_n)$ axis will summarize the aggregate supply plans of businesses. Being equidistant from the two axes, this line is necessarily the 45-degree line. We conclude that the 45-degree line is the aggregate supply schedule. This schedule shows the various outputs which businesses will offer at each of the various levels of spending that might prevail.

To get the $C + I_n$ or aggregate demand schedule in Figure 13–1, we simply graph the consumption schedule of Figure 12–3a and add to it vertically the constant $20 billion amount from Figure 12–5, which, we assume, businesses will want to invest at each possible level of NNP. More directly, we can plot the $C + I_n$ data of column 6 in Table 13–1.

The question: What is the equilibrium level of NNP? The answer: that NNP at which the aggregate quantity demanded and the aggregate quantity supplied are equal. And this must be where the aggregate supply schedule (the 45-degree line) and the aggregate demand schedule ($C + I_n$) intersect. Because our graphed schedules are based on the data of Table 13–1, we once again find the equilibrium output to be at the $470 billion level. It is evident from Figure 13–1 that no levels of NNP above the equilibrium level are sustainable, because $C + I_n$ falls short of NNP. For example, at the $510 NNP level $C + I_n$ is only $500. Inventories of unsold goods rise to undesired levels. This unhappy state of affairs will prompt businesses to readjust their production sights downward in the direction of the $470 billion output level. Conversely, at all possible levels of NNP less than the $470 billion level, the economy desires to spend in excess of what businesses are producing. $C + I_n$ exceeds the value of the corresponding output. At the $410 billion NNP, for example, $C + I_n$ totals $425 billion. Inventories decline as the rate of spending exceeds the rate of

production, prompting businessmen to raise their production sights in the direction of the $470 billion NNP. Unless there is some change in the consumption-saving plans of households or the investment plans of businesses, the $470 billion level of NNP will be sustained indefinitely.

SAVING-EQUALS-INVESTMENT APPROACH

The aggregate demand–aggregate supply approach to the determination of NNP has the advantage of spotlighting total spending as the immediate determinant of the levels of output, employment, and income. Though the $S = I_n$ approach is less direct, it does have the advantage of giving emphasis to the reason why $C + I_n$ and NNP are unequal at all levels of output except the equilibrium level.

The saving schedule (columns 2 and 4) and the investment schedule (columns 2 and 5) of Table 13–1 are pertinent. Our $C + I_n = $ NNP approach has just led us to conclude that all levels of NNP less than $470 billion are unstable because the corresponding $C + I_n$ exceeds these NNPs, driving them upward. A comparison of the amounts households and businesses want to save and invest at each of these below-equilibrium NNP levels explains these excesses of total spending. In particular, at each of these relatively low NNP levels businesses desire to invest more than households plan to save. For example, at the $410 billion level of NNP, households will save only $5 billion, thereby spending $405 of their $410 billion incomes. Supplemented by $20 billion of business investment, total spending $(C + I_n)$ is obviously $425 billion. Total spending exceeds NNP by $15 billion ($= $425 - 410) *because* the amount businesses desire to invest at this level of NNP exceeds the amounts households plan to save by $15 billion. It is the fact that a very small "leakage" of saving at this relatively low income level will be more than compensated for by the relatively high level of investment spending which causes $C + I_n$ to exceed NNP and induce the latter upward.

Similarly, all levels of NNP above the $470 level are also unstable, because here NNP exceeds $C + I_n$. The reason for this insufficiency of total spending lies in the fact that at all NNP levels above $470 billion households will attempt to save in excess of the amount businesses desire to invest. That is, the saving leakage is not compensated for by the level of investment. For example, households will choose to save at the high rate of $30 billion at the $510 billion NNP. Businesses, however, will only invest $20 billion at this NNP. This $10 billion excess of saving over investment will cause total spending to fall $10 billion short of the value of total output. And this deficiency will cause NNP to decline.

Again we verify that the equilibrium NNP is at the $470 billion level. It is only at this point that the saving desires of households and the investment plans of businesses are equal. And only when businesses and households attempt to invest and save at equal rates will $C + I_n = $ NNP. Only here will the annual rates of production and spending be in balance; only here will unplanned changes in inventories be absent. One can think of it in this way: If saving were zero, consumer spending would always be sufficient to clear the market of any given NNP; that is, consumption would equal NNP. But saving can and does occur, causing consumption to fall short of NNP. Hence, only when businesses are willing to invest at the same rate at which households attempt to save will the amount by which consumption falls short of NNP be precisely compensated for.

The $S = I_n$ approach to determining the equilibrium NNP can be readily demonstrated graphically. In Figure 13–2 we have merely combined the saving schedule of Figure 12–3b and the simplified investment schedule of Figure 12–5. The numerical data for these schedules are repeated in

FIGURE 13–2. THE SAVING-EQUALS-INVESTMENT APPROACH TO THE EQUILIBRIUM NNP.
A second approach is to view the equilibrium NNP as determined by the intersection of the saving (S) and investment (I_n) schedules. Only at the point of equilibrium will households plan to save the amount businesses want to invest. It is the consistency of these plans which causes NNP and $C + I_n$ to be equal.

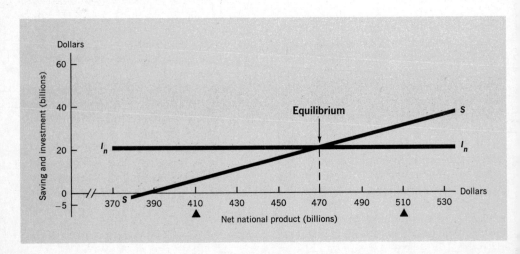

columns 2, 4, and 5 of Table 13–1. It is evident that the equilibrium level of NNP is at $470 billion, where the saving and investment schedules intersect. Only here do households and businesses plan to save and invest at the same rates; therefore, only here will NNP and $C + I_n$ be equal. At all higher levels of NNP households will attempt to save at a rate higher than businesses are willing to invest. This causes $C + I_n$ to fall short of NNP, driving the latter downward. At the $510 billion NNP, for example, saving of $30 billion will exceed investment of $20 billion by $10 billion with the result that $C + I_n$ is $500 billion—$10 billion short of NNP. At all levels of NNP below the $470 billion equilibrium level businesses will desire to invest at a rate in excess of the amount households plan to save. The result is that $C + I_n$ exceeds NNP, driving the latter upward. To illustrate: At the $410 level of NNP the $5 billion leakage of saving is more than compensated for by the $20 billion businesses desire to invest. The result is that $C + I_n$ exceeds NNP by $15 billion, inducing businesses to produce a larger NNP.

PLANNED VERSUS ACTUAL SAVING AND INVESTMENT

We have emphasized that because savers and investors are essentially different groups and are differently motivated, discrepancies in saving and investment can occur and these differences bring about changes in the equilibrium NNP. Now we must recognize that in another sense saving and investment must always be equal to one another! This apparent contradiction concerning the equality of saving and investment is resolved when we distinguish between *planned* or *intended* saving and investment (which need not be equal) and *actual* or *realized* saving and investment (which by definition must be equal). The catch essentially is that actual investment consists of both intended and unintended investment (unintended changes in inventory investment),

and the latter functions as a balancing item which always equates the actual amounts saved and invested in any period of time.

Consider, for example, the $490 billion above-equilibrium NNP (Table 13–1). What would happen if businesses produced this output, thinking they could sell it? At this level households save $25 billion of their $490 billion DI, so consumption is only $465 billion. *Intended* investment is $20 billion; that is, businessmen want to buy $20 billion worth of capital goods. This means aggregate demand $(C + I_n)$ is $485 billion, and sales therefore fall short of production by $5 billion. This extra $5 billion of goods is obviously retained by businesses as an *unintended* or involuntary increase in inventories. It is unintended because it results from the failure of total spending to take total output off the market. Remembering that national income accountants include changes in inventories as a part of investment, we note that actual or *realized* investment of $25 billion ($20 intended or planned *plus* $5 unintended or unplanned) equals *realized* saving of $25 billion, even though *intended* saving exceeds *intended* investment by $5 billion. Businessmen, obviously not anxious to accumulate unwanted inventories at this annual rate, will react by cutting back on production.

Now look at the below-equilibrium $450 billion output (Table 13–1). Because households save only $15 billion of their $450 billion DI, consumption is $435 billion. Businesses want or intend to invest $20 billion, so aggregate demand is $455 billion. That is, sales exceed production by $5 billion. How can this be? The answer is that an unplanned or unintended decline in business inventories has occurred. More specifically, businesses have unintentionally *dis*invested $5 billion in inventories. Note once again that *realized* investment is $15 billion ($20 intended or planned *minus* $5 unintended or unplanned) and equal to *realized* saving of $15 billion, even though intended investment exceeds intended saving by $5 billion. This unintended decline in investment in inventories due to the excess of sales over production will induce businessmen to increase the NNP by expanding production.

To summarize: At all above-equilibrium levels of NNP (where intended saving exceeds intended investment) realized investment and realized saving are equal because of unintended increases in inventories, which, by definition, are included as a part of actual or realized investment. Graphically (Figure 13–2) the unintended inventory increase is measured by the vertical distance by which the (intended) saving schedule lies above the (intended) investment schedule. At all below-equilibrium levels of NNP (where intended investment exceeds intended saving), realized investment will be equal to realized saving because of unintended decreases in inventories which must be subtracted from intended investment to determine actual investment. These unintended inventory declines are shown graphically as the vertical distance by which the (intended) investment schedule lies above the (intended) saving schedule.

These distinctions are important because they correctly suggest that it is the equality of intended investment and intended saving which determines the equilibrium level of NNP. We can think of the process by which equilibrium is achieved as follows:

1. A difference between intended saving and intended investment causes a difference between the production and spending plans of the economy as a whole.

2. This difference between aggregate production and spending plans results in unintended investment or disinvestment in inventories.

3. As long as unintended investment in inventories persists, businessmen will revise their production plans downward and thereby reduce the NNP. Conversely, as long as unintended disinvestment in inventories exists, firms will revise their production plans upward and increase the NNP.

Both types of movements in NNP are toward equilibrium in that they tend to bring about the equality of intended saving and intended investment.

4. Only where intended saving and intended investment are equal will the level of NNP be stable or in equilibrium; that is, only where intended investment equals intended saving will there be no unintended investment or disinvestment in inventories to drive the NNP downward or upward.

CHANGES IN EQUILIBRIUM NNP AND THE MULTIPLIER

Thus far we have been concerned with explaining the equilibrium levels of total output and income. But we saw in Chapter 11 that actually the NNP of American capitalism is seldom stable: rather it is characterized by long-run growth punctuated by cyclical fluctuations. Let us turn to the questions of *why* and *how* the equilibrium level of NNP fluctuates.

The equilibrium level of NNP will change in response to changes in the investment schedule or the saving-consumption schedules. Because investment spending generally is less stable than the consumption-saving schedules, we shall assume that changes in the investment schedule occur. The impact of changes in investment can be readily envisioned through Figure 13–3a and b. If technological advance, population growth, or simply business optimism enhances profit expectations, investment spending by businesses will increase by, say, $5 billion. This is indicated in Figure 13–3a as an upward shift in the aggregate demand schedule from $(C + I_n)_0$ to $(C + I_n)_1$ and in Figure 13–3b as an upward shift in the investment schedule from I_{n_0} to I_{n_1}. In each of these portrayals the result is a rise in the equilibrium NNP from $470 to $490 billion.

Conversely, a $5 billion decline in investment stemming from such considerations as high acquisition and maintenance costs on capital, a high interest rate, a low rate of technological advance, or general business pessimism will shift the investment schedule downward from I_{n_0} to I_{n_2} in Figure 13–3*b* and the aggregate demand schedule from $(C + I_n)_0$ to $(C + I_n)_2$ in 13–3*a*. In each case these shifts cause the equilibrium NNP to fall from the original $470 billion level to $450 billion. The reader should verify these conclusions in terms of Table 13–1 by substituting $25 billion and then $15 billion for the $20 billion investment figure given in the table.

When changes in the consumption-saving schedules occur, they will have similar effects. If households want to consume more (save less) at each level of NNP, the aggregate demand schedule will shift upward and the saving schedule downward in Figure 13–3*a* and *b*, respectively. In either portrayal these shifts will mean an increase in the equilibrium NNP. If households want to consume less (save more) at each possible NNP, the resulting drop in the consumption schedule and increase in the saving schedule will in turn reduce the equilibrium NNP.

The Multiplier Effect

You have undoubtedly detected a curious feature of the above examples: A $5 billion change in investment spending has given rise to a $20 billion change in the output-income level. This surprising result is called the *multiplier effect*. It is based upon two seemingly innocent facts. On the one hand, the economy is characterized by repetitive, continuous flows of expenditures and income wherein the dollars spent by Smith are received as income by Jones. On the other hand, any change in income will cause both consumption and saving to vary in the same direction as, and by a fraction of, the change in income.

It follows from these two facts that an initial change in the rate of spending will cause a chain reaction which, although of diminishing importance at each successive step, will cumulate to a multiple change in NNP. The multiplier effect is illustrated numerically in Table 13–2 for a $5 billion increase in investment spending. We assume that the MPC is three-fourths; the MPS is therefore one-fourth.

The initial increase in investment generates an equal amount of wage, rent, interest, and profit income for the simple reason that spending and receiving income are two sides of the same transaction. This $5 billion income increase causes consumption to rise by $3.75 billion and saving by $1.25 billion. The $3.75 billion which is spent is received by other households as income. They in turn consume three-fourths, or $2.81 billion, of this $3.75 billion and save one-fourth, or $0.94 billion. The $2.81 billion which is consumed flows to

TABLE 13–2. THE MULTIPLIER: A TABULAR ILLUSTRATION
(in billions of dollars; hypothetical data)

	Change in income	Change in consumption (MPC = ¾)	Change in saving (MPS = ¼)
Assumed increase in investment	$ 5.00	$ 3.75	$1.25
Second round	3.75	2.81	0.94
Third round	2.81	2.11	0.70
Fourth round	2.11	1.58	0.53
Fifth round	1.58	1.19	0.39
All other rounds	4.75	3.56	1.19
Totals	$20.00	$15.00	$5.00

(a)

(b)

still other households as income. Though the spending and respending effects of the initial increase in investment diminish with each successive round of spending, the cumulative increase in the output-income level will be $20 billion if the process is carried through to the last dollar.

It is no coincidence that the multiplier effect ends at the point where exactly enough saving has been generated to offset the initial $5 billion increase in investment spending. It is only then that the disequilibrium created by the investment increase will be corrected. In this case NNP and total incomes must rise by $20 billion to create $5 billion in additional saving to match the $5 billion increase in investment spending. Income must increase by four times the initial excess of investment over saving, because households save one-fourth of any increase in their incomes. In this case the multiplier—the number of times the ultimate increase in income exceeds the initial increase in investment spending—is 4.

Characteristics of the multiplier. Several noteworthy characteristics of the multiplier are not sufficiently emphasized by mere illustrations of its mechanics:

1. Remember that a change in any of the components of the aggregate demand schedule will give rise to a multiplier effect. In practice, economists usually associate the multiplier with changes in investment because of the relative instability of the investment schedule as compared with the consumption schedule. But keep in mind that a shift in the consumption schedule or, as we shall see shortly, a shift in the schedule of government spending will also prompt a similar chain reaction.

2. Keep in mind too that the multiplier works in both directions. That is, a small increase in spending can give rise to a multiple increase in NNP, or a small decrease in spending can be magnified into a much larger decrease in NNP by the multiplier.

3. You may have sensed from Table 13–2 that a relationship of some sort must exist between the MPS and the size of the multiplier. There is such a relationship: The fraction of an increase in income which is saved—that is, the MPS—determines the cumulative respending effects of any initial change in I_n, G, or C, and therefore the multiplier. More specifically, *the size of the MPS and the size of the multiplier are inversely related.* The smaller the fraction of any change in income which is saved, the greater the respending at each round and the greater the multiplier. If the MPS is one-fourth, as in our example, the multiplier is 4. If the MPS were one-third, the multiplier would be 3. If the MPS were one-fifth, the multiplier would be 5. We can summarize these and all other possibilities by simply saying that *the multiplier is equal to the reciprocal of the MPS.* The reciprocal of any number is the quotient you obtain by dividing 1 by that number. In short, we can say that

$$\text{The multiplier} = \frac{1}{\text{MPS}}$$

This formula provides us with a shorthand method of determining the multiplier. All we need to know is the MPS (or MPC) to calculate the size of the multiplier quickly.[1]

[1] Since MPS + MPC = 1, it is also true that MPS = 1 − MPC. Substituting in the above

FIGURE 13–3. CHANGES IN THE EQUILIBRIUM NNP CAUSED BY SHIFTS IN (a) THE AGGREGATE DEMAND SCHEDULE AND (b) THE INVESTMENT SCHEDULE.
An upshift in the aggregate demand schedule from, say, $(C + I_n)_0$ to $(C + I_n)_1$ will increase the equilibrium NNP. Conversely, a downshift in the aggregate demand schedule from, say, $(C + I_n)_0$ to $(C + I_n)_2$ will lower the equilibrium NNP. In the saving-investment figure an upshift in the investment schedule (I_{n_0} to I_{n_1}) will raise, and a downshift (I_{n_0} to I_{n_2}) will lower, the equilibrium NNP.

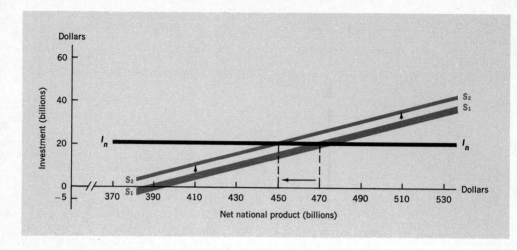

FIGURE 13–4. THE PARADOX OF THRIFT.
Unless offset by an upshift in the investment schedule, any attempt by households to save more (S_1 to S_2) will be frustrated by a multiple decline in the equilibrium NNP.

Significance of the multiplier. The significance of the multiplier is almost self-
_____
formula, we can say that

$$\text{The multiplier} = \frac{1}{1 - \text{MPC}}$$

Furthermore, the importance of footnote 7 in Chapter 12 now becomes clear. There we noted that the MPS measures the slope of the saving schedule. In terms of the saving-equals-investment approach this means that if the MPS is relatively large (say, one-half) and the slope of the saving schedule is therefore relatively steep (one-half), any given upward shift in investment spending will be subject to a relatively small multiplier. For example, a $5 billion increase in investment will entail a new point of intersection of the S and I_n schedules only $10 billion to the right of the original equilibrium NNP. The multiplier is only 2. But if the MPS is relatively small (say one-sixth), the slope of the saving schedule will be relatively gentle. Therefore, a $5 billion upward shift in the investment schedule will provide a new intersection point some $30 billion to the right of the original equilibrium NNP. The multiplier is 6 in this case. The reader should verify these two examples by drawing appropriate saving and investment diagrams.

evident. A relatively small change in the investment plans of business or the consumption-saving plans of households can trigger a much larger change in the equilibrium level of NNP. The multiplier magnifies the fluctuations in business activity initiated by changes in spending. Estimates of the size of the multiplier for the United States suggest a figure of from 2 to 4.

Paradox of Thrift

A curious paradox is suggested by the saving-investment approach to NNP determination and by our analysis of the multiplier. The paradox is that if society attempts to save more, it may end up actually saving the same amount, or even less. Figure 13–4 is relevant. Suppose I_n and S_1 are the current investment and saving schedules which determine a $470 billion equilibrium NNP. Now assume that households, perhaps anticipating a recession, attempt to save, say, $5 billion more at each income level in order to provide a nest egg against the expected bad times. This attempt to save more is reflected in an upward shift of the saving schedule from S_1 to S_2. But this very upshift creates an excess of planned saving over planned investment at the current $470 equilibrium output. And we know that the multiplier effect will cause this small increase in saving (decline in consumption) to be reflected in a much larger—$20 billion ($5 times 4) in this case—decline in equilibrium NNP.

There is a paradox here in several different senses. First, note that at the new $450 equilibrium NNP households are saving the same amount they did at the original $470 billion NNP. Society's attempt to save more has been frustrated by the multiple decline in the equilibrium NNP which that attempt itself caused. Second, this analysis suggests that thrift, which has always been held in high esteem in our economy, now becomes something of a social vice. From the individual point of view a penny saved may be a penny earned. But from the social point of view a penny saved is a penny not spent and therefore a decline in someone's income. The act of thrift may be virtuous from the individual's point of view but disastrous from the social point of view because of its undesirable effects upon total output and employment. Third, it is ironic, if not paradoxical, that households may be most strongly induced to save more (consume less) at the very time when increased saving is most inappropriate and economically undesirable, that is, when the economy seems to be backsliding into a recession. An individual fearing the loss of his job will hardly be inclined to go on a spending spree.

The reader will find it challenging and rewarding to pursue his analysis of the paradox of thrift and the multiplier by substituting an upsloping investment schedule for the simplified investment schedule we have employed. In the case of the paradox of thrift you should conclude that the attempt of households to save more will not simply be frustrated but will actually give rise to a decline in the amount actually saved. You should also find that a positively

sloped investment schedule will increase the size of the multiplier and in effect make it a "supermultiplier."[2]

EQUILIBRIUM VERSUS FULL-EMPLOYMENT NNP

We now turn from the task of explaining to that of evaluating the equilibrium NNP.

Too much emphasis cannot be placed upon the fact that the $470 billion equilibrium NNP embodied in our analysis (Table 13–1 and Figures 13–1 and 13–2) may or may not entail full employment. Remember: The basic theme of Keynes's "new economics" is that capitalism contains no mechanisms capable of automatically creating that particular level of aggregate demand which will induce businessmen to produce a full-employment noninflationary level of output. For example, if we assume the full-employment noninflationary output to be $490 billion, it would only be by chance that the aggregate demand schedule would be at the $(C + I_n)_0$ level in Figure 13–5 to intersect the aggregate supply schedule at this desired level of output. Aggregate demand might very well lie below this ideal location at, say, the $(C + I_n)_2$ level, or above the full-employment noninflationary output at, say the $(C + I_n)_1$ level.

Deflationary Gap

Suppose in Figure 13–5 that the aggregate demand schedule is at $(C + I_n)_2$, which, incidentally, happens to be the aggregate demand schedule developed and employed in this chapter. This schedule intersects aggregate supply to the left of the full-

[2] *Hints:* (1) Substitute the investment schedule of columns 1 and 3 in Table 12–2 in column 5 of Table 13–1; (2) assume a $5 billion increase in saving; (3) compute (estimate) the new equilibrium point at which intended saving equals intended investment; (4) compare the original and the new amounts saved; and (5) calculate the size of the multiplier.

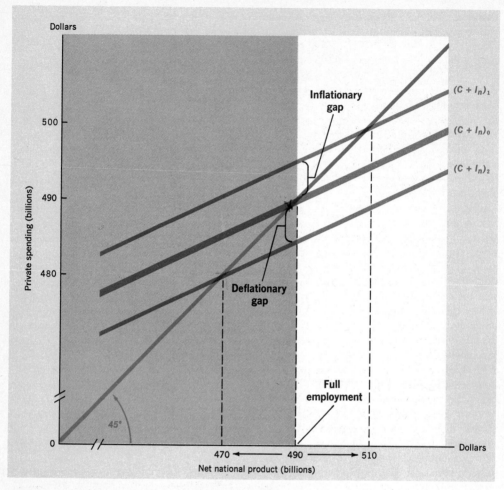

FIGURE 13–5. DEFLATIONARY AND INFLATIONARY GAPS.
In a capitalistic system the equilibrium and full employment NNPs may not coincide.
Deflationary and inflationary gaps refer to the deficiency or excess of total spending
which may exist at the full employment NNP. A deflationary gap will cause a multiple
decline in the real NNP, whereas an inflationary gap will give rise to a multiple
increase in the money NNP.

employment output, causing the economy's aggregate production to fall $20 billion short of its capacity production. In terms of Table 13–1 the economy is failing to employ 5 million of its 70 million available workers and, as a result, is sacrificing $20 billion worth of output. Looked at from a slightly different vantage point, we find that

total spending is deficient by $5 billion (see Table 13–1) at the $490 billion level of NNP. This deficiency is called a *deflationary gap* for the simple reason that it has a deflationary, depressing, or contractionary impact upon the economy. This $5 billion deficiency of total spending, subject to a multiplier of 4, accounts for the $20 billion difference between the equilibrium and the full-employment NNP.

Inflationary Gap

Now let us suppose that the aggregate demand schedule happens to be at $(C + I_n)_1$ in Figure 13–5, intersecting the aggregate supply schedule at some point to the right of the $490 billion full-employment output. In this case there exists $5 billion of excess spending at the full-employment output, which economists call an *inflationary gap*. Because $490 billion is the economy's full-employment or maximum output (as valued at current or existing prices), it is quite obvious that a *real* NNP of $510 billion, indicated by the intersection of $(C + I_n)_1$ and the aggregate supply schedule, is unobtainable. The effect of the excess spending—the inflationary gap—will be to pull up the prices on the economy's fixed physical volume of production. More specifically, the $5 billion inflationary gap, subject to a multiplier of 4, will cause *money* NNP to rise by $20 billion while *real* NNP remains unchanged. Businesses as a whole cannot respond to the $5 billion in excess spending by expanding their real outputs for the simple reason that all available resources are already employed; the economy is already operating at some point on its production possibilities curve. Putting the matter quite bluntly, NNP changes to the left of the full-employment output (the shaded area of Figure 13–5) are *real* changes; NNP changes to the right of the full-employment output (the white area) are merely monetary or "paper" changes in NNP.[3]

---

[3] The alert reader will have detected a simplification or two in our deflationary-inflationary gap analysis. We have implicitly assumed that the price level is perfectly constant until full employment is reached; that is, up to the $490 billion NNP, increases in total spending would simply bring about proportionate increases in output and employment. Then, further in-

The main objective of Chapter 14 is to understand how governmental fiscal (taxation and expenditure) policy might be used to close deflationary or inflationary gaps.

SUMMARY

1. The equilibrium level of NNP is that at which the aggregate quantity demanded and the aggregate quantity supplied are equal or, graphically, where the $C + I_n$ line intersects the 45-degree line. At any NNP greater than the equilibrium NNP, aggregate quantity supplied will exceed the aggregate quantity demanded, resulting in unsold goods, depressed profits, and eventual declines in output, employment, and income. At any below-equilibrium NNP the aggregate quantity demanded will exceed the aggregate quantity supplied, thereby resulting in substantial profits, declining inventories, and eventual increases in NNP.

2. An alternative, complementary approach determines the equilibrium NNP at the point where the amount households plan to save and the amount businesses plan to invest are equal. This is at the point where the saving and investment schedules

---

creases in spending beyond the full-employment output are purely inflationary. Actually, we know that increases in total spending *near* the full-employment level will usually cause both the price level and the level of real NNP to increase. In the context of Figure 11–1 we are here assuming that the price-level line is ⌐-shaped rather than ⌐-shaped. The transition from the dark to the light area is not so abrupt as in Figure 13–5, but is actually rather blurred. Similarly, full employment (or capacity production) itself is something of an elastic concept because a given number of workers can increase their hours of work by simply working overtime, or, as a matter of fact, persons who are not ordinarily in the labor force may be induced to offer their services when job opportunities are abundant. The general validity of our analysis is not impaired by ignoring these refinements.

intersect. Any excess of planned saving over planned investment will cause a shortage of total spending, forcing NNP to fall. Any excess of planned investment over planned saving will cause an excess of total spending, inducing NNP to rise. These changes in NNP will in both cases correct the assumed discrepancies in investment and saving plans.

3. Shifts in the saving-consumption schedules or in the investment schedule will cause the equilibrium output-income level to change by several times the amount of the initial change in spending. This phenomenon, which accompanies both increases and decreases in spending, is called the *multiplier effect*. The multiplier is equal to the reciprocal of the marginal propensity to save.

4. The *paradox of thrift* is that the attempt of society to save more may be frustrated by the multiple decline in the equilibrium NNP which the increased saving will cause.

5. The equilibrium level of NNP and the full-employment noninflationary NNP need not coincide. The amount by which aggregate demand falls short of the full-employment NNP is called the deflationary gap; this gap prompts a multiple decline in real NNP. The amount by which aggregate demand exceeds the full-employment NNP is the inflationary gap; it causes a multiple increase in money NNP.

QUESTIONS AND STUDY SUGGESTIONS

1. Explain graphically the determination of the equilibrium NNP by (*a*) the aggregate demand-aggregate supply approach and (*b*) the saving-equals-investment approach for the private sector of the economy. Why must these two approaches always yield the same equilibrium NNP?
2. Explain in detail the difference between planned saving and investment and realized saving and investment. Why is the distinction significant?
3. "The fact that households may try to save more than businesses want to invest is of no consequence, because events will in time force households and businesses to save and invest at the same rates." Critically evaluate.
4. "It is socially desirable for households to attempt to increase their rate of saving whenever a recession begins. In this way households will be able to accumulate the financial resources to pay their way through bad times." Critically evaluate.
5. What is the multiplier effect? What relationship does the MPC bear to the size of the multiplier? The MPS? What will the multiplier be when the MPS is 0, 0.4, 0.6, and 1? When the MPC is 1, ⅚, ⅔, ½, and 0? How much of a change in NNP will result if businesses increase their rate of investment by $8 billion and the MPC in the economy is four-fifths? If the MPC is two-thirds?
6. What effect will each of the changes designated in question 7 at the end of Chapter 12 have upon the equilibrium level of NNP? Explain your answers.
7. Explain the paradox of thrift, indicating its significance.
8. Assuming the level of investment is $16 billion and independent of the level of total output, complete the following table and determine the equilibrium level of output and income which the private sector of the economy would provide.

Possible levels of employment, millions	Aggregate supply (NNP = NI = PI = DI), billions	Consumption, billions	Saving, billions
40	$240	$244	$ _-4_
45	260	260	_0_
50	280	276	_4_
55	300	292	_8_
60	320	308	_12_
65	340	324	_16_
70	360	340	_20_
75	380	356	_24_
80	400	372	_28_

a. If this economy has a labor force of 70 million, will there exist an inflationary or deflationary gap? Explain the consequences of this gap.
b. Will an inflationary or deflationary gap exist if the available labor force is only 55 million? Trace the consequences.
c. What are the sizes of the MPC and the MPS?
d. Use the MPC and MPS concepts to explain the increase in the equilibrium NNP which will occur as the result of an increase in investment spending from $16 to $20 billion.

SELECTED REFERENCES

Clemence, Richard V.: *Income Analysis* (Reading, Mass.: Addison-Wesley Publishing Company, Inc., 1951).

Dillard, Dudley: *The Economics of John Maynard Keynes* (Englewood Cliffs, N.J.: Prentice-Hall, Inc., 1948).

Hansen, Alvin: *A Guide to Keynes* (New York: McGraw-Hill Book Company, 1953).

Heilbroner, Robert L.: *Understanding Macroeconomics* (Englewood Cliffs, N.J.: Prentice-Hall, Inc., 1965).

McKenna, Joseph P.: *Aggregate Economic Analysis*, rev. ed. (New York: Holt, Rinehart and Winston, Inc., 1965).

Peterson, Wallace C.: *Income, Employment, and Economic Growth* (New York: W. W. Norton & Company, Inc., 1962), chaps. 5–9.

CHAPTER 14

THE ECONOMICS OF FISCAL POLICY

This chapter is a continuation of Chapters 12 and 13. Its fundamental purpose is to add the public sector to our analysis of the equilibrium NNP.

FISCAL POLICY

In particular we want to assess the impact of fiscal policy, that is, the manipulation of taxes and government spending for the expressed purpose of achieving the full-employment noninflationary level of NNP. But first we must pause for some preliminary considerations.

Rationale

The rationale underlying government spending and taxation decisions—particularly at the Federal level—differs in one crucial respect from the consumption-saving and investment decisions of the private sector of the economy. The consumption-saving decisions of households and the investment decisions of businesses are based upon what each group feels to be the course of action that will best further its own self-interest. Households divide their disposable incomes between consumption and saving in the manner most satisfying to them; businesses will invest only when they feel prospective profits to be lucrative enough to justify such spending. A basic notion of modern employment theory is that the sum of these individual decisions, motivated by self-interest, need not provide for the full-employment noninflationary level of NNP.

Millions of individual consumption and investment decisions, based on private self-interest, need not necessarily provide for the realization of the social goal of full employment. Government, however, is an instrument of society as a whole, and within limits its spending and taxation decisions can be made to influence the equilibrium NNP in terms of the general welfare. Indeed, the task of fiscal policy is to manipulate government spending and taxation to close deflationary or inflationary gaps.

Employment Act of 1946

The notion that governmental fiscal actions can exert an important stabilizing influence upon the economy began to gain widespread acceptance during the Depression crisis of the 1930s. As previously noted, Keynesian employment theory played a major role in emphasizing the importance of remedial fiscal measures. But it was not until 1946, when the end of hostilities re-created the specter of unemployment, that the Federal government formalized in law its area of responsibility in promoting economic stability. The Employment Act of 1946 proclaims:

The Congress hereby declares that it is the continuing policy and responsibility of the Federal Government to use all practicable means consistent with its needs and obligations and other essential considerations of national policy, with assistance and cooperation of industry, agriculture, labor and State and local governments, to coordinate and utilize all its plans, functions, and resources for the purpose of creating and maintaining, in a manner calculated to foster and promote free competitive enterprise and the general welfare, conditions under which there will be afforded useful employment opportunities, including self-employment, for those able, willing, and seeking to work and to promote maximum employment, production, and purchasing power.

Note that the act recognizes explicitly and by implication that America's economic goals are manifold: We seek not only full employment, but also price stability, growth, and the preservation of economic freedom. We know that to some degree these various goals may conflict (Chapter 1); the achievement of one goal—full employment—may be at the cost of other goals. Fiscal policy will therefore reflect the system of priorities which Congress establishes for the various economic objectives.

DISCRETIONARY FISCAL POLICY

Let us first focus attention upon *discretionary* fiscal policy. Discretionary fiscal policy is the deliberate changing of taxes and government spending by the Congress for the purpose of offsetting cyclical fluctuations in output and employment. To keep a potentially complex discussion as simple as possible, three simplifying assumptions are invoked. First, we continue to employ the simplified investment schedule in our analysis. Second, we shall suppose that the initial impact of government spending is such that it neither depresses nor stimulates private spending. That is, government spending will not cause any upward or downward shifts in the consumption and investment schedules. Third, it will be presumed that the government's net tax revenues[1] are derived entirely from personal taxes. The significance of this is that although DI will fall short of PI by the amount of govern-

[1] By net taxes we mean total tax revenues less negative taxes in the form of transfer payments.

ment's tax revenues, NNP, NI, and PI will remain equal.

In Figure 14–1a and b we have repeated our equilibrium NNP models for the private sector (Figures 13–1 and 13–2). The intersection of private aggregate demand $(C + I_n)$ and aggregate supply in Figure 14–1a indicates the equilibrium NNP as does the intersection of I_n and S in Figure 14–1b. You will recall from our gap analysis of Chapter 13 that the $470 billion equilibrium NNP is short of the assumed $490 billion full-employment noninflationary NNP.

In our discussion of the private sector of the economy we implicitly assumed that government purchases of goods and services (G) and tax revenues (T) were both zero. Now let us suppose that G and T both increase from zero to, say, $20 billion, and note the impact of each and then the combined impact of the two. As before, we pursue our analysis both graphically and tabularly.

Government Spending and Equilibrium NNP

Suppose that government decides to purchase $20 billion worth of goods and services regardless of what the level of NNP might be. By adding this amount of public spending G to the level of private spending, $C + I_n$, in Figure 14–1a we find that the total spending schedule (public plus private) has been increased to $C + I_n + G$. That is, the aggregate demand schedule now has a third component, which gives us a new and higher aggregate demand schedule. And this means a new and higher equilibrium level of NNP. In particular, the equilibrium level of NNP has increased from $470 to $550 billion. Increases in public spending, as increases in private spending, will boost the aggregate demand schedule in relation to the aggregate supply schedule and result in a higher equilibrium NNP. Note, too, that government spending is subject to the multiplier.

FIGURE 14–1. GOVERNMENT SPENDING AND THE EQUILIBRIUM NNP.
(*a*) The aggregate demand–aggregate supply approach. The addition of government expenditures G to our analysis raises the aggregate demand $(C + I_n + G)$ schedule and increases the equilibrium level of NNP as would an increase in C or I_n. Note that changes in government spending are subject to the multiplier effect. (*b*) $S = I_n$ approach. In terms of the saving-equals-investment approach, government spending supplements private investment spending $(I_n + G)$, increasing the equilibrium NNP.

(a)

(b)

Figure 14–1b shows the same change in the equilibrium NNP in terms of the $S = I_n$ analysis. With G added to our discussion, the equilibrium level of NNP is now determined where the amount households plan to save is offset exactly by the amount which businesses plan to invest plus the amount government desires to spend on goods and services. That is, the equilibrium NNP is determined by the intersection of the S schedule and the $I_n + G$ schedule. Note that either approach indicates the same new equilibrium NNP.

What of the effect of a decline in government spending? Obviously, a decline in G will cause the aggregate demand schedule to fall or the $G + I_n$ schedule to fall. In either case the result is a multiple *decline* in the equilibrium NNP.

Taxation and Equilibrium NNP

But government also collects tax revenues. How do tax collections affect the equilibrium level of NNP? Obviously, if government increases its tax revenues from zero to $20 billion, the immediate effect will be to lower DI by $20 billion. And, because DI is made up of consumer spending and saving, we can expect a decline in DI to lower both consumption and saving. But by how much will each decline? The MPC and the MPS hold the answer: The MPC tells us what fraction of a decline in DI will come at the expense of consumption, and the MPS indicates what fraction of a drop in DI will come at the expense of saving. Assuming that the MPC equals three-fourths and the MPS equals one-fourth, we can conclude that if government collects $20 billion in taxes at each possible level of NNP, the amount of consumption forthcoming at each level of NNP will drop by $15 billion (three-fourths of $20 billion), and the amount of saving at each level of NNP will fall by $5 billion (one-fourth of $20 billion).

The impact of a $20 billion increase in taxes is shown graphically in Figure 14–2a

and b. In Figure 14–2a the $20 billion increase in taxes shows up as a $15 billion decline in the aggregate demand ($C + I_n + G$) schedule. Under our simplifying assumptions this decline is solely the result of a decline in the consumption component of the aggregate demand schedule.

The equilibrium NNP shifts from $550 billion to a $490 billion level as a result of this tax-caused drop in consumption. The imposition of $20 billion in taxes has a two-fold effect in Figure 14–2b. First, the taxes reduce DI by $20 billion and, with the MPS at one-fourth, cause saving to fall by $5 billion at each level of NNP. In Figure 14–2b this is shown as a shift from S_b (saving before taxes) to S_a (saving after taxes). Then the $20 billion in taxes as such appear as a $20 billion additional leakage at each NNP level which must be added to S_a, giving us $S_a + T$. Equilibrium now exists at the $490 billion NNP where the total amount which households plan to save plus the amount of taxes government intends to collect are equal to the total amount businesses desire to invest plus the amount government plans to spend. The equilibrium condition is then $S_a + T = I_n + G$. Graphically, it is the intersection of the $S_a + T$ and the $I_n + G$ schedules which determines the equilibrium NNP.

A decline in existing taxes will cause the aggregate demand schedule to rise as a result of an upward shift in the consumption schedule or it will cause a decline in the $S_a + T$ schedule. The result in either case is a multiple *increase* in the equilibrium NNP.

Spending and Taxation: Balanced-budget Multiplier

Table 14–1 shows the net impact of government spending and taxation upon the equilibrium NNP in terms of simple arithmetic data. This table is merely Table 13–1 adjusted to allow for $20 billion worth of tax revenues (column 3) and $20 billion of government spending (column 8)

FIGURE 14-2. TAXES AND THE EQUILIBRIUM NNP.
(a) The aggregate demand—aggregate supply approach. If the MPC is three-fourths, the
imposition of $20 billion of taxes will lower the consumption schedule by $15 billion and
thereby cause a decline in the equilibrium NNP. (b) The $S = I_n$ approach. Here taxes have
a twofold effect. First, with an MPS of one-fourth, the imposition of taxes of $20 billion
will reduce disposable income by $20 billion and saving by $5 billion at each level
of NNP. This is shown by the shift from S_b (saving before taxes) to S_a (saving after taxes).
Second, the $20 billion of taxes constitute an additional $20 billion leakage at each
NNP level, giving us $S_a + T$. By adding government, the equilibrium condition
changes from $S = I_n$ to $S_a + T = I_n + G$.

(a)

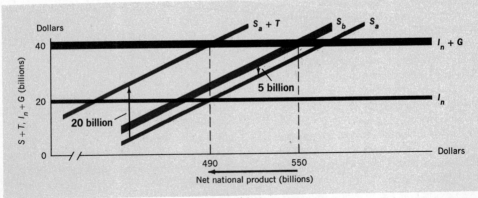

(b)

at each possible level of NNP. The immediate effect of taxes is shown in column 4: DI falls by $20 billion. Supposing the MPC and MPS are three-fourths and one-fourth, respectively, we find in columns 5 and 6 that the amounts of consumption and saving forthcoming at each level of NNP are $15 and $5 billion less, respectively.

Thus, for example, before the imposition of taxes, where NNP equaled DI, consumption was $420 billion and saving $10 billion at the $430 billion level of NNP (Table 13–1). After taxes are imposed, DI is $410 billion, obviously $20 billion short of the $430 billion NNP, with the result that consumption is only $405 billion and saving is $5 billion. It is in this manner that columns 4, 5, and 6 of Table 14–1 are determined. Column 7 carries over investment from Table 13–1, and column 8 adds government spending.

What is the equilibrium level of output now that taxation and government spending have been brought into the picture? The aggregate demand–aggregate supply, or $C + I_n + G =$ NNP, approach tells us to compare columns 2 and 9. It is apparent that the aggregate amounts demanded and supplied are equal only at the $490 billion NNP. At all higher levels businesses will attempt to produce in excess of what the economy, including both the private and the public sectors, plans to spend. The resulting deficiency of total spending will force these higher levels of NNP downward back to the $490 billion level. Conversely, at all levels of NNP below the $490 billion level the economy will spend at a rate in excess of NNP, inducing businesses to expand NNP. We can conclude that $490 billion is the equilibrium NNP.

Our alternative approach must and does yield the same results. With the public sector added to the private sector, equilibrium will prevail where $S_a + T = I_n + G$. And this is at the $490 billion level. At all lower levels you should verify that investment and government spending will more than compensate for the saving and taxation

leakages, causing $C + I_n + G$ to exceed NNP and thereby inducing the latter to rise. Conversely, at all levels of NNP above the $490 level, you should note that the saving and taxation leakages are not offset by investment and government spending, thus causing $C + I_n + G$ to fall short of NNP and forcing declines in NNP.

Note an important and curious thing about our tabular and graphic illustrations. *Equal increases in government spending and taxation increase the equilibrium NNP.* The $20 billion increase in G and T causes the equilibrium NNP to increase from $470 to $490 billion. The rationale for this so-called *balanced-budget multiplier* is revealed in our example. The $20 billion increase in personal taxes only reduces consumption by $15 billion, the extra $5 billion in tax revenues coming at the expense of saving. Thus the *net* effect is a $5 billion increase in total spending—the combination of a $20 billion increase in public spending and a $15 billion decline in private spending. Being subject to the multiplier, the $5 billion net increase in spending boosts NNP by $20 billion.

Fiscal Policy over the Cycle

In our illustration—thanks to the net expansionist effect of a balanced budget—fiscal policy has moved the economy from the unemployment NNP of $470 billion to the full-employment noninflationary NNP of $490 billion. The net $5 billion increase in spending afforded by equal increases in government spending and taxation has closed the existing $5 billion deflationary gap.

More generally, a level of private spending which fails to provide the full-employment noninflationary NNP calls for an *expansionary* fiscal policy. An expansionist policy obviously entails (1) increased government spending, (2) lower taxes, or (3) a combination of the two. In other words, if the budget is balanced at the outset, fiscal policy should move in the

TABLE 14–1. DETERMINATION OF THE EQUILIBRIUM LEVELS OF EMPLOYMENT, OUTPUT, AND INCOME: PRIVATE AND PUBLIC SECTORS (hypothetical data)

(1) Possible levels of employment, millions	(2) Possible levels of aggregate supply (NNP = NI = PI), billions	(3) Taxes, billions	(4) Possible levels of disposable income, billions, or (2) − (3)	(5) Consumption, billions
40	$370	$20	$350	$360
45	390	20	370	375
50	410	20	390	390
55	430	20	410	405
60	450	20	430	420
65	470	20	450	435
70	490	20	470	450
75	510	20	490	465
80	530	20	510	480

direction of a government budget *deficit* during a recession or depression to close the existing deflationary gap. Conversely, a level of private spending which threatens to cause inflation, that is, a spiraling up of the money GNP, calls for a restrictive or *contractionary* fiscal policy. A contractionary policy is composed of (1) decreased government spending, (2) higher taxes, or (3) a combination of these two policies. Stated differently, fiscal policy calls for a *surplus* in the government's budget when the economy is faced with the problem of closing an inflationary gap.[2]

NONDISCRETIONARY FISCAL POLICY: BUILT-IN STABILIZERS

To some extent appropriate changes in tax receipts and government spending occur automatically over the business cycle. Such changes are labeled *nondiscretionary fiscal policy* because they arise from the kinds of taxes and disbursement programs built into

[2] Minor qualification: Because, as we have just noted, a balanced budget is actually expansionary, a relatively small budget surplus might be slightly expansionary rather than deflationary.

our fiscal system and do not require congressional action. That is, the existing tax structure and existing spending programs are such that declines in the levels of output and national income automatically tend to create budget deficits, and increases in output and income automatically tend to cause budget surpluses. Let us examine the main automatic stabilizers.

Personal and Corporate Income Taxes

Because both personal and corporate income taxes entail progressive tax rates, any rise in the national income will result in more than proportionate increases in government tax receipts, which puts the brakes on an economic expansion or boom. Conversely, as the national income falls, tax collections will fall more than proportionately, thereby cushioning a recession.

Transfers and Subsidies

Certain government disbursements also change automatically in such a way as to diminish cyclical instability. During recession incomes do not decline as much as otherwise because unemployed workers

(6) Saving, billions, or (4) − (5)	(7) Investment, billions	(8) Government expenditures, billions	(9) Aggregate demand $(C + I_n + G)$, billions, or (5) + (7) + (8)	(10) Tendency of employment, output, and income
$−10	$20	$20	$400	Increase
−5	20	20	415	Increase
0	20	20	430	Increase
5	20	20	445	Increase
10	20	20	460	Increase
15	20	20	475	Increase
20	20	20	490	Equilibrium
25	20	20	505	Decrease
30	20	20	520	Decrease

receive unemployment compensation payments under our social security system. Relief payments flow to those who do not qualify for unemployment compensation or who have used up their benefits. During prosperity when unemployment is low, unemployment compensation and relief payments obviously will decline. Similarly, falling farm prices during recession cause the volume of price support subsidies to agriculture to increase; rising farm prices during the cyclical upswing cause these subsidies to diminish.

Consequences. The net effect of tax revenues moving directly with and transfer payments and farm subsidies varying inversely with national income is that changes in disposable income and consumption will be less than proportionate to the changes in national income (see Table 10–7). Automatic changes in tax receipts and transfer payments partially insulate disposable income, and therefore consumption, from changes in national income. Because a decline in national income causes tax collections to decline and transfer payments to rise, disposable income will decline by less than does national income. This means

in turn that consumption declines by less than would otherwise be the case and therefore the cumulative downward movement is less than it otherwise would be. Similarly, because an increase in national income automatically causes tax receipts to rise and transfers to decline, disposable income will rise less than does national income. In turn this means that consumption will increase less than would otherwise be the case, cushioning the cumulative upward movement in national income. The reader can verify the operation of these automatic stabilizers by observing the course of personal and corporate income taxes (lines 11 and 14) and transfer payments (line 13) during the 1949, 1954, and 1958 recessions on the table inside the covers of this book. The important point is that an element of *built-in stability* is injected into our economy by these nondiscretionary changes in tax receipts and transfer payments. In technical terms, nondiscretionary fiscal policy reduces the size of the multiplier effect.

Limitations. Although they have served the economy well, it must be emphasized that these automatic, or built-in, stabilizers are not sufficiently strong to offset any serious variations in the level of economic activity. Discretionary action—that is, changes in tax rates, tax structure, and expenditure programs—by Congress is required to alleviate inflation or recession of any appreciable magnitude. In particular, automatic stabilizers do not correct inflation or unemployment, but merely reduce their magnitude and severity. It is estimated that in the United States built-in stabilizers are currently strong enough to reduce fluctuations in national income by about one-third. In other words, a $1 billion drop in national income will cause an automatic decline in tax revenues and an automatic increase in government transfer payments to the extent that a $333 million government deficit will occur to offset partially the given decline in incomes.[3]

SOME REFINEMENTS

Because the built-in stabilizers are inadequate to cope with serious economic fluctuations, discretionary action by Congress is required. A recession-ridden economy can be stimulated by cutting taxes and increasing government spending, that is, by incurring a budget deficit. Higher taxes and decreased government spending can be used to fight inflation; that is, inflations call for surpluses. In addition, the greater a deficit, the greater its expansionary effect. And the greater a surplus, the greater the contractionary impact of government. Now we must add one or two embellishments to these cursory statements of fiscal policy.

Financing Deficits and Disposing of Surpluses

Given the size of a deficit, its expansionary effect upon the economy will depend upon

[3] R. A. Musgrave and M. H. Miller, "Built-in Flexibility," *American Economic Review*, March, 1948, pp. 122–128.

the method by which it is financed. Similarly, given the size of a surplus, its deflationary impact will depend upon its disposition.

Financing deficits: borrowing versus creating new money. One usually thinks of borrowing as the obvious means by which government can spend in excess of its receipts or income. That is, government can finance a deficit by selling bonds to the public—to households and to business firms.

Borrowing from individuals will reduce total spending to the degree that households use disposable income which would otherwise be consumed to buy government bonds. Similarly, a portion of the funds used by businesses to buy bonds might otherwise be spent on capital goods or paid out as dividend income which households then might consume. However, the purchase of government bonds is a voluntary act in so far as buyers are concerned. And it is not likely that households will greatly restrict their standard of living, or businesses their investment plans, in order to buy government bonds.[4] The poor man simply will not be able or willing to purchase bonds, and the bond purchases of the rich man will be made mostly out of funds which otherwise would have been saved in some other form. The point is this: Borrowing from the public reduces the antidepression impact of a government deficit to the extent that consumption and investment spending are reduced by the borrowing. But in all probability these declines in private spending will not be particularly great.

Government has a second basic means of financing a deficit. This method of finance is to *create new money*. In its simplest terms we can think of Congress authorizing

[4] In wartime the story is different. A strong sense of patriotism increases the likelihood of bond sales reducing the levels of consumption and investment.

the printing of the paper money needed to finance the deficit. By financing in this way government can avoid the depressing effects upon consumption and investment which borrowing from the public may have. Printing and spending new money permit increased government spending which does not entail direct reductions in private spending. For this reason it is a more expansionary method than borrowing in financing a deficit.

It is noteworthy that past experiences of the United States and of other nations have led the public to look upon the financing of deficits by running the printing presses with profound distrust. Government, however, accomplishes substantially the same results by borrowing from (selling bonds to) central banks.

Disposing of a surplus: debt retirement versus an idle surplus. Inflation calls for fiscal action by government which will result in a budget surplus. However, the anti-inflationary effect of this surplus depends upon what government does with it. Generally speaking, government can dispose of a surplus in one of two ways.

First, in view of the fact that the Federal government has an outstanding debt of some $319 billion, it is logical that government should use a surplus to retire outstanding debt. The anti-inflationary impact of a surplus, however, may be reduced somewhat by this. In retiring debt held by the general public, the government transfers its surplus tax revenues into the hands of households and businesses that *might* in turn spend these funds on consumer and capital goods. But this potential increase in private spending should not be exaggerated. In all probability a sizable portion of the surplus funds received by households and businesses as their bonds mature will be used to purchase private securities rather than goods and services. In brief, debt retirement will lessen the anti-inflationary impact of a surplus to the degree that

holders of maturing bonds spend the surplus funds they receive. In all likelihood these increases in private spending will not be very large.

On the other hand, government can realize a greater anti-inflationary impact from its budgetary surplus by literally destroying the surplus funds or by allowing them to stand idle. An idle surplus means that the government is extracting and withholding purchasing power from the income-expenditure stream. If surplus tax revenues are not reinjected into the economy, there is no possibility of the surplus being spent. That is, there is no chance that the funds will create inflationary pressure to offset the deflationary impact of the surplus itself. Because the general public views the actual destruction of paper money as an act of considerable obscenity, a surplus will typically be held by the central banks of the economy as an idle Treasury deposit.

Types of Expenditures and Taxes

The expansionary impact of a deficit and the anti-inflationary significance of a surplus depend in part upon the types of taxes and expenditures employed. Unfortunately, this particular aspect of fiscal policy is clouded with inconclusive and conflicting evidence. Economists are not in agreement as to the expansionary effects of various types of government spending and the relative deflationary effects of various taxes. Our conclusions then must be very tentative.

Purchases versus transfers. Generally speaking, there are two types of government expenditures: expenditures on goods and services and transfer payments. The former includes defense spending and what the man in the street terms "public works" projects—the building of dams, highways, parks, and public buildings. Transfer payments refer to unemployment compensation payments, subsidies to businesses, and interest on the public debt.

It is generally felt that public works expenditures are somewhat more expansionary in their effect on NNP and employment than are transfer payments. The reasons are basically twofold. First, public works spending stimulates the construction and capital goods industries, which are typically those hardest hit by depression. Second, as opposed to relief payments and subsidies, public works expenditures guarantee that government funds will be spent at least once. In contrast, the mere transfer of funds to needy families or faltering businesses through relief payments and subsidies does not directly account for any production and employment. Production is stimulated only to the extent that the recipients of these transfer payments spend them on goods and services. If the recipients of transfer payments use them to pay off existing debts or simply hoard the funds (expecting further price declines), the expansionary effect will be relatively small.

There are other advantages and shortcomings of public works spending which merit mentioning. By providing jobs, helping to maintain skills, and bolstering the morale of the labor force, public works projects seem preferable to government doles in the form of transfer payments. And, of course, very worthwhile social goods are the end result of carefully planned public works programs. On the other hand, as we shall see shortly, public works programs are typically inflexible and, too, if government is not careful in its selection of such projects, they may compete with and thereby reduce private investment. Furthermore, it can be argued that government expenditures on dams, highways, parks, and public buildings at a time when the economy needs a greater output of basic consumer goods constitute a misallocation of resources.

The deflationary impacts of different taxes. What about taxes? Because they tap potential purchasing power from the income-expenditures stream, all taxes tend to be deflationary. But, given the size of government's tax collections, some taxes seem to be more deflationary than others. Most economists feel that consumption taxes—excises and sales taxes—are more deflationary than are personal and corporate income taxes. In other words, regressive taxation is thought to depress private spending more than does progressive taxation. It must be added, however, that this conclusion is not universally accepted. Some authorities contend that although regressive taxation may dampen consumer spending more than does progressive taxation, heavy taxes on corporate income might entail considerable reduction in business investment. Hence, they conclude that corporate and personal income taxation cause a greater decline in consumption and investment combined than do sales and excise taxes.

SOME COMPLICATIONS

Unfortunately, there is a great deal of difference between fiscal policy on paper and fiscal policy in practice. It is therefore imperative that we examine some specific problems which may be encountered in enacting and applying appropriate fiscal policy.

Problems of Timing

Several problems of timing may arise in connection with fiscal policy.

1. It is very difficult to predict accurately the future course of economic activity. Business forecasting is a very imperfect science. The result is that fiscal policy is typically put into effect only after recession or inflation is upon us. The inability to predict upswings and downswings injects a time lag between the economic illness and the fiscal medicine.

2. The expenditure aspect of fiscal policy

is lacking in flexibility. Spending on public works—the construction of dams, interstate highways, and so forth—entails long planning periods and even longer periods of construction. Such spending is of questionable usefulness in offsetting short—for example, six- or eighteen-month—periods of recession.

3. The wheels of democratic government are often slow in turning. Indeed, Congress has on occasion consumed so much time in adjusting fiscal policy that the economic situation has taken a turnabout in the interim, thereby rendering the policy action completely inappropriate. The $11 billion tax cut which became law in February of 1964 was first proposed by President Kennedy in early 1963. But let us now consider the more basic question as to whether Congress will initiate appropriate fiscal action at all.

Political Problems

Fiscal policy is created in the political arena. Will political considerations outweigh economic factors in the formation of fiscal policy? Given the general unpopularity of tax increases, can Congress be expected to increase tax rates quickly and sufficiently when severe inflation is encountered? Even if Congress quickly agrees upon needed tax increases, might its efforts founder on disagreement as to what specific types of taxes are to be raised? Can Congress reasonably be expected to reach agreement as to what specific types of expenditures should be trimmed (for example, highway construction, agricultural research, education) during inflation? More generally put, is the public willing to accept, and the politician to enact, the fiscal cures which inflation and deflation require? There is no simple answer here. But at a minimum it must be noted that the democratic political processes simply do not lend themselves to the making of such decisions quickly and smoothly. "Ineffectual or unde-

sirable changes, or more likely, fiscal inertia, may often result from the interaction of political considerations."[5]

What does the historical record show? While it is generally agreed that the built-in stabilizers have functioned well in the post–World War II period, the record of discretionary fiscal policy has been the subject of debate and substantial criticism. A fair share of this criticism undoubtedly stems from an imperfect functioning of the democratic political processes. A recent report to the Joint Economic Committee of Congress concludes that our postwar use of discretionary fiscal policy has been "disappointing" for several reasons:

1. Except for the Korean conflict, government has failed to employ discretionary tax changes for countercyclical purposes.

2. The discretionary increases in government spending which have been employed during recessions have been too modest in size and too tardy in timing.

3. Primarily because of sudden and substantial changes in defense expenditures which are uncompensated for by appropriate tax adjustments, discretionary fiscal policy has on balance actually exerted a *destabilizing* influence on the economy.[6] It must be emphasized that the postwar record of fiscal policy is subject to other interpretations; some might argue that on numerous occasions Congress has clearly recognized appropriate fiscal policy and has acted with reasonable firmness and certainty. Fortunately, the postwar years have provided us with no sieges of unemployment comparable to the 1930s and no really drastic and prolonged periods of inflation to put discretionary fiscal policy to really severe tests.

In the hope of improving the timing of fiscal policy President Kennedy in 1962

[5] Joint Economic Committee, *Staff Report on Employment, Growth, and Price Levels* (Washington: 1960), p. 209.
[6] *Ibid.*, chap. 8.

asked the Congress for legislation which would give the President limited authority, subject to congressional veto, to adjust tax rates upward during inflation and downward during recession. Though this delegation of power has not been realized, some economists feel that such action is the most obvious and effective means of strengthening discretionary fiscal policy.

State and Local Finance

From the viewpoint of the economy as a whole it would be desirable for the fiscal policies of all levels of government—Federal, state, and local—to be of a countercyclical nature. Unfortunately, this is not the case. State and local finance tend to reinforce, rather than alleviate, cyclical fluctuations. State and local governments do most of their spending for schools, libraries, and streets and highways during prosperity. As is true of households and private businesses, they cut expenditures and sometimes even retire debt during depression. The 1930s provide an excellent illustration of how declines in state and local expenditures partially negated increases in Federal spending designed to boost the economy from the Great Depression. In the 1930–1934 period total state and local expenditures declined steadily from $8.2 billion to $6.4 billion, thereby canceling a sizable portion of the $3.6 billion increase in Federal spending which occurred in the same period. At the other extreme, state and local governments have on occasion cut taxes during periods of inflationary pressure.

The reasons for the perverse nature of state and local finance are many: the weaker credit standings of state and local governments, the relative instability of state and local tax systems, statutory or constitutional limits on their debts, and a rather widespread belief in the alleged virtues of an annually balanced budget all contribute to the procyclical character of state and local finance.

Private Investment

The business community sometimes expresses the fear that government spending may impair the incentives of private businesses to invest. Although it is undoubtedly true that government expenditures which are competitive with individual enterprise could lead to a more than counterbalancing decline in private investment, there is no reason why this need be the case. Government expenditures on social goods clearly outside the sphere of private enterprise—for example, irrigation and flood control projects, superhighways, parks, recreational areas, and so forth—will not interfere with the flow of private investment, but rather are likely to induce increases in private investment spending. Judicious government spending can and should be a stimulus to private investment.

Social Priorities: Inflation and Allocation

As the Employment Act of 1946 clearly indicates, full employment is one of many economic goals we seek. Certain of these goals may conflict with the objective of full employment.

1. Price stability. We know that as the economy approaches (but has not yet achieved) full employment, the general price level will begin to rise (Figure 11–2). What to do? Cutting aggregate demand will promote price stability but keep the economy short of full employment. Increasing aggregate demand will promote full employment but accelerate inflation. This is essentially a problem of social priorities: Do we prefer full employment with some inflation or price stability with some unemployment?

2. Social goods. A second problem has to do with the allocation of resources between private and social goods. Fiscal policy (in particular the policy of varying government spending inversely with the level of private spending) puts social goods in the position of being expendable or of a lower priority than private goods. More precisely, if the private sector of the economy is exuberant and consumption and investment are at high levels, fiscal policy will call for a cutting back of government spending as an anti-inflationary measure. If prolonged, the result might be an undue restraint or sacrifice of such vital social goods and services as education, basic technological research, and preventive medicine. In other words, the notion that public expenditures should be of a compensatory character, that is, that they should be adjusted downward or upward in accordance with the exuberance or lethargy of the private sector, may not be conducive to an efficient allocation of resources between private and public goods (see Chapter 38).

Countercyclical fiscal policy suggests the possibility of budget deficits. And, as a matter of fact, sizable and quite persistent deficits have given rise to a large public debt. In the next chapter we probe the causes and consequences of this debt.

SUMMARY

1. Government responsibility for achieving and maintaining full employment is set forth in the Employment Act of 1946. In practice the economy simultaneously seeks several related objectives—full employment, price stability, full production, and economic freedom.

2. Increases in government spending expand, and decreases contract, the equilibrium NNP. Conversely, increases in taxes reduce, and decreases expand, the equilibrium NNP. Appropriate fiscal policy therefore calls for increases in government spending and decreases in taxes—that is, for

a budget deficit—to correct for unemployment. Decreases in government spending and increases in taxes—that is, a budget surplus—is appropriate fiscal policy for correcting inflation.

3. In view of the balanced-budget multiplier, equal increases in government spending and taxation will increase the equilibrium NNP.

4. Built-in flexibility refers to the automatic and appropriate changes in transfer payments and tax revenues which occur over the course of the business cycle. However, these nondiscretionary changes must be supplemented by discretionary fiscal action to mitigate inflation or unemployment of any severity.

5. Financing a government deficit through the creation of new money is more expansionary than financing the same deficit by borrowing. A surplus is more deflationary when held by government as an idle money balance than it is when used to retire outstanding public debt.

6. Generally speaking, public works expenditures are more expansionary than are transfer payments. Similarly, sales and excise taxes are generally felt to be more deflationary than are personal and corporate income taxes.

7. The enactment and application of appropriate fiscal policy are subject to certain problems and questions. Some of the most important are these: **a.** Can the enactment and application of fiscal policy be better timed so as to maximize its effectiveness in heading off economic fluctuations? **b.** Can the economy rely upon Congress to enact appropriate fiscal policy? **c.** State and local finance generally work to intensify rather than alleviate the cycle. **d.** Injudicious government spending may result in a curtailment of private investment. **e.** The use of fiscal policy to achieve full employment may conflict with other social goals such as price stability and achieving the desired allocation of resources to social goods.

QUESTIONS AND STUDY SUGGESTIONS

1. Explain graphically the determination of equilibrium NNP through both the aggregate demand–aggregate supply approach and the saving-equals-investment approach for the private sector. Now add government spending and taxation, showing the impact of each upon the equilibrium NNP.

2. Explain how discretionary fiscal policy can be used to close inflationary and deflationary gaps. How effective are the built-in stabilizers in controlling the business cycle? Adjust the appropriate schedules in Figures 14–1 and 14–2 for the existence of the built-in stabilizers. Use these new graphs to show that a given increase or decrease in autonomous investment will cause smaller changes in the equilibrium NNP with the built-in stabilizers than without.

3. What is the balanced-budget multiplier? Explain: "Equal increases in government spending and tax revenues of *n* dollars will increase the equilibrium NNP by *n* dollars." Does this hold true regardless of the size of the MPS?

4. Refer to the tabular data for question 8 at the end of Chapter 13. Now, assuming investment is $16 billion, incorporate government into the table by assuming that it plans to tax and spend $20 billion at each possible level of NNP. Assume all taxes are personal taxes and that government spending does not entail shifts in the consumption and investment schedules. Explain the change in the equilibrium NNP which the addition of government entails.

5. What is the best method of financing a government deficit during depression? What is the best means of disposing of a surplus during inflation? Explain your answers.

6. Suppose the economy encounters a severe and prolonged period of depression. What variations in the levels of taxes and expenditures would be appropriate? What variations in the tax structure and government expenditure programs would be desirable?

7. "If the economy needs $10 billion with which to finance the expansion and improvement of its highways, it should simply print up the needed money to finance the undertaking. In this way we'll get the roads, and no one will be hurt by having to pay higher taxes." Evaluate this suggestion, first under conditions of full employment, and second under depressed conditions.

8. Briefly state and evaluate the major problems encountered in enacting and applying fiscal policy. Which do you feel are the most significant?

9. Prof. Alvin H. Hansen has recently endorsed the following proposals as means of strengthening our fiscal policies:[7]
   a. "We should introduce an automatic or semiautomatic system of tax-rate adjustment in the first income tax bracket, so that the rate would rise and fall according to agreed-upon criteria of employment . . . or rates of investment."

[7] Alvin H. Hansen, *Economic Issues of the 1960's* (New York: McGraw-Hill Book Company, 1961), chap. 4.

b. The rate of depreciation allowable on capital goods for tax purposes should be made countercyclical. That is, businesses should be permitted to make larger depreciation charges in calculating taxable income during a period of unemployment, but smaller depreciation charges during an inflationary boom.

c. ". . . [A special] tax on investment could be employed to choke off such unhealthy and abnormal investment spurts as that of 1955–1957."

d. ". . . advertising expenditures tend to fluctuate *with* the cycle and thus serve to intensify instability. . . . Consideration might be given to countercyclical adjustment of advertising as an allowable business expense in calculating income taxes."

e. "The public should be represented at every important collective-bargaining table."

To which of these proposals would you adhere? Why? Which would you reject? Why? Discuss any administrative problems that might arise with each proposal. Assess as best you can the political feasibility of each.

10. Comment and evaluate:

a. "Full employment must be achieved and maintained at all costs."

b. "Rising prices cause real incomes to fall. In such circumstances all levels of government should cut taxes. This will permit the American people to maintain their standard of living."

SELECTED REFERENCES

Culbertson, J. M.: *Full Employment or Stagnation?* (New York: McGraw-Hill Book Company, 1964), particularly chaps. 1–8.

Due, John F.: *Government Finance*, 3d ed. (Homewood, Ill.: Richard D. Irwin, Inc., 1963), chaps. 27–31.

Hansen, Alvin H.: *Economic Issues of the 1960's* (New York: McGraw-Hill Book Company, 1961), particularly chaps. 4 and 6.

Hansen, Alvin H.: *The Postwar American Economy* (W. W. Norton & Company, Inc., 1964), chaps. 1–3.

Sharp, Ansel M., and Bernard F. Sliger: *Public Finance* (Homewood, Ill.: The Dorsey Press, 1964), chaps. 7, 8, and 10.

Strayer, Paul J.: *Fiscal Policy and Politics* (New York: Harper & Row, Publishers, Incorporated, 1958).

CHAPTER 15

FISCAL POLICY AND
THE PUBLIC DEBT

Fiscal policy is a cause of great concern to the populace because it suggests the some-time economic desirability of deficits. Deficits mean debt, and debt—particularly when measured in terms of hundreds of billions of dollars—is a most worrisome phenomenon. It is the basic purpose of this chapter to explore the causes and consequences of the public debt and, more particularly, to explode many of the fallacies associated with its existence. As a preliminary matter, we want to trace the evolution of several alternative budget policies and assess their capacities to stabilize the economy.

THREE BUDGET PHILOSOPHIES

A basic tenet of modern fiscal policy is that unbalanced budgets are helpful in stabilizing the economy. Surpluses are appropriate in tempering inflation; deficits are needed to cushion recessions. We can deepen our understanding of unbalanced budgets by exploring several alternative budget philosophies.

Generally speaking, there are three prevailing budget philosophies. The most conservative—not to say reactionary—policy is that which advocates an *annually* balanced budget. At the other extreme is *functional finance*, the most liberal view; it assigns a secondary priority to balancing the Federal

budget annually or over any other time period. Standing between the two is the idea of a *cyclically* balanced budget, wherein the Federal budget is to be balanced over the course of the business cycle rather than annually.

Annually Balanced Budget

Until the Great Depression of the 1930s the annually balanced budget was generally accepted without question as a desirable goal of public finance. An incorrect identification of private and public finance and widespread belief in the classical theory of employment both fostered this acceptance.

Upon examination, however, it becomes evident that an annually balanced budget rules out government fiscal activity as a countercyclical force. Worse yet, an annually balanced budget actually intensifies the business cycle. To illustrate, suppose that the economy encounters a siege of unemployment and falling incomes. As we have already noted, in such circumstances tax receipts will automatically decline. In seeking to balance its budget, government must either (1) increase tax rates, (2) reduce government expenditures, or (3) employ a combination of these two. It is obvious that all these policies are deflationary; each one further dampens rather than stimulates the level of aggregate demand.

Similarly, an annually balanced budget will intensify inflation. As money incomes rise during the course of inflation, tax collections will automatically increase. To avoid the impending surplus, government must either (1) cut tax rates, (2) increase government expenditures, or (3) adopt a combination of both. It is clear that all three of these policies will add to inflationary pressures.

The basic conclusion, then, is evident: *An annually balanced budget is not economically neutral; the pursuit of such a policy is procyclical, not countercyclical.*

Cyclically Balanced Budget

The Great Depression, general acceptance of Keynesian employment theory, and the recognition that public and private finance are not comparable all contributed to the development of the idea of a cyclically balanced budget. This budget philosophy envisions government's exerting a countercyclical influence and at the same time balancing its budget. In this case, however, the budget would not be balanced annually—after all, there is nothing sacred about twelve months as an accounting period—but rather over the course of the business cycle.

The rationale of this budget philosophy is simple, plausible, and appealing. To offset depression government should lower taxes and increase spending, thereby purposely incurring a deficit. During the ensuing inflationary upswing taxes would be raised and government spending slashed. The resulting surplus could then be used to retire the Federal debt incurred in financing the depression. In this way government fiscal operations would exert a positive countercyclical force, and the government could still balance its budget—not annually, but over a period of years.

A little reflection will reveal one big shortcoming of this budget philosophy which goes far to rob it of much of its luster: The upswing and downswing of the cycle may not be of equal magnitude and duration. Figure 11–3 makes this strikingly clear. In particular the very real possibility of persistent government deficits and a growing public debt arises. For example, should a long and severe depression be followed by a rather modest and brief prosperity, there would be little chance of obtaining surpluses in the good years sufficient to retire the deficits incurred in alleviating the bad years. Or the period of prosperity may be one wherein military considerations call for high levels of government spending, thereby ruling out the possibility of government's realizing a surplus. In brief, although the idea of a cyclically balanced budget looks fine on paper, there is some real question as to whether or not it is workable in practice.

Functional Finance

Out of the problems associated with any application of the cyclically balanced budget has evolved the idea of functional finance. As this budget philosophy sees it, the question of a balanced budget—either annually or cyclically—is of secondary importance. The primary purpose of Federal finance is to provide for noninflationary full employment. If the attainment of this objective entails either persistent surpluses or a large and growing public debt, so be it. The problems involved in government deficits or surpluses are relatively minor compared with the extremely unsavory alternatives of prolonged depression or severe inflation. The Federal budget is first and foremost an instrument for achieving and maintaining a noninflationary full-employment level of output. Government should not hesitate to incur any deficits and surpluses required in achieving this goal. In response to those who express concern about the large Federal debt which the pursuit of functional finance might entail, proponents of this budget philosophy offer two arguments. First, they contend that the problems of a large Federal debt are not as burdensome as most people think. In particular, public debt does not involve the same problems as does private debt. Second, the government's ability to finance deficits is almost unlimited. The credit standing of the government is exceedingly good; hence, the government should have no difficulty in borrowing. Furthermore, if its credit standing should somehow deteriorate, the government has the power to create money for the financing of deficits by running the printing presses.

Over the years tremendous changes have occurred in our thinking concerning public finance. Worship of a small and annually balanced budget has given way to the notion that government expenditures and taxes should be manipulated so as to compensate for any deficiency or excess of private spending in promoting full employment without inflation. Further, the budget should be balanced cyclically, or, if this is not feasible, not at all. In general the contention that government finance should be based upon "sound financial principles"—implicitly those principles which apply to private finance—has been largely supplanted by a recognition of the fact that public and private finance are so different as to be incomparable.

THE PUBLIC DEBT

Because modern fiscal policy stresses unbalanced budgets, its application will quite possibly lead to substantial growth in the public debt. Let us consider the public debt and the real and imaginary problems associated with its growth.

It has been said in reference to the public debt that "Never have so many understood so little about so much." To a very considerable degree this statement is true. The public debt is surrounded by awe, ignorance, and, in the extreme, outright fear. It is vital that we accurately comprehend the size, significance, and real problems

associated with it. In doing so we must be particularly alert for false impressions and inappropriate analogies and comparisons.

Dimensions of Debt

Growth of the public debt, as Table 15–1 indicates, has been substantial since 1930. *The primary cause of this expansion was the financing of World War II, rather than deficits incurred as a result of countercyclical fiscal policy.* In 1929, on the eve of the Great Depression, the public debt stood at $16.3 billion. At the end of the depressed thirties (1940) the debt had grown to $50.9 billion. The debt clearly expanded by a considerable amount as the result of deficit spending during the 1930s. But this growth is dwarfed by the more than fivefold increase during the World War II era.

There is no denying it: The absolute size of the public debt is so large—$318.7 billion in 1964—as to be almost beyond comprehension. But we must not fear large numbers per se. Let us therefore put the size of the public debt in better perspective.

1. A bald statement of the absolute size of the debt glosses over the fact that the wealth and productive ability of our economy have also increased tremendously over the years. It is safe to say that a wealthy nation has greater ability to incur and carry a large public debt than does a poor nation. In other words, it seems more realistic to measure changes in the public debt *in relation to* changes in the economy's GNP. Column 5 in Table 15–1 presents such data. Note that instead of the more than sixfold increase in the debt between 1940 and 1964 shown in column 2, we now find that the debt has not grown at all! As a matter of fact, the *relative* size of the debt has *declined* very considerably since 1946. Note, too, that the per capita size of the public debt has diminished since the close of World War II.

2. As we shall see momentarily, many

TABLE 15–1. QUANTITATIVE SIGNIFICANCE OF THE PUBLIC DEBT: THE PUBLIC DEBT AND INTEREST PAYMENTS IN RELATION TO GNP, 1929–1964

(1) Year	(2) Public debt, billions	(3) Gross national product,* billions	(4) Interest payments, billions	(5) Public debt as per cent of GNP, (2) ÷ (3)	(6) Interest payments as per cent of GNP, (4) ÷ (3)	(7) Per capita public debt
1929	$ 16.3	$104.4	$ 0.68	16%	0.6%	$ 134
1940	50.9	100.6	1.06	51	1.0	382
1942	112.5	159.1	1.27	71	0.8	833
1946	259.5	210.7	4.82	123	2.3	1,827
1950	256.7	284.6	5.82	90	2.0	1,689
1954	278.8	363.1	6.47	77	1.8	1,404
1958	283.0	444.5	7.69	64	1.7	1,617
1960	290.4	502.6	9.27	58	1.8	1,604
1962	304.0	556.2	9.20	55	1.7	1,626
1964	318.7	622.6	10.76	51	1.7	1,651

* In current dollars.
Source: Economic Report of the President (Washington: Government Printing Office, 1965).

economists feel that the primary burden of the debt is the annual interest charge that accrues as a result of the debt. The absolute size of these interest payments is shown in column 4. Interest charges as a percentage of GNP are presented in column 6. In these latter terms the burden of the debt has increased by very small amounts over the last four decades, and has actually declined since 1946.

3. Although the size and growth of public debt are looked upon with awe and alarm, private debt has grown much faster and is now twice as large—over $850 billion as compared to $319 billion—as the public debt. If one insists upon worrying about debt, you will do well to concern yourself with private rather than public indebtedness.

Let us turn now from the causes and size of the debt to the question of ownership. The basic point here is that the public debt is *internally* held; that is, it is held by American citizens and American institutions.

This, as we shall see shortly, is of considerable importance, because the problems posed by an *externally* held debt, that is, a public debt which is held by foreign individuals, foreign institutions, and foreign governments, are different from those of an internally held debt.

Public and Private Debt

But this brings us to another consideration: The debts of individuals and the public debt are not readily comparable. Public debt is basically a macroeconomic concept and private debt a microeconomic concept. The fallacy of composition reminds us that different principles may govern macro and micro concepts. More specifically, one must be very cautious in applying the principles and practices surrounding private debt to the public debt. Much misunderstanding of the significance and burden of the public debt stems from such a misguided application. Let us be more specific.

Characteristics of private debt. The debts of private individuals are owed by one person to some other individual or organization. In incurring such debt, the individual obtains funds which expand his dollar claims over output and permit him to currently increase his standard of living. But individuals are mortal, and creditors will demand repayment of loans at some future date. This repayment obviously involves a decline in the debtor's ability to obtain goods and services and a reduction in his standard of living.

Characteristics of public debt. Public debt differs on all counts. First, the public debt is a debt which we—American citizens and institutions—owe to ourselves. Whereas a private debt is one between distinct economic units, a public debt is one held within a single economic unit. Strictly speaking, the public debt is owed by the United States government to bondholding citizens and institutions—banks, insurance companies, and businesses—within the United States. But should the government decide to retire this debt, how would the needed funds be obtained? By collecting taxes from American citizens and institutions. Hence, the public debt is one which we owe to one another. Were the public debt externally held, that is, held by foreigners, it would be like a private debt—a debt between distinct economic units—and this owe-it-to-ourselves characteristic would not be applicable.

Second, nations are quite immortal, and there is no compelling reason why their debt need be retired. Indeed, as Table 15-1 suggests, no serious attempt has been made in recent decades to reduce the public debt. As a relatively small portion of the total debt falls due each month or year, the government does not cut expenditures or boost taxes to provide funds for *retiring* the debt.

(Indeed, we know with depressed economic conditions this would be a most unwise fiscal policy.) Rather, the government sells new bonds and uses the proceeds to pay off holders of the maturing bonds. Debt *refunding* is a less troublesome task both economically and politically than is debt retirement.

Furthermore, the owe-it-to-ourselves character of the public debt tells us that even if the public debt were to be retired, there would be no direct loss of wealth for the economy as a whole. Retirement of the public debt would call for a gigantic transfer payment whereby American individuals and institutions would pay higher taxes and the government in turn would pay out those tax revenues to those same taxpaying individuals and institutions in the aggregate in redeeming the bonds which they hold. Although a redistribution of wealth would result from this gigantic financial transfer, it need not entail any immediate decline in the economy's aggregate wealth or standard of living. The repayment of an internally held public debt entails no leakage of purchasing power from the economy of the country as a whole.

There is a final significant distinction between individual and public debt. If you or I as individuals were to increase or reduce our indebtedness, the impact of so doing upon the economy would be negligible. But the Federal government is obviously so large relative to the economy that changes in its debt can and do have very substantial effects upon the economic health of society. Indeed, fiscal policy is predicated upon this fact.

Debt Burdens and War Finance

There are many gross misconceptions concerning the burden or disadvantages associated with the public debt. The crucial question is: What costs or disadvantages are imposed upon the economy when government expenditures are financed by borrowing rather than taxation?

The cost of an increase in the public debt depends upon the economic conditions under which it is incurred. If the public debt is increased during a period of substantial unemployment, the real cost of the debt is zero. Why? Because the expansionary effect of the deficit puts idle resources back to work, and the resulting increase in the national output is all a net gain. No alternative products are sacrificed, and therefore no real costs are involved in putting idle resources back to work by increasing the debt. We have noted in Table 15–1 that both the absolute size of the debt and the strength of the economy have grown historically. As a matter of fact, *some of the economy's healthiest periods of expansion and growth in real output have occurred at times when the public debt was increasing most rapidly.* It is no mystery why this is so: A budget deficit means a net injection of purchasing power into the economy by government, and this, of course, is expansionary.

Deficit spending during full employment is a different matter. In the first place we know that such spending is completely inappropriate in so far as stabilization policy is concerned. Yet during the full-employment years of World War II, when the bulk of our present public debt was incurred, government found that it was neither politically nor economically feasible to finance the war on a pay-as-you-go basis through taxation. Borrowing was chosen as the best alternative to supplement taxes that were considered to be at the upper limit of the economy's tolerance. This spending pulled resources from the production of private goods to the production of armaments. The burden of deficit spending during full employment is that alternative private goods —in this case automobiles, refrigerators, vacuum cleaners, and a host of other consumer goods—were not produced.

These observations answer a frequently heard question: Does government borrowing as a method of finance permit society to pass a portion of the economic cost of a war to future generations? Certainly not if government borrows internally, that is, from people and institutions within the country. It is the wartime generation itself which must tighten its civilian standard of living in order to free scarce resources for the production of armaments. There is no way of sidestepping or postponing these costs. Putting the matter in specific terms, it was the population living during 1941–1946 which did without a multitude of consumer durables to permit the United States to arm itself and its allies.

In money, or financial, terms the waging of World War II increased the public debt by well over $200 billion. Is this not a financial burden for future generations to bear? For the economy as a whole, no. The making of interest and principal payments on the war-born portion of the public debt will constitute transfers of funds from future Americans as taxpayers to future Americans as bondholders. Such a financial transfer, as we have already seen, does not entail a direct decline in the total wealth of that future generation. The fact that each American baby born in 1970 may be, say, $1,800 or $2,000 in debt at the time he enters the world is not quite as disturbing as it sounds. Each member of the 1970 baby crop will also inherit, on the average, ownership of that same amount in government bonds. The higher taxes *paid* by our grandchildren in paying interest and principal on the war-incurred public debt will be *received* by that same group of grandchildren. In short, the real economic cost of a war must be shouldered at the time the war is being fought.

There is one notable exception: The emergency of wartime production may cause a nation's stock of capital to cease to grow or to dwindle as precious resources are taken from the production of capital goods and shifted to the production of war goods. As a result, future generations inherit a smaller stock of capital goods than would otherwise be the case. This occurred in the United States during World War II (see table on inside covers, line 2). But this shifting of costs is independent of how a war is financed.

Whereas an internally held public debt is a debt existing within an economic unit (a nation), an externally held public debt is a debt between distinct economic units (two nations). As a result, an externally held public debt has the characteristics of a private debt. Hence, a nation can ease the immediate economic burden of a war by obtaining loans from other nations and spending the proceeds on the goods and services of the lending nation. Imports thus received supplement the borrowing nation's standard of living and ease the wartime strain on its own resources. But the tables are turned when time for repayment of the loan rolls around, say, twenty years later. The borrowing nation must then make enough of its currency available to the lending nation to retire its matured bonds. The lending nation then spends these funds in acquiring a portion of the borrowing nation's GNP. In other words, the generation living at the time the bonds fall due must tighten their belts to make goods and services available for repayment of a loan incurred some twenty years earlier. A portion of the real economic cost of a war has been shifted two decades into the future by increasing a nation's externally held public debt.

Real Burden of the Debt

But we must be careful not to whitewash the public debt. The existence of a large public debt does pose real and potential problems.

Incentives. Table 15–1 makes evident the fact that the present public debt necessitates an annual interest payment of almost $11 billion. With no increase in the size of the debt, this annual interest charge must be paid out of tax revenues. Taxes may tend to dampen incentives to bear risk, to innovate, to invest, and to work. In this indirect way the existence of a large debt can impair economic growth.

Income inequality. In all probability the payment of interest and principal on the public debt contributes to income inequality. Common sense and available statistical evidence concerning the income status of savers suggest that most government bondholders are in the middle- and upper-income brackets. On the other hand, under the prevailing tax structure the revenue needed to pay interest and principal on the debt would come rather evenly from all income groups (see Table 9–6). In all probability the net result of interest or principal repayment is greater income inequality, held by many to be undesirable on equity grounds.

A word of caution: In weighing the possible impact of the public debt upon incentives and the personal distribution of income, two points should be kept in mind. First, the size of the annual interest charge on the debt is relatively small—about 1.7 per cent of the GNP. Second, the relative size of this interest charge has been fairly stable for the last fifteen years. As a matter of fact, it has declined somewhat in the postwar era.

Debt, liquidity, and inflation. The very existence of a large debt tends to be inflationary. This is so for at least two reasons:

1. Because they are highly liquid assets, the possession of government bonds makes consumers feel wealthier. This feeling of wealth leads to greater consumption out of their incomes. In short, the existence of a large public debt tends to shift the consump-

tion schedule upward. If the economy is already at full employment, this shift will be inflationary.

2. Furthermore, government bonds can be converted into money easily and with little or no risk of loss. Government bonds, therefore, constitute a potential backlog of purchasing power which can add materially to inflationary fires. During periods of inflation it is very tempting for consumers to dig into this reserve of purchasing power in an attempt to beat rising prices. Such an attempt to beat inflation will cause more inflation. Something like this happened at the end of World War II; the inflation-causing buying spree of 1946–1947 was financed partly by the cashing in of bonds purchased during the war.

But the contention that a large public debt has an inflationary bias must be qualified. First, *changes* in the size of the public debt have a much greater impact upon employment, output, and the price level than does the *absolute size* of the existing debt. Thus a $5 billion increase in the debt can be expected to exert a much greater expansionary or inflationary effect on the economy than the mere presence of an existing debt of, say, $319 billion. Furthermore, remember that deficit spending is inflationary only if it is inappropriate fiscal policy. Deficit spending under full-employment conditions is inflationary; but this is ill-advised fiscal policy. Deficit spending during recession is expansionary; it increases employment and output and is therefore well advised.

Debt management dilemma. Every month several billion dollars worth of outstanding government bonds mature and must be refinanced. Decisions made in managing the public debt may have a significant impact upon the stability of the economy and may be at odds with countercyclical fiscal policy. The basic dilemma is between the Treasury's desire for low interest costs, on the one hand, and economic stabilization, on the

other. For example, because interest rates tend to fall during the downswing of the cycle, the Treasury can minimize its interest costs by selling long-term bonds during recession periods. But such sales are likely to intensify the recession by driving up interest rates and drawing scarce money capital away from potential private spenders. Similarly, in Chapter 18 we shall find that during inflation the Treasury's desire for low interest rates conflicts with the desire of the monetary authorities to raise interest rates for the purpose of limiting investment and consumer spending.

Advantages of a Public Debt

There is a brighter side to the public debt. Indeed, in at least three respects the existence of a large debt can be desirable.

1. Because government bonds are highly liquid and virtually risk-free securities, they make an excellent purchase for small and conservative savers.

2. It should also be noted that although a large debt may pose inflationary problems in a full-employment economy, that same debt can cushion a cyclical downswing. That which is potentially undesirable in a full-employment economy may be very desirable in a less-than-full-employment economy. A large public debt may prove to be a kind of built-in stabilizer in so far as recessions are concerned.

3. Finally, Chapter 18 will reveal the important role which government bonds play in effectuating monetary policy. The sale and purchase of government bonds by the economy's central banks influence the money supply, the level of spending, and hence the level of economic activity.

SUMMARY

1. Historically, the concept of an annually balanced budget has given ground to that of the cyclically balanced budget and,

more recently, to the idea of functional finance.

2. The public debt is now $318.7 billion, about 51 per cent of the GNP. The main source of the debt was the financing of World War II.

3. Public debt has different characteristics from private debt. Public debt **a.** is owed by Americans to Americans, **b.** need not be retired, and **c.** does not entail a reduced standard of living for the economy as a whole when payment of interest or principal is made.

4. The real cost of a war or of a depression cannot be shifted to future generations by increasing the internally held public debt.

5. A large public debt may **a.** impair incentives to innovate and invest, **b.** contribute to income inequality, **c.** add to inflationary pressures, and **d.** entail knotty problems of debt management.

QUESTIONS AND STUDY SUGGESTIONS

1. Explain each of the following statements:
a. "No budget-balancing principle can be as important as maintaining full employment and preventing inflation."
b. "A national debt is like a debt of the left hand to the right hand."
c. "Find an individual who is steadily accumulating debt, and you have probably found one who is in trouble; find one who is paying off his debts, and you have probably found one in good economic health. But find a nation whose domestic debts are mounting, whose mortgages year by year are increasing, whose corporate debentures are proliferating, whose state and local and federal bond issues are growing, and chances are that you have found a nation whose rate of growth is high, whose economy is buoyant, whose savings are abundant, whose business is booming."[1]

2. Explain the three major budget philosophies. To which do you subscribe? Why? Why is an annually balanced budget not economically neutral?

3. How do private and public debts differ? How does an internally held public debt differ from an externally held public debt? What would be the effects of retiring an internally held public debt?

4. In what ways might the mere existence of a large public debt contribute to inflationary pressures? "Incurring a public debt is more inflationary than carrying an existing public debt." Do you agree?

5. Distinguish clearly between refunding and retiring public debt.

6. Explain: "As a society becomes wealthier saving increases. If prosperity is to be sustained, the private and public sectors together must borrow and spend an amount sufficient to offset this saving. The expansion of debt is therefore a prerequisite of full employment."

[1] Robert L. Heilbroner and Peter L. Bernstein, *A Primer on Government Spending* (New York: Vintage Books, Inc., Random House, Inc., 1963), p. 45.

SELECTED REFERENCES

Bowen, William G., Richard G. Davis, and David H. Kopf: "The Public Debt: A Burden on Future Generations?" *American Economic Review,* September, 1960, pp. 701–706.

Buchanan, James M.: *Public Principles of Public Debt* (Homewood, Ill.: Richard D. Irwin, Inc., 1958).

Heilbroner, Robert L., and Peter L. Bernstein: *A Primer on Government Spending* (New York: Vintage Books, Inc., Random House, Inc., 1963).

Peterson, Rudolph A.: "Debt in the New Economic Environment," *Challenge,* December, 1964, pp. 15–19.

Sharp, Ansel M., and Bernard F. Sliger: *Public Finance* (Homewood, Ill.: The Dorsey Press, 1964), chaps. 11 and 12.

PART THREE: MONEY, MONETARY POLICY,
AND ECONOMIC STABILITY

CHAPTER 16

MONEY AND BANKING IN AMERICAN CAPITALISM

Money—one of the truly great inventions of man—constitutes a most fascinating aspect of economic science.[1]

Money bewitches people. They fret for it, and they sweat for it. They devise most ingenious ways to get it, and most ingenuous ways to get rid of it. Money is the only commodity that is good for nothing but to be gotten rid of. It will not feed you, clothe you, shelter you, or amuse you unless you spend it or invest it. It imparts value only in parting. People will do almost anything for money, and money will do almost anything for people. Money is a captivating, circulating, masquerading puzzle.

Money is also one of the most crucial elements of economic science. It is much more than a passive component of the economic system—a mere tool for facilitating the economy's operation. When operating properly, the monetary system is the lifeblood of the circular flows of income and expenditure which typify all economies. A well-behaved money system is conducive to both full production and full employment. Conversely, a malfunctioning monetary system can make major contributions to severe fluctuations in the economy's levels of output, employment, and prices.

In this chapter we are concerned with the nature and functions of money and the basic institutions of the American banking system.

[1] Federal Reserve Bank of Philadelphia, "Creeping Inflation," *Business Review*, August 1957, p. 3.

Chapter 17 looks into the methods by which individual commercial banks and the banking system as a whole can vary the money supply. In Chapter 18 we discuss how the central banks of the economy attempt to regulate the supply of money so as to promote full employment and full production.

The specific objectives of the present chapter are fourfold. We begin with a review of the functions of money. Next we designate and assess the relative importance of the various types of money used in American capitalism. Third, we pose a query: What "backs" money in the United States? Finally, the institutional structure and the basic functions of the American banking system will be described.

THE FUNCTIONS OF MONEY

What is money? Money is what money does. Anything that performs the functions of money is money. There are three functions of money:

1. First and foremost, money is a *medium of exchange;* that is, money is usable in buying and selling goods and services. As a medium of exchange, money allows society to escape the complications of barter and to thereby reap the benefits of geographic and human specialization (see Chapter 3).

2. Money is also a *standard of value.* Society finds it convenient to use the monetary unit as a yardstick for measuring the relative worth of heterogeneous goods and resources. Two related advantages are in-

volved here. On the one hand, with a money system, the price of each product need only be stated in terms of the monetary unit rather than in terms of each of the other products for which it might be exchanged. This very substantially reduces the number of prices in the economy. On the other hand, with money prices as a common denominator of value, transactors can readily compare the relative worth of various commodities and resources. Such comparisons facilitate rational decision making. Money is also used as a standard of value for transactions involving future payments. Debt obligations of all kinds are measured in terms of money.

3. Finally, money serves as a *store of value*. Because money is the most liquid of all assets, it is a very convenient form in which to store wealth. Though it is not likely to yield monetary returns such as one gets by storing wealth in the form of real assets (property) or paper assets (stocks, bonds, and so forth), money does have the advantage of being immediately usable by a firm or a household in meeting any and all financial obligations.

MONEY IN AMERICAN CAPITALISM

Historically, such diverse items as whale's teeth, elephant tail bristles, circular stones, nails, slaves, cattle, beer, cigarettes, and pieces of metal have functioned as media of exchange. More recently, the debts of governments and of banks have been employed as money.

In so far as the United States is concerned, the money supply is composed of only three items: (1) coins, (2) paper money, and (3) demand deposits, or checking accounts. The first two items are debts of government and governmental agencies; the third represents a debt of commercial banks. Table 16–1 shows the quantitative importance of each money item in both absolute and relative terms. Let's comment briefly on each of these components of the money supply.

Coins

Ranging from copper pennies to silver dollars, coins constitute the "small change" of our money supply. As Table 16–1 indicates, coins constitute a very small portion of our total money supply. Coins are essentially "convenience money" in that they permit us to make all kinds of very small purchases.

It is notable that all the coins in circulation in the United States are token money. This simply means that the intrinsic value—that is, the value of the bullion contained in the coin itself—is less than the face value of the coin. This is purposely the case so as to avoid the melting down of token money for profitable sale as bullion. If a 50-cent piece contained, say, 75 cents' worth of silver bullion, it would be highly profitable to melt these coins for sale as bullion. Despite the illegality of such a procedure, 50-cent pieces would tend to disappear from circulation. This is one of the potential defects of commodity money: Its worth as a commodity may come to exceed its worth as money, causing it to cease functioning as a medium of exchange.

Paper Money

Much more significant than coins, paper money constitutes about one-fifth of the economy's money supply. You have undoubtedly noticed that there are several different types of paper money currently in

TABLE 16–1. MONEY IN THE UNITED STATES, MARCH, 1965

Money	Billions of dollars	Per cent of total
Coins	$ 2	1
Paper money	33	21
Demand deposits	126	78
Total	$161	100

Source: Federal Reserve Bulletin, May, 1965.

circulation in the United States. By far the most important are *Federal Reserve Notes.* These notes, which constitute about $32 billion of the $33 billion worth of paper money in circulation, are issued by the Federal Reserve Banks with the authorization of Congress. The remaining $1 billion are made up of silver certificates plus a few very minor forms of paper money such as National Bank Notes, Treasury Notes of 1890, and so forth. All of these forms of paper money other than Federal Reserve Notes have been issued by the Treasury and are therefore called *Treasury currency.* In the interest of a more uniform currency the various types of Treasury currency are in the process of retirement in favor of Federal Reserve Notes. The coin and paper money components of the money supply are frequently lumped together and simply labeled *currency.*

Demand Deposits

The safety and convenience of using checks, or bank money, have made demand deposits the most important type of money in the United States. Despite the efficiency of the Post Office Department and the integrity of its employees, one would not think of stuffing, say, $4,896.47 in an envelope and dropping it in a mailbox in paying a debt; but to write and mail a check for a large sum is very commonplace. A check must be endorsed by the person cashing it; the drawer of the check subsequently receives the canceled check as an endorsed receipt attesting to the fulfillment of his obligation. Similarly, because the writing of a check requires endorsement by the drawer, the theft or loss of one's bank book is not nearly so calamitous as would be the losing of an identical amount of currency. It is, furthermore, simply more convenient to write a check in many cases than it is to transport and count out a large sum of currency. For all these reasons checkbook money has come to be the dominant form of money in Ameri-

can capitalism. Even Table 16–1 belittles the significance of bank money; it is estimated that dollarwise about 90 per cent of all transactions are carried out by the use of checks.

It might seem strange that demand deposits or checking accounts are a part of the money supply. But the reason for their inclusion is clear: Checks, which are nothing more than a means for transferring the ownership of demand deposits, are generally acceptable as a medium of exchange. Furthermore, demand deposits can be immediately converted into paper money and coins on demand; demand deposits are for all practical purposes the equivalent of currency.

In short,

$$\text{Money} = \text{demand deposits} + \text{currency}$$

Currency is essentially government-created money, and demand deposits, we shall discover in Chapter 17, are bank-created money.

Near-monies and Bank and Treasury Holdings

Two qualifications of our definition of money must be noted.

1. The line between what we have defined as money and certain highly liquid assets called *near-monies* is a very fine one. The two most important near-monies are time deposits, or savings accounts, and United States government bonds. Households and businesses currently hold about $90 billion worth of government bonds and own in the neighborhood of $185 billion worth of savings deposits in commercial banks, mutual savings banks, and in the postal savings system. Time deposits come very close to being money. But they must be excluded from the definition of money because they are not a medium of exchange. You cannot write checks on a savings account in making purchases or in paying

debts.[2] Much the same can be said of United States government bonds: most are highly marketable and can be readily converted into currency or demand deposits with little fear of loss. As a matter of fact, your Series E bonds can be converted into currency or demand deposits at commercial banks at a stipulated price upon demand. Yet, as such, government bonds are not a medium of exchange.

Near-monies are important to our discussion for three related reasons. First, the fact that people have such highly liquid assets available affects their consuming-saving habits. Generally speaking, the greater the amount of wealth people have in the form of near-monies, the greater is their willingness to spend out of their money incomes. Second, a sudden conversion of easily cashable near-monies into money adds significantly to the money supply and, if not offset, can pose serious problems during inflationary periods. Finally, the existence of near-monies points up the fact that the definition of money is somewhat arbitrary. In modern complex economies there is no clear-cut distinction between money and certain highly liquid assets.

2. The second qualification of our definition of money is of a somewhat technical nature. In the definition of the money supply, currency and demand deposits owned by government and by Federal Reserve or commercial banks are excluded. This exclusion is partly to avoid overstating the money supply and partly because money in the possession of households and businesses is more relevant to the level of spending in the economy.[3]

[2] Yet, although bankers may legally require thirty or sixty days' notice of withdrawal, time deposits are in practice immediately convertible into demand deposits or currency.

[3] A paper dollar in the hands of John Doe obviously constitutes just $1 of the money supply. But, if we were to count dollars held by banks as a part of the money supply, that same $1 would count for $2 when deposited in a commercial bank. It would count for a $1

WHAT "BACKS" THE MONEY SUPPLY?

This is a slippery question; any reasonably complete answer is likely to be at odds with the preconceptions many of us hold with respect to money.

Money As Debt

The first point to recognize is that the major components of the money supply—paper money and demand deposits—are simply debts, or promises to pay. Paper money is the debt of the Treasury and the Federal Reserve Banks.[4] Paper currency is merely the circulating IOUs of the government and the central banks. Demand deposits are simply the debts of commercial banks.

Furthermore, paper currency and demand deposits have no intrinsic value. A $5 bill is just a piece of paper, and a demand deposit is merely a bookkeeping entry. And coins, we already know, have an intrinsic value less than their face value. Nor will government redeem the paper money you hold for anything tangible such as gold. In so far as our domestic money supply is concerned the supplies of gold which the

demand deposit owned by Doe and also for $1 worth of currency resting in the bank's vault. This problem of double counting can be avoided by excluding currency resting in commercial banks (and currency redeposited in the Federal Reserve Banks or other commercial banks) in determining the total money supply. The exclusion of currency held by, and demand deposits owned by, government is somewhat more arbitrary. The major reason for this exclusion is that it permits us better to gauge the money supply and rate of spending which occurs in the private sector of the economy apart from spending initiated by government policy.

[4] Federal Reserve Notes in circulation are the debts or obligations of the Federal Reserve Banks, and all other forms of paper money (Treasury currency) are debts of the United States Treasury.

government has hidden away in assorted holes in the ground are of little consequence; the supply of money is linked to our stocks of precious metals only in a very loose and flexible manner. In effect, American capitalism has wisely chosen to "manage" its money supply in seeking to provide the amount of money needed for that particular volume of business activity which will foster full employment, price level stability, and a healthy rate of economic growth. Such management of the money supply is eminently more sensible than linking the money supply to gold or any other commodity whose supply might arbitrarily and capriciously change. After all, a substantial increase in the nation's gold stock as the result of mining or importation might increase the money supply far beyond that amount needed to transact a full-employment level of business activity and therefore result in sharp inflation. Conversely, the loss of gold in settling international transactions (Chapter 39) could reduce the domestic money supply to the point where economic activity was choked off and unemployment and a retarded growth rate resulted. The important point is that paper money cannot be converted into gold but is only exchangeable for other pieces of paper money. For example, Federal Reserve Notes, the major component of our paper money supply, boldly proclaim that "the United States of America will pay to the bearer on demand" the number of dollars stated on the note. But what form will these dollars which the government promises to pay assume? They will be in the form of other paper currency, that is, other paper promises to pay![5] The government will swap one paper $5 bill for another bearing a different serial number. That is all you can get should you ask the government to redeem some of the paper

money you hold. Similarly, demand deposit money cannot be exchanged for gold but only for paper money, which, as we have just seen, will not be redeemed by the government for anything tangible.

Value of Money

Now don't get discouraged and tear up the $5 bill you have in your pocket. Actually, the fact that the government does not stand ready to hand you a lump of gold for every dollar you possess really is not as significant as it might first sound. *Paper money does have value, because you can exchange it for the goods and services you wish to obtain in order to satisfy your wants.* Although the government will not give you anything tangible for your $5 bill, businesses and households are willing to exchange goods, services, and resources for it. Suppose you swap a $10 bill for a sweater at a clothing store. Why does the merchant accept this piece of paper in exchange for one of his products? The answer is tricky: The merchant accepts paper money because he is confident that others will also be willing to accept it in exchange for goods and services. He knows that he can purchase the services of his clerks, acquire products from wholesalers, pay the rent on his store, and so forth. Each of us accepts paper money in exchange because he has confidence that it will be exchangeable for real goods and services when he chooses to spend it.

This confidence in the acceptability of paper money is partly a matter of law; currency has been designated as *legal tender* by government. This means that paper currency must be accepted in the payment of a debt or the creditor forfeits the privilege of charging interest and the right to sue the debtor for nonpayment. Put more bluntly, the acceptability of paper dollars is bolstered by the fact that government says these dollars are money. The paper money in our economy is basically *fiat money;* it is money because the government says it is, not because of redeemability in terms of some

---

[5] The government will give you coins, if you insist, for silver certificates. But remember that the bullion value of these coins falls considerably short of their face value, so they too in part are debts.

precious metal. The general acceptability of currency is also bolstered by the willingness of government to accept it in the payment of taxes and other obligations due the government.

Lest we be overimpressed by the power of government, it should be noted that the fact that paper currency is generally accepted in exchange is decidedly more important than government's legal tender decree in making these pieces of paper function as money. Indeed, the government has not decreed checks to be legal tender, but they nevertheless successfully perform the vast bulk of the economy's exchanges of goods, services, and resources.

But let us consider the value of money in more positive terms. The value of money, as the economic value of anything else, is essentially a supply and demand phenomenon. That is, money derives its value from its scarcity relative to its usefulness. The usefulness of money, of course, lies in its unique capacity to be exchanged for goods and services, either now or in the future. The economy's demand for money thus depends upon its total dollar volume of transactions in any given time period plus the amount of money individuals and businesses want to hold for possible future transactions. Given a reasonably constant demand for money, the value or "purchasing power" of the monetary unit will be determined by the supply of money. Let us see why this is so.

The real value or purchasing power of money is simply the amount of goods and services a unit of money will buy. It is obvious, furthermore, that the amount a dollar will buy varies inversely with the price level; stated differently, a reciprocal relationship exists between the general price level and the value of the dollar. Figure 16–1 allows us to visualize this inverse relationship.[6] When the consumer's price index or "cost-of-living" index goes up, the purchasing power of the dollar necessarily goes down, and vice versa. Higher prices lower the value of the dollar because it will now take more dollars to command a given amount of goods and services. Conversely, lower prices increase the purchasing power of the dollar because you will now need fewer dollars to obtain a given quantity of goods and services. If the price level doubles, the value of the dollar will decline by one-half or 50 per cent. If the price level falls by one-half or 50 per cent, the purchasing power of the dollar will double.

You have probably heard or read of situations wherein a nation's currency became worthless and unacceptable in exchange. Indeed, we noted several in Chapter 11. With few exceptions these were situations where government issued so many pieces of paper currency that the value of each of these units of money was almost totally undermined. The infamous post–World War I inflation in Germany is a most notable example. In December of 1919 there were about 50 billion marks in circulation. Exactly four years later this figure had expanded to 496,585,345,900 billion marks! The result? The German mark in 1923 was worth an infinitesimal fraction of its 1919 value.[7] Inflation, you will recall, is the consequence of society's spending beyond its capacity to produce. Other things being equal, increases in the money supply will increase total spending. Once full employment is reached and total output becomes virtually fixed, this added spending can only serve to make prices spiral up. The sweater which sold for $10 in our previous illustration may, after severe inflation, cost $100. This means that the dollar which was formerly worth one-tenth of a sweater is now worth just one-hundredth of a sweater. The dollar's value, or purchasing power, has obviously been

---

[6] Figure 16–1 is called a "ratio" or "semi-log" chart, because equal vertical distances measure equal percentage changes rather than equal absolute changes.

[7] Frank G. Graham, *Exchange, Prices and Production in Hyper-inflation Germany, 1920–1923* (Princeton, N.J.: Princeton University Press, 1930), p. 13.

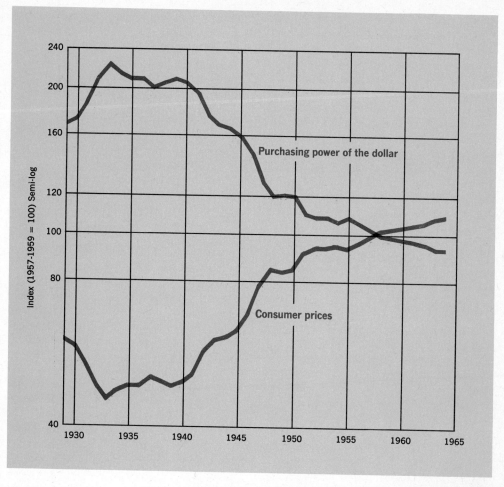

FIGURE 16–1. THE PRICE LEVEL AND THE VALUE OF MONEY.
A reciprocal or inverse relationship exists between the general price level
and the purchasing power of the dollar.

reduced to 10 per cent of its former value by inflation.

How might inflation and the accompanying decreases in the value of the dollar affect the acceptability of paper dollars as money? Households and businesses are willing to accept paper currency as a medium of exchange so long as they know it can in turn be spent by them without any noticeable loss in its purchasing power. But with spiraling inflation this is not the case. Runaway inflation, such as Germany faced in the early 1920s, may significantly depreciate the value of money between the time of its receipt and its expenditure. Money will be "hot" money. It is as if the government were constantly taxing away the purchasing power of dollars. Rapid depreciation of the value of the dollar may cause it to cease functioning as a medium of exchange. Businesses and households may refuse to accept paper money in exchange, because they do not want to bear the loss in its value which will occur while it is in their possession. (All this despite the fact that government says the paper currency is legal tender.) Without an acceptable medium of exchange the economy will be thrown into disorder.

Similarly, people are willing to use money as a store of value so long as there is no unreasonable deterioration in the value of those stored dollars because of inflation. And the economy can effectively employ the monetary unit as a standard of value only when its purchasing power is relatively stable. A yardstick of value which is subject to drastic shrinkage no longer permits buyers and sellers to establish clearly the terms of trade. When the value of the dollar is declining rapidly, sellers will not know what to charge and buyers will not know what to pay for the various goods and services.

Managing Money

Now the overriding implication of this discussion of the value of money is this: The major "backing" of paper money is the public's confidence in the government's ability to keep the value of money reasonably stable. This entails (1) appropriate fiscal policy, as explained in Chapter 14, and (2) intelligent management or regulation of the money supply, as noted above. The acceptability of paper money depends in part upon sound management of the monetary system and the pursuit of appropriate fiscal measures by government. Businesses and households accept paper money in exchange for goods so long as they know it will command a roughly equivalent amount of goods when they in turn spend it. In our economy a blending of legislation, government policy, and social practice serves as a bulwark against any imprudent expansion of the money supply which might jeopardize money's value in exchange.

What we have said with respect to paper currency also applies to demand deposit money. In this case money is the debt of the commercial banks. If you have a checking account worth $100, this simply means that your commercial bank is indebted to you for that number of dollars. You can collect this debt in one of two ways. You can go to the bank and demand paper currency for your demand deposit; this simply amounts to changing the debts you hold from bank debts to government-issued debts. Or, and this is more likely, you can "collect" the debt which the bank owes you by transferring this claim by check to someone else. For example, if you buy a $100 suit from your clothier, you can pay for it by writing a check, which transfers the bank's indebtedness from you to your clothier. The bank now owes your clothier the $100 which it previously owed to you. Why does the clothier accept this transfer of indebtedness (the check) as a medium of exchange? Because he can convert it into currency on demand or can in turn transfer the debt to others in making purchases of his choice. Thus checks, as means of transferring bank debts, are acceptable as money because of the public's confidence in commercial banks' ability to honor these claims.

In turn, the ability of commercial banks to honor claims against them depends upon their not creating too many of these claims. We shall find in a moment that a decentralized system of private, profit-seeking banks does not contain sufficient safeguards against the creation of too much check money. Hence, the American banking system has a substantial amount of governmental control to guard against the imprudent creation of check money by commercial banks.

Let us now summarize the major points of this section:

1. In the United States and other advanced economies, all money is essentially the debts of government and commercial banks.

2. These debts efficiently perform the functions of money so long as their value, or purchasing power, is relatively stable.

3. The value of money is no longer rooted in carefully defined quantities of precious metals, but rather in the amount of goods and services money will purchase in the market place.

4. Government's responsibility in stabilizing the value of the monetary unit involves (1) the application of appropriate fiscal policies and (2) effective control over the supply of money.

INSTITUTIONAL FRAMEWORK OF THE AMERICAN BANKING SYSTEM

We have noted that the major component of the money supply, demand deposits, is created by commercial banks and that government-created money, coins and paper currency, typically comes into circulation through the commercial banks. It is essential then that we take a thorough look at the framework of the American banking system prior to a detailed analysis in Chapter 17 of how commercial banks create money.

Need for Centralization

It became painfully apparent rather early in American history that, like it or not, centralization and public control were prerequisites of an efficient banking system. Congress became increasingly aware of this around the turn of the twentieth century. Decentralized banking fostered the inconvenience and confusion of a heterogeneous currency, monetary mismanagement, and an inflexible supply of money. This latter problem was particularly acute. A dynamic and growing economy demands a flexible money supply—one which will respond to the economy's varying needs. The volume of trade expands and contracts unevenly and irregularly; hence, the supply of money must be elastic in meeting the needs of the economy. "Too much" money can precipitate dangerous inflationary problems; "too little" money can stunt the economy's growth by hindering the production and exchange of goods and services. The United States and innumerable foreign countries have learned through bitter experience that a decentralized banking system is not likely to provide that particular money supply which is most conducive to the welfare of the economy as a whole.

An unusually acute money panic in 1907 was the straw that broke Congress's back. A National Monetary Commission was established to study the monetary and banking problems of the economy and to outline a course of action for Congress. The end result was the Federal Reserve Act of 1913.

Structure of the Federal Reserve System

The banking system which has developed under the frequently amended Federal Reserve Act is sketched in Figure 16–2. It is important that we understand the nature and functions of the various segments which compose the banking system and the relationships which the parts bear to one another.

Board of Governors. The kingpin of our money and banking system is the Board of Governors of the Federal Reserve System. The seven members of this Board are appointed by the President with the confirmation of the Senate. Terms are long—fourteen years—and staggered so that one member is replaced every two years. The Board is staffed by appointment rather than elections in an attempt to divorce monetary policy from partisan politics. Long and staggered terms are intended to provide the Board with continuity and experienced membership.

The Board of Governors has the responsibility of exercising general supervision and control over the operation of the money and banking system of the nation. The Board's actions, which are to be in the public interest and designed to promote the general economic welfare, determine the basic policies which the commercial banking system is to follow. These basic policy decisions are made effective through the twelve Federal Reserve Banks and entail the use of two sets of control techniques which are at the disposal of the Board. *Quantitative credit controls,* consisting of (1) the reserve requirement, (2) open-market operations,

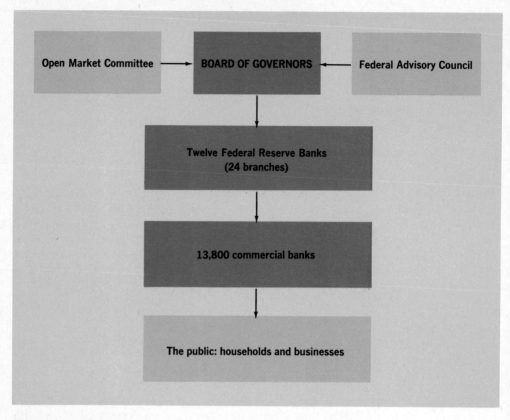

FIGURE 16–2. FRAMEWORK OF THE FEDERAL RESERVE SYSTEM AND ITS RELATIONSHIP TO THE PUBLIC.
With the advice and counsel of the Open Market Committee and the Federal Advisory Council, the Board of Governors makes the basic policy decisions which regulate our money and banking systems. These decisions are made effective through the twelve Federal Reserve Banks.

and (3) the discount rate, are designed to negotiate those changes in the money supply which the Board deems most conducive to a stable and expanding economy. From time to time the Board invokes *selective* or *qualitative credit controls* to regulate the availability of certain specific types of credit, for example, consumer credit in the purchase of housing or durables and credit in buying securities in the stock market. Much of Chapter 18 will be concerned with a discussion of these two types of credit controls and the manner in which they permit the Board

of Governors to influence the activities of commercial banks.

Two important bodies assist the Board of Governors in determining basic banking policy. On the one hand, the Federal Open Market Committee, made up of the seven members of the Board plus five of the presidents of the Federal Reserve Banks, sets the System's policy with respect to the purchase and sale of government bonds in the open market. These open-market operations constitute the most significant technique by which the monetary authorities can affect the money supply. On the other hand, the Federal Advisory Council is composed of twelve prominent commercial bankers, one selected annually by each of the twelve Federal Reserve Banks. The Council meets periodically with the Board of Governors to voice its views on banking policy. However, as its name indicates, the Council is purely advisory; it has no policy-making powers.

The twelve Federal Reserve Banks. The twelve Federal Reserve Banks have three major characteristics. They are (1) central banks, (2) quasi-public banks, and (3) bankers' banks.

1. Americans are blessed with a more or less inherent fear of centralization. As a result, the American banking system is less centralized than most of the other advanced economies of the world. As a matter of fact,

the Federal Reserve Act was a compromise between exponents of centralization and advocates of decentralization. Hence, instead of creating a single central bank, the act divided the nation into twelve districts and provided for a Federal Reserve Bank to function as a central bank in each of these districts. Figure 16–3 shows these twelve Federal Reserve districts. Geographic considerations were also of significance in the creation of the twelve Federal Reserve Banks. It was felt that a single central bank would be unresponsive to the peculiar economic problems faced by the various regions of the economy. In any event the net result is that the twelve Federal Reserve Banks make up the central banking system of the economy. It is through these central banks that the basic policy directives of the Board of Governors are made effective. The Fed-

FIGURE 16–3. THE TWELVE RESERVE DISTRICTS.
The Federal Reserve System divides the United States into twelve districts, each of which has one central bank and in some instances one or more branches of the central bank. Hawaii and Alaska are included in the twelfth district. *(Federal Reserve Bulletin.)*

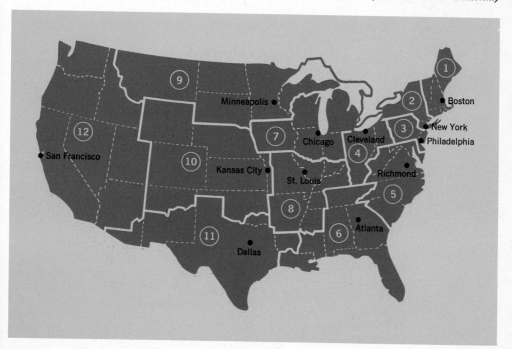

eral Reserve Bank of New York City is by far the most important of these central banks.

2. The twelve Federal Reserve Banks are quasi-public banks. They reflect an interesting blend of private ownership and public control. The Federal Reserve Banks are owned by the member banks in their districts. Upon joining the Federal Reserve System commercial banks are required to purchase shares of stock in the Federal Reserve Bank in their district. But the basic policies which the Federal Reserve Banks pursue are set by a public body—the Board of Governors. The central banks of American capitalism are privately owned but governmentally controlled.

The fact that the Federal Reserve Banks are essentially public institutions is vitally important to an understanding of their operation. In particular it must be emphasized that the Federal Reserve Banks are not motivated by profits as are private enterprises. The policies followed by the central bank are those which tend to promote the economic well-being of the economy as a whole. Hence, the activities of the Federal Reserve Banks will frequently be at odds with the profit motive.[8] Furthermore, the Federal Reserve Banks are not in competition with commercial banks. With rare exceptions, the Federal Reserve Banks do not deal with the public, but rather with the government and the commercial banks.

3. Finally, the Federal Reserve Banks are frequently called "bankers' banks." This is a shorthand way of saying that the Federal Reserve Banks perform essentially the same functions for commercial banks as commercial banks perform for the public. Just as commercial banks accept the deposits of

[8] Though it is not their basic goal, the Federal Reserve Banks have actually operated profitably. A part of the profits has been used to pay 6 per cent dividends to member banks on their holdings of stock; the bulk of the remaining profits has been turned over to the United States Treasury.

and make loans to the public, so the central banks accept the deposits of and make loans to commercial banks. But the Federal Reserve Banks have a third function which commercial banks no longer perform: the function of issuing currency. Congress has authorized the Federal Reserve Banks to put into circulation Federal Reserve Notes, which constitute the bulk of the economy's paper money supply.

The commercial banks. The work horses of the American banking system are its 13,761 commercial banks. The majority of these are *state banks,* that is, private banks operating under state charters. But a good many have received their charters from the Federal government; that is, they are *national banks.* Roughly one-half of all existing commercial banks are members of the Federal Reserve System. The 4,773 national banks in our economy are required by law to join the Federal Reserve System; the remaining 8,988 state banks have the option of joining or declining to do so. As Figure 16–4 indicates, 1,452 of the state banks have chosen to join the Federal Reserve System.

These statistics, however, tend to underestimate grossly the significance of the Federal Reserve System. Virtually all the larger commercial banks are members of the System, nonmembers being the smaller "country banks" for the most part. Thus, about 85 per cent of all deposits held by the commercial banking system rest in member banks. In addition, nonmember banks can participate on a limited basis in the functioning of the Federal Reserve System. For example, nonmember banks can avail themselves of the Federal Reserve System's program for the efficient collection of checks. Nonmember banks are not entirely disassociated from the Federal Reserve System or immune to its policy decisions.

Commercial banks, as already noted, have two basic functions. First, they hold the money deposits of businesses and households. Second, commercial banks make loans to the public and, in so doing, increase the

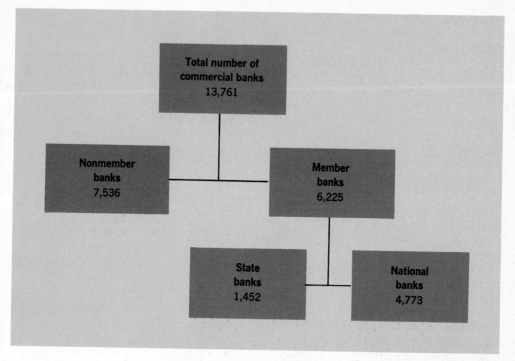

FIGURE 16–4. THE CLASSIFICATION OF COMMERCIAL BANKS, 1964.
Slightly less than half of all commercial banks are members of the Federal Reserve
System. However, these member banks hold about 85 per cent of all commercial
bank deposits. *(Federal Reserve Bulletin.)*

economy's supply of money. Detailed analysis of these functions is the main objective of Chapter 17.

Although the present analysis will be concerned only with ordinary commercial banks, it is important to recognize that the commercial banking system is thoroughly supplemented by a diverse group of specialized banking and financial institutions. For example, savings banks and savings and loan associations accept the funds of relatively small savers as time deposits and make these funds available to investors by extending mortgage loans or by purchasing marketable securities. Investment banks, on the other hand, perform the task of marketing the newly issued bonds and stocks of corporations which desire funds for capital expansion. Insurance companies accept huge

volumes of savings in the form of premiums on insurance policies and annuities and use these funds, wholly or in part, to buy a variety of private, corporate, and government securities. These banking and financial institutions are merely representative; the list is by no means exhaustive.

All banking and financial institutions, including commercial banks, have one point in common: They are all dealers in credit or debt. *These individual institutions lend the savings deposited with them or acquired by them, receiving credit instruments— bonds, stocks, mortgages, or promissory notes—in return.*[9] Hence, these institutions

[9] Or, as is sometimes the case with insurance companies, the institution itself may invest the savings it receives.

play a significant role in the economy, functioning as *intermediaries between savers and investors*. But from the social point of view, you will recall, their operation falls short of perfection (Chapter 12). These banking and financial institutions do not provide for an exact and continuing balance of investment spending and the full-employment volume of saving. Why? Because savers and investors are essentially different groups, which make their decisions in response to different motivations.

Commercial banks, accepting both time and demand deposits and using the proceeds wholly or in part to acquire income-earning securities, also function as intermediaries between savers and investors. But commercial banks perform an additional function which other banking and financial institutions do not. That function is *to create money by extending bank credit*—that is, *by making loans—to businesses and households*. Other financial institutions can only *transfer* money from savers to spenders. In doing so they do not affect the total supply of money available. Commercial banks, however, can *create* demand deposit money and make it available for use by potential spenders. Banks are by no means totally dependent upon the deposits of savers in making money available to spenders. Within limits commercial banks can create the money that spenders desire. Generally speaking, it works this way: Banks accept the credit of borrowing individuals and businesses (their promissory notes) and give these borrowers bank credit (demand deposits) in return. By exchanging debts that are not money (promissory notes) for debts that are money (demand deposits), commercial banks perform the unique function of increasing the money supply. In retiring bank credit, commercial banks decrease the money supply. The mechanics of these transactions will be studied in some detail in the ensuing chapter. At this juncture, the basic point to recognize is this: *Because of their money-creating and money-destroying abilities, commercial banks are highly strategic insti-*

tutions in our economy. Commercial banks play a particularly vital role in affecting the volume of money and, hence, the levels of spending, output, employment, and prices. Therefore, our attention is centered upon the functioning of commercial banks as opposed to the more specialized banking and financial institutions mentioned above.

Functions of the Federal Reserve System [10]

The Federal Reserve System—in particular, the twelve Federal Reserve Banks and the Board of Governors—was established to achieve certain definite objectives. These goals largely stem from the defects inherent in the system of uncoordinated state and national banks which prevailed prior to the passage of the Federal Reserve Act.

Holding the deposits of member banks.

Federal Reserve banks hold the deposits, or "reserves," of member banks. Private businesses and individuals find it convenient to establish checking accounts at commercial banks. These accounts are simply reserves of funds which the owner more or less regularly draws upon and occasionally replenishes. In the same manner member banks keep reserves—that is, money deposits —with the Federal Reserve Bank of their district. When in need of currency, the commercial banks can, within limits, draw upon these reserves. When in possession of surplus cash, commercial banks may deposit this extra currency in their reserves. Or, just as you may buy a bond or fulfill an obligation by drawing a check on your bank account, so may a commercial bank buy a government bond or honor some claim against itself by drawing down its reserves at the Federal Reserve Bank. Much of the daily work of the Federal Reserve Banks is concerned with

[10] For a more detailed look at the service functions of the Federal Reserve Banks see Board of Governors of the Federal Reserve System, *The Federal Reserve System: Purposes and Functions*, 4th ed. (1961), chaps. 8 and 14.

increasing and decreasing the reserves of commercial banks as routine banking transactions occur.

Providing for the collection of checks. As previously noted, a check is merely a written order which the drawer may use in making a purchase or paying a debt. A check is collected, or "cleared," when one or more banks negotiate a transfer of part of the drawer's checking account, or demand deposit, to the demand deposit of the recipient of the check. If Jones and Smith have checking accounts in the same commercial bank and Jones gives Smith a $10 check, Smith can collect this check by taking it to the commercial bank, where his account will be increased by $10 and Jones's reduced by $10. In many cases, however, the drawer and receiver of a check will be located in different towns or different states and therefore have their accounts in commercial banks far distant from one another. An important function of the Federal Reserve Banks is to provide facilities for the collection of checks where the banks of the drawer and receiver are geographically remote.

Though routine, this function is important because the bulk of the exchange which occurs in our economy is transacted by the use of check money. A money system so heavily committed to the use of check money obviously needs some mechanism for the quick and cheap collection of checks, particularly if payer and payee are geographically remote from one another. A basic function of the Federal Reserve Banks is to fulfill this need. At present the maximum time for collecting a check through the Federal Reserve System is three days, and the service is performed free of charge to all member banks. The mechanics of check collecting and the effect it has upon the financial position of commercial banks will be outlined in detail in the next chapter.

Supplying the economy with paper currency. It is also the responsibility of the Federal Reserve Banks to supply the economy with most of its paper currency. The bulk of the economy's paper money—Federal Reserve Notes—is issued directly by the central banks. As the fountainhead of the economy's paper money supply, the Federal Reserve Banks function as a reservoir of cash. When the economy needs more currency, the reservoir is opened and currency spills into the economy. When the economy has more currency than it desires to hold, the excess is channeled back into the reservoir. The commercial banks act as intermediaries between the public and the Federal Reserve Banks in each case. Specifically, it works something like this: During the Christmas buying rush, for example, the public wants more currency in circulation. To get this additional cash, individuals and businesses cash checks at the commercial banks. This lowers the amounts of currency resting in bank vaults. Commercial banks then turn to the bankers' banks and draw checks against their deposits (reserves) with the Federal Reserve Banks to replenish their vault cash. After the Christmas rush has subsided, less currency is needed. The public deposits this extra currency in their bank accounts. As a result, commercial banks find they have an overabundant stock of currency in their vaults. They deposit their surplus cash in the Federal Reserve Banks, thereby increasing their reserves.

Acting as fiscal agents for government. The Federal Reserve Banks act as fiscal agents for the Federal government. As we have seen, government—the Federal government in particular—is an exceedingly big business. As such, it collects huge sums through taxation, spends equally astronomical amounts, and sells and redeems bonds. Naturally, the government wants to avail itself of banking facilities in carrying out these functions. The Federal Reserve Banks function as bankers for the Federal government. The bankers' banks hold a part of the Treasury's checking accounts, aid the government in collecting various tax revenues, and administer the sale and redemption of government bonds.

Supervising member banks. The Federal Reserve Banks supervise the operations of member banks. A banking system stands or falls on the financial soundness of the individual commercial banks of which it is composed. Unsound banking practices can have widespread repercussions to the point of threatening the financial structure of the entire economy. Since commercial banking is "vested with a public interest," it has been subject to government supervision.

The Federal Reserve has supervisory powers over all member commercial banks.[11] This supervision usually takes the form of periodic unannounced examinations of the commercial banks. Banks which do not conform to the standards set forth by the Federal Reserve authorities may be denied the privilege of borrowing from the Federal Reserve Banks, and in extreme cases the officers and directors of offending banks may be removed by the Board of Governors.

Regulating the supply of money. Finally—and most important of all—the Federal Reserve System has ultimate responsibility for regulating the supply of money. The major task of the Federal Reserve authorities is to manage the money supply in accordance with the needs of the economy as a whole. In the dynamic and expanding economy of American capitalism, this task entails making that amount of money available which is consistent with high and steadily rising levels of output and employment and a relatively constant price level. It is through the previously mentioned quantitative and qualitative credit controls that the Federal

[11] The Federal Reserve is not alone in the task of supervision. The individual states supervise all banks which they charter. The Comptroller of the Currency supervises all national banks. Finally, the Federal Deposit Insurance Corporation has the power to supervise all banks whose deposits it insures. Hence, a member national bank which belongs to the FDIC will be subject to three supervisory agencies—the Federal Reserve, the Comptroller of the Currency, and the FDIC.

Reserve authorities attempt to manipulate the supply of money in terms of short-run stability and long-run economic growth.

In addition to being the most vital objective of the Federal Reserve System, the regulation of the money supply differs from the other Federal Reserve functions in another significant respect: Whereas all the other functions are of a more or less routine or service nature, the goal of correctly managing the money supply entails the making of basic and unique policy decisions of a nonroutine character. Chapter 18 is concerned with Federal Reserve monetary policy and its effectiveness in achieving economic stability in a growing economy.

SUMMARY

1. Anything that functions as **a.** a medium of exchange, **b.** a standard of value, and **c.** a store of value is money.

2. In the United States money is defined as demand deposits plus currency (coins and paper money) in circulation. By far the most important component of the money supply is demand deposits. Demand deposits are money because they can be spent if checks are written against them. Currency and demand deposits owned by the Treasury or by commercial or central banks are not "in circulation."

3. Money, which is essentially the debts of government and commercial banks, has value because of the goods and services which it will command in the market. Maintenance of the purchasing power of money depends to a considerable degree upon the effectiveness with which government manages the money supply.

4. The American banking system is composed of **a.** the Board of Governors of the Federal Reserve System, **b.** the twelve Federal Reserve Banks, and **c.** some 13,800 commercial banks. The Board of Governors is the basic policy-making body for the entire banking system. The directives of the Board are made effective through the twelve Federal Reserve Banks, which are simultaneously **a.** central banks, **b.** quasi-public banks, and **c.** bankers' banks. The commercial banks of the economy perform the tasks of accepting money deposits and making loans. In lending, commercial banks create demand deposits; these deposits are money. Commercial banks, then, are money-creating institutions.

5. The major functions of the Federal Reserve System are **a.** to hold the deposits or reserves of commercial banks, **b.** to provide facilities for the rapid collection of checks, **c.** to supply the economy's needs for paper currency, **d.** to act as fiscal agent for the Federal government, **e.** to supervise the operations of member banks, and **f.** to regulate the supply of money in terms of the best interests of the economy as a whole.

QUESTIONS AND STUDY SUGGESTIONS

1. What are the three basic functions of money? Describe how drastic inflation can undermine the ability of money to perform these functions.

2. What are the disadvantages of commodity money? What are the advantages of (*a*) paper money and (*b*) check money as compared to commodity money?

3. "Money is only a bit of paper or a bit of metal that gives its owner a lawful claim to so much bread or beer or diamonds or motorcars or what not. We cannot eat money, nor drink money, nor wear money. It is the goods that money can buy that are being divided up when money is divided up."[12] Evaluate and explain.

4. Fully evaluate and explain the following statements:
  a. "The invention of money is one of the great achievements of the human race, for without it the enrichment that comes from broadening trade would have been impossible."
  b. "Money is whatever society says it is."
  c. "When prices of everything are going up, it is not because everything is worth more, but because the dollar is worth less."
  d. "The difficult questions concerning paper [money] are . . . not about its economy, convenience or ready circulation but about the amount of the paper which can be wisely issued or created, and the possibilities of violent convulsions when it gets beyond bounds."[13]

5. What items constitute the money supply in American capitalism? What is the most important component of the money supply? What are near-monies? Of what significance are they? Why is the face value of a coin greater than its intrinsic value?

6. "In most modern industrial economies of the world the debts of government and of commercial banks are used as money." Explain.

7. What "backs" the money supply in the United States? Be as specific as you are able.

8. What determines the value of money? Who is responsible for maintaining the value of money? Why is it important for the money supply to

[12] George Bernard Shaw, *The Intelligent Woman's Guide to Socialism and Capitalism* (New York: Brentano's, Inc., 1928), p. 9. Used by permission of the Public Trustee and the Society of Authors.
[13] F. W. Taussig, *Principles of Economics,* 4th ed. (New York: The Macmillan Company, 1946), pp. 247–248.

be elastic, that is, capable of increasing or decreasing in size? What is meant by (*a*) "sound money" and (*b*) a "52-cent dollar"?

9. What is the major responsibility of the Board of Governors? Discuss the major characteristics of the Federal Reserve Banks. Of what significance is the fact that the Federal Reserve Banks are quasi-public?

10. What are the two basic functions of commercial banks? How do commercial banks differ from other financial institutions?

11. State and briefly discuss the major functions of the Federal Reserve System.

SELECTED REFERENCES

Board of Governors of the Federal Reserve System: *The Federal Reserve System: Purposes and Functions,* 4th ed. (1961), particularly chaps. 1 and 4.

Chandler, Lester V.: *The Economics of Money and Banking,* 4th ed. (New York: Harper & Row, Publishers, Incorporated, 1964), chaps. 1–3, 7 and 8.

Pritchard, Leland J.: *Money and Banking,* 2d ed. (Boston: Houghton Mifflin Company, 1964), chaps. 1–4 and 12–15.

Robertson, D. H.: *Money,* 6th ed. (New York: Pitman Publishing Corporation, 1948).

Thomas, Rollin G.: *Our Modern Banking and Monetary System* (Englewood Cliffs, N.J.: Prentice-Hall, Inc., 1964), chaps. 1–5, 15, and 16.

HOW BANKS CREATE MONEY

In Chapter 16 we saw that the Federal Reserve Banks are the primary source of the economy's paper money. However, we shall find in the present chapter that commercial banks are the fountainhead of the major component of the money system—demand deposits.

More specifically, in this chapter we want to explain and compare the money-creating abilities of:

1. A single commercial bank which is part of a multibank system.
2. A monopoly bank.
3. The commercial banking system as a whole.

It will be convenient for us to seek these objectives through the commercial bank's balance sheet. An understanding of the basic items which make up a bank's balance sheet and the manner in which various transactions change these items will provide us with a valuable analytical tool for grasping the workings of our monetary and banking systems.

THE BALANCE SHEET OF A COMMERCIAL BANK

What is a *balance sheet?* It is merely a statement of assets and claims which portrays or summarizes the financial position of a firm—in this case a commercial bank—at some specific point in time. Every balance sheet has one overriding virtue: by definition, it must balance. Why? Because each and every known *asset,* being something of economic value, will be claimed by someone. Can you think of an asset—something of monetary value—which no one claims? A balance sheet balances because assets equal claims. The claims shown on a balance sheet are divided into two groups: the claims of the owners of a firm against the firm's assets, called *net worth,* and the claims of nonowners, called *liabilities.* Thus, it can be said that a balance sheet balances because

Assets = liabilities + net worth

A balance-sheet approach to our study of the money-creating ability of commercial banks is invaluable in two specific respects: On the one hand, a bank's balance sheet provides us with a convenient point of reference from which we can introduce new terms and concepts in a more or less orderly manner. On the other hand, the use of balance sheets will allow us to quantify certain strategic concepts and relationships which would defy comprehension if discussed in verbal terms alone.

A SINGLE COMMERCIAL BANK IN A BANKING SYSTEM

Our immediate goal is an understanding of the money-creating potential of a single bank which is part of a multibank banking system. How does a single commercial bank create and destroy money? What factors govern the money-creating abilities of such a bank?

Formation of a Commercial Bank

The answers to these questions demand that we understand the ins and outs of a commercial bank's balance sheet and how certain rather elementary transactions affect that balance sheet. We start with the organization of a local commercial bank.

vault cash or *till money*. The outstanding shares of stock, however, constitute an equal amount of claims which the owners have against the bank's assets. That is, the shares of stock are obviously the net worth of the bank, though assets from the viewpoint of those who possess these shares. Hence, the bank's balance sheet would read as follows:

BALANCE SHEET 1: WAHOO BANK

Assets	Liabilities and net worth
Cash $250,000	Capital stock $250,000

Transaction 1: the birth of a bank. Let us start from scratch. Suppose some farsighted citizens of the metropolis of Wahoo, Nebraska, decide that their town is in need of a new commercial bank to provide all the banking services needed by that growing community. Assuming these enterprising individuals are able to secure a state charter for their bank, they then turn to the task of selling, say, $250,000 worth of capital stock to buyers, both in and out of the community. These financing efforts having met with success, the Merchants and Farmers Bank of Wahoo, Nebraska, now exists—at least on paper. How does the Wahoo bank's balance statement appear at its birth?

The new proprietors of the bank have sold $250,000 worth of shares of stock in the bank—some to themselves, some to other

Transaction 2: becoming a going concern. The newly established board of directors must now breathe life into their infant enterprise. They must get the newborn bank off the drawing board and make it a living reality.

The first step will be to acquire property and equipment. Suppose the directors, confident of the success of their venture, purchase a building for $220,000 and some $20,000 worth of office equipment. This simple transaction merely changes the composition of the bank's assets. The bank now has $240,000 less in cash and $240,000 worth of new property assets. Using an asterisk to denote those accounts which are affected by each transaction, we find that the bank's balance sheet at the conclusion of transaction 2 appears as follows:

BALANCE SHEET 2: WAHOO BANK

Assets	Liabilities and net worth
Cash* .... $ 10,000	Capital stock $250,000
Property* 240,000	

people. As a result, the bank now has $250,000 in cash on hand and $250,000 worth of capital stock outstanding. Obviously the cash is an asset to the bank. The cash held by a bank is sometimes dubbed

Note that the balance sheet still balances, as indeed it must.

Transaction 3: accepting deposits. We have already emphasized that commercial banks have two basic functions: to accept deposits of money and to make loans. Now that our bank is in operation, let us suppose that the citizens of Wahoo decide to deposit some $100,000 in the Merchants and Farmers Bank. What happens to the bank's balance sheet?

The bank receives cash, which we have already noted is an asset to the bank. Suppose this money is placed in the bank in the form of demand deposits (checking accounts), rather than time deposits (savings accounts). These newly created demand deposits constitute claims which depositors have against the assets of the Wahoo bank. Thus the depositing of money in the bank creates a new liability account—demand deposits. The bank's balance sheet now looks like this:

Reserve System. Suppose the directors of the bank decide in favor of joining. To accomplish this, the bank must meet a very specific requirement: It must keep a *legal reserve deposit* in the Federal Reserve Bank of its particular district.

This legal reserve deposit is *an amount of cash equal to a specified percentage of its own deposit liabilities which a member bank must keep on deposit with the Federal Reserve Bank in its district.*[1]

The "specified percentage" is known as the *reserve ratio.* Why? Because that is exactly what it is—a ratio between the size of the deposits which the commercial bank must keep in the Federal Reserve Bank and the commercial bank's own outstanding deposit liabilities. This ratio is as follows:

BALANCE SHEET 3: WAHOO BANK

Assets		Liabilities and net worth	
Cash*	$110,000	Capital stock	$250,000
Property	240,000	Demand deposits*	100,000

You should note that, although there is no change in the total supply of money, a change in the composition of the economy's money supply has occurred as a result of transaction 3. Bank money, or demand deposits, have *increased* by $100,000 and currency in circulation has *decreased* by $100,000. Currency held by a bank, you will recall, is not considered to be a part of the economy's money supply.

It is obvious that a withdrawal of cash will reduce the bank's demand deposit liabilities and its holdings of cash by the amount of the withdrawal. This, too, changes the composition, but not the total supply, of money.

Transaction 4: joining the Federal Reserve System. Being a state bank, the Merchants and Farmers Bank of Wahoo will have the option of joining or not joining the Federal

$$\text{Reserve ratio} = \frac{\substack{\text{commercial bank's} \\ \text{required deposit in} \\ \text{Federal Reserve Bank}}}{\substack{\text{public's deposits} \\ \text{in commercial bank}}}$$

Hence, if the reserve ratio were 10 per cent, our bank, having accepted $100,000 in deposits from the public, would be obligated to bundle up $10,000 and send it as a deposit, or reserve, to the Federal Reserve Bank in Kansas City. If the ratio were 20 per

[1] Since 1960 banks have been permitted to count vault cash as a part of reserves. As a matter of banking practice, however, the vast bulk of bank reserves are in the form of deposits in the Federal Reserve Banks. We shall simplify our discussion by supposing that our bank keeps its legal reserve *entirely* in the form of deposits in the Federal Reserve Bank of its district.

cent, $20,000 would have to be deposited in the Federal Reserve Bank. If 50 per cent, $50,000, and so forth.

How is the exact size of the reserve ratio determined? Congress has the responsibility for setting the upper and lower limits within which the ratio may vary. These legal limits differ, depending upon the size and location of commercial banks, as Table 17–1 indicates. The Board of Governors can vary the ratio at its discretion within these limits.[2] To avoid a lot of messy computations, we shall suppose that the reserve ratio for all banks is 20 per cent. This is a nice round

ings of the public's deposits will grow in the future. Hence, instead of sending the minimum amount, $20,000, they send an extra $90,000, making a total of $110,000. In so doing, the bank will avoid the inconvenience of sending additional reserves to the Federal Reserve Bank each time its own deposit liabilities increase by some small amount. And we shall see shortly that it is upon the basis of extra reserves that banks can lend and thereby earn interest income.[3]

At the completion of this transaction, the balance sheet of the Merchants and Farmers Bank will appear as follows:

BALANCE SHEET 4: WAHOO BANK

Assets		Liabilities and net worth	
Cash*	$ 0	Capital stock	$250,000
Property	240,000	Demand deposits	100,000
Reserves (deposits in the Federal Reserve Bank)*	110,000		

figure and is reasonably close to reality. It is to be emphasized that reserve requirements are *fractional*, that is, less than 100 per cent. This consideration will be vital in the ensuing analysis of the lending abilities of various possible banking systems.

The Wahoo bank will just be meeting the required 20 per cent ratio between its deposit in the Federal Reserve Bank and its own deposit liabilities by depositing $20,000 in the Federal Reserve Bank. To distinguish this deposit from the public's deposits in commercial banks, we shall use the term *reserves* in referring to these funds which commercial banks deposit in the Federal Reserve Banks.

But let us suppose that the directors of the Wahoo bank anticipate that their hold-

There are several points relevant to this transaction which must still be explained:

1. A note on terminology: The amount by which the bank's actual reserves exceed its required reserves is the bank's *excess* reserves. In this case,

Actual reserves	$110,000
Required reserves	−20,000
Excess reserves	$ 90,000

[2] State nonmember banks are required by state laws to keep reserves. These reserves usually take the form of cash and deposits in other commercial banks. Though the reserve ratio varies considerably among the states, 15 per cent is about the average.

[3] Actually, of course, the bank would not deposit all its cash in the Federal Reserve Bank. However, because (1) banks as a rule only hold vault cash in the amount of 1½ or 2 per cent of their total assets and (2) vault cash can be counted as reserves (footnote 1), we shall find it expedient to assume that all the bank's cash is deposited in the Federal Reserve Bank and therefore constitutes the commercial bank's total reserves. The cumbersome process of adding two assets—"cash" and "deposits in the Federal Reserve Bank"—to determine "reserves" is thereby avoided.

TABLE 17–1. LEGAL RESERVE REQUIREMENTS OF MEMBER BANKS

Type of bank	Reserve ratio against demand deposits	
	Upper and lower legal limits, per cent	Actual ratio, per cent
Reserve city banks (member banks in large and medium-sized cities)	10–22	16½
All other member banks (country or small town)	7–14	12

Source: *Federal Reserve Bulletin*, **May, 1965.**

The only reliable way of computing excess reserves is to multiply the bank's demand deposit liabilities by the reserve ratio ($100,000 times 20 per cent equals $20,000) to obtain required reserves, then to subtract this figure from the actual reserves listed on the asset side of the bank's balance sheet. To ensure an understanding of this process, the reader should compute excess reserves for the bank's balance sheet as it stands at the end of transaction 4 on the assumption that the reserve ratio is (a) 10 per cent, (b) 33⅓ per cent, and (c) 50 per cent.

Because the ability of a commercial bank to make loans depends upon the existence of excess reserves, this concept is of vital importance in grasping the money-creating ability of the banking system.

2. What is the rationale underlying the requirement that member banks deposit a reserve in the Federal Reserve Bank of their district? One might think that the basic purpose of reserves is to enhance the liquidity of a bank and thereby protect commercial bank depositors from losses; that is, it would seem that reserves constitute a ready source of funds from which commercial banks can meet large and unexpected withdrawals of cash by depositors. But this reasoning does not hold up under close scrutiny. Although historically reserves were looked upon as a source of liquidity and therefore protection for depositors, *legal*, or required, reserves cannot be used for the purpose of meeting unexpected cash withdrawals. If a banker's nightmare materialized—that is, if everyone

having a demand deposit in his bank appeared on the same morning to demand his deposits in cash—the banker could not draw upon his required reserves to meet this crisis without violating the legal reserve ratio and thereby incurring the wrath and penalties of the Federal Reserve authorities. In practice, legal reserves are not an available pool of liquid funds upon which commercial banks can rely in times of emergency.[4] As a matter of fact, even if legal reserves were accessible to commercial banks, they would not be sufficient to meet a serious "run" on a bank. Why? Because, as we shall soon discover, demand deposits may be three, four, or five times as large as a bank's required reserves.

It is not surprising that commercial bank

[4] This amendment must be added: As depositors withdraw cash from a commercial bank, the bank's demand deposit liabilities will obviously decline. This lowers the absolute amount of required reserves which the bank must keep, thereby freeing some of the bank's actual reserves for use in meeting cash withdrawals by depositors. To illustrate: Suppose a commercial bank has reserves of $20 and demand deposit liabilities of $100. If the legal reserve ratio is 20 per cent, all the bank's reserves are obviously required. Now, if depositors withdraw, say, $50 worth of their deposits as cash, the bank will only need $10 as required reserves to support the remaining $50 of demand deposit liabilities. Thus $10 of the bank's actual reserves of $20 is no longer required. The bank can draw upon this $10 in helping to meet the cash withdrawals of its depositors.

depositors are protected by other means. As noted in Chapter 16, periodic bank examinations are an important device for promoting prudent commercial banking practices. Furthermore, the Federal Deposit Insurance Corporation was established in 1933 to insure the deposit liabilities of member banks and qualified nonmember banks that voluntarily become members of the FDIC. At the present time about 99 per cent of all depositors have their deposits insured up to a maximum of $10,000 by the FDIC. FDIC members pay insurance premiums equal to one-twelfth of 1 per cent of their total deposits, from which the FDIC has built up a substantial insurance fund.

If the purpose of reserves is not to provide for commercial bank liquidity, what is their function? *Control* is the answer. Legal reserves are a means by which the Board of Governors can influence the lending policies of commercial banks. The next chapter will explain in detail how the Board of Governors can invoke certain policies which either increase or decrease commercial bank reserves and thereby affect the ability of banks to grant credit. The object is to prevent banks from *over*extending or *under*extending bank credit. To the degree that they are successful in influencing the volume of commercial bank credit, the Board of Governors can help the economy avoid the business fluctuations which give rise to bank runs, bank failures, and collapse of the monetary system. It is in this indirect way—as a means of controlling commercial bank credit—that reserves protect depositors, not as a source of liquidity.

3. Let us pause to note a rather obvious accounting matter which transaction 4 entails. Specifically, *the reserve created in transaction 4 is an asset to the depositing commercial bank but a liability to the Federal Reserve Bank receiving it.* To the Wahoo bank the reserve is an asset. Why? Because it is a claim which this commercial bank has against the assets of another institution—the Federal Reserve Bank. To the Federal Reserve Bank this reserve is a

liability, that is, a claim which another institution—the Wahoo bank—has against it. Just as the demand deposit you get by depositing money in a commercial bank is an asset to you and a liability to your commercial bank, so the deposit or reserve which a commercial bank establishes by depositing money in a banker's bank is an asset to the commercial bank and a liability to the Federal Reserve Bank. An understanding of this relationship is necessary in pursuing transaction 5.

Transaction 5: a check is drawn against the bank. Now let us tackle a very significant and somewhat more complicated transaction. Suppose that Clem Bradshaw, a Wahoo farmer who deposited a substantial portion of the $100,000 in demand deposits which the Wahoo bank received in transaction 3, purchases $50,000 worth of farm machinery from the Ajax Farm Implement Company of Beaver Crossing, Nebraska. Bradshaw very sensibly pays for this machinery by writing a $50,000 check, against his deposit in the Wahoo bank, in favor of the Ajax company. We want to determine (1) how this check is collected or "cleared" and (2) the effect that the collection of the check has upon the balance sheets of the banks involved in the transaction.

To accomplish this, we must consider the Wahoo bank, the Beaver Crossing bank, and the Federal Reserve Bank of Kansas City.[5] Let us suppose that both the commercial banks are members of the Federal Reserve System. And to keep our illustration as clear as possible, we shall deal only with the changes which occur in those specific accounts affected by this transaction.

Let us trace this transaction in three related steps, keying the steps by letters to Figure 17–1.

a. Mr. Bradshaw gives his $50,000 check, drawn against the Wahoo bank, to the Ajax

---

[5] Actually the Omaha Branch of the Federal Reserve Bank of Kansas City would handle the process of collecting this check.

FEDERAL RESERVE BANK OF KANSAS CITY

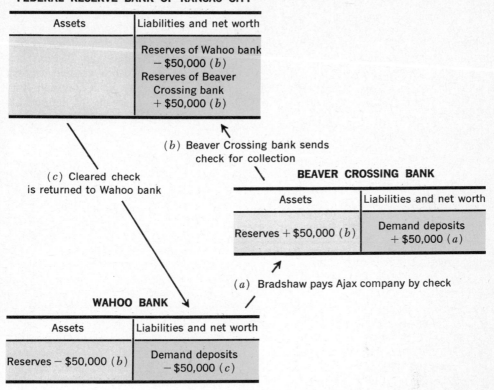

Assets	Liabilities and net worth
	Reserves of Wahoo bank − $50,000 (*b*) Reserves of Beaver Crossing bank + $50,000 (*b*)

(*b*) Beaver Crossing bank sends
check for collection

(*c*) Cleared check
is returned to Wahoo bank

BEAVER CROSSING BANK

Assets	Liabilities and net worth
Reserves + $50,000 (*b*)	Demand deposits + $50,000 (*a*)

(*a*) Bradshaw pays Ajax company by check

WAHOO BANK

Assets	Liabilities and net worth
Reserves − $50,000 (*b*)	Demand deposits − $50,000 (*c*)

FIGURE 17–1. THE COLLECTION OF A CHECK THROUGH A
FEDERAL RESERVE BANK.

company. The Ajax company in turn deposits the check in its account with the Beaver Crossing bank. The Beaver Crossing bank increases the Ajax company's demand deposit by $50,000 when it deposits the check. (The Ajax company is now paid off.) Bradshaw is elated over his new machinery, for which he has now paid.

b. But now the Beaver Crossing bank has Bradshaw's check in its possession. This check is simply a claim against the assets of the Wahoo bank. How will the Beaver Crossing bank collect this claim? By sending this check—along with checks drawn on other banks—to the Federal Reserve Bank of Kansas City. Here a clerk will clear, or collect, this check for the Beaver Crossing

bank by increasing its reserve in the Federal Reserve Bank by $50,000 and by decreasing the Wahoo bank's reserve by a like amount. The check is collected simply by making a few pen-and-ink notations to the effect that the Wahoo bank's claim against the Federal Reserve Bank has been reduced by $50,000 and the Beaver Crossing bank's claim increased accordingly. Note these changes on the balance sheets.[6]

---

[6] Here is an interesting sidelight: The collection of Bradshaw's check by the Beaver Crossing bank through the Federal Reserve Bank involves the same type of procedure as the collection of a check between two individuals who

c. Finally, the cleared check is sent back to the Wahoo bank, and for the first time the Wahoo bank discovers that one of its depositors has drawn a check for $50,000 against his demand deposit. Accordingly, the Wahoo bank reduces Mr. Bradshaw's demand deposit by $50,000 and recognizes that the collection of this check has entailed a $50,000 decline in its reserves at the Federal Reserve Bank. Note that the balance statements of all three banks will still balance. The Wahoo bank will have reduced both its assets and liabilities by $50,000. The Beaver Crossing bank will have $50,000 more in

receives a check drawn on another bank, the bank receiving the check will, in the process of collecting it, have its reserves and deposits increased by the amount of the check. In our example, the Wahoo bank loses $50,000 in both reserves and deposits to the Beaver Crossing bank. But there is no loss of reserves or deposits for the banking system as a whole. What one bank loses another bank gains.

Bringing all the other assets and liabilities back into the picture, the Wahoo bank's balance sheet looks like this at the end of transaction 5:

BALANCE SHEET 5: WAHOO BANK

Assets		Liabilities and net worth	
Property	$240,000	Capital stock	$250,000
Reserves*	60,000	Demand deposits*	50,000

reserves and in demand deposits. The ownership of reserves at the Federal Reserve Bank will have changed, but total reserves will stand the same.

The point we are making is this: *Whenever a check is drawn against a bank and deposited in another bank, the collection of that check will entail a loss of both reserves and deposits by the bank upon which the check is drawn.* Conversely, if a bank

---

have deposits in the same commercial bank. Suppose you and I both have checking accounts in the Wahoo bank. I owe you $10 and I pay this debt by check. You deposit the $10 check in the bank. Here a bank clerk collects the check for you by noting a "+$10" in your account and a "−$10" in my account. And that's that. The same thing happens at the Federal Reserve Bank of Kansas City when the Beaver Crossing bank clears a $50,000 check against the Wahoo bank. The banker's bank increases the Beaver Crossing bank's deposit in the Federal Reserve Bank—that is, its reserve—by $50,000 and lowers the Wahoo bank's reserve by the same amount. The check is then cleared.

The reader should verify that with a 20 per cent reserve requirement the bank's *excess* reserves now stand at $50,000.

This transaction indicates the manner in which commercial banks acquire the bulk of their reserves and deposits: from other banks through the check-clearing process. While most of us in our personal dealings with banks think of demand deposits as being created by customer deposits of cash, and of reserves arising as the result of the bank's redepositing some of this cash with the Federal Reserve Banks, this is not actually the case. Most bank deposits and reserves are received from other banks in the way the Beaver Crossing bank has acquired new reserves and deposits in the present transaction.

Transaction 5 is obviously reversible. If a check drawn against another bank is deposited in the Wahoo bank, the Wahoo bank will receive both reserves and deposits equal to the amount of the check as it is collected.

Let us designate here some of the salient conclusions from the first five transactions we have analyzed:

1. When a bank accepts deposits of cash, the composition of the money supply is changed, but the total supply of money is not altered.

2. Commercial banks which are members of the Federal Reserve System are required to keep legal reserve deposits, or simply "reserves," equal to a specified percentage of their own deposit liabilities on deposit with the Federal Reserve Bank of their district. The reserve ratio indicates the size of this "specified percentage." Reserves are a means by which the monetary authorities can control the lending policies of commercial banks.

3. The amount by which a bank's actual reserves exceed its required reserves is called "excess reserves."

4. Commercial bank reserves are an asset to the commercial bank but a liability to the Federal Reserve Bank holding them.

5. A bank which has a check drawn and collected against it will lose both reserves and deposits equal to the value of the check to the bank receiving the check.

Money-creating Transactions of a Commercial Bank

The next two transactions are particularly crucial because they explain how a single commercial bank can literally create money by making loans to individuals and businesses and by purchasing government bonds. Though these transactions are similar in many respects, we treat them separately.

Transaction 6: granting a loan. You will recall that in addition to accepting deposits a basic function of commercial banks is the granting of loans to borrowers. What effect does commercial bank lending have upon the balance sheet of a commercial bank?

Suppose that the Grisley Meat Packing Company of Wahoo decides that the time is ripe to expand its facilities. Suppose, too, that the company needs exactly $50,000—which, by some unexplained coincidence, just happens to be equal to the Wahoo bank's excess reserves—to finance this project.

The company approaches the Wahoo bank and requests a loan for this amount. The Wahoo bank is acquainted with the Grisley company's fine reputation and financial soundness and is convinced of its ability to repay the loan. So the loan is granted. The president of the Grisley company hands a promissory note—a high-class IOU—to the Wahoo bank. The Grisley company, as all other modern firms, is interested in paying its obligations by check. Hence, instead of receiving a bushel basket full of cash from the bank, the Grisley company will simply get a $50,000 increase in its demand deposit in the Wahoo bank.

In short, the Grisley company has swapped an IOU for the right to draw an additional $50,000 worth of checks against its demand deposit in the Wahoo bank. Both parties are pleased with themselves. The Wahoo bank now possesses a new asset—an interest-bearing promissory note which it happily files under the general heading of "Loans." The Grisley company, sporting a fattened demand deposit, is now in a position to expand its operations.

At the moment the loan is negotiated, the balance sheet of the Wahoo bank looks like this:

BALANCE SHEET 6a: WAHOO BANK (when loan is negotiated)

Assets		Liabilities and net worth	
Property	$240,000	Capital stock	$250,000
Reserves	60,000	Demand deposits*	100,000
Loans*	50,000		

All this looks innocent enough. But a closer examination of the Wahoo bank's balance statement will reveal a startling fact: *When a bank makes loans, it creates money.* The president of the Grisley company went to the bank with something which is not money—his IOU—and walked out with something that is money—a demand deposit.[7] When banks lend, they create demand deposits which are money. By extending credit the Wahoo bank has "monetized" an IOU. The Grisley company and the Wahoo bank have created and then swapped claims. The claim created by the Grisley company and given to the bank is not money; an individual's IOU is not generally acceptable as a medium of exchange. But the claim created by the bank and given to the Grisley company is money; checks drawn against a demand deposit are acceptable as a medium of exchange. It is through the extension of credit by commercial banks that the bulk of the money used in our economy is created.

But there are important forces which cir-

able if needed. Let us assume that the Grisley company awards a $50,000 contract to the Quickbuck Construction Company of Omaha. Quickbuck, true to its name, completes the expansion job and is rewarded with a check for $50,000 drawn by the Grisley company against its demand deposit in the Wahoo bank. The Quickbuck company, having its headquarters in Omaha, does not deposit this check back in the Wahoo bank but instead deposits it in the Fourth National Bank of Omaha. The Fourth National Bank now has a $50,000 claim against the Wahoo bank. This check is collected in the manner described in transaction 5. As a result, the Wahoo bank *loses* both reserves and deposits equal to the amount of the check; the Fourth National Bank *acquires* $50,000 of reserves and deposits. In short, assuming a check is drawn by the borrower for the entire amount of the loan ($50,000) and given to a firm which deposits it in another bank, the Wahoo bank's balance sheet will read as follows *after the check has been cleared against it:*

BALANCE SHEET 6b: WAHOO BANK (after a check drawn on the loan has been collected)

Assets		Liabilities and net worth	
Property	$240,000	Capital stock	$250,000
Reserves*	10,000	Demand deposits*	50,000
Loans	50,000		

cumscribe the ability of a commercial bank to create demand deposits—that is, "bank money"—by lending. In the present case, the Wahoo bank can expect the newly created demand deposit of $50,000 to be a very active account. The Grisley company would not borrow $50,000 at, say, 8 per cent for the sheer joy of knowing the funds were avail-

---

[7] In transaction 3 demand deposits were created, but only by currency's going out of circulation. Hence, there was a change in the composition of the money supply but no change in the total supply of money.

You will note immediately that, after the check has been collected, the Wahoo bank is just barely meeting the legal reserve ratio of 20 per cent. The bank has *no excess reserves.* This poses an interesting question: Could the Wahoo bank have safely lent an amount greater than $50,000—an amount greater than its excess reserves—and still have met the 20 per cent reserve requirement if a check for the full amount of the loan cleared against it? The answer is "No." For example, suppose the Wahoo bank had loaned $55,000 to the Grisley company. Collection of the check against the Wahoo bank would have lowered its reserves to $5,000 (equal to $60,000 minus $55,000) and deposits would again stand at $50,000 (equal to $105,000 minus $55,000). The ratio of actual reserves to deposits would now be only $5,000/$50,000, or 10 per cent. The Wahoo bank could thus not safely have lent $55,000. By experimenting with other figures in excess of $50,000, the reader will find that the maximum amount which the Wahoo bank could safely lend at the outset of transaction 6 is $50,000. This figure is identical with the amount of excess reserves which the bank had available at the time the loan was negotiated. We can conclude that *a single commercial bank in a multibank banking system can safely lend only dollar for dollar with its excess reserves.* Why? Because when it lends, it faces the likelihood that checks for the entire amount of the loan may be drawn and cleared against the lending bank. A lending bank can anticipate the loss of reserves to other banks equal to the amount it lends.

There is a qualification to this discussion: When a bank makes a loan, some of the checks drawn by the borrower *may* be redeposited back in the lending bank. To the extent that this happens, the bank is able to lend an amount greater than its excess reserves. You might try this problem: Suppose a bank with $1,000 in excess reserves knows from past experience that for every loan it negotiates, checks drawn on that loan equal to one-tenth of the value of the loan will be redeposited in the bank. Thus, if the bank makes a $100 loan, the borrower promptly draws 10 checks for $10 each. Nine of these wind up in other banks. The tenth is redeposited by its recipient in the lending bank. Knowing this in advance, what is the maximum amount this bank can safely lend on the basis of $1,000 of excess reserves?

Now that you are convinced that this credit-creating business can be complicated, let us accept our original conclusion that commercial banks can safely lend dollar for dollar with their excess reserves as being accurate enough for our purposes. It is a pretty good approximate statement of a single commercial bank's credit-creating potential.

If commercial banks create demand deposits—that is, money—when they make loans, it seems logical to inquire as to whether money is destroyed when the loans are repaid. The answer is "Yes." Using Balance Sheet 6b, let us see what happens when the Grisley company repays the $50,000 it borrowed.

To simplify, we shall (1) suppose that the loan is repaid not in installments but rather in one lump sum three years after the date of negotiation and (2) ignore interest charges on the loan. Repayment may take two forms. Most likely the Grisley company will write a check for $50,000 against its demand deposit, which assumedly has been fattened by extra profits resulting from the company's expanded operations. As a result the Wahoo bank's demand deposit liabilities decline by $50,000; the Grisley company has given up $50,000 worth of its claim against the bank's assets. In turn the bank will surrender the Grisley company's IOU which it has been patiently holding these many months. The bank and the company have reswapped claims. But the claim given up by the Grisley company is money; the claim it is repurchasing—its IOU—is not. The supply of money has therefore been reduced by $50,000; that amount of demand deposits has been destroyed, unaccompanied by any increase in the money supply elsewhere in the economy. The Grisley company's IOU has been "demonetized." On the Wahoo bank's balance sheet demand deposits and loans both fall by $50,000. You will note that the decline in demand deposits increases the bank's holdings of excess reserves; this provides the basis for new loans to be made.

The second repayment alternative open to the Grisley company is to repay by cash. It would be very unlikely that the company would want to bear the risk of accumulating such a large sum of money in its safe. But even if it did, the supply of money would still decline by $50,000 when cash repayment was made. In this case, the Grisley company would repurchase its IOU by handing over $50,000 in cash to the bank. This causes loans to fall on the bank's balance sheet by $50,000 and, obviously, cash to increase by $50,000. Remember that we specifically excluded currency held by banks from the money supply on the ground that to include such cash would be double counting; it is apparent that this constitutes

needed $50,000 from the Wahoo bank, the Grisley company borrows just $25,000 and obtains an additional $25,000 by selling government bonds which it holds to the bank. The Wahoo bank pays for the Grisley company's IOU and the IOUs (bonds) of the government in the same way, by increasing the Grisley company's demand deposit. Demand deposit liabilities increase by $50,000, and the bank's assets of securities and loans increase by $25,000 each. Immediately after negotiating the loan and bond purchase, the Wahoo bank's balance sheet will appear as follows:

BALANCE SHEET 7a: WAHOO BANK (when loan is negotiated and bonds purchased)

Assets		Liabilities and net worth	
Property	$240,000	Capital stock	$250,000
Reserves	60,000	Demand deposits*	100,000
Securities*	25,000		
Loans*	25,000		

a $50,000 reduction in the supply of money. The Wahoo bank would probably use this additional cash either to enhance its reserves so as to permit new lending or to purchase securities.

Transaction 7: buying government securities. When a commercial bank buys government bonds[8] from individuals and business concerns, the effect is substantially the same as that of lending. New money is created. To illustrate, let us assume that the Wahoo bank's balance sheet initially stands as it did at the end of transaction 5. Now let us suppose that instead of borrowing all the

[8] Commercial banks are restricted by law in their purchase of private securities. It is felt that banks should be restricted to the performance of recognized banking functions and not permitted to become holding companies or speculative institutions.

The important point is that demand deposits, that is, the supply of money, have been increased by a total of $50,000 as in transaction 6. *Commercial bank bond purchases from the public increase the supply of money in the same way as does lending to the public.* The bank accepts government bonds—which are not money—and gives the Grisley company an increase in its demand deposits—which is money. The only real difference between selling a government bond to a commercial bank and negotiating a loan is that in the first case one gives the banker a claim against someone else (the United States Treasury), and in the second case a claim against one's own assets (one's IOU).

As in transaction 6, the effect of the Grisley company's drawing a $50,000 check in favor of the Quickbuck company will be for the Wahoo bank to lose reserves and demand deposits of $50,000 to the bank in which

Quickbuck deposits the check. When the check is cleared against the Wahoo bank, the balance sheet will appear as follows:

such liquid assets as cash and excess reserves. Banks must be on guard for depositors' transforming their demand deposits

BALANCE SHEET 7b: WAHOO BANK (after collection of check)

Assets		Liabilities and net worth	
Property	$240,000	Capital stock	$250,000
Reserves*	10,000	Demand deposits*	50,000
Securities	25,000		
Loans	25,000		

As you must now suspect, the selling of government bonds by a commercial bank will reduce the supply of money. If the Grisley company were to repurchase $25,000 worth of securities at some future date, it would in all probability pay by check. This, of course, reduces the quantity of demand deposits or bank money. If payment were made in cash, the quantity of currency in circulation would decline, thereby reducing the supply of money. The only difference between a commercial bank's selling a government bond and receiving payment on a loan is that in the former case the bank gives up a claim against the government, and in the latter a claim against a private borrower.

The impact of buying and selling government bonds upon the commercial bank's balance sheet will be explored in greater detail in Chapter 18.

Profits and Liquidity

The relative importance of the various asset items on a commercial bank's balance sheet is the result of the banker's pursuit of two conflicting goals. One goal is profits. Commercial banks, as any other business, are seeking profits. To this end the bank is desirous of holding loans and securities. These two items are the major earning assets of commercial banks. On the other hand, a commercial bank must seek safety. For a bank, safety lies in liquidity—specifically

into cash. Similarly, the possibility exists that more checks will be cleared against a bank than are cleared in its favor, causing a net outflow of reserves. Bankers are thus seeking a proper balance between prudence and profits. The compromise that is achieved determines the relative size of earning assets as opposed to highly liquid assets.

A MONOPOLY BANK

We have just gauged the lending ability of a single commercial bank which is part of a multibank banking system. Our conclusion is that such a bank can only lend an amount equal to its excess reserves. This is so because a single bank faces the prospect of losing reserves equal to the demand deposits it creates by lending. The drawing of a check equal to the amount of a loan will whisk reserves and demand deposits off to the bank in which the check is deposited.

Let us now consider for a moment the lending, or money-creating, potential of a monopoly bank. Suppose that instead of some fourteen thousand commercial banks in our economy there existed just one huge commercial bank. This is admittedly unrealistic, but there is an important lesson to be learned from studying the lending ability of such a bank. Suppose that the balance sheet of this gigantic monopoly bank were as shown at the top of page 312.

If the reserve ratio is 20 per cent, we find that our monopoly bank is "loaned up." It is

MONOPOLY BANK OF THE UNITED STATES (in billions)

Assets		Liabilities and net worth	
Property	$ 5	Capital stock	$25
Reserves	5	Demand deposits	25
Securities	20		
Loans	20		

just barely meeting its reserve requirement and consequently has no excess reserves upon which to make loans. But suppose that some citizens decide to exchange $1 billion in cash for some government bonds which the monopoly bank is willing to sell. When the public buys these bonds from the monopoly bank, the bank's holdings of securities fall to $19 billion. The monopoly bank acquires in return $1 billion in cash. Assuming the bank has on hand sufficient cash to meet the day-to-day withdrawals of people cashing checks against their deposits, the bank adds the $1 billion to its reserves. Reserves will now stand at $6 billion. As a result of this transaction, it is obvious that the bank now has $1 billion in excess reserves. On the basis of this excess reserve, by how much can the monopoly bank increase the economy's supply of money by lending?

Careful consideration of the situation reveals that on the basis of this $1 billion in excess reserves the monopoly bank can support an additional $5 billion in new loans. Why? *The monopoly bank with a 20 per cent reserve ratio can lend $5 for every $1 of excess reserves, because it has no fear of losing reserves when it lends.* Indeed, by assumption, there are no other banks to

which reserves can be lost! In lending $5 billion, the bank increases its outstanding loans from $20 to $25 billion, and its demand deposits will increase from $25 to $30 billion. And remember: This $5 billion increase in demand deposits constitutes a $5 billion increase in the supply of money. Now what if the borrowers draw $5 billion worth of checks against these new deposits as they purchase various goods and services? Will the monopoly bank face the loss of reserves and deposits as did the single bank? No, because the recipients of these checks *must* deposit them back in the monopoly bank. Checks drawn against the demand deposits of the monopoly bank must come directly home to roost. These checks are cleared by simply transferring the ownership of demand deposits from the drawer of the check to the recipient of the check. But the total volumes of the monopoly bank's reserves and demand deposits are unchanged when checks are drawn and used to finance purchases and sales of goods and services. With a 20 per cent reserve ratio the monopoly bank's $1 billion in excess reserves will permit a $5 billion expansion of loans from $25 to $30 billion. At the end of this transaction, the monopoly bank's balance sheet will stand as follows:

MONOPOLY BANK OF THE UNITED STATES (in billions)

Assets		Liabilities and net worth	
Property	$ 5	Capital stock	$25
Reserves*	6	Demand deposits*	30
Securities*	19		
Loans*	25		

The astute reader will recognize that the ability of the monopoly bank to lend by a multiple—five, in this case—of its excess reserves is related to the size of the reserve ratio. Suppose for the moment that the monopoly bank's reserve ratio is just 10 per cent and that at the outset its reserves are $2 billion and its outstanding demand deposits $20 billion. Again, the bank would be loaned up; it would have no excess reserves. Now the public buys $1 billion of securities and pays by cash. As before, the cash is added to reserves, giving the bank $1 billion in excess reserves. With a 10 per cent reserve ratio, how much can the monopoly bank safely lend? The answer is clear: It can lend $10 billion, thereby increasing demand deposits by $10 billion. In this case, we find that with a 10 per cent reserve ratio the monopoly bank can lend by a multiple of 10 for every dollar's worth of excess reserves it acquires.

If you are suspicious that a generalization is lurking in these two examples, you are absolutely right. A 10 per cent reserve ratio— that is, a ratio between reserves and demand deposits of 1:10—permits the monopoly bank to lend by a multiple of 10. A 20 per cent reserve ratio—that is, a 1:5 ratio between reserves and deposits—allows the monopoly bank to create new money by a multiple of 5 for each dollar's worth of excess reserves. If the ratio were 33⅓ per cent, the multiple would be 3. If 50 per cent, it would be 2. If 100 per cent, just 1. There is obviously an inverse relationship between the size of the reserve ratio and the multiple by which the monopoly bank can lend; the smaller the reserve ratio, the greater the multiple. More specifically, our generalization is this: *The multiple by which a monopoly bank can create new money by lending is the reciprocal of the reserve ratio.* The reciprocal of any number is the quotient you obtain by dividing that number into 1. Keep in mind, however, that the ability of the monopoly bank to lend anything at all is dependent upon the existence of excess reserves. No excess reserves, no lending—regardless of the size of the multiple.

Is this process of multiple credit creation reversible? Yes, it is. Suppose the monopoly bank has $4 billion in reserves and $25 billion in outstanding demand deposits. If the reserve ratio is 20 per cent, the bank would be faced with a $1 billion deficiency in reserves. It would have to call in $5 billion in loans and extend no new credit to get its house back in order. The needed contraction in the supply of bank money is five times the deficiency of reserves.

In short, we can say that the monopoly bank can lend by a multiple of its excess reserves for two reasons. First, the monopoly bank, in sharp contrast to the single bank in the banking system, cannot lose reserves. When the recipients of new loans draw checks to make purchases or pay debts, these checks must be redeposited back in the monopoly bank. The bank clears these checks by merely transferring claims against its assets—the payer's deposit is reduced and the payee's deposit increased by the amount of the check. The total volumes of demand deposits and reserves remain unchanged. Second, the monopoly bank's ability to lend by a multiple of its excess reserves hinges on the fact that the reserve ratio is fractional— that is, less than 100 per cent. A 100 per cent ratio would permit the monopoly bank to lend only dollar for dollar with its excess reserves.

THE COMMERCIAL BANKING SYSTEM AS A WHOLE

Thus far we have discovered that:

1. A single bank in a banking system can safely lend dollar for dollar with its excess reserves.

2. A monopoly bank, if one existed, could lend by a multiple of its excess reserves.

Now what of the lending ability of all commercial banks taken as a group? Jumping to our conclusions, we find that *the commercial banking system, as is true of a monopoly bank, can lend by a multiple of its excess reserves. This multiple lending is accomplished despite the fact that each bank in the system can only lend dollar for dollar with its excess reserves.* The immediate task is to uncover how these seemingly paradoxical conclusions come about.

To do this it is necessary that we keep our

the central banks are a part of their deliberate policy to increase the excess reserves of commercial banks and ultimately the supply of money through bank lending.) Since we are recording only *changes* in the balance sheets of the various commercial banks, bank A's balance sheet now appears as follows (a_1):

BALANCE SHEET: COMMERCIAL BANK A

Assets		Liabilities and net worth	
Reserves	$+100 (a_1)$ $- 80 (a_3)$	Demand deposits	$+100 (a_1)$ $+ 80 (a_2)$
Loans	$+ 80 (a_2)$		$- 80 (a_3)$

analysis as simple as possible. Therefore, we shall rely upon three simplifying assumptions. First, suppose that the reserve ratio for all commercial banks is 20 per cent. Second, assume initially that all banks are exactly meeting this 20 per cent reserve requirement. No excess reserves exist; all banks are "loaned up." Third, we shall suppose that if any bank becomes able to increase its loans as a result of acquiring excess reserves, an amount equal to these excess reserves will be loaned to one borrower, who will write a check for the entire amount of the loan and give it to someone else, who deposits the check in another bank. This messy assumption simply means that we are assuming the worst thing possible that can happen to any lending bank—a check for the entire amount of the loan is drawn and cleared against it and in favor of another bank.

The Banking System's Lending Potential

To get the ball rolling, suppose that one of the twelve Federal Reserve Banks buys a $100 government bond in the open market from a private individual or business firm. The seller of the bond deposits the $100 check he receives in bank A and, having ample till money, bank A adds this $100 to its reserves. (We shall find in Chapter 18, incidentally, that such bond purchases by

How much *excess reserves* does bank A now have? It has acquired $100 in new reserves, but in the process it has also acquired $100 in new demand deposits. This means that 20 per cent of the new reserves must be earmarked as required reserves to offset the new deposits. In short, $20 of the new reserves will be required, freeing the remaining $80 as excess reserves. Remembering that a single commercial bank such as bank A can only lend an amount equal to its excess reserves, we conclude that bank A can safely lend a maximum of $80. When a loan for this amount is negotiated, bank A's loans will increase by $80, and the borrower will get an $80 demand deposit. Let us add these figures to bank A's balance sheet (a_2).

But now we must invoke our third assumption: The borrower draws a check for $80—the entire amount of the loan—and gives it to someone who deposits it in another bank, bank B. As we saw in transaction 6, bank A *loses* both reserves and deposits equal to the amount of the loan (a_3). The net result of all the transactions is that bank A's reserves now stand at $20 (equal to $100 minus $80), loans at $80, and demand deposits at $100 (equal to $100 plus $80 minus $80). Note that when the dust has settled, bank A is just meeting the 20 per cent reserve ratio.

Bank B *acquires* both the reserves and the

deposits which bank A has lost. Bank B's balance sheet looks like this (b_1):

BALANCE SHEET: COMMERCIAL BANK B

Assets	Liabilities and net worth
Reserves .... $+80 ($b_1$) −64 ($b_3$) Loans .... +64 (b_2)	Demand deposits .... $+80 ($b_1$) +64 ($b_2$) −64 ($b_3$)

When the check is drawn and cleared, bank A *loses* $80 in reserves and deposits and bank B *gains* $80 in reserves and deposits. But 20 per cent, or $16, of bank B's newly acquired reserves must be kept as required reserves against the new $80 in demand deposits. This means that bank B has $64 (equal to $80 minus $16) in excess reserves. It can therefore lend $64 ($b_2$). When the borrower draws a check for the entire amount and deposits it in bank C, the reserves and deposits of bank B both fall by the $64 ($b_3$). As a result of these transactions, bank B's reserves will now stand at $16 (equal to $80 minus $64), loans at $64, and demand deposits at $80 (equal to $80 plus $64 minus $64). Note that, after all this has transpired, bank B is just meeting the 20 per cent reserve requirement.

We are off and running again. Bank C has acquired the $64 in reserves and deposits lost by bank B. Its balance statement appears as follows (c_1):

BALANCE SHEET: COMMERCIAL BANK C

Assets	Liabilities and net worth
Reserves .... $+64.00 ($c_1$) −51.20 ($c_3$) Loans .... +51.20 (c_2)	Demand deposits .... $+64.00 ($c_1$) +51.20 ($c_2$) −51.20 ($c_3$)

Exactly 20 per cent, or $12.80, of this new reserve will be required, the remaining $51.20 being excess reserves. Hence, bank C can safely lend a maximum of $51.20. Suppose it does ($c_2$). And suppose the borrower draws a check for the entire amount and gives it to someone who deposits it in another bank (c_3).

Bank D—the bank receiving the $51.20 in reserves and deposits—now notes these changes on its balance sheet (d_1):

BALANCE SHEET: COMMERCIAL BANK D

Assets	Liabilities and net worth
Reserves .... $+51.20 ($d_1$) −40.96 ($d_3$) Loans .... +40.96 (d_2)	Demand deposits .... $+51.20 ($d_1$) +40.96 ($d_2$) −40.96 ($d_3$)

It can now lend $40.96 ($d_2$). The borrower draws a check for the full amount and deposits it in another bank (d_3).

Now if we wanted to be particularly obnoxious, we could go ahead with this procedure by bringing banks E, F, G, H, . . . , N into the picture. We shall simply suggest that the student check through computations for banks E, F, and G, to ensure that he has the procedure firmly in mind.

The nucleus of this analysis is summarized in Table 17–2. Data for banks E through N are supplied so you may check your computations. Our conclusion is a rather startling

TABLE 17–2. EXPANSION OF THE MONEY SUPPLY BY THE COMMERCIAL BANKING SYSTEM

Bank	(1) Acquired reserves and deposits	(2) Required reserves	(3) Excess reserves, or (1) − (2)	(4) Amount which the bank can lend, = (3)
Bank A	$100.00 (a_1)	$20.00	$80.00	$ 80.00 (a_2)
Bank B	80.00 (a_3, b_1)	16.00	64.00	64.00 (b_2)
Bank C	64.00 (b_3, c_1)	12.80	51.20	51.20 (c_2)
Bank D	51.20 (c_3, d_1)	10.24	40.96	40.96 (d_2)
Bank E	40.96	8.19	32.77	32.77
Bank F	32.77	6.55	26.22	26.22
Bank G	26.22	5.24	20.98	20.98
Bank H	20.98	4.20	16.78	16.78
Bank I	16.78	3.36	13.42	13.42
Bank J	13.42	2.68	10.74	10.74
Bank K	10.74	2.15	8.59	8.59
Bank L	8.59	1.72	6.87	6.87
Bank M	6.87	1.37	5.50	5.50
Bank N	5.50	1.10	4.40	4.40
Other banks	21.97	4.40	17.57	17.57
Total amount loaned				$400.00

one: On the basis of the $80 in excess reserves (acquired by the banking system when someone deposited the $100 received from the sale of a government bond in bank A), the *commercial banking system* is able to lend $400. Lo and behold, the banking system is able to lend by a multiple of 5 when the reserve ratio is 20 per cent! Yet you will note that each single bank in the banking system is only lending an amount equal to its excess reserves. How do we explain these seemingly conflicting conclusions? Why is it that the *banking system* can lend by a multiple of its excess reserves, but *each individual bank* can only lend dollar for dollar with its excess reserves?

The answer lies in the fact that reserves lost by a single bank are not lost to the banking system as a whole. The reserves lost by bank A are acquired by bank B. Those lost by B are gained by C. C loses to D, D to E, E to F, and so forth. Hence, although reserves can be and are lost by *individual* banks in the banking system, there can be no

loss of reserves for the banking *system* as a whole. Remember that the monopoly bank was able to lend by a multiple of its excess reserves because it could not lose reserves. For the same reason the banking system as a whole can lend by a multiple of its excess reserves. This contrast, incidentally, is a fine illustration of why it is imperative that we keep the fallacy of composition firmly in mind. Commercial banks *as a group* can create money by lending in a manner much different from that of the individual banks in that system.

The rationale involved in this bank money, or deposit, multiplier is not unlike that underlying the income multiplier discussed in Chapter 13. The income multiplier was based on the fact that the expenditures of one household are received as income by another; the deposit multiplier rests on the fact that the reserves and deposits lost by one bank are received by another bank. And, just as the size of the income multiplier is determined by the reciprocal of the MPS, that is, by the leakage into saving which occurs at each round of spending, so the deposit multiplier is determined by the reciprocal of the reserve ratio, that is, by the leakage into required reserves which occurs at each step of the lending process. But keep in mind that, despite the similar rationale, one of these processes has to do with creating income and the other with creating money.

The reader might experiment with these teasers in testing his understanding of multiple credit expansion by the banking system:

1. Rework the preceding analysis (at least three or four steps of it) on the assumption that the reserve ratio is 10 per cent. What is the maximum amount of money the banking system could create upon acquiring $100 in new reserves and deposits? (No, the answer is not $800!)

2. Explain how a banking system which is "loaned up" and faced with a 20 per cent reserve ratio might be forced to *reduce* its outstanding loans by $400 as a result of a Federal Reserve Bank's *selling* a $100 bond to a private individual or business.

Some Modifications

Our discussion of credit expansion has been conducted in a somewhat rarefied atmosphere. There are certain complications which might modify the quantitative preciseness of our analysis.

Other leakages. Aside from the leakage of required reserves at each step of the lending process, certain other leakages of money from the commercial banks might occur, thereby dampening the money-creating potential of the banking system.

1. A borrower may request that a part of his loan be paid in cash. Or the recipient of a check drawn by a borrower may present it at his bank to be redeemed partially or wholly in currency rather than added to his account. Thus, if the person who borrowed the $80 from bank A in our illustration asked

for and got $16 of it in cash and the remaining $64 as a demand deposit, bank B would only receive $64 in new reserves (of which only $51.20 would be excess) rather than $80 (of which $64 was excess). This decline in excess reserves reduces the lending potential of the banking system accordingly. As a matter of fact, if the first borrower had taken the entire $80 in cash, and this currency remained in circulation, the multiple expansion process would have stopped then and there. But the convenience and safety of demand deposits make this unlikely.

2. Our analysis of the commercial banking system's ability to expand the money supply by lending is based on the supposition that commercial banks are willing to meet precisely the legal reserve requirement. In practice bankers are more prudent than this. They arrange to have a "safety margin" of excess reserves to avoid the embarrassment of falling below the legal reserve ratio in the event that an unusually large amount of checks is cleared against them. Therefore, bank A, upon receiving $100 in new cash, might choose to add $25 rather than the legal minimum of $20 to its reserves, the extra $5 serving as a buffer, or cushion, against adverse check clearings. The overall credit expansion potential of the banking system would obviously be reduced by such additions to a bank's excess reserves.

Willingness versus ability to lend. It is only fair to emphasize that our illustration of the banking system's ability to create money rests upon the supposition that commercial banks are willing to exercise their abilities to create money by lending and that households and businesses are willing to borrow. In practice, this need not be the case. Bankers, you will recall, seek a proper balance between prudence and profits. When prosperity reigns, banks may expand credit to the maximum of their ability. Why not? Loans are interest-earning assets, and in good times there is little fear of borrowers defaulting. But if depression clouds appear on the economic horizon, bankers may hastily withdraw their invitations to borrow, seeking the safety of liquidity even if it involves the sacrifice of potential interest income. Bankers may fear the large-scale withdrawal of deposits by a panicky public and simultaneously doubt the ability of borrowers to repay. It is not too surprising that during some years of the Great Depression of the 1930s banks had considerable excess reserves but lending was at a low ebb. Obviously, if the amount actually loaned by each commercial bank falls short of its excess reserves, the resulting multiple expansion of credit will be curtailed.

The fact that bankers may not expand the supply of money to their maximum ability is of more than passing interest. It may be a factor which contributes significantly to business fluctuations. By holding back on credit expansion as the economy begins to slip into a depression, commercial banks may further inhibit total spending and intensify that cyclical downswing. Indeed, we noted in Chapter 11 that a rapid shrinkage of the money supply contributed to the Great Depression of the 1930s. Conversely, by lending and thereby creating money to the maximum of their ability during prosperity, commercial banks may contribute to an excess of total spending and to the resulting inflationary pressures. In Chapter 18 the means by which the Board of Governors attempts to influence the lending policies of commercial banks, so that they will offset rather than enforce cyclical fluctuations, will be explored.

SUMMARY

1. Commercial banks create money—that is, demand deposits, or bank money—when they make loans. The creation of demand deposits by bank lending is the most important source of money in American capitalism.

2. The ability of a single commercial bank to create money by lending depends upon the size of its *excess* reserves. Generally speaking, a commercial bank can safely lend only an amount equal to the size of its excess reserves. It is thus limited because, in all likelihood, checks drawn by borrowers will be deposited in other banks, causing a loss of reserves and deposits to the lending bank equal to the amount it has loaned.

3. A monopoly bank would be in a position to lend by a multiple of any excess reserves which it might acquire. This is so because **a.** a monopoly bank could not lose reserves as the result of checks drawn by borrowers and **b.** the reserve ratio is assumed to be less than 100 per cent. The multiple by which a monopoly bank could expand the money supply through lending is the reciprocal of the reserve ratio.

4. The commercial banking system as a whole can also lend by a multiple of its excess reserves. As is the case with the monopoly bank, the banking *system* cannot lose reserves, although individual banks can lose reserves to other banks in the system. The multiple by which the banking system can lend is, once again, the reciprocal of the reserve ratio. This multiple credit expansion process is reversible.

QUESTIONS AND STUDY SUGGESTIONS

1. Why must a balance sheet always balance? What are the major assets and claims on a commercial bank's balance sheet?
2. Why are commercial banks required to have reserves? Explain why reserves are assets to commercial banks but liabilities to the Federal Reserve Banks. What are excess reserves? How are they calculated? What is their significance?

3. "Whenever currency is deposited in a commercial bank, cash goes out of circulation and, as a result, the supply of money is reduced." Do you agree? Explain.

4. "When a check is drawn against bank A and deposited in another bank, bank A will lose reserves as the check is cleared. Yet the collection of checks entails no loss of reserves by the commercial banking system." Explain. Of what significance is this for the lending ability of the banking system?

5. "When a commercial bank makes loans, it creates money; when loans are retired, money is destroyed." Explain.

6. Explain why a single commercial bank can safely lend only an amount equal to its excess reserves but the commercial banking system can lend by a multiple of its excess reserves. Why is the multiple by which the banking system can lend equal to the reciprocal of its reserve ratio?

7. Assume that Jones deposits $500 in currency in the First National Bank. A half hour later Smith negotiates a loan for $750 at this bank. By how much and in what direction has the money supply changed? Explain.

8. Suppose the Continental Bank has the following simplified balance sheet. The reserve ratio is 20 per cent.

Assets			Liabilities and net worth		
	(1)	(2)		(1)	(2)
Reserves $22,000	___	___	Demand de-		
Securities 38,000	___	___	posits $100,000	___	___
Loans 40,000	___	___			

a. What is the maximum amount which this bank can safely lend? Show in column 1 how the bank's balance sheet will appear after the bank has loaned this amount.

b. By how much has the supply of money changed? Explain.

c. How will the bank's balance sheet appear after checks drawn for the entire amount of the new loans have been cleared against this bank? Show this new balance sheet in column 2.

d. Answer parts a, b, and c on the assumption that the reserve ratio is 15 per cent.

9. Suppose the National Bank of Commerce has excess reserves of $8,000 and outstanding demand deposits of $150,000. If the reserve ratio is 20 per cent, what is the size of the bank's actual reserves?

10. Suppose the Fourth National Bank has the following simplified balance sheet. The reserve ratio is 20 per cent.

Assets			Liabilities and net worth		
	(1)	(2)		(1)	(2)
Reserves $40,000	___	___	Demand de-		
Securities 90,000	___	___	posits $200,000	___	___
Loans 70,000	___	___			

Assume that households and businesses deposit $5,000 worth of currency in this bank and that this currency is added to the bank's reserves.

a. In column 1 show how the bank's balance sheet would appear after this transaction. Has there been a change in the supply of money as a result of these deposits?

b. How much excess reserves does this bank now have? By how much can it safely expand its loans? In column 2 show the bank's balance sheet as it appears after those loans have been made.

c. To what extent, if at all, will this lending alter the supply of money? Explain.

11. Suppose the following is a simplified consolidated balance sheet for the commercial banking system. All figures are in billions. The reserve ratio is 20 per cent.

Assets		(1)	Liabilities and net worth		(1)
Reserves	$40	_____	Demand deposits ... $186		_____
Securities	56	_____			
Loans	90	_____			

a. How much excess reserves does the commercial banking system have? How much can the banking system lend? Show in column 1 how the consolidated balance sheet would look after this amount has been lent.

b. Answer question 11a on the assumption that the reserve ratio is 15 per cent. Explain the resulting difference in the lending ability of the commercial banking system.

12. The Third National Bank has reserves of $20,000 and demand deposits of $100,000. The reserve ratio is 20 per cent. Households deposit $5,000 in currency in the bank. This $5,000 is added by the bank to its reserves. How much excess reserves does the bank now have?

13. Suppose again that the Third National Bank has reserves of $20,000 and demand deposits of $100,000. The reserve ratio remains at 20 per cent. The bank now sells $5,000 in securities to the Federal Reserve Bank in its district, receiving a $5,000 increase in reserves in return. How much excess reserves does the bank now have? Why does your answer differ (yes, it does!) from the answer to question 12?

14. What are "leakages"? How might they affect the money-creating potential of the banking system? Be specific.

SELECTED REFERENCES

Chandler, Lester V.: *The Economics of Money and Banking*, 4th ed. (New York: Harper & Row, Publishers, Incorporated, 1964), chaps. 4 and 5.

Duesenberry, James S.: *Money and Credit: Impact and Control* (Englewood Cliffs, N.J.: Prentice-Hall, Inc., 1964), chaps. 3–5.

Federal Reserve Bank of Chicago: *Modern Money Mechanics* (May, 1961).

Halm, George N.: *Economics of Money and Banking*, rev. ed. (Homewood, Ill.: Richard D. Irwin, Inc., 1961), chaps. 5, 13, and 14.

Pritchard, Leland J.: *Money and Banking*, 2d ed. (Boston: Houghton Mifflin Company, 1964), chaps. 5–11.

CHAPTER 18

THE FEDERAL RESERVE BANKS
AND MONETARY POLICY

In Chapter 17 our attention was focused upon the money-creating ability of individual banks and the commercial banking system. Our discussion ended on a disturbing note: Unregulated commercial banking might contribute to cyclical fluctuations in business activity. That is, commercial banks will find it profitable to expand the supply of money during inflationary prosperity and to restrict the money supply in seeking liquidity during depression. It is the task of this chapter to see how the monetary authorities of American capitalism attempt to reverse the procyclical tendencies of the commercial banking system through a variety of control techniques.

More specifically, the goals of the present chapter are these: First, the objectives of monetary policy, the roles of participating institutions, and the route by which monetary policy affects the operation of the economy are detailed. Next, the balance sheet of the Federal Reserve Banks is surveyed, because it is through these central banks that monetary policy is largely effectuated. Third, the quantitative and qualitative techniques of monetary control are analyzed in considerable detail. Then the monetary aspects of Treasury gold transactions are explained. Fifth, a monetary approach to output- and price-level determination, based upon the so-called equation of exchange, is presented. Finally, monetary policy is evaluated as to its overall effectiveness in restraining fluctuations in economic activity.

OBJECTIVE OF MONETARY POLICY

Before analyzing the techniques through which monetary policy is effectuated, it is essential that we clearly understand the objectives of monetary policy and locate the institutions responsible for the formulation and implementation of that policy. Certain key points made in Chapter 16 merit reemphasis at the outset of our discussion. The Board of Governors of the Federal Reserve System has the responsibility of supervising and controlling the operation of our monetary and banking systems. It is this Board which formulates the basic policies which the banking system follows. Because it is a public body, the decisions of the Board of Governors are made in the interests of the general economic welfare of society as a whole. The twelve Federal Reserve Banks—the central banks of American capitalism—implement the policy decisions of the Board. As quasi-public banks, the Federal Reserve Banks are not guided by the profit motive, but rather pursue those measures which the Board of Governors recommends.

However, to say that the Board follows policies which "promote the general economic welfare" is not enough. We must pinpoint the goal of monetary policy. It will come as no great surprise that *the objective of monetary policy is to assist the economy in achieving a full-employment noninflationary level of total output.*

But precisely how does monetary policy work toward this goal? The process is complicated, but essentially it boils down to this:

1. By invoking certain control techniques, the Board of Governors and the Federal Reserve Banks can influence the size of the reserves—and therefore the excess reserves—of commercial banks.

2. Because excess reserves are the basis upon which commercial banks can expand the money supply by lending, any manipulations of excess reserves through the control techniques of the Board of Governors will affect the supply of money, that is, the amounts which commercial banks will be able and willing to lend at various possible interest rates.

3. Given the demand for money, changes in the supply of money will affect the cost and availability of money. That is, changes in the supply of money will affect the interest rate and the amount of credit bankers are willing to make available to borrowers.

4. Changes in the cost and availability of bank credit will in turn have an impact upon the spending decisions of society, particularly upon investment decisions, and therefore upon the levels of output, employment, income, and prices.

The cause-effect chain between monetary policy and output and employment is summarized in the outline below.

Federal monetary policy influences commercial bank reserves
    which
Influences the supply of money
    which
Influences the interest rate (the cost) and the availability of bank credit
    which
Influences investment spending, output, employment, and the price level

Let us examine the operation of monetary policy through a simple example. Suppose the economy is operating below the full-employment mark. Side-stepping troublesome complications and qualifications for the moment, we find that monetary policy would work something like this:

1. The Board of Governors would direct the Federal Reserve Banks to pursue certain policies designed to increase the (excess) reserves of commercial banks.

2. Finding themselves with abundant excess reserves, commercial banks are now in a position to make available a greater supply of money by granting bank credit. The banking *system* can expand the supply of money by a multiple of its excess reserves.

3. With an increase in the supply of money relative to the demand for it, interest rates will decline, and the quantity of bank credit (money) taken by borrowers will increase.

4. Low interest rates and the ready availability of bank credit will induce increases in spending. These increases in spending will be subject to the multiplier, driving the equilibrium NNP upward by a multiple of the increase in total spending.

Economists are in general agreement that the investment component of total spending is more likely to be affected by changes in the interest rate than is consumer spending. The interest rate does not seem to be a very crucial factor in determining how households divide their disposable income between consumption and saving. Indeed, it is not clear whether decreases in the interest rate will tend to increase or decrease the amount of consumption. On the one hand, a lower interest rate may induce some households, particularly those operating small businesses, to save less, because it is now cheap to finance by borrowing. On the other hand, we have noted that those who save to provide a given retirement income or to provide funds for the education of their children find that a lower interest rate will mean that a larger volume of saving will be required to earn the needed income. Then, too, the effect of higher interest rates on consumer installment buying is not great, because considerable increases or decreases in the interest rate have little impact on the size of each monthly payment; that is, the consumer is not impressed by the total interest charge but only by how much interest he must pay per month. Furthermore, any tendency for higher interest charges to diminish consumer installment buying can be largely canceled by extending the repayment period from, say, twenty-four to thirty-six months.

The impact of changing interest rates upon investment spending is greater because of the size and long-term nature of such purchases. Capital equipment, factory buildings, warehouses, and so forth, are tremendously expensive purchases. In absolute terms the interest charges on funds borrowed for these purchases will be very considerable. Similarly, the interest cost on a house purchased on a long-term contract will be very large: A ½ per cent change in the interest rate could easily amount to hundreds or even thousands of dollars on the total cost of a home. It is important to note as well that changes in the interest rate may also affect investment spending by changing the relative attractiveness of capital equipment purchases and bond purchases. If the interest rate rises on bonds, then, given the profit expectations on capital good purchases, businesses will be more inclined to purchase securities than to buy capital equipment. Conversely, given profit expectations on investment spending, a fall in the interest rate makes capital purchases more attractive than bond ownership. In short, the impact of changing interest rates will be primarily upon investment spending and, through this channel, upon output, employment, and the level of prices.

The above comments detail the ideal operation of an "easy money" policy. A "tight money" policy follows the same route, but the procedure is to lower commercial bank reserves, reduce the supply of money, raise the cost and lessen the availability of bank credit, and thereby curtail investment spending. Tight money should obviously be invoked when an excess of total spending is causing inflation in the economy.

So much for the objectives of monetary policy and the cause-effect chain which its application entails. We now seek an understanding of the techniques by which the Board of Governors can manipulate the size of commercial bank reserves.

CONSOLIDATED BALANCE SHEET OF THE FEDERAL RESERVE BANKS

Because monetary policy is implemented by the twelve Federal Reserve Banks, it is essential to consider the nature of the balance sheet of the Federal Reserve Banks. Some of the assets and liabilities found here are considerably different from those found on the balance sheet of a commercial bank. Table 18–1 is a consolidated balance sheet which shows all the pertinent assets and liabilities of the twelve Federal Reserve Banks as of April 28, 1965.

TABLE 18–1. TWELVE FEDERAL RESERVE BANKS' CONSOLIDATED BALANCE SHEET, APRIL 28, 1965 (in billions)

Assets		Liabilities and net worth	
Cash	$ 0.1	Reserves of member banks	$17.4
Gold certificates	14.1	Treasury deposits	1.0
Securities	37.4	Federal Reserve Notes (outstanding)	34.0
Loans to commercial banks	0.3	All other liabilities	6.9
All other assets	7.4	Total	$59.3
Total	$59.3		

Source: Federal Reserve Bulletin, May, 1965.

Assets

Cash. This is the Federal Reserve Banks' holdings of Treasury currency. The Federal Reserve Banks may have received this cash as a result of Treasury or commercial bank deposits.

Gold certificates. Two things should be noted about gold certificates. First, these certificates are simply warehouse receipts for the gold bullion held by the Treasury. The law requires that newly mined gold or gold coming into the United States as a result of international trade must be sold to the Treasury. The Treasury pays for such gold by drawing checks against its deposit in the Federal Reserve Banks. The clearing of these checks reduces Treasury deposits in the Federal Reserve Banks. To replenish these deposits the Treasury issues gold certificates—claims or warehouse receipts against the newly obtained gold—and deposits them in the Federal Reserve Banks. Second, gold certificates constitute the reserves which the Federal Reserve Banks are required by law to keep against outstanding Federal Reserve Notes. Table 18–1 reveals that required reserves are $8.5 billion (25 per cent of $34 billion) and excess reserves are $5.6 ($14.1 minus $8.5) billion.

Securities. This refers to the government bonds which the Federal Reserve Banks are holding. Some of these bonds may have been purchased directly from the Treasury, but most are bought in the open market from commercial banks or the public. Although these bonds are an important source of income to the Federal Reserve Banks, they are not bought and sold primarily for income. Rather they are bought and sold primarily to influence the size of commercial bank reserves and therefore their ability to create money by lending.

Loans to commercial banks. Commercial banks occasionally borrow from the Federal Reserve Banks. The IOUs which the com-mercial banks give to the bankers' banks in negotiating loans are listed as loans to commercial banks. From the Federal Reserve Banks' point of view these IOUs are assets, that is, claims against the commercial banks that have borrowed from them. To the commercial banks these IOUs are liabilities. In borrowing, the commercial banks obtain increases in their reserves in exchange for their IOUs.

Before shifting to the liability side of the Federal Reserve Banks' balance sheet, one note on terminology: "Securities" and "loans to commercial banks" are sometimes called "Reserve Bank credit." These two accounts represent credit which the bankers' banks have extended to (1) the government by buying government securities and (2) commercial banks by accepting their IOUs in return for increases in their reserves.

Liabilities

On the liability side we find three major items:

Reserves of member banks. We are already familiar with this account. It is an asset from the viewpoint of the member banks but a liability to the Federal Reserve Banks.

Treasury deposits. Just as businesses and private individuals find it convenient and desirable to pay their obligations by check, so does the United States Treasury. It keeps deposits in the various Federal Reserve Banks and draws checks on them in paying its obligations. To the Treasury such deposits are obviously assets; to the Federal Reserve Banks, liabilities. The Treasury creates and replenishes these deposits by depositing tax receipts, money borrowed from the public or the banks through the sale of bonds, and gold certificates.

Federal Reserve Notes. The basic portion of our paper money supply is Federal Reserve Notes. These notes are issued by the Federal Reserve Banks. When in circulation, these pieces of paper money constitute circulating claims against the assets of the Federal Reserve Banks and are therefore treated by them as liabilities. Just as your own IOU is neither an asset nor a liability to you when it is in your own possession, so Federal Reserve Notes resting in the vaults of the various Federal Reserve Banks are neither an asset nor a liability. Only those notes in circulation are liabilities to the bankers' banks. These notes, which come into circulation through commercial banks, are not a part of the money supply until they are in the hands of the public.

MONETARY POLICY: QUANTITATIVE CONTROLS

With this cursory understanding of the Federal Reserve Banks' balance sheet, we are now in a position to explore how the Board of Governors of the Federal Reserve System can influence the money-creating abilities of the commercial banking system. What devices can be employed at the discretion of the Board of Governors to influence commercial bank reserves?

The general, or quantitative, controls of the monetary authorities are three in number: (1) changing the reserve ratio, (2) open-market operations, and (3) changing the discount rate. These controls are general, or quantitative, in that they seek to manipulate the total quantity of bank credit. Later we shall discuss selective, or qualitative, controls, which are aimed at influencing the volume of specific types of credit.

The Reserve Ratio

How can the Board of Governors influence the ability of commercial banks to lend through manipulation of the legal reserve ratio? A simple example will supply a clear answer to this query. Suppose a commercial bank's balance sheet is such that reserves are $5,000 and demand deposits $20,000. If the legal reserve ratio stands at 20 per cent, the bank's *required* reserves are $4,000. Since *actual* reserves are $5,000, it is apparent that the *excess* reserves of this bank are $1,000. On the basis of this $1,000 of excess reserves we have seen that this single bank can lend $1,000, but the banking system as a whole could create a maximum of $5,000 in new bank money by lending (Table 18–2). Now what if the Board of Governors raised the legal reserve ratio from 20 to 25 per cent? Required reserves would jump from $4,000 to $5,000, shrinking excess reserves from $1,000 to zero. It is obvious that *raising the reserve ratio increases the amount of required reserves banks must keep. Either banks lose excess reserves, diminishing their ability to create money by lending, or else they find their reserves deficient and are*

TABLE 18–2. THE EFFECTS OF CHANGES IN THE RESERVE RATIO UPON THE LENDING ABILITY OF COMMERCIAL BANKS (hypothetical data)

(1) Legal reserve ratio, per cent	(2) Demand deposits	(3) Actual reserves	(4) Required reserves	(5) Excess reserves, or (3) − (4)	(6) Money-creating potential of single bank, = (5)	(7) Money-creating potential of banking system
10	$20,000	$5,000	$2,000	$ 3,000	$ 3,000	$ 30,000
20	20,000	5,000	4,000	1,000	1,000	5,000
25	20,000	5,000	5,000	0	0	0
30	20,000	5,000	6,000	−1,000	−1,000	−3,333

forced to contract the money supply. In the above case, excess reserves are transformed into required reserves, and the money-creating potential of our bank is reduced from $1,000 to zero.

What if the Board of Governors announced a forthcoming increase in the legal reserve requirement to 30 per cent? The commercial bank would be faced with the embarrassing prospect of failing to meet this requirement. To protect itself against such an eventuality, the bank would be forced to lower its outstanding demand deposits and at the same time to increase its reserves. To reduce its demand deposits, the bank would be prone to let outstanding loans mature and be repaid without extending new credit. To increase reserves, the bank might sell some of its holdings of securities, adding the proceeds to its reserves. Both courses of action will reduce the supply of money (see transactions 6 and 7, Chapter 17).

What would be the effect if the Board of Governors lowered the reserve ratio from the original 20 to 10 per cent? In this case required reserves would decline from $4,000 to $2,000, and as a result excess reserves would jump from $1,000 to $3,000. We can conclude that *lowering the reserve ratio changes required reserves to excess reserves, thereby enhancing the ability of banks to create new money by lending.* Table 18–2 summarizes all the reserve-ratio changes just discussed.

Table 18–2 reveals that a change in the reserve ratio actually affects the money-creating ability of the banking *system* in two ways. First, it affects the size of excess reserves. Second, it changes the multiple by which the banking system can lend. Thus, raising the reserve ratio from 10 to 20 per cent reduces the money-creating potential of the banking system from $30,000 to $5,000.

Open-market Operations

The buying and selling of government bonds by the Federal Reserve Banks in the open market—that is, from or to commercial banks and the general public—also affect the excess reserves of commercial banks.

Buying securities. Suppose the Board of Governors orders the Federal Reserve Banks to buy government bonds in the open market. From whom may these securities be purchased? In general, from commercial banks and the public. In either case the overall effect is basically the same—commercial bank reserves are increased.

Let us trace through the situation in which the Federal Reserve Banks buy government bonds *from commercial banks.* This transaction is a simple one.

a. The commercial banks give up a part of their holdings of securities to the bankers' banks.

b. The Federal Reserve Banks pay for these securities by increasing the reserves of the commercial banks by the amount of the purchase.

Just as the commercial bank may pay for a bond bought from a private individual by increasing the seller's demand deposit, so the bankers' bank may pay for bonds bought from commercial banks by increasing the bank's reserves. In short, the consolidated balance sheets of the commercial banks and the Federal Reserve Banks will change as follows:

FEDERAL RESERVE BANKS

Assets	Liabilities and net worth
+ Securities (*a*)	+ Reserves of member banks (*b*)

↑ (*a*) Securities | (*b*) + Reserves ↓

COMMERCIAL BANKS

Assets	Liabilities and net worth
− Securities (*a*) + Reserves (*b*)	

The most important aspect of this transaction is that, when Federal Reserve Banks purchase securities from commercial banks, the reserves—and therefore the lending ability—of the commercial banks are increased.

If the Federal Reserve Banks should purchase securities *from the general public,* the effect on commercial bank reserves would be substantially the same. Suppose that the Grisley Meat Packing Company possesses some negotiable government bonds which it sells in the open market to the Federal Reserve Banks. The transaction goes like this:

a. The Grisley company gives up securities to the Federal Reserve Banks and gets in payment a check drawn by the Federal Reserve Banks on themselves.

b. The Grisley company promptly deposits this check in its account with the Wahoo bank.

c. The Wahoo bank collects this check against the Federal Reserve Banks by sending it to the Federal Reserve Banks for collection. As a result the Wahoo bank receives an increase in its reserves.

Balance sheet changes are shown below.

Two aspects of this transaction are noteworthy. First, as with Federal Reserve purchases of securities directly from commercial banks, the reserves and lending ability of the commercial banking system have been increased. Second, in this instance the supply of money is directly increased by the central banks' purchase of government bonds aside from any expansion of the money supply which may occur as the result of the increase in commercial bank reserves.

You may detect a slight difference be-

FEDERAL RESERVE BANKS

Assets	Liabilities and net worth
+ Securities (*a*)	+ Reserves of member banks (*c*)

(*a*) Securities   (*a*) Check

GRISLEY COMPANY

Assets	Liabilities and net worth
+ Demand deposits (*b*) − Securities (*a*)	

(*c*) + Reserves   (*c*) Check

(*b*) + Deposits   (*b*) Check

WAHOO BANK

Assets	Liabilities and net worth
+ Reserves (*c*)	+ Demand deposits (*b*)

tween the Federal Reserve Banks' purchases of securities from the commercial banking system and from the public. Assuming all commercial banks are "loaned up" initially, Federal Reserve bond purchases from commercial banks will increase the actual reserves and excess reserves of the commercial banks by the entire amount of the bond purchases. Thus a $1,000 bond purchase from commercial banks would increase both the actual and excess reserves of the commercial banks by $1,000. On the other hand, Federal Reserve Bank purchases of bonds from the public increase actual reserves but also increase demand deposits. Thus a $1,000 bond purchase from the public would increase actual reserves of the "loaned-up" banking system by $1,000; but with a 20 per cent reserve ratio the excess reserves of the banking system would only amount to $800. In the case of bond purchases from the public it is *as if* the commercial banking system had already used one-fifth or 20 per cent of its newly acquired reserves to support $1,000 worth of new demand deposit money.

However, in each transaction the basic conclusion is the same: *When the Federal Reserve Banks buy securities in the open market, commercial banks' reserves will be increased*

Selling securities. We should now be highly suspicious that Federal Reserve Bank sales of government bonds will reduce commercial bank reserves. Let us confirm these suspicions.

Suppose the Federal Reserve Banks sell securities in the open market *to commercial banks:*

a. The Federal Reserve Banks give up securities which the commercial banks obviously acquire.

b. The commercial banks pay for these securities by drawing checks against their deposits—that is, their reserves—in the Federal Reserve Banks. The Federal Reserve Banks collect these checks by reducing commercial banks' reserves accordingly.

In short, the following balance sheet changes occur:

FEDERAL RESERVE BANKS

Assets	Liabilities and net worth
− Securities (*a*)	− Reserves of member banks (*b*)

(*a*) Securities   (*b*) − Reserves

COMMERCIAL BANKS

Assets	Liabilities and net worth
− Reserves (*b*) + Securities (*a*)	

Note specifically the reduction in commercial bank reserves.

Should the Federal Reserve Banks sell securities *to the public*, the overall effect is substantially the same. Let us put the Grisley company on the buying end of government bonds which the Federal Reserve Banks are selling.

a. The Federal Reserve Bank sells government bonds to the Grisley company, the latter paying for these securities by a check drawn on the Wahoo bank.

b. The Federal Reserve Banks clear this check against the Wahoo bank by reducing its reserves.

c. The Wahoo bank returns the Grisley company's check to it, reducing the company's demand deposit accordingly.

The balance sheets change as shown at the top of page 329.

Note that Federal Reserve bond sales of $1,000 to the commercial banking system reduce the system's actual and excess reserves by $1,000. But a $1,000 bond sale to the public reduces excess reserves by $800 because demand deposit money is also reduced by $1,000 by the sale. In the case of bond sales to the public it is *as if* the commercial banking system had reduced its outstanding demand deposits by $1,000 to cushion the decline in excess reserves to the extent of $200.

In each of the two variations of the

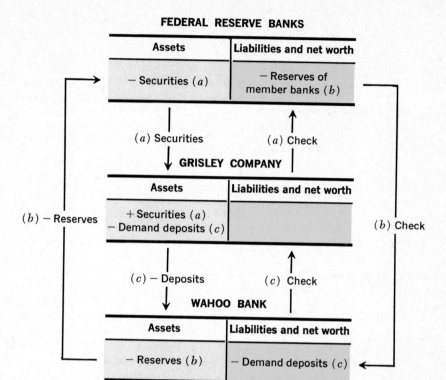

Federal Reserve bond sale transaction, however, the basic conclusion is the same: *When the Federal Reserve Banks sell securities in the open market, commercial bank reserves are reduced.*

The Discount Rate

The Federal Reserve Banks perform essentially the same functions for commercial banks as the commercial banks perform for the public. One of these functions is the making of loans. Just as commercial banks extend credit to the public, so the bankers' banks may lend to the commercial banks.

When commercial banks borrow from Federal Reserve Banks, they may turn over to the bankers' banks either IOUs drawn against themselves or the promissory notes of businesses and individuals which they hold as security against loans granted to the public. Just as commercial banks charge interest on their loans, so do the Federal Reserve Banks charge interest on the loans

they grant to commercial banks. This interest rate is called the *discount rate*, the interest on such loans being discounted at the time the loan is negotiated, rather than collected at the time the loan is repaid.

Let us suppose commercial banks borrow from the Federal Reserve Banks by drawing IOUs against themselves. These IOUs, being claims against the commercial banks, are assets to the Federal Reserve Banks and appear on their balance sheet as "loans to commercial banks." To the commercial banks these IOUs are liabilities, appearing as "loans from the Federal Reserve Banks" on the commercial banks' balance sheets. In payment of the loan the Federal Reserve Banks will increase the reserves of the borrowing commercial banks. Since no required reserves need be kept against loans from the Federal Reserve Banks, *all* new reserves acquired by borrowing from the Federal Reserve Banks would be excess reserves. These changes are reflected in the balance sheets of the commercial banks and the bankers' banks as shown below:

FEDERAL RESERVE BANKS

Assets	Liabilities and net worth
+ Loans to commercial banks	+ Reserves of commercial banks

IOUs ↑   + Reserves ↓

COMMERCIAL BANKS

Assets	Liabilities and net worth
+ Reserves	+ Loans from the Federal Reserve Banks

It is interesting to note that this transaction is analogous to a private person's borrowing from a commercial bank (see transaction 6, Chapter 17).

The important point, of course, is that *commercial bank borrowing from the Federal Reserve Banks increases the reserves of commercial banks, thereby enhancing their ability to extend credit to the public.*

The Board of Governors of the Federal Reserve System has the power to establish and manipulate the discount rate at which commercial banks can borrow from the Federal Reserve Banks. From the commercial banks' point of view, the discount rate obviously constitutes a cost entailed in acquiring reserves. Hence, a *decrease* in the discount rate encourages commercial banks to build up their reserves by borrowing. Although not obligated to do so, the Federal Reserve Banks usually stand ready to extend credit to borrowing banks that can offer acceptable collateral. But if the discount rate is high, this means that commercial banks that borrow must in turn boost the interest rate at which they lend to the public to make such transactions profitable. If a commercial bank has to pay 3 per cent for

the attainment of new reserves, it may have to charge 8 per cent for loans made on these new reserves to the public in order to earn an acceptable profit. Such a high rate discourages the public from increasing the money supply by borrowing from the commercial banks. Conversely, a low discount rate permits commercial banks to acquire new reserves cheaply from the Federal Reserve Banks. This allows the commercial banks to lend profitably at relatively low interest rates to the public, thereby encouraging an expansion in the supply of money. Apart from these quantitative considerations, changes in the discount rate may well have significant psychological effects upon the credit policies of banks and the public. Changes in the discount rate are a very explicit means by which the Board of Governors can communicate the overall direction of monetary policy to banks and the public.

As evidenced by the consolidated balance sheet of the Federal Reserve Banks (Table 18–1), commercial banks borrow rather infrequently from the Federal Reserve Banks. For this reason the discount rate is a relatively weak instrument of monetary policy.

Reserve Bank Credit

Early in this chapter we noted that the sum of loans to commercial banks and securities appearing on the Federal Reserve Banks' balance sheet constitutes Reserve Bank credit. Loans to commercial banks represent credit extended to the commercial banks, and the Federal Reserve Banks' holdings of securities indicate credit granted to the government.

Obviously, when the Federal Reserve Banks increase the volume of loans to commercial banks by lowering the discount rate and buy securities in the open market, Reserve Bank credit increases. An expansion of Reserve Bank credit increases the reserves of commercial banks and thereby enhances their ability to increase the supply of money by lending to the public. On the other hand, if the Federal Reserve Banks choose to decrease loans to commercial banks by boosting the discount rate and sell securities in the open market, Reserve Bank credit will decline. This decline in Reserve Bank credit destroys commercial bank reserves and limits further increases in the supply of money. It may even force a contraction in the money supply. In short, *there is a direct relationship between the volume of Reserve Bank credit and the size of commercial bank reserves.*

Easy Money and Tight Money

Suppose the economy is faced with unemployment and deflation. The monetary authorities correctly decide that an increase in the supply of money is needed to stimulate the volume of spending in order to help absorb the idle resources. To induce an increase in the supply of money, the Board of Governors must see to it that the excess reserves of commercial banks are expanded. What specific policies will bring this about?

1. The reserve ratio should be reduced, automatically changing required reserves into excess reserves.

2. The Board of Governors should order the Federal Reserve Banks to buy securities in the open market. This will build up the size of commercial bank reserves.

3. The discount rate should be lowered to induce commercial banks to add to their reserves by borrowing from the Federal Reserve Banks. The second and third policies can be combined by simply saying that Reserve Bank credit should be expanded.

For obvious reasons, this set of policy decisions is called an *easy money policy.* Its purpose is to make credit easily available, so as to increase the volumes of spending and employment.

Suppose, on the other hand, an excess of spending is pushing the economy into an inflationary spiral. The Board of Governors should attempt to reduce total spending by limiting or contracting the supply of money.

The key to this goal lies in reducing the reserves of commercial banks. How is this done?

1. Increasing the reserve ratio will automatically strip commercial banks of excess reserves.

2. The Federal Reserve Banks should sell government bonds in the open market to tear down commercial bank reserves.

3. A boost in the discount rate will discourage commercial banks from building up their reserves by borrowing at the Federal Reserve Banks. These latter two policies constitute a reduction in Reserve Bank credit.

This group of directives is appropriately labeled a *tight money policy.* The objective is to tighten the supply of money in order to reduce spending and inflationary pressures.

MONETARY POLICY: QUALITATIVE CONTROLS

The major techniques of monetary control are (1) changing the reserve ratio, (2) changing the discount rate, and (3) open market operations. These devices are quantitative controls; they are designed to control the quantity of bank credit generally available. But these instruments of monetary management are supplemented periodically by certain other less important credit controls in the form of (1) qualitative, or selective, credit controls and (2) moral suasion.

Selective Credit Controls

On occasion the monetary authorities have restricted certain specific types of credit:

1. Stock market credit. In some instances the overall flow of money and credit in the economy has been fairly serene, and at the same time speculative stock market purchases threaten to precipitate economic difficulties. To thwart this possibility the Board of Governors has the authority to specify the *margin requirement,* or minimum percentage down payment which purchasers of stock must make. Thus a margin requirement of 70 per cent means that only 30 per cent of the purchase price of a security may be borrowed, the remaining 70 per cent being paid "cash on the barrel head." This rate will be raised when it is deemed desirable to restrict speculative stock purchases and lowered to revive a sluggish market.

2. Consumer credit. Congress occasionally has authorized the Board of Governors to invoke specific restraints on consumer credit. During World War II money incomes were increasing at a time when the output of civilian goods was declining because of the drastic rechanneling of resources to the production of war goods. The result was sharp inflationary pressure in certain consumer goods industries. To dampen this pressure Congress gave the Board of Governors temporary authority to specify down payments and maximum repayment periods on loans involving the purchase of real estate and a variety of consumer durables.

Moral Suasion

The monetary authorities sometimes use the less tangible technique of moral suasion to influence the lending policies of commercial banks. Moral suasion simply means the employment by the monetary authorities of "friendly persuasion"—policy statements, public pronouncements, or outright appeals —warning that excessive expansion or contraction of bank credit might involve serious consequences for the banking system and the economy as a whole. Such pronouncements are not limited to bank credit in general; they may call for the curtailment of specific types of bank credit. For example, in attempting to relieve inflationary pressures during the Korean conflict in 1951, the public statements and publicity releases of the monetary authorities pleaded for the curtailment of bank lending not essential to the war effort and the general exercise of voluntary restraint by commercial bankers in

creating money by lending. Private bankers' associations often aid the Federal monetary authorities in the application of moral suasion by echoing the pleas of the Board of Governors.

RELATIVE EFFECTIVENESS OF CONTROLS

It is generally agreed that the most important single credit control device is open-market operations—the reserve ratio, the discount rate, and selective controls being of less significance. The reasons for this are somewhat complex. As things now stand, actual reserve ratios are pushing the upper limits set by Congress (see Table 17–1). This means that the anti-inflationary influence of higher reserve ratios is definitely limited in terms of future effectiveness. The obvious suggestion is that Congress raise the upper limits on the reserve ratio to permit further boosts in the actual ratio when inflation threatens. But this is more easily said than done. Further boosts in the actual reserve ratio would mean that commercial banks must keep more of their assets in reserves and therefore less as earning assets (loans and securities). This might work rather severe hardships on those banks whose profits are not particularly large.

The importance of the discount rate has not been particularly great in recent years, simply because commercial banks have not needed to borrow very extensively from the Federal Reserve Banks.

But why the great importance of open-market operations as such? A glance at the consolidated balance sheet for the Federal Reserve Banks (Table 18–1) reveals very large holdings of government bonds ($37.4 billion) the sales of which could easily reduce commercial bank reserves from $17.4 billion to zero! In short, the ability of the Federal Reserve Banks to affect commercial bank reserves through bond sales and purchases is potentially very great.

Note finally that the manipulation of commercial bank reserves through open-market operations is accomplished at the initiative of the Federal Reserve System. By way of contrast the discount rate, to be influential as a technique of monetary policy, depends on commercial bank initiative in borrowing from the Federal Reserve Banks.

TREASURY GOLD TRANSACTIONS

In going off the gold standard in 1934, Congress passed legislation which retired all gold coins and gold certificates from circulation in the economy. This legislation also specified that newly mined gold or gold flowing into the United States in payment for exported goods and services must be sold to the Treasury at the legally established price of $35 per ounce. In turn the Treasury will sell gold to licensed buyers: dentists, jewelers, American firms desiring to use gold in paying for the purchases of imported goods, and foreign governments that need gold to pay for goods and services purchased in international markets.

Now we are about to discover that Treasury gold purchases and sales affect the supply of money and commercial bank reserves. Furthermore, these purchases and sales are made on the basis of long-standing legislation which is *not* subject to alteration or control by the Board of Governors. Hence, Treasury gold transactions may cause changes in the supply of money and in bank reserves which are quite undesirable in so far as the objectives of our monetary authorities are concerned.

Treasury Purchases of Gold

The question is this: How do the Treasury's purchases of gold affect the demand deposits and reserves of commercial banks? The answer is quite simple. Let us suppose American exporters are selling more goods and services to foreigners than American importers are buying from foreigners, and foreigners pay for the difference by sending

gold to the United States. As just noted, the law requires that recipients of this gold must sell it to the Treasury. The Treasury pays for the gold by checks which American exporters deposit in their commercial banks, thereby directly increasing the supply of money. The banks send these checks to the Federal Reserve Banks for collection (transaction 5 in Chapter 17) and in the process have their reserves increased. To the extent that these reserves are excess, they will support a multiple expansion of the money supply by the commercial banking system.

Treasury Sales of Gold

The effect of Treasury gold sales is to reduce directly the supply of money and, more significantly, to reduce commercial bank reserves. Suppose the United States imports more than it exports and American importers buy gold from the Treasury and ship it abroad to finance the difference. These buyers, paying the Treasury by check, give up demand deposits in return for gold bullion, thereby directly reducing the supply of money in the economy. The Treasury deposits these checks in the Federal Reserve Banks; this increases the Treasury's deposits in the Federal Reserve Banks at the expense of commercial bank reserves. This loss of reserves will restrain commercial banks in creating new money and might even give rise to a multiple contraction of the money supply.

The important point is that these gold transactions are not controlled by the Board of Governors and may therefore either facilitate or conflict with monetary policy. Purchases of gold by the Treasury obviously reinforce an easy money policy but conflict with tight money; gold sales facilitate a tight money policy but are at odds with easy money. The Board of Governors must use its control techniques to offset any potentially undesirable changes in the money supply caused by Treasury gold transactions.

MONEY, OUTPUT, AND PRICES: A SECOND APPROACH

The cause-and-effect chain outlined at the start of this chapter suggests how changes in the supply of money may affect the level of NNP and the price level through their effect upon aggregate demand or, alternatively stated, upon the saving-investment relationship. The possible impact of changes in the supply of money upon output, employment, and prices can be seen more directly through a second, complementary approach, which centers upon the equation of exchange.

Equation of Exchange

The equation of exchange is essentially a restatement of a truism which we encountered earlier in our analysis of national income accounting (Chapter 10). Specifically, the total amount spent by buyers is equal to the total amount that is received by sellers. Buying and selling are two sides of the same transaction and the equation of exchange is merely a useful way of presenting this identity. According to this second approach, total spending or aggregate demand is equal to the supply of money M multiplied by V, the income or circuit velocity of money, that is, the number of times per year the average dollar is spent on final goods. Because MV is aggregate demand or total spending on all final goods in one year, it is obviously equal to the NNP. On the other hand, the total dollar amount received from the sale of any year's output can be thought of as the physical volume of all goods produced Q multiplied by P, the price level or, more specifically, the average price at which each unit of final goods is sold. In short, we may state the identity between the value of what is bought and what is sold as:

$$MV = PQ$$

Consider an extremely simple illustration. If the supply of money is $150 and each of these dollars on the average is spent 4 times a year, total expenditures will be $600. If the economy produced 200 units of only one commodity, the price level or price per unit would be $3. That is,

$$M \cdot V = P \cdot Q$$
$$\$150 \cdot 4 = \$3 \cdot 200$$

What lessons can be learned from the equation of exchange? More particularly for our purposes, what does the equation tell us about changes in the money supply and the other terms in the equation, specifically output and the price level? It is quite obvious, for example, that if the supply of money M increases and the velocity of money V is constant, the price level P *or* the quantity of goods Q *or* both P and Q must increase. The effects on P and Q will depend upon whether the economy is experiencing recession or full employment at the time M is increased. Recalling Figure 11–2, an increase in M will raise Q proportionately with virtually no change in P if substantial unemployment exists initially. As full employment is approached, P and Q may both rise somewhat as M is increased. At full employment Q becomes constant because the economy is producing its capacity or maximum output; hence, increases in M will be purely inflationary and will cause P to increase proportionately.

Velocity of Money

Whereas the expenditures approach to output- and price-level determination of Chapters 12 and 13 emphasizes the importance of saving and investment decisions, the above illustrations make it abundantly clear that the equation of exchange or monetary approach puts the spotlight upon the supply of money as the immediate determinant of output and the price level.

And *M*, we know, is subject to manipulation by public policy decisions. If we have a recession, the monetary authorities should increase *M* by such an amount that *Q* will increase to the full-employment level. If the economy is faced with serious inflation, the monetary authorities should restrict *M* in order to stabilize *P* the price level. But, alas, all of our illustrations and policy prescriptions rely upon the assumption that *V* is constant. Actually, statistical evidence shows that *V* has varied substantially from year to year. For example, *V* was 4 in 1929, 2.5 in 1946 and 4 once again in 1964. Changes of this magnitude can clearly complicate and decidedly "loosen" any relationship between changes in *M*, on the one hand, and changes in *Q* and *P*, on the other, which the equation of exchange might otherwise suggest. We must therefore explore more fully the determinants of *V* and the reasons why it might vary.

Velocity and the Demand for Money

We know that the velocity of money is the number of times per year that the representative or average dollar flows around the circular flow—that is, the number of times it is spent on final goods and received as income—each year. Furthermore, the velocity of money is intimately linked to the fact that both households and businesses demand money; rather than immediately spend all the income they receive, these decision makers will choose to hold a certain amount of money—a cash balance—on hand. Thus we can think of dollars being detained temporarily in both the household and business sectors as they make their way around the circular flow. The amount of time they are delayed in each sector obviously determines the velocity of money. For example, suppose every household and every business on the average held each dollar received for two months. This would mean that the average dollar would make one complete trip around

the circular flow every four months or one-third of a year. *V* would therefore be 3. If the "resting time" of the average dollar in each sector is longer, it will complete the income-expenditure circuit fewer times each year. If households and businesses each held the average dollar three months, the typical dollar would be spent on final goods and received as income just twice each year, and *V* would be only 2. If the resting time of money in each sector were just one and a half months, *V* would obviously be 4. *It is quite clear that the greater the demand for money, that is, the longer the "resting time of money" in the household and business sectors, the lower will be the velocity of money, and vice versa.*

Why can't *V* be regarded as constant? Why might *V* increase or decrease? Or, differently stated, why might households and businesses want to hold money for shorter or longer periods? The answer depends largely upon expectations. For example, if households and businesses feel optimistic about the economic future and therefore more certain about the regularity of their incomes and receipts or if they feel that inflation is going to occur and thereby erode the value of the dollar, these decision makers will be inclined to hold smaller cash balances. Dollars will be detained for shorter periods in each sector, and *V* will obviously increase. The opposite circumstances—a poor economic outlook and the expectation of deflation—will cause households and businesses to hold larger cash balances, and *V* will decline as a result. Such changes in *V* are important because they may either reinforce or conflict with monetary policy. To illustrate: An easy money policy designed to increase *M* by some desired amount may result in too large an increase in aggregate demand if accompanied by an unanticipated increase in *V;* or the increase in *M* may result in too small an increase in aggregate demand—perhaps in no increase at all—if *V* should decline.

One other point of interest is suggested

by our discussion of V. The impact of the multiplier effect (Chapter 13) in any time period—say, a year—will depend upon V. For example, Table 13–2 demonstrates how a multiplier of 4 will cause a $5 billion increase in investment to boost the equilibrium NNP by $20 billion. But this increase will not occur instantaneously; it takes time for each of the "rounds" of spending and receiving income to occur. How much time? This obviously depends upon the velocity of money. Thus in Table 13–2 if we assume V is 3, the first three expenditure-income rounds will occur in a year, and the total increase in NNP realized in that year will be $11.56 (= $5.00 + $3.75 + $2.81) rather than $20 billion.

The Two Approaches

The saving-investment and equation-of-exchange approaches to analyzing the levels of output and prices are quite compatible with each other. Indeed, the saving-investment approach can be easily reinterpreted in terms of the equation of exchange. For example, assume businesses plan to invest more than households plan to save. Our expenditures model (Figure 13–3), based upon the imbalance of saving and investment, tells us this will mean an increase in the equilibrium NNP. But the equation of exchange suggests the same result. How can businesses invest more than households save? By borrowing from banks (which increases M) or by digging into their past accumulations or stocks of savings (which increases V). With M or V or both increasing, the level of aggregate demand $(= MV)$ is obviously rising. The result is the same as what the saving-investment approach would suggest—a rising NNP. If the economy has substantial unemployment, the rise in NNP will be real; that is, Q will increase, and P will be virtually unchanged. If full employment already exists, the rise in NNP will be purely monetary; the increase in MV will leave Q unchanged and serve only to increase P. Conversely, if households plan to save more than businesses intend to invest, our expenditures approach would predict a decline in NNP (Figure 13–3). So, too, would the equation of exchange. If households use their saving to retire existing bank debts, M will obviously fall. If the saving is held as idle cash balances, V will fall. In either case MV or aggregate demand will decline, and so will P or Q or both P and Q.

A concluding word of caution: The fact that all four components of the equation of exchange are variable suggests that we must avoid the pitfall of imputing a tight relationship between any two components. The classical economists, for example, took the position that Q was constant because the economy always operated at the full-employment level and that the money-holding decisions of households and businesses were so strongly circumscribed by habit that V could be regarded as constant. With both Q and V constant, an increase or decrease in the supply of money M would cause the price level P to increase or decrease *proportionately*. A doubling of the money supply would double the price level! But as explained above, the facts of economic life are far less simple than the classical economists presumed. Nevertheless, despite the variability of all four components, the equation of exchange is a useful way of organizing one's thinking about the forces which bear upon the levels of output and prices. In particular, by focusing attention upon the supply of money and the desires of households and businesses to hold money, the equation of exchange stresses considerations which are underemphasized or suggested only indirectly and obliquely by the saving-investment approach. In a sense each approach is incomplete without some understanding of the other. The saving-investment approach fails to stress the influence of a changing money supply upon the levels of output and prices. The monetary approach, on the other hand, does not bring to the fore the underlying changes in saving-investment decisions which cause variations in V.

EFFECTIVENESS OF MONETARY POLICY

How well does monetary policy work? Actually the effectiveness of monetary policy is subject to considerable debate.

The Case for Monetary Policy

There are those who argue that monetary policy is an effective stabilization device which has proved its worth in recent years, helping to offset, for example, the recessions of 1949 and 1954 and to restrain inflationary tendencies throughout a good portion of the 1950s. Furthermore, monetary policy enjoys a degree of flexibility which fiscal policy does not enjoy: The decisions of the Board of Governors are not subject to the time-consuming procedures which characterize congressional action or to the time lapse which may occur between the enacting and the applying of fiscal policy. In short, it is argued that monetary policy can be altered quickly and is of considerable effectiveness in promoting economic stability.

Shortcomings of Monetary Policy

It must be recognized, on the other hand, that monetary policy entails certain inherent limitations and encounters a number of real-world complications.

1. Cyclical asymmetry. If pursued vigorously enough, tight money can actually destroy commercial bank reserves to the point where banks are *forced* to contract the volume of loans. As tight money eliminates excess reserves, banks will be forced to allow outstanding loans to mature without making offsetting loans to other borrowers. This means a contraction in the money supply. But an easy money policy suffers from a "You can lead a horse to water, but you can't make him drink" kind of problem. An easy money policy can do no more than see to it that commercial banks have the ability—that is, the excess reserves needed—to make loans. It cannot guarantee, however, that loans will

actually be negotiated and the supply of money increased. If the public does not want to borrow, or commercial banks, seeking liquidity, are unwilling to lend, the easy money efforts of the Board of Governors will be to little avail. An easy money policy can do no more than create excess reserves upon which loans may or may not be made.[1] During the first few years of the Great Depression an easy money policy did little to expand the supply of money and stimulate investment. Commercial banks, fearful of becoming insolvent, built up substantial excess reserves in the late 1930s to ensure their liquidity rather than risk holding the less liquid assets of loans and securities.

2. Private offsets and financial intermediaries. Within limits monetary policy can be offset by the actions of banks, private businesses, or financial intermediaries. To illustrate: Both commercial banks and businesses hold large quantities of "near-monies" in the form of government bonds. Hence, commercial banks can sell off some of their securities and add the proceeds to their reserves, thereby offsetting the efforts of a tight money policy to reduce bank reserves. Similarly, corporations can sell their bond holdings or convert savings accounts into demand deposits and use the proceeds for investment purposes or to extend credit to customers. Both these actions were taken during the 1955–1957 upswing, complicating the Board of Governors' efforts to tighten up on credit and spending. Conversely, the tendency of banks and businesses to purchase government bonds during recession collides with an easy money policy. Banks and corporations bought a substantial volume of government securities during the 1958 recession, cancel-

---

[1] *Qualification:* Remember that Federal Reserve purchases of securities *from the public* directly increase the supply of money apart from any expansion of bank credit which commercial banks may make available on the basis of the reserves they acquire as the result of these bond purchases.

ing in part the easy money efforts of the monetary authorities.

It may also be noted that our economy is characterized by a myriad of nonbank lending institutions in the form of savings and loan associations, personal finance companies, mutual savings banks, credit unions, and so forth. These institutions are called *financial intermediaries* because, although they do not create money as do commercial banks, they do gather or mobilize savings and make them available by lending to spenders. During economic expansion these institutions, prompted by rising interest rates, pursue more aggressively and more effectively the task of getting funds from savers into the hands of spenders. To the extent they are successful, they offset the objectives of a tight money policy. Some economists feel that a more effective monetary policy depends upon making these financial intermediaries directly subject to control by the Board of Governors.

3. Changes in velocity. A related point is that a tight money policy might be partially frustrated by increases, and an easy money policy by decreases, in the velocity of money. This possibility, you will recall, is clearly suggested by the equation of exchange. Indeed, empirical evidence bears out the fear that changes in V have been at odds with policy-instigated changes in M. During inflation, when M is restrained by policy, V tends to increase. Conversely, when policy measures are taken to increase M during a recession, V may very well fall! This tendency of changes in V to frustrate changes in M becomes quite clear if one recalls the determinants of V. During a boom period, economic optimism and expectations of rising prices make businesses and households less anxious to hold money, so V rises. During recession, a pessimistic outlook and expected deflation increase the demand for money and cause V to fall.

4. Conflict with Treasury goals. The United States Treasury is the world's greatest, and most renowned, debtor. As such, it is naturally interested in low interest rates: An increase in interest rates of 1 per cent on government bonds can cost the Treasury approximately $3 billion in interest payments each year. But we know that during periods of inflation the Board of Governors is obligated to undertake a tight money policy for the purpose of raising interest rates. Hence, a conflict arises during inflation between the Treasury's desire for low interest rates and the monetary authority's obligation to boost interest rates. During such periods these two agencies attempt to work out an acceptable compromise or "accord" which, as the case might be, could weaken the effectiveness of a tight money policy.

5. Cost-push inflation. As is the case with fiscal policy, monetary policy is designed to control inflation by restraining excess total spending. That is, an anti-inflationary monetary policy is geared to alleviate or correct demand-pull inflation. It is not very relevant in getting at the causes of inflation which might lie on the cost or supply side of the market. As a matter of fact, given the downward inflexibility of resource and product prices, the vigorous use of a tight money policy in an inflationary situation where total demand is not excessive (and possibly is deficient) might increase unemployment and retard the growth rate (Chapter 21).

6. The investment impact. As noted earlier in this chapter, it is generally agreed that tight money has little direct effect upon consumer spending. Some economists also doubt its ability to curtail investment. And for several reasons: First, the interest rate is only one of some half-dozen determinants of the level of investment spending, and it is far from the most significant. It is very possible that changes in the noninterest determinants of investment, for example, technological advance or favorable business expectations, will cause the level of investment spending to increase *despite* increases in the interest rate. Of particular importance is the fact that the rising product and stock prices which are part of inflation give rise to business optimism and a strong incentive to invest at the very time this investment will be most inflationary. Second, large monopolistic firms—the very firms which do the bulk of the investing—are in a position to pass on any increase in interest costs to consumers in the form of higher product prices. Indeed, in many cases monopolistic firms are able to finance substantial portions of their investment programs internally and therefore will not be hindered by the unavailability of credit for investment purposes. However, tight money is likely to have a considerable impact upon smaller firms in competitive industries. This is another criticism of tight money: it discriminates against such firms.

A final word: It is *not* to be deduced from this discussion of its limitations that monetary policy is a hopelessly weak and ineffectual technique for economic stabilization. What our analysis does suggest is that monetary policy is subject to practical limitations in attacking both inflation and unemployment. And, although most economists would take the position that monetary policy is a less powerful stabilization

technique than is fiscal policy, there is no doubt that monetary control is a useful and important facet of our overall stabilization policy.

SUMMARY

1. The goal of monetary policy is full employment without inflation. The route, or cause-effect chain, through which monetary policy functions is complex: **a.** Policy decisions affect commercial bank reserves; **b.** changes in reserves affect the supply of money; **c.** changes in the supply of money influence the interest rate and the availability of bank credit; and **d.** changes in the interest rate and availability of credit affect investment, the equilibrium NNP, and the price level.

2. For a consideration of monetary policy the most important assets of the Federal Reserve Banks are cash, gold certificates, securities, and loans to commercial banks. The basic liabilities are the reserves of member banks, Treasury deposits, and Federal Reserve Notes.

3. Table 18–3 draws together all the

TABLE 18–3. A SUMMARY OF MONETARY POLICY

I. Problem: unemployment and deflation	I. Problem: inflation
II. Remedy: to induce an expansion in the supply of money, and therefore spending, by reducing the cost and increasing the availability of bank credit	II. Remedy: to induce a contraction in the supply of money, and therefore spending, by increasing the cost and reducing the availability of bank credit

III. Techniques:
  A. General, quantitative controls: easy money policy
    1. Lower reserve ratio.
    2. Buy bonds in the open market.
    3. Lower discount rate.
  B. Selective, qualitative controls
    1. Lower margin requirements.
    2. Ease credit regulations on consumer durables and real estate.
    3. Use moral suasion to induce banks to lend.
	III. Techniques:
	  A. General, quantitative controls: tight money policy
	    1. Raise reserve ratio.
	    2. Sell bonds in the open market.
	    3. Raise discount rate
	  B. Selective, qualitative controls
	    1. Raise margin requirements.
	    2. Tighten credit regulations on consumer durables and real estate.
	    3. Use moral suasion to encourage banks to be more selective in lending.

IV. Possible complication: Treasury sales of gold bullion	IV. Possible complication: Treasury purchases of gold bullion

basic notions relevant to the application of tight and easy money policies. It therefore merits careful study.

4. The equation of exchange, $MV = PQ$, provides a convenient way of viewing the possible effects of changes in the supply and circuit velocity of money upon the level of economic activity or, more specifically, upon the levels of output and prices.

5. Monetary policy is subject to a number of limitations. a. The excess reserves which an easy money policy provides may not be used by banks to expand the supply of money. b. The converting of near-monies into money or reserves and the functioning of financial intermediaries may partially offset monetary policy. c. Policy-instigated changes in the supply of money may be partially offset by changes in the velocity of money. d. The Treasury's desire for low interest rates conflicts with the higher rate of interest which tight money entails. e. A tight money policy is of questionable relevance in correcting cost-push inflation. f. The weight of the many noninterest determinants of investment, the ability of monopolistic firms to pass increases in interest costs on to consumers through price increases, and internal financing may all weaken the ability of tight money to curtail investment spending.

QUESTIONS AND STUDY SUGGESTIONS

1. Suppose you are a member of the Board of Governors of the Federal Reserve System. The economy is experiencing a sharp and prolonged inflationary trend. What changes in (*a*) the reserve ratio, (*b*) the discount rate, and (*c*) open-market operations would you recommend? Explain in each case how the change you advocate would affect commercial bank reserves and influence the money supply.

2. Specify the impact of each of the following transactions upon commercial bank reserves:

   a. The Federal Reserve Banks purchase securities from private businesses and consumers.

   b. Commercial banks borrow from the Federal Reserve Banks.

   c. The Board of Governors reduces the reserve ratio.

   d. The Treasury sells gold bullion.

3. Evaluate the overall effectiveness of monetary policy. Why are open-market operations regarded as a more effective credit control technique than changes in the rediscount rate and the reserve ratio? Discuss the specific limitations of monetary policy.

4. What is the basic objective of monetary policy? Describe the cause-effect chain through which monetary policy is made effective. Critics of monetary policy assert that this cause-effect chain contains too many "loose links." What do they mean?

5. The following are simplified consolidated balance sheets for the commercial banking system and the twelve Federal Reserve Banks. In columns 1 through 4 indicate how the balance sheets would read after each of the four ensuing transactions is completed. Do not cumulate your answers; that is, analyze each transaction separately, starting in each case from the given figures. All accounts are in billions of dollars.

CONSOLIDATED BALANCE SHEET: ALL COMMERCIAL BANKS

		(1)	(2)	(3)	(4)
Assets:					
Reserves	$ 33				
Securities	60				
Loans	60				
Liabilities and net worth:					
Demand deposits	$150				
Loans from the Federal Reserve Banks	3				

CONSOLIDATED BALANCE SHEET: TWELVE FEDERAL RESERVE BANKS

		(1)	(2)	(3)	(4)
Assets:					
Gold certificates	$20				
Securities	40				
Loans to commercial banks	3				
Liabilities and net worth:					
Reserves of commercial banks	$33				
Treasury deposits	3				
Federal Reserve Notes	27				

a. Assume foreigners ship $2 billion in gold to American exporters who have sold goods abroad. The gold, as required by law, is then sold to the United States Treasury. To replenish its deposits with the Federal Reserve Banks, the Treasury deposits $2 billion in gold certificates with the Federal Reserve Banks. Show the new balance sheet figures in column 1.

b. Suppose a decline in the discount rate prompts commercial banks to borrow an additional $1 billion from the Federal Reserve Banks. Show the new balance sheet figures in column 2.

c. The Federal Reserve Banks sell $3 billion in securities to private business firms and consumers, who pay for the bonds with checks. Show the new balance sheet figures in column 3.

d. The Federal Reserve Banks buy $2 billion of securities from commercial banks. Show the new balance sheet figures in column 4.

e. Now review each of the above four transactions, asking yourself these three questions: (1) What change, if any, took place in the money supply as a direct and immediate result of each transaction? (2) What increase or decrease in commercial banks' reserves took place in each transaction? (3) Assuming a reserve ratio of 20 per cent, what change in the money-creating potential of the commercial banking *system* occurred as a result of each transaction?

6. What is the significance of the equation of exchange? What conditions must prevail for an increase in the money supply to cause (*a*) a rise in output and employment and (*b*) an increase in the price level? What determines the velocity of money? Explain why a change in *M* might be accompanied by a change in *V* in the opposite direction.

SELECTED REFERENCES

Board of Governors of the Federal Reserve System: *The Federal Reserve System: Purposes and Functions,* 4th ed. (1961), particularly chaps. 1–3, 6, and 7.

Carson, Deane (ed.): *Banking and Monetary Studies* (Homewood, Ill.: Richard D. Irwin, Inc., 1963), particularly chaps. 4, 6, and 8.

Chandler, Lester V.: *The Economics of Money and Banking* (New York: Harper & Row, Publishers, Incorporated, 1964), chaps. 20–25.

Commission on Money and Credit: *Money and Credit: Their Influence on Jobs, Prices, and Growth* (Englewood Cliffs, N.J.: Prentice-Hall, Inc., 1961), particularly chap. 3.

Federal Reserve Bank of Chicago: *Workbook on Bank Deposits, Bank Reserves, and Currency* (Chicago).

Federal Reserve Bank of New York: *A Day's Work at the Federal Reserve Bank of New York,* 2d ed. (New York, 1953).

Hansen, Alvin H.: *The American Economy* (New York: McGraw-Hill Book Company, 1957), particularly chaps. 3 and 4.

Jacoby, Neil H. (ed.): *United States Monetary Policy,* rev. ed. (New York: Frederick A. Praeger, Inc., 1964).

Ritter, Lawrence S. (ed.): *Money and Economic Activity: Readings in Money and Banking,* 2d ed. (Boston: Houghton Mifflin Company, 1961), particularly chaps. 8–11.

CHAPTER 19

ECONOMIC STABILITY: THEORY AND POLICY

This very short chapter is a recapitulation and synthesis of the theory of employment and the public policies designed to achieve the full-employment noninflationary level of output. In the preceding nine chapters we have examined the components of macroeconomics and the policy aspects thereof in considerable detail; this chapter is to ensure that we understand how the components and policies fit together.

EMPLOYMENT THEORY

Figure 19–1 embodies the "big picture" we seek. The overriding virtue of this diagram is that it does remind us that the many concepts and relationships discussed in Parts Two and Three are something more than a series of unrelated principles and notions. On the contrary, these concepts are related to one another and constitute a coherent and meaningful theory of what determines the level of resource use in a market economy. The coherence and relevance of this theory are reflected in its acceptance as a framework for the formulation of national economic policy.

Now let us review the substance of Figure 19–1. Reading from left to right, the key point, of course, is that the levels of output, employment, income, and prices are all directly related to the level of total spending. The decisions of business firms to produce goods and therefore to employ resources depend upon the total amount of money spent on these goods. To discover what determines the level of aggregate spending, we must examine its three major components.[1]

Consumption

The absolute level of consumption spending depends upon the position of the consumption schedule and the level of net national product or disposable income. Although the determinants of the consumption schedule are quite numerous, economists are convinced that the schedule is quite stable. Therefore, the absolute level of consumption spending usually can be thought of as changing in response to changes in NNP brought about by fluctuations in other components of aggregate demand.

Furthermore, the seemingly innocent fact that households will consume part and save part of any change in their incomes is actually of great significance because the exact division of a change in income between consumption and saving determines the size of the multiplier. Specifically, the size of the multiplier effect and the marginal propensity to save are inversely related; the smaller the MPS, the greater will be the change in NNP due to a given change in aggregate demand.

Investment

Investment spending is the most volatile component of aggregate demand and there-

[1] We assume a closed economy, that is, net exports are zero.

343

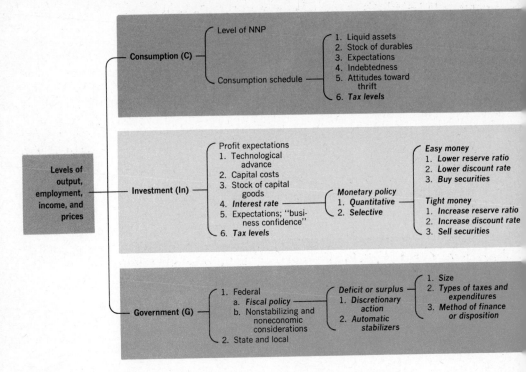

FIGURE 19–1. THE THEORY OF EMPLOYMENT AND STABILIZATION POLICIES.
This figure integrates the various components of employment theory and stabilization policy. Note that determinants which constitute, or are strongly influenced by, public policy are shown in bold italics.

fore the most likely cause of fluctuations in the levels of output, employment, and prices. The instability of investment lies in its determinants: Business confidence is subject to frequent and substantial revision; technological progress occurs at an uneven rate; and the durability of capital goods makes their purchase postponable. Furthermore, business profits—an increasingly important source of funds for investment—are highly variable. It is reasonably correct to think of changes in investment as the main source of output and price-level instability in our economy and to regard changes in consumption largely as the result of moving from one equilibrium NNP to another along a quite stable consumption schedule.

Government Spending

Government purchases of goods and services are the third major component of total spending. But this component differs from consumption and investment in that it is determined by public policy. Consumption and investment decisions are made in the self-interest of the household and business sectors, respectively. Government spending decisions, on the other hand, are made, at least in part, to fulfill society's interest in high levels of output and employment and a stable price level. With this motivational distinction in mind, let us examine the major components and characteristics of stabilization policy.

STABILIZATION POLICY

Government seeks to stabilize the economy primarily through (1) fiscal policy and (2) monetary policy.

Fiscal Policy

Fiscal policy refers, of course, to changes in government spending and tax revenues which are designed to eliminate either an inflationary or a deflationary gap. Figure 19–1 makes the potential stabilizing role of government quite evident; government spending, as one of the three major components of aggregate demand, directly affects output, employment, and the price level. Tax policy, on the other hand, works through the other two major components of total spending; taxation is a determinant of both consumption and investment. In particular, reductions in the personal income tax tend to shift the consumption schedule upward; tax increases tend to shift it downward. Corporation income tax cuts tend to improve profit expectations and stimulate investment; tax increases weaken profit expectations and reduce the willingness to invest.

Fiscal policy is both *discretionary* and *automatic*. The automatic or built-in stabilizers—the progressiveness of the Federal tax structure, unemployment compensation payments, subsidies to farmers—cause tax collections to vary directly, and government disbursements inversely, with the level of national income. Discretionary policy consists of the changing of spending levels and the manipulation of tax rates or the tax structure by Congress for the explicit purpose of achieving greater stability in the economy. The impact of discretionary fiscal policy depends upon (1) the size of the budgetary deficit or surplus, (2) the specific types of taxes and government expenditures invoked, and (3) the manner in which a deficit is financed and the method of disposing of a surplus (Figure 19–1).

Monetary Policy

Although monetary policy may have some impact upon consumption, the primary effect is undoubtedly upon investment spending, where the interest rate is a determinant of some importance. Other things being equal, the pursuit of an easy money policy by the Board of Governors will reduce the interest rate and make bank credit (money) more readily available, thereby stimulating investment and the levels of output and employment. A tight money policy will have the reverse effects and presumably will be invoked only when the level of aggregate demand is excessive and inflation is feared.

COMPLICATIONS AND PROBLEMS

As a summary view of employment theory and stabilization policy, Figure 19–1 is useful. But it does not reveal all. It does not make explicit the many problems of achieving the proper timing of fiscal policy or mention the fact that congressmen are often subject to economically irrational demands from pressure groups and individual voters (Chapter 14). Nor does it point out the cyclical asymmetry of monetary policy, or the complicating role of financial intermediaries and changes in the velocity of money (Chapter 18). But there are even further complications and problems associated with Figure 19–1 which we must consider.

Complexity of Interrelationships

Cause-effect relationships are much more complicated and intermixed than Figure 19–1 suggests. In the first place, some of the relationships suggested by this figure may actually be quite loose. Recall, for example, that the relationship between a change in total spending, on the one hand, and the resulting changes in the levels of output, employment, and prices, on the other, depends itself upon the level of employment that currently exists in the economy (Figure 11-2). Furthermore, we shall soon discover (Chapter 21) that structural unemployment and cost-push inflation complicate the relationship between aggregate demand and the levels of output, employment, and prices. Secondly, the various determinants of output and employment are actually interdependent. Examples: A reduction in personal income taxes may give rise to an increase in consumption and expand the levels of output and employment and, perhaps, the price level too. But in turn this expansion may well have a favorable effect upon "business confidence" and stimulate investment spending. Or an increase in the rate of technological progress might increase the demand for money capital on the part of investors and, unless offset by appropriate monetary policy, cause interest rates to rise. In brief, there are many behind-the-scenes interrelationships of an intricate and complicated character at work which Figure 19-1 fails to reveal. Stated differently, Figure 19-1 is a summary statement of a theory and cannot be expected to mirror the full bloom of reality.

Quantification and Policy

We must also recognize that there exist important problems in quantifying the interrelationships of Figure 19-1 and therefore in formulating quantitatively precise stabilization policies. To illustrate: Suppose a deflationary gap exists. Let us say that the level of NNP is $30 billion below the full-employment noninflationary level. We know the general character of the monetary and fiscal policies needed to close the gap. What we do *not* know—or at least do not know with great accuracy—is the size of the deficit needed or the extent to which bank credit should be eased. We are not certain of the size of the multiplier effect, that is, of the magnitude of the chain reaction which an increase in government spending or a decline in taxes would precipitate. Nor are we certain of the size of the impacts which changes in government spending and tax collections

might have upon the consumption or investment schedules. All of this is not to say that the policy implications of our theoretical framework cannot be made operational. It does suggest, however, that it is not realistic to expect stabilization policy to work perfectly so as to provide continuous full employment and absolute price stability.

Noneconomic Goals

There is another reason why we should not expect stabilization policy to function perfectly. Fiscal policy is governed by objectives other than stabilization (Chapter 1). For example, a stepping up of the cold war may necessitate increases in government military spending at a time when the economy is threatened with inflation. Or a political party's commitment to relieve certain social problems—to ameliorate the poverty problem or expand public school facilities—may call for changes in spending or the tax structure that destabilize the economy. Indeed, Figure 19-1 reminds us that the fiscal operations of state and local governments simply do not have an anticyclical orientation at all, but one concerned with the allocation of resources between private and public uses. In brief, budgetary policy is designed and altered not only with stability in mind, but also in response to international political-military factors, pressing domestic needs, and considerations of equity and social justice.

Appropriate Policy-mix

The great variety of fiscal devices available and the problem of coordinating monetary and fiscal policy are implicit in Figure 19-1. Should a deflationary gap, for example, be closed with a tax cut or an increase in government spending? Or with a combination of the two? What kind of tax cuts? Corporate income taxes? Personal income taxes? Federal excise taxes? And what kind of spending is best? Should the government spend on tangibles—slum clearance, highways, and hospitals—or on intangibles—education and welfare programs? And how can monetary and fiscal policy be best coordinated to achieve stability? A "strong" fiscal policy may make a "weak" monetary policy quite appropriate, and vice versa. On the other hand, strong fiscal and monetary policies combined could overcompensate or overcorrect for unemployment or inflation. Priorities must be applied not only to goals but also to policies designed to achieve those goals.

SUMMARY

1. The levels of output, income, employment, and prices are determined by the level of spending. Of the three major components of total spending, investment is relatively unstable as compared to consumption. Government spending is policy-determined.

2. Stabilization policy consists of fiscal policy, which may be either discretionary or automatic, and monetary policy.

3. Although the various components of employment theory fit together in a coherent framework which is useful for policy formulation, it must be recognized that **a.** the cause-effect interrelationships between the components are complex; **b.** the interrelationships are difficult to quantify precisely; **c.** noneconomic goals may interfere with the attainment of economic stability; and **d.** there are serious problems involved in determining the most appropriate policy-mix in correcting any specific inflationary or deflationary gap.

QUESTIONS AND STUDY SUGGESTIONS

1. Summarize the theory of employment graphically, using the aggregate demand—aggregate supply approach. Show in detail how monetary and fiscal policies might affect the various components of aggregate demand.

2. Why is it unrealistic to expect fiscal and monetary policies to result in complete economic stability? What might be done to improve monetary and fiscal policies?

SELECTED REFERENCES

Dillard, Dudley: *The Economics of John Maynard Keynes* (Englewood Cliffs, N.J.: Prentice-Hall, Inc., 1948), pp. 48–51.

Heilbroner, Robert L.: *Understanding Macroeconomics* (Englewood Cliffs, (N.J.: Prentice-Hall, Inc., 1965).

Schlesinger, James R.: "Emerging Attitudes toward Fiscal Policy," *Political Science Quarterly*, March, 1962, pp. 6–18.

PART FO

ACHIEV

In less than 200 years our economy has grown from an industrial infant to a vigorous productive giant. This long-run growth has not occurred at a steady pace. On the contrary, it has been punctuated by periods of instability—unemployment and inflation. Parts Two and Three of this book have dealt with the causes and cures of short-run economic instability. The business cycle, the theory of employment, and fiscal and monetary policy have been the focal points of our analysis. The task of this chapter is to take a very long-run look at the economic growth which our economy has experienced, largely ignoring the occasional cyclical deviations from that historical trend. Our basic objective is to explain the long-run economic growth which has driven American capitalism from the clutches of poverty toward the arms of opulence. Specific objectives are several. First, we want to define economic growth, assess its significance, and note those factors which underlie it. Next we shall examine the growth record of our economy. Then we turn to an analysis of those several factors which have caused economic growth to occur. Finally, the public policy implications of economic growth are briefly noted. We defer until Chapter 21 any direct discussion of the costs and problems which rapid economic growth might entail.

DEFINING ECONOMIC GROWTH

"Economic growth" is a much-used and much-abused term. Indeed, it is a slippery concept. What is economic growth? And why need we be concerned about it?

Two definitions of economic growth are commonly offered. First, economic growth may be defined in terms of the total physical output, or real income, of the economy. Or, to be more sophisticated about it, economic growth refers to increases in the economy's *real* gross national product, or *real* national income. An expanding real output means that the economy is growing. A stable or declining output means that the economy is static or declining. Note that this definition hinges upon *real* and not *money* output. The production of a larger amount of goods and services signifies growth; paying a larger number of dollars for a fixed or declining quantity does not.

A second and somewhat more refined definition links economic growth to real *per capita* output. This definition correctly recognizes that the standard of living of any economy is best measured in terms of real output per person. The actual standard of living could decline in an economy if the population increased at a faster rate than the volume of real output.

Which of these definitions is best? It depends upon the specific problem with which one is dealing. If one is concerned with the question of military potential, for example, total real output is the more appropriate measure of growth. On the other hand, per capita real income is superior for comparisons of living standards between regions or nations. Both definitions suffer from a major limitation: they are material measures and do not reflect important nonmaterial considerations. The good life involves political, spiritual, and cultural as well as material objectives. Nevertheless, our definitions of economic growth will be useful because (1) our immediate concern as students of economics is with material well-being and (2) as a matter of fact a free nation which is wealthy in material things is in a strategic position to realize, if it chooses, the non-material aspects of the good life.

Importance of Growth

Why be concerned with economic growth? The specific reasons are numerous, but four stand out:

1. Economic growth means a higher standard of living. It is obvious that an increase in per capita real output means a higher standard of living. The primary goal of the economic system is the provision of material abundance. In the long run it is an economy's growth which determines its degree of success in attaining that goal.

2. Economic growth is a solvent for domestic problems. The acuteness of domestic issues—economic, social, and political—is intimately related to economic growth. Increased production and improved standards of living diminish the social and political tensions surrounding such problems as poverty, income inequality, and economic insecurity. These and other domestic problems can be managed more effectively and even largely resolved in an environment of economic growth. Conversely, the lack of growth—economic stagnation—may well cause these same problems to assume explosive proportions.

3. Economic growth is a source of aid to underdeveloped countries. The specter of poverty and starvation haunts many nations of the world. The advanced nations—the United States in particular—have a tremendous moral obligation to relieve the abject poverty of less fortunate peoples. The numerous problems of the underdeveloped nations are of such vital significance that a detailed analysis is reserved for a later chapter.

4. Economic growth is essential in meeting the ideological challenge of Soviet Russia. The Soviet Union not only poses a military threat to American capitalism but also has issued an explicit ideological challenge. Soviet leaders have made clear their opinion that the superiority of the communist ideology over capitalism will be proved "in the field of peaceful production." The ideological paths of many nations, particularly the underdeveloped nations, will be influenced by the course and eventual outcome of this challenge. A later chapter is devoted to a discussion of economic growth in the Soviet Union.

Ingredients of Growth

What are the cornerstones of economic growth? Basically, there are six strategic ingredients in the growth of any economy. Four of these factors relate to the physical ability of an economy to grow. They are (1) the quantity and quality of its natural resources, (2) the quantity and quality of its human resources, (3) the supply or stock of capital goods, and (4) technology. These four items may be termed the *permissive factors* in economic growth. These are the physical agents of greater production. It is the availability of more and better resources, including the stock of technological knowledge, which permits an economy to produce a greater real output.

But the ability to grow and the actual realization of economic growth are two different things. The permissive factors in growth must be accompanied by two basic *implemental factors*. They are (1) the full-employment level of aggregate demand and (2) continuing efficiency in the allocation of resources. To realize its productive potential, a nation must provide for the full employment and full production of its avail-

able resources. The ability to expand
production is not a sufficient condition for
the expansion of total output; the actual
utilization of available resources and the
allocation of those resources in such a way
as to get the maximum amount of useful
goods produced are also required.

These factors can be placed in proper
perspective by recalling the production
possibilities curve, reproduced in Figure
20–1. This is a best-performance curve in
that it indicates the various *maximum* combinations of products the economy can
produce, given the quantity and quality of
its natural, human, and capital resources,
and its stock of technological know-how.
Obviously an improvement in any of the
permissive factors will push the production
possibilities curve to the right, as indicated
by the shift from *AB* to *CD* in Figure 20–1.
Increases in the quantity or quality of
resources and technological advances push
the curve to the right. But the implemental
factors remind us that the economy need not
realize its maximum productive potential;
the curve may shift to the right and leave the
economy behind at some level of operation
inside the curve. In particular, an increase
in the productive *potential* of the economy
will not be realized if the economy fails to
generate a level of aggregate demand sufficient to provide full employment and the
flexibility to adjust to those changes in the
allocation of resources demanded by changes
in the relative supplies of resources or technological information. That is, to stay on the
rightward-shifting production possibilities
curve, the economy must avoid *un*employment (apparent unemployment) and *under*-
employment (disguised unemployment).

Example: The net increase in the labor
force of the United States is over 1 million
workers per year. As such this increases the
productive capacity, or potential, of the
economy. But the realization of the extra
output these additional workers are capable
of producing presumes an appropriate increase in aggregate money demand. Further-

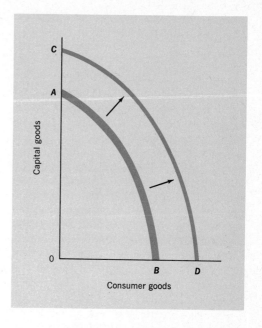

**FIGURE 20–1. ECONOMIC GROWTH AND
THE PRODUCTION POSSIBILITIES CURVE.**
Economic growth is indicated by an outward
shift of the production possibilities curve, as
from *AB* to *CD*. Increases in the quantity and
quality of resources and technological advance
permit this shift; full employment and allocative
efficiency are essential to its realization.

more, achieving the maximum additional
output from this increase in the labor force
presumes that these new workers will be
efficiently allocated within the economy; that
is, additions to the labor force should be
apportioned to those industries and firms
wherein the value of their contribution to
total output will be greatest.

It is notable that the permissive and implemental factors in growth are *not* unrelated.
For example, unemployment tends to retard
the rate of capital accumulation and may
slow expenditures for research. And, conversely, a low rate of innovation and
investment can be a basic cause of unemployment.

GROWTH RECORD OF AMERICAN CAPITALISM

Now let us orient our discussion of economic growth to the American economy. What level of economic growth has been achieved in American capitalism? How can this growth be explained in terms of the six ingredients or causes of growth?

Table 20–1 gives us a rough idea of economic growth in the United States over the last century as viewed through our two proposed definitions of growth. Column 2 gives us a decade-by-decade account of the economy's growth as measured by national income. Note that these figures are adjusted for price differences, and, hence, reflect *real* national income. Though not steady, the upsurges of national income are rather remarkable. Except for the 1910–1930 period, *real national income has tended to*

double every two decades. When the population figures of column 3 are divided into the real national income data, the result is a per capita picture of real national income. We find that, even after suitable allowance has been made for an expanding population, economic growth is impressive. *Over the last century per capita real income has almost quadrupled.*

A number of recent statistical studies estimate that the growth rate of real GNP has been about 3 to 4 per cent per year, while the annual increase in real GNP per person has been about 1½ to 2 per cent.

For at least two reasons these quantitative conclusions understate the economic growth which American capitalism has actually experienced. First, these figures do not take into account improvements in product quality. Purely quantitative data do not provide an accurate comparison between an era of

TABLE 20–1. REAL NATIONAL INCOME AND PER CAPITA NATIONAL INCOME, 1850–1964

(1) Year	(2) National income, billions of 1950 dollars	(3) Population, millions	(4) Per capita national income, 1950 dollars, or (2) ÷ (3)
1850	$ 9.4	23.2	$ 405
1860	14.4	31.4	459
1870	18.6	39.8	467
1880	25.6	50.2	510
1890	44.3	62.9	704
1900	63.3	76.0	833
1910	86.4	92.0	939
1920	94.7	105.7	896
1930	118.5	122.8	965
1940	147.0	131.7	1,116
1950	240.6	150.7	1,597
1956	296.2	168.1	1,761
1958	296.0	174.1	1,700
1961	330.9	182.7	1,811
1964	378.1	192.1	1,968

Source: Data from J. Frederic Dewhurst and Associates, *America's Needs and Resources: A New Survey* (New York: The Twentieth Century Fund, Inc., 1955), pp. 40–41, 51. Data for 1958, 1961, and 1964 calculated by the author from U.S. Department of Commerce and U.S. Census Bureau figures.

crystal sets and one of stereophonic phonographs. Second, the increases in real national income and per capita national income shown in Table 20–1 were accomplished despite very sizable increases in leisure. The seventy-hour work week is a thing of the distant past. The standard work week is now less than forty hours, with the more aggressive unions, much to the dismay of American housewives, whetting their appetites for a thirty-five- or thirty-hour week.

On the other hand, there are a couple of considerations which take a bit of the luster off our growth statistics. First, the United States' growth rate has been substantially less than that of a number of other industrially advanced nations. Soviet Russia, Japan, and many of the nations of Western Europe are experiencing larger annual increases in their real GNPs than we are (see Table 21–2). Second, as column 4 of Table 20–1 suggests, the growth of per capita real output has been modest in the post–World War II period. We shall discover in Chapter 21 that considerations such as these have stimulated considerable debate concerning the adequacy of our growth rate and public policies designed to accelerate our growth.

PERMISSIVE FACTORS

Now let us explain the impressive record of American capitalism in terms of the six basic ingredients of economic growth. We look first to the permissive factors, that is, to the supply side of economic growth.

Natural Resources

Climate, soil, rainfall, mineral deposits, and sources of power are all important facets of any nation's natural resource base. These natural resource endowments constitute an obvious but fundamental factor in its capacity to expand, because, in contrast to the quantity and quality of labor and capital resources, the quantity and quality of a nation's natural resources are relatively fixed in supply. Note that we say "relatively"

fixed: within limits *available* natural resources can be increased in supply. True, given a nation's territorial limits, its mineral deposits of, for example, lead, copper, and zinc are present only in fixed amounts. The same holds true for petroleum and natural-gas deposits. Yet the discovery and appropriation of existing deposits can add significantly to available, or usable, supplies of these resources. Similarly, arable land, pasture land, and timberland which have been exploited can frequently be renewed by modern conservation practices. Irrigation and drainage can and have added significantly to the supply of arable land. And, as we shall soon discover, technological advancement has added significantly to available resource supplies.

For present purposes, the major question is this: Are the supplies of natural resources with which the United States is endowed sufficient to permit continued economic growth? There is no simple, unqualified answer to this question. But in so far as the majority of natural resources are concerned, the United States has been most generously endowed in terms of both quantity and quality. It is generally agreed that, with the possible exception of Soviet Russia, the United States has a larger variety and greater quantities of resources than any other nation. Actually, we are not sure of the exact quantities available—as noted, exploration and discovery continue. We are aware that known reserves of most resources insure us against scarcities in the foreseeable future.

But there is a gloomy side to the picture: The possibility of shortages and bottlenecks is also evident in so far as certain specific resources are concerned. In recent years the production and consumption of certain strategic metals—for example, lead, zinc, copper, and bauxite—indicate the need for conservation in the use of these resources. In other words, the natural resource picture is a varied and changing one. General abundance and evidence of approaching exhaustion of specific resources exist side by side. It seems fairly safe to say that the overall resource picture at the present time is favorable to future economic growth. Bottlenecks, however, may occur in specific industries.[1]

Alleviating scarcities. It is noteworthy that two alleviating factors have almost invariably come to the rescue when the United States has encountered serious shortages of specific raw materials.

1. Technological advance, in addition to being a basic determinant of economic growth in and of itself, has bailed American capitalism out of resource difficulties on many occasions. On the one hand, technological advance has led to greater economy in the *use* of scarce materials. For example, the development of electroplating as a substitute for the hot-dip method of manufacturing tin plate saves 60 per cent of this scarce metal. Furthermore, technology has permitted greater efficiency in the *acquisition* of natural resources. Evidence?[2]

Sixty years ago copper deposits of less than 3 per cent metal content would have been considered poor; now the average grade is less than one per cent. A few decades ago aluminum was so difficult to extract and so costly that it was scarcely used at all; now it ranks second only to steel in terms of metal volume. . . . The deepest oil well drilled in 1900 was about 3,000 feet; by 1950 the world's deepest well went down more than 20,000 feet—about four miles.

The development of new instruments in the fields of geology, geophysics, and geochemistry—for example, magnetometers, scintillometers, and electromagnetic surveyors—are undoubtedly of great long-run significance in the discovery of new sources of raw

materials. Lastly, technological advances have developed *new materials* to replace resources in particularly scarce supply. The development of plastics and synthetic rubber to supplement strategic materials during the war years provides standard and outstanding examples.

In brief, technological advance has played a key role (*a*) in achieving greater economy in the use of available supplies of resources, (*b*) in developing means for the economical recovery of known sources of raw materials, and (*c*) in the discovery of new, substitute materials.

2. Foreign supplies of resources can be used to supplement domestic supplies. As a matter of fact, the United States has historically changed from a world supplier to an importer of raw materials. Despite dramatic increases in the domestic *production* of most basic raw materials, simultaneous and more than proportionate increases in the domestic *consumption* of these materials have caused our economy to become a net importer of raw materials. The important point is this: Foreign resources acquired through international trade can and have effectively combated specific raw-material shortages.

Conservation and the price system. A final but highly important point: The price system plays a very vital role in prompting the conservation and prudent use of our scarcest resources. For example, should a mineral resource, say, copper, come to be in particularly scarce supply in relation to the demand for it, its price will rise. This higher price has two related effects.

First, it signals manufacturers to "go easy" in the use of copper and to employ substitute materials in production where this is feasible. Stated differently, a high price for copper will tend to ration the available supply to those uses deemed most vital by society; only the manufacturers of products wanted most intensely by consumers will be able to pay the high price for copper and achieve a profit in the sale of their finished products. In addition, manufacturers who are depend-

[1] See Hans H. Landsberg, *Natural Resources for U.S. Growth* (Baltimore: The Johns Hopkins Press, 1964).

[2] J. Frederic Dewhurst and Associates, *America's Needs and Resources: A New Survey* (New York: The Twentieth Century Fund, Inc., 1955), p. 757.

ent upon copper may be prompted by its high price to direct research activities toward the more efficient use of copper or the seeking of suitable substitute materials. If successful, this will tend to take pressure off the price of copper from the demand side of the market.

Second, the high price of copper induces suppliers of copper to step up production to overcome the shortage. The high price may now make possible the mining of lower-grade ores, not economically feasible at a lower price. Similarly, the high price for copper may well induce technological advances in the mining and smelting of copper. Success in such ventures will tend to reduce the price of copper from the supply side of the market. The basic point is that the price mechanism simultaneously promotes conservation in the use of particularly scarce resources and may induce means for alleviating such severe shortages.[3]

Human Resources

The productive capacity of a nation depends not only upon the size of its labor force but also upon its quality. The size of any nation's labor force is determined primarily by the overall size of its population. The quality of the labor force depends upon its education and training, its personal health and vigor, its morale, and its attitude toward work.

Population and the labor force. Let us first explore the *quantitative* aspect of human resources. An increase in the quantity of human resources will obviously enhance the economy's productive potential, permitting an outward shift of the production possibilities curve. Because the size of the economy's labor force[4] is obviously related

[3] See the President's Materials Policy Commission, *Resources for Freedom* (Washington: Government Printing Office, 1952), pp. 17–18.
[4] The term "labor force" is used in this instance in its broadest sense, so as to include entrepreneurs.

directly to the size of its total population, the first question to ask is this: What long-run changes, if any, have occurred in the size of the population of the United States? Column 3 of Table 20–1 gives us the answer. A high birth rate, a declining death rate, and heavy immigration have teamed to provide the United States with a rapidly expanding population through most of its history. The population quadrupled during the first half of the nineteenth century. It more than trebled during the last half and has increased 2½ fold since 1900. There are over eight times as many Americans today as there were in 1850.

But the population has grown at varying rates. The high rates of increase of the decades prior to the 1920s began to fade in the roaring twenties and depressed thirties. The sharp population increases prior to the 1920s were accounted for in part by high immigration rates. But the 1920s saw the enactment of government policies which severely restricted this facet of population growth; in the 1930s government clamped a virtually airtight lid on the great American melting pot. Furthermore, the Great Depression of the 1930s forced many people to postpone marriage, and those who married tended to defer having children. As a result, the rate of population increase hit a new low in the 1930–1940 decade. Experts predicted a leveling off of population growth to be climaxed by a plateau or even a decline.

But much to the surprise of demographers, a combination of factors reversed this trend in the 1940s. The war and postwar years have featured a rather startling upsurge in population growth. Prosperity is undoubtedly a partial explanation. And Uncle Sam's need for able-bodied and preferably unmarried fighting men clearly played a role. The outbreak of World War II and the creation of Selective Service caused a stream of confirmed bachelors to embrace the holy bonds of matrimony. And, of course, in recent years significant medical advances have continued to reduce infant mortality and increase the average life span. Finally, it simply seems to have become fashionable once again to have larger families. These and a variety of other factors have all contributed to the "population explosion" of the last two decades which has brought our population to the 192 million level currently. Where will it all end? Demographers differ on this point. "Low" estimates envision a population of 248 million by 1985; "high" estimates call for 276 million. There is little prospect that future American economic growth will be retarded by an inadequate labor supply.

Optimum population. It must be emphasized that an expanding population is not always a boon to economic growth as defined in terms of real per capita output. To explain why this is so, let us assume for the moment that a nation's stock of natural resources, capital equipment, and technological information is fixed. Now suppose that the population, which is initially very small relative to these other resources, begins to expand. As more and more labor is combined with the fixed quantities of the other resources, we can expect that for a time output and therefore real income per person will rise. Why? The answer lies in increased specialization and the more efficient utilization of the nonlabor resources.

With a very small labor force there will be little opportunity for specialization; each worker will be required to divide his time among a number of tasks. But as population expands, each man can concentrate on that job for which he is best suited. As a matter of fact, by concentrating on one job, workers will tend to become more proficient than when performing a variety of jobs. Furthermore, an expanding population will permit a fuller utilization of the economy's other resources—in particular its capital facilities. Modern or even somewhat archaic technology requires that capital facilities be of certain minimum size, whether output is relatively small or large. If a small quantity of labor is combined with this capital equipment, production will be relatively ineffi-

cient. Even the most modern automobile assembly line will be inefficient if it is grossly undermanned. For both these reasons output per head will rise for a time as population expands.

However, in time an opposing tendency will arise to diminish per capita output. As population continues to expand, a point will finally be reached where capital and natural resources are overutilized. That is, each worker will be equipped with smaller and smaller amounts of materials and capital goods. This will cause output per capita, and therefore real income per capita, to decline. In a later chapter we shall find that excessively large and still expanding populations which continuously press upon the available capital and natural resources keep living standards close to the subsistence level in many of the so-called underdeveloped countries.

As Figure 20–2 suggests, if an expanding population entails an expanding real output per head up to a point and then a decline in output per person, there must be some point of maximum output and therefore real income per person. In purely economic terms the corresponding population can be regarded as of optimum size. But two points must be noted. First, our figure is hypothetical; practical problems of measurement make it virtually impossible to determine the optimum population size with any degree of accuracy. Second, increases in the nation's stocks of natural or capital resources and in its technological know-how which may accompany population growth will tend to extend the range of increasing output per capita and forestall the range of declining output per capita. That is, an expansion of nonlabor resources will shift the point of optimum population to the right, as from L_1 to L_2 in Figure 20–2.

Quality of the labor force. Man for man the American labor force is qualitatively superior to that of any other nation in the world. The physical strength, health, education and

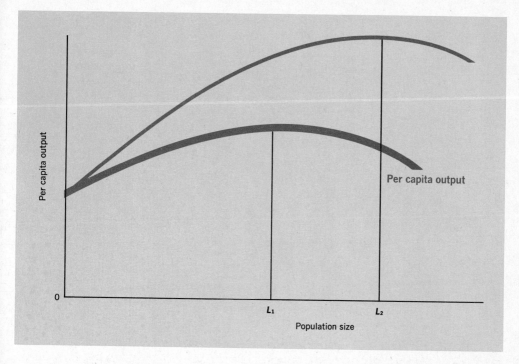

FIGURE 20–2. THE OPTIMUM POPULATION SIZE.
Given the quantity and quality of the nation's nonhuman resources, there is some optimum population size such as L_1 at which real per capita output is at a maximum. Increases in the quantity and quality of property resources will shift the point of optimum population size to the right, for example, from L_1 to L_2.

training, and versatility of our labor force all contribute to this superiority. One eminent scholar has concluded that if the age composition and state of health of the population of underdeveloped countries could be "Westernized," per capita incomes in these countries might rise by 20 to 30 per cent or more above existing levels.[5]

A rough indication of the improvement in the quality of the labor force is reflected in educational statistics. In 1870 only 57 per cent of the school age (five to seventeen years, inclusive) population was enrolled in elementary and secondary schools. By 1900 this figure had climbed to over 72 per cent, and by 1960 it was approximately 94 per cent. Furthermore, the number of persons receiving college degrees currently is almost twenty times greater than it was in 1900. The current illiteracy rate in the United States is about 2 per cent. And, of course, these statistics conceal improvements in the quality of education. Figure 20–3 indicates the occupational shifts which have occurred since 1870 and generally reflects an upgrading of the labor force. Note the relative decline in agriculture and the corresponding gains in professional and public services and the transportation, trade, and finance occupations.

[5] J. J. Spengler, "The Population Obstacle to Economic Betterment," *American Economic Review, Proceedings*, May, 1951, p. 344.

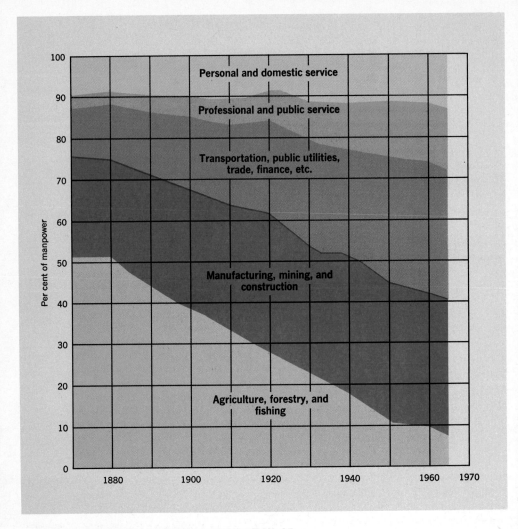

FIGURE 20–3. CHANGING INDUSTRIAL COMPOSITION OF
AMERICAN MANPOWER, 1870–1964.
Long-term occupational shifts generally reflect an upgrading of the labor force.
[J. Frederic Dewhurst and Associates, *America's Needs and Resources: A
New Survey* (New York: The Twentieth Century Fund, Inc., 1955), p. 733.
Estimates for 1964 by this author.]

But here are some less encouraging considerations which tend to tarnish this glowing
picture.

1. Despite substantial evidence of teacher
and classroom shortages, total annual expenditures on public education are only
about 3 per cent of the GNP.

2. We apparently do a rather poor job of
recruiting our best brains for higher education; only about half of our ablest youth go
on to college.

3. Serious problems seem to be arising
with respect to the composition of our labor
force; workers who lose their jobs in declin-

ing industries generally do not have the brainpower or skills needed for reemployment in expanding industries.

Although we defer any detailed discussion of these problems until Chapter 21 it should be emphasized that most authorities on economic growth feel that brainpower and the technological advances to which it gives rise are the most valuable resources of all. If this is accurate, our economy may be failing to invest sufficient amounts in the development of its human resources.

Technological Advance

Technological advance and capital formation are closely related processes. Technological advance, the development and application of new products or new productive techniques, typically entails investment in new machinery and equipment. The idea that there is a more efficient way to catch a rabbit than running it down led to investment in the bow and arrow. Yet in a few instances technological advance and capital accumulation are distinct. Example: Modern crop rotation practices and contour plowing are ideas which contribute greatly to output, although they do not necessarily entail the use of more capital equipment. In any event we shall find it rewarding to discuss technological advance and capital formation separately, recognizing that the two are usually birds of a feather.

What has been the rate of technological advance in the United States? It is very difficult to say with any real degree of precision. Simple observation recalls gas and diesel engines, conveyor belts, and assembly lines as some of the more profound historical technological advances. More recently, the lamp of technology has freed the automation jinni and with it the wonders of the electronic brains and the push-button factory. Indeed, the far-flung frontiers of technological advance are almost beyond the comprehension of the average man. Yet an examination of historical facts makes it clear that technological advance has not

occurred at a balanced rate among various industries: the electronics, chemical, and metal fabrication industries, for example, have outdistanced service industries and land transportation.

Recent empirical studies[6] suggest that technological advance is now the major factor underlying the growth record of American capitalism and that its importance is on the increase. Of the 3.5 per cent per annum increase in output which American capitalism has averaged since the early 1870s, approximately half is the result of increases in the stock of capital and in the supply of labor. Technological advance, abetted by concomitant increases in the quality of labor, accounts for the remaining half.

Research and invention. Technological advance involves both *invention*—the discovery and development of a new product or technique of production—and *innovation*—the practical application of the method, or commercial production of the product, which invention has provided.

Generally speaking, invention depends upon the quality and availability of scientific education and the provision of monetary and physical resources for basic research. We do have a rough indicator of the discovery aspect of technological advance—total research and development expenditures for the economy as a whole. Table 20–2 summarizes this data for the postwar era and provides an estimate for 1969. In absolute terms the picture to date looks very impressive, but much less so in relative terms. It is more than a bit disconcerting to find that American capitalism—the acclaimed fountainhead of technological progress—currently devotes a mere 3 per cent of its total output to research! It is noteworthy, too, that a very substantial portion of our research expendi-

---

[6] See, in particular, Moses Abramovitz, *Resources and Output Trends in the United States Since 1870* (New York: National Bureau of Economic Research, 1956).

TABLE 20–2. SOURCES OF FUNDS FOR RESEARCH AND DEVELOPMENT IN THE UNITED STATES, 1945–1963 (in millions)

Year	(1) Total expenditures, or (2) + (3) + (4)	(2) Govern- ment	(3) Industry	(4) Universities and nonprofit institutions	(5) Total research expenditures as a per cent of GNP
1945	$ 1,520	$ 1,070	$ 430	$ 20	0.7
1950	2,870	1,610	1,180	80	1.0
1954	5,660	3,120	2,365	175	1.6
1957	9,810	6,150	3,455	250	2.2
1959	12,430	8,070	4,070	290	2.6
1963	17,350	11,340	5,565	445	3.0
1969*	22,200	12,000	9,000	2,500	—

* Estimated figures for 1969 from Dexter Keezer, *American Economic Review*, May, 1960, pp. 363–365.
Source: U.S. Department of Defense and National Science Foundation.

tures originate in the public sector of the economy; private research expenditures as a per cent of GNP provide an even less impressive figure. Worst of all, a significant portion of research expenditure is not for basic research but rather for applied research of an ofttimes trivial nature. It is debatable whether highly competent technicians should devote their waking hours to making Rusty Dusties the noisiest breakfast food on the market rather than to basic chemical, electronics, or space research. Brainpower is too precious a resource to squander on research of trivial importance. When political and military considerations are considered the situation becomes more acute. As early as 1947 Soviet Russia spent as much as the United States did on research. But, because the Soviet national income was only about one-fourth that of the United States, Russia clearly devoted a relatively larger portion of her resources to the development and application of new technology.[7]

The point is this: By any reasonable

[7] Report by the President's Scientific Research Board, *Science and Public Policy*, vol. I, August, 1947, pp. 5–6.

absolute standard, American capitalism has done a most creditable job in achieving technological progress. Relative comparisons, however, are a bit less encouraging. For a wealthy nation the United States may be considerably myopic in devoting resources to technological research and development.

Innovation. But the discovery of new technological knowledge is only half the battle. The commercial application of such discoveries in the production of goods is equally essential in achieving economic growth through technological advance. It is here that the size, vigor, and ability of the entrepreneurial class become all-important. Certainly other factors are vital. The costliness of financing the application of a technological improvement and its anticipated profitability undoubtedly play major roles in determining whether or not a new bit of technological know-how gets off the drawing board and is commercially applied. Yet in the long pull the most fundamental determinant of the commercial application of new technological knowledge is the character of the entrepreneur. Insight, foresight, vision, courage, adventuresomeness, the desire to make good—call it what you may, the leadership and vigor of the entrepreneurial class play the key role in determining how much new technological know-how gets out of the research department and into the assembly line. In a later section on allocative efficiency we shall note that the overall social-cultural-political environment of our economy generally has been highly receptive to the introduction of new products and new methods of production.

The future significance of technological advance—both invention and innovation—as an instrument of economic growth is visualized by a 1947 report of the President's Scientific Research Board: [8]

Throughout most of our history, the living standards of our people were raised by expanding our land areas and by bringing more and more acres under cultivation. That route has now been substantially closed for more than a generation, and we have increased our productivity through an advancing technology. The processes and machines we use in factories, the ways in which we raise and preserve food, all derive from theoretical discoveries in the basic sciences. The technology in which we excel and which has transformed us in some 80 years from a backward agricultural nation to a world power rests upon progress in the basic sciences. Only through research and more research can we provide the basis for an expanding economy and continued high levels of employment.

Capital Formation

To a very considerable degree workers, regardless of their skills and training, are no better than the capital goods with which they are equipped. The indirect or roundabout production which capital goods affords is a basic means of enhancing productive efficiency. A nation's stock of capital goods is clearly a crucial factor in its growth

potential.[9] Our American capitalism has managed to accumulate a larger stock of real capital than has any other nation of the world. Surprisingly, we are not exactly sure how much capital our economy has managed to accumulate in its lifetime. The difficulties of taking such an inventory are great; in particular, the problem of defining what is meant by "capital goods" is a difficult one.

We do know that on the average the American worker is better equipped with capital goods in his productive efforts than is the worker of any other nation. The average American worker in manufacturing is equipped with approximately $24,000 worth of capital equipment. We also know that the growth in capital facilities has been very rapid in recent years. During the war-postwar decade of the 1940s American capitalism ". . . doubled the aggregate manufacturing capacity of 1939–40 which had taken nearly three centuries to develop and build."[10] A recent and conservative estimate for 1961 sets the value of America's stock of fixed business capital at $532 billion, measured in 1954 prices.[11]

In 1964 private businesses in the economy spent over $58 billion on capital facilities—machinery, equipment, and nonresidential construction. This means that about 9 per cent of the economy's GNP is currently devoted to maintaining and expanding the productive facilities of private industry. Were we to add the basic "social capital" constructed by government—highways, hydroelectric dams, harbor and waterway improvements, and so forth—another $20 billion would be added to this $58 billion

[8] *Science and Public Policy,* vol. I, p. 4.

[9] It has recently been argued, however, that the role of capital, as opposed to human and institutional factors, in growth has been exaggerated. See Colin Clark, *Growthmanship* (London: Institute of Economic Affairs, 1961).
[10] Dewhurst, *op. cit.,* p. 813.
[11] George Jaszi, Robert C. Wasson, and Lawrence Grose, "Expansion of Fixed Business Capital in the United States," *Survey of Current Business,* November, 1962, p. 11.

figure. Residential construction would involve another $26 billion.

IMPLEMENTAL FACTORS

So much for the permissive factors which expand the productive potential of the economy. Will the economy's actual performance keep pace with its expanding ability to produce? Is the economy sufficiently flexible to negotiate the continuous resource reallocations which economic growth demands?

Aggregate Demand

The permissive factors constitute the "supply side" of economic growth; they establish the productive capacity of the economy. We now want to examine the demand side of growth.

The essence of the problem is that in an economy whose productive capacity is expanding, the full-employment noninflationary NNP will obviously be increasing over time. Therefore, the realization or achievement of that desired output is clearly dependent upon an expanding level of aggregate demand. We discovered in Chapter 13 that whether or not an economy achieves full employment depends upon the interaction of its saving and investment plans. Businesses must be willing to invest an amount equal to the full-employment volume of saving if full employment is to be attained. In a static or stationary economy, that is, an economy whose permissive factors are such that its productive potential is fixed and unchanging, this is largely a matter of sustaining a constant level of investment year after year. But in a growing economy—one whose real national income is expanding—the problem is decidedly more complex. Why? Because in an expanding economy saving increases. Remember: Households save a larger proportion of a large income than they do of a small income. This obviously means that if the expanding productive capacity of a growing economy is to be realized, investment spending must increase by the same amount as the full-employment level of saving increases. Let is now consider the specifics of the demand side of growth in two slightly different ways.

1. Consider, first, the very simple model presented in Table 20–3. Suppose that the economy is initially (in year 1) at the full-employment noninflationary level of output. Assume this entails a $500 billion NNP and a $50 billion level of investment. Suppose, secondly, that the economy is capable of expanding its total real output by 4 per cent per annum. And, finally, let us assume as in Chapter 13 that the MPS is one-fourth. Column 2 of Table 20–3 indicates that a 4 per cent rate of growth means that the economy is capable of producing $520 billion in year 2 ($500 billion plus 4 per cent of $500 billion). If businessmen attempt to utilize this increase in the economy's pro-

TABLE 20–3. INVESTMENT REQUIREMENTS IN A GROWING ECONOMY
(hypothetical data in billions)

(1) Year	(2) Full-employment NNP at 4 per cent annual growth rate	(3) Annual increase in saving	(4) Investment required to achieve full-employment NNP
1	$500.0	—	$50.0
2	520.0	$5.0	55.0
3	540.8	5.2	60.2
4	562.4	5.4	65.6
	etc.	etc.	etc.

ductive potential—that is, if businessmen produce the $520 billion NNP—will the economy spend enough to sustain this output? The answer hinges upon the rate of investment. The $20 billion increase in output and income will cause saving to increase by $5 billion (one-fourth of $20 billion). Investment spending must expand by a like amount in year 2 to compensate for this increase. Investment spending must expand from $50 to $55 billion for the growth potential of the economy to be realized in year 2. In year 3 the investment requirement is even greater. The economy is capable of producing an output of $540.8 billion. But the $20.8 billion increase in output and income which occurs between years 2 and 3 gives rise to $5.2 billion in additional saving. This means that investment spending must rise from an annual rate of $55 billion in year 2 to a $60.2 billion rate in year 3. And so it goes for succeeding years. The basic lesson of this simplified illustration is clear: *The maintenance of a given rate of growth requires a constantly expanding volume of investment spending.* Needless to say, to increase the rate of growth requires that investment increase at an even more rapid rate.

2. A related and somewhat more sophisticated view of the demand side of growth focuses attention upon the growth-inducing role of investment. This approach can be presented graphically as an extension of the tools of Keynesian employment theory.[12]

Consider Figure 20–4, wherein we have drawn the now familiar consumption schedule and the aggregate supply (45-degree line) schedule. For simplicity's sake we ignore government and consider only the private sector. Assume initially—in year 1— that capacity production, that is, the full-employment noninflationary NNP as determined by the permissive factors, is ON_1 (say, $470 billion, as shown by the equilib-

rium position in Table 13–1). We know that the production of this output will bring forth consumption of C_1N_1 (say, $450 billion). Planned saving, which you will recall from Chapter 12 is the vertical distance between the consumption schedule and the 45-degree line, is S_1C_1 ($20 billion). Let us suppose happily that intended investment is the same amount, S_1C_1 or $20 billion, so saving equals net investment and initially the full-employment noninflationary output is being realized.

But now a new consideration comes to the fore. In our earlier analysis of output determination we looked only at the *income-creating* aspect of investment spending. That is, in Chapters 12 and 13 we were interested in investment only as a component of aggregate demand which helped to generate and sustain some level of NNP. Our discussion of capital formation in this chapter, however, tells us that net investment also has a *capacity-creating* aspect; net investment, by expanding the nation's stock of capital facilities, will enhance the economy's productive capacity. Simply stated, because net investment has occurred in year 1, the economy has the capacity to produce a still larger full-employment noninflationary NNP in year 2.

How much larger? This depends upon what economists call the *capital-output ratio*, that is, the relationship between net investment and the resulting increase in the productive or output capacity of the economy. Let us suppose this ratio is 2:1; every $2 of net investment in year 1 makes the economy capable of producing $1 of additional output in year 2 and succeeding years. Specifically, $20 billion of net investment will increase the economy's productive capacity by $10 billion, from $470 to $480 billion. In Figure 20–3 the amount added to the full-employment noninflationary or capacity NNP as the result of year 1's net investment is N_1N_2. Note that because the capital-output ratio is 2:1 N_1N_2 equals $\frac{1}{2}S_1C_1$.

Will this new, higher NNP which the economy is capable of producing in year 2

[12] See William Fellner, *Trends and Cycles in Economic Activity* (New York: Holt, Rinehart and Winston, Inc., 1956), chap. 4.

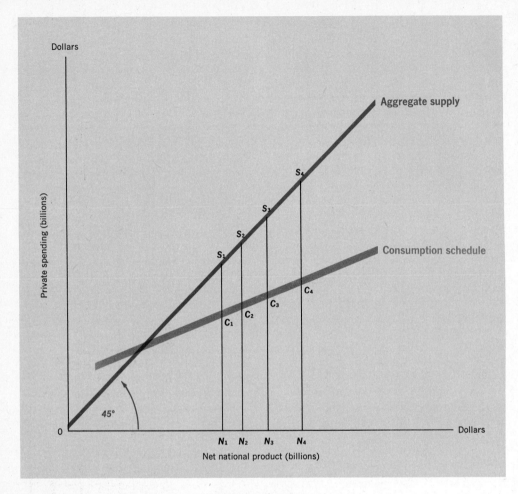

FIGURE 20–4. THE DEMAND SIDE OF ECONOMIC GROWTH.
Achievement of the full-employment noninflationary NNP of N_1 in year 1 will require
net investment equal to saving of S_1C_1. But this investment will raise the economy's
productive capacity by N_1N_2. To achieve this higher level of production net
investment must rise to S_2C_2. But this level of investment will increase capacity
by N_2N_3, which, to be realized, calls for a still-higher investment level of
S_3C_3, and so forth.

be realized? It depends, as in year 1, on
whether planned investment is equal to the
new and higher level of planned saving S_2C_2
that occurs in year 2. Specifically, if we
assume the marginal propensity to save is,
say, one-fifth, S_2C_2 will be $22 billion in
year 2. Planned investment must then be
equal to S_2C_2 or $22 billion if year 2's

expanded productive capacity is to be realized. But, once again, if planned investment
is actually S_2C_2, the economy's productive
potential will be larger by N_2N_3 ($= \frac{1}{2}S_2C_2$)
in year 3. Specifically, with a capital-output
ratio of 2:1 the economy will be capable of
producing a $491 billion NNP in year 3.
For this greater productive capacity to be

realized, businesses must be prepared to invest at the higher S_3C_3 level in year 3 to absorb that same volume of saving. The same reasoning applies to years 4, 5, and so on. The basic conclusion is quite evident: *The maintenance of economic growth relies upon an expanding level of investment.*

What will happen if intended investment fails to equal intended saving at each of the successively higher levels of full-employment noninflationary NNP? The answer obviously is that the economy will be faced with unemployment and underutilized productive facilities. Furthermore, the lower than desired rate of investment will cause the economy to grow less rapidly than depicted in Figure 20–4. If planned investment is persistently in excess of planned saving at the various full-employment levels of NNP, the economy will realize rapid growth accompanied by chronic inflation. Appropriate monetary and fiscal measures would be called for in either case. We shall have more to say about policies to achieve economic growth in Chapter 21.

Allocative Efficiency

The social environment of an economy can be every bit as significant as its physical environment in influencing economic growth. The social environment of any society must meet two requirements to facilitate economic growth. First, it must encourage those changes in products, productive techniques, and capital facilities which are vital to economic growth. Second, it must provide a suitable mechanism for negotiating with reasonable efficiency the reallocation of resources which are appropriate to the development of new products, new productive techniques, and changes in the stock of capital goods.

The social environment. The overall social-cultural-political environment of the United States has been very conducive to economic growth. Several interrelated factors contribute to this favorable environment. First,

as opposed to many other nations, there are virtually no social or moral taboos upon production and material progress. The free and individualistic nature of our economy has been generally conducive to the development of new products and new methods of production. Consumers are free and ordinarily willing to try new products. Indeed, American social philosophy has embraced the notion that material advance is an attainable and highly desirable economic goal. The inventor, the innovator, and the business executive are accorded high degrees of prestige and respect in American society. Second, Americans have traditionally possessed healthy attitudes toward work and risk taking; our society has benefited from a willing labor force and an ample supply of entrepreneurs. Third, our economy has been characterized by a stable political system wherein internal order, the right of property ownership, the legal status of enterprise, and the enforcement of contracts have been fostered. Though not subject to quantification, this bundle of characteristics has undoubtedly provided an excellent foundation for American economic growth.

The price system. Furthermore, historical observation suggests that the price system of American capitalism has performed reasonably well as a mechanism for negotiating the reallocations of resources which economic growth demands. New methods and new products call for realignments of resources. And the price system, we have seen, provides the carrot of profits and the stick of losses to induce the expansion of innovating industries and to force the contraction of those industries whose products have been rendered obsolete or less desirable by these advances. The ebb and flow of economic progress shove old industries into oblivion and create whole new industries to replace the old. The demise of the steam locomotive industry and the more or less simultaneous rise of the diesel locomotive industry are one of innumerable examples. The tremendous stimulus which the automobile industry gave to the steel, rubber, and petroleum industries has already been cited. The death blow which the automobile industry dealt the carriage makers is the other side of the picture.

Figure 20–3 provides a rough outline of some of the reallocations of labor which the price system has negotiated over a long period of years. Most obvious is the relative shift of labor from agricultural pursuits to other types of productive endeavor—particularly to trade, transportation, and white-collar work. Agriculture accounted for over half of the economy's employment in 1870, but only about 7 per cent in 1964. In contrast professional and public service engaged about 3½ per cent of the economy's labor force in 1870; by 1964 this figure was about 16 per cent. These are clearly significant shifts in the allocation of manpower.

Impediments to allocative efficiency. But economic change is not an unmixed blessing. The rise of new prosperous industries and the decline of old unprosperous industries is an essential feature of economic progress, desirable from the viewpoint of society as a whole. Businesses and resource suppliers caught in declining industries are adversely affected by economic growth; they face declining incomes and the prospect of painful and costly readjustments to other expanding lines of production. It is not surprising that adversely affected groups have sought to impede the reallocations of resources essential to economic growth. Illustrations are rather numerous.

Monopolies in both product and resource markets have retarded the reallocations of resources required for economic growth. Business monopolies may find it more profitable to suppress a newly discovered product or productive technique than to have their present capital facilities rendered obsolete before they have been fully depreciated. Furthermore, remember that the expansion of prosperous industries is a self-limiting process; as new firms enter growing indus-

tries, economic profits are competed away. Therefore, firms now established in these prosperous industries may contrive monopolistic restrictions upon the entry of new firms in an effort to preserve economic profits for themselves. Some labor unions have followed similar policies, resisting new work methods which threaten to cause unemployment by making workers more productive. To illustrate: Unions in the building trades have staunchly resisted the use of spray guns, fearing that workers will paint themselves out of jobs. And some unions, following restrictive membership policies, such as limiting the number of apprentices or charging high initiation fees, have created an artificial obstacle to labor mobility and have therefore limited the reallocation of human resources demanded by economic growth. Example: A growing economy typically wants more and better housing and relatively less food. This calls for fewer farmers and more carpenters, that is, a rechanneling of labor from the farm to housing projects. But the restrictive membership practices of certain building trades unions have impeded this shift.[13]

Other groups adversely affected by economic growth have been unable to resist its effects by their own tactics. Many of these have exerted political pressure for assistance, and some have received it. For example, a variety of forces (which will be detailed in a later chapter) have made agriculture a declining industry; that is, a smaller number of farmers can now produce more than enough food and fiber for the economy. This calls for a reallocation of resources from agriculture to relatively more productive

---

[13] It should be emphasized that many unions have been receptive to technological advance, demanding only that (1) new machines and methods be introduced in an orderly way to facilitate the reabsorption of technologically unemployed workers and (2) the business community and society as a whole share in the costs of technological unemployment.

uses in industry. However, public policy in the form of price supports and other subsidies have bolstered farmers' incomes and impeded the price system in reallocating farmers from agriculture to other industries where their productivity and incomes would be considerably higher. Similarly, the American watch industry has long been faced with the prospect of extinction because of the severe competition provided by foreign watches. But the American industry—manufacturers supported by the unions—has retarded this decline by seeking and getting a measure of relief from this competition through governmental enactment of higher tariffs (excise taxes) on imported watches.

These artificial impediments to growth are enforced by certain inherent resource immobilities. Apart from union and business monopolies, resources are far from perfectly mobile. The obstacles to labor mobility, for example, are many and varied. Geographic immobility stems from the reluctance of workers to break existing social ties, move to a new community, meet new people, and take roots. Moreover, in so far as occupational mobility is concerned, it is no easy chore to abandon one's life work at, say, middle age and assume the responsibility, costs, and inconvenience of learning a new trade. Immobility is even more evident when it comes to property resources. To use an extreme example, a wheat combine is completely immobile in the sense that it has only one use, and, price system or no price system, a combine cannot be shifted to the manufacture of automobiles or plastic toys.

But over time resource immobilities become less important. The sixty-year-old farmer who has worked the land since he was sixteen is not likely to obey the dictates of the price system to take a factory job in the city. But his son, particularly if he goes to college, will probably not go back to the farm. Instead, he is likely to seek out employment in more profitable, expanding, and therefore higher-paying industries. Many a farmer's son is now in engineering college,

and if he ever comes into contact with a John Deere tractor, it will probably be on a drafting board and not in a corn field. Figure 20–3 makes it clear that decades may be involved in negotiating significant transfers in the employment of human resources.

Furthermore, even durable capital wears out in time and may go unreplaced. A farm combine is useless in automobile manufacturing, but in time the combine may wear out and not be replaced. Money capital formerly flowing into farm equipment may now finance new and expanded capital facilities for the automobile industry. Hence, over the years the composition of the economy's stock of real capital changes; capital goods are in effect shifted among alternative uses.

PUBLIC POLICY

It will come as no surprise that public policy may have a very profound effect upon the growth process. Public policy affects not only the implemental factors, but also the permissive factors which underlie economic growth. Government can either tighten the reins or apply the whip to economic growth. The broad sweep of history reveals that government has actually done much to facilitate growth in the United States. Free or cheap land policies hastened westward expansion. Subsidies to railroads widened the domestic market and laid the framework for huge volumes of investment spending. Government's contributions to highway construction and communications provided a similar stimulus. More recently, we find government sharing the spotlight with private industry in financing research activity (Table 20–2). And, needless to say, the monetary and fiscal policies of government can have a crucial bearing upon the ability of the economy to achieve the level of aggregate demand required to realize fully its growth potential. In Chapter 21 we shall have occasion to outline a number of specific policies through which government might accelerate the growth rate. This is not to deny that there have been political blunders. But even from the vantage point of the present, it is fairly evident that government policies again and again have cut a clear path for economic development.

Not only does public policy affect economic growth; economic growth may also involve significant implications for the scope and character of public policies. For example, a wealthy, expanding economy can afford certain public policies—a very comprehensive social security system—which would be an intolerable burden for a less opulent society. Furthermore, as was suggested in Chapter 6, the wants of an expanding economy may change in favor of relatively larger amounts of social goods and relatively smaller amounts of private goods, implying an expanding economic role for government. Finally, growth and affluency may allow government to use certain techniques in the implementation of public policy which would be intolerable in a poorer society. To illustrate: Traditionally the use of the sales tax has been strongly resisted by Congress because of its regressivity and the relatively heavy burden it imposes upon low-income families. This objection is substantially weakened, however, as economic growth causes low-income families virtually to disappear.

SUMMARY

1. Economic growth may be defined either in terms of **a.** an expanding real national output (income) or **b.** an expanding per capita real output (income).

2. Economic growth **a.** provides a higher standard of living, **b.** lessens the acuteness of domestic economic problems, **c.** is a source of aid to less developed nations, and **d.** is essential in meeting the Soviet economic challenge.

3. The permissive factors in economic growth are **a.** the quantity and quality of a nation's natural resources, **b.** the quantity

and quality of its human resources, **c.** its stock of capital facilities, and **d.** its technology. Two implemental factors—a sufficient level of aggregate demand and allocative efficiency—are essential if the economy is to realize its growth potential.

4. In general the economy of the United States is amply endowed with natural resources. Scarcities of specific resources have been largely overcome by technological advances which have permitted the more efficient use and acquisition of such resources and the development of new substitute materials. Furthermore, in some cases abundant foreign supplies have been tapped to relieve specific scarcities. Lastly, the price system automatically tends to conserve on those resources which are most scarce.

5. Historically the American population has grown rapidly. At any point in time there is some specific optimum population which, given the nation's supplies of other resources, will provide a maximum output per person. Although the education and training of the American labor force is relatively good, there is ample room for improvement.

6. Economists are assigning an increasingly crucial role to technological progress—research and innovation—in the process of economic growth. Currently the United States devotes only about 3 per cent of its GNP to research, some of which is not of a very fundamental character.

7. In relation to other nations, American workers are very well equipped with capital facilities. However, growth in our stock of capital goods has been very irregular.

8. An expanding productive potential will not be achieved unless aggregate demand expands at an appropriate rate. In particular, investment spending not only generates income and sustains output, but it also adds to productive capacity. As capacity and the economy's full-employment noninflationary NNP rises, so does saving, and this means still more investment is needed to sustain this expanded output.

9. The American social-cultural-political environment has been conducive to economic growth. The price system has been a reasonably efficient mechanism for negotiating those resource reallocations which economic progress invariably entails. However, impediments to reallocations do exist, particularly in the form of product and resource market monopolies and the more or less inherent immobilities of both human and property resources.

10. Public policy affects the growth process through both the permissive and the implemental factors in the growth process. In turn economic growth can influence the scope and character of public policies.

QUESTIONS AND STUDY SUGGESTIONS

1. Define economic growth. Describe the rate of growth achieved in American capitalism.
2. What difficulties are involved in measuring economic growth? Specifically, what roles do leisure and improvements in product quality play in the growth process?
3. What are the major causes of economic growth? "There are both a demand and a supply side to economic growth." Explain. Why might it be important to distinguish between the "permissive" and the "implemental" factors underlying growth? Illustrate the operation of both sets of factors in terms of the production possibilities curve.
4. How do you account for the rapid increase in the rate of population growth which began in the early 1940s? "Population might increase but at the same time the labor force might shrink." Explain. Define and explain the concept of an optimum population.
5. What major occupational shifts have occurred in the allocation of labor resources? How are they to be explained?
6. "The greatest conserver of scarce natural resources is the price mechanism." Explain. In what ways has technological advance alleviated acute resource shortages? Be specific.
7. "If we want economic growth in a free society, we may have to accept a measure of instability." Evaluate. The noted philosopher Alfred North Whitehead once remarked that ". . . the art of progress is to preserve order amid change and to preserve change amid order." What did he mean? Is this contention relevant for economic growth? What implications might this have for public policy? Explain.
8. "Technological advance is bound to play a more important role in economic growth in the future than it has in the past." Do you agree? Explain and evaluate: "The American economy invests too much in machinery and not enough in people."
9. Discuss the importance of the income-creating and the capacity-creating aspects of investment for economic growth. What is the importance of the capital-output ratio? Using a diagram similar to Figure 20–4, illustrate what differences an increase or decrease in (*a*) the MPS and (*b*) the capital-output ratio would make for the rate of growth and the volume of investment required to maintain the full-employment noninflationary NNP over time.
10. Why is resource mobility essential to economic growth? "Resource

immobilities are less in the long run than they are in the short run."
Explain.
11. What role do social, cultural, political, and institutional forces play in
economic growth? Be as specific as you can.
12. "Public policy affects and is affected by economic growth." Explain
and illustrate.

SELECTED REFERENCES

Danière, André: *Higher Education in the American Economy* (New York:
Random House, Inc., 1964).

Economic Growth in the United States: Its Past and Future (New York:
Committee for Economic Development, February, 1958).

Gill, Richard T.: *Economic Development: Past and Present* (Englewood
Cliffs, N.J.: Prentice-Hall, Inc., 1963), particularly chaps. 1–4.

Joint Economic Committee: *Staff Report on Employment, Growth, and
Price Levels* (Washington, D.C., 1960), chaps. 1 and 2.

Landsberg, Hans H.: *Natural Resources for U.S. Growth* (Baltimore: The
Johns Hopkins Press, 1964).

Morris, Bruce R.: *Problems of American Economic Growth* (Fair Lawn,
N.J.: Oxford University Press, 1961), chaps. 1–7.

Phelps, Edmund S. (ed.): *The Goal of Economic Growth* (New York:
W. W. Norton & Company, Inc., 1962).

Problems of United States Economic Development (New York: Committee
for Economic Development, January, 1958).

Rostow, W. W.: *The Stages of Economic Growth* (New York: Cambridge
University Press, 1960).

Villard, Henry H.: *Economic Development,* rev. ed. (New York: Holt,
Rinehart and Winston, Inc., 1963), chaps. 1–12.

CHAPTER 21

GROWTH IN AMERICAN CAPITALISM: COSTS, PROBLEMS, AND POLICIES

We discovered in Chapter 20 that economic growth is a highly desirable state of affairs. Growth means a higher standard of living domestically; it is a palliative for domestic economic problems; and growth can provide the wherewithal for meeting the Soviet challenge and the acute needs of the under-developed nations. Other things being equal, there is no question but that rapid growth is clearly preferable to slow or modest growth. But we must now recognize that rapid economic growth is not free for the asking; nor is it a panacea for all our problems. Indeed, rapid growth may entail certain costs and may create, or contribute to, a number of economic problems.

It is the purpose of this chapter to examine some of these less pleasant facets of economic growth. First, some of the reasonably evident costs or sacrifices which the attainment of rapid growth may involve are enumerated. Second, the troublesome problem posed by the chronically depressed areas will be given rather detailed treatment. Third, the very controversial question of whether United States economic growth has been sufficiently rapid will be analyzed. Finally, we shall explore the contention that the causes and character of inflation may change as an expanding economy reaches an advanced stage of growth and study the implications of this eventuality for public policy.[1] All this

discussion is placed in the context of American capitalism. That is, we are addressing ourselves to the growth problems of an advanced economy rather than to those great obstacles faced by underdeveloped nations (Chapter 41).

THE COSTS OF ECONOMIC GROWTH

Despite the many desirable aspects of an expanding economy, it must be acknowledged that the pursuit of almost any economic objective—including rapid economic growth—entails certain costs and sacrifices. For the most part these costs, once mentioned, are sufficiently obvious to merit only brief comment. First, our production possibilities analysis of Chapter 2 reminds us that provision for the necessary research, education, capital equipment, and so forth, which are so essential to rapid growth must come at the expense of current consumption. More "goods for the future" can be provided only at the cost of fewer "goods for the present." Second, rapid growth means an accelerated tempo of industrial life. Declines in leisure, or sacrifices of potential increases in leisure, are involved. And a higher participation rate in the labor force may be required, that is, more women, oldsters, and youngsters may be required to hold jobs. It is of interest to note that the ulcer rate is said to be extremely

---

[1] Another problem associated with a growing, increasingly affluent economy will be deferred until Chapter 38. This is the problem of social

balance—the question of whether an expanding economy tends to produce too many private goods and not enough social goods.

high among Soviet plant managers who are under great pressure from the government to fulfill or overfulfill their assigned production targets. Third, history suggests that rapid growth may be accompanied and nurtured by the wasteful exploitation of natural resources. Fourth, a growing, changing economy may be increasingly susceptible to instability. For example, since a high level of total demand is requisite to full employment and vigorous economic expansion, it may be more difficult to achieve price stability. Finally, brisk growth implies rapid changes in the structure and character of the economic system; these changes may result in insecurity and unemployment for adversely affected businessmen and workers. This final point has been of increasing consequence for the United States in the postwar years and now merits detailed examination.

STRUCTURAL UNEMPLOYMENT AND DISTRESSED AREAS

In Chapter 11 we noted that the United States has encountered no serious depressions since World War II; massive unemployment has been avoided. On the other hand, postwar growth has been disrupted by a series of recessions wherein unemployment rates have been roughly double the 3 per cent "hard core" unemployment rate we have associated with "full employment" (Chapter 11). Indeed, since 1947 the average annual rate of unemployment has been about 4.9 per cent of the labor force (see Table 21–1.) The addition of part-time workers who would prefer longer hours and those discouraged workers who are no longer actively seeking employment might easily bring the above figure to 7 or 8 per cent.

There are several less evident aspects of postwar unemployment which add to the seriousness of the situation. On the one hand, there is evidence (Table 21–1) to suggest that persistent unemployment may be on the increase. The recovery from each of the postwar recessions seems to have been less vigorous and less complete. As Table 21–1

TABLE 21–1. THE UNEMPLOYMENT RATE, 1947 TO 1964

Year	Per cent of civilian labor force unemployed
1947	3.9
1948	3.8
1949	5.9
1950	5.3
1951	3.3
1952	3.1
1953	2.9
1954	5.6
1955	4.4
1956	4.2
1957	4.3
1958	6.8
1959	5.5
1960	5.6
1961	6.7
1962	5.6
1963	5.7
1964	5.2

Source: U.S. Department of Labor.

suggests, the postwar era may be bringing us face to face with a problem of "creeping unemployment." Second, unemployment seems to be of a longer duration. The portion of the unemployed who have been without work for six months or more has been on the increase. Third, only about one-half of those unemployed in years of overall prosperity are explainable as those temporarily unemployed because of the seasonability of their industry or because they have voluntarily quit their old jobs to seek something better. In other words, about half the unemployed are clearly those who are involuntarily unemployed and who may encounter serious and prolonged difficulties in finding new jobs.

Structural Unemployment

Many economists feel that this growing residue of unemployment is to be associated not solely with a deficiency of total spending, but rather with the failure of the economy to adjust fully and efficiently to certain basic changes associated with economic growth. More specifically, such factors as rapid changes in technology, shifts in the pattern of consumer demand, and the geographic relocation of industry call for substantial occupational and geographic shifts on the part of adversely affected workers if they are to be reemployed. The failure of adjustments of the required magnitude to occur has resulted in a number of chronically depressed areas—areas where unemployment rates are substantially and persistently higher than the national average. These are very adversely affected by downswings in the national economy and recover only slowly and partially during a national economic upswing. In late 1964 there were seventeen areas in the United States characterized by "substantial and persistent" unemployment. Most of the major chronically depressed areas are in the Northeastern United States.

Causes of Structural Unemployment

How did these chronically depressed areas get that way? Generally speaking, these are areas which have been highly dependent upon one or maybe two firms or industries as sources of income and employment. These firms or industries have been adversely affected, that is, they have become declining industries because of one or more of the previously cited basic changes associated with the dynamic nature of a growing economy. Some illustrations will be helpful.[2] A number of chronically distressed areas in West Virginia, Pennsylvania, Kentucky, and southern Illinois are the result of the decline of the coal mining industry. This decline has a number of diverse causes: coal has lost out to gas and oil in home heating; technological advances in coal mining equipment have substantially reduced the need for labor;

[2] These examples are taken from Committee for Economic Development, *Distressed Areas in a Growing Economy* (New York, June, 1961), pp. 24–28.

export markets for coal have dwindled because of increases in foreign trade barriers. In the cotton and wool textile manufacturing industries, firms have found it economically justified to migrate from New England and the Middle Atlantic states and relocate in North and South Carolina and Georgia, resulting in large numbers of stranded workers in the former areas. Competition from newer synthetic products and increased foreign competition have also contributed to the overall decline of the textile industry. Certain areas heavily dependent upon the manufacture and repair of railway equipment, for example, Centralia, Illinois, and Altoona, Pennsylvania, have become distressed areas largely as the result of the shift from steam to diesel engines, the persistent decline in railway passenger traffic, and inroads made on freight traffic by truck lines. Automation, changes in emphasis in government defense spending, alterations in the pattern of consumer preferences as between various automobile makes and models, and the decentralization of automobile manufacturing facilities have all contributed to chronic unemployment in Detroit and a number of other Michigan communities. It is of considerable significance that most of these chronically depressed areas are heavily populated areas. Hence, the unemployment situation—the decline in the absolute number of job opportunities—is seriously aggravated by a rapidly expanding population and labor force.

In short, the changes which characterize a growing, dynamic economy—technological changes as reflected in both products and capital equipment, changes in consumer preferences, and so forth—cause some industries and sectors of the economy to decline significantly and rapidly in importance. This has meant substantial amounts of noncyclical unemployment in adversely affected areas.

From Brawn to Brains

But, you might ask, won't a growing economy create enough new jobs to absorb the unemployed of the depressed areas? Shouldn't a readjustment or reallocation process such as described in Chapter 5 resolve this type of problem? The answer is that the effectiveness of the reallocation process is seriously hampered by two facts: (1) The rapidly expanding industries (electronics, plastics, antibiotics, synthetic fibers) are generally located in areas geographically distant from the distressed areas; and (2) the new jobs provided by these expanding industries typically call for more skill and

training than unemployed workers in the distressed areas possess. The "men available" ads are placed by the unskilled and semi-skilled, while the "help wanted" ads come from companies seeking professional people, scientists, executives, and technicians. A very remarkable change in the structure of employment opportunities is illustrated in Figure 21–1. Employment in goods-producing industries has been declining relative to employment in service industries. Absolutely the number of jobs in goods-producing

FIGURE 21–1. EMPLOYMENT IN GOODS-PRODUCING INDUSTRIES AND IN SERVICE INDUSTRIES.
In the last three and one-half decades employment has increased rather steadily in the service industries. The goods-producing industries, on the other hand, provide about the same number of jobs now as they did at the end of World War I. [Joint Economic Committee, *Staff Report on Employment, Growth, and Price Levels* (Washington, D.C., 1959), p. 174, and U.S. Department of Labor data.]

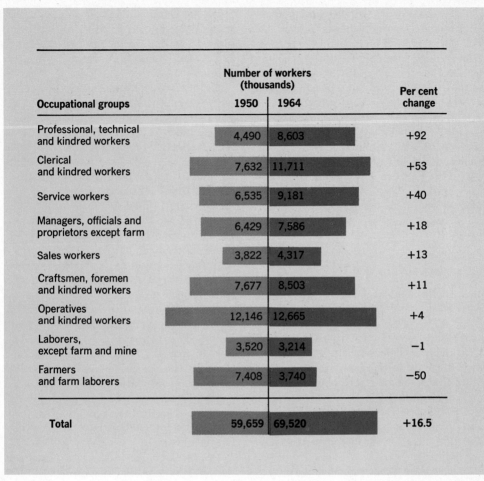

FIGURE 21–2. SHIFTS IN THE SIZE OF MAJOR OCCUPATIONAL GROUPS BETWEEN 1950 AND 1964.
National requirements for higher skills have been increasing, while automation has been replacing workers in many of the less skilled occupations. The shifts toward higher proportions of professional, technical, and highly trained workers are expected to continue into the 1970s. (U.S. Department of Labor data.)

industries was slightly less in 1964 than in 1919, whereas the number of jobs in service industries has increased from about 14 million in 1919 to almost 37 million in 1964. Figure 21–2 provides a more detailed portrayal of this phenomenon.

Why has this dramatic shift from blue-collar to white-collar labor—from brawn to brains—occurred? The answer, most simply stated, is "automation." The use of more and better capital equipment has put a ceiling on the number of material goods-producing jobs, *despite* rapid population growth and massive government spending on military goods. Automation has permitted us to meet an expanding demand for material goods with a constant or a slightly declining number of material goods workers. But at the same time the development and application of increasingly complex productive equipment has expanded greatly the job opportunities for all breeds of scientists, for technicians, for supervisory personnel, and for high-caliber managers. Here's the nub of the structural unemployment problem: The machine-displaced blue-collar workers frequently do not have the skills or education prerequisite for reemployment in most available white-collar jobs. The labor supply has failed to adjust adequately to the change in the composition or structure of labor demand.

Public Policy and the Distressed Areas

What is the outlook for the chronically depressed areas? What remedies are appropriate?

Though it is not easy to generalize, we must frankly recognize that the outlook for many of the distressed areas is not particularly favorable. Chronic unemployment tends to create conditions which impede recovery. New industries (which, remember, seek mostly skilled, technical, and professional labor) are not likely to locate in depressed areas where manual and semiskilled labor are in surplus. Indeed, the labor force of a depressed area may deteriorate qualitatively as the younger, more capable workers move to other areas, leaving the older, less capable workers behind. A depressed regional market is obviously not an attractive place in which a consumer goods producer might locate. Furthermore, there is the bald fact that those declining areas which owe their former prosperity to now-declining extractive industries—for example, coal—may offer no locational advantages for other types of industry. There are no compelling reasons why new industries will be attracted to the hills of West Virginia as the mines afford fewer and fewer jobs. Finally, community services upon which industry depends may also seriously deteriorate as unemployment persists: bond issues and tax increases for the maintenance,

much less the improving, of public utilities, school systems, streets, and so forth, are increasingly unlikely to be realized. All this makes the community less attractive to new industry.

Now what about remedies? Most obviously, overall national prosperity helps, but does not erase, structural unemployment. The nature of structural unemployment calls for more selective remedies. These take two general forms: (1) the relocation of unemployed workers and (2) the economic rehabilitation of the area. Or, in other words, remedies lie in moving the unemployed to new jobs in more prosperous areas or moving the new jobs (that is, new industries) into the areas of unemployment.

If the prospects for economic rehabilitation are dismal, special policies to induce a more rapid geographic outmigration of workers from the distressed areas are in order. Publicly sponsored programs to recruit and relocate the surplus labor of the chronically depressed areas through an expansion of the activities of the United States Employment Service are a frequently recommended policy. This action might be supplemented by legislation which provides for government payment of transportation and moving costs for those families willing to leave the distressed areas in favor of more prosperous regions. If area rehabilitation seems feasible, proposals such as the following might be helpful:

1. The Federal government might provide financial and technical assistance in helping local authorities evaluate their circumstances and formulate realistic redevelopment programs.

2. The Federal government might provide financial assistance to depressed municipalities and regions for the revitalization of their public facilities and services—schools, roads, water and electric utilities, and so forth—which are so essential to the attraction of new industries.

3. The Federal government in cooperation with state and local governments may make available long-term low-interest loans to prospective employers who are will-

ing to establish themselves in distressed areas.

4. Provided minimum requirements of economic and locational efficiency can be met, the depressed areas should be given special consideration in the granting of public contracts and in the location of public facilities.

Whether the solution for a distressed area entails worker migration or area rehabilitation, vocational retraining will typically be required to match now-unemployed workers to new job opportunities (see Figure 21–2). Hence, most aid programs advocate the use of Federal funds to support vocational training. And it is often recommended that unemployed workers undergoing vocational retraining who are not already receiving unemployment compensation payments should be extended these benefits through their retraining period. Until relocation or area rehabilitation is realized, the immediate needs of unemployed workers might be met by such measures as extending unemployment compensation benefits to those who do not qualify or who have exhausted their claims, by free distribution of government-owned food surpluses, and so forth. Advocates of the several specific aid proposals here outlined point out that the required

government outlays on these programs should be large enough to work effectively toward a solution of the problem; these programs, if adopted, may be costly. But then, it is argued, the economic and social costs of unemployment are also very great.

It must be emphasized that these programs are a subject of considerable controversy. Some opponents contend that proposals designed to attract new industries into depressed areas may only interfere with the operation of market forces and thereby encourage unemployed workers to remain in areas which can never again support them at reasonable income levels. Others flatly argue that all such aid programs, by going far beyond the dictates of the Employment Act of 1946, entail an unjustified and undesirable extension of government action and the welfare state.

IS GROWTH RAPID ENOUGH?

We noted in Chapter 20 that over a long period of years the United States has achieved an enviable growth record. Yet, oddly enough, there currently exists a basic controversy concerning the adequacy of the United States' growth. There are a number of reasons for this debate. As Table 21–2

TABLE 21–2. AVERAGE ANNUAL RATE OF GROWTH IN REAL GNP IN SELECTED COUNTRIES

Country	Actual growth rate, per cent per year, 1950–1960	Projected growth rate, per cent per year, 1960–1970
Japan	8.8	7.0–7.5
West Germany	7.5	4.5–5.0
U.S.S.R.	6.8	6.0–6.5
Italy	5.9	5.0–5.5
France	4.3	5.0–5.5
United States	3.3	4.0–4.5
United Kingdom	2.6	3.5–4.0

Source: Stanley H. Cohn, "The Gross National Product in the Soviet Union: Comparative Growth Rates," in Joint Economic Committee, *Dimensions of Soviet Economic Power* (Washington, D.C., 1962), pp. 75, 87.

indicates, the growth rates of a number of other nations are substantially in excess of ours. Most notable and most ominous is the Soviet rate, variously estimated by Western experts at 6 to 8 per cent per year. Furthermore, in the postwar era our per capita increases in real output have been rather modest; that is, increases in total output have been substantially eaten up by rapid population growth (Table 20–1). Finally, there is some evidence to support the view that American growth has been slowing in the 1950s and early 1960s, primarily because of higher unemployment rates and a decrease in the rate of productivity increases.[3] Though innumerable specific views exist as to the adequacy of American economic growth, there are two general positions.

Case for the Affirmative

A number of highly respected economists[4] feel that our growth rate is quite adequate and that any attempt to accelerate it might do little to solve the problems we face, on the one hand, and impose intolerable costs upon our society, on the other. In more detail the rationale of this viewpoint runs something like this: Our economy is already affluent. Hence, the production of more goods for domestic use is generally not a high priority goal. Internationally it is doubtful that the size and rate of growth in our GNP are particularly crucial. It is not so much the size of the GNP, but rather its composition, which determines our military position vis-à-vis the Soviet Union. After all, the Soviet military posture is roughly the equivalent of ours, although their GNP is only about 50 per cent of ours.[5] Nor is it clear that the

future of the underdeveloped nations will be determined primarily by bald comparisons of U.S. and U.S.S.R. growth rates.[6]

In short, there is little to show that the issues between us and the rest of the world will be governed predominantly by our economic successes, or that we can buy safe survival with an additional per cent or two of economic growth.

Of even greater long-run significance, it is argued that the policies which would be required to increase our growth rate are politically and ideologically unacceptable. That is, more rapid growth implies in general an expanding role for government and in particular greater restraints upon consumers to free resources for investment, the direct allocation of materials and manpower to growth-oriented sectors of the economy, and wage-price controls to contain the inflation that such a high-pressure economy inevitably generates. In brief, any significant acceleration of the growth rate—from, say, 3 to 5 or 6 per cent—necessitates the use of techniques and controls which are incompatible with a free society. Accelerated growth can be achieved only at the cost of freedom. This, it is argued, is much too high a price to pay for a percentage point or two increase in our growth rate.

Case for the Negative

Other highly regarded voices envision the situation much differently.[7] Despite our overall national wealth, there are compelling reasons why growth must be accelerated. First, the lowest 20 per cent of the income receivers in our society have yet to partake adequately of the overall affluence of our nation. Growth will tend to raise the entire income distribution absolutely and will also

---

[3] Joint Economic Committee, *Staff Report on Employment, Growth, and Price Levels* (Washington, D.C., 1959), chap. 3.

[4] The present discussion is based primarily upon Henry C. Wallich, *The Cost of Freedom* (New York: Harper & Row, Publishers, Incorporated, 1960).

[5] Cynics point out that the GNP of the barbarians was undoubtedly much less than that of the Romans.

[6] Wallich, *op. cit.*, p. 158.

[7] For example, see the Joint Economic Committee, *op. cit.*, chaps. 1–4, and Alvin H. Hansen, *Economic Issues of the 1960's* (New York: McGraw-Hill Book Company, 1961), particularly chap. 5.

enhance the ability and willingness of society to provide public assistance to these low-income groups. Second, the increasingly acute international situation demands an expanded rate of American growth. The reputation or image of our economy—indeed, of our entire society—as evaluated by under-developed nations is highly dependent upon our growth performance. Economic growth, rightly or wrongly, *is* widely accepted as an index of a nation's vitality, efficiency, and capacity for survival in the cold war. Growth rates *do* impress the uncommitted under-developed nations. Furthermore, a growing capitalism obviously has a greater capacity and probably a greater willingness to extend aid to the underdeveloped nations and to improve its own military posture. This is so because the real output gains from an accelerated growth rate may be substantial. Example: A $600 billion GNP economy with a 2 per cent growth rate will add $12 billion to its GNP in a year; that same economy will add $30 billion if it achieves a 5 per cent rate of growth. These figures also suggest that growth helps any nation avoid a crude clash between consumer goods production, on the one hand, and capital, military, or foreign aid goods, on the other (Chapter 2).[8]

Accelerated growth is not only desirable, but it is also said to be obtainable within the present institutional-ideological frame-work of capitalism. Thus, after detailed analysis, the Joint Economic Committee has concluded that our economy is capable of growing at a rate of 4½ per cent per year "without changing our economic system in any fundamental way."[9] We need not embrace forced draft techniques or accept an erosion of our freedom to achieve a significantly better growth rate than is now enjoyed.

Those who feel that past American growth is inadequate and that it can be accelerated

note several policies which would promote more rapid growth and simultaneously be compatible with the institutions and ideology of a free society.

POLICIES TO ACCELERATE GROWTH

There are three policies generally recognized as crucial to the acceleration of American economic growth: (1) the achievement of continuous full employment; (2) expanded expenditures on basic scientific research; and (3) increased spending on education.

Continuous Full Employment

Achieving and maintaining full employment is a basic implemental factor in economic growth. Total demand must increase at a rate equal to the expansion of the economy's productive capacity, or potential growth will not be realized. If total spending is not growing appropriately, all other efforts to raise total output will be frustrated.

The immediate impact of unemployment upon the growth rate is clear. For example, because of the 1957–1958 recession, the annual realized growth rate of the United States in the 1955–1958 period was about 0.5 per cent, short of the 3 or 3½ per cent which the United States has achieved over a long span of years and far short of the 4 or 5 per cent rate which many economists feel to be attainable without any significant changes in our institutions or economic way of life. It is notable, too, as analysis of the production possibilities curve reminds us, that to move from a position of unemployment to one of full employment entails no cost or sacrifice for society; on the contrary, it is unemployment itself which imposes the cost of forgone production upon society.

A thorough grasp of the significance of full employment for economic growth requires the understanding of two additional points. On the one hand, the movement from less than full employment to full employment provides a one-shot stimulus to the economy's growth rate. Thus a movement from a

---

[8] In Chapter 38 another point will be considered: Economic growth facilitates the production of much-needed social goods and services.
[9] Joint Economic Committee, *op. cit.*, pp. xxvi and 101.

6 per cent to a 3 per cent unemployment rate will stimulate the GNP and the growth rate in the year this is achieved. But afterward, as full employment is maintained, there will occur no further windfall increases in output and the rate of growth in succeeding years.

On the other hand, cyclical *un*employment can have certain harmful "carry over" effects upon the growth rate in subsequent years of full employment through the adverse effects it might have upon the permissive factors in growth. For example, unemployment depresses investment and capital accumulation; it may give rise to a decline in the work week which is frequently demanded by organized labor as a technique to more equitably apportion the burden of unemployment; the expansion of research budgets may be slowed by recession; union resistance to technological change may stiffen, and so forth. Though it is impossible to quantify the impact of these considerations upon the growth rate, they undoubtedly can be of considerable importance.

Growth and Research Revolution

We emphasized in the previous chapter that research and its end result—technological advance—are widely recognized as the most significant ingredient in economic growth.[10]

Fundamentally, economic growth means growth in a nation's underlying ideas and skills. The immediate generator of economic growth is investment . . . but . . . investment arises from new ideas, new developments in science and technology, from education, research, innovations—new products, new processes, new resources—all of these are the real seeds of long-term economic growth.

If we accept the basic role of research as a determinant of the growth rate, it is obvious that a major policy step in accelerating economic growth is to increase expenditures upon research and development activities.

[10] Leonard S. Silk, *The Research Revolution* (New York: McGraw-Hill Book Company, 1960), p. 203.

But at this juncture some serious questions and problems arise.

1. Most importantly, can American capitalism generate the research expenditures needed to achieve the desired acceleration in the growth rate? It is very difficult to answer with authority. We do know that a number of forces have been operating in the postwar period to accelerate research spending—to foster a "research revolution": (*a*) Our World War II experience demonstrated the feasibility of organizing and carrying through to completion large-scale basic research projects and also created a backlog of technological information applicable to peacetime products; (*b*) research and development activity has generally proven to be highly profitable; (*c*) 1954 revisions of our tax laws make research expenditures deductible as a current expense; and (*d*) research spending tends to be cumulative; that is,[11]

Research feeds upon itself: Discovery breeds discovery; innovation breeds innovation; and with each new discovery or innovation, the total body of scientific and technological knowledge increases.

And, indeed, we know that the absolute level of research and development spending has grown substantially (Table 20–3) and now stands at over $17 billion per year.

All this is impressive. But there are some less encouraging factors to consider. Absolutely, the Soviets spend somewhat more on research than we do, and, with a GNP approximately half the size of ours, they spend relatively much more. And qualitatively Soviet research ranks high because more emphasis is placed upon basic or pure scientific research in contrast with greater American emphasis upon applied research and what some would classify as trivia. Thus, it is not at all clear that the quantity and quality of American research efforts will be adequate to achieve the desired acceleration of our rate of growth.

2. An advancing technology as reflected

[11] *Ibid.*, pp. 162–163.

in automation is feared and resisted by groups who stand to be adversely affected. Thus, for example, organized labor does not accept with complete equanimity the widespread and rapid introduction of new labor-replacing machinery. Indeed, we have seen that the whole problem of structural unemployment is bound up with automation as it destroys unskilled and semiskilled jobs, on the one hand, while creating jobs for the skilled, the technician, and the professional person, on the other.

3. There is the knotty problem of providing the brainpower upon which research activity so heavily depends. In analyzing this problem we turn to the third policy for increasing the growth rate—devoting more resources to education.

Education: Investment in Human Capital

Can our educational system provide the brainpower to accelerate the flow of technological advance, on the one hand, and provide better-trained workers to fit the changing labor force needs of an advancing economy, on the other (Figure 21–2)? Probably the greatest social need of the United States for coming decades is a sufficient quantity and quality of educated people. Can we meet that need? The numerous current appraisals of our educational needs and resources almost invariably reach pessimistic conclusions. Future demands upon the educational system will be great. Our rapidly expanding population means greatly expanded enrollments. Elementary and high school enrollments, which were 25 million in 1950 are over 44 million in 1965. And, despite the fact that overcrowded schools are now commonplace, it is estimated that we are currently constructing only about 60 per cent of the extra classrooms needed to house the annual increases in enrollment. That isn't all: If the demand for a better-trained work force is to be met, a larger percentage of our young people will have to receive higher education—and education of increasing quality—than is now the case.

Another frequent conclusion is that we do a poor job of recruiting our best brains for higher education. Evidence: An estimated 50 per cent of our ablest young people do not go on to college primarily because of a lack of financial resources. In other words, we seriously underutilize or misallocate brainpower, our most valuable resource. In the crucial area of scientific and engineering personnel the annual number of graduates is known to be lagging seriously behind that of the U.S.S.R. Finally, at the core of our educational problems is the teacher shortage. It is estimated that we need to recruit about 100,000 teachers per year for our public schools, but are actually recruiting only about half that number. Fulfillment of the estimated need for teachers in the decade of the 1960s will require nearly 2 million college graduates—over half the total estimated 3.7 million college graduates forthcoming in that period!

There are, of course, some potential alleviating factors which *may* increase the productivity of teachers: instruction by television, relieving trained teachers of routine tasks, expanding class sizes, and so forth. But, even assuming such devices do not dilute the quality of education, there is clearly a tremendous task ahead in meeting the demands put upon the educational system. Meeting these needs and simultaneously upgrading the quality of education will undoubtedly require much thought, much effort, and substantial amounts of human and property resources.[12]

Research, Education, and Social Revenues

Although private expenditures for research and education are large and on the increase, a substantial number of economists and public officials feel that increased public sup-

[12] The interested student might consult Seymour E. Harris, *More Resources for Education* (New York: Harper & Row, Publishers, Incorporated, 1960) and André Danière, *Higher Education in the American Economy* (New York: Random House, Inc., 1964).

port in these two crucial areas is increasingly necessary if we seek to accelerate our rate of growth. A report of the Joint Economic Committee of Congress concludes that:[13]

A program of Federal aid to education, designed to help the poorer school districts, is the single most important step that can be taken to raise our longrun economic growth . . . [and] the Federal government must continue to exercise financial responsibility for our scientific establishment . . . the Government must make sure that sufficient scientific resources are put into basic, rather than applied, research.

Can expansion of governmental activity in the areas of basic scientific research and education be justified on economic grounds? Though there are no universally accepted answers here—witness the endless and heated debate on Federal aid to education—proponents of expanded government spending in these two areas generally base their case on the grounds that basic research and education entail substantial social revenues or that they have the primary characteristics of social goods (Chapter 6).

Let us examine the area of basic scientific research. The first point to note is that basic research may entail benefits or revenues which go far beyond those realized by the sponsoring firm, that is, substantial social revenues or benefits may accrue to society as a whole. For example, provided the new knowledge is made freely available, the development of a new heat-resistant material might yield substantial benefits for, say, the electronics industry which sponsored the development, but also for a host of other industries ranging from automobiles and home appliances to our national space program. This means that, because it is geared to private benefit as measured by profitability, research activity of this type carried on by private firms will be deficient in amount. In other words, the demand for basic research facilities will understate the total benefits derivable from resulting discoveries. You will recall from Chapter 6 that

[13] Joint Economic Committee, *op. cit.*, p. 31.

the correction of such an underallocation calls for government subsidization.

Secondly, in some instances—for example, atomic energy, space exploration, oceanography, meteorology, preventive medicine, and so forth—the required scope of the research undertaking is simply beyond the means of private enterprise. That is, research in these areas is a social good. The price system would allocate few or no resources to such projects, despite their obvious real and potential significance. Finally, resources may also be underallocated to basic research activities because of the great uncertainty as to profitability and the potentially long payoff period on successful research which may cause risk-avoiding and conservative firms to shun basic research in favor of more practical applied research undertakings.

Similar arguments can be, and have been (Chapter 6), made in justifying public support of education. All these arguments, however, do not deny the existence of legitimate disagreement as to the specific level at which public spending for research and education should be determined.

GROWTH, UNEMPLOYMENT, AND INFLATION

Having analyzed structural unemployment and the debate over the adequacy of our growth rate, we now turn to a final growth-related problem: Have the causes and characteristics of inflation changed substantially as long-run growth has enhanced the opulence of our economy?

Traditionally, inflation has been regarded as the result of excess total demand. That is, the *demand-pull theory* of inflation states that once the economy is operating at the full-employment level and the total output therefore becomes fixed, an excess of total demand will necessarily have the effect of pulling up the price level. Because the demand-pull theory assumes considerable flexibility of resource and product prices, changes in the composition or structure—but not the size—of total demand will leave the price level unchanged. In those sectors of the economy in which demand is increasing, prices will rise; but these increases will be offset by compensating price declines in those segments of the economy in which demand has fallen. On balance, then, a change in the structure of demand should change the *structure* of prices yet leave the overall price *level* constant.

Policies for dealing with demand-pull inflation are evident and familiar to us (Chapters 14 and 18). The policy goal is to eliminate the excess of total demand which is pulling the price level upward. Appropriate fiscal policy calls for tax increases and reductions in government spending, whereas monetary policy demands tight money.

The New Inflation: Two Theories

The demand-pull theory of inflation is widely accepted by economists, and over the years it has provided a useful and accurate explanation of our inflationary experiences. At least, it did until the late 1950s. In the 1955–1958 period in particular, price-level–employment fluctuations occurred which were not readily explainable in terms of a simple demand-pull theory. During the 1957–1958 recession, for example, economists were embarrassed to find that employment and output were *declining*, while at the same time the general price level was *rising*. Between 1956 and 1958 the consumer price index rose by 6 points, while in the same period the index of industrial production fell by 6 points, and unemployment jumped from 4.2 to 6.8 per cent of the labor force (see table on inside covers). Major industries, such as automobiles and steel, found themselves with excess capacity and partially employed labor forces; yet wages and prices continued to creep upward. This oddity prompted economists to restudy in detail the whole inflationary problem and has resulted in two possible explanations of the "new" inflation: the cost-push theory and the theory of structural inflation. Both these new explanations are closely associated with institutional changes—particularly the development of strong labor unions and monopolistic businesses—which have accompanied the process of growth in our economy.

Cost-push inflation. The cost-push theory explains inflation in the absence of full employment in this way: Unions have considerable control over wage rates; that is, they possess considerable market power. Indeed, they have so much market power that even with a moderate deficiency of total demand, some unemployment, and some excess industrial capacity, the stronger unions can demand and obtain wage increases. Large employers, faced now with increased costs but also in the possession of considerable market power, push their increased wage costs and "something extra" on to consumers by raising the prices of their products. This theory is obviously based on the presumption that both unions and businesses typically possess some significant degree of market power and therefore can within limits manipulate wages and prices independent of overall conditions of total demand. Thus it is that we find cost-push inflation sometimes labeled "administered price" inflation or simply "seller's inflation."

Not surprisingly, management contends that wage increases initiate price increases, and therefore unions are obviously the villain, nudging wages and necessarily prices upward at a time when inflation otherwise would not occur. Labor counters by charging that the power of big businesses to adjust or administer prices results in price increases which are neither initiated nor justified by increases in wage costs.

Structural inflation.[14] A second, more recent explanation of the inflation-with-unemployment situation centers upon the effects of a change in the structure, though not the size, of total demand. Briefly stated, the rationale

[14] See Charles L. Schultze, *Recent Inflation in the United States*, Study Paper No. 1 for the Joint Economic Committee (Washington, D.C., 1959) and also Professor Schultze's "Creeping Inflation: Causes and Consequences," *Business Horizons*, Summer, 1960, pp. 65–77.

is based on the fact that for a number of reasons—a basic one of which is the market power of businesses and unions—prices and wages tend to be flexible upward but inflexible downward (Chapters 11 and 12). Now let us suppose that total demand is not excessive; as a matter of fact, let us assume that it is slightly deficient, resulting in, say, 5 per cent unemployment. Now a rather sharp change in the structure or composition of this total demand occurs. This structural change in demand means that prices and wages will rise in those segments of the economy experiencing an expanding demand. However, because of their downward stickiness, wages and prices will not fall, or at least will not fall by much, in those sectors of the economy witnessing a declining demand. The result is a net increase in the price and wage levels; that is, inflation will occur. Remember: This inflation arises despite the fact that there is less than full employment and the economy is failing to realize its growth potential.

But this is not all. Secondary effects may intensify structural inflation by transmitting wage and price rises from the increasing-demand segments of the economy to other sectors where demand might be unchanged or even falling. Suppose, for example, that one of the industries most favorably affected by our assumed change in the structure of total demand is the steel industry. The result will be a tendency for steel prices and profits to rise. But now the big steel firms are a lucrative target for the United Steelworkers of America, which demands and receives wage increases. At this point the secondary, transmitting effects enter the picture. On the one hand, a host of industries using significant quantities of steel—including those unaffected and adversely affected by the change in the structure of total demand—find themselves faced with higher material costs. So they raise their prices to cover these cost boosts. And, as it happens, the wage increases which occur in the steel industry tend to create pressures for wage increases in other related industries such as aluminum, copper, and other fabricated metal product

industries—even though these industries may be among those faced with a constant or sagging product demand. Wage rates in these related industries are traditionally patterned after wages in steel. Hence, when steel wages go up, union leaders in these related industries will be under pressure to secure comparable increases for their constituents. And, of course, the fact that the cost of living is rising provides the basis for demanding these increases. As a matter of fact, if existing collective bargaining agreements in these related or, indeed, in other unrelated industries, contain "escalator clauses," wage rates will automatically go up as the consumer price index rises.

Oddly enough, employers in the related industries may feel obligated to grant wage increases because the severing of a traditional relationship between wages in the steel industry and the related industries may undermine worker morale and impair productivity in the latter. Firms in the related industries then recover these wage increases by raising product prices. The point is this: Through these several avenues, wage and price increases originating in those sectors of the economy which are prosperous because of the favorable change in the composition of demand spill over into other sectors of the economy where the change in the structure of demand has caused unemployment and excess productive capacity. In short, a sharp change in the composition of a given level of total demand may be inflationary in both favorably and unfavorably affected segments of the economy. This explains the paradox of inflation with unemployment; changes in the composition of demand may cause the price level to rise even though total demand is deficient and unemployment is increasing.

It must be emphasized that these three theories—demand-pull, cost-push, and structural inflation—are not unrelated or mutually exclusive. All three can operate simultaneously. For example, a rising level of total demand whose composition is significantly changing can cause both demand-pull and structural inflation simultaneously.

And the exertion of market power may cause cost-push forces to accentuate this inflation, particularly in those industries where unions are strong and demand most favorably affected. Thus, a careful analysis of the late 1950s reveals all three types of inflationary pressure present in varying degrees.

Public Policy and the New Inflation

To the extent that the new inflation—cost-push and structural inflation—occurs in a growing economy, a serious public policy dilemma is posed. The reason: The new inflation can occur when total demand is deficient. And our major anti-inflationary weapons—monetary policy and fiscal policy—are designed to halt inflation by restraining total demand and forcing it into balance with the current value of the full-employment level of total output. In other words, available stabilization techniques are simply not very relevant in dealing with inflation, the source of which is not excess total demand, but rather cost-push forces and structural changes in total demand.

As a matter of fact, it is just possible that the application of a tight money policy to the new inflation might do more harm than good. Tight money, you will recall, has a *general* contractionary impact upon the economy. Now the only way tight money can be at all effective in getting at the new inflation is the indirect one of restricting the market demand for products in order to force employers to resist wage increases more vigorously. This restriction of demand, if sufficiently large, may ultimately curb the new inflation. But the accompanying costs may be great—increased unemployment and a retarded rate of economic growth. Some economists feel this sort of thing occurred during the 1957–1958 recession when cost-push and structural factors accounted for a significant share of the price-level increases. The government applied a tight money policy to an inflationary situation which tight money is simply not equipped to handle. The resulting restriction of total demand simply added to existing unem-

ployment and slowed expansion of the GNP, but accomplished little by way of halting inflation.

New Policy: The Productivity Rule

If unions and businesses possess considerable market power, and if currently available stabilization techniques cannot halt inflation except at the prohibitive cost of unemployment and impeded growth, what techniques, if any, can be invoked to halt the new inflation? The answer put forward by the Federal government in recent years is that as a general rule wage increases should be limited to the overall rate of increase in the nation's productivity.[15] The rationale of this guidepost is simply that if the average hourly output of workers increases by, say, 2 per cent, employers can increase wages by 2 per cent without experiencing any increase in labor costs per unit of output. Because wage increases of this magnitude keep labor costs per unit of output constant, there is no cost-push pressure to increase product prices.

But what mechanism can be used to make such a guidepost to noninflationary wage increases effective?[16] How can labor and management be made to recognize and abide by this rule?

1. Voluntary restraint. One suggested approach is to have the President, the Secretary of Labor, and other respected public officials make appeals and admonitions to labor and business leaders, encouraging them to exercise self-restraint in reaching wage-price decisions. Now although the use of this form of moral suasion with respect to collective bargaining and price setting may be of some effectiveness in some situations, some observers seriously discount its overall useful-

[15] *Economic Report of the President* (Washington, D.C., 1962), pp. 185–190.
[16] See Abraham L. Gitlow, *The National Wage Policy: Antecedents and Application* (New York: New York University Press, 1964), for an excellent summary of the many conceptual and statistical problems which arise in applying the productivity rule.

ness. The basic weakness of "creeping admonitionism," as cynics label it, is that it asks businessmen and labor leaders to abandon their primary functions—to forgo the goals of higher wages and profits.

2. Reducing market power. A second avenue for attacking the new inflation embraces the rationale that, if the market power of business and labor is causing inflation, this market power must be reduced or eliminated. Unions and businesses must be made to face such vigorous competition that they will be unable to increase wage rates ahead of productivity. But how? One recommendation is to apply our antitrust laws more vigorously to big business, and possibly to unions too. Or another proposal is to prohibit unions from bargaining on a centralized, nationwide level, forcing each local union to bargain with its own immediate employer. This decentralization of union power and authority, it is hoped, will ameliorate cost-push inflation.

But serious questions can be raised about such proposals. Antitrust legislation, we shall discover (Chapter 34), has not been particularly successful in restricting the power of big business. Nor is it clear that antitrust can be applied to labor without virtually destroying unions and the institution of collective bargaining. Finally, there is little evidence to suggest that localized wage setting results in more socially acceptable wage rates than does centralized bargaining. Indeed, interlocal union rivalries, petty grievances, and less ability to realize the social consequences of its actions may all tend to make local bargaining more aggressive and potentially more inflationary than centralized bargaining.

3. Increased government participation and control. A number of observers have reluctantly come to the conclusion that some degree of government participation in, or regulation of, wage-price determination in key industries—for example, steel and automobiles—must be invoked if the new inflation is to be controlled without depressing the level of employment and the rate of growth. A variety of techniques might be employed. For example, the Federal government might simply establish a "study group" to publicize wage and price changes. Or a fact-finding board might hold hearings on proposed wage and price increases in key industries, and possibly issue a report or recommendations based thereon. Others suggest that, because major wage agreements affect the price level, and therefore the public interest, the public interest should be represented by having public officials participate in key collective bargaining negotiations. Or the government may legislate the right to suspend or delay wage or price increases which are significantly in excess of productivity increases. Finally, government, at the extreme, might simply establish public control over wages and prices in crucial industries such as steel, where the inflationary potential of substantial wage and price increases is great. These wage-price controls would be reminiscent of those exercised by the government during World War II to contain the strong inflationary pressures then existing.

These various proposals clearly entail considerable gradations in the degree of government control and participation. In particular, government participation in wage negotiations, public authority to reject proposed wage-price increases, and direct wage-price controls embody far-reaching changes in our economic way of life. Hence, many economists feel these techniques to be of a "last resort" character, to be used only if less drastic means are ineffective and if the inflationary problem becomes severe. At the same time it is important to note that many of these as yet relatively untried and unexplored means of getting at the causes of the new inflation are being accorded serious consideration by both economists and public officials.

SUMMARY

1. Though rapid economic growth is a desirable social objective, it does entail certain costs and can contribute to and create socioeconomic problems.

2. The main costs of growth include: the forgoing of current consumption; less leisure and a more rapid pace of economic life; wasteful exploitation of natural resources; enhanced short-run instability; and economic insecurity for those adversely affected by economic change.

3. Such growth-associated factors as **a.** technological advance as reflected in the automation of production and the development of new products; **b.** changes in consumer demand; and **c.** the geographic relocation of industry have resulted in structural unemployment and chronically depressed areas.

4. The readjustment or reallocation process is seriously impeded in chronically depressed areas because **a.** labor is relatively immobile geographically and **b.** most structurally unemployed workers in, say, the coal, automobile, textile, and railway equipment industries do not have the education or skills for reemployment in such new growing industries as electronics, plastics, synthetics, and so forth.

5. Proposals of aid for depressed areas entail either or both of two approaches: **a.** the geographic and occupational relocation of structurally unemployed workers and **b.** the economic revitalization of depressed areas by the attraction of new industries.

6. Some respected observers feel the United States' growth rate is quite adequate and that, given the size of our GNP, little would be gained in military power or in improving the impression we make on underdeveloped nations by more rapid growth. Indeed, the policy measures necessary to the acceleration of our growth rate might seriously threaten our way of economic life. Others feel more rapid growth is vital in order to **a.** take care of our low-income people; **b.** more strongly illustrate the vitality and efficiency of our economy to the rest of the world; and **c.** enhance our ability and willingness to increase our military strength

and foreign aid programs. More rapid growth, it is argued, will strengthen, not weaken, our institutions and ideology.

7. Basic policies for accelerating United States growth include **a.** the maintenance of full employment, **b.** increased spending on research, and **c.** expanded outlays on education. The fact that research and education entail substantial social revenues or are social goods underlies the argument that substantial public support in these areas is justified.

8. Although the demand-pull theory still provides the basic explanation of inflation, our unemployment-with-inflation experience of the late 1950s has caused economists to talk of a "new inflation" explainable in terms of cost-push forces and changes in the structure of total demand. The theory of cost-push inflation asserts that the market power of unions and big businesses may cause wages and prices to rise even when total demand is somewhat short of the full-employment level. The concept of structural inflation indicates that, because wages and prices are inflexible downward but flexible upward, a sharp change in the structure of total demand will cause prices to rise in demand-increasing sectors but to remain constant in demand-decreasing sectors of the economy. The resulting net increases in the price level may be reinforced by secondary effects—for example, pattern bargaining, escalator clauses, the transmission of higher material costs to other industries, and so forth.

9. The Federal government has advanced the "rule" that wage increases should not exceed productivity increases as an anti-inflationary guidepost. Possible means of implementing the productivity rule include **a.** inducing voluntary restraint by labor and management in wage-price determination; **b.** reducing the market power of businesses and unions through vigorous antitrust action and the decentralization of collective bargaining; and **c.** increased government control of, or participation in, the wage- and price-setting processes.

QUESTIONS AND STUDY SUGGESTIONS

1. Identify the costs of economic growth. Which do you feel are the most significant? To what degree, if any, are these various costs avoidable? "Growth contributes to instability and insecurity, but also provides the means to provide for those adversely affected by instability and insecurity." Comment.

2. What is structural unemployment? "There are both a demand and a supply side to the problem of chronic unemployment." Explain. How does structural unemployment differ from cyclical unemployment? What implications do these differences have for the formulation of policies to deal with structural unemployment? Outline and evaluate the two basic policy approaches for dealing with chronic unemployment.

3. Do you feel our economy has been experiencing "creeping unemployment" in the postwar era? "The 'hard core' of unemployment can and should be substantially reduced." Do you agree? If so, formulate an appropriate program.

4. "The problem of reemploying the workers of the chronically depressed areas is, in a sense, an aspect of the law of increasing costs." Do you agree? Explain.

5. Explain the problems implied in the following two statements:
   a. "The production of 6.1 million cars required 928,900 workers in 1953, but only 786,300 in 1957."
   b. "In the last forty years there has been hardly any employment growth in the goods-producing sectors of the economy; by contrast in the same period the number of jobs in the service-producing sectors has more than doubled."

6. Contrast and evaluate the following two statements:
   a. "Government measures to reverse or slow down such declines in employment in particular sectors of the economy are not likely to be successful and are likely to be extremely costly. . . . We should beware of becoming involved in a . . . hopeless and . . . costly program for rescuing distressed areas."[17]
   b. "It does not seem fair to deny progress to a society in order to protect a few. Nor does it seem fair for society to accept all the gain at the expense of a few. Therefore, it would seem that society should find some way of caring for those who lose out by progress."[18]

7. What programs might be employed to accelerate our economic growth? Can an expansion in the role of government necessitated by these programs be justified on economic grounds? Evaluate: "The relationship between economic growth and individual liberties is such that one can be achieved only at the expense of the other."

8. Briefly analyze and evaluate:
   a. ". . . human capabilities do not stay abreast of physical capital, and they do become limiting factors in economic growth."

[17] *Unemployment: Causes and Cures* (New York: National Association of Manufacturers, April, 1961), pp. 8–9.
[18] Bruce R. Morris, *Problems of American Economic Growth* (Fair Lawn, N.J.: Oxford University Press, 1961), p. 219.

b. ". . . we should consider creating government-sponsored productivity institutes to stimulate research for industries where increases in output appear particularly necessary."

c. ". . . under our present economic structure the social benefits of basic research are not adequately reflected in opportunities for private profit. Indeed, there is a basic contradiction between the conditions necessary for efficient basic research—few or no constraints on the direction of research with full and free dissemination of research results—and full appropriation of the gains from sponsoring basic research in a competitive economy."[19]

d. "The best way to stimulate growth is to fight inflation. This is so for several reasons. First, inflation will undermine incentives to save and therefore limit investment. Furthermore, only with price stability is healthy, maintainable growth possible. Finally, creeping inflation inevitably accelerates to a gallop and precipitates economic collapse."

9. Discuss and compare the assumptions and operations of (*a*) demand-pull, (*b*) cost-push, and (*c*) structural inflation. Outline a program to deal with an inflation which occurs when 5 per cent of the labor force is unemployed. Briefly evaluate the "productivity rule" as a guide for noninflationary wage increases.

10. "In the contemporary institutional setting of our economy, the principal effect of tight money is not to control inflation, but to create unemployment and the underutilization of capacity, and to slow down the rate of growth." Explain and evaluate.

SELECTED REFERENCES

The American Assembly: *Automation and Technological Change* (Englewood Cliffs, N.J.: Prentice-Hall, Inc., 1962).

Distressed Areas in a Growing Economy (New York: The Committee for Economic Development, June, 1961).

Gutmann, Peter M. (ed.): *Economic Growth: An American Problem* (Englewood Cliffs, N.J.: Prentice-Hall, Inc., 1964).

Hansen, Alvin H., *Economic Issues of the 1960's* (New York: McGraw-Hill Book Company, 1961), chaps. 1–8.

Joint Economic Committee: *Staff Report on Employment, Growth, and Price Levels* (Washington, D.C., 1960), chaps. 1–6.

Knorr, Klaus, and William J. Baumol (eds.): *What Price Economic Growth?* (Englewood Cliffs, N.J.: Prentice-Hall, Inc., 1961).

Morris, Bruce R.: *Problems of American Economic Growth* (Fair Lawn, N.J.: Oxford University Press, 1961).

Silk, Leonard S.: *The Research Revolution* (New York: McGraw-Hill Book Company, 1960).

Thorp, Willard L., and Richard E. Quandt: *The New Inflation* (New York: McGraw-Hill Book Company, 1959).

U.S. Department of Labor: *Manpower Report of the President* (Washington, D.C., 1965).

[19] Richard R. Nelson, "The Simple Economics of Basic Scientific Research," *Journal of Political Economy*, June, 1959, p. 305.

PART FIVE: THE ECONOMICS OF THE FIRM
AND RESOURCE ALLOCATION

CHAPTER 22

THE MARKET STRUCTURES OF
AMERICAN CAPITALISM

Scarce resources and unlimited wants, you will recall, are the foundation of economic science. The efficient management of scarce resources is the social goal of all economic processes. Furthermore, there are two major facets to the problem of achieving efficient resource use. The first, which we have examined in Parts Two and Three and, to some degree, in Part Four of this book, centers upon the full employment of available resources. The second aspect of the economizing problem—the one to which we now turn—has to do with allocating employed resources among alternative uses in the most efficient manner. Stated differently, Parts Two, Three, and Four focused upon the last of the Five Fundamental Questions posed in Chapter 2: "Can the economy achieve the full employment of its available resources?" Part Five deals with the first four questions: "Can the economy produce that output most desired by society?" "Will the production of that output be organized in the most efficient manner?" "Can the economy successfully distribute that output?" "Is the economy capable of maintaining efficiency in the use of its resources in the face of changes in the relative supplies of resources, changes in consumer tastes, and changes in technology?" All four of these questions obviously have an important bearing on the problem of achieving and maintaining an efficient allocation of available resources.

We are well aware that one of the major characteristics of capitalistic economies is their heavy reliance upon a price system as a means for allocating resources (Chapter 5). Our major topics of discussion, then, are prices and the price system. Specifically, our basic goal in the ensuing chapters is to acquire a comprehensive understanding of the operation and relative efficiency of the *price system* in allocating resources within the framework of American capitalism. As a means to achieving this primary goal, we also seek a thorough analysis of *individual prices* under a variety of contrasting market arrangements.

Using the product market as a point of reference, the present chapter defines and describes the various market arrangements we propose to examine. In the subsequent chapters in Part Five we review and apply our previous analysis of demand and supply, enhance our understanding of the demand side of the market, explore the production (supply) side of the market through a discussion of production costs—the major determinant of a firm's willingness to supply a given product—and examine in some detail the interaction of supply and demand under the various market arrangements described in the present chapter. Our attention will then shift to the functioning of prices in the resource market. Finally, the overall operation of the price system in American capitalism is evaluated.

FOUR BASIC MARKET MODELS

There is no such thing as an "average" or "typical" industry. Detailed examination of the business sector of American capitalism reveals an almost infinite number of different market situations; no two industries are alike. At one extreme we may find a single producer completely dominating a particular market. At the other we discover thousands upon thousands—yes, even millions—of firms, each of which supplies a minute fraction of total or market output. Between these extremes lies an almost unlimited variety of market arrangements, most of which shade into one another.

Obviously, any attempt to examine each specific industry would be an endless and impossible task. There are simply too many of them. Hence, we seek a more realistic objective—to define and discuss several basic market structures, or models. In so doing we shall acquaint ourselves with the *general* way in which price and output are determined in most of the market types which characterize American capitalism.

But the use of a few market models as typifying most of American industries calls for a word or two of caution. First, the market models to be considered are necessarily abstractions. They are merely first approximations and as such do not purport to present a clear or complete picture of reality (see Chapter 1). In no case will the market models we are about to define provide a *detailed* explanation of the functioning of any specific firm. Yet they will do a reasonably good job of outlining the operation of many firms.

Furthermore, some firms and industries will not fall neatly within any of the market models we are about to outline; rather they will bear characteristics of two or more of these models. This means that the classification of a given firm or industry might entail an element of arbitrariness. This is the same type of problem which other scientists encounter. The botanist, for example, classifies all plants under three family groups—algae and fungi (thallophytes), moss plants (bryophytes), and vascular plants (tracheophytes). Yet many forms of plant life do not neatly fit into any one of these families but rather

are borderline cases. So it is with the economist in classifying industries.

Finally, it is important to recognize at the outset that the economist's definitions of the basic market models do not coincide with those typically employed by businessmen and laymen. The definitions which follow are not of common-sense vintage. "Competition," for example, has a much more precise meaning to the economist than it does to the average businessman.

Economists envision four relatively distinct market situations. These are (1) pure competition, (2) pure monopoly, (3) monopolistic competition, and (4) oligopoly. The immediate task is to describe the major characteristics of each of these four market models. In doing so we shall use the seller's side of the product market as a point of reference. We shall see later that the same general models also are relevant for the buying side of the market.

Pure Competition

A purely competitive market has several distinct characteristics which set it off from other market structures.

1. A main feature of a purely competitive market is the presence of a large number of independently acting sellers, usually offering their products in a highly organized market.

2. Competitive firms are producing a standardized or virtually standardized product. Given price, the consumer is indifferent as to the seller from which he purchases. In a competitive market the products of firms B, C, D, E, and so forth are looked upon by the buyer as perfect substitutes for that of firm A.

3. In a purely competitive market *individual firms* exert no significant control over product price. This characteristic follows from the preceding two. Under pure competition each firm produces such a small fraction of total output that increasing or decreasing its output will have no perceptible influence upon total supply or, therefore,

product price. To illustrate, assume there are 10,000 competing firms, each of which is currently producing 100 units of output. Total supply is obviously 1,000,000. Now suppose one of these 10,000 firms cuts its output to 50 units. Will this affect price? No. And the reason is clear: This restriction of output by a single firm has an almost imperceptible impact on total supply—specifically, the total quantity supplied declines from 1,000,000 to 999,950. This is obviously not enough of a change in total supply to affect product price noticeably. In short, the individual competitive producer cannot adjust market price; he can only adjust to it.

Stated differently, pricewise the individual competitive producer is at the mercy of the market; to him product price is a given datum over which he exerts no influence. He can get the same price per unit for a large output as he can for a small output. To ask a price higher than the going market price would be futile. Consumers will not buy anything from firm A at a price of $2.10 when his 9,999 competitors are selling an identical and therefore perfect substitute product at $2 per unit. Conversely, because firm A can sell as much as it chooses at $2 per unit, there is no reason for it to charge some lower price, say, $1.95. Indeed, to do so would shrink its profits.

Finally, a subtle but highly important point: Although the *individual* firm cannot influence product price by varying its output, all firms in a competitive industry taken *as a group* can cause market price to vary. Should all 10,000 firms cut their outputs from 100 to 50 units, the total quantity supplied will decline from 1,000,000 to 500,000 units. This is most certainly a very significant change and can be expected to boost product price considerably. In brief, the individual firm cannot significantly influence price, but all firms as a group can. Although product price to an individual competitive seller is fixed, that price is free to move up or down in accordance with changes in either *total* demand or *total* supply.

4. New firms are free to enter and existing firms are free to leave purely competitive industries. In particular, no significant obstacles—legal, technical, financial, or other—exist to prohibit new firms from coming into being and selling their outputs in competitive markets.

5. Because purely competitive firms are producing a standardized product, there is virtually no room for *nonprice competition*, that is, competition on the basis of differences in product quality, advertising, or sales promotion. By definition each firm in a competitive market is producing an identical product. Hence, no firm has a quality edge over its rivals. Advertising by individual firms will be to no avail, because each firm's product has no distinguishing features to be advertised or promoted. Buyers will know that the products of all firms in the industry have the same features. Advertising has virtually no chance of convincing them otherwise.

What about examples? Really precise examples of pure competition are few and far between. If we neglect the government's farm program, agriculture provides us with most of the good illustrations. Thus, we find, for example, that there are literally millions of farmers producing class I corn—a product which is obviously standardized or uniform. Class I corn is class I corn! Each firm supplies such a small fraction of the total that no single farmer has any control over the market price for class I corn. He accepts the market price which exists in the highly organized market as a datum over which he has no influence; the individual farmer can sell as much or as little as he wants without affecting that price. He does not squander his financial resources on advertising or sales promotion. Farmer Jones knows that millions of other farmers are producing an identical product and that buyers are well aware of this. Hence, advertising would be futile, a sheer waste of time, effort, and money. The markets for wheat, cotton, barley, oats, the various types of livestock, and a good many other farm staples also fit rather well into the competitive mold we have outlined.

Pure Monopoly

Now we turn to the other extreme of the spectrum. Pure monopoly provides us with the sharpest contrast to pure competition.

1. A pure, or absolute, monopolist is a one-firm industry. A single firm is the only producer of a given product; hence, the firm and the industry are synonymous.

2. It follows from this first characteristic that the monopolist's product is unique in the sense that there are no good, or close, substitutes available. From the buyer's point of view this means that he has no reasonable alternatives to which he can turn. He must buy the product from the monopolist or do without.

A question arises at this point: When are products "good" substitutes? There is no clear answer to this query. In a very broad sense all goods and services which compete for the consumer's dollar are substitutes. A down payment on a house may be a substitute for a new automobile. A two-week vacation may be a substitute for a television set. A pair of shoes may be a substitute for a new pair of slacks. A symphony concert may be a substitute for a fraternity dance. Yet in a more restricted sense of the term it is clear that some products and services simply do not have reasonably good substitutes. Candles and kerosene lamps are not good substitutes for electric lights. Other spices are poor substitutes for salt. Bus or train transportation may be a poor substitute for owning one's own automobile. To many, a symphony concert is no substitute at all for the Signa Phi Nothing formal.

In our discussion we shall employ the idea of substitution in the narrower sense of the term. Hence, we can agree that, as most consumers see it, there are no good substitutes for the water piped into our homes by the municipal water works or the electric power provided by the local power company. Digging a well or importing water from a neighboring community is not a realistic substitute for running water in one's home. And few would regard candles and kerosene lighting as acceptable substitutes for electric lights. In any event your television set will not run on kerosene. Up to World War II manufacturers whose products entailed the need for a strong but lightweight metal had little choice but to purchase aluminum from Alcoa; no competing aluminum producers were in existence prior to the war.

3. We have emphasized that the individual firm operating under pure competition exercises no influence over product price. This is so because he contributes only a negligible portion of total supply. In vivid contrast the pure monopolist exercises considerable control over price. And the reason is obvious: He is responsible for, and therefore controls, the total quantity supplied. By manipulating the amount supplied he can cause product price to change. If it is to his advantage, we can expect him to use his power in this way.

4. If, by definition, a pure monopolist has no immediate competitors, there must be a reason for this lack of competition. And there is: The existence of monopoly depends upon the existence of barriers to entry. Be they economic, technological, legal, or other, certain obstacles must exist to keep new competitors from coming into the industry if monopoly is to persist. Entry is not easy under conditions of pure monopoly; on the contrary, it is blocked. More of this in Chapter 27.

5. Depending upon the type of product or service involved, monopolists may or may not engage in extensive advertising and sales promotion activity. Local public utilities see no point in large expenditures for advertising; any local citizen who wants water, gas, and electric power and telephone service already knows from whom he must buy.

If pure monopolists do advertise, such advertising is likely to be of a public relations, or good-will, character rather than highly competitive, as is the advertising associated with, say, cigarettes, soap flakes, and beer.

Because they have no immediate rivals, monopolists, in trying to induce more people to buy their products, need not invoke the ours-is-better-than-theirs type of advertising which plagues radio, television, and otherwise scenic highways. Rather the monopolist's pitch is likely to be "We're really nice fellows and certainly wouldn't do anything to exploit other firms, our beloved employees, or, heaven forbid, consumers." Or the monopolist may be anxious for the public to recognize that at least 90 per cent of the firm's stock is held by destitute widows and orphans. Or, finally, the monopolist may be content simply to point out the technological progress for which the firm has been responsible.

Because pure monopoly is admittedly an extreme market model, we once again find relatively few precise illustrations. Most local public utilities are pure monopolists for the municipalities which they serve. Thus consumers either purchase their water, electricity, gas, and telephone service from the local utility or do without. Much the same may hold true of railway service in rural areas. On a nationwide basis American Telephone and Telegraph approximates a pure monopoly. Pullman Standard is the sole manufacturer of sleeping cars for the nation's railroads. Until World War II, Alcoa was a virtual monopolist in the production of most basic aluminum products; now it faces some competition from Reynolds and Kaiser. The United Shoe Machinery Company is the only manufacturer of certain equipment used in the production of shoes. IBM is the only source of certain calculating machines.

This is not to say that the pure monopolist will charge the highest price he can get for his product or service. Consumers may find it impossible to do without some amount of water and highly inconvenient to do without some quantity of electricity. But the amounts they purchase will vary inversely with price. If the prices of electricity and water were extremely high, the poor (but cheap) substitutes of kerosene lamps and digging a well would become relevant. And an extremely high price on office machines might induce firms to substitute bookkeepers for the machines.

Monopolistic Competition

As its name indicates, monopolistic competition stands between the extremes of pure competition and pure monopoly. It embraces characteristics of both, but for the most part it stands closer to pure competition.

1. As is the case with pure competition, monopolistic competition entails a large number of sellers acting independently. This does not mean that there need be 1,000, 10,000, or 1,000,000 firms in the industry; 30, 40, or 100 firms of more or less equal size may prevail. The important point is that each firm produces a fairly small share of the total output.

2. In contrast to pure competition, wherein the product is standardized, *product differentiation* is a major characteristic of monopolistically competitive industries. Product differentiation entails not only physical differences in the products of various producers or sellers in the industry, but also differences in such factors as the location and "snob appeal" of the seller's store, the packaging of the product, the cordiality of the firm's salespeople, the effectiveness of its advertising, the availability of credit, the company's reputation for servicing or "making good on" defective products, and so forth. The net result is that, although all firms in such an industry are producing the same general type or class of product, the particular product of each firm will have certain distinguishing features which set it off to some extent from those of other firms in the industry. In other words, the products of monopolistically competitive firms are close, but not perfect, substitutes. Just as the presence of a relatively large number of firms makes for competition, product differentiation gives rise to a measure of monopoly power. Indeed, monopolistic competition is sometimes called "the case of differentiation and large numbers."

3. Monopolistically competitive producers have a limited amount of control over product price. The control that exists depends essentially upon the degree of product differentiation and the number and proximity of competitors. The monopolistically competitive producer can raise his price modestly without having his sales fall to zero. Why? Because buyers recognize some differences between the products of various sellers. In the presence of product differentiation consumers are likely to have definite preferences for the products of specific sellers, and relatively small price increases by one firm will not cause all buyers to seek out the close substitute products of rival firms in that industry. Generally, when the rivals of a monopolistically competitive firm are many in number and in close proximity, each firm's control over price will be less than would otherwise be the case.

4. Entry into monopolistically competitive industries is typically easy. Nevertheless, entry may be a bit more difficult under monopolistically competitive conditions than when pure competition prevails. This is so because of product differentiation. A new firm must not only obtain the capital necessary to go into business but must also win clients away from existing firms. Securing a share of the market might entail considerable research and product development costs by the new firm to ensure that its product will have features which distinguish it from products already on the market. Similarly, considerable advertising outlays may be necessary to inform consumers of the existence of a new brand and to convince a number of them that it will be to their advantage to switch to the new product. In short, greater financial obstacles may face the potential newcomer under monopolistic competition than under pure competition.

5. Because products are differentiated, monopolistically competitive industries are ordinarily characterized by vigorous competition in other areas than price. Economic rivalry, as we have already noted, may be based not only on price, but also on product quality, advertising, and conditions or services associated with the sale of a product. Great emphasis is placed upon trademarks and brand names as means for convincing the consumer that the products of one's rivals are not as good substitutes for brand X as might first seem to be the case. Indeed, quality and advertising competition go hand in hand. Advertising proclaims and, if possible, magnifies real differences in product quality. While quality competition manipulates the firm's product, advertising and sales promotion attempt to manipulate the consumer.

A considerable number of industries approximate the conditions of monopolistic competition (see Table 28–1). At the manufacturing level the women's dress industry provides a good example; New York City and a few other large metropolitan areas are the locations of the large number of small manufacturers which constitute this industry. The shoe industry also has features which make it reasonably close to being monopolistically competitive. A good many types of retail trade, particularly in cities of any size, occur under conditions which approximate monopolistic competition. Most cities will contain a fairly large number of grocery stores, cleaning establishments, clothing shops, gasoline stations, restaurants, barber shops, and so forth, all of which are providing differentiated products and services.

Oligopoly

The remaining market model—oligopoly—is less precisely defined by economists than are the three market structures just discussed. Two reasons go far to explain this lack of preciseness. On the one hand, oligopoly includes a wider range of market structures than do the other three market models; in effect it embraces all the remaining market situations which do not fit the rather clearly defined market models of pure competition, monopolistic competition, and pure monopoly. On the other hand, as we shall discover in a moment, oligopoly has certain characteristics which make it difficult to make hard and fast predictions about the behavior of oligopolistic industries.

1. The basic characteristic of oligopoly is "fewness." Oligopoly exists whenever a few firms dominate the market for a product. When we hear of the "Big Three," "Big Four," or "Big Six," we can be relatively certain that the industry is oligopolistic. This does not mean, of course, that the Big Three or Four necessarily share the total market. The dominant few may control, say, 70 or 80 per cent of a market, with a competitive fringe—a group of smaller firms—sharing the remainder.

When a few firms dominate a market, each of these firms will have a share of the market sufficiently large so that its actions and policies will have repercussions on the other firms. Because each firm supplies a large portion of the total industry output, actions taken by any one firm to improve its share of the market will directly and immediately affect its rivals. Hence, each firm must carefully weigh the expected reactions of its rivals when considering changes in product price, advertising outlays, product quality, and so forth. Such clear-cut *mutual interdependence* is peculiar to oligopoly. It is not present in pure competition or monopolistic competition because of the large numbers of firms involved. The pure monopolist has no need to worry about the reactions of rivals because he has none. Indeed, it can be said that oligopoly exists whenever the number of sellers is so few that the actions of one will have obvious and significant repercussions on the others. The firms of an oligopolistic industry are all in the same boat. If one rocks the boat, the others will be affected and in all probability will know the identity of the responsible firm and can retaliate.

2. Oligopolists may be producing virtually standardized products or differentiated products. Speaking very generally, those oligopolistic industries which are producing raw materials or semifinished goods are typically offering virtually uniform products to buyers.

For example, most metal products—steel, copper, zinc, lead, and aluminum—along with cement, rayon, explosives, industrial alcohol, and some building materials, are virtually uniform goods produced in markets in which a few large firms are dominant. On the other hand, oligopolistic industries producing finished consumer goods are typically offering differentiated products to buyers. Automobiles, tires, petroleum products, soap, cigarettes, fountain pens, breakfast foods, aircraft, farm implements, plus a host of electrical appliances—refrigerators, radios, electric razors, and so forth—are produced by oligopolistic industries wherein product differentiation is considerable.[1]

3. An individual oligopolistic firm's control over price tends to be closely circumscribed by the mutual interdependence which characterizes such markets. Specifically, if a given firm lowers price, it will initially gain sales at the expense of its several rivals. However, these adversely affected rivals will have little choice but to retaliate to recover their shrinking shares of the market; they will match or even undercut the given firm to preserve their market share. The result may be a price war and possibly losses for all firms. Conversely, if a given oligopolist increases his price, rival firms stand to gain sales and profits by adhering to their present prices. That is, a price-boosting oligopolist runs the risk of "pricing himself out of the market" to the benefit of his rivals. For both these reasons there is a strong tendency for firms in oligopolist markets not to alter their prices very frequently.

The potentially adverse effects of price warring or pricing oneself out of the market can be largely avoided by a group of oligopolistic firms through the establishment of some sort of collusive agreement by which all firms either increase or decrease their prices as a group. Under such a collusive arrangement

[1] Illustrations are from Joe S. Bain, *Pricing, Distribution, and Employment,* rev. ed. (New York: Holt, Rinehart and Winston, Inc., 1953), pp. 273–274, 333.

the firms as a group can exert control over price in much the same way as can a pure monopolist.

4. Obstacles to entry are typically formidable in oligopolistic industries. The ownership of strategic patents or essential raw materials by existing firms may virtually prohibit the entry of new firms. Furthermore, the technology of heavy industry may demand that a new competitor be a large-scale producer from the outset, thus ruling out the possibility of a new firm's starting on a small-scale basis and in time expanding into a significant rival of existing firms. In addition, certain advantages of being established —that is, the mere fact that existing firms are producing well-known, highly advertised products and selling them through long-established marketing outlets—may work against the successful entrance of new firms into the industry. Yet, in contrast to pure monopoly, entry is not usually blocked completely in oligopolistic industries. For example, the relatively recent entry of Sylvania Electric into the electrical equipment industry presents a formidable rival for General Electric and Westinghouse. Entry into oligopolistic industries is very difficult, but by no means impossible.

5. Oligopolistic industries frequently channel considerable amounts of resources into advertising and other promotional activities. But the type and amount of advertising will depend upon whether or not the firms are producing standardized or differentiated products.

Advertising competition is likely to be strong among oligopolists who are producing differentiated products. For example, each major automobile producer or cigarette manufacturer will have a large budget for convincing the consumer that his particular product is in all ways superior to those of his rivals. Such advertising is likely to be of a highly competitive ours-is-better-than-theirs nature. On the other hand, public relations advertising is the bill of fare for oligopolists who are producing virtually standardized products. United States Steel does not try to convince the public that its sheet steel is superior to that produced by Republic, Bethlehem, or any of its other rivals. Skilled buyers who purchase the raw or fabricated steel products from these firms know that any differences are negligible. Hence, advertising in such industries is to keep the company in the public's eye, to convince the public that big business is an essential cog in the American economy, and so forth.

Quality competition may be intense under oligopoly, particularly so when product differentiation prevails. The research and design departments of many oligopolistic industries are becoming increasingly important over the years. Indeed, it is through research and rapid product development that the entry of potential rivals into the industry may be thwarted.

A good many American industries fall under the heading of oligopoly. As a matter of fact, most of those industries which come to mind when we think of big business are some form or another of oligopoly. In addition to the specific examples previously mentioned, Table 29–1 contains a list of industries which are oligopolistic.

Imperfect Competition

We shall find it convenient from time to time to distinguish between the characteristics of a purely competitive market and those of all other basic market arrangements—pure monopoly, monopolistic competition, and oligopoly. To facilitate such comparisons we shall employ "imperfect competition" as a generic term to designate all those market structures which deviate from the purely competitive market model.

THE BUYER'S SIDE OF THE MARKET

The preceding definitions of the four basic market models are couched in terms of the seller's side of the market. The same variety of market arrangements can and does exist on the buying or demand side. Here, however, the classification is almost exclusively based on the number of buyers. For example, a very large number of purchasers obviously means pure competition on the buying side of the market. *Monopsony* describes the situation in which there is only one buyer. When a few buyers dominate a market, *oligopsony* exists. *Monopsonistic competition* designates the presence of a fairly large number of buyers.

With the selling and buying sides of the market placed together as in Figure 22–1, it is easy to recognize that an almost infinite number of seller-buyer relationships can exist. A few representative examples will help underscore this point. The public utilities field is usually characterized by pure monopoly on the selling side and pure competition on the buying side. The market for raw tobacco links a large number of purely competitive tobacco farmers on the selling side with a few large buyers—American, Liggett and Myers, Lorillard, and Reynolds—dominating the demand side. Where a strong union exists, specific labor markets often approximate *bilateral monopoly*—pure monopoly on one side and pure monopsony on the other. The local union is the "seller" of labor services, and the company is the single buyer. In the "original equipment" segment of the automobile tire market we have oligopsonistic buyers—General Motors, Ford, and Chrysler—linked with oligopolistic sellers—Goodyear, Firestone, U.S. Rubber, and B. F. Goodrich. A similar arrangement exists in the market for tin plate—a few large steel companies are the sole producers, and two large tin-can manufacturers are the major buyers. And so it goes. When all the hybrid cases falling between the four basic market models are taken into account, it is clear that the number of possible market arrangements can be and actually is extremely large.

OTHER COMPETITIVE DIMENSIONS

It is important that we qualify and amend the foregoing definitions and explanations of the various market models in several ways.

Geographic Factor

In practice the competitiveness of an industry or firm is a geographic phenomenon. That is, the degree of competition in a particular industry depends upon the size of the market. Although a given city may have seventy or eighty grocery stores, a particular supermarket in a suburban area may, for all practical purposes, be competing only with

FIGURE 22–1. SOME BASIC MARKET RELATIONSHIPS.
The four basic market models are pertinent to both the selling and buying sides
of markets; this suggests the existence of a very large number
of selling-buying relationships.

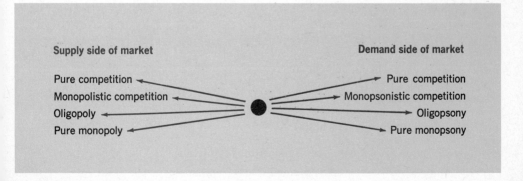

Supply side of market

Pure competition
Monopolistic competition
Oligopoly
Pure monopoly

Demand side of market

Pure competition
Monopsonistic competition
Oligopsony
Pure monopsony

three other chain stores and one or two independent corner groceries. Similarly, commercial banking appears to be highly competitive at first glance—after all, there are over 13,000 banks in our economy providing essentially identical services. But to the farmer in Podunk Center, Iowa, borrowing from the Chase National Bank in New York City or the Bank of America in California is out of the question. In negotiating a loan Farmer Jones will look to the Podunk Center State Bank or possibly one or two of the larger banks in a nearby city.

In short, before hastily labeling an industry as "competitive" or "monopolistic," we must be very sure that we have properly delineated the geographic boundaries of the market. The number of firms alone is not a sufficient criterion by which to gauge the competitiveness of an industry; proximity is important, too.

Interindustry Competition

It is important to recognize the significance of interindustry or interproduct competition. Although a few firms may be the only ones producing a specific product, they may face rather severe rivalry from other somewhat distinct products. Illustrations of such interproduct competition are numerous. The aluminum industry is a strong oligopoly with three firms—Alcoa, Reynolds, and Kaiser—dominating the market. Buyers who must use aluminum have no choice but to do business with one of these three industrial giants. However, in many cases other materials—steel, copper, and even wood or plastics—are suitable substitutes for aluminum. Hence, steel competes with aluminum in the manufacturing of many automobile parts. Aluminum and copper hotly contest the market for transmission lines. Aluminum battles both steel and wood in the construction field. Pricewise, these comments add up to the fact that the control over price which the Big Three of the aluminum industry possesses is subject to limitations dictated by the prices of distinct but nevertheless competing products. Another example: The Big Two of the tin-can industry—American Can and Continental Can—dominate over 80 per cent of their market. From within the industry they face little serious competition. But from without they face the competition of glass, plastic, and paper containers.

Nonprice Competition

This is a convenient juncture at which to restate a point emphasized earlier: Competition is something more than the willingness and ability to cut prices. Competition in other areas than price may be vigorous and important in an industry. Variations in product quality, advertising and promotional activities, and so forth are important elements of competition which may supplement or, in some cases, supplant price competition.

Technological Advance

The previous explanations of the four basic market models tend to classify the various markets at some particular *point* in time. Hence, they neglect an important competitive force which only functions over a *period* of time. That competitive force is technological advance. The development of new products and new techniques of production can result in new competition for producers who previously enjoyed a considerable degree of monopoly power. Thus the leading proponent of the role of technological advance as a competitive force has argued that[2]

. . . in capitalist reality . . . it is . . . competition from the new commodity, the new technology, the new source of supply, the new type of organization (the largest-scale unit of control for instance)—competition which commands a decisive cost or quality advantage and which strikes not at the margins of the profits and the

[2] Joseph A. Schumpeter, *Capitalism, Socialism, and Democracy*, 3d ed. (New York: Harper & Row, Publishers, Incorporated, 1950), pp. 84–85.

outputs of the existing firms but at their foundations and their very lives. This kind of competition is . . . so . . . important that it becomes a matter of comparative indifference whether competition in the ordinary sense functions more or less promptly; the powerful lever that in the long run expands output and brings down prices is in any case made of other stuff.

. . . that competition of the kind we now have in mind acts not only when in being but also when it is merely an ever-present threat. It disciplines before it attacks. The businessman feels himself to be in a competitive situation even if he is alone in his field. . . . In many cases, though not in all, this will in the long run enforce behavior very similar to the perfectly competitive pattern.

An example or two may help to underscore this point. For over a decade a single firm enjoyed the position of a pure monopolist in the production of rayon. Its profits, enormous by any standard, were the results of the successful competition this innovation provided for other textiles. But more recently the development of acetates, nylon, acrilon, and other "miracle fibers" has in turn provided considerable competition for rayon.[3] In a similar manner the rapid development of the dehydrated and quick-frozen food industries during World War II has permitted an intensification of the competition which paper, fiber, and plastic containers provides for the Big Two of the tin-can industry.

DETERMINANTS OF MARKET STRUCTURE

Agriculture is an almost purely competitive industry. The clothing industry fits roughly into the mold of monopolistic competition. The steel and automobile industries are obviously oligopolistic. American Telephone and Telegraph nationally, and public utilities locally, approximate pure monopolies. What forces explain the emergence of these different market structures? What factors have

[3] A. D. H. Kaplan, *Big Enterprise in a Competitive System* (Washington: The Brookings Institution, 1954), p. 193.

caused agriculture to remain highly competitive and the automobile industry, spiced in its infancy with seventy-odd producers, now to be a tight oligopoly dominated by the Big Three? Although there exists no short, easy answer to these questions, we can put our fingers on some of the more important forces which historically have played significant roles in determining the competitive structures of the various American industries. Generally speaking, such factors as (1) legislation and government policy, (2) the policies and practices of business firms, (3) technological considerations, and (4) institutions and characteristics inherent in the capitalistic ideology go far to explain the variety of market structures which characterizes American capitalism.

Legislation and Government Policy

Government has promoted both monopoly and competition. By issuing *exclusive franchises* to so-called natural monopolies (for example, public utilities), government has purposely created many pure monopolies in industries which might otherwise have attained some degree of competition. Federal government commissions—the Interstate Commerce Commission, Civil Aeronautics Board, and Federal Communications Commission—play the major role in determining the degree of competition in the land and air transportation, radio, and television industries. Similarly, *patent laws* have promoted monopoly by giving innovating firms the exclusive right to manufacture a product for extended periods of time. *High tariffs* have promoted and preserved monopoly power in many domestic industries. On the other hand, there is but little doubt that the liberal Homestead Act of 1862 provided a competitive base for American agriculture. *Antitrust legislation*—the Sherman and Clayton Acts—is explicitly designed to curb the abuses of monopoly power.

We find here seemingly inconsistent government policies; but this inconsistency can be at least partly explained. Although government has pursued a generally antimonopolistic social policy, it simultaneously seeks other social objectives. One of these goals is the promotion of technological advance—an aim which patent legislation tends to promote. And in the case of public utilities, competition has simply not functioned effectively; here government has condoned and promoted monopoly, but has then provided regulatory commissions designed to prevent the abuse of this government-sponsored monopoly power.

Business Policies and Practices

The practices and policies pursued by various firms and industries can also be critical in determining the structure of industry. In some industries mergers, consolidations, and the development of holding companies have pushed in the direction of oligopoly or monopoly. The evolution of the corporate form of business enterprise and collusive practices between legally independent firms have played a similar role. In other industries cutthroat competition has resulted in some firms driving others from existence, thereby lowering the number of competitors in the industry. In still other instances firms have acquired ownership or control over vital raw materials so as to eliminate present rivals and destroy the possibility of new firms coming into being. These practices and developments, however, have occurred unevenly among various industries, causing some to move in the direction of monopoly and others to remain rather highly competitive.

Technology

Technology has undoubtedly become an increasingly important determinant of industrial structure. In a good many industries technology has developed to the point where the existence of large industrial giants is necessary if efficient low-cost production is to be achieved. Technology has given rise to economies of mass production which only large producers can realize. This means that, given consumer demand, efficient production

necessitates the existence of a small number of large producers rather than a large number of small producers. It is thus that technological advance has "forced" the market structure of many "heavy" industries—for example, the automobile, steel, and aluminum industries—in the direction of oligopoly. Economists differ in evaluating the extent to which technological factors require bigness; we shall examine the conflicting views in greater detail in Chapter 34.

In some industries technological advance has worked toward the same end but in a somewhat different manner. Superior research on product development has permitted some firms to outgrow and often eliminate less progressive rivals. Furthermore, this tendency is frequently cumulative; by gaining a larger share of the market through its superior research, a firm realizes the financial rewards that facilitate a widening of the technological advantages which it possesses over its rivals.

Capitalistic Institutions

We must be reminded that the institutions of American capitalism are permissive of the concentration of economic power and the development of oligopoly and monopoly. The relatively free, individualistic economic environment of the economy is a fertile ground for the most efficient, the most courageous, the most fortunate, or the most crafty producer to conquer his rivals in an effort to free himself from the regulatory powers of competition. Freedom of contract, private property, and inheritance rights have also contributed to the concentration of economic power. And, too, the business cycle has probably abetted the tendency toward monopoly. As one scholar puts it:[4]

Weaklings may still fail, and disappear, especially in more difficult times. Good times make it easy to finance consolidations, and

[4] John K. Galbraith, *American Capitalism*, rev. ed. (Boston: Houghton Mifflin Company, 1956), p. 35.

tempting for the strong company to expand and the weak to sell out. Thus, both adversity and prosperity work alike to reduce the number of firms in an industry.

SUMMARY

1. American industry is characterized by differing degrees of competition. The market models of **a.** pure competition, **b.** pure monopoly, **c.** monopolistic competition, and **d.** oligopoly are classifications into which most industries can be fitted with reasonable accuracy. These market models, however, are merely first approximations of reality.

2. Table 22–1 provides a convenient

summary of the major characteristics of these four market models.

3. Similar market classifications, based essentially upon numbers, are applied to the buying, or demand, side of the market.

4. The economist's definitions of the four market models focus attention upon **a.** the number of firms, **b.** the degree of product differentiation, and **c.** the ease or difficulty encountered by new firms in entering the industry. However, certain other important factors which have a bearing upon the competitive nature of an industry must also be considered:

a. In practice any meaningful description of the market structure of an industry requires

TABLE 22–1. CHARACTERISTICS OF THE FOUR BASIC MARKET MODELS

Characteristic	Market Model			
	Pure competition	Monopolistic competition	Oligopoly	Pure monopoly
Number of firms	A very large number	Many	Few	One
Type of product	Standardized	Differentiated	Standardized or differentiated	Unique; no close substitutes
Control over price	None	Some, but within rather narrow limits	Circumscribed by mutual interdependence; considerable with collusion	Considerable
Conditions of entry	Very easy, no obstacles	Relatively easy	Significant obstacles present	Blocked
Nonprice competition	None	Considerable emphasis on advertising, brand names, trademarks, etc.	Typically a great deal, particularly with product differentiation	Mostly public relations advertising
Example	Agriculture	Retail trade, dresses, shoes	Steel, automobiles, farm implements, meat packing, many household appliances	AT&T, local utilities

a proper definition of the geographic limits of the market.

b. Interindustry or interproduct competition is a significant force in many markets which might otherwise appear to be lacking in competition.

c. Nonprice competition may be an important supplement to price competition.

d. Technological advance, working as a competitive force through time, often undermines existing industries characterized by strong monopolistic elements.

5. Legislation, government policies, research and technological development, industry practices, and a variety of other factors have all played significant roles in determining the present structure of American industry.

QUESTIONS AND STUDY SUGGESTIONS

1. Under which of the four market classifications discussed in the chapter do each of the following most accurately fit: (*a*) a supermarket located in your home town; (*b*) the steel industry; (*c*) a Kansas wheat farm; (*d*) the commercial bank in which you or your family has an account; (*e*) the automobile industry. In each case justify your classification. In making your classifications, specify any assumptions you have made about the geographic limits of the various markets.

2. "Purely competitive producers have no price policy, but monopolistically competitive, oligopolistic, and purely monopolistic firms do." Explain.

3. In 1950 Crawford H. Greenewalt, president of E. I. du Pont de Nemours & Company, made the following statements before a House committee which was studying the monopoly problem:

> The difference between three and one [firms] is very substantial. It is the difference between monopoly and no monopoly.
>
> Oligopoly . . . to me is meaningless, because there is either competition or there is not. If there is competition, the public interest is being served.

What differences, if any, can you detect between Mr. Greenewalt's definition of "competition" and the economist's definition of "pure competition"? Do you feel that all industries can be meaningfully categorized as competitive or not competitive? Explain your answers.

4. A single farmer is "at the mercy of the market" in that he must regard the market price for his products as being fixed. Yet agricultural prices are very flexible. Reconcile these two statements.

5. What is interindustry competition? How important is it in each of the following industries? In each case specify the competing products or industries.

    a. Automobile   **b.** Cement   **c.** Coal

    d. Railway   **e.** Steel   **f.** Glass container

6. What is nonprice competition? How prevalent do you think nonprice competition to be in the industries mentioned in questions 1 and 5?

7. Why doesn't a purely competitive producer advertise his product?

8. "Competition should be judged solely on the basis of the number of firms in the industry; the larger the number, the greater the competition." Critically evaluate.

9. What are some of the major forces which determine the market structure of industries? Drawing on your knowledge of American history, what is the relative significance of these forces in explaining the market structures of the following industries?

a. Automobile   **b.** Steel   **c.** Agriculture
d. Television   **e.** Petroleum   **f.** Chemical
g. Tobacco

Be as specific as you can in your answers.

10. "Technological advance has both encouraged and limited the development of monopoly." Do you agree? Explain.

SELECTED REFERENCES

Dean, Joel: *Managerial Economics* (Englewood Cliffs, N.J.: Prentice-Hall, Inc., 1951), chap. 2.

Due, John F., and Robert W. Clower: *Intermediate Economic Analysis*, 4th ed. (Homewood, Ill.: Richard D. Irwin, Inc., 1961), chap. 4.

Enke, Stephen: *Intermediate Economic Theory* (Englewood Cliffs, N.J.: Prentice-Hall, Inc., 1950), chap. 15.

Fellner, William: *Modern Economic Analysis* (New York: McGraw-Hill Book Company, 1960), chap. 17.

Hague, Douglas C., and Alfred W. Stonier: *The Essentials of Economics* (New York: Longmans, Green & Co., Inc., 1955), chaps. 1–4.

Heilbroner, Robert L.: *The Making of Economic Society* (Englewood Cliffs, N.J.: Prentice-Hall, Inc., 1962), chap. 5.

Weiss, Leonard W.: *Economics and American Industry* (New York: John Wiley & Sons, Inc., 1961), chap. 1.

CHAPTER 23

DEMAND, SUPPLY, AND ELASTICITY: SOME APPLICATIONS

In Chapter 4 we familiarized ourselves with the rudiments of demand and supply analysis. In the present chapter we seek a more sophisticated understanding of demand and supply. Specifically, the tasks of this chapter are threefold. First, a brief summary of the elements of demand and supply analysis is presented. Second, we shall consider the concept of elasticity as applied to both demand and supply. Third, some specific applications of demand and supply analysis are discussed.

DEMAND, SUPPLY, AND MARKET PRICE[1]

Demand and supply both refer to schedules. The demand schedule shows the relationship between various possible prices of a product and the quantities which consumers will purchase at each of these prices (columns 1 and 2, Table 23–1). The price–quantity-demanded relationship thus portrayed is an inverse one. Consumers typically buy less at a high price than at a low price. This common-sense relationship is called the *law of demand*. Graphically the demand curve is downsloping (*DD* in Figure 23–1).

The supply schedule embodies the relationship between possible product prices and

the quantities which producers will supply at each of those prices (columns 2 and 3, Table 23–1). The relationship between price and quantity supplied is a direct one. The *law of supply* states that producers will find it profitable to devote more resources to the production of a good when its price is high than they will when it is low. When graphed, this direct relationship results in an upsloping supply curve (*SS* in Figure 23–1).

The intersection of demand and supply determines the market, or equilibrium, price and quantity. Both Table 23–1 and Figure 23–1 clearly show that the demand and supply data here assumed result in an equilibrium price of $3 and an equilibrium quantity of 7,000 units. Competition guarantees that any other price will be unstable. The surpluses which result at any above-equilibrium price will induce competing sellers to shade their prices to work off these excess stocks. The shortages which accompany below-equilibrium prices will prompt competing buyers to bid up the price, as consumers want to avoid doing without the product. At the equilibrium price the market will be cleared. The tendency of a competitive market to establish a price at which quantity demanded will just equal quantity supplied is called the *rationing function* of competitive prices.

Changes in the determinants of either demand or supply can cause the demand and supply schedules (curves) to shift. Vari-

---

[1] This brief review is not a substitute for Chapter 4. The student is strongly urged to reread Chapter 4 at this point.

TABLE 23–1. THE DEMAND FOR, AND SUPPLY OF, CORN (hypothetical data)

(1) Total quantity demanded per week	(2) Price per bushel	(3) Total quantity supplied per week	(4) Surplus (+) or shortage (−) (arrow indicates effect on price)
2,000	$5	12,000	+ 10,000↓
4,000	4	10,000	+ 6,000↓
7,000	3	7,000	0
11,000	2	4,000	− 7,000↑
16,000	1	1,000	− 15,000↑

ations in consumer tastes, incomes, the prices of related goods, consumer expectations, and the number of buyers in the market all will account for shifts in demand. Changes in any of those factors which affect produc-

tion costs will cause supply to shift. The relationship between a change in demand and the resulting changes in equilibrium price and quantity is a direct one. An inverse relationship exists between a change in

FIGURE 23–1. THE EQUILIBRIUM PRICE FOR CORN AS DETERMINED BY MARKET DEMAND AND MARKET SUPPLY.

Equilibrium price and equilibrium quantity are determined by the intersection of demand *DD* and supply *SS*.

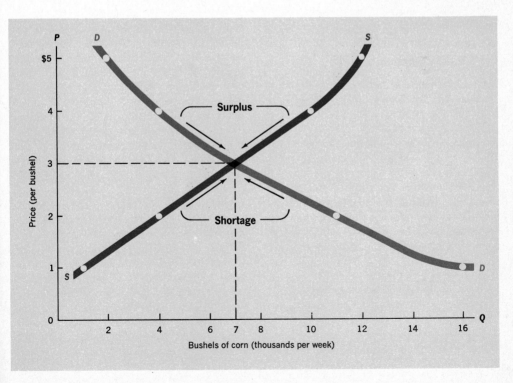

supply and the ensuing change in price. However, the relationship between a change in supply and the ensuing change in quantity is direct.

ELASTICITY OF DEMAND

The law of demand tells us that consumers will respond to a price decline by buying more of a product. But the degree of responsiveness of consumers to a price change may vary considerably from product to product. Economists measure how responsive, or sensitive, consumers are to a change in the price of a product by the concept of *elasticity*.

The demand for some products is such that consumers are relatively responsive to price changes; price changes give rise to very considerable changes in the quantity purchased. The demand for such products is said to be *elastic*. For other products consumers are relatively unresponsive to price changes; that is, price changes result in modest changes in the amount purchased. In such cases demand is *inelastic*.

The Elasticity Formula

Economists measure the degree of elasticity or inelasticity by the *elasticity coefficient*, or E_d in this formula:

$$E_d = \frac{\text{percentage change in quantity demanded}}{\text{percentage change in price}}$$

One calculates these *percentage* changes, of course, by dividing the change in price by the original price and the change in quantity demanded by the original quantity demanded. Thus we can restate our formula as:

$$E_d = \frac{\text{change in quantity demanded}}{\text{original quantity demanded}}$$
$$\div \frac{\text{change in price}}{\text{original price}}$$

But why use percentages rather than absolute amounts in measuring consumer responsiveness? The answer is that if we simply use absolute changes, our impression of buyer responsiveness will be arbitrarily affected by the choice of units. To illustrate: If the price of product X falls from $3 to $2 and consumers, as a result, increase their purchases from 60 to 100 pounds, we get the impression that consumers are quite sensitive to price changes and therefore that demand is elastic. After all, a price change of "one" has caused a change in the amount demanded of "forty." But by changing the monetary unit from dollars to pennies (why not?) we find a price change of "one hundred" causes a quantity change of "forty," giving the impression of inelasticity. The use of percentage changes avoids this problem. The given price decline is 33 per cent whether measured in terms of dollars ($1/ $3) or pennies (100¢/300¢).

Now let us interpret our formula. Demand is *elastic* if a given percentage change in price results in a larger percentage change in quantity demanded. Example: If a 2 per cent decline in price results in a 4 per cent increase in quantity demanded, demand is elastic. In all such cases, where demand is elastic, the elasticity coefficient will obviously be greater than 1. If a given percentage change in price is accompanied by a relatively smaller change in the quantity demanded, demand is *inelastic*. Illustration: If a 3 per cent decline in price gives rise to a 1 per cent increase in the amount demanded, demand is inelastic. It is apparent that the elasticity coefficient will always be less than 1 when demand is inelastic. The borderline case which separates elastic and inelastic demands occurs where a percentage change in price and the accompanying percentage change in quantity demanded chance to be equal. For example, a 1 per cent drop in price causes a 1 per cent increase in the amount sold. This special case is termed *unit elasticity*, because the elasticity coefficient is exactly 1, or unity.

It must be emphasized that when economists say demand is "inelastic," they do not mean consumers are completely unresponsive to a price change. The term *perfectly inelastic* demand designates the extreme situation wherein a change in price results in no change whatsoever in the quantity demanded. Approximate example: An acute diabetic's demand for insulin. A demand curve parallel to the vertical axis would show this situation graphically. Conversely, when economists say demand is "elastic," they do not mean that consumers are completely responsive to a price change. In the extreme situation, wherein there is some small price reduction which would cause buyers to increase their purchases from zero to all they could obtain, we say that demand is *perfectly elastic*. We shall find later in this chapter that such a demand curve applies to a firm which is selling in a perfectly competitive market. Graphically such a demand curve is parallel to the horizontal axis (see Figure 23–6).

Refinement: Mid-points Formula

An annoying problem arises in applying the elasticity formula. To illustrate: In calculating the elasticity coefficient for corn for the $5–$4 price range in Table 23–2, should we use the $5–2,000-bushel price-quantity combination or the $4–4,000-bushel combination as a point of reference in calculating the percentage changes in price and quantity which the elasticity formula requires? Our choice will influence the outcome. Using the $5–2,000-bushel reference point, we find that the percentage decrease in price is 20 per cent and the percentage increase in quantity is 100 per cent. Substituting in the formula, the elasticity coefficient is 100/20 or 5. But using the $4–4,000-bushel reference point, we find that the percentage increase in price is 25 per cent and the percentage decline in quantity is 50 per cent. The elasticity coefficient is therefore 50/25 or 2, in this case. Although the formula indicates that demand is elastic in both cases,

the two solutions involve a considerable difference in the degree of elasticity. In other instances—experiment, for example, with the $3–$2 price range—the formula may indicate a slightly elastic demand for one price-quantity combination and slight inelasticity of demand for the other.

Economists have reached a workable compromise to this problem by using the averages of the two prices and the two quantities under consideration for reference points. In the $5–$4 price range case the price reference is $4.50 and the quantity reference 3,000 bushels. The percentage change in price is now about 22 per cent and the percentage change in quantity about 67 per cent, giving us an elasticity coefficient of 3. Instead of gauging elasticity at either one of the extremes of this price-quantity range, this solution estimates elasticity at the mid-point of the $5–$4 price range. More positively stated, we can refine our earlier statement of the elasticity formula to read:

$$E_d = \frac{\text{change in quantity}}{\text{sum of quantities}/2} \div \frac{\text{change in prices}}{\text{sum of prices}/2}$$

Substituting data for the $5–$4 price range, we get

$$E_d = \frac{2,000}{6,000/2} \div \frac{1}{9/2} = 3.00$$

In column 5 of Table 23–2 we have calculated the elasticity coefficients for the demand data of Table 23–1, using the mid-points formula. The reader should verify each of these calculations.

The Total-revenue Test

Perhaps the easiest way to gauge whether demand is elastic or inelastic is to note what happens to total revenue or receipts—total expenditures from the buyer's viewpoint—when product price changes.

1. If demand is *elastic*, a decline in price

TABLE 23–2. ELASTICITY OF DEMAND AS MEASURED BY THE TOTAL-RECEIPTS TEST AND THE ELASTICITY COEFFICIENT (hypothetical data)

(1) Total quantity demanded per week	(2) Price per bushel	(3) Total revenue (expenditures)	(4) Total-revenue test	(5) Elasticity coefficient E_d (approximate)
2,000	$5	$10,000		
			Elastic	$\dfrac{2,000}{6,000/2} \div \dfrac{1}{9/2} = 3.00$
4,000	4	16,000		
			Elastic	$\dfrac{3,000}{11,000/2} \div \dfrac{1}{7/2} = 1.91$
7,000	3	21,000		
			Elastic	$\dfrac{4,000}{18,000/2} \div \dfrac{1}{5/2} = 1.11$
11,000	2	22,000		
			Inelastic	$\dfrac{5,000}{27,000/2} \div \dfrac{1}{3/2} = 0.56$
16,000	1	16,000		

will result in an increase in total revenue. Why? Because even though a lesser price is being received per unit, enough additional units are now being sold to more than make up for the lower price. This is illustrated in Figure 23–2a for the $5–$4 price range of our demand curve from Table 23–1. Total revenue, of course, is price times quantity. Hence, the area shown by the rectangle OP_1AQ_1 is total revenue ($10,000) when price is P_1 ($5) and quantity demanded is Q_1 (2,000 bushels). Now when price declines to P_2 ($4), causing the quantity demanded to increase to Q_2 (4,000 bushels), total revenue changes to OP_2BQ_2 ($16,000), which is obviously larger than OP_1AQ_1. It is larger because the *loss* in revenue due to the lower price per unit (area P_2P_1AC) is *less* than the *gain* in revenue due to the larger sales (area Q_1CBQ_2) which accompanies the lower price. This reasoning is reversible: If demand is elastic, a price increase will reduce total revenue. Why? Because the *gain* in total revenue caused by the higher unit price (area P_2P_1AC) is less than the *loss* in revenue associated with the accompanying fall in sales (Q_1CBQ_2).

2. If demand is *inelastic*, a price decline

will cause total revenue to fall. The modest increase in sales which occurs will be insufficient to offset the decline in revenue per unit, and the net result is that total revenue declines. This situation exists for the $2–$1 price range of our demand curve as shown in Figure 23–2b. Initially total revenue is OP_4FQ_4 ($22,000) when price is P_4 ($2) and quantity demanded is Q_4 (11,000 bushels). If we reduce price to P_5 ($1), quantity demanded will increase to Q_5 (16,000 bushels). Total revenue will change to OP_5GQ_5 ($16,000), which is obviously less than OP_4FQ_4. It is smaller because the loss in revenue due to the lower unit price (area P_5P_4FH) is larger than the *gain* in revenue due to the accompanying increase in sales (area Q_4HGQ_5). Again our analysis is reversible: If demand is inelastic, a price increase will increase total revenue.

3. In the special case of unit elasticity an increase or decrease in price will leave total revenue unchanged. The loss in revenue due to a lower unit price will be exactly offset by the gain in revenue brought about by the accompanying increase in sales. Conversely, the gain in revenue due to a higher unit price will be exactly offset by the loss in

(a) *(b)*

FIGURE 23–2. ELASTICITY AND TOTAL REVENUE.
If demand is elastic as in the $5–$4 price range in (*a*), a change in price will cause
total revenue to change in the opposite direction. Conversely, if demand is
inelastic as in the $2–$1 price range in (*b*), price and total revenue will move
in the same direction.

revenue associated with the accompanying decline in the amount demanded.

Column 4 of Table 23–2 applies the total-revenue test to the entire demand curve for corn.

Characteristics

The alert reader may have detected two subtle but notable characteristics of elasticity from our applications of the elasticity formula and the total-revenue tests. First, as Table 23–2 indicates, elasticity typically varies over the different price ranges of the same demand schedule or curve. In the case of the demand curve for corn, demand is considerably more elastic at higher prices than at low prices. This correctly suggests that as the price of a product falls, sales will increase to the saturation point at which consumers are virtually "filled up" on the product. When this is the case, further price cuts will not induce buyers to take much more. Conversely, when prices are already relatively high, further price increases will induce buyers to seek out substitute products or do without, causing relatively sharp declines in sales. There is a tendency for most demand curves to be elastic at high prices and inelastic at low prices.

In the second place, the graphic appearance of a demand curve is *not* a sound basis upon which to judge its elasticity. For example, in Figure 23–2 we find that because the demand curve has a steeper slope at relatively higher prices and a flatter slope at relatively lower prices, one is tempted to associate an inelastic demand with high prices and an elastic demand with low prices. But this is dangerous reasoning. Have we not just discovered that the elasticity formula and the total-revenue test indicate that the reverse is true? The catch lies in the fact that the flatness or steepness of a demand curve is based upon absolute changes in price and quantity while elasticity has to do with relative changes in price and quantity.

Determinants of Elasticity of Demand

What makes the demand for any specific product elastic or inelastic? Generally speaking, the elasticity of demand for any product is greater (1) the larger the number of good substitutes available, (2) the larger the item as a part of one's total budget, and (3) the more the product is regarded as a luxury item and therefore dispensable. A couple of illustrations will help.

The demand for salt tends to be highly inelastic on all three counts. There are simply no good substitutes for salt to which consumers can turn if its price rises from, say, 15 cents to 20 cents per pound. Furthermore, a household's expenditures on salt are such a small fraction of a family's weekly or monthly budget that the total impact of this price increase is negligible for all practical purposes. And, finally, the product is a necessity; unsalted cooking leaves much to be desired. On the other hand, the demand for a brand X stereophonic phonograph may be relatively elastic. There are many good substitutes available in the form of competing brands of stereo, not to mention FM radios. The price of the item is large in relation to one's budget, so a given percentage change in price will have a very significant impact dollarwise upon that budget. And to most families a stereo phonograph is a luxury and therefore an expendable item in their budget.

Other factors also influence elasticity. Consumers are creatures of habit. It is only over a period of time that they alter their customary expenditure patterns in response to given price changes. Demand therefore tends to be more elastic in the long run than in the short run. Furthermore, the durability of some products has a bearing upon the elasticity of the demand for them. Few consumers actually face the choice of doing without a refrigerator or automobile. The question is rather one of repairing your old refrigerator or car or buying new ones. Repairing older durable goods is frequently a very good substitute for buying a new model. Durability therefore tends to make demand more elastic than would otherwise be the case.

In Chapter 30 we shall discover that a somewhat different group of factors determines the elasticity of demand for resources.

Some Practical Applications

The concept of elasticity of demand is something more than a theoretical notion designed to confuse unwary students. It is a notion of great practical significance. Some examples will make this evident.

In August of 1957 Walter Reuther, UAW president, contended that automobile manufacturers should raise wages and simultaneously cut automobile prices. Reuther, arguing that the elasticity of demand for automobiles was about 4, concluded that a price cut would help check inflation, boost the total receipts of manufacturers, and preserve or even increase the profits of producers. A spokesman for the Ford Motor Company, however, claimed that available studies suggest an elasticity of demand for automobiles in the 0.5–1.5 range. He held that price cuts would therefore shrink profits or result in losses for manufacturers. In this case, the elasticity of demand for automobiles was a strategic factor in labor-management relations and wage bargaining.[2]

Another example: Studies indicate that the demand for most farm products is highly inelastic. As a result, increases in the output of farm products due to a good growing season or productivity increases depress both the prices of farm products and the total receipts (incomes) of farmers. For farmers the inelastic nature of the demand for their products means that a bumper crop may be

[2] See the statement by Theodore Yntema, vice president of finance, Ford Motor Company, before the Subcommittee on Antitrust and Monopoly of the Committee on the Judiciary, United States Senate, February 4–5, 1958.

a mixed blessing. For policy makers it means that higher farm incomes depend upon the restriction of farm output.

Finally, the impact of automation, that is, of rapid technological advance, upon the level of employment depends in part upon the elasticity of demand for the product being manufactured. Suppose a firm installs new laborsaving machinery, resulting in the technological unemployment of, say, 500 workers. Suppose too that a part of the cost reduction resulting from this technological advance is passed on to consumers in the form of reduced product prices. Now the effect of this price reduction upon the firm's sales and therefore the quantity of labor it needs will obviously depend upon the elasticity of product demand. An elastic demand might increase sales to the extent that some, all, or even more than the 500 displaced workers are reabsorbed by the firm. An inelastic demand will mean that few, if any, of the displaced workers will be reemployed, because the increase in the volume of the firm's business will be small.

These examples could be multiplied, but the main point is clear. Elasticity of demand is vitally important to businessmen, farmers, labor, and government policy makers.

Elasticity of Supply

The concept of price elasticity can also be applied to supply. If producers are responsive to price changes, supply is elastic. If they are relatively insensitive to price changes, supply is inelastic.

The elasticity formula is pertinent in determining the degree of elasticity or inelasticity of supply. The only obvious alteration is the substitution of percentage change in quantity supplied for percentage change in quantity demanded.

The main determinant of the elasticity of supply is the amount of time which a producer has to respond to a given change in product price. Generally speaking, we can expect a greater output response—and there-fore greater elasticity of supply—the longer the amount of time a producer has to adjust to a given price change. Why? Because a producer's response to an increase in the price of product X depends upon his ability to shift resources from the production of other products[3] to the production of X. And the shifting of resources takes time: the greater the time, the greater the resource "shiftability." Hence, the greater will be the output response and the elasticity of supply.

An example may help at this point: Suppose a small truck farmer brings his entire season's output of tomatoes—one truckload—to market. His supply curve will be perfectly inelastic; he will sell the truckload whether the price is high or low. Why? Because he cannot offer more tomatoes than his one truckload if the price of tomatoes should be higher than he had anticipated. Even though he might like to offer more, tomatoes simply cannot be produced overnight. It will take him another full growing season to respond to a higher-than-expected price by producing more than one truckload. Similarly, because his product is perishable, he cannot withhold it from the market. If the price is lower than he had anticipated, he will still sell the entire truckload. Costs of production, incidentally, will not be important in making this decision. Even though the price of tomatoes may fall far short of his production costs, he will nevertheless sell out to avoid a total loss through spoilage. In a very short period of time, then, our farmer's supply of tomatoes is fixed; he can offer one truckload no matter how high the price. The perishability of his product forces him to sell all no matter how low the price.

In a longer period of time—say, two or three growing seasons—our farmer can make extensive adjustments to, say, an increase in the price of tomatoes. He can cultivate his tomatoes more intensively by applying more labor, capital, and fertilizer to the land

---

[3] The prices of which assumedly remain constant.

planted in tomatoes. Similarly, in time he can transfer some of his land from the production of other crops to the growing of tomatoes or can even purchase additional land to be used in tomato production. Therefore, in this longer period of time we can expect a considerable change in the amount supplied in response to the assumed price increase. In Chapter 26 we shall discover that costs become an important consideration in deciding how much to offer at various prices in these longer time periods.

We have made no mention of a total-revenue test for elasticity of supply. Indeed, there is none. Supply shows a direct relationship between price and the amount supplied; that is, the supply curve is upsloping. This means that, regardless of the degree of elasticity or inelasticity, price and total receipts will always move together.

APPLICATIONS OF SUPPLY AND DEMAND ANALYSIS

Supply and demand analysis and the elasticity concept will be applied repeatedly in the remainder of this book. Let us strengthen our understanding of these analytical tools and their significance by examining two important applications: (1) legal prices and (2) demand from the viewpoint of the individual firm.

Legal Prices

The "facts" of the market may not always be consistent with what society feels they *ought* to be. The free market is an impersonal mechanism which does not judge the fairness of the manner in which a product is distributed to consumers or how equitable are the incomes which flow to resource suppliers. Specifically, the prices of certain products and resources may be judged by society as being "too high" or "too low." Acting through government, society may attempt to bring a "proper" adjustment in such prices. Let us examine in turn the cases in which prices are felt to be unduly high and unjustly low

and, in the process, explore some of the complications entailed in correcting these errant prices.

Price ceilings and shortages. With few exceptions ceiling prices in the United States have been a wartime phenomenon. Government expenditures for war goods invariably cause the general level of product prices to rise. On the other hand, government spending has varying effects upon the money incomes of households. Generally speaking, those supplying human and property resources essential to the war effort will find their money incomes booming. Those offering nonessential resources may experience modest increases or, conceivably, decreases in their money incomes. The net effect of these distortions in money incomes in the midst of product price inflation is obviously an arbitrary redistribution of real incomes. Those essential resource suppliers whose money incomes race ahead of the level of product prices realize sharply increasing real incomes. Those offering nonessential resources find that the price level spurts ahead of their money incomes to the end that their real incomes are curtailed. Government imposition of ceiling prices is a means of alleviating this arbitrary redistribution of real income so that the real economic cost of the war will be more equitably distributed among the citizenry.

Let us examine the effect of a ceiling price upon a specific product—say, butter. Suppose that the war severely disrupts agriculture in allied countries, obliging the United States to provide large amounts of foodstuffs for foreign peoples and their armies. This obviously increases the demand for American butter in relation to its supply. The resulting market price, let us assume, is $1.20 per pound. The government then imposes a legal price of, say, 90 cents per pound. What will be the effects of this price ceiling? The rationing ability of the market mechanism will be rendered ineffective. Although the equilibrium price ($1.20) would bring quantity demanded and quantity supplied into balance, the imposition of the ceiling price will prompt producers to cut back on the rate of production and will induce consumers to step up their rate of purchase. The net result will be a persistent shortage of the product.[4]

Figure 23–3 illustrates graphically the effect of a ceiling price. Let *SS* and *DD* be

[4] When a shortage exists in a free market, competition among buyers will bid up price. This induces a greater output and simultaneously rations some buyers out of the market, thereby bringing quantity demanded and quantity supplied into equality at the equilibrium price. But with an effective ceiling price it is of course illegal to bid price up to the equilibrium point.

the supply and demand curves for butter. The equilibrium price and quantity will be *P* and *Q*, respectively. If government now makes it illegal to sell butter at any price above the ceiling price of P_c, the quantity forthcoming onto the market would be only Q_s despite the fact that consumers would be willing to purchase Q_d at the ceiling price. The shortage is measured by the excess of Q_d over Q_s.

But ceiling prices pose problems of government. First, effective ceiling prices invite the development of black markets. Such illegal markets, wherein sales take place at prices above the ceiling price, can be exceedingly difficult to detect and eliminate.

FIGURE 23–3. CEILING PRICES RESULT IN PERSISTENT SHORTAGES.
Because the imposition of a price ceiling such as P_c results in a persistent product shortages as indicated by the distance Q_sQ_d, government must undertake the job of rationing the product in order to achieve an equitable distribution.

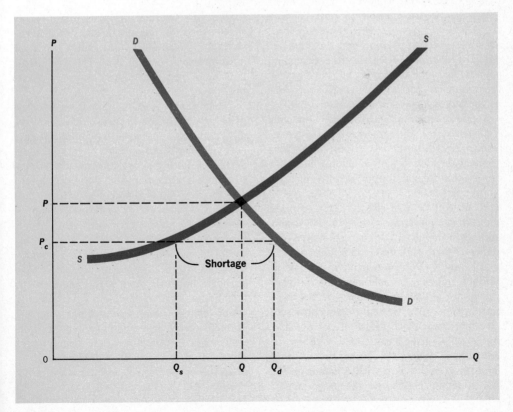

Second, government must undertake the job of rationing butter to consumers. Should government take no formal step to ensure a fair distribution of butter, it would probably be sold on a first-come-first-served basis. But such unregulated shortages may result in some consumers doing without any butter while others—those who are first in line or who manage to cultivate a friendship with the corner grocer—get as much or more than they want. An unregulated shortage may foster the very problem the ceiling price was designed to solve—the inequitable distribution of a product. To avoid a catch-as-catch-can distribution of the product, government must undertake the task of fairly distributing it to consumers. This is done by issuing ration coupons to consumers on an equal basis.

Price supports and surpluses. While the imposition of price ceilings in the United States has been a wartime proposition, this has not been the case with price supports. Minimum wage legislation and the supporting of agricultural prices are the two most widely discussed examples of government price supports. Let us examine price supports as applied to a specific farm commodity.

Suppose the going market price for corn is $1 per bushel, and, as a result of this price, farmers realize extremely low incomes. Government decides to lend a helping hand by establishing a legal supported price of, say, $1.50 per bushel.

What will be the effects? At any price above the equilibrium price, quantity supplied will obviously exceed quantity demanded; there will be a persistent surplus of the product. Farmers will be willing to produce and offer for sale more than private buyers are willing to purchase at the supported price. The size of this surplus will vary directly with the elasticity of demand and supply. The greater the elasticity of demand and supply, the greater the resulting surplus. As is the case with a ceiling price, the rationing ability of the free market

obviously has been disrupted by the imposition of a legal price.

Figure 23–4 provides us with a graphic illustration of the effect of a supported price. Let SS and DD be the supply and demand curves for corn. Equilibrium price and quantity are obviously P and Q, respectively. If government imposes a supported price of P_s, farmers will be willing to produce Q_s, but private buyers will only take Q_d off the market at that price. The surplus entailed is measured by the excess of Q_s over Q_d.

Government inherits the unsavory task of coping with the surplus which a supported price entails. There are two general approaches open to government. First, it might invoke certain programs to restrict supply (for example, acreage allotments) or to increase demand (for example, research on new uses for agricultural products) in order to reduce the difference between the equilibrium price and the supported price and thereby the size of the resulting surplus. If these efforts are not wholly successful, then, secondly, government must simply purchase and store or dispose of the surplus. We shall have more to say about agricultural surpluses in Chapter 35.

Government imposes price ceilings or price supports when hyperinflation or unusually depressed prices are working undue economic hardships on some buyers or sellers and are resulting in arbitrary windfall gains to others. But ceiling and supported prices rob the free market forces of supply and demand of their ability to bring the supply decisions of producers and the demand decisions of buyers into accord with one another. Freely determined prices automatically ration products to buyers; legal prices do not. Therefore, government must accept the administrative problem of rationing which stems from price ceilings and the problem of buying or eliminating surpluses which price supports entail. Legal prices simply do not work unless accompanied by programs to control consumption or production.

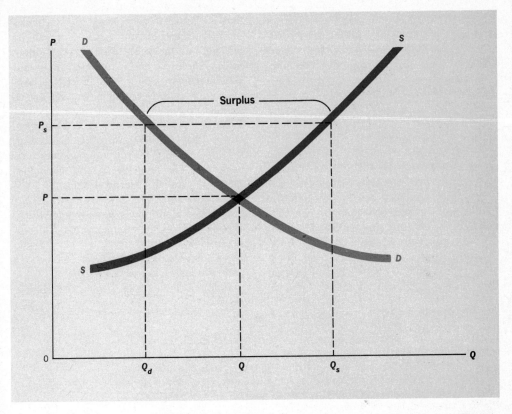

FIGURE 23–4. SUPPORTED PRICES RESULT IN PERSISTENT SURPLUSES.
A price support such as P_s gives rise to a persistent product surplus as indicated by
the distance Q_dQ_s. Government must either purchase these surpluses or take
measures to eliminate them by restricting product supply.

Although legal prices involve knotty problems for government by upsetting the rationing ability of the market mechanism, one must be careful not to prejudge ceilings or supports as undesirable. Remember: Legal prices are designed to correct alleged inequities which free market prices entail.

Demand from the Individual Firm's Viewpoint

Thus far we have emphasized the concepts of demand and elasticity primarily from the buyer's point of view. But these concepts are also of vital importance from the seller's point of view. Whereas demand indicates price and amount purchased from the consumer's standpoint, it simultaneously reflects revenue per unit and sales from the seller's standpoint. We first seek to examine the demand or average-revenue curve of an individual competitive producer.

Demand to a purely competitive seller. You will recall (Chapter 22) that a purely competitive market entails a very large number of producers selling a standardized product. Because he offers a negligible fraction of total supply, the individual competitive seller exerts no influence whatever on market price.

Price is set by the market, and the individual firm can sell as much or as little as it chooses at that price. Stated differently, the demand schedule is perfectly elastic to the individual competitive firm.

But let us digress here for a moment to voice a word of caution. We are not saying that the *market* demand curve is perfectly elastic in a competitive market. Indeed, it is not, but rather it is typically a downsloping curve as shown in Figure 23–5b. As a matter of fact, the total-demand curves for most agricultural products are quite *in*elastic, even though agriculture is the most competitive industry in our economy. We are saying that the demand schedule faced by the *individual firm* in a purely competitive industry is perfectly elastic. The distinction comes about in this way. For the industry—

that is, for all firms producing a particular product—a larger volume of sales can be realized only by accepting a lower product price. All firms, acting independently but simultaneously, can and do affect total supply and therefore market price. But not so for the individual firm. If a single producer increases or decreases his output, the outputs of all other competing firms being constant, the effect on total supply and market price is negligible. The single firm's sales schedule is therefore perfectly elastic. Figure 23–5a is illustrative. This is an instance in which the fallacy of composition is worth remembering. What is true for the group of firms (a downsloping, less than perfectly elastic demand curve), is *not* true for the individual firm (a perfectly elastic demand curve).

Columns 1 and 2 of Table 23–3 show a

FIGURE 23–5. THE INDIVIDUAL COMPETITIVE FIRM'S DEMAND CURVE (a) AND DEMAND TO A COMPETITIVE INDUSTRY (b).
Industry demand is downsloping, such as *DD* in (b); that is, firms as a group must accept a lower price in order to sell a greater output. However, the product price which is determined by market demand and supply is given to the individual firm, making his demand curve *dd* perfectly elastic at that price, as shown in (a).

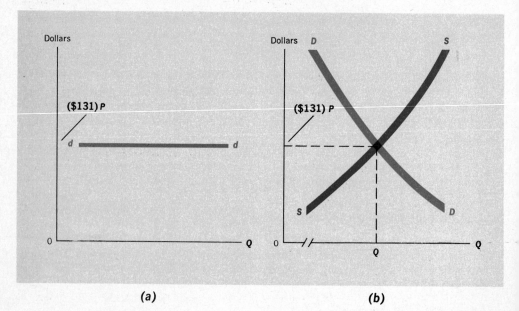

(a)   (b)

TABLE 23–3. THE DEMAND AND REVENUE SCHEDULES FOR AN INDIVIDUAL PURELY COMPETITIVE FIRM (hypothetical data)

Firm's demand or average-revenue schedule		Revenue data	
(1) Product price (average revenue)	(2) Quantity demanded (sold)	(3) Total revenue	(4) Marginal revenue
$131	0	$ 0	
			$131
131	1	131	
			131
131	2	262	
			131
131	3	393	
			131
131	4	524	
			131
131	5	655	
			131
131	6	786	
			131
131	7	917	
			131
131	8	1,048	
			131
131	9	1,179	
			131
131	10	1,310	

perfectly elastic demand curve where market price is assumed to be $131. Note that the firm cannot obtain a higher price by restricting output; nor need it lower price in order to increase its volume of sales.

Average, total, and marginal revenue to a purely competitive seller. A moment's reflection reveals that this demand schedule is simultaneously a revenue schedule. What appears in column 1 as price per unit to the purchaser is obviously revenue per unit, or *average revenue*, to the seller. To say that a buyer must pay a price of $131 per unit is to say that the revenue per unit, or average

revenue, received by the seller is $131. Price and average revenue are the same thing looked at from different points of view.

Total revenue for each level of sales can obviously be determined by multiplying price by the corresponding quantity which the firm can sell. Multiply column 1 by column 2, and the result is column 3. In this case total receipts increase by a constant amount, $131, for each additional unit of sales. Each unit sold adds exactly its price to total revenue.

Whenever a firm is pondering a change in its output, it will be concerned with how its revenue will change as a result of that change in output. What will be the additional revenue from selling another unit of output? *Marginal revenue* is the addition to total revenue, that is, the extra revenue, which results from the sale of one more unit of output. In other words, in Table 23–3 marginal revenue is simply the rate of change in total revenue. In column 3 we note that total revenue is obviously zero when zero units are being sold. The first unit of output sold increases total revenue from zero to $131. Marginal revenue—the increase in total revenue resulting from the sale of the first unit of output—is therefore $131. The second unit sold increases total revenue from $131 to $262, so marginal revenue is again $131. Indeed, you will note in column 4 that marginal revenue is a constant figure of

$131. Why? Because total revenue increases at a constant rate with every extra unit sold. Under purely competitive conditions product price is constant to the individual firm; added units therefore can be sold without lowering product price. This means that each additional unit of sales adds exactly its price—$131 in this case—to total revenue. And marginal revenue is this rate of increase in total revenue. Marginal revenue is constant under pure competition, because additional units can be sold at a constant price.

The competitive firm's demand curve and total and marginal revenue curves are shown graphically in Figure 23–6. The demand or average-revenue curve is perfectly elastic. The marginal-revenue curve coincides with the demand curve because the market is a

FIGURE 23–6. DEMAND, MARGINAL REVENUE, AND TOTAL REVENUE OF A PURELY COMPETITIVE FIRM.
Because it can sell additional units of output at a constant price, the marginal revenue curve (MR) of a purely competitive firm coincides with its perfectly elastic demand curve (*D*). The firm's total revenue curve (TR) is a straight upsloping line.

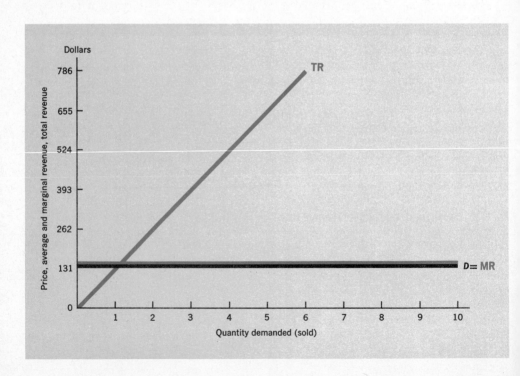

purely competitive one and, as a result, product price is constant to the single firm. Each extra unit of sales increases total revenue by $131. Total revenue is a straight line up to the right. Its slope is constant—that is, it is a straight line—because marginal revenue is constant.

In order to test his grasp of these new concepts, the reader should pause at this point and explain both tabularly and graphically what happens to average, total, and marginal revenue if price were, say, increased to $151 or lowered to $81.

Let us now consider the nature of the demand and revenue schedules faced by imperfectly competitive producers, that is, firms which are pure monopolies, monopolistically competitive, or oligopolistic.

Demand to an imperfectly competitive seller.

Though they differ in details, the demand schedules facing imperfectly competitive firms have one basic point in common: they are downsloping. The demand curve of a pure monopolist, a monopolistically competitive producer, and an oligopolist may differ considerably in elasticity; yet all are less than perfectly elastic and therefore downsloping.

Why? An imperfectly competitive producer sells a significant percentage of the industry's total output. Therefore any decision one firm makes to increase or reduce its output will have a noticeable effect on total supply and therefore market price. This is most obvious in the case of the pure monopolist, where the firm and the industry are synonymous. Here the firm's output and market output are identical.

Specifically, when an imperfectly competitive producer attempts to sell more, market supply increases in relation to market demand, and price falls. As a result, the demand schedule faced by the individual firm is downsloping, that is, less than perfectly elastic. The firm must accept a lower price to achieve a larger volume of sales. Columns 1 and 2 of Table 23–4 portray

this situation. Here we assume that the firm must accept a $10 price cut in order to sell each succeeding unit of output.

Average, total, and marginal revenue to an imperfectly competitive seller.

As for the purely competitive firm, price and average revenue are identical to the imperfectly competitive producer. Total revenue is again the product of price and the corresponding volume of sales. Note, however, that the rate of increase in total revenue is not constant, as it was under purely competitive conditions. As a matter of fact, total revenue reaches a maximum of $738 with the ninth unit sold and declines thereafter.

Under pure competition each successive unit sold adds the same amount—its price—to total revenue. Marginal revenue is constant under competition because price is constant to the individual firm. But with imperfect competition price declines as sales increase. Hence, we should expect marginal revenue to decline. It does, and as a glance at columns 1 and 4 reveals, it falls *faster* than does price. Why? The catch is this: *When an imperfectly competitive firm cuts price to increase its volume of sales, this lower price will apply not only to the extra unit sold but also to all other units of sales.* For example, when our imperfectly competitive firm is selling 1 unit at $162, total revenue is obviously $162. To increase its sales to 2 units price must be cut by $10 to $152. This new price applies not only to the extra (second) unit of sales but also to the first unit, which could have been sold at $162. In short, the second unit adds $152 (its price) less $10 (the price cut which the firm must take on the first unit), or $142, to total revenue. Similarly, to sell 3 units the firm must lower price from $152 to $142. The resulting marginal revenue will be just $122—the $142 addition to total revenue which the third unit of sales provides less $10 price cuts on the first 2 units of output. These calculations are shown in the marginal-revenue column in Table 23–4.

TABLE 23–4. THE DEMAND AND REVENUE SCHEDULES FOR AN INDIVIDUAL IMPERFECTLY COMPETITIVE FIRM (hypothetical data)

Firm's demand or average-revenue schedule		Revenue data	
(1) Product price (average revenue)	(2) Quantity demanded (sold)	(3) Total revenue	(4) Marginal revenue
$172	0	$ 0	
			$162
162	1	162	
			142 (152 − 10)
152	2	304	
			122 (142 − 20)
142	3	426	
			102 (132 − 30)
132	4	528	
			82 (122 − 40)
122	5	610	
			62 etc.
112	6	672	
			42
102	7	714	
			22
92	8	736	
			2
82	9	738	
			−18
72	10	720	

Note that with the tenth unit of sales marginal revenue becomes negative. Why?

Graphically the data of Table 23–4 appear as in Figure 23–7. The points of contrast with Figure 23–6 are clear. The demand or average-revenue curve is, of course, downsloping. Total revenue increases but at an ever-declining rate. In time total revenue reaches a maximum and then actually declines. Aside from the first unit of sales, marginal revenue lies below the demand curve. The reason? Marginal revenue is derived from total revenue and therefore reflects price declines not only on the extra unit sold but also on all prior units of output which otherwise could have been sold at a higher price.

SUMMARY

1. The present chapter extends the rudiments of demand and supply analysis developed in Chapter 4. The summarizing statements pertinent to that chapter should be reviewed at this point.

2. Elasticity of demand measures the responsiveness of consumers to price changes. If consumers are sensitive to price changes, demand is elastic. If consumers are unresponsive to price changes, demand is inelastic.

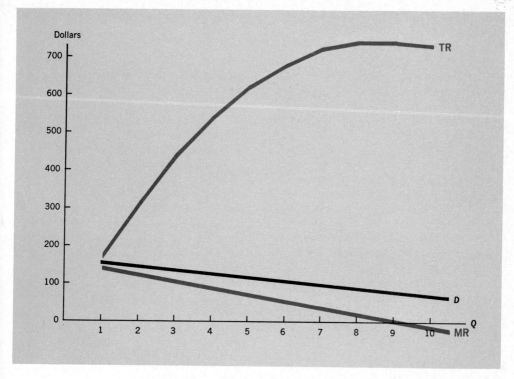

FIGURE 23–7. DEMAND, MARGINAL REVENUE, AND TOTAL REVENUE OF AN IMPERFECTLY COMPETITIVE FIRM.
Because it must lower price to increase its sales, the marginal revenue curve (MR) of an imperfectly competitive firm lies below its downsloping demand curve (D). Total revenue (TR) increases at a decreasing rate, reaches a maximum, and then declines.

3. The price elasticity formula measures the degree of elasticity or inelasticity of demand. The formula is

$$E_d = \frac{\text{percentage change in quantity demanded}}{\text{percentage change in price}}$$

The averages of the prices and quantities under consideration are used as reference points in determining the percentage changes in price and quantity. If E_d is greater than 1, demand is elastic. If E_d is less than 1, demand is inelastic. Unit elasticity is the special case in which E_d equals 1.

4. Price elasticity of demand can be determined by observing the effect of a price change upon total receipts from the sale of the product. If price and total receipts move

in opposite directions, demand is elastic. If price and total receipts move in the same direction, demand is inelastic.

5. The number of available substitutes, the size of an item in one's budget, whether the product is a luxury or necessity, the time period involved, and the durability of a product are all considerations which influence elasticity of demand.

6. Elasticity varies at different price ranges on a demand curve. Furthermore, it is not safe to judge elasticity by the steepness or flatness of a demand curve on a graph.

7. The elasticity concept is also applicable to supply. Elasticity of supply depends upon the shiftability of resources between alternative employments. This shiftability in

turn varies with the amount of time producers have to adjust to a given price
change.

8. Legal prices upset the rationing function of free market prices. Effective price
ceilings result in persistent product shortages, and if an equitable distribution of the
product is sought, government will have to
ration the product to consumers. Price
supports give rise to product surpluses;
government must purchase these surplus
products or take what measures are possible
to eliminate them by imposing restrictions on production or by increasing demand.

9. The demand or average-revenue curve
faced by a purely competitive seller is
perfectly elastic. In contrast the demand
curve facing an imperfectly competitive

seller is downsloping, that is, less than perfectly elastic.

10. Under pure competition product price
is constant to the individual seller; therefore,
each extra unit of output adds exactly the
same amount (its price) to total revenue. In
other words, marginal revenue is constant
and equal to price. Graphically, the marginal
revenue curve coincides with the firm's perfectly elastic demand curve. Total revenue
is a straight upsloping line.

11. The imperfectly competitive seller
must lower price to sell more, and this lower
price will apply to all prior units of sales. As
a result, marginal revenue is less than price.
Graphically, the firm's marginal revenue
curve lies below its demand curve. Total
revenue increases at a declining rate, reaches
a maximum, and finally declines.

QUESTIONS AND STUDY SUGGESTIONS

1. Answer questions 3, 4, and 10 at the end of Chapter 4.
2. In many oligopolistic industries, for example, the petroleum industry, producers justify their reluctance to lower prices by arguing that the demand for their products is inelastic. Explain.
3. How will the following changes in price affect total receipts (expenditures)—that is, will total receipts *increase, decline,* or *remain unchanged?*
   a. Price falls and demand is inelastic.
   b. Price rises and demand is elastic.
   c. Price rises and supply is elastic.
   d. Price rises and supply is inelastic.
   e. Price rises and demand is inelastic.
   f. Price falls and demand is elastic.
   g. Price falls and demand is of unit elasticity.
4. Determine the elasticity of demand and supply for the following demand and supply schedules. Use the total-revenue test to check the answers given by the E_d formula.

E_s	Quantity supplied	Product price	Quantity demanded	Total revenue	E_d
	28,000	$10	10,000	$_____	
_____	22,500	9	13,000	_____	
_____	17,000	8	17,000	_____	_____
_____	15,500	7	22,000	_____	_____
_____	11,000	6	25,000	_____	_____

5. What are the major determinants of elasticity of demand? Use these determinants in judging whether the demand for the following products is elastic or inelastic.
   a. Oranges   **b.** Salt
   c. Cigarettes   **d.** Chesterfield cigarettes
   e. Automobiles   **f.** Football games
   g. Gasoline   **h.** Diamond bracelets
   i. Butter   **j.** This textbook

6. Why is it difficult to judge elasticity of demand or supply by simply observing the appearance of a demand or supply curve on a graph?

7. Why is it necessary for ceiling prices to be accompanied by government rationing? Price supports by surplus-purchasing or output-restricting or demand-increasing programs? Show graphically why price ceilings entail shortages and price supports result in surpluses. What effect, if any, does the elasticity of demand and supply have upon the size of these shortages and surpluses? Explain.

8. How would you expect the elasticity of supply of product X to differ as between a situation of full employment in industry X, on the one hand, and considerable unemployment in the industry, on the other? Explain.

9. "If the demand for farm products is highly inelastic, a bumper crop may reduce farm incomes." Evaluate and illustrate graphically.

10. Suppose you are chairman of a state commission charged with the responsibility of establishing a program to raise new revenue through the use of excise taxes. Would elasticity of demand be important to you in determining those products upon which excises should be levied? Explain.

11. Use the following demand schedule to determine total and marginal revenue for each possible level of sales.

Product price	Quantity demanded	Total revenue	Marginal revenue
$2	1	$_____	
			$_____
2	2	_____	
			_____
2	3	_____	
			_____
2	4	_____	
			_____
2	5	_____	
			_____
2	6	_____	

a. What can you conclude about the structure of the industry in which this firm is operating? Explain.

b. Graph the demand, total-revenue, and marginal-revenue curves for this firm.

c. Why do the demand and marginal-revenue curves coincide?

d. "Marginal revenue is the rate of change in total revenue." Do you agree? Explain verbally and graphically, using the above data.

12. Now determine total and marginal revenue for each level of sales for this set of data:

Product price	Quantity demanded	Total revenue	Marginal revenue
$7	0	$_____	
			$_____
6	1	_____	
			_____
5	2	_____	
			_____
4	3	_____	
			_____
3	4	_____	
			_____
2	5	_____	
			_____
1	6	_____	

a. What can you conclude about the structure of the industry in which this firm is operating? Explain.
b. Graph the demand, total-revenue, and marginal-revenue curves for this firm.
c. Why does the marginal-revenue curve lie below the demand curve?

SELECTED REFERENCES

Boulding, Kenneth E.: *Economic Analysis,* 3d ed. (New York: Harper & Row, Publishers, Incorporated, 1955), chaps. 4, 5, 7, and 8.

Lipsey, Richard G.: *An Introduction to Positive Economics* (London: Weidenfeld and Nicolson, 1963), chap. 8.

Warner, Aaron W., and Victor R. Fuchs: *Concepts and Cases in Economic Analysis* (New York: Harcourt, Brace & World, Inc., 1958), chap. 5 and pp. 173–182.

Watson, Donald S.: *Price Theory and Its Uses* (Boston: Houghton Mifflin Company, 1963), chap. 3.

Watson, Donald S.: *Price Theory in Action* (Boston: Houghton Mifflin Company, 1965), part 1.

CHAPTER 24

FURTHER TOPICS IN THE THEORY OF CONSUMER DEMAND[1]

In Chapter 23 we extended our understanding of demand and supply by introducing the concept of price elasticity and by discussing some specific applications of demand and supply analysis. The present chapter is devoted to further consideration of the demand side of the market. In Chapter 25 we shall discuss production costs, which, we shall discover, are the major determinant of supply. The goal of Chapters 26 to 29 is to use our understanding of demand and supply in analyzing pricing and output decisions under the various market structures which were outlined in Chapter 22.

Now for a more detailed look at the two main objectives of the present chapter. First, we seek a more sophisticated explanation of the law of demand. Second, we want to understand how consumers allocate their money incomes among various goods and services. Why does a consumer buy some specific bundle of goods rather than any one of a number of other collections of goods which are available to him?

TWO EXPLANATIONS OF THE LAW OF DEMAND

Thus far we have accepted the law of demand as a common-sense notion. We have simply appealed to observation in claiming an inverse relationship between price and quantity demanded. A high price usually

[1] To the instructor: This is an optional chapter which may be omitted without impairing the continuity and meaning of ensuing chapters.

does discourage consumers from buying; a low price typically does encourage them to buy. Now let us explore two complementary explanations of the downsloping nature of the demand curve which will back up our everyday observations.[2]

Income and Substitution Effects

One explanation of the law of demand says in essence that as the price of a product declines, consumers will be both *able* and *willing* to buy more of it.

As the price of steak declines, you are obviously able to buy more of it with your money income. With a constant money income of, say, $10 per week you can purchase 10 pounds of steak at a price of $1 per pound. But if the price of steak falls to 50 cents per pound and 10 pounds of steak is bought, $5 per week is freed for buying more of this and other commodities. A decline in the price of steak increases the real income of the consumer. This is called the *income effect*.

[2] A third explanation, based upon *indifference curves*, is in some respects more precise than the two we now discuss. The complexities of this approach, however, make it more suitable for an intermediate course in economic theory. The interested reader should refer to Richard H. Leftwich, *The Price System and Resource Allocation*, rev. ed. (New York: Holt, Rinehart and Winston, Inc., 1960), chap. 5, or John F. Due and Robert W. Clower, *Intermediate Economic Analysis*, 4th ed. (Homewood, Ill.: Richard D. Irwin, Inc., 1961), chap. 5.

But being able to buy more steak at a lower price is not a complete explanation of why you actually do buy more. As the price of steak falls—the prices of other products being unchanged—steak will become more attractive to the buyer. At 50 cents per pound it is a "better buy" than at $1 per pound. Consequently, the lower price will induce the consumer to substitute steak for some of the now less attractive items in his budget. Steak may well be substituted for pork, mutton, veal, and a variety of other foods. A lower price increases the relative attractiveness of a product and makes the consumer willing to buy more of it. This is known as the *substitution effect*.

The income and substitution effects combine to make a consumer able and willing to buy more of a specific good at a low price than at a high price.

Law of Diminishing Marginal Utility

A second explanation centers upon the notion that, although consumer wants in general may be insatiable, wants for specific commodities can be fulfilled. In a given span of time, wherein the tastes of buyers are unchanged, consumers can get as much of specific goods and services as they want. The more of a specific product a consumer obtains, the less anxious he is to get more units of the same product. This can be most readily seen for durable goods. A consumer's want for an automobile, when he has none, may be very strong; his desire for a second car is much less intense; for a third or fourth, very weak. Even the wealthiest of families rarely have more than a half dozen cars, despite the fact that their incomes would allow them to purchase and maintain a whole fleet of them.

Economists put forth the idea that specific consumer wants can be fulfilled with succeeding units of a commodity in the *law of diminishing marginal utility*. Let us dissect this law to see exactly what it means. A product has utility if it has the power to satisfy a want. Utility is want-satisfying power. Two characteristics of this concept must be emphasized: First, "utility" and "usefulness" are by no means synonymous. Diamond rings and paintings by Picasso may be useless in the functional sense of the term yet be of tremendous utility to senior coeds and art connoisseurs, respectively. Second—and implied in the first point —utility is a subjective notion. The utility of a specific product will vary widely from person to person. A nip of Old Tennisshoes will yield tremendous utility to the Skid Row alcoholic, but zero or negative utility to the local WCTU president.

By marginal utility we simply mean the extra utility, or satisfaction, which a consumer gets from one additional unit of a specific product. In any relatively short period of time, wherein the consumers' tastes can be assumed not to change, the marginal utility derived from successive units of a given product will decline.[3] Why? Because a consumer will eventually become saturated, or "filled up," with that particular product. The fact that marginal utility will decline as the consumer acquires additional units of a specific product is known as the *law of diminishing marginal utility*.

We have noted that utility is a subjective concept. As a result it is not susceptible to precise quantitative measurement. But for purposes of illustration, let us assume that we can measure satisfaction with units we shall call "utils." This mythical unit of satisfaction is merely a convenient pedagogical device which will allow us to quantify our thinking about consumer behavior. Thus in Table 24–1 we can illustrate the relationship between the quantity obtained of a product— say, product A—and the accompanying extra

[3] For a time the marginal utility of successive units of a product may increase. A third cigarette may yield a larger amount of extra satisfaction than the first or second. But beyond some point we can expect the marginal utility of added units to decline.

$$\frac{\text{MU of A: 10 utils}}{\text{price of A: \$1}} > \frac{\text{MU of B: 18 utils}}{\text{price of B: \$3}}$$

The last dollar spent on A provides 10 utils of satisfaction and the last dollar spent on B only provides 6. On a per dollar basis, units of A provide more extra satisfaction than units of B. The consumer will obviously increase his total satisfaction by purchasing more of A and less of B. As dollars are reallocated from B to A, the marginal utility from additional units of A will decline as the result of moving down the diminishing marginal utility schedule for A, and the marginal utility of B will rise as the consumer moves up the diminishing marginal utility schedule for B. At some new combination of A and B—specifically, 4 of A and 2 of B—the equality of the two ratios and therefore consumer equilibrium will be achieved. As we already know, the net gain in utility is 6 utils $(79 - 73)$.

Now there are admittedly a number of criticisms of this theory of consumer behavior. Most obviously, we have no "utilometer" by which the consumer's preferences can be set down precisely as in Table 24–2. Nor is it easy to incorporate large, indivisible products such as houses, automobiles, pianos, or a college education in our analysis. Nevertheless, there is little doubt that the theory accurately describes the basic rationale underlying consumer behavior. In a general way the theory does explain how consumers behave. Albeit in a loose fashion, consumers do seek to maximize their satisfaction. And though the process may be crude, consumers do make marginal comparisons in allocating their limited incomes. In formulating its budget, a family must choose between, say, a food freezer, a television set, and building a recreation room in the basement. And the college student must weigh the relative satisfaction to be derived from spending $10 on a Saturday-night date as opposed to a new pair of shoes or a couple of shirts. Despite its limitations, the utility-maximizing rule is a meaningful general statement of how consumers behave.

SUMMARY

1. The law of demand can be explained on the basis of the income and substitution effects or the law of diminishing marginal utility.

2. The income effect says that a decline in the price of a product will enable the consumer to buy more of it with his fixed money income. The substitution effect points out that a lower price will make a product relatively more attractive and therefore increase the consumer's willingness to substitute it for other products.

3. The law of diminishing marginal utility states that beyond some point additional units of a specific commodity will yield ever-declining amounts of extra satisfaction to a consumer. It follows that a lower price will be needed to induce the consumer to increase his purchases of such a product.

4. We may assume that the typical consumer is rational and acts on the basis of rather well-defined preferences; consumers act sensibly and know roughly the satisfaction they will derive from successive units of various products available to them. Because his income is limited and goods have prices on them, the consumer cannot purchase all the goods and services he might like to have. He should therefore select that attainable combination of goods which will maximize his utility or satisfaction.

5. The consumer's utility will be maximized when he is allocating his income so that the last dollar spent on each product purchased yields the same amount of extra satisfaction. Algebraically, the utility-maximizing rule is fulfilled when

$$\frac{\text{MU of product A}}{\text{price of A}} = \frac{\text{MU of product B}}{\text{price of B}}$$

and the consumer's income is spent. Though subject to limitations, this rule is a meaningful guide in explaining consumer behavior.

QUESTIONS AND STUDY SUGGESTIONS

1. Explain the law of demand through the income and substitution effects, using a price increase as a point of departure for your discussion.
2. Explain the law of diminishing marginal utility. Explain the law of demand in terms of diminishing marginal utility.
3. Mrs. Peterson buys loaves of bread and quarts of milk each week at prices of 20 cents and 30 cents, respectively. At present she is buying these two products in amounts such that the marginal utilities from the last units purchased of the two products are 40 and 70 utils, respectively. Is Mrs. Peterson currently buying the best, that is, the utility-maximizing, combination of bread and milk? If not, in what manner should she reallocate her expenditures between the two goods?
4. Columns 1 through 4 of the following table show the marginal utility, measured in terms of utils, which Mr. Black would get by purchasing various amounts of products A, B, C, and D. Column 5 shows the marginal utility Black gets from saving. Assume that the prices of A, B, C, and D are $24, $4, $6, and $18, respectively, and that Black has a money income of $106.

Column 1		Column 2		Column 3		Column 4		Column 5	
								Number of	
Units of A	MU	Units of B	MU	Units of C	MU	Units of D	MU	dollars saved	MU
1	36	1	15	1	24	1	72	1	5
2	30	2	12	2	15	2	54	2	4
3	24	3	8	3	12	3	45	3	3
4	18	4	7	4	9	4	36	4	2
5	13	5	5	5	7	5	27	5	1
6	7	6	4	6	5	6	18	6	½
7	4	7	3½	7	2	7	15	7	¼
8	2	8	3	8	1	8	12	8	⅛

    a. What quantities of A, B, C, and D will Black purchase in maximizing his satisfactions?
    b. How many dollars will Black choose to save?
    c. Check your answers by substituting in the algebraic statement of the utility-maximizing rule.
5. "Nothing is more useful than water: but it will purchase scarce any thing; scarce any thing can be had in exchange for it. A diamond, on the contrary, has scarce any value in use; but a very great quantity of other goods may frequently be had in exchange for it."[6] Explain.

[6] Adam Smith, *The Wealth of Nations* (New York: Modern Library, Inc., originally published in 1776), p. 28.

6. "In the long run it may be irrational to purchase goods on the basis of habit; but in the short run habitual buying may prove to be a very sensible means of allocating income." Do you agree? Explain.

SELECTED REFERENCES

Bober, M. M.: *Intermediate Price and Income Theory,* rev. ed. (New York: W. W. Norton & Company, Inc., 1962), chap. 3.

Fellner, William: *Modern Economic Analysis* (New York: McGraw-Hill Book Company, 1960), chap. 14.

Leftwich, Richard H.: *The Price System and Resource Allocation,* rev. ed. (New York: Holt, Rinehart and Winston, Inc., 1960), chap. 4.

Watson, Donald S.: *Price Theory and Its Uses* (Boston: Houghton Mifflin Company, 1963), chaps. 4 and 5.

CHAPTER 25

SUPPLY AND THE COSTS OF PRODUCTION

Product prices are determined by the interaction of the forces of demand and supply. Preceding chapters have focused our attention upon the factors underlying demand. The basic factor underlying the ability and willingness of firms to supply a product in the market is the cost of production. The production of any good requires the use of economic resources which, because of their relative scarcity, bear price tags. The amount of any product which a firm is willing to supply in the market depends upon the prices, or costs, of the resources essential to its production, on the one hand, and the price which the product will bring in the market, on the other. The present chapter is concerned with the general nature of production costs. Product prices are introduced in the following several chapters, and the supply decisions of producers are then explained.

ECONOMIC COSTS IN REAL AND MONEY TERMS

Economic costs are those payments which must be received by resource owners in order to assure that they will continue to supply them in a particular line of production. This definition goes back to the basic fact that resources are scarce and have alternative uses. First in real (physical) terms, the economist's definition of costs simply suggests that to use a resource in producing one product entails giving up some alternative product. The real cost of producing 5 units of X is the number of units of Y or Z which

the resources used in X could otherwise have produced. The production possibilities curve of Chapter 2 clearly embodies this notion of costs. Note at point *C* in Table 2–1 that the real cost of producing 100,000 more units of bread is the 3,000-unit decrease in the production of drill presses which will necessarily be entailed. A final illustration: Suppose an assembly-line worker can be used in producing automobiles, washing machines, and refrigerators. The real cost of using this worker in producing automobiles is the contribution which he might otherwise have made in the production of washing machines and refrigerators.

When expressed in money terms, the notion of economic costs is a bit more elusive. The main reason for this is that we, as the accountant or businessman, typically think of costs as being essentially money payments, that is, cash outlays, which a firm makes to the "outsiders" who supply labor services, materials, fuel, transportation services, power, and so forth, to the firm. These expenditures, or *explicit costs*, are certainly a part of the economist's definition of costs; but they are only a part. The economist would also include any nonexpenditure, or *implicit*, costs, that is, the value of any resources which are owned and employed by an enterprise. The economist's reasoning is simple and very pertinent: Regardless of whether a resource is owned or hired by an enterprise, there is a cost involved in using that resource in a specific employment. In real terms that cost is the units of alternative products which are forgone. In money terms it is the money payment which the self-employed resource could have earned in its best alternative employments. For example, suppose Brooks operates a corner grocery as a sole proprietor. He owns his store building and supplies all his own labor and money capital. Though his enterprise has no explicit rental or wage costs, implicit rents and wages are incurred. By using his own building for a grocery, Brooks sacrifices the $200 monthly rental income which he could otherwise have earned by renting it to someone else. Similarly, by using his money capital and labor in his own enterprise, Brooks sacrifices the interest and wage incomes which he otherwise could have earned by supplying these resources in their best alternative employments. And, finally, by running his own enterprise, Brooks forgoes the earnings he could realize by supplying his entrepreneurial efforts in someone else's firm.

The minimum payment required to keep Brooks's entrepreneurial talents engaged in this enterprise is sometimes called a *normal profit.* As implicit rent or implicit wages, this normal return for the performing of entrepreneurial functions is an implicit cost. If this minimum, or normal, return is not realized, the entrepreneur will withdraw his efforts from this line of production and reallocate them to some alternative line of production. Or the individual may cease being an entrepreneur in favor of becoming a laborer.

In short, the economist includes as costs all payments—explicit and implicit, the latter including a normal profit—required to retain resources in a given line of production.

Economic, or Pure, Profits

Our discussion of economic costs correctly suggests that economists and accountants use the term "profits" differently. By "profits" the accountant generally means total receipts less explicit costs. But to the economist "profits" means total receipts less *all* costs (explicit and implicit, the latter including a normal return to the entrepreneur). Therefore, when an economist says that a firm is just covering its costs, he means that all explicit and implicit costs are being met and that the entrepreneur is therefore receiving a return just large enough to retain his talents in his present line of production. If a firm's total receipts exceed all its economic costs, any residual accrues to the entrepreneur. This residual is called an *economic,* or *pure, profit.* It is not a cost, because by definition it is a return in excess of the normal profit required to retain the entrepreneur in this particular line of production. In Chapter 32 we shall find that economic profits are associated with risk bearing and monopoly power.

Short Run and Long Run

The costs which a firm or industry incurs in producing any given output will depend upon the types of adjustment it is able to make in the amounts of the various resources it employs. The quantities employed of many resources—labor, raw materials, fuel, power, and so forth—can be varied easily and quickly. But the amounts of other resources demand more time for adjustment. For example, the capacity of a manufacturing plant, that is, the size of the factory building and the amount of machinery and equipment therein, can only be varied over a considerable period of time. In some heavy industries it may take several years to alter plant capacity.

These differences in the time necessary to vary the quantities of the various resources used in the productive process make it essential to distinguish between the short run and the long run. The *short run* refers to a period of time too short to permit an enterprise to alter its plant capacity yet long enough to permit a change in the level at which the fixed plant is utilized. The firm's plant capacity is fixed in the short run, but output can be varied by applying larger or smaller amounts of manpower, materials, and so forth, to that plant. Existing plant capacity can be used more or less intensively in the short run.

From the viewpoint of existing firms the *long run* refers to a period of time long enough to allow these firms to change the quantities of *all* resources employed, including plant capacity. From the viewpoint of an industry the long run also encompasses enough time for existing firms to dissolve and leave the industry and for new firms to be created and enter the industry. While the short run is a "fixed-plant" time period, the long run is a "variable-plant" time period.

Some examples will make clear the distinction between the short run and the long run. If a General Motors plant were to hire an extra 100 workers or to add an entire shift of workers, these would be short-run adjustments. If the same GM plant were to add a new wing to its building and install more equipment, this would be a long-run adjustment. Studebaker's abandonment of its South Bend, Indiana, plant in 1964 was a long-run adjustment.

It is important to note that the short run and the long run are conceptual rather than specific calendar time periods. In light manufacturing industries, changes in plant capacity may be negotiated almost overnight. A small firm making men's clothing can increase its plant capacity in a few days or less simply by ordering and installing a couple of new cutting tables and several extra sewing machines. But heavy industry is a different story. It may take Ford or General Motors several years to construct a new assembly plant and to install elaborate assembly-line equipment.

We turn now to the task of analyzing production costs in the short-run, or fixed-plant, period. Following this we consider costs in the long-run, or variable-plant, period.

PRODUCTION COSTS IN THE SHORT RUN

A firm's costs of producing any output will depend not only upon the prices of needed resources, but also upon technology—the quantity of resources it takes to produce that output. It is the latter, technological aspect of costs with which we are concerned for the moment. In the short run a firm can change its output by adding variable resources to a fixed plant. Question: How does output change as more and more variable resources are added to the firm's fixed resources?

Law of Diminishing Returns

The answer is provided in general terms by the *law of diminishing returns*. This engineering law states that *as successive units of a variable resource (say, labor) are added to a fixed resource (capital), beyond some point the extra, or marginal, product attributable to each additional unit of the variable resource will decline.* Stated somewhat differently, if additional workers are applied to a given amount of capital equipment, as is the case in the short run, eventually output will rise less than in proportion to the increase in the number of workers employed. A couple of examples will illustrate this law.

Suppose a farmer has a fixed amount of land—say, 80 acres—which he has planted in corn. Assuming the farmer does not cultivate his cornfields at all, his yield will be, say, 40 bushels per acre. If he cultivates the land once, output may rise to 50 bushels per acre. A second cultivation may increase output to 57 bushels per acre, a third to 61, and a fourth to, say, 63. But further cultivations will add little or nothing to total output. Successive cultivations add less and less to the land's yield. If this were not the case, the world's needs for corn could be fulfilled by extremely intense cultivation of this single 80-acre plot of land. Indeed, if diminishing returns did not occur, the world could be fed out of a flowerpot.

The law of diminishing returns also holds true in nonagricultural industries. Assume a small planing mill is manufacturing unupholstered furniture. The mill has a given amount of equipment in the form of lathes, planers, saws, sanders, and so forth. If this firm hired just one or two workers, total output and production per man would be very low. These workers would have a number of different jobs to perform, and the advantages of specialization would be lost. Time would also be lost in switching from one job operation to another, and the machines would stand idle most of the time. In short, the plant would be undermanned, and production therefore would be inefficient. These difficulties would disappear as more workers were added. Equipment would be more fully utilized, and workers could now specialize on a single job. Thus as more workers are added to the initially undermanned plant, the extra or marginal product of each will tend to rise as a result of more efficient production. But this cannot go on indefinitely. As still more workers are added, problems of overcrowding will arise. Workers must wait in line to use the machinery, so now *workers* are underutilized. The extra, or marginal, product of additional workers declines because the plant is overmanned. In the extreme the continuous addition of labor to the plant would use up all standing room, and production would be brought to a standstill!

Table 25–1 illustrates the law of diminishing returns numerically. In this instance diminishing marginal product is incurred with the hire of the third worker. Total product is found by simply accumulating the extra, or marginal, product attributable to each successive worker. Total product will increase so long as marginal product is positive.

Fixed, Variable, and Total Costs

The production data described by the law of diminishing returns must be coupled with resource prices to determine the total and per unit costs of producing various outputs. We have already emphasized that in the short run some resources—those associated with the firm's plant—are fixed. Others are variable. This correctly suggests that in the short run costs can be classified as either fixed or variable.

Fixed costs are those costs which in total do not vary with changes in output. Fixed costs are associated with the very existence of a firm's plant and therefore must be paid even if the firm's rate of output is zero. Such costs as interest on a firm's bonded indebtedness, rental payments, a portion of depreciation on equipment and buildings, insurance premiums, and the salaries of top management and key personnel are generally fixed costs. In column 2 of Table 25–2

TABLE 25–1. THE LAW OF DIMINISHING RETURNS (hypothetical data)

(1) Inputs of the variable resource (labor)	(2) Extra, or marginal, product	(3) Total product
0		0
	5	
1		5
	8	
2		13
	5	
3		18
	4	
4		22
	3	
5		25
	2	
6		27

TABLE 25–2. TOTAL- AND AVERAGE-COST SCHEDULES FOR AN INDIVIDUAL FIRM IN THE SHORT RUN (hypothetical data)

	Total-cost data, per week			Average-cost data, per week			
(1)	(2)	(3)	(4)	(5)	(6)	(7)	(8)
Total product	Total fixed cost	Total variable cost	Total cost	Average fixed cost, or (2) ÷ (1)	Average variable cost, or (3) ÷ (1)	Average total cost, or (4) ÷ (1)	Marginal cost, or Δ(4)
0	$100	$ 0	$ 100				
							$ 90
1	100	90	190	$100.00	$90.00	$190.00	
							80
2	100	170	270	50.00	85.00	135.00	
							70
3	100	240	340	33.33	80.00	113.33	
							60
4	100	300	400	25.00	75.00	100.00	
							70
5	100	370	470	20.00	74.00	94.00	
							80
6	100	450	550	16.67	75.00	91.67	
							90
7	100	540	640	14.29	77.14	91.43	
							110
8	100	650	750	12.50	81.23	93.73	
							130
9	100	780	880	11.11	86.67	97.78	
							150
10	100	930	1,030	10.00	93.00	103.00	

we have assumed that the firm's fixed costs are $100. Note that this fixed-cost figure prevails at all levels of output, including zero.

Variable costs are those costs which increase with the level of output. Variable costs include payments for labor, materials, fuel, power, transportation services, and similar variable resources. In column 3 of Table 25–2 we find that the total of variable costs changes with output, but note that the rate of increase in variable costs is not constant. As production begins, variable costs will for a time increase at a decreasing rate; this is true through the fourth unit of output. Beyond the fourth unit, however, variable costs increase at an increasing rate. The explanation of this behavior of variable costs

lies in the law of diminishing returns. Because of increasing marginal product, smaller and smaller increases in the amounts of variable resources will be needed for a time to get successive units of output produced. This means that total variable costs will increase at a decreasing rate. But when marginal product begins to decline as diminishing returns are encountered, it will be necessary to use larger and larger additional amounts of variable resources to produce each successive unit of output. Total variable costs will therefore increase at an increasing rate.

Total cost is self-defining: it is the *sum of fixed and variable costs at each level of output.* It is shown in column 4 of Table 25–2.

At zero units of output total cost is equal to the firm's fixed costs. Then for each unit of production—1 through 10—total cost varies at the same rate as does variable cost.

Figure 25–1 shows graphically the fixed-, variable-, and total-cost data of Table 25–2. Note that total variable cost is measured from the horizontal axis and total fixed cost is added vertically to total variable cost in locating the total cost curve.

The distinction between fixed and variable costs is of no little significance to the businessman. Variable costs are those costs which the businessman can control or alter in the short run by changing his level of production. On the other hand, fixed costs are

FIGURE 25–1. TOTAL COST IS THE SUM OF FIXED AND VARIABLE COSTS. Variable costs (VC) vary with output. Fixed costs are independent of the level of output. The total cost (TC) of any output is the (vertical) sum of the fixed and variable costs of that output.

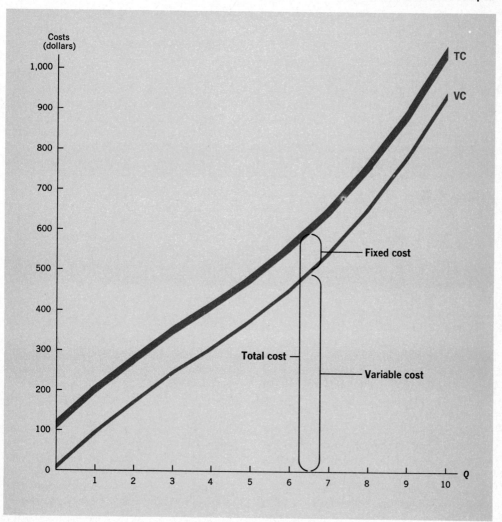

clearly beyond the businessman's control; such costs are incurred and must be paid regardless of output level.

Per Unit, or Average, Costs

Producers are certainly interested in their total costs, but they are equally concerned with their per unit, or average, costs. In particular, average-cost data are more usable for making comparisons with product price, which is always stated on a per unit basis. Average fixed cost, average variable cost, and average total cost are shown in columns 5 to 7 of Table 25–2. It is important that we know how these unit-cost figures are derived and how they vary as output changes.

Average fixed cost (AFC) is found by dividing total fixed costs by the corresponding output. AFC declines as output increases. Whereas total fixed costs are, by definition, independent of output, AFC will decline as output increases. As output increases, a given total fixed cost of $100 is obviously being spread over a larger and larger output. When output is just 1 unit, total fixed costs and AFC are equal—$100. But at 2 units of output, total fixed costs of $100 become $50 worth of fixed costs per unit; then $33.33, as $100 is spread over 3 units; $25, when spread over 4 units; and so forth. This is what businessmen commonly refer to as "spreading the overhead." We find in Figure 25–2 that AFC graphs as a continually declining figure as total output is increased.

Average variable cost (AVC) is found by dividing total variable cost by the corresponding output. AVC declines initially, reaches a minimum, and then increases again. Graphically, this provides us with a U-shaped AVC curve, as is shown in Figure 25–2.

Because total variable cost reflects the law of diminishing returns, so must the AVC figures, which are derived from total variable cost. Because of increasing returns it takes fewer and fewer additional variable resources to produce each of the first 4 units of output. As a result, variable cost per unit will decline. AVC hits a minimum with the fifth unit of output, and beyond this point AVC rises as diminishing returns necessitate the use of more and more variable resources to produce each additional unit of output. In more direct terms, at low levels of output production will be relatively inefficient and costly, because the firm's fixed plant is undermanned. Not enough variable resources are being combined with the firm's plant; production is inefficient, and per unit variable costs are therefore relatively high. As output expands, however, greater specialization and a more complete utilization of the firm's capital equipment will make for more efficient production. As a result, variable cost per unit of output will decline. As more and more variable resources are added, some point will eventually be reached where diminishing returns are incurred. The firm's capital equipment will now be overmanned, and the resulting overcrowding and overutilization of machinery impairs efficiency. This means that AVC will increase.

Average total cost (ATC) can be found by dividing total cost by total output or, more simply, by adding AFC and AVC for each of the ten levels of output. These data are shown in column 7 of Table 25–2. Graphically, ATC is found by adding vertically the AFC and AVC curves, as in Figure 25–2. Thus the vertical distance between the ATC and AVC curves reflects AFC at any output.

Marginal Cost

There remains one final and very crucial cost concept—marginal cost. *Marginal cost (MC) is the extra, or additional, cost of producing one more unit of output.* MC can be determined for each additional unit of output simply by noting the change in total cost which that unit's production entails. In Table 25–2 we find that production of the first unit of output increases total cost from $100 to $190. Therefore, the additional, or marginal, cost of that first unit is $90. The marginal cost of the second unit is $80 ($270 − $190); the MC of the third is $70

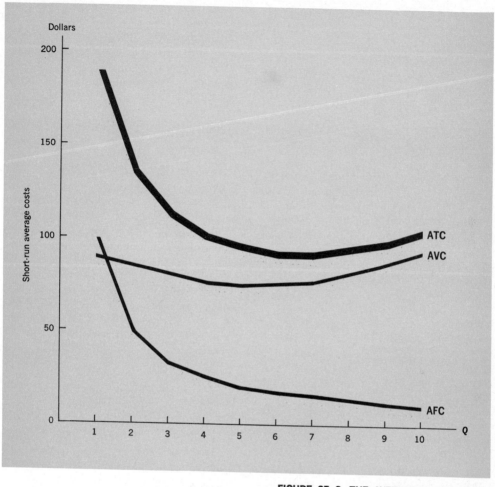

FIGURE 25–2. THE AVERAGE-COST CURVES.
Average total cost (ATC) is the vertical sum of average variable cost (AVC) and
average fixed cost (AFC). AFC necessarily falls as a given amount of fixed costs is
apportioned over a larger and larger output. AVC initially falls because of
increasing physical returns but then rises because of diminishing physical returns.

($340 − $270); and so forth. MC for each of the ten units of output is shown in column 8 of Table 25–2. MC can also be calculated from the total-variable-cost column. Why? Because the only difference between total cost and total variable cost is the constant amount of fixed costs. Hence, the change in total cost and change in total variable cost associated with each additional unit of output is the same.

Marginal cost is a very strategic concept, because it designates those costs over which the firm has the most direct control. More specifically, MC indicates those costs which are incurred in the production of the last unit of output and, simultaneously, the cost which can be "saved" by reducing total output by the last unit. Average-cost figures do not provide this information. For example, suppose the firm is undecided as to whether it should produce 3 or 4 units of output. At 4 units of output Table 25–2 indicates that ATC is $100. But the firm does not increase its total costs by $100 by producing, nor does it "save" $100 by not producing, the fourth unit. Rather the change in costs involved here is only $60, as the MC column of Table 25–2 clearly reveals. A firm's decisions as to what output to produce are marginal decisions, that is, decisions to produce a few more or a few less units. Marginal cost reveals the change in costs which one more unit or one less unit of output entails. When coupled with marginal revenue, which we found in Chapter 23 indicates the change in revenue from one more or one less unit of output, marginal cost allows a firm to determine whether it is profitable to expand or contract its level of production. The analysis in the next four chapters centers upon these marginal calculations.

Marginal cost is shown graphically in Figure 25–3. Note that marginal cost declines sharply, reaches a minimum, and then rises rather sharply. This mirrors the fact that variable cost, and therefore total cost, increases first at a decreasing rate and then at an increasing rate (see Figure 25–1 and columns 3 and 4 of Table 25–2). This, you will recall, is in accord with the law of diminishing returns.

Furthermore, it is notable that marginal cost cuts both AVC and ATC at their minimum points. This marginal-average relationship is a matter of mathematical necessity, which a common-sense illustration can make readily apparent. Suppose a baseball pitcher has allowed his opponents an average of 3 runs per game in the first three games he has pitched. Now whether his average falls or rises as a result of pitching a fourth (marginal) game will depend upon whether the additional runs he allows in that extra game are fewer or more than his current 3-run average. If he allows fewer than 3 runs—for example, 1—in the fourth game, his total runs will rise from 9 to 10, and his average will fall from 3 to 2½ (10 ÷ 4). Conversely, if he

allows more than 3 runs—say, 7—in the fourth game, his total will rise from 9 to 16 and his average from 3 to 4 (16 ÷ 4). So it is with costs. When the amount added to total cost (marginal cost) is less than the average of total cost, ATC will fall. Conversely, when marginal cost exceeds ATC, ATC will rise. This means in Figure 25–3 that so long as MC lies below ATC, the latter will fall, and where MC is above ATC, ATC will rise. Therefore at the point of intersection where MC equals ATC, ATC has just ceased to fall but has not yet begun to rise. This, by definition, is the minimum point on the ATC curve. Because MC can be defined as the addition either to total cost or to total variable cost resulting from one more unit of output, this same rationale explains why MC also cuts AVC at the latter's minimum point. No such relationship exists for MC and average fixed cost, because the two are simply not related; marginal cost embodies only those costs which change with output, and fixed costs by definition are independent of output.

PRODUCTION COSTS IN THE LONG RUN

In the long run all desired resource adjustments can be negotiated by an industry and the individual firms which it comprises. The firm can alter its plant capacity; it can build a larger plant or revert to a smaller plant than that assumed in Table 25–2. The industry can also change its plant size; the long run is an amount of time sufficient for new firms to enter or old firms to leave an industry. The impact of the entry and exodus of firms from an industry will be discussed in the next chapter; here we are concerned only with changes in plant capacity made by a single firm. And in considering these adjustents, we couch our analysis in terms of ATC, making no distinction between fixed and variable costs for the obvious reason that all resources and therefore all costs are variable in the long run.

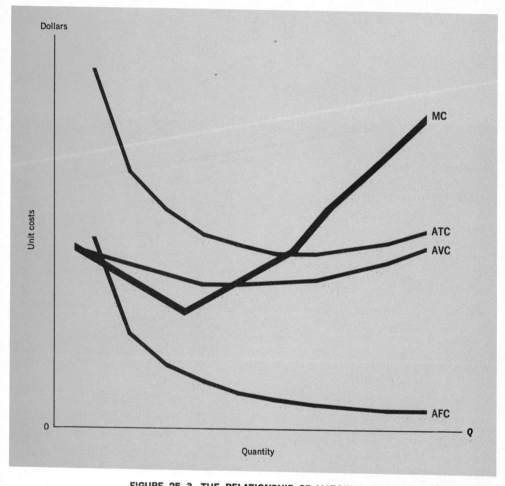

FIGURE 25–3. THE RELATIONSHIP OF MARGINAL COST TO AVERAGE TOTAL COST AND AVERAGE VARIABLE COST.
Marginal cost (MC) cuts both ATC and AVC at their minimum points. This is so because whenever the extra or marginal amount added to total cost (or variable cost) is less than the average of that cost, the average will necessarily fall. Conversely, whenever the marginal amount added to total (or variable) cost is greater than the average of total cost, the average must rise.

Suppose a single-plant manufacturing enterprise starts out on a small scale and then, as the result of successful operations, expands to successively larger plant sizes. What will happen to average total costs as this growth occurs? The answer is this: For a time successively larger plants will bring lower average total costs. However, even-

tually the building of a still larger plant will cause ATC to rise.

Figure 25–4 illustrates this situation for five possible plant sizes. ATC-1 is the average-total-cost curve for the smallest of the five plants, and ATC-5 for the largest. The relationship of the five plant sizes to one another is clearly that stated above. Con-

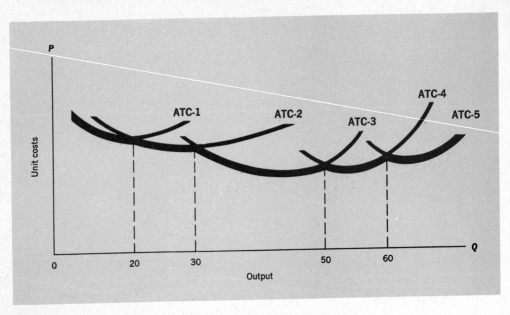

FIGURE 25–4. THE LONG-RUN AVERAGE-COST CURVE: FIVE POSSIBLE PLANT SIZES.
The long-run average-cost curve is made up of segments of the short-run cost curves (ATC-1, ATC-2, etc.) of the various-sized plants from which the firm might choose. Each point on the bumpy planning curve shows the least unit cost attainable for any output when the firm has had time to make all desired changes in its plant size.

structing a larger plant will entail lower per unit costs through plant size 3. But beyond this point a larger plant will mean a higher level of average total costs.

The dotted lines perpendicular to the output axis are crucial. They indicate those points at which the firm should change plant size in order to realize the lowest attainable per unit costs of production. To illustrate in terms of Figure 25–4: For all outputs up to 20 units the lowest per unit costs are attainable with plant size 1. However, if the firm's volume of sales expands to some level greater than 20 but less than 30 units, it can achieve lower per unit costs by constructing a larger plant—plant size 2. For any output between 30 and 50 units plant size 3 will yield the lowest per unit costs. For the 50–60-unit range of output, plant size 4 must be built to achieve the lowest unit costs. Lowest per unit costs for any output in

excess of 60 units demand the construction of the still larger plant of size 5.

Tracing these adjustments, we can conclude that the long-run ATC curve for the enterprise will comprise segments of the short-run ATC curves for the various plant sizes which can be constructed. *The long-run ATC curve shows the least per unit cost at which any output can be produced after the firm has had time to make all appropriate adjustments in its plant size.* In Figure 25–4 the heavy, bumpy curve is the firm's long-run ATC curve or, as it is often called, the firm's planning curve. In most lines of production the choice of plant sizes is much wider than that assumed in our illustration. In fact, in many industries the number of possible plant sizes is virtually unlimited. This means that in time very small changes in the volume of output (sales) will prompt appropriate changes in the size of the plant.

Graphically this means that the planning curve will be smooth rather than bumpy. Figure 25–5 is illustrative.

Economies and Diseconomies of Scale

We have patiently accepted the contention that for a time a larger and larger plant size will entail lower unit costs but that beyond some point successively larger plants will mean higher average total costs. Now we must explain this point. Exactly why is the long-run ATC curve U-shaped? It must be emphasized, first of all, that the law of diminishing returns is not applicable here, because it presumes that one resource is fixed in supply and, as we have seen, the long run assumes that all resources are variable. What then is our explanation? The U-shaped long-run average-cost curve is explainable in terms of what economists call "economies and diseconomies" of large-scale production.

Economies of large scale. Economies of scale or, more commonly, economies of mass production, explain the downsloping part of the long-run ATC curve. As the size of a plant increases, a number of considerations will for a time give rise to lower average costs of production.

1. Increased specialization in the use of labor is feasible as a plant increases in size. The hire of more workers means that jobs can be divided and subdivided. Instead of performing five or six distinct operations in the productive process, each worker may now have just one task to perform. Workers can be used full time on those particular operations at which they have special skills. In a small plant a skilled machinist may spend half his time performing unskilled tasks. This makes for high production costs. Further, the dividing of work operations which large scale allows will give workers the opportunity to become very proficient at

FIGURE 25–5. THE LONG-RUN AVERAGE-COST CURVE: UNLIMITED NUMBER OF PLANT SIZES.

If the number of possible plant sizes is very large, the long-run average-cost curve approximates a smooth curve. Economies and diseconomies of scale cause the curve to be U-shaped.

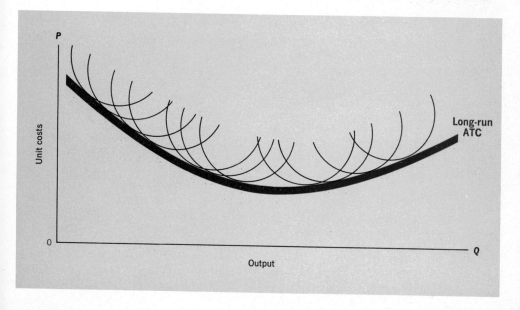

the specific tasks assigned them. The Jack-of-all-trades who is burdened with five or six jobs will not be likely to become very efficient in any of them. When allowed to concentrate on one task, the same worker may become highly efficient. Finally, greater specialization tends to eliminate the loss of time which accompanies the shifting of workers from one job to another.

2. *Large-scale production also permits better utilization of, and greater specialization in, management.* A foreman capable of handling fifteen or twenty men will be underutilized in a small plant hiring only eight or ten men. The production staff can be doubled with no increase in administrative costs. In addition, small firms will not be able to use management specialists to best advantage. In a small plant a sales specialist may be forced to divide his time between several executive functions—for example, sales, personnel, and finance. A larger scale of operations will mean that the sales expert can devote full time to supervising sales while appropriate specialists are added to perform other managerial functions. Greater efficiency and lower unit costs are the net result.

3. *Small firms are often not able to utilize the most efficient productive equipment.* In many lines of production the most efficient machinery is available only in very large and extremely expensive units. Furthermore, effective utilization of this equipment demands a high volume of production. This means only large-scale producers are able to afford and operate efficiently the best available equipment.

To illustrate: In the automobile industry the most efficient fabrication method entails the use of extremely elaborate assembly-line equipment. The efficient use of this equipment demands an annual output of thousands of automobiles per year. Only very large-scale producers can afford to purchase and use this equipment efficiently. The small-scale producer is between the devil and the deep blue sea. To fabricate automobiles with the use of other equipment is inefficient and

therefore more costly per unit. The alternative of purchasing the most efficient equipment and underutilizing it with a small level of output is equally inefficient and costly.

4. *The large-scale producer is in a better position to utilize by-products than is a small firm.* The large meat-packing plant makes glue, fertilizer, pharmaceuticals, and a host of other products from animal remnants which would be discarded by smaller producers.

All these technological considerations—greater specialization in the use of labor and management, the ability to use the most efficient equipment, and the effective utilization of by-products—will contribute to lower unit costs for the smaller producer who is able to expand his scale of operations.

Diseconomies of large scale. But in time the expansion of a firm will likely give rise to diseconomies and therefore higher per unit costs.

The main factor causing diseconomies of scale has to do with certain managerial problems which typically arise as a firm becomes a large-scale producer. In a small plant a single key executive may render all the basic decisions relative to his plant's operation. Because of the firm's smallness he is close to the production line. He can therefore comprehend the various aspects of the firm's operations and digest the information fed to him by his subordinates to the end that efficient decision making is possible.

This neat picture changes, however, as a firm grows. The management echelons between the executive suite and the assembly line become many; top management is far removed from the actual production operations of the plant. It becomes impossible for one man to assemble, understand, and digest all the information essential to rational decision making in a large-scale enterprise. Authority must be delegated to innumerable vice-presidents, second vice-presidents, and so forth. This expansion in the depth and width of management entails problems of coordination and bureaucratic red tape which can eventually impair the efficiency of a firm and lead to higher costs.

Significance of economies and diseconomies of scale.

Economies and diseconomies of scale are something more than a plausible pipedream of economic theorists. Indeed, in most American manufacturing industries economies of scale have been of great significance. Firms which have been able to expand their scale of operations to realize the economies of mass production have survived and flourished. Those unable to achieve this expansion have found themselves in the unenviable position of high-cost producers, doomed to a marginal existence or ultimate insolvency.

Diseconomies of scale, when encountered, can be equally significant. The organizational structure of General Motors, for example, is designed to avoid managerial diseconomies which its gigantic size would otherwise entail. This industrial colossus has subdivided itself into some thirty-four operating subdivisions, each of which is basically autonomous and in some cases—for example, its five automobile-producing divisions (Chevrolet, Buick, Oldsmobile, Pontiac, and Cadillac)—competing. A degree of decentralization has been sought which will allow full realization of the economies of mass production yet help to avoid diseconomies of scale.[1] Another example: Some economists feel that U.S. Steel has declined in relative importance in the steel industry because of diseconomies of scale. One authority has described U.S. Steel as[2]

. . . a big sprawling inert giant, whose production operations were improperly coordinated; suffering from a lack of a long-run planning agency; relying on an antiquated system of cost

[1] See Leonard W. Weiss, *Economics and American Industry* (New York: John Wiley & Sons, Inc., 1961), pp. 347–350.
[2] Statement by George Stocking, cited in Walter Adams (ed.), *The Structure of American Industry*, 3d ed. (New York: The Macmillan Company, 1961), p. 180.

accounting: with an inadequate knowledge of the costs or of the relative profitability of the many thousands of items it sold; with production and cost standards generally below those considered everyday practice in other industries; with inadequate knowledge of its domestic markets and no clear appreciation of its opportunities in foreign markets; with less efficient production facilities than its rivals had; slow in introducing new processes and new products.

These comments correctly imply that economies and diseconomies of scale are a fundamental determinant of the structure of any industry. Where economies of scale are many and diseconomies are remote, the long-run ATC curve will decline over a long range of output as in Figure 25–6*a*. Such is the case in the automobile, aluminum, steel, and a host of other heavy industries. This means that, given consumer demand, efficient production will be achieved only with a small number of large producers. On the other hand, where economies of scale are few and diseconomies quickly encountered, minimum unit costs will be achieved at a modest level of production. The long-run ATC curve for such a situation is shown in Figure 25–6*b*. In such industries a given level of consumer demand will support a large number of relatively small producers. Many of the retail trades and some types of farming fall into this category. So do certain types of light manufacturing, for example, the baking, clothing, and shoe industries. Fairly small firms are as efficient as, or more efficient than, large-scale producers in such industries.

In some industries we find a mixture of large and small producers operating with roughly the same degree of efficiency—the meat-packing, household-appliance, and furniture industries are representative. In such industries the long-run ATC curve may be such that there exists a wide range of output between the point at which available economies of scale are exhausted and the point at which diseconomies of scale are encountered. Or, alternatively, economies and diseconomies of scale may be largely self-canceling over an extended range of output. Figure

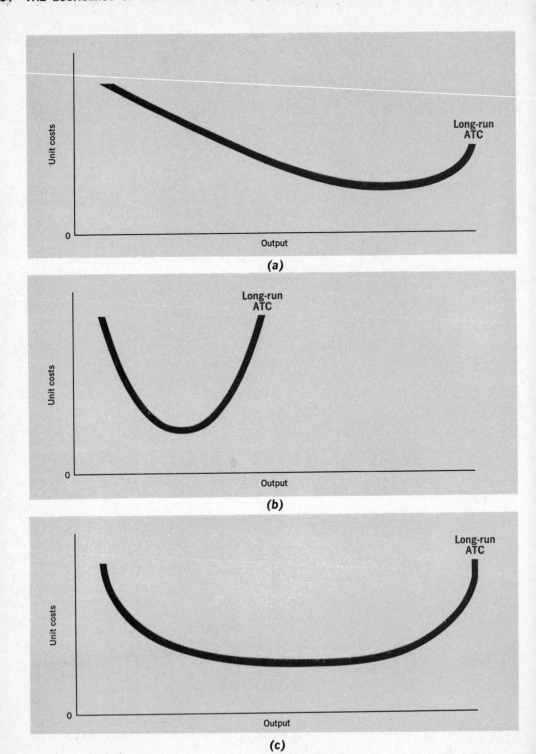

25–6c illustrates the situation in which average costs are relatively constant over a wide range of output.

Caution: We are not implying here that long-run unit costs are the only determinant of the structure of industry. Indeed, it was stressed in Chapter 22 that the major determinants of the competitiveness of industry are several and varied. We are saying that there is considerable evidence that cost considerations are one important force in determining the number and size of firms in a particular industry.

SUMMARY

1. Economic costs include all payments which must be received by resource owners in order to assure their continued supply in a particular line of production. This definition includes explicit costs which flow to resource suppliers who are separate from a given enterprise and also implicit costs which are the remuneration of self-owned and self-employed resources. One of the implicit cost payments is a normal profit to the entrepreneur for the functions he performs.

2. In the short run a firm's plant capacity is fixed. The firm can use its plant more or less intensively by adding or subtracting units of variable resources, but the firm does not have sufficient time to alter its plant size.

3. The law of diminishing returns describes what happens to output as a fixed plant is used more intensively. The law states that, as successive units of a variable resource such as labor are added to a fixed plant, beyond some point the resulting marginal product associated with each additional worker will decline.

4. Because some resources are variable and others fixed, costs can be classified as variable or fixed in the short run. Fixed costs are those which are independent of the level of output. Variable costs are those which vary with output. The total cost of any output is the sum of fixed and variable costs at that output.

5. Average fixed, average variable, and average total costs are simply fixed, variable, and total cost per unit of output. Average fixed costs decline continuously as output increases, because a fixed sum is being apportioned over a larger and larger number of units of production. Average variable costs are U-shaped, reflecting the law of diminishing returns. Average total cost is the sum of average fixed and average variable cost; it too is U-shaped.

6. Marginal cost is the extra, or additional, cost of producing one more unit of output. Graphically, marginal cost cuts ATC and AVC at their minimum points.

7. The long run is a period of time sufficiently long for a firm to vary the amounts of all resources used, including plant size. Hence, in the long run all costs are variable. The long-run ATC, or planning, curve is composed of segments of the short-run ATC curves, which represent the various plant sizes a firm is able to construct in the long run.

8. The long-run ATC curve is generally U-shaped. Economies of scale are first encountered as a small firm expands. A number of considerations—greater specialization in the use of labor and management, the ability to use the most efficient equipment, and the more complete utilization of by-products—contribute to these economies of scale. Dis-

FIGURE 25–6. VARIOUS POSSIBLE LONG-RUN AVERAGE-COST CURVES.
(*a*) When economies of scale are many and diseconomies remote, the ATC will fall over a wide range of production. (*b*) If economies of scale are few and diseconomies are quickly incurred, minimum unit costs will be encountered at a relatively low output. (*c*) Where economies of scale are rather rapidly exhausted and diseconomies not encountered until a considerably large scale of output has been achieved, long-run average costs will be relatively constant over a wide range of output.

economies of scale stem from the managerial complexities which accompany large-scale production.

9. The relative importance of economies and diseconomies of scale in an industry is often an important determinant of the structure of that industry. Generally speaking, where economies of scale extend to large levels of output, an industry tends to be comprised of a small number of large-scale producers. When economies of scale are exhausted at relatively low levels of output, there tends to be a large number of small firms in an industry.

QUESTIONS AND STUDY SUGGESTIONS

1. Assume a firm has fixed costs of $60 and variable costs as indicated below. Complete the table. When finished, check your calculations by referring to question 9 at the end of Chapter 26.

Total product	Total fixed cost	Total variable cost	Total cost	Average fixed cost	Average variable cost	Average total cost	Marginal cost
0	$___	$ 0	$___	$___	$___	$___	
							$___
1	___	45	___	___	___	___	
							___
2	___	85	___	___	___	___	
							___
3	___	120	___	___	___	___	
							___
4	___	150	___	___	___	___	
							___
5	___	185	___	___	___	___	
							___
6	___	225	___	___	___	___	
							___
7	___	270	___	___	___	___	
							___
8	___	325	___	___	___	___	
							___
9	___	390	___	___	___	___	
							___
10	___	465	___	___	___	___	

a. Graph fixed cost, variable cost, and total cost. Explain how the law of diminishing returns influences the shapes of the variable-cost and total-cost curves.

b. Graph AFC, AVC, ATC, and MC. Explain the derivation and shape of each of these four curves and the relationships which they bear to one another. Specifically, explain in nontechnical terms why MC cuts both AVC and ATC at their minimum points.

2. Distinguish between the short run and the long run. Which of the following are short-run and which are long-run adjustments?
   a. General Motors builds a new assembly plant; **b.** Acme Steel Corporation hires 200 more workers; **c.** a farmer increases the amount of fertilizer used on his corn crop; and **d.** an Alcoa plant adds a third shift of workers.
3. State and explain the law of diminishing returns. What bearing does this law have upon short-run costs? Be specific.
4. Distinguish between fixed and variable costs. Why can this distinction be made in the short run? Classify the following as fixed or variable costs: advertising expenditures, fuel, interest on company-issued bonds, shipping charges, payments for raw materials, real estate taxes, executive salaries, insurance premiums, wage payments, depreciation and obsolescence charges, sales taxes, and rental payments on leased office machinery. "There are no fixed costs in the long run; all costs are variable." Explain.
5. How do economists define costs? Distinguish between explicit and implicit costs, giving examples of each. What are the explicit and implicit costs of going to college? What are "normal profits"? Why does the economist classify normal profits as a cost? What are "economic profits"?
6. What are economies and diseconomies of scale? How do they affect the shape of a firm's long-run ATC curve? What bearing may the exact shape of this curve have upon the structure of an industry?

SELECTED REFERENCES

Bain, Joe S.: *Industrial Organization* (New York: John Wiley & Sons, Inc., 1959), pp. 145–169.

Bober, M. M.: *Intermediate Price and Income Theory*, rev. ed. (New York: W. W. Norton & Company, Inc., 1962), chaps. 5–7.

Colberg, M. R., and W. C. Bradford: *Business Economics: Principles and Cases*, 3d ed. (Homewood, Ill.: Richard D. Irwin, Inc., 1962), chap. 4.

Haynes, Warren W.: *Managerial Economics: Analysis and Cases* (Homewood, Ill.: The Dorsey Press, Inc., 1963), chaps. 7–9.

Robinson, E. A. G.: *The Structure of Competitive Industry* (Chicago: The University of Chicago Press, 1958).

Stigler, George J.: *The Theory of Price* (New York: The Macmillan Company, 1947), chap. 8.

Watson, Donald S. (ed.): *Price Theory in Action* (Boston: Houghton Mifflin Company, 1965), Part 3.

CHAPTER 26

PRICE AND OUTPUT DETERMINATION: PURE COMPETITION

We now have at our disposal the basic tools of analysis needed to understand how product price and output are determined. These analytical tools are applicable to all four basic market models—pure competition, pure monopoly, monopolistic competition, and oligopoly. In this chapter we focus attention upon price and output determination in a purely competitive industry.

CONCEPT AND OCCURRENCE OF PURE COMPETITION

Pure competition, you will recall, presupposes that certain specific conditions are fulfilled.

1. A purely competitive industry is composed of a large number of independent sellers.

2. The firms offer a standardized product. This feature rules out nonprice competition, that is, advertising, sales promotion, and so forth.

3. No individual firm supplies enough of the product to influence its market price noticeably.

4. In a competitive industry no artificial obstacles prevent new firms from entering or old firms from leaving the industry. Firms and the resources they employ are shiftable, or mobile.

The third characteristic is particularly important. The individual competitive firm has nothing to say about determining market price. Because it supplies a negligible portion of total output, the competitive firm cannot significantly influence the market price

which the forces of total demand and supply have established. The competitive firm does not have a price policy, that is, the ability to adjust price. Rather the firm can merely *adjust* to the market price, which it must regard as a given datum determined by the market.

Pure competition is rare in practice. This does not mean, however, that an analysis of how competitive markets work is a useless and irrelevant exercise in logic. In the first place, there are a few industries which more closely approximate the competitive model than they do any other market structure. For example, much can be learned about American agriculture by understanding the functioning of competitive markets. Secondly, pure competition provides the simplest context in which to apply the revenue and cost concepts developed in previous chapters. Pure competition is a simple and meaningful starting point for any discussion of price and output determination. Finally, in the concluding section of this chapter we shall discover that the operation of a purely competitive economy provides us with a standard, or norm, against which the efficiency of the real-world economy can be compared and evaluated. Though pure competition is a relatively rare market structure in our economy, it is one of considerable analytical and some practical importance.

Our analysis of pure competition centers upon three major objectives. First, we seek an understanding of how a competitive producer adjusts to market price in the short run. Next, the nature of long-run adjustments in a competitive industry is explored. Finally, we seek to evaluate the efficiency of competitive industries from the standpoint of society as a whole.

PROFIT MAXIMIZATION IN THE SHORT RUN

In the short run the competitive firm has a fixed plant and is attempting to maximize its profits or, as the case may be, minimize its losses by adjusting its output through changes in the amounts of variable resources (materials, labor, and so forth) it employs. The economic profits its seeks are obviously the difference between total revenue and total costs. Indeed, this points out the direction of our analysis. The revenue data of Chapter 24 and the cost data of Chapter 25 must be brought together in order that the profit-maximizing output for the firm can be determined.

There are two complementary approaches to determining the level of output at which a competitive firm will realize maximum profits or minimum losses. The first involves a comparison of total revenue and total costs; the second, a comparison of marginal revenue and marginal cost. Both approaches, incidentally, can be applied not only to a purely competitive firm but also to firms operating in any of the other three basic market structures. To ensure an understanding of output determination under pure competition, we shall invoke both approaches, emphasizing the marginal approach. Furthermore, both hypothetical data and graphic analysis will be employed to bolster our understanding of the two approaches.

Total-receipts–Total-cost Approach

Given the market price of its product, the competitive producer is faced with three related questions: (1) Should I produce? (2) If so, what amount? (3) What profit (or loss) will be realized?

At first glance the answer to question 1 seems obvious: "You should produce if it is

profitable to do so." But the situation is a bit more complex than this. In the short run a part of the firm's total costs is variable costs, and the remainder is fixed costs. The latter will have to be paid "out of pocket" even when the firm is closed down. In the short run a firm takes a loss equal to its fixed costs when it is producing zero units of output. This means that, although there may be no level of output at which the firm can realize a profit, the firm might still produce, provided that in so doing it can realize a loss less than the fixed-cost loss it will face in closing down. In other words, the correct answer to the "Should I produce?" question is this: *The firm should produce in the short run if it can realize an economic profit or a loss which is less than its fixed costs.*

Assuming the firm *will* produce, the second question becomes relevant: "How much should be produced?" The answer here is fairly obvious: *In the short run the firm should produce that output at which it maximizes profits or minimizes losses.*

Now let us examine three cases which will demonstrate the validity of these two generalizations and answer our third query by indicating how profits and losses can be readily calculated. In the first case the firm will maximize its profits by producing. In the second case it will minimize its losses by producing. In the third case the firm will minimize its losses by closing down. Our plan of attack is to assume given short-run cost data for all three cases and to explore the firm's production decisions when faced with three different product prices.

Profit-maximizing case. In all three cases we employ cost data with which we are already familiar. Columns 3 through 5 of Table 26–1 merely repeat the fixed-, variable-, and total-cost data which were developed in Table 25–2. Assuming that market price is $131, we can derive total revenue for each level of output by simply multiplying output times price, as we did in Table 23–3. These data are presented in column 2. Then in column 6 the profit or loss which will be encountered

TABLE 26–1. THE PROFIT-MAXIMIZING OUTPUT FOR A PURELY COMPETITIVE FIRM: TOTAL-REVENUE–TOTAL-COST APPROACH (PRICE = $131) (hypothetical data)

(1) Total product	(2) Total revenue	(3) Total fixed cost	(4) Total variable cost	(5) Total cost	(6) Profit (+) or loss (−), = (2) − (5)
0	$ 0	$100	$ 0	$ 100	$−100
1	131	100	90	190	− 59
2	262	100	170	270	− 8
3	393	100	240	340	+ 53
4	524	100	300	400	+124
5	655	100	370	470	+185
6	786	100	450	550	+236
7	917	100	540	640	+277
8	1,048	100	650	750	+298
9	1,179	100	780	880	+299
10	1,310	100	930	1,030	+280

at each output is found by subtracting total cost from total revenue. Now we have all the data needed to answer the three questions.

Should the firm produce? Yes, because it can realize a profit by doing so. How much? Nine units, because column 6 tells us that this is the output at which profits will be at a maximum. The size of that profit? $299.

Figure 26–1a compares total revenue and total cost graphically. Total revenue is a straight line, because under pure competition each additional unit adds the same amount—its price—to total revenue (Chapter 23). Total costs increase with output; more production requires more resources. But the rate of increase in total costs varies with the relative efficiency of the firm. For a time the rate of increase in total cost is less and less as the firm utilizes its fixed resources more efficiently. Then, after a time, total cost begins to increase at an ever-increasing rate because of the inefficiencies which accompany overutilization of the firm's plant. A break-even point occurs at about 2 units of output. And, if our data were extended beyond 10 units of output, another such point would be incurred where total cost would catch up with total revenue, as is

shown in Figure 26–1a. Any output within these break-even points will entail an economic profit. The maximum profit is obviously achieved where the vertical difference between total revenue and total cost is greatest. For our data this is at 9 units of output.

Loss-minimizing case. Assuming no change in costs, the firm may not be able to realize economic profits if the market yields a price considerably below $131. To illustrate: Suppose the market price is $81. As column 6 of Table 26–2 indicates, at this price all levels of output will entail losses. But the firm will not close down. Why? Because by producing the firm can realize a loss very considerably less than the fixed-cost loss it will incur by closing down. Specifically, the firm will minimize its losses by producing 6 units of output. The resulting $64 loss is clearly preferable to the $100 loss which closing down will involve. Stated differently, by producing 6 units the firm earns a total revenue of $486 sufficient to pay all the firm's variable costs ($450) and also a substantial portion—$36 worth—of the firm's fixed costs. There are, you will note, several other outputs which entail a loss less than the firm's $100 fixed

**FIGURE 26–1. THE PROFIT-MAXIMIZING, LOSS-MINIMIZING, AND CLOSE-DOWN
CASES AS SHOWN BY THE TOTAL-REVENUE–TOTAL-COST APPROACH.**
A firm's profits are maximized in (*a*) at that output at which total revenue exceeds
total cost by the maximum amount. A firm will minimize its losses in (*b, see
page 462*) by producing at that output at which total cost exceeds total revenue by
the smallest amount. However, if there is no output at which total revenue exceeds
variable costs, the firm will minimize losses in the short run by closing down.

(a)

FIGURE 26–1   *(continued)*

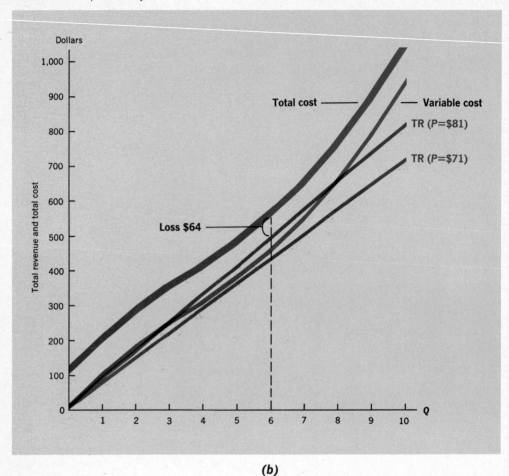

(b)

costs; but at 6 units of output the loss is minimized.

Close-down case. Assume finally that the market price is a mere $71. Given short-run costs, column 9 of Table 26–2 clearly indicates that at all levels of output losses will exceed the $100 fixed-cost loss the firm will incur by closing down. Obviously, then, the firm will minimize its losses by closing down, that is, by producing zero units of output.

Figure 26–1*b* demonstrates the loss-minimizing and close-down cases graphically. In the loss-minimizing case the total-revenue line *TR* (*P* = $81) exceeds

total variable cost by the maximimum amount at 6 units of output. Here total revenue is $486, and the firm recovers all of its $450 of variable costs and also $36 worth of its fixed costs. The firm's minimum loss is $64, clearly superior to the $100 fixed-cost loss involved in closing down. In the close-down case the total-revenue line *TR* (*P* = $71) lies below the total-variable-cost curve at all points; there is no output at which variable costs can be recovered. Therefore, by producing, the firm would incur losses in excess of its fixed costs. The firm's best choice therefore is to close down and pay its $100 fixed-cost loss out of pocket.

TABLE 26–2. THE LOSS-MINIMIZING OUTPUTS FOR A PURELY COMPETITIVE FIRM: TOTAL-REVENUE–TOTAL-COST APPROACH (PRICES = $81 AND $71) (hypothetical data)

	Product Price = $81					Product Price = $71		
(1)	(2)	(3)	(4) Total vari-	(5)	(6) Profit (+) or loss (−),	(7)	(8)	(9) Profit (+) or loss (−),
Total prod- uct	Total reve- nue	Total fixed cost	able cost	Total cost	= (2) − (5)	Total reve- nue	Total cost	= (7) − (8)
0	$ 0	$100	$ 0	$ 100	$−100	$ 0	$ 100	$−100
1	81	100	90	190	−109	71	190	−119
2	162	100	170	270	−108	142	270	−128
3	243	100	240	340	− 97	213	340	−127
4	324	100	300	400	− 76	284	400	−116
5	405	100	370	470	− 65	355	470	−115
6	486	100	450	550	− 64.	426	550	−124
7	567	100	540	640	− 73	497	640	−143
8	648	100	650	750	−102	568	750	−182
9	729	100	780	880	−151	639	880	−241
10	810	100	930	1,030	−220	710	1,030	−320

Marginal-revenue–Marginal-cost Approach

An alternative means for determining the amounts which a competitive firm will be willing to offer in the market at each possible price is for the firm to determine and compare the amounts that each additional unit of output will add to total revenue, on the one hand, and to total cost, on the other. That is, the firm should compare the *marginal revenue* (MR) and the *marginal cost* (MC) of each successive unit of output. Any unit whose marginal revenue exceeds its marginal cost should obviously be produced. Why? Because on each such unit the firm is gaining more in revenue from its sale than it adds to costs in getting that unit produced. The unit of output is adding to profits or, as the case may be, subtracting from losses. Similarly, if the marginal cost of a unit of output exceeds its marginal revenue, the firm should avoid producing that unit. It will add more to costs than to revenue; such a unit will not "pay its way." In the initial stages of production, where

output is relatively low, marginal revenue will usually (but not always) exceed marginal cost. It is therefore profitable to produce through this range of output. But at later stages of production, where output is relatively high, rising marginal costs will cause the reverse to be true. Marginal cost will exceed marginal revenue. Production of units of output falling in this range is obviously to be avoided in the interest of maximizing profits. Separating these two production ranges will be a unique point at which marginal revenue equals marginal cost. This point is the key to the output-determining rule: *The firm will maximize profits or minimize losses by producing at that point where marginal revenue equals marginal cost.* For convenience we shall call this profit-maximizing guide the MR = MC rule. For most sets of MR and MC data there will be no nonfractional level of output at which MR and MC are precisely equal. In such instances the firm should produce the last complete unit of output whose MR exceeds its MC.

Two features of this MR = MC rule merit

comment. First, a qualification: The rule presumes that the firm will choose to produce rather than close down. Shortly we shall note that marginal revenue must be equal to or exceed average variable cost, or the firm will find it preferable to close down rather than produce the MR = MC output.

Second, it is to be emphasized that the MR = MC rule is an accurate guide to profit maximization for all firms, be they purely competitive, monopolistic, monopolistically competitive, or oligopolistic. The rule's application is not limited to the special case of pure competition. At the same time it is noteworthy that the MR = MC rule can be conveniently restated in a slightly different form when being applied to a purely competitive firm. You will recall that product price is determined by the broad market forces of supply and demand, and although the competitive firm can sell as much or as little as it chooses at that price, the firm cannot manipulate the price itself. In technical terms the demand, or sales, schedule faced by a competitive seller is perfectly elastic at the going market price. The result is that product price and marginal revenue are equal; that is, each extra unit sold adds precisely its price to total revenue (Chapter 23). Thus under pure competition—and *only* under pure competition—we may substitute price for marginal revenue in the rule, so it reads as follows: *To maximize profits or minimize losses the competitive firm should produce at that point where price equals marginal cost* $(P = MC)$.

Now let us apply the MR = MC or, if you prefer, MR (P) = MC rule, using the same three prices employed in our total-revenue–total-cost approach to profit maximization.

Profit-maximizing case. Table 26–3 reproduces the unit- and marginal-cost data derived in Table 25–2. It is, of course, the marginal-cost data of column 5 in Table 26–3 which we wish to compare with price (equal to marginal revenue) for each unit of output. Suppose first that market price, and therefore marginal revenue, is $131 as shown in column 6. What is the profit-maximizing output? It is readily seen that each and every unit of output up to and including the ninth adds more to total revenue than to total cost. That is, price, or marginal revenue, exceeds marginal cost on all of the first 9 units of output. Each of these units therefore adds to the firm's profits and should obviously be produced. The tenth unit, however, will not be produced because it would add more to costs—$150—than to revenue—$131.

The level of economic profits realized by the firm can be readily calculated from the unit-cost data. Multiplying price ($131) times output (9), we find total revenue to be $1,179. Total cost of about[1] $880 is found by multiplying average total cost ($97.78) by output (9). The difference of $299 is economic profits. An alternative means of calculating economic profits is to determine profit *per unit* by subtracting average total cost ($97.78) from product price ($131) and multiplying the difference (per unit profits of $33.22) by the level of output (9). The skeptical reader should calculate profits at outputs other than those indicated most profitable by the MR (P) = MC rule to verify that they entail either losses or profits less than $299.

Figure 26–2 makes the comparison of price and marginal cost graphically. Here per unit economic profit is indicated by the distance AP. When multiplied by the profit-maximizing output, the resulting total economic profit is shown by the white rectangular area.

It should be noted that the firm is seeking

---

[1] In most instances the unit-cost data are rounded figures. Therefore, economic profits calculated from them will typically vary by a few cents from the profits determined in the total-revenue–total-cost approach. We here ignore the few cents differentials and make our answers consistent with the results of the total-revenue–total-cost approach.

TABLE 26–3. THE PROFIT-MAXIMIZING OUTPUTS FOR A PURELY COMPETITIVE FIRM: MARGINAL-REVENUE-EQUALS-MARGINAL-COST APPROACH (PRICE = $131) (hypothetical data)

(1) Total product	(2) Average fixed cost	(3) Average variable cost	(4) Average total cost	(5) Marginal cost	(6) Price = marginal revenue
0					
				$ 90	$131
1	$100.00	$90.00	$190.00		
				80	131
2	50.00	85.00	135.00		
				70	131
3	33.33	80.00	113.33		
				60	131
4	25.00	75.00	100.00		
				70	131
5	20.00	74.00	94.00		
				80	131
6	16.67	75.00	91.67		
				90	131
7	14.29	77.14	91.43		
				110	131
8	12.50	81.23	93.73		
				130	131
9	11.11	86.67	97.78		
				150	131
10	10.00	93.00	103.00		

to maximize its *total* profits, not its *per unit* profits. Per unit profits are largest at 7 units of output, where price exceeds average total cost by $39.57 ($131 minus $91.43). But by producing only 7 units, the firm would be forgoing the production of additional units of output which would clearly contribute to total profits. The firm is happy to accept lower per unit profits if the resulting extra units of sales more than compensate for the lower per unit profits.

Loss-minimizing case. Now let us apply the same reasoning on the assumption that market price is $81 rather than $131. Should the firm produce? If so, how much? And what will the resulting profits or losses be?

The answers, respectively, are: "Yes," "Six units," and "A loss of $64."

Column 6 of Table 26–4 shows the new price (equal to marginal revenue) alongside the same unit- and marginal-cost data presented in Table 26–3. Comparing columns 5 and 6, we find that the first unit of output adds $90 to total cost but only $81 to total revenue. One might be inclined to conclude: "Don't produce—close down!" But this would be hasty. Remember that in the very early stages of production marginal physical returns are low, making marginal cost unusually high. The price–marginal-cost relationship might improve with increased production. And it does. On the next five units—2 through 6—price exceeds marginal

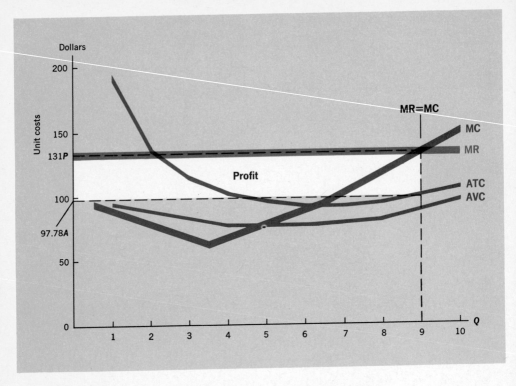

**FIGURE 26–2. THE SHORT-RUN PROFIT-MAXIMIZING POSITION OF A PURELY
COMPETITIVE FIRM.**
The $P = MC$ output allows the competitive producer to maximize profits or minimize
losses. In this case price exceeds average total cost at the $P = MC$ output of 9
units. Economic profits per unit of AP are realized; total economic profits are indicated
by the white rectangle.

cost. Each of these 5 units adds more to
revenue than to cost, more than compensating for the "loss" taken on the first unit.
Beyond 6 units, however, MC exceeds
MR (P). The firm should therefore produce
at 6 units. In general, the profit-seeking
producer should always compare marginal
revenue (price) with the rising portion of
his marginal-cost schedule or curve.

Will production be profitable? No, it will
not. At 6 units of output average total costs
of $91.67 exceed price of $81 by $10.67 per
unit. Multiply by the 6 units of output, and
the firm's total loss is about $64. Then why
produce? Because this loss is less than the

firm's $100 worth of fixed costs—the $100
loss the firm would incur in the short run by
closing down. Looked at differently, the firm
receives enough revenue per unit ($81) to
cover its variable costs of $75 and also pro-
vide $6 per unit, or a total of $36, to apply
against the payment of fixed costs. Therefore, the firm's loss is only $64 ($100 minus
$36), rather than $100.

This case is shown graphically in Figure
26–3. Whenever price exceeds the minimum
average variable cost but falls short of
average total cost, the firm can pay a part of,
but not all, its fixed costs by producing. In
this instance total variable costs are shown

TABLE 26–4. THE LOSS-MINIMIZING OUTPUTS FOR A PURELY COMPETITIVE FIRM: MARGINAL-REVENUE-EQUALS-MARGINAL-COST APPROACH (PRICES = $81 AND $71) (hypothetical data)

(1) Total product	(2) Average fixed cost	(3) Average variable cost	(4) Average total cost	(5) Marginal cost	(6) $81 price = marginal revenue	(7) $71 price = marginal revenue
0						
				$ 90	$81	$71
1	$100.00	$90.00	$190.00			
				80	81	71
2	50.00	85.00	135.00			
				70	81	71
3	33.33	80.00	113.33			
				60	81	71
4	25.00	75.00	100.00			
				70	81	71
5	20.00	74.00	94.00			
				80	81	71
6	16.67	75.00	91.67			
				90	81	71
7	14.29	77.14	91.43			
				110	81	71
8	12.50	81.23	93.73			
				130	81	71
9	11.11	86.67	97.78			
				150	81	71
10	10.00	93.00	103.00			

by the area *OVGF*. Total revenue, however, is *OPEF*, greater than total variable costs by *VPEG*. This excess of revenue over variable costs can be applied against total fixed costs, represented by area *VACG*.

Close-down case. Suppose now that the market yields a price of only $71. In this case it will pay the firm to close down, to produce nothing. Why? Because there is no output at which the firm can cover its average variable costs, much less its average total cost. In other words, the smallest loss it can realize by producing is greater than the $100 worth of fixed costs it will lose by closing down. The smart thing is obviously to close down. This can be verified by comparing

columns 3 and 7 of Table 26–4 and can be readily visualized in Figure 26–4. Price comes closest to covering average variable costs at the MR $(P) = $ MC output of 5 units. But even here price or revenue per unit would fall short of average variable cost by $3 ($74 minus $71). By producing at the MR $(P) = $ MC output the firm would lose its $100 worth of fixed costs *plus* $15 ($3 on each of the five units) worth of variable costs, for a total loss of $115. This clearly compares unfavorably with the $100 fixed-cost loss the firm would incur by choosing to close down. In short, it will obviously pay the firm to close down rather than operate at a $71 price or, for that matter, at any price less than $74.

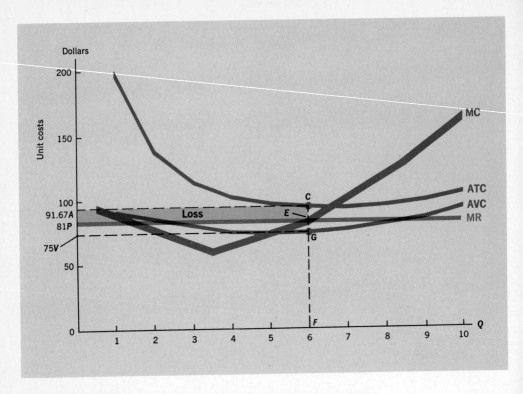

FIGURE 26–3. THE SHORT-RUN LOSS-MINIMIZING POSITION OF A PURELY COMPETITIVE FIRM.
If price exceeds the minimum AVC but is less than ATC, the $P = MC$ output of 6 units will permit the firm to minimize its losses. In this instance losses are AP per unit; total losses are shown by area APEC.

The close-down case obligates us to modify our MR $(P) = $ MC rule for profit maximization or loss minimization. *A competitive firm will maximize profits or minimize losses in the short run by producing at that output at which MR $(P) = $ MC, provided that price exceeds the minimum average-variable-cost figure.*

Marginal cost and the short-run supply curve. Now the astute reader will recognize that we have simply selected three different prices and asked how much the profit-seeking competitive firm, faced with certain costs, would choose to offer or supply in the market at each of these prices. This information—

price and corresponding quantity supplied—obviously constitutes the supply schedule for the competitive firm. Table 26–5 summarizes the supply-schedule data for the three prices we have chosen—$131, $81, and $71. The reader is urged to apply the MR $(P) = $ MC rule (as modified by the close-down case) to verify the quantity-supplied data for the $151, $111, $91, and $61 prices and calculate the corresponding profits or losses. The supply schedule is obviously upsloping. In this instance price must be $74 (equal to minimum average variable cost) or greater before any output is supplied. The profit-seeking firm is induced to offer more of the product as higher and higher prices

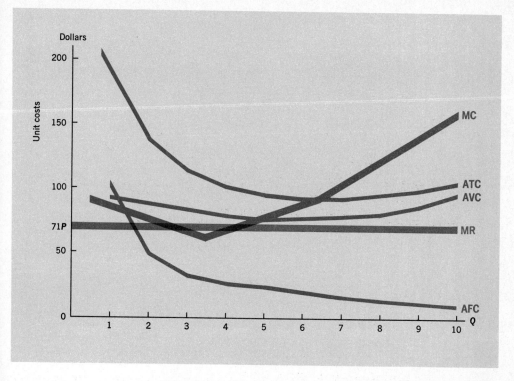

FIGURE 26–4. THE SHORT-RUN CLOSE-DOWN POSITION OF A PURELY COMPETITIVE FIRM.

If price falls short of minimum AVC, the competitive firm will minimize its losses in the short run by closing down. There is no level of output at which the firm can produce and realize a loss smaller than its fixed costs.

TABLE 26–5. THE SUPPLY SCHEDULE OF A COMPETITIVE FIRM CONFRONTED WITH THE COST DATA OF TABLE 26–3 (hypothetical data)

Price	Quantity supplied	Maximum profit (+) or minimum loss (−)
$151	10	$
131	9	+299
111	8	
91	7	
81	6	− 64
71	0	−100
61	0	

are equated with the marginal cost of larger and larger outputs in the cost table.

Figure 26–5 generalizes upon our application of the MR (P) = MC rule. Here we have drawn the appropriate cost curves. Then from the vertical axis we have extended a series of marginal-revenue lines from some of the various possible prices which the market might set for the firm. The crucial prices are P_2 and P_4. Our close-down case reminds us that at any price *below* P_2—that price equal to the minimum average variable cost—the firm should close down and supply nothing. Actually, by producing Q_2 units of output at a price of P_2, the firm will just

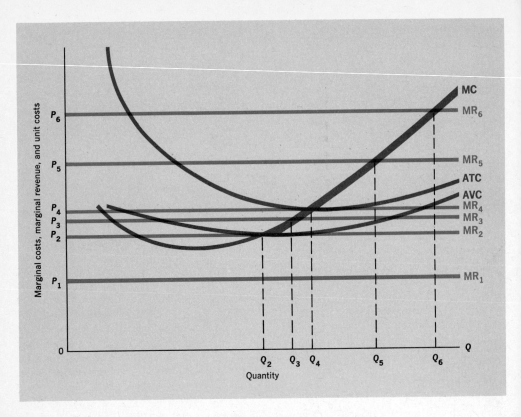

FIGURE 26–5. MARGINAL COST AND THE COMPETITIVE FIRM'S SHORT-RUN SUPPLY CURVE.
Application of the $P = $ MC rule, as modified by the close-down case, reveals that the segment of the firm's MC curve which lies above AVC is its short-run supply curve. At any price between P_2 and P_4, such as P_3, losses will be minimized by producing the $P = $ MC output. At any price above P_4, such as P_5 or P_6, profits will be maximized at the $P = $ MC output.

cover its variable costs, and its losses will be equal to its fixed costs. The firm, therefore, would be indifferent as between closing down and producing Q_2 units of output. But at any price below P_2, such as P_1, the firm will close down and supply zero units of output. P_4 is strategic because it is the price at which the firm will just break even by producing Q_4 units of output, as indicated by the MR $(P) = $ MC rule. Here total revenue will just cover total costs (including a normal profit). At P_3 the firm supplies Q_3 units of output and in so doing minimizes its losses.

At any other price between P_2 and P_4 the firm will minimize its losses by producing to the point where MR $(P) = $ MC. At any price above P_4 the firm will maximize its economic profits by producing to the point where MR $(P) = $ MC. Thus at P_5 and P_6 the firm will realize the greatest profits by supplying Q_5 and Q_6 units of output.

Now the basic point is this: Each of the various MR $(P) = $ MC intersection points (shown by the dots in Figure 26–5) indicates a possible product price and the corresponding quantity which the profit-seeking firm would supply at that price. These points, by definition, constitute the supply curve of the competitive firm. Because nothing would be produced at any price below the minimum average variable cost, we can conclude that *that portion of the firm's marginal-cost curve which lies above its average-variable-cost curve is its short-run supply curve.* This is the link between production costs and supply in the short run.

Short-run Competitive Pricing

Let us now pause to summarize the main points we have made concerning short-run competitive pricing. Table 26–6 provides a convenient check sheet on the total-revenue–total-cost and MR = MC approaches to determining the competitive firm's profit-maximizing output. This table warrants careful study by the reader. In the MR = MC approach it is noteworthy that in deciding whether or not to produce, it is the comparison of price with minimum average variable cost which is all-important. Then, in determining the profit-maximizing or loss-minimizing amount to produce, it is

the comparison or, better yet, the equality of MR (P) and MC which is crucial. Finally, in determining the actual profit or loss associated with the MR (P) = MC output, price and average total cost must be contrasted. A final basic conclusion implied in Table 26–6 is that that segment of the short-run marginal-cost curve which lies above the average variable cost curve is the competitive firm's short-run supply curve. This conclusion stems from the application of the MR (P) = MC rule and the necessary modification suggested by the close-down case.

Firm and Industry: Equilibrium Price

Now one final wrap-up step remains. Having developed the competitive firm's short-run supply curve through the application of the MR (P) = MC rule, we must determine which of the various price possibilities will actually be the equilibrium price. Recalling Chapter 4, we know that in a purely competitive market equilibrium price is determined by *total,* or market, supply and total demand. To derive total supply we know that the sales schedules or curves of the individual competitive sellers must be

TABLE 26–6. SUMMARY OF THE TOTAL-REVENUE–TOTAL-COST AND MARGINAL-REVENUE–MARGINAL-COST APPROACHES TO COMPETITIVE OUTPUT DETERMINATION IN THE SHORT RUN

	Total-revenue–total-cost approach	Marginal-revenue–marginal-cost approach
Should the firm produce?	Yes, if TR exceeds TC or if TC exceeds TR by some amount less than total fixed costs.	Yes, if price is equal to, or greater than, minimum average variable cost.
What quantity should be produced to maximize profits?	Produce where the excess of TR over TC is a maximum or where excess of TC over TR is a minimum (and less than total fixed costs).	Produce where MR or price equals MC.
Will production result in an economic profit?	Yes, if TR exceeds TC. No, if TC exceeds TR.	Yes, if price exceeds average total cost. No, if average total cost exceeds price.

TABLE 26–7. FIRM AND MARKET SUPPLY AND MARKET DEMAND (hypothetical data)

(1) Quantity supplied, single firm	(2) Total quantity supplied, 1,000 firms	(3) Product price	(4) Total quantity demanded
10	10,000	$151	4,000
9	9,000	131	6,000
8	8,000	111	8,000
7	7,000	91	9,000
6	6,000	81	11,000
0	0	71	13,000
0	0	61	16,000

summed. Thus in Table 26–7, columns 1 and 3 repeat the individual competitive firm's supply schedule just derived in Table 26–5. Let us now conveniently assume that there are a total of 1,000 competitive firms in this industry, each having the same total and unit costs as the single firm we have been discussing. This allows us to calculate the total or market supply schedule (columns 2 and 3) by multiplying the quantity-supplied figures of the single firm (column 1) by 1,000.

Now in order to determine equilibrium price and output, this total supply data must be compared with total demand data. For purposes of illustration, let us assume total demand data are as shown in columns 3 and 4 of Table 26–7. Comparing the total quantity supplied and total quantity demanded at the seven possible prices, we readily determine that the equilibrium price is $111 and that equilibrium quantity is 8,000 units for the industry and 8 units for each of the 1,000 identical firms.

Will these conditions of market supply and demand make this a prosperous or unprosperous industry? Multiplying product price ($111) by output (8), we find the total revenue of each firm to be $888. Total cost is $750, found by multiplying average total

cost of $93.73 by 8 or simply by looking at column 5 of Table 26–1. The $138 difference is the economic profit of each firm. Another way of calculating economic profits is to determine *per unit* profit by subtracting average total cost ($93.73) from product price ($111) and multiplying the difference (per unit profits of $17.27) by the firm's equilibrium level of output (8). For the industry, total economic profit is obviously $138,000. This, then, is a prosperous industry.

Figure 26–6a and b shows this analysis graphically. The individual supply curves of each of the 1,000 identical firms—one of which is shown as *ss* in Figure 26–6a—are summed horizontally to get the total-supply curve *SS* of Figure 26–6b. Given total demand *DD*, equilibrium price is found to be $111, and equilibrium quantity for the industry is 8,000 units. This equilibrium price is given and unalterable to the individual firm; that is, the typical firm's demand curve is perfectly elastic at the equilibrium price as indicated by *dd*. Because price is given and constant to the individual firm, the marginal-revenue curve coincides with the demand curve. Price obviously exceeds average total cost at the firm's equilibrium MR (P) = MC output, resulting in a situ-

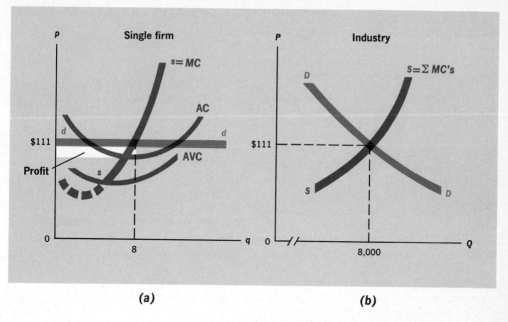

(a)   (b)

FIGURE 26–6. SHORT-RUN COMPETITIVE EQUILIBRIUM FOR A
REPRESENTATIVE FIRM (*a*) AND THE INDUSTRY (*b*).
The horizontal sum of the 1,000 firms' supply curves (*ss*) determines the industry
supply curve (*SS*). Given industry demand (*DD*), the short-run equilibrium price and
output for the industry are $111 and 8,000 units. Taking the equilibrium price as
given datum, the representative firm establishes its profit-maximizing output at 8
units and, in this case, realizes the economic profit shown by the white area.

ation of economic profits similar to that already portrayed in Figure 26–2.

Assuming that no changes in costs or market demand occur, these diagrams reveal a genuine short-run equilibrium situation. There are no shortages or surpluses in the market to cause price or total quantity to change. Nor can any of the firms making up the industry improve themselves profitwise by altering their output. Note, too, that higher unit and marginal costs, on the one hand, or a weaker market demand situation, on the other, could have posed a loss situation similar to Figure 26–3. The student is urged to sketch in Figure 26–6*a* and *b* how higher costs and a less favorable demand could cause a short-run equilibrium situation entailing losses.

Figure 26–6*a* and *b* brings out a final notable point. We have emphasized that product price is a given datum to the *individual* competitive firm. But at the same time the supply plans of all competitive producers *as a group* are a basic determinant of product price. If we recall the fallacy of composition, we find there is no inconsistency here. Though each firm, supplying a negligible fraction of total supply, cannot affect price, the sum of the supply curves of all the many firms in the industry constitutes the industry supply curve, and this curve does have an important bearing upon price. In short, under competition, equilibrium price is a given datum to the individual firm and simultaneously is the result of the production (supply) decisions of all firms taken as a group.

PROFIT MAXIMIZATION
IN THE LONG RUN

The long run permits firms to make certain adjustments which time does not allow in the short run. In the short run there is a given number of firms in an industry, each of which has a fixed, unalterable plant. True, firms may close down in the sense that they produce zero units of output in the short run; but they do not have sufficient time to liquidate their assets and go out of business. By contrast, in the long run firms already in an industry have sufficient time either to expand or to contract their plant capacities, and, more importantly, the number of firms in the industry may either increase or decrease as new firms enter or old firms leave. We want to discover how these long-run adjustments modify our conclusions concerning short-run output and price determination.

It will facilitate our analysis greatly to make certain simplifying assumptions, none of which will impair the general validity of our conclusions.

1. We shall suppose that the only long-run adjustment is the entry and exodus of firms. Furthermore, for simplicity's sake we ignore the short-run adjustment already analyzed, in order to grasp more clearly the nature of long-run competitive adjustments.

2. It will also be assumed that all firms in the industry have identical cost curves. This allows us to talk in terms of an "average," or "representative," firm with the knowledge that all other firms in the industry are similarly affected by any long-run adjustments which occur.

3. We assume for the moment that the industry under discussion is a constant-cost industry. This means simply that the entry and exodus of firms will not affect resource prices or, therefore, the locations of the unit-cost schedules of the individual firms.

Now the job is to describe long-run competitive adjustments both verbally and through simple graphic analysis. It will be well to state in advance the basic conclusion we seek to explain: *After all long-run adjustments are completed, that is, when long-run equilibrium is achieved, product price will be exactly equal to, and production will occur at, each firm's point of minimum average total cost.* This conclusion follows from two basic facts: (1) firms seek profits and shun losses, and (2) under competition firms are free to enter and leave industries. If price exceeds average total costs, the resulting economic profits will attract new firms to the industry. But this expansion of the industry will increase product supply until price is brought back down into equality with average total cost. Conversely, if price is less than average total cost, the resulting losses will cause firms to leave the industry. As they leave, total product supply will decline, bringing price back up into equality with average total cost.

Our conclusion can best be demonstrated and its significance evaluated by assuming that the average or representative firm in a purely competitive industry is initially in long-run equilibrium. This is shown in Figure 26–7a, where price and minimum average total cost are equal at $50. Economic profits here are zero; hence, the industry is in equilibrium or "at rest," because there is no tendency for firms to enter or leave the industry. As we know, the going market price is determined by total, or industry, demand and supply, as shown by D_1D_1 and S_1S_1 in Figure 26–7b. (The market supply schedule, incidentally, is a short-run schedule; the industry's long-run supply schedule will be developed in our discussion.) By examining the quantity axes of the two graphs, we note that if all firms are identical, there must be 1,000 firms in the industry, each producing 100 units, to achieve the industry's equilibrium output of 100,000 units.

Entry of Firms Eliminates Profits

Now our model is set up. Let us upset the serenity of this long-run equilibrium situation and trace the subsequent adjustments.

FIGURE 26–7. TEMPORARY PROFITS AND THE REESTABLISHMENT OF LONG-RUN EQUILIBRIUM IN A REPRESENTATIVE FIRM (*a*) AND THE INDUSTRY (*b*).
A favorable shift in demand (D_1D_1 to D_2D_2) will upset the original equilibrium and cause economic profits. But profits will cause new firms to enter the industry, increasing supply (S_1S_1 to S_2S_2) and lowering product price until economic profits are once again zero.

Suppose that a change in consumer tastes increases product demand from D_1D_1 to D_2D_2. This favorable shift in demand obviously makes production profitable; the new price of $60 exceeds average total cost. *These economic profits will lure new firms into the industry.* Some of the entrants will be newly created firms; others will shift from less prosperous industries. But as the firms enter, the market supply of the product will increase, causing product price to gravitate downward from $60 toward the original $50 level. Assuming, as we are, that the entry of new firms has no effect upon costs, economic profits will persist, and entry will therefore continue until short-run market supply has increased to S_2S_2. At this point price is again equal to minimum average total cost at $50. The economic profits caused by the boost in demand have been competed away to zero, and as a result the previous incentive for more firms to enter the industry has disappeared. Long-run equilibrium has been restored at this point.

Figure 26–7 tells us that upon the reestablishment of long-run equilibrium, industry output is 110,000 units and that each firm in the now expanded industry is producing 100 units. We can therefore conclude that the industry is now composed of 1,100 firms; that is, 100 new firms have entered the industry.

Exodus of Firms Eliminates Losses

To strengthen our understanding of long-run competitive equilibrium, let us throw our analysis into reverse. In Figure 26–8*a* and *b* the heavy lines show once again the initial long-run equilibrium situation used

(a)   (b)

FIGURE 26–8. TEMPORARY LOSSES AND THE REESTABLISHMENT OF LONG-RUN EQUILIBRIUM IN A REPRESENTATIVE FIRM (*a*) AND THE INDUSTRY (*b*).
An unfavorable shift in demand (D_1D_1 to D_3D_3) will upset the original equilibrium and cause losses. But losses will cause firms to leave the industry, decreasing supply (S_1S_1 to S_3S_3) and increasing product price until all losses have disappeared.

as a point of departure in our previous analysis of how the entry of firms eliminates profits.

Now let us suppose that consumer demand falls from D_1D_1 to D_3D_3. This forces price down to $40, making production unprofitable. In time these losses will force firms to leave the industry. As capital equipment wears out and contractual obligations expire, some firms will simply toss in the sponge. As this exodus of firms proceeds, however, industry supply will decrease, moving from S_1S_1 toward S_3S_3. And as this occurs, price will begin to rise from $40 back toward $50. Assuming costs are unchanged by the exodus of firms, losses will force firms to leave the industry until supply has declined to S_3S_3, at which point price is again exactly $50, barely consistent with minimum average total cost. The exodus of firms continues until losses are eliminated and long-run equilibrium is again restored.

The reader will note from Figure 26–8*a* and *b* that total quantity supplied is now 90,000 units and each firm is producing 100 units. This obviously means that the industry is now populated by only 900 firms rather than the original 1,000. Losses have forced 100 firms out of business.

Our prestated conclusion has now been verified. Competition, as reflected in the entry and exodus of firms, forces price into equality with the minimum long-run average total cost of production, and each firm produces at the point of minimum long-run average total cost.

Long-run Supply for a Constant-cost Industry

Even though our discussion is concerned with the long-run, we have noted that the market supply curves of Figures 26–7*b* and 26–8*b* are short-run curves. However, our analysis itself permits us to sketch the nature of the long-run supply curve for this competitive industry. The crucial factor in determining the shape of the industry's long-run supply curve is the effect, if any, which changes in the number of firms in the industry will have upon the costs of the individual firms which the industry comprises.

In the foregoing analysis of long-run competitive equilibrium we assumed the industry under discussion was a *constant-cost industry*. By definition, this means that the expansion of the industry through the entry of new firms will have no effect upon resource prices or, therefore, upon production costs. Graphically, the entry of new firms does not change the position of the long-run average-cost curves of the individual firms in the industry. When will this be the case? For the most part when the industry's demand for resources is small in relation to the total demand for those resources. And this is most likely to be the situation when the industry is employing unspecialized resources which are being demanded by many other industries. In short, when the particular industry's demand for resources is a negligible component of the total demand, the industry can expand without significantly affecting resource prices and costs.

What will be the nature of the long-run supply curve for a constant-cost industry? The answer is contained in our previous discussion of the long-run adjustments toward equilibrium which profits or losses will initiate. Here we assumed that the entry or exodus of firms would not affect costs. The result was that the entry or exodus of firms would alter industry output but always bring product price back to the original $50 level, where it is just consistent with the unchanging minimum average total cost of production. Specifically, we discovered that the industry would supply 90,000, 100,000, or 110,000 units of output, all at a price of $50 per unit. In technical terms the long-run supply curve of a constant-cost industry is perfectly elastic.

This is demonstrated graphically in Figure 26–9. Suppose that product demand for the industry is originally at D_1D_1, industry output is Q_1, and product price is Q_1P_1. This situation, let us suppose, is one of long-run equilibrium. Now assume that demand increases to D_2D_2, upsetting this equilibrium. The resulting economic profits will attract new firms. Because this is a constant-cost industry, entry will continue and industry output will expand until price is driven back down to the unchanged minimum average-total-cost level. This will be at price Q_2P_2 and output Q_2. The long-run industry supply curve SS, which connects these equilibrium points, is obviously perfectly elastic.

Long-run Supply for an Increasing-cost Industry

But constant-cost industries are a special case. In most instances the entry of new firms will affect resource prices and therefore unit costs for the individual firms in the industry. When an industry is using a relatively large portion of some resource whose total supply is not readily increased, the entry of new firms will increase resource demand in relation to supply and boost resource prices. This is particularly so in industries which are using highly specialized resources whose initial supply is not readily augmented. The result of higher resource prices will be higher long-run average costs for firms in the industry. These higher costs, it should be noted, take the form of an upward shift in the long-run average-cost curve for the representative firm.

The net result is that when an increase in product demand causes economic profits and attracts new firms to the industry, a two-way squeeze on profits will occur to eliminate those profits. On the one hand, the entry of new firms will increase market supply and lower product price, and, on the other, the entire average-total-cost curve of the representative firm will shift upward. This means that the equilibrium price will now be higher than it was originally. The industry will only produce a larger output at a higher price. Why? Because expansion of the industry has increased average total costs, and in the long

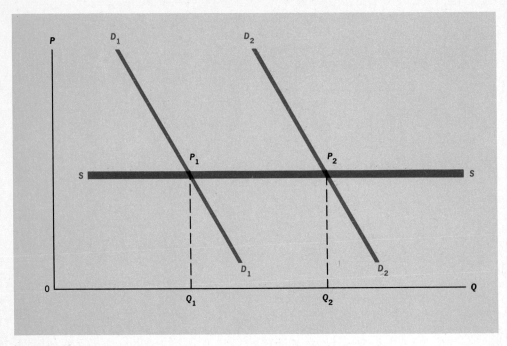

FIGURE 26–9. THE LONG-RUN SUPPLY CURVE FOR A CONSTANT-COST INDUSTRY IS PERFECTLY ELASTIC.
Because the entry of new firms does not affect resource prices or, therefore, unit costs, an increase in demand (D_1D_1 to D_2D_2) will cause an expansion in industry output (Q_1 to Q_2) but no alteration in price ($Q_1P_1 = Q_2P_2$). This means that the long-run industry supply curve (SS) will be perfectly elastic.

run product price must cover these costs. A greater industry output will be forthcoming at a higher price, or, more technically, the industry supply curve for an increasing-cost industry will be upsloping. Instead of getting either 90,000, 100,000, or 110,000 units at the same price of $50, in an increasing-cost industry 90,000 units might be forthcoming at $50; 100,000 at $55; and 110,000 at $60. The higher price is required to induce more production because costs increase as the industry expands.

This can be seen graphically in Figure 26–10. Original market demand, industry output, and price are D_1D_1, Q_1 and Q_1P_1, respectively. An increase in demand to D_2D_2 will upset this equilibrium and give rise to economic profits. As new firms enter, (1)

industry supply will increase, driving price down, and (2) resource prices will rise, causing the average total costs of production to rise. Because of these average-total-cost increases, the new long-run equilibrium price will be established at some level above the original price, such as Q_2P_2.

Which situation—constant or increasing costs—is characteristic of American industry? It is hard to say. Agriculture and extractive industries such as mining and lumbering are increasing-cost industries, because each utilizes a very large portion of some basic resource—farmland, mineral deposits, and timberland. Expansion will significantly affect the demand for these resources and result in higher costs. It is almost impossible to generalize with respect to manufacturing

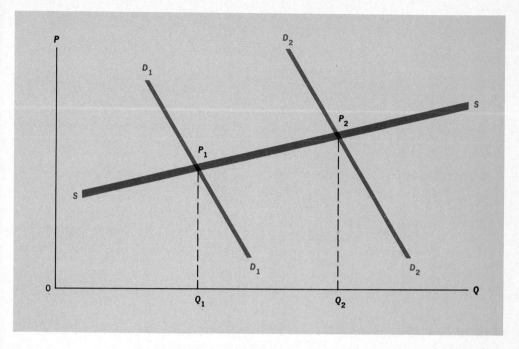

FIGURE 26–10. THE LONG-RUN SUPPLY CURVE FOR AN INCREASING-COST
INDUSTRY IS UPSLOPING.
In an increasing-cost industry the entry of new firms in response to an increase in
demand (D_1D_1 to D_2D_2) will bid up resource prices and thereby increase unit costs.
As a result, an increased industry output (Q_1 to Q_2) will be forthcoming only at a
higher price (Q_2P_2 is greater than Q_1P_1). The long-run industry supply curve (SS) is,
therefore, upsloping.

industries. In their early stages of development such industries may well be relatively
constant-cost industries.[2] But as continued

[2] Under certain very special circumstances an
industry may be for a time a *decreasing-cost
industry*. For example, as more mines are established in a given locality, each firm's costs in
pumping out water seepage may decline. With
more mines pumping, the seepage into each is
less, and pumping costs are therefore reduced.
Furthermore, with only a few mines in an area,
industry output might be so small that only
relatively primitive and therefore costly transportation facilities are available. But as the
number of firms and industry output expand, a
railroad might build a spur into the area and
thereby significantly reduce transportation costs.
Under such special conditions we get a long-run
supply curve which is *down*sloping.

expansion increases the importance of these
industries in resource markets, they may in
time become increasing-cost industries.

AN EVALUATION OF
COMPETITIVE PRICING

Whether a purely competitive industry is
one of constant or increasing costs, the final
long-run equilibrium position for each firm
will have the same basic characteristics. As in
Figure 26–11, price (and marginal revenue)
will settle at the level where it is equal to
minimum average cost. However, we discovered in Chapter 25 that the marginal-cost
curve intersects, and is therefore equal to,
average cost at the point of minimum average
cost. In the long-run equilibrium position

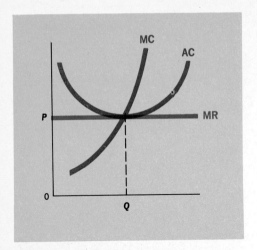

FIGURE 26–11. FOR THE COMPETITIVE FIRM IN LONG-RUN EQUILIBRIUM, $P = AC = MC$.
The equality of price and minimum average cost indicates that the firm is using the most efficient known technology and is charging the lowest price P and producing the greatest output Q consistent with its costs. The equality of price and marginal cost indicates that resources are being allocated in accordance with consumer preferences.

"everything is equal." MR $(P) = AC = MC$. This triple equality is of more than geometric interest. It tells us that, although a competitive firm may realize economic profits or losses in the short run, it will barely break even by producing in accordance with the MR $(P) = MC$ rule in the long run. Furthermore, this triple equality suggests certain conclusions concerning the efficiency of a purely competitive economy which are of great social significance. It is to an evaluation of competitive pricing from society's point of view that we now turn.

You will recall that the overview of the price system found in Chapter 5 yielded some general conclusions with respect to the efficiency of any economy characterized by a competitive price system. Equipped now with a better understanding of costs and of price-output determination under competition, we are in a position to sharpen our understanding of the efficiency of a competitive price economy. Specifically, we want

to see how our analysis of long-run competitive equilibrium implies certain highly desirable features of a competitive price system.

Efficient Allocation of Resources

Most economists argue that, subject to certain limitations and exceptions, a purely competitive economy will lead to the most efficient, or "ideal," allocation of resources. That is, *a competitive price economy will tend to allocate the fixed supplies of resources available to society in such a way as to maximize the satisfactions of consumers.* Actually, there are two related points which underlie this conclusion. First, it is argued that under pure competition firms will be forced to produce those goods which consumers want the most. Second, competition forces firms to use the most efficient methods in the production of these goods. To facilitate our discussion we shall examine the second point first.

1. P = AC. We have just noted that in the long run competition forces firms to produce at the point of minimum average total cost of production and to charge that price which is just consistent with these costs. This is obviously a most desirable situation from the consumer's point of view. It means that firms must use the best available (least-cost) technology or they will simply not survive. And, too, it means that consumers benefit from the highest volume of production and the lowest product price which are possible under the cost conditions which currently prevail. Furthermore, the costs involved in each instance are only those costs essential in producing a product. Because products are standardized in competitive industries, there will be no selling or promotional costs which must be added to production costs in determining product price.

2. P = MC. But the competitive production of *any* collection of goods does not necessarily make for an efficient allocation of resources. Production must not only be technologically efficient, but it must also entail the "right goods," that is, the goods that consumers want the most. The competitive price system will see to it that resources are allocated so as to result in a total output whose composition best fits the preferences of consumers.

Let us see precisely how this comes about. We must first grasp the social meaning of competitive product and resource prices. The money price of any product—product X—is society's measure, or index, of the relative worth of that product at the margin. Similarly, the marginal cost of producing X measures the value, or relative worth, of the other goods that the resources used in the production of an extra unit of X could otherwise have produced. In short, product price measures the benefit, or satisfaction, which society gets from additional units of X, and the marginal cost of an additional unit of X measures the sacrifice, or cost to society, of other goods in using resources to produce more of X. Now, under competition the production of each product will occur up to that precise point at which price is equal to marginal cost (Figure 26–11). The profit-seeking competitor will only realize the maximum possible profit by equating price and marginal cost. To produce short of the MR $(P) =$ MC point will mean less than maximum profits to the individual firm and an *under*allocation of resources to this product from society's standpoint. The fact that price exceeds marginal cost indicates that society values additional units of X more highly than the alternative products which the appropriate resources could otherwise produce.

For similar reasons, the production of X should not go beyond the output at which price equals marginal cost. To do so would entail less than maximum profits for producers and an *over*allocation of resources to X from the standpoint of society. To produce X at some point at which marginal cost exceeds price means that resources are being used in the production of X at the sacrifice of alternative goods which society values more highly than the added units of X. In

brief, *under pure competition producers will be forced to produce each commodity up to that precise point at which price and marginal cost are equated. This means that resources are efficiently allocated under competition.* Each good is produced to the point at which the value of the last unit is equal to the value of the alternative goods sacrificed by its production. To alter the production of X would necessarily reduce consumer satisfactions. To produce X beyond the $P =$ MC point would result in the sacrifice of alternative goods whose value to society exceeds that of the extra units of X. To produce X short of the $P =$ MC point would involve the sacrifice of units of X which society values more than the alternative goods resources can produce.

A further attribute of the competitive price system is its ability to negotiate appropriate adjustments in resource use as changes occur in basic data of the economy. In a competitive economy any changes in consumer tastes, resource supplies, or technology will automatically set in motion appropriate realignments of resources. For example, an increase in consumer demand for product X will increase its price. Disequilibrium will occur, in that at its present output the price of X will now exceed its marginal cost. This will create economic profits in industry X and stimulate its expansion. Its profitability will permit the industry to bid resources away from less pressing uses. Expansion in this industry will end only when the price of X is again equal to its marginal cost, that is, when the value of the last unit produced is once again equal to the value of the alternative goods society forgoes in getting that last unit of X produced. Similarly, changes in the supplies of particular resources or in the techniques pertinent to various industries will upset existing price–marginal-cost equalities by either raising or lowering marginal cost. These inequalities will cause businessmen in either pursuing profits or shunning losses to reallocate resources until price once again equals marginal cost in each line of production. In so doing, they correct any inefficiencies in the allocation of resources which changing economic data may temporarily impose upon the economy.

A final appealing feature of a purely competitive economy is that the highly efficient allocation of resources which it fosters comes about because businesses and resource suppliers freely seek to further their own self-interests. That is, the "invisible hand" (Chapter 5) is at work in a competitive market system. In a competitive economy, businessmen employ resources until the extra, or marginal, costs of production equal the price of the product. This not only maximizes the profits of the individual producers but simultaneously results in a pattern of resource allocation which maximizes the satisfactions of consumers. The competitive price system organizes the private interests of producers along lines which are fully in accord with the interests of society as a whole.

Shortcomings of Competitive Price System

Despite these several virtues, economists acknowledge certain limitations of the price system which may impair its ability to allocate resources efficiently. Some of these criticisms have been previously noted in Chapter 5.

1. The competitive price system does not accurately reflect the needs of consumers. There are two major facets of this criticism. On the one hand, the price system registers and responds only to those wants which can be expressed by individuals in the market. The competitive price system therefore ignores certain important social goods and services—for example, education, highways, and national defense—which consumers need and want. On the other hand, it is also argued that the market demand for various goods does not reflect the needs of consumers very accurately, because income is unequally distributed in a competitive price economy. This uneven distribution of "dollar votes" will lead to the production of trifles for the rich and deny the most basic needs of the very poor. The price system adjusts resources in accordance with a given un-

equal distribution of income. Some economists argue that the needs of society might be better served by altering the distribution of income which pure competition provides. More will be said on this point in a later chapter.

2. The competitive price system does not accurately measure costs and revenues where social costs and social revenues are significant. Competition forces each producer to assume only those costs which he must pay. This correctly implies that in some lines of production there are significant costs which producers can and do avoid. These avoided costs accrue to society and are aptly called *social costs.* Firms may avoid the cost of properly disposing of waste materials or of buying smoke- and dust-abatement equipment. The result is significant social costs in the form of polluted rivers, smog, and a generally debased community. Similarly, unbridled competition may cause profit-seeking firms to exploit brutally farmland, timberland, and mineral deposits through the use of the cheapest production methods. The cost to society is the permanent loss of irreproducible natural resources. On the other hand, you will recall from Chapter 6 that the consumption of certain goods and services such as chest X rays and polio shots yields widespread satisfactions, or "revenues," to society as a whole. These satisfactions are called *social revenues.*

Now the significance of social costs and social revenues for present purposes is this: The profit-seeking activities of producers will bring about an allocation of resources which is efficient from society's point of view only if marginal cost embodies *all* the costs which production entails and product price accurately reflects *all* the benefits which society gets from a good's production. Only in this case will competitive production at the MR $(P) =$ MC point balance the total sacrifices and satisfactions of society and result in an efficient allocation of resources. To the extent that price and marginal cost are not accurate indexes of sacrifices and satisfactions, that is, to the extent that social costs and revenues exist, production at the

MR (P) = MC point will not signify an efficient allocation of resources.

3. *The competitive price system may not always entail the use of the most efficient productive techniques or the development of improved techniques.* There are both a static or "right now" aspect and a dynamic or "over time" aspect of this general criticism. The static aspect argues that in certain lines of production existing technology may be such that a firm must be a large-scale producer in order to realize the lowest unit costs of production. Given consumer demand, this suggests that a relatively small number of efficient, large-scale producers is needed if production is to be carried on efficiently. In other words existing mass production economies might be lost if such an industry were populated by the large number of small-scale producers which pure competition requires. This point was discussed in some detail in Chapter 25.

The dynamic aspect of this criticism concerns the willingness and ability of purely competitive firms to undertake technological advance. The progressiveness of pure competition is debated by economists. For present purposes we simply call attention to the fact that some authorities feel that a purely competitive economy would not foster a very rapid rate of technological progress. They argue, first, that the incentive for technological advance may be weak under pure competition, because the profit rewards accruing to an innovating firm as the result of a cost-reducing technological improvement will be quickly competed away by rival firms who readily adopt the new technique. Second, the small size of the typical competitive firm raises serious questions as to whether or not such producers could finance substantial programs of organized research.

4. *The competitive price system may not provide for a sufficient range of consumer choice or for the development of new products.* This criticism, like the previous one, has both a static and a dynamic aspect. Pure competition, it is contended, entails product standardization, whereas other market structures—for example, monopolistic competition and, frequently, oligopoly—entail a wide range of types, styles, and quality gradations of any product. This product differentiation widens the consumer's range of free choice and simultaneously allows his preferences to be more completely fulfilled. Similarly, critics of pure competition point out that, just as pure competition is not likely to be progressive with respect to the development of new productive techniques, neither is this market structure conducive to the improvement of existing products or the creation of completely new ones.

The question of the progressiveness of the various market structures in terms of both productive techniques and product development will be a recurring one in the following three chapters.

SUMMARY

1. A purely competitive industry comprises a large number of independent firms producing a standardized product. Pure competition assumes that firms and resources are mobile as between different industries. No single firm can influence market price in a competitive industry; price, therefore, equals marginal revenue.

2. Short-run profit maximization by a competitive firm can be analyzed by a comparison of total revenue and total cost or through marginal analysis. A firm will maximize profits by producing that output at which total revenue exceeds total cost by the greatest amount. Losses will be minimized by producing where the excess of total cost over total revenue is at a minimum and less than total fixed costs.

3. Provided price exceeds minimum average variable cost, a competitive firm will maximize profits or minimize losses by producing at that output at which price or marginal revenue is equal to marginal cost. If price is less than average variable cost, the firm will minimize its losses by closing down. If price is greater than average variable cost but less than average total cost, the firm will minimize its losses by producing

the $P = MC$ output. If price exceeds average total cost, the $P = MC$ output will provide maximum economic profits for the firm.

4. Applying the $MR(P) = MC$ rule at various possible market prices leads to the conclusion that the segment of the firm's short-run marginal cost curve which lies above average variable cost is its short-run supply curve.

5. In the long run, competitive price will tend to equal the minimum average cost of production. This is so because economic profits will cause firms to enter a competitive industry until those profits have been competed away. Conversely, losses will force the exodus of firms from the industry until product price once again barely covers unit costs.

6. The long-run supply curve of a constant-cost industry is perfectly elastic. However, for an increasing-cost industry the long-run supply curve is upsloping.

7. In a purely competitive economy the profit-seeking activities of producers will result in an allocation of resources which maximizes the satisfactions of consumers. The long-run equality of price and minimum average cost indicates that competitive firms will use the most efficient known technology and charge the lowest price consistent with their production costs. The equality of price and marginal cost indicates that resources will be allocated in accordance with consumer tastes. The competitive price system will reallocate resources in response to a change in consumer tastes, technology, or resource supplies so as to maintain allocative efficiency over time.

8. Economists recognize four possible deterrents to allocative efficiency in a competitive economy. **a.** Income inequality and the unresponsiveness of the price system to social wants suggest that the competitive price economy does not accurately reflect the needs of consumers. **b.** In allocating resources, the price system does not allow for social costs and revenues. **c.** A purely competitive industry may preclude the use of the best known productive techniques and foster a slow rate of technological advance. **d.** A competitive system provides neither a wide range of product choice nor an environment conducive to the development of new products.

QUESTIONS AND STUDY SUGGESTIONS

1. Strictly speaking, pure competition never has existed and probably never will. Then why study it?

2. Why is the equality of marginal revenue and marginal cost essential for profit maximization in all market structures? Explain why price can be substituted for marginal revenue in the MR = MC rule when an industry is purely competitive.

3. Explain: "A competitive producer must look to average variable cost in determining whether or not to produce in the short run, to marginal cost in deciding upon the best volume of production, and to average total cost to calculate his profits or losses." Explain why a firm might produce at a loss in the short run rather than close down.

4. Using diagrams for both the industry and a representative firm, illustrate competitive long-run equilibrium. Employing these diagrams, show how (a) an increase and (b) a decrease in market demand will upset this long-run equilibrium. Trace graphically and describe verbally the adjustment processes by which long-run equilibrium is restored. Assume the industry is one of constant costs.

5. Distinguish carefully between a constant-cost and an increasing-cost industry. Answer question 4 on the assumption that the industry is one

of increasing costs. Compare the long-run supply curves of a constant-cost and an increasing-cost industry.

6. Suppose a decrease in demand occurs in a competitive increasing-cost industry. Contrast the product price and industry output which exist after all long-run adjustments are completed with those which originally prevailed.

7. In long-run equilibrium $P = AC = MC$. Of what significance for the allocation of resources is the equality of P and AC? The equality of P and MC?

8. Explain why some economists feel that an unequal distribution of income might impair the efficiency with which a competitive price system allocates resources. What other criticisms can be made of a purely competitive economy?

9. Assume the following unit-cost data for a purely competitive producer:

Total product	Average fixed cost	Average variable cost	Average total cost	Marginal cost
0				
				$45
1	$60.00	$45.00	$105.00	
				40
2	30.00	42.50	72.50	
				35
3	20.00	40.00	60.00	
				30
4	15.00	37.50	52.50	
				35
5	12.00	37.00	49.00	
				40
6	10.00	37.50	47.50	
				45
7	8.57	38.57	47.14	
				55
8	7.50	40.63	48.13	
				65
9	6.67	43.33	50.00	
				75
10	6.00	46.50	52.50	

a. At a product price of $32, will this firm produce in the short run? Why, or why not? If it does produce, what will be the profit-maximizing or loss-minimizing output? Explain. Specify the amount of economic profit or loss per unit of output.

b. Answer the questions of 9a on the assumption that product price is $41.

c. Answer the questions of 9a on the assumption that product price is $56.

d. Complete the following short-run supply schedule for the same firm, and indicate the profit or loss incurred at each output (columns 1 to 3).

(1) Price	(2) Quantity supplied, single firm	(3) Profit (+) or loss (−)	(4) Quantity supplied, 1,500 firms
$26	___	$___	___
32	___	___	___
38	___	___	___
41	___	___	___
46	___	___	___
56	___	___	___
66	___	___	___

e. Explain: "That segment of a competitive firm's marginal cost curve which lies above its average variable cost curve constitutes the short-run supply curve for the firm." Illustrate graphically.

f. Now assume there are 1,500 identical firms in this competitive industry; that is, there are 1,500 firms, each of which has the same cost data as shown above. Calculate the industry supply schedule (column 4).

g. Suppose the market demand data for the product are as follows:

Price	Total quantity demanded
$26	17,000
32	15,000
38	13,500
41	12,000
46	10,500
56	9,500
66	8,000

What will equilibrium price be? What will equilibrium output be for the industry? For each firm? What will profit or loss be per unit? Per firm?

SELECTED REFERENCES

Bain, Joe S.: *Pricing, Distribution, and Employment*, rev. ed. (New York: Holt, Rinehart and Winston, Inc., 1953), chap. 4.

Bober, M. M.: *Intermediate Price and Income Theory*, rev. ed. (New York: W. W. Norton & Company, Inc., 1962), chap. 9.

Due, John F., and Robert W. Clower: *Intermediate Economic Analysis*, 4th ed. (Homewood, Ill.: Richard D. Irwin, Inc., 1961), chap. 9.

Stigler, George J.: *The Theory of Price*, rev. ed. (New York: The Macmillan Company, 1952), chap. 10.

Stonier, Alfred W., and Douglas C. Hague: *A Textbook of Economic Theory*, 3d ed. (New York: Longmans, Green & Co., Inc., 1964) chaps. 6 and 7.

CHAPTER 27

PRICE AND OUTPUT DETERMINATION:
PURE MONOPOLY

Let us now jump to the opposite end of the industry spectrum and examine the characteristics, the bases, the price-output behavior, and the social desirability of pure monopoly.

CONCEPT AND OCCURRENCE OF PURE MONOPOLY

Pure or absolute monopoly exists when a single firm is the sole producer of a product for which there are no close substitutes. By the absence of close substitutes we mean that there are no other firms producing the same product or products varying only in very minor ways from that of the monopolist. Thus there is no close substitute for the electricity or water supplied by local utilities. And, if there existed only one manufacturer of automobiles, consumers would have no reasonably good alternative to buying from the monopolistic producer. Of course, as mentioned earlier, there may be competition in the broad sense that a food freezer or color television set is a "substitute" for a down payment on an automobile. But these products are clearly distinct from automobiles and do not fulfill the consumer's need for convenient local transportation. The important point is that the monopolist is the only supplier of a certain product for which there are no close substitutes available. Defined in this way, pure monopoly is a rare phenomenon.

Yet a brief analysis of pure monopoly is important for two related reasons. First, some industries are reasonable approximations of pure monopoly. The behavior of firms with 80, 70, or even 60 per cent of a market can often be explained with considerable accuracy through the pure monopoly market model. For all practical purposes the dominant firm *is* the industry in such instances. Second, a study of pure monopoly provides us with valuable insights concerning the more realistic market structures of monopolistic competition and oligopoly, which will be discussed in Chapters 28 and 29. These two market situations combine in differing degrees the characteristics of pure competition and pure monopoly.

BARRIERS TO ENTRY

It was noted in Chapter 22 that the absence of competitors which characterizes pure monopoly is largely explainable in terms of barriers to entry, that is, considerations which prohibit additional firms from entering an industry. These barriers are also pertinent in explaining the existence of oligopoly and monopolistic competition between the market extremes of pure competition and pure monopoly. In the case of pure monopoly entry barriers are sufficiently great to block completely all potential competition. Somewhat less formidable barriers permit the existence of oligopoly, that is, a few firms. Still weaker barriers permit the fairly large number of firms which characterize monopolistic competition. The virtual absence of entry barriers helps explain the very large number of competing firms which is the basis of pure competition. The important point is this: Barriers to entry are pertinent not only to the extreme case of pure monopoly but also to the "partial monopolies" which are so characteristic of American capitalism.

What forms do these entry barriers assume?

Economies of Scale

Modern technology is such in many industries that efficient, low-cost production can be achieved only if producers are extremely large both absolutely and in relation to the market (see Chapter 25). Where economies of scale are very significant, a firm's average-cost schedule will decline over a wide range of output. Given product demand, the achieving of low unit costs and therefore low unit prices for consumers depends upon the existence of a small number of firms or, in the extreme case, only one firm. The automobile, aluminum, and steel industries are a few of many heavy industries which reflect such conditions. If three firms currently enjoy all available economies of scale and each has roughly one-third of a market, it is easy to see why new competitors may find it extremely difficult to enter this industry. On the one hand, new firms entering the market as small-scale producers will have little or no chance to survive and expand. Why? Because as small-scale entrants they will be unable to realize the cost economies enjoyed by the existing "Big Three" and therefore will be unable to realize the profits necessary for survival and growth. New competitors in the steel and automobile industries will not come about as the result of the successful operation and expansion of small "back-yard" producers. They simply will not be efficient enough to survive. The other option is to start out big, that is, to enter the industry as a large-scale producer. In practice, this is virtually impossible. It is extremely unlikely that a new and untried enterprise will be able to secure the money capital needed to obtain capital facilities comparable to those accumulated by any of the Big Three in the automobile industry.

The financial obstacles in the way of starting big are so great in many cases as to be prohibitive.

Public Utilities: Natural Monopolies

In a few industries economies of scale are particularly pronounced, and at the same time competition is impractical, inconvenient, or simply unworkable. Such industries are called *natural monopolies,* and most of the so-called public utilities—the electric and gas companies, bus and railway firms, and water and communication facilities—can be so classified. These industries are generally given exclusive franchises by government. But in return for this sole right to supply electricity, water, or bus service in a given geographic area, government reserves the right to regulate the operations of such monopolies to prevent abuses of the monopoly power it has granted.

Let us examine some illustrations. It would be exceedingly wasteful for a community to have a number of firms supplying water or electricity. Technology is such in these industries that heavy fixed costs on generators, pumping and purification equipment, water mains, and transmission lines are required. This is aggravated by the fact that capital equipment must be sufficient to meet the peak demands which occur on hot summer days when lawns are being watered and air conditioners turned on. These heavy fixed costs mean that unit costs of production decline with the number of cubic feet of water or kilowatt hours of electricity supplied by each firm. The presence of a number of water and electricity suppliers would divide the total market and reduce the sales of each competitor. Each firm would be pushed back up its declining average-cost curve. Firms would underutilize their fixed plants with the result that unit cost and therefore electricity and water rates would necessarily be high. In addition, competition might prove to be highly inconvenient. For example, the presence of a half dozen telephone companies in a municipality would entail the inconvenience of having six telephones and six telephone books—not to mention six telephone bills—to ensure communications with all other residents in the same town.

Because firms are eager to spread their fixed costs and thereby achieve lower unit costs, cutthroat price competition tends to break out when a number of firms exist in these public utilities industries. The result may be losses, the bankruptcy of weaker rivals, and the eventual merger of the survivors. The evolving pure monopoly may be anxious to recoup past losses and to profit fully from its new position of market dominance by charging exorbitant prices for its good or service.

To spare society from such disadvantageous results, government will usually grant an exclusive franchise to a single firm to supply water, natural gas, electricity, telephone service, or train or bus transportation. In return government reserves the right to designate the monopolist's geographic area of operation and the prices which it may charge. The result is a regulated or government-sponsored monopoly—monopoly designed to achieve low unit costs but regulated to guarantee that consumers will benefit from these cost economies.

Ownership of Essential Raw Materials

The institution of private property can be used by a monopoly as a means of achieving an effective obstacle to potential rivals. A firm owning or controlling a raw material which is essential in production can obviously prohibit the creation of rival firms. There are several classic examples. The Aluminum Company of America retained its monopoly position in the aluminum industry for many years by virtue of its control of all basic sources of bauxite, the major ore used in aluminum fabrication. The International Nickel Company of Canada controls approximately 90 per cent of the world's known nickel reserves. Most of the world's

diamond mines are owned by the De Beers Company of South Africa. About 95 per cent of the world's molybdenum reserves are owned by the Climax Molybdenum Company.

Patents and Research

By granting an inventor the exclusive right to control a product for some seventeen years, American patent laws are aimed at protecting an inventor from having his product or process usurped by rival enterprises which have not shared in the time, effort, and money outlays which have gone into its development. By the same token, of course, patents may provide the inventor with a monopoly position for the life of the patent. Patent control figures prominently in the growth of many modern-day industrial giants—National Cash Register, General Motors, General Electric, du Pont, to name a few. The United Shoe Machinery Company provides a notable example of how patent control can be abused to achieve monopoly power. In this case United Shoe became the exclusive supplier of certain essential shoemaking machines through patent control. It extended its monopoly power to other types of shoemaking machinery by requiring all lessees of its patented machines to sign a "tying agreement" in which shoe manufacturers agreed also to lease all other shoemaking machinery from United Shoe. This allowed United Shoe to monopolize the market until partially effective antitrust action was taken by the government in 1955.

Research, of course, underlies the development of patentable products. Firms which gain a measure of monopoly power by their own research or by purchasing the patents of others are in a strategic position to consolidate and strengthen their market position. The profits provided by one important patent can be used to finance the research required to develop new patentable products. Monopoly power achieved through patents may well be cumulative.

Unfair Competition

A firm's rivals may be eliminated and the entry of new competitors blocked by aggressive, cutthroat tactics. Familiar techniques entail product disparagement, pressure on resource suppliers and banks to withhold materials and credit, the hiring away of strategic personnel, and aggressive price cutting designed to bankrupt competitors. Though many of these facets of unfair competition are now illegal or fringe upon illegality, they are of more than historical interest. For example, although Federal legislation prohibits price cutting intended to reduce competition, how is one to distinguish in practice between legitimate price competition based upon cost advantages and price competition designed to bankrupt rivals?

Economies of Being Established

A bit of reflection will reveal that for a variety of reasons an established, going concern has numerous advantages over new, embryonic rivals. There are good reasons why existing firms should survive and prosper, whereas new firms have every reason to founder and fail. Established firms which have proved themselves by their continued existence and prosperity will have relatively easy access to the capital market, on favorable terms. This advantage is not unrelated to the fact that an established concern will tend to have a relatively efficient administrative framework staffed by competent and experienced personnel. The firm's longevity will have allowed it to eliminate inappropriate policies and to have screened the dolts from its administrative ranks. It must be added that going concerns will also be in a position to expand their size and market share by internal financing.

The new concern may have great difficulties in securing needed money capital. Its personnel and policies are untried and untested; it is an industrial question mark. If funds are available to newcomers, the added risks of investing in a new concern are likely to make the terms unattractive to the firm.

In addition, an established firm will be likely to have a widely known and highly advertised product, which it sells through well-established marketing channels to long-standing customers. A new firm faces serious financial obstacles in developing and advertising a product, in establishing marketing outlets, and in building up a clientele.

Two Implications

Our discussion of barriers to entry suggests two noteworthy points. First, barriers to entry are rarely complete; indeed, this is simply another way of stating our earlier point that pure monopoly is rare. Although, as we have seen, research and technological advance may strengthen the market position of a firm, technology may also undermine existing monopoly power. Existing patent advantages may be circumvented by the development of new and distinct, yet substitutable, products. New sources of strategic raw materials may be found. It is probably not an overstatement to say that monopoly in the sense of a one-firm industry only persists over time with the sanction or aid of government.

Second, it is implied in our discussion that monopolies may be desirable or undesirable from the standpoint of economic efficiency. The public utilities and economies-of-scale arguments suggest that market demand and technology may be such that efficient low-cost production presupposes the existence of monopoly. On the other hand, our comments upon materials ownership, patents, and unfair competition as sources of monopoly imply more undesirable connotations of business monopoly.

With these points in mind let us analyze the price-output behavior of a pure monopolist. Important insights with respect to the social desirability of monopoly will be revealed by this analysis.

PRICE AND OUTPUT DETERMINATION

Let us assume a pure monopolist who through, say, patent and materials control is able to block the entry of new firms to the market. Suppose, too, that the monopolist is unregulated; he is unhampered by the existence or the prospect of a regulatory commission. In short, we have a monopolist who is ideally situated to exploit his market fully. The pure monopolist will determine his profit-maximizing output on the basis of his cost and demand data.

Monopoly Demand

The crucial difference between a pure monopolist and a purely competitive seller lies on the demand side of the market. We recall from Chapter 26 that the purely competitive seller faces a perfectly elastic demand schedule at the market price determined by industry supply and demand. The competitive firm can sell as much or as little as it wants at the going market price. It follows that each additional unit sold will add a constant amount—its price—to the firm's total revenue. In other words, for the competitive seller marginal revenue is constant and equal to product price. But the competitive seller can do nothing about market price; he has no price policy. For better or worse, he must accept the market-determined price.

The monopolist's demand curve is much different. Because the pure monopolist *is* the industry, his demand, or sales, curve is the industry demand curve. And the industry demand curve is not perfectly elastic but rather is downsloping.[1] This is illustrated by columns 1 and 2 of Table 27–1.

There are two implications of a downsloping demand curve which must be understood. In the first place, a downsloping demand curve means that a pure monopoly can increase its sales only by charging a lower unit price for its product. *Furthermore, the fact that the monopolist must lower price to boost sales causes marginal revenue to be less than price (average revenue) for every level of output save the first.* The reason? Price cuts will apply not only to the extra output sold but also to all other units of output which otherwise could have been sold at a higher price. Each additional unit sold will add to total revenue its price less the sum of the price cuts which must be taken on all prior units of output.[2] The marginal revenue of the second unit of output in Table 27–1 is $142 rather than its $152 price, because a $10 price cut must be taken on the first unit to increase sales from 1 to 2 units. It is this rationale which explains why the marginal-revenue data of column 4 of Table 27–1 fall short of product price in column 2 for all levels of output save the first.

The second implication of a downsloping demand curve is this: In all imperfectly competitive markets in which such demand curves are relevant—that is, purely monopolistic, oligopolistic, and monopolistically competitive markets—firms have a price policy. By virtue of their ability to influence total supply, the output decisions of such firms necessarily affect product price. This is most evident, of course, in the present case of pure monopoly, where one firm controls total output. Faced with a downsloping demand curve, wherein each output is associated with some unique price, the monopolist unavoidably determines price in

---

[1] Beware of this pitfall: Because the individual competitive firm's demand curve is perfectly elastic, it does not follow that the monopolist's demand curve will be perfectly *in*elastic. Remember: Even though the individual competitor regards his demand as perfectly elastic, the demand curve for a competitive *industry* is downsloping. The pure monopolist's demand curve is downsloping, but not perfectly inelastic, because here the firm *is* the industry. As with competitive industry demand, the degree of elasticity or inelasticity which characterizes the pure monopolist's demand curve depends upon those elasticity-determining factors discussed in Chapter 23.

[2] At this point it may be helpful to reread the discussion of the mechanics of this process in Chapter 23.

TABLE 27–1. REVENUE AND COST DATA OF A PURE MONOPOLIST (hypothetical data)

	Revenue data				Cost data			
(1) Quantity of output	(2) Price (average revenue)	(3) Total revenue	(4) Marginal revenue		(5) Average total cost	(6) Total cost	(7) Marginal cost	(8) Profit (+) or Loss (−)
0	$172	$ 0				$ 100		$−100
			$162				$ 90	
1	162	162			$190.00	190		− 28
			142				80	
2	152	304			135.00	270		+ 34
			122				70	
3	142	426			113.33	340		+ 86
			102				60	
4	132	528			100.00	400		+128
			82				70	
5	122	610			94.00	470		+140
			62				80	
6	112	672			91.67	550		+122
			42				90	
7	102	714			91.43	640		+ 74
			22				110	
8	92	736			93.73	750		− 14
			2				130	
9	82	738			97.78	880		−142
			−18				150	
10	72	720			103.00	1,030		−310

deciding what volume of output to produce. The monopolist simultaneously chooses both price and output. In columns 1 and 2 of Table 27–1 we find that the monopolist can sell only an output of one unit at a price of $162, only an output of two units at a price of $152, and so forth.[3]

But all this is not to imply that the monopolist is "free" of market forces in establishing price and output or that the

[3] The notion of a supply curve does not apply in a purely monopolistic (or any other imperfectly competitive) market because of the ability of the seller to control product price. A supply curve shows the amounts producers will offer at various *given* prices which may confront them in the market. But prices are not "given" to the pure monopolist; he does not respond to a fixed price, but rather sets the price himself.

consumer is somehow completely at the monopolist's mercy. In particular, the monopolist's downsloping demand curve means that high prices are associated with low volumes of sales and, conversely, low prices with larger outputs. The monopolist cannot raise price without losing sales or gain sales without charging a lower price. The question which now arises is this: What specific price-quantity combination on his demand curve will the pure monopolist choose? This depends not only upon demand and marginal-revenue data but also upon costs.

Cost Data

On the cost side of the picture we shall assume that, although the firm is a monopolist in the product market, it hires resources

competitively and employs the same technology as our competitive firm in the preceding chapter. This permits us to use the cost
data developed in Chapter 25 and applied
in Chapter 26, thereby facilitating a comparison of the price-output decisions of a
pure monopoly with those of a pure competitor. Columns 5 through 7 of Table 27–1
merely restate the pertinent cost concepts
of Table 25–2.

Equating Marginal Revenue
and Marginal Cost

A profit-seeking monopolist will employ the
same rationale as a profit-seeking firm in a
competitive industry. He will produce each
successive unit of output so long as it adds
more to his total revenue than it does to his
total costs. In technical language, the firm

will produce up to that output at which
marginal revenue equals marginal cost.

A comparison of columns 4 and 7 in Table
27–1 indicates that the profit-maximizing
output is 5 units; the fifth unit is the last unit
of output whose marginal revenue exceeds
its marginal cost. What price will the
monopolist charge? His downsloping demand
curve of columns 1 and 2 shows there is only
one price at which 5 units can be sold: $122.

This same analysis is presented graphically in Figure 27–1, where the demand,
marginal-revenue, average-total-cost, and
marginal-cost data of Table 27–1 have been
drawn. A comparison of marginal revenue
and marginal cost again indicates that the
profit-maximizing output is 5 units or, more
generally, Q_m. The unique price at which
Q_m can be sold is found by extending a
perpendicular up from the profit-maximizing

FIGURE 27–1. THE PROFIT-MAXIMIZING POSITION OF A PURE MONOPOLIST.
The pure monopolist maximizes profits by producing the MR = MC output. In this
instance profit is AP_m per unit; total profits are measured by the white rectangle.

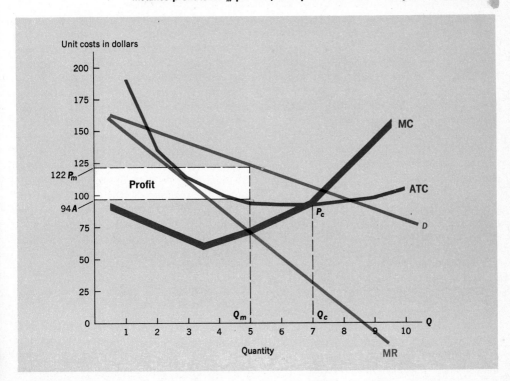

point on the output axis and then at right angles from the point at which it hits the demand curve to the vertical axis. The indicated price is P_m. By charging a price higher than P_m, the monopolist must move up his demand curve, and this means that his sales will fall short of the profit-maximizing level Q_m. To charge less would involve a volume of sales in excess of the profit-maximizing output.

Columns 2 and 5 of Table 27–1 indicate that, at five units of output, product price of $122 exceeds average total cost of $94. Economic profits are therefore $28 per unit; total economic profits are then $140 (or 5 times $28). In Figure 27–1 per unit profit is indicated by the distance AP_m, and total economic profits—the white area—are found by multiplying this unit profit by the profit-maximizing output Q_m.

The same profit-maximizing combination of output and price can also be determined by comparing the total revenue and total costs incurred at each possible level of production. The reader should employ columns 3 and 6 of Table 27–1 to verify all the conclusions we have reached through the use of marginal-revenue–marginal-cost analysis. Similarly, an accurate graphing of total revenue and total cost against output will also show the greatest differential (the maximum profit) at 5 units of output.

Misconceptions Concerning Monopoly Pricing

Our analysis explodes some popular fallacies concerning the behavior of monopolies.

1. Because a monopolist can manipulate output and price, it is often alleged that a monopolist "will charge the highest price he can get." This is clearly a misguided assertion. There are many prices above P_m in Figure 27–1, but the monopolist shuns them for the simple reason that they entail a smaller than maximum profit. Total profits are the difference between total revenue and total costs, and each of these two determi-

nants of profits depends upon quantity sold as much as upon price and unit cost.

2. The monopolist seeks maximum *total* profits, not maximum *unit* profits. In Figure 27–1 a careful comparison of the distance between average cost and price at various possible outputs indicates that per unit profits are greater at a point slightly to the left of the profit-maximizing output Q_m. This is more readily seen in Table 27–1, where unit profits are $32 at 4 units of output as compared to $28 at the profit-maximizing output of 5 units. In this instance the monopolist is accepting a lower-than-maximum per unit profit for the simple reason that the additional sales more than compensate for the lower unit profits. A monopolist would obviously rather sell 5 units at a profit of $28 per unit than sell 4 units at a profit of $32 per unit.

3. It must also be emphasized that pure monopoly does not guarantee economic profits. True, the likelihood of economic profits is greater for a pure monopolist than for a purely competitive producer. In the long run the latter is doomed by the free and easy entry of new firms to a normal profit; barriers to entry permit the monopolist to perpetuate economic profits in the long run. Of course, like the pure competitor, the monopolist cannot persistently operate at a loss. The monopolist must realize a normal profit or better in the long run or will simply not survive. However, if the demand and cost situation faced by the monopolist is less favorable than that shown in Figure 27–1, the monopolist may realize short-run losses. Despite his dominance in the market, the monopolist shown in Figure 27–2 realizes a loss in the short run by virtue of a weak demand and high costs.

Possible Restraints upon Profit Maximization

The comments just made indicate that certain restraints are imposed upon the monopolist by the market. Cost and demand considerations set restrictions upon the

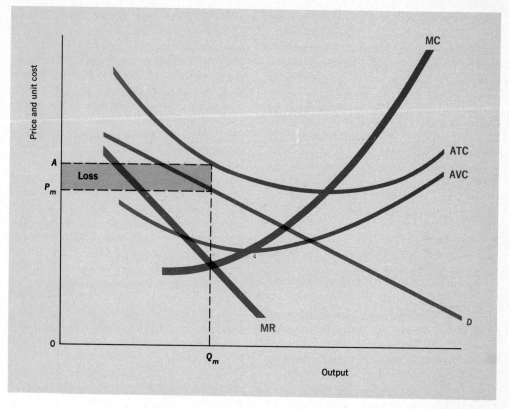

FIGURE 27–2. THE LOSS-MINIMIZING POSITION OF A PURE MONOPOLIST.
If demand D is weak and costs AC are high, the pure monopolist may be unable to make
a profit. He will minimize his losses in the short run by producing at that output where
MR = MC. Loss per unit is AP_m and total losses are indicated by the gray rectangle.

monopolist's price-output behavior. Actually certain other forces may cause the monopolist to exercise restraint; these forces may cause the monopolist purposely to charge a lower price and produce a greater output than is consistent with maximum profits. Two such restraints merit comment.

In the first place, the monopolist does not enjoy anonymity; the identity of monopolistic sellers is typically well known. It follows that the monopolist who fully exploits his market position may find himself the target of public criticism. After all, in Figure 27–1 there are many prices less than P_m which will entail outputs greater than Q_m and still yield substantial economic profits

to the monopolist. If widespread and persistent, such criticism can lead to a loss of good will or, worse yet from the firm's viewpoint, some form of governmental intervention—antitrust action, rate regulation, government stimulation of new competitors or, at the extreme, nationalization of the firm. Thus, from a very long-run standpoint it may be very sensible for the monopolist to avoid unfavorable comment with respect to its market behavior even at the sacrifice of some profits.

Secondly, the monopoly may deliberately limit its profits so as not to attract new competitors. A highly profitable monopoly may cause potential rivals to double their efforts to overcome the monopolist's barriers. And remember: Barriers to entry are rarely insurmountable over time. Full exploitation of a monopolist's position in the short run may destroy that monopolistic position in the long pull.

The importance of these "voluntary" restraints is subject to heated debate. It would be a mistake to say that they undermine our profit-maximizing analysis; at best they probably cause minor deviations from the most profitable price-output combination.

ECONOMIC EFFECTS

Let us now evaluate pure monopoly from the standpoint of society as a whole. Our emphasis will be upon (1) price, output, and resource allocation, (2) the distribution of income, and (3) economic progress, that is, technological advance. To sharpen our analysis we ignore any possible restraints upon the monopolist's policies and presume that the monopolist seeks the maximum profit that his cost-revenue situation permits.

Price, Output, and Resource Allocation

In Chapter 26 we concluded that pure competition would result in a highly efficient, or "ideal," allocation of resources. In the long run the free entry and exodus of firms would force firms to operate at the optimum rate of output where unit costs of production were at a minimum. Product price would be at the lowest level consistent with average total costs. To illustrate: In Figure 27–1 the competitive firm would sell Q_c units of output at a price of Q_cP_c. Furthermore, long-run competitive equilibrium would also entail an efficient allocation of resources, in that production would occur up to that point at which price (the measure of a product's value to society) equals marginal cost (the measure of the alternative products forgone by society in the production of any given commodity).

Figure 27–1 indicates that, given the same costs, a purely monopolistic firm will give

much less desirable results. As we have already discovered, the pure monopolist will maximize his profits by producing an output of Q_m and charging a price of P_m. It can be readily seen that the monopolist will find it profitable to sell a smaller output and to charge a higher price than would a competitive producer. Furthermore, it is clear that, at Q_m units of output, product price is considerably greater than marginal cost. This means that society values additional units of this monopolized product higher than it does the alternative products which resources could otherwise produce. In other words, the monopolist's profit-maximizing output results in a misallocation of resources; the monopolist finds it profitable to restrict output and therefore employ fewer resources than are justified from society's standpoint.

Given identical costs, a purely monopolistic firm will find it profitable to charge a higher price, produce a smaller output, and foster an allocation of economic resources inferior to that of a purely competitive firm. These contrasting consequences are rooted in the barriers to entry which characterize monopoly.

There is one basic exception to these conclusions: The assumption that the unit costs available to the purely competitive and the purely monopolistic firm are the same does not always hold in practice. Given production techniques and therefore production costs, consumer demand may simply not be sufficient to support a large number of competing firms, each producing at an output which permits it to realize all known economies of scale. In such instances a firm must be large in relation to the market—that is, it must be monopolistic—to produce efficiently (at low unit cost). Our previous discussion of economies of scale as a barrier to entry and the desirability of establishing public utilities in certain fields is based primarily upon such cost considerations (see Chapter 25).

How important is this exception? Most economists feel that it applies for the most part only to public utilities and is therefore not significant enough to undermine our general conclusions concerning the restrictive nature of monopoly. The best available evidence (see footnote 6 in Chapter 8) suggests that the giant corporations which populate many manufacturing industries now have more monopoly power than can be justified on the grounds that these firms are merely availing themselves of existing economies of scale.

Income Distribution

Business monopoly probably contributes to inequality in the distribution of income in our society. By virtue of their market power monopolists charge a higher price than would a purely competitive firm with the same costs; monopolists are in effect able to levy a "private tax" upon consumers and thereby realize substantial economic profits. These monopolistic profits, it should be noted, are not widely distributed for the simple reason that corporate stock ownership is largely concentrated in the hands of upper income groups. The owners of monopolistic enterprises thereby tend to be enriched at the expense of the rest of society.

Assuming monopoly does contribute to income inequality, is this necessarily undesirable? There is no agreement here, and no scientifically correct answer will ever be found because any view entails a value judgment with respect to what one feels the distribution of income ought to be. Nevertheless, there is a rather widespread feeling in our society that the extreme degrees of income inequality to which pure monopoly frequently contributes are undesirable (see Chapter 37).

Technological Advance

We have already qualified our condemnation of pure monopoly by noting that in a few instances *existing* mass-production economies may be lost if an industry comprises a large number of small, competing firms. There is also a dynamic aspect to this line of reasoning. To be specific, will competition or monopoly foster the more rapid improvement of products and productive techniques? This is fertile ground for honest differences of opinion.

Competitive firms certainly have the incentive—indeed, a market mandate—to employ the most efficient *known* productive techniques. We have seen that their very survival depends upon being efficient. But at the same time competition tends to deprive firms of economic profit—an important means and a major incentive to develop *new* products and *new* improved productive techniques. The profits of technological advance will be short-lived to the innovating competitor. An innovating firm in a competitive industry will find that its many rivals will soon duplicate or imitate any technological advance it may achieve; rivals will share the rewards but not the costs of successful technological research.

In contrast we have seen that a monopolist may persistently realize substantial economic profits. Hence, the pure monopolist will have greater financial resources for technological advance than will competitive firms. But what about the monopolist's incentives for technological advance? Here the picture is clouded.

There is one imposing argument which suggests that the monopolist's incentives to develop new products and new techniques will be weak: the absence of competitors means that there is no automatic stimulus to technological advance in a monopolized market. Because of its sheltered market position, the pure monopolist can afford to be inefficient and lethargic. The keen rivalry of a competitive market penalizes the inefficient; an inefficient monopolist does not face this penalty for the simple reason that he has no rivals. The monopolist has every reason to become satisfied with the *status quo,* to become complacent. It might well pay the monopolist to withhold or "file" technological improvements in both product and productive techniques in order to exploit existing capital equipment fully. New and improved products and techniques, it is argued, may be suppressed by monopolists to avoid any losses caused by the sudden obsolescence of existing machinery and equipment. And, even when improved techniques are belatedly introduced by monopolists, the accompanying cost reductions will accrue to the monopolist as increases in profits and only partially, if at all, to consumers in the form of lower prices and an increased output. Proponents of this view point out that in a number of industries which approximate pure monopoly—for example, steel and aluminum—the interest in research has been minimal. Such advances as have been realized have come largely from outside the industry or from the smaller firms which make up the "competitive fringe" of the industry.

Basically there are three offsetting arguments:

1. Any gross failure to achieve some minimum level of technological advance will induce public criticism and, in time, government control.

2. Technological advance is a means of lowering unit costs and thereby expanding profits. As our analysis of Figure 27–1 implies, lower costs will give rise to a profit-maximizing position which involves a larger output and a lower price than previously. Furthermore, any expansion of profits will not be of a transitory nature; barriers to entry protect the monopolist from profit encroachment by rivals.

3. Research and technological advance may be one of the monopolist's barriers to entry; hence, the monopolist must persist and succeed in the area of technological advance or eventually fall prey to new competitors.

Which view is more accurate? Frankly, economists are not sure. Most economists do not envision pure monopoly as a particularly progressive market structure. At the same time they acknowledge that agriculture, the industry which most nearly fits the competitive model, has only on rare occasion provided itself with new innovations in product

and method. Government research and the oligopolistic firms which produce farm equipment have provided this competitive industry with most of its improvements in products and techniques. As we shall see in Chapter 29, some respected economists seem to feel that oligopolistic industries, wherein firms are large enough to have the ability to finance research and at the same time are compelled to engage in such research because of the presence of a moderate number of rivals, may be more conducive to technological advance than any other market structure.

Now what can be offered by way of a summarizing generalization as to the economic efficiency of pure monopoly? Simply this: In a static economy, wherein economies of scale are equally accessible to purely competitive and monopolist firms, pure competition will be superior to pure monopoly in that pure competition forces use of the best-known technology and allocates resources in accordance with the wants of society. On the other hand, when economies of scale available to the monopolist are not attainable by small competitive producers, or in a dynamic context in which changes in the rate of technological advance must be considered, the economic inefficiencies of pure monopoly are not so evident.

REGULATED MONOPOLY

Most purely monopolistic industries are "natural monopolies" and therefore subject to social regulation. In particular, the prices or rates which public utilities—railroads, telephone companies, natural gas and electricity suppliers—can charge are determined by a Federal, state, or local regulatory commission or board. Can such regulation improve the social acceptability of monopoly?

Socially Optimum Price

Figure 27–3 is informative. We know that P_m and Q_m are the profit-maximizing price and output which the unregulated monopo-

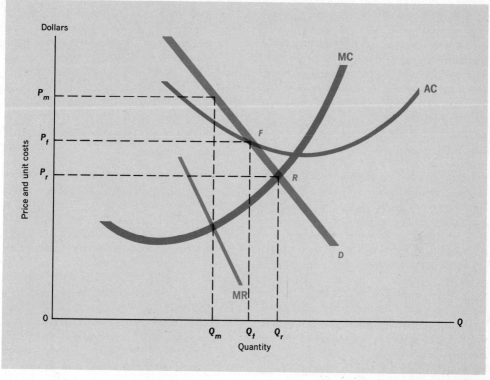

FIGURE 27–3. REGULATED MONOPOLY.
Price regulation can improve the social consequences of a natural monopoly.
The socially optimum price P_r will result in an efficient allocation of resources but
is likely to entail losses and therefore call for permanent public subsidies. The
"fair return" price P_f will allow the monopolist to break even, but will not fully
correct the underallocation of resources.

list would choose. Because price exceeds average total cost, the monopolist enjoys a substantial economic profit which is likely to contribute to income inequality. Furthermore, price exceeds marginal cost, which designates a substantial underallocation of resources to this product or service.

Now if the objective of our regulatory commission is to achieve an efficient allocation of resources, it should obviously establish a legal (ceiling) price for the monopolist that is equal to marginal cost. Remembering that each point on the market demand curve designates a price-quantity combination and noting that marginal cost cuts the demand

curve only at point R, it is quite obvious that P_r is the only price which is equal to marginal cost. The imposition of this maximum or ceiling price causes the monopolist's effective demand curve to become P_rRD; the demand curve becomes perfectly elastic, and therefore $P_r = MR$ out to point R, where the regulated price ceases to be effective. The important point is that, given the legal price P_r, the monopolist will maximize profits by producing Q_r units of output because it is at this output that MR $(P_r) = MC$. By making it illegal to charge more than P_r per unit, the regulatory agency has eliminated the monopolist's incentive to restrict output in order to benefit from a higher price. In short, by imposing the legal price P_r and letting the monopolist choose his profit-maximizing output, the allocative results of pure competition can be simulated. Production takes place where $P = MC$, and this equality indicates an efficient allocation of resources to this product or service.

"Fair-return" Price

But the socially optimum price P_r is likely to pose a problem of losses for the regulated firm. The price which equals marginal cost is likely to be so low that average total costs are not covered. The inevitable result is losses. The reason for this lies in the basic character of public utilities. Because they are required to meet "peak" demands (both daily and seasonally) for their product or service, they tend to have substantial excess productive capacity when demand is relatively "normal." This high level of investment in capital facilities means that unit costs of production are likely to decline over a wide range of output. In technical terms the market demand curve in Figure 27–3 cuts marginal cost at a point to the left of the marginal-cost–average-total-cost intersection, so the socially optimum price is necessarily below AC. Therefore, to enforce a socially optimum price upon the regulated monopolist would mean short-run losses and in the long run bankruptcy for the utility.

What to do? In practice regulatory commissions have tended to back away somewhat from the objective of allocative efficiency and marginal-cost pricing. Most regulatory agencies in the United States are concerned with establishing a "fair-return" price. This is so in no small measure because, as the courts have envisioned it, an unembellished socially optimum price would lead to losses and eventual bankruptcy and thereby deprive the monopoly's owners of their private property without "due process of law." Indeed, the Supreme Court has held that the regulatory agencies must permit a "fair return" to owners.

Remembering that total costs include a normal or "fair" profit, the "fair" or "fair-return" price in Figure 27–3 would obviously be P_f. Because the demand curve cuts average cost only at point F, it is clear that P_f is the only price which permits a fair return. The corresponding output at regulated price P_f will be Q_f.

Dilemma of Regulation

A comparison of the results of the socially optimum price and the "fair-return" price suggests a policy dilemma. When price is set to achieve the most efficient allocation of resources ($P = MC$), the regulated utility is likely to suffer losses. Survival of the firm would presumably depend upon permanent public subsidies out of tax revenues. On the other hand, although a fair price allows the monopolist to cover costs, it only partially resolves the underallocation of resources which the unregulated monopoly would foster. That is, the fair-return price would only increase output from Q_m to Q_f, whereas the socially optimum output is Q_r. Despite this knotty problem, the basic point is that regulation can improve upon the results of monopoly from the social point of view. Price regulation can simultaneously reduce price, increase output, and reduce the economic profits of monopolies.[4]

SUMMARY

1. A pure monopolist is the sole producer of a commodity for which there are no close substitutes.

2. Barriers to entry, in the form of **a.** economies of scale, **b.** natural monopolies, **c.** the ownership or control of essential raw materials, **d.** patent ownership and research,

---

[4] The interested reader should consult Clark Lee Allen, James M. Buchanan, and Marshall R. Colberg, *Prices, Income, and Public Policy*, 2d ed. (New York: McGraw-Hill Book Company, 1959), chap. 30, from which the above discussion has benefited.

e. unfair competition, and **f.** economies of being established, help explain the existence of pure monopoly and other imperfectly competitive market structures. Barriers to entry which are very formidable in the short run may prove to be surmountable in the long run.

3. The pure monopolist's market situation differs from that of a competitive firm in that the monopolist's demand curve is down-sloping, causing the marginal-revenue curve to lie below the demand curve. Like the competitive seller, the pure monopolist will maximize profits by equating marginal revenue and marginal cost. Barriers to entry may permit a monopolist to acquire economic profits even in the long run. It is noteworthy, however, that **a.** the monopolist does not charge "the highest price he can get"; **b.** the maximum total profit sought by the monopolist rarely coincides with maximum unit profits; and **c.** high costs and a weak demand may prevent the monopolist from realizing any profit at all.

4. Given the same costs, the pure monopolist will find it more profitable to restrict output and charge a higher price than would a competitive seller. This restriction of output causes resources to be misallocated, as is evidenced by the fact that price exceeds marginal cost in monopolized markets.

5. Monopoly tends to increase income inequality.

6. Economists disagree as to how conducive pure monopoly is to technological advance. Some feel that pure monopoly is more progressive than pure competition because its ability to acquire economic profits provides for the financing of technological research. Others, however, argue that the absence of rival firms and the monopolist's desire to exploit fully his existing capital facilities weaken the monopolist's incentive to innovate.

7. Price regulation can be invoked to eliminate wholly or partially the tendency of monopolists to underallocate resources and to earn economic profits.

QUESTIONS AND STUDY SUGGESTIONS

1. "No firm is completely sheltered from rivals; all firms in fact compete for the dollars of consumers. Pure monopoly, therefore, simply does not exist." Do you agree? Explain.

2. Discuss the major barriers to entry. In particular, what are "the economies of being established"? Explain how each barrier can foster monopoly or oligopoly. Which barriers, if any, do you feel give rise to monopoly that is socially justifiable?

3. Critically evaluate and explain:
    a. "Because they can control product price, monopolists are always assured of profitable production by simply charging the highest price consumers will pay."
    b. "The pure monopolist seeks that output which will yield the greatest per unit profit."
    c. "An excess of price over marginal cost is the market's way of signaling the need for more production of a product."
    d. "The more profitable a firm, the greater its monopoly power."
    e. "The monopolist has a price policy; the competitive producer does not."
    f. "With respect to resource allocation the interests of the seller and of society coincide in a purely competitive market but conflict in a monopolized market."

g. "In a sense the monopolist makes a profit for not producing; the monopolist produces profits more than he does goods."

4. Carefully evaluate the following widely held viewpoint. Can you offer any arguments to the contrary?[5]

Competition is congenial to material progress. It keeps the door open to new blood and new ideas. It communicates to all producers the improvements made by any one of them. Monopoly, as such, is not conducive to progress. The large firm may engage in research and invent new products, materials, methods and machines. But when it possesses a monopoly, it will be reluctant to make use of these inventions if they would compel it to scrap existing equipment or if it believes that their ultimate profitability is in doubt. The monopolist may introduce innovations and cut costs, but instead of moving goods by reducing prices he is prone to spend large sums on alternative methods of promoting sales. His refusal to cut prices deprives the community of any gain.

5. Suppose a pure monopolist is faced with the following demand schedule and the same cost data as the competitive producer discussed in question 9 at the end of Chapter 26. Calculate marginal revenue and determine the profit-maximizing price and output for this monopolist. Verify your answer graphically.

Price	Quantity demanded	Marginal revenue
$100	1	
		$_____
83	2	
		_____
71	3	
		_____
63	4	
		_____
55	5	
		_____
48	6	
		_____
42	7	
		_____
37	8	
		_____
33	9	
		_____
29	10	

6. Explain verbally and graphically how price (rate) regulation may improve the performance of monopolies. What is the "dilemma of regulation"?

[5] Clair Wilcox, *Public Policies toward Business* (Homewood, Ill.: Richard D. Irwin, Inc., 1955), p. 12.

one or more respects. Indeed, it must be emphasized that product differentiation has more dimensions than are immediately apparent. "Real," or physical, differences involving functional features, materials, design, and workmanship are obviously important aspects of product differentiation. But "imaginary" differences created through advertising, packaging, and the use of trademarks and brand names can be equally significant. Finally, the conditions of sale make for differentiation; the location of a store, the courteousness of its clerks, the firm's reputation for servicing its products, and the availability of credit are all facets of product differentiation.

The significance of product differentiation is basically twofold. On the one hand, despite the presence of a relatively large number of firms, monopolistically competitive producers have limited amounts of control over the prices of their products because of differentiation. Consumers have preferences for the products of specific sellers and *within limits* will pay a higher price to satisfy those preferences. Sellers and buyers are no longer linked at random as in a purely competitive market. On the other hand, the fact that products are differentiated adds a new and complicating factor to our analysis: *nonprice competition.* Because products are differentiated, it can be supposed that products can be varied over time and that the differentiating features of each firm's product will be susceptible to advertising and other forms of sales promotion. In a monopolistically competitive market economic rivalry centers not only upon price but also upon product variation and product promotion.

Entry into monopolistically competitive industries tends to be relatively easy. The fact that monopolistically competitive producers are typically small-sized firms both absolutely and relatively suggests that economies of scale and capital requirements are few. On the other hand, as compared to pure competition, there may be some added financial barriers posed by the need for deriving a product different from one's rivals and the obligation to advertise that product. Existing firms may hold patents on their products and copyrights on their brand names and trademarks, enhancing the difficulty and cost of successfully imitating them.

In short, monopolistic competition refers to industries that comprise a relatively large number of firms, operating noncollusively, in the production of differentiated products. Nonprice competition accompanies price competition. Ease of entry makes for competition by new firms in the long run.

It is difficult to find clear-cut illustrations of monopolistically competitive industries. Many industries which approximate monopolistic competitions also embody one or more characteristics of oligopoly. Table 28–1 contains a group of manufacturing industries which approximate monopolistic competition. Retail stores in larger cities and metropolitan areas are generally monopolistically competitive; grocery stores, gasoline stations, barber shops, dry cleaners, clothing stores, and so forth, operate under conditions similar to those we have described.

PRICE AND OUTPUT DETERMINATION

Let us now analyze the price-output behavior of a monopolistically competitive firm. To facilitate this task we assume initially that the firms in the industry are producing *given* products and are engaging in a *given* amount of promotional activity. Later we shall note how product variation and advertising modify our discussion.

The Firm's Demand Curve

Our explanation is couched in terms of Figure 28–1a. The basic feature of this diagram, which sets it off from our analyses of pure competition and pure monopoly, is the elasticity of the firm's individual demand, or sales, curve. The demand curve faced by a monopolistically competitive seller is highly, but not perfectly, elastic. It is much more elastic than the demand curve of the pure

TABLE 28–1. PERCENTAGE OF OUTPUT* PRODUCED BY FIRMS IN SELECTED LOW-CONCENTRATION MANUFACTURING INDUSTRIES, 1958

Industry	Four largest firms	Four next largest firms	Twelve next largest firms
Plywood	19%	9%	14%
Paperboard boxes	17	10	18
Upholstered furniture	14	4	7
Metal house furniture	14	8	16
Costume jewelry	12	6	14
Men's and boys' suits and coats	11	8	13
Wood furniture	9	4	9
Millinery	6	4	9
Dresses	4	3	5
Women's suits, coats, and skirts	4	2	6

* As measured by value of shipments.
Source: Senate Subcommittee on Antitrust and Monopoly, *Concentration Ratios in Manufacturing Industry, 1958* (Washington, D.C., 1962), part I, table 2.

monopolist, because the monopolistically competitive seller is faced with a relatively large number of rivals producing close-substitute goods. The pure monopolist, of course, has no rivals at all. Yet, for two reasons, the monopolistically competitive seller's sales curve is not perfectly elastic as is the purely competitive producer's:

1. The monopolistically competitive firm has a smaller number of rivals.

2. The products of these rivals are close but not perfect substitutes.

Generally speaking, the precise degree of elasticity embodied in the monopolistically competitive firm's demand curve will depend upon the exact number of rivals and the degree of product differentiation. The larger the number of rivals and the weaker the product differentiation, the greater will be the elasticity of each seller's demand curve, that is, the closer the situation will be to pure competition.

The Short Run: Profits or Losses

The firm will maximize its profits or minimize its losses in the short run by producing that output designated by the intersection of marginal cost and marginal revenue, for reasons with which we are now familiar. The representative firm of Figure 28–1a produces an output Q, charges a price P, and is fortunate enough to realize a total profit of the size indicated. But a less favorable cost and demand situation may exist, putting the monopolistically competitive firm in the position of realizing losses in the short run. This is illustrated in Figure 28–1b. In the short run the monopolistically competitive firm may either realize an economic profit or be faced with losses.

The Long Run: Break-even

In the long run, however, the tendency is for monopolistically competitive firms to earn a normal profit, that is, to break even. In the short-run profits case, Figure 28–1a, we can expect the economic profits to attract new rivals, because entry is relatively easy. As new firms enter, the demand curve faced by the typical firm will fall (shift to the left) and become more elastic. Why? Because each firm has a smaller share of the total demand and now faces a larger number of close-substitute products. This in turn tends to cause the disappearance of economic profits. When the demand curve is tangent to the average-cost curve at the profit-maximizing output, as shown in Figure 28–1*c*, the firm is just breaking even. Output *Q* is the equilibrium output for the firm; as Figure 28–1*c* clearly indicates, any deviation from that output will entail average costs which exceed product price and, therefore, losses for the firm. Furthermore, economic profits have been competed away, and there is no incentive for additional firms to enter. In the short-run losses case, Figure 28–1*b*, we can expect an exodus of firms to occur in the long run. Faced with fewer substitute products and blessed with an expanded share of total demand, surviving firms will find that their losses disappear and gradually give way to approximately normal profits.[1]

Note that we have been very careful in designating our long-run analysis as a statement of a tendency. The representative firm in a monopolistically competitive market *tends* to break even in the long run. There are certain complicating factors which prevent us from being more dogmatic. First, some firms may achieve a measure of product differentiation which cannot be duplicated by rivals even over a long span of time. A given gasoline station may have the only available location at the busiest intersection in town. Or a firm may hold a patent which gives it a slight and more or less permanent advantage over imitators. Such firms may realize a sliver of economic profits even in the long run. Second, remember that entry is not completely unrestricted. Because of product differentiation, there are likely to be greater financial barriers to entry than otherwise would be the case. This again suggests that some economic profits may persist even in the long run. A third consideration may work in the opposite direction, causing losses—below-normal profits—to persist in the long run. The proprietor of a corner delicatessen persistently accepts a return less than he could earn elsewhere,

[1] For simplicity's sake we assume constant costs; shifts in the cost curves as firms enter or leave would complicate our discussion but not alter the conclusions.

(a)

(b)

(c)

FIGURE 28–1. MONOPOLISTICALLY COMPETITIVE FIRMS TEND TO REALIZE A NORMAL PROFIT IN THE LONG RUN.

The economic profits shown in (*a*) will induce new firms to enter, causing the profits to be competed away. The losses indicated in (*b*) will cause an exodus of firms until normal profits are restored. Thus in (*c*), where price just covers unit costs at the MR = MC output, the firm's long-run equilibrium position is portrayed.

because his business is a way of life to him. The suburban barber ekes out a meager existence, because cutting hair is "all he wants to do." With all things considered, however, the long-run profitless equilibrium of Figure 28–1c is probably a reasonable portrayal of reality.

WASTES OF MONOPOLISTIC COMPETITION

Recalling our evaluation of competitive pricing in Chapter 26, we know that economic efficiency requires the triple equality of price, marginal cost, and average cost. The equality of price and marginal cost is necessary for a correct allocation of resources to the product. The equality of price with minimum average total cost entails the use of the most efficient (least-cost) technology; this equality means that consumers will enjoy the largest volume of product and the lowest price which prevailing cost conditions will allow.

An examination of Figure 28–1c suggests that the monopolistic element in monopolistic competition causes a modest underallocation of resources to goods produced under this market structure. Price exceeds marginal cost in long-run equilibrium, thereby indicating that society values additional units of this commodity more than the alternative products which the needed resources can otherwise produce.

Furthermore, in contrast to purely competitive firms, as suggested in Figure 28–1c, monopolistically competitive firms produce somewhat short of the most efficient (least unit cost) output: Production entails higher unit costs than the minimum attainable. This in turn means a somewhat higher price than would result under pure competition. Consumers do *not* benefit from the largest output and lowest price which cost conditions permit. Indeed, monopolistically competitive firms must charge a higher than competitive price in the long run in order to manage a normal profit. Looked at differently, if each firm were able to produce at the most effi-cient output, a smaller number of firms could produce the same total output, and the product could be sold to consumers at a lower price. Monopolistically competitive industries tend to be overcrowded with firms, each of which is underutilized, that is, operating short of optimum capacity. This is typified by retail establishments, for example, the highway intersection adorned with four gleaming gasoline stations all operating far short of capacity. Underutilized plants, consumers penalized through higher than competitive prices for this underutilization, and producers just making a normal return in the long run—these are the so-called "wastes" of monopolistic competition.

But we must not be hypercritical of monopolistic competition. Some economists argue that in many monopolistically competitive industries the price and output results are not drastically different from those of pure competition. The highly elastic nature of each firm's demand curve guarantees that the results are nearly competitive. Furthermore, it must be kept in mind that any deviations from the purely competitive output and price may be offset by the fact that with monopolistic competition the consumer now can choose from a variety of products; he is not faced with a homogeneous commodity.

NONPRICE COMPETITION

For reasons cited above, we can conclude that the situation portrayed in Figure 28–1c may not be particularly beneficial to society. It can also be surmised that it is not very satisfying to the monopolistically competitive producer who barely captures a normal profit for his efforts. We can therefore expect monopolistically competitive producers to take steps to improve upon the long-run equilibrium position. But how can this be accomplished? The answer lies in product differentiation. Each firm has a product which is currently distinguishable in some more or less tangible way from those of his rivals. The product is assumedly subject to further variation, that is, to product development. Then, too, the emphasis of real product differences and the creation of imaginary differences may be achieved through advertising and related sales promotion. In short, the profit-realizing producer of Figure 28–1a is loath to stand by and watch new competitors encroach upon his profits by duplicating or imitating his product, copying his advertising, and matching his services to consumers. Rather, he will attempt to sustain these profits and "stay ahead" of competitors through further product development and by enhancing the quantity and quality of advertising. In this way he might prevent the long-run tendency of Figure 28–1c from becoming a reality. True, product development and advertising will add to the firm's costs. But they can also be expected to increase the demand for his product. If demand increases by more than enough to compensate for development and promotional costs, the firm will have improved its profit position. As Figure 28–1c suggests, the firm may have little or no prospect of increasing profits by price cutting. So why not practice nonprice competition?

Product Differentiation and Product Development

The likelihood that easy entry will promote product variety and product improvement is possibly a redeeming feature of monopolistic competition which may offset, wholly or in part, the "wastes" associated with this market structure. There are really two somewhat distinct considerations here: (1) product differentiation at a point in time and (2) product improvement over a period of time.

1. Product differentiation means that at any point in time the consumer will be offered a wide range of types, styles, brands, and quality gradations of any given product. As compared with the situation under pure competition, this correctly suggests possible advantages to the consumer. His range of free choice is widened, and variations and shadings of consumer tastes are more fully met by producers. But skeptics warn that product differentiation is not an unmixed blessing. Product proliferation may reach the point where the consumer becomes confused and rational choice is highly unlikely. Variety may add spice to the consumer's life, but only up to a point. Worse yet, some observers fear that the consumer, faced with a myriad of similar products, may rely upon such a dubious expedient as judging product quality by price; that is, the consumer may irrationally assume that price is an index of product quality.

2. Product competition is an important avenue of technological innovation and product betterment over a period of time. Such product development may be cumulative in two different senses. (a) A successful product improvement by one firm obligates rivals to imitate or, if they can, improve upon this firm's temporary market advantage or suffer the penalty of losses. (b) Profits realized from a successful product improvement can be used to finance further improvements. Again, however, there are notable criticisms of the product development which may occur under monopolistic competition. Critics point out that many product alterations are more apparent than real, consisting of frivolous and superficial changes in the product which do not improve its durability, efficiency, or usefulness. A more exotic container, bright packaging, or "shuffling the chrome" are frequently the focal points for product development. It is argued, too, that particularly in the cases of durable and semidurable consumer goods, development seems to follow a pattern of "planned obsolescence," wherein firms improve their product only by that amount necessary to make the average consumer dissatisfied with last year's model.

Do the advantages of product differentiation, properly discounted, outweigh the "wastes" of monopolistic competition? It is difficult to say, short of examining specific cases, and even then concrete conclusions are difficult to come by. For example, a recent study of the (oligopolistic) automobile industry attempts to measure the cost of model changes in recent years.[2] Specifically, this question was posed: What has been the aggregate annual cost of the increases in automobile size, increases in horsepower, increased gasoline consumption caused by the "horsepower race," "power" accessories, and the cost of factory retooling required by such model changes? The investigators concluded that "the estimated costs of model changes since 1949 . . . run about 5 billion dollars per year over the 1956–60 period. . . ." Thus, although there is no question that the automobile today is a better product than it was in 1949, it is nevertheless quite legitimate to inqure: Is it *that much* better?

Advertising

A monopolistically competitive producer may gain at least a temporary edge on his rivals by manipulating his product. He may achieve the same result by manipulating the consumer through advertising and sales promotion. While product differentiation adapts the product to consumer demand, advertising adapts consumer demand to the product. In practice these two aspects of nonprice competition may be difficult to disentangle. Does a new and colorful method of packaging a product constitute a change in the product, or is it a means of advertising and promotion?

Though we might tentatively agree that product development is a desirable feature of monopolistic competition, the advertising which accompanies it is more difficult to evaluate. The social desirability of extensive advertising expenditures is a very controversial and clouded topic. A basic reason for this is the fact that some advertising is *informative,* that is, accurately descriptive of the qualities and prices of products, while

[2] F. M. Fisher, Z. Griliches, and C. Kaysen, "The Costs of Automobile Model Changes since 1949," *Journal of Political Economy,* October, 1962, pp. 433–451.

other advertising is *competitive,* consisting of unsubstantiated ours-is-better-than-theirs exhortation. Local newspaper advertising is informative; the cigarette and soap advertisements that the television industry funnels into American living rooms are competitive.

This controversy is not an unimportant one. Currently advertising and promotional expenditures in American capitalism have been about $14 billion per year. This is roughly equal to the nation's annual outlay on primary and secondary public education. Hence, if advertising is generally wasteful, any potential virtues of monopolistically competitive markets are thereby dimmed, and the need for corrective public policies is indicated.

Extreme arguments are prevalent. Some economists are prone to write off all advertising as sheer economic waste. Others—the admen themselves—manage to associate all that is just and good in American society with advertising. An accurate picture lies in the middle ground. Let us survey the basic claims for and the charges against advertising.

The case for advertising. Some of the arguments in favor of advertising follow:

1. Advertising allegedly provides the information which assists consumers in making rational choices. In a dynamic, complex economy there is an acute need for the consumer to be closely acquainted with new firms, new products, and improvements in existing products. Advertising is the medium which disperses such information.

2. Advertising supports national communications. Radio, television, magazines, and newspapers are supported wholly or in part through advertising.

3. It has been argued more recently that advertising is a stimulant to product development. Successful advertising is frequently based upon unique and advantageous features of a firm's product. Hence, a firm is obligated to improve its product to provide "sales points" for competing successfully in the advertising sphere.

4. Through successful advertising a firm can expand its production and thereby realize greater economies of scale. As shown in Figure 28–2, by shifting the firm's demand curve to the right through advertising, production will expand from, say, Q_1 to Q_2. Despite the fact that advertising outlays will shift the firm's average-cost curve upward, unit costs will nevertheless decline from, say, AC_1 to AC_2. Greater productive efficiency resulting from economies of scale more than offsets the increase in unit costs due to advertising. Consumers will therefore get the product at a lower price with advertising than they would in its absence.

5. It is also contended that advertising promotes full employment by inducing high levels of consumer spending. This is particularly crucial, it is argued, in a wealthy society such as that of American capitalism, where much of total production takes the form of luxury or semiluxury goods which fulfill no basic wants. One need not advertise to sell food to a hungry man, but advertising and sales promotion are essential in persuading families that they need a

FIGURE 28–2. THE POSSIBLE EFFECTS OF ADVERTISING UPON A FIRM'S OUTPUT AND AVERAGE COSTS.

Proponents of advertising contend that resulting economies of scale will expand the firm's production from, say, *a* to *b* and lower unit costs as economies of scale are realized. Some critics argue that advertising is more likely to increase costs and leave output largely unchanged, as is suggested by the movement from *a* to *c*. Others point out that expansion realized through advertising may force diseconomies of scale upon the firm, as the movement from *a* to *d* indicates.

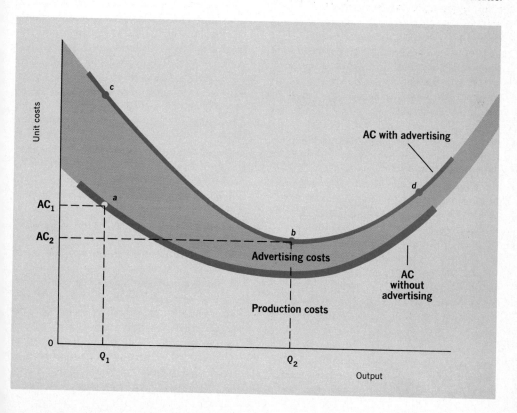

second car, color television, or an automatic dishwasher. Stability in an opulent society calls for want-creating activities—in particular, advertising—or high levels of production and employment will not be sustainable.

The case against advertising. Some of the arguments on the other side of the picture debunk the claims for advertising; others raise new points.

1. Critics of advertising point out that the basic objective of advertising is to persuade, not to inform. Competitive advertising is based upon misleading and extravagant claims which serve to confuse and frequently insult the intelligence of the consumer, not enlighten him. Little of real value in the rendering of rational choices can be garnered from the soap and cigarette advertising which crowds our television screens and adds bulk to our slick magazines. Indeed, advertising may well persuade consumers in some cases to pay high prices for much-acclaimed but inferior products, forgoing better but unadvertised products selling at lower prices. The Pure Food and Drug and Federal Trade Commission Acts, which are aimed at protecting consumers from product misrepresentation and misleading advertising, testify as to past and present abuses by modern-day hucksters.

2. Advertising expenditures as such are relatively unproductive; they add little or nothing to the well-being of society. Advertising diverts human and property resources from other, more pressing areas. For example, lumber which is sorely needed in the production of low- and medium-priced housing is squandered on the construction of unsightly billboards. In short, advertising gives rise to a gross misallocation of resources.

In recent years the general criticism that advertising promotes a misallocation of resources has assumed a special form: advertising allegedly contributes to *social imbalance*. That is, advertising, in conjunction with a number of other considerations, has given rise to the overproduction of private goods relative to public or social goods. It is argued that advertising is peculiar to, and an integral part of, the production and sale of private goods. Gigantic advertising campaigns extol the merits of electric can openers, self-propelled lawnmowers, and eight-speaker stereophonic phonographs. But no similar force proclaims the virtues of social goods and services; similar persuasion does not exist to whet the consumer's appetite for better schools, improved streets and highways, increased expenditures for medical research, and so forth. The net result, it is contended, is a misallocation of resources; resources are overallocated to private goods and underallocated to public goods. Private goods are superabundant; the quantity and quality of social goods are remarkably deficient. The problem of social imbalance will be pursued at length in Chapter 38.

3. Significant social costs are entailed by advertising. Billboards blot out roadside scenery and generally debase the countryside. Sound trucks disrupt suburban serenity. Of potentially greater importance are the effects which advertising's support of national communications may have upon the accuracy and quality of those communications. Will a newspaper present an unprejudiced report of the labor dispute in which its major advertiser is involved? Will a television newscast conveniently ignore the fact that antitrust action has been initiated against its sponsor? Will a firm which distributes its product nationally permit the television playhouse it sponsors to present an honest and frank portrayal of the integration problem? In more general terms, it is charged that competitive advertising offends the common sense and tries the patience of society. The fact that water consumption rises enormously during television commercials adds credulity of this latter contention.

4. Critics of advertising are very dubious of the argument that advertising permits firms to expand, to achieve lower unit costs, and to offer their products at lower prices to consumers. Reasons for this doubt are several. First, it is contended that advertising

tends to be self-canceling. The million-dollar advertising campaign of one cigarette manufacturer is largely offset by equally expensive campaigns waged by its rivals. Few additional people smoke cigarettes. Each firm has about the same portion of the market as it had originally. And the cost, and therefore the price, of cigarettes is higher. In Figure 28–2 self-canceling advertising may move the firm from point *a* to point *c*, not from *a* to *b*. Second, if advertising can cause a firm to realize economies of scale through growth, can it not also cause a firm to encounter diseconomies? Might not advertising shift the firm's level of output from point *a* to point *d* in Figure 28–2? Third, are there not more desirable and less costly alternative means by which a firm might expand output and achieve economies of scale? Would not product development or research on productive methods permit a firm to achieve economies of scale and at the same time avoid the upshift in its average-cost schedule which advertising entails? Finally, even if a firm achieves lower units costs through advertising, will the consumer benefit through proportionate price reductions? This point is particularly pertinent in view of the fact that the expansion of those firms whose advertising is most successful implies that less successful advertisers will fall by the wayside, causing the industry to move away from monopolistic competition and in the direction of oligopoly, wherein firms have greater control over product price.

5. Most economists are reluctant to accept advertising as an important determinant of the levels of output and employment. There has been little evidence of economic stagnation in the postwar years that would seem remediable by advertising and promotional outlays. Furthermore, the most volatile aspect of aggregate demand is not so much highly advertised consumer goods as it is little-advertised investment goods. The consensus seems to be that advertising probably affects the composition more than it does the volume of spending. And those economists who do accept the contention that advertising now has an impact upon consumer spending suggest that at some future time its effect on the level of spending may diminish to zero.[3]

On some not distant day, the voice of each individual seller may well be lost in the collective roar of all together. Like injunctions to virtue and warnings of socialism, advertising will beat helplessly on ears that have been conditioned by previous assault to utter immunity. . . . It will be worth no one's while to speak, for since all speak none can hear.

At this point an economy whose level of spending is supported by effective advertising will be plagued by serious instability. If consumer wants and consumer spending are contrived through advertising, the future failure of that contrivance could materially contribute to recession and unemployment.

At least one critic has contended that advertising expenditures are procyclical, that is, they fluctuate *with* total spending, intensifying unemployment during bad times and adding to inflationary pressures during prosperous times.[4]

6. There is evidence that in some industries advertising has become such a large part of the cost of doing business that it constitutes an important financial barrier to entry. This is generally recognized to be the case in the cigarette industry, where producers as a group may spend considerably in excess of $150 million per year on advertising and related promotional activities.

Where do these arguments and counter-arguments leave us? Certainly without a clear-cut conclusion. However, even though both cases are interspersed with partial truths and arguments that are valid in specific instances but not generally, we are at least in a better position to form a personal judgment upon the social worth of adver-

---

[3] John K. Galbraith, *The Affluent Society* (Boston: Houghton Mifflin Company, 1958), p. 202.
[4] Alvin H. Hansen, *Economic Issues of the 1960's* (New York: McGraw-Hill Book Company, 1961), p. 36.

tising.[5] This much can be ventured: Most economists are inclined to conclude that the consumer benefits much more from nonprice competition in the form of product development than he does from advertising.

Monopolistic Competition and Economic Analysis

Our discussion of nonprice competition correctly infers that the equilibrium situation of a monopolistically competitive firm is actually much more complex than the previous graphic analysis indicates. Figure 28–1a, b, and c assumes a given product and a given level of advertising expenditures. But, alas, these we now know are not given in practice. The monopolistically competitive firm must actually juggle three variable considerations—price, product, and promotion—in seeking maximum profits. What specific variety of product, selling at what price, and supplemented by what level of promotional activity will result in the greatest level of profits attainable? This complex situation is not readily expressed in a simple, meaningful economic model. At best we can note that each possible combination of price, product, and promotion poses a different demand and cost (production plus promotion) situation for the firm, some one of which will allow him maximum profits. In practice, this optimum combination cannot be readily forecast but must be sought by the process of trial and error. And even here certain limitations may be imposed by the actions of rivals. A firm may not risk the elimination of advertising expenditures for fear his share of the market will decline sharply to the benefit of his rivals who do advertise. Similarly, patents held by rivals will rule out certain choice product variations.

[5] The student who feels compelled to pursue this controversy should compare Vance Packard, *The Hidden Persuaders* (New York: David McKay Company, Inc., 1957), and Steuart Henderson Britt, *The Spenders* (New York: McGraw-Hill Book Company, 1960).

DOES MONOPOLISTIC COMPETITION BREED OLIGOPOLY?

Monopolistic competition presumes a relatively large number of independently acting firms producing differentiated products in a market environment into which entry is relatively easy. Many economists feel that there are few industries in modern American capitalism in which these requirements are strictly fulfilled. Further, in those industries in which monopolistic competition does exist, certain dynamic aspects of this market situation tend to push monopolistic competition in the direction of oligopoly. Let us explain these contentions.

1. Many retail industries which outwardly fulfill the conditions of monopolistic competition are actually much more localized than they appear to be. A city may have forty or fifty grocery stores, but each store is only in direct competition with a *few* nearby rivals. Suburban stores do not compete greatly with their downtown counterparts; northside and southside grocers do not compete, and so forth. This means that, although a large number of firms exist, they are usually subdivided into smaller, *interdependent* groups.

2. Combination has caused monopolistic competition to give ground to oligopoly in some important retail industries. For example, vertical integration by large petroleum producers has pushed the oligopolistic structure of the petroleum industry forward to the retail level. Instead of thirty independent gasoline stations, we now have groups of gasoline stations affiliated with, say, four or five different brands of gasoline. Horizontal combinations in the form of chain stores at the retail level have also had the effect of reducing the number of independent firms in the areas of retail automobile supplies, groceries, and drugs. By, in effect, reducing the number of independent firms, these two tendencies give rise to mutual interdependence among sellers—a basic characteristic of oligopoly.

3. Of greatest importance is the belief

that nonprice competition is a dynamic facet of monopolistic competition through which such industries evolve into the less competitive market structure of oligopoly. More specifically, it is argued that product development and advertising simultaneously work to reduce the number of firms in monopolistically competitive industries and to create entry barriers which discourage their replacement by new firms. This merits some explanation.

Product differentiation and development can lead to significant entry barriers over time. This is particularly pertinent because product development is likely to be cumulative; that is, a firm which gains a temporary advantage over its rivals through a successful change in its product can employ the resulting profits to finance the research needed to widen that advantage. Temporary product advantages have a tendency to become permanent, to the end that less alert or less fortunate rivals fall by the wayside. All this is reinforced when product variations are significant enough to result in patent and copyright protection. Similarly, if the fruits of successful product variation are used to finance the development of more efficient productive techniques, the resulting economies of scale and lower unit costs provide a basis for eliminating high-cost rivals and restricting the entry of new firms.

Advertising may also reduce the number of firms in a monopolistically competitive industry over a span of time. In a few instances some firms may simply "outadvertise" and thereby eliminate their rivals. On the other hand, if the advertising campaigns of monopolistically competitive rivals are largely self-canceling between firms and have little impact upon industry demand, the rising unit costs attributable to advertising may press upon price and eliminate the least efficient firms. Or possibly this price-cost squeeze will precipitate aggressive price cutting—a price war—which will have substantially the same effect. Finally, we have already noted that large advertising budgets can pose a substantial barrier to

entry, thereby also undermining a basic characteristic of monopolistic competition.

If these arguments are reasonably accurate, we can conclude that the basic reasons for studying the behavior of monopolistically competitive industries are:

1. A knowledge of such industries provides important information concerning the evolution and growth of oligopoly.

2. Many industries in American capitalism blend features of both monopolistic competition and oligopoly.

It is with oligopolistic markets that the next chapter is concerned.

SUMMARY

1. The distinguishing features of monopolistic competition are: **a.** There is a large enough number of firms so that each has little control over price, mutual interdependence is absent, and collusion is virtually impossible; **b.** products are characterized by real and imaginary differences and by varying conditions surrounding their sale; and **c.** entry to the industry is relatively easy. Many aspects of retailing, and some industries wherein economies of scale are few, approximate monopolistic competition.

2. Monopolistically competitive firms may earn economic profits or incur losses in the short run. The easy entry and exodus of firms gives rise to a long-run tendency for them to earn a normal profit.

3. The long-run equilibrium position of the monopolistically competitive producer is less socially desirable than that of a purely competitive firm. Under monopolistic competition price exceeds marginal cost, suggesting an underallocation of resources to the product, and price exceeds minimum average total cost, indicating that consumers do not get the product at the lowest price which cost conditions would allow. However, because the firm's demand curve is highly elastic, these "wastes" of monopolistic competition should not be overemphasized.

4. Product differentiation provides a means by which monopolistically competitive firms can offset the long-run tendency for economic profits to approximate zero. Through product development and advertising, a firm may strive to increase the demand for its product more than nonprice competition increases its costs.

5. Although subject to certain dangers and problems, product differentiation affords the consumer a greater variety of products at any point in time and improved products over time. Whether these features fully compensate for the wastes of monopolistic competition is a moot question.

6. There is sharp disagreement as to the economic benefits of advertising. Proponents justify advertising on the grounds that it **a.** aids consumers in exercising rational choices, **b.** supports national communications, **c.** speeds product development, **d.** permits firms to realize economies of scale, and **e.** encourages spending and a high level of employment. Critics assert that advertising **a.** confuses rather than informs, **b.** misallocates resources away from more urgent employments (particularly from the production of social goods), **c.** involves a variety of social costs, **d.** results in higher, not lower, costs and prices, **e.** is not a strategic determinant of spending and employment, and **f.** often constitutes a significant financial barrier to entry.

7. In practice the monopolistic competitor seeks largely through trial and error that specific combination of price, product, and promotion which will maximize his profits.

8. There is evidence to suggest that monopolistically competitive market situations tend to give way to oligopoly. Product development and advertising may well tend to eliminate existing firms and create barriers to the entry of new ones. Vertical and horizontal combination and the localized nature of retail markets have tended to undermine monopolistic competition in retailing.

QUESTIONS AND STUDY SUGGESTIONS

1. How does monopolistic competition differ from pure competition? From pure monopoly? Explain fully what product differentiation entails.
2. Compare the elasticity of the monopolistically competitive producer's demand curve with that of (a) a pure competitor and (b) a pure monopolist. Assuming identical long-run costs, compare graphically the prices and output which would result under pure competition and monopolistic competition. "Monopolistically competitive industries are characterized by too many firms, each of which produces too little." Explain.
3. "Monopolistic competition is monopoly up to the point at which consumers become willing to buy close substitute products and competitive beyond that point." Explain.
4. What is nonprice competition? "Competition in quality and in service may be quite as effective in giving the buyer more for his money as is price competition." Do you agree? Explain why monopolistically competitive firms frequently prefer nonprice to price competition.
5. Critically evaluate and explain:
   a. "In monopolistically competitive industries economic profits are competed away in the long run; hence, there is no valid reason to criticize the performance and efficiency of such industries."
   b. "Monopolistic competition is merely a way station on the road to oligopoly."
   c. "In the long run monopolistic competition leads to a monopolistic price but not to monopolistic profits."

6. Do you agree or disagree with the following statements? Why?
  a. "The amount of advertising which a firm does is likely to vary inversely with the real differences in its product."
  b. "If each firm's advertising expenditures merely tend to cancel the effects of its rivals' advertising, it is clearly irrational for these firms to maintain large advertising budgets."
7. Carefully evaluate the two views expressed in the following statements:
  a. "It happens every day. Advertising builds mass demand. Production goes up—costs come down. More people can buy—more jobs are created. These are the ingredients of economic growth. Each stimulates the next in a cycle of productivity and plenty which constantly creates a better life for you."
  b. "Advertising constitutes 'inverted education'—a costly effort to induce people to buy without sufficient thought and deliberation and therefore to buy things they don't need. Furthermore, advertising intensifies economic instability because advertising outlays vary directly with the level of consumer spending. Indeed, by contributing to inflation during prosperous periods, advertising may foster political pressures for the curtailment of government spending on much-needed social goods and services, thereby promoting a misallocation of resources."
  Which view do you feel is the more accurate? Justify your position.

SELECTED REFERENCES

Adams, Walter (ed.): *The Structure of American Industry,* 3d ed. (New York: The Macmillan Company, 1961), chap. 2.

Bain, Joe S.: *Industrial Organization* (New York: John Wiley & Sons, Inc., 1959), chap. 7.

Bober, M. M.: *Intermediate Price and Income Theory,* rev. ed. (New York: W. W. Norton & Company, Inc., 1962), chap. 11.

Due, John F., and Robert W. Clower: *Intermediate Economic Analysis,* 4th ed. (Homewood, Ill.: Richard D. Irwin, Inc., 1961), chap. 10.

McKenna, Joseph P.: *Intermediate Economic Theory* (New York: Holt, Rinehart and Winston, Inc., 1958), chap. 11.

Watson, Donald S.: *Price Theory and Its Uses* (Boston: Houghton Mifflin Company, 1963), chap. 21.

Weiss, Leonard W.: *Economics and American Industry* (New York: John Wiley & Sons, Inc., 1961), chaps. 4 and 9.

CHAPTER 29

PRICE AND OUTPUT DETERMINATION: OLIGOPOLY

In many of the manufacturing, mining, wholesaling, and retailing industries of American capitalism a few firms are dominant. Such industries are called *oligopolies*. It is with such industries that the present chapter is concerned. Specifically, we have four objectives. We seek first to define oligopoly, assess its occurrence, and note the reasons for its existence. The second and major goal is to survey the possible courses of price-output behavior which oligopolistic industries might follow. Third, the role of nonprice competition, that is, competition on the basis of product development and advertising, in oligopolistic industries is discussed. Finally, some comments with respect to the economic efficiency and social desirability of oligopoly are offered.

CONCEPT AND OCCURRENCE OF OLIGOPOLY

What are the basic characteristics of oligopoly? How frequently is it encountered in American capitalism? Why has this industry structure developed?

The outstanding feature of oligopoly is "fewness." When a relatively small number of firms dominates the market for a good or service, the industry is oligopolistic. But what specifically is meant by "a few" firms? This is necessarily vague, because the market model of oligopoly covers a great deal of ground, ranging from pure monopoly, on the one hand, to monopolistic competition, on the other. Thus oligopoly encompasses the tin-can industry, in which two firms virtually

dominate an entire national market, and the situation in which, say, fifteen or twenty gasoline stations may enjoy roughly equal shares of the petroleum products market in a medium-sized town. Table 29–1 lists a number of industries in which fewness is present in varying degrees. This table correctly suggests that the market structure of oligopoly is very common in American capitalism. And we remember from Chapter 28 that many aspects of the retail trades are characterized by oligopoly.

Rivalry between a small number of firms interjects a new and complicating factor into our discussion: *mutual interdependence*. Imagine three firms, A, B, and C, each of which has about one-third of the market for a particular product. If A cuts price, its share of the market will increase. But B and C will be directly, immediately, and adversely affected by A's price cutting. Hence, we can expect some *reaction* on the part of B and C to A's behavior: B and C may match A's price cut or even undercut A, thereby precipitating a price war. This correctly suggests that no firm in an oligopolistic industry will dare to alter its price policies without attempting to calculate the most likely reactions of its rivals. To be sure, cost and demand data are important to the oligopolist in establishing price, but to these we must add the reaction of rivals, a highly uncertain factor. The situation faced by oligopolistic producers resembles that of participants in games of strategy such as poker, bridge, or chess. There is no way of knowing beforehand the best way of playing your cards, because this depends upon the way in which other participants play theirs! Each player must pattern his actions according to the actions and expected reactions of his rivals. In recent years economists have sought to develop and apply a "theory of games" to the behavior of oligopolies.[1]

It is to be emphasized that the mutual interdependence resulting from fewness, and the consequent need for a firm to weigh the possible reactions of rivals in altering its price policy, are unique features of oligopoly. The large number of rivals which characterizes pure competition and monopolistic competition and the absence of rivals which is the earmark of pure monopoly rule out mutual interdependence in these market structures. Indeed, a good, workable definition of oligopoly is this: Oligopoly exists when the number of firms in an industry is so small that each must consider the reactions of rivals in formulating its price policy.

The existence of a small number of firms correctly suggests that barriers to entry characterize oligopolistic industries. In some oligopolistic industries—for example, automobiles, agricultural machinery, and steel—technological considerations as reflected in economies of large-scale production constitute the basic barrier to entry. Many industries start out with a large number of firms, but then as technology improves, each firm attempts to expand in order to achieve the lower costs which economies of scale provide. For example, estimates suggest that as many as 70 to 80 firms populated the automobile industry in its infancy. Then the introduction of mass-production techniques reduced the field through failure and combination. Now the Big Three of the automobile industry have over 90 per cent of the

[1] The interested reader should consult two informative and delightful books on the subject: John D. Williams, *The Compleat Strategyst* (New York: McGraw-Hill Book Company, 1954), and John McDonald, *Strategy in Poker, Business and War* (New York: W. W. Norton & Company, Inc., 1950).

TABLE 29–1. PERCENTAGE OF OUTPUT* PRODUCED BY FIRMS IN SELECTED HIGH-CONCENTRATION MANUFACTURING INDUSTRIES, 1958

Industry	Per cent of industry output produced by first four firms
Primary aluminum	100
Passenger cars	99
Linoleum	96
Locomotives and parts	95
Electric lamps (bulbs)	92
Telephone and telegraph equipment	92
Gypsum products	88
Steam engines and turbines	87
Sewing machines	81
Tin cans and tinware	80
Cigarettes	79
Typewriters	79
Synthetic fibers	78
Phonograph records	76
Tires and inner tubes	74
Tractors	69
Distilled liquor	60

* As measured by value of shipments.
Source: Senate Subcommittee on Antitrust and Monopoly, *Concentration Ratios in Manufacturing Industry, 1958* (Washington, D.C., 1962), part I, table 2. Aluminum and sewing machine data are for 1954.

market. The existence of other oligopolies, for example, the electronics, chemical, and aluminum industries, is grounded basically upon the ownership of patents or the control of strategic raw materials. Less frequently the advantages of being established as reflected particularly in prodigious advertising outlays may present a significant financial obstacle to entry. The cigarette industry is the classic illustration.

Finally, oligopolies may produce either standardized or differentiated products. Many industrial products—steel, zinc, copper, aluminum, lead, cement, industrial alcohol, and so forth—are virtually standardized products in the physical sense and are produced under oligopolistic conditions. Of course, even here slight physical differences may exist, and the service, credit, and speed of delivery may differ between sellers, making for a measure of differentiation. But for most practical purposes these are standardized products. On the other hand, many consumer goods industries—automobiles, tires, typewriters, petroleum products, soap, cigarettes, fountain pens, and a host of electrical appliances—are differentiated oligopolies.

PRICE DETERMINATION

Now at first glance one might suspect that price-output determination similar to that of a pure monopoly would be possible for an oligopolistic firm. The only notable difference might be that the oligopolist's sales curve would be somewhat more elastic, because he is plagued by a few close substitute goods, whereas the pure monopolist faces no good substitutes at all. Marginal-cost and marginal-revenue comparisons would then determine the profit-maximizing output and the unique price at which this output could be sold. Unfortunately, this is too simple a picture of the situation. Indeed, more and more economists are reluctantly coming to the conclusion that formal economic theory simply does not take us very far in explaining the price-output policies of oligopolies.

There are two major reasons why it is difficult to use formal economic analysis in explaining the price behavior of oligopolies.

1. The previously noted fact that oligopoly encompasses many specific market situations works against the development of a single, generalized explanation or model of how an oligopoly determines price and output. Pure competition, monopolistic competition, and pure monopoly all refer to rather clear-cut market arrangements; oligopoly does not. It includes the situation in which two or three firms dominate an entire market as well as the market in which twelve or fifteen firms compete. It includes both product differentiation and standardization.

It encompasses the situations in which firms are acting in collusion and in which they are not. It embodies the situations in which barriers to entry are very strong and in which they are not quite so strong. In short, the many breeds, or strains, of oligopoly work against the development of any simple market model which provides a general explanation of oligopolistic behavior.

2. The element of mutual interdependence which fewness adds to the analysis is a most significant complication. To be specific, the inability of a firm to predict with certainty the reactions of its rivals makes it virtually impossible to estimate the demand and marginal-revenue data faced by an oligopolist. And without such data firms cannot determine their profit-maximizing price and output even in theory, as we shall presently make clear.

Despite these analytical difficulties, two interrelated characteristics of oligopolistic pricing stand out. On the one hand, oligopolistic prices tend to be inflexible, or "sticky." Prices change less frequently in oligopoly than they do under pure competition, monopolistic competition, and, in some instances, pure monopoly. Figure 11–4 provides some interesting data on this point. On the other hand, when oligopolistic prices do change, firms are likely to change their prices together. There is a decided absence of price competition in most oligopolistic industries. However, when price competition does occasionally break out, it is likely to take the form of aggressive price warring.

Let us now explore several oligopolistic pricing policies to help explain these introductory comments.

"Independent Action" and Price Inflexibility

Again suppose an oligopolistic industry comprised of just three firms, A, B, and C, each having about one-third of the total market for a differentiated product. Assume the firms are "independent" in the sense that they do not engage in collusive practices in setting prices. Suppose, too, that the going price for firm A's product is QP and its current sales are Q, as shown in Figure 29–1. Now the question is "What does the firm's demand, or sales, curve look like?" We have just noted that mutual interdependence and the uncertainty of rivals' reactions which it entails make this question difficult to answer. The location and shape of an oligopolist's demand curve depends upon how the firm's rivals will react to a price change introduced by A. There are two plausible assumptions

about the reactions of A's rivals with which we might experiment.

One possibility is that firms B and C will exactly match any price change initiated by A. In this case A's demand and marginal-revenue curves will look something like D_1D_1 and MR_1MR_1 in Figure 29–1. If A cuts price, its sales will increase very modestly, because its two rivals will follow suit and thereby prevent A from gaining any price advantage over them. The small increase in sales which A (and its two rivals) will realize

FIGURE 29–1. THE KINKED DEMAND CURVE.
The nature of an oligopolist's demand and marginal-revenue curves will depend upon whether his rivals will match (D_1D_1 and MR_1MR_1) or ignore (D_2D_2 and MR_2MR_2) any price changes which he may initiate from the current price QP. In all likelihood an oligopolist's rivals will ignore a price increase but follow a price cut. This causes the oligopolist's demand curve to be kinked (as D_2PD_1) and his marginal revenue curve to have a vertical break, or gap (as rust MR_2MR_1).

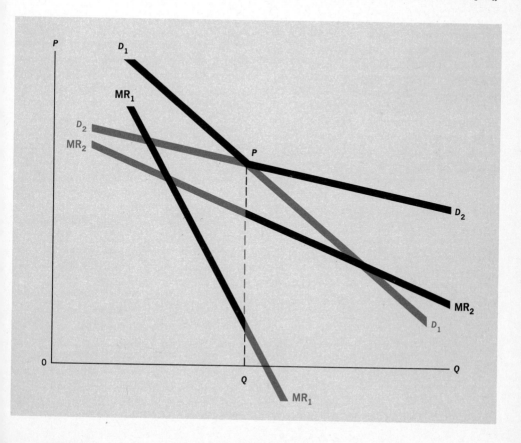

is at the expense of other industries; A will gain no sales from B and C. If A raises the going price, its sales will fall only modestly. Why? Because B and C match its price increase, so A does not price itself out of the market. The industry now loses some sales to other industries, but A loses no customers to B and C.

The other obvious possibility is that firms B and C will simply ignore any price change invoked by A. In this case the demand and marginal-revenue curves faced by A will resemble D_2D_2 and MR_2MR_2 in Figure 29–1. The demand curve in this case is considerably more elastic than under the assumption that B and C will match A's price changes. The reasons are clear. If A lowers its price and its rivals do not, A will gain sales sharply at the expense of its two rivals because it will obviously be underselling them. Conversely, if A raises price and its rivals do not, A will be pricing itself out of the market and will lose many customers to B and C, which are now underselling it. Because of product differentiation, however, A's sales do not fall to zero when it raises price; some of A's customers will pay the higher price because they have strong preferences for A's product.

Now, which is the most logical assumption for A to make as to how its rivals will react to any price change it might initiate? The answer is "some of each"! Common sense and observation of oligopolistic industries suggest that price declines will be matched as a firm's competitors act to prevent the price cutter from taking their customers, but that price increases will be ignored, because rivals of the price-increasing firm stand to gain the business lost by the price booster. In other words, the D_2P segment of the "rivals ignore" demand curve seems relevant for price increases, and the PD_1 segment of the "rivals follow" demand curve is more realistic for price cuts. It is logical, or at least a good guess, that an oligopolist's demand curve is "kinked" on the order of D_2PD_1. The curve is highly elastic above the going price but much less elastic or even inelastic below the current price. Note, too, that if it is correct

to suppose that rivals will follow a price cut but ignore an increase, the marginal-revenue curve of the oligopolist will also have an odd shape. It, too, will be made up of two segments—a part of the marginal-revenue curve appropriate to D_1D_1 and a chunk of the marginal-revenue curve appropriate to D_2D_2. Because of the sharp differences in elasticity of demand above and below the going price, there occurs a gap, or what we can treat as a vertical segment, in the marginal-revenue curve. In Figure 29–1 the marginal-revenue curve is shown by the two rust lines connected by the dotted vertical segment, or gap.

This analysis is important in that it goes far to explain why price changes are infrequent in noncollusive oligopolistic industries. On the one hand, the kinked demand schedule gives each oligopolist good reason to believe that any change in price will be for the worse. A firm's customers will desert it in quantity if it raises price. If it lowers price, its sales at best will increase very modestly. Even if a price cut increases its total revenue somewhat, the oligopolist's costs may well increase by a more than offsetting amount. Should the PD_1 segment of its sales schedule be inelastic in that E_d is less than 1, the firm's profits will surely fall. A price decrease will lower the firm's total receipts, and the production of a somewhat larger output will increase total costs. Worse yet, a price cut by A may be *more than* met by B and C. That is, A's initial price cut may precipitate a price war; so the amount sold by A may actually decline as its rival firms charge still lower prices. These are all good reasons on the demand side of the picture why noncollusive oligopolies might seek "the quiet life" and follow live-and-let-live and don't-upset-the-applecart price policies.

A second reason for price inflexibility under noncollusive oligopoly works from the cost side of the picture. The broken marginal revenue curve which accompanies the kinked demand curve suggests that within limits substantial cost changes will have no effect upon output and price. To be specific, any shift in marginal cost between MC_1 and MC_2 as shown in Figure 29–2 will result in no change in price or output, because the oligopolist fears a price war, on the one hand, and pricing himself out of the market, on the other.

All this is not to say that the prices of noncollusive oligopolists are completely inflexible, but rather that they are likely to change only when significant and mutually applicable cost changes occur. For example,

price adjustments may await wage, tax, or interest-rate increases which collective bargaining or government imposes uniformly upon the firms. Knowing its rivals are also afflicted with these cost increases, each firm boosts price with considerable certainty that each and every rival will follow suit. The practice of linking price increases to wage or tax hikes has the further advantage of shielding oligopolies from public criticism. To many the price increase—even if in excess

FIGURE 29–2. COST CHANGES AND PRICE STABILITY UNDER OLIGOPOLY.
The kinked demand curve *DPD* and the accompanying broken marginal revenue curve MRMR help explain the price inflexibility which characterizes oligopoly. Because any shift in marginal costs between MC_1 and MC_2 will cut the vertical (dotted) segment of the marginal revenue curve, no change in either price *QP* or output *Q* will occur.

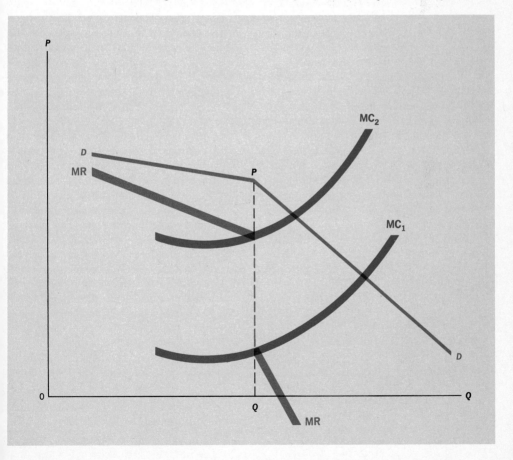

of cost increases—will clearly seem the fault of irresponsible unions and the insatiable appetite of government for tax revenues.

The astute reader will undoubtedly have detected a crucial shortcoming of our kinked demand analysis: It simply does not explain how the going price gets to be at PQ in the first place. Rather it merely helps to explain why oligopolists may be reluctant to deviate from any existing price which yields them a "satisfactory" or "reasonable" profit. The kinked demand curve explains price inflexibility but not price itself.

The kinked demand situation described above may be decidedly unappealing to oligopolists. It is surrounded by an air of uncertainty. Although there may be a strong disposition toward price stability, the possibility always does exist that a firm may shade its price to expand its share of the market and thereby precipitate disastrous rounds of price cutting. This is particularly likely if firms have excess capacity because of, say, a general business recession; under these circumstances a firm can lower unit costs by increasing its market share. Then, too, the possibility is always present that new firms may surmount barriers to entry and initiate aggressive price cutting to gain a foothold in the market. In addition, the tendency toward rigid prices may adversely affect profits if general inflationary pressures increase costs. All this is conducive to the establishment of some sort of collusive action by oligopolists as a means of avoiding disastrous price warring, on the one hand, and of achieving orderly price increases, on the other.

Formal Collusion

There are many forms of collusion. At one extreme a number of oligopolistic firms may form a *cartel*. Under this arrangement firms may enter into a formal written agreement which fixes product price and divides the market, the latter possibly on a geographic basis. In the United States such an arrangement is clearly at odds with our antitrust laws and, hence, a most rare occurrence.

Somewhat less formal *gentlemen's agreements* undoubtedly enjoy greater currency in American capitalism. Such agreements arise when competing oligopolists reach a verbal agreement on product price, market shares almost invariably being left to the ingenuity of each seller as reflected in nonprice competition. Gentlemen's agreements arise at trade conventions, on the golf course, or at cocktail parties, not in a lawyer's office. Although they too collide with the antitrust laws, their *sub rosa* and intangible character make them more difficult to detect and prosecute successfully.[2]

What will be the economic consequences of a gentlemen's agreement? Assuming the entry of new firms is blocked, the price-output consequences of a gentlemen's agreement are likely to be very much like those of a pure monopoly. Output will be restricted in the interest of maximizing profits for the several firms, and this will mean higher prices and underutilized plants. As a matter of fact, the price-output results of collusive oligopoly may from the consumer's standpoint be inferior to those of pure monopoly for several reasons.

1. Pure monopoly in the United States is almost invariably subject to government regulation to mitigate abuses of such market power. A *sub rosa* gentleman's agreement may create an approximation of pure monopoly, yet it maintains the outward appearance of several independent and "competing" firms.

2. It is possible that the existence of several distinct oligopolistic producers will cause the industry and society to forgo some economies of scale which those firms, combined as a pure monopoly, could realize. For example, a multiplant pure monopolist can ship to customers from that plant which is closest to the buyer. But under a gentlemen's agreement on price, wasteful crosshauling

[2] For a fascinating case study of collusive pricing, read Clarence C. Walton and Frederick W. Cleveland, Jr., *Corporations on Trial: The Electric Cases* (Belmont, Calif.: Wadsworth Publishing Company, Inc., 1964).

may result. The oligopolist located in California ships to a customer in New Jersey, while the New York oligopolist ships to an Oregon buyer.

3. Collusive oligopolists may engage in extensive competitive advertising and sales promotion which is of little benefit to the public. This is particularly so when products are differentiated. Under pure monopoly this would be largely, if not fully, eliminated.

4. Because price agreements are difficult to negotiate, oligopolists may be inclined to maintain the existing agreed-upon price even though cost-reducing technological advances would make it profitable for the firms to lower this price. Fearing the inability to reach precise agreement on a new and lower price and a possible breakdown of the gentlemen's agreement, the firms may simply let well enough alone and accept a less-than-maximum profit. This will mean that consumers are deprived of the lower price and the greater output that lower unit costs now justify. The pure monopolist, unhampered by the problem of price negotiation with rivals, would cut price and increase output to his own benefit and to the benefit of consumers.[3]

Informal, Tacit Collusion

The illegality of gentlemen's agreements has prompted many oligopolistic industries to seek still less formal means of avoiding the uncertainties of independent, noncollusive action. Many important American industries have long followed the practice of *price leadership*, that is, one firm—usually the largest in the industry—initiates price changes, and all other firms more or less automatically follow that price change. In some cases—for example, the oil and cigarette

industries—the identity of the price leader may vary over time, whereas in other industries—the steel industry—a single firm may persistently enjoy the position of price leader. The importance of price leadership is evidenced in the fact that such industries as farm machinery, anthracite coal, cement, copper, gasoline, newsprint, tin cans, lead, sulfur, rayon, fertilizer, glass containers, and nonferrous metals are practicing or have in the recent past practiced price leadership. Because price leadership is an informal, tacit agreement involving no written or spoken commitments, it is generally accepted as a legal technique by the courts in interpreting the antitrust laws.

Why do firms follow the leader? There is no simple answer here. On the one hand, the situation clearly obligates smaller firms to do so. Followers are obliged to match a price cut, or they will lose sales to the price leader. They must match price increases or else find themselves in effect in the position of a price cutter and exposed to the unhappy prospect of provoking a price war with the price leader. An intermixture of custom and convenience also helps to explain price leadership. In some industries the practice has achieved the status of a deeply ingrained custom which is accepted by all participants with little or no question. Then, too, small followers may be ill equipped to determine their present and estimate their future cost and demand situations; hence they find it convenient to follow the estimates and the judgment of the price leader on these matters. If the price set by the leader yields a reasonable profit for the followers, the latter are not likely to stray from the price-leadership pattern. The belief is professed by followers in many industries that profits will be greater in the long run under price leadership than could be obtained under alternative pricing arrangements. In other words, price leadership largely avoids the uncertainties of independent pricing and, at the same time, usually results in substantial profits for both leader and followers.

A final question remains: How will the price leader determine price? If the position

---

[3] It must be acknowledged that arguments 2 and 4 are reversible; that is, the combining of several oligopolists into a pure monopoly may lead to *dis*economies of scale, and it is more certain that cost increases will cause *higher* prices and greater output restriction with pure monopoly than with oligopoly.

of the price leader is well established, chances are good that he will seek out the price he feels will maximize his own profits. If the price leader's position is less secure or he is of a benevolent nature, he may seek a price which is mutually satisfactory to price followers and therefore unlikely to upset the price-leadership arrangement. And, too, the price leader may be subject to restraints similar to those facing the pure monopolist. Price must not be "too high" or new rivals will enter, or adverse public opinion and governmental interference may be induced.

Multiproduct Firms and Cost-plus Prices

Thus far our discussion of price and output determination has proceeded on the assumption that each oligopolistic firm produces a single product. In practice, this is the exception, not the rule. Most oligopolistic manufacturers produce a variety of products. And this is not merely a matter of one major product being supplemented by a number of side-line products. To illustrate: Besides producing about half the nation's passenger cars, General Motors is listed in government reports as one of the four largest companies in some twenty-three different lines of production including diesel engines, trucks, buses, railroad locomotives, bicycles, aircraft engines and propellers, household refrigerators, electric ranges, storage batteries, cast iron heating boilers, and air-conditioning equipment.[4] There are some manufacturers that produce literally hundreds and others thousands of separate products.

Motives for product proliferation. A moment's reflection reveals several good reasons for this proliferation of products by manufacturers.

1. In some cases the same productive process necessarily turns out several different products; some products are *joint prod-*ucts. Meat-packing concerns necessarily produce a variety of products ranging from fillets and frankfurters to hides, glue, fertilizers, and pharmaceuticals. Gasoline and kerosene both result from the process of cracking petroleum; coke and gas are jointly created in the distillation of coal.

2. Firms seek product diversification to lessen the effects of fluctuations in demand. The local coal dealer sells ice in the summer and the furnace manufacturer produces air conditioners to lessen seasonal variations in demand. Automobile manufacturers would be more significantly affected by cyclical fluctuations in consumer spending were it not for the fact that they produce a variety of makes and models. Specifically, the demand for the low-priced models holds up better during recession than does that for luxury models.

3. The long-run quest for profits also induces product proliferation. A firm which now has a decided advantage over rivals in the production of a given product will likely find that that advantage and the accompanying profits will decline over time as competitors successfully imitate or duplicate the product. It thus behooves each firm to develop new products as a means of sustaining profits. To this it must be added that a firm is more likely to incur adverse public opinion and risk an antitrust suit by expanding its share of the market for a given product than it will by channeling its efforts to the production of other existing products or the development of new products.[5]

4. Product diversification is also a means by which a firm can more fully utilize its plant capacity. At any point in time excess plant capacity is likely to plague oligopolistic producers as a result of the tendency of such firms to restrict output in order to realize economic profits. It is tempting for a firm thus situated to devote its excess capacity to some related product to which its capital facilities are adaptable. A television manu-

---

[4] Senate Committee on the Judiciary, *Administered Prices: Automobiles* (Nov. 1, 1958), pp. 25–28.

[5] See A. D. H. Kaplan, *Big Enterprise in a Competitive System* (Washington: The Brookings Institution, 1954), pp. 187–188.

facturer, for example, may have excess plant capacity because fuller utilization in television-set production would call for lower prices (and hence the risk of price warring) and lower profits. The firm therefore uses its excess facilities to produce radios, electric clocks, and parts for radar equipment. Incidentally, a firm's research department is in effect a part of its plant capacity. Failure to produce any promising new products which this department develops will obviously mean it is underutilized.

Complexities of multiproduct pricing. For reasons already noted, it may be difficult for a single-product firm to practice marginal-cost-equals-marginal-revenue pricing. The task is virtually impossible for the multiproduct firm. This is partially so for the obvious reason that there are so many more prices to be determined and then redetermined when cost and revenue conditions change. But complex problems also arise because it is difficult for a multiproduct firm to allocate its costs accurately among the many specific products it produces. Some costs are *separable* costs; that is, they can be associated with the production of specific products. For example, labor and materials used exclusively in the production of a specific product are separable costs. These pose no great problem. But other costs—costs which we have previously classified both as fixed and variable—are *common* costs; that is, they are costs which are associated with the firm's many products as a group. Most fixed costs will be common costs: rental payments, salaries of management, some depreciation charges, interest charges, and insurance costs are good illustrations. And some variable costs will be common costs: the materials and labor used in the production of joint products are examples. How is the cost of a steer to be apportioned among the many meat products, the hide, the fertilizer, and the pharmaceuticals which will result from its slaughter? What about the cost of the labor employed in the rendering process? Because there is no precise way to allocate variable common costs among specific prod-

ucts, it is impossible to calculate the marginal costs of these many products.

Multiproduct pricing poses a second problem: Product proliferation contains the seeds of price warring. Unless oligopolistic firms allocate common costs to the various products in some more or less uniform way, they will establish significantly different costs and hence different prices on their products. But under oligopoly, firms producing high-priced products will of necessity be forced to meet the lower prices of competitors. To illustrate: Firm A charges a low price on its refrigerators and a high price on its air conditioners because it has arbitrarily apportioned most of its common costs to its air conditioners. Firm B, however, has arbitrarily allocated most of its common costs to refrigerators and therefore charges a high price for refrigerators and a low price for air conditioners. This means that A will have to cut its air-conditioner price to meet B's and, conversely, B will need to slice its refrigerator prices to meet A's low prices. Price cutting and possibly price warring will result in this situation. To the benefit of consumers and the dismay of producers such aggressive price competition, caused by nonuniform allocations of common costs, may result in losses for both firms.

Cost-plus pricing. To circumvent both these problems oligopolistic multiproduct firms very frequently employ cost-plus pricing. There are two basic steps in this pricing technique.[6] First, the firm simply estimates the separable costs per unit on its various products when it is producing at some average or typical rate of output, for example, two-thirds or three-fourths of capacity. The resulting figure is the "standard cost" of the

---

[6] There are many variations of and qualifications to the simple technique here explained. The interested reader is referred to Joel Dean, *Managerial Economics* (Englewood Cliffs, N.J.: Prentice-Hall, Inc., 1951), pp. 444–457, and Milton H. Spencer and Louis Siegelman, *Managerial Economics* (Homewood, Ill.: Richard D. Irwin, Inc., 1959), p. 292ff.

product. Second, price is determined by adding some "markup," or "margin," to the standard cost figure to allow for common costs and a "fair," or "reasonable," profit. To illustrate: If the standard cost of product X is estimated to be $10 and the markup is 20 per cent, the product's price will be set at $12.

Though cost-plus pricing may be an accurate picture of how many multiproduct businesses set prices, it is not a very satisfactory theory of oligopolistic pricing, because it does not explain why the markup is 10, 15, 25, or 35 per cent. In many instances the markup is "customary"; that is, it is a figure which has been evolved through trial-and-error experimentation by the industry and which seems to yield a satisfactory profit to firms.

The simplicity of this rule-of-thumb pricing technique need hardly be elaborated. Cost-plus pricing is a workable and expedient means of price determination. However, its usefulness as a means of avoiding oligopolistic price warring is not quite so evident. If a group of oligopolists employ essentially the same productive techniques, as is often the case, the application of cost-plus pricing will provide each firm with approximately the same standard cost figure. The application of a common markup figure which is customary to the industry will then result in identical or at least very similar prices. In other words, cost-plus pricing is a means by which multiproduct oligopolists can successfully avoid price competition and price warring. When a group of firms employ standard or similar cost-accounting techniques and apply the same markup figure to the resulting standard cost estimates, they have at their disposal, in the form of cost-plus pricing, a subtle and tacit technique of price collusion.

BASIC ROLE OF NONPRICE COMPETITION

We have noted that, for several reasons, oligopolists have a notable aversion to price competition. This aversion may lead to some more or less informal type of collusion on price. In the United States, however, price collusion is usually accompanied by nonprice competition. It is typically through nonprice competition that each firm's share of the total market is determined. This emphasis upon nonprice competition has its roots in two basic facts.

1. Price cuts can be quickly and easily met by a firm's rivals. Because of this the possibility of significantly increasing one's share of the market through price competition is small; rivals will promptly cancel any potential gain in sales by matching price cuts. And, of course, the risk is always present that price competition will precipitate disastrous price warring. More positively stated, oligopolists seem to feel that more permanent advantages can be gained over rivals through nonprice competition, because product variations, improvements in productive techniques, and successful advertising gimmicks cannot be duplicated so quickly and so completely as can price reductions. And there is less likelihood of nonprice competition's forcing all firms to the wall profitwise in the manner of unbridled price competition. Nonprice competition is less likely to get out of hand. It might be added that many oligopolistic producers of consumer goods apparently are of the opinion that consumers are more product- and advertising-conscious than they are price-conscious.

2. There is a more obvious reason for the tremendous emphasis which oligopolists put upon nonprice competition: Manufacturing oligopolists are typically blessed with substantial financial resources with which to support advertising and product development. Hence, although nonprice competition is a basic characteristic of both monopolistically competitive and oligopolistic industries, the latter are in a financial position to indulge more fully.

We need not restate the pros and cons of advertising. The arguments stated in Chapter 28 with respect to advertising under monopolistic competition are pertinent when applied to oligopoly. However, the implications of the rather prodigious outlays which manufacturing oligopolies sometimes make for technological research on both product quality and productive techniques are a matter of major concern.

OLIGOPOLY AND ECONOMIC EFFICIENCY

The troublesomeness of evaluating the economic efficiency of oligopoly is matched only by the importance of such an evaluation. The root difficulty is that of deciding whether it is more realistic to look at the probable effects of oligopoly in a short-run (static) or in a long-run (dynamic) environment.

Restrictive Oligopoly

The more or less traditional view holds that, because oligopoly is close to pure monopoly in structure, we should expect it to operate in a similar way. Being characterized by barriers to entry, oligopoly can be expected, according to this view, to result in a restriction of output short of the point of lowest unit costs and a corresponding market price which yields substantial, if not maximum, economic profits. These points usually rest upon an analysis similar to that shown in Figure 29–3a. Facing a *given* demand and a *given* cost situation, the oligopolist will find that it pays him to be restrictive. As indicated in Figure 29–3a, higher unit costs will soon arise if output is expanded far beyond Q_1, and the lowering of price which such an expansion requires courts the disaster of a price war. Other things being equal, the price and output results under such an oligopoly would be clearly inferior to those of pure competition. Worse yet, for reasons noted earlier, the results of oligopoly might even be inferior to those of a pure monopoly. If pure monopoly impairs the efficient allocation of resources by producing short of the $P = MC$ point, so then does oligopoly.

At the level of macroeconomics we have previously noted that cost-push and structural inflation are based upon the existence of market power. Therefore, oligopoly may also be criticized as a potential source of inflationary pressure.

Progressive Oligopoly

The above view of oligopoly seems at odds with the historical facts surrounding the operation of many oligopolistic manufacturing industries such as the automobile, farm-equipment, electronics, home-appliance, and steel industries. These industries have been characterized by falling product prices, improvements in product quality, and expanding levels of output and employment over a period of years. But caution is required here. The basic issue is whether this progress would have been even greater had these industries been organized on a purely competitive basis. And, lacking the ability to conduct controlled laboratory experiments, the economist cannot offer a clear-cut answer. It is evident, however, that there has been significant progress in some oligopolistic industries, and the possibility does exist that in the long run some oligopolistic industries may well have fostered lower unit costs, lower prices, and a greater output than the same industry would have provided if organized competitively. Graphically, the restrictive situation portrayed in Figure 29–3a may give way over time to the progressive situation reflected in Figure 29–3b, wherein demand and output have been substantially increased and unit cost and price reduced as compared with Figure 29–3a.[7]

Technological progress: the argument. Generally speaking, the reasons for this possible progressiveness lie in the fact that many oligopolistic industries focus their competi-

---

[7] This comparison of restrictive and progressive oligopoly and the graphic presentation of Figure 29–3 are based upon Henry Grayson, *Price Theory in a Changing Economy* (New York: The Macmillan Company, 1965).

FIGURE 29–3. RESTRICTIVE AND PROGRESSIVE OLIGOPOLY.

Restrictive oligopoly (a): Faced with given demand and marginal revenue data (such as DP_1D and MRMR) and given cost data (such as AC and MC), the oligopolist will maximize profits by restricting output to Q_1 and charging price Q_1P_1. In expanding output beyond Q_1, the oligopolist must accept considerable price reductions and run the risk of starting a price war. Furthermore, by expanding the output, the producer may soon encounter rising average costs AC.

Progressive oligopoly (b): In fact some oligopolists have been progressive, achieving lower average costs AC and marginal costs MC through technological advance. Similarly, demand DP_2D and marginal revenue MRMR have been pushed far to the right as a result of product development and want-creating activities. As compared to the restrictive oligopoly of (a), the net result of progressive oligopoly has frequently been a larger output (Q_2 as compared to Q_1) and a lower price (Q_2P_2 as compared to Q_1P_1).

(a)

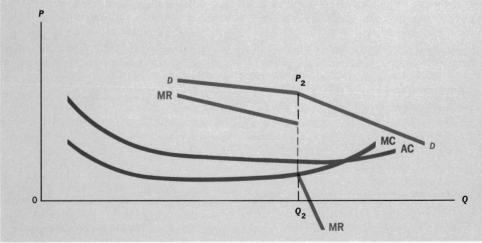

(b)

tive energies upon technological competition as reflected in both the development of productive techniques and improvement of product quality. The betterment of productive techniques will have the effect of expanding the range of constant or, better yet, declining unit costs. Advances in product quality, accompanied by advertising and related want-creating activities, will shift the firm's demand curve to the right. As indicated in Figure 29–3b, product price is very likely to decline with declines in unit costs.

At present there is a rather widely held presumption that modern oligopolies have both greater means and a stronger inclination for technological advance than does any other market structure. Let us summarize the arguments underlying this presumption and then test them against such statistical data as are available.

First, oligopolies typically possess the *means*—substantial profits—with which to undertake the incredibly expensive task of modern research. Technological progress, it is contended, is no longer in the domain of the back-yard Edison or the basement Whitney. Rather, it is the result of highly organized and cooperative efforts of a variety of scientists and engineers housed in the elaborate research departments of such giant oligopolies as du Pont and General Electric. Purely and monopolistically competitive firms, being smaller and less prosperous, are decidedly less progressive.

Second, oligopolistic producers have a host of good *incentives* for accelerating technological advance:

1. Given their disposition to avoid price competition, technological, or cost, competition provides an obvious alternative means for enlarging total profits through an expanded product demand and lower unit costs. Like advertising and product development, the discovery of more efficient productive techniques is less certainly and less quickly matched by one's rivals than is a price cut.

2. Technological superiority is a basic

means by which an oligopolist can ensure survival in the event that a price war should somehow plague the quiet life of the industry.

3. In contrast to an unrivaled, pure monopolist, the presence of several strong rivals puts the oligopolist under considerable pressure to seek maximum productive efficiency. Failure to do so may mean that his several competitors will in time drive him out of business. The pure monopolist, being devoid of rivals, is under no competitive spur to technical progress. But the oligopolist, having a few rivals, clearly is in an environment of technological competition.

4. The existence of barriers to entry gives the progressive oligopolist some assurance that he will actually realize the profit rewards to which his research expenditures may give rise. This is in contrast to a monopolistically competitive market, wherein the rewards of a new productive technique will be shared by many competitors who will quickly copy or imitate a progressive firm without bearing any of the research and development costs. And the presence of a large number of rivals will hasten price reductions to consumers, based upon the cost reductions stemming from the advance. The presence of fewer rivals and the proclivity of oligopolists not to cut price enhance the possibility of the innovating oligopolist's realizing greater profit rewards from his technical progress. The importance of this point is evident in an economy such as American capitalism, wherein the basic drive wheel is profits.

Technological progress: the evidence.[8] Such data as are available do considerable damage to the image of the oligopolistic industry as a mainspring of research and development

[8] This section draws heavily upon Daniel Hamberg, "Size of Firm, Monopoly, and Economic Growth," in *Employment, Growth, and Price Levels, Hearings of the Joint Economic Committee, Part 7* (Washington, 1959), pp. 2337–2352, and "Invention in the Industrial Research Laboratory," *Journal of Political Economy*, April, 1963, pp. 95–115.

activity. Available statistics suggest that the research laboratories of giant corporate oligopolies are *not* the fountainhead of technological advance. A recent study[9] of sixty-one important inventions made since 1900 indicates that over half were the work of independent inventors, quite disassociated from the industrial research laboratories of corporate enterprise. Such substantial advances as air conditioning, power steering, cellophane, the jet engine, insulin, the helicopter, and the catalytic cracking of petroleum have this individualistic heritage. Other equally important advances have been provided by small- and medium-sized firms. According to this study, about two-thirds— 40 out of 61—of the basic inventions of this century have been fathered by independent inventors or the research activities of relatively small firms. Other studies—for example, analyses of patent statistics—reinforce the conclusion that a large proportion of basic technological advances originates outside the laboratories of giant oligopolies.

This, of course, is the overall picture and does not in any way repudiate the fact that in a number of oligopolistic industries—for example, the aircraft, chemical, petroleum, and electrical-equipment industries—research activity has been pursued vigorously, fruitfully, and on an expanding scale. But even here we must amend at least two important qualifications. In the first place, there are a number of other oligopolistic industries wherein it is generally agreed that the interest in research and development activity has been modest at best; the steel, cigarette, and aluminum industries are cases in point. Secondly, a very substantial portion of the research carried on by oligopolistic industries is actually financed with public funds. For example, about 90 per cent of the research performed in the aircraft-missile industry is government sponsored, over 60 per cent in the electrical-equipment industry, 71 per

cent in the communications industry, and so forth. Despite the increased interest of businesses, the Federal government remains the most important source of funds for research and development activity.

Countervailing Power

There is a second consideration which brightens somewhat the traditional dim view of oligopoly. John K. Galbraith of Harvard has developed the notion that many oligopolies (and monopolies) tend to induce the development of oligopolies (and monopolies) on the opposite side of the market.[10] That is, the existence of a monopolistic (or oligopolistic) seller tends to stimulate the growth of a monopsonistic (or oligopsonistic) buyer, and vice versa. More specifically, there is a tendency for "countervailing power" to evolve on the opposite side of those markets in which strong positions of "original power" have already developed. The development of countervailing power is not a matter of chance. It stems, on the one hand, from the desire of resource suppliers or customers to protect themselves from any abuses of the original-power position and, on the other hand, from the desire to share in the profits of the original-power position. Stated differently, for both defensive and offensive reasons, countervailing power is self-generating. Oligopoly begets oligopoly on the opposite side of the market. Oligopoly, in effect, generates its own antidote.

The significance of countervailing power is implicit in the concept itself. Countervailing power, or "across-the-market" competition, can be an important competitive force in those very markets in which "same-side-of-the-market" rivalry is weak. Oligopolistic sellers may be restrained by a few large buyers. The Big Four of the tire industry face the Big Three of the automobile industry; chain grocery stores and

[9] John Jewkes, David Sawers, and Richard Stillerman, *The Sources of Invention* (New York: St Martin's Press, Inc., 1958).

[10] John Kenneth Galbraith, *American Capitalism,* rev. ed. (Boston: Houghton Mifflin Company, 1956), particularly chap. 9.

mail order houses buy in quantity from oligopolistic food processors and manufacturers. Oligopsonistic buyers may be faced with a small number of sellers. Labor unions face gigantic employers; agricultural marketing cooperatives sell to large food processors. Now, to the degree that these opposed positions of market power are successful in checking or restraining the power of one another, the successful operation of a market system characterized by oligopoly will be furthered. Buyer and seller may cancel the power and negate the potential market abuses of one another. The monopolistic seller who seeks a high monopolistic price is faced with a monopsonistic buyer who obviously is interested in a low monopsonistic price. That is, each seeks to use his market power to raise or depress price to his own advantage. The market power of each may be largely self-canceling, and the resulting compromise price close to the competitive level. Furthermore, given the compromise price, the monopolist will have no incentive to restrict his output and sales as he would be obligated to do in establishing a monopolistic price. Thus the net result of monopoly on both sides of the market may be a price and output closer to those of pure competition than if monopoly existed on only one side of the market. This is true of oligopoly as well. Countervailing power is an important regulatory force in American capitalism and makes the economy more competitive than any discussion limited to same-side-of-the-market competition would lead one to conclude.

Countervailing power, however, is not devoid of shortcomings and criticisms. One shortcoming is that it is not universally present. In the automobile industry, for example, dealers are highly dependent upon manufacturers and thus in a poor position to bargain for lower automobile prices which may benefit both themselves and consumers. In other cases—for example, the petroleum industry—manufacturers are integrated vertically down to the consumer, thus excluding the possibility of countervailing power. Be-

cause the residential-construction industry is composed of thousands of small and unorganized contractors, no countervailing power is exerted against oligopolistic suppliers of building materials.

Even where countervailing power is firmly established, it does not function with equal effectiveness under all economic conditions. In particular, during periods of inflation countervailing power does not operate effectively as a competitive force, because with excess demand buyers are no longer able to restrain sellers. When a resource buyer enjoys a seller's market for his product, he is not apt to offer stiff resistance to the demands of resource suppliers. This is best exemplified in the labor market, where unions as "sellers" of labor are in a most strategic position in bargaining with employers during inflation. Management does not want to risk a work stoppage when consumer demand is burgeoning. Why resist? Increases in wage costs (and more) can be readily passed on to the consumer through price increases with no loss of sales, and profits thereby can be maintained or even expanded. The results of this situation are anything but socially desirable.

Finally, it has been pointed out that the two power positions may both benefit at the expense of the rest of the economy by combining their forces rather than by offsetting one another. Across-the-market rivals may find mutual advantages in collusive action or outright merger rather than in expending their energies in negating the market power of one another.

Oligopoly: Tentative Appraisal

Having surveyed these two viewpoints, what, if anything, can we conclude about the economic efficiency of oligopolistic industries? Not much more than this: Assuming *given* long-run costs of production, an oligopolistic industry will produce less, provide fewer jobs, and charge a higher product price than would the same industry organized competitively. But to the extent that oligopoly results in lower unit costs and improvements in product quality, this conclusion must be altered in a manner less condemnatory of oligopoly. That is, *if* large oligopolistic producers are in a better position than competitive firms to realize existing (known) economies of scale or are more able and willing to develop improved productive techniques and better products, then oligopoly *may* be more desirable socially than competition. However, despite plausible arguments why oligopoly may be progressive, such empirical evidence as is available suggests that giant oligopolistic corporations are not the basic source of technological advance in our society. Furthermore, there are many known instances (see footnote 2) in which oligopolists, unbridled by countervailing power, have sorely abused their market power to the detriment of society as a whole. Indeed, the picture is a mixed one: when oligopolies are good, they may be very good; when they are bad, they tend to be very bad. The examination of specific cases will reveal both restrictive and progressive oligopolies. This tentative conclusion is worth venturing: Oligopolistic industries may be much more palatable over time, that is, in the long run, than they seem to be at a particular point in time.

SUMMARY

1. Oligopolistic industries are characterized by few firms, each of which has a significant fraction of the market. Firms thus situated are mutually interdependent; the behavior of any one firm directly affects and is affected by the actions of rivals. Products may be virtually uniform or significantly differentiated; entry is substantially restricted, frequently by technological considerations.

2. The wide variety of oligopolistic markets and the uncertainty which stems from mutual interdependence limit the applicability of formal economic analysis to oligopolistic markets. The factual record indicates, however, that **a.** oligopolistic prices tend to be inflexible, or "sticky," and **b.** the price changes which do occur are "orderly" in the sense that firms tend to change their prices together.

3. Independent (noncollusive) oligopolists in effect face a kinked demand curve. This curve and the accompanying marginal-revenue curve help explain the price rigidity which characterize such markets; they do not, however, explain the level of price.

4. The uncertainties inherent in independent pricing are conducive to collusion. Gentlemen's agreements on price may entail economic consequences even less desirable to society than pure monopoly because **a.** the oligopolists are likely to escape public regulation, **b.** economies of scale may be sacrificed, **c.** wasteful competitive advertising may persist, and **d.** the resulting price rigidity may forestall price reductions which cost-reducing technological advances justify.

5. Price leadership, whereby all firms in the industry follow the price changes of a dominant firm, is a less formal and widely practiced form of price collusion.

6. Many oligopolistic producers are multiproduct firms. There are many reasons behind product proliferation: **a.** Some products are jointly produced, **b.** product diversification provides insurance against demand fluctuations, **c.** the initial advantage of being the sole producer of a newly developed product is conducive to high profits, and **d.** a firm can more fully utilize its plant through product diversification.

7. In multiproduct firms some costs are separable, that is, associated exclusively with the production of specific goods, whereas others are common, associated with many products taken as a group. This poses two difficulties: **a.** It is extremely difficult to calculate marginal costs for each product, and **b.** significant price differences and price warring may result from the lack of a uniform technique in allocating common costs to different products.

8. Cost-plus pricing is used to side-step these difficulties. By this rule-of-thumb pricing technique, per unit separable costs are calculated, or estimated, for a typical rate of output; a customary markup which includes common costs and a fair profit is then added to this standard-cost figure in determining price.

9. Market shares in oligopolistic industries are usually determined on the basis of nonprice competition. Oligopolists emphasize nonprice competition because **a.** advertising and product variations are less easy for rivals to match and **b.** oligopolists frequently have ample financial resources to finance nonprice competition.

10. There is no clear-cut conclusion as to the social desirability of oligopoly; oligopoly may be either restrictive or progressive. Where oligopoly is restrictive, abuses of its market power may sometimes be curbed by countervailing power.

QUESTIONS AND STUDY SUGGESTIONS

1. What features distinguish oligopoly from monopolistic competition? Be specific.
2. "Fewness of rivals means mutual interdependence and mutual interdependence means uncertainty as to how those few rivals will react to a price change by any one firm." Explain. Of what significance is this for determining demand and marginal revenue? Other things being equal, would you expect mutual interdependence to vary directly or inversely with the degree of product differentiation? Explain.
3. What are the basic characteristics of oligopolistic prices? How are these characteristics best explained?
4. What assumptions concerning a rival's responses to price changes underlie the kinked demand curve? Why is there a gap in the marginal-revenue curve? How does the kinked demand curve help explain oligopolistic price rigidity?
5. What is price leadership? Explain its operation. Why, from society's standpoint, might the economic consequences of collusive oligopoly be inferior to those of pure monopoly?
6. What advantages might accompany product diversification? Why do oligopolists prefer nonprice to price competition?
7. "If each firm knows that the price of each of its few rivals depends on its price, how can the prices be determined?" Explain.
8. What is cost-plus pricing? What might its advantages be to the oligopolist?
9. "Oligopolistic industries have both the means and the inclination for technological progress." Do you agree? Explain.
10. Under what conditions will oligopoly be economically efficient? Economically inefficient? Which set of conditions do you feel better describes oligopoly in American capitalism? Justify your answer.
11. What is countervailing power? How does it differ from ordinary competition? Why is it self-generating? What are its limitations?

SELECTED REFERENCES

Adams, Walter (ed.): *The Structure of American Industry,* 3d ed. (New York: The Macmillan Company, 1961), chaps. 5, 6, 8–10, and 12.

Bain, Joe S.: *Pricing, Distribution, and Employment,* rev. ed. (New York: Holt, Rinehart and Winston, Inc., 1953), chap. 6.

Bober, M. M.: *Intermediate Price and Income Theory,* rev. ed. (New York: W. W. Norton & Company, Inc., 1962), chap. 12.

Colberg, M. R., and W. C. Bradford: *Business Economics,* 3d ed. (Homewood, Ill.: Richard D. Irwin, Inc., 1962), chaps. 6–9.

Galbraith, John K.: *American Capitalism,* rev. ed. (Boston: Houghton Mifflin Company, 1956), chaps. 7 and 9.

Grayson, Henry: *Price Theory in a Changing Economy* (New York: The Macmillan Company, 1965), chap. 9.

Joint Economic Committee: *Employment, Growth, and Price Levels, Hearings, Part 7, The Effects of Monopolistic and Quasi-monopolistic Practices* (Washington, D.C., 1959), papers by James S. Duesenberry, William J. Fellner, and Daniel Hamberg.

Kaplan, A. D. H.: *Big Enterprise in a Competitive System* (Washington, D.C.: The Brookings Institution, 1954).

Weiss, Leonard W.: *Economics and American Industry* (New York: John Wiley & Sons, Inc., 1961), chaps. 7 and 8.

CHAPTER 30

PRODUCTION AND THE DEMAND
FOR ECONOMIC RESOURCES

The preceding four chapters have been concerned with the pricing and output of goods and services under a variety of product market structures. In producing any commodity, a firm must hire productive resources which, directly or indirectly, are owned and supplied by households. It is appropriate that we now turn from the pricing and production of goods to the pricing and employment of resources needed in accomplishing production. In terms of our circular flow diagram of the economy we now shift our attention from the bottom loop of the diagram, where firms supply and households demand products, to the top loop, where households supply and businesses demand resources. It is in part this reversal of roles which makes necessary a separate discussion of resource pricing.

SIGNIFICANCE OF RESOURCE PRICING

The importance of studying resource pricing is almost self-evident. The most basic fact about resource prices is that they constitute a major determinant of money incomes. The expenditures which businesses make in acquiring economic resources flow as wage, rent, interest, and profit incomes to those households which in turn supply the human and property resources at their disposal. Here we are concerned with explaining the resource prices which play such a crucial role in determining the distribution of income.

Another important aspect of resource pricing is that, just as product prices ration finished goods and services to consumers,

so resource prices allocate scarce resources among various industries and firms. An understanding of the manner in which resource prices negotiate the allocation of resources is particularly significant in view of the fact that in a dynamic economy such as American capitalism the efficient allocation of resources over time calls for continuing shifts in resources among alternative uses.

A very special aspect of the resource allocation problem faces the individual firm. To the firm, resource prices are costs, and to realize maximum profits a firm must produce the profit-maximizing output with the most efficient (least costly) combination of resources. Given technology, it is resource prices which play the major role in determining how much land, labor, capital, and entrepreneurial ability are to be combined in the productive process.

Finally, aside from these objective facets of resource pricing, there are a myriad of ethical questions and public policy issues surrounding the resource market. In particular, the amoral nature of resource prices results in considerable inequality in the personal distribution of income. Too, the age-old question of the sizes of the income shares going to specific groups is still very much alive. What is the proper distribution of the national income between profits and wages? What shares should go to farmers, factory workers, white-collar employees? Indeed, the pursuit of these questions leads into a consideration of the alternative economic ideologies. Most of Part Six of this book is concerned with endeavors—both public and private—to alter the distribution of income. Chapter 37 is concerned specifically with the ethics of income distribution.

COMPLEXITIES OF RESOURCE PRICING

Economists are in substantial agreement as to the basic principles of resource pricing. Yet there exist considerable disagreement and sometimes an element of confusion as to the variations in these general principles which must be made as they are applied to specific resources and particular markets. While economists are in general agreement that the pricing and employment of economic resources, or factors of production, are a supply and demand phenomenon, they also recognize that in particular markets resource supply and demand may assume strange and often complex dimensions. This is further complicated by the fact that the operation of supply and demand forces may be muted or even largely supplanted by the policies and practices of government, business firms, or labor unions, not to mention a host of other institutional considerations.

Our major objective in this chapter is a limited one: to explain the basic factors which underlie the demand for economic resources. We shall couch our discussion in terms of labor, recognizing that the principles outlined in our discussion are also generally applicable to land, capital, and entrepreneurial ability. In Chapter 31 we shall combine our understanding of resource demand with a discussion of labor supply in analyzing wage rates. Then in Chapter 32 we shall emphasize the supply side of the market for property resources.

DEMAND FOR A SINGLE RESOURCE

The simplest approach to resource demand is that which assumes a firm is hiring a single resource in a competitive market and in turn is selling its product in a competitive market. The simplicity of this situation lies in the fact that under competition the firm can dispose of as little or as much output as it chooses at the going market price. The firm is selling such a negligible fraction of total output that it exerts no influence whatever on product price. Similarly, in the resource market, competition means that the firm is hiring such a small fraction of the total supply of the resource that its price is unaffected by the quantity the firm purchases.

Resource Demand As a Derived Demand

Having specified these simplified conditions, the most crucial point to note is that the demand for resources is a *derived* demand, that is, derived from the finished goods and services which resources help produce. Resources do not directly satisfy consumer wants, but do so indirectly by producing goods and services. No one wants to consume an acre of land, an International Harvester tractor, or the labor services of a farmer, but households do want to consume the various products which these resources help produce.

Marginal Revenue Product (MRP)

The derived nature of resource demand correctly implies that the strength of the demand for any resource will depend upon (1) the capability of the resource in producing a good and (2) the value of the good it is producing. In other words, the demand for a resource depends upon its productivity and the market price of the commodity it is producing. A resource which is highly productive in turning out a commodity highly valued by society will be in great demand. On the other hand, demand will be very weak for a relatively unproductive resource which is only capable of producing some good not in great demand by households. There will be no demand for a resource which is phenomenally efficient in the production of something which no one will buy!

The roles of productivity and product value in determining resource demand can be brought into sharper focus through Table 30–1. Here it is assumed that a firm is

TABLE 30–1. THE DEMAND FOR A RESOURCE: PURE COMPETITION IN THE SALE OF THE PRODUCT (hypothetical data)

(1) Units of resource	(2) Total product	(3) Marginal physical product (MPP) or Δ(2)	(4) Product price	(5) Total revenue, or (2) × (4)	(6) Marginal revenue product (MRP), or Δ(5)
1	15		$1	$15	
		15			$15
2	27		1	27	
		12			12
3	36		1	36	
		9			9
4	42		1	42	
		6			6
5	45		1	45	
		3			3
6	46		1	46	
		1			1

adding one variable resource—labor—to its fixed plant. Columns 1 through 3 remind us that the law of diminishing returns will be applicable in this situation, causing the marginal physical product (MPP) of labor to fall beyond some point. For simplicity's sake it is here assumed that diminishing marginal physical product sets in with the first worker hired. But we have already emphasized that the derived demand for a resource depends not only upon the productivity of that resource but also upon the price of the commodity it produces. Column 4 adds this information. Note that product price is constant at $1 because we are supposing a competitive product market. Multiplying column 2 by column 4, we get the total-revenue data of column 5. From these total-revenue data we can readily compute *marginal revenue product (MRP)—the increase in total revenue resulting from the use of each additional input of labor.* This is indicated in column 6.

Rule for Employing Resources

The MRP schedule—columns 1 and 6—is crucial in that it constitutes the firm's

demand schedule for labor. To explain why this is so we must first discuss the rule which guides a profit-seeking firm in hiring any resource. To maximize profits a firm should hire additional units of any given resource so long as each successive unit adds more to the firm's total revenue than it does to its total costs. Economists have special terms which designate what each additional unit of a resource adds to total cost and what it adds to total revenue. We have just noted that MRP measures how much each successive worker adds to total revenue. The amount which each additional unit of a resource adds to the firm's total (resource) cost is called *marginal resource cost (MRC).* Thus we can restate our rule for hiring resources as follows: *It will be profitable for a firm to hire additional units of a resource up to the point at which that resource's MRP is equal to its MRC.* If the number of workers a firm is currently hiring is such that the MRP of the last worker exceeds his MRC, the firm can clearly profit by hiring more workers. But if the number being hired is such that the MRC of the last worker exceeds his MRP, the firm is hiring workers who are not "paying their way," and it can thereby increase its profits by laying off some workers. The reader will recognize that this MRP = MRC rule is very similar to the MR = MC rule employed throughout our discussion of product pricing. The rationale of the two rules is the same, but the point of reference is now inputs of resources, not outputs of product.

MRP Is a Demand Schedule

Just as product price and marginal revenue are equal in a competitive product market, so resource price and marginal resource cost are equal when a firm is hiring a resource competitively. In a competitive labor market the wage rate is set by the total, or market, supply of, and the market demand for, labor. Because it hires such a small fraction of the total supply of labor, a single firm cannot influence this wage rate. This means that total resource cost increases by exactly the amount of the going wage rate for each additional worker hired; the wage rate and MRC are equal. It follows that so long as it is hiring labor competitively, *the firm will hire workers to the point at which their wage rate (or MRC) is equal to their MRP.*

Accordingly, employing the data in column 6 of Table 30–1, we find that if the wage rate is $14.95, the firm will hire only one worker. This is so because the first worker adds $15 to total revenue and slightly less—$14.95—to total costs. For each successive worker, however, we find that his MRC exceeds his MRP, indicating that it will not be profitable to hire him. If the wage rate is $11.95, we apply the same reasoning and discover that it will pay the firm to hire both the first and second workers. Similarly, if the wage rate is $8.95, three will be hired. If $5.95, four. If $2.95, then five. And so forth. It is evident that *the MRP schedule constitutes the firm's demand for labor, because each point on this schedule (curve) indicates the number of workers which the firm would hire at each possible wage rate which might exist.* This is shown graphically in Figure 30–1.

Resource Demand under Imperfect Competition

Our analysis of labor demand becomes slightly more complex when we assume that the firm is selling its product in an imperfectly competitive market. Pure monopoly, oligopoly, and monopolistic competition in the product market all mean that the firm's product demand curve is downsloping; that is, the firm must accept a lower price in order to increase its sales. Table 30–2 takes this into account. The productivity data of Table 30–1 are retained, but it is now assumed in column 4 that product price must be lowered in order to sell the marginal product of each successive worker. The MRP of the competitive seller falls for one reason: marginal physical product diminishes. But the MRP of the imperfectly competitive seller falls for two reasons: marginal product diminishes, and product price falls as output increases.

It must be emphasized that the lower price which accompanies every increase in output applies in each case not only to the marginal product of each successive worker but also to all prior units which otherwise could have been sold at a higher price. To illustrate: The second worker's marginal product is 12 units. These 12 units can be sold for $1.20 each or, as a group, for $14.40. But this is not the MRP of the second worker. Why? Because in order to sell these 12 units the firm must take a 10-cent price cut on the 15 units produced by the first worker—units which could have been sold for $1.30 each. Thus the MRP of the second worker is only $12.90 [$14.40 − (15 × 10 cents)]. Similarly, the third worker's MRP is $7.20. Although the 9 units he produces are worth $1.10 each in the market, the third worker does not add $9.90 to the firm's total revenue when account is taken of the 10-cent price cut which must be taken on the 27 units produced by the first two workers. In this case the third worker's MRP is only $7.20 [$9.90 − (27 × 10 cents)]. And so it is for the other figures in column 6.

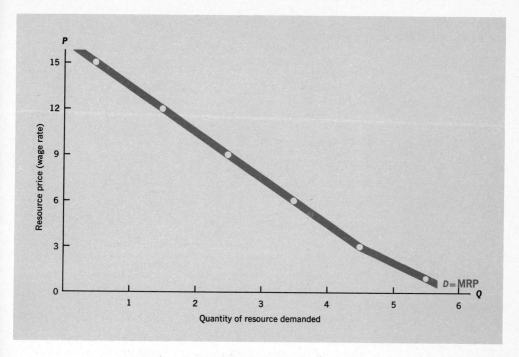

FIGURE 30–1. THE PURELY COMPETITIVE SELLER'S DEMAND FOR A RESOURCE.
The MRP curve is the resource demand curve. The location of the curve depends upon
the marginal productivity of the resource and the price of the product. Under pure
competition product price is constant; therefore, it is solely because of diminishing
marginal productivity that the resource demand curve is downsloping.

The net result is obvious: The MRP curve
—the resource demand curve—of the imperfectly competitive producer tends to be less
elastic than that of a purely competitive
producer. At a wage rate or MRC of $11.95
both the purely competitive and the imperfectly competitive seller will hire two
workers. But at $8.95 the competitive
firm will hire three and the imperfectly
competitive firm only two. And at $5.95 the
purely competitive firm will take four and
the imperfect competitor only three. This
difference in elasticity can be readily
visualized by graphing the MRP data of
Table 30–2 as in Figure 30–2 and comparing
them with Figure 30–1. It is not surprising
that the imperfectly competitive producer
is less responsive to wage cuts in terms of
workers employed than is the purely com-

petitive producer. The relative reluctance
of the imperfect competitor to employ more
resources and thereby produce more output
when resource prices fall is merely the
resource market reflection of the imperfect
competitor's tendency to restrict output in
the product market. Other things being
equal, the imperfectly competitive seller will
produce less of a product than would a
purely competitive seller. In producing this
smaller output, he will demand fewer
resources.

But one qualification is pertinent. We
noted in Chapters 27 and 29 that in some
instances the market structures of oligopoly
and pure monopoly might be progressive
rather than restrictive. That is, they might
give rise to a higher level of production,
more employment, and lower prices in the

TABLE 30–2. THE DEMAND FOR A RESOURCE: IMPERFECT COMPETITION IN THE SALE OF THE PRODUCT (hypothetical data)

(1) Units of resource	(2) Total product	(3) Marginal physical product (MPP), or Δ(2)	(4) Product price	(5) Total revenue, or (2) × (4)	(6) Marginal revenue product (MRP), or Δ(5)
1	15	15	$1.30	$19.50	$19.50
2	27	12	1.20	32.40	12.90
3	36	9	1.10	39.60	7.20
4	42	6	1.05	44.10	4.50
5	45	3	1.00	45.00	0.90
6	46	1	0.95	43.70	−1.30

long run than would a purely competitive market arrangement. This, you will recall, seems more likely in the case of oligopoly. The resource demand curve for progressive oligopoly and monopoly would not be so restricted.

Market Demand for a Resource

Can we now derive a market demand curve for a resource? Yes, we can. You will recall that the total, or market, demand curve for a product is developed by summing the demand curves of all individual buyers in the market. Similarly, the market demand curve for a particular resource can be derived in essentially the same fashion, that is, by summing the individual demand or MRP curves for all firms hiring that resource.[1]

[1] The matter is actually not quite this simple. The resource demand, or MRP, curve *for each firm* is drawn on the assumption that product price is constant. However, if a lowering of resource price causes *all firms* in the industry to hire more of the resource and thereby expand total output, we can expect product price to decline. The result is that the resource market

CHANGES IN RESOURCE DEMAND

What will alter the demand for a resource, that is, shift the demand curve? The very derivation of resource demand immediately suggests two related factors—the resource's productivity and the market price of the product it is producing. And our previous analysis of changes in product demand (Chapter 4) indicates another factor— changes in the prices of other resources.

1. Because resource demand is a derived demand, it is obvious that any change in the demand for the product will affect product price and therefore the MRP of the resource. An increase in the demand for automobiles will increase automobile prices and therefore cause the demand for the services of

demand curve will not be quite identical with the sum of the individual firms' demand curves for that resource. The whole will not equal the sum of the parts. We shall ignore this complication in our discussion and accept the approximation in the text. If interested, consult Neil W. Chamberlain, *The Labor Sector* (New York: McGraw-Hill Book Company, 1965), pp. 378–381.

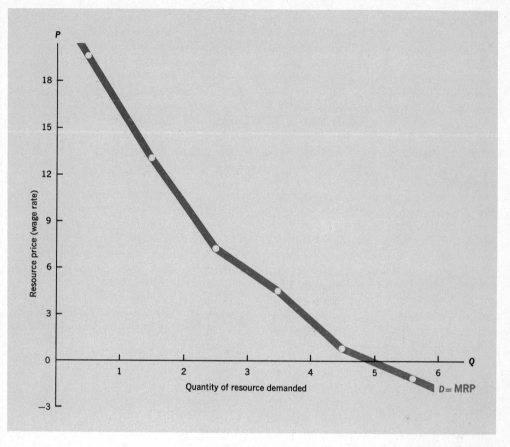

**FIGURE 30–2. THE IMPERFECTLY COMPETITIVE SELLER'S DEMAND
FOR A RESOURCE.**
An imperfectly competitive seller's resource demand curve slopes downward because
marginal product diminishes and product price falls as output increases.

automobile workers to shift to the right; a decline in the demand for automobiles will reduce automobile prices and thereby shift the demand for automobile workers to the left.

2. Changes in productivity will also cause resource demand to shift. The productivity of any resource can be altered in several ways. (*a*) The marginal productivity data for, say, labor will depend upon the quantities of other resources with which it is combined. The greater the amount of capital and land resources with which labor is com-

bined, the greater will be the marginal productivity and the demand for labor. (*b*) Technological improvements will have the same effect. The better the quality of the capital, the greater the productivity of labor. A worker equipped with a power shovel is very much more productive than the same worker armed with a spade. (*c*) Improvements in the quality of the variable resource itself—labor—will increase the marginal productivity and therefore the demand for labor.

All these considerations, incidentally, are important in explaining why the average level of (real) wages is higher in the United States than in foreign nations. American workers are generally healthier and better trained than those of foreign nations, and in most industries they work with a larger and more efficient stock of capital goods and more abundant natural resources than do the workers of most foreign nations. This spells a strong demand for labor. On the supply side of the market labor is *relatively* scarce as compared to most foreign nations. A strong demand and a relatively scarce supply result in high wage rates. This will be discussed further in Chapter 31.

3. Just as changes in the prices of other products will change the demand for a specific commodity, so changes in the prices of other resources can be expected to alter the demand for a particular resource. And just as the effect of a change in the price of product X upon the demand for product Y depends upon whether X and Y are substitute or complementary goods, so the effect of a change in the price of resource A upon the demand for resource B will depend upon their substitutability or their complementariness.

Within limits resources are typically substitutes for one another. A drop in the price of machinery may prompt a firm to substitute machinery for labor; this is the obvious adjustment to make if the firm seeks to produce any given output in the least costly fashion. At given wage rates, less labor will now be employed. The demand for labor will have fallen. But this *substitution effect* may be offset wholly or in part by an accompanying *output effect*. Because the price of machinery has fallen, the cost of producing various outputs will also have declined. And with lower costs the firm will produce and sell a larger output. This greater output will tend to increase the demand for all resources, including labor. The net effect of a decline in the price of machinery upon the demand for labor will depend upon the sizes of these two opposed effects. If the substitution effect outweighs the output effect, the demand for

labor will decline. If the reverse holds true, the demand for labor will increase.

When resources are complementary or jointly demanded, the situation is a bit more clear-cut. In some situations the nature of the productive process allows little or no room for substituting resources; resources are combined in fixed proportions. Suppose, for example, that a small manufacturer of metal products uses punch presses as its basic piece of capital equipment. Each press is designed to be operated by one worker; the machine is not automated—it won't run itself—and a second or third worker would be wholly redundant. Now assume that a significant technological advance in the production of these presses substantially reduces their cost. Other things being unchanged, this reduction in the price of capital goods will induce our manufacturer to use more presses. However, because labor and capital are required in fixed proportions—one man for one machine—there will be no substitution of capital for labor. On the contrary, the purchase of more machines will increase the firm's demand for punch-press operators. The output effect will bolster this increase in labor demand. To the extent that the firm's metal products are reduced in price because of the drop in the cost of the presses, its volume of sales and therefore its demand for labor will increase.

ELASTICITY OF RESOURCE DEMAND

The considerations just discussed are responsible for shifts in the location of resource demand curves. Such changes in demand are to be carefully distinguished from a change in the quantity of a resource demanded. The latter, you will recall, does not entail a shift in the resource demand curve but rather a movement from one point to another on a stable resource demand curve, because of a change in the price of the specific resource under consideration. To illustrate: An increase in the wage rate from $5.95 to $8.95 will reduce the quantity of labor demanded from four to three workers, as can be readily seen in Table 30–1 and Figure 30–1.

This raises a question: What determines the sensitivity of producers to changes in resource prices? Or, more technically, what determines the elasticity of resource demand? Several long-standing generalizations provide some important insights in answering this question.

1. A purely technical consideration is of importance to us—the rate at which the marginal physical product of the variable resource declines. If the marginal product of labor declines slowly as it is added to a fixed amount of capital, the MRP, or demand curve for labor, will decline slowly and tend to be highly elastic. A small decline in the price of such a resource will give rise to a relatively large increase in the amount demanded. Conversely, if the marginal productivity of labor declines sharply, the MRP, or labor demand curve, will decline rapidly. This means that a relatively large decline in the wage rate will be accompanied by a very modest increase in the amount hired; resource demand will be inelastic.

2. The degree to which resources are substitutable for one another is a highly important determinant of elasticity. The larger the number of good substitute resources available, the greater will be the elasticity of demand for a particular resource. If a furniture manufacturer finds that some five or six different types of wood are equally satisfactory in making coffee tables, a rise in the price of any one type of wood may cause a very sharp drop in the amount demanded as the producer readily substitutes other woods. At the other extreme, it may be impossible to substitute: bauxite is absolutely essential in the production of aluminum ingots. This means that the demand for it tends to be very inelastic.

3. The elasticity of demand for any resource will depend upon the elasticity of demand for the product which it helps produce. The greater the elasticity of product

demand, the greater the elasticity of resource demand. The derived nature of resource demand would lead us to expect this relationship. A small rise in the price of a product with great elasticity of demand will give rise to a sharp drop in output and therefore a relatively large decline in the amounts of the various resources demanded. Indeed, our comparisons of resource demand when output is being sold competitively (Table 30–1 and Figure 30–1), on the one hand, and under imperfectly competitive conditions (Table 30–2 and Figure 30–2), on the other, have already suggested that, other things being the same, the greater the elasticity of product demand, the greater the elasticity of resource demand.

4. Finally, the larger the portion of production costs accounted for by a resource, the greater will be the elasticity of demand for that resource. The rationale here is rather evident. If labor costs account for, say, three-fourths of the total cost of a product, a given increase in wage rates will alter total cost and therefore product price by a relatively large amount, resulting in a significant increase in product price. Given the elasticity of product demand, this will cause a relatively large decline in sales and a sharp decline in the amount of labor demanded. But if labor cost is only 5 or 10 per cent of total cost, the same given increase in wage rates will have little effect upon total cost and product price. Given the same elasticity of product demand, a small decline in sales and therefore in the amount of labor demanded will result.

A FIRM'S DEMAND FOR SEVERAL RESOURCES

So much for the character of the demand for a single resource. Now we must examine resource demand from the standpoint of an individual firm that is employing several different resources for which, within limits, there are substitutes. The problem faced by the producer is much like that confronting the consumer. You will recall from Chapter 24 that the consumer seeks that combination of goods which gives him the maximum utility for his given money income. In achieving the utility-maximizing collection of goods, the consumer considers both his preferences as reflected in (diminishing) marginal-utility data and the prices of the various products. The producer is in a similar boat. He seeks that combination of resources which will provide the maximum output and, given product price, the maximum total revenue for a given money outlay, or cost. The producer obviously wants to maximize his profits, just as the consumer seeks to maximize his utility. In pursuing this combination of resources, the producer must consider both the productivity of the resource as reflected in (diminishing) marginal-physical-product data and the prices (costs) of the various resources. A firm may very well find it profitable to employ very small amounts of a highly productive resource if its price is high. Conversely, it may be sensible to hire large amounts of a relatively unproductive resource if its price is sufficiently low.

In effect two related questions face the producer in hiring resources.

1. What relative amounts, or what *proportions*, of two or more resources should be employed?

2. What *absolute amounts* of these variable resources should be hired?

These questions are analogous to those faced by a painter who wants to paint a room a very light pink. He is faced, first, with the question of combining white and red paint in the correct proportions to achieve the desired shade of pink. Should quarts of white and red paint be combined on a 2-to-1, 3-to-1, or 4-to-1 basis to get the correct shade of pink? Then, secondly, he must determine what absolute amounts of white and red will provide just enough paint to complete the room. For example, the painter may find that 3 quarts of white and 1 of red provide the right shade of pink. But then he must determine what absolute amounts of white and red

paint—6 of white to 2 of red, 9 white to 3 red, or 15 white to 5 red—will be just enough to do the room.

Resources in Best Proportions

Suppose a farmer is adding two resources—labor and capital—to a fixed amount of land. (Though we limit our discussion to just two variable resources to simplify the exposition, our analysis can readily be extended to any number of resources.) Assume, too, that the farmer purchases labor and capital competitively, so that the prices of these resources are given to him. The law of diminishing returns tells us that as labor and capital are added to a fixed amount of land, their marginal physical products will diminish beyond some point.

In what proportions, or relative amounts, should the farmer hire labor and capital? The answer is this: *The producer should allocate his money outlays on labor and capital so that the last dollar spent on each adds the same amount to his total revenue.* This rule should have a familiar ring. It is simply a variation of the utility-maximizing rule which is a cornerstone of the theory of consumer behavior. Note that the farmer is balancing the relative, or proportionate, contributions of labor and capital. That is, he is comparing and balancing the contributions of labor and capital in relation to, or in proportion to, their prices (what they cost). In simple algebraic terms the rule for employing labor and capital in the best proportion is

$$\frac{\text{Marginal revenue product of labor}}{\text{price of labor}} = \frac{\text{marginal revenue product of capital}}{\text{price of capital}} \quad (1)$$

Verbally, this equation merely says that the ratio of the MRP of any resource to its price should be the same for each variable resource employed. These two ratios simply show the amounts that the last dollars spent on labor and on capital add to the farmer's total revenue. Their equation, then, indicates that the last dollar spent on labor and the last dollar spent on capital each add the same amount to the firm's total revenue.

We can verify that this rule indicates the best relative amounts of labor and capital to employ by assuming that the farmer is initially violating the best-proportion rule and discovering that he can increase his total revenue for the same total outlay, thereby increasing his profits. To illustrate: Suppose that labor costs $10 per man per day and capital costs $20 per unit per day. Suppose, too, that labor and capital are currently being employed in such relative amounts that the MRP of the last worker hired is $20 and the MRP of the last unit of capital is $60. It is obvious that our ratios are now unequal:

$$\frac{\text{Labor MRP: \$20}}{\text{Labor price: \$10}} < \frac{\text{capital MRP: \$60}}{\text{capital price: \$20}} \quad (2)$$

The last dollar spent on labor adds $2 to the farmer's total revenue, while the last dollar spent on capital adds $3. Because capital is more profitable than labor at the margin, it will pay the farmer profitwise to substitute capital for labor.

As dollars are channeled from labor to capital, the MRP of capital will fall as the result of moving down the declining MRP schedule for capital, and the MRP of labor will rise as the farmer moves up the declining MRP schedule for labor. At some new combination of more capital and less labor, the equality of the above ratios will be restored. This may be, for example, where

$$\frac{\text{Labor MRP: \$25}}{\text{Labor price: \$10}} = \frac{\text{capital MRP: \$50}}{\text{capital price: \$20}} \quad (3)$$

Here the last dollars spent on both labor and capital contribute the same amount—$2.50—to the firm's total revenue. When this point is reached, there is no further possibility of increasing total revenue with the same total outlay by substituting between the two resources. Given the farmer's money outlay, there is no possible way for the farmer to increase profits by substituting labor for capital or capital for labor.

Resources in Best Absolute Amounts

But using labor and capital in the correct proportions does not mean that the farmer is employing these two variable resources in the right absolute amounts. Three quarts of white and one quart of red paint may provide the right shade of pink; but four quarts of paint may be too much or not enough to paint a room. If the farmer finds that he should use about three times as many units of capital as he does labor in order for the MRP of the last dollar spent on each to be equal, the question remains as to what is the best—that is, the profit-maximizing—number of units of capital and labor to employ. Stated differently, what output of product, and therefore outlay of cost, will maximize the firm's profits? Note that the problem now is not simply that of apportioning a given total outlay (cost) but that of determining what level of output, and therefore level of outlay on resources, will permit the firm to achieve the maximum attainable profit.

From our analysis of the product market we know that a firm will maximize its profits by supplying a product up to the point at which marginal revenue equals marginal cost. To produce less is to forgo profitable units of output; to produce more is to produce units of output which are simply not profitable. The problem is one of balancing how much an extra unit of *output* adds to the firm's total revenue and how much that unit adds to total costs. This same question can be readily reformulated in terms of *inputs* of resources. Because a product is produced with the use of several inputs, the question becomes one of how much each extra input of resource adds to total revenue and how much it adds to total cost. In looking at the profit-maximizing problem from the supply side of the product market, we compare the marginal revenue and marginal cost of each additional unit of output to find what level of output should be produced. In viewing the same question from the demand side of the resource market, we contrast the marginal revenue and marginal cost of *each* of the resources used in the production of that good to find how much of each should be employed. We have already found that the marginal revenue of any resource is its MRP, and its marginal cost under competitive conditions is simply the price of the resource. (Remember: When hiring resources under pure competition, resource price and marginal resource cost are equal.) By the rule for employing a resource, the firm will find it profitable to hire each variable resource up to the point at which its MRP equals its price. Glancing back at equation (3), we see that the firm is using the right relative amounts of labor and capital; that is, the last dollar spent on each adds the same amount to total revenue. We now know that this combination of labor and capital involves insufficient absolute amounts of both resources for the attainment of maximum profits. How do we know this? Because with the absolute amounts of labor and capital involved in equation (3), the MRP of each resource exceeds its price. The farmer can therefore increase his profits by hiring more of both labor and capital, because extra units of each will add more to his revenue than to his costs. When does the farmer stop adding the two resources? When the MRP of each resource equals its (constant) price. In other words, to use labor and capital in the right proportions *and* in the right absolute amounts, labor and capital should be hired up to the point where

$$\frac{\text{Labor MRP: \$10}}{\text{Labor price: \$10}} = \frac{\text{capital MRP: \$20}}{\text{capital price: \$20}} = 1 \ (4)$$

This is merely an application of the rule for employing resources to more than one resource.

The reader will readily recognize that changes in the productivity or price of either resource will tend to change both the relative and the absolute amounts of the resources which a firm will find it most profitable to employ.

SUMMARY

1. Resource prices are a major determinant of money incomes, and simultaneously perform the function of rationing resources to various industries and firms.

2. Though economists agree that resource pricing is a supply and demand phenomenon, they frequently disagree as to the exact characteristics of, and the operation of, supply and demand in particular resource markets.

3. The fact that the demand for any resource is derived from the product it helps produce correctly suggests that the demand for a resource will depend upon its productivity and the market value of the good it is producing.

4. The marginal-revenue-product schedule of any resource is the demand schedule for that resource. This follows from an application of the rule that a firm operating under competitive conditions will find it most profitable to hire a resource up to the point at which the price of the resource equals its marginal revenue product.

5. The demand curve for a resource is downsloping, because the marginal physical product of additional inputs of any resource declines in accordance with the law of diminishing returns. When a firm is selling in an imperfectly competitive market, the resource demand curve will fall, too, because product price must be reduced in order to permit the firm to sell a larger output.

6. The market demand for a resource can be derived by summing the demand curves of all firms hiring that resource.

7. The demand for a resource will change, that is, a resource demand curve will shift, as the result of **a.** a change in the demand for, and therefore the price of, the product the resource is producing, **b.** changes in the productivity of the resource due either to increases in the quantity or improvements in the quality of the resources with which a given resource is being combined, or improvements in the quality of the given resource itself, and **c.** changes in the prices of other resources.

8. A decline in the price of resource A will typically give rise to a substitution effect; that is, resource A will tend to be substituted for resources B and C. But these declines in the demand for resources B and C may be partially, wholly, or more than offset by an output effect; that is, the decrease in cost which the decline in the price of resource A entails will increase output and tend to increase the demand for resources B and C. When resources are not substitutes but are complementary, a decline in the price of resource A will increase the demand for complementary resource B.

9. The elasticity of resource demand depends upon **a.** the rate at which the marginal physical product of the resource declines, **b.** the number of good substitute resources available, **c.** the elasticity of demand for the product, and **d.** the portion of total production costs attributable to the resource.

10. A firm will employ several variable resources in the best relative amounts when the last dollar spent on each resource adds the same amount to total revenue, or, algebraically, when

$$\frac{\text{MRP of resource A}}{\text{Price of A}} = \frac{\text{MRP of resource B}}{\text{price of B}}$$
$$= \frac{\text{MRP of resource N}}{\text{price of N}}$$

These several resources will also be used in the right absolute amounts (in profit-maximizing amounts) when the MRP of each resource is equal to its price, that is, when the above ratios are equal to 1.

QUESTIONS AND STUDY SUGGESTIONS

1. Explain or define the following terms: (*a*) marginal physical product, (*b*) marginal revenue product, (*c*) marginal resource cost, (*d*) output effect, and (*e*) substitution effect.
2. Complete the following labor demand table for a firm which is hiring labor competitively and selling its product in a competitive market.

Units of labor	Total product	Marginal physical product	Product price	Total revenue	Marginal revenue product
1	17		$2	$_____	
		_____			$_____
2	31		2	_____	
		_____			_____
3	43		2	_____	
		_____			_____
4	53		2	_____	
		_____			_____
5	60		2	_____	
		_____			_____
6	65		2	_____	

a. How many workers will the firm hire if the going wage rate is $27.95? $19.95? Explain why the firm will not hire a larger or smaller number of workers at each of these wage rates.

b. Show in schedule form and graphically the labor demand curve of this firm.

c. Now redetermine the firm's demand curve for labor on the assumption that it is selling in an imperfectly competitive market and that, although it can sell 17 units at $2.20 per unit, it must lower product price by 5 cents in order to sell the marginal physical product of each successive worker. Compare this demand curve with that derived in question 2b. Explain any differences.

3. What is the significance of resource pricing? Explain in detail how the factors determining resource demand differ from those underlying product demand.

4. Explain the meaning and significance of the notion that the demand for a resource is a *derived* demand. Why do resource demand curves slope downward?

5. Distinguish between a change in resource demand and a change in the quantity of a resource demanded. What specific factors might give rise to a change in resource demand? A change in the quantity of a resource demanded?

6. Using the substitution and output effects, explain how a decline in the price of resource A *might* cause an increase in the demand for substitute resource B.

7. What factors determine the elasticity of resource demand? What effect will each of the following have upon the elasticity or the location of the demand for resource C, which is being used in the production of commodity X? Where there is any uncertainty as to the outcome, specify the causes of that uncertainty.

   a. An increase in the demand for product X.

   b. An increase in the price of substitute factor D.

   c. An increase in the number of resources which are substitutable for C in producing X.

   d. A technological improvement in the capital equipment with which resource C is combined.

   e. A decline in the price of complementary resource E.

   f. A decline in the elasticity of demand for product X due to a decline in the competitiveness of the product market.

8. Assume that a manufacturer of machine tools is employing variable resources A and B in his fixed plant in such amounts that the MRP of the last units of A and B employed are $70 and $45, respectively. Resource A can be hired at $20 and B at $15 per unit. Is the firm hiring A and B in the best relative amounts? Are the two resources being employed in the absolute amounts which will provide the firm with maximum profits? In each instance explain the precise nature of any required substitutions or changes in the absolute amounts of A and B purchased.

9. Answer question 10 at the end of Chapter 5.

SELECTED REFERENCES

Bober, M. M.: *Intermediate Price and Income Theory*, rev. ed. (New York: W. W. Norton & Company, Inc., 1962), chap. 13.

Due, John F., and Robert W. Clower: *Intermediate Economic Analysis*, 4th ed. (Homewood, Ill.: Richard D. Irwin, Inc., 1961), chap. 13.

Chamberlain, Neil W.: *The Labor Sector* (New York: McGraw-Hill Book Company, 1965), chaps. 17 and 18.

Heneman, Herbert G., Jr., and Dale Yoder: *Labor Economics*, 2d ed. (Cincinnati: South-Western Publishing Company, 1965), chaps. 5 and 21.

Hyde, Francis E., et al.: *A New Prospect of Economics* (Liverpool: Liverpool University Press, 1958), chap. 7.

CHAPTER 31

THE PRICING AND
EMPLOYMENT OF RESOURCES:
WAGE DETERMINATION

Armed with some understanding of the strategic factors underlying resource demand, we must now combine this information with the supply situations which characterize the markets for labor, land, capital, and entrepreneurial ability to see how wages, rents, interest, and profits are determined. For two reasons we discuss wage rates prior to other resource prices.

1. The marginal-productivity explanation of resource demand is probably more applicable to an explanation of wage rates than it is to the pricing of other resources.

2. To most households the wage rate is the most important price in the economy; it is the sole or basic source of income. At least two-thirds of the national income is in the form of wages and salaries.

Our basic objectives in discussing wage determination are fourfold:

1. To understand the forces underlying the general level of wage rates in the United States.

2. To see how wage rates are determined in particular labor markets and therefore to discuss several representative labor market models.

3. To explain wage differentials.

4. To raise a question: What effect, if any, do wage changes have upon employment?

Throughout this chapter we shall rely upon the marginal-productivity theory of Chapter 30 as an explanation of labor demand.

MEANING OF WAGES

Wages, or wage rates, are the price paid for the use of labor. Economists often employ the term "labor" broadly to apply to the payments received by (1) workers in the narrow sense of the term, that is, blue- and white-collar workers of infinite variety, (2) professional people—physicians, lawyers, dentists, teachers, and so forth, and (3) small-business men—barbers, plumbers, television repairmen, and a host of retailers—for the labor services they provide in operating their own businesses. This broad definition of labor, incidentally, encompasses individuals who would be considered as profit receivers in national income accounting. Hence, under this definition, wages would clearly amount to more than two-thirds of the national income.

Though in practice wages may take the form of bonuses, royalties, commissions, and monthly salaries, we shall use the term "wages" to mean wage rates per unit of time—per hour, per day, and so forth. This designation has the advantage of reminding us that the wage rate is a price paid for the use of units of labor service. It also permits us to distinguish clearly between "wages" and "earnings," the latter depending upon wage rates and the number of hours or weeks of labor service supplied in the market. It is important, too, to make a distinction between money wages and real wages. *Money wages* are simply the amount of money received per hour, per day, per week, and so forth. *Real wages,* on the other hand, are the quantity of goods and services which one can obtain with his money wages; real wages are the "purchasing power" of money wages. Obviously one's real wages depend upon his money wages and the prices of the goods and services he buys. Note that money wages and real wages need not move together. For example, money wages may rise and real wages simultaneously decline if product prices rise more rapidly than do money wages. Unless otherwise indicated, our discussion will be couched in terms of real wage rates by making the simple assumption that the level of product prices is constant.

GENERAL LEVEL OF WAGES

Wages tend to differ among nations, among regions, among various occupations, and among individuals. Wage rates are vastly higher in the United States than in China or India; wage rates are generally higher in the North and East of the United States than in the South; plumbers are paid more than cotton pickers; physician Abrams may earn three times as much as physician Bennett for the same number of hours of work.

Our approach will involve moving from the general to the specific. In this section we are concerned with explaining why the general level of wages is higher in the United States than in foreign nations. This explanation will be largely applicable to regional wage differences within nations. In the following section we seek to explain wages in terms of markets for specific types of labor. In both these discussions a supply and demand approach will offer the most fruitful results.

The general level of wages, like the general level of prices, is a composite concept encompassing a wide range of different specific wage rates. This admittedly vague concept is a useful point of departure in making and explaining international and interregional wage comparisons. Statistical data indicate that the general level of real wages in the United States is higher than that of any other nation. The simplest explanation of this fact is that in the United States the demand for labor has been great in relation to the supply.

Let us look behind these forces of demand and supply. We know that the demand for labor—or any other resource—depends upon its productivity. The greater the productivity of labor, the greater the demand for it. And, given the total supply of labor, the stronger the demand, the greater the level of real wages. The demand for American labor has been high because American labor is highly productive. But why the high productivity? The reasons are several:

1. American workers are used in conjunction with large amounts of capital equipment. For example, the average American worker in manufacturing is assisted by some $24,000 worth of machinery and equipment.

2. Natural resources are very abundant in relation to the size of the labor force. The United States is richly endowed with arable land, basic mineral resources, and ample sources of industrial power.

3. The level of technological advance is generally higher in the United States than in foreign nations. American workers in most industries not only use more capital equipment but better, that is, technologically superior, equipment than do foreign workers. Similarly, work methods are steadily being improved through detailed scientific study and research.

4. The health, vigor, education and training, work attitudes, and adaptability of American workers to the discipline of factory production are generally superior to those of the labor of other nations. This means that, even with the same quantity and quality of natural and capital resources, American workers typically would be somewhat more efficient than their foreign brethren.

5. Less tangible yet important items underlying the high productivity of American labor are (*a*) the efficiency and flexibility

of American management, (*b*) a business, social, and political environment which puts great emphasis upon production and productivity, and (*c*) the vast size of the domestic market, which provides the opportunity for firms to realize mass-production economies.

The reader will recall that the aforementioned factors are merely a restatement of the cornerstones. of economic growth

(Chapter 20). It is also. notable that the productivity of labor depends to a very great degree upon considerations other than the quality of labor itself. A worker's productivity is determined largely by the quantity and quality of the property resources at his disposal.

The dependence of real hourly wages upon the level of productivity is indicated in Figure 31–1. Note the close relationship in

FIGURE 31–1. OUTPUT PER HOUR AND REAL AVERAGE HOURLY EARNINGS.
Over a long period of years there has been a close relationship between real hourly wages and output per man-hour in nonfarm private industries. [*Economic Report of the President* (Washington, D.C., 1964), p. 89.]

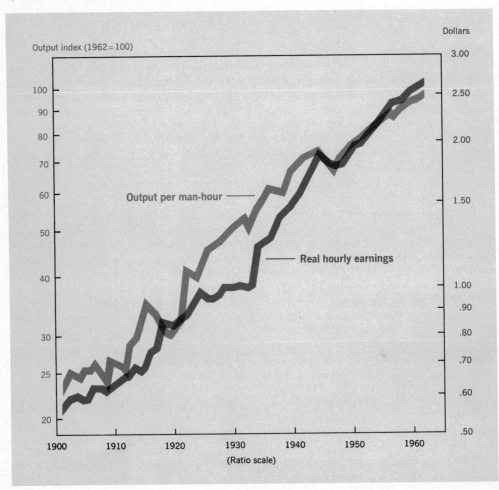

the long run between real hourly wages and output per man-hour in nonfarm private industries. When one recalls that real income and real output are two ways of viewing the same thing, it is no surprise that income per worker can only increase at about the same rate as output per worker.

But simple supply and demand analysis suggests that, even if the demand for labor is strong in the United States, increases in the supply or labor will cause the general level of wages to decline over time. It is certainly true that the American population and the labor force have grown significantly over the decades. However, these increases in the supply of labor have been more than offset by increases in the demand for labor

stemming from the productivity-increasing factors discussed above. The result has been a long-run, or secular, increase in wage rates as suggested by Figure 31–2.

WAGES IN PARTICULAR LABOR MARKETS

We now turn from the general level of wages to the wage structure, that is, to the system of specific wage rates which the general level of wages comprises. The question now is this: What determines the wage rate received by some specific type of worker? Demand and supply analysis again provides the most revealing approach. Our analysis covers some half dozen basic market models.

FIGURE 31–2. THE SECULAR TREND OF REAL WAGES IN THE UNITED STATES.
The productivity of American labor has increased substantially in the long run, causing the demand for labor to increase in relation to the supply. The result has been increases in real wages.

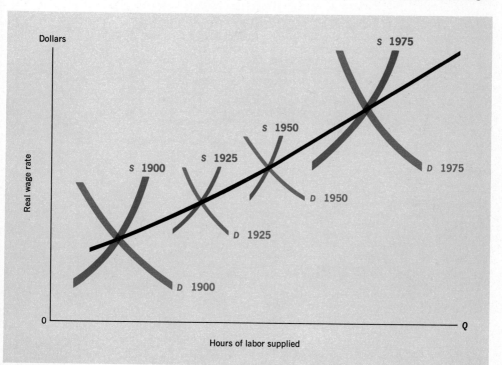

Competitive Model

Let us suppose that there are many—say, 200—firms demanding a particular type of semiskilled or skilled labor.[1] The total, or market, demand for this labor can be determined by summing the labor demand curves (the MRP curves) of the individual firms as suggested in Figure 31–3a and b. On the supply side of the picture we assume there is no union; workers compete freely for available jobs. The supply curve for a particular

[1] These firms need not be in the same industry; industries are defined in terms of the products they produce and not the resources they employ. Thus firms producing unupholstered furniture, window and door frames, and cabinets will all demand carpenters.

type of labor will be upsloping, reflecting the fact that, in the absence of unemployment, hiring firms as a group will be forced to pay higher wage rates to obtain more workers. Why? Because the firms must bid these workers away from other industries and other localities. Within limits workers have alternative job opportunities; that is, they may work in other industries in the same locality, or they may work in their present occupations in different cities or states. In a full-employment economy the group of firms in this particular labor market must pay higher and higher wage rates to attract this type of labor away from these alternative job opportunities.

The equilibrium wage rate and the equilibrium level of employment for this type of labor are obviously determined by the inter-

FIGURE 31–3. THE SUPPLY OF, AND DEMAND FOR, LABOR TO A SINGLE COMPETITIVE FIRM (a) AND IN A COMPETITIVE MARKET (b).
In a competitive labor market the equilibrium wage rate W_c and number of workers employed Q_c are determined by supply SS and demand DD, as shown in (b). Because this wage rate is given to the individual firm hiring in the market, its labor supply curve, $S = MRC$, is perfectly elastic as in (a). The firm finds it most profitable to hire workers up to the MRP = MRC point.

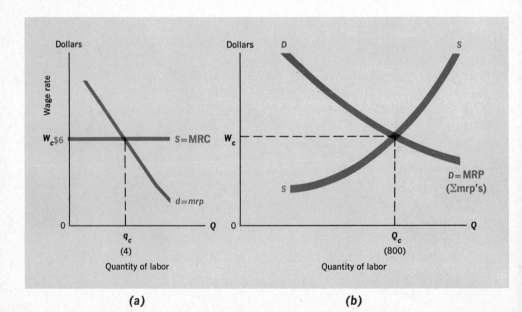

(a)   (b)

section of the labor demand and labor supply curves. In Figure 31–3b the equilibrium wage rate is W_c ($6), and the number of workers hired is Q_c (800). To the individual firm the wage rate W_c is given. Each of the many hiring firms employs such a small fraction of the total available supply of this type of labor that none can influence the wage rate. Technically, the supply of labor is perfectly elastic to the individual firm, as shown by S in Figure 31–3a. Each individual firm will find it profitable to hire workers up to the point at which the going wage rate is equal to labor's MRP. This is merely an application of the MRP = MRC rule developed in Chapter 30. (Indeed, the demand curve in Figure 31–3a is based upon Table 30–1.) As Table 31–1 indicates, if the resource price is given to the individual firm, the marginal cost of that resource (MRC) will be constant and equal to resource price. In this case the wage rate and hence the marginal cost of labor are constant to the individual firm. Each additional worker hired adds precisely his wage rate to the firm's total resource cost. The firm then will maximize its profits by hiring workers to the point at which their wage rate and therefore

marginal resource cost equal their marginal revenue product. In Figure 31–3a the "typical" firm will hire q_c (4) workers.

Monopsony Model

But in many labor markets workers are not hired competitively. Rather, employers are *monopsonists;* that is, they have some monopolistic buying power. In some instances the monopsonistic power of employers is virtually complete in the sense that there is only one major employer in a labor market. For example, the economies of some towns and cities depend almost entirely upon one major firm. A silver mining concern may be the basic source of employment in a remote Colorado town. A New England textile mill, a Wisconsin paper mill, or a farm-belt food processor may provide a large proportion of the employment in its locality. In other cases *oligopsony* may prevail; three or four firms may each hire a large portion of the supply of labor in a particular market. Our study of oligopoly correctly suggests that there is a strong tendency for oligopsonists to act in concert—much like a monopsonist—in hiring labor.

TABLE 31–1. THE SUPPLY OF LABOR: PURE COMPETITION IN THE HIRE OF LABOR (hypothetical data)

(1) Units of labor	(2) Wage rate	(3) Total labor cost (wage bill)	(4) Marginal resource (labor) cost
1	$6	$ 6	
			$6
2	6	12	
			6
3	6	18	
			6
4	6	24	
			6
5	6	30	
			6
6	6	36	

The important point is this: When a firm hires a considerable portion of the total available supply of a particular type of labor, his decision to employ more or fewer workers will affect the wage rate paid to that labor. Specifically, if a firm is large in relation to the labor market, it will have to pay a higher wage rate in order to obtain more labor. For simplicity's sake let us suppose there is only one employer of a particular type of labor in a specified geographic area. Obviously, the labor supply curve to that firm and the total supply curve for the labor market are identical. This supply curve, for reasons already made clear, is upsloping, indicating that the firm must pay a higher wage rate to attract more workers. This is shown by SS in Figure 31–4. The supply curve is in effect the average-cost-of-labor curve from the firm's point of view; each point on it indicates the wage rate (cost) per worker which must be paid to attract the corresponding number of workers.

But the higher wages involved in attracting additional workers will also have to be paid to all workers currently employed at lower wage rates. If not, labor morale will surely deteriorate, and the employer will be

FIGURE 31–4. THE WAGE RATE AND LEVEL OF EMPLOYMENT IN A MONOPSONISTIC LABOR MARKET.

In a monopsonistic labor market the employer's marginal resource (labor) cost curve (MRC) lies above the labor supply curve (S). Equating MRC with labor demand MRP at point b, the monopsonist will hire Q_m workers (as compared to Q_c under competition) and pay the wage rate W_m (as compared to the competitive wage W_c).

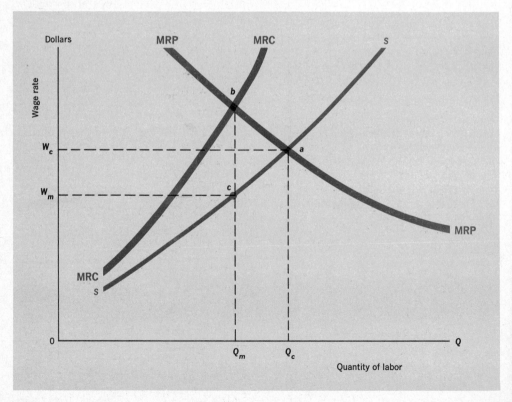

plagued with serious problems of labor unrest because of the wage-rate differentials existing for the same job. Costwise the payment of a uniform wage to all workers will mean that the cost of an extra worker—the marginal resource (labor) cost (MRC)—will exceed the wage rate by the amount necessary to bring the wage rate of all workers currently employed up to the new wage level. Table 31–2 illustrates this point. One worker can be hired at a wage rate of $6. But the hire of a second worker forces the firm to pay a higher wage rate of $7. Marginal resource (labor) cost is $8—the $7 paid the second worker plus a $1 raise for the first worker. Similarly, the marginal labor cost of the third worker is $10—the $8 which must be paid to attract him from alternative employments plus $1 raises for the first two workers. The important point is that to the monopsonist marginal resource (labor) cost will exceed the wage rate. Graphically, the MRC curve (columns 1 and 4 in Table 31–2) will lie above the average cost, or supply, curve of labor (columns 1 and 2 in Table 31–2). This is shown graphically in Figure 31–4. How much labor will the firm hire, and what wage rate will it pay? To maximize profits the firm will equate mar-

ginal resource (labor) cost with the MRP. The number of workers hired by the monopsonist is indicated by Q_m, and the wage rate paid, W_m, is indicated by the corresponding point on the resource supply, or average-cost-of-labor, curve. It is particularly important to contrast these results with those which a competitive labor market would have yielded. With competition in the hire of labor the level of employment would have been greater (Q_c), and the wage rate would have been higher (W_c). It simply does not pay the monopsonist to hire workers up to the point at which the wage rate and labor's MRP are equal. Other things being equal, he maximizes his profits by hiring a smaller number of workers and thereby paying a less than competitive wage rate. In the process society gets a smaller output,[2] and workers get a wage rate less by bc than their marginal revenue product. Just as a monopolistic seller finds it profitable to restrict product

[2] This is analogous to the monopolist's restricting output as he sets product price and output on the basis of marginal revenue, not product demand. In this instance resource price is set on the basis of marginal labor cost, not resource supply.

TABLE 31–2. THE SUPPLY OF LABOR: MONOPSONY IN THE HIRE OF LABOR
(hypothetical data)

(1) Units of labor	(2) Wage rate	(3) Total labor cost (wage bill)	(4) Marginal resource (labor) cost
			$ 6
1	$ 6	$ 6	
			8
2	7	14	
			10
3	8	24	
			12
4	9	36	
			14
5	10	50	
			16
6	11	66	

output to realize an above-competitive price for his goods, so the monopsonistic employer of resources finds it profitable to restrict employment so as to depress wage rates and therefore costs, that is, to realize below-competitive wage rates.

Will a monopsonistic employer also be a monopolistic seller in the product market? Not necessarily. The New England textile mill may be a monopsonistic employer yet face severe domestic and foreign competition in selling its product. In other cases—for example, the automobile and steel industries—firms have both monopsonistic and monopolistic (oligopolistic) power. How does the presence of monopoly or oligopoly power affect our analysis of a monopsonistic labor market? Through the labor demand curve. If the monopsonistic employer is also a restrictive monopoly or oligopoly, we can expect the resource demand curve of Figure 31–4 to be depressed. The result will be a wage rate even lower than W_m and a volume of employment less than Q_m. On the other hand, a progressive monopoly or oligopoly may entail a resource demand curve to the right of that shown in Figure 31–4, with the result that the wage rate and level of employment will exceed W_m and Q_m. In short, monopoly (oligopoly) power will depress or increase labor demand, depending upon whether the monopoly is restrictive or progressive.

Some Union Models

Thus far we have been content to assume that workers are actively competing in the sale of their labor services. In a good many markets workers sell their labor services collectively through unions. To envision the economic impact of unions in the simplest context, let us suppose a union is formed in an otherwise competitive labor market. That is, a union is now bargaining with a relatively large number of employers. Later we shall consider the case where the union faces a large single employer.

Unions seek many goals. Their basic objective, however, is to raise wage rates. The union can pursue this objective in several different ways.

Increasing the demand for labor. The most desirable technique for raising wage rates from the union's point of view is to increase the demand for labor. As shown in Figure 31–5, an increase in the demand for labor will result in both higher wage rates and a larger number of jobs. The relative sizes of these increases will depend upon the elasticity of labor supply. Classic examples are the International Ladies' Garment Workers Union and the Amalgamated Clothing Workers Union, both of which have positively assisted clothing firms to increase their productivity. The New York locals of the ILGWU have even assisted employers in financing advertising campaigns to bolster the demand for their products. And it is no accident that some unions have vigorously supported their employers in seeking to maintain protective tariffs designed to exclude competing foreign products. The American Watch Workers Union is a case in point. Some unions have sought to expand the demand for labor by forcing make-work, or "featherbedding," rules upon employers. The Railway Brotherhoods force railroads to hire train crews of a certain minimum size; diesel engines must have a fireman even though there is no fire.

But the opportunity for unions to increase the demand for labor is limited. The main reason is obvious: As noted in our earlier discussion of the general level of wages, the basic forces underlying the productivity and therefore the demand for labor are largely outside the control of labor unions. The quantity and quality of the capital equipment with which labor is combined are the basic determinant of labor productivity in most firms, and this is a matter over which unions typically have little or no control. It should be noted, too, that in many of the instances in which unions have pleaded for tariff protection and have practiced featherbedding, the situation has been that of a

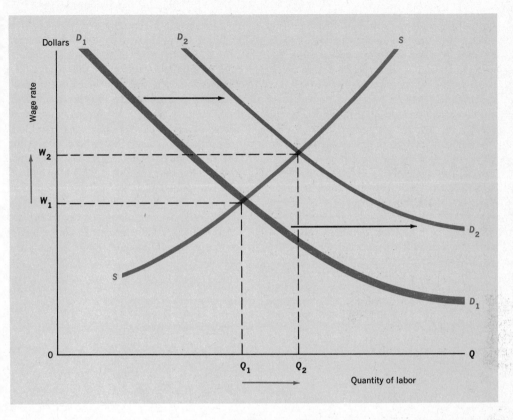

FIGURE 31–5. UNIONS AND THE DEMAND FOR LABOR.
When unions can increase the demand for labor (D_1D_1 to D_2D_2), higher wage rates
(W_1 to W_2) and a larger number of jobs (Q_1 to Q_2) can be realized.

union's attempting to forestall anticipated declines in the demand for labor rather than actually increasing the existing demand for a particular type of labor. This comment seems pertinent to the watchmakers and the Railway Brotherhoods, both of which find themselves in the unfortunate position of being employed in declining industries. In view of these comments it is not surprising that union efforts to increase wage rates have concentrated upon the supply side of the market.

Exclusive or craft unionism. Unions may boost wage rates by reducing the supply of labor, that is, by shifting the supply curve of a particular type of labor to the left. Historically, the labor movement has favored

policies designed to restrict the supply of labor to the economy as a whole in order to bolster the general level of wages. Labor unions have supported legislation which has (1) restricted immigration, (2) reduced child labor, (3) encouraged compulsory retirement, (4) enforced a shorter work week, and so forth.

More relevant for present purposes is the fact that specific types of workers have adopted through unions a host of techniques designed to restrict their numbers. This has been especially true of *craft unions*—that is, unions that comprise workers of a given skill, such as carpenters, bricklayers, plumbers, and printers. These unions have in many instances forced employers to agree to hire only union workers, thereby giving the union virtually complete control of the supply of labor. Then, by following restrictive membership policies—long apprenticeships, exorbitant initiation fees, the limitation or flat prohibition of new members—the union causes an artificial restriction of the labor supply. As indicated in Figure 31–6, this results in higher wage rates. For obvious reasons this approach to achieving wage increases might be called "exclusive" unionism. Higher wages are the result of excluding workers from the union and therefore from the supply of labor.

Inclusive or industrial unionism. Most unions, however, do not attempt to limit their membership. On the contrary, they seek to organize all available or potential workers. This is characteristic of the so-called *industrial unions*—unions such as the automobile workers and steelworkers which include all unskilled, semiskilled, and even skilled workers in a given industry. A union can afford to be exclusive when its members are skilled craftsmen for whom substitute workers are not readily available in quantity. But a union that comprises largely unskilled and semiskilled workers will undermine its own existence by limiting its membership and thereby causing numerous highly substitutable nonunion workers to be readily available for employment.

FIGURE 31–6. EXCLUSIVE OR CRAFT UNIONISM.
By reducing the supply of labor (S_1S_1 to S_2S_2) through the use of restrictive membership policies, exclusive unions achieve higher wage rates (W_1 to W_2). However, the restriction of labor supply also reduces the number of workers employed (Q_1 to Q_2).

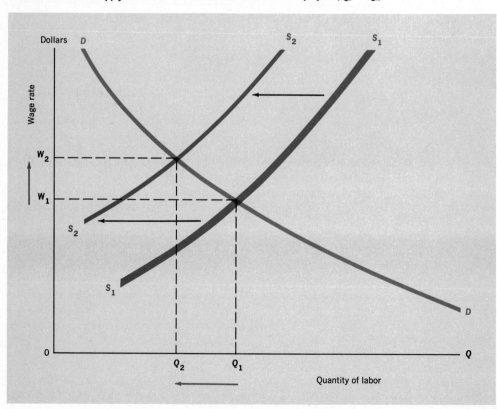

If an industrial union is successful in including virtually all workers in its membership, firms will be under great pressure to come to terms at the wage rate demanded by the union. Why? Because the union can obviously deprive the firm of its entire labor supply.

Inclusive unionism is illustrated graphically in Figure 31–7. Initially the competitive equilibrium wage rate is W_c, and the level of employment is Q_c. Now an industrial union is formed, and it imposes a higher, above-equilibrium wage rate of, say, W_u. The imposition of this wage rate changes the supply curve of labor to the firms from

the pre-union SS curve to the post-union $W_u aS$ curve shown by the heavy line.[3] No workers will be forthcoming at a wage rate

[3] Technically, the imposition of the wage rate W_u makes the labor supply curve perfectly elastic over the $W_u a$ range in Figure 31–7. If employers hire any number of workers within this range, the union-imposed wage rate is effective and must be paid, or the union will supply no labor at all—the employers will be faced with a strike. If the employers want a number of workers in excess of $W_u a$ (which they never will when the union sets an above-equilibrium wage rate), they will have to bid up wages above the union's minimum.

FIGURE 31–7. INCLUSIVE OR INDUSTRIAL UNIONISM.
By organizing virtually all available workers and thereby controlling the supply of labor, inclusive industrial unions may impose a wage rate, such as W_u, which is above the competitive wage W_c. The effect is to change the labor supply curve from SS to $W_u aS$. At the W_u wage rate employers will cut employment from Q_c to Q_u.

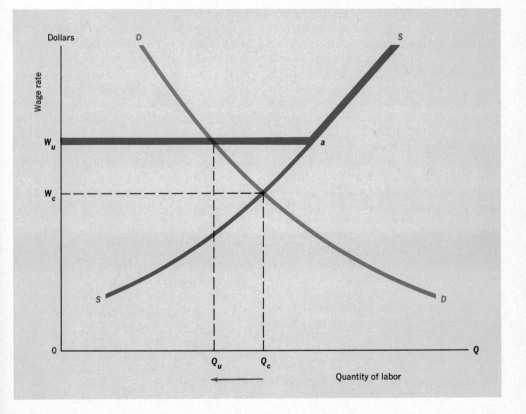

less than that demanded by the union. If the employers decide it is better to pay this higher wage rate than to suffer a strike, they will cut back on employment from Q_c to Q_u. In other words, the above-equilibrium wage rate will cause some unemployment of union workers in this particular labor market.

Needless to say, this unemployment effect constitutes an important restraining influence upon the union in formulating its wage demands. A union cannot expect to maintain the solidarity of its members if it seeks a wage rate so high that the result will be joblessness for 20, 30, or 40 per cent of its members. The elasticity of labor demand is the basic consideration in determining the amount of unemployment which will accompany a wage hike: The more inelastic the demand for labor, the smaller will be the resulting unemployment. You will recall from Chapter 30 that the determinants of the elasticity of labor demand include the elasticity of demand for the product, the portion of total costs for which wages account, and the substitutability of other resources for labor. It is notable that substitutability and hence elasticity vary directly with time. That is, over a short period of time—say a few weeks or months—a firm may hire about the same number of workers after a pay hike as it did before. But then, as the months pass, employers have sufficient time to substitute laborsaving capital equipment for workers. The practical significance of this is that, as substitution occurs, workers will be *gradually* unemployed and typically will drift into other jobs and other geographic areas. And with the absence of job opportunities new workers entering the labor force will be discouraged from entering this line of work. For these reasons the unemployment restraint upon union wage demands may be less pressing than it first appears to be. Even though industrial unions encourage rather than restrict membership, there is clearly a restrictive aspect to this analysis. But in contrast to the practices of exclusive unionism the restriction of employment is here made

not by directly influencing labor supply but by enforcing an above-equilibrium wage rate and allowing the market to restrict the number of jobs available.

The United Mine Workers provide an excellent illustration of how an industrial union can achieve substantial wage increases, but only at the cost of a reduction in the number of jobs the industry has to offer. The UMW has clearly done an outstanding job of raising wage rates for miners. In January, 1965, the average weekly earnings of bituminous coal workers were $138.80 as compared to $105.93 for all manufacturing industries. However, employment in January, 1965, stood at only 133,000 in bituminous coal as compared to a peak figure of almost 705,000 in 1923. There is little doubt that UMW wage pressure has been a major cause of this decline in the number of jobs. Labor costs constitute about 70 per cent of total costs in bituminous coal production. Hence, union-imposed wage increases have increased the total cost of coal sharply in relation to those of oil and gas, causing a sharp drop in coal output and in the number of jobs the industry can offer. Simultaneously, the increased cost of labor has accelerated the substitution of machinery for labor, causing further diminutions in the number of miners employed. The UMW has explicitly taken the position that the fattening of pay envelopes which it has brought about more than compensates for the sacrifice of jobs that these high wages have entailed.[4]

Bilateral Monopoly Model

Now let us suppose that a union is formed in a labor market that is not competitive but monopsonistic. Let us assume further that the union is a strong industrial union. In

[4] See Gordon F. Bloom and Herbert R. Northrup, *Economics of Labor Relations*, 3d ed. (Homewood, Ill.: Richard D. Irwin, Inc., 1958), pp. 389–392.

other words, let us combine the monopsony model with the inclusive unionism model. The result is a case of *bilateral monopoly*. The union is a monopolistic "seller" of labor, in that it can exert an influence over wage rates; it faces a monopsonistic employer (or combination of oligopsonistic employers) of labor who can also affect wages. Is this an extreme or special case? Not at all. In such important industries as steel, automobiles, meat packing, and farm machinery, "big labor"—one huge industrial union—bargains with "big business"—a few huge industrial giants.

This situation can be shown graphically as in Figure 31–8, which merely superimposes Figure 31–7 upon 31–4. The monopsonistic employer will seek the wage rate W_m and the union presumably will press for some above-equilibrium wage rate such as W_u. Which of these two outcomes will result? We cannot say with any certainty. The outcome is logically indeterminate in the sense that economic theory does not explain what the resulting wage rate will be. We should expect the resulting wage to lie somewhere between W_m and W_u. Beyond that, about all we can say is that the party with the most bargaining power and the most effective bargaining strategy will be able to

FIGURE 31–8. BILATERAL MONOPOLY IN THE LABOR MARKET.
When a monopsonistic employer seeks the wage rate W_m and the inclusive union he faces seeks an above-equilibrium wage rate such as W_u, the actual outcome is logically indeterminate.

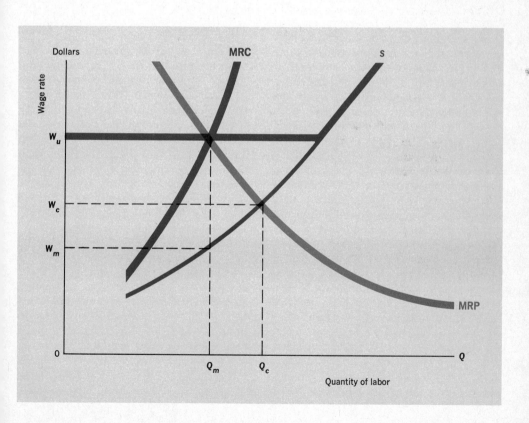

get his opponent to agree to a wage close to that which he seeks.[5]

These comments suggest another important feature of the bilateral monopoly model. The kind of labor market we are here describing may be an important manifestation of countervailing power. If either the union or management prevailed in this market—that is, if the actual wage rate were determined at W_u or W_m—employment would be restricted to Q_m, which is obviously below the competitive level. But now let us suppose the countervailing power of the union roughly offsets the original monopsony power of management and a bargained wage rate of about W_c, which is the competitive wage, is agreed upon. Once management agrees to this wage rate, its incentive to restrict employment disappears; no longer can the employer depress wage rates by restricting employment. Thus management equates the bargained wage rate W_c (= MWC) with MRP and finds it most profitable to hire Q_c workers. In short, with monopoly on both sides of the labor market it may be possible that the resulting wage rate and level of employment will be closer to competitive levels than if monopoly existed on only one side of the market.

Do Unions Raise Wages?

Consideration of the three union models and the bilateral monopoly model raises an interesting question: Do unions actually raise wages? This is not an easy question to answer conclusively because empirical studies of relative wage gains in organized and unorganized industries or areas are subject to severe obstacles and shortcomings. Analysis of a number of detailed studies would suggest, however, that unions have probably achieved a 10 to 15 per cent wage advantage

for their members as compared with non-union workers.[6] Although this is not an insignificant accomplishment, the advantage is not so large as to imply that the formation of unions and the determination of wages through collective bargaining somehow permit labor to break free of market restraints and to establish wage rates largely at their discretion.

WAGE DIFFERENTIALS

We have discussed the general level of wages and the role of supply and demand in a series of specific labor market situations. Yet to be explained are the wage differences which persist between different occupations and different individuals in the same occupations. Why does a corporate executive or a movie star receive $200,000 per year while garbage collectors and retail clerks get a paltry $2,000 per year? Table 31–3 indicates the substantial wage differentials which exist among certain common occupational groups. Our problem is to explain these differences.

Once again the forces of supply and demand provide a general answer. If the supply of a particular type of labor is very great in relation to the demand for it, the resulting wage rate will be low. But if demand is great and the supply very small, wages will be very high. Though a good starting point, this supply and demand explanation is not particularly revealing. We want to know *why* supply and demand conditions differ in various labor markets. To do this we must probe those factors which lie behind the supply and demand of particular types of labor.

If (1) all workers were homogeneous, (2) all jobs were equally attractive to workers, and (3) labor markets were perfectly competitive, all workers would receive precisely the same wage rate. As such, this is not a particularly startling statement. It merely

---

[5] Economists are now actively developing a number of bargaining theories. The ambitious reader should consult Carl M. Stevens, *Strategy and Collective Bargaining Negotiation* (New York: McGraw-Hill Book Company, 1963).

[6] Albert Rees, *The Economics of Trade Unions* (Chicago: The University of Chicago Press, 1962), p. 79.

TABLE 31–3. AVERAGE HOURLY AND WEEKLY EARNINGS IN SELECTED INDUSTRIES, JANUARY, 1965

Industry	Average hourly gross earnings	Average weekly gross earnings
Contract construction	$3.62	$131.41
Bituminous coal	3.47	138.80
Motor vehicles	3.31	149.28
Petroleum refining	3.24	133.81
Printing and publishing	3.00	114.60
Chemicals	2.84	117.86
Fabricated metals	2.72	113.42
Food products	2.44	99.55
Retail trade	1.92	70.85
Apparel and finished textiles	1.81	65.16
Laundries	1.47	56.60

Source: Monthly Labor Review, May, 1965.

suggests that, in an economy having one type of labor and in effect one type of job, competition will result in a single wage rate for all workers. The statement is important in that it does suggest the reasons why wage rates do differ in practice. (1) Workers are not homogeneous. They differ in capacities and in training and, as a result, fall into noncompeting occupational groups. (2) Jobs vary in attractiveness; the nonmonetary aspects of various jobs are not the same. (3) Labor markets are typically characterized by imperfections.

Noncompeting Groups

Workers are not homogeneous; they differ tremendously in their mental and physical capacities and in their education and training. Hence, at any point in time the labor force can be thought of as falling into a number of *noncompeting groups,* each of which may be composed of several or possibly just one occupation for which the members of this group qualify. For example, a relatively small number of workers have the ability—the capacity and the training— to be brain surgeons, concert violinists, and research chemists. Few people have the

inherent capacity to enter these occupations, and even fewer have the financial means of acquiring the necessary training. The result is obviously that the supplies of these particular types of labor are very small in relation to the demand for them and the resulting wages and salaries are high. These and similar groups do not compete with each other or with other skilled or semiskilled workers. The violinist does not compete with the surgeon, nor does the garbage collector or retail clerk compete with either the violinist or the surgeon.

This is not to say that each of the thousands of specific occupations in the United States constitutes a noncompeting group of workers or that workers fall into isolated occupational compartments. A number of unskilled or semiskilled occupations may well fall into one noncompeting group. For example, gasoline station attendants, farm hands, and unskilled construction workers may all fall into the same group, because each is capable of doing the others' jobs. Yet none of the workers in this group currently offer severe competition for printers or electricians, who find themselves in other, more exclusive groups.

It should be noted, too, that the lack of

competition between noncompeting groups of workers is actually a matter of degree. *Within limits* unskilled construction workers can be substituted for printers and electricians. Furthermore, this substitutability will be greater over a period of time than it will be in the short run; over time workers may move from one noncompeting group to another as they are able to develop their native capacities through education and training. The assembly-line worker who has an IQ of 140 may become an accountant or lawyer by going to night school. But here another obstacle arises: education is a costly business. Our ambitious but low-income laborer does not have the same opportunity of entering the higher-paid occupational groups as do the offspring of the lawyers and accountants who are already in those groups. And, needless to say, differences in inherent capacities provide an even more permanent obstacle to occupational mobility. In short, both native capacity and the opportunity to train oneself are unequally distributed, causing the wage differentials of noncompeting groups to persist.

The concept of noncompeting groups is a flexible one; it can be applied to various subgroups and even to specific individuals in a given group. Some especially skilled surgeons are able to command wages considerably in excess of their run-of-the-mill colleagues who perform the same operations. Mickey Mantle, Willie Mays, and a few others demand and get salaries many times that of the average major-league ballplayer. Why? Because in each instance their colleagues are only imperfect substitutes.

Equalizing Differences

Now if a group of workers in a particular noncompeting group are equally capable of performing several different jobs, one might expect that the wage rate would be identical for each of these jobs. But this is not the case. A group of high school graduates may be equally capable of becoming bank clerks or unskilled construction workers. But these jobs pay different wages. In virtually all localities construction laborers receive better wages than do beginning bank clerks.

These differences can be explained on the basis of the *nonmonetary aspects* of the two jobs. The construction job involves dirty hands, a sore back, the hazard of accidents, and irregular employment both seasonally and cyclically. The banking job entails a white shirt, pleasant air-conditioned surroundings, and little fear of injury or layoff. Other things being equal, it is easy to see why workers will prefer picking up a deposit slip rather than a shovel. The result is that construction contractors must pay higher wages than banks to compensate for the unattractive nonmonetary aspects of construction jobs. These wage differentials are sometimes called *equalizing differences,* because they must be paid to compensate for the nonmonetary differences in various jobs.

Market Imperfections

The notion of noncompeting groups helps explain wage differentials between different jobs for which limited numbers of workers are qualified. Equalizing differences aid in understanding wage differentials on different jobs for which workers in the same noncompeting group are equally qualified. Market imperfections in the form of various immobilities help explain wage differences paid on identical jobs.

1. Geographic immobilities. Workers take root geographically. They are reluctant to leave friends, relatives, and associates, to force their children to change schools, to sell their houses, and to incur the costs and inconveniences of adjusting to a new job and a new community. Geographical mobility is likely to be particularly low for older workers who have seniority rights and substantial claims to pension payments upon retirement. Then, too, workers who may be willing to move may simply be ignorant of job opportunities and wage rates in other geographic areas. As Adam Smith noted almost two centuries ago, ". . . a man is of all sorts of luggage the most difficult to be transported."

2. Artificial institutional immobilities. Geographic immobilities may be reinforced by artificial restrictions on mobility which are imposed by institutions. In particular, we have already noted that craft unions find it to their advantage to restrict their membership. After all, if carpenters and bricklayers become plentiful, the wages they can command will decline. Thus the low-paid nonunion carpenter of Brush, Colorado, may be willing to move to Chicago in the pursuit of higher wages. But his chances of successfully doing so are slim. He will be unable to get a union card, and no card, no job. The professions impose similar artificial restraints. For example, at most universities individuals lacking advanced degrees are simply not considered for employment as teachers. Quite apart from one's competence as a teacher and command of the subject matter, a "union card"—an M.A. or Ph.D.—is the first requisite for employment.

3. Sociological immobilities. Finally, we must acknowledge sociological immobilities. Despite recent regulatory legislation to the contrary, women workers frequently receive less pay than men working at the same job. Negroes, Mexicans, Jews, and other minority groups are often forced to accept lower wages on given jobs than fellow workers receive.

A final point: It is more than likely that all three considerations—noncompeting groups, equalizing differences, and market imperfections—will play a role in the explanation of actual wage differentials. For example, the differential between the wages of a physician and a construction worker are largely explainable on the basis of noncompeting groups. Physicians fall into a noncompeting group where, because of mental and financial requisites to entry, the supply of labor is small in relation to demand, and wages are

therefore high. In construction work, where mental and financial prerequisites are much less significant, the supply of labor is great in relation to demand and wages low as compared to those of physicians. However, were it not for the unpleasantness of the construction worker's job and the fact that his craft union pursues restrictive membership policies, the differential would probably be even greater than it is.

EFFECT OF WAGE CHANGES ON EMPLOYMENT

Thus far we have been concerned with explaining the general level of wages, wage rates in particular labor markets, and the reasons why wage rates might differ between specific labor markets. Emphasis has been largely placed upon wage rates apart from any detailed consideration of accompanying levels of employment. We must now examine the relationship between wage rates and employment. In so doing, it is crucial to distinguish between an individual firm's or industry's demand for a particular type of labor and the demand for labor of the economy as a whole.

Single Firm or Industry

The fact that a particular firm's demand curve for labor is downsloping correctly suggests that, *given its demand for labor,* the wage rate and the number of workers the firm employs will be inversely related. An increase in the wage rate will reduce and a decrease in the wage rate will increase the number of workers the firm will hire. This relationship was evident in our discussions of both exclusive (craft) and inclusive (industrial) unionism. Though their techniques differ, both types of unionism will tend to reduce the number of jobs available by moving back up the given labor demand curve (see Figures 31–6 and 31–7).

There are several recognized exceptions to the general rule, however. Under certain circumstances higher wage rates will not cause unemployment in a specific labor market.

1. During periods of inflationary prosperity a firm faced with a union-imposed wage increase will find it opportune and relatively easy to pass the increase in wage costs on to consumers in the form of higher prices. This is particularly true of oligopolistic producers, who tend to boost prices only when some significant increase in costs has occurred which assumedly justifies higher prices. Because of the expanding money demand for goods which prosperity entails, the firm will suffer no decline in sales for its price-increasing efforts. Higher prices have the effect of increasing the demand for labor, because product price, along with productivity data, is the main component of the demand for labor. And wage boosts need not cause unemployment when the labor demand curve is shifting to the right.

2. A related possibility is that the prospect of higher wage rates will force firms to operate more efficiently, that is, to increase the productivity of their resources through greater managerial efficiency. This so-called "shock effect," by increasing the demand for labor through the productivity component, can offset the unemployment which normally accompanies higher wage rates. Labor economists, however, feel that the possibility of such productivity increases is limited.

3. We have seen that where labor is being hired under monopsonistic conditions, the employer will find it profitable to restrict his employment of labor. By restricting employment, the monopsonist can depress wage rates and therefore costs. This was demonstrated in Figure 31–8, where the monopsonist would hire Q_m workers at a wage rate of W_m. Now, if a union is organized and succeeds in imposing a higher wage rate upon the monopsonist—say, a wage rate in the vicinity of W_c—the result may be an *increase* in the number of workers the monopsonist will hire. By refusing to work at the monopsonistic rate of W_m, the union has eliminated the monopsonist's incentive to restrict employment. Where monopsony

exists, a union can increase wages up to their marginal revenue product without causing any unemployment.

These and similar exceptions do not destroy the notion that there is an inverse relationship between the price of a particular type of labor and the number of workers who will be hired. They do, however, suggest that this relationship is not a hard and fast rule, but rather a statement of a general tendency.

Economy As a Whole

Reasoning in terms of an individual firm or industry, we have come to the conclusion that, with exceptions, a decline in the wage rate causes a movement down any given labor demand curve and results in more employment. But this reasoning is not applicable to the entire economy; that is, general wage cuts will not necessarily increase employment in the economy as a whole. Why? Because of the fallacy of composition: The wage-rate–employment relationship which exists for an individual firm or industry is simply not relevant to the economy as a whole.

In talking about an individual firm's demand for labor, it is reasonable to suppose that a decline in the wage rate paid by the firm will have little or no effect upon the demand for its product and hence upon its demand for labor. After all, a firm's or industry's own workers account for a negligible portion of the total demand for its product; this is true even in the largest industries. This means in turn that it is proper to regard a firm's or industry's demand curve for labor as stable when it alters the wage rate it pays. We therefore can and do conclude that wage cuts can reduce unemployment in particular labor markets.

Businessmen have seized upon this reasoning to argue that general wage decreases are an effective means of combating general (cyclical) unemployment. However, this reasoning loses its validity when couched in terms of general wage decreases which permeate the economy as a whole. If the wage rates of *all* workers were reduced, a significant decline in the (money) national income would result. Remember: Wages account for over two-thirds of the national income. This would bring about a general decline in the demand for goods and services, which would then be mirrored in the resource market as a decline in the demand for labor. Employers might, as a result, hire no more (and possibly less) labor than originally, even though wage rates would now be lower.

In short, the individual firm can ignore the impact of lower wages upon national income and upon his product and resource demand curves, but employers as a group cannot. They must recognize that a general lowering of wages will adversely affect product and labor demand. As a matter of fact, if employers feel that a given general wage cut is indicative of further wage declines, unemployment may increase as firms postpone current production in anticipation of future cost reductions.

Labor leaders have reasoned that, if general wage *reductions* are of doubtful efficacy in reducing unemployment, the obvious solution is general wage *increases*. By putting more money into the hands of workers, they argue, one can increase total spending and the level of employment. But a closer examination of this policy also reveals possible pitfalls. Will higher wages actually bring about significant increases in consumption during a recession? During a cyclical downswing, households might use wage increases to retire outstanding indebtedness, or they may hoard this extra income in anticipation of job losses or declines in product prices. And, even if higher wages do boost consumption, businessmen, faced with higher costs, may simultaneously reduce their investment spending. This could leave total spending unchanged or even diminished. The interrelationships involved here are very complex, and much depends upon the pessimism or optimism of households and businesses and the precise stage of the business cycle at which a general wage change is invoked.[7] Awaiting the time when economic theory clarifies the repercussions of general wage changes, most economists are content to accept the tentative conclusion that general wage decreases or increases are not likely to have significant or certain effects upon the general level of employment. At least the anticyclical measures described in Parts Two and Three of this book are much more dependable means of seeking full employment.

SUMMARY

1. Wages are the price paid per unit of time for the services of labor.

2. The general level of wages in the United States is higher than in foreign nations, because the demand for labor is great in relation to the supply. The strong demand for American labor is based upon its high productivity, which in turn depends upon the quantity and quality of the capital equipment and natural resources used by labor, the quality of the labor force itself, the efficiency of management, a favorable sociopolitical environment, and the vast size of the domestic market. Over time these factors have caused the demand for labor to increase in relation to the supply, accounting for the long-run rise of real wages in the United States.

3. The determination of specific wage rates depends upon the structure of the particular labor market. In a competitive market the equilibrium wage rate and level of employment will be determined by the intersection of labor supply and demand.

4. Under monopsony, however, the marginal-resource-cost curve will lie above the resource supply curve, because the monopsonist must bid up wage rates in hiring extra workers and pay that higher wage to *all*

---

[7] The interested reader should consult Gordon F. Bloom and Herbert R. Northrup, *Economics of Labor Relations*, 5th ed. (Homewood, Ill.: Richard D. Irwin, Inc., 1965), chap. 13.

workers. The monopsonist will hire fewer workers than under competitive conditions in order to achieve less than competitive wage rates (costs) and thereby greater profits.

5. A union may raise competitive wage rates by **a.** increasing the derived demand for labor, **b.** restricting the supply of labor through exclusive unionism, and **c.** directly enforcing an above-equilibrium wage rate through inclusive unionism.

6. In many important industries the labor market takes the form of bilateral monopoly; that is, a strong union "sells" labor to a monopsonistic employer. Although the outcome of this labor market model is logically indeterminate, it might entail an important manifestation of the concept of countervailing power.

7. Statistical studies suggest that unions have perhaps gained a wage advantage on the order of 10 to 15 per cent over unorganized workers.

8. Wage differentials are largely explain-able in terms of **a.** noncompeting groups, that is, differences in the capacities and training of different groups of workers, **b.** equalizing differences, that is, wage differences which must be paid to offset nonmonetary differences in jobs, and **c.** market imperfections in the form of geographic, artificial, and sociological immobilities.

9. A particular firm or industry's downsloping labor demand curve will be unaffected by a change in wage rates paid by that firm, because its workers demand a negligible portion of the good they produce. Hence, a lower wage rate will increase the number of workers employed by that firm or industry. A general lowering of wage rates, however, will reduce the national income and therefore reduce product and labor demand. As a result, no more (or even fewer) workers will be hired at lower wage rates than originally. Most economists feel that general wage changes are neither a significant nor a certain means of altering the level of employment for the economy as a whole.

QUESTIONS AND STUDY SUGGESTIONS

1. Explain why the general level of wages is higher in the United States than in foreign nations. What is the most important single factor underlying the long-run increase in the average real wage rates in the United States? What, if anything, does this suggest concerning the ability of unions to raise real wages?

2. a. Describe wage determination in a labor market in which workers are unorganized and many firms are actively competing for the services of labor. Show this situation graphically, using W_1 to indicate the equilibrium wage rate and Q_1 to show the number of workers hired by the firms as a group.

b. Suppose now that the formerly competing firms form an employer's association which hires labor as would a monopsonist. Describe verbally the impact upon wage rates and employment. Adjust the graph drawn for question 2a, showing the monopsonistic wage rate and employment level as W_2 and Q_2, respectively.

3. Describe the techniques which unions might employ to raise wages. Evaluate the desirability of each from the viewpoint of (a) the union and (b) society as a whole. Explain: "Craft unionism directly restricts the supply of labor; industrial unionism relies upon the market to restrict the number of jobs."

4. Assume a monopsonistic employer is paying a wage rate of W_m and hiring Q_m workers, as is indicated in Figure 31–8. Now suppose that an industrial union is formed and that the union forces the employer to accept a wage rate of W_c. Explain verbally and graphically why in this instance the higher wage rate will be accompanied by an *increase* in the number of workers hired.

5. Complete the following labor supply table for a firm hiring labor competitively.

Units of labor	Wage rate	Total labor cost (wage bill)	Marginal resource (labor) cost
			$_____
1	$14	$_____	
			_____
2	14	_____	
			_____
3	14	_____	
			_____
4	14	_____	
			_____
5	14	_____	
			_____
6	14	_____	

a. Show graphically the labor supply and marginal resource (labor) cost curves for this firm. Explain the relationships of these curves to one another.

b. Compare these data with the labor demand data of question 2 in Chapter 30. What will the equilibrium wage rate and level of employment be? Explain.

c. Now redetermine this firm's supply schedule for labor on the assumption that it is a monopsonist and that, although it can hire the first worker for $14, it must increase the wage rate by $1 to attract each successive worker. Show the new labor supply and marginal labor cost curves graphically and explain their relationships to one another. Compare these new data with those of question 2 for Chapter 30. What will be the equilibrium wage rate and the level of employment? Why does this differ from your answer to question 5b?

6. What are the basic considerations which help explain the wage differentials between particular labor markets?

7. Evaluate and explain these two statements:

a. "Wage differentials can be explained in terms of two factors: first, vertical immobilities, that is, obstacles to the movement of workers from one occupational level to another, and, second, horizontal immobilities, that is, factors which prevent workers from being perfectly mobile geographically."

b. "If all workers were of equal capacity and training, all jobs equally attractive to workers, and labor markets were free of imperfections, all workers would receive the same wage rate."

8. "Wage cuts lower costs, and lower costs tend to increase output and the employment of labor. Therefore, general wage reductions will help eliminate general unemployment." Evaluate critically.

SELECTED REFERENCES

Bloom, Gordon F., and Herbert R. Northrup: *Economics of Labor Relations,* 5th ed. (Homewood, Ill.: Richard D. Irwin, Inc., 1965), chaps. 8–15.

Bober, M. M.: *Intermediate Price and Income Theory,* rev. ed. (New York: W. W. Norton & Company, Inc., 1962), chap. 14.

Burtt, Everett Johnson, Jr.: *Labor Markets, Unions, and Government Policies* (New York: St Martin's Press, Inc., 1963), chaps. 4, 15–18.

Maher, John E.: *Labor and the Economy* (Boston: Allyn and Bacon, Inc., 1965), chaps. 12–16.

McKenna, Joseph P.: *Intermediate Economic Theory* (New York: Holt, Rinehart and Winston, Inc., 1958), pp. 215–222.

Rothschild, K. W.: *The Theory of Wages* (Oxford: Basil Blackwell & Mott, Ltd., 1956).

The discussion of wages in Chapter 31 is rather lengthy. In contrast the discussions of the other income shares—rent, interest, and profits—found in the present chapter are relatively brief. There are two reasons for this difference in emphasis.

1. Wage incomes are clearly the major component of the national income. Statistics tell us that about 70 per cent of the national income is in the form of wage and salary incomes, the remainder accruing as rent, interest, and profit incomes. And because economists define wages more broadly and interest, rent, and profits more narrowly than do national income accountants, labor's share is understated in national income figures, and the size of the other three shares is overstated.

2. The economic theories of rent, interest, and profit are very unsettled; there are honest differences among authorities as to definitions, explanations, and implications where nonwage incomes are concerned. For these two reasons we shall concentrate upon the basic features of rent, interest, and profit determination and forgo the many controversial points and the often ambiguous details which are encountered in more advanced discussions of these income shares.

ECONOMIC RENT

To most people the term "rent" means the seemingly exorbitant sum one must pay for a two-bedroom apartment or a dormitory room. To the businessman "rent" is a payment made for the use of a factory building, machinery, or warehouse facilities. Closer examination finds these common-sense definitions of rent to be confusing and ambiguous. Dormitory room rent, for example, includes interest on the money capital the university has borrowed from the government or private individuals in financing the dormitory's construction, wages for custodial and maid service, and so forth. Economists therefore use the term "rent" in a narrower but less ambiguous sense: *Economic rent is the price paid for the use of land and other natural resources which are completely fixed in total supply.* It is the unique supply conditions of land and other natural resources—their fixed supply—which makes rental payments distinguishable from wage, interest, and profit payments.

Let us examine this feature and some of its implications through simple supply and demand analysis. To avoid complications, assume, first, that all land is of the same grade or quality, that is, that each available acre of land is equally productive. Suppose, too, that all land has just one use, that is, that all land is capable of producing just one product—say, corn. And assume that land is being rented in a competitive market—that many corn farmers are demanding and many landowners offering land in the market.

In Figure 32–1 SS indicates the supply of

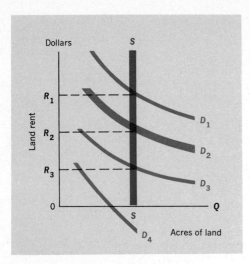

FIGURE 32–1. THE DETERMINATION OF LAND RENT.
Because the supply of land and other natural resources is perfectly inelastic (SS), demand is the sole active determinant of land rent. An increase (D_2 to D_1) or decrease (D_2 to D_3) in demand will cause considerable changes in rent (R_2 to R_1 and R_2 to R_3). If demand is very small (D_4) relative to supply, land will be a "free good."

arable farm land available in the economy as a whole and D_2 the demand of farmers for the use of that land. As with all economic resources, demand is a derived demand. It is downsloping because of the law of diminishing returns and the fact that, for farmers as a group, product price must be diminished to sell additional units of output.

The unique feature of our analysis is on the supply side: for all practical purposes the supply of land is perfectly inelastic, as reflected in SS. Land has no production cost; it is a "free and nonreproducible gift of nature." The economy has so much land, and that's that. It is true, of course, that within limits existing land can be made more usable by clearing, drainage, and irrigation. But these programs constitute capital improvements and not changes in the amount

of land as such. Furthermore, such variations in the usability of land are a very small fraction of the total amount of land in existence and therefore do not undermine the basic argument that land and other resources are in virtually fixed supply.

The fixed nature of the supply of land means that demand is the only active determinant of land rent; supply is passive. And what determines the demand for land? Those factors discussed in Chapter 30—the price of the product grown on the land, the productivity of land (which depends in part upon the quantity and quality of the resources with which land is combined), and the prices of those other resources which are combined with land. If in Figure 32–1 the demand for land should increase from D_2 to D_1 or decline from D_2 to D_3, land rent would change from R_2 to R_1 or R_3, but the amount of land supplied would remain unchanged at OS. In technical terms there is a large price effect and no quantity effect when the demand for land changes. If the demand for land is only D_4, land rent will be zero; that is, land will be a "free good," because it is not scarce enough in relation to the demand for it to command a price. This situation was approximated in the free-land era of American history. Changes in economic rent will have no impact upon the amount of land available; the supply of land is simply not augmentable.

Land Rent Is a Surplus

The perfect inelasticity of the supply of land must be contrasted with the relative elasticity of such property resources as apartment buildings, machinery, and warehouses. These resources are not fixed in total supply. A higher price will give entrepreneurs the incentive to construct and offer larger quantities of these property resources. Conversely, a decline in their prices will induce suppliers to allow existing facilities to depreciate and not be replaced. The same general reasoning applies to the total supply of labor. Within limits a higher average level of wages will induce more workers to enter the labor force, and lower wages will cause them to drop out of the labor force. In other words, the supplies of nonland resources are upsloping, or, stated differently, the prices paid to such resources perform an *incentive function*. A high price provides an incentive to offer more; a low price, to offer less.

Not so with land. Rent serves no incentive function, because the total supply of land is fixed. If rent is $10,000, $500, $1, or $0 per acre, the same amount of land will be available to society to make a contribution to production. Rent, in other words, could be eliminated without affecting the productive efficiency of the economy. For this reason economists consider rent to be a *surplus*, that is, a payment which is not necessary to ensure that land will be available to the economy as a whole.

Should Rent Be Paid?

If land is a free gift of nature, costs nothing to produce, and would be available even in the absence of rental payments, why should rent be paid to those who by historical accident or inheritance happen to be land-owners? Socialists have long argued that all land rents are unearned incomes. Therefore, they argue, land should be nationalized—owned by the state—so that any payments for its use can be utilized by the state in furthering the well-being of the entire population rather than a landowning minority. In the United States criticism of rental payments has taken the form of a *single-tax movement* which gained considerable support in the late 1800s. Spearheaded by Henry George's provocative book, *Progress and Poverty* (1879), this reform movement centered upon the notion that economic rent might be taxed away completely without impairing the available supply of land or therefore the productive potential of the

economy as a whole. If the relevant supply and demand conditions for land are as shown by D_2 and SS in Figure 32–1, land rent will be R_2. A land tax of that same amount—R_2 per acre—will obviously confiscate this land rent but will leave the amount of land available for productive purposes unchanged at OS. The complete inelasticity of land supply makes it impossible for the landowner to shift this tax to renters.

The simplicity and apparent justice of a single tax gained considerable support for the single-tax movement. But glaring defects become apparent upon closer analysis:

1. As noted earlier, in practice most income payments combine elements of interest, rent, wages, and profits. As a practical matter, it would be virtually impossible to determine how much of any given income payment is economic rent.

2. A single tax on land rent would not be capable of financing modern government. It is estimated that only 2 or 3 per cent of the national income takes the form of economic rent. Modern governments spend in excess of 20 per cent of the national income in peacetime and much more during war. In short, it is no longer realistic to espouse a tax on land as a *single* tax.

3. The apparent justice of a single tax on land disappears once it is recognized that in the course of history virtually all pieces of land have changed hands many times. Hence, a single tax would fall not upon the original settlers or expropriators who claimed nature's free gift but rather upon recent purchasers who have bought the land at prices reflecting the capitalized rental income of the land.

4. Although rent performs no incentive function, it does perform a rationing function. In the absence of a single tax, land-owners will supply land to those renters who are willing to pay the highest rent for it. And, under competitive conditions, it will be those producers for whom the marginal revenue product of land is greatest who will be

able to pay the highest rent. In other words, rent will ration the available supply of land to the most productive uses. On the other hand, landowners would be completely indifferent as to which producers obtained the use of their land if government stood ready to tax away the entire rental payment.

Productivity Differences and Alternative Uses

Our analysis thus far has proceeded upon the assumption that all units of land are of the same grade. In practice, this simply is not so. Different acres vary greatly in productivity. These productivity differences stem primarily from differences in soil fertility and such climatic factors as rainfall and temperature. It is these factors which explain why Iowa soil is excellently suited to corn production, the plains of eastern Colorado are much less so, and desert wasteland of New Mexico is incapable of corn production. These differences in productivity will be reflected in resource demand. Competitive bidding by farmers will establish a high rent for the very productive Iowa land. The less productive Colorado land will command a much lower rent, and the New Mexico land no rent at all. Location may be equally important in explaining differences in land rent. Other things being equal, renters will pay more for a unit of land which is strategically located with respect to materials, labor, and customers than for a unit of land whose location is remote from these markets.

The rent differentials to which quality differences in land would give rise can be easily seen by looking at Figure 32–1 from a slightly different point of view. Suppose, as before, that only one agricultural product, say corn, can be produced on four grades of land, *each* of which is available in the fixed amount OS. When combined with identical amounts of capital, labor, and other cooperating resources, the productivity—or, more specifically, the marginal revenue produc-

tivity—of each grade of land is reflected in demand curves D_1, D_2, D_3, and D_4. Grade 1 land is the most productive, as reflected in D_1, whereas grade 4 is the least productive, as is shown by D_4. The resulting rents for grades 1, 2, and 3 land will obviously be R_1, R_2, and R_3, respectively, the rent differentials mirroring the differences in the productivity of the three grades of land. Grade 4 land is so poor in quality that it would simply not pay farmers to bring it fully into production; it would be a "free" and only partially used resource.

We have also supposed thus far that land has only one use. Actually, we know that land usually has a number of alternative uses. An acre of Iowa farmland may be useful in raising not only corn, but also wheat, oats, milo, and cattle, or it may be useful as a site for a house or factory. What is the importance of this obvious point? It indicates that, although land is a free gift of nature and has no production cost from the viewpoint of society as a whole, the rental payments of individual producers are *costs*. The total supply of land will be available to society even if no rent at all is paid for its use, but, from the standpoint of individual firms and industries, land has alternative uses, and therefore payments must be made by specific firms and industries to attract that land from those other uses. Such payments by definition are costs. Once again the fallacy of composition has entered our discussion. From the standpoint of society there is no alternative but for land to be used by society. Therefore to society rents are a surplus, not a cost. But because land has alternative uses, the rental payments of corn farmers or any other individual user are a cost, because such payments are required to attract land from alternative uses.

INTEREST

Interest is the price paid for the use of money or, better yet, for the use of loanable funds. Three related aspects of this income payment are immediately notable:

1. Because it is paid in kind, interest is typically stated as a percentage of the amount of money being borrowed rather than as an absolute amount. It is less clumsy to say that one is paying 5 per cent interest than to proclaim that interest is "$50 per year per $1,000." Furthermore, stating interest as a percentage facilitates the comparison of interest paid on loans of much different absolute amounts. By expressing interest as a percentage we can immediately compare an interest payment of, say, $144 per year per $2,880 and one of $600 per year per $12,000. In this case both interest payments are 5 per cent—a fact not at all obvious from the absolute figures.

2. Money is not an economic resource. As such, money is not productive; it is incapable of producing goods and services. However, businessmen "buy" the use of money, because money can be used to acquire capital goods—factory buildings, machinery, warehouses, and so forth. And these facilities clearly do make a contribution to production. Thus in hiring the use of money capital, businessmen are ultimately buying the use of real capital goods. As a matter of fact, it is the expected marginal revenue productivity of capital goods which sets an upper limit upon the rate of interest businessmen will pay to obtain the funds needed for the purchase of those capital goods.

3. Though economists find it convenient to talk as if there existed a single interest rate, it must be recognized that there are actually many different rates of interest. The Federal government currently borrows at 3½ to 4 per cent on most of its securities. Corporate bonds may pay 4½ to 5½ per cent. FHA mortgage loans may entail interest rates of 5½ to 6 per cent. Bank loans to consumers for automobile or refrigerator purchases may run 10 or 14 per cent. Those whose credit standing forces them to borrow from consumer finance companies may pay

extremely high rates—24 or 36 per cent is not uncommon.

Why the differences?

1. The varying degrees of *risk* on loans are important. The greater the chance the borrower will not repay the loan, the more interest the lender will charge to compensate for this risk.

2. The *length* of a loan also affects the interest rate. Other things being equal, long-term loans usually command higher rates of interest than do short-term loans, because the long-term lender suffers the inconvenience and possible financial sacrifice of forgoing alternative uses for his money for a greater period of time.

3. Given two loans of equal length and risk, the interest rate will be higher on the smaller of the two loans. This is so because the *administrative costs* of a large and a small loan are about the same absolutely.

4. *Market imperfections* are also important in explaining some interest rate differentials. The small-town bank which monopolizes the local money market may charge high interest rates on loans to consumers because households find it inconvenient to "shop around" at banks in somewhat distant cities. The large corporation, on the other hand, is able to survey rival investment houses in disposing of a new bond issue and thereby secure the lowest obtainable rate.

To circumvent the difficulties involved in discussing the whole structure of interest rates, economists talk of "the" interest rate or the "pure" rate of interest. This pure rate is best approximated by the interest paid on long-term, virtually riskless bonds such as the long-term bonds of the United States government or of American Telephone and Telegraph. This interest payment can be thought of as being made solely for the use of money over an extended time period, because the risk factor and administrative costs are negligible and the interest on such securities is not distorted by market imperfections. The pure interest rate in the fall of 1965 was about 4 per cent.

If the interest rate can be defined as the price paid for the use of loanable funds, it is clear that to understand the determination of the rate of interest we must understand the factors which underlie the demand for, and the supply of, loanable funds.

Demand for Loanable Funds

Who borrows money? For what purposes? Generally speaking, businesses, households, and government are the primary demanders of loanable funds.

The great bulk of loanable funds is borrowed by *businesses* for use in the purchase of more and better capital goods. Businesses seek the use of capital goods (Chapter 3) because "roundabout production" through the use of tools and equipment increases productivity. Hence, we can draw a marginal-revenue-product curve—a capital demand curve—for the various specific types of capital goods. Like other resource demand curves, this MRP curve will diminish because of the law of diminishing returns. However, this resource demand curve is more complex than other resource demand curves because capital goods are durable. A lathe or drill press may have a life of ten or fifteen years. Therefore, businessmen must assess as best they can the uncertainties of the future and estimate the return above acquisition, maintenance, and operating costs which the purchase of additional units of capital will probably yield. This net *expected* return can be expressed as a percentage of the cost of the capital goods and compared with the rate of interest.

Now we found in Chapter 30 that under competition it is profitable for a firm to purchase any resource up to the point at which the price of that resource equals its marginal revenue product. In this instance the marginal revenue productivity of a capital good is measured by the expected net

return on the capital good expressed as a percentage of its cost. The price of the loanable funds required to purchase the capital good is obviously the interest rate. Hence, it will pay businessmen to demand loanable funds up to the point at which the expected net rate of return on the capital good equals the rate of interest.

Households also demand loanable funds when they wish to make purchases in excess of their current incomes and cash resources. The long-run relative increase in the production of durable goods which has taken place in our economy has encouraged the growth of consumer credit. Automobiles, refrigerators, and television sets are typically purchased on credit.

Governments—Federal, state, and local— are also major borrowers. Although this borrowing is at its zenith during wartime, governments are rather persistently borrowing against future tax revenues to finance highways, education, welfare programs, and so forth (Chapter 9). The Federal government is almost continuously in the money market as it refinances the public debt.

The demand for loanable funds is clearly downsloping. Businessmen will find it profitable to purchase large amounts of capital goods when the price of loanable funds declines. Similarly, lower interest rates may encourage some increase in consumer and governmental borrowing. Economists are in general agreement, however, that the demand for loanable funds is inelastic. The reasons for this are several. Interest costs are usually a relatively small portion of the total cost of any capital goods purchase; hence, the demand for loanable funds for investment purposes tends to be insensitive to changes in the interest rate. Consumer short-term borrowing is also interest-inelastic. Consumers are interested more in the size of their "small monthly payments" than in their interest charges. On long-term housing loans, on the other hand, interest rates undoubtedly exert a significant influence on consumer borrowing. The amount of loanable funds demanded by government is also relatively insensitive to interest-rate fluctuations—particularly for heavy Federal borrowing, which is usually associated with wartime emergencies. Here interest charges are a very secondary consideration. With everything taken into account, the demand for loanable funds is downsloping and in all probability interest-inelastic.

Potential Supply of Loanable Funds

There are three basic sources of loanable funds.

1. The current saving and the past savings accumulated by households are one potential source of loanable funds. In any reasonably prosperous year households as a group will consume less than their disposable incomes, the difference being personal saving. These funds may be augmented by decreases in the liquid savings which households now hold as idle hoards; these accumulations may be drawn down and offered in the money market.

2. The current saving and accumulated savings of businesses are a major source of loanable funds. In each prosperous year businesses save very substantial amounts in the form of depreciation charges and undistributed corporate profits. And, as with households, current business saving may be supplemented by declines in the cash hoards or bank balances of businesses. These business sources of loanable funds are often demanded for investment purposes by the firms themselves and therefore do not enter the market for loanable funds.

3. A potential source of loanable funds is newly created money, that is, money created by commercial bank lending.

Actual Supply of Loanable Funds

We have been careful to designate the current saving and past savings of households

and businesses and commercial bank lending as the *potential* supply of loanable funds. The reason is that households, businesses, and banks may not actually be willing to make these funds available to borrowers. Money, remember, is a store of value. Households and businesses may not want to offer either their current saving or any of their accumulated savings to borrowers. On the contrary, they may choose to add a portion of their current saving to their accumulated savings balances.

Having made choices as to how to divide their incomes and receipts between spending and saving, households and businesses must then decide the specific form in which to hold their savings. The basic choice is between money in the form of either idle cash or bank accounts, on the one hand, and securities of some sort, on the other. Idle cash and bank accounts are highly liquid assets; securities acquired from borrowers are somewhat less liquid. That part of savings (current or accumulated) which households and businesses want to hold as securities flows into the money market as the supply of loanable funds. That part which households and businesses want to hold as cash obviously does not. This division depends upon the *liquidity preferences* of households and businesses. More specifically, there are three main reasons why households and businesses prefer to hold cash rather than securities:

1. There is a *transaction motive* for holding money rather than securities. Households and businesses both need a stock of cash on hand to make the ordinary day-to-day purchases. Households, for example, receive a sizable chunk of income every two weeks or every month. Disbursements, on the other hand, occur more or less evenly over time. This means that households have an average money balance of some size bridging the gap between paydays. And it is simply more convenient to have one's assets in their most liquid form, that is, as idle cash balances or bank accounts, than in the form of securi-

ties. Liquidity permits one to avail himself readily of any extraordinarily good buys or bargains he may chance upon. Furthermore, there are costs—brokerage fees—in transferring cash into securities and back again.

2. There is a *precautionary motive* for holding money. Households and businesses may hold cash balances to meet any rainy day contingencies which might arise. Particularly relevant are those risks which one cannot protect himself against by purchasing insurance policies—prolonged illness, unemployment, unfavorable shifts in consumer demand, and so forth.

3. There is a *speculative motive* for holding money. At any point in time there is a certain rate of interest which households and businesses as potential suppliers of loanable funds consider to be about "normal." If the rate of interest is currently low, that is, "below normal," households and businesses may withhold a part of their savings which would otherwise flow into the money market as a part of the supply of loanable funds. They hold more money and less securities than they normally would. Why? Because they expect that the current below-normal interest rate will probably rise in the future. Hence, households and businesses refrain from supplying their current loanable funds in anticipation of a higher interest return in the future. Conversely, if the current interest rate is unusually high, that is "above normal," households and businesses will choose to hold less money and more securities to take advantage of high current interest rates as opposed to the lower normal rate expected to prevail again in the future.

The supply of loanable funds is clearly upsloping. Though the interest rate probably does not exert a very strong influence upon the amount households and businesses save, higher and higher interest rates will induce households and businesses to be less liquid. At relatively high interest rates households and firms will prefer to hold their assets in the form of interest-bearing securities rather than as non-interest-bearing checking ac-

counts and idle cash balances. There is little clear-cut evidence as to how sensitive or insensitive the supply of loanable funds is to changes in the interest rate.

The interaction of the upsloping supply-of-loanable-funds curve and the downsloping demand-for-loanable-funds curve determines the equilibrium rate of interest.

Interest Rate: An Administered Price

Though we have concluded that the interest rate is determined by the demand for, and the supply of, loanable funds, few would argue that the interest rate is genuinely a free market price. The interest rate is actually an administered price—a price which is profoundly and purposely influenced by government. Government's influence is apparent on both the demand and the supply sides of the picture. As previously noted, government is an important borrower. Fiscal policies appropriate to recession and depression call for Federal deficits. During wartime government assumes the dominant role on the demand side of the market for loanable funds. Finally, the Treasury is constantly refunding portions of the public debt as outstanding government bonds mature. On the supply side, the Federal Reserve authorities influence the supply of loanable funds and therefore the interest rate through the application of tight and easy money policies (Chapter 18).

The reasons why government is interested in administering the interest rate are apparent upon examination of the ways in which the interest rate may influence the operation of the economy. Specifically, the interest rate affects both the *level* and the *composition* of investment goods production.

Interest, capital accumulation, and employment. The interest rate affects the level of investment and therefore the level of employment in the economy. Other things being equal, a lowering of the interest rate will induce businessmen to increase their purchases of investment goods. This stimulates total spending and the volume of employment. Conversely, other things being equal, an increase in the interest rate will cause businessmen to cut their expenditures for capital goods, thereby causing total spending and employment to fall.

This is not to say, however, that adjustments in the interest rate brought about by changes in either the private or public components of the demand for, and supply of, loanable funds will be sufficient to alter investment spending to the level required for achieving full employment. Recall that the interest rate is only one of many forces which have a bearing upon the investment plans of businesses. The rate of technological advance, population growth, the acquisition and operating costs of capital goods, government tax and expenditure policies, the stocks of capital goods on hand, anticipated market conditions, and business confidence are all important determinants of investment. Changes in any of or all these factors may easily offset any alterations in the interest rate which government may initiate in seeking to influence investment spending and employment. Stated differently, frequent and significant fluctuations in all those factors which affect the expected marginal revenue productivity of capital goods are considerably more important than changes in the interest rate in determining the actual level of investment spending. It is also notable that if interest rates are initially low, as they typically are in industrially advanced nations, it simply is not possible for significant declines in the interest rate to occur. For all these reasons we must conclude that there is nothing inherent in the market for loanable funds or, more specifically, the interest rate—even as influenced by government—which gives rise to the level of investment required for achieving full employment.

Interest and the allocation of capital. Prices, you will recall, are rationing devices. The interest rate, being the price of loanable funds, is no exception. The interest rate performs the function of allocating money capital and therefore real capital to various firms and investment projects. It rations the available supply of loanable funds to those investment projects whose rate of return or expected profitability is sufficiently high to warrant payment of the going interest rate. If the expected marginal revenue productivity of additional real capital in industry X is 10 per cent and the required loanable funds can be secured at an interest rate of 6 per cent, industry X will be in a position to borrow and expand its capital facilities. On the other hand, if the marginal productivity of additional capital in industry Y is expected to be only 3 per cent, it will be unprofitable for this industry to accumulate more capital goods. In short, the interest rate allocates money and ultimately real capital to those industries in which it will be most productive and therefore most profitable. Such an allocation of capital goods is obviously in the interest of society as a whole.

But the interest rate does not perform perfectly the task of rationing capital to its most productive uses. Many firms finance their capital expansions internally and therefore are not subject to screening by the interest rate. Similarly, large oligopolistic borrowers are in a better position than competitive borrowers to pass interest costs on to consumers by virtue of their ability to manipulate their prices. And, too, the sheer size and prestige of large industrial concerns might allow them to obtain money capital on favorable terms, whereas the market for loanable funds screens out less well-known firms whose profit expectations might actually be superior.

BUSINESS PROFITS AND ECONOMIC PROFITS

As is the case with rent, economists find it advantageous to define profits more narrowly than do businessmen or accountants. To most businessmen "profit" is what remains of a firm's total revenue after it has paid other individuals and firms for materials, capital, and labor supplied to the firm. To the economist this definition is too broad and therefore ambiguous. The difficulty, as the economist sees it, is that this view of profits takes into account only *explicit* costs, that is, payments made by the firm to outsiders. It therefore ignores *implicit* costs, that is, payments to similar resources which are owned and self-employed by a firm. In other words, the businessman's concept of profits fails to allow for implicit wage, rent, and interest costs. *Economic,* or *pure, profits* are what remain after both explicit and implicit wage, rent, and interests costs and a normal profit have been subtracted from a firm's total revenue (Chapter 25). Economic profits may be either positive or negative (losses).

An example may sharpen these comments. As the economist sees it, a farmer who owns his land and equipment and provides all his own labor is grossly overstating his economic profits if he merely subtracts his payments to outsiders for seed, fertilizer, gasoline, and so forth, from his total receipts. Actually, much or possibly all of what remains are the implicit rent, interest, and wage costs which the farmer forgoes in deciding to self-employ the resources he owns rather than make them available in alternative employments. Interest on the capital or wages for the labor contributed by the farmer himself are no more profits than are the payments which would be made if outsiders had supplied these resources. In short, the businessman's definition and the economist's definition of profits are compatible only if the businessman includes both explicit and implicit costs in determining total costs. Economic profits are a residual—the total revenue remaining after *all* costs are paid.

Economic Profits and the Entrepreneur

Speaking very generally, the economist views profits as the return to a very special type of human resource—entrepreneurial ability. A part of this return, you will recall, is called a *normal profit*. This is the minimum return or payment necessary to retain the entrepreneur in some specific line of production. By definition, this normal profit payment is a cost (Chapter 25). However, we know that a firm's total revenue may exceed its total costs (explicit, implicit, and inclusive of a normal profit). This extra or excess revenue above all costs is an *economic,* or *pure, profit.* This residual—which is not a cost because it is in excess of the normal profit required to retain the entrepreneur in the industry—accrues to the entrepreneur. The entrepreneur, in other words, is the residual claimant.

Economists offer several theories to explain why this residual of economic profit might occur. As we will see in a moment, these explanations relate to:

1. The risks which the entrepreneur necessarily bears as he functions in a dynamic and therefore uncertain environment or as he undertakes innovational activity.

2. The possibility of attaining monopoly power.

Sources of Economic Profit

Our understanding of economic profits and the entrepreneur's functions can be both deepened and widened by describing an artificial economic environment within which pure profits would be zero. Then, by noting real-world deviations from this environment, we can lay bare the sources of economic profit.

In a purely competitive, static economy pure profits would be zero. By a static economy we mean one in which all the basic data—resource supplies, technological knowledge, and consumer tastes—are constant and unchanging. A static economy is a changeless one in which all the determinants of cost and supply data, on the one hand, and demand and revenue data, on the other, are constant. Given the static nature of these data, the economic future is perfectly foreseeable; economic uncertainty is nonexistent. The outcome of price and production policies is accurately predictable. Furthermore, the static nature of such a society precludes any type of innovational change. Under pure competition any pure profits (positive or negative) which might have existed initially will disappear with the entry or exodus of firms in the long run. All costs—both explicit and implicit—will therefore be precisely covered in the long run, leaving no residual in the form of pure profits.

The notion of zero economic profits in a static, competitive economy enhances our understanding of profits by suggesting that the presence of profits is linked to the dynamic nature of real-world capitalism and the accompanying uncertainty. Furthermore, it indicates that economic profits may arise from a source apart from the directing, innovating, risk-bearing functions of the entrepreneur. And that source is the presence of some degree of monopoly power.

Uncertainty, risk, and profits. In a dynamic economy the future is always uncertain. This means that the businessman necessarily assumes risks. Profits can be thought of in part as a reward for assuming these risks.

In linking pure profits with uncertainty and risk bearing, it is important to distinguish between risks which are insurable and those which are not. Some types of risks— for example, fires, floods, theft, and accidents to employees—are measurable in the sense that actuaries can estimate their occurrence with considerable accuracy. As a result, these risks are insurable. Firms can avoid, or at least provide for, these risks by incurring a small known cost in the form of an insurance premium. It is the bearing of uninsurable risks, then, which is a potential source of economic profits.

What are such uninsurable risks? Basically, they are uncontrollable and unpredictable changes in demand (revenue) and supply (cost) conditions facing the firm.

Some of these uninsurable risks stem from unpredictable changes in the general economic environment or, more specifically, from the business cycle. Prosperity brings substantial windfall profits to most firms, whereas depression means widespread losses. But, in addition, changes are constantly taking place in the structure of the economy. Even in a full-employment noninflationary economy changes are always occurring in consumer tastes, resource supplies, and so forth. These changes continually alter the revenue and cost data faced by individual firms and industries, leading to changes in the structure of the business population as favorably affected industries expand and adversely affected industries contract. Changes in government policies are pertinent at both levels. Appropriate fiscal and monetary policies of government may reverse a recession, whereas a tariff may significantly alter the demand and revenue data of the protected industry.

The point is this: Profits and losses can be associated with the assumption of uninsurable risks stemming from both cyclical and structural changes in the economy.

Uncertainty, innovations, and profits. The uncertainties just discussed are external to the firm; they are beyond the control of the individual firm or industry. One other extremely important dynamic feature of capitalism—innovation—occurs at the initiative of the entrepreneur. Business firms deliberately introduce new methods of production and distribution to affect their costs favorably and new products to influence their revenue favorably. The entrepreneur purposely undertakes to upset his existing cost and revenue data in a way he hopes will be profitable to him.

But once again uncertainty enters the picture. Despite exhaustive market surveys, entrepreneurs do not know in advance whether consumers actually want more horsepower in their automobiles, clothing made of paper, color television sets, three-dimensional movies, and ball-point pens. Nor do they know certainly whether a new machine will actually provide the cost economies predicted for it while it is still in the blueprint stage. Innovations purposely undertaken by entrepreneurs entail uncertainty, just as do those changes in the economic environment over which an individual enterprise has no control. In a sense, then, innovation as a source of profits is merely a special case of risk bearing.

Under competition and in the absence of patent laws innovational profits will be temporary. Rival firms will imitate successful (profitable) innovations, thereby competing away all economic profits. Nevertheless, innovational profits may always exist in a progressive economy as new successful innovations replace those older innovations whose associated profits have been competed away.

Monopoly profits. Thus far we have emphasized that profits are related to the uncertainties and uninsurable risks surrounding dynamic events which enterprises are exposed to or initiate themselves. The existence of monopoly in some form or another is a final source of economic profits. As explained previously, because of his ability to restrict entry, a monopolist may persistently enjoy economic profits provided demand is strong relative to costs. This profit stems from the monopolist's ability to restrict output and influence product price to his own advantage.

There are both a causal relationship and a notable distinction between uncertainty, on the one hand, and monopoly, on the other, as sources of profits. The causal relationship involves the fact that an entrepreneur can reduce uncertainty, or at least manipulate its effects, by achieving monopoly power. The competitive firm is unalterably exposed to the vagaries of the market; the monopolist, however, can control the market to a degree and thereby offset or minimize potentially adverse effects of uncertainty. Furthermore,

innovation is an important source of monopoly power; the short-run uncertainty associated with the introduction of new techniques or new products may be borne for the purpose of achieving a measure of monopoly power.

The notable distinction between profits stemming from uncertainty and from monopoly has to do with the social desirability of the two sources of profits. Bearing the risks inherent in a dynamic and uncertain economic environment and the undertaking of innovations are socially desirable functions. The social desirability of monopoly profits, on the other hand, is subject to very great doubt. Monopoly profits typically are founded upon output restriction, above-competitive prices, and a contrived misallocation of resources.

Functions of Profits

Profit is the prime mover, or energizer, of the capitalistic economy. As such, profits influence both the level of resource utilization and the allocation of resources among alternative uses. It is profits—or better, the *expectation* of profits—which induce firms to innovate. And innovation stimulates investment, total output, and employment. Innovation is a fundamental aspect of the process of economic growth, and it is the pursuit of profit which underlies innovation. We know from our previous analysis of the determination of national income that profit expectations are highly volatile, with the result that investment, employment, and the rate of growth have been unstable. Profits have functioned imperfectly as a spur to innovation and investment.

Profits perform more effectively the task of allocating resources among alternative lines of production. Businessmen seek profits and shun losses. The occurrence of economic profits is a signal that society wants that particular industry to expand. Indeed, profit rewards are more than an inducement for an industry to expand; they also are the financial means by which firms in such industries can add to their productive capacities. Losses, on the other hand, signal society's desire for the afflicted industries to contract; losses penalize those who fail to adjust their productive efforts to those goods and services most preferred by consumers. This is not to say that profits and losses result in an allocation of resources which is now and forever attuned to consumer preferences. In particular the presence of monopoly in both product and resource markets impedes the shiftability of firms and resources, as also do the various geographic, artificial, and sociological immobilities discussed in Chapter 31.

SUMMARY

1. Economic rent is the price paid for the use of land and other natural resources whose total supplies are fixed.

2. Rent is a surplus in the sense that land would be available to the economy as a whole even in the absence of all rental payments.

3. The notion of rent as a surplus gave rise to the single-tax movement of the late 1800s, which advocated a confiscatory single tax on land rent. This proposal, however, is subject to serious limitations. **a.** It overlooks the administrative difficulties of determining what portion of specific income payments constitutes economic rent. **b.** A single tax on land will not provide enough revenue to finance modern government. **c.** The tax would unjustly penalize those who have purchased land. **d.** A confiscatory tax on land rent would undermine the rationing function of rent.

4. Differences in land rent are explainable in terms of differences in productivity due to the fertility and climatic features of land and in its location.

5. Land rent is a surplus rather than a cost to the economy as a whole; however,

because from the viewpoint of individual firms and industries land has alternative uses, rental payments of firms and industries are correctly regarded as costs.

6. Interest is the price paid for the use of loanable funds. Specific interest rates vary because of differences in the degree of risk loans entail, the length of loans, the relative size of administrative costs associated with lending, and market imperfections.

7. Businesses, households, and government are the principal demanders of loanable funds. The current and past savings of businesses and households and commercial bank credit are the major potential sources of loanable funds. However, the actual supply of loanable funds may differ from the potential supply because of changes in the liquidity preference of households, businesses, and banks. The intersection of the supply of loanable funds and the demand for them determines the equilibrium interest rate.

8. Because of the borrowing activities of the Treasury and the Board of Governors' control over the loan-creating activities of commercial banks, the price of loanable funds is largely administered by government.

9. The interest rate influences the level of capital accumulation and helps ration capital goods to specific firms.

10. Economic, or pure, profits are the difference between a firm's total revenue and its total costs, the latter defined to include implicit costs and a normal profit.

11. Profits accrue to entrepreneurs for assuming the uninsurable risks associated with the organizing and directing of economic resources and innovating. Profits also result from monopoly power.

12. Profit expectations influence the innovating and investment activities and therefore the level of employment. The basic function of profits and losses, however, is to induce that allocation of resources which is in general accord with the tastes of consumers.

QUESTIONS AND STUDY SUGGESTIONS

1. Define economic rent. How does the economist's usage of the term "rent" differ from everyday usage? "Though rent need not be paid by society to make land available, rental payments are very useful in guiding land into the most productive uses." Explain.

2. Explain why economic rent is a surplus to the economy as a whole but a cost of production from the standpoint of individual firms and industries. Explain: "Rent performs no 'incentive function' in the economy." What arguments can be made for and against a single tax on land?

3. How is interest defined? What considerations account for the fact that interest rates differ greatly on various types of loans? Use these considerations to explain the relative size of the interest rates charged on the following:
   a. A long-term $1,000 government bond, b. A $20 pawnshop loan, c. An FHA mortgage loan on a $17,000 house, d. A $2,000 commercial bank loan to finance the purchase of an automobile, and e. A $100 loan from a personal finance company.

4. If money capital, as such, is not an economic resource, why is interest paid and received for its use? Answer from the standpoint of both borrower and lender, and from the borrower's standpoint distinguish between business and consumer borrowing.

5. What are the three sources of the demand for loanable funds? What are the three potential sources of the supply of loanable funds? Explain liquidity preference in terms of its underlying motives. Use this concept to explain the difference between saving and the supply of loanable funds.

6. What are the major economic functions of the interest rate? Of economic profits? How might the fact that more and more businesses are financing their investment activities internally affect the efficiency with which the interest rate performs its functions?

7. How do the concepts of business profits and economic profits differ? Why are economic profits smaller than business profits?

8. What are the three basic sources of economic profits? Classify each of the following in accordance with these sources:
   a. The profits acquired by a firm from developing and patenting a ballpoint pen containing a permanent ink cartridge, b. The profit of a restaurant which results from construction of the interstate highway past its door, c. The profit received by a firm benefiting from an unanticipated change in consumer tastes.

9. Distinguish between insurable and uninsurable risks. Why is this distinction significant for the theory of profits? Carefully evaluate: "All economic profits can be traced to either uncertainty or the desire to avoid it."

10. Explain the absence of economic profit in a purely competitive static economy. Realizing that the major function of profits is to allocate resources in accordance with consumer preferences, evaluate the allocation of resources in such an economy.

SELECTED REFERENCES

Bober, M. M.: *Intermediate Price and Income Theory,* rev. ed. (New York: W. W. Norton & Company, Inc., 1962), chaps. 15–17.

Due, John F., and Robert W. Clower: *Intermediate Economic Analysis,* 4th ed. (Homewood, Ill.: Richard D. Irwin, Inc., 1961), chaps. 16–19.

Hansen, Alvin: *A Guide to Keynes* (New York: McGraw-Hill Book Company, 1953), chaps. 6 and 7.

Meyers, Albert L.: *Elements of Modern Economics,* 4th ed. (Englewood Cliffs, N.J.: Prentice-Hall, Inc., 1956) chaps. 14–16.

Stonier, Alfred W., and Douglas C. Hague: *A Textbook of Economic Theory,* 3d ed. (New York: Longmans, Green & Co., Inc., 1964), chaps. 13–15.

CHAPTER 33

GENERAL EQUILIBRIUM: THE PRICE SYSTEM AND ITS OPERATION IN AMERICAN CAPITALISM

This chapter is a way station in our study of economics. Here we seek to gain perspective—to envision "the big picture"—in two different senses.

1. It is imperative that, at the conclusion of our detailed analysis of the various categories of product and resource markets, we reemphasize that these many diverse markets are interwoven into a *price system.*

2. This is a convenient juncture for an overall evaluation of the operation of American capitalism—to ask ourselves what the major accomplishments and the basic defects of our economy are.

These two objectives are not unrelated. The dominant feature of American capitalism is that it relies primarily upon a price system in organizing its resources for production. In evaluating the operation of American capitalism, we are largely evaluating the efficiency of the price system in the economy of the United States. Furthermore, we shall find that only when the interrelatedness of individual markets and prices is understood can the major and secondary shortcomings of American capitalism be fully appreciated.

GENERAL EQUILIBRIUM: PRICE INTERRELATIONSHIPS

The preceding eleven chapters have provided us with a rather detailed analysis of how prices are established in several particular types of product markets and how

the prices of specific categories of resources are determined. Thus far our discussion of prices has been compartmentalized; we have examined representative product and resource prices one at a time and apart from any detailed interrelationships each may bear to the other. In the jargon of the economist, we have been concerned with *partial equilibrium analysis*—a study of equilibrium prices and outputs in the many specific markets which are the component *parts* of the price system.

But the economy is not merely a myriad of isolated and unrelated markets. On the contrary, it is an interlocking network of prices wherein changes in one market are likely to elicit numerous and significant changes in other markets. Hence, our vantage point now shifts from individual markets and prices in isolation to an analysis of the price system as a whole. In technical language, our discussion now shifts to *general equilibrium analysis*—an overall big-picture view of the interrelationships between all the various prices (parts) which make up the price *system.*

The interrelatedness of individual prices can best be grasped through an illustration.[1] Suppose initially that general equilibrium exists, that is, that all product and resource

[1] This illustration follows the excellent example discussed in Francis E. Hyde et al., *A New Prospect of Economics* (Liverpool: Liverpool University Press, 1958), chap. 9.

markets are "at rest." Now assume there occurs an increase in the demand for automobiles. What will be the effects?

The immediate impact is obviously an increase in automobile prices. As automobile manufacturers react by increasing production, an increase will occur in the derived demands for, and therefore the prices of, all those resources used in the production of automobiles. These interrelationships between product and resource prices are not new to us; they were a key point in our analysis of resource demand (Chapter 30). In any event, the prospect of higher earnings in the automobile industry will attract resources to it. Industries losing labor to the automobile industry may find it necessary to pay higher wages to counteract this loss, and these higher wage costs imply declining profits for the affected industries. Furthermore, if the shift of labor to the automobile industry involves a geographic relocation of workers and their families, we can expect repercussions upon a number of other industries. For example, the residential construction industry—and therefore cement, lumber, and glass suppliers in the area—will experience an increase in the demand for their products. And, too, the demand for the services of various skilled and semiskilled construction workers will increase, imposing still additional changes on other labor markets. A similar analysis would apply to nonlabor resources. An increase in the demand for automobiles will increase the demand for steel, and we know that the list of firms and industries using substantial amounts of steel reads like a *Who's Who* of American industry. In brief, innumerable other industries using the same types of land, labor, and capital as the automobile industry will find that their costs have increased. This will give rise to increases in the prices and declines in the sales of the products produced by these industries.

But we must not conclude that the effects of an increase in the demand for automobiles emanate solely from the resource market. An increase in the price of automobiles will affect the demand for, and prices of, other goods. The character of these effects depends primarily upon whether these "other goods" happen to be complementary to, or substitutes for, automobiles (Chapter 4). The demand for, and prices of, such complementary products as gasoline, motor oil, and tires will increase in response to the initial increase in the demand for automobiles. The demand for, and prices of, substitute goods, on the other hand, will tend to decline. Bus lines, interurban railways, and taxis will be so affected. These changes in the prices of complementary and substitute goods will be communicated back into the resource markets relevant to all these industries. The initial change in the price of automobiles will have little or no impact upon the prices of such independent goods as, for example, potatoes, wrist watches, razor blades, and file cabinets.

This is still not all: An equally subtle series of price alterations will emanate in the resource market from the initial price increases of those resources used by the automobile industry. As the prices and employment of resources used in automobile production rise, the prices of both substitute and complementary resources will be affected. To illustrate: If the increase in the automobile industry's derived demand for steel significantly increases the price of steel, automobile manufacturers may substitute aluminum where possible for engine and body parts. All other industries using steel may make similar substitutions. As the prices of resources change, all industries and firms employing these resources will tend to shuffle the quantities of the various resources used to reachieve the least costly combination of resources (Chapter 30). This will affect the demand for, and prices of, these resources.

Noteworthy, too, is the fact that all the changes in resource prices which we have sketched will affect the personal distribution of income. In our example, automobile workers will find themselves moving into higher income brackets as the result of the initial increase in the demand for automobiles. They may well react by demanding more superior, or normal, goods such as butter and steak and less of such inferior goods as oleomargarine and potatoes. Indeed, they may even decide to buy still more automobiles, prompting a whole new series of price interactions such as we have already outlined.

The reader will readily note many loose ends in our discussion. If one had the patience and inclination, these price interrelationships could be pursued almost indefinitely. But our discussion is sufficiently detailed to emphasize our major point. Individual prices are interrelated in a number of both evident and subtle ways. Any initial disturbance such as a change in demand, a change in technology, or a change in resource supply will set off a highly complex economic chain reaction.

GENERAL EQUILIBRIUM: INPUT-OUTPUT ANALYSIS

Further appreciation of the intricate interrelationships between the various sectors or industries of the economy can be gained through an input-output table. Table 33–1 is a very highly simplified hypothetical input-output table for an economy.[2] Listed

[2] Wassily W. Leontieff is largely responsible for input-output analysis. See his simplified discussion of "Input-Output Economics," *Scientific American*, October, 1951, pp. 15–21. Table

down the left side of the table are the five producing sectors (industries) of the economy. Column 6 shows the total output associated with each of the five sectors; the metal sector produces 100 units, the machine sector 200 units, and so forth. These same five sectors are also the consuming sectors of the economy and are shown in this capacity across the top of the table. Looking across each of the horizontal rows of figures, we can see how the total output of each sector is disposed of, or consumed, among the five sectors. For example, of the 200 units of output of the machinery sector, 40 units go to the metal sector, 25 to the machinery sector itself (because it takes machines to produce machines!), and 35, 75, and 25 units go to the fuel, agriculture, and household sectors, respectively, thereby exhausting the units produced.

Following through on this disposition-of-output procedure for all five sectors, we find that each vertical column must and does show the units of output of each producing sector which are consumed as inputs by the five sectors. For example, we find in column 2

33–1 and portions of the accompanying discussion are from Francis M. Boddy, "Soviet Economic Growth," in Robert T. Holt and John E. Turner (eds.), *Soviet Union: Paradox and Change* (New York: Holt, Rinehart and Winston, Inc., 1962), pp. 77–79, with permission of the publisher.

TABLE 33–1. A SIMPLIFIED INPUT-OUTPUT TABLE (hypothetical data)

| | Consuming or using sectors | | | | | |
Producing sectors	(1) Metal	(2) Machinery	(3) Fuel	(4) Agriculture	(5) Households (labor)	(6) Total output
(1) Metal	10	65	10	5	10	100
(2) Machinery	40	25	35	75	25	200
(3) Fuel	15	5	5	5	20	50
(4) Agriculture	15	10	50	50	525	650
(5) Labor (households)	100	200	100	550	50	1000

that to produce 200 units of machinery, an input of 65 units of metal, 25 of machinery, 5 of fuel, 10 of agricultural products, and 200 of labor is required. In this way the table vividly reveals the highly interdependent character of the various sectors or industries. Any given industry or sector employs the outputs of other sectors—and indeed some of its own output—as its inputs! And the outputs of that given sector are similarly the inputs of the other sectors. To cite a real-world example: While outputs of steel are inputs in the production of railroad cars, these railroad cars are, in turn, used to transport both steel and the various inputs—coke, pig iron, and so forth—which are necessary to its production.

The interdependence of the economy's sectors or industries can be further demonstrated by tracing through the repercussions of an assumed change in the output of some commodity. Consider, for example, the repercussions of a 20-unit (10 per cent) increase in machinery production. This means that a 10 per cent increase in the production of all of the outputs which are used as inputs in the production of machinery is required.[3] These inputs, as we know, are listed in column 2 of the table. Applying the 10 per cent figure, we find that 6.5 additional units (outputs) of metal, 0.5 unit of fuel, 1 unit of agricultural products, 20 units of labor, and 2.5 units of machinery will be needed to produce another 20 units of machinery. But this is just the beginning: obviously, a myriad of further adjustments are also required. Because each sector which supplies inputs to the machinery sector must expand its output, these supplying sectors in turn will require more inputs from other sectors. Example: The additional 6.5 units of metal needed as inputs to produce the extra 20 units of machinery will in turn call for an appropriate—6.5 per cent in this case—increase in

the production of all the inputs shown in column 1 to be needed in producing metal. The same reasoning, of course, is applicable to the fuel, agriculture, and labor sectors. That is, the 0.5-unit increase in fuel production required in producing the extra 20 units of machinery will call for an appropriate (1 per cent) increase in the production of all the inputs listed in column 3, and similarly for the agricultural and labor sectors. Example: We noted earlier that the production of 20 more units of machinery output requires as inputs the production of 2.5 units of machinery. This 2.5-unit increase will require "second-round" increases (of 1.25 per cent in this case) in the inputs of all the resources shown in column 2 in the same general fashion as did the initial 20-unit increase in machinery output. The reader will clearly recognize that the chain reaction is by no means at an end. All the repercussions cited in these examples call themselves for still further adjustments similar to those already described. The crucial point, of course, is that, because of the high degree of interrelatedness between the sectors of the economy, a change in the figure in any one "cell" or "box" of the input-output table will precipitate an almost endless series of adjustments in other figures. In our illustration, the expansion of production in one sector has nearly innumerable repercussions which reach into virtually every nook and cranny of the economy.

GENERAL EQUILIBRIUM AND ECONOMIC UNDERSTANDING

In what respects, if any, is a knowledge of general equilibrium analysis important? Is an understanding of the interrelationships of prices or sectors useful? Up to a point, at least, an understanding of these interrelationships is an indispensable tool in evaluating the overall operation of the economy, in understanding specific economic problems, and in formulating policies. A failure to recognize price and sector interrelationships is an important source of

---

[3] We invoke here one of the simplifying assumptions underlying the input-output table, namely, that production occurs under conditions of constant returns to scale (see Chapter 25).

misunderstanding and faulty reasoning about major economic problems. Furthermore, input-output analysis lends itself to an abundance of practical applications.

Some examples will clarify these points. In Chapter 31 we noted that the immediate effect of a general wage cut is to reduce the costs of specific firms. And, other things being equal, lower costs will cause a firm to lower prices, increase production, and hire more workers. But general equilibrium analysis tells us that this seemingly obvious conclusion is of very doubtful validity. Lower wages mean lower incomes, which are communicated into the product market as general declines in the demand for, and prices of, products. These price declines are then projected back into the resource market once again as declines in resource demand. And these declines in resource demand will mean unemployment. The immediate impact of wage cuts (more employment) which partial equilibrium analysis suggests may be swallowed up by the secondary effects (less employment), which are discernible only by an understanding of general equilibrium analysis.

Another example: Many people favor protective tariffs levied on, say, Japanese or German toys, because the immediate and obvious effect is to increase the price of foreign toys and therefore increase the demand for American-made toys. The result is that output and employment rise in the American toy industry. But this ignores the fact that incomes in Japan and Germany will decline as a result of their inability to sell toys in the United States. And with smaller incomes they will be less able to buy from American industries exporting machine tools, chemicals, grains, and so forth. The obvious increase in employment in the protected industry may well be offset, wholly or in part, by the indirect, subtle declines in employment in American export industries. As a matter of fact, apart from any decline in domestic employment stemming from tariff-induced declines in exports, general equilib-

rium analysis reminds us that the extra resources which are shifted into the expanding toy industry must come from other industries. That is, in a full-employment economy the tariff-inspired expansion of the toy industry will entail a contraction in the production of other goods. A final illustration: It would not be legitimate to consider the impact of a general sales tax upon the production of one industry in isolation, thereby ignoring its simultaneous effects upon related products. In analyzing the effects of the imposition of a sales tax upon the butter industry one must not ignore the fact that oleomargarine will also be subject to the same tax.

While our interest in input-output analysis has centered upon the pedagogical goal of emphasizing that "everything depends upon everything else" in the economy, it should be noted that input-output analysis has resulted in empirical measurement of the various interactions between sectors of the economy, and these measurements have proven of considerable value as an instrument of economic forecasting and prediction. Assume for the moment a much more detailed input-output table containing 50 or even 500 individual sectors with each box filled with accurate empirical data. Now, for example, if the government should decide to increase the production of Polaris submarines by 25 per cent, the impact of this decision upon affected sectors could be quite accurately predicted; we can forecast quantitatively "what it will take" in terms of the outputs of all the many affected industries to fulfill this goal. Input-output analysis also has great relevance for the underdeveloped nations, virtually all of which seek growth through some form of planning (Chapter 41), and for more advanced centrally planned systems such as the Soviet Union (Chapter 42). By revealing the quantitative interrelationships between various sectors of the economy, input-output analysis allows the planners to determine how realistic—how feasible—planned production targets actually are. By tracing the repercussions of, say, a planned increase in steel production of 10 per cent, the Central Planning Board of the U.S.S.R. can determine what outputs of coal, iron ore, transportation, manpower, relevant capital equipment, and all other inputs used in the production of steel will be needed to fulfill this target. In this way potential bottlenecks to the realization of this goal (or others) may be uncovered; for example, transportation problems may be uncovered, or it may be found that the additional plant capacity required conflicts severely with the planned production of housing or the planned expansion of the chemicals industry. Appropriate adjustments may therefore be made in the production targets for steel or other products to make the plan more realistic and more consistent with the constraints imposed by technology and overall scarcities of economic resources.

General equilibrium analysis provides a broader perspective for analyzing the effects of given economic disturbances or policies than does partial equilibrium analysis. Partial equilibrium analysis shows merely "the big splash" of an initial disturbance; general equilibrium analysis traces the waves and ripples emanating from the big splash. In some instances the waves and ripples are relatively unimportant; in others they may prove to be a tidal wave which changes completely conclusions one would draw from the big splash viewed in isolation. As we noted in Chapter 1, a basic task of the economist is that of ascertaining which waves and ripples are important to the analysis of a given question and which can be safely ignored. In any event a grasp of the general equilibrium point of view is essential in understanding and evaluating our economy.

AN EVALUATION OF AMERICAN CAPITALISM

Equipped with this overview of the price system and an appreciation of the economy's interrelatedness, let us now turn to the task of evaluating the price system as it has operated in American capitalism. At the outset we must note that the price system of American capitalism is a far cry from the purely competitive system described earlier, which tended to allocate resources in a highly efficient manner. Rather our economy is based upon an interrelated network of imperfectly competitive markets and prices. Oligopoly and monopolistic competition, not pure competition, pervade American product and resource markets. The question then is this: How well has American capitalism—based upon an imperfectly competitive price system whose operation is modified by government—managed to reconcile the fact of resource paucity with the insatiability of human material wants?

Problems of Evaluation

It is no easy task to evaluate objectively those individuals and institutions with which one is closely associated. This also holds true in attempting to evaluate the performance of our economy. As participants in American capitalism, we find it quite difficult to stand back and assess objectively its shortcomings and accomplishments. In the first place, biases are likely to plague our analysis in many subtle and almost imperceptible ways. And, too, most of us have no firsthand experience with the operation of alternative economic systems as background in attempting the evaluating process. Another significant stumbling block lies in the fact that it is virtually impossible to determine whether a particular achievement or shortcoming of American capitalism stems from the capitalistic ideology as such (see Chapter 3) or the specific environmental setting of the United States in which it functions. Is it the quantities and characteristics of American resources or is it the particular set of assumptions and institutions constituting the capitalistic ideology which account for American capitalism's successes and failures? Obviously, any analysis of American capitalism cannot clearly distinguish between the two. The present discussion can do no more than evaluate capitalism as it has actually operated in the environment of the United States.

If we wanted to be finicky and detailed, it would be possible to sketch innumerable virtues and vices associated with American capitalism. At this juncture such hair-splitting will be avoided in favor of an overall evaluation which concentrates upon the economy's major accomplishments and defects. Such an evaluation will kill two birds with one stone: It will provide us with a thumbnail assessment of our economy and simultaneously focus attention upon some of the specific problems and issues which are to be explored in Parts Six and Seven of this book. Our evaluation will be both a look backward and a look forward.

Accomplishments of American Capitalism

Generally speaking, there is rather clear-cut agreement that American capitalism has been successful in two respects:

1. The economy has been remarkably productive, providing its citizenry with a high and rising standard of living.

2. American capitalism has provided for a high degree of individual freedom.

Expanding production and a rising standard of living. Over a century ago an intense and vitriolic man penned the greatest tribute to the productivity of capitalism that will probably ever be offered:

The bourgeoisie (capitalist class), during its rule of scarce one hundred years, has created more massive and more colossal productive forces than have all preceding generations together. Subjection of nature's forces to man, machinery, application of chemistry to industry and agriculture, steam navigation, railways, electric telegraphs, clearing of whole continents for cultivation, canalization of rivers, whole populations conjured out of the ground—what earlier century had even a presentiment that

such productive forces slumbered in the lap of social labor?

The time? 1848. The writer? Karl Marx, founding father of the Communist ideology. The document? The *Communist Manifesto*. And capitalism's most ardent opponents continue to admire the productive capabilities of capitalism. Current propaganda emanating from the Kremlin boasts of the Soviet Union's *catching up* with the productive performance of American capitalism.

Needless to say, more sympathetic scholars are also cognizant of the affluency of our economy: [4]

Make no mistake about it, capitalism has performed exceedingly well in the United States and it holds every promise of being able to surpass its own performance . . . if the trend of the past continues into the future for another twenty years, we may within our lifetimes usher into being the first economy of universal sufficiency the world has ever seen.

These testimonials by both friend and foe can be readily fortified with a myriad of facts. Example: It is estimated that the real GNP (in terms of 1960 prices) which was $235 billion in 1940, $363 billion in 1950, and $503 billion in 1960, will soar to $780 billion by 1970, and approach 1 trillion— $955 billion to be exact—by 1975. [5] Example: The real per capita national income of the United States has expanded from a meager $405 in 1850 to a creditable $833 by 1900, and subsequently to a remarkable $1,968 by 1964. Example: The aggregate real national income has tended to double every two decades (Table 20–1). Improvements in product quality and tremendous increases in the amount of leisure with which to enjoy this higher standard of living make these

[4] Robert L. Heilbroner, *The Worldly Philosophers* (New York: Simon and Schuster, Inc., 1953), pp. 282–283.

[5] Arnold B. Barach, *U.S.A. and Its Economic Future* (New York: The Macmillan Company, 1964), pp. 30 and 135.

figures all the more impressive. International comparisons also underscore the prolificness of the American economic machine. The living standard of the average American citizen exceeds that of any other nation of the world (Table 41–1). In terms of aggregates the population of the United States is about 6 per cent of the world's population, its land area is about 7 per cent of the world's total, yet its economy annually produces over 33 per cent of the world's goods and services and almost one-half of the world's factory-produced goods.[6]

As noted earlier, it would be impossible to prove that the opulence of American society has been caused by that particular set of institutions which the capitalist ideology comprises rather than by the fact that an abundance of natural resources is embraced by our national boundaries. On the other hand, it is equally difficult to discount the contention that these institutions have played an important role in making the United States the wealthiest nation the world has ever known. It is hard to shrug aside the argument that the capitalist ideology has been highly successful in harnessing the incentives of individuals. Nor can one readily ignore the assertion that the capitalist ideology has assisted the economy in remaining remarkably flexible over time, helping it adapt itself, for example, to varying rates of technological advance and from a situation of "a fabulously rapid exploitation of virgin resources" to a condition of "a paucity of undeveloped resources."[7]

Individual freedom. The great emphasis which American capitalism puts upon individual freedom is held to be a virtue in and of itself and, at the same time, an important

causal factor underlying its other successes.

One of the most creditable features of our economy is that freedom of choice has persisted largely unscathed despite the many problems which have arisen as the economy has matured and become increasingly complex in its structure and operation. Consumers are still free to choose that collection of goods and services which they feel best satisfies their wants. Resource suppliers are free to choose among the alternative employment opportunities available to them. Further, resource suppliers are free to become entrepreneurs, to assume the uncertainties and risks inherent in forming and operating a business. And the entrepreneur can go into whatever line of production he wishes and freely choose among various methods of production.

Freedom, of course, is a relative concept. Through both legislative action and institutional forces, freedom of choice is limited somewhat. The freedom of individuals is purposely curtailed by government when the exercise of such freedom may impair the freedom or well-being of others. For example, consumers are not free to purchase narcotics because of the great social costs involved. Institutional factors also limit freedom of choice: The required discipline of modern factory production requires that individual workers forgo the freedom to choose the precise number of hours they want to work each day. And, as we have seen, the imperfectly competitive price system puts artificial barriers upon the choices of resource suppliers and potential entrepreneurs. Despite the increasing role of government in regulating economic affairs and the many nongovernmental deterrents to free choice which have developed in modern capitalism, free individual choice is still a dominant characteristic of our society. Democratic government, the political counterpart of this freedom, still flourishes.

This emphasis upon individualism has undoubtedly played a causal role in accounting

[6] Thomas R. Carskadon and George Soule, *U.S.A. in New Dimensions* (New York: The Macmillan Company, 1957), p. 4.
[7] William N. Loucks, *Comparative Economic Systems,* 7th ed. (New York: Harper & Row, Publishers, Incorporated, 1965), p. 45.

for the achievements of American capitalism. Individual freedom has permitted capitalism to harness very effectively the incentives of both workers and entrepreneurs. An individualistic environment is certainly an important stimulant to technological advance and innovation. Similarly, freedom of choice has been at least a permissive factor in inducing the accumulation of property resources.

Having paid our compliments to American capitalism, let us now turn to the less palatable chore of stating and discussing the United States economy's more apparent defects.

Defects of American Capitalism

Two basic shortcomings of our economy are frequently cited:

1. The economy has been characterized by instability. Periods of unemployment and sieges of inflation have characterized American capitalism, giving rise to serious economic insecurity for its citizenry.

2. The growth of monopoly power in both product and resource markets has impaired the allocative efficiency of the price system.

These are the major defects. In addition there are numerous more specific trouble spots in American capitalism.

The business cycle: unemployment, inflation, and insecurity. Capitalism's most vehement critics and its staunchest defenders generally have one point in common: Both groups acknowledge that the performance of American capitalism has been characterized by frequently severe instability. Serious and prolonged unemployment, on the one hand, and troublesome inflation, on the other, have plagued our economy. In particular, the historical record makes it painfully clear that the long-run climb to higher living standards has been punctuated by periodic setbacks (Figure 11–3).

The economic costs of general unemployment are tremendous. For example, in 1929 our economy was riding the crest of prosper-

ity; GNP was a then record-setting $85.9 billion. Unemployment in that year was extraordinarily low—429,000 workers, less than 1 per cent of the labor force. The picture was reversed a scant four years later. The economy's 1933 GNP was a meager $61.5 billion.[8] And by 1933 pay lines had changed to bread lines crowded with some 12 million workers—some 23 per cent of the labor force was out of work! Worse yet, unemployment fluctuated between 6 and 14 million workers all during the 1932–1939 period. About 10½ million workers were still looking for work during the first quarter of 1940. Total cost of the Great Depression? An estimated $650 billion worth of goods and services measured in terms of 1956 prices.

But dollars and cents are not the whole story. There is no way to measure the deterioration of morale, the loss of skills, the undermining of incentives, the loss of self-respect, and the decline in loyalty to the capitalistic ideology which accompany extended periods of unemployment. No nation —not even the wealthiest—can afford the economic and human costs of depression. The potential effects of an inflationary boom can be every bit as serious. By unevenly changing resource and product prices, inflation capriciously penalizes some income receivers and rewards others, and if severe enough, inflation can undermine the value of money to the extent that the economy is thrown into utter chaos. All this is not to say that the historical record of capitalism is a hodgepodge of inflation and unemployment. There have been remarkable periods of stability and growth. But the long pull has been punctuated by periods of severe unemployment and price instability.

Perhaps the most distressing aspect of the business cycle is the fact that some of the basic causal factors lie within the capitalistic ideology itself. Decentralized, individualistic decision making based upon profit and loss

---

[8] Both GNP figures are in terms of 1939 dollars and hence measure real output.

is the ultimate determinant of the level of employment in a capitalistic economy. There is no central agency continually forcing the economy to operate at the full-employment mark. Thus it is possible for millions of individual decisions, grounded on self-interest, not to coincide with society's interest in fully utilizing all its available resources. Furthermore, there are several tendencies within American capitalism which have increased the possibility of recurring periods of instability. On the one hand, the increasing opulence of our society has been accompanied by a marked increase in the production of durable goods for both businesses and consumers. These goods are expensive, and their replacement is typically postponable. Hence, the threat or beginning of a recession might cause investors and consumers to forgo these optional purchases, thereby contributing greatly to the economy's instability. And, further, because investment expands the economy's productive capacity, a higher and higher level of investment is thereby required each year to maintain a given rate of growth; failure to do so means unemployment and stagnation (Chapter 20). Finally, rapid technological progress may contribute to structural unemployment and the persistence of economically distressed areas.

Yet there is a brighter side to this bleak picture. Most economists feel that in fiscal and monetary policy American capitalism has the means for correcting economic instability without scrapping the major cornerstones of the capitalist ideology. Indeed, despite several recessions and disconcerting signs of semistagnation in the late fifties and early sixties, the post–World War II performance of the American economy has been commendable. But guarded optimism is required: remember that in the booming twenties many thinking people were convinced that American capitalism was a depression-proof economy.

The growth of monopoly power. Competition is the organizing and controlling mechanism in a purely capitalistic economy. Economic rivalry forces producers to acknowledge and obey the preferences of consumers (society). It obligates them to employ the most efficient productive techniques in meeting consumer preferences. In short, competition is conducive to an efficient allocation of resources, to full production.

But the price system of American capitalism is permeated with varying degrees of imperfect competition. Monopolistic competition, oligopoly, and sometimes pure monopoly characterize the product and resource markets. As a result of his ability to influence total output, the imperfectly competitive producer can resist the dictates of consumer sovereignty and likely finds it profitable to do so. By artificially blocking or restricting entry to both product and resource markets, imperfect competition deprives the economy of the flexibility required to achieve and maintain an efficient allocation of resources. In brief, it is argued that the imperfectly competitive price system of American capitalism impedes the attainment of full production. Imperfect competition means higher prices and economic profits for those possessing monopoly power, but artificial and economically undesirable distortions of the composition of total output.

As with deviations from full employment, the causal factors underlying the development of monopoly in the economy are not unrelated to the capitalist ideology. In the first place, although competition may be highly desirable from society's point of view, it is most irksome to the individual producer or resource supplier subject to its rigors. It is inherent in the free, individualistic environment of the capitalistic system that the profit-seeking producer will attempt to break free of the restraining force of competition in trying to better his position. Combination, conspiracy, cutthroat competition, and sheer productive efficiency are all means to the end of eliminating competition.

Technological advance has also contributed to the demise of competition in some product markets. Modern technology frequently requires the existence of large-scale monopolistic producers. In other words, the achievement of maximum productive efficiency through the employment of the best available technology often presupposes the concentration of economic power. Technological advance has brought abundance to American capitalism, but in so doing has sometimes contributed significantly to the decline of competition.

As we have seen (Chapter 29), one of the potential redeeming features of imperfect competition may lie in the area of technological advance. Many objective observers are willing to grant that, within limits, imperfect competition has provided the incentive and the financial wherewithal to foster the relatively rapid development of new products and new productive methods. But it would be naïve to suppose that each and every case of monopoly or oligopoly can be justified in terms of technological imperatives. And it would be shortsighted to ignore the possibility that pure competition in these very same industries would have been equally or more progressive.

Another, and noneconomic, aspect of the monopoly problem merits emphasis: Some competent economists feel that the most fundamental danger of monopoly power lies not in its distortion of resource allocation away from the most efficient pattern, but rather in its political implications.[9]

Monopoly . . . is an abomination in a free society. It can come into existence only by the destruction of economic freedom; it can perpetuate itself only by the continued suppression of economic freedom. . . . But monopoly, in order to preserve itself, can do more than merely destroy the free market and restrict competition; it can, transcending the narrow confines of the market place, reach out to suppress both social and political freedom. Monopoly is not, as many assume, strictly an *economic* phenomenon, the

influence of which is limited to the market. On the contrary, it is a power system—and power is a social institution, indivisible and all-pervasive. . . . And herein lies the ultimate danger of unchecked monopoly power—the prospect that it might eventually dominate the entire society and suppress all freedom.

The state, it is argued, must control or be controlled by monopolies.

In Chapter 34 the monopoly problem is explored in terms of the product market. Chapter 36 examines the monopolistic aspects of labor unions in the resource market. In each instance emphasis is upon public policy toward monopoly.

Specific trouble spots: a brief statement. Aside from economic instability and the monopoly problem, there are several other, more specific problem areas in American capitalism which will be accorded detailed treatment in Part Six.

Agriculture. As in most nations, American agriculture has been an economic trouble spot. Ironically, the problem in American agriculture is not underproduction as in most other nations but rather overproduction. Rapid technological advance and relatively stable demand conditions have given rise to the production of voluminous amounts of products which consumers are not willing to purchase at existing prices. The price system—sometimes assisted and sometimes hampered by government programs—has failed to negotiate adjustments appropriate to the correction of these difficulties. This is one area wherein the price system has not provided the flexibility demanded by changing conditions. The "farm problem" will receive detailed treatment in Chapter 35.

Poverty and income inequality. The fruits of America's economic progress have not been equally shared by all participants. The problems of income inequality and, more specifically, of poverty amidst general abundance have their roots firmly embedded in the capitalist ideology. Private property, inheritance rights, the role of self-interest as a motivating force, and the largely impersonal nature of the price system all con-

[9] Walter Adams and Horace M. Gray, *Monopoly in America* (New York: The Macmillan Company, 1955), p. 5. See also Henry C. Simons, *Economic Policy for a Free Society* (Chicago: The University of Chicago Press, 1948).

tribute to income inequality and permit the persistence of poverty. Furthermore, recalling earlier analyses of structural unemployment (Chapter 21), we know that poverty for some can be the unsavory by-product of overall economic progress. Chapter 37 is devoted to the economics of income inequality and the poverty problem.

Social imbalance. In recent years a number of leading economists[10] have contended that the evolution of capitalism in the United States, whereby a nation of relative poverty has become one of relative abundance, has been accompanied by a serious distortion in the composition of total output. A problem of "social imbalance" has allegedly arisen: resources are inefficiently allocated as between private goods and social goods. More specifically, private goods—automobiles, television sets, and electric can openers—abound, while public goods and services—education, police and fire protection, and other basic community services—are remarkably deficient in quantity and quality. In more general terms it is argued that the phenomenal output performance of our economy behooves society to pay somewhat less attention to *how much* we produce and more attention to *what* we produce. As Harvard's Alvin Hansen has so succinctly put it, "We have learned to make a living; we have still to learn how to live." The social imbalance issue is aired in Chapter 38.

International economic problems. Domestic economic problems must share the spotlight with a host of equally important problems in the international sphere. Most evident are the many problems which are associated with international commerce and finance. Some of these problems stem from fundamental imbalances in the structures and needs of the industrially advanced nations and the underdeveloped nations; others can be readily traced to questionable

international economic policies. Of increasingly grave concern is the many-sided problem of the underdeveloped nations. American capitalism affects and is affected by this problem. In these underdeveloped areas lie vast potential markets and sources of raw materials crucial to the sustaining of American economic growth. And in these areas reside people whom we are morally obligated to assist in achieving higher levels of material well-being. Finally, the economic challenge of the Soviet Union presents perhaps the most acute international problem of our times. All these international economic problems are explored in Part Seven of this book.

Two Qualifying Comments

Two final observations must supplement our evaluation of American capitalism:

1. The defects of American capitalism are not necessarily peculiar to economies which embrace the capitalist ideology. For example, many socialist countries are plagued by unemployment and inflation. These are real problems, for example, in the liberal socialism of Great Britain. And the authoritarian brand of socialism characteristic of the Soviet Union has failed to eradicate these problems. The Soviet economy has faced rather severe inflationary pressures, and although cyclical unemployment as such does not exist, underemployment is a serious problem. Similarly, the relative inequality with which income is distributed in other nations rivals and in some cases surpasses that in the United States. In short, the present discussion of American capitalism's defects is not meant to imply that these difficulties are the exclusive heritage of capitalism. Much the same can be said of capitalism's successes. We shall discover in a later chapter that the Soviet Union's rate of growth in recent years has exceeded that of the United States.

2. The reader will undoubtedly have noted that certain of our economy's shortcomings are related to its successes. For example, technological advance, a major

---

[10] See Alvin H. Hansen, *The American Economy* (New York: McGraw-Hill Book Company, 1957), chap. 8, and John K. Galbraith, *The Affluent Society* (Boston: Houghton Mifflin Company, 1958).

driving force behind the economy's high standard of living, has undoubtedly been a contributing factor in the development of monopoly power and has intensified the problem of structural unemployment. Similarly, as we have already noted, capitalism's emphasis upon freedom of choice and decentralized decision making has provided an environment permissive of both the business cycle and the development of monopoly power.

It may appear that the preceding discussion has unduly manhandled our beloved capitalism. This is very possibly true, but there is reason in our bluntness. Our evaluation has purposely emphasized the weak spots in our economy, because a strong statement of the defects and shortcomings of the economy helps to drive home the point that American capitalism is by no means a perfect, or ideal, economic system. Certainly we are justified in generally praising our economy's performance, but there is plenty of room for improvement; and it is through stating and analyzing the economy's defects, not through praising its accomplishments, that improvement is brought about. Our present evaluation of American capitalism is analogous to a physical examination. The main purpose is to put the spotlight on defects and weak spots, not to dwell on strong points.

It is most dangerous to ignore or to understate American capitalism's shortcomings on the implicit assumption that they will somehow correct themselves and blow away. The improvement and strengthening of the economy demands that we emphasize the economy's failures.

SUMMARY

1. General equilibrium analysis is concerned with the operation of the entire price system and the interrelationships between different markets and prices. These interrelationships are important in that they might modify or negate the immediate effects of economic disturbances or policies which partial equilibrium analysis reveals. The input-output table provides a kind of general equilibrium analysis which reveals the overall fabric of the economy by focusing upon the interdependencies or linkages that exist between the various sectors or industries which it comprises. Input-output analysis has many practical applications to economic forecasting and planning.

2. The major accomplishments of American capitalism have been **a.** its tremendous productive capacity and the high standard of living which has resulted therefrom and **b.** the high degree of individual freedom which prevails in the economy.

3. The basic shortcomings of our economy are **a.** its susceptibility to cyclical fluctuations and **b.** the development of monopoly power in both product and resource markets.

4. More specific problem areas in the domestic economy have to do with overproduction in the agricultural segment, income inequality and poverty, and social imbalance. International economic problems entail certain fundamental imbalances between the advanced and the underdeveloped nations, faulty international economic policies, the economic development of the underdeveloped nations, and the economic challenge of Soviet Russia.

QUESTIONS AND STUDY SUGGESTIONS

1. Compare partial and general equilibrium analysis. In what respect is each useful?
2. Trace through the price system the economic effects of:
   a. The development of a man-made fiber which never wears out, fades, or stains
   b. A permanent increase in the demand for leather
   c. A sharp decline in the size of the labor force

   d. The development of a new production technique which cuts the cost of color television by 30 per cent

3. What is an input-output table? Using Table 33–1, trace through some of the repercussions of a 5-unit (10 per cent) increase in fuel production. What insights might input-output provide as to the operation of a capitalistic system? How might input-output analysis be used as a "mechanism of coordination" in a centrally planned system?

4. Cite examples other than those given in the text which indicate the contribution general equilibrium analysis can make to the understanding of economic problems and policies.

5. What are some of the difficulties involved in attempting to evaluate objectively the operation of any economic system? Be specific. By what means, if any, can these difficulties be overcome?

6. In your opinion what is capitalism's most important success? Why? What is its most significant shortcoming? Why?

7. In what ways do the shortcomings of capitalism affect the noneconomic aspects of our society? Be specific.

8. Explain in detail how the institutions and ideology of American capitalism have played at least a permissive role in (*a*) causing business fluctuations and economic insecurity, (*b*) contributing to income inequality, and (*c*) abetting the growth of monopoly.

9. "The most striking successes of American capitalism bear the seeds of its most significant shortcomings." Critically evaluate. Do you agree?

10. "The elimination of inequality and instability would entail the undermining and destruction of the capitalistic ideology." Evaluate critically but fairly.

SELECTED REFERENCES

Bowen, Howard R.: *Toward Social Economy* (New York: Holt, Rinehart and Winston, Inc., 1948), particularly chaps. 15 and 16.

Due, John F., and Robert W. Clower: *Intermediate Economic Analysis*, 4th ed. (Homewood, Ill.: Richard D. Irwin, Inc., 1961), chaps. 20 and 23.

Loucks, William: *Comparative Economic Systems*, 7th ed. (New York: Harper & Row, Publishers, Incorporated, 1965), chaps. 3 and 4.

Phelps-Brown, E. H.: *The Framework of the Pricing System* (London: Chapman & Hall, Ltd., 1936).

Stigler, George J.: *The Theory of Price*, rev. ed. (New York: The Macmillan Company, 1952), chap. 16.

PART SIX: CURRENT DOMESTIC

ECONOMIC PROBLEMS

CHAPTER 34

THE MONOPOLY PROBLEM:
THE SOCIAL CONTROL OF INDUSTRY

Previous chapters have made these two contrasting points:

1. Many important American industries are characterized by considerable monopoly power. Some of these industries were shown in Table 29–1.

2. It was noted in Chapter 6 that one of the basic economic functions of government is to preserve competition as a key mechanism of control in the economy.

It is the overall objective of the present chapter to describe and evaluate governmental policies toward business monopolies. More specifically, the objectives of this chapter are threefold:

1. To review briefly the case against, and then state the case for, business monopolies

2. To understand and appraise government policies toward business monopolies

3. To explore several possible future public policy alternatives

BIG BUSINESS AND MONOPOLY

Before considering the pros and cons of business monopoly, we must pause to define our terminology. In Chapters 22 and 27 we developed and applied a very strict definition of monopoly. A *pure*, or *absolute*, monopoly, we said, is a one-firm industry— a situation in which a unique product is produced entirely by one firm, entry to the industry being blocked by certain insurmountable barriers. When a single firm controls an entire market, pure monopoly exists.

In the present chapter we shall find it convenient to use the term "monopoly" in a broader sense. *Monopoly exists whenever a small number of firms controls all or a large portion of the output of a major industry.* This definition, which comes closer to the way the man in the street understands monopoly, includes many industries which we have heretofore designated as oligopolies.

What is the difference between monopoly (as we have just defined it) and big business? The term "big business" may be defined either in terms of a firm's share of the total market for its product or in terms of some absolute measure such as the volume of its assets, sales, or profits, the number of workers employed, or the number of stockholders. A firm can obviously be large *in relation to* the size of the total market but small in an *absolute* sense. The Weeping Water General Store may almost completely dominate the local market for a good many products yet be exceedingly small by any meaningful absolute standard. Conversely, a firm might be very large in the absolute sense but small in relation to the total market. For example, American Motors is large by most absolute standards one can employ. In 1964 its net sales revenue was $1,132,356,298, some 32,983 employees were on its payroll, and net income after taxes totaled $37,807,-205. Yet American Motors sells only about 5 per cent of all automobiles in the United States. In so far as the automobile industry is concerned, American Motors is a small producer. However, *in a good many instances absolute and relative bigness go hand in hand.* A firm which is large in absolute terms very frequently controls a significant portion of the market for its product. Thus, although "big business" and "monopoly" are not necessarily synonymous, they frequently do go together. The present chapter is concerned with the type of situation in which absolute and relative bigness are both present. In using the term "business monopoly" in this chapter, we refer to those industries in which firms are large in absolute terms and in relation to the total market. Examples are the electrical equipment industry, where General Electric and Westinghouse, large by any absolute standard, dominate the market; the automobile industry, where General Motors, Ford, and Chrysler are similarly situated; the chemical industry, dominated by du Pont, Union Carbide, and Allied Chemical; the aluminum industry, where three industrial giants— Alcoa, Reynolds, and Kaiser—reign supreme; and the cigarette industry, where four giant firms of Reynolds, Liggett and Myers, American Tobacco, and Lorillard have the lion's share of the market.[1]

MONOPOLY: CASES FOR AND AGAINST

It is not at all clear whether business monopolies are on balance advantageous or disadvantageous to the functioning of American capitalism. Note these two statements—one bitterly opposed to monopoly in any form or context and the other viewing business monopoly as an integral part of modern American capitalism:

Monopoly power must be abused. It has no use save abuse. . . . There must be an outright dismantling of our gigantic corporations and persistent prosecution of producers who organize, by whatever methods, for price maintenance or output limitation.
. . . Legislation must prohibit, and administration effectively prevent, the acquisition by any private firm, or group of firms, of substantial monopoly power.[2]

[1] See George J. Stigler, "The Case against Bigness in Business," *Fortune*, May, 1952, p. 123.
[2] Henry C. Simons, *Economic Policy for a Free Society* (Chicago: The University of Chicago Press, 1948), pp. 129, 158.

In our economy big business undertakes the major role of coordinating individual efforts and resources into collective achievement. This is a function that must be undertaken under modern technology, whether by private enterprise or by the state. In the United States it has been possible so to mix dispersion with centralization that the major job can be left to private competition, under government regulation. Big business has not merely been kept effectively subject to a competitive system; on the whole it has also made an essential contribution to its scope, vitality, and effectiveness.[3]

These are not propaganda blasts sponsored by antimonopoly and promonopoly pressure groups. Rather they are the well-considered arguments of respected scholars. These two assertions accurately reflect that there is ample room for serious disagreement as to the desirability of business monopolies in American capitalism. Almost endless debate on this issue has precipitated a series of rather well-defined arguments on both sides. Our immediate goal is to outline these divergent views.

Case against Monopoly

The case against business monopoly was largely stated in Chapter 27 and may be summarized as follows:

1. Monopolists find it possible and profitable to restrict output and charge higher prices than would competitive producers.

2. The monopolist's profit-maximizing output entails a misallocation of economic resources. It is through his ability to block or retard the entry of new firms and resources into an industry that the monopolist can realize economic profits in the long run. These profits are an indication that consumers want more resources allocated to the production of the monopolized commodity. More technically, monopolists maximize profits by producing an output at which price (society's measure of product X's relative

[3] A. D. H. Kaplan, *Big Enterprise in a Competitive System* (Washington, D.C.: The Brookings Institution, 1954), p. 248.

worth) exceeds marginal cost (society's measure of the worth of the alternative products which the resources used in producing an extra unit of X could otherwise have produced).

3. The persistent economic profits which monopolists realize contribute to greater inequality in the distribution of income.

4. Monopoly is conducive to a slow rate of technological advance. The sheltered position of the monopolist is conducive to inefficiency and lethargy; there is no competitive spur to productive efficiency. Furthermore, monopolists are inclined to resist or suppress technological advances which may cause the sudden obsolescence of their existing machinery and equipment.

5. Monopoly is an obstacle to the achievement of economic stability, that is, full employment with reasonable price stability. Two somewhat distinct assertions underlie this point. On the one hand, it was noted in Chapter 18 that business monopolies are in a position of relative immunity in so far as an anti-inflationary (tight) money policy is concerned. Indeed, the ability of monopolists to manipulate prices may cause a tight money policy to contribute indirectly to inflation as monopolists pass interest rate increases on to consumers through product price increases. On the other hand, we saw in Chapter 21 that business monopolies, in conjunction with labor monopolies, can cause cost-push inflation in the absence of full employment through the exertion of their market power. Business monopolies are allegedly active agents in an inflationary process which is not directly remedied by the demand-restricting efforts of a tight money policy or a fiscal surplus.

6. Finally, we noted in Chapter 33 that business monopoly may pose serious political dangers. The growth of monopoly, it is argued, must result in one of two possible outcomes: Monopoly may come to exert undue influence upon government and therefore the formation of public policy, or government will be forced to regulate monopoly. In other words, government must control monopoly or be controlled by it. In either

instance the result will be a basic alteration in the structure of our economy or the free political institutions which now characterize it.

Case for Monopoly

But business monopoly is not without defense. A series of plausible arguments with which we are only partially familiar have been evolved to explain and justify the existence of the giant business enterprises which dominate various markets.

1. The presence of *workable competition* effectively regulates the operations of big businesses. It is argued that there exist certain types of competition, more subtle than the mere presence of a large number of rival producers, which in fact make so-called monopolistic industries "workably competitive." This contention suggests that any judgment of the competitiveness of an industry which rests solely on the number of existing producers is incomplete and misleading, because it overlooks other important dimensions of competition.

The general argument has several more specific facets. (*a*) All products are in competition for the dollars of consumers. A down payment on a house is often a good substitute for a new automobile. A new dress and accessories are sometimes in strong competition with a new vacuum cleaner for the housewife's dollars. Refrigerators compete with washing machines, television sets, and air conditioners. This argument shades into (*b*) interproduct competition as a factor to be considered in judging the competitiveness of an industry. The fact that only three firms are responsible for the nation's output of aluminum belies the competition which aluminum faces in specific markets from steel, copper, wood, plastics, and a variety of other products. These first two aspects of workable competition both suggest that the demand for the products of a monopolistic industry may be considerably more elastic than the number of firms in that specific industry would imply. (*c*) Competition in the form of countervailing power must not be ignored (Chapter 29). An original position of monopoly power tends to induce the growth of monopoly power on the opposite side of the market. This across-the-market competition provides effective checks, or restraints, on both the original and the countervailing power position. Countervailing power effectively prevents abuses of monopoly power in those very markets in which traditional same-side-of-the-market competition is weak. (*d*) It is argued that *potential* competition and the fear of censure can regulate the behavior of monopolists almost as effectively as does the actual presence of a large number of rivals. The possibility that new rival firms will be formed or that other industrial giants will branch out works against the monopolist's exploiting his market power. The fear of public censure, the embarrassment of an antitrust suit, or the possibility of government regulation may also contribute to the monopolist's disinclination to exert his monopoly power. (*e*) Of greatest importance is the competitive role of technological progress. Technological advance operates over a period of time so as to circumscribe and undermine existing monopoly positions. Innovation, in particular the development of new products, is a force which persistently destroys the market power of individual firms, making monopoly power a precarious and transitory phenomenon.

Those who emphasize the importance of workable competition feel that firms and industries should be judged not on the basis of their market structure but rather in terms of their performance. Such characteristics as the number of firms in the industry and the importance of barriers to entry should be supplanted by criteria of performance—price, efficiency of production, and rate of technological advance—in gauging the social desirability of an industry or specific firm. Defenders of business monopoly contend that many industries which fall short of the large-numbers no-barriers criteria nevertheless perform very well, efficiently producing a quality product at a low price.

As a matter of fact, probably the main cornerstone of the case for monopoly centers upon technology as an aspect of efficient performance. Two related arguments are made: The utilization of the most efficient technologies demands the existence of large monopolistic producers, and the rate of technological advancement is more rapid when an industry is characterized by a few large producers than would be the case if a large number of small competing firms existed.

2. Existing mass-production economies can be realized only by big businesses. Where existing technology is highly advanced, only large producers—firms which are large both absolutely and in relation to the market—can realize low unit costs and therefore sell to consumers at relatively low prices. This line of reasoning is used to counter the contention that monopoly means less output, higher prices, and an inefficient allocation of resources. Critics of monopoly, it is argued, incorrectly overlook economies of scale in their price-output comparisons of competitive and monopolistic producers.

Antimonopoly economists, although generally recognizing an element of truth in this technological defense of monopoly, offer several noteworthy counterarguments. (*a*) Many existing monopolies allegedly have attained a size far beyond that necessary for the realization of all existing economies of scale. It is contended, for example, that the Chevrolet, Pontiac, Oldsmobile, Buick, and Cadillac divisions of General Motors are for operating purposes independent producers. How then can their legal unification be justified on the basis of mass-production economies? And how do economies of scale justify the expansion of General Motors into the appliance and locomotive fields? How can technology justify the existence of U.S. Steel, a giant business corporation composed of a number of geographically distinct plants? Furthermore, if economies of scale are so significant, how can relatively small firms successfully persist in many industries dominated by a few very large firms? (*b*) A second counterargument emphasizes that the low unit costs achieved by big producers are not so much the result of any *real* advantages over smaller firms in combining resources as they are the consequence of the larger firms' exerting their superior bargaining power as large buyers to depress resource prices. The existence of business monopolies does not make for an expansion of the real output and income of the economy but rather for a redistribution of income in favor of business monopolists and at the expense of resource suppliers. (*c*) It is argued that empirical studies fail to indicate that the largest firms are the most efficient. Critics of monopoly conclude that available evidence suggests that medium-sized producers are most efficient in many industries.

3. Monopolistic industries—in particular, three- or four-firm oligopolies—are conducive to a high rate of technological advance. Such firms, it is contended, have both the financial resources and the incentive to undertake technological research.[4]

. . . The modern industry of a few large firms [is] an excellent instrument for inducing technical change. It is admirably equipped for financing technical development. Its organization provides strong incentives for undertaking development and for putting it into use. . . . In the modern industry shared by a few large firms, size and the rewards accruing to market power combine to insure that resources for research and technical development will be available. The power that enables the firm to have some influence on prices insures that the resulting gains will not be passed on to the public by imitators (who have stood none of the costs of development) before the outlay for development can be recouped. In this way market power protects the incentive to technical development.

4. Business monopolies exert a stabilizing influence upon the economy because of both their investment policies and their pricing policies. Concerning investment policies, it is argued that the absolute and relative size of business monopolies permits them to gear

their investment spending to long-run business prospects rather than to the short-term cyclical upswings and downswings which are so influential in determining the investment outlays of smaller, competitive firms. Thus it has been argued that a part of the stability achieved in the 1950s arose from the fact that the long-term investment programs of large monopolies were continued despite short-term changes in inventory investment and consumer spending. A more debatable assertion is that the ability of business monopolies to resist price reductions during recession (coupled with the propensity of unions to resist wage cuts) helps thwart the development of a cumulative wage-price deflationary spiral and the accompanying declines in output and employment.

5. A few economists and most business groups suggest that business leaders are blessed with a strong sense of social responsibility which will mitigate, if not eliminate entirely, abuses of monopoly power. Although industry leaders command tremendous economic power, we are assured that they have the social maturity not to wield this power in a manner detrimental to the public interest. The public-be-damned attitude of business monopolies in earlier decades is allegedly a thing of the past.

PUBLIC POLICY TOWARD MONOPOLY

In view of the sharp conflict of opinion over the relative merits of business monopoly, it is not surprising to find that government policy toward business monopolies has been something less than clear-cut and consistent. As reflected in major pieces of legislation, the Federal government's stated policy objective is the maintenance of competition. Yet the government has passed legislation and at times pursued policies which have furthered the development of monopoly power. As one scholar has aptly phrased it,[5]

---

[4] John Kenneth Galbraith, *American Capitalism*, rev. ed. (Boston: Houghton Mifflin Company, 1956), pp. 86–88.

[5] Fritz Machlup, *The Political Economy of Monopoly* (Baltimore: Johns Hopkins Press, 1952), p. 182.

Governments, apparently, have never been able to make up their minds as to which they dislike more, competition or monopoly. . . . Whether government activities, on the basis of the presently existing body of law, are on balance more favorable to monopoly or competition is controversial.

Government, in short, has both restrained business monopoly and promoted it.

Legislation and Policies Restricting Monopoly

Historically, American capitalism, steeped in the philosophy of free, competitive markets, has been a fertile ground for the development of a suspicious and fearful public attitude toward business monopolies. Though relatively dormant for many decades, this fundamental distrust of monopoly came into full bloom in the decades following the Civil War. The widening of local markets into national markets as transportation facilities improved, the ever-increasing mechanization of production, and the increasingly widespread adoption of the corporate form of business enterprise were important forces giving rise to the development of "trusts"— that is, business monopolies—in the 1870s and 1880s. Trusts developed in the petroleum, meat-packing, sugar, lead, coal, whisky, and tobacco industries, among others, during this era. Not only were questionable tactics employed in monopolizing the various industries, but the resulting market power was almost invariably exerted to the detriment of all who did business with these monopolies. Farmers and small-business men, being particularly vulnerable to the growth and tactics of the giant corporate monopolies, were among the first to censure their development. Consumers and labor unions were not far behind.

The Sherman Act of 1890. The acute public resentment of the trusts culminated in the passage of the Sherman Antitrust Act in 1890. This cornerstone of antitrust legislation

is surprisingly brief and, at first glance, directly to the point. The core of the act is embodied in two major provisions:

In Section 1:

Every contract, combination in the form of a trust or otherwise, or conspiracy, in restraint of trade or commerce among the several states, or with foreign nations is hereby declared to be illegal. . . .

In Section 2:

Every person who shall monopolize, or attempt to monopolize, or combine or conspire with any person or persons, to monopolize any part of the trade or commerce among the several states, or with foreign nations, shall be deemed guilty of a misdemeanor. . . .

The act had the effect of making monopoly and "restraints of trade" criminal offenses against the Federal government. Either the government or parties injured by business monopolies could file suits under the Sherman Act. Firms found in violation of the act could be ordered dissolved by the courts, or injunctions could be issued to prohibit practices deemed unlawful under the act. Fines and imprisonment were also possible results of successful prosecution. Further, parties injured by illegal combinations and conspiracies could sue for triple the amount of damages done them. The Sherman Act seemed to provide a sound foundation for positive government action against business monopolies.

A study of key antitrust cases indicates that at times the Sherman Act has been applied with great verve and effectiveness, whereas at other times it has lain dormant. Two considerations go far to explain this inconsistency:

1. The Federal government has varied considerably in its willingness to apply the act. Administrations "friendly" toward big business have sometimes emasculated the act by the simple process of ignoring it or by

cutting the budget appropriations of enforcement agencies.

2. The courts have run hot and cold in interpreting the Sherman Act and its various amendments. At times the courts have applied the Sherman Act with vigor, adhering closely to the spirit and objectives of the law. In other cases, the courts have interpreted the act in such ways as to render it all but completely innocuous.

These varying interpretations of the act by the courts undoubtedly arose in good measure from its loose and general wording. Not too many years after the passage of the Sherman Act it was quite evident that a more explicit statement of the government's antitrust sentiments was in order.

The Clayton Act and the Federal Trade Commission Act, 1914. This needed elaboration of the Sherman Act took the form of the 1914 Clayton Antitrust Act. The following sections of the Clayton Act were designed to strengthen and make explicit the intent of the Sherman Act:

Section 2 outlaws price discrimination between purchasers when such discrimination is not justified on the basis of cost differences.

Section 3 forbids exclusive, or "tying," contracts, whereby a producer would sell a product only on the condition that the buyer acquire other products from the same seller and not from competitors.

Section 7 prohibits the acquisition of stocks of competing corporations when the effect is to lessen competition.

Section 8 prohibits the formation of interlocking directorates in large corporations where the effect will be to reduce competition.

Actually there was little in the Clayton Act which had not already been stated by implication in the Sherman Act. The Clayton Act merely attempted to sharpen and make clear the general provisions of the Sherman Act. Furthermore, the Clayton Act attempted to outlaw the techniques by which monopoly might develop and, in this sense, was a preventive measure. The Sherman Act, by contrast, was aimed at the punishment of existing monopolies.

The Federal Trade Commission Act was also passed in 1914. It too was based on the belief that preventive rather than mere punitive measures were needed to sustain competition. Specifically, the act was designed to prevent competition from assuming certain aggressive forms which would tend to undermine competition and bring about the development of monopoly power. The act created the Federal Trade Commission, a permanent five-man board, and charged it with the power to investigate unfair competitive practices on its own initiative or at the request of injured firms. The Commission could hold public hearings on such complaints and, if necessary, issue cease-and-desist orders where "unfair methods of competition in commerce" were discovered.

The antitrust potential of the FTC has been limited by subsequent court rulings which have restricted the investigatory powers of the Commission and made it clear that the courts, not the FTC, have the final authority in interpreting the meaning of the antitrust laws. Then in 1938 the Wheeler-Lea Act amended the Federal Trade Commission Act by prohibiting "unfair or deceptive acts or practices in commerce." As a result, a primary task of the FTC now is the prohibition of false and misleading advertising and the misrepresentation of products.

More recent antitrust legislation. More recent antitrust legislation has taken the form of amendments designed to plug loopholes in—and thereby strengthen—the Clayton Act.

The Robinson-Patman Act of 1936 amended Section 2—the price discrimination section—of the Clayton Act. This section, you will recall, attempted to eliminate the practice by which producers charged different prices to different buyers, where the objective was to drive competing producers from business. The various trusts frequently employed such cutthroat tactics—charging extremely low prices in markets in which small competitors persisted but higher prices in markets where competition had already been eliminated—as a method of improving and strengthening their monopoly positions. The Robinson-Patman Act, or "Chain Store Law," had a different background. It was aimed at the growing number of chain stores which, so argued independent retailers, were obtaining large and unjustified price discounts from wholesalers because of their strong bargaining positions as large buyers. By passing some of these cost savings on to consumers in the form of price reductions, the chains allegedly were driving their independent competitors to the wall. The Robinson-Patman Act outlaws quantity discounts to large buyers when such discounts are not justified on the basis of actual cost economies arising from mass buying. And, in turn, the act prohibits retailers from selling "at unreasonably low prices" when the purpose is to eliminate competitors. Many economists feel that the effect of the act has been not so much to deter the growth of monopoly but rather to stifle price competition, particularly at the retail level, and therefore to sustain inefficient retailers who would otherwise succumb to more vigorous competition.

Finally, the Celler Antimerger Act of 1950 amended Section 7 of the Clayton Act, the section which prohibits one firm from acquiring the *stock* of competitors when the effect is to reduce competition. This provision had been weakened by court decisions and had been dodged by firms who merged with competitors by acquiring their *assets* rather than their stock. The Celler Act attempted to tighten the stock acquisition ban and also prohibited the acquisition of the assets of competitors when the effect was to lessen competition.

Effectiveness of antitrust legislation. How effective has antitrust legislation been in restricting the growth of monopoly? It is hard to say. Although there is sharp and often violent disagreement on this question, the consensus seems to be that antitrust

legislation has generally helped to slow the growth of business monopoly in the economy but has accomplished little or nothing by way of restoring competition. Many economists are of the opinion that stronger antitrust laws coupled with more vigorous and more discriminating enforcement could do much to make our economy even more competitive. It is felt in some quarters that faulty judicial interpretations, legal loopholes, and indifferent Federal administrations have undermined and considerably weakened antitrust policy. Most importantly, there is rather widespread agreement that many of the government's most notable legal victories in applying the antitrust laws have proven to be economic defeats. That is, the guilty firms have agreed to cease-and-desist orders or have been subject to minor penalties rather than forced to dissolve. Indeed, even when dissolution has occurred, the economic benefits have been dubious: When it comes to price and output policies, a tight three- or four-firm oligopoly is likely to behave much as the absolute monopoly which once comprised it.

On the positive side, it must be recognized that there currently exists widespread interest in antitrust. Examples: The Senate Subcommittee on Antitrust and Monopoly has conducted detailed investigations of administered prices in the automobile, steel, and drug industries; the Department of Justice indicted the nation's principal electrical equipment producers in late 1960 for conspiracy in violation of the Sherman Act; and, finally, economists have reasserted their long-standing interest in the monopoly problem as the cost-push and structural theories of inflation have emphasized market power as a cause of rising prices.

Legislation and Policies Promoting Monopoly

Let us now consider briefly the other side of the picture. Government has directly and indirectly promoted the growth of monopoly in several different ways.

Industry exemptions to the antitrust laws.
Over the years government has enacted certain laws which have either exempted certain specific industries or, alternatively, have excluded certain trade practices from antitrust prosecution. In doing so, the government has tended indirectly to foster the growth of monopoly power.

In 1918 the Webb-Pomerene Act exempted American exporters from the antitrust laws by permitting them to form export trade associations. Although the act was intended to put American exporters in a stronger competitive position with international cartels, the effect has probably been to reduce competition in both international and domestic markets.

We have already noted too that the Robinson-Patman Act of 1936 had the effect of dampening price competition at the retail level. The Miller-Tydings Act of 1937, amending the Sherman Act, moved in the direction of eliminating this competition. This so-called fair-trade law exempts from antitrust laws *resale price maintenance contracts* for branded and trademarked goods when such contracts are permitted by state legislation. Price maintenance contracts allow manufacturers to set the retail prices of their products by signing contracts to this effect with retailers. The Miller-Tydings Act has operated so that these agreements have applied not only to those retailers who actually enter into such contracts but also to all other "nonsigner" retailers in the state. This means that if one retailer signs a price maintenance contract, the agreement is binding on *all* other retailers in the state. The net effect has been to restrict price competition on branded products at the retail level; a monopolistic practice—price fixing—has been injected by legislation into an otherwise highly competitive segment of the economy.

It should be noted, too, that labor unions and agricultural cooperatives have been exempt, subject to limitations, from the antitrust laws. We shall see in the next chapter that Federal legislation and policy have attempted to provide some measure of monopolistic power for agriculture, feeling that this

would help alleviate the farm problem. Similarly, in a subsequent chapter we shall discover that since 1930 Federal legislation on balance has generally promoted the growth of strong labor unions. This Federally sponsored growth has resulted, according to some authorities, in the development of union monopolies. This will later be discussed further.

Public utility legislation. The Interstate Commerce Act of 1887 was the first of several Federal laws which had the effect of declaring certain aspects of the transportation, communications, and power industries to be "public utilities," or "natural monopolies."

The Interstate Commerce Act was based on the supposition that competition was unworkable in the railroad industry. Certain industry characteristics ruled out the possibility of effective competition:

1. Relatively large fixed costs entailed the necessity of large-scale operations by each firm in order to achieve efficient, low-cost service.

2. The existence of several firms would entail the wasteful duplication of very costly capital facilities.

3. The service supplied—transportation—was essential to many firms and individuals.

And, as a matter of fact, "competition" had not worked well in this industry. Price competition aimed at the fuller realization of economies of scale often degenerated into cutthroat competition and losses for all participants. The results would be either the elimination of the weaker competitors and the evolution of monopoly or the establishment of a collusive price agreement of some sort by which the competitors sought to improve their lot. If monopoly resulted, the exploitation of that power through discriminatory pricing—that is, charging what the traffic would bear—was likely. If a collusive price resulted, the industry would then operate in much the same manner as a pure monopoly, at least until another round of price warring was precipitated.

In view of such circumstances the Interstate Commerce Act was passed by Congress to make railroads regulated monopolies. Although their management and actual operation remained in private hands, an Interstate Commerce Commission was established to regulate the rates and the services of railroads. Similar legislation has established public utilities in the fields of air transportation, power, and radio and television and has also created appropriate regulatory commissions.

The intent of this "natural monopoly" legislation is to regulate such industries effectively and for the benefit of the public to the end that consumers might be assured quality service at reasonable rates. The rationale is this: If competition is inappropriate, *regulated* monopolies should be established to avoid possible abuses of uncontrolled monopoly power. In particular, regulation should guarantee that consumers benefit from the economies of scale—that is, the lower per unit costs—which their natural-monopoly position allows public utilities to achieve. Few would quarrel with this reasoning.

But there is serious disagreement as to whether or not the government's control over the various public utility monopolies has been at all effective. Some reputable scholars feel that the various regulatory commissions have not only created, but have also protected and subsidized, the so-called natural monopolies.[6] Though willing to note that public regulation has been something less than perfect, many other economists feel that public regulation has been at least reasonably effective and that it is clearly preferable to the obvious alternatives of no regulation or public ownership. A poorly regulated monopoly, it is reasoned, is superior to private monopoly and may well be more conducive to expansion and technological advance than would be public ownership. There is no simple generalization here.

[6] Walter Adams and Horace M. Gray, *Monopoly in America* (New York: The Macmillan Company, 1955), p. 71.

Patent laws. Technological research is a costly and risky procedure. American patent laws—the first of which was passed in 1790—are aimed at providing sufficient monetary incentive for innovators by granting them exclusive rights to produce and sell a new product or machine for a period of seventeen years. Patent grants have the effect of protecting the innovator from competitors who would otherwise quickly imitate his product and share in the profits, though not the cost and effort, of his research. Few contest the desirability of this particular aspect of our patent laws.

However, patents are a mixed blessing. The granting of a patent frequently amounts to the granting of monopoly power in the production of the patented item. Many economists feel that the length of patent protection—seventeen years—is much too long. Such an extended period of protection from competitors is likely to allow the innovator to entrench himself firmly in a monopoly position to the extent that he is able to block successfully any potential competition after his patent expires. This is particularly true if the innovating firm extends its patent rights longer than seventeen years by patenting improved models of the original innovation. By this and similar procedures innovating firms have often been able to extend their exclusive jurisdiction over a product for three or four decades!

When patents are licensed to competitors, the innovating firm has the right to specify the prices which these competitors may charge for the product, the markets in which they may sell, and even the amounts which they may produce. The result is that the innovator faces no genuine competition. The worst abuses of patent rights occur when one firm accumulates by research or purchase a large number of related patents or, alternatively, several firms in an industry "pool" the patents which they own and exclude potential rivals from their use. In such situations patents can constitute a very formidable barrier to entry and thereby create and perpetuate monopoly power.

And, finally, a patent monopoly is an excellent basis for a tying agreement and the subsequent extension of monopoly power. The classic case is that of the United Shoe Machinery Corporation, which leased the machinery over which it had exclusive patents only on the condition that shoe manufacturers would purchase all their other machinery from United. This practice stripped United's competitors of their customers and firmly entrenched United as the dominant firm in the industry.

The importance of patent laws in the growth of business monopoly must not be underestimated. Such well-known firms as du Pont, General Electric, American Telephone and Telegraph, Eastman Kodak, Alcoa, and innumerable other industrial giants have attained various measures of monopoly power in part through their ownership of certain patent rights.

Protective tariffs. Although we must postpone any detailed discussion of tariffs until a later chapter, it is most relevant at this point to recognize that tariffs and similar trade barriers have the effect of shielding American producers from foreign competition. Protective tariffs are in effect discriminatory taxes against the goods of foreign firms. These taxes make it difficult and often impossible for foreign producers to compete in domestic markets with American firms. The result? A less competitive domestic market and an environment frequently conducive to the growth of domestic business monopolies.

FUTURE POLICY ALTERNATIVES

Now let us look ahead. What is the most desirable path for public policy to follow in the future? There are three general positions and a host of hybrid views on this important question. There are those who are satisfied with the structure and performance of American industry and therefore generally content with the *status quo* or even in favor of some relaxation of antitrust enforcement.

There are those who feel that American capitalism has no choice but to move in the direction of increased governmental regulation and/or ownership of monopolized industries. There are those who believe that it is both desirable and possible to make American industry more competitive.[7] The serious consequences of any choice between these sharply contrasting policy alternatives demand that we weigh each rather carefully.

Maintaining the Status Quo

Those who advocate maintaining the *status quo* are convinced that the presence of business monopolies and the degree of concentration of economic power which now exists are not only essential but also desirable. Supporting arguments are generally those made earlier in this chapter as the case for business monopoly.

Competition of all products for the dollars of consumers, interproduct competition, nonprice competition, countervailing power, potential competition and the fear of government regulation, and technological advance all render "workably competitive" industries which appear at first glance to be monopolistic. Then, too, it is contended that business leaders have attained levels of maturity and social responsibility far beyond those attained by their predecessors. Business leaders are trustees of economic power and can be expected not to abuse that trust.

But the most significant and the most frequently heard claim for preservation of the *status quo* is the doctrine of *technological determinism*. The current advanced stage of technological development, it is argued, makes it imperative that big businesses prevail. Business monopolies are necessary if the economy is to realize the productive efficiencies which modern technology now

[7] The present discussion follows the general pattern outlined in Walter Adams (ed.), *The Structure of American Industry*, 3d ed. (New York: The Macmillan Company, 1961), chap. 15.

makes available. A return to competition, in the sense of a large number of small producers, would be to forgo economies of scale. Any restoration of large-numbers competition is a step in the direction of economic *in*efficiency and the misuse of scarce resources.

Toward Public Regulation and Ownership

There are many observers who are less satisfied with the current structure of American industry. Public regulation or even public ownership and operation are envisioned as inevitable consequences of the need to control private monopoly power.

This position rests on three points:

1. Modern technology, it is assumed, is such that business monopoly is here to stay if we are to achieve and maintain productive efficiency.

2. The arguments underlying the *status quo* position are discounted by those who view public regulation as the only course for future public policy. It is naïve to assume that monopolists will exercise self-restraint in using the economic power at their disposal. Workable competition is more a myth than a reality; it does not function as an effective regulatory device. Further, countervailing power is subject to many exceptions, and in many instances it functions in a very imperfect manner.

3. Present antitrust laws are deemed too weak to curb abuses of monopoly power, and if strengthened and vigorously enforced, antitrust laws would entail the loss of the productive efficiencies which modern technology now provides.

It is concluded that the only real alternative is the social control of business monopolies through government regulation. Only in this way can business monopoly be operated in the public interest.

Restoring Vigorous Competition

A final alternative seeks the restoration of "effective" competition in what now are monopolistic industries. The objective sought is not the establishment of *pure* competition; this is recognized as unrealistic and in some instances economically undesirable. Rather the goal is the establishment of markets wherein (1) the number of producers is sufficiently large so that no individual firms possess considerable market power, (2) collusion is absent, and (3) the entry to markets is relatively unrestricted.

Proponents of this policy alternative contend that the goal of effective competition is realistic, attainable, and highly desirable. They argue that the *status quo* is intolerable. Monopoly power exists, workable competition and countervailing power to the contrary, and it is being sorely abused. No effective market or moral forces exist to protect consumers from business monopolies. Hence, the restoration of competition to such industries is highly desirable.

In the second place, it is felt that in most industries the growth of big-business monopolies has far exceeded that necessary for the attainment of all the economies of scale which modern technology allows. A considerable degree of competition can be reestablished in many now-monopolized markets with little or no impairment of productive efficiency.

And it is argued that past experience indicates that public regulation of monopoly has generally failed to function in the public interest. Public monopolies can abuse their power in the same way as can private monopolies.

Through what techniques is competition to be restored? On the one hand, antitrust laws should be strengthened and vigorously applied. A rear-guard defensive application of antitrust legislation to retard the rate of monopoly growth is wholly inadequate. The restoration of effective competition calls for positive action designed to *increase* the degree of competition in industries in which monopoly power is considerable. And, too, it is imperative that all exceptions to the antitrust laws be eliminated. Similarly, legislation and policies which now promote the growth of monopoly—for example, patent laws and protective tariffs—must be either eliminated or modified.

SUMMARY

1. The role of business monopolies in American capitalism is a highly controversial one. The case against business monopoly centers upon the contentions that business monopoly **a.** results in high prices and output restriction, **b.** contributes to the misallocation of resources, **c.** promotes income inequality, **d.** retards the rate of technological advance, **e.** is an obstacle to the achievement of economic stability, and **f.** poses a threat to political democracy.

2. The defense of business monopoly is built around the following points: **a.** "Workable competition" prevails in many industries in which large-numbers competition is absent, **b.** the realization of mass-production economies often necessitates the presence of business monopolies, **c.** monopoly provides both the means and incentives for rapid technological advance, **d.** the investment and price policies of monopolies tend to stabilize the economy, and **e.** business monopolies are socially responsible.

3. Government has not followed a consistent, one-sided policy in dealing with business monopolies. It has both restrained and promoted the growth of monopoly power.

4. Government has attempted to retard the growth of monopoly through the antitrust laws. The cornerstone of antitrust policy consists in the Sherman Act of 1890 and the Clayton Act of 1914.

5. The Sherman Act specifies that "Every contract, combination . . . or conspiracy in the restraint of interstate trade . . . is . . . illegal . . ." and that any person who monopolizes or attempts to monopolize interstate trade is guilty of a misdemeanor. The general wording of the act, however, has resulted in a variety of court interpretations, many of which have served to limit the effectiveness of the act.

6. The Clayton Act was designed to bolster and make more explicit the provisions of the Sherman Act. To this end the Clayton Act declared that price discrimination, tying contracts, intercorporate stockholdings, and interlocking directorates are illegal when the effect of their use is the lessening of competition.

7. The Federal Trade Commission Act of 1914 created the Federal Trade Commission to investigate antitrust violations and to prevent the use of "unfair methods of competition." Empowered to issue cease-and-desist orders, the Commission now serves as a watchdog agency for the false and deceptive representation of products.

8. Though designed to sustain competition between retail distributors, the Robinson-Patman Act of 1936 has stifled retail price competition by prohibiting chain stores from **a.** acquiring "unjustified" discounts in buying from wholesalers and **b.** selling to consumers at "unreasonably" low prices.

9. The Celler Antimerger Act of 1950 prohibits one firm from acquiring the assets of another firm where the result is a lessening of competition.

10. Government, however, has also done much to promote both directly and indirectly the concentration of economic power and the growth of monopoly. Industrial exceptions to antitrust laws include: **a.** the exclusion of exporters by the Webb-Pomerene Act of 1918, **b.** partial exclusion of retailers by the Robinson-Patman Act (1936) and the Miller-Tydings Act (1937), and **c.** the exemption of unions and agricultural cooperatives.

11. Through public utility legislation Federal and state governments have created regulated monopolies in such industries as railway and air transportation, radio and television, telephone and telegraph, and electric power.

12. Patent laws and protective tariffs also constitute bases for the development of business monopoly.

13. Possible future policies for dealing with business monopolies include **a.** maintenance of the *status quo*, **b.** increasing public regulation and ownership of industry, and **c.** the restoration of effective competition.

QUESTIONS AND STUDY SUGGESTIONS

1. "All big firms are monopolistic, but not all monopolistic firms are big." Appraise critically.
2. Suppose you are president of one of the Big Three automobile producers. Discuss critically the case against business monopoly.
3. Now suppose you are a spokesman for a farm organization and are attempting to convince a congressional committee that the presence of business monopolies is a significant factor contributing to the farm problem. Critically evaluate the case for business monopoly.
4. Distinguish between "pure," "workable," and "effective" competition.
5. Briefly identify each of the following acts, specifying the manner in which each has restrained or contributed to the development of business monopoly:
    a. Webb-Pomerene Act, 1918
    b. Robinson-Patman Act, 1936
    c. Sherman Act, 1890
    d. Miller-Tydings Act, 1937
    e. Interstate Commerce Act, 1887
    f. Clayton Act, 1914
    g. Federal Trade Commission Act, 1914
    h. Celler Antimerger Act, 1950
6. What stake do you, as a consumer, have in the application of antitrust legislation? Do you feel that antitrust legislation should be applied to labor unions? Explain.
7. Which of the three policies outlined at the end of this chapter do you feel is the most desirable? What criticisms can be made of each of the three positions? Be as specific as you can.
8. Define the concept of countervailing power. Explain its operation. How does countervailing power differ from competition as we defined it in Chapter 26? What implication, if any, does countervailing power have for the application of antitrust policy?
9. Explain the meaning and significance of each of the following:
    a. Resale price maintenance contracts
    b. Tying agreements
    c. Interlocking directorates
    d. Cease-and-desist orders
10. What proposals can you make to strengthen the antitrust laws in their application to business monopolies? Be specific.
11. "The social desirability of any given business enterprise should be judged not on the basis of the structure of the industry in which it finds itself, but rather on the basis of the market performance of that firm." Analyze critically.
12. A much-discussed policy alternative in dealing with the business monopoly problem suggests that (a) government should establish and maintain "effectively competitive conditions in all industries where competition can function as a regulative agency . . . ," and (b) government should gradually assume the "ownership and operation in the case of all industries where competition cannot be made to function effectively as an agency of control."[8] Evaluate these suggestions as to their social desirability and political feasibility. What practical problems do you think might be encountered in the application of these recommendations?

[8] Henry C. Simons, *Economic Policy for a Free Society* (Chicago: The University of Chicago Press, 1948), p. 57.

SELECTED REFERENCES

Adams, Walter (ed.): *The Structure of American Industry,* 3d ed. (New York: The Macmillan Company, 1961), particularly chap. 15.

Adams, Walter, and Horace M. Gray: *Monopoly in America* (New York: The Macmillan Company, 1955).

Caves, Richard: *American Industry: Structure, Conduct, Performance* (Englewood Cliffs, N.J.: Prentice-Hall, Inc., 1964).

Kaplan, A. D. H.: *Big Enterprise in a Competitive System* (Washington, D.C.: The Brookings Institution, 1954).

Mansfield, Edwin (ed.): *Monopoly Power and Economic Performance* (New York: W. W. Norton & Company, Inc., 1964).

Simons, Henry C.: *Economic Policy for a Free Society* (Chicago: The University of Chicago Press, 1948), particularly chap. 2.

Stigler, George J.: "The Case against Bigness in Business," *Fortune,* May, 1952.

Wilcox, Clair: *Public Policies towards Business,* rev. ed. (Homewood, Ill.: Richard D. Irwin, Inc., 1960), particularly chaps. 3–5, 11, 12, and 18.

CHAPTER 35

AMERICAN AGRICULTURE: THE FARM PROBLEM

American agriculture is a chronic soft spot in an otherwise prosperous and expanding economy. Agriculture is a sick and, at least in relative terms, a declining industry. It is maladjusted, out of step with the rest of the economy.

The major objectives of this chapter are:

1. To describe and assess the severity of the farm problem
2. To outline the causes of the farm problem
3. To describe government policy toward American agriculture
4. To evaluate critically the effectiveness of public policy
5. To outline a positive program for American agriculture

HISTORY OF THE FARM PROBLEM

The two decades prior to World War I were exceedingly prosperous ones for agriculture; indeed, this period has been dubbed "the golden age of American agriculture." The demand for farm products, farm prices, and farm incomes all rose. World War I intensified these good times. Foreign demand for the output of American farmers skyrocketed during, and immediately following, the war. Foreign countries, diverting resources from agriculture to war goods production, turned to American agriculture for needed food and fiber. High prices and an almost insatiable demand were the happy lot of American farmers.

These highly favorable conditions were not to last. A sharp postwar depression in 1920 was a sudden and severe shock to agriculture. In particular, the large volume of mortgage indebtedness incurred during the previous years of prosperity proved a heavy burden. The economy as a whole quickly recovered from this downturn, however, and by 1921 the booming twenties were upon us. But agriculture failed to share in this prosperity to the extent that did other segments of the economy.

The reasons for this were several. European agriculture not only recovered from the war but also began to expand rapidly under the impetus of new technological advances. Hence, foreign demand for American farm goods began to level off and decline. American foreign trade policies also contributed to this deterioration in foreign demand. High tariffs on goods imported to the United States helped undermine foreign demand for American farm products. To the extent that foreigners could not sell to us because of trade restrictions, they were unable to earn the funds they needed to buy from American producers. Furthermore, the domestic demand for farm products simply did not rise very much in the twenties. American stomachs were full, and as a result income increases were used to buy automobiles, refrigerators, and a host of new products of industry. Finally, on the supply side of the picture technological advances boosted farm output markedly. The net result of a lagging, inelastic demand and a sharply increasing supply of farm products was low farm prices and incomes.

The Great Depression of the 1930s was a

particularly acute blow to American agriculture. The competitive nature of agriculture makes it especially vulnerable to bad times. Unlike sellers who possess a modicum of monopoly power, farmers are unable to influence their prices. They are at the mercy of the market. Therefore, when market demand declines as it did during the Depression, farm prices and farm incomes fall sharply. Ironically, farmers buy in markets which are basically noncompetitive. Hence, while their incomes fell by very large amounts, the prices of farmers' purchases declined very modestly. As Figure 35–1 indicates, farmers in the 1920s and 1930s found themselves in a harsh price-cost squeeze.

World War II provided welcome but temporary relief for the farmer. Both domestic and foreign demand for agricultural products boomed during the war, and prosperity returned to agriculture. Except for the 1948–1949 slump, the middle and late forties were peak years for American farmers. Then in the 1950s a slow but certain relapse became evident, and agriculture was once again encountering difficulty. As farm prices faltered and declined, other prices inched upward. The farmer again found himself in the unenviable position of paying more and more for what he bought and getting less and less for what he sold.

The relative deterioration of the economic position of the farmer can be readily seen through income statistics. Indeed, low incomes are the most obvious symptom of the farm problem. Table 35–1 provides us with a comparison of per capita farm and nonfarm incomes since the mid-thirties. Note

FIGURE 35–1. PRICES PAID AND RECEIVED BY FARMERS, 1910–1964.
Throughout the twenties and thirties and again since the mid-fifties,
the prices received by farmers have lagged behind the prices paid by them.
(U.S. Department of Agriculture, *Agriculture Outlook Charts.*)

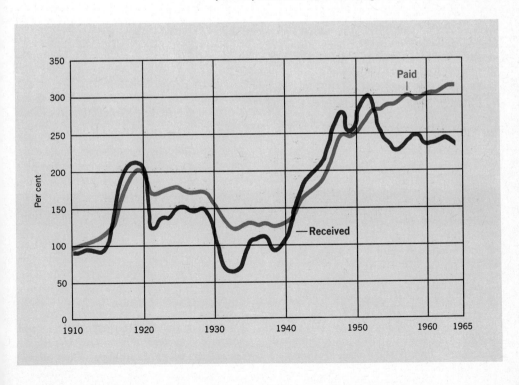

TABLE 35–1. PER CAPITA DISPOSABLE
INCOME OF FARM AND NONFARM
PEOPLE, SELECTED YEARS, 1934–1964

Year	Farm people	Nonfarm people
1934	$ 163	$ 496
1937	283	637
1940	246	675
1942	477	979
1944	625	1,156
1946	743	1,222
1948	900	1,369
1950	841	1,464
1952	961	1,610
1954	915	1,670
1956	925	1,844
1958	1,119	1,904
1960	1,165	2,008
1962	1,309	2,121
1964	1,405	2,318

Source: U.S. Department of Agriculture, *Farm Income Situation.*

that farm income has been persistently less than nonfarm income over the entire period and that the differential has been large. Per capita farm income is currently about 60 per cent of per capita nonfarm income.

We must be careful to note that the data of Table 35–1 are average figures. Do not jump to the false conclusion that all farmers are poor. This is most certainly not the case; a good many farmers are well off by any relevant standard. A motor trip through the corn belt of the Middle West provides sufficient evidence to support this point. It is the "tobacco roader" of the Deep South, the "two-cow, twenty-chicken, 40-acre" Appalachian sharecropper, the marginal farmer of the Southwest, and the 6-acre tobacco farmer of North Carolina who cling to the bottom rung of the farm income ladder. It is with these people that the low-income symptoms of the farm problem are most evident.

Table 35–2 gives us a rough idea of the degree of income disparity *within* agriculture. These figures show that in 1960, 3.2 per cent of the farms in the United States accounted for 33.3 per cent of total farm output. At the other extreme, cumulating the figures for the bottom two economic classes makes it clear that 39.8 per cent of all farms sold less than $2,500 worth of farm products in 1960 and that the output of these farms was a mere 4.7 per cent of the total amount of farm products sold in that year. Were we to arbitrarily label those farms which market $5,000 worth or more of products each year as "efficient" and those marketing less than $5,000 worth as "inefficient," or "marginal," it could then be concluded that the 43.5 per cent of our farms which are "efficient" produce 89 per cent of all marketed farm products. The 56.5 per cent which are "inefficient" account for the remaining 11 per cent of marketed farm output. It is in this latter group that extremely low incomes—the main symptom of the difficulties which plague American agriculture—are predominant.

In addition to wide income disparities within agriculture, the data of Table 35–2 suggest a second point about which more will be said later: A substantial amount of human and property resources could leave agriculture without causing a very significant decline in total farm output.

CAUSES OF THE FARM PROBLEM

It is a bit misleading to talk of "the" farm problem. Actually, the changes which have occurred in farm incomes suggest the presence of both a long-run problem and a short-run problem. The long-run problem concerns those forces which have caused farm prices and incomes to decline over a period of years. The short-run problem has to do with the extreme year-to-year instability of farm incomes.

The Long-run Problem

Complex problems can rarely be stated accurately in brief terms. This is certainly true of the long-run problem which plagues

TABLE 35–2. DISTRIBUTION OF COMMERCIAL FARMS BY ECONOMIC CLASS, 1960

Value of farm products sold	Number of farms (thousands)	Per cent of total farms	Dollar output, millions	Per cent of total output
$40,000 or more	106	3.2	$10,050	33.3
$20,000–$39,999	228	7.0	5,920	19.7
$10,000–$19,999	490	15.1	6,668	22.1
$5,000–$9,999	591	18.2	4,188	13.9
$2,500–$4,999	543	16.7	1,914	6.3
$50–$2,499	307	9.4	424	1.4
Other farms*	998	30.4	982	3.3
Total	3,253	100.0	$30,146	100.0

* Most of these are "residential farms" where the value of products sold is $50–$2,499 per year. Also included, however, are institutional, experimental, and community-project farms. *Source: United States Census of Agriculture: 1959, 1960 Sample Survey of Agriculture.*

American agriculture. Nevertheless a workable picture of the problem can be portrayed through the economic tools of demand and supply. In these terms, we may say that the causes of the long-run farm problem are embodied in

1. *The price inelasticity* of the demand for agricultural products

2. The *shifts* which have occurred over time in the demand and supply curves for farm products

3. The relative immobility of agricultural resources

The inelastic demand for agricultural products. In most developed societies the price elasticity of demand for agricultural products is low. For farm products in the aggregate the elasticity coefficient is estimated to be from .20 to .25.[1] These figures suggest that the prices of agricultural products would have to fall by 40 to 50 per cent in order for consumers to increase their purchases by a mere 10 per cent. Consumers apparently put

[1] Dale E. Hathaway, *Problems of Progress in the Agricultural Economy* (Chicago: Scott, Foresman and Company, 1964), p. 10. This short book is an incisive and highly readable survey of the farm problem.

a low value on additional agricultural output as compared with alternative goods. Why is this so? You will recall that the basic determinant of elasticity of demand is substitutability. That is, when the price of a product falls, the consumer will tend to substitute *that* product for other products the prices of which presumably have not fallen. But in wealthy societies this "substitution effect" (Chapter 24) is very modest. People simply do not switch from three to six or eight meals each day in response to declines in agricultural prices. An individual's capacity to substitute food for other products is subject to very real biological constraints. The inelasticity of agricultural demand can also be explained in terms of diminishing marginal utility. In a wealthy society the population by and large is well fed and well clothed, that is, relatively saturated with the food and fiber of agriculture. Therefore, additional agricultural output entails rapidly diminishing marginal utility. Thus it takes very large price cuts to induce small increases in consumption. Curve *D* in Figure 35–3 portrays an inelastic demand.

Technological advance and rapid increases in agricultural supply. An inelastic demand for farm products is, in and of itself, innocent enough. It is the accompanying fact that the supply of agricultural products has increased in relation to the demand for them that has spelled declining farm incomes.

On the supply side of the picture a rapid rate of technological advance, particularly since World War I, has caused significant increases in the supply of agricultural products. This technological progress has many roots: the virtually complete electrification and mechanization of farms, improved techniques of land management and soil conservation, irrigation, the development of hybrid crops, improvements in the breeding and care of livestock, and so forth.

How significant have these technological advances actually been? Very! The simplest index is the increasing number of people which a single farmer's output will support. Table 35–3 pictures the long-run trend. In 1820 each farm worker produced enough feed and fiber to support four persons. By 1964 each farmer produced enough to support thirty-two! There can be no question but that productivity in agriculture has risen significantly.

Two more significant points must amend

TABLE 35–3. PERSONS SUPPORTED BY PRODUCTION OF ONE FARM WORKER, SELECTED YEARS, 1820–1964

Year	Persons supported per farm worker
1820	4
1870	5
1900	7
1910	7
1920	9
1930	10
1940	11
1950	15
1954	19
1957	24
1961	28
1964	32

Source: U.S. Department of Agriculture, *Agricultural Outlook Chartbook, 1964.*

this discussion of the increasing productivity in American farming:

1. Most recent technological advances have not been initiated by farmers but are rather the result of government-sponsored programs of research and education and the work of farm machinery producers. Land-grant colleges, experimental stations, county agents of the Agricultural Extension Service, the inexhaustible supply of educational pamphlets issuing from the U.S. Department of Agriculture, and the research staffs of John Deere and International Harvester are the sources of technological advance in American agriculture.

2. Technological advance has not occurred evenly throughout agriculture. Many farmers—particularly those resting on the bottom rung of the income ladder—are undermechanized, uninformed, and startlingly inefficient.

Lagging demand for agricultural products. Increases in the demand for agricultural commodities have failed to keep pace with technologically inspired increases in their supply. Why? The answer lies in the two major determinants of agricultural demand—incomes and population.

In underdeveloped countries consumers must devote the bulk of their meager incomes to the products of agriculture—food and clothing—to sustain themselves. But as income expands beyond the subsistence level and the problem of hunger gives way to one of obesity, consumers will increase their outlays on food and clothing at ever-declining rates. Once a consumer's stomach is filled, his thoughts turn to the amenities of life which industry, not agriculture, provides. Economic growth in the United States has boosted average per capita income far beyond the level of bare subsistence. As a result, *increases in the incomes of American consumers lead to less than proportionate increases in expenditures on farm products.* In brief, the demand for farm products is income-inelastic. Recent estimates indicate that a 10 per cent increase in real per capita disposable income entails at the most an increase in the consumption of farm products of only 2 per cent.[2]

Population is a somewhat different proposition. Despite the fact that, after a minimum income level is reached, each individual consumer's intake of food and fiber will become relatively fixed, more consumers will mean an increase in the demand for farm products. And it has. But population increases added to the relatively small increase in the purchase of farm products which occurs as incomes rise have simply not been great enough to match the concomitant increases in farm output.

When coupled with the inelastic demand for agricultural products, these shifts in supply and demand have resulted in declining farm incomes. This is illustrated in Figure 35–2, where a large increase in supply is shown against a very modest increase in demand. Because of the very inelastic demand for farm products, these shifts have resulted in a sharp decline in farm prices accompanied by relatively small increases in sales. This means that farm incomes decline. Diagrammatically, income before the increase in supply occurs (measured by rectangle $OPAQ$) will exceed farm income after supply increases (OP_1BQ_1). The income "loss" of P_1PAC is not fully offset by the income "gain" of $QCBQ_1$. In summary, *given an inelastic demand for farm products, an increase in the supply of farm products relative to the demand for them can result, and has resulted, in declining farm incomes.*

All this is not to say that farm prices and incomes are always declining. Figure 35–1 indicates that farm prices rose sharply during the 1940s, but the abnormal demand for farm products which accompanied World War II, European reconstruction, and the Korean conflict largely explains these increases. The price declines which farmers faced in the prosperous twenties and early

[2] Joint Economic Committee, *Staff Report on Employment, Growth, and Price Levels* (Washington, D.C., 1960), p. 190.

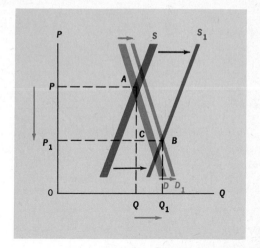

FIGURE 35–2. A GRAPHIC SUMMARY OF THE LONG-RUN FARM PROBLEM.
In the long run, increases in the demand for agricultural products (D to D_1) have not kept pace with the increases in supply (S to S_1) which technological advances have permitted. Coupled with the fact that agricultural demand is inelastic, these shifts have tended to depress farm prices (as from P to P_1) and incomes (as from $OPAQ$ to OP_1BQ_1).

fifties are indicative of the persistent tendency of farm prices to fall.

Immobility of resources. Our previous discussion of the workings of the price system would certainly suggest an obvious and automatic solution to the long-run problem faced by agriculture. In a price-directed economy one would expect declining farm prices and incomes to signal an exodus of resources from agriculture. Prices and incomes which are low in relation to the rest of the economy would seemingly prompt farmers to leave their farms in favor of more lucrative occupations. The adjustments of a competitive industry as outlined in Chapters 5 and 26 indicate that this exodus of farmers would reduce industry supply in relation to demand, thereby boosting farm prices and incomes. This reallocation of resources away from agriculture and toward industry, one can assume, would bring farm incomes into closer accord with those of the rest of the economy.

But, despite its competitiveness, agriculture has not behaved quite in the fashion economic analysis suggests. It is quite easy to understand why falling farm prices and incomes have not caused capital and land to move rapidly out of agriculture. These resources, after all, are highly specialized, and their value in alternative uses is very low. Except for the minute portion of total farm land which borders on metropolitan areas, farm land has no real alternative uses. Similarly, dairy barns, silos, and chicken coops are also physically fixed and have virtually no value in alternative employments. Although farm machinery is physically mobile, we must also recognize that combines and corn pickers are highly specialized and have no alternative uses.

It is extremely significant that farmers themselves have also become *relatively* fixed resources in agriculture. Now it is true that over the years many farmers have left agriculture for industry. But this outmigration has been insufficient to solve the farm problem. Farmers have been mobile, but not mobile enough. Table 35–4 clearly reflects the long-run trend for the farm population to decline in both absolute and relative terms (see also Figure 20–3). Nevertheless—and this is the important point—the net outmigration of human resources away from agriculture has not been great enough to alleviate the low-income crisis in American agriculture. *High birth rates and a relatively slow rate of outmigration of farmers have resulted in too many people trying to make a living in an industry which will not support them at an income level comparable with that of the rest of the economy.* Statistics underscore this point. In 1910 the farm population was about 35 per cent of the total population and received about 19 per cent of the national income; by 1964 the farm population had declined to about 7 per cent of the total, but farm income was about 4 per cent of national income. It is a fact that agri-

TABLE 35–4. THE DECLINING FARM POPULATION, SELECTED YEARS, 1910–1964

Year	Farm population, millions	Percentage of the total population
1910	32.1	35
1920	31.9	30
1930	30.5	25
1935	32.2	25
1940	30.5	23
1945	24.4	18
1950	23.0	15
1954	19.0	12
1958	17.1	10
1962	14.3	8
1964	13.0	7

Source: Statistical Abstract of the United States, 1962, p. 613, and 1965 Economic Report of the President, p. 280.

culture's share of the national income has fallen roughly in proportion to the farm population, and this has caused low per capita incomes to persist in the agricultural segment of the economy.

In a broad sense, the relative slowness of the reallocation of farmers from agriculture to industry is the crux of the farm problem. Ironically enough, in an industry long associated with the word "surplus," we find that the biggest and most fundamental farm surplus of all is the number of farmers. Indeed, the farm problem can best be envisioned as a problem of resource misallocation. It is the fact that too many farmers are sharing agriculture's shrinking slice of the national income pie that makes income per farmer small. Later in the chapter this point will be discussed further.

If the relative immobility of the farm population is a major dimension of the farm problem, it is certainly legitimate to inquire why farmers have been relatively slow in moving out of agriculture. There is no simple answer. Economic considerations certainly play a role. Of greatest importance is the fact that in a less than full-employment economy the farmer has little or no alternative but to stay on the farm. Why move to the city when industry has no jobs to offer? And the costs of moving and retraining oneself for industrial employment may be significant, especially if the move occurs at a time when the farmer's financial plight is particularly acute. Similarly, the high fixed costs associated with farming work against any hasty decision to quit farming. Noneconomic and institutional factors are also significant: Any suggested movement from the farm to a metropolitan area, and the assembly-line environment it implies, strikes fear into the hearts of most farm families.

Then, too, the Negro sharecropper of the South is restricted by his color from many of the more desirable jobs available in urban areas; minority groups are all too often the last hired and the first fired by industry. In other cases restrictive membership practices by unions are pertinent. Or the mere lack of information about the availability of urban employment may be the vital factor.

The Short-run Problem

The fact that farm incomes lag behind the rest of the economy is evidence of the long-run agricultural problem. Extreme year-to-year fluctuations in farm incomes reflect a short-run problem. This short-run instability can be traced back to the inelastic demand for agricultural products. This inelastic demand contributes to the instability of farm prices and incomes in two different ways.

Fluctuations in output. On the production side of the picture, the inelastic demand for farm products causes small changes in agricultural production to be magnified into relatively larger changes in farm prices and incomes. To understand this point we must first note that farmers possess only limited control over their production. Floods, droughts, insect damage, and similar disasters can mean short crops. Conversely, an excellent growing season may mean bumper crops. Weather factors are beyond the con-

trol of farmers, yet they exert an important influence upon production. Furthermore, the highly competitive nature of agriculture makes it virtually impossible for farmers to form a huge combination to control their production. Agriculture is a highly competitive industry, made up of millions of widely scattered and independent producers. If all should by chance plant an unusually large or abnormally small portion of their land, extra large or small outputs would result even if the growing season were normal.

Now, putting the instability of farm production together with an inelastic demand for farm products, we can readily discover why farm prices and incomes are highly unstable. Figure 35–3 is pertinent. Even if we assume that the market demand for agriculture products is stable at D, the inelastic nature of demand will magnify small changes in output into relatively large changes in farm prices and income. For example, assume that a "normal" crop of Q_n results in a "normal" price of P_n and a "normal" farm

FIGURE 35–3. THE EFFECT OF OUTPUT CHANGES ON FARM PRICES AND INCOMES. Because of the inelasticity of demand for farm products, a relatively small change in output (Q_n to Q_s or Q_b) will cause relatively large changes in farm prices (P_n to P_s or P_b) and incomes (OP_nNQ_n to OP_sSQ_s or OP_bBQ_b).

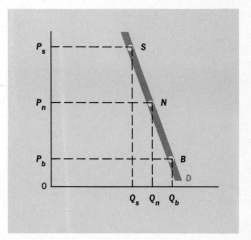

income of OP_nNQ_n. But a bumper crop or a short crop will cause large deviations from these normal prices and incomes; these results stem from the inelasticity of demand for farm products.

If an unusually good growing season occurs, the resulting bumper crop of Q_b will cause farm incomes to *fall* from OP_nNQ_n to OP_bBQ_b. Why? Because when demand is inelastic, an increase in the quantity sold will be accompanied by a more than proportionate decline in price. The net result is that total receipts, that is, total farm income, will decline. Similarly, for farmers as a group a short crop caused by, say, a drought may boost farm incomes. A short crop of Q_s will raise total farm income from OP_nNQ_n to OP_sSQ_s. Why? Because a decline in output

will cause a more than proportionate increase in price when demand is inelastic. Ironically, for farmers as a group a short crop may be a blessing and a bumper crop a hardship. Our conclusion is this: Given a stable market demand for farm products, the inelasticity of that demand will turn relatively small changes in output into relatively larger changes in farm prices and incomes.

Fluctuations in demand. The other aspect of the short-run instability of farm incomes has to do with shifts in the demand curve for agricultural products. Let us suppose that somehow agricultural output is stabilized at the "normal" level of Q_n in Figure 35–4. Now, because of the inelasticity of the demand for farm products, short-run fluctuations in the demand for farm products will cause markedly different prices and incomes to be associated with this level of production that we assume to be constant. That is, a slight drop in demand from D_1D_1 to D_2D_2 will cause farm incomes to fall from OP_1aQ_n to OP_2bQ_n. A relatively small decline in demand gives farmers a drastically reduced money reward for the same amount of production. Conversely, a slight increase in demand will bring an equally sharp increase in farm incomes for the same volume of output. These large price-income changes are linked to the fact that demand is inelastic. This can be grasped by observing the much smaller price-income changes which accompany an equal shift in demand from the more elastic demand curve D_3D_3.[3] If demand drops from D_3D_3 to D_4D_4, price will fall very modestly from P_1 to P_4 and income will only fall from OP_1aQ_n to OP_4cQ_n.

It is tempting to argue that the sharp declines in farm prices which accompany a decrease in demand will cause many farmers to close down in the short run, thereby

FIGURE 35–4. THE EFFECT OF DEMAND CHANGES ON FARM PRICES AND INCOMES. Because of the highly inelastic demand for agricultural products, a small shift in demand (D_1D_1 to D_2D_2) will cause drastically different levels of farm prices (P_1 to P_2) and farm incomes (OP_1aQ_n to OP_2bQ_n) to be associated with a given level of production Q_n. Note that equal changes in a more elastic demand curve (D_3D_3 to D_4D_4) will be accompanied by much smaller price (P_1 to P_4) and income (OP_1aQ_n to OP_4cQ_n) alterations.

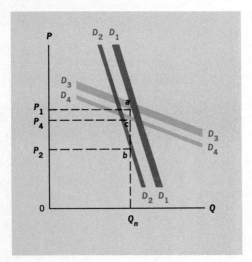

[3] Though they may not appear so graphically, these two shifts in demand are equal in the sense that in each instance buyers want to purchase the same amount less at each possible price.

reducing total output and alleviating these price-income declines. But farm production is relatively insensitive to price changes, because the farmer's fixed costs are high as compared with his variable costs. Interest, rental, tax, and mortgage payments on buildings and equipment are the major costs faced by the farmer. These are clearly fixed charges. Furthermore, the labor supply of the farmer and his family can also be regarded as a fixed cost. So long as he stays on his farm, the farmer cannot reduce his costs by firing himself! This means that his variable costs are the small amounts of hired help he may employ plus expenditures for seed, fertilizer, and fuel. As a result of this high volume of fixed costs, the farmer is almost invariably better off by working his land than he is by sitting idle and attempting to pay his fixed costs out of pocket. The other factors, noted previously, which contribute to the relative immobility of farmers are also pertinent. In particular, if a decline in the demand for farm output is part of an overall recession, there will be no real incentive for farmers to stop production in order to seek nonexistent jobs in industry. As a matter of fact, a migration in the opposite direction—from the city to the farm—often accompanies a full-scale depression. Note in Table 35–4 the absolute *increase* in the farm population which occurred between 1930 and 1935. Note, too, in Figure 11–4 that between 1929 and 1933 farm prices fell by 63 per cent and farm output by a mere 6 per cent.

Let us pause at this point to bring our knowledge of the causes of the long- and short-run farm problems into sharper focus. The long-run problem is the result of the unhappy combination of four factors.

1. The demand for agricultural commodities is inelastic.

2. Rapid technological advance has given rise to significant increases in the supply of farm products.

3. The demand for agricultural commodities has increased very modestly. This consideration, combined with factors 1 and 2, has resulted in falling farm prices and incomes.

4. The relatively fixed nature of agricultural resources—land, capital, and farmers themselves—has caused low prices and incomes to persist; resources have not been reallocated from agriculture rapidly enough to offset the tendency for agricultural prices and incomes to decline.

In the short run the extreme sensitiveness of farm prices and incomes is based upon the inelastic demand for agricultural products which transforms small changes in farm output and demand into much larger changes in farm prices and incomes.

An alternative explanation correctly puts emphasis upon resource misallocation as the core of the long-run farm problem and couches the problem in terms of a growing economy. Of necessity primitive or underdeveloped countries have essentially agrarian economies. The total population of such a nation must devote its efforts to agricultural endeavors to provide enough food and fiber to sustain itself. But as technological advance increases productivity per farmer, the economy can maintain or even increase its consumption of food and clothing and simultaneously transfer a portion of its population into nonagricultural pursuits. This is the path which any expanding, progressive economy follows. Indeed, the shift of resources from agricultural to industrial pursuits is the earmark of a growing economy. The experience of the United States is illustrative. About 90 per cent of our population was devoted to agriculture in the eighteenth century. At present about 7 per cent of the population is in farming, the remaining 93 per cent being free to produce refrigerators, armaments, automobiles, and the thousand and one other goods and services which make up a high standard of living. But in American capitalism, the actual shift of resources to nonagricultural employments has not kept pace with the rate of reallocation which rapid technological advance permits.

The economy has thereby failed to realize the increases in nonfarm output which technological progress in farming has made available. In short, we need *less* than 7 per cent of our population in agriculture.

PUBLIC POLICY TOWARD AGRICULTURE

Many clouded and confused issues surround agricultural policy in the United States. Yet one basic point is clear: Farmers have been highly successful in the political arena. The farm bloc has succeeded in establishing a comprehensive and many-sided program of public aid to agriculture.

Agriculture's Appeal for Aid

The claims to assistance voiced by individual farmers and by the major farm groups—the Farm Bureau, the Farmers Union, the National Farmers Organization, and the National Grange—are many and varied. They include the following:

1. Farming, and particularly the family farm, is a fundamental American institution—a way of life which is to be nurtured and preserved for the virtues it entails. What could be more puritanical than working the soil, living close to nature, and being one's own master in an environment untainted by the evils of modern urban life?

2. Agriculture is a major cog in the American economy; prosperity for farmers is essential for prosperity in the economy as a whole.

3. Farmers face certain hazards—floods, droughts, hailstorms, and invasion by hordes of insects—to which other industries are not exposed.

4. Society as a whole, not individual farmers, should bear the cost of soil conservation, that is, of maintaining the nation's soil resources.

5. The highly competitive nature of agriculture makes it more vulnerable to changes in the market forces of demand and supply than the less competitive industries which characterize American capitalism. While selling in competitive markets, farmers must buy from monopolistic sellers.

6. A more recent and ironic claim: Past farm policies are alleged to have been so faulty and misguided that the government is obliged to bless the farmer with improved farm programs in the future.

Several words of caution: These arguments for public aid to agriculture are not presented on the assumption that they are correct or valid. It is up to you as a thinking individual to make such an evaluation and to decide whether the public assistance programs about to be described are justified or not. Two points are clear.

1. Most of these claims can be applied in somewhat modified forms to a host of other industries.

2. Whether our background is rural or metropolitan, as taxpayers we have a direct interest in any program of aid to agriculture or any other industry.

Yet there also exists a more general claim for aid which is perhaps of greater substance: While agriculture has made great contributions to the nation's economic growth, it has had to bear a disproportionately large share of the costs associated with this progress. The high degree of progressiveness of American agriculture has resulted in substantial and widespread benefits to the economy as a whole. The population has been able to get more and better food and fiber from agriculture in exchange for a smaller portion of its money income. Furthermore, over the years agriculture has been a major source of labor for industry (Table 35-4).[4]

Farm families have for years produced children well in excess of the numbers needed to replace retiring members of the farm labor force. This, together with the absolute decline in the number of people on farms, means that a very substantial portion of our present productive nonfarm labor force was raised on a farm, educated in schools heavily dependent upon farm taxes, and migrated to the cities after finishing school.

[4] Hathaway, *op. cit.*, p. 5.

On the other hand, the peculiar combination of economic circumstances already discussed—an inelastic demand for farm products, rapid technological progress, the slow growth of demand, and the relatively fixed nature of agricultural resources—has caused farm people to bear a large share of the costs of agricultural progress in the form of incomes substantially below those of nonfarm income receivers.

In any event, on the basis of these arguments and the disproportionately large voice which farms have had historically in Congress, a detailed farm program has been established. Let us consider the main elements of this program.

The Farm Program

"The farm program" actually refers to a whole series of more or less related government programs concerning (1) farm prices, incomes, and output, (2) soil conservation, (3) agricultural research, (4) farm credit, (5) crop insurance, and so forth. However, for the last thirty or thirty-five years the typical American farmer and the average politician have both viewed the farm problem as essentially a price-income problem. Low farm prices and the depressed farm incomes resulting therefrom are held to be the cause of the farmer's plight. As a consequence, the American farm program has become "price-centered." The major aim of agricultural policy is to raise farm incomes by raising the prices of farm products.

The enactment of the Agricultural Adjustment Act in 1933—at the depth of the Great Depression—set the pattern for American agricultural policy. This act established a framework for farm policy which has persisted down to the present time.

Briefly, the major policy goals and techniques embodied in American agricultural policy growing out of the AAA are (1) the concept of parity, (2) price supports for farm products, (3) the disposal of surplus farm output, and (4) the restriction of agricultural production.

These four aspects of farm policy are in fact closely intertwined. Application of the parity concept, we shall find, demands that government support farm prices at above-equilibrium levels. The result is surpluses of farm products and subsequent storage or disposal problems. The complexities of disposing of agricultural surpluses and the costliness of storing them lead to the establishment of programs to restrict production in the hope of preventing surpluses from arising.

The concept of parity. Established in the Agricultural Adjustment Act of 1933 as the major objective of American farm policy, the concept of parity has acquired a degree of holiness over the last quarter of a cer It is something of a symbol to Amc agriculture.

The simple rationale of the parity concept can be readily envisioned in both real and money terms. In real terms, parity simply says that year after year for a given output of farm products a farmer should be able to acquire a given total amount of goods and services. A given real output should always result in the same real income. "If a man could take a bushel of corn to town in 1912 and sell it and buy himself a shirt, he should be able to take a bushel of corn to town today and buy a shirt."

In money terms the parity concept alleges that it is only fair that a certain relationship be maintained between (1) the prices which farmers *receive* for the products they sell and (2) the prices which they must *pay* for the goods and services they purchase. The money income which a farmer receives from a given volume of output should have the same purchasing power over the years. This implies that if the prices of the goods farmers purchase increase, the prices which farmers receive for their products should be increased accordingly.

Let us examine the simplest possible example to lay bare the parity principle and the manner in which parity prices are determined. Table 35–5 is relevant. Suppose a

TABLE 35-5. PARITY PRICING: A SIMPLE CASE (BASE: YEAR 1) (hypothetical data)

Year	Bushels of wheat	Price per bushel	Money income	Price per suit	Real income, suits
1	50	$2	$100	$25	4
2	50	4	200	50	4
3	50			65	

farmer produces 50 bushels of wheat in both year 1 and 2. If the *market price* for wheat is $2 per bushel in year 1, the farmer's money income will obviously be $100. Suppose now that the farmer spends this money income entirely on one product—say, dress suits. If suits are selling at $25 each in year 1, the farmer will obviously be able to buy four of them. Using year 1 as our point of reference, or *base year,* the parity concept says that for the same output—50 bushels of wheat—the farmer should be able to acquire the same real income—four suits—in succeeding years as he did in the base year.

What if in year 2 the farmer finds that the price of suits has doubled because of inflation and now stands at $50 per suit? This means that 50 bushels of wheat selling at $2 per bushel will only provide the farmer with enough income to buy two suits. Assuming the market price for wheat remains at $2, the farmer's real income has been halved, because the prices of the goods he buys have doubled. Obviously, the concept of parity applied to year 2 would entail a $4 *parity price* for wheat. The price of the given quantity of wheat must be doubled in order for the farmer to maintain his real income in the face of a doubling in his cost of living. The reader can complete Table 35–5 by determining the parity price for wheat in year 3.

Now an important word on the mechanics of calculating parity price. Note that it is the ratio of the price of suits in the current year (year 2) to the price of suits in the base year (year 1) that determines the multiple by which the price of wheat should be changed—increased in this case—to achieve

parity. In our simple example, this ratio is $50/$25, or 2. Thus, multiplying the $2 base-period price of wheat by 2, we get the parity price of $4. In other words, the formula for determining the parity price for wheat in this example is

Base period price of wheat

$$\times \frac{\text{current price of suits}}{\text{base year price of suits}}$$

$$= \text{parity price of wheat}$$

Substituting the figures from our illustration, we get

$$\$2 \times \frac{\$50}{\$25} = \$4$$

In practice, of course, farmers purchase a wide variety of products and services. As a result, we must substitute an *index* of prices paid for the price of suits. The formula for determining parity thus becomes

Base period price of wheat

$$\times \frac{\text{current prices paid index}}{\text{prices paid index in base year}}$$

$$= \text{parity price of wheat}$$

Let us illustrate with actual data for wheat. In the 1910–1914 base period used in determining parity prices, the average price for wheat was 88.4 cents per bushel. The 1965 index of prices paid by farmers was about 330. In the 1910–1914 base period this index was, of course, 100 per cent. In effect, the prices paid by farmers had increased 3.30 times between the base period and 1965. Therefore, wheat farmers must receive 3.30 times as much per bushel of wheat in 1965 as they did in 1910–1914 to achieve 100 per cent parity. Substituting in the above formula, it is discovered that the parity price of wheat in 1965 was $2.92:

$$88.4 \text{ cents} \times \frac{330}{100} = \$2.92$$

In many instances government has supported prices at something less than 100 per cent of parity. Legislation might give the Secretary of Agriculture the authority to establish the price of, say, wheat or corn at some level within, say, 70 to 90 per cent of parity.

Three points are vital to a complete appreciation of the parity concept:

1. Despite the seemingly "scientific" manipulations involved in establishing parity prices, parity is actually an ethical concept. Parity is a notion concerning what the economic position of farmers *should,* or *ought to,* be.

2. A bit of reflection will make clear that, in any application of the parity concept, the choice of the base year, or base period, is all-important. If the base period were one wherein the farmer's economic position was good (prices received were relatively high and prices paid relatively low), a strict application of parity would guarantee farmers that the favorable situation would be perpetuated. Conversely, if the choice were a base period where farmers were squeezed between getting low prices and paying high prices, the application of parity would simply sustain the farmer's misery. In view of the strong political voice of agriculture it is not surprising to find that a prosperous farm era—the 1910–1914 so-called "golden age" of American agriculture—is the actual base period for determining parity.[5]

[5] Recent modifications have adjusted some parity prices from the 1910–1914 base so as to allow for more recent price trends.

3. Also, it is notable that price parity is not income parity. For example, if price parity is rigidly maintained over a period of time wherein productivity is increasing significantly, price parity will mean rising rather than parity incomes for farmers.

Price supports. The practical importance of the notion of parity prices lies in the fact that it is the focal point for government price-support programs designed to bolster farm incomes. Indeed, it is the concept of parity which provides the rationale and justification for government price supports on farm products. The fact that in the long run the actual market prices received by farmers have not kept abreast of prices paid by them means that to achieve parity or some percentage thereof the government is likely to be required to establish above-equilibrium prices on farm products. The 1920–1941 period in Figure 35–1 reflects the tendency of prices received to fall behind prices paid, as, indeed, does our hypothetical illustration in Table 35–5. Government must take action to boost prices received above the level established by the market to prevent the real income position of the farmer from deteriorating. In short, government must support farm prices.

Effective price supports invariably result in product surpluses. Let us illustrate, using the data from Table 35–5. In this simple example the parity price for wheat in year 2 is $4 per bushel. Suppose that the market forces of supply and demand establish an equilibrium price of only $2.40 per bushel, as shown in Figure 35–5. Assuming the farmer's costs and productivity have not changed sufficiently to offset this below-parity market price, the farmer's income from the sale of a bushel of wheat will fail to keep his real income at the level of year 1. If 100 per cent of parity is the objective of public policy, it is up to government to establish a legal, or supported, price of $4 per bushel for wheat in year 2. But it is all too evident from Figure 35–5 that private buyers will not be willing to consume the quantity of wheat

FIGURE 35–5. EFFECTIVE PRICE SUPPORTS RESULT IN FARM SURPLUSES.
Application of the parity concept obligates government to support farm prices at above-equilibrium levels. These supported prices result in persistent surpluses of farm products.

forthcoming at this supported price. There will be a market imbalance; specifically, a *surplus* of wheat will result at the supported price of $4. The competitive price mechanism will no longer perform the rationing function of automatically equating quantity demanded and quantity supplied when a higher than equilibrium legal price is imposed.

What happens to the surplus, that is, the quantity of wheat which private buyers will not take at the $4 price? It is the government's headache. To make the above-equilibrium supported price effective, government must buy what private purchasers will not.

In some cases government purchases surplus output directly in the market to maintain the supported price. In many cases,

however, the surpluses are handled through the use of *nonrecourse loans* to farmers. These loans, which are often the equivalent of the outright purchase of surpluses by the government, work something like this: The Commodity Credit Corporation (CCC), affiliated with the U.S. Department of Agriculture, has the power to make loans to farmers equal to the supported value of their wheat, corn, cotton, tobacco, and so forth. For example, if a farmer has 50 bushels of wheat and the supported price is $4, as in our prior illustration, the farmer can obtain a CCC loan of $200 (or $4 times 50), the 50 bushels of wheat serving as security on the loan. The farmer will often store the collateral—the wheat—on his own farm. Should the market price of wheat rise above $4— say, to $5—the farmer has the right to sell his wheat and pocket the $50 difference between the revenue from his sale ($250) and the amount of his CCC loan ($200). If the market price fails to climb above the supported price, the farmer simply defaults on the loan, turning his wheat over to the CCC. In this case, the farmer in effect has sold his wheat to the CCC at $4 per bushel.

This program is clearly aimed at bolstering farmers' incomes. The plan is a "heads the farmer wins, tails the government loses" proposition. The $4 price support guarantees the farmer an income of $200 for his wheat and leaves the door open for favorable market conditions to better that figure. As the program has worked in practice, however, the farmer very typically ends up selling a considerable portion of his output to the CCC. The result? Government-owned farm surpluses.

In 1948 the CCC had $294 *million* tied up in inventories of surplus farm products and nonrecourse loans. By 1954 this figure had jumped to $3.7 *billion,* and at mid-1964 it stood at a whopping $7.6 billion. And had it not been for a drought and two wars, these figures would be much larger. These ever-growing surpluses of farm products are by no means a goal of public policy; rather they are a troublesome consequence of the government's attempt to bolster sagging farm incomes through the use of price supports.

Farm surpluses are undesirable on several counts. First and foremost, the very existence of these surpluses indicates a gross misallocation of the economy's resources. Government-held surpluses reflect the fact that the economy is devoting large amounts of resources to the production of commodities which, *at existing supported prices,* are simply not wanted by consumers. And, of course, surpluses are politically embarrassing. The CCC storage bins which one cannot help but encounter on a Sunday drive in the country are impeccable evidence that neither political party has made substantial progress in resolving the basic resource imbalance which lies at the heart of America's farm troubles. Furthermore, the storing of surplus products is a costly proposition which has added to the cost of the farm program and ultimately to the consumer's tax bill. Currently storage costs on existing surpluses are about $1 billion per year!

Disposing of surpluses. In view of these facts it is not at all surprising that Congress has attempted in a variety of ways to reduce farm surpluses. The possible courses of action are (1) to dump the surpluses on foreign markets, (2) to dump them on domestic markets, (3) to destroy the surpluses, and (4) to restrict agricultural production so as to avoid the accumulation of the surpluses in the first place.

The first alternative—selling the surpluses on foreign markets at low prices or even giving them away—is enticing. On the surface it would seem a policy destined to create international good will. But there are weighty objections. American taxpayers, docile as they are, may object to having their tax money used to subsidize foreign buyers while simultaneously having to pay above-market prices domestically for the same products. On the other hand, in practice foreign dumping is almost invariably a source of international ill will. Foreign producers violently resent the government-subsidized competition of American food and fiber. How are Argentinians to get a fair international price for their wheat or Egyptians for their cotton when they are in competition with American wheat and cotton substantially subsidized by the United States government? Therefore, instead of friendship, foreign dumping may easily breed retaliatory trade policies and the shrinking of foreign markets for American exporters. Our current Food for Peace program is an attempt to overcome these problems by distributing our farm surpluses to the hungry people of the underdeveloped countries in ways which will not depress the domestic agricultural markets of the recipient countries.

Dumping at home embraces a variety of programs. Food stamp plans have been invoked to distribute surpluses to low-income families. School lunch programs and the distribution of surpluses to welfare and charitable institutions are other variations of domestic dumping. Or, after buying the surplus crops at high supported prices, the government may sell them back to farmers at low token prices as feed for livestock.[6] While helpful, these programs have only had a modest impact upon the aggregate level of farm surpluses. Domestic dumping is restricted by the fact that such programs are self-defeating in the task of reducing surpluses if they provide products to those who would otherwise obtain them through the market.

A third disposal technique is appallingly simple and at the same time destined to fan the flames of public resentment. This solution is to destroy the surpluses—burn them, dump them in the ocean, or simply let them rot. This is not an easy solution politically.

[6] The late Senator Joseph R. McCarthy of Wisconsin once received this letter from a constituent: "I have six children. My brother-in-law lives outside the town. He is raising hogs. He can buy Grade A potatoes at 25 cents a bushel to feed to his hogs. But when I go to the grocery store I have to pay 85 cents a peck for No. 2 potatoes. My question is, are his hogs more important to the nation than my children are?"

The most persuasive orator will find himself incapable of explaining to the public why potatoes, grains, and dairy products are deliberately destroyed when large portions of the world's population go hungry.

Despite domestic and foreign disposal, surpluses continue to grow. Aside from CCC storage bins, such unlikely installations as Liberty ships and abandoned airplane hangars bulge with farm surpluses. This suggests the need for a more positive approach to the problem of farm surpluses.

Restricting farm production. Why not create programs designed to manipulate market demand and supply so as to prevent farm surpluses from occurring in the first place? That is, by increasing demand or reducing supply, one could bring the market prices of farm products up to the desired supported prices. As a result, no surpluses will appear at the supported prices. Much public and private money has been spent to uncover new uses for agricultural commodities. The results have been very modest. Most agricultural economists agree that such research ventures will result in slight increases in demand at best and will prove a complete waste of time and effort at worst.

But on the supply side of the market public policy has long been aimed at restricting farm output in order to bolster market prices. The programs center upon taking farmland out of the production of certain basic crops.

The *soil conservation* program provides direct income subsidies to farmers who do not plant certain soil-depleting crops. Aside from its conservation objective, this program has bolstered farm incomes and at the same time restricted farm production.

Of greater significance is the *acreage allotment* program, which accompanies the application of price supports. In return for the privilege of getting CCC nonrecourse loans on their crops, farmers must agree to limit the number of acres planted in those crops whose prices are supported. Attempting to bring quantity supplied and quantity demanded into balance, the Department of Agriculture estimates the amount of each product which private buyers will take at the supported price. This amount is then translated into the number of acres of planting which will produce this amount. The total acreage figure is apportioned among states, counties, and ultimately individual farmers.

Under the *soil bank* program, inaugurated in 1956, the Department of Agriculture has been authorized to get farmland entirely out of production by "renting" land from farmers. Such idle land is to be planted in cover crops or in timber, not in other cash crops. This program ties together the restriction of output, soil conservation, and income subsidies to farmers in one package.

But these programs have proved to be relatively unsuccessful, as is evidenced by the continued growth of surpluses. The basic reason lies in the fact that acreage reduction invariably results in less than proportionate declines in production. Why? Farmers retire their worst land and keep the best in production. Those acres which are used are cultivated more intensively. The use of better seed, more and better fertilizer and insecticides, and more manpower will enhance output per acre. And, of course, the fortuitous occurrence of a good growing season will mean large per acre outputs. For these and other reasons the supply of farm products may actually *increase*, although acreage is reduced. To illustrate: In 1953 some 78.9 million acres of wheat were planted, and the resulting total output was about 1.2 billion bushels. Approximately 54.9 million acres wheat were planted in 1960, and output was 1.4 billion bushels. A 30 per cent *reduction* in wheat acreage was accompanied by a 17 per cent *increase* in output!

It is to be emphasized that production restricting programs are in substance a government-sponsored attempt to give some measure of monopoly power to the last major industry in American capitalism which approximates pure competition. Restricting supply in relation to demand in order to increase receipts is the stock in trade of the monopolist. And this is precisely what the farm program has attempted to do in seeking to solve the surplus problem.

EVALUATING THE FARM PROGRAM

How successful has public policy been in resolving the chronic imbalances which plague American agriculture? Not very. Evidence is abundant: Farm incomes continue to sag, agriculture surpluses continue to accumulate, and the costs of the farm program persist in rising. What specific criticisms can be made?

Symptoms and Causes

First and foremost, the farm program has failed to get at the causes of the farm problem. Public policy toward agriculture is designed to treat symptoms and not causes. The root *cause* of the farm problem is a misallocation of resources between agriculture and the rest of the economy. Simply put, the problem is one of too many farmers. The effect or symptom of this misalllocation of resources is low farm incomes. *For the most part, public policy in agriculture has been oriented toward supporting farm prices and incomes rather than alleviating the resource allocation problem, which is the fundamental cause of these sagging farm incomes.* As a matter of fact, the income-oriented farm program which both political parties have pursued has probably deterred the migration of resources out of agriculture, thereby fostering the resource misallocation it should seek to alleviate. Price-income supports encourage people to stay in agriculture who might otherwise migrate to industry. On the other hand, were the farm program reoriented to speed the movement of resources out of agriculture, the resulting reduction in the supplies of agricultural products would boost farm prices and thereby increase the average incomes of those who remained in agriculture.

Misguided Subsidies

A second criticism is this: The price-income support schemes which have been the focal point of our farm program tend to benefit most those farmers who least need government assistance. Assuming the goal of our farm program is to be the bolstering of low farm incomes, it follows that any program of government aid should be aimed at farmers at the bottom of the farm income distribution. It is the "inefficient" low-income farmer of Table 35–2 who desperately needs income subsidies. But such farmers get very little help from price supports. Why? Because the "inefficient" farmer simply does not produce and sell enough in the market. The "inefficient" 56.5 per cent of American farmers who produce only 11 per cent of the total marketed output cannot gain much from any income subsidy based upon the quantity produced. It is the "efficient" farmers—the 43.5 per cent of the farmers who supply 89 per cent of the marketed farm output—who reap the benefits of price supports. Individual subsidy checks running into hundreds of thousands of dollars are not easy to justify. If public policy must be designed to supplement farm incomes, a strong case can certainly be made for making those benefits vary inversely with one's position in the income distribution. An income-support program should be geared to *people*, not *commodities*. It is not too difficult to understand why the farm program entails misguided income subsidies: the poverty-stricken farmer of the Deep South and subsistence farmer of the West are rarely members of the major agricultural interest groups—the Farm Bureau, the Farmers Union, the National Farmers Organization, and the National Grange.

Policy Conflicts

A final criticism is that there are certain embarrassingly evident inconsistencies within the farm program and between the farm program and other public policies. In particular, at the same time that government is making attempts to cut back on agricultural production, other government policies are aimed at boosting farm output. Specifically, acreage allotment, soil conservation, and soil bank programs work at cross purposes with government-sponsored research designed to increase farm output and Federal irrigation-reclamation programs tailored to increase the supply of arable land. There clearly exists a real dilemma here in public policy. As we have seen, in the long run technological advance in agriculture is a basic permissive force in economic growth. Furthermore, future population growth and the ever-present prospect of war demand that we develop both our land resources and our agricultural technology. Yet in the short run, given the lagging exodus of human resources from agriculture and government's commitment to a price-centered farm program, it is desirable to restrict farm production to avoid the problems and costs associated with ever-expanding surpluses.

A POSITIVE PROGRAM FOR AGRICULTURE

Many individuals and groups, including some of the major farm organizations, are convinced that fundamental difficulties, such as those just outlined, plague the present farm program. But these groups disagree sharply as to what *ought* to be done to remedy the farm problem. Let us pause to consider the challenging program suggested by the Committee for Economic Development (CED).[7] To choose this particular program for discussion is not to earmark it necessarily as the best of all possible pro-

[7] The CED is a "non-profit, non-partisan, and non-political" organization of businessmen and scholars. The brevity of the present discussion does not do justice to the CED's program. The interested student is urged to read *An Adaptive Program for Agriculture* (New York: CED, 1962) and *Toward a Realistic Farm Program* (New York: CED, 1957).

grams. This is a judgment which the reader must make for himself. However, the program does lay bare the nub of the farm problem, and it does make some thought-provoking suggestions aimed at a permanent solution to the economy's farm troubles.

The policy statements of the CED are based upon the contention that the current farm program has been grossly unsuccessful in achieving the objective of stabilizing and supporting the incomes of farmers. The government, it is pointed out, has spent over $50 billion over the last twenty-five years on programs of direct and indirect assistance to American agriculture, but farm incomes continue to decline, and agricultural surpluses continue to accumulate. If anything, the present farm program has perpetuated the misallocation of resources which is the core of agricultural difficulties. The positive program suggested by the CED centers around the following five points:

Return to Free Markets

Free markets should ultimately be restored in agriculture by the *gradual* elimination of price and income supports. The economic position of farmers should be bettered by means which are consistent with free markets. The key to success in achieving this goal is to bring agricultural supply (ultimately the number of farmers) and demand into balance at prices which yield reasonable incomes for the farm population.

Adaptive Approach

The implementation of a return to free markets is not to be achieved as the result of a sudden and complete withdrawal of all public aid to agriculture but rather through an *adaptive approach* to the farm problem.[8]

The adaptive approach calls for action by government working with the free market, not against it. It seeks to achieve the results of the

[8] *An Adaptive Program for Agriculture*, p. 12.

free market more quickly and easily, rather than to keep those results from occurring. The adaptive approach works by permitting full production, rather than by limiting production. And, government adaptive programs applied to particular industries can ordinarily be temporary, whereas protectionist government actions generate the need for their own indefinite continuance.

An adaptive program for agriculture is designed to accelerate the movement of human and property resources out of agriculture to the end that resulting farm prices would yield per family farm incomes comparable to those of nonfarm families. The adaptive or adjustment program for agriculture proposed by the CED entails policies designed to (1) attract excess resources out of agriculture and (2) cushion the effects of such adjustments upon those adversely affected.

Human Exodus

The exodus of human resources from agriculture is to be accelerated through substantial improvements in the labor market. This is to be accomplished in two general ways. First, statistics make clear that farm youth get less education and therefore less preparation for alternative nonfarm employment than do nonfarm youth. And, ironically, about 45 per cent of the nation's vocational education funds are for training in agriculture and therefore tend to retard the outflow of human resources from farming. The CED recommends programs designed to upgrade the overall quality of rural education and a revamping of vocational education to provide the training and skills needed to obtain employment in expanding (nonfarm) industries.

Second, the exodus of human resources from agriculture should be stimulated by increasing the mobility of farm labor through (1) providing better information to rural people about the availability, requirements, and rewards from off-farm employment and (2) subsidizing both the retraining and mov-

ing costs of farm workers who seek nonfarm jobs. It is explicitly recognized by the CED that the success of an accelerated exodus of labor from agriculture depends heavily upon the maintenance of a high level of employment in the economy as a whole.

The movement of labor from agriculture envisioned by the CED is quite massive: about 2 million workers—roughly one-third of the agricultural labor force—over a five-year period.

Establishing Adjustment Prices

Supported farm prices fail to signal farmers as to how much output and what composition of output are wanted by society. Therefore, the present structure of price supports should be abandoned through a price adjustment program and replaced by "adjustment prices." The adjustment price for any commodity is

1. "A price at which the total output of the commodity can be sold to domestic consumers or in commercial export markets without government subsidy"

2. ". . . a price at which resources efficiently employed in agriculture, after a period of maximum freedom to move out, could earn incomes equivalent to those earned in the nonfarm economy."[9]

It is important to note that these adjustment prices are envisioned to be *below* the current level of supported prices but *above* the free competitive market prices which would result if all existing government farm programs were immediately terminated. The adjustment prices are below supported prices because government would no longer supplement private demand by buying the surpluses needed to keep prices at supported levels and because present restrictions on farm output would be removed. On the other hand, adjustment prices would be above present free market prices because during a five-year adjustment or transitional period substantial amounts of agricultural resources

[9] *Ibid.,* pp. 40–41.

—labor, as described earlier, and land, as will be discussed momentarily—would have left agriculture. In other words, given agricultural demand, the withdrawal of resources from agriculture will reduce supply relative to what it would have been in the absence of these reallocations, and the resulting market prices will be higher.

Land Retirement

Two temporary land retirement programs are recommended to cushion the adverse effects on farm incomes during the adjustment period when labor resources are leaving agriculture at an accelerated rate. A cropland adjustment program is recommended for the Western Plains and Mountain region to convert some 20 million acres of land from crops back to grassland. This conversion would be induced by temporary subsidies to cooperating farms. But then the downward drift of crop prices during the adjustment period would presumably cause farmers to continue using the land for grazing rather than crops. A temporary soil bank would also be employed to cut back on grain production. Land would be retired on a "whole farm" basis because, first, it retires both labor and capital from agriculture, and, second, this approach avoids a fundamental difficulty in current acreage allotment programs: Farmers cultivate their remaining land more intensely and thereby produce a larger output per cultivated acre.

As the CED sees it, the net result of its adaptive program would substantially correct the overallocation of resources to agriculture which now exists. The free market prices which would prevail at the end of the five-year period of adjustment would involve *lower* average prices but *higher* average incomes per farmer because of the substantial decrease in the number of farmers. The CED acknowledges that its program would not immediately reduce government agricultural expenditures. But, it is contended, because its program gets at the cause of the farm problem, costs would be substantially reduced over time. In particular, the elimination of our price-support, surplus-storage programs would entail very significant declines in government outlays.

Regardless of whether one accepts or rejects the CED's proposals as a workable solution to our farm troubles, this much is reasonably certain: In the immediate years ahead we can expect our present farm policies to come under intense scrutiny. Existing farm programs have become very costly, and it is increasingly evident that they have accomplished remarkably little in resolving the causes of our farm problem. Furthermore, as the farm population has declined in numbers, so has its political power diminished. Sweeping changes in our agricultural policies seem quite likely in the not too distant future.

SUMMARY

1. Agriculture is a maladjusted industry. The major symptom of this maladjustment is relatively low farm incomes.

2. The core of the long-run farm problem is a misallocation of resources between agriculture and the rest of the economy. Rapid technological advance coupled with a highly inelastic and relatively constant demand for agricultural output has caused low farm incomes. Because of the relatively fixed nature of both property and human resources, the price system has failed to correct the farm problem by reallocating sufficient amounts of resources out of agriculture.

3. In the short run the highly inelastic nature of agricultural demand translates small changes in output and small shifts in demand into large fluctuations in prices and incomes.

4. Agriculture's claims for public assistance are manifold: **a.** Farming is a way of life. **b.** Agriculture is the backbone of the economy. **c.** Farmers face special risks and hazards. **d.** The community should bear the costs of soil conservation. **e.** Farmers are in an unfavorable market position in relation to the rest of the economy. **f.** The inadequacies of past farm programs obligate the government to establish more effective forms of public assistance in the future. **g.** Perhaps the most substantial argument for government assistance is that agriculture has made substantial contributions to economic growth but has borne a disproportionate share of the costs of this progress in the form of low incomes.

5. The farm program is price-centered and based upon the concept of parity. Parity is the notion that a given real output should always result in the same real income. Parity price can be determined by the following formula:

Base year price

$$\times \;\; \frac{\text{current prices paid index}}{\text{prices paid index in base year}}$$

$$= \text{parity price}$$

6. The application of parity prices results in farm surpluses. Attempts to dispose of these surpluses by **a.** dumping them on foreign markets, **b.** dumping them on domestic markets, and **c.** destroying them have fallen far short of success. Productivity increases have reduced the effectiveness of acreage allotment programs in restricting output. Surpluses therefore continue to accumulate.

7. Basic shortcomings of the current farm program are several. Foremost is the fact that the program treats symptoms rather than causes; public policy is designed to boost farm incomes rather than to speed the reallocation of resources away from agriculture. More specific criticisms concern **a.** the inverse relationship between the size of income subsidies and need and **b.** certain inconsistencies which exist between short-run and long-run aspects of farm policy.

8. The CED has offered a thought-provoking adaptive program for agriculture. It envisions the return to free markets over a five-year adjustment period. During this time the exodus of labor from agriculture is to be accelerated through the general improvement of rural education and the subsidization of retraining and moving costs. Land retirement programs are proposed to cut back on grain production. The goal is to achieve higher farm incomes with lower free market prices through the substantial outmigration of resources (particularly labor) from agriculture.

QUESTIONS AND STUDY SUGGESTIONS

1. "The whole process of economic growth is one of making agriculture less fundamental in the economic system. The fewer people the nation needs to employ in the production of food and fiber, the better off it is—and the better off farm people are."[10] Evaluate this statement.

2. The CED concludes that in American agriculture "Lower average prices can be made consistent with higher average income." Explain the assumptions which underlie this conclusion.

3. Reconcile these two statements: "The farm problem is one of over-production." "Despite the tremendous productive capacity of American agriculture, plenty of Americans are going hungry." What assumptions about the price system are implied in your answer?

4. Explain how each of the following contributes to the farm problem:
   a. The inelasticity of the demand for farm products
   b. Rapid technological progress in farming
   c. The modest long-run growth in the demand for farm commodities

[10] Lauren Soth, *Farm Trouble* (Princeton, N.J.: Princeton University Press, 1957), p. 40.

    d. The competitiveness of agriculture

    e. The relative fixity or immobility of agricultural resources

5. The key to efficient resource allocation is the shifting of resources from low-productivity to high-productivity uses. Given the high and expanding physical productivity of agricultural resources, explain why many economists want to get resources out of farming in the interest of greater allocative efficiency.

6. "Industry complains of the higher taxes it must pay to finance subsidies to agriculture. Yet the fact that the trend of agricultural prices has been downward while industrial prices have been moving upward suggests that on balance agriculture is actually subsidizing industry." Explain and evaluate.

7. "To reduce agricultural output by a certain percentage an even larger percentage reduction in acres planted is required." Explain.

8. "Because consumers as a whole must ultimately pay the total incomes received by farmers, it makes no real difference whether this income is paid through free farm markets or through supported prices supplemented by subsidies financed out of tax revenues." Analyze this statement very carefully.

9. "Uncle Sam should dispose of troublesome farm surpluses by selling them at special low prices to those Americans who are in the lower income brackets." Evaluate this proposal.

10. "The supply and demand for agricultural products are such that small changes in agricultural supply will result in drastic changes in prices. However, large changes in farm prices have modest effects on agricultural output." Carefully evaluate. *Hint:* a brief review of the distinction between *supply* and *quantity supplied* may be of assistance.

11. What relationship, if any, can you detect between the fact that the farmer's fixed costs of production are large and the fact that the supply of most agricultural products is generally inelastic? Be specific in your answer.

12. "The long-run demand for farm products depends more upon future growth in the size of our population than it does upon the growth which occurs in average family or per capita incomes." Do you agree? Explain.

13. Suppose you are the president of a local chapter of one of the major farm organizations. You are directed by the chapter's membership to formulate policy statements for the chapter which cover the following topics: (*a*) antitrust policy, (*b*) monetary policy, (*c*) fiscal policy, and (*d*) tariff policy. Briefly outline the policy statements which will best serve the interests of farmers. What is the rationale underlying each statement? Do you see any conflicts or inconsistencies in your policy statements?

14. Explain and evaluate the following statements:

    a. "Price supports intensify rather than resolve the farm problem."

    b. "The best farm program is the Employment Act of 1946."

    c. "The trouble with parity prices in agriculture is that they strip the price mechanism of its ability to allocate resources."

15. The price of wheat was 88.4 cents per bushel in the 1910–1914 base period. Assume in 1966 the prices paid index is 335. If the government decided to support the price of wheat at 90 per cent of the parity in 1966, what would the supported price be?

SELECTED REFERENCES

An Adaptive Program For Agriculture (New York: Committee for Economic Development, 1962).

Hathaway, Dale E: *Problems of Progress in the Agricultural Economy* (Chicago: Scott, Foresman and Company, 1964).

Higbee, Edward: *Farms and Farmers in an Urban Age* (New York: The Twentieth Century Fund, 1963).

Keyserling, Leon H.: *Agriculture and the Public Interest* (Washington, D.C.: Conference on Economic Progress, 1965.)

Smith, Mervin G., and Carlton F. Christian (eds.): *Adjustments in Agriculture: A National Basebook* (Ames, Iowa: The Iowa State University Press, 1961).

Snodgrass, Milton M., and Luther T. Wallace: *Agriculture, Economics, and Growth* (New York: Appleton-Century-Crofts, Inc., 1964).

Sorenson, Vernon L. (ed.): *Agricultural Market Analysis* (East Lansing, Mich.: The Michigan State University Press, 1964).

Soth, Lauren: *Farm Trouble* (Princeton, N.J.: Princeton University Press, 1957.)

Toward a Realistic Farm Program (New York: Committee for Economic Development, 1957).

CHAPTER 36

LABOR UNIONS AND COLLECTIVE BARGAINING

Almost 18 million workers—roughly one-third of the nonagricultural labor force—now belong to labor unions. Bare statistics, however, understate the importance of unions. The wage rates, hours, and working conditions of nonunionized firms and industries are influenced by those determined in organized industries. Unions are clearly permanent and powerful institutions of American capitalism.

In this chapter we seek, first, an understanding of the historical background and the present status of labor unions. Attainment of this objective necessarily involves a discussion of government policy toward organized labor, because labor legislation and union growth are intimately related. A friendly government and prolabor legislation cause unions to flourish and grow; an indifferent government and unfavorable legislation can result in stagnation and decay of the labor movement. Second, we want to analyze labor-management relations. Here our discussion will center upon the process of collective bargaining. Finally, we must examine carefully the economic impact of unions upon the operation of American capitalism—what effect do they have on economic stability and efficient resource allocation?

BRIEF HISTORY OF AMERICAN UNIONISM

The history of the labor movement in America is long, colorful, and flavored with violence.[1]

In terms of national labor policy the American labor movement has gone through three phases: repression (1790 to 1930), encouragement (1930 to 1947), and intervention (1947 to date). Though the dates are somewhat arbitrary, these three phases serve as an excellent guide for our discussion.

Repression Phase: 1790 to 1930

Labor unions have existed in the United States for well over 150 years. The shoemakers, carpenters, printers, and other skilled craftsmen formed unions of some permanence in the early 1790s. As Figure 36–1 indicates, despite this early start, union growth was relatively slow and sporadic until the 1930s. Two considerations go far to account for this meager progress: (1) the hostility of the courts toward labor unions and (2) the extreme reluctance of American businessmen to recognize and bargain with unions.

Unions and the courts. It was not until the 1930s that legislation spelled out the Federal government's policy toward labor unions. In the absence of a national labor policy it was up to the courts to decide upon specific union-management conflicts. And,

---

[1] The following are highly recommended: U.S. Department of Labor, *Brief History of the American Labor Movement* (1964), and Foster Rhea Dulles, *Labor in America*, 3d ed. (New York: Thomas Y. Crowell Company, 1960).

much to the dismay of organized labor, the courts were generally hostile toward unions. This court hostility had two sources.

1. Most judges had propertied-class backgrounds.

2. The courts are inherently conservative institutions charged with the responsibility of protecting *established* rights. Unions, throughout the 1800s and the early decades of the 1900s, were in the unenviable position of seeking rights for labor at the expense of the *existing* rights of management.

The hostility of the courts was first given vent in the *criminal conspiracy doctrine.* This doctrine, "imported" by the American courts from English common law at the turn of the nineteenth century, was unbelievably narrow by modern standards. The doctrine flatly concluded that combinations of workmen to raise wages were criminal conspiracies and hence illegal. Though weakened by subsequent court rulings in the 1840s, the shadow of the conspiracy doctrine hung heavy over organized labor throughout most of the 1800s. Although unions, as such, were later recognized by the courts as legal organizations, the techniques employed by unions to enforce their demands—strikes, picketing, and boycotting—were generally held to be illegal. And in the latter part of the 1800s the courts employed both antitrust laws and injunctions in such a way as to impede the labor movement significantly.

Although Congress passed the Sherman Act of 1890 for the express purpose of thwarting the growth of business monopolies, the courts interpreted the loose wording of the act to include labor unions as conspiracies in restraint of trade and frequently so applied the act.

A simpler and equally effective anti-union device was the *injunction.* An injunction, or restraining order, is a court order which directs that some act not be carried out, on the grounds that irreparable damage will be done to those affected by the action. The attitude of the courts toward unions was such that it was extremely simple for an employer to obtain injunctions from the courts, prohibiting unions from enforcing their demands by striking, picketing, and boycotting. Stripped of these weapons, unions were relatively powerless to obtain the status and rights they sought.

In brief, the courts employed the criminal conspiracy doctrine, the Sherman Act, and injunctions to the end that union growth was greatly retarded during the 1790–1930 period.

Anti-union techniques of management. American businessmen did not rely entirely upon the courts in their attempt to impede the growth of unions. The business community, hostile to unions from their inception, developed a group of anti-union techniques to undermine unions. A startlingly simple anti-union technique was that of ferreting out and firing pro-union workers. Too, the average employer felt it his Christian duty to inform fellow employers that the discharged workers were "troublemakers" and "labor agitators" and not fit to be hired. This combination of *discriminatory discharge* and *blacklisting* made it extremely risky for workers even to think in terms of organizing a union. One's present and future employment opportunities were at stake.

Another potent weapon in management's struggle to keep unions down was the *lockout,* management's counterpart of the strike. By closing up shop for a few weeks employers were frequently able to bring their employees to terms and to destroy any notions they might have about organizing a union. In some cases this might prove a bit costly to the employer in the short run. In other cases, when business was slack, the lockout was a good means of killing two birds with one stone—working off excess inventories and undermining worker attempts to organize. Remember: Workers of the late 1800s and early 1900s were not blessed with savings accounts or multi-million-dollar strike funds to draw upon in such emergencies.

Where workers were determined to organize, pitched battles often ensued. Rocks, clubs, shotguns, and an occasional stick of dynamite were the shadowy ancestors of collective bargaining. Some of the darkest pages of American labor history concern the violent clashes between workers and company-hired *strikebreakers*. The Homestead strike of 1892, the Pullman strike of 1894, and the Ludlow Massacre of 1914 are cases in point. Less dramatic skirmishes erupt down to the present time.

But management tactics were often more subtle than a cracked skull. The *yellow-dog contract* was one of the more ingenious anti-union devices fostered by management. In such contracts workers agreed to remain nonunion as a condition of employment. Workers had little choice but to sign such contracts—no contract, no job. Violation of a yellow-dog contract exposed a worker to a lawsuit by his employer, the result of which might be a court-imposed fine or even imprisonment.

As a last resort, an employer might shower his work force with such amenities as group insurance and pension programs, stock ownership and profit-sharing schemes, and even company magazines to convince them that employers would look after the interests of the workers as effectively as would unions established by "outsiders." The next step beyond such *paternalism* was employee representation schemes or *company unions*, that is, employer-dominated "dummy" unions which it was hoped would discourage the establishment of genuine unions. Paternalism and company unions were decidedly effective in retarding union growth as late as the 1920s.[2]

[2] During a prolonged strike in the bituminous coal industry in 1902, a spokesman for the mine operators, George F. Baer, issued the classic statement of business paternalism: "The rights and interests of the laboring man will be protected and cared for—not by the labor agitators, but by the Christian men to whom God in His infinite wisdom has given the control of the property interests of this country."

Evolution of business unionism. The growth which occurred in the labor movement during the 1800s not only was modest, but it also embodied a variety of union philosophies. The mid-1800s were in effect a laboratory wherein American labor experimented with alternative forms of unionism—Marxism, utopianism, reformism, and a host of other isms. But such unions usually foundered in the span of a few short years because of the internal conflict between the workers' interest in short-run practical goals (higher wages and shorter hours) and the long-run utopian goals (producer cooperatives, creation of a labor party, and so forth) of the union leaders.

Then in 1886, a new labor organization—the American Federation of Labor—which was to dominate the labor movement for the next fifty years was formed. Under the leadership of Samuel Gompers, labor charted a conservative course which has been very influential down to the present date.[3] Appropriately honored as "the father of the American labor movement," Gompers preached three fundamental ideas: (1) practical business unionism, (2) political neutrality for labor, and (3) the autonomy of each trade or craft.

Gompers was firmly convinced that "safe and sane" business unionism was the only course for American labor to follow. In 1903 he declared[4]

[3] This is not to say that all unions have followed conservative paths since Gompers first espoused the virtues of business unionism. The Industrial Workers of the World, founded in 1905, advocated a decidedly revolutionary brand of left-wing unionism. And in the late thirties and early forties Communists infiltrated a number of CIO unions. In 1949 and 1950 the CIO expelled eleven affiliated unions whose leaderships had come to be dominated by Communists.
[4] From the *Proceedings* of the 1903 AFL convention, reprinted in George P. Shultz and John R. Coleman, *Labor Problems: Cases and Readings,* 2d ed. (New York: McGraw-Hill Book Company, 1959), pp. 16–17.

I want to tell you, Socialists, that I have studied your philosophy; read your works on economics . . . studied your standard works. . . . I have heard your orators and watched the work of your movement the world over. I have kept close watch upon your doctrines for thirty years; have been closely associated with many of you, and know how you think and what you propose. I know, too, what you have up your sleeve. And I want to say that I am entirely at variance with your philosophy. I declare it to you, I am not only at variance with your doctrines, but with your philosophy. Economically, you are unsound; socially, you are wrong; industrially, you are an impossibility.

Gompers flatly rejected long-run idealistic schemes entailing the overthrow of the capitalistic system. He spurned intellectuals and theorizers and emphasized that unions should be concerned with practical short-run economic objectives—higher pay, shorter hours, and improved working conditions. In the words of one scholar, Gompers felt that ". . . you must offer the American working man bread and butter in the here and now instead of pie in the sky in the sweet by and by."[5]

In addition to espousing "bread and butter" unionism, Gompers had strong opinions on labor's role in politics and the basis upon which workers should be organized. In so far as politics was concerned, Gompers was convinced that government should keep its nose out of labor-management relations and collective bargaining. Although he recognized that governmental interference on behalf of labor might be a boon to union growth, Gompers was equally certain that anti-union government policies could stifle the progress of the entire labor movement. In pursuing the idea of political neutrality, Gompers cautioned organized labor not to align itself with any political party. Preoccupation with

long-run political goals, he argued, merely causes labor to lose sight of the short-run economic objectives it ought to seek. Gompers admonished organized labor to follow one simple principle in the political arena: rewarding labor's friends and punishing its enemies at the polls without regard to political affiliation.

Finally, Gompers was firmly convinced that "autonomy of the trade," that is, unions organized on the basis of specific crafts, was the only permanent foundation for the labor movement. Unions composed of many different crafts lack the cohesiveness, he argued, that is essential to strong, hard-hitting, business unionism. These craft unions should then be affiliated in a national federation. "One union to each trade, affiliated for one labor movement."

This philosophy—conservative business unionism, political "neutrality," and the craft principle of union organization—was destined to dominate the AFL and the entire labor movement for the next half century. Indeed, the AFL, operating under Gompers' leadership, met with considerable success— at least for a time. AFL membership hit a highwater mark of about 4 million members by the end of World War I. Then a combination of circumstances arose in the 1920s which forced the AFL into an eclipse (see Figure 36–1). One factor was a strong anti-union drive by employers. Spearheaded by the National Association of Manufacturers, businesses waged a last-ditch effort to stem the rising tide of organized labor. Then, too, many firms introduced employee representation plans, company unions, and a host of paternalistic schemes to convince workers that employers were better prepared to look out for their employees' interests than were labor leaders. Finally, the AFL clung tenaciously to the craft principle of union organization, thereby ignoring the ever-increasing number of unskilled workers employed by the rapidly expanding mass-production industries—the automobile and steel industries in particular.

[5] Charles C. Killingsworth, "Organized Labor in a Free Enterprise Economy," in Walter Adams (ed.), *The Structure of American Industry*, 3d ed. (New York: The Macmillan Company, 1961), p. 570.

Encouragement Phase: 1930 to 1947

Two significant events occurred in the 1930s which revived the labor movement and inaugurated a period of rapid growth. Most importantly, the attitude of the Federal government toward unions changed from one of indifference, not to say hostility, to one of encouragement. Also, a major structural change in the labor movement accompanied the founding of the Committee (later the Congress) of Industrial Organizations in 1936. Both events, coupled with the wartime prosperity of the 1940s, greatly swelled the ranks of organized labor.

Prolabor legislation of the 1930s. Against the background of the depressed thirties, the Federal government enacted two decidedly prolabor acts. In part the passage of these acts reflects the violent opposition of organized labor to the previously described weapons employed by the courts and by management to suppress unions. In part they reflect a Democratic administration replacing a Republican administration. In part they echo the widely held opinion that strong unions, by achieving higher wages through collective bargaining, would increase total spending and help alleviate the Great Depression.

The *Norris–La Guardia Act* of 1932 did much to clear the path for union growth by outlawing two of the more effective anti-union weapons. Specifically, the act

1. Made it decidedly more difficult for employers to obtain injunctions against unions
2. Declared that yellow-dog contracts were unenforceable

Three years later, in 1935, the Federal government took more positive steps to encourage union growth. The *Wagner Act* (officially the National Labor Relations Act) guaranteed the "twin rights" of labor: the right of self-organization and the right to bargain collectively with employers. The act listed a number of "unfair labor practices" on the part of management. Specifically it

1. Forbade employers from interfering with the right of workers to form unions
2. Outlawed company unions
3. Prohibited anti-union discrimination by employers in hiring, firing, and promoting
4. Outlawed discrimination against any worker who files charges or gives testimony under the act
5. Obligated employers to bargain in good faith with a union duly established by their employees

The Wagner Act was clearly "labor's Magna Charta."

A National Labor Relations Board was established by the act and charged with the authority to investigate unfair labor practices occurring under the act, to issue cease-and-desist orders in the event of violations, and to conduct worker elections in deciding which specific union the workers wanted to represent them. The NLRB, you will note, is reminiscent of the Federal Trade Commission discussed in Chapter 34.

The Wagner Act was tailored to accelerate union growth. It was extremely successful in achieving this goal. The protective umbrella provided to unions by this act in conjunction with the Norris–La Guardia Act played a major role in causing the ranks of organized labor to mushroom from about 4 million in 1935 to 15 million in 1947.

Industrial unionism. We have already noted that one of the causes of stagnation in the AFL during the 1920s was its unwillingness to organize the growing masses of unskilled assembly-line workers. Though the majority of AFL leaders chose to ignore the unskilled workers, a vocal minority under the leadership of John L. Lewis contended that craft unionism would be completely ineffective as a means of organizing the hundreds of thousands of workers in the growing mass-production industries. According to Lewis and his followers, the basis for organization should be shifted from *craft unionism* to *industrial unionism*, that is, away from unions which only encompass a specific type of skilled workers to unions which include all workers—both skilled and unskilled—in a given industry or group of related industries. This conflict came to a head, and in 1936 Lewis and his sympathizers withdrew their unions (and were simultaneously expelled) from the AFL.

The withdrawing unions established themselves as the Congress of Industrial Organizations. The CIO met with rather startling success in organizing the automobile and steel industries. So great was this success that the AFL also moved in the direction of organizing on an industrial basis. By 1940 total union membership approximated 9 million workers.

Intervention Phase: 1947 to Date

In recent years there has been a decided increase in government regulation of, and intervention in, labor-management relations. It is important to understand the background of this governmental interference.

The prolabor legislation of the 1930s, the birth of industrial unionism, and the booming prosperity of the war years brought rapid union growth (see Figure 36–1). As unions gathered strength—both numerical and financial—it became increasingly evident that labor unions could no longer be regarded as the weak sister or underdog in their negotiations with management. Just as the

FIGURE 36–1. THE GROWTH OF UNION MEMBERSHIP.
Most of the growth in organized labor has occurred since 1935.
(U.S. Bureau of the Census and Bureau of Labor Statistics.)

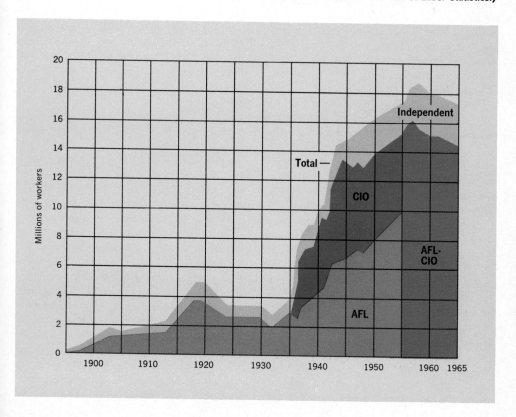

growing power of business monopolies brought a clamor for public control in the 1870s and 1880s, the upsurge of union power in the 1930s and 1940s brought a similar outcry for regulation. This pressure for union control came to a head in the postwar years.

Many people felt that the wartime strike record of American labor left much to be desired. Despite no-strike pledges, work stoppages reached a new high at the height of the war effort in 1944. Equally harmful to the favorable climate of public opinion which labor enjoyed in the 1930s was the series of nationwide strikes which broke out during the reconversion period in such basic industries as steel, coal, meat packing, and railway transportation. The man in the street felt that these strikes not only slowed the reconversion process but also inaugurated the severe wage-price inflationary spiral which was to plague the immediate postwar years (see Chapter 11). Businessmen, needless to say, were happy to fan the flames of public resentment. By the mid-forties the prolabor climate of the prior decade had done a virtual turnabout.

Taft-Hartley Act of 1947. This growing public hostility toward unions was crystallized in the Taft-Hartley Act (officially the Labor-Management Relations Act) in 1947. A very detailed piece of legislation, this act mirrors the increasing complexity of labor-management relations. Generally its specific provisions fall under four headings: (1) provisions which designate and outlaw certain "unfair union practices"; (2) provisions which regulate the internal administration of unions; (3) provisions which specify collective bargaining procedures and regulate the actual contents of bargaining agreements; and (4) provisions for the handling of strikes imperiling the health and safety of the nation.

1. You will recall that the Wagner Act outlined a number of "unfair labor practices" on the part of management. A new and crucial feature of the Taft-Hartley Act was that it introduced a number of "unfair labor practices" on the part of unions. These unfair practices, which constitute some of the most controversial sections of the act, are as follows: (*a*) Unions are prohibited from coercing employees to become union members. (*b*) *Jurisdictional strikes* (disputes between unions over the question of which has the authority to perform a specific job) are forbidden, as are *secondary boycotts* (refusing to buy or handle products produced by another union or group of workers) and certain *sympathy strikes* (strikes designed to assist some other union in gaining employer recognition or some other objective). (*c*) Unions are prohibited from charging excessive or discriminatory initiation fees or dues. (*d*) *Featherbedding*, a mild form of extortion wherein the union or its members receive payment for work not actually performed, is specifically outlawed. (*e*) Unions cannot refuse to bargain in good faith with management.

2. Taft-Hartley also imposes significant controls on the internal processes of labor unions: (*a*) Unions are obligated to make detailed financial reports to the National Labor Relations Board and to make such information available to its members. (*b*) Unions are prohibited from making political contributions in elections, primaries, or conventions which involve Federal offices. (*c*) Originally, union officials were required to sign non-Communist affidavits.

3. Other Taft-Hartley provisions are designed to control the actual collective bargaining process and the contents of the work agreement resulting therefrom: (*a*) The *closed shop* (which requires that a firm hire only workers who are already union members) is specifically outlawed; that is, a closed shop arrangement cannot be written into a collective bargaining agreement. (*b*) The *checkoff* (whereby union dues are deducted from the workers' pay checks by the employer and turned over to the union in a lump sum) cannot be written into a bargaining agreement unless authorized in writing by individual workers. (*c*) Collective bargaining agreements must provide that,

where they exist, welfare and pension funds are kept separate from other union funds and jointly administered by the union and management. (*d*) Bargaining agreements must contain termination or *reopening clauses* whereby both labor and management must give the other party 60 days' notice of their intent to modify or terminate the existing work agreement.

4. Finally, the Taft-Hartley Act outlines a procedure for avoiding major strikes which might disrupt the entire economy and thereby imperil the health or safety of the nation. According to this procedure, the President may obtain an injunction to delay such strikes for an 80-day "cooling-off" period. Within this period the involved workers are polled by the NLRB as to the acceptability of the last offer of the employer. If the last offer is rejected, the union can then strike. The government's only recourse— one of questionable legality—is seizure of the industry.

The Taft-Hartley Act is difficult to evaluate.[6] It has been a subject of heated debate since its enactment. Unions have condemned Taft-Hartley as a "slave labor act," claiming that it has undermined the status of unions and imperiled many of organized labor's basic weapons. Most employers feel that the act is merely a step in the right direction— a long-overdue attempt to restore a better balance of power between labor and management.

This much is agreed upon: The Taft-Hartley Act represents a marked shift in public policy. This shift is essentially one from "government-sponsored" collective bargaining to "government-regulated" collective bargaining. The underlying philosophy of the Wagner Act was that a balance of bargaining power between labor and management should be established. This balance would be conducive to effective collective bargaining free of government intervention. The

Taft-Hartley Act, however, envisions a need for detailed and continuous government control of collective bargaining to assure labor-management relations which are not unduly injurious to the welfare of the general public. Most objective observers feel that this shift in public policy toward labor has been a necessary one. Disagreement is strong, however, with respect to the form these controls should take and the manner in which they should be applied.

Landrum-Griffin Act of 1959. Government regulation of the internal processes of unions has been recently extended by passage of the Landrum-Griffin Act (officially the Labor-Management Reporting and Disclosure Act) in the fall of 1959. This act places regulations upon union elections and union finances and guarantees certain rights of union members. Specifically, the act regulates union elections by requiring regularly scheduled elections of officers and the use of secret ballots; restrictions are placed upon ex-convicts and Communists in holding union offices. Furthermore, union officials are now held strictly accountable for union funds and property. Officers handling union funds must be bonded, the embezzlement of union funds is made a Federal offense, and close restrictions are placed upon union loans to its officers and members. The act is also aimed at preventing autocratic union leaders from infringing upon certain rights of their constituents. The individual worker's rights to attend and participate in union meetings, to vote in union proceedings, and to nominate officers are guaranteed. The act permits a worker to sue his union if it denies him these rights. Under the act the Secretary of Labor is given broad powers in investigating violations of the act.

Labor Unity

In 1955 unity was formally reestablished in the American labor movement with the merger of the AFL and CIO. Many forces were significant in closing the breach which

---

[6] See "The Taft-Hartley Act after Ten Years: A Symposium," *Industrial and Labor Relations Review,* April, 1958.

existed between the two for almost two decades:

1. The AFL's increased willingness to accept and practice industrial unionism lessened the original structural differences between the AFL and the CIO.

2. The political and legislative setbacks which labor has encountered since the pro-labor era of the 1930s convinced labor leaders that unity in the labor movement is a necessary first step toward bolstering the political influence of organized labor.

3. Failure to achieve the desired rate of growth in the ranks of organized labor in the postwar years made evident to organized labor that a concerted, unified effort is needed to organize currently nonunion firms and industries.

4. The 1949 expulsion of eleven Communist-infiltrated unions made the CIO more palatable to the AFL and, at the same time, made the CIO more interested in unification by reducing the latter's numerical and financial strength.

5. Then, too, considerable turnover in top leadership in both the AFL and CIO pushed into the background certain personality conflicts which had proved to be a significant obstacle to reunification of the labor movement at an earlier date.

At present the AFL-CIO boasts 14.6 million members. Independent unions, of which the Teamsters and the United Mine Workers are the major ones, add another 3 million members. Hence, the ranks of organized labor now embody close to 18 million workers, or roughly one-third of the nonfarm labor force.

The labor movement remains basically conservative, and, assuming reasonably full employment, we can expect organized labor to remain concerned with the practical topics of the collective bargaining agenda rather than schemes designed to alter radically the framework of American capitalism. One point is clear: History has demonstrated that effective political action by organized labor is essential to union welfare and growth. Although there is little likelihood that a labor party will evolve in the United States, the upsurge of union activity in the political arena which has occurred in recent years is likely to continue in the future.

Labor Stagnation?

A number of prominent labor economists are currently talking of an "organizational plateau" and "stagnation" in the labor movement. Noting that union membership has been approximately 25 per cent of the civilian labor force in the entire post–World War II period, they predict a relative decline in the economic and political importance of organized labor. A number of factors underlie this thinking.

1. The previously noted (Chapter 21) shift in the composition of the labor force from blue- to white-collar employment has tended to reduce the potential membership base of organized labor.

2. The remaining unorganized blue-collar workers are in smaller plants, in agriculture, in service industries, and in the South—all of which are "hard-to-organize" jobs and areas.

3. Legislative reversals—namely, the shift of public policy from encouragement to intervention—pose a more hostile legal environment for organized labor.

4. The evolution of public apathy or hostility toward organized labor which has resulted from (a) the corrupt and fraudulent union practices uncovered by the investigations of the Senate's McClellan Committee, (b) prolonged strikes such as the 1959 steel strike, and (c) the implication of the cost-push inflation concept that unions are inflation-causing institutions, may work against future union growth.

5. Finally, it is frequently alleged that complacency and internal squabbles in the AFL-CIO are retarding expansion of the labor movement. The labor movement and its leaders have become complacent as the result of past successes. Organized labor has

"arrived" and has no place to go; the labor movement has been reduced from a "cause" to a day-to-day way of life. Furthermore, differences between various labor leaders and specific unions have diverted attention and energy away from the task of organizing the unorganized. To what extent these problems will impair future growth in the labor movement is difficult to ascertain; it is safe to conclude that in the future expansion will not be as easy to come by as it has been in the past.[7]

COLLECTIVE BARGAINING

As a result of the rapid growth of unions in recent decades, collective bargaining has become "a way of life" in labor-management relations. It is estimated that over 140,000 collective bargaining agreements are now in force in the United States.

The Bargaining Process

To the outsider, collective bargaining is a dramatic once-a-year clash between labor and management. Chief participants are a John L. Lewis type character with baggy suit, bushy eyebrows, and calloused hands, and on the other side of the table a Daddy Warbucks with diamond stickpin and formal attire. Furthermore, one gets the impression from the newspapers that labor and management settle their differences only with strikes, picketing, and not infrequent acts of violence.

These impressions are largely inaccurate. Collective bargaining is a somewhat less colorful process than most people believe. In negotiating important contracts, the union will be represented by top local and national officials, duly supplemented with lawyers and research economists. Management representatives include top policy-making execu-

[7] For a contrasting view consult Irving Bernstein, "Don't Count the Unions Out," *Challenge*, November, 1961, pp. 17–19.

tives, plant managers, personnel and labor relations specialists, lawyers, and staff economists. The union usually takes the initiative, outlining its demands. These take the form of specific adjustments in the current work agreement. The merits and demerits of these demands are then debated. Typically a compromise solution is reached and written into a new work agreement. Strikes, picketing, and violence are clearly the exception and not the rule. A rough indication of this is mirrored in the fact that only about one-fifth of 1 per cent of all working time was lost in 1964 as a result of work stoppages resulting from labor-management disputes! *Labor and management display a marked capacity for compromise and agreement.* We must keep in mind that strikes and labor-management violence are newsworthy, while the peaceful renewal of a work agreement hardly rates a page-5 column.

The Work Agreement

Collective bargaining agreements assume a variety of forms. Some agreements are amazingly brief, covering two or three typewritten pages; others are highly detailed, involving two hundred or more pages of fine print. Some agreements involve only a local union and a single plant; others set wages, hours, and working conditions for entire industries. There is no such thing as an "average" or "typical" collective bargaining agreement. Nevertheless, the following skeleton agreement, based on an actual contract, provides a fairly accurate notion of the scope and content of collective bargaining.

CONTRACT AND AGREEMENT

Sample Agreement

Article I. Intent, union status, management prerogatives. *Section 1.* This agreement entered into June 30, 1966, between the Deep South Manufacturing Company, hereinafter referred to as the "Employer," and the

International Brotherhood of Boilermakers, Iron Shipbuilders, and Helpers of America, Local No. 167, hereinafter referred to as the "Union." It is the intent and purpose of the parties hereto that this Agreement will promote and improve industrial relations between the Employer and the Union.

Section 2. The Employer recognizes the Union as the sole and exclusive bargaining agency for the purpose of determining rates of pay, hours of employment, and all other conditions of employment for all the Employer's production and maintenance employees. It is understood and agreed that the Union shall designate a representative who is duly authorized and will be consulted in all matters pertaining to the application of this work agreement.

Section 3. There shall be in each unit no less than one (1), nor more than two (2), Shop Stewards, these Stewards to be appointed by the Union. A unit shall be defined as any part of the Company Organization that provides for a foreman. Shop Stewards may leave their work during their regular working hours, without loss of pay, for the purpose of adjusting grievances.

Section 4. The Employer shall have the sole right of determining plant layout, the means of manufacturing and distributing products, the scheduling of production operations, and the setting of work shifts.

Section 5. Upon receipt of a written authorization by any employee the Employer shall deduct from the first pay each month and remit to the local Union such sum as the employee shall specify in said authorization.

Article II. Wages, hours of work, holidays.

Section 1. The minimum wage rates per hour shall be as follows:

Layout man	$2.40
Welders	1.98
Tackers	1.98
Painters	1.96
Riveting machine operator	1.85
Truck drivers	1.76
Helpers	1.59

When employees are transferred to a new job, their rate of pay shall not be changed for a period of fifteen (15) working days. If they are retained on the new job after this probationary period, the job rate called for by this agreement shall then be paid to them. If such job change involves a pay raise, the new rate shall be retroactive to the date the job was assigned.

Section 2. Wage rates shall be adjusted every three (3) months in accordance with changes in the U.S. Department of Labor's Index of Consumer Prices. For each one (1) point change upward in the index there shall be a one (1) cent per hour raise in wages. For each one (1) point downward change in the Index, there shall be a one (1) cent per hour decrease in wages. Wages in no case shall fall by more than five (5) cents per hour in any three-month period.

Section 3. All employees shall receive a two (2) per cent longevity increase in hourly wages for each year of service. This two (2) per cent shall be based on the previous year's hourly base rates.

Section 4. Forty (40) hours shall constitute the work week, from Monday to Friday, inclusive. The established schedule of hours shall be from 8 A.M. to 12 noon and from 12:30 noon to 4:30 P.M. The employer shall provide thirty-eight (38) weeks of employment per year.

Section 5. Time and one-half shall be paid for work performed in excess of eight hours in one day and for hours worked on Saturday. Double time shall be paid for hours worked on Sunday.

Section 6. When the following legal holidays—New Year's Day, Memorial Day, Fourth of July, Labor Day, Thanksgiving Day, and Christmas Day—occur or are celebrated during the employee's work week, he shall receive said holidays off duty with his regular straight-time pay, provided that he shall have been in the employ of the Employer at least thirty (30) calendar days. If said holiday falls on Saturday, it shall be celebrated on Friday, and if it falls on Sunday, celebration shall be on Monday. In the event an employee is required to work on one of the above-named holidays, he shall receive double time for such time worked in addition to his regular holiday pay. However, if any employee shall refuse to work on a holiday if he is requested by the Employer, he shall forfeit his holiday pay, but only if he refuses for other than a legitimate reason.

Section 7. All overtime work shall be divided among the workers according to seniority.

Section 8. All employees within the bargaining unit of the Union who shall have been in the service of the company one year and less than three years shall receive a paid vacation of five (5) days; those who have been in the service of the company three (3) years or more shall receive a paid vacation of ten (10) days.

Article III. Seniority and job opportunities.

Section 1. Seniority is defined as the principle that if, because of lack of work, the employer deems it advisable to reduce his work force, the last man hired shall be the first man laid off, and, in rehiring, the last man laid off shall be the first man rehired, until the list of former employees is exhausted.

Section 2. Seniority shall be on the basis of job classification. If an employee is transferred to another classification, he shall carry his seniority with him.

Section 3. Seniority shall be the determining factor regarding layoff and reemployment, transfers, demotions, promotions, or other job changes where the necessary skill and ability are present to perform the work required.

Section 4. Seniority shall be lost for the following reasons: (*a*) voluntary quitting; (*b*) discharge for cause; (*c*) layoff for twelve (12) consecutive months; (*d*) if laid-off employee is notified by the Employer by registered mail sent to his last known address to return and fails to do so within five (5) days of mailing the letter, unless a reasonable excuse shall be established.

Section 5. A seniority list shall be maintained and kept up to date by the Employer and shall be available to the Union at all times.

Article IV. Grievance procedure. *Section 1.*

In the event a grievance arises between an employee or group of employees and the Employer, such grievance shall be handled according to the following procedure.

Section 2. The employee or employees having a grievance shall report the same in a signed statement to the Shop Steward, who will in turn take up the grievance with the Foreman verbally. The Foreman will attempt to make a satisfactory settlement and will advise the Steward of his decision.

Section 3. If the Steward and employee are not satisfied with the decision of the Foreman, the Steward shall then submit the grievance to the Plant Superintendent verbally. The Superintendent shall make his decision within ten (10) days of the time the grievance is submitted to him. If the Steward or employee is not satisfied with the decision of the Superintendent, the Steward shall report the grievance to the Union's President, who shall submit the grievance to the management within ten (10) days and endeavor to reach an agreement.

Section 4. If no agreement is reached within ten (10) days, the grievance shall be submitted to an impartial arbitrator. The arbitrator shall be jointly selected by the Employer and the Union. The arbitrator shall be required to hand down a decision within thirty (30) days. This decision shall be binding, so long as it does not change the terms of this Agreement in any way.

Article V. Termination. *Section 1.* This

Agreement shall remain in full force and effect until June 30, 1967, and thereafter from year to year unless, within the ten (10) day period immediately preceding the sixty (60) days prior to the day of expiration, notice is given in writing to the other party indicating a desire to change the agreement.

Section 2. Anything in this Agreement found to be contrary to any state or national law shall be automatically voided.

....

International Brotherhood of Boilermakers, Iron Shipbuilders, and Helpers of America, Local 167
Deep South Manufacturing Company

Basic Contract Areas

This contract is representative in that it covers four basic areas: (1) the degree of recognition and status accorded the union and the prerogatives of management (Article I); (2) wages and hours (Article II); (3) seniority and job opportunities (Article III); and (4) a procedure for settling grievances (Article IV).

Union status. Unions enjoy differing degrees of recognition from management. Listed in order of the union's preference are (1) the closed shop, (2) the union shop, and (3) the open shop.

Prior to being outlawed by the Taft-Hartley Act, the *closed shop* afforded the greatest security to a union. Under a closed shop a worker must be a union member before the employer can hire him. A *union shop*, on the other hand, permits the employer to hire nonunion workers but provides that these workers must join the union in a specified period—say, thirty days—or relinquish their jobs. Since it is not specified to the contrary, we may assume in our sample contract that an *open shop* exists (Article I, Section 2). Management may apparently hire union or nonunion workers. Those who are nonunion are not obligated to join the union; they may continue on their jobs indefinitely as nonunion workers. In this contract, the union is the bargaining agent for *all* the firm's production and maintenance workers. In other cases the union may bargain only for union members. Finally, we must also mention the *nonunion shop.* Here

no union exists, and the employer makes a conscious effort to hire those workers who are least inclined to form or join a union.

Interesting variations of these basic types of union status have been developed. During World War II the *maintenance of membership shop* was evolved. Under this arrangement workers have the choice of joining or not joining the union. Those who join are obligated to maintain their membership in the union for the duration of the contract or sacrifice their jobs. Those who choose not to join the union can work indefinitely as nonunion employees. In some instances union or open-shop status will be supplemented with *preferential hiring.* Management agrees to hire union members so long as they are available, then it can hire nonunion workers.

Finally, in an *agency shop* union and non-union workers may be hired and continue on their jobs indefinitely as in an open shop. But in an agency shop nonunion workers must pay regular union dues and fees. These payments are in effect charges by the union for acting as the nonunion workers' agent in bargaining and enforcing a work agreement. From the union's standpoint the agency shop has the advantage of eliminating "free riders"—workers who benefit from, but do not financially support, the union.

Many businessmen fear that in time the expansion of the scope of collective bargaining may reach the point where certain fundamental management decisions will become matters to be decided jointly by management and labor. It is felt by businessmen that such an eventuality will "tie the hands" of management to the extent that efficient business operation may be jeopardized. For this reason at the insistence of management an increasing number of work agreements contain clauses which outline certain decisions which are to be made solely by management. These *managerial prerogatives* usually cover such matters as the size and location of plants, products to be manufactured, types of equipment and materials used in production, and the scheduling of production (Article I, Section 4). Frequently the hiring, transfer, discipline, discharge, and promotion of workers are decisions made solely by management but subject to the general principle of seniority and to challenge by the union through the grievance procedure.

Wages and hours. The focal point of any bargaining agreement is wages and hours. Our skeleton agreement is representative of most contracts in that basic hourly pay rates, length of work week, overtime rates, holidays, and vacations are all specified (Article II).

Both labor and management tend to be highly pragmatic in wage bargaining. The standards, or "talking points," most frequently invoked by labor in demanding (and by management in resisting) wage boosts are (1) "what others are getting"; (2) productivity, (3) ability to pay, (4) cost of living, and (5) economic stability. If a given firm has basic pay rates below those of comparable firms, the union is likely to stress that wages should be increased to bring them into line with what workers employed by other firms are getting. Similarly, if the firm has had a banner year, the union is likely to demand high wages on the grounds that the company has ample ability to grant such increments. In recent years unions have achieved considerable success in tying wages to the cost of living. It is estimated that work agreements covering about 3.7 million workers embody some kind of "escalator clause." This is true of our sample agreement (Article II, Section 2). And, many contracts link wage rates to productivity; wages automatically increase in terms of an estimated "improvement factor." Finally, when the economy flirts with unemployment, unions argue that wage increases are the best means of bolstering purchasing power and alleviating the economic slump.

Three points should be mentioned in connection with these wage criteria. In the first place, they are clearly two-edged propositions. For example, the cost-of-living criterion is only invoked by the union when prices are hurrying upward; unions conveniently ignore this criterion when prices are stable or declining. Similarly, the union only considers the ability-to-pay argument to be of importance when profits are large. The economic-stability argument is conveniently forgotten when the economy is besieged by inflation rather than unemployment. Management is equally inconsistent in the evaluation it places on the various wage-bargaining standards.

It must be emphasized, too, that these wage criteria are considerably less objective than might first appear. Most people might agree that it is only just that wage rates be adjusted for increases in productivity and the cost of living. But then arises the difficult question "By how much?" What wage boost should accompany, say, a 2-point increase in the Consumer's Price Index? Similarly, not only are productivity increases difficult to gauge, but, once gauged, how does one determine how much of the increase should accrue to labor and how much to capital?

Another noteworthy point: Wage changes —either increases or declines—based on these criteria are not necessarily desirable on either economic or equity grounds. Many economists fear, for example, that the widespread use of the cost-of-living criterion will cause a wage-price inflationary spiral to be built into our economy. In like manner, indiscriminate application of the what-others-are getting standard may push a relatively inefficient firm out of business, causing considerable hardship for affected workers.

Seniority and the control of job opportunities. The uncertainty of employment in a capitalistic economy coupled with the fear of anti-union discrimination on the part of employers has made workers and their unions decidedly "job-conscious." The explicit and detailed provisions covering job opportunities which most work agreements contain reflect this concern. The importance of seniority as the guiding principle in controlling job opportunities is apparent from Article III of our work agreement. It should be noted, however, that in many cases seniority is not rigidly applied. Strategic workers, or "key" personnel, will often be exempt from seniority regulations. And unions are typically willing to recognize that, particularly where promotion is concerned, ability must take precedence over seniority (Article III, Section 3).

Grievance procedure. It has been quipped that a collective bargaining agreement is to labor relations what the wedding ceremony is to domestic relations—only the beginning. Despite formal agreements, it is the "living together" that counts. It is unthinkable that even the most detailed and comprehensive work agreement can anticipate all the issues and problems which might occur during its life. What if Local 167 members show up for work on a Monday morning to find that for some reason the plant is closed down? Should they be given "show-up" pay amounting to, say, two or four hours' pay? This event is not covered in the contract and would therefore be a problem which might be ironed out through the grievance machinery. Then, too, there may be some disagreement in interpreting points covered in the work agreement. For example, the abbreviated work agreement upon which our discussion is centered poses some possible questions of interpretation because of which it may be necessary to invoke the grievance procedure. What is a "legitimate reason" for refusing to work on a holiday (Article II, Section 6)? Exactly how is "necessary skill and ability" to be defined in specific cases (Article III, Section 3)? What is meant by "discharge for cause" (Article III, Section 4)?

As a result, virtually all agreements contain a more or less explicit procedure for the handling of disputes which arise during the life of an agreement. In our sample agree-

ment a very complete four-step procedure is clearly outlined. In this instance the grievance machinery culminates in arbitration, that is, a neutral third party is designated to render a decision by which both labor and management must abide.

Three Implications

Three points, implicit in our discussion of collective bargaining, merit emphasis:

1. Collective bargaining is not only concerned with wage rates but also with the security and status of workers and of the union itself. Man does not live by bread alone. Workers seek protection from arbitrary actions by management; they seek a voice in determining the conditions under which they must work; they seek a means of voicing their grievances; they seek the status and dignity which accompany membership in economically powerful institutions. These objectives are fulfilled wholly or in part by membership in unions.

2. Also worthy of emphasis is the fact that collective bargaining is a continuous process. True, the *negotiation* of an agreement is an important and often dramatic point of departure. But this is followed by the equally important and continuing tasks of *administering* and *interpreting* (through the grievance procedure) the agreement. Collective bargaining is much more than a once-a-year clash of labor and management.

3. Finally, labor-management relations occur in a dynamic climate. Technological advance, business fluctuations, population changes, changes in the legislative framework, and changes in the character of businesses and unions themselves constitute some of the obvious dynamic aspects of the environment in which bargaining occurs. Changes such as these virtually preclude the reaching of final, once-and-for-all solutions to labor-management problems. At best collective bargaining provides short-run, temporary adjustments to labor-management conflicts—adjustments which the changing

economic milieu is likely to render obsolete in a relatively short span of time. In view of this observation the previously cited paucity of work stoppages due to labor-management disputes is all the more remarkable.

ECONOMIC IMPLICATIONS OF LABOR UNIONS

We must now look beyond the day-to-day dealings of a specific union and a specific firm and assume a broader perspective. What is the impact of strong unions upon the operation of American capitalism? More specifically, what implications do unions have for *full production*—that is, the efficient allocation of resources—and *full employment*—that is, economic stability and growth?

Widely divergent opinions exist on this question. To achieve the clearest picture of this controversy, let us sketch the extreme views on the question of the role of unions in modern capitalism.

The Case against Unions

Some economists and most businessmen take a decidedly dim view of labor unions. They envision unions as uncontrollable, socially irresponsible monopolies whose operation is inimical to efficient resource allocation and economic stability.

Character of unions. The anti-union view holds that, by either restricting the supply of labor (exclusive unionism) or imposing above-equilibrium wage rates (inclusive unionism), unions impair the operation of the price mechanism in labor markets. Unions are monopolies, it is argued, in that they rig the labor market to their own advantage and to the detriment of the rest of the economy. By achieving above-equilibrium wage rates, unions restrict employment either directly (in the case of exclusive unionism) or indirectly (in the case of inclusive unionism). Workers deprived of job opportunities by these union tactics drift into nonunionized labor markets, causing wage rates there to fall.

Unions and resource allocation. By thus distorting the wage structure, it is contended, unions alter the allocation of resources away from the ideal pattern which competitive labor markets would foster. We learned in a previous chapter that under competition the wage rates paid to labor would tend to equal labor's marginal revenue productivity. Now, assuming labor markets are competitive, labor will tend to move from low-wage, low-productivity jobs to high-wage, high-productivity jobs. Labor mobility, of course, is not perfect even under pure competition; but the tendency for this shifting to occur exists, and at least in the long run it would work with reasonable efficiency. The movement of labor from low- to high-productivity jobs which competition fosters is all to the good. Such shifting entails an expansion of total output; that is, it makes for an efficient allocation of labor resources.

The anti-union view contends that both exclusive and inclusive unionism impede the movement of labor from low- to high-marginal-productivity employments and therefore interfere with the efficient allocation of labor. By making a particular type of labor scarce in relation to the demand for it, exclusive unions move back up the MRP, or labor demand, curve and in so doing achieve above-competitive wages (see Figure 31–6). These high wages are sustained by restrictive membership policies which block the reallocation of workers into this occupation from other low-wage, low-productivity employments. Inclusive unionism accomplishes the same end indirectly by imposing above-equilibrium wage rates and allowing the market to restrict the number of jobs (see Figure 31–7). In this case the reallocation of workers from low-wage, low-productivity jobs to high-wage, high-productivity jobs is impeded not by the inability to get a union card but rather by the unwillingness of employers to take on more workers at the union-imposed wage rates. The basic conclusion is that by rigging wage rates, unions distort the allocation of labor away from the most efficient pattern.

But this is only half the story. The growth of union monopolies induces the further development of business monopolies. This is particularly true where union power forces business firms to band together in employer associations for purposes of collective bargaining. It is only a short step from here to industry cartelization. Furthermore, union monopolies are not to be viewed as counterpoises to business monopoly; rather they are "ominously complementary" to industrial concentration. In short, ". . . each tends to foster and to strengthen the other, fighting together to maximize joint exactions from the public while also fighting each other over division of the spoils."[8] By rigging resource prices and by contributing to the growth of business monopoly, unions contribute to an inefficient allocation of labor resources.

Unions and economic stability. The anti-union position envisions unions as having highly undesirable implications for economic stability. It is contended that there exist no effective internal or external restraints upon the monopoly power of unions. It is naïve, according to the anti-union view, to argue that labor unions will not use their power; unions and their leaders are not socially responsible. Similarly, there are no external restraints sufficient to contain strong unions. In particular, business firms have neither the ability nor the desire to resist the demands of aggressive union monopolies. And, if the experience of the last three decades is meaningful, government has done more to promote than to curb the monopoly power of unions.

This unrestrained union power is allegedly a major cause of unemployment and inflation. The attainment of high wages, it is

[8] Henry C. Simons, *Economic Policy for a Free Society* (Chicago: The University of Chicago Press, 1948), p. 35.

argued, will restrict the demand for labor, thereby causing unemployment and a slowing down of the growth rate. Marginal firms, finding it impossible to operate profitably in the face of above-competitive wage rates, will cease production and dismiss their labor forces. In addition, aggressive union wage policies can be expected to affect business profit expectations adversely. As a result, the levels of investment spending, aggregate demand, and employment will be reduced.

On the other hand, if the economy manages to achieve full employment despite irresponsible union wage policies, unions will then cause inflationary pressure to arise. For example, suppose that government activates the monetary and fiscal tools at its disposal so as to sustain a full-employment level of spending. Blessed with a high level of aggregate demand, businessmen will find it a relatively simple matter to pass wage boosts on to consumers through price increases. But this rise in the cost of living will prompt unions to demand and receive another round of wage hikes. The wage-price spiral will then be on its way, causing a cumulative inflation problem for the economy.

Government policy toward unions. Those who embrace the anti-union position conclude that either unemployment or inflation will eventually prove inimical to capitalism; either is held to be a sufficient cause for the demise of the free enterprise system. A variety of policy recommendations have been offered to deal with the threat posed by union monopolies. There are those who feel that the only real remedy is the outright destruction of unions. Unions simply cannot be allowed to endure. Others call for increased governmental regulation of collective bargaining. It is felt that the Taft-Hartley Act is a step in the right direction but that it fails to go far enough in regulating unions. It might be helpful, it is suggested, to subject unions once again to the antitrust laws. Or three-party bargaining involving labor, management, and the public as represented by government officials may be necessary to avoid the disruptive economic effects of strong unions. Still others envision the need for wage-price controls by government if economic stability is to be maintained.

The Case for Unions

The anti-union view just outlined is hardly a happy one. However, there exists an equally important school of thought which paints a cautiously optimistic picture of unions as being compatible with economic efficiency, stability, and growth. Let us sketch this pro-union position.

Character of unions. The pro-union view holds that, although unions have a degree of monopoly power, there are effective internal and external restraints which guard against the abuse of that power. Internal restraints are several. It is argued that the larger unions in particular represent their constituents not only as wage earners but also as consumers and savers; hence, unions are obligated to concern themselves with the effects which their wage demands might have upon job opportunities and the cost of living. And, as collective bargaining tends to become more mature, labor leaders are acquiring a greater sense of social responsibility. In addition to these internal restraints on union power there exist significant external restraints. Because of the extreme reluctance of unions to accept wage cuts, it is felt that in periods of both high and low aggregate demand employers can and do exhibit considerable resistance to union wage demands. It must be remembered, too, that, while a businessman stands to lose only a small fraction of his market as the result of a price increase, a union risks a work stoppage and the loss of income for *all* its members when it demands a wage increase. Unions may actually be subject to greater restraints in the resource market than are business monopolies in the product market.

Unions and resource allocation. The pro-union position holds that the anti-union view

rests on the faulty assumption that labor markets would be highly competitive in the absence of unions. It is contended that this is simply not the case; labor markets would be imperfect ones even in the absence of unions. In particular, large business firms would exert considerable monopsonistic power in hiring workers (Figure 31–4).

More positively, the pro-union view argues that the monopoly power of unions operates so as to offset or neutralize the monopsonistic power of large employers. Because the strongest unions have generally developed in the most highly monopolized industries, unions are felt to be a primary manifestation of countervailing power. By counterbalancing the economic power of business monopolies, unions contribute to a more efficient allocation of labor resources. In short, the presence of union monopoly power on the seller's side of the labor market may serve to cancel the monopsonistic power of large employers on the buyer's side. The result is a near-competitive wage rate accompanied by an allocation of labor resembling that which would have existed if competition had prevailed in the labor market. In terms of wage rates and resource allocation, monopoly power on both sides of the labor market is allegedly superior to the presence of such power only on the buying side (see Figure 31–8).

Unions and economic stability. The pro-union view alleges that it is flatly incorrect to make unions the scapegoat for unemployment and inflation. As previously explained, unions cannot and do not seek higher wages in a manner oblivious to employment and price implications. Both internal and external forces limit the exertion of economic power by unions. The wage-price spiral is a descriptive characteristic of inflation which would exist in modern capitalism with or without unions and collective bargaining. Stated differently, it is the myriad of forces which determine the level of aggregate demand, and not simply the existence of labor unions, which govern the amount of unemployment or inflation the economy experiences. Strong unions are compatible with economic stability and growth; collective bargaining is not inherently inflationary, nor is it a significant cause of unemployment. More positively, the role of unions in American capitalism may be such as to make them an integral force in the complex of balances and counterbalances which permits the relatively smooth functioning of our economy despite its many market imperfections.

Government policy toward unions. The pro-union school of thought concludes that government policy should be generally aimed at the goal of encouraging the growth of unions where they constitute positions of countervailing power. Furthermore, increasing maturity is envisioned in labor-management relations. As a result, less control over collective bargaining will be needed in the future.

Although each of the two views just sketched can be applied with little or no modification to specific unions, both represent the extremes. Hence, neither is acceptable as a general explanation of the economic impact of unions. Their value lies in the fact that the contrast they provide serves as an important point of reference for policy makers and an informed citizenry.

SUMMARY

1. The growth of labor unions was slow and irregular until the 1930s. The repression of unions by the courts and by management was an important factor in accounting for this retarded growth. The courts employed the conspiracy doctrine, injunctions, and the antitrust laws against unions. Management invoked such varied anti-union techniques as discriminatory discharge, blacklisting, lockouts, strikebreakers, yellow-dog contracts, paternalism, and company unions in slowing the development of unions.

2. The AFL dominated the American labor movement from 1886 until the CIO

was formed in 1936. Its philosophy was essentially that of Samuel Gompers—business unionism, political neutrality, and craft unionism.

3. Union growth was rapid in the 1930s and 1940s. The shift toward industrial unionism triggered by the formation of the CIO in 1936 was a significant factor in this growth. Equally important were the wartime prosperity of the 1940s and the prolabor legislation passed by the Federal government in the 1930s.

4. The Norris-La Guardia Act of 1932 rendered yellow-dog contracts unenforceable and sharply limited the use of injunctions in labor disputes.

5. The Wagner Act of 1935—"labor's Magna Charta"—guaranteed labor the rights to organize and to bargain collectively with management. The act prohibited certain "unfair labor practices" on the part of management, thereby paving the way for unions to organize, unimpeded by management.

6. The Taft-Hartley Act of 1947 brought about a shift from government-sponsored to government-regulated collective bargaining. The act **a.** specifically outlaws certain "unfair practices" of unions; **b.** regulates certain internal operations of unions; **c.** controls the content of collective bargaining agreements; and **d.** outlines a procedure for handling "national health and welfare" strikes.

7. The Landrum-Griffin Act of 1959 was designed to regulate the internal processes of unions—in particular the handling of union finances and the union's relationships with its members.

8. At the present time almost 18 million workers are union members; this constitutes about one-third of the nonfarm labor force. A number of economists feel that, for a variety of reasons, future growth in the labor movement will be modest.

9. Labor and management "live together" under the terms of collective bargaining agreements. These work agreements cover four major topics: **a.** union status and managerial prerogatives; **b.** wages and hours; **c.** seniority and job control; and **d.** a grievance procedure. Experience indicates that both labor and management are very willing to compromise and reach agreement short of work stoppages.

10. There is considerable disagreement as to the economic impact of strong unions. The anti-union view holds that unions are potent labor market monopolies. Exertion of their monopoly power allegedly contributes to a misallocation of resources and causes instability in the levels of employment and prices. The destruction of unions, increased public regulation of unions, three-party bargaining, and wage-price controls are possible public policy alternatives that have been suggested by various writers who embrace the anti-union position.

11. The pro-union view contends that unions are socially responsible organizations which can be expected to temper their wage demands if unemployment or inflation looms as a probable consequence. The monopoly power which unions exert allegedly serves to counterbalance the monopsonistic power of large employers. The result is that labor allocation and wage rates are likely to be closer to the competitive situation than would be the case in the absence of unions. Collective bargaining is not a basic cause of instability; rather instability stems from all those factors which influence the components of aggregate demand. The pro-union view envisions increasing maturity in collective bargaining and a decline in the need for government controls over labor-management relations.

QUESTIONS AND STUDY SUGGESTIONS

1. The first unions to develop in the United States were composed of skilled craftsmen rather than unskilled workers. Can you explain why?
2. Identify the following terms:
   a. Injunction
   b. Blacklisting
   c. Lockout
   d. Checkoff
   e. Featherbedding
   f. Company unions
   g. Criminal conspiracy doctrine
   h. Secondary boycott
   i. Sympathy strike
   j. Discriminatory discharge
   k. Jurisdictional strikes
   l. Yellow-dog contract
3. Distinguish clearly between craft and industrial unionism. Which is generally associated with the AFL? The CIO?
4. Distinguish between a closed shop, a union shop, an open shop, an agency shop, and a nonunion shop.
5. "There are legislative, executive, and judicial aspects to collective bargaining." Explain.
6. What are the major provisions of the Norris-La Guardia Act? The Wagner Act? How do you account for the passage of these prolabor acts? What are the functions of the National Labor Relations Board? Briefly indicate the nature of the Landrum-Griffin Act.
7. "In the 1930s public opinion was prolabor, but by the mid-1940s the public was of an antilabor disposition." Account for this turnabout.
8. What are the major provisions of the Taft-Hartley Act? If you had the power to revise this act, what changes would you make? In what ways has the Taft-Hartley Act directly or indirectly affected the sample work agreement studied in this chapter? Be specific.
9. It has been said that the Taft-Hartley Act was passed to achieve three major goals: (*a*) to reestablish an equality of bargaining power between labor and management to maintain industrial peace; (*b*) to protect

"neutrals," that is, third parties who are not directly concerned with a given labor-management dispute; (c) to protect the rights of individual workers in their relations with unions. Review the Taft-Hartley provisions as outlined in this chapter, and relate each to these three major goals.

10. Suppose you are the president of a newly established local union which is about to bargain with an employer for the first time. Make a list of those points which you would want to be covered explicitly in the work agreement.

11. Suppose you are a union president bargaining for higher wages. Assuming the economic climate which exists at this moment, what wage criteria would you use in backing your demands? Explain.

12. Briefly contrast the anti-union and pro-union views of organized labor. To what degree does the anti-union view depend upon an affirmative answer to the question "Do unions raise wages?" Which of the two views do you feel is the more accurate? Outline a compromise position less extreme than either the anti-union or the pro-union view sketched in this chapter.

SELECTED REFERENCES

Bloom, Gordon F., Herbert R. Northrup, and Richard L. Rowan: *Readings in Labor Economics* (Homewood, Ill.: Richard D. Irwin, Inc., 1963).

Bloom, Gordon F., and Herbert R. Northrup: *Economics of Labor Relations,* 5th ed. (Homewood, Ill.: Richard D. Irwin, Inc., 1965).

Bowen, William G. (ed.): *Labor and the National Economy* (New York: W. W. Norton & Company, Inc., 1965).

Chamberlain, Neil W., and James W. Kuhn: *Collective Bargaining,* 2d ed. (New York: McGraw-Hill Book Company, 1965).

Chamberlain, Neil W.: *Sourcebook on Labor* (New York: McGraw-Hill Book Company, 1958).

Lester, Richard A.: *Labor: Readings on Major Issues* (New York: Random House, Inc., 1965).

Rees, Albert: *The Economics of Trade Unions* (Chicago: The University of Chicago Press, 1962).

Reynolds, Lloyd G.: *Labor Economics and Labor Relations,* 4th ed. (Englewood Cliffs, N.J.: Prentice-Hall, Inc., 1964).

CHAPTER 37

THE ECONOMICS OF
INEQUALITY AND POVERTY

In his January, 1964, State of the Union Message President Johnson declared war on poverty:

Unfortunately, many Americans live on the outskirts of hope. . . .

Our task is to replace their despair with opportunity.

And this Administration today, here and now, declares unconditional war on poverty in America. . . .

It will not be a short or easy struggle, no single weapon or strategy will suffice, but we shall not rest until that war is won.

The richest nation on earth can afford to win it.

We cannot afford to lose it.

Our basic task in this chapter is to examine the dismal economics of poverty: Who are the poor? What are their numbers? Why does poverty persist amidst general abundance? Can the poverty problem be resolved and, if so, by what means?

INCOME INEQUALITY

The first step in approaching the poverty problem is to analyze carefully available factual data on income inequality. Average income in the United States is the highest of any nation in the world; the median income for all consumer units was $6,140 in 1963. But now we must envision how it is distributed around the average. Table 37–1 tells the story: *Income inequality in the United States is considerable.* At the low end of the scale we find that 11 per cent of all consumer units, that is, families and unat-

tached individuals, received about 2 per cent of total personal income. A mere 9 per cent of the total income went to the 29 per cent of the consumer units receiving an annual income of less than $4,000 per year in 1963. At the top of the income pyramid we find that 21 per cent of the consumer units received incomes of $10,000 or more per year; this group got about 47 per cent of total personal income. These figures clearly point to considerable income inequality.

Causes of Income Inequality

The price system is an impersonal mechanism. It has no conscience, and it does not cater to any set of ethical standards concerning what is an "equitable," or "just," distribution of income. As a matter of fact, the basically individualistic environment of the capitalist economy is more than permissive of a high degree of income inequality. Some of the more specific factors contributing to income inequality include:

1. Native abilities. Nature has been very arbitrary in apportioning mental, physical, and aesthetic talents. Some individuals have had the good fortune to inherit the exceptional mental qualities essential to entering the relatively high-paying fields of medicine, dentistry, and law. Others, rated as "dull normals" or "mentally retarded," are assigned to the most menial and low-paying occupations or are incapable of earning income at all. Some are blessed with the physical capacity and coordination to become highly

TABLE 37–1. THE DISTRIBUTION OF PERSONAL INCOME BY CONSUMER UNITS, 1963

(1) Personal income class	(2) Per cent of all consumer units in this class	(3) Per cent of total personal income received by consumers in this class	(4) Per cent of all consumer units in this class and all lower classes	(5) Per cent of income received by this class and all lower classes
Under $2,000	11	2	11	2
$2,000–$3,999	18	7	29	9
$4,000–$5,999	20	13	49	22
$6,000–$7,999	18	17	67	39
$8,000–$9,999	12	14	79	53
$10,000 and over	21	47	100	100
	100	100		

Source: U.S. Department of Commerce, *Survey of Current Business*, April, 1964.

paid professional athletes. The clumsy and frail must settle for much less. Some have the aesthetic qualities prerequisite to becoming great artists or musicians. Others could not carry a tune or paint a discernible likeness if their lives depended upon it. In brief, native talents put some individuals in a position to make contributions to total output which command very high incomes. Others are in much less fortunate circumstances.

2. Training, education, and opportunities to advance. Despite high-sounding claims to the contrary, opportunities to develop latent talents and to acquire new abilities are not equally available to all. Discrimination on the basis of race, religion, and sex block many paths to self-betterment. Similarly, the inability to finance extended periods of training and the virtual closing of certain occupational doors by unions or professional associations are equally effective obstacles. Thus, even if everyone were blessed with identical physical and mental talents, income inequality would still result because of the fact that opportunities to develop and employ those talents are not equally available.

3. Property ownership. The ownership of property resources, and hence the receipt of property incomes, is very unequal. The vast majority of households own little or no property resources, while the remaining few supply very great quantities of machinery, real estate, farmland, and so forth. Basically, property incomes account for the position of those households at the very pinnacle of the income pyramid. The right of inheritance and the fact that "wealth begets wealth" reinforce the role played by unequal ownership of property resources in determining income inequality.

4. Ability to exert market power. Ability to "rig the market" on one's own behalf is undoubtedly a major factor in accounting for income inequality. Certain unions and professional groups have adopted policies which limit the supplies of their productive services, thereby boosting the incomes of those "on the inside." Exorbitant initiation fees, prolonged apprenticeship periods, flat refusal to accept new members, or the setting of unrealistic standards of performance are well-known and frequently employed tactics for manipulating the market on the behalf of a particular group. The same holds true in the product market: profit receivers in particular stand to benefit when their firm develops some degree of monopoly power.

5. Unequal distribution of misfortune. Many of the households are at the base of the income pyramid as a result of economic misfortune. A host of economic hazards in such forms as prolonged illness, serious accident, death of the family breadwinner, or unemployment may plunge a family into relative poverty. The burden of such misfortunes is borne very unevenly by the population and hence contributes to the degree of income inequality.

6. Miscellaneous factors. There are obviously other important forces which play a part in explaining income inequality. Luck, chance, and "being in the right place at the right time" have all caused individuals to stumble into fortunes. Discovering oil on a run-down farm, meeting the right press agent, or making a favorable impression on the boss's daughter have accounted for many high incomes. Nor can personal contacts and political influence be discounted as means of attaining the higher income brackets.

Trends in Income Inequality

We know from Chapter 20 that economic growth has brought increases in incomes:

Absolutely the entire distribution of income has been moving upward over time. Changes in the *relative* distribution of income are quite another thing. Incomes can move up absolutely, and the degree of inequality may or may not be affected. Table 37–2 is instructive on this point. Here we divide the total number of income receivers into five numerically equal groups, or *quintiles*, and show the percentage of total personal income received by each.

These data suggest, first, that a significant reduction in income inequality occurred between 1929 and 1944. Note in Table 37–2 the declining percentage of personal income going to the top quintile and the increasing percentage received by the other four quintiles during this period. Many of the forces at work during World War II undoubtedly contributed to this decline in inequality. War-born prosperity eliminated the many low incomes caused by the severe unemployment of the 1930s, brought a reduction of wage and salary differentials, boosted depressed farm incomes through sharp increases in farm prices, was accompanied by a decline in property incomes as a share of the national income, and so forth.

The second notable feature of these data is that income inequality has *not* diminished significantly since World War II; indeed, it has been remarkably constant. The forces making for greater equality during the war ceased to be of great import after the war.

TABLE 37–2. PERCENTAGE OF TOTAL PERSONAL INCOME RECEIVED BY EACH ONE-FIFTH, AND BY THE TOP 5 PER CENT, OF CONSUMER UNITS, 1929, 1935–1936, 1944, 1962

Quintile	1929	1935–1936	1944	1962
Lowest }	12.5	4.1	4.9	4.6
Second }		9.2	10.9	10.9
Third	13.8	14.1	16.2	16.3
Fourth	19.3	20.9	22.2	22.7
Highest	54.4	51.7	45.8	45.5
Total	100.0	100.0	100.0	100.0
Top 5 per cent	30.0	26.5	20.7	19.6

Source: **U.S. Department of Commerce,** *Survey of Current Business,* **April, 1964.**

The Case against Income Inequality

The desirability of income inequality is anything but a new subject for debate. Indeed the long-standing nature of the controversy has resulted in the development of a more or less standardized set of arguments that condemn and an equally traditional group of contentions that defend income inequality.

Five points constitute the case against inequality in the distribution of income:

1. Maximizing satisfactions. It is alleged that income inequality is a large obstacle in maximizing consumer satisfaction. The underlying reasoning is this: Money income is subject to the principle of diminishing marginal utility. In any time period income receivers spend the first dollars received on those products which they value most, that is, on products whose marginal utility is high. As their most pressing wants become satisfied, consumers will spend additional dollars of income on increasingly frivolous, lower-marginal-utility items. Suppose, for example, that $10,000 worth of annual income is unequally distributed between Brooks and Anderson—the former getting $8,000 and the latter $2,000. As a result, the last, or marginal, dollars spent by Brooks will yield him relatively small increments of satisfaction or utility. Why? Because these dollars will be spent in satisfying less urgent needs; that is, they will be spent on frivolous products or on extra units of items already possessed in abundance. In either event the marginal utility of these dollars will be relatively low.

But, alas, $2,000-a-year Anderson is in a much different situation. His annual pittance is such that his marginal dollars are spent on very basic, high-marginal-utility products. He is able to buy such small quantities of most products that the marginal utility of added units is still relatively high. It is concluded that any transfer of money income from high-income Brooks to low-income Anderson will increase the satisfactions or utility of the latter by more than it will

decrease those of the former. The result is a net increase in *total* consumer satisfaction. Greater income equality has moved the economy closer to the goal of maximizing aggregate satisfaction. In a somewhat altered form this argument contends that income inequality causes economic resources to be misallocated. Inequality results in inefficient resource use by drawing resources into the production of frivolous, unimportant products at the expense of more essential products that low-income groups desire but are unable to afford.

This is a very persuasive argument. But there is a major loophole: The argument assumes that Brooks and Anderson have equal capacities to enjoy income. In fact, however, *interpersonal* comparisons of the subjective concept of utility cannot be scientifically made. Although the above argument against inequality rests on the supposition that Brooks and Anderson are equally capable of enjoying income, that is unlikely. The chances are at least fifty-fifty[1] that Brooks has a greater capacity to derive satisfaction from spending money income than does Anderson. Were this actually the case, an *unequal* distribution of income would be required to achieve maximum consumer satisfaction. So, although this argument for greater income equality cannot be disproved, it also cannot be proved valid. The ability to derive satisfaction from the expenditure of money income eludes quantitative measurement.

2. Productivity. It is also argued that excessive income inequality impairs productivity. In the first instance, laborers who find themselves at the base of the income pyramid may not be able to obtain that minimum of food and shelter needed to maintain their physical

---

[1] They may be better than fifty-fifty. It is plausible to argue that the ability to enjoy income varies directly with the size of one's income. A high income provides (and presupposes!) the education prerequisite to the intelligent allocation of money income and the greater enjoyment of the goods and services thereby obtained.

and mental vigor, not to mention the effects which poverty may have upon their morale. And, ironically enough, inequality may impair the productivity of those at the pinnacle of the pyramid. Leveling off the income peak might induce the "idle rich" and the "I retired at thirty-five" segment of the economy's human resources back into harness.

3. Opportunity. Income inequality means unequal opportunities for training and education. The sons of the poor are at a decided handicap in getting the education required for entering many occupations. To overstate the situation, an individual must be an M.D. in order to finance a medical education for his son. The implications for resource allocation are clear: the unequal distribution of opportunities fostered by income inequality distorts the allocation of resources. Resources should be allocated in terms of ability and productivity, not by accident of birth.

4. Political inequality. Another pillar in the case against inequality links income inequality to political and social inequality. Money talks in politics. Theoretically, of course, the rich man and the poor man have equal voices in politics; that is, each has one vote. In practice, it is no secret that the rich man, by virtue of his wealth, is in a position to influence many other votes. How? By financing the campaigns of "right-minded" politicians, by "recommending" candidates to subordinates, by using his resources to support lobbyists, and so forth. A similar set of arguments can be offered to support the view that there is a direct relationship between wealth and social inequality.

5. Ethics. A final argument against income inequality is the ethical judgment that social justice cannot be realized with substantial income inequality.

The Case for Income Inequality

Three long-standing arguments anchor the defense of income inequality.

1. Capital formation. Income inequality gives rise to sizable amounts of private savings, which, when invested, provide the capital goods which are the core of economic growth. Indeed, it is primarily as a result of this expanding stock of capital which the savings of the wealthy finance that the productivity and standard of living of the entire economy are bettered. The savings of the very wealthy, it is argued, provide the means for improving the lot of the very poor.

But proponents of greater income equality are quick to point out a major loophole in this capital formation argument: The alleged relationship between inequality and capital formation is not at all clear. Norway, for example, has moved far in the direction of income equality; yet in the postwar era it achieved a high rate of capital formation. In contrast low rates of capital formation persist in those Middle Eastern nations in which income inequality is particularly great.

2. Disincentive effects. Income inequality is also defended on the grounds that it furnishes the incentives to work, produce, and innovate which are the driving forces of any economy. Monetary gain—the opportunity to better oneself financially—is alleged necessary to induce workers and entrepreneurs to rise above mediocrity. Income inequality is essential if risky ventures are to be undertaken and workers are to perform effectively and faithfully over time. An unequal distribution of income is a necessary and desirable consequence of the price system in allocating resources in terms of their productivity.

Skeptics feel that this justification of income inequality has been overdrawn. They question, in particular, whether there is any firm relationship between income and productivity. Business executives, enthralled by their work and anxious to be heralded as "top men" in their field, may put out the same effort at $20,000 per year as they will at $50,000. Nor is it clear that the unskilled assembly-line worker will be more productive after his union negotiates a $150 increase in his annual income than before.

3. The "good life." Defenders of inequality also claim that high-income consumers have played a crucial role in the development of new products. The rich, it is said, support new industries in their high-cost, high-price infancies. This support allows low-cost mass production to evolve, bringing the products within the financial means of the masses of consumers. Stated differently, in the face of a drastic leveling of incomes, "The production of all first-quality goods would cease. The skill they demand would be lost and the taste they shape would be coarsened." A closely related and more general point is that the sociocultural fiber and viability of any society are directly related to, and dependent upon, income inequality. In short, it is alleged that the highly egalitarian society promises to be intellectually uncreative, culturally unappealing, technologically unprogressive, and socially unrewarding.[2]

Other points bolster the case for inequality. A most pragmatic point is this: Because of the relatively small number of people at the top of the income pyramid and the extremely large number at the base, a redistribution of income from rich to poor would only raise the income of the latter by minute amounts. And it is invariably argued that the philanthropic actions of the very wealthy devote resources to cultural and educational pursuits and to humanitarian activities—a reallocation of resources which greater income equality would not foster.

Thus go the cases for and against income inequality. Each of us must weigh the relative merits of the two positions and judge for himself which is superior.

A final comment must be appended to this discussion. Few would advocate complete equality or very extreme inequality in the distribution of income. The real problem is to find the optimum degree of income inequality. That is, we seek that particular distribution of income which will allow us to realize substantially the desirable aspects of income inequality without encountering to a serious degree the problems and disadvantages which accompany extreme income inequality.

THE DISMAL ECONOMICS OF POVERTY

With this background information on income inequality in mind, let us now turn to the poverty problem. How extensive is poverty in the United States? What are the characteristics of the poor? And what is the best strategy of attack in a war on poverty?

Who Are the Poor?

Poverty does not lend itself to precise definition. But as a broad generalization, we might say that a family lives in poverty when its basic needs exceed its available means of satisfying them. A family's needs have many determinants: its size, its health, the ages of its members, and so forth. Its means include currently earned income, transfer payments, past savings, and so on. The definition of poverty more or less officially accepted by concerned government agencies is that any family which receives from all sources an income less than $3,000 per year, or any unattached individual who receives less than $1,500 per year, is poor. Applying this definition to income data for the United States, it is found that *nearly one-fifth of the nation lives in poverty.*[3]

Who are these 35 million or so souls—the "forgotten fifth" of the population—who live in poverty? Unfortunately for purposes of public policy, the poor are heterogeneous; they can be found in all geographic regions, they are whites and nonwhites, they include large numbers of both rural and urban people, they are both old and young. Yet, despite this pervasiveness, some useful—though overlapping—guidelines serve to

[2] Bertrand de Jouvenel, *The Ethics of Redistribution* (New York: Cambridge University Press, 1952), pp. 41, 46, 54.

[3] *Economic Report of the President* (Washington, D.C., 1964), pp. 57–61.

identify the greatest concentrations of poverty.[4]

1. The amount of education and size of income are directly related; some 4 million poor families are headed by individuals who have had eight or less years of education. Sixty-one per cent of the breadwinners of poor families did not get beyond the eighth grade. A substantial portion of the working population possesses neither the education nor the skills to hold a decent-paying position. Examples: the 8,954,000 workers in retail stores earned an average of $71 per week in early 1965. Workers employed in laundry and dry cleaning plants received only $57 per week. Hotel and motel workers averaged the appalling sum of $49 per week.

2. The incidence of poverty is much greater among nonwhites than it is among whites. Seventeen per cent of all white families are poor; forty-four per cent of all nonwhite families are poor.

3. Poverty is common to the aged; one-third of all poor families are headed by a person sixty-five years old or over.

4. Poverty is very common in agriculture—particularly in the South—where the tenant farmer, the small marginal farmer, and farm laborers are afflicted. In excess of 40 per cent of all farmers are poor.

5. Families headed by women—because, for example, of divorce or death of the husband—are very apt to be poor. About one-half of all families headed by women are poor.

6. Health deficiencies—both physical and mental—are highly correlated with low incomes.

7. A very high percentage of the families of the unemployed and the partially employed are living in poverty.

The "Invisible" Poor

The facts and figures we have just summarized may be a bit difficult to accept. After

[4] These characteristics and supporting data are largely from the *Economic Report of the President* (1964), especially pp. 56–57.

all, ours is presumably the affluent society. How does one square the depressing statistics on poverty which permeate both government and private reports with everyday observations of abundance? The answer lies in good measure in the fact that much American poverty is hidden; it is largely invisible. First of all, poverty is increasingly isolated in the hearts of large cities because the middle and upper classes have migrated away from them to suburbia. Poverty persists in the slums and ghettos not readily visible from the freeway or subway. Secondly, much poverty embraces the aged and infirm who rarely venture from their meager rented rooms. Similarly, rural poverty and the chronically depressed areas of Appalachia and Kentucky are all off the beaten path. Fourthly, and quite ironically, "America has the best dressed poverty the world has ever known"; the relative cheapness of clothing means that the poor can be reasonably well dressed and therefore *look* prosperous, although they are inadequately housed, fed, and doctored. Finally, and perhaps most importantly[5]

The poor are politically invisible.... [They] do not, by far and large, belong to unions, to fraternal organizations, or to political parties. They are without lobbies of their own; they put forward no legislative program. As a group they are atomized. They have no face; they have no voice.

Indeed, the American poor have been labeled "the world's least revolutionary proletariate."

Paradox of the Welfare State

Although not as comprehensive as those of, say, Great Britain or Sweden, the American economy embodies a reasonably well-devel-

[5] Michael Harrington, *The Other America* (Baltimore: Penguin Books, Inc., 1963), p. 14. This admirable and disturbing little book is required reading for anyone seriously interested in the poverty problem.

oped welfare state, which treats the poverty problem in a variety of ways. For example, the social security system, legislated in 1935 and put into operation in 1937, is an accepted feature of our society and consists of three parts.

1. *Old age and survivors insurance* (OASI) is essentially a gigantic program of compulsory saving. The program is financed by compulsory taxes (premiums) levied upon both employers and employees. In 1966 these taxes are each 4.2 per cent upon the first $6,600 of annual income. Legislative provisions have been made which will increase the tax on both employer and employee to 5.65 per cent by 1987. The self-employed now pay a tax of 6.15 per cent, a figure which will rise to 7.8 per cent by 1987. Benefit payments are made to those reaching the retirement age of sixty-five; if the worker dies before sixty-five, benefits accrue to his survivors. Widows can retire and collect old age benefits at age sixty-two. Currently over 90 per cent of all employed persons in the United States are covered by OASI.

The actual size of benefit payments varies according to the amount the worker has contributed to the program, the number of dependents, and so forth. At the beginning of 1965 almost 20 million people were receiving OASI checks averaging about $80 per month. Benefit payments redistribute income to some degree; small contributors get relatively more in comparison with their contributions than do large contributors. On the other hand, benefit payments are not based upon the recipient's need; a participant's contribution gives him the right to benefits regardless of whether or not he would be otherwise financially secure.

2. The Social Security Act does not provide for a federally operated program of *unemployment insurance.* But it does provide the incentive for the states to establish and operate such programs:[6] All fifty states

[6] The incentive: Congress levied a tax on employers, returning the tax collections only to those states willing to set up an unemployment insurance program.

now have them. Though the same in principle, the programs of the various states differ considerably with respect to details.

The programs are financed by taxes on employers; these taxes probably average about 1½ per cent of covered payrolls. Any insured worker who finds himself unemployed can, after a short waiting period (usually a week), become eligible for benefit payments. The size of the payments and the number of weeks they may be received vary considerably from state to state. In 1963 some 3 million workers received a total of $2.6 billion in benefits; the average check was about $35 per week. Of course, the number of people receiving benefits at any time will vary with the overall health of the economy. In 1965 about 45 million people were covered by unemployment compensation. It is to be recalled that unemployment compensation benefits are one of the important built-in stabilizers of American capitalism.

3. Needy persons who do not qualify for OASI or unemployment compensation are assisted by a variety of special *public assistance* programs. These programs—for the needy aged and blind, the permanently and totally disabled, and dependent children—are administered by the state governments and financed out of state tax revenues and Federal grants-in-aid. In 1964 about 7.6 million persons were receiving benefits under the various assistance programs. In addition, all the states have passed legislation providing for workmen's compensation. These programs assure medical expenses and partial wages to workers who are victims of industrial accidents.

Now there can be no doubt that the social security system—not to mention local relief, public housing, minimum wage legislation, agricultural subsidies, and private transfers through charities, pensions, supplementary unemployment benefits, and so forth—are important means of alleviating poverty. Indeed, transfer payments account for over 40 per cent of the income of the lowest one-fifth of our consumer units. Poverty would be more prevalent and more severe were it not for such programs. Yet with considerable justification, a salient criticism of our welfare programs is that *they frequently tend to be of least benefit to those who need economic assistance the most.* Aside from serious questions concerning the adequacy of social security payments, there is compelling evidence that millions of needy Americans are outside of the welfare state. Some 3 or 4 million, for example, are not currently covered by OASI; some 14 million are not eligible for unemployment compensation payments. Only about 60 per cent of all wage earners are protected by Federal minimum wage legislation; those excluded include many people in intrastate occupations, which pay notoriously low wages. *Only about one-half of those families and individuals now classified as poor receive any transfer payments at all.* Furthermore, it has been charged that public housing projects have benefited middle-income groups more than the poor and that the main beneficiaries of the farm program are wealthy corporate farms rather than the small or tenant farmer. The "fundamental paradox of the welfare state," Michael Harrington laments, is "that it is not built for the desperate, but for those who are already capable of helping themselves. . . . The poor get less out of the welfare state than any group in America."[7]

Vicious Circle of Poverty

Having noted the incidence of poverty, described its "invisible" nature, and appraised the perverted tendency of many welfare programs, we must now emphasize an additional characteristic of poverty—the fact that it tends to be self-perpetuating.[8]

Poverty breeds poverty. A poor individual or family has a high probability of staying poor. Low incomes carry with them high risks of illness; limitations on mobility; limited access to education, information, and training. Poor parents cannot give their children the opportunities

[7] Harrington, *op. cit.*, p. 172.
[8] *Economic Report of the President* (1964), pp. 69–70.

for better health and education needed to improve their lot. Lack of motivation, hope, and incentive is a more subtle but no less powerful barrier than lack of financial means. Thus the cruel legacy of poverty is passed from parents to children.

THE ATTACK ON POVERTY

As a prelude to any systematic discussion of public policy toward the poverty problem, we must recognize at the outset that, while multidimensional, poverty is a legitimate economic problem.[9]

Our Nation's most precious resource is its people. We pay twice for poverty: once in the production lost in wasted human potential, again in the resources diverted to coping with poverty's social by-products [delinquency, crime, immorality, etc.]. Humanity compels our action, but it is sound economics as well.

President Johnson has put it quite succinctly: "One thousand dollars invested in salvaging an unemployable youth today can return $40,000 or more in his lifetime."

Two Philosophies

But even if we grant that the poverty problem is an economic issue, the question remains: Is the problem of poverty primarily a matter for government or individual action? A fundamental philosophical disagreement exists on this point.

One view holds that most of the poor are ultimately responsible for their circumstances. They have forfeited or frittered away their educational opportunities. They lack salable skills and won't enroll in retraining programs. They live in now-depressed areas and, instilled with a "homing instinct," refuse to move. They have large families and are too shortsighted to use contraceptives. They have been spendthrifts in the days of youth and high earning power and now, in their old age, are unable to supplement their social security benefits or relief payments.

[9] *Ibid.*, p. 56.

Some are poor because they are slothful or lazy. The Bohemian, the beatnik, and the skidrow alcoholic have willfully, and perhaps even joyously, chosen poverty as a way of life. In short, poverty is largely a matter of personal inadequacies, "attitudes of shiftlessness," shortsightedness, and, in some instances, a matter of preference. Poverty is therefore deserved and should be dealt with, if at all, through private charity and philanthropy.

The virtually diametrically opposed position is that poverty is essentially the result of self-perpetuating cultural and social deficiencies which are beyond the capacities of individuals to remedy through self-help. The very characteristics of poverty suggest that poor families are by and large the victims of society and their environment. Some are the victims of rapid technological change; others can't find employment because of a lagging rate of economic growth. Why should workers retrain in the quest of nonexistent jobs? Others are arbitrarily penalized by race discrimination. And the 11 million children who are members of poor families can hardly be held responsible for their plight. Furthermore, the current poor by and large bear a history of poverty; the old-age pensioner who now survives on minimal OASI benefits is likely to have no income supplement in the form of savings or other assets. Can those suffering from physical or mental infirmities be held responsible for these tragedies? In brief, for the most part poverty is the social by-product of a complex, highly interdependent, dynamic economy; therefore, responsibility for alleviating this poverty rests primarily upon society as opposed to the individuals so afflicted.

Anti-poverty Program

Though individual cases can be readily cited to support either philosophy, the latter view is more widely accepted in our society. What specific forms, then, might public policy assume in dealing with the poverty problem? The fact that the roots of poverty are manifold suggests that the strategy of an attack on poverty must operate on many fronts. Let us mention the general types of programs and policies that would seem appropriate.

1. Full employment and rapid growth. Perhaps the most general measure for alleviating poverty is to achieve a prosperous and rapidly expanding economy. Job opportunities for the unemployed, the partially employed, and those employed in extremely low-paying positions will obviously improve in such an environment.

2. Direct income reinforcement. Poverty would undoubtedly be alleviated as the result of expanding, modernizing, and generally strengthening our entire social security system. The objective, of course, is to eliminate the "paradox of the welfare state" by increasing the payments and extending the coverage of unemployment insurance and OASI, improving existing programs of public assistance, and enlarging the coverage and increasing the level of the minimum wage. The reorientation of our farm program away from the subsidization of commodities and toward the subsidization of people, as suggested in Chapter 35, could do much to alleviate rural poverty. The recently legislated "medicare" program—medical care for the aged under social security—is perhaps the most controversial extension of the welfare state.

3. Area redevelopment and urban renewal. A significant portion of America's poverty lies in certain chronically depressed areas—most notably Appalachia—where natural resource depletion, changes in consumer tastes, and technological progress have caused these regions to be bypassed by the general advance of the economy. Vast cooperative programs sponsored by Federal and state governments are proposed to rehabilitate these areas. Similarly, urban renewal and slum clearance are proposed to help the poor of blighted metropolitan areas break out of the "culture of poverty" which now severely limits their chances for improving their economic opportunities and incomes.

4. Enlarging economic opportunities. A number of programs are relevant here. Public aid to education can be instrumental in helping the children of the poor more fully realize their inherent abilities and enhance their earning power. Programs of vocational training, perhaps supplemented by relocation allowances, can be made available to the structurally unemployed. Knowledge of existing job opportunities can be made more readily available through the strengthening of the U.S. Employment Service. The thorough implementation of civil-rights legislation will clearly assist those who are in the lowest income classes because of discrimination in employment.

A final point: Men of good will can agree that poverty in America clearly exists as a problem of substantial magnitude. They may also disagree with respect to specific remedies and as to how massive and extensive the assault on poverty should be. The kinds of proposals just outlined will entail heavy costs.[10] But to do nothing at all—which after all is a "policy" of sorts—also imposes heavy costs upon society.

SUMMARY

1. The distribution of personal income in American capitalism reflects considerable inequality. Though income inequality les-

[10] Economists are inclined to remind each other that there is no such thing as a "free lunch."

sened between 1929 and the end of World War II, little change has occurred in the postwar period.

2. Five arguments constitute the case against income inequality. Income inequality **a.** impedes the maximization of consumer satisfaction; **b.** impairs productivity; **c.** limits the occupational opportunities of the poor; **d.** fosters noneconomic inequalities; and **e.** is ethically undesirable.

3. Income inequality is defended as follows: **a.** income inequality is conducive to a high rate of saving and a rapid rate of capital accumulation; **b.** income inequality is essential as an incentive to work and invest; and **c.** income inequality is essential to a viable, progressive society.

4. Current statistics suggest that about one-fifth of the nation lives in poverty. Although the poor are a heterogeneous group, poverty is concentrated among the poorly educated, nonwhites, the aged, farmers, and families headed by women. There is evidence to indicate that poverty is self-regenerating.

5. Most existing social welfare programs exclude, or provide for at very minimal levels, those families and individuals whose incomes are lowest.

6. The basic types of programs and policies embodied in a "war on poverty" include **a.** achieving full employment and rapid growth; **b.** direct income reinforcement through the modernization and expansion of existing social welfare programs; **c.** area redevelopment and urban renewal; and **d.** the enlargement of economic opportunities for the poor.

QUESTIONS AND STUDY SUGGESTIONS

1. What are the major causes of income inequality? Outline and critically evaluate the arguments for and against income inequality. Which position do you favor? Why?
2. Are the issues of "equity" and "equality" in the distribution of income synonymous? To what degree, if any, is income inequality equitable?
3. Explain: "To endow everyone with equal income will certainly make for very unequal enjoyment and satisfaction."

4. "Poverty [in America] is not an economic malady so much as it is a social disgrace." Interpret and explain. Do you agree?
5. Who are the poor? Explain and comment: "We have socialism for the rich and free enterprise for the poor."
6. Outline the main characteristics of a comprehensive "war on poverty." Explain and evaluate: "The impact of a carefully conceived war on poverty will not be an increase in costs but rather a redistribution and more rational budgeting of costs which are now being met in a haphazard and inequitable way."
7. Explain and evaluate: "Some freedoms may be more important in the long run than freedom from want on the part of every individual."

SELECTED REFERENCES

Bagdikian, Ben H.: *In the Midst of Plenty* (Boston: Beacon Press, 1964).

Carlson, Valdemar: *Economic Security in the United States* (New York: McGraw-Hill Book Company, 1962).

Economic Report of the President (Washington, D.C., 1964), chap. 2.

Gordon, Margaret S.: *The Economics of Welfare Policies* (New York: Columbia University Press, 1963).

Harrington, Michael: *The Other America* (Baltimore: Penguin Books, Inc., 1962).

Keyserling, Leon H.: *Progress or Poverty* (Washington, D.C: Conference on Economic Progress, 1964).

Miller, Herman P.: *Rich Man, Poor Man* (New York: Thomas Y. Crowell Company, 1964).

Will, Robert E., and Harold G. Vatter (eds.): *Poverty in Affluence* (New York: Harcourt, Brace & World, Inc., 1965).

CHAPTER 38

THE SOCIAL
IMBALANCE CONTROVERSY

A number of well-known economists[1] currently argue that the evolution of the United States from a nation of relative poverty to one of relative abundance has created a distortion in the composition of the economy's total output. It is asserted that the increasing affluence of American capitalism has been accompanied by a lack of social balance. That is, an inefficient allocation of resources between private goods and services, on the one hand, and social goods and services, on the other, has arisen. Television sets, automobiles, and a profligacy of gadgetry are produced in abundance, while education, police and fire protection, streets and highways, and a myriad of basic community services are slighted. In short, it is contended that the development of our economy has fostered the poverty-amidst-plenty problem in a new guise: Private goods abound, but social goods are remarkably deficient.

The primary purposes of this chapter are to

1. Present the arguments of those economists who feel a serious social imbalance exists in the composition of our total output

2. Outline a number of criticisms of, and counterarguments to, the social imbalance position

3. Note briefly various policy means of alleviating social imbalance should it exist now or in the future

THE NATURE OF SOCIAL IMBALANCE

It must be acknowledged at the outset that the question as to whether social imbalance actually exists is ultimately an ethical one; that is, it is a question of what the proper or optimum balance of private and social goods *ought* to be. It is impossible to compare scientifically the marginal utility of an extra dollar spent on an electric can opener or power mower with that of a marginal dollar of expenditures on education or space research. Yet it can be argued that there is substantial evidence which lends credence to the position that social imbalance now exists as a basic economic problem. Simple observation—evidence of the eye—is said to be abundant: overcrowded and ill-equipped schools, a paucity of parks and recreation areas, overcrowded streets and inadequate highways, underpaid and undermanned police forces, and so on. Simple statistical comparisons may also be invoked as evidence. In 1964 United States consumers spent $23 billion on recreation as compared with the $18.7 billion which all state and local governments spent on education. Approximately $14 billion was spent on advertising, over $8 billion on tobacco products, and over $20 billion on automobile purchases, as opposed to total (public and private) spending of $17 billion for research and development.[2]

[1] See, in particular, the works of John Kenneth Galbraith, Alvin H. Hansen, W. W. Rostow, and Francis M. Bator listed at the end of this chapter.

[2] Data from U.S. Department of Commerce, *Survey of Current Business*, July, 1964, and August, 1965.

Can one present more comprehensive statistical information on the question of social imbalance? This is one of many instances wherein the choice of statistics and their manipulation can support about any conclusion one desires. It is perhaps most relevant to compare government purchases of nondefense goods and services with the size of the nondefense GNP over a period of years, thereby envisioning what share of the "civilian" GNP has been in the form of social goods and services.[3] This comparison reveals that government's nondefense spending as a percentage of the civilian GNP rose from 7.5 per cent in 1929 to 13.5 per cent in 1939, only to decline to 11 per cent in 1964. We seem currently to be committing a smaller share of the civilian GNP to collective goods and services than in 1939.[3]

SOCIAL IMBALANCE AS AN ECONOMIC PROBLEM

Those who embrace the social imbalance thesis argue that it constitutes a first-rank economic problem because it embodies a misallocation of resources, constitutes a threat to economic stability and full employment, and has critical implications for the economy's rate of economic growth.

The Allocation of Resources

As already noted, social imbalance suggests a misallocation of economic resources and, therefore, a failure of the economic system to maximize the satisfactions of society. More specifically, private goods, because of their very superabundance, are now relatively low-priority (low-marginal-utility) goods; the production of additional private

[3] See Francis M. Bator, *The Question of Government Spending* (New York: Harper & Row, Publishers, Incorporated, 1960), pp. 21–22. National Planning Association, *National Investment for Economic Growth* (Washington, D.C., 1957) reaches a similar conclusion.

goods is not a matter of very high urgency. In contrast, the very paucity of social goods makes them relatively high-priority (high-marginal-utility) goods; the production of more social goods *is* a matter of relatively high urgency. It is argued, in brief, that given an initial position of social imbalance—too much private and not enough public goods—a reallocation of resources in favor of the latter is a rechanneling of resources away from low- toward high-marginal-utility employments. This obviously accomplishes an increase in the total satisfaction (utility) of society.

Economic Stability

Social imbalance is also a crucial economic problem because of the contribution it might make to economic instability and unemployment. Professor Galbraith has emphasized that a sustained demand for private consumer goods has become highly dependent upon want-creating activities (advertising) and the willingness and ability of consumers to increase their indebtedness. Now, if a point is reached at which the myriad of claims and counterclaims of advertisers renders consumers immune to the claims of all, or, if any of the innumerable uncertainties which characterize our economy should interrupt the expansion of consumer credit, consumption spending would decline and unemployment would result. The reduction or amelioration of social imbalance would lessen the possibility of these difficulties arising.[4]

Since public wants are not contrived, they are not subject to a failure of contrivance. Since they are not sold on the installment plan, they are not subject to curtailment by any of the factors which make people unwilling or unable to incur debt. Thus the better the social balance the more immune the economy to fluctuations in private demand.

[4] John Kenneth Galbraith, *The Affluent Society* (Boston: Houghton Mifflin Company, 1958), p. 279.

To these contentions can be added the simple fact that social balance might contribute to stability for the simple reason that the production of public goods is not motivated by profit considerations.

Economic Growth

The final reason for the great significance of social imbalance as an economic problem may well be the most crucial of all. The manner in which a nation chooses to divide its *current* output between public and private goods may well have a bearing upon the size of that economy's *future* output (Chapter 2). More specifically, the present relationship between private and social goods may be an important determinant of the nation's economic growth potential. This is so because many basic social goods—for example, education, basic scientific research, and preventive medicine—are important factors contributing to the process of economic growth. Thus a current public-private goods choice which puts heavy emphasis upon such private consumer goods as automobiles, television sets, and air conditioners and therefore slights the aforementioned social goods is tending to reduce its potential rate of growth in so doing. Bluntly put, a nation which becomes overly obese with consumer goods may, by that very act, undermine its future economic health.

Some International Implications

In view of the current Soviet challenge (Chapter 42) the economic, political, and military overtones of these three points cannot be minimized. The misallocation-of-resources aspect of the social imbalance problem is highly relevant with respect to the Soviet military threat. By choosing a higher ratio of public to private goods than the United States, the Soviet Union has created a military force which rivals or, in the opinion of some military experts, surpasses that of the United States. This fact is particularly disconcerting when it is acknowledged that the nuclear instruments of modern warfare bar the United States from having the time necessary to reallocate resources away from private (civilian) goods to social (war) goods. Assuming the distinction between "winners" and "losers" is meaningful in an age of nuclear rocketry, it is safer to suppose that future major wars will be won by those nations whose existing stock of military goods is quantitatively and technologically superior, rather than by those countries which can amass the greatest gross national product.

Similarly, on the politicoeconomic front we find the emerging and uncommitted underdeveloped nations closely observing the productive performances of American capitalism and Soviet communism in an effort to ascertain which model to pursue in structuring their own political and economic institutions. To the extent that social imbalance may actually contribute to unemployment and retard economic growth in the United States, the destiny of the free world may be impaired.

ALLEGED CAUSES OF SOCIAL IMBALANCE

How has this alleged paucity of social goods developed amidst an affluence of private goods? It would seem that mixed capitalism embodies the mechanisms necessary for obtaining a reasonably good balance between private and public output. Consumers govern the production of private goods by the dollar votes they register in the market place. Through political means—the process of political voting—consumers in effect select the amount of social goods they desire. In brief, in a democracy is not the considered judgment of the majority of the citizenry transformed through dollar and political voting into a choice as to how total output is to be divided among private and social goods? How, then, can social imbalance arise?

Economists who envision a social imbalance in current GNP argue that the matter is not as simple as that just described. True, mechanisms exist in mixed capitalism by which the citizenry can render a private-social goods decision. But it is argued that in practice certain historical, attitudinal, and politicoeconomic forces bear upon this decision so as to cause the production of social goods to fall seriously out of balance with the production of private goods.

What are these distorting forces? In examining the alleged causes of social imbalance, we are in effect asking, "What happens to the amounts of social goods and services demanded and supplied in an expanding economy?"[5] If the amount of social goods demanded seems to increase ahead of the amount supplied, a "disequilibrium" in the form of social imbalance will result. Let us first consider the demand for social goods; then we shall turn to supply considerations.

DEMAND FOR SOCIAL GOODS: WAGNER'S LAW

The forces underlying the growing demand for social goods and services are well known: hot and cold wars, population growth, industrialization and the subsequent urbanization and socioeconomic complexity which it entails, and so forth. Also, of course, as real incomes rise, the demand for both private and social goods can be expected to increase. There are plausible reasons to argue that as real per capita incomes rise, the pattern of consumer wants may alter in favor of relatively more social goods and relatively fewer private goods. This alleged alteration of wants in the growing economy is labeled *Wagner's Law*, so-named for the nineteenth-century German economist Adolph Wagner who first emphasized this phenomenon.

[5] This is loose terminology because there is no market for social goods and services in the sense in which there is a market for private goods and services.

The rationale underlying Wagner's Law is relatively simple. The poor society, dominated by agriculture, must consume its entire real income in the form of such basic private goods as food, shelter, and clothing. After these basic wants have been largely fulfilled, the growing wealth of society permits it to turn its attention more and more to the satisfaction of somewhat less urgent but nevertheless important "new needs." Many of these new wants entail social goods—for example, education, streets and highways, police and fire protection. Economic growth is characterized by increasing industrialization and urbanization. This creates a demand for sanitation and sewerage facilities, a water supply, extensive police and fire protection, and similar social goods which in a poorer and simpler agrarian society would be provided by each family for itself or simply not provided at all. Similarly, the industrialization and urbanization which characterize an expanding economy lead to increasing interdependence and greater socioeconomic complexity. Government's regulatory role may therefore be expected to expand markedly. Further, the increased leisure which is typically a component of economic growth can be expected to enhance the demand for educational facilities. And, too, the poor society spends little or nothing on national defense for the simple reason it has little wealth to protect from external aggression; opulence changes this and makes armament expenditures an important social good. All these considerations may give rise to a tendency for the demand for social goods to increase, not only absolutely, but also relative to the demand for private goods.

SUPPLY OF SOCIAL GOODS

Economists who view social imbalance as an acute issue feel there are a number of considerations which prevent the supply of social goods from keeping pace with the growing demand for them.

The Mechanisms and Mores of Capitalism

The very nature of the capitalistic ideology and the attitudes of large numbers of Americans concerning the public sector of the economy have fostered obstacles to an expanding volume of social goods production. A number of related points are involved here.

1. The ideology of pure capitalism embraces the concepts of consumer sovereignty, free competitive markets, and a highly restricted economic role for government. This long-obsolete portrayal of capitalism provides that virtually all resources are channeled into the production of private goods and services. Furthermore, as the economy evolves and becomes more affluent, the capitalistic ideology obviously provides both the philosophical basis and the mechanism—consumer sovereignty and the price system—to provide for ever-increasing amounts of private goods. No such philosophy or mechanism exists to provide automatically for the additional social goods which a growing and more opulent nation may require. Indeed, the provision of additional social goods requires that government somehow take positive steps to divert resources from private to public uses. In practice, government must convince the citizenry—government must "prove"—that particular social goods are needed and are clearly to be preferred to the private goods at whose expense their production must come in a full-employment economy. An individual need not justify his purchase of a new car, an automatic dishwasher, or a color television set to his community or to the nation. Yet the burden of proof is on government to justify increases in expenditures on highways, educational facilities, urban renewal, or expanded police and fire protection.

2. In fulfilling its role as a provider of social goods, government is typically viewed as an intruder upon the private sector of the economy and therefore as a threat to individual freedoms. Tax payments needed to finance social goods are compulsory as, indeed, is the consumption of certain social goods and services—education, for example. And at any point in time the provision of more social goods in a full-employment economy necessarily entails a restriction of private goods production. Implicit in these observations is the frequently voiced contention that governmental provision of social goods necessarily impinges upon individual liberties. There is little doubt that this view of government as a freedom-limiting agency is partially a public reaction to the upsurges of governmental activity during the Great Depression and World War II.

3. The attitude of much of the business community, large parts of the citizenry, and some political leaders envisions private goods as sacrosanct while public goods are held to be wasteful, of secondary significance, or at best a necessary evil. "The public, as a general rule . . . gets less production in return for a dollar spent by government than from a dollar spent by private enterprise."[6] The closely related notion that "economy in government" is synonymous with minimal public expenditures is also widely accepted (Chapter 6); believers are apparently oblivious of the fact that "economy" is concerned with the employment and efficient allocation of resources.

Ironically, the assumption of modern fiscal policy that public expenditure should accommodate itself to changes in the level of private spending has probably fostered such thinking indirectly and inadvertently by implying that public spending is expendable so long as the private sector is sufficiently exuberant to provide full employment. The notion that public expenditures should be of a compensatory character is an obstacle to a careful evaluation of the composition of total output as between private and public goods.

4. Social imbalance may also reflect in

[6] National Association of Manufacturers, *The American Individual Enterprise System* (New York: McGraw-Hill Book Company, 1946), p. 952.

part certain attitudes widely held in our society. Professor Hansen, for example, envisions social imbalance as a deeply rooted "frame of mind."[7]

We are living in a tumultuous age—an age of disillusionment. The World War, the Korean conflict, the cold war. We are trying to escape from reality. We do not like to face the cold facts of the world we live in. We are caught up in a wave of escapism and comfortable complacency.

Political Realities

Because they are overweighted with the representatives of sparsely populated, rural areas, the Federal legislature and many state legislatures are relatively insensitive to the acute social goods needs of the heavily populated metropolitan areas. Although recent Supreme Court decisions may provide the necessary corrective, "we do not [now] have majority rule in many of our State legislatures," with the result that rapidly expanding urban areas are denied even the traditional types of community services.[8] The dire social needs of the Negro have been clearly underrepresented in the Southern states. At the level of local government, it will be noted later, heavy dependence upon property taxes works against the expansion of social goods production.

Character of Social Goods

The inherent characteristics of public goods, as opposed to private goods, also tend to impede their production (Chapter 6). Private goods are sold on the basis of this-for-that transactions in the market place. The

[7] Alvin H. Hansen, *Economic Issues of the 1960's* (New York: McGraw-Hill Book Company, 1961), p. 82.
[8] *Ibid.*, pp. 111–112.

consumer knows precisely how much he pays for a private good, and the benefits he receives from such a purchase are immediate and certain; private goods entail a close link between costs and benefits. Not so with social goods and services. Here benefits are both more remote and less certain than in the case of private goods, and, with minor exceptions, the production of social goods is divorced from specific tax revenues (costs). The production of social goods is undertaken by the government and financed through taxes levied on the community or society as a whole. These differences in the characteristics of social goods and private goods tend to restrict the output of social goods in at least two ways.

1. The remoteness and uncertainty of the benefits derived from social goods prejudice the consumer (voter) against their production. In a realm of goods and services, individuals prefer the immediate and certain benefits of automobiles, television sets, and automatic dishwashers to the remote benefits of public education, municipal libraries, streets and highways, a boost in the budget of the local park department, or the highly uncertain benefits of aid to underdeveloped countries, space research, and a continuing arms race. It is particularly lamentable that investment in individuals (that is, in education) is slighted relative to investment in capital goods primarily because the former is in the public and the latter is in the private domain. In general, in any expression of choice between public and private goods which the electorate may render, public goods find themselves at a decided psychological disadvantage because of the remoteness and uncertainty of their benefits.

Unfortunately, there appear to be no alleviating factors or correctives in the picture. As a matter of fact, as the economy matures and becomes more affluent and complex, the benefits of additional social goods may well become increasingly remote and uncertain, further threatening their production. That is, the benefits of the highways, sanitation programs, and public schools provided by the government of a semideveloped economy are less remote and less uncertain than are the benefits of the foreign aid and space research programs undertaken by the governments of those nations which are most highly advanced economically.

It is tempting to argue that, if the tax payments which finance social goods were as vague to the citizenry as are their benefits, this would constitute a compensating factor by stimulating the flow of social goods. This is not felt to be the case, however. Relatively few taxes are really hidden taxes.[9] Income and property taxes entail explicit and often detailed consideration by the taxpayer, assuring his awareness of the cost of social goods to him. In contrast, the greatly expanded use of consumer credit in the postwar era has undoubtedly made the total cost of private durable consumer goods less immediate and less explicit to buyers, thereby increasing consumer preferences for private as opposed to social goods. In short, the remoteness and uncertainty of the benefits associated with the production of social goods coupled with the immediacy of their tax costs tends to prejudice the production of social goods.

2. Another characteristic of social goods or, more precisely, of the public sector, allegedly impedes the achievement of social balance. In the private sector of the economy each individual consumer exercises a great deal of selectivity in his purchases. He considers the marginal utility of various commodities relative to their prices and, subject to his budget restraint, achieves consumer equilibrium by freely selecting those goods and services which yield the greatest marginal utility per dollar and rejecting those yielding less (Chapter 24).

However, the individual's economic deal-

ings with government are on a nonselective basis. The consumer cannot select and therefore contribute financially only to those programs in the public sector's budget which he favors, thereby rejecting and withholding tax payments for programs he disfavors. Thus, assuming realistically that the policy mix of the government is so complex that it will not precisely match the social goods preferences of any specific consumer, it follows that there will invariably be a number of social goods and services which he is compelled to help finance, but of which he does not approve. The practical conclusion is that each voter feels that the public budget is too high relative to the benefits he derives from it; that is, each taxpayer feels that a cut in government spending is warranted. Government, therefore, is persistently faced with significant pressure to reduce the flow of social goods and services.

Tax Obstacles

It is also asserted that a number of tax problems contribute to social imbalance.

Tax levels. Over a period of time the existing level of taxation tends to become acceptable—to become "proper"—to large numbers of households and businesses for the simple reason that they have had time to adjust to it. As a result, it becomes politically feasible to maintain existing levels of taxation, while at the same time it becomes extremely dangerous politically to raise tax levels. As the existing tax level acquires a measure of sanctity with the passage of time, it becomes exceedingly difficult—short of an obvious and acute military or domestic crisis—to raise the tax level in order to finance an increased flow of social goods production. No doubt the fact that added tax costs are not linked to specific social goods programs and their benefits contributes to this difficulty. Such thinking with respect to the tax level has been more or less formalized by a number of proposals seeking to limit the level of taxes and

---

[9] Sales taxes, which are usually thought of as "hidden," constitute only about 15 per cent of total governmental revenues.

expenditures to a fixed proportion of the national income. For present purposes the important point is that allegiance to existing tax levels works against the expansion of social goods production.

Allocating tax burdens. Even where voters are in general agreement as to the desirability of having more of particular social goods and are willing to accept a higher tax level to finance them, the problem of allocating the tax costs of these goods may still impede their production. For example, a majority of the voters of a community may be convinced of the need for street improvements and repairs, but they may be deadlocked with respect to what taxes should be used to finance these repairs. Should a special tax (for example, a wheel tax) be assessed on automobile and truck owners? Or should property taxes be raised? Or should a city sales tax be used? At the national level the citizenry might be convinced of the need to hasten the development of domestic natural resources or to strengthen our national defense posture. Again, these projects might be blocked by disagreement as to how the tax cost should be distributed. Most liberals are likely to favor progressive (for example, individual and corporate income) taxes, whereas conservatives plump for regressive (for example, sales and excise) taxes. Inability to reach agreement on the distribution of tax costs may cause the community and the nation to forgo sorely needed social goods and services.

Tax competition. A special tax obstacle to the increased production of social goods exists at the state level. States compete for industry on the basis of low tax rates or preferential tax structures—for example, a tax structure which omits the income tax. "States compete in niggardliness. . . . The result inevitably is that community services are starved."[10]

[10] Hansen, *op. cit.*, pp. 112–113.

Advertising and Emulation

Advertising and sales promotion activities, which are an integral part of the production and sale of private goods, are almost entirely absent with respect to social goods. For example, while gigantic advertising campaigns by automobile manufacturers operate to convince consumers of the virtues of being a two-car family, no similar persuasion extols to the citizenry the need for more and better roads on which to operate the ever-expanding mass of automobiles. While advertising stresses the merits of stereophonic phonographs, no similar persuasion suggests that better education may be a prerequisite to appreciating the fine recorded music playable thereon. The public sector, under persistent pressure to reduce expenditures, is prohibited from use of the exhortative techniques which characterize the private sector. The result is a tendency for private to expand ahead of social goods.

Like advertising, emulation also favors greater production of private goods. Families witness the new gadgetry of their neighbors—a second car, an automatic dishwasher, a food freezer, a backyard swimming pool—and feel compelled to "keep pace" by also acquiring these amenities. Emulative inducements work very weakly, if at all, between towns and between states in stimulating the output of social goods and services.

Inflation

The contribution of persistent inflation to the relative shrinkage and deterioration of public goods and services is twofold.

1. Inflation causes product and resource prices to rise in a very uneven and irregular fashion. While the incomes of most profit receivers (stockholders and proprietors) and many wage earners rise rapidly and significantly, the wages and salaries of public employees typically rise belatedly and by considerably less than the general level of

prices. That is, inflation tends to reduce the real incomes of many government employees. This seems to be particularly true of the employees of state and local governments, where pay scales are highly formalized and quite insensitive to the overall economic environment. Thus, as a practical matter, it is particularly difficult for governmental agencies to match the increasingly lucrative salaries offered by private industries, which, in the mainstream of inflation, are generally in a good position to raise their prices and revenues in pace with or ahead of the general level of prices. In brief, inflation tends to divert human resources from public services to private industry. Through this diversion, inflation discriminates in favor of private goods at the expense of public goods.

2. Inflation may contribute to social imbalance in another way. By creating inflationary pressure, a burgeoning private sector tends to create strong political pressures to retrench on government spending as an anti-inflationary technique. The dogma of price-level stability is invoked to hold down government expenditures. Given the previously noted disposition to hold taxes at present levels and the questionable effectiveness of a tight money policy, the obvious and politically least offensive means of ameliorating inflation is to restrain government purchases of social goods and services. Thus it is that, when the rate of production of private goods is very high and inflation occurs, the pressure may be greatest for the output of social goods to be constrained. The congressman who, under these circumstances, advocates greater social balance finds himself in the embarrassing position of a "friend of inflation," no matter how crucial the need for the social goods he seeks.

SOME COUNTERARGUMENTS

There are those who seriously question that social imbalance exists or, at least, that it is a pressing problem; and, even if it were to assume acute dimensions, it is argued that the suggested remedies may be both ineffective and very costly.[11]

Does Social Imbalance Really Exist?

Critics of the social imbalance thesis have raised a number of points in questioning whether or not social imbalance actually exists.

Affluence and the average consumer. Over-infatuation with the notion of an affluent society and the conception of extravagant and frivolous consumer spending do not square very well with the fact that the median family income in the United States is currently $6,140, not to mention the fact that nearly one-fifth of the nation lives in poverty. The vast majority of consumers are not in a position to overindulge in unessential goods and trivia. It is inaccurate and misleading to classify any substantial portion of consumer spending as being devoted to low-priority goods or sheer gadgetry. Furthermore, because total spending for consumer durables is only about 14 per cent of personal consumption, one must be cautious in exaggerating the emphasis our society puts upon such goods as color television sets, heavily chromed automobiles, and electric can openers.

Growing expenditures on "the new needs." The rates of increase in spending on the allegedly neglected "new needs" of the social imbalance position—for example, education, research, health and welfare services, and so forth—have been very substantial and, in general, have exceeded the rate of growth in the GNP. Note, for example, that in the 1950–1960 decade expenditures on research

---

[11] The counterarguments of this section stem primarily from the writings of Henry C. Wallich cited at the end of this chapter.

increased by 336 per cent, expenditures for highway construction by 146 per cent, and state and local spending for education rose by 161 per cent, while GNP increased by only 77 per cent. Although other social needs—for example, urban renewal and the economic revitalization of depressed areas—have admittedly been neglected, the overall conclusion must be that many of the "new needs" of the social imbalance position have not been ignored by our society at all; on the contrary, they have been accorded substantial attention.

Forces accelerating social goods production. Though the aforementioned obstacles which allegedly impede the expansion of social goods production infer the existence of social imbalance, there are important counterbiases which facilitate the growth of social goods output at the expense of private goods.

1. The apparent unrelatedness of taxation and public spending decisions has admittedly caused the citizenry to view taxes only in the negative sense, that is, as a cost which entails no observable benefits. However, this same unrelatedness has encouraged the public attitude that government spending is costless, that is, the benefits of social goods and services are relatively free. It is argued that the latter attitude has encouraged public goods production more than the former has inhibited it.

2. Assuming that taxing and public spending decisions are related by the citizenry, it is admittedly true that some citizens rebel at paying taxes whose benefits to them as individuals are uncertain. By the same token, others are very willing to vote for expenditures from which they expect to benefit, although they have not contributed. Indeed, our progressive Federal income tax structure means that most of the taxpayers who are in the lower income brackets obtain many social goods at bargain prices; hence, there is every reason for them as a political majority to be inclined to favor and vote for the expansion of social goods.

3. Finally, political reality is such that vocal and active minorities constantly press for and achieve increased public expenditures.

The conclusion, then, is that, considering both the obstacles which inhibit *and* the forces which accelerate social goods production, it is difficult to determine whether, on balance, the public sector is expanding too slowly or too rapidly.

Public Spending: A Corrective?

Assuming social imbalance actually exists, will the advocated increases in public spending resolve this imbalance? It is argued that for at least two related reasons this need not be the case. First, the complexity of the problem is such that it is misleading to pose it simply as a "public-versus-private expenditure" issue. To suggest that more public and less private spending will resolve social imbalance invokes the implicit assumption that the reallocation of resources from private to public uses will necessarily entail less "unwise" private expenditure and more "wise" public spending, given the value schema of those who insist social imbalance now exists. Is it not possible that reductions in private spending may come more at the expense of adequate housing, medical care, education, and cultural pursuits rather than at the expense of television sets, automobiles, and microscopic radios? Might not a disproportionate share of any increase in public expenditures on, say, education be for gymnasiums and stadiums as opposed to laboratories and classrooms? There is no reason to suppose that public spending is inherently "wise" (on high-priority goods) and more conducive to growth, whereas private spending is "unwise" (on low-priority goods) and not conducive to rapid growth. As one critic has put it: "I do not see why transferring expenditures to a government no wiser than the voters who elect it . . . would solve the problem. It would probably replace private folly with official silli-ness."[12]

Secondly, it is not at all evident that the "new needs" of society are social goods and therefore clearly fall within the public sector. That is, education, research, providing for old age, health services, and so forth lie in the twilight zone between the public and private sectors of the economy. For example, about one-third of the nation's total research expenditures originates in private industry, and the remaining two-thirds in government. And a very substantial portion of total expenditures on education, particularly higher education, is private. Expenditures on health services are predominantly private.

For both these reasons it is allegedly a misleading oversimplification to say that our major scarcities of specific goods and services can be corrected by merely expanding the public sector at the expense of the private sector of the economy.

Social Balance, Growth, and International Problems

It was noted earlier that those economists who envision the existence of social imbal-ance feel that it is detrimental to growth and may therefore impair the United States' chances of meeting the Soviet challenge. Professor Wallich is dubious, arguing, on the one hand, that military posture depends as much on the composition of gross national output as it does on the size and rate of growth of output and, on the other, that percentage growth rates are not likely to be the ultimate determinant of the ideo-logical evolution of the underdeveloped nations.[13]

[12] Ernest van den Haag, "Private and Public Expenditures: A Reappraisal," *Modern Age*, Spring, 1962, p. 148.
[13] Henry C. Wallich, *The Cost of Freedom* (New York: Harper & Row, Publishers, Incor-porated, 1960), p. 158.

In short, there is little to show that the issues between us and the rest of the world will be governed predominantly by our economic suc-cesses, or that we can buy survival with an additional per cent or two of economic growth.

Indeed, if one accepts the previous argument that public expenditures are not necessarily more conducive to growth than private spending, the production of more social and less private goods is simply not very perti-nent to the issue of economic growth.

The Cost of Social Balance

Even if social imbalance is really an acute problem, certain very substantial costs may be involved in its resolution—costs which may well be prohibitive.

1. In the first place, the provision of tax-financed public services is a crude and ineffi-cient way of meeting consumer needs. This is so because, in contrast to the market, there is no neat this-for-that adjustment of benefits and costs. This poor adjustment means that the taxpayer is likely to get more or less of some public service than he desires. Further-more the apparently "free" character of social goods and services provides no incentive for the taxpayer to economize in their use.

2. Short of a military emergency the balance of interest in our society works against any marked shifts in the composition of public spending. This "balance of inter-ests" effect causes components of the govern-ment budget to increase and decrease, not selectively, but rather on an across-the-board basis. Politicians, it is contended, have a low propensity for setting priorities on various social goods and services. If not all public expenditures are conducive to the elimination of social imbalance, the consequence is that increased spending on "desirable" public programs entails a heavy political surcharge in the form of increased spending on other "less desirable" programs. This means that

the overall cost of those public programs which are essential in rectifying a condition of social imbalance may be inordinately high. In effect, the dollar of public spending is typically subject to a discount; it only buys, say, 75 or 80 cents' worth of needed, high-priority social goods and services.

3. Of greatest significance is the argument that the expansion of the public sector advocated as a corrective for social imbalance may come at the very high cost of freedom. The cumulative effect of expanding a number of particular government programs could be a serious threat to freedom, despite the fact that each individual program may be of merit. In drawing a line between the public and the private sectors, it must be recognized that not only economics, but also freedom, is involved. "The centralized economy puts a strain upon democracy and freedom; the free economy does not." As a practical guide, Professor Wallich suggests that, because the expansion of government impinges upon freedom and causes[14]

. . . the cumulative discouragement of private and local initiative . . . , it would have to be shown that the people could do something only very imperfectly, and the government very substantially better, before the government should step in.

CORRECTIVES FOR SOCIAL IMBALANCE

It is not the purpose of this chapter to argue that social imbalance does or does not exist in our economy, but rather to pose the controversy for the reader's understanding and evaluation. Nevertheless, it is interesting to examine what might be done to remedy social imbalance if it now exists or arises in the future as a significant economic problem. A number of events and policies would be helpful in redressing social imbalance. Unfortunately, the simplest and most effective correctives tend to be either the least likely to occur or the least palatable politically.

[14] *Ibid.,* pp. 57 and 71.

Disarmament

Potentially the happiest solution to the problem of social imbalance would be an effective disarmament agreement. The assumption here is that a cessation of the arms race would set the stage for a rechanneling of government military spending to such non-military social goods and services as research, education, urban renewal, and so forth. This transfer of government expenditures from defense to nondefense categories has the virtue of imposing no direct constraints upon private goods output; a crude, direct clash between private and public wants is happily avoided. In fact, in the absence of the huge backlog of consumer and business demand and the condition of overemployment which facilitated reconversion after World War II, increased spending on public goods might be imperative in sustaining full employment.

Most obviously, the main difficulty with demobilization as a remedy for social imbalance is the fact that its potential pleasantness as a corrective is exceeded by its unlikeliness of occurrence. Even waiving this, there is a further possible problem. Disarmament could generate tremendous public pressures for tax cuts; tax rates which are acceptable during hot or cold wars might prove highly objectionable when peace breaks out. Our post–World War II experience suggests that it might be naïve to expect any easy or automatic transfer of resources from armaments production to the production of "civilian" social goods and services.

Growth As a Palliative

It must also be noted that the extent to which the provision of more social goods collides with the production of private goods depends upon the rate of growth achieved by the economy. The correcting of social imbalance in a static economy—that is, an economy whose GNP is unchanging—obviously implies a painful retrenchment in consumer goods production both absolutely and relatively. However, if the economy continues to achieve the 3 to 4 per cent annual growth rate of past full-employment years, an annual increment of $19 billion to $25 billion in output will result, as the simple application of these percentages to the 1964 GNP of $623 billion quickly reveals. A division of this increment which favors social goods can clearly alleviate social imbalance and simultaneously provide for modest increases in total consumption. Moreover, it is of no little significance that such a distribution of the increment might contribute to an acceleration of the growth rate.

Again, this solution is not devoid of problems. Even with a favorable annual growth rate, the correcting of fairly acute social imbalance may require an absolute decline in private consumption. Then, too, the growth process itself may intensify certain aspects of a social imbalance problem. Has it not been noted earlier that the industrialization and urbanization which characterize economic growth are basic factors underlying the increasing demand for social goods and services?

Acknowledging that demobilization is a pleasant but unlikely answer and that economic growth is a palliative in correcting social imbalance, let us consider two more concrete and more immediate proposals.

Increased Use of Sales Taxes

Some economists have strongly endorsed the greater use of sales taxation as a means of attacking social imbalance.[15] Because they are shifted to consumers, sales taxes raise the prices of consumer goods. The result is that a given total amount of consumer spending commands less private goods and automatically provides more government revenues to reabsorb the released resources through larger purchases of social goods. As private production expands, public revenues and therefore public goods increase on a pro rata basis. Furthermore, given the present high level of marginal income tax rates and the fact that sales taxes are effectuated through the price mechanism, the financing of increased public expenditures by sales rather than income taxation is less likely to blunt incentives. Finally, to the degree that sales taxes are hidden in prices and paid in relatively small amounts spread more or less evenly over a period of time, the cost of the social goods financed thereby is neither very explicit nor very immediate to the taxpayer. To the extent that this remoteness or vagueness of tax costs offsets the remoteness of social goods benefits, the cause of social balance may be furthered.

A New Budget Philosophy?

Current conceptions of fiscal policy—in particular, the cyclically balanced budget and functional finance (Chapter 15)—embrace the notion of compensatory spending by government. That is, the public sector, and especially the level of government spending, should be adjusted to compensate for the exuberance or lethargy of the private sector of the economy. This implies that social goods and services are expendable, or of a lower urgency, than private goods. Hence, if private consumption and investment spending are at high levels, it is held that government purchases of social goods can and

---

[15] Galbraith notes that the personal and corporate income taxes which provide about 70 per cent of Federal tax revenues are progressive and thus admirable agents of social balance. That is, an increase in the national income will result in more than proportionate increases in tax revenues for Federal use. At the same time, he emphasizes that (1) over half of Federal revenues are committed to defense expenditures and (2) social imbalance is more crucial at state and local levels. Galbraith rejects property taxes as a means to social balance because, in contrast to the sales tax, the property tax base is relatively insensitive to changes in the overall level of economic activity. This means that property tax rates must be raised to finance additional social goods, resulting in a conflict with the aforementioned resistance to increases in tax rates. Galbraith, *op. cit.*, pp. 311–315; Hansen, *Economic Issues of the 1960's,* pp. 104–110.

should be sacrificed in the interest of restraining inflationary pressures. As already noted, the application of such a fiscal policy over time can contribute to social imbalance.

The most direct and most obvious assault upon a social imbalance problem would therefore seem to be the development and acceptance of a new budget philosophy whereby private and social goods would somehow be evaluated on their own merits and neither would be considered inherently inferior and therefore expendable in the pursuit of economic stability. The goal is a *socially optimum budget* wherein government spending is aligned more closely with the long-run goal of social balance and less closely with the short-run goal of alleviating cyclical variations in output, employment, and the price level. In other words, if social imbalance actually exists, there may be a need for a new budget philosophy which pays attention not only to the full-employment but also to the resource allocation aspect of the economizing problem. Under this philosophy the public and private sectors would compete on a more nearly equal footing for the economy's scarce resources. Depending upon the initial presence or absence of social imbalance, this new budget philosophy may or may not call for an expansion of the public sector of the economy.

There can be no doubt that the problems involved in the acceptance and application of a socially optimum budget would be considerable in both number and severity. Two of the more obvious ones require special mention.

1. The political and administrative obstacles to the adoption and application of this new budget philosophy are obvious. Indeed, many of these are essentially the same obstacles to the production of social goods and services which we have already discussed in this chapter.

2. Would the adoption of a socially optimum budget philosophy seriously weaken the government's role in providing for full employment and reasonable price stability?

Would discretionary fiscal policy as we now know it cease to be an important stabilizing force in our economy? More specifically, if government spending is fixed at a level designed to fulfill society's demands for social goods, does this not rule out the compensatory changes in government spending which current fiscal philosophies require?

Although a weakening of fiscal policy *might* be involved, a number of offsetting considerations must be noted. First, in practice government spending has sometimes exerted a *destabilizing* influence upon the economy (Chapter 14), reflecting sudden and significant changes in military outlays. Thus, the stabilization of government spending might in fact make a contribution to stability. In the second place, it is possible that taxation may be strengthened as a fiscal device. In Chapter 14 it was noted that postwar discretionary fiscal policy had been criticized because of failure to invoke countercyclical tax changes. Greater flexibility in altering taxes could make up for any possible weakening of fiscal policy arising from an increase in the rigidity of government spending which a socially optimum budget might demand. Third, because of the many political problems which impede the enacting of appropriate fiscal policy (Chapter 14), a number of economists have taken the position that we should do well to strengthen our automatic or built-in stabilizers and thereby reduce our dependence upon discretionary fiscal policy. Still other economists have called for the consideration of new stabilizing techniques to supplement existing fiscal policy.[16] Such changes will tend to compensate for any potential weakening of discretionary fiscal policy which a socially optimum budget philosophy might entail. And, to the extent that future inflations are of the "new" cost-push and structural varieties, traditional fiscal policy will be inappropriate in any event. In summary, although at first glance a budget philosophy which pays greater attention to the achieving

[16] See question 9 at the end of Chapter 14.

of social balance would thereby seem to be less effective in providing for economic stability, there are a number of offsetting considerations which make this something less than a clear-cut conclusion.

SUMMARY

1. Economists are currently debating whether economic growth and the affluence it has brought to our economy have created a social imbalance problem, that is, an over-allocation of resources to private goods and an underallocation to social goods. In addition to having an obvious and direct bearing upon the problem of efficiently allocating resources, the social imbalance issue also has implications for economic stability and economic growth.

2. Those who feel that a social imbalance problem now exists argue that the amount of social goods and services demanded has increased ahead of the amount supplied. On the one hand, Wagner's Law asserts that as an economy becomes increasingly wealthy, the demand for social goods and services increases both absolutely and relative to the demand for private goods. On the other hand, there exist in our society a number of obstacles which inhibit social goods production. **a.** The ideological framework of capitalism and the attitudes fostered thereby are not conducive to an expansion of social goods production. **b.** The growing urban population whose social goods needs are most acute is allegedly underrepresented politically. **c.** The remoteness and uncertainty of the benefits from social goods puts them at a psychological disadvantage as compared with private goods. **d.** A number of tax problems make it difficult to finance social goods production. **e.** Advertising and emulation are forces which tend to pull resources toward private goods production and away from social goods production. **f.** Inflation draws resources from the public to the private sector and simultaneously creates political pressures to cut government spending because private spending is high.

3. Equally respected economists take the opposite position, and in so doing offer a number of counterarguments. **a.** Statistical evidence and a careful consideration of both those forces which retard and those which accelerate social goods production do not bear out the contention that social imbalance exists; they may even suggest that, in general, society's "new needs" are receiving ample attention. **b.** Increased public spending may not correct social imbalance because, first, this falsely assumes that all private goods are low-priority goods and all social goods are high-priority goods, and, second, it is not correct to suppose that all the "new needs" of society entail public, as opposed to private, goods. **c.** It is very questionable that the implications of a social imbalance problem for American economic growth and United States–Soviet competition for the allegiance of the new emerging nations are as clear-cut or dramatic as those who embrace the social imbalance position would suggest. **d.** The economic and political costs of correcting a social imbalance problem might be more substantial than the problem itself: The nonmarket and "free" character of social goods means that they might easily be overproduced; the tendency of public spending to increase "across the board" rather than selectively imposes a heavy surcharge on the production of high-urgency social goods; and, finally, a substantial increase in the production of social goods may seriously impair individual freedoms.

4. If social imbalance exists now or is encountered in the years ahead, disarmament and the achievement of rapid economic growth are potential means of redressing this imbalance. More realistic remedies are an increased use of sales taxation and the adoption of a socially optimum budget philosophy which removes social goods from the stigma of being "expendable." All these potential correctives entail serious questions concerning likelihood of occurrence and substantial problems of political and administrative feasibility.

QUESTIONS AND STUDY SUGGESTIONS

1. What is social imbalance? Why is it an economic problem? Why is social imbalance more likely to arise in a wealthy, growing economy than in a poor, static economy?
2. What is Wagner's Law? Do you think this law is valid? Explain how (a) the character of social goods, (b) advertising, and (c) inflation might contribute to a social imbalance problem.
3. Explain why one might argue that an increase in government spending may not resolve a social imbalance problem.
4. What are the possible economic and political costs of correcting social imbalance? How important do you estimate these costs to be? In your opinion are these costs prohibitive?
5. Carefully evaluate the following statement:[17]

   The root cause of our difficulty lies not in our income or our growth potential but in certain American habits of mind, carried over from earlier phases of our history, and in the workings of the political process, as they affect the allocation of resources. This interplay of intellectual conception and conventional politics conspires to make it difficult for Americans to increase the scale of public outlays except at moments of acute crises. Here lies a danger to the national interest as well as a threat to the quality of American society.

6. Why is the greater use of sales taxes, as opposed to income or property taxes, recommended as a corrective for social imbalance? Why might disarmament and rapid economic growth help correct a social imbalance?
7. What are the basic characteristics of a socially optimum budget? How does it differ from functional finance? To what degree, if any, do you think a socially optimum budget philosophy would impair achievement of the goals of full employment and price level stability? Explain.

SELECTED REFERENCES

Bator, Francis M.: *The Question of Government Spending* (New York: Harper & Row, Publishers, Incorporated, 1960).

Downs, Anthony: "Why the Government Budget Is Too Small in a Democracy," *World Politics*, July, 1960, pp. 541–563.

Galbraith, John Kenneth: *The Affluent Society* (Boston: Houghton Mifflin Company, 1958), particularly chaps. 18, 19, and 22.

Hansen, Alvin H.: *The American Economy* (New York: McGraw-Hill Book Company, 1957), chap. 8.

Hansen, Alvin H.: *Economic Issues of the 1960's* (New York: McGraw-Hill Book Company, 1961), chaps. 7 and 8.

[17] W. W. Rostow, "Summary and Policy Implications," in Joint Economic Committee, *Comparisons of the United States and Soviet Economics* (Washington, D.C., 1960), p. 601.

Rostow, W. W.: *The United States in the World Arena* (New York: Harper & Row, Publishers, Incorporated, 1960), Book 6.

Wallich, Henry C.: *The Cost of Freedom* (New York: Harper & Row, Publishers, Incorporated, 1960), particularly chap. 5.

Wallich, Henry C.: "Private vs. Public: Could Kenneth Galbraith Be Wrong?" *Harper's Magazine,* October, 1961, pp. 12–25.

PART SEVEN: INTERNATIONAL ECONOMICS,
THE UNDERDEVELOPED COUNTRIES,
AND THE SOVIET ECONOMIC CHALLENGE

CHAPTER 39

INTERNATIONAL TRADE AND
INTERNATIONAL EQUILIBRIUM

Thus far our analysis of American capitalism has been based upon the assumption that it is a "closed," or isolated, economy. This obviously is not true. Our economy is linked to other nations of the world through a complex network of international trade and financial relationships. It is the purpose of this and the following chapter to describe and analyze these relationships.

The specific objectives of the present chapter are fourfold:

1. To explain the bases of international trade, noting the ways in which it is similar to, and dissimilar to, domestic trade

2. To introduce the monetary aspects of international trade

3. To define, analyze, and interpret the international balance of payments

4. To discuss international disequilibrium and the mechanisms for restoring international equilibrium

INTERNATIONAL SPECIALIZATION

The same basic rationale underlies both domestic and international trade. We recall from Chapter 3 that individuals or regions can achieve a greater real output and therefore a higher standard of living by specializing according to comparative advantage; that is, each individual or region should specialize in those goods which it can produce with the greatest relative advantage or the least relative disadvantage.[1] This results

in a more efficient allocation of resources, as is evidenced in the fact that more output will result from the same volume of resources. The same reasoning extends beyond international boundaries. The world can achieve a more efficient allocation of resources and a higher real output by specializing according to comparative advantage and trading.

We must recognize, however, that there are limitations upon international specialization. Only in very rare instances is a single nation responsible for the world's production of some product. South Africa's role as the sole producer of diamonds is the exception which helps illustrate the rule. Even in the "one-crop" economies, for example, the sugar economy of Cuba and the coffee economy of Brazil, we find that many other goods are produced for both export and domestic use. In short, most products of international trade are produced by several, if not many, nations. Specialization is less than complete.

Why is this so? The first limitation upon specialization is economic and goes back to the production possibilities curve and the law of increasing costs. As a nation expands its production of any particular commodity, it must employ resources which are less and less suited to that commodity's production. To illustrate: Farmers in Iowa, Illinois, and a few other Midwestern states can probably produce corn at a lower cost than can farmers in any other nation. Yet the United States does not produce the world's total supply of corn, because to do so would necessitate the use of more land in the South, New England, and the Far West for corn

[1] The student should reread the examples given in Chapter 3, substituting, say, the United States for Anderson and Brazil for Brooks.

production. Since land and climate in these latter areas are not particularly suitable to corn, costs would be considerably higher. Therefore, some foreign farmers in, say, Canada or South America may produce corn at lower costs than it can be produced in some parts of the United States. In short, the comparative advantage of the United States in corn does not apply to *all* levels of output. This means that many nations may export the same product. As a matter of fact, a given nation may both export and import the same product.

Secondly, there are political limitations upon international specialization. These limitations, which often stem from the disadvantages that specialization entails (Chapter 3), usually take the form of governmentally imposed trade restrictions which limit the size of the export market for a product. In particular, the United States flatly prohibits the export of military equipment and strategic raw materials to the Soviet Union and has attempted to persuade allied nations and friendly neutrals to follow similar policies. Furthermore, the United States has placed import quotas and embargoes upon certain foreign farm products to avoid disruption of the domestic farm price support programs. Finally, political pressures exerted by domestic producers of certain goods have resulted in trade barriers which restrict the amounts foreign firms can sell in the United States and thereby limit the extent to which those nations can specialize. High tariffs on watches imported to the United States limit the degree to which the Swiss can specialize in watchmaking.

Domestic and International Trade

If the basic principle of comparative advantage underlies both domestic and international trade, why do we devote special attention to the topic of international trade? There are several reasons:

1. Though the difference is a matter of degree, the mobility of resources is considerably less between nations than it is within nations. American workers, for example, are free to move from Iowa to California or from Maine to Texas. Of course, there are sociological limits on this mobility, but otherwise there are no serious obstacles. If a worker wants to move, he can do so. Crossing international boundaries is a different story. Immigration laws, not to mention language and cultural barriers, put severe restrictions upon the migration of labor between nations. Different tax laws, different governmental regulations, different business practices, and a host of other institutional barriers limit the migration of real capital over international boundaries.

International trade is a substitute for the international mobility of resources. If human and property resources do not move readily between nations, the movement of goods and services can serve as an effective substitute.

2. Each nation uses a different currency. This poses complications. For example, in buying a British automobile you must first buy British pounds sterling (£) and then spend these pounds on the Hillman or Austin of your choice.

3. As already noted, international trade is subject to political interferences and controls which differ markedly in degree and kind from those applying to domestic trade.

American Trade

In 1964 United States exports of goods and services were about 6 per cent and imports about 5 per cent of the GNP. These figures clearly understate the significance of international trade to the United States and, in particular, to the nations with which we deal, for several reasons:

1. A 5 or 6 per cent figure is very large in absolute terms. In 1964, for example, American exports of goods and services totaled in excess of $36 billion, and imports were over $28 billion. Though other nations may derive as high as 30 or 40 per cent or more of their national incomes from international trade, the absolute volume of American imports and exports exceeds that of any other nation.

2. Despite the versatility of American capitalism, we are almost entirely dependent upon other nations for our supplies of specific commodities. Bananas, coffee, spices, tea, raw silk, nickel, tin, natural rubber, and diamonds are cases in point. Similarly, a host of American industries are highly dependent upon foreign markets. Almost all segments of agriculture rely heavily upon foreign markets—rice, wheat, cotton, and tobacco exports vary from one-fourth to more than one-half of total output. The chemical, automobile, machine tool, and textile industries are only a few of many American industries which sell significant portions of their output in international markets. Table 39–1 shows the major commodity exports and imports of the United States.

3. Changes in net exports, that is, in the difference between the value of a nation's exports and imports, will have multiple effects upon the level of national income in roughly the same fashion as will fluctuations in the various types of domestic spending. A small change in the volume of American imports and exports can have magnified repercussions upon the domestic levels of income, employment, and prices.

With these points in mind we need not belabor the significance of international trade for such nations as the Netherlands, Japan, Australia, and Great Britain, whose volumes of international trade range from one-fourth to over one-half their national incomes.

So much for the volume and composition of American trade. Let us now survey its financial aspects.

FOREIGN EXCHANGE

Though the particular techniques of financing international transactions are rather detailed, their general nature can be readily grasped. To simplify our discussion of international finance, we shall treat trade on a nation-to-nation basis, recognizing that in practice most trade is carried on by private businesses. Thus in talking about "United States exports" we really mean the sales of thousands of private American businesses to foreign buyers and do not imply that American export trade has been nationalized. Furthermore, we shall couch much of the remainder of this chapter in terms of a two-nation world. Again this is to simplify; bilateral trade can be discussed more readily

TABLE 39–1. PRINCIPAL COMMODITY EXPORTS AND IMPORTS OF THE UNITED STATES, 1964 (in millions)

Exports	Amount	Per cent of total	Imports	Amount	Per cent of total
Machinery	$ 6,344	25	Petroleum and products	$ 1,872	10
Grains and preparations	2,580	11	Coffee and cocoa	1,331	7
Chemicals	2,326	9	Paper and newsprint	1,158	6
Automobiles, tractors	2,268	9	Iron and steel products	820	4
Iron and steel manufactures	895	3	Nonferrous ores and metals	778	4
Textiles	805	3	Sugar	458	3
Unmanufactured cotton	690	3	Rubber	200	1
All other exports	9,364	37	All other imports	11,983	65
Total	$25,272	100	Total	$18,600	100

Source: U.S. Department of Commerce, *Survey of Current Business,* June, 1965, pp. S-22 and 23.

than can multilateral trade. Now, how are international transactions financed?

When the United States purchases goods and services from foreign nations, Americans must exchange dollars for foreign currencies in negotiating these purchases. For example, suppose an American firm wants to buy £10,000 worth of woolens from a British manufacturer. Because the British firm must pay its own obligations in pounds rather than dollars, the American firm must somehow exchange its dollars for pounds in order to make payment to the British firm. How is this accomplished? Suppose the *rate of exchange*—that is, the rate or price at which dollars can be exchanged for pounds, and vice versa—is $3 for £1. The American importer can go to an American bank and purchase for $30,000 a check for £10,000. This check can then be sent to the British woolens manufacturer in payment for the desired woolens. But where does the American bank get pounds sterling? It buys pounds from a British bank for $30,000, and in so doing makes American dollars available to the British bank. Our basic conclusion is this: American import transactions simultaneously create a demand for foreign exchange (pounds in this case) and make a supply of domestic currency (dollars) available to foreigners.

American export transactions have precisely the opposite results. Suppose a British manufacturer wants to purchase $30,000 worth of American-made machinery. At a $3-for-£1 exchange rate, the British manufacturer can buy $30,000 for £10,000 at a British bank and use this $30,000 check to make payment to the American machine manufacturer. The British bank gets the needed $30,000 from an American bank by buying it for £10,000. Our conclusion: American export transactions create a foreign demand for dollars and simultaneously make a supply of foreign currency available to Americans.

We can say, then, that American exports make available a supply of foreign currencies, and American imports create a demand for these foreign monies. Similarly, British exports to the United States earn a supply of dollars and British imports create a demand for these dollars. Briefly, *any nation's exports finance, or "pay for," its imports*. By selling to foreign nations a given country earns the foreign exchange it needs in order to buy from those nations.

INTERNATIONAL BALANCE OF PAYMENTS

Nations of the world systematically record and summarize *all* the transactions which take place between their residents (including individuals, businesses, and governmental units) and the residents of all other foreign nations and present them in an annual accounting statement called the *international balance of payments*. Despite its name, this statement is more like a business firm's profit and loss statement than a balance sheet. Like a profit and loss statement, a nation's balance of payments records its sales to, and purchases from, all other nations, and it accounts for any differences between its sales (receipts) and its purchases (expenditures). A simplified balance of payments for the United States in 1964 is presented in Table 39–2. Let us analyze this accounting statement to see what it reveals about American international trade and finance.

Balance of Trade

In items 1 and 2 on the United States international balance of payments, it is important to note that exports and imports are defined rather broadly. There is no question about the inclusion of items 1*a* and *b* as a part of American exports. As with domestic trade, international trade involves the exchange of both goods and services. The United States exports not only machinery, automobiles, and farm products, but also sells transportation services, insurance, and brokerage services to residents of foreign nations. Note, however, that one of the very special services which foreigners get from the United States

TABLE 39–2. THE UNITED STATES INTERNATIONAL BALANCE OF PAYMENTS, 1964 (in billions)

(1) United States exports		$+36.5
(*a*) Goods	$+25.2	
(*b*) Services	+6.1	
(*c*) Income from United States investments abroad	+5.2	
(2) United States imports		−28.3
(*a*) Goods	$−18.6	
(*b*) Services	−8.4	
(*c*) Income from foreign investments in United States	−1.3	
(3) Net balance due United States on exports and imports		$ +8.2
(4) Financial and balancing transactions:		
(*a*) Net unilateral transfers		−2.7
(*b*) Net capital movements (short- and long-term)		−4.8
United States capital outflow	$ −8.0	
Capital inflow to United States	+3.2	
(*c*) Net gold flow from the United States		+0.2
(*d*) Errors and omissions		−0.9
		0.0

Source: U.S. Department of Commerce, *Survey of Current Business,* March, 1965, p. 14. Details may not add to totals because of rounding.

consists of the services of American money capital which has been invested abroad. As item 1*c* indicates, the dividend and interest income received from the use of this American capital which has been invested in foreign nations is a payment for the American "export" of the services of this capital. United States imports, item 2, obviously include three analogous items. Americans import goods and services, including the services of foreign money capital which has been invested in the United States.

A comparison of items 1 and 2 reveals that United States exports of $36.5 billion exceeded United States imports of $28.3 billion by about $8.2 billion in 1964. Economists call the difference between a nation's total exports and its total imports the *balance of trade.* If a nation's exports exceed its imports, as is the case here, a nation is said to have a balance of trade *surplus.* On the other hand, if a country's imports exceed its exports, it is incurring a trade *deficit.* Note that, because United States exports are the rest of the world's imports and United States imports

are the rest of the world's exports, an American trade surplus of $8.2 billion obviously appears as a trade deficit to the rest of the world in its trade with the United States.

In Table 39–2 we have designated American exports with plus signs and American imports with minus signs. You will recall from our earlier discussion of foreign exchange that American exports entail payments of dollars from foreign buyers to the United States. These transactions, which involve dollar "inpayments" to the United States, have been marked plus. Conversely, American imports require that Americans make dollars available to foreigners. Such transactions, which involve dollar "outpayments" from the United States, have been marked minus. Thus the fact that the balance-due figure is a *plus* $8.2 billion indicates the United States incurred a trade surplus, and as a result net inpayments of that amount are due the United States from the rest of the world. This $8.2 billion balance due the United States correctly suggests that the rest of the world had to enter into some additional transactions so as to get the extra dollars needed to finance its trade deficit with the United States.

Financial and Balancing Transactions

These extra dollars were obtained through the three transactions shown as item 4 on the balance of payments. The net result of these transactions must be to make dollars available to foreigners; that is, overall they must be minus transactions. Item 4a, net unilateral transfers, indicates that the United States made net dollar gifts of some $2.7 billion to the rest of the world during 1964.

A small portion of the gifts were private, for example, immigrants' remittances to their families in the "old country." The bulk of these grants, however, were United States government grants made for purposes of providing military assistance to allies or aid in the economic growth of the underdeveloped nations. Item 4b indicates that the United States made net investments in, and extended net loans to, foreign nations in the amount of $4.8 billion dollars. These loans and investments were both public and private.

These two balancing transactions plus the $0.9 billion "errors and omissions" item totaled $8.4 billion and therefore provided foreign nations with more than enough dollars to settle their balance of trade deficit with the United States. Foreign nations used the extra dollars to purchase gold bullion from the United States. Because gold bullion is readily acceptable as a medium of international exchange, we can say that foreign nations added to their international monetary (gold) reserves by receiving American grants, investments, and loans which were more than sufficient to cover their trade deficit with the United States. From the American point of view the trade surplus of the United States in 1964 was inadequate to cover the flow of American grants, loans, and investments abroad, causing the United States to lose gold reserves. We shall have more to say about this gold outflow in Chapter 40.

Though a trade imbalance—a trade deficit or surplus—may occur, the balance of payments must always balance. It must balance for the simple reason that every transaction must be settled in one way or another. If an individual or nation sells (exports) more than it purchases (imports), it must provide a net amount of its currency through gifts and lending to cover the difference. Similarly, a nation can only purchase (import) more than it sells (export) by being on the receiving end of grants and loans.

INTERNATIONAL DISEQUILIBRIUM

Though a balance of payments statement always balances, nations are not always in equilibrium in achieving that balance. Nations can and do incur balance of payments deficits and surpluses. Although international equilibrium is a rather slippery concept, we can say that *international equilibrium exists when a nation's "normal" needs for foreign exchange are met by its "normal," or "dependable," sources of supply.* International equilibrium implies a stable, or maintainable, situation. Conversely, disequilibrium means that a nation is achieving a balance in its balance of payments through some abnormal, undependable sources of foreign currencies which are of a temporary, or stopgap, nature and therefore not maintainable.

Now at first glance it might appear that international equilibrium exists only when a nation's exports (item 1) equal its imports (item 2), eliminating the need for any balancing transactions. But this is not the case, because long-term private capital flows can be regarded as a normal source of foreign currencies for certain nations. That is, private long-term loans and investments can and do flow rather persistently into some nations, providing a regular and dependable source of foreign currencies. Thus we can say that, if a nation's exports and its net long-term capital inflows equal its imports, it is in international equilibrium. A young, expanding economy in which there are many opportunities for profitable investment and lending may achieve international equilibrium in its balance of payments even though its imports are persistently greater than its exports. Indeed, the United States was in precisely this position throughout much of its early history, receiving large capital inflows from Great Britain in particular to offset an American trade deficit.

A nation incurs a balance of *payments deficit* when its imports exceed the sum of its exports and net private capital inflows. The best evidence of such a condition is that the nation must invoke such temporary nonmaintainable measures as selling gold reserves for foreign exchange, obtaining short-term foreign credit, or receiving grants and loans from foreign governments to cover the deficit and make the balance of payments balance. These transactions are temporary and nonmaintainable, because a nation's gold stock and its ability to get credit from exporters and foreign banks will be limited. Similarly, a nation cannot depend upon the receipt of loans and grants from foreign governments. In short, such transactions are evidence that a nation is not "paying its way" internationally; that is, it is living beyond its income. An outstanding example of a balance of payments disequilibrium occurred in the immediate post–World War II period, when most nations of Europe incurred large and persistent payments deficits in their trade with the United States. Of course, such deficits appear as balance of *payments surpluses* to the United States, evidence of which took the form of American government loans and grants, the granting of short-term credit by American firms and banks, and the receipt of gold from abroad. The causes and cures of the postwar "dollar shortage" will be examined in detail in the next chapter.

RESTORING INTERNATIONAL EQUILIBRIUM

Because it is a nonmaintainable situation, some adjustments must occur to correct a balance of payments disequilibrium. There are three basic monetary mechanisms for restoring international equilibrium: (1) freely flexible exchange rates, (2) the international gold standard, and (3) exchange controls.

Freely Flexible Exchange Rates

When foreign currencies can be freely bought and sold, the rate of exchange between any two currencies will be determined by the forces of supply and demand. Let us examine the rate, or price, at which American dollars might be exchanged for British pounds sterling. As indicated in Figure 39-1, the demand for pounds will be downsloping, and the supply of pounds will be upsloping. Why? The downsloping demand for pounds shown by D_0D_0 reflects the fact that, if pounds become less expensive to Americans, British goods will become cheaper to Americans. This causes Americans to demand larger quantities of British goods and therefore larger amounts of pounds with which to buy those goods. The supply of pounds is upsloping, as S_1S_1, because, as the dollar price of pounds rises, the British will be inclined to purchase more American goods. The reason, of course, is that at higher and higher dollar prices for pounds, the British can obviously get more American dollars and therefore more American goods per pound. In other words, American goods become cheaper to the British, inducing the British to buy more American goods. Such purchases, we have seen, will make larger and larger quantities of pounds available to Americans. The intersection of the supply and demand for pounds will determine the dollar price of pounds. Suppose that the equilibrium rate of exchange is $3 to £1. At this rate American-British trade is in balance; American imports from Great Britain create a demand for the precise quantity of pounds which American exports to Great Britain make available.

Now let us assume that American tastes change so that they begin to import more British goods. Americans want more Hillman automobiles, more Scotch whisky, and more Harris tweeds. This increase in imports causes an American trade deficit, and if it is not offset by long-term private loans and investments from Britain, an American balance of payments deficit results. The immediate impact of the increase in American imports from Britain is an increase in the American demand for pounds, as indicated by the shift from D_0D_0 to D_1D_1 in Figure 39–1. Because of this shift, a shortage of pounds equal to AB now appears at the existing $3-for-£1 exchange rate. Since this is a free competitive market, the shortage will change the exchange rate (the dollar

price of pounds) from $3 for £1 to, say, $4 for £1. This obviously means that the value of the dollar has depreciated—it is worth less—in international trade.

This change in the exchange rate will alter the relative attractiveness of American imports and exports in such a way as to restore equilibrium in the balance of payments of the United States. From the American point of view, as the dollar price of pounds changes from $3 to $4, the Hillman automobile priced at £500, which formerly cost an

FIGURE 39–1. ADJUSTMENTS UNDER FLEXIBLE EXCHANGE RATES, THE GOLD STANDARD, AND EXCHANGE CONTROLS.
Under flexible rates an American trade deficit at the $3-for-£1 rate would be corrected by an increase in the rate to $4 for £1. Under the gold standard the deficit would cause changes in domestic prices and incomes, which would shift the demand for (D_1D_1) and the supply of (S_1S_1) pounds into equilibrium at the $3-for-£1 rate. Under exchange controls the government would ration the available supply of pounds XA among persons demanding the quantity XB.

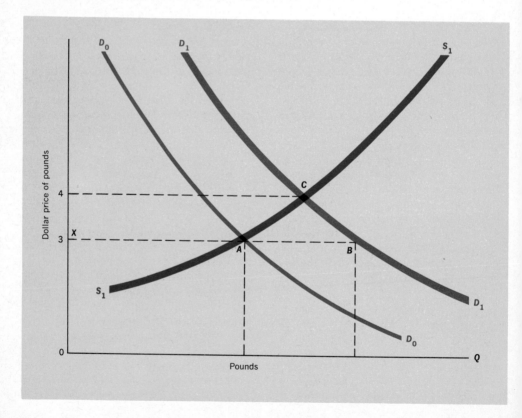

American $1,500, now costs $2,000. Also other British goods will be more expensive to Americans. Hence, American imports of British goods will tend to decline. Graphically, this is shown as a move from point *B* toward point *C* in Figure 39–1.

Conversely, from Britain's standpoint the exchange rate, that is, the pound price of dollars, has fallen. The international value of the pound has appreciated. The British previously got only $3 for £ 1; now they get $4 for £ 1. American goods are therefore cheaper to the British, and as a result American exports to Great Britain tend to rise. In Figure 39–1 this is indicated by the move from point *A* toward point *C*. These two adjustments—a decrease in American imports from Great Britain and an increase in American exports to Great Britain—are precisely what are needed to correct the American balance of payments deficit. The reader should reason through the operation of freely fluctuating exchange rates in correcting an initial American balance of payments surplus in its trade with Great Britain.

Though freely flexible exchange rates automatically correct a balance of payments disequilibrium, they may entail several serious problems:

1. The risks associated with flexible exchange rates are likely to discourage the flow of trade. To illustrate: Suppose an American automobile dealer contracts to purchase ten Hillman cars for £ 5,000. At the current exchange rate of, say, $3 for £ 1, the American importer expects to pay $15,000 for these automobiles. But if in the two- or three-month shipping period the rate of exchange changes to $4 for £ 1, the £ 5,000 payment contracted by the American importer will now amount to $20,000. Obviously, this unheralded increase in the dollar price of pounds may easily turn the American importer's anticipated profits into substantial losses. Aware at the outset of the possibility of an adverse change in the exchange rate, the American importer may simply not be willing to assume the risks involved. He therefore confines his operations to domestic

automobiles with the result that international trade does not occur on this item. Note, too, that contracting for payment in terms of dollars rather than pounds does not solve the risk problem, but merely shifts the risk to the British exporter.

2. A nation's terms of trade will tend to be worsened by a decline in the international value of its currency. For example, an increase in the dollar price of pounds will mean that the United States must export a larger volume of goods and services to finance a given level of imports from Britain.

3. Flexible exchange rates may also have some destabilizing effects upon the domestic economy as widely fluctuating exchange rates stimulate and then depress those industries producing internationally traded goods. Furthermore, if the American economy is operating at full employment and the international value of its currency depreciates as in our illustration, the subsequent rise in American exports and decline in imports will tend to increase net exports and cause domestic price inflation.

For all these reasons nations of the world have sought a means of stabilizing exchange rates. For a half century prior to World War I and again for a period in the 1920s, most of the major trading nations looked to the international gold standard for that stability.

The Gold Standard

A nation is on the gold standard when it fulfills two conditions:

1. It must define its monetary unit in terms of a certain quantity of gold and stand ready to convert gold into paper money and paper money into gold at the rate stipulated in its definition of the monetary unit.

2. It must allow gold to be freely exported and imported.

If each nation defines its monetary unit in terms of gold, the different currencies will have a fixed relationship to one another. For example, suppose the United States defines a dollar as being worth, say, 25 grains of gold and Britain defines its pound sterling as being worth 75 grains of gold. This means that a British pound is worth 75/25 dollars or, simply, £1 equals $3.

Now, if we momentarily ignore the costs of packing, insuring, and shipping gold between countries, under the gold standard the rate of exchange would not vary from this $3-for-£1 rate. And the reason is clear: No one in the United States would pay more than $3 for £1, because he could always buy 75 grains of gold for $3 in the United States, ship it to Britain, and sell it for £1. Nor would an Englishman pay more than £1 for $3. Why should he, when he could buy 75 grains of gold in England for £1, send it to the United States, and sell it for $3?

Of course, in practice the costs of packing, insuring, and shipping gold must be taken into account. But these costs would only amount to a few cents per 75 grains of gold. For example, if these costs were 3 cents for 75 grains of gold, Americans wanting pounds would pay up to $3.03 for a pound rather than buy and export 75 grains of gold to get that pound. Why? Because it would cost them $3 for the 75 grains of gold plus 3 cents to send it to England to be exchanged for £1. This $3.03 exchange rate at which gold would flow out of the United States is called the *gold export point.* Conversely, the exchange rate would fall to $2.97 before gold would flow into the United States. Englishmen wanting dollars would accept as little as $2.97 in exchange for £1, because from the $3 which they could get by buying 75 grains of gold in England and reselling it in the United States 3 cents must be subtracted to pay shipping and related costs. This $2.97 exchange rate at which gold would flow into the United States is called the *gold import point.* Our basic conclusion is that under the gold standard the flow of gold between nations would result in exchange rates which for all practical purposes are fixed.

But these gold flows would do more than stabilize exchange rates. They would also cause internal adjustments within the domestic economies which would tend to restore equilibrium in the balance of payments. These adjustments involve both (1) price changes and (2) income and employment changes.

Suppose that, as in our analysis of freely fluctuating exchange rates, the United States incurs a balance of payments deficit by importing more from, than it exports to, Great Britain. The immediate result is that the dollar price of pounds will move up to the $3.03 gold export point, and gold will flow from the United States to Great Britain to settle the deficit. But as gold is purchased in the United States, bank reserves and the supply of money will tend to decline. Other things being unchanged, this is conducive to a decline in total spending and a fall in the price level in the United States. The reverse occurs in Great Britain; the inflow of gold expands bank reserves and the money supply. Spending tends to increase and inflation occurs in Great Britain. Declining American prices and rising British prices will encourage American exports to, and discourage American imports from, Great Britain, thereby tending to correct the initial American payments deficit. These price-level changes were envisioned by the classical economists as the only adjustment necessary under the gold standard in restoring equilibrium in the balance of payments. The classical economists (Chapter 12) reasoned that Say's Law would provide perpetual full employment. Therefore, changes in spending would affect only prices and, through these changes, would restore international equilibrium.

Modern economists, on the other hand, know that changes in spending will cause not only price changes but also changes in the levels of employment and income. In our illustration, the decline in spending which accompanies the outflow of gold from the United States will cause incomes and employment to decline in the United States. Conversely, the increase in spending which follows the inflow of gold to Great Britain will increase incomes and employment in

Great Britain. These income changes will also tend to correct the balance of payments disequilibrium. As their incomes fall, Americans import less British goods. As their incomes rise, the British buy more American exports. In reality the corrective process of the gold standard is a combination of changes in price and income levels.

Gold standard adjustments can be envisioned in terms of Figure 39–1. You will recall that under a system of freely fluctuating exchange rates an American payments deficit would be corrected by a rise in the exchange rate from $3 to $4. In the case of the gold standard, gold flows between the two nations hold the exchange rate approximately at the $3 level. But gold flows result in changes in the price, income, and employment levels of the nations receiving and losing gold. These domestic adjustments shift the demand for and supply of foreign exchange so as to achieve equilibrium at the fixed $3-for-£1 exchange rate. Specifically, given the initial American payments deficit and the resulting American pound shortage of *AB* at the $3 exchange rate, gold will flow from the United States to Great Britain. The contractionary impact in the United States will tend to lower the American demand for pounds, and the expansionary impact in Great Britain will tend to increase the available supply of pounds. These shifts continue until equilibrium is restored at the $3-for-£1 gold standard rate. Graphically, this means the D_1D_1 curve of Figure 39–1 will shift to the left, and the S_1S_1 curve to the right, providing a new intersection (equilibrium) point somewhere on the dotted black line between points *A* and *B*.

The gold standard entails obvious advantages:

1. The stable exchange rates which it fosters reduce the riskiness and thereby stimulate the volume of international trade.

2. The gold standard automatically corrects balance of payments disequilibria. International equilibrium under the gold

standard does not require the action of governmental bodies; inevitable gold flows adjust trade deficits or surpluses to the end that a balance of payments disequilibrium will be resolved.

The basic drawback of the gold standard is apparent from our discussion of the adjustment processes it entails. Nations on the gold standard must accept domestic adjustments in such distasteful forms as deflation, unemployment, and falling incomes, on the one hand, or inflation, on the other. These adjustments may obviously collide with monetary and fiscal programs designed to foster domestic economic stability.

Exchange Controls

Another means of resolving a balance of payments deficit is through government control of the exchange rate. To see how exchange controls work let us suppose the United States government has fixed the legal dollar price of pounds at $3 to £1, as in Figure 39–1. Now assume as before that American imports increase, resulting in an American trade deficit. The main symptom of this deficit is an American foreign exchange shortage of *AB* in Figure 39–1. Under exchange controls the government handles this problem by requiring that all foreign exchange obtained by American exporters and other recipients be sold to the government. Then, in turn, the government allocates or rations this short supply of pounds (*XA*) among the various American importers and other users, who demand the quantity *XB*. In this way government can restrict American imports to the amount of foreign exchange earned by American exports. In effect government rationing of foreign exchange "forces" a balance of payments equilibrium by restricting imports to the value of exports. The rationing process necessarily involves government discrimination between different importers, typically denying foreign exchange for the importation of luxury, or nonessential, goods in order to make the short supply available for necessary, or essential, goods.

Exchange controls may permit nations to achieve stable exchange rates when they do not have the gold required to achieve exchange rate stability under the gold standard. But exchange controls do not free nations from internal price and income adjustments. Specifically, the restriction of imports in the control nation leads to domestic scarcities of certain goods and materials ordinarily imported. The prices of these products and resources therefore tend to rise. This is reinforced by the fact that the restricting of imports to the value of exports will increase national income in the control economy; expenditures formerly made on imported goods are now reallocated to domestically produced goods.

On the other hand, deflation tends to occur in other nations as the exchange controls tend to curtail their export markets and the production of goods normally exported begins to depress the domestic markets of these foreign nations. Furthermore, the loss of export markets which the imposition of exchange controls forces upon foreign nations will cause the incomes of those nations to decline. The decline in the net exports of these nations will have a contractionary impact upon their economies.

If government has the legal power to establish exchange rates, it obviously also has the power to alter those rates. Historically, when faced with (1) persistent trade deficits or (2) domestic unemployment, individual nations have *devaluated* their currencies for the specific purpose of overcoming these difficulties. For example, if the United States should find itself faced with a persistent deficit in its trade, it might increase the dollar price of pounds from $3 for £1 to $3.50 or $4 for £1. This would make American goods cheaper to the British and British goods dearer to Americans, increasing American exports and decreasing American imports to the end that the deficit be alleviated or corrected. During the Great Depression most nations devaluated their currencies in the hope of alleviating domestic unemployment. They reasoned that the increase in exports and decline in imports which devaluation would bring would stimulate their domestic economies. That is, by increasing international sales and reducing international purchases, it was felt that domestic income and employment would be bolstered. However, most nations found that the resulting stimuli to their domestic economies were short-lived, as other nations embraced the same rationale and in turn devaluated their currencies.

SUMMARY

1. Nations can achieve a more efficient allocation of economic resources, in essentially the same way as can regions and individuals, by specializing in accordance with comparative advantage. The degree of international specialization is limited by the law of increasing costs and by political considerations.

2. International and domestic trade differ in that **a.** resources are less mobile internationally than domestically; **b.** each nation uses a different currency; and **c.** international trade is subject to more political controls.

3. International trade is vital to the United States in several respects. **a.** The absolute volumes of American imports and exports exceed those of any other single nation. **b.** The United States is completely dependent upon trade for certain commodities and materials which cannot be obtained domestically. **c.** Changes in the volume of net exports can have magnified effects upon the domestic levels of output and income.

4. American imports simultaneously create a demand for foreign exchange and make a supply of dollars available to foreigners. Conversely, American exports create a foreign demand for dollars and make a supply of foreign exchange available to Americans. It follows that each nation's exports earn the foreign currencies needed to pay for its imports.

5. The balance of payments is an annual accounting statement of all of a nation's international trade and financial transactions. A nation's balance of trade is the difference between its exports and its imports. An excess of exports over imports is a trade surplus; an excess of imports over exports is a trade deficit.

6. A balance of payments equilibrium exists when a nation's normal needs for foreign exchange are met by its normal and dependable sources of supply. Generally speaking, the purchase of imports constitutes a nation's normal needs for foreign exchange, and its exports and its net long-term private capital inflows are its dependable sources of supply. Disequilibrium calls for temporary adjustments such as selling gold reserves, obtaining short-term foreign credit, and receiving aid in the form of grants and loans from foreign governments.

7. Freely flexible exchange rates, the gold standard, and exchange controls are mechanisms by which a balance of payments disequilibrium can be adjusted. Flexible exchange rates restore equilibrium primarily by affecting the relative attractiveness of internationally traded goods. The gold standard entails stable exchange rates but brings about international equilibrium through changes in the price, income, and employment levels of trading nations. Under exchange controls government forces imports into equality with exports by rationing foreign exchange.

QUESTIONS AND STUDY SUGGESTIONS

1. In what ways are domestic and foreign trade similar? In what ways do they differ? What are the limitations upon international specialization?
2. "The United States is the world's most efficient producer of primary steel. Yet other nations of the world produce and export steel." Explain. The United States can produce product X more efficiently than can Great Britain. Yet we import X from Great Britain. Explain.
3. What is the rate of exchange? "A rise in the dollar price of pesos necessarily means a fall in the peso price of dollars." Do you agree?
4. Why are resources less mobile internationally than domestically? Of what significance is this for international trade?
5. "Exports pay for imports. Yet in 1964 the rest of the world imported about $8.2 billion more worth of goods and services from the United States than were exported to the United States." Resolve the apparent inconsistency of these two statements.
6. Define and compare (*a*) the balance of payments and the balance of trade and (*b*) a balance of trade deficit and a balance of payments deficit. Explain how a nation can incur a balance of trade deficit or surplus and yet achieve an equilibrium in its balance of payments.
7. Explain in detail the adjustments which must occur to resolve a balance of payments surplus under (*a*) the gold standard (*b*) flexible exchange rates and (*c*) exchange controls. Now trace the adjustments entailed by a payments deficit. Evaluate the virtues and shortcomings of the gold standard and flexible exchange rates.
8. "The operation of the international gold standard undermines domestic full-employment policies, and, conversely, the active pursuit of full employment domestically is inimical to the operation of the gold standard." Explain and evaluate this statement.

SELECTED REFERENCES

Balassa, Bela (ed.): *Changing Patterns in Foreign Trade and Payments* (New York: W. W. Norton & Company, Inc., 1964).

Kenen, Peter B.: *International Economics* (Englewood Cliffs, N.J.: Prentice-Hall, Inc., 1964), particularly chaps. 1, 2, and 4.

Kindleberger, Charles P.: *International Economics*, 3d ed. (Homewood, Ill.: Richard D. Irwin, Inc., 1963), chaps. 1–4.

Krause, Walter: *International Economics* (Boston: Houghton Mifflin Company, 1965), chaps. 1–5.

U.S. Department of Commerce: *U.S. Balance of Payments* (Washington, D.C., 1964).

CHAPTER 40

THE BREAKDOWN AND RECONSTRUCTION OF INTERNATIONAL TRADE

With the elements of international trade and finance in mind we are now in a position to explore international economic problems and the economic policies which have sometimes alleviated and sometimes contributed to these problems. In particular we seek, first, to explain how depression, war, and political tensions caused world trade to disintegrate in the 1929–1946 period. Next, we examine the real and financial problems posed by this breakdown of world trade. In accomplishing this objective we emphasize national and international policies designed to remedy both the financial and real impediments to trade. Third, the perennial problem of protectionism versus free trade is discussed. Finally, the changing position of the United States in the world economy is outlined. The increasingly acute problems which are associated with the underdeveloped nations are discussed in Chapter 41.

DISINTEGRATION OF INTERNATIONAL TRADE

During most of the nineteenth century a harmonious network of international trade and finance linked the nations of the world. Some nations—particularly those of northwestern Europe—quickly grasped the new techniques of the Industrial Revolution, while others remained almost completely unaffected. These differences formed the basis for a highly complementary pattern of trade wherein underdeveloped nations exported raw materials to the manufacturing nations. The latter in turn came to depend upon the expanding markets of the semi-developed and underdeveloped nations in selling their manufactured goods. This trade pattern was accompanied by relatively large flows of private long-term capital from the manufacturing to the raw material nations. These flows increased the production of raw materials and simultaneously strengthened overseas markets in the raw materials nations. Furthermore, *laissez faire* was the dominant ideology during this golden age of international trade. Governmental interference with the composition and volume of trade was at a minimum. Each nation accepted any and all internal adjustments which inevitable changes in the structure and terms of trade demanded. The international gold standard worked automatically and effectively during this period to resolve balance of payments disequilibria. The world of the last half of the nineteenth century was a closely knit economic unit wherein the volume of trade was large and generally in accord with the principle of comparative advantage. Events of the twentieth century—the Great Depression, World War II, and the cold war—brought changes that have resulted in the demise of this golden age of international trade.

World Trade in the Thirties

The Great Depression of the 1930s severely disrupted the volume and composition of international trade. Nations heavily dependent upon foreign trade found that the Depression caused their overseas markets to collapse, preventing them from earning the foreign monies needed to finance the importation of essential goods. Nations which imported more than they exported witnessed the disappearance of the long-term capital flows which financed this difference as the Depression undermined profit expectations. Furthermore, drastic and uneven changes in the price levels of the various nations rendered existing exchange rates unrealistic and raised serious questions about the terms of trade. It is easy to see why many nations faced severe balance of payments difficulties during the thirties.

In addition to upsetting the international flow of goods and capital and posing exchange rate problems, the Great Depression prompted a myriad of trade controls. Domestic unemployment invariably gives rise to trade barriers designed to create more employment domestically. A most obvious means of bolstering domestic employment and production is to increase exports and cut imports. Success in this endeavor expands net exports, which through the multiplier effect promises a magnified expansionary effect upon the domestic economy. In seeking this trade surplus, the nations of the world imposed high tariff barriers, created import quotas and export subsidies, established government controls upon foreign exchange, and devalued their currencies. Unfortunately, because the exports of one nation are the imports of another, all nations could not succeed in stimulating their domestic economies by exporting more than they imported. But most tried. And the trade barriers which accompanied the attempts further distorted and choked off the declining flow of international trade.

World War II: Disruption of Trade

Following on the heels of the Great Depression, World War II completed the disintegration of world trade. The impact of war upon international trade is manifold:

1. Most obviously, the pattern of trade is altered so that it is in accord with military objectives rather than comparative advantage. At the outset of World War II Great Britain and France sought to mobilize as many resources as possible—both domestic and foreign—for war goods production. On the one hand, this means cutting exports, that is, shifting resources from export goods to war goods production. On the other hand, it means increasing imports to supplement the productive capacity of the domestic economy. The resulting excess of imports over exports poses an obvious balance of payments problem: How can a warring nation, when restricting exports, obtain enough foreign exchange to expand greatly its volume of imports?

2. War invariably means inflationary pressures, and, like depression, inflation affects different nations in differing degrees. Some encounter creeping inflation, and others are maligned with the galloping variety. Those nations which experience the greatest amount of inflation find that at existing exchange rates their goods are less attractive to foreign buyers and, unhappily, domestic consumers are attracted to foreign goods. Down go that nation's exports and up go its imports. This again contributes to a balance of payments deficit and a shortage of foreign monies.

3. World War II had dramatically different effects upon the productive capacities of nations. The capital facilities of some—particularly Great Britain, France, and Germany —were seriously reduced as the result of physical destruction through invasion, bombings, and the inability to replace depreciated capital during the wartime emergency. Those nations whose capital facilities are seriously impaired by war will want to achieve an excess of imports over exports to supplement domestic productive capacity in the postwar reconstruction period. But how is this trade deficit to be financed?

For example, Great Britain was the unwilling victim of all these war-born difficulties during the 1940s. The war itself called for persistent trade deficits. Inflationary pressures, though admirably contained, were strong, complicating domestic and international postwar adjustments. Finally, Great Britain faced the gigantic task of restoring its productive capacity at the cessation of hostilities. All these considerations meant long-term balance of payments deficits and posed in this instance the specific problem of a *dollar shortage.*

The Cold War

The Great Depression and World War II destroyed the harmonious trade structure of earlier decades. The cold war of the postwar period has proved a hostile environment in which to rebuild world trade. This has been so for a variety of reasons:

1. The World War II victors are ideologically divided. The cessation of hostilities brought forth no common ideological basis upon which world trade could be reconstructed. On the contrary, the end of the war merely ushered in the cold war and brought to the fore the ideological cleavages of the Communist bloc and the Western nations. More practically, the cold war has brought a virtual embargo upon American-Communist trade. And the nationalization of industry in both Communist nations and some nations of Western Europe injects *political* objectives into any evolving trade pattern, making it difficult to restore an *economically* desirable pattern of world trade.

2. The nationalistic emotions aroused by war are not easily abated with the end of hostilities. Mutual distrust, fear, and insecurity tend to linger on. Furthermore, the effect of the Great Depression on these nationalistic tendencies continues to operate. As a result of the chaos of the 1930s, the governments of most nations now explicitly accept responsibility to maintain domestic full employment and reasonable price stability. The pursuit of domestic stability can

and frequently does collide with the goal of rebuilding international trade and finance.

3. Fired by a rising spirit of nationalism, the underdeveloped nations now seek to reduce their economic dependence upon the industrially advanced nations and to improve their domestic living standards. Industrialization and diversification of their domestic economies are held by these nations to be the best means of accomplishing these ends. Tariffs, import quotas, and similar impediments to the flow of international trade have been techniques by which industrialization and diversification have been sought.

REBUILDING THE WORLD ECONOMY

In short, at the close of World War II world trade was in a shambles. Old trade patterns were almost completely destroyed, the productive capacity of Europe was at a very low level, the price levels of the various nations had changed in a disjointed fashion as a result of the war, and the Depression had imposed a myriad of restrictions upon the flow of trade. The problem of rebuilding the world economy in the postwar period was clearly a formidable one.

The postwar programs and institutions concerned with reconstructing world trade sought three closely related objectives:

1. To assist in European economic recovery

2. To provide an international monetary system capable of providing relatively stable exchange rates and the supplies of foreign exchange needed for trade

3. To liberalize trade by reducing artificial barriers to the flow of trade

The most pressing postwar problem in the reconstruction of world trade was that of rebuilding the economy of Europe. The end of World War II found the nations of Europe near economic prostration. The victorious and the conquered both paid heavily in terms of forgone consumption and tremendous physical destruction of their industries. The major economic problem of the postwar period was all too clear: to rebuild European economies and facilitate their transition to peacetime production. Europe was destitute; it needed crucial goods and services but had nothing to sell in financing their importation. American capitalism, on the other hand, emerged from the holocaust more vigorous and with a greater productive capacity than when it had entered. Thus the solution to reconstruction was almost as evident as the immediate problem: American economic aid to the needy nations. The fact that the United States had contributed some $37 billion to its allies through Lend-Lease during the war was indicative of the postwar role it was to play.

Foreign Aid in Postwar Years

American postwar aid to foreign nations has assumed several different forms and has been extended with a number of different objectives in mind. Table 40–1 indicates that in the 1945–1963 period some $89 billion worth of aid in the form of military grants, eco-

nomic grants, and loans has been extended by the United States. The bulk of this aid has been received by Western Europe. In the immediate postwar years foreign aid was aimed at reconstructing the war-torn economies of Europe. Later, however, aid was designed to provide the military and economic strength needed by foreign nations to resist the spread of communism. Though specific aid programs are difficult to classify in terms of these varying objectives, our present discussion will focus upon immediate postwar aid for the economic revival of Europe and more recent programs of military assistance. Then in the ensuing chapter we shall survey those aid programs whose primary objective is the economic development of underdeveloped nations.

Immediate postwar aid. The immediate, basic needs of postwar Europe were met through the United Nations Relief and Rehabilitation Administration (UNRRA). The aid extended by UNRRA amounted to almost $4 billion, centering for the most part upon

TABLE 40–1. UNITED STATES POSTWAR FOREIGN AID EXPENDITURES, JULY 1, 1945– JUNE 30, 1963 (millions of dollars)

Net United States military grants		$32,075
Western Europe	$15,463	
Far East and Pacific	10,103	
Near East, Africa, and South Asia*	5,343	
Latin America	802	
Rest of world	364	
Net United States economic grants		$42,454
Western Europe	$17,751	
Far East and Pacific	11,355	
Near East, Africa, and South Asia*	8,689	
Latin America	1,536	
Rest of world	3,123	
Net United States loans		$14,958
Western Europe	$ 6,359	
Far East and Pacific	1,591	
Near East, Africa, and South Asia*	3,823	
Latin America	2,757	
Rest of world	428	
Net total military and economic aid		$89,487

* Includes Greece and Turkey.
Source: U.S. Department of Commerce, *Foreign Grants and Credits,* 1964, table 2-A.

the provision of food, clothing, and medical services. About three-fourths of the total cost of this program was met through the contributions of the United States. Though successful in providing temporary relief, UNRRA did not provide in any significant way for the economic recovery of Europe.

Other American aid programs, however, supplemented UNRRA.

1. The United States distributed over $3.2 billion in emergency relief aid through the armed forces located in occupied countries.

2. Loans were made to specific foreign nations, the most notable of these being a $3.75 billion loan made by the United States Treasury to Great Britain in 1946 to help ease the acute dollar shortage then faced by the British.

3. Piecemeal grants of aid were made in 1947 to specific nations threatened by economic and political disorder. Austria, France, Italy, Greece, and Turkey were among the recipients of these grants.

All told the United States extended some $16.8 billion in foreign aid between the end of World War II and early 1948. This aid was almost evenly divided between outright grants and loans.

The Marshall Plan (ERP). Though substantial, it became increasingly clear that this immediate postwar aid was simply not sufficient to cope with the economic and political crises of the postwar era. On the economic front, European recovery was lagging. American inflation in the late 1940s made serious inroads on the purchasing power of American loans and grants. Trade between European nations was stifled by serious balance of payments problems. Drought, crop failures, and material and fuel shortages added to these economic woes. It was more apparent than ever that a freer and an expanding volume of international trade depended upon European recovery. On the international political front, Soviet Russia was becoming increasingly aggressive in seeking the world-wide spread of communism. And the Rus-

sians found a potentially fertile ground for this advance in the destitute and hungry peoples of Europe. On the domestic political front, there was a growing desire to abandon piecemeal aid programs designed to meet each individual economic and political crisis in favor of a comprehensive and coordinated aid program designed to restore the economic health and the political stability of Europe once and for all.

Out of this background the United States established in 1948 the European Recovery Program (ERP), called the "Marshall Plan" for its progenitor, Secretary of State George Marshall. The fundamental objective was to restore the productive capacity of European industry and agriculture. Related objectives were domestic political stability, the establishment of sound monetary and fiscal systems in the reviving nations of Europe, and the overcoming of the serious balance of payments problems which hampered trade between the nations of Europe in particular and world trade in general. In the four years of its existence the Marshall Plan channeled well over $10 billion in American aid to Europe, virtually all of which was in the form of outright grants.

Although comprehensive aid programs such as the Marshall Plan are elusive of precise evaluation, most experts agree that ERP was highly successful both economically and politically. In 1951 the average level of industrial production in all participating nations was 55 per cent above the 1947 level. Though far from completely successful in resolving balance of payments difficulties, considerable progress was made in this area. A very rough indicator of the political success of ERP lies in the fact that after 1948 no European nations succumbed to communism. The political ties of the United States and Western Europe were strengthened immeasurably by the Marshall Plan.

Mutual Security programs. Aid to Europe did not end with the expiration of the Marshall Plan in 1951. ERP in effect has been superseded by the Mutual Security

Agency, which continues through a variety of specific programs to provide large amounts of military, economic, and technical assistance to both European and non-European nations.

Several brief statements concerning the volume, objectives, and direction of American aid must be made:

1. Since the outbreak of World War II the United States has extended about $126 billion worth of foreign aid. This aid includes Lend-Lease during the war and the variety of postwar aid programs just outlined.

2. American aid has been primarily in the form of grants rather than loans.

3. Whereas American aid in the immediate postwar years was for economic reconstruction, the volume and direction of aid has been dominated by political and military security objectives since the early 1950s.

4. With the economic revival of Europe the direction of American aid has shifted to the Near East, Africa, Asia, and Latin America in more recent years.

RESTORING THE INTERNATIONAL MONETARY SYSTEM

It was well recognized at the end of World War II that the reconstruction of world trade would depend upon some satisfactory international monetary system to encourage the flow of international trade. In particular it was felt that relatively *stable exchange rates* and *exchange convertibility* were essential monetary prerequisites to the revival of the world economy. Fluctuating exchange rates would discourage the flow of trade; inconvertibility, that is, the inability of any nation to obtain needed supplies of foreign monies, would obviously pose a serious financial obstacle to trade.

In particular, it was evident that some means of providing an adequate volume of *international monetary reserves* was essential. As suggested in Chapter 39, a nation's balance of payments is not likely to be in equilibrium year after year. A nation might occasionally or rather persistently incur significant balance of payments deficits. This is

true not only during a period of economic reconstruction, such as that following World War II, but also during more normal times. When it incurs deficits, a nation in effect has two choices. First, it may finance its payments deficit by paying out some kind of international money, or international monetary reserves, to the nations which are realizing payments surpluses at its expense. As among the free world nations, gold and two "key currencies"—American dollars and British pounds—have come to be acceptable as international money in settling payments deficits. In time a nation incurring persistent payments deficits must overcome them through internal economic adjustments, for example, by halting domestic inflation, increasing productivity and accelerating the economy's growth rate, or altering the structure of its domestic industry. Such adjustments, if they are not to be acutely painful, may be time-consuming; they may take several years to accomplish. Hence, in the meantime deficits will persist, and the need for international monetary reserves will continue.

The second alternative for a deficit nation is to undertake rapid, and therefore very painful, domestic readjustments or to invoke exchange controls and trade barriers which, as we have already seen, have the very undesirable effect of choking off the flow of international trade. (Remember that the increasing of trade barriers by one nation may induce retaliatory action by other nations.) This second means of adjustment, then, is clearly less desirable than the first. But—and this is the important point—the first alternative is only relevant when an adequate volume of international monetary reserves is available. Hence, the need for an effective international monetary system was, and continues to be, an obvious prerequisite to the restoration and expansion of world trade.

The International Monetary Fund (IMF)

Against this background an international conference of Allied nations was held at Bretton Woods, New Hampshire, in 1944.

Out of this conference there was created the International Monetary Fund (IMF), an organization designed to deal with problems of the type just described. More specifically, the Fund was designed to assist nations in meeting financial problems posed by both temporary and fundamental disequilibria in their balance of payments.

The IMF was empowered, in the first place, to make short-term loans to nations faced with temporary, or short-run, balance of payments deficits. These loans were to be made out of currencies and gold contributed by the participating nations on the basis of size of national income, population, and volume of trade. The United States was the major contributor, providing about $2.75 billion, or roughly one-third of the total. If Great Britain or France, for example, faces a temporary shortage of dollars, it can borrow the needed dollars from the Fund by supplying its own currency as collateral. The dollars so acquired are in the form of a loan, not a grant, and must be repaid with interest in a relatively short period of time. The maximum a nation can borrow in any year is an amount equal to one-fourth of its own contribution to the Fund.

The Fund provides for the orderly alteration of exchange rates to cope with international disequilibrium stemming from long-run, or fundamental, causes. It was recognized that, if a nation's currency was overvalued in relation to other currencies, that nation would encounter severe difficulties in exporting. Hence, it would persistently be faced with a payments deficit. To cope with such situations the Fund allows each member nation to alter the value of its currency by 10 per cent without explicit permission from the Fund to correct a deeply rooted balance of payments deficit. Further exchange rate changes require the sanction of the Fund's board of directors. This procedure for changing exchange rates is more significant than first appears. By requiring approval of significant rate changes, the Fund attempts to guard against arbitrary and competitive currency devaluation prompted by nations seeking a tem-

porary stimulus to their domestic economies or the solution to a payments deficit.

As originally instituted, the IMF had neither sufficient authority nor sufficient financial resources to cope with the postwar international financial problems, which loomed more severe and prolonged than had originally been anticipated. But with the economic reconstruction of Western Europe and the rebuilding of world trade in general, the IMF has proved itself to be a very useful institution.

New Proposals: Triffin Plan

There is good reason to expect that the authority, the financial resources, and therefore the role of the IMF in facilitating free world trade will increase in the years ahead. Indeed, the need for international monetary reserves is clearly on the increase. There are a number of reasons why this is so; let us explore two of the more important ones.

1. In the postwar period the volume of world trade increased rapidly. This has been the result of both the economic reconstruction of Europe and a general reduction in artificial trade barriers such as tariffs and import quotas. Hence, because the flow of trade is greater, the likelihood that various nations will incur larger deficits in the future is also greater.

2. Payments deficits may be less temporary in the future than they have been in the past. Aside from the immediate postwar period, past deficits were typically the result of the business cycle; for example, substantial domestic inflation might make a nation's exports less attractive and its imports more attractive, thereby causing a payments deficit. The arresting of this inflation through appropriate monetary and fiscal policies could usually be accomplished in a relatively short period of time, say, one or two years. Some recent payments deficits, however, are of a more long-run character because they entail basic structural changes in the domestic economies of the trading nations. To illustrate: In the last section of this chapter we shall find that the rapid economic growth

of the economies of Western Europe and Japan have cut substantially into many of the United States' export markets and have been a major cause of persistent and sizable American payments deficits in the late 1950s and 1960s. A proper adjustment of this chronic deficit calls for policies (for example, the modernization of our productive facilities and changes in the structure of American industry) which may only prove effective over a substantial period of time. In the meantime the United States may incur more or less chronic payments deficits. In short, free nations have faced, and will encounter in the future, balance of payments deficits larger and more chronic than those originally anticipated when the IMF was created.

In view of this it is not surprising that a bevy of proposals has been offered in recent years to strengthen the international monetary system—that is, to increase the volume of international monetary reserves—by bolstering the IMF. Professor Robert Triffin of Yale has made one of the most far-reaching proposals. Skirting the many technical details, he suggests that the IMF be made an international bank which would perform the same functions for the international economy that the commercial banking system performs for a domestic economy, that is, accept deposits and make loans. Specifically, instead of holding key currencies as monetary reserves, surplus nations would be required to deposit a portion of these reserves in the IMF. On the basis of these deposits the IMF could *create* needed international monetary reserves by lending to deficit nations. In essence, the IMF's ability to provide needed monetary reserves would no longer be limited to the pools of currencies and gold received as the required subscriptions of its members. Rather, like a commercial banking system, the Fund could create credit (international monetary reserves) as required to meet payments deficits, and in so doing greatly facilitate the flow of international trade and investment.

Whether the world community of free nations is ready to accept the Triffin Plan or some similar proposal remains to be seen. The fact that in early 1962 ten leading free world nations agreed to increase the reserves of the IMF by $6 billion is indicative of current strong interest in improving the present international monetary system.

LIBERALIZING WORLD TRADE

A final aspect of the problem of rebuilding world trade has to do with the lessening or abolishing of artificial obstacles to trade. Though nations of the world retard the flow of international trade in many ways, the basic means are protective tariffs and import quotas.

Protective Tariffs and Import Quotas

Tariffs are simply excise taxes on imported goods; they may be imposed for purposes of revenue or protection. Revenue tariffs are usually applied to products which are not produced domestically, for example, tin, coffee, and bananas in the case of the United States. Rates on revenue tariffs are typically modest. Protective tariffs, on the other hand, are designed to shield domestic producers from foreign competition. Although protective tariffs are usually not high enough to prohibit the importation of foreign goods, they obviously put foreign producers at a competitive disadvantage in selling in domestic markets.

Import quotas specify the maximum amounts of specific commodities which may be imported in any period of time. Frequently import quotas are more effective in retarding international commerce than are tariffs. A given product might be imported in relatively large quantities despite high tariffs; low import quotas, on the other hand, completely prohibit imports once the quota is fulfilled.

The imposition of protective tariffs and import quotas is rooted in several different factors.

1. Throughout history, special-interest groups have sought to preserve or improve

their economic positions by persuading government to use tariffs and quotas to protect them from foreign competition.

2. As we have already noted, during depression nations are inclined to seek a trade surplus by imposing tariff and quota barriers upon imports.

3. Postwar international tensions have prompted nations to use tariffs and quotas to protect domestic producers of materials and goods essential to mobilization and war.

4. We have earlier called attention to the fact that underdeveloped nations have turned to tariffs and quotas in attempting to industrialize and diversify their economies.

Protectionism versus Free Trade

The issue of protectionism versus free trade has long been a subject of academic and political debate. Let us survey the basic cases for and against protectionism.

The case for free trade. The case for free trade rests on one potent argument: *Through free trade based upon the principle of comparative advantage, the world economy can achieve a more efficient allocation of resources and a higher level of material well-being.* The resource mixes and technological knowledge of each country are different. Therefore, each nation can produce particular commodities at different real costs. Each nation should therefore produce those goods for which its costs are low relative to those of other nations and exchange these specialties for those products for which its costs are high relative to those of other nations. If each nation does this, the world can fully realize the advantages of geographic and human specialization. That is, the world—and each free-trading nation—can realize a larger real income from the given supplies of resources available to it. The analytical underpinnings of the case for free world trade are the same as those developed in Chapter 3 within a context of free domestic trade. Protection—barriers to free trade—

lessens or eliminates the gains from specialization. If nations cannot freely trade, they must shift resources from efficient (low-cost) to inefficient (high-cost) uses in order to satisfy their diverse wants.

A collateral benefit of free trade also should be noted: Unimpeded international trade deters the establishment of domestic business monopolies. As opposed to free trade, protection from foreign competition creates a domestic economic environment more conducive to the development of monopoly and the host of restrictive practices associated therewith.

It is a fair statement to say that the vast majority of economists embrace the case for free trade as an economically valid position. However, economists do, as we shall note shortly, acknowledge the relevance of short-run and politically motivated exceptions to the case for free trade.

The case for protection. Though large in number, the arguments for protection vary greatly in quality. The first two arguments are of some validity under certain conditions and within certain limits. The remaining arguments vary from subtle half-truths to outright fallacies.

1. The *infant industry* argument contends that protective tariffs are needed for the purpose of allowing new domestic industries to establish themselves. Temporarily shielding young domestic firms from the severe competition afforded by more mature and therefore currently more efficient foreign firms will give the infant industries a chance to develop and become efficient producers. This argument for protection rests upon an alleged exception to the case for free trade. The exception is that all industries have not had and, in the presence of mature foreign competition, will never have the chance to make long-run adjustments in the direction of larger scale and greater efficiency in production. The provision of tariff protection for infant industries will therefore correct a current misallocation of world resources now perpetuated by historically different levels of

economic development between domestic and foreign industries.

Though the infant industry argument has logical validity, these qualifying points must be noted. (a) This argument is simply not pertinent to industrially advanced nations such as the United States. (b) In the underdeveloped nations it is very difficult to determine which industries are the infants capable of achieving economic maturity and therefore deserving of protection. (c) Unlike old soldiers, protective tariffs rarely fade away but rather tend to persist and increase even after industrial maturity has been realized. (d) Most economists feel that, if infant industries are to be subsidized, there are better means than tariffs for doing it. Outright subsidies, or "bounties," for example, have the advantage of making clear what industries are being aided and to what degree.

2. The *military self-sufficiency* argument contends that protective tariffs are needed to strengthen industries producing strategic goods and materials essential for war. Unlike the infant industry argument, the present argument is of a political-military nature. It very plausibly contends that in an uncertain world political-military objectives (self-sufficiency) must take precedence over economic goals (efficiency in the allocation of world resources). Unfortunately, there is no objective criterion for weighing the relative worth of the increase in national security, on the one hand, and the decrease in productive efficiency, on the other, which accompany the reallocation of resources toward strategic industries when such tariffs are imposed. The economist can only call the politician's attention to the fact that certain economic costs are involved when tariffs are levied to enhance military self-sufficiency.

This argument is also guilty of abuses. Virtually every industry can directly or indirectly claim a contribution to national security. Can you name an industry which did not contribute in some small way to the execution of World War II? Aside from abuses, are there not means superior to tariffs which will provide for needed strength in

strategic industries? Achieved through tariffs, self-sufficiency gives rise to costs in the form of higher domestic prices on the output of the shielded industry. Hence, the cost of enhanced military security is apportioned arbitrarily upon those consumers who buy the industry's product. Virtually all economists agree that a subsidy to strategic industries, financed out of general tax revenues, would entail a more equitable distribution of these costs.

Apart from the infant-industry and military self-sufficiency arguments, the case for restricted trade is very weak. Yet we must outline the remaining contentions in order to explore their shortcomings.

3. The *increase-domestic-employment* argument for tariffs becomes increasingly fashionable as an economy encounters a recession. The core of this argument has already been noted: A trade surplus, that is, an excess of goods and services exports over imports, stimulates the domestic economy. By reducing imports, protective tariffs and import quotas will give rise to such a surplus, bolstering domestic employment.

The shortcomings of this argument are several and serious. First, although the immediate effect of an export surplus is to bolster domestic employment, it is obvious that all nations cannot simultaneously succeed in this endeavor. The exports of one nation must be the imports of another. To the extent that one country is able to stimulate its economy through an export surplus, some other economy's unemployment problem is worsened by the resulting trade deficit. It is no wonder that tariff boosts and the imposition of import quotas for the purposes of achieving domestic full employment are termed "beggar my neighbor" policies.

In the second place, nations adversely affected by tariffs and quotas are likely to retaliate, causing a competitive raising of trade barriers which will choke off trade to the end that all nations are worse off. It is not surprising that the Hawley-Smoot Tariff Act of 1930, which imposed the highest tariffs ever enacted in the United States, backfired miserably. Rather than stimulate the American economy, this tariff act only induced a series of retaliatory restrictions by adversely affected nations. This caused a further contraction of international trade and tended to lower the income and employment levels of all nations.

Lastly, in the long run a trade surplus is doomed to failure as a device for stimulating domestic employment. Remember: It is through American imports that foreign nations earn dollars with which to purchase American exports. In the long run a nation must import in order to export. Hence, the long-run impact of tariffs is not to increase domestic employment but at best to reallocate workers away from export industries and toward protected domestic industries. This shift implies a less efficient allocation of resources, that is, an increase in disguised unemployment. Tariffs shift resources away from those industries in which production is so efficient as to provide a comparative advantage. There is little doubt that intelligent, well-timed monetary and fiscal policies are far superior to tariff and quota adjustments as anticyclical techniques.

4. Closely related to the increase-domestic-employment argument for tariff protection is the *diversification-for-stability* argument. The point here is that highly specialized economies—for example, Brazil's coffee economy or Cuba's sugar economy—are highly dependent upon international markets for their incomes. Wars, cyclical fluctuations, and adverse changes in the structure of industry will force large and frequently painful readjustments upon such economies. It is therefore alleged that tariff and quota protection is needed in such nations to induce greater diversification and therefore less dependence upon foreign markets. This will insulate the domestic economy from wars and depressions abroad and from random fluctuations in world supply and demand for one particular commodity, thereby providing greater domestic stability.

There is undoubtedly some truth in this argument. There are also serious qualifications and shortcomings. (*a*) The argument has little or no relevance to the United States and other advanced economies. (*b*) The economic costs of diversification may be great; one-crop economies are likely to be highly inefficient in manufacturing. (*c*) Might it not be better to seek full employment through monetary and fiscal measures?

5. Proponents of tariff protection frequently argue that tariffs are essential to *protect high wages and the high standard of living* now enjoyed in American capitalism. Cheap foreign labor, it is contended, will cause cheap foreign goods to flow into the United States. As a result, the prices of American goods and ultimately wage rates and the level of living will be driven down by this competition.

This appeal is tempting but fallacious. The argument falsely presumes that low foreign wages will necessarily mean low prices on foreign goods and high domestic wages mean high prices on domestic goods. This is not necessarily the case. Indeed, the argument conveniently ignores the fact that wage rates and per unit production costs are related through productivity. Hourly wage rates may be high and unit costs and product price low, if productivity is high. And what determines the productivity of labor? Basically the quality of labor and the quality and quantity of the capital with which it is equipped. As compared to most other nations, American labor is of a high quality and is extremely well equipped. The consequence is that high wages in the United States usually are accompanied by low unit costs and low product prices. As we have already discovered, wages are high in the United States for the simple reason that productivity is high!

These comments, of course, do not rule out the fact that in the production of certain articles higher American productivity is more than offset by the low money wages paid foreign workers. This is particularly likely to be the case where production of a commodity requires much hand labor and little capital equipment, for example, Swiss watches or Japanese toys. Is protection warranted under these circumstances? Certainly not on economic grounds. These nations will simply have a comparative advantage in these lines of production. Limiting American imports of these goods by imposing tariffs will also curtail American exports. The result is that American workers will be released from efficient, high-productivity export industries and absorbed in relatively inefficient, low-productivity industries which can only survive under an umbrella of protective tariffs. This reallocation will lower, not increase, real wages domestically and impair the domestic standard of living.

Though the arguments for protection are many and varied, they fail to overshadow the case for free trade: Unimpeded international trade permits greater specialization and a more efficient allocation of world resources. Under proper conditions, the infant-industry argument stands as a valid exception, justifiable on economic grounds. And on political-military grounds, the self-sufficiency argument can be used to validate protection. Both arguments, however, are susceptible to severe abuses, and both neglect alternative means of fostering industrial development and military self-sufficiency. Most other arguments are semiemotional appeals in the form of half-truths and outright fallacies. These arguments only note the immediate and direct consequences of protective tariffs. They ignore the simple truth that in the long run a nation must import in order to export.

American Policies

Since the enactment of the first American tariff in 1789 and up to 1934, the long-run trend was in the direction of higher tariffs on American imports. This trend, however, encompasses periods of tariff boosting and tariff cutting—the Republicans usually doing the boosting and the Democrats the cutting. Intense foreign competition after World War I and the Great Depression led to significant tariff increases in the 1920s and 1930s. The previously noted Hawley-Smoot

Tariff Act of 1930 enacted the highest tariffs ever imposed by the United States.

In view of the foregoing evaluation of the case for protection, this trend toward higher tariffs may be a bit surprising. If tariffs are economically undesirable, why has Congress been so willing to employ them? The answer lies in the political realities of tariff making. Those interest groups who stand to benefit from protection have done an effective job of lobbying for tariffs. And in a sense the pressure for protection is cumulative. With some tariff protection domestic producers increase their economic strength. This means they have greater financial resources to plead for more protection and also more to lose if they fail in their efforts to sustain protection. Most consumers, ignorant of all the economic implications of tariffs, are impressed not only by the vigor but also the plausibility ("Cut imports and prevent domestic unemployment") and the patriotic ring ("Buy American!") of the protectionists. Alleged tariff benefits seem immediate and clear-cut to the public. The adverse effects cited by economists seem ever so obscure and widely dispersed over the economy. Then, too, the public is likely to trip on the fallacy of composition: "If a protective tariff on Swiss watches will preserve profits and employment in the American watch industry, how can it be detrimental to the economy as a whole?" Those relatively few individuals who do recognize that the benefits gained by protected industries come at the expense of the general welfare are incapable of financing lobbyists to offset the protectionists. When political logrolling is added in—"You back tariffs for industry X in my state and I'll do the same for industry Y in your state"—the sum is protective tariffs and import quotas.

In the last twenty-five years there has occurred a reversal of the trend toward higher tariffs. This turnabout in American tariff policy was inaugurated with the Reciprocal Trade Agreements Act of 1934.

Specifically aimed at tariff reduction, this act has two main features:

1. It authorizes the President to negotiate

agreements with foreign nations which reduce American tariffs up to 50 per cent of the existing rates. Such negotiations occur on the assumption that the other nation will reciprocate by lowering tariffs on American exports.

2. By incorporating "most favored nation" clauses in these agreements, the resulting tariff reductions apply not only to the specific nation negotiating with the United States but would be *generalized* so as to apply to all nations.

Tariff reductions under Reciprocal Trade have been very substantial. Today the United States stands as one of the leading free-trade nations of the world. This is not to deny, of course, that substantial tariffs persist on many foreign goods. Nor is it to deny that the Reciprocal Trade Act has led a precarious existence. Congress has frequently threatened not to renew the act and has in several ways limited the tariff-cutting authority of the President. The fact remains, however, that the United States has gone far in the direction of freer trade since 1934.

American policies in establishing import quotas are also explained largely in terms of political considerations. Specifically, the United States imposes import quotas primarily upon agricultural products to avoid upsetting the operation of the domestic farm program. Supported farm prices make foreign producers eager to sell in the high-price American market. Permission to do so would only add to American surpluses which already embarrass congressmen and burden the taxpayer. On the other hand, as with tariffs, import quotas work against the most efficient allocation of world resources and, at the same time, conflict with the avowed United States policy of promoting freer trade.

International Policies

In the post–World War II era the United States spearheaded a drive for freer trade. This objective was to be sought through a proposed International Trade Organization (ITO). This organization was to foster international economic cooperation in general and to promote freer multilateral trade in particular. Out of much open debate by the representatives of some fifty-seven nations there evolved a charter for this proposed organization—a charter unacceptable to the United States Congress. American rejection spelled defeat for the ITO, and the organization has simply never come into being.

However, out of the negotiations which led to the ITO charter, a General Agreement on Tariffs and Trade (GATT) was signed in 1947 by some twenty-three nations, including the United States. GATT is based upon three cardinal principles: (1) equal, nondiscriminatory treatment for all trading nations, (2) the reduction of tariffs by negotiations similar to those carried out under the Reciprocal Trade Act, and (3) the elimination of import quotas. The nations participating in GATT have increased significantly in number, and the resulting tariff and quota agreements have done much to lower artificial trade barriers. Table 40–2 provides a rough indication[1] of the extent to which tariffs have been reduced under Reciprocal Trade and GATT.

AMERICA'S CHANGING POSITION IN THE INTERNATIONAL ECONOMY

In the late 1950s and the 1960s two highly important and related developments occurred which have profound implications for American international trade and trade policies. These developments are (1) the changing of our balance of payments position from a surplus to a deficit and (2) the emergence of an integrated European economy in the form of the Common Market. Let us examine these developments in the order stated.

[1] These figures understate the importance of tariffs by not accounting for the fact that some goods are *excluded* from American markets because of existing tariffs. Then, too, average figures conceal the extremely high tariffs on particular items: watches, china, hats, woolens, scissors, wine, jewelry, glassware, and so forth.

TABLE 40–2. AVERAGE RATES OF DUTY UNDER UNITED STATES TARIFF LAWS, 1913–1963

Year	Tariff law	Duties collected, per cent of value of dutiable imports
1913–1921	Underwood Law	27.0
1922–1929	Fordney-McCumber Law	38.5
1930–1933	Hawley-Smoot Law	52.8
1939	Reciprocal Trade Agreements Law	37.3
1947	GATT	15.3
1963	GATT, Trade Expansion Act	11.9

Source: Walter Krause, *The International Economy* (Boston: Houghton Mifflin Company, 1955), p. 237, and U.S. Department of Commerce.

AMERICA'S CHANGING PAYMENTS POSITION

For many years prior to 1950 the United States balance of payments was characterized by a payments surplus. But the 1950s brought a marked change in America's payments position. Since 1958 the United States has incurred substantial and persistent balance of payments deficits, the ultimate consequence of which has been a significant decline in American international gold reserves. Our gold stock, which totaled $25 billion in 1948, was slightly less than $15 billion in early 1965. Why has this turnabout occurred? What can be done to correct our payments deficit?

Causes

The underlying causes of the United States' balance of payments deficit are manifold. Let us examine several of the more prominent considerations.

1. Foreign productivity increases. The productivity of the nations of Western Europe and Japan has increased rapidly in recent years. This is partly a reflection of the success of postwar economic recovery programs. The economies of Western Europe and Japan have been rebuilt and strengthened with new and modern productive facilities, increasing the capacities of these nations to compete successfully with the United States in world

markets. In the case of the Western European nations, productivity increases have been fostered by the transformation of Western Europe from a number of small, localized markets into a single, growing mass market through the Common Market. This has permitted European producers to realize greater economies of scale, lower unit costs, and sell their products at lower prices.

2. Domestic inflation. American trade surpluses have tended to decline because of domestic inflation. The prices of American export goods generally rose faster in the 1950s than did those of our closest competitors for world markets. In short, inflation has priced American producers out of certain export markets.

These two considerations—rapid productivity gains in Japan and the Common Market nations and domestic price rises in excess of those experienced by foreign nations—have had the effect of narrowing our balance of trade surplus. Yet we do have a substantial *trade* surplus—$8.2 billion in 1964 as Table 39–2 indicates. Why, then, despite this trade surplus, does the United States have a *payments* deficit? The answer lies in two additional considerations.

3. Growing capital outflows. The outflow of American investment capital has expanded very rapidly since the mid-1950s. This growth has occurred in response to the burgeoning profit opportunities available in

the more rapidly expanding economies of the world, particularly those of Western Europe. Americans have found that the expected return on foreign investment has exceeded that on domestic investment, so they have invested abroad. In so doing, they have supplied the rest of the world with a growing quantity of American dollars. Note in Table 39–2 that net capital outflows were $4.8 billion in 1964.

4. Foreign aid. As Table 39–2 makes clear, the United States grants a substantial amount of economic and military assistance to foreign nations each year. These grants obviously involve an outflow of dollars. In 1964 this aid outflow amounted to $2.7 billion (Table 39–2). One might think at first glance that American dollar aid would tend to increase our trade surplus and therefore not contribute to our payments deficit. But it has only worked this way to a limited degree. Some American aid dollars have been spent on American goods, thereby increasing our exports and our trade surplus. But other American aid dollars have been spent on, say, German and French goods and ultimately hoarded by the central banks of these countries and therefore not respent on American exports. Thus foreign aid has entailed dollar outflows not fully matched by dollar inflows resulting from aid-induced expenditures on American exports. In this way aid has contributed to our payments deficit.

To summarize: In the immediate post–World War II period the United States enjoyed a trade surplus of such a great magnitude that outflows of aid and private capital were quite easily covered. But the economic recovery and rapid productivity increases of Western Europe and Japan, coupled with American inflation, have caused our trade surplus to fall from early postwar levels. At the same time foreign aid has remained at a substantial level, and outflows of American investment capital have grown sharply. Thus our shrinking trade surplus has failed to cover our outflows of investment dollars and aid dollars. Foreign nations have used the extra dollars thus

received to purchase American gold, or they have held these dollars as idle balances which are convertible to gold upon demand.

Cures

The changing world trade position of the United States obviously poses a problem. No nation can indefinitely lose gold reserves at rates which have averaged close to $1 billion per year in recent years. Because there is little evidence to suggest that the payments difficulties of the United States will resolve themselves, some adjustments must be made in our international trade accounts to restore equilibrium. The crucial question involves the character of these adjustments. The most immediate techniques are to expand the American trade surplus by restricting American imports through the raising of tariff barriers, the tightening of import quotas, or devaluation of the dollar. Use of these techniques, however, would seem ill-advised. These methods are likely to induce retaliatory actions of a similar nature by adversely affected nations. This would not only reduce the effectiveness of these techniques in solving the American payments problem but, more importantly, would tend to reverse the current trend toward a larger and freer volume of international trade.

This suggests that a more responsible program by the United States is needed. Several lines of attack are suggested by the very nature of the problem:

1. Redistributing aid and defense burdens. Western Europe might well assume a larger share of the costs of the mutual defense effort and of economic aid programs designed to benefit the underdeveloped nations. The balance of payments problem of the United States stems in a sense from the fact that American military and economic assistance and capital outflows are considerably in excess of its trade surplus, causing an outflow of gold. European recovery and the resulting substantial shrinkage of the American trade surplus suggest that Europe can now share more fully in the free world's defense against communism and in the vital programs which assist the underdeveloped nations in improving their economic lot. This is not to suggest an overall cut in mutual defense spending or in economic assistance to less fortunate nations; rather, the aim is to redistribute the financial burden of these programs.

2. Increase American productivity. A second line of attack is for American producers to intensify their efforts to increase productivity as a means of making American goods more competitive in international markets. This is obviously more easily said than done. It implies the maintenance of full employment and a high level of net investment spending. It suggests increased activity in technological research by both industry and government. It demands farsightedness by labor and management in introducing automation and in eliminating obsolete work rules.

3. Restrict domestic inflation. The effective use of monetary and fiscal policies to restrain domestic inflationary pressures may help in resolving our payments problem. Further increases in the domestic price level will cause further shrinkage in the trade surplus of the United States. Sufficient restraint by domestic labor and management in increasing wages and prices might even allow American productivity increases to be reflected in lower product prices. This, of course, would clearly tend to bolster American exports.

4. Anti-American discrimination. The United States might bolster its trade surplus by negotiating the reduction or elimination of discriminatory trade restrictions which still apply to some American goods. These restrictions developed during the turbulent thirties and forties. Now that most European nations have substantially overcome their "dollar shortages," the United States might well press for the relaxation of these discriminatory restrictions.

All these programs call for adjustments which are likely to be unpalatable either to our Allies or to specific groups within the

domestic economy. But inconvenient and painful adjustments are an inevitable by-product of resolving balance of payments difficulties. The most important point is that such alternatives as import restrictions and devaluation of the dollar are not likely to provide an effective long-run solution to the problem and may well prove to be a major roadblock in the expansion of international trade.

ECONOMIC INTEGRATION: THE COMMON MARKET

A second development of major significance for the United States' world trade position has been the emergence of an integrated economy in Western Europe. The reconstruction of the postwar years attempted to do more than simply restore the prewar economic structure of Europe; *economic integration* of the nations of Western Europe was also sought. Economic integration entails (1) the removal of barriers to trade and to the making of payments between nations and (2) the free flow of labor and capital resources across national boundaries.

The most dramatic step in efforts to achieve European economic integration came in 1958 with the establishment of the European Economic Community (EEC), or the Common Market, as it is popularly called. The European Common Market, composed of France, West Germany, Italy, Belgium, the Netherlands, and Luxembourg, calls for (1) the abolishment of tariffs and import quotas on all products traded among the six participating nations over a twelve- to fifteen-year period and (2) the establishment of a common system of tariffs applicable to all goods received from nations outside the Common Market, and envisions (3) the eventual free movement of capital and labor within the Market and (4) the creation of common policies with respect to monopoly and agriculture. If fully realized, the Common Market has tremendous implications. The result will be a huge free-trade market with a population of some 173 million, more than ample to remove any market limitations upon the achievement of mass-production economies by European industry.

Achievements of Common Market

The Common Market nations have achieved considerable success in working toward these stated goals, particularly so with respect to the first two objectives. Member nations have actually accelerated their scheduled internal tariff reductions, and common external tariffs are to be completed in 1967. Future expansion of Common Market membership is on the horizon; Great Britain, Denmark, Norway, and Ireland are possible candidates.

The tangible success of the Common Market is reflected in the high levels of output and growth and the dramatic expansion of both internal and external trade which have been enjoyed.[2]

. . . the Six [member nations] as a group have been growing faster than the United States . . . and . . . their share of world trade has been expanding. . . . From 1953 to 1960, the [Common Market] area's total product grew 45 percent, while that of other European countries . . . expanded by 26 percent, and that of the United States by only 15 percent. In per capita terms, the contrast between the United States and the Community during the 1953–1960 period is even greater: per capita output rose by 36 percent in the community as compared with only 6 percent in the United States. . . . [The Common Market's] share of total world trade rose continuously throughout the 1950's. From 16 percent in 1950, it reached 26 percent in 1960, while the shares of the United States and the rest of Europe remained constant at 18 percent and 17 percent.

What are the causes of this outstanding economic performance? It is impossible to determine with any degree of accuracy how much of the Common Market's economic success has been due to economic integration

[2] Robert R. Bowie and Theodore Geiger, *The European Economic Community and the United States,* for the Joint Economic Committee (Washington, D.C., 1961), pp. 23–25.

as such; one can plausibly argue that the gradual reconstruction of the European economy and world trade would have brought an expansion of output and trade to Europe even if the Common Market had never been formed. On the other hand, the potential benefits of economic integration in Europe are very great. Two merit explicit comment. First, economic integration generally promotes a more rational allocation of Europe's economic resources in accordance with the principle of comparative advantage. Second, integration of the national economies of Western Europe creates a large-scale mass market which is essential for European industries in realizing economies of large-scale production. More efficient production for a large-scale market permits European industries to realize the lower costs which small, localized markets have historically denied them. Indeed, it is this greater productive efficiency on the part of European firms that has contributed to the United States' balance of payments difficulties.

All things considered, there can be but little doubt that the Common Market as an institution has been a significant factor in the buoyancy and expansion of the economies of its member nations.

Economic Potential of an Atlantic Alliance

Prior to the Common Market, the United States was the leader of a number of industrially advanced nations allied by the ties of international trade and devoted to the common causes of political and economic freedom. With the growth and success—past and anticipated—of the Common Market, this picture is now changing to one in which two economic giants—the United States and the Common Market—are dominant in the free world. Table 40–3 summarizes two of the major economic aggregates for the present and potential Common Market membership, the United States, and Canada. There is little doubt that these giants, with a combined national income of over $878 billion, embrace a tremendous amount of economic power.

If we assume effective political and eco-

TABLE 40–3. ECONOMIC AGGREGATES FOR THE ENLARGED COMMON MARKET, CANADA, AND THE UNITED STATES, 1962

Country or area	Population, millions	National income, billions
Common Market nations	173.1	$217.4
Prospective Common Market members*	84.4	123.6
Subtotal	257.5	$341.0
Canada	18.6	35.1
United States	186.6	502.2
Grand total	462.7	$878.3

* England, Austria, Denmark, Ireland, Norway, Sweden, and Switzerland.
Source: United Nations, *Yearbook of National Accounts Statistics, 1963*, p. 329.

nomic ties and reasonable unity of action between the United States and the Common Market, this new "Atlantic Alliance" could be in a very strategic position to meet the most crucial problems now faced by the free world. In particular, such a partnership could (1) provide the military strength needed to deter or meet Communist aggression, (2) afford the resources for effective aid programs to the underdeveloped countries, and (3) create the institutions and unity of policies and efforts to assure continuing prosperity and economic growth within such a partnership.[3]

. . . the European Community . . . offers an effective means to enable the developed countries of the West to join together in discharging their common obligations and responsibilities. In tandem, the European Community and the United States can work for the creation of a more viable world order which can accommodate the needs and interests of the less developed countries as well. Together they can assure the growth of their own economies, provide their own people rising standards of life, and help the less developed nations in the gigantic effort to modernize. And finally they can concert more effectively for military defense against Communist aggression and for a common political

[3] *Ibid.*, p. 12.

approach designed to bring about ultimate changes in Soviet purposes and objectives.

Achieving Economic Harmony

But it is by no means a foregone conclusion that such objectives will be achieved. Many problems exist for both the Common Market nations and for the United States in establishing an effective Atlantic Alliance.

Comparable growth rates. It is well known that the prospects for an expanding level of mutually advantageous trade between any two nations or groups of nations are greater if both are realizing adequate rates of growth. Vigorous growth means rising incomes, new products and production techniques, rising productivity, and an environment conducive to the lowering of existing trade barriers. We have seen that the growth rates of the Common Market nations have generally exceeded those of the United States. Hence, it is important that the United States achieve both short-run economic stability and an adequate growth rate if the opportunities for increased trade and investment between the United States and the Common Market are to be fully realized.

Trade policies. The trade policies adopted by the United States toward the Common Market, and in turn the Common Market's trade policies toward the United States, will be most crucial in determining the degree of unity and harmony realized by these two economic giants. Upon these policies might also hinge the fate of the free world.

Most economists feel it is imperative that the United States seize the initiative and forge policies which will closely link our economy with that of the Common Market. The most obvious and most effective policy in establishing close economic ties would be for the United States to negotiate substantial reciprocal tariff reductions with the Common Market nations. There are a number of compelling reasons why it is felt such a policy should be pursued vigorously by the United States.

1. Given our position as the leading nation in world trade and our current policy commitment to more liberalized trade, any other policy would be detrimental to the prestige and image of the United States and might split the Free World economically and politically.

2. The basic economic argument for freer international trade is applicable: The more efficient allocation of the world's resources resulting from freer trade based upon comparative advantage will be mutually beneficial to the United States and the Common Market.

3. Unless substantial reciprocal tariff reductions are negotiated, the United States faces the prospect of future losses of export markets and therefore a worsening of its balance of payments position. The loss of export markets is anticipated for several reasons. First, the Common Market embodies a rapidly growing, but as yet relatively unsaturated, market for our manufactured goods. European incomes and living standards are rising, and the Common Market nations are generally entering the "high mass consumption" stage of their economic development. The lowering of European tariffs on imports from the United States would make increasingly accessible to United States manufacturers a growing mass market for consumer durables and semidurables—those very products which American firms produce with such great efficiency.

In the second place, as the Common Market reduces internal tariffs toward zero and simultaneously establishes a common external tariff, it will necessarily become more difficult for the United States and other free world nations to sell in the Common Market. For example, *before* the establishment of the Common Market, American, German, and French automobile manufacturers all faced the same tariff in selling their products to, say, Belgium. However, *after* the establishment of the Common Market, Belgian tariffs on German Volkswagens and French Renaults fell to zero, but an external tariff of, say, 25 or 30 per cent applies to all nonmember nations such as the United States.

This obviously puts American firms at a serious competitive disadvantage. And, of course, to the extent that this disadvantage results in a growing mass market for European producers, they may realize greater economies of scale (lower unit costs) and find themselves increasingly able to compete with American manufacturers in the export market of nations outside the Common Market. It is obvious that such declines in our ability to export to the Common Market will intensify the United States' balance of payments difficulties.

In brief, the successful negotiation of reciprocal tariff reductions with the Common Market will

1. Provide for the more rational use of free world resources which liberalized trade generally promotes

2. Prove consistent with the United States' free trade philosophy and its role as the leading trading nation

3. Make the Common Market more accessible to American exporters and thereby tend to alleviate American balance of payments problems.

These reasons for achieving an Atlantic Alliance are all the more compelling because the only real alternative may be the United States' economic isolation from the Common Market nations and the potential political-military disunity which might very well be involved: [4]

. . . if the challenges and opportunities immediately ahead are constructively seized for united free world action on trade, payments, and aid—the tide can indeed lead on to fortune. But if the challenges and opportunities are *not* taken, or are postponed out of calculations of tactical advantage, there is a good chance that we shall be "bound in shallows and miseries"—new recession and protectionism and isolationism at home; abroad, a fractured free world for . . . [communism] to divide and conquer.

[4] Henry S. Reuss, *The Task for 1962: A Free World Community,* for the Joint Economic Committee (Washington, D.C., 1961), p. 1.

Trade Expansion Act of 1962

In the fall of 1962 Congress took a major step toward the achievement of close economic ties between the United States and the Common Market by passing the Trade Expansion Act. This act provides the President with broad powers to negotiate reciprocal tariff reductions. More specifically, the act gives the President authority to

1. Lower or eliminate entirely all tariffs on products where the Common Market and the United States together have 80 per cent or more of the world's trade

2. Lower tariffs up to 50 per cent on other goods over a five-year period.

The reductions are to be made by reciprocal negotiations and are to embody "most-favored-nation" clauses, automatically extending the lower tariffs to many other countries.

The Trade Expansion Act explicitly acknowledges that the sweeping tariff reductions required for a close alignment of the Common Market and the United States economies will entail certain costs. These costs are of two general types. On the one hand, a number of domestic industries, when relieved of tariff protection, will be faced with declining markets, falling profits, and unemployment. The act therefore provides for "trade adjustment assistance" to those who are adversely affected. Specifically, workers who lose their jobs because of increased import competition can get vocational training, relocation allowances, and cash payments up to $61 per week for as long as 78 weeks of unemployment. Adversely affected businessmen can get tax relief and loans and technical assistance for the modernization and reorganization of plants.

There is a second type of "cost" implicit in the act. Any close linking of the United States and Common Market economies will call for a closer harmonization of national economic policies and conditions among participating nations. As the economies of nations in an Atlantic Alliance become increasingly interdependent through expand-ing trade and financial relationships and through integration, the issues, problems, and policies which were once of a purely domestic character will now become of international importance. For example, the monetary and fiscal policies, agricultural policy, and antitrust policy of the United States or of any other participating nations will now necessarily become increasingly important to all other participating nations. Despite these costs, there can be little doubt of the overriding merits of the Trade Expansion Act as a mechanism for achieving closer economic and political harmony among free world nations.

SUMMARY

1. In the 1929–1945 period the Great Depression and World War II severely disrupted the volume and pattern of world trade. The cold war has posed serious obstacles to the rebuilding of international trade.

2. Postwar reconstruction of world trade has centered upon resolving three related problems: **a.** European economic recovery, **b.** providing exchange rate stability and exchange convertibility, and **c.** reducing trade barriers.

3. In the postwar years the United States has provided some $89 billion worth of economic and military aid to foreign nations. Much of this aid was channeled to Europe through UNRRA, the Marshall Plan, and more recently, the Mutual Security Program.

4. The International Monetary Fund is designed **a.** to make short-term loans to help nations meet temporary payments deficits and **b.** to provide for an orderly adjustment of exchange rates to help correct fundamental payments deficits. The Triffin Plan is designed to strengthen the IMF by making it in effect an international bank, that is, by empowering it to create international monetary reserves by lending to nations with payments deficits.

5. Artificial trade barriers usually take the form of protective tariffs and import quotas. The basic argument for free trade is that it fosters a more efficient allocation of resources and a higher standard of living for the world as a whole. When applicable, the strongest arguments for protection are the infant-industry and military self-sufficiency arguments. Most of the other arguments for protection are half-truths, emotional appeals, or fallacies which typically emphasize the immediate effects of trade barriers while ignoring long-run consequences.

6. The long-run trend of American tariffs to rise has been reversed by the Reciprocal Trade Agreements Act of 1934.

7. The proposed International Trade Organization sought to increase economic cooperation and to promote freer multilateral trade. In 1947 the General Agreement on Tariffs and Trade was formed **a.** to encourage nondiscriminatory treatment for all trading nations, **b.** to achieve tariff reductions, and **c.** to eliminate import quotas.

8. Since 1958 the United States has been faced with large and persistent balance of payments deficits. The growing productivity of Western Europe and Japan, American inflation, large outflows of investment capital, and a substantial American foreign aid program have all contributed to this deficit. American productivity increases, restraints against inflation, the reduction of discriminatory trade barriers against American exports, and a redistribution of the costs of Western military and economic aid programs are possible remedial measures.

9. One of the remarkable international developments of the postwar period has been the move toward European economic integration in the form of the Common Market. Member nations seek the gradual elimination of internal trade barriers, the establishment of common external tariffs, and the eventual free movement of labor and capital resources within the Common Market area. The Common Market nations have achieved very substantial economic success as reflected in rapidly growing GNPs, expanding per capita outputs, and a rising share of world trade.

10. Most economists take the position that close economic and political ties between the United States and the Common Market can provide the resources for **a.** the military strength required to deter Communist aggression, **b.** more effective aid programs for the underdeveloped countries, and **c.** continuing prosperity and growth of all nations participating in such an Atlantic Alliance. Reciprocal tariff reduction is the most obvious path to this alliance. In addition to providing for a more rational allocation of free world resources, tariff reduction entails a special advantage to the United States: Lower tariffs will make the expanding market of Western Europe more accessible to American exporters and thereby help alleviate our balance of payments deficit. The Trade Expansion Act of 1962 is an important step toward the achievement of these objectives.

QUESTIONS AND STUDY SUGGESTIONS

1. What factors underlay the disintegration of international trade? Explain the impact of each.
2. What were the character and size of American postwar economic aid? Describe and evaluate the Marshall Plan and the Mutual Security Program. What changes have occurred in the volume, character, and direction of American foreign aid since the end of World War II?
3. What is "economic integration"? Why do many economists feel that European economic integration is an essential measure in reconstructing world trade? Use the "economies of scale" analysis of Chapter 25 to explain why the Common Market has enabled many European industries to compete more effectively in international markets.
4. Identify and discuss the International Monetary Fund, indicating the nature of its goals and its operation. What is the Triffin Plan?

5. Identify and discuss each of the following:
   a. The Hawley-Smoot Tariff Act of 1930, **b.** The Reciprocal Trade Agreements Act of 1934, **c.** ITO, **d.** GATT, and **e.** The Trade Expansion Act of 1962.
6. Explain the existence of artificial barriers to international trade.
7. Carefully evaluate the following statements:
   a. "Protective tariffs limit both the imports and the exports of the nation levying tariffs."
   b. "The extensive application of protective tariffs destroys the ability of the international price system to allocate resources efficiently."
   c. "Apparent unemployment can often be reduced through tariff protection, but by the same token disguised unemployment typically increases."
   d. "American imports and exports since World War II are higher than they have ever been. This indicates that tariffs are not restricting the volume of trade."
8. "The most valid arguments for tariff protection are also the most easily abused." What are these arguments? Why are they susceptible to abuse?
9. Suppose the currently high American tariffs on Swiss watches were abolished. What would be the short-run economic effects upon the American and Swiss watch industries? Upon total American exports to and imports from Switzerland? What would the long-run effects of this abolishment be upon (*a*) the volume of employment, (*b*) the allocation of resources, and (*c*) the standard of living in the two nations?
10. Carefully evaluate the use of artificial trade barriers such as tariffs and import quotas as a means of achieving and maintaining full employment.
11. In view of the fact that the United States is running a trade (export) surplus, how do you explain recent American gold outflows? How should this loss of gold be corrected?
12. What economic and noneconomic advantages might accrue to the free world from an Atlantic Alliance? To the United States in particular?

SELECTED REFERENCES

Balassa, Bela (ed.): *Changing Patterns in Foreign Trade and Payments* (New York: W. W. Norton & Company, Inc., 1964).

Bowie, Robert R., and Theodore Geiger: *The European Economic Community and the United States*, for the Joint Economic Committee (Washington, D.C., 1961).

Ellsworth, P. T.: *The International Economy*, 3d ed. (New York: The Macmillan Company, 1964), chaps. 11–13 and 23–30.

Hansen, Alvin H.: *The Dollar and the International Monetary System* (New York: McGraw-Hill Book Company, 1965).

Harris, Seymour E. (ed.): *The Dollar in Crisis* (New York: Harcourt, Brace & World, Inc., 1961).

Jensen, Finn B., and Ingo Walter: *The Common Market* (Philadelphia: J. B. Lippincott Company, 1965).

Kenen, Peter B.: *Giant among Nations* (Chicago: Rand McNally & Company, 1963).

Krause, Walter: *International Economics* (Boston: Houghton Mifflin Company, 1965), particularly chaps. 6–8, 14–21, and 26–29.

TABLE 41-1. AVERAGE INCOME PER CAPITA IN SELECTED COUNTRIES, 1949 AND 1961

Country	1949	1961	Country	1949	1961
United States	$1,453	$2,308	Barbados	$...	$245
Switzerland	849	1,463	Yugoslavia	146	223
Canada	870	1,459	Colombia	132	222
Sweden	780	1,445	British Guiana	...	218
New Zealand	856	1,313	Syria	100	218
Australia	679	1,237	Algeria	...	217
Luxembourg	553	1,153	Malaya	...	215
United Kingdom	773	1,149	Dominican Republic	75	205
Denmark	689	1,148	Mauritius	...	203
West Germany	320	1,072	Philippines	44	200
Norway	587	1,036	Honduras	83	182
Belgium	582	1,035	Turkey	125	180
France	482	1,034	Ghana	...	179
Iceland	476	925	El Salvador	92	176
Finland	348	889	Rhodesia and Nyasaland	...	156
Netherlands	502	864	Guatemala	77	151
Soviet Union	308	800	Peru	100	145
Austria	216	736	Ecuador	40	143
Puerto Rico	...	685	Tunisia	...	141
Venezuela	322	671	Jordan	...	139
Israel	389	627	Brazil	112	129
Ireland	420	570	Ceylon	67	122
Italy	235	561	Formosa	...	122
Trinidad and Tobago	...	503	Morocco	...	120
Japan	100	402	China	27	117
South Africa	264	396	Paraguay	84	113
Malta	...	391	Sudan	...	91
Argentina	346	378	Thailand	36	88
Chile	188	377	Kenya	...	72
Jamaica	...	373	India	57	69
Panama	183	367	Congo (Leopoldville)	...	67
Greece	128	364	Nigeria	...	66
Cyprus	...	359	Uganda	...	57
Costa Rica	125	291	Pakistan	51	54
Mexico	121	279	Tanganyika	...	50
Spain	...	271	Burma	36	50
Portugal	250	251	Indonesia	25	49

Source: Charles P. Kindleberger, *Economic Development,* 2d ed. (New York: McGraw-Hill Book Company, 1965), pp. 12–13, compiled from United Nations data.

people of the highly developed countries. They suffer much of the time from malaria, dysentery, tuberculosis, trachoma, or other ills. . . . Their food supply is about one-third less, measured in calories, than that of the developed countries, and when account is taken of the needs of the human body for the relatively expensive "pro-tective" foods, such as milk and meat, the extent of malnutrition is found to be very great indeed. The opportunity to attend school is limited to a small minority. . . . Only one person in four or five, again on a broad average of underdeveloped countries, knows how to read or write. The supply of cloth for clothing, home furnishing, and other purposes is about one-fourth as great per person in underdeveloped as in highly developed countries. Nonhuman energy to supplement the labor of human beings in industry, agriculture, transport, and household tasks is less than one-twentieth as plentiful, measured in horsepower-hours per person. Incomes, on the average, are less than one-tenth as high.

Viewpoint of Underdeveloped Nations

The income disparities revealed in Table 41–1—great as they are—conceal the discontent harbored by the people of the underdeveloped nations. The bulk of these people are not resigned to their fate. Far from it. Most seek and feel they have a right to a better life. As they see it, poverty is not inescapable.

Two recent developments—one economic and the other political—have fanned the desire of the underdeveloped nations for material and social betterment:

1. The per capita income gap between the economically advanced nations and the underdeveloped nations has not merely persisted, but in many instances it has widened. As between nations, the rich have been getting richer and the poor have been getting relatively poorer.[2]

This widening has intensified the discontent of the peoples of the underdeveloped countries. The equation for social unrest is no secret:

Aspirations − standard of living = social unrest

As the living standards of the advanced nations have improved, the economic goals and aspirations of the underdeveloped na-

[2] The grim jokes of the day mirror the widening economic gap between the United States and the underdeveloped nations:

Polish Communist party secretary: "Hear you've got a brother out of work in Detroit. Why don't you write him and tell him to come home?"

Warsaw automobile worker: "Sure, but who'd send us the food parcels?"

tions have increased accordingly. But their actual standard of living in most instances has shown meager growth. The differential—social unrest—has clearly been on the increase. One need only review the political and military crises of the post–World War II era to validate this point.

2. In recent years many of the underdeveloped lands have achieved or are in the process of achieving political independence. Accompanying this freedom from colonial status has been a tremendous upsurge of nationalistic spirit. The underdeveloped nations seek the economic independence, the respect, and the social status which they feel are due them as independent nations.

Viewpoint of Advanced Nations

Like it or not, the advanced nations, the United States in particular, have a great stake in the future of the underdeveloped nations. This interest has several roots. The *humanitarian* aspect of this interest is obvious: The wealthier nations have a tremendous moral obligation to relieve the stark poverty of the less fortunate peoples. The *political-military* importance of the underdeveloped nations is also clear: The ideological conflict between the Western world and communism may well be won or lost according to the paths of development pursued by the underdeveloped countries. Then, too, for purely *economic* reasons the United States has a vital interest in these less advanced nations: In selfish terms, these nations provide us with vital raw materials and, simultaneously, with markets for a portion of our finished goods. Through trade with these nations all participants can reap a portion of the benefits of international specialization.

Dubious Lessons of History

It is disarmingly tempting for the advanced nations to offer less fortunate nations a simple formula for economic development: "Do what we did." Such a formula is glib, inaccurate, and, to the informed citizens of poor nations, downright insulting. This advice is akin to advising an undernourished, one-legged youngster that he too can bat cleanup for the Yankees if he will just follow Mickey Mantle's training schedule. The simple fact of the matter is that the now advanced nations initiated their development in an environment vastly different from that currently faced by the underdeveloped countries. Witness the favorable setting for American economic development: abundant and diverse mineral resources, opulent sources of power, navigable rivers, fertile and free farm land, a temperate climate, a small but energetic and (for the time) intelligent labor force, and, finally, the virtual absence of social and moral taboos on business and commerce. This is an environment ripe for economic growth.

Throw these characteristics into reverse and you have the typical underdeveloped nation: a niggardly resource base, a lack of power, low-quality land, a teeming and untrained population, and a host of fetishes narrowly circumscribing any existing spirit of enterprise. The spontaneous growth arising from the favorable environs of the North American continent is not likely to blossom forth in such a briar patch. In most cases growth, if and when it is to be achieved, must be forced by a degree of government planning and nurtured by the aid of the more advanced nations. This is not to imply that communism or socialism is the modern-day path to economic development, or to say foreign aid is the primary fountainhead of economic growth. We are saying that economic growth must be actively pursued and not merely awaited. We are also saying that many underdeveloped countries cannot pull themselves up by their own bootstraps without external assistance.

BREAKING THE POVERTY BARRIER

The avenues of economic growth are essentially the same for both advanced and underdeveloped nations:

1. Existing supplies of resources must be used more efficiently. This entails not only the elimination of unemployment but also the achievement of greater efficiency in the allocation of resources.

2. The supplies of productive resources must be altered—typically, increased. By expanding the supplies of raw materials, capital equipment, effective manpower, and technological knowledge, a nation can push its production possibilities curve to the right (Chapter 20).

Why have some nations been so successful in pursuing these avenues of growth while other countries have lagged far behind? The answer, as noted above, lies in differences in the physical and sociocultural environments of the various nations. Our plan of attack is to examine the obstacles in the underdeveloped countries to altering the quantities and improving efficiency in the use of (1) natural resources, (2) human resources, (3) capital goods, and (4) technological knowledge. Emphasis here will be upon the private sector of the economy. In addition, social and institutional impediments to growth will be illustrated. And, finally, the roles of government and foreign aid in the development process will be analyzed.

Natural Resources

A nation's endowments of natural resources constitute an obvious but crucial element in its capacity for economic development. Poor nations are frequently burdened with an adverse climate, a paucity of arable land, very scarce mineral resources, and few sources of power. An inadequate resource base poses a more serious obstacle to growth than does, say, a lack of capital goods or a qualitatively inferior labor force. The reason for this lies in the fact that there is little or nothing that can be done to overcome a weak resource base. Certainly swamps can be drained and jungles cleared, but the prospects here are usually very limited and the process exceedingly slow. As a matter of fact, faulty soil conservation practices and the application of wasteful technologies in mining often cause a premature shrinkage in an underdeveloped nation's natural resources. Then, too, there is the ever-present possibility that technological improvements in the advanced nations will impair the economic value of the underdeveloped nation's natural resources. Witness the impact of synthetic rubber upon the natural rubber industries of Malaya and Indonesia.

The crucial limiting role of natural resources must be kept clearly in mind in programing the economic development of any nation. Though an inviting and pleasant mental exercise, it is flatly unrealistic for many of the underdeveloped nations to envision an economic destiny comparable to that of the United States, Canada, or the Soviet Union. Automated steel, automobile, and aluminum plants are simply not a part of the foreseeable economic futures of most underdeveloped nations. This is not, of course, to rule out future development for those underdeveloped nations plagued with severe scarcities of natural resources. Switzerland, Israel, and Japan, for example, have achieved relatively high levels of living despite narrow resource bases. At the same time, other nations with more affluent natural resources—for example, Bolivia—have not done so well. In almost all underdeveloped nations, despite the lack of natural endowments, there is ample room for growth. But it must be recognized that the relatively unaugmentable character of natural resources may set very real limits on this growth.

Employment of Human Resources

Three statements describe the typical underdeveloped nation's circumstances with respect to human resources:

1. It is overpopulated.
2. Disguised unemployment is widespread.
3. The quality of the labor force is exceedingly low.

Overpopulation. Ironically, many of the nations with the most meager natural and capital resources have the largest populations to support. Table 41–2 compares the population of some selected nations with that of the United States. Overpopulation in some of these nations approaches the point at which population actually presses upon the food supply to the extent that per capita food consumption is pulled down perilously close to the subsistence level. In the worst instances it is only the despicable team of malnutrition and disease and the high death rate they provide which keep incomes near subsistence.

It would seem at first glance that, since

$$\text{Per capita standard of living} = \frac{\text{consumer goods (food) production}}{\text{population}}$$

the standard of living could be raised simply by boosting consumer goods—particularly food—production. But in reality the problem is much more complex than this, because any increase in consumer goods production which initially raises the standard of living is likely to induce a population increase. This increase, if sufficient in size, will dissipate the increase in living standards, and sub-

TABLE 41–2. POPULATION PER SQUARE MILE OF SELECTED COUNTRIES, 1962

Country	Population per square mile
United States	52
Cuba	161
China	186
Philippines	256
Pakistan	264
India	376
Haiti	395
Ceylon	418
Japan	664
South Korea	687
Puerto Rico	819

Source: National Industrial Conference Board, *The Economic Almanac, 1964* (New York: Thomas Y. Crowell Company, 1964), pp. 20–21. The datum for China is for 1960.

sistence living levels will again prevail. But why does population growth tend to accompany increases in output?

First, the nation's death rate will decline with initial increases in production. This decline is the result of (1) a higher level of per capita food consumption and (2) the basic medical and sanitation programs which almost invariably accompany the initial phases of economic development. Second, the birth rate will remain high or may even increase, particularly so as the medical and sanitation programs cut the rate of infant mortality. The cliché that "the rich get richer and the poor get children" is uncomfortably accurate for many of the underdeveloped nations of the world. In short, an increase in the per capita standard of living may give rise to a population upsurge which will cease only when the standard of living has again been reduced to the level of bare subsistence.

Most authorities advocate birth control as the obvious and most effective means for breaking out of this dilemma. But the obstacles to this solution are typically great. Those nations which stand to gain most by accepting birth control as a release from this cycle of poverty are often those least willing, for religious and sociocultural reasons, and least able, for literacy reasons, to accept the practice.

Caution: Not all underdeveloped nations suffer from overpopulation, nor is it to be concluded that a large population necessarily means underdevelopment. The points to note are: (1) an initially large population may pose a special obstacle to initiating economic development, and (2) many of the underdeveloped and semideveloped nations are so burdened.

Disguised unemployment. Aside from the drag of overpopulation, the underdeveloped countries are faced with a serious underemployment problem. In contrast to the unemployment in advanced nations the problem is not so much cyclical fluctuations—most underdeveloped nations are simply too poor to afford a business cycle!—but rather a chronic

and large-scale overallocation of labor to agriculture.

How has this problem of disguised unemployment come about? The predominance of agriculture is common to virtually all the underdeveloped nations. It is very likely that two-thirds to four-fifths of an underdeveloped nation's labor force will be engaged in agricultural pursuits. Much— possibly 25 to 30 per cent—of this farm labor is underemployed, or surplus, labor,[3] that is, labor which contributes little or nothing to total agricultural output. In terms of our earlier discussion of the principle of diminishing returns, the agricultural "plant" (the fixed supply of arable land) of most underdeveloped nations is hopelessly overmanned, to the extent that the marginal product of one-fourth or one-third of the nation's agricultural labor force may be zero or even negative! This means that a large fraction of an underdeveloped nation's labor force might be reallocated from agricultural to industrial pursuits with little or no decline, and possibly an increase, in food production.

But, as a matter of fact, this shift of human resources, which we recall is the earmark of a growing economy, has simply not come to pass. Why not? The most important and most obvious reason is that there are very few industrial jobs available in these underdeveloped nations to attract surplus labor from agriculture. The people of underdeveloped nations farm because there is nothing else to do. In addition, ignorance of alternative employments plus a host of religious and sociocultural factors may bind the worker to his land. It is apparently more pleasant to starve while busy (though unproductive) in familiar surroundings than to suffer the same fate in total idleness amidst the impersonal environment of a city. A final factor also retards any potential migration of surplus labor from agriculture to industry: The qual-

[3] See Ragnar Nurkse, *Problems of Capital Formation in Underdeveloped Countries* (Fair Lawn, N.J.: Oxford University Press, 1953), p. 35.

ity of the labor force may prohibit workers from accepting industrial employment even if it were readily available. A minimum level of training and education is necessary in operating the most simple machines; the labor forces of many underdeveloped nations have not as yet achieved that level. The result is that labor immobility is pronounced in most underdeveloped countries, and disguised unemployment persists.

Quality of the labor force. Though long on numbers, the populations of the underdeveloped nations are pitifully short on quality. Malnutrition, the absence of proper medical care, and insufficient educational facilities all contribute to populations ill equipped for economic development and industrialization. Particularly vital is the absence of a vigorous entrepreneurial class willing to bear risks, accumulate capital, and provide the organizational requisites essential to economic growth. Closely related is the dearth of labor prepared to handle the routine supervisory functions basic to any program of development.

Capital Accumulation

Most economists feel that an important focal point of economic development is the accumulation of capital goods. There are several reasons for this emphasis upon capital formation:

1. All underdeveloped countries do suffer from a critical shortage of capital goods—factories, machinery and equipment, public utilities, and so forth. There can be no doubt that better-equipped labor forces would greatly enhance the productivity of the underdeveloped nations and help to boost the per capita standard of living.

2. Increasing the stock of capital goods is crucial because of the very limited possibility of increasing the supply of arable land. If there is little likelihood of offsetting the law of diminishing returns in agriculture by increasing the supply of land, the obvious alternative is to counter its operation by

better equipping the available agricultural manpower or by providing industrial capital to which agricultural labor can be reallocated.

3. Once initiated, the process of capital accumulation can be cumulative. If capital accumulation can increase output ahead of population growth, a margin of saving will arise which permits further capital formation. In a sense capital accumulation can feed upon itself.

Let us first consider the prospects for underdeveloped nations to accumulate capital domestically. Then we shall examine the possibility of foreign capital's flowing into them. In each case we are concerned with private capital; public investment will be considered later.

Domestic capital formation. How does an underdeveloped nation—or any nation for that matter—accumulate capital? The answer: through the processes of saving and investing. A nation must save, that is, refrain from consumption, to release resources from consumer goods production. Investment spending must then occur to absorb these released resources in the production of capital goods. But the impediments to saving and investing are much greater in an underdeveloped nation than in an advanced economy.

The savings potential. Consider first the savings side of the picture. The savings potential of the underdeveloped countries is low. Statistics indicate that the underdeveloped countries manage to save at best some 5 per cent of their national incomes, while the advanced nations save about 10 per cent. In explaining this point it is important to distinguish between (1) the masses of people, who are unable or unwilling to save, and (2) the very wealthy who can save but do not make their savings available for the accumulation of productive capital goods.

1. Saving is a luxury far beyond the reach of the masses of people in the underdeveloped nations; most consume their entire incomes to keep body and soul intact. In-

comes are simply too low to permit the masses to save.

But this is only half the picture. There is serious doubt as to whether significant increases in per capita incomes will generate much saving. Most experts agree that the propensities of underdeveloped nations to consume—that is, their willingness to spend—depend not only upon their own levels of income but also upon the relationship of their income levels to those of the advanced nations. Better communications, increased literacy, expanding hordes of American tourists, and, in some instances, the presence of foreign troops have made the peoples of the underdeveloped nations increasingly aware of the superior consumption levels of the advanced nations. This whets the appetites of the poverty-ridden and intensifies their dissatisfaction with their own standard of living. New wants and higher aspirations lead to a high propensity to consume.[4] The underdeveloped nations, in short, are most anxious to consume, not save, any forthcoming increases in their national incomes.

2. This is not to say that no one saves in an underdeveloped nation. We have noted that saving might be as high as 5 per cent of the national income. This saving stems from the highly unequal distribution of income which characterizes most of the underdeveloped nations. Ironically, both the poorest and the richest families of the world reside in the most underdeveloped countries. Those fortunate few with astronomical incomes—the tribal chieftains, the kings, and the religious leaders—do have ample capacity to save. Unfortunately, these high-income receivers frequently squander their wealth on luxury goods, trivialities, foreign travel, the hoarding of precious metals, or the purchase of existing properties in the form of land or urban real estate. The monetary saving which does occur often flows abroad for safekeeping or to take advantage of the more convenient saving outlets provided by the securities markets of the advanced nations.

[4] *Ibid.,* p. 584.

The important point is that those few who have the ability to save are unwilling to do so or, if they are willing, do not make their savings available for investment in productive facilities.

The investment side. The investment side of the capital formation process abounds with equally serious obstacles. These obstacles serve to undermine the rate of capital formation even when a sufficient volume of savings is available to finance the needed investment. *The major obstacles to investment fall into two categories: the lack of investors and the lack of incentives to invest.*

Oddly enough, in some underdeveloped countries—Turkey and Pakistan, for example—the major obstacle to investment is simply the lack of businessmen who are willing to assume the risks associated with investment. This, of course, is a special case of qualitative deficiencies of the labor force previously discussed.

But even if substantial savings and a vigorous entrepreneurial class are present, an essential ingredient in capital formation—the incentive to invest—may be weak. And clearly a host of factors may combine in an underdeveloped nation to cripple investment incentives. Political and social instability—in particular, the fear of nationalization of industry—may dampen the incentive to invest. Similarly, very low incomes mean a limited domestic market for most nonagricultural goods. This factor is especially crucial when it is recognized that the chances of successfully competing with the mature industries of the advanced nations in international markets are typically nil. Then, too, the previously cited lack of trained administrative and operating personnel may be a vital factor in retarding investment. Finally, many of the underdeveloped countries simply do not have a sufficient accumulation of the *basic social capital,* that is, the public utilities, which are prerequisite to private investment of a productive nature. Poor roads, inadequate railways, little gas and electricity production, antiquated communications, unsatisfactory housing, and meager educational and public health facilities hardly provide an inviting environment for investment spending.

The absence of basic social capital presents more of a problem than one might first surmise. The dearth of social capital means that a great deal of investment spending which does not *directly* result in the production of goods and which may not be capable of bearing profits must take place prior to, and simultaneously with, productive investment in manufacturing machinery and equipment. Statistics for the advanced nations indicate that about 60 per cent of gross investment goes for housing, public works, and public utilities, leaving about 40 per cent for directly productive investment in manufacturing, agriculture, and commerce.[5] These figures probably understate the percentage of total investment which must be devoted to social capital in the underdeveloped nations. The volume of investment required to initiate economic development may be much greater than it first appears.

There is one potential bright spot in this otherwise dismal picture: The possibility of accumulating capital through *nonfinancial investment*, or investment in kind. Given the prerequisite leadership and willingness to cooperate, capital can be accumulated by simply transferring surplus agricultural labor to the improvement of agricultural facilities or to the construction of basic social capital. If each agricultural village would allocate its surplus manpower to the construction of irrigation canals, wells, schools, sanitary facilities, and roads, significant amounts of capital might be accumulated at no sacrifice of consumer goods production. Nonfinancial investment simply bypasses the problems embodied within the financial aspects of the capital accumulation process. Such investment does not require consumers to save portions of their money income, nor does it

presume the presence of an entrepreneurial class anxious to invest. In short, provided the leadership and cooperative spirit are present, nonfinancial investment is a promising avenue for the accumulation of basic capital goods.

External capital formation. Can flows of private capital from the advanced to the underdeveloped nations avoid the obstacles to internal capital formation and thereby compensate for the paucity of investment spending in the underdeveloped nations? Most underdeveloped nations have received considerable assistance from such capital flows. But extreme caution is required lest we regard external capital as a panacea for economic underdevelopment. The obstacles to foreign flows of private capital are serious. Virtually all the deterrents to private domestic investment apply to foreign capital flows. In addition, there are certain unique barriers:

1. The underdeveloped countries seek to make their economies more diversified. They want to develop home markets, on the one hand, and to reduce their dependence upon the economic well-being of the advanced nations, on the other. Foreign private capital, however, seeks out those industries which are currently the most profitable, that is, the ones which are now producing for the export market. In brief, while the underdeveloped nations strive for less dependence on world markets, flows of foreign private capital tend to enhance that dependence.

2. The growing spirit of nationalism in the underdeveloped nations has made them increasingly reluctant to have their domestic economies dominated by foreign interests. Having won political independence, the typical underdeveloped nation seeks control over its own economic machinery. The result has been a maze of policies detrimental to the international flow of private capital into the underdeveloped regions. Discriminatory taxation, limits or prohibitions upon the withdrawal of profits, and cumbersome governmental regulations and red tape concerning incoming capital are some of the more com-

[5] W. Arthur Lewis, *The Theory of Economic Growth* (Homewood, Ill.: Richard D. Irwin, Inc., 1955), p. 210.

mon barriers. To this must be added the ever-present danger of confiscation which political instability entails. This is not to deny that considerable private foreign investment does occur. But, relatively speaking, the flow is not large, and over the years it has failed to keep pace with the rising national incomes of the advanced nations.

Technological Advance

Technological advance and capital formation are frequently part of the same process. Yet there are advantages in treating technological advance, or the accumulation and application of new ideas concerning methods of producing, and capital formation, or the accumulating of capital goods, as separate processes.

This is particularly so in discussing the underdeveloped countries. We view technological advance in the industrially advanced nations as a slow, evolutionary process wherein researchers first inch forward the boundaries of technological knowledge. Then follows the financing and construction of the ever-larger amounts of complex capital equipment which the technological advance demands. But this picture is not accurate for the underdeveloped countries. The rudimentary state of their current technology puts these nations far from the frontiers of technological advance. There already exists a huge body of technological knowledge accumulated by the advanced nations which the underdeveloped countries might adopt and apply without undertaking the expensive tasks of basic research. For example, the adoption of modern crop rotation practices and the introduction of contour plowing require no additional capital equipment, and they may contribute very significantly to productivity. By raising grain storage bins a few inches above the ground, significant grain spoilage can be avoided. Such changes may sound minor to people of advanced nations. However, the resulting gains in productivity can mean the difference between subsistence and starvation in many poverty-ridden nations.

In most instances the application of either existing or new technological knowledge entails the use of new and different capital goods. But, within limits, this capital can be obtained without an increase in the rate of capital formation. That is, if the annual flow of replacement investment is rechanneled from technologically inferior to technologically superior capital equipment, productivity can be increased out of a constant level of investment spending. As a matter of fact, some technological advances may be *capital-saving* rather than *capital-using*. A new fertilizer, better adapted to a nation's topography and climate, might be cheaper than that currently employed. A simple metal plow which will last ten years may be cheaper in the long run than a technologically inferior wooden plow which requires annual replacement.

All this is not to deny that, before a nation's development program is far along, further technological progress will call for an expanding flow of investment in capital goods. However, even here we must keep in mind that the productivity increases which the most fundamental technological advances permit may provide an increase in the standard of living sufficient to generate a part of the saving prerequisite to meeting the nation's expanding capital goods requirements. By boosting incomes, basic technological advances may provide for the capital accumulation upon which still further technological progress depends. To a degree, technological advance and capital formation may feed upon one another. But we must guard against overoptimism even when this mutual reinforcement of technological and capital accumulation occurs. Remember that the lack of entrepreneurs, of qualified industrial labor, or of essential natural resources can block technological progress as effectively as can a dearth of capital equipment.

Social and Institutional Aspects

Purely economic considerations are not sufficent to explain the occurrence or the absence of economic growth. Massive social and institutional readjustments are usually an integral part of the growth process. Economic development entails not only changes in a nation's physical environment (that is, new transportation and communications facilities, new schools, new housing, new plants and equipment) but also drastic changes in the ways in which people think, behave, and associate with one another. The emancipation from custom and tradition is frequently the fundamental prerequisite of economic development. Possibly the most crucial but least tangible ingredient in economic development is "the will to develop." Economic growth may hinge upon ". . . what individuals and social groups *want*, and *whether they want it badly enough to change their old ways of doing things* and to work hard at installing the new."[6]

Eugene Staley, chief economist of a 1950 economic survey mission to Cuba, has outlined an excellent case study of the key role of social and institutional changes in economic growth. Cuba was found to have a relatively high growth potential based upon excellent natural resources, an abundant supply of technical and industrial personnel, sufficient investment capital, and proximity to the vast United States market. Yet Cuba's actual rate of development had been meager. The cause for this poor showing lay in social and institutional barriers to growth.[7]

Public administration was ineffective and often corrupt. The nation received much less than full value for monies invested in public works. These lacked a coherent plan related to development needs and were often left incomplete because of a change in administration. A mass of overly rigid labor regulations, erratically and politically administered, acted as a drag on enterprise, new and old. Like many other countries, Cuba has tried to legislate modern standards of social security without building up the productivity to sustain them. Agricultural experiment and extension services, mining, and other resource surveys, vocational training, current information on economic and social trends, and

other potent aids to economic expansion were inadequate and poorly supported. The tax system was cumbersome and unjust, unnecessarily discouraging constructive initiative. . . . the public school system had been weakened and demoralized by maladministration and large-scale misappropriation of funds. . . .

Commerce and manufacturing mostly followed the old pattern of high markups, low turnover, limited markets. Personnel management, with outstanding exceptions, was 25 to 50 years behind modern practice. This fact, the lack of competent and responsible trade union leadership, the sense of insecurity resulting from an unstable economy, and the lingering resentment in the ranks of labor over past abuses were largely responsible for the extremely bad labor relations which were probably the major obstacle to industrial development. . . .

Though it [Cuba] has ample resources and opportunities, it is caught in a mesh of vicious circles. It could cut its way out if somehow improvement could be brought about in the organizing factors—government, business leadership, labor leadership—and if there could be a stronger sense of social cohesiveness and civic responsibility throughout the community. Here we are at the heart of the social problems of economic development.

Because of the predominance of farming in the underdeveloped nations, the problem of achieving that institutional environment in agriculture which is most conducive to increasing production must be a vital consideration in any growth program. More specifically, the institutional problem of *land reform* demands attention in virtually all underdeveloped nations. But the needed reform may vary tremendously as between specific nations. In some underdeveloped countries the problem assumes the form of excessive concentration of land ownership in the hands of a few wealthy families. This situation is demoralizing for the tenants, weakening their incentive to produce, and is typically not conducive to capital improvements. At the other extreme is the absurd arrangement whereby each and every family owns and farms a minute fragment of land far too small for the application of modern agricultural technology. An important complication to the problem of land reform lies

[6] Staley, *op. cit.*, p. 218.
[7] *Ibid.*, pp. 208–210.

in the fact that political considerations often push land reform in that direction which is least defensible on economic grounds. Land reform may well be the most acute institutional problem to be resolved in initiating the process of economic development.

Crucial Role of Government

One of the most debated aspects of economic development concerns the role of government. What should be the size and nature of the role of an underdeveloped nation's government in the growth process? Such a complex question is not susceptible to a simple answer. Each case must be evaluated separately. The circumstances of one nation may call for vigorous, widespread, and persistent governmental action. In a neighboring nation growth may best be achieved through major reliance upon private enterprise and the price system.

This much can be said with reasonable certainty: At least during the initial stages of economic growth we can expect government to play a more important role in the underdeveloped countries than did the governments of, say, the United States and Great Britain in the initial phases of industrial development in those countries.[8] The economic development of Japan, Germany, and Soviet Russia have all entailed governmental sponsorship and/or direction of the growth process. As a matter of fact, economic development and the level of governmental participation in economic life are positively correlated.[9]

There are several closely related reasons for the expectation that government's role in the development of the underdeveloped

[8] The student of history will recognize that the role of government was considerably greater in the development of the United States and Great Britain than most people recognize or care to admit.

[9] Charles P. Kindleberger, *Economic Development* (New York: McGraw-Hill Book Company, 1958), p. 139.

nations is likely to be a major one. These reasons stem from the character of the obstacles facing these nations.

1. The absence of a sizable and vigorous entrepreneurial class, ready and willing to accumulate capital and initiate production, indicates that in many cases private enterprise is simply not capable of spearheading the growth process.

2. Many of the basic obstacles to economic growth center upon deficiencies of social goods and services. Sanitation and basic medical programs, education, irrigation and soil conservation projects, and the construction of highways and transportation-communication facilities are all essentially indivisible goods and services yielding widespread benefits throughout a nation. These characteristics preclude their production by private enterprise and distribution to consumers through the price system. Government is the sole institution in a position to provide these goods and services in required quantities.

3. Government action may also be required to break through the saving-investment dilemma which impedes capital formation in the underdeveloped nations. We have noted that when the ability to save does exist, the desire to emulate the consumption standards of the advanced nations may make an underdeveloped nation's citizenry unwilling to save. And, when an entrepreneurial class exists, the deficiency of domestic markets and the temptation to invest in the advanced nations may similarly slow capital formation.

It may well be that only governmental action can provide a solution by forcing the economy to accumulate capital. The alternatives here are essentially twofold. One is to force the economy to save by increasing taxes. These tax revenues can then be channeled into top-priority investment projects. The problems of honestly and efficiently administering the tax system and achieving a relatively high degree of compliance with tax laws are frequently very great.

The other alternative is to force the economy to save through inflation; that is, the government can finance capital accumulation by printing and spending new money or by selling bonds to banks and spending the proceeds. The resulting inflation, you will recall, is the equivalent of an arbitrary tax upon the economy. There are serious arguments against the advisability of saving through inflation. In the first place, inflation tends to distort the composition of investment away from productive facilities to such items as luxury housing, precious metals and jewels, or foreign securities, which provide a better hedge against rising prices. Furthermore, significant inflation may reduce voluntary saving as potential savers become less willing to accumulate depreciating money or securities payable in money of declining value. Internationally, inflation may boost the nation's imports and retard its flow of exports, creating balance of payments difficulties.

4. Government is obviously in the key position to deal effectively with the social-institutional obstacles to growth. Population growth—in particular the persistence of high birth rates—is a basic problem which calls for the broad approach that only government can provide. The same can be said for the particularly crucial problem of land reform and the difficulties entailed in inducing the migration of labor from agriculture to industrial pursuits. And government is in an advantageous position to stimulate the will to develop, to change a "Heaven and faith will determine the course of events" philosophy to a "God helps those who help themselves" point of view.

5. The underdeveloped nations seek *rapid* economic growth. The surging spirit of nationalism and the widening gap between the aspirations and the economic positions of the peoples of the underdeveloped nations constantly fan this passion to catch up with the advanced nations. The price system, you will remember, operates slowly, without certainty, and often with little regard for considerations of equity. It may be that government is the only mechanism through which the development process can be accelerated with certainty and with a reasonably equitable distribution of costs.

But all this must not blind us to certain potential problems and disadvantages which a governmentally directed development program may entail. If entrepreneurial talent is lacking in the private sector, can we expect men of quality to be present in the ranks of government? Is there not a real danger that government bureaucracy will prove an impediment, not a stimulus, to much-needed social and economic change? And, too, what of the tendency of centralized economic planning to favor the spectacular "show-piece" projects at the expense of less showy but more productive programs? Might not political objectives take precedence over the economic goals of a governmentally directed development program? Finally, did we not see in our brief notation of the social obstacles to growth in Cuba in 1950 that maladministration, corruption, and a lack of leadership on the part of public officials were major problems?

It must also be emphasized strongly that we are not here advocating socialism or communism as the most likely paths to opulence. The point to be made is that government might well be obligated by the environmental characteristics of an underdeveloped country to provide the incentive and the means of *initially* breaking the poverty barrier. With economic growth there may evolve a price system, an entrepreneurial class, and all the institutions and attitudes prerequisite to a strong private economy. Government may then relinquish its key role, assured that the private sector of the economy is capable of sustaining the growth process. Such has been the role of government in the economic development of Turkey and Japan.

ROLE OF THE ADVANCED NATIONS

Experience suggests that economic development depends primarily upon the capacity and will to develop that are present in a nation's economy. In virtually every case of significant and sustained economic growth most of the initiative and means for development have been provided by that nation's domestic economy. Yet external aid can serve as a vital supplement to any country's development process and may be the deciding factor in the success or failure of its endeavor to grow.

As the most advanced industrial nation of the world, the United States has a very great responsibility to assist in the development of the underdeveloped countries. The United States and the Common Market nations are the only free world sources of economic assistance sufficient to help the underdeveloped nations break the poverty barrier and initiate economic growth. And for both altruistic and selfish reasons we are obligated to provide such assistance. What are the ways in which American capitalism can assist the underdeveloped nations? And to what degree has each of these avenues of assistance been pursued?

The United States has aided the underdeveloped nations through a variety of American programs and through participation in international institutions designed to stimulate economic development.

Loans and Grants

The most obvious way of assisting the underdeveloped nations is to extend credit or simply make outright grants to them. In this way the underdeveloped nations can obtain dollars without having to export; foreign aid permits the underdeveloped nations to offset their low domestic saving potential. Expenditure of foreign loans and grants on American capital goods and technical assistance permits the underdeveloped nations to expand their productive capacity without current curtailment of their domestic standard of living. This correctly implies the vital role which foreign aid can play in the early, crucial years of an underdeveloped nation's growth program. Provided foreign capital is channeled into sufficiently productive uses, loan repayment can be made out of increases which occur in the underdeveloped country's

national income. As noted at the outset of this chapter, there are humanitarian, political-military, and economic reasons underlying American aid to underdeveloped areas.

It is generally recognized that there is a need for both public and private financial assistance to the underdeveloped countries; private capital cannot be expected to do the job itself. This is so for two basic reasons:

1. Many of the underdeveloped nations lack the basic social capital—irrigation and public health programs and educational, transportation, and communications systems —prerequisite to the attraction of either domestic or foreign private capital. Foreign public aid is needed to tear down this major roadblock to the flow of private capital to the underdeveloped countries.

2. In those nations in which the political-military reasons for economic aid are most compelling, the climate for private capital is likely to be least appealing. That is, those nations which are the most undecided as to their ideological allegiance will attract little or no private capital from the West. But at the same time keeping these nations in the free world camp may well depend upon the amount of aid which they can obtain from the West.

After appraising other means by which the advanced nations have helped the underdeveloped nations, we shall discuss the quantitative aspects of American foreign aid.

Export-Import Bank and the World Bank

In 1934 the Export-Import Bank of Washington was created as an agency of the United States government to help in the financing of American exports to ease the domestic unemployment problem of the 1930s. Over the years, the bank's financial resources have been increased substantially and its objectives reoriented in the direction of lending to underdeveloped nations. Such loans have been extended not only to the governments of underdeveloped countries but also to private enterprises for the undertaking of specific development projects. Currently the bank has over $3.5 billion in loans outstanding.

The United States has also been a major participant in the International Bank for Reconstruction and Development. The World Bank, as it is often called, grew out of the same Bretton Woods Conference which gave birth to the International Monetary Fund (IMF). Though its first loans in 1947 were for postwar reconstruction, the World Bank's major objective now is to assist underdeveloped nations in achieving growth. The 102 member nations have subscribed to the bank's $21 billion worth of capital stock roughly in proportion to their economic strength. The share of the United States is approximately one-third of the total. In a sense the $21 billion capital stock figure is misleading. Only a small fraction, about 10 per cent, of the capital stock subscribed has actually been paid in, the remaining 90 per cent being on call. On the other hand, the World Bank not only lends out of its own capital funds but also (1) sells bonds and lends the proceeds and (2) guarantees and insures private loans.

Several characteristics of the World Bank merit comment.

1. The World Bank is in a sense a "last resort" lending agency; that is, its loans are limited to productive projects for which private funds are not readily available.

2. Because many World Bank loans have been for basic development projects—multipurpose dams, irrigation projects, health and sanitation programs, communications and transportation facilities—it has been hoped that the bank's activities will provide the basic social capital prerequisite to substantial flows of private capital.

3. The bank has played a significant role in providing technical assistance to underdeveloped nations by helping them discover what avenues of growth seem most appropriate for their economic development.

The World Bank has met with at least limited success in promoting economic development. Since its operation began in 1947 the World Bank has lent about $8 billion to

nations which can be classified as underdeveloped or semideveloped. Yet two basic criticisms have been levied at the bank. Some economists feel that it has been overly conservative in its lending policies; $8 billion spread over two decades is a relatively small amount of lending in view of the tremendous needs of the underdeveloped nations. Furthermore, the bank has only been mildly successful in stimulating the flow of private capital to the underdeveloped nations.

The Point Four Program

Underdevelopment cannot be remedied by capital formation alone; technical assistance is equally essential and in many cases more productive dollar for dollar than is the acquisition of real capital. Earlier American aid programs that provided tractors, but not knowledge of how to operate them, brought home the urgency of American exports of technological "know-how."

In his inaugural address of 1949, President Truman laid the basis for a program designed to encourage the growth of underdeveloped nations through the extending of technical assistance by the United States.

Fourth, we must embark on a bold new program for making the benefits of our scientific advances and industrial progress available for the improvement and growth of underdeveloped areas.

The United States is pre-eminent among nations in the development of industrial and scientific techniques. The material resources which we can afford to use for the assistance of other peoples are limited. But our imponderable resources in technical knowledge are constantly growing and are inexhaustible.

I believe that we should make available to peace-loving peoples the benefits of our store of technical knowledge in order to help them realize their aspirations for a better life. . . .

Our aim should be to help the free peoples of the world, through their own efforts, to produce more food, more clothing, more materials for housing, and more mechanical power to lighten their burdens.

Point Four was put into effect in 1950. Currently several thousand American technicians are scattered about the globe, increasing the stocks of knowledge in the underdeveloped nations. In general this grass-roots approach to economic development has met with considerable success; results in particular instances have been startling.

Expanding the Volume of Trade

Some authorities contend that the simplest and most effective means by which the United States can aid the underdeveloped nations is by lowering trade barriers. "Trade, not aid," they say, will promote economic development. The easing of American protective tariffs and the elimination of import quotas will allegedly enable foreign nations to expand their national incomes through an increased volume of trade with the United States.

Though there is undoubtedly a kernel of truth in this view, it is easily exaggerated. It is true that some nations—for example, Iraq, Saudi Arabia, and Venezuela—need only obtain large foreign markets for their raw materials to achieve some measure of growth. Other underdeveloped nations, however, clearly need trade *and* aid. Their problem is not that of obtaining markets for the utilization of existing productive capacity or the sale of relatively abundant raw materials, but rather the more fundamental one of getting the capital and technical assistance needed to produce something for export! An expansion of international trade will help most of the underdeveloped nations, but it will not prove a panacea for the problems of most of them. Ironically, while condemning the trade restrictions of the industrially advanced nations, many of the underdeveloped nations have simultaneously invoked higher tariffs, import quotas, and exchange controls to encourage the growth of their domestic industries.

American Economic Stability

In absolute terms the United States is the leading trading nation of the world. Like it or not, many other nations—both underdeveloped and semideveloped—find their economies closely linked to the health of American capitalism. The old quip that "When Uncle Sam gets his feet wet, the rest of the world gets pneumonia" is of some accuracy.[10]

A recession both in the United States and in Europe, though relatively mild, will typically cause serious suffering and hardship in the underdeveloped countries. Indeed in the 1958 recession the losses sustained by the underdeveloped countries by reason of the decline in raw-material prices by far outweighed any foreign aid given over several years.

The implication of these comments is clear: The maintenance of domestic full employment and relative price stability may be the greatest contribution which American capitalism can make to the progress of the underdeveloped nations. This suggests in turn that the United States should seek full employment through domestic fiscal and monetary policies, not through the artificial manipulation of imports and exports. The inappropriate and self-defeating character of attempts to "export unemployment" was illustrated all too clearly by the Hawley-Smoot Tariff Act in 1930. Any American attempt to increase domestic employment by restricting imports in relation to exports will greatly intensify, not relieve, the weighty problems of economic development faced by our less fortunate neighbors.

Too Little, Too Late?

How much economic aid is needed to provide a noticeable increase in the standard of

[10] Alvin H. Hansen, *Economic Issues of the 1960's* (New York: McGraw-Hill Book Company, 1961), p. 136.

living of the underdeveloped nations of the free world? A recent estimate indicates that a reasonable rate of growth—a 1 to 2 per cent annual increase in per capita incomes—will require from $5 to $10 billion of foreign capital per year over the next 10 or 15 years. After this time, it is hoped that the underdeveloped nations would be off dead center and growth would be self-sustaining.[11]

How much aid has the United States provided for underdeveloped nations? Though any answer to this question will depend upon the breadth of one's definition of "aid," the statistical data of Table 40–1 provide a partial answer. Although United States foreign aid totaled about $89 billion in the postwar period (1945 to 1963), only $57 billion of this was for economic assistance; the remaining $32 billion was in the form of military assistance. Furthermore, the relatively advanced nations of Europe received about $24 billion—about 42 per cent—of this $57 billion worth of American aid, much of it under the Marshall Plan. Of the remaining $33 billion, $2.6 billion went to Japan, whose level of economic growth and industrialization is relatively great; another $3.5 billion went to underdeveloped nations for disaster relief. This leaves $27 billion worth of aid actually available for economic development —slightly less than $1.5 billion each year. In relative terms this amounts to about ⅓ to ¼ of one per cent of the United States' GNP! Of course, private capital flows and international lending agencies have helped some. But at best the annual total flow of aid for economic development is currently at about the $3 billion level, clearly short of the minimum goal noted above. One has little choice but to conclude that American economic aid to the underdeveloped nations has been anything but extravagant. And, as one authority has put it,[12]

There is practically no danger that the United States government will spend more than our national interest requires on economic aid to underdeveloped countries. The danger is all the other way. Underdeveloped countries are not represented in Congress where the appropriation logs are rolled, and the compelling American interest in the advancement of the underdeveloped parts of the free world is less easy for statesmen to explain than for narrowmindedness and shortsightedness to obscure.

The implications of the relative paucity of American aid to the underdeveloped nations are many. In particular, the ideological clash between the "free world" and communism may well be won or lost on the basis of the relative rates of growth achieved by the underdeveloped nations of the free world and their communist-dominated brethren.

Soviet Aid Offensive[13]

Until 1953 the free world nations, and the United States in particular, were the sole source of aid to the underdeveloped nations. But in that year the Soviet Union inaugurated a competitive aid offensive. Several factors underlay the development of this program.

1. Russia's post-Stalin leaders have been more interested in a growing international role for the U.S.S.R. than was their predecessor.

2. By 1953 the Soviet Union had recovered from the war and was achieving substantial economic growth; hence, it now had the economic capacity to extend foreign aid.

3. Finally, the Soviet aid program was designed to offset the effectiveness of

[11] Delbert A. Snider, *Introduction to International Economics,* rev. ed. (Homewood, Ill.: Richard D. Irwin, Inc., 1958), p. 543.
[12] Staley, *op. cit.,* p. 372.

[13] This section has benefited greatly from Franklyn D. Holzman, "Moscow's Motives—Profits or Politics?" *Challenge,* April, 1961, pp. 13–17, and G. S. Carnett and M. H. Crawford, "The Scope and Distribution of Soviet Economic Aid," and Leon M. Herman, "The Political Goals of Soviet Foreign Aid," in Joint Economic Committee, *Dimensions of Soviet Economic Power* (Washington, D.C., 1962), pp. 461–485.

American aid in thwarting the spread of communism in both the underdeveloped countries and Europe.

As is the case with Russian foreign trade, Soviet aid is motivated by both economic and political considerations. At least two facts underscore the importance of political considerations. First, Soviet aid conflicts with the tremendous emphasis which the U.S.S.R. puts upon its own domestic industrialization program. Soviet foreign aid entails the exportation of machinery, equipment, and highly skilled human resources which the Soviet Union could well use at home to fulfill the ambitious targets of its Five- and Seven-year Plans. Secondly, in payment for its loans the U.S.S.R. has frequently been willing to accept certain raw materials and foodstuffs which it has in ample supply domestically. The political-ideological return which the Soviet Union anticipates from its aid may take the form of a genuine political friendship with the underdeveloped nations wherein aid is followed by trade missions, educational and cultural exchanges, and the export of Soviet "technicians," or aid may lead to close economic ties and ultimately economic and political dependence upon the Soviet Union.

Although the Soviet aid program has expanded substantially since 1953, it is currently modest in comparison to the United States program. Aid from the entire Soviet bloc now amounts to $1 billion per year while our total aid averages about $3 or $4 billion per year. However, the political-ideological and propaganda impacts of Soviet aid have been out of proportion to its volume. A number of factors explain why the propagandist and political impact of Soviet aid has been so very substantial. Consider briefly three of the more significant:

1. The Soviet aid program has attracted favorable comment because of its relative newness. To many underdeveloped nations Soviet aid is novel; United States aid is "old hat." Uncle Sam suffers from a "what have you done for us that's new?" effect in its aid competition with the U.S.S.R.

2. The Soviets have been more willing to go along with the whims and desires of the recipient nations for specific projects than have the Americans. Soviet aid has catered to the underdeveloped nations' desire for industrial development; Soviet aid has tended to emphasize the construction of facilities for heavy industry, for example, steel plants. United States aid, on the other hand, has been more concerned with the economic soundness of development projects and, therefore, has been directed toward less spectacular projects involving agricultural development, sanitation, and the providing of basic social capital.

3. Soviet aid has generally taken the form of low-interest (2 per cent) "businesslike" loans, while American aid has been largely in the form of grants or, less frequently, relatively high-interest (4 to 5 per cent) loans. Soviet propaganda has managed with some success to decry our grants as a debasing form of charity which implies political, ideological, and military commitments from the recipients and, at the same time, to criticize our loans because of the "exploitative" interest rates they entail!

"Key Countries" Approach[14]

American aid to the underdeveloped countries has been subjected to critical appraisal in recent years. This criticism has diverse roots. First, the ideological-political impact of Soviet aid has often seemed great relative to that of our aid. Second, substantial segments of the public feel that other advanced nations such as West Germany and Japan, now fully recovered from World War II and achieving growth rates in excess of ours, should shoulder a greater share of the foreign aid burden. Third, our heavy foreign aid commitments clearly complicate our balance of payments difficulties; a decline in United States' aid would help correct our payments

[14] See Walter Krause, *Economic Development* (San Francisco: Wadsworth Publishing Company, Inc., 1961), chaps. 23 and 24.

deficit (Table 39–2). Fourth, many people object to extending aid to nations whose ideologies are seriously at odds with those of the United States. Fifth, the Johnson Administration's emphasis upon "The Great Society" has refocused attention upon long-neglected domestic problems and, at least relatively, this has tended to downgrade our international obligations. Finally, the most telling criticism perhaps is that United States' foreign aid programs have had at best a minor impact upon the recipient nations. The growth rates of most recipient countries are about the same as they were a decade ago. Assuming that humanitarian, economic, and political considerations preclude any suggestion that the United States abandon its aid program, what are the alternatives?

On the one hand, given the level of our GNP, we have ample resources with which to expand the volume of our foreign aid. But, as we have already noted, domestic political considerations make unlikely any dramatic increases in our foreign aid budget. Indeed, we have been tightening the purse strings on foreign aid the last few years. A second alternative is to restructure and reorient the use of the available funds in an effort to increase the economic effectiveness of our aid. In particular, it has been argued that the basic flaw in the present program is that we spread a relatively modest amount of aid very thinly over some ninety-five recipient nations and territories with the result that no significant growth is achieved anywhere. We are trying, it is argued, to do "too much for too many too soon." (The Russians, incidentally, concentrate the vast bulk of their aid on only ten or twelve nations.) Hence, it is contended that the United States should redistribute the bulk of its aid in the direction of a relatively few "key countries." The key countries would be those which

1. Have the greatest economic potential for achieving growth

2. Possess the "will to develop" as reflected in their willingness to initiate land and tax reform, establish sound fiscal and monetary policies, and maintain a stable,

honest, and reasonably efficient government

3. Are strategic politically, geographically, or in terms of land and population size

Thus, for example, Brazil in South America, Turkey in the Middle East, and India in Asia might readily be labeled as key countries.

Advocates of the key country approach to American aid cite two potential merits of such a reorientation. First and foremost, this approach has a greater chance of success than our present one. Because they now will receive a substantially larger amount of aid, the key countries are in a better position to establish the conditions necessary for getting off dead center and into a process of self-sustaining economic growth. Furthermore, this approach puts the underdeveloped nations in a position in which they must display a will to develop and to make necessary institutional and policy changes in order to qualify as key countries. A second and more selfish merit is this: The key countries approach might effectively meet the Soviet aid challenge. We shall find in Chapter 42 that the Soviet Union itself is an outstanding example of rapid industrialization and economic growth achieved under a system of totalitarian central economic planning. The economic achievements of the U.S.S.R. have favorably impressed many underdeveloped nations. The free world would benefit substantially if it were able to demonstrate by example to the uncommitted nations of the world that an underdeveloped country can achieve economic progress through non-totalitarian techniques.

The main weakness of the key countries approach lies in the fact that for a time many underdeveloped countries—the non-key countries—would receive less aid than they do now. But there are possible offsets: Assuming the current key countries will achieve self-sustaining growth, aid to these advancing countries could be reduced in the future and reallocated to other nations, which could then be reclassified as key countries. That is, the nations which get less aid now would conceivably get a larger amount of aid in the long run. In addition, the total volume of aid coming from the free world—the United States and the Common Market nations in particular—may hopefully be expected to increase modestly in the future, thereby mitigating the declines in aid to non-key countries.

Alliance for Progress

Some of the thinking underlying the key countries approach to foreign aid is reflected in the Alliance for Progress program. Established in 1961, the Alliance obligated the United States to provide some $20 billion worth of aid to South America over the next ten years. The program simultaneously obligates the recipient Latin American nations to undertake a number of self-help measures which are felt to be prerequisite to the effective utilization of American aid. Specifically, such institutional changes as tax reform, land reform, and the establishment of a stable and reasonably efficient political system (conditions which would be characteristic of key countries) are required of the South American nations. Although it is too early to evaluate the effectiveness and potential of the Alliance for Progress, many close observers are of the opinion that the economic and political destinies of the Latin American nations may well be intimately related to the fate of the Alliance.

SUMMARY

1. Most nations of the world are underdeveloped (low per capita income) nations. Spurred by **a.** the widening gap between their incomes and those of the advanced nations and **b.** the rising spirit of nationalism, the people of the underdeveloped nations are far from content with their current economic status.

2. Initial scarcities of natural resources and the limited possibility of augmenting existing supplies may impose a rigid limitation upon a nation's capacity to develop.

3. The presence of large populations in the underdeveloped countries contributes to low per capita incomes. In particular, increases in per capita incomes frequently induce rapid population growth to the end that per capita incomes again deteriorate back to near-subsistence levels.

4. Disguised unemployment in the form of surplus agricultural labor exists in most of the underdeveloped nations. This underemployment stems from the absence of alternative job opportunities, on the one hand, and the occupational and geographic immobility of agricultural labor, on the other.

5. In the underdeveloped nations both the saving and investment aspects of the capital formation process are impeded by formidable obstacles. The vast majority of households in the underdeveloped nations receive incomes too small to permit them to save. Furthermore, little saving may be forthcoming out of incomes considerably higher than those currently received by this group. A high propensity to consume accounts for this expectation. The very wealthy have considerable ability to save but prefer to spend lavishly or to invest their savings unproductively.

6. The absence of a vigorous entrepreneurial class and the weakness of investment incentives are the major obstacles to capital accumulation when money capital is readily available. Political and social instability, the lack of large domestic markets, shortages of operating and administrative personnel, and deficiencies of basic social capital all contribute to an uninviting environment for private investment. Some degree of capital accumulation can usually be achieved, however, through nonfinancial investment.

7. Discriminatory taxation, limits and prohibitions upon profit withdrawals, and a host of diverse government regulations are additional obstacles which impair the flow of private capital from the advanced to the underdeveloped nations.

8. Within limits the underdeveloped nations may achieve a degree of technological advance with little or no increase in their expenditures for research and- capital accumulation. It must be acknowledged, however, that severe limitations may be imposed upon such advance by capital accumulation and the requirements of natural and human resources.

9. Appropriate alterations in the quantity and quality of a nation's economic resources will not guarantee economic growth. Appropriate social and institutional arrangements and, in particular, the presence of "the will to develop" are essential ingredients in economic development.

10. The role of government in the development of the underdeveloped nations is likely to be considerable. The nature of the obstacles to growth—the absence of an entrepreneurial class, the dearth of social capital, the saving-investment dilemma, and the presence of social-institutional obstacles to growth—and the fact that the underdeveloped nations seek rapid growth suggest the need for government action in initiating the growth process.

11. The United States can assist the underdeveloped nations in their quest for growth in several ways. **a.** The United States can extend aid in the form of grants, loans, and technical assistance directly through American programs and institutions—for example, the Export-Import Bank and the

Point Four program—or indirectly through participation in international institutions—for example, the World Bank. **b.** By reducing its trade barriers, the United States can help the underdeveloped nations increase their national incomes through an expanding volume of international trade. **c.** Finally, the United States can help provide a world environment conducive to economic development by maintaining domestic economic stability. American economic aid to the underdeveloped nations has been modest in relative terms.

12. In 1953 the Soviet Union inaugurated a competing program of aid to the underdeveloped nations which has strong political-ideological overtones. Although the volume of Soviet aid relative to United States aid has been small, the political and propagandist impact of the Soviet program has been substantial. This success has prompted a number of American experts to advocate a new "key countries" approach to our own aid program in an effort to enhance its effectiveness in promoting self-sustaining growth in the underdeveloped nations.

13. The Alliance for Progress obligates the United States to extend $20 billion in aid to Latin America over the decade of the 1960s and requires the recipient nations to negotiate a number of domestic reforms.

QUESTIONS AND STUDY SUGGESTIONS

1. What are the major characteristics of an underdeveloped nation? List the major avenues of economic development available to such a nation. State and explain the obstacles which face the underdeveloped nations in breaking the poverty barrier. Now outline in detail the steps which an underdeveloped country might take to initiate economic development.

2. "The path to economic development has been clearly blazed by American capitalism. It is only for the underdeveloped nations to follow this trail." Critically evaluate.

3. "Economic inequality is conducive to saving, and saving is the prerequisite of investment. Therefore, greater inequality in the income distribution of the underdeveloped countries would be a spur to capital accumulation and growth." Critically evaluate.

4. "The spirit of nationalism sometimes aids and sometimes impedes the process of economic growth." Explain and illustrate.

5. "The underdeveloped nations are hurting themselves by seeking too quickly living standards and social legislation which their productive potential is now incapable of producing. They must resign themselves to 'less now' to get 'more later.'" To what degree is this position valid? What problems might its application entail?

6. "The advanced economies fear the complications which stem from over-saving; the underdeveloped countries bear the yoke of undersaving." Explain.

7. "The core of the development process involves changing human beings more than it does altering a nation's physical environment." Critically evaluate.

8. Much of the initial investment in an underdeveloped country must be devoted to basic social capital which does not directly or immediately result in a greater production of goods and services. What bearing might this have upon the degree of inflation which results as government finances capital accumulation through the printing and spending of new money? Be specific.

9. "The nature of the problems faced by the underdeveloped nations creates a bias in favor of a governmentally directed as opposed to a decentralized development process." Do you agree? Substantiate your position. If you do agree, specify the implications of your position for the foreign aid programs of the United States.

10. Contrast United States and Soviet aid programs as to characteristics of the aid. Given its modest size as compared with the United States program, why has the Soviet program yielded substantial political and propagandist returns to the U.S.S.R?

11. What is the "key countries" approach to foreign aid? What are its advantages and disadvantages? Would you recommend such a reorientation of our present aid program? Describe briefly the Alliance for Progress.

12. Explain and evaluate: "Poverty and freedom cannot persist side by side; one must triumph over the other."

SELECTED REFERENCES

Bauer, Peter T., and Basil S. Yamey: *The Economics of Underdeveloped Countries* (Chicago: The University of Chicago Press, 1957).

Gill, Richard T.: *Economic Development: Past and Present* (Englewood Cliffs, N.J.: Prentice-Hall, Inc., 1963), chaps. 2, 3, 5, and 6.

Heilbroner, Robert L.: *The Great Ascent* (New York: Harper & Row, Publishers, Incorporated, 1963).

Kindleberger, Charles P.: *Economic Development*, 2d ed. (New York: McGraw-Hill Book Company, 1965).

Krause, Walter: *Economic Development* (San Francisco: Wadsworth Publishing Company, Inc., 1961).

Mikesell, Raymond F., and Robert Loring Allen: *Economic Policies toward Less Developed Countries*, for the Joint Economic Committee (Washington, D.C., 1961).

Millikan, Max F., and Donald L. M. Blackmer (eds.): *The Emerging Nations* (Boston: Little Brown and Company, 1961).

Novack, David E., and Robert Lekachman (eds.): *Development and Society* (New York: St Martin's Press, Inc., 1964).

Randall, Laura (ed.): *Economic Development: Evolution or Revolution?* (Boston: D. C. Heath and Company, 1964).

Ranis, Gustav (ed.): *The United States and the Developing Economies* (New York: W. W. Norton & Company, Inc., 1964).

Singer, Hans W.: *International Development: Growth and Change* (New York: McGraw-Hill Book Company, 1964).

Staley, Eugene: *The Future of Underdeveloped Countries* (New York: Harper & Row, Publishers, Incorporated, for the Council on Foreign Relations, 1954).

THE UNDERDEVELOPED COUNTRIES:
A SPECIAL PROBLEM
IN ECONOMIC GROWTH

It is exceedingly difficult for the typical American family, whose 1964 average income was $6,140, to grasp the simple fact that some two-thirds of the world's population is persistently on the brink of starvation. The typical American is too busy waging a loud but losing battle against obesity or watching his television set to acknowledge the abject poverty which characterizes much of our planet. A five-room suburban home, a new Buick, and a healthy bank account all tend to make the hunger, squalor, and disease which prevail in most nations of the world seem remote.

UNDERSTANDING THE UNDERDEVELOPED NATIONS

This ignorance and lack of concern cannot be condoned. We must

1. Identify the underdeveloped nations
2. Appreciate the attitudes of the peoples of the underdeveloped nations toward their economic circumstances
3. Understand the interest of the advanced nations in the development of these nations

Low per Capita Income

The underdeveloped nations of the world bear a common brand: poverty—low per capita incomes as compared with such industrially advanced countries as the United States, Great Britain, and Canada. Table

41–1 clearly identifies most of the underdeveloped nations. Of course, where one draws the line between "developed," "semideveloped," and "underdeveloped" is an arbitrary matter. Nevertheless, in Table 41–1 we can roughly envision these three classifications. Looking at the 1961 data, we might tag those nations with per capita incomes of $700 or more as developed, or advanced, nations. Included here, primarily, are the United States, Canada, Australia, New Zealand, and the countries of Western Europe. Next is the semideveloped group, whose per capita incomes vary from, say, $350 to $699 per year. This heterogeneous group includes several Latin American nations, several countries of Eastern and Southern Europe, South Africa, and Japan, Ireland, and Israel. The rest of the world—including most of Asia, Africa, Latin America, and Southeastern Europe—bear the designation "underdeveloped."

We need not belabor the pitifully low per capita annual incomes evidenced in Table 41–1. However, the implications of the poverty reflected by these figures merit emphasis.[1]

The poverty of underdeveloped countries means that their people, on a broad average, have a life expectancy only about half that of the

[1] Eugene Staley, *The Future of Underdeveloped Countries* (New York: Harper & Row, Publishers, Incorporated, for the Council on Foreign Relations, 1954), pp. 15–18.

CHAPTER 42

THE ECONOMIC CHALLENGE
OF SOVIET RUSSIA[1]

In November of 1957 Nikita Khrushchev declared economic war on the United States with these rather immodest assertions:

We declare war upon you—excuse me for using such an expression—in the peaceful field of trade. We declare war. We will win over the United States. The threat to the United States is not the ICBM, but in the field of peaceful production. We are relentless in this and it will prove the superiority of our system.

This Soviet challenge—which, of course, has military, political, and sociocultural as well as economic aspects—is not simply a propaganda blast or an idle threat. It is a well-acknowledged reality. Furthermore, there is no serious doubt that the new Soviet leadership remains committed to this boast. We turn, then, in this final chapter to an analysis of this competing economy. We want to survey its institutions, understand its goals, evaluate its performance, and appreciate the challenge it poses for the West. There are two notable by-products of this endeavor. First, the Soviet economy is a fascinating case study in forced economic growth; the accomplishments and shortcomings of the Soviet system in vigorously pursuing economic growth provide invaluable

[1] This chapter is necessarily a brief survey of a very complex economy. Space simply does not permit a detailed analysis of many important and interesting aspects of Soviet economic life. The interested reader is urged to consult the highly recommended references cited at the end of the chapter and in the pages that follow.

lessons. Second, by examining an economy at the opposite end of the ideological spectrum, we cannot help but deepen our understanding of the capitalistic system.

INSTITUTIONS OF THE COMMAND ECONOMY

There are two outstanding institutional characteristics of the Soviet economy: (1) the public ownership of property resources and (2) central economic planning.

Public Ownership

The Soviet constitution of 1936 makes the pervasiveness of public ownership of property resources quite clear:

Article IV. The economic foundation of the U.S.S.R. is the socialist system of economy and the socialist ownership of the instruments and means of production, firmly established as a result of the liquidation of the capitalist system of economy, the abolition of private ownership of the instruments and means of production, and the elimination of the exploitation of man by man.

Article V. Socialist property in the U.S.S.R. exists either in the form of state property (belonging to the whole people) or in the form of cooperative and collective-farm property (property of collective farms, property of cooperative societies).

The Soviet state owns all land, natural resources, transportation and communication facilities, the banking system, and virtually all of industry. Most retail and wholesale enterprises and most urban housing are governmentally owned. In agriculture many farms are state owned; most, however, are government-organized collective farms, that is, essentially cooperatives. The main exception to public ownership is the small plot of land which each collective farm family has set aside for its personal use: "Every household on a collective farm . . . has for its personal use a small plot of household land and, as its personal property, a subsidiary husbandry on the plot, a dwelling house, livestock, poultry, and minor agricultural implements. . . ." And, of course, clothing, household furnishings, and small tools and implements used by craftsmen are privately owned. Workers in rural areas and farmers typically own their homes as do over one-third of all urban families.

Central Economic Planning

Despite a highly democratic constitution, in practice the government of Soviet Russia is a strong dictatorship. The Communist party, although its membership includes only 4 or 5 per cent of the total population, stands unchallenged. Indeed, the party and the government can be regarded as virtually synonymous.

As the constitution makes clear, the Soviet government, through economic planning, sets the objectives of the economy and directs resources toward the attainment of these goals:

Article XI. The economic life of the U.S.S.R. is determined and directed by the state national economic plan, with the aim of increasing the public wealth, of steadily raising the material and cultural standards of the working people, and of consolidating the independence of the U.S.S.R. and strengthening its defensive capacity.

In contrast with the decentralized market economy of the United States, that of the Soviet Union is a centralized, "command" economy which functions in terms of a detailed economic plan. The economy of the Soviet Union is government-directed rather than price-directed.

Circumscribed Freedom

The dominant roles of public ownership and central planning correctly imply that it is not the free decisions of consumers and businessmen which determine the allocation of resources and the composition of total output in the Soviet Union. Yet we must recognize that, subject to the overall restraints imposed by the central planners, consumers and laborers have a degree of free choice.

The concept of consumer sovereignty as we know it does not exist in the Soviet Union. The preferences of individual consumers, as reflected in the size and structure of consumer demand, do *not* determine the volume and composition of consumer goods production in Soviet Russia; this determination is made by the government. However, consumers are free to spend their money incomes as they see fit on those consumer goods for which the central plan provides.

Similarly, although the Soviet Union has a history of compulsory job assignment, harsh labor codes, and, in the extreme, slave labor, much greater reliance has been put upon free occupational choice in recent years. But, again, there are overall restraints imposed by the central plan. The composition of output as determined by the plan establishes the number and kinds of jobs available. Then the government planners set wage rates so as to attract the needed number and types of workers to the various occupations. If the plan assigns great importance to steel and a low priority to shoes, jobs will be plentiful and wage rates established at a high level in the steel industry. Conversely, few jobs will be available and wages will be low in the shoe industry. In short, workers are largely free to change jobs in response to wage differentials; the differentials, however, are designed and manipulated to bring about an allocation of labor both geographically and occupationally which is consistent with the goals of the plan.

CENTRAL PLANNING

Perhaps the most dramatic feature of the Soviet economy is its use of central planning. In the Soviet Union the means of answering the Five Fundamental Questions is central planning. Choices made primarily through the market in our economy must be consciously made by bureaucratic decision in the U.S.S.R. The overall character of the Soviet Five- and Seven-year Plans has been succinctly described in these words: [2]

The Soviet economic plan is a gigantic, comprehensive blueprint that attempts to govern the economic activities and interrelations of all persons and institutions in the U.S.S.R., as well as the economic relations of the U.S.S.R. with other countries. To the extent that the plan actually controls the development of events, all the manifold activities of the Soviet economy are coordinated as if they were parts of one incredibly enormous enterprise directed from the central headquarters in Moscow.

Now let us probe below the surface. What are the goals of the plans? How are the plans constructed and implemented? What problems does central planning entail?

Planning Goals

The Soviet government—in reality the Communist party—sets the basic objectives for the Russian economy. These objectives have varied somewhat as succeeding Five-year Plans have been formulated, but emphasis has been upon rapid economic growth through the development of heavy industry. The attainment of a high level of military strength is a closely correlated goal. Lip service is invariably accorded the goal of a

[2] Harry Schwartz, *Russia's Soviet Economy*, 2d ed. (Englewood Cliffs, N.J.: Prentice-Hall, Inc., 1954), p. 146.

higher standard of living for consumers, but the lower priority assigned to this goal means that it is frequently sacrificed to achieve the objectives of industrial expansion and military strength.

Basic Planning Problem: Coordination

It is no simple matter to sweep away the market system, as the Soviet Union has done, and replace it with an effective central plan. After all, we have found that the market system is a powerful organizing force which coordinates millions upon millions of individual decisions by consumers, entrepreneurs, and resource suppliers and fosters a reasonably efficient allocation of resources. Is central planning a satisfactory substitute for the market?

The core of the planning problem is revealed by the input-output table (Table 33–1). Input-output analysis, you will recall, reveals the highly interdependent character of the various industries or sectors of the economy. Each industry employs the outputs of other industries as its inputs; in turn its outputs are inputs to still other firms. This means that a planning decision to increase the production of machinery by, say, 10 per cent is not a single, isolated directive, but rather a decision which implies a myriad of related decisions for fulfillment. For example, in terms of Table 33–1, if planners do not make the related decisions to increase metal output by 6.5 units, fuel by 0.5 unit, agricultural products by 1 unit, and to provide an extra 20 units of labor (not to mention additional second-round increases in all these inputs because 2.5 more inputs of machinery are also needed to increase machinery output!), bottlenecks will develop, and the planned increase in machinery output cannot be realized.

Let us look at the matter from a slightly different vantage point: Even if an internally consistent set of decisions—a perfectly coordinated plan—could be constructed by the central planners, the failure of any single industry to fulfill its output target would cause an almost endless chain of adverse repercussions. If iron mines—for want of machinery or labor or transportation inputs— fail to supply the steel industry with the required inputs of iron ore, the steel industry in turn will be unable to fulfill the input needs of the myriad of industries dependent upon steel. All of these steel-using industries will be unable to fulfill their planned production goals. And so the bottleneck chain reaction goes on to all those firms which use steel parts or components as inputs.

It must be emphasized that our illustrative input-output table (Table 33–1) is a gross oversimplification of the problem of coordinating a command economy. There are now some 200,000 industrial enterprises producing goods in the Soviet Union. The central planners must see to it that all of the resources needed by these enterprises to fulfill their assigned production targets are somehow allocated to them.[3]

The literally billions of planning decisions that must be made to achieve consistency result in a complex and complete interlocking of macro- and micromanagement. . . . The number of planned interconnections increases more rapidly than the size of the economy, and since 1953 the Soviet economy has doubled in terms of national production. . . . Even with the most sophisticated mathematical techniques and electronic computers, the task of interrelating demands and factor inputs for every possible item by every possible subcategory becomes impossible for the central planners alone.

Coordination Techniques

Despite the gargantuan character of the coordination problem, Soviet central planning has worked and in some respects has functioned remarkably well. It is certainly legitimate to inquire: Why? What techniques do Soviet planners employ to achieve the level of coordination sufficient to make central planning workable? The answers lie substantially in the way the plans are constructed and implemented.

1. Planning by negotiation. Given the overall economic objectives established by the Communist party, it is the task of the state planning commission, or *Gosplan*, to construct a detailed economic blueprint designed to bring about the realization of these goals. In formulating a plan, the Gosplan collects voluminous amounts of statistical data from a host of subordinate ministries, each of which is concerned with the operation of certain industries. From these data, a tentative plan is constructed. The plan is then submitted to the various units of the Soviet administrative hierarchy for study, evaluation, and criticism. This criticism, it must be noted, concerns the specific details of the economic plan and not the overall goals which the plan seeks.

Let us illustrate this procedure. Note, first, that there are two obvious organizational alternatives for a planned economy: geographical (regional) and functional (industrial). All enterprises in a given region may be grouped for planning purposes or all enterprises in a given industry may be grouped for planning regardless of their location. Over time the Soviet Union has used both alternatives and mixtures of the two. Currently the emphasis is upon the regional approach and some 47 regional economic councils (called *sovnarkhozy*) are subordinate to Gosplan in the planning hierarchy. The important point is that relevant segments of the overall plan are submitted to the subordinate agencies, which exercise operational control. Thus the plans are evaluated at the regional level, by the trusts and combines—that is, groups of plants which are combined for administrative purposes—and ultimately by the individual plants or enterprises. At each level the plan is analyzed, suggestions are made for revision, and perhaps alterations are proposed in production goals or planned allocations of inputs. These evaluations are passed back up

[3] Barry M. Richman, *Soviet Management* (Englewood Cliffs, N.J.: Prentice-Hall, Inc., 1965), p. 17.

the planning hierarchy to Gosplan. Taking into account those suggestions and criticisms which it feels are worthy, Gosplan then draws up a final plan. When rubber-stamped by the party and the government, this becomes the Five- or Seven-Year Plan.

The point to be emphasized is this: By breaking the overall plan into its component parts and subjecting these detailed segments to considerable critical examination by sub-ministries, combines, and plants, the Gosplan is able to establish a final plan which is more realistic and workable than would otherwise be the case. Soviet planners apparently recognize their limitations in obtaining and digesting masses of detailed information. The "down-and-up" evaluation of the tentative plan by the administrative hierarchy and its subsequent revision is aimed at obtaining on-the-spot knowledge and an understanding of immediate, detailed facts and circumstances which a relatively small group of planners could not otherwise grasp. To the extent that the resulting plan is more realistic and feasible, the chance is less that problems of coordination—in particular, bottlenecks—will arise to jeopardize plan fulfillment.

2. The priority principle. A second means of making central planning workable is embodied in the priority principle of resource allocation. Not all production goals established by Gosplan are held to be of equal importance. The goals of certain "leading links" sectors or industries (machinery, chemicals, steel) are given high priority; other industries (agriculture, automobiles) in effect are assigned low priorities. Thus, when bottlenecks arise in the actual operation of the national plan, resources or inputs are shifted from low-priority to high-priority sectors of the economy. Coordination and plan fulfillment are sacrificed in low-priority production in order to maintain coordination and fulfill production targets in high-priority sectors. This accounts for the unevenness with which the goals of the various central plans have been fulfilled. Planned increases

in housing and consumer goods are typically sacrificed to realize the planned increases in industrial and military goods production.

3. Reserve stocks. To some extent coordination problems—bottlenecks and the chain reactions they precipitate—can be avoided by drawing upon reserve stocks of various inputs. Inventories, in other words, are used as a cushion or buffer to resolve specific bottlenecks or input deficiencies before they can trigger a serious chain of production shortfalls.

Although all of these techniques contribute in varying degrees to the workability of Soviet central planning, they by no means ensure a high degree of efficiency. There is a great amount of evidence gathered from Soviet sources to indicate that bottlenecks do occur with rather alarming regularity:[4]

The Byelorussian Tractor Factory, which has 227 suppliers, had its production line stopped 19 times in 1962 because of the lack of rubber parts, 18 times because of ball bearings, and 8 times because of transmission components. The pattern of breakdowns continued in 1963. During the first quarter of 1963 only about one-half of the plant's ball bearing and rubber needs were satisfied, and only half of the required batteries were available. One supplier shipped 19,000 less wheels than called for in the contract. In total, they were short of 27 different items. . . .

It is not surprising that 90 enterprises out of 100 surveyed in the Chelyabinsk region blamed their underfulfillment of production plans in 1962 on supply deficiencies.

Executing the Plan: Control Agencies

The proof of the pudding is in the eating. Setting up detailed production goals and making some provision for their internal balance are one thing; achieving those objectives may be something else again.

The Soviet government is not inclined to sit back, after each industrial plant and farm has been assigned its production targets, and

[4] *Ibid.*, p. 123.

hope for favorable results. On the contrary, an abundance of control agencies supervise the carrying out of each plan. Most obvious, of course, is the Gosplan and the regional and local planning groups affiliated with it. These administrative units keep a running check on the progress of the plan. The Central Committee of the Communist party and a variety of subordinate party organizations function as watchdog agencies by uncovering, reporting, and helping to correct deviations from the plan. The control functions of the infamous secret police are well known. And, too, a less formal type of control is exercised through a much-publicized program of "criticism and self-criticism," whereby the Soviet citizenry is encouraged to register complaints concerning deviations from, and violations of, the plan.

Perhaps the most vital enforcement agency is the state banking system, or *Gosbank*. The Gosbank with its thousands of branches supervises the financial aspects of each plant's production activities and in this manner has a running account of each plant's performance. More precisely, this supervision—"control by the ruble"—works something like this: The government establishes prices on all resources and finished products. For a greatly simplified example, the Leningrad Machine Tool Plant may require 1,000 tons of steel and 100 workers to produce 5,000 units of output per year. If steel costs 60 rubles per ton and each worker is paid 1,000 rubles per year, the total cost of the 5,000 units of output will be 160,000 rubles. Gosplan then directs the Gosbank to make this amount of credit available to the plant over the course of the year. Now, because all the plant's financial transactions—both receipts and expenditures—must be completed through the use of checks, the Gosbank will have an accurate record (in effect, a running audit) of the plant's progress, or lack thereof, in fulfilling the production targets assigned by the Five-year Plan. Should the plant achieve its assigned output at an expense less than 160,000 rubles, it will have overfulfilled its production goal. Inefficient,

wasteful production will cause the plant to exhaust its bank credit before its production goal is reached. Either eventuality will be reflected in the plant's account with the Gosbank.

Incentives

How are the various economic units motivated toward fulfillment of the Five-year Plan? A combination of monetary and nonmonetary incentives, on the one hand, and coercive techniques, on the other, are employed to this end.

Monetary incentives. The Soviet government relies heavily upon monetary incentives to obtain the maximum productive effort from labor. In particular, wages are geared to skill and productivity. The resulting wage differentials are considerable. Great emphasis is put upon piecework, more so than in the United States. Probably as much as four-fifths of the Soviet labor force works under a piecework plan of one sort or another. Elaborate systems of bonuses and premiums induce workers to exceed normal production rates. Most competent observers conclude that wage incomes in the Soviet Union are as unequally distributed as in the United States. Keep in mind, too, that Soviet income receivers, though not free to determine the portion of total output which is to take the form of consumer goods, are able to spend their incomes as they wish on the consumer goods which the Gosplan makes available to them. This means that differences in money incomes are generally reflected in real income differentials.

Nonmonetary incentives. A variety of nonmonetary inducements also exist to stimulate labor to greater productivity. A rather comprehensive system of awards and decorations exists to cite exemplary workers. These are closely correlated with material rewards. For example, a "Hero of Socialist Labor" is likely to be accorded certain tax exemptions, monthly bonuses, low rental on state housing, free use of transportation facilities, government-supplied vacations at a Crimean resort, and so forth. The real standard of living of the average Soviet worker is about one-fourth that of his American counterpart, so that the value of such benefits is considerable. Much publicity accompanies these awards. A member of the "Order of Lenin" may enjoy fame and prestige comparable to that of a professional baseball player or movie star in the United States. In addition, "socialist competitions" are encouraged by the party, pitting the productive capacities of various groups of workers against one another.

The labor unions to which the vast majority of Soviet workers belong bear little or no resemblance to their American counterparts. In effect, Russian labor unions are functionaries of the state whose basic goals are to encourage a high rate of productivity among their members in carrying out the economic plan, to train new workers, to aid in the solution of labor discipline problems, and to administer the social security system. Wage rates are set by the government. Collective bargaining as we know it does not exist, and strikes simply do not occur. Soviet labor unions do, however, prevent undue exploitation of their members by plant managers eager to fulfill their assigned production quotas. They also play an active role in providing recreational and cultural programs for workers.

Coercion. Monetary and nonmonetary inducements are duly supplemented by a variety of coercive techniques. Indeed, Article XII of the Soviet constitution of 1936 flatly states that "Work in the U.S.S.R. is a duty and a matter of honor for every able-bodied citizen, in accordance with the principle 'He who does not work, neither shall he eat.'" But labor discipline has at times been very poor: absenteeism, tardiness, and worker indifference are common problems. The rate of labor turnover has also been a major problem. Plant managers frequently "pirate" the personnel of one another to ensure a labor force adequate for fulfillment of their output targets. Workers seem very

willing to change jobs, however slight the resulting improvement in their standard of living might be.

Soviet authorities have taken action to cope with such problems. Fines, pay reductions, dismissal, eviction from state housing, the freezing of workers to their jobs, and discriminatory treatment with respect to social insurance benefits all hang over the head of the bungling, the lazy, the indifferent, and the overly mobile worker. "Spies" and "wreckers" may be subject to the wrath of the secret police and assigned to "correctional labor camps" in Siberia or similarly remote areas.

Comparable monetary and nonmonetary inducements and compulsory techniques bear upon plant managers. High salaries, bonuses, awards, and promotion await those who fulfill their production targets. Failure exposes the plant manager to investigation and reassignment to a less palatable position. A good many plant managers are party members and therefore inspired by party doctrines.

Planning and Prices

To say that the Soviet system is a command economy rather than a market economy is not to say that prices have no role to play in the centrally planned system. Although Soviet prices are not employed as a guiding mechanism in determining the structure of output, they are used in implementing the production objectives established by the state. *Soviet prices are government-manipulated to aid in the achievement of state-established goals; capitalistic prices are market-established and induce the fulfillment of individually determined goals.*

Actually, the function of prices in the Soviet Union differs considerably as between the production process, on the one hand, and the sale of final products to consumers, on the other. In the first instance prices are simply accounting devices which facilitate checking the efficiency with which products are manufactured. In the latter case prices are employed as rationing devices to distribute products to consumers without the use of government rationing.

Producer prices. In producing, say, a television set, a Soviet plant will be faced with certain governmentally established prices for component parts, labor, and other needed resources. And, similarly, government will determine the price of the final product. Generally speaking, the basic principle in establishing these prices is that a plant or industry of average efficiency should realize total receipts from its production which will just cover its total costs; that is, it should break even. If production is less efficient than that deemed average by the plan, losses will result. Greater-than-average efficiency will result in unplanned profits.[5] In short, the prices of resources and components are used as accounting costs to assess the efficiency with which various plants and industries operate. Except for the fact that capitalistic prices are market-determined rather than government-determined, this role of the Soviet price system parallels that of its capitalistic counterpart. But here—for two reasons—the similarity ends.

In the first place, in a capitalistic economy losses call for a contraction of output and a release of resources by the affected industry; profits signal industry expansion and the absorption of resources. Not so in the Soviet Union. Expansion and contraction of industry are determined by the government, not the price system. Therefore a relatively inefficient industry which is considered vital by the state may be expanded despite losses. Similarly, a highly efficient, profit-realizing industry may be purposely contracted by state planning.

Secondly, market-determined input prices in a capitalistic system reflect the relative

scarcity of resources and their value in alternative uses. Thus, to minimize money costs in the production of a product is to minimize real costs, that is, to get a given good produced with a minimum sacrifice of alternative goods (Chapter 26). But in the Soviet Union prices are governmentally determined and therefore do not accurately reflect the relative scarcity of resources. Hence, the minimization of money costs in a Soviet enterprise does not mean that real costs of production are being minimized.

Consumer prices. Whereas prices in the production process are essentially accounting devices used to gauge plan fulfillment, the prices of finished goods are established to serve as rationing devices. In other words, the government attempts to set consumer goods prices at levels which will clear the market so there will be no persistent shortages or surpluses. As a result, the price of television sets which is used for accounting purposes may vary considerably from the price which is charged consumers who purchase them. The difference typically takes the form of a sales tax or what the Russians call a turnover tax.

To illustrate: Suppose the accounting price of a finished television set is 1,500 rubles. This price is used by the Gosplan in judging the efficiency of the assembly plant. But, because of the low priority assigned to consumer goods, consumer demand in the Soviet Union has persistently exceeded the available supply of consumer goods. This means that, if shortages and government rationing are to be avoided, the price charged by the state in selling television sets to consumers must be higher than the accounting price. Suppose the government estimates that the consumer price of television sets must be 3,000 rubles to bring the quantity demanded into balance with the quantity of television sets currently available. This is accomplished by adding a 100 per cent turnover tax to television sets. At this price the market will be cleared and government rationing avoided.

Turnover taxes—which, incidentally, are

---

[5] For the most part, these profits will accrue to the government as revenue from state-owned enterprises. A part may be used to expand the industry, if such expansion is consistent with the objectives of the plan. Another portion may be shared by the plant's workers and executives as a bonus for their efficiency.

the major source of government revenue in Russia—vary widely among various products. High turnover taxes on particularly scarce goods greatly discourage their consumption and force the amounts demanded into accord with the skimpy quantities allowed by the plan. Lower rates on consumer staples—for example, potatoes and other vegetables—available in relative abundance encourage their consumption. The greater the relative scarcity of a product, the higher the turnover tax placed upon it. The total prices of such products will necessarily be higher and purchases discouraged. Lower tax rates on more abundant products give them lower relative prices and encourage their consumption. In this way inflation-causing income is taxed away, and the pattern of consumer spending is forced into rough accord with the planned composition of consumer goods output.[6]

Efficiency: Micro versus Macro

How efficient is the Soviet economy? The answer to this crucial question hinges upon the goal structure one assumes. On the one hand, efficiency can be defined in essentially microeconomic terms to mean full production, that is, the maximization of consumer wants through the optimum allocation and organization of scarce resources. Given this notion of efficiency, we must say that Soviet planning is probably not very efficient; a strong case could be made to back the assertion that Soviet communism is less efficient in terms of this goal than is American capitalism. In Soviet Russia consumer wants are assigned a relatively low priority; we have seen that allocative bottlenecks are commonplace; and least-cost production is virtually impossible in the absence of market

or scarcity prices. Furthermore, the Soviet press persistently denounces the poor quality of both consumer and producer goods.

But there are other goals in terms of which an economy's efficiency might be judged. The alternative and essentially macroeconomic goal which has been paramount with the Soviet leadership is *rapid* economic growth. Soviet Russia has pursued with great vigor the goal of rapid growth and the political-military strength derived therefrom. These two concepts of efficiency may be in conflict in certain important ways.[7] In particular, it is the fact that Soviet planning seeks very rapid growth which results in highly ambitious production targets and the overcommitment of resources. And ambitious targets and overcommitted resources are the source of many of the coordination problems discussed earlier. In any event, we know that the Soviet economy has performed well in terms of the objective of growth. Let us now consider the rate of growth achieved by the Soviet Union, the sources of this growth, and the prospect of its maintenance.

SOVIET ECONOMIC GROWTH[8]

Authoritative estimates put the Soviet GNP at about one-half that of the United States. Figure 42–1 shows this relationship and indicates the relative composition of the national outputs of the two nations. Experts also agree that the Soviet economy has been realizing a growth rate about twice that of the United States. Western economists estimate that *the Soviet GNP has been expanding at about 6 to 7 per cent per year as compared to 3 to 3½ per cent per year for the United States* (Table 21–2).

---

[6] For an authoritative discussion of Soviet pricing see Morris Bornstein, "The Soviet Price System," in Morris Bornstein (ed.), *Comparative Economic Systems: Models and Cases* (Homewood, Ill.: Richard D. Irwin, Inc., 1965), pp. 278–309.

[7] The interested reader should consult Albert O. Hirschman, *The Strategy of Economic Development* (New Haven, Conn.: Yale University Press, 1959).

[8] This section is based upon Campbell R. McConnell, "Perspectives on Soviet Economic Growth," *Business Topics*, Autumn, 1964, pp. 7–16.

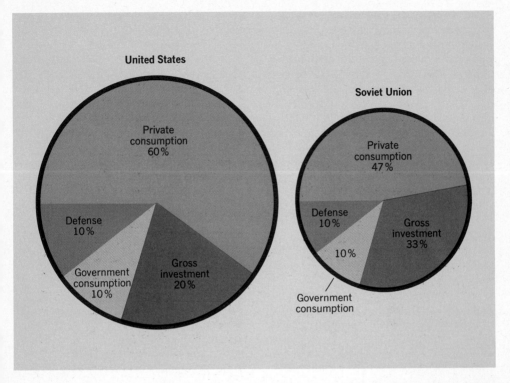

FIGURE 42–1. SIZE AND COMPOSITION OF GNP IN THE UNITED STATES AND THE SOVIET UNION.
Soviet Russia's GNP is roughly one-half the size of the United States' GNP. As compared with the United States, the Soviet Union puts relatively greater emphasis on investment goods than consumer goods. [Stanley H. Cohn, "The Gross National Product in the Soviet Union: Comparative Growth Rates," in Joint Economic Committee, *Dimensions of Soviet Economic Power* (Washington, D.C., 1962), p. 72, data for 1960.]

Sources of Soviet Growth

The Soviet Union's enviable growth record has a number of roots.

1. Natural resource base. The Soviet Union has a generous and varied natural resource base. Although differing significantly in composition, it is not inaccurate to say that the natural resource endowments of the U.S.S.R. are roughly comparable to those of the United States. The major exception to this generalization is agricultural resources.

Most of Russia's most fertile soil lies in regions susceptible to drought and short growing seasons.

2. Totalitarianism and allocation. It follows from the fact that the Soviet Union is a totalitarian state that the government can and does exercise tight political control over the allocation of resources. That the government has, with little hesitation or reservation, exerted a strong and often brutal "will to develop" is reflected in its efforts to indoctrinate, regiment, push and prod its citizenry, and to structure its institutions to the overriding goal of economic growth. The Soviet economy has aptly been described as "totalitarianism harnessed to the task of industrialization and economic growth."[9] To be more specific, we may say that the will to develop has been expressed most explicitly in the high-volume and growth-oriented composition of Soviet investment. The Soviet Union devotes one-third of its total output to investment as compared to one-fifth for the United States (Figure 42–1). Furthermore, the composition of Soviet investment has put emphasis upon those industries most crucial to the growth process. Retail and wholesale distributional facilities and housing, for example, have been largely ignored in favor of steel, petroleum, chemicals, and machine tools.

3. Surplus farm labor.

You will recall from Chapter 41 that it is characteristic of underdeveloped countries to have a sizable amount of surplus or underemployed labor in agriculture. This was true of the Soviet Union at the time of the revolution. Under central planning much of this low-productivity farm labor was shifted to newly created industries, where its productivity was substantially higher. In 1925, 84 per cent of the Soviet labor force was in agriculture; currently about 40 per cent are so employed. The result of this reallocation has been significant increases in the Soviet GNP.

4. Technological gap.

Rapid expansion in Soviet production has stemmed in good measure from the adoption of the superior technological knowledge pioneered by the Western nations. The Soviet Union has eagerly, unashamedly, and quite effectively borrowed and skillfully applied the superior techniques of other nations. In this manner the U.S.S.R. has quickly and very inexpensively bridged a long period of research and development activity in many key industries.

5. Full employment.

The Soviet economy's growth rate, unlike those of the United States and other capitalistic nations, has benefited in that since about 1930 Soviet economic planning has virtually eliminated cyclical unemployment. Unlike the United States, the Soviet Union has *not* had to count years of zero or negative growth due to recession in calculating its long-term rate of growth.

Possible Retarding Factors

What of future Soviet growth? One can readily offer a number of quite plausible reasons why a slowing down of the Soviet growth rate might be anticipated.

1. Diversion of resources.

One line of thought suggests that mounting pressures from consumers, the acute need to modernize agriculture and certain long-neglected components of the system's social overhead capital, burgeoning military demands, and a reasonably ambitious foreign aid program will all have the effect of diverting resources to less growth-effective uses. In particular, the proliferation and intensification of the aforementioned claimants may reduce the volume and alter the composition of Soviet investment, with the result that the growth rate is lowered. On the supposition that even totalitarian regimes are significantly influenced by the will of their constituents, optimists in the West feel that modest concessions to the consuming sector may merely whet consumer appetites and result in an irresistible spiraling of consumer demands with the result that a substantial growth-retarding reallocation of resources will be inevitable.

The claims of the military and foreign aid have also been increasing. The Soviet Union's military effort relative to its GNP is comparable to that of the United States. Both economies assign about 10 per cent of their

[9] Robert W. Campbell, *Soviet Economic Power* (Boston: Houghton Mifflin Company, 1960), p. 8.

GNP to defense (Figure 42–1), a figure substantially higher than that of other advanced nations. Soviet military-space programs have been subject to sharply increasing costs and entail types of research and development activity, the relevance of which for the civilian economy is highly questionable. The diversion of Soviet scientists, engineers, and managerial resources to military research and production may prove to be in strong competition with the objective of growth. Although foreign aid is of modest proportions, it must be recognized once again that the specific resources involved are quite crucial to the Soviet Union's domestic growth effort.

2. Replacement investment. A less spectacular point of a more technical nature is that, as the size and age of the Soviet Union's stock of capital increases, replacement investment necessarily increases. That is, a growing proportion of gross investment will be for depreciation, leaving a smaller share as net investment to contribute to growth. Other things being the same, an increasing volume of gross investment will be required to maintain a constant rate of growth.

3. Closing of technological gap. While a technological gap remains between the Soviet Union and the West, it is quite clear that the gap has narrowed appreciably and in some instances may have been eliminated. And it is significant that the closing of the gap has generally occurred more fully in heavy industry than in sectors of the Soviet economy less crucial to growth. The important point is that, as the USSR begins to draw abreast technologically, windfall productivity gains from technological borrowing will diminish, and the Soviet Union will be faced with the highly resource-absorbing task of pushing forward its own technological frontiers.

4. Labor shortage. In recent years the Soviet Union has encountered a significant tightening of the market for industrial labor. This manpower shortage has several dimensions. First, for the last four or five years the Soviet economy has been experiencing a below-average number of labor force entrants because of the wartime birth deficit of the early 1940s. Second, whereas earlier Soviet growth was attributable in substantial amount to shifts of surplus labor from agriculture to industry, the Soviet Union is finding it increasingly difficult to make additional shifts without significantly imperiling the output of an already troubled agricultural sector. A final consideration is that a promised shortening of the workweek has been realized in recent years, and this, of course, has had the effect of reducing the labor force.

5. Agricultural drag. By Western standards Soviet agriculture is something of a monument to inefficiency and now constitutes a drag upon economic growth, engulfing as it does over 40 per cent of the labor force. The low productivity of Soviet agriculture is attributable to many factors: the relative scarcity of good land; the neglect of agriculture as reflected in scarcities of farm capital and the limited use of chemical fertilizers; serious errors in planning and administration; the failure to construct an effective incentive system; and vagaries in rainfall and length of growing season.

6. Planning problems. There are forces at work in the U.S.S.R. which may be tending to reduce the relative efficiency of Soviet planning and thereby to retard the growth rate. Indeed, the chronic and sweeping revisions of the planning hierarchy are *prima facie* evidence of party dissatisfaction with the performance of planning institutions. Mounting planning problems are closely linked to the development of the Soviet economy itself. Early planning under Stalin was not unlike the wartime planning of Western nations: A limited number of key production goals were established, and resources were centrally directed toward the fulfillment of these goals regardless of costs or consumer welfare. But the past success of such "campaign planning" has resulted in an industrially advanced economy. This new, more modern economy is vastly different from that of the earlier period of war-economy planning. The proliferation and realignment of priorities has already been noted. In short, planning techniques which were more or less adequate for the Stalinist era of limited production goals are decreasingly relevant and less workable in the more sophisticated economy of the 1960s. With growth the economy, and therefore planning, become decidedly more complex. Neither labor nor capital is as relatively abundant as a scant decade or so ago. The expansion of a relatively few standard product lines with a blatant disregard for costs is relatively simple; production of a much larger variety of products, each of which is more complex, within a context of growing cost-consciousness is quite a different matter. To state the situation quite simply, the Soviet economy has tended to outgrow its planning mechanisms. This fact has posed serious questions concerning the allocative efficiency of the system and its capacity to sustain its growth rate.

Possible Accelerating Factors

But we must not embrace too readily the view that the Soviets have reached the end of the road growthwise. There are factors which suggest that the Soviet Union may be able to sustain its enviable growth record. Two general reminders are in order before we examine these specific growth-accelerating factors.

In the first place, we must acknowledge that there exists no generalization in the economics of growth to indicate that, once realizing the take-off into economic growth, a nation will achieve vigorous expansion—a kind of economic adolescence—for a time, only to face middle age and an inevitable hardening of the economic arteries. Such vague biological analogies are of doubtful relevance to economic growth. There is no reason to anticipate an *automatic* or *inevitable* retardation of Soviet growth.

Secondly, we must not fall into the delusion that growth rates are unimportant. One often hears the consoling assertion that, because the United States has a GNP roughly twice that of the Soviet Union, there is no cause to be alarmed about the fact that the Soviet growth rate is twice ours. This is simply not true. It must be clearly recognized that *any* growth rate differential favorable to the U.S.S.R., despite its smaller GNP base, implies an inevitable catching up in terms of absolute GNPs. Table 42–1 makes this point strikingly clear. It is assumed here that the Soviet GNP initially is 45 per cent of ours. Then by comparing various possible growth rates for the United States, shown across the top of the table, and possible Soviet rates, shown down the left, we can find in the body of the table the number of years required for the Soviet GNP to equal ours. For example, if our rate is 3 per cent and their rate is 7 per cent, the Soviet GNP will equal our GNP in 24 years.

Consider now a number of specific factors which suggest the maintainability of the Soviet growth rate.

1. GNP increments. An already rapidly expanding economy is in a most advantageous position even in the face of insistent new

TABLE 42–1. YEARS REQUIRED FOR SOVIET OUTPUT TO MATCH UNITED STATES OUTPUT

Soviet annual growth rate	United States annual growth rate		
	2%	3%	4%
7%	19	24	32
8%	16	19	24
9%	14	16	20

Source: Robert W. Campbell, *Soviet Economic Power* (Boston: Houghton Mifflin Company, 1960), p. 195.

demands upon its resources to sustain its growth. The Soviet Union is now realizing annual increments in its GNP on the order of $16 to $19 billion per year. A 6 per cent growth rate compounded will double the Soviet GNP in a scant twelve years! Increases of this size certainly provide the potential out of which rising demands from consumers, the military-space effort, and the foreign aid program *might* be met.

2. Education and technology. It must also be recognized that the Soviet regime has historically put great emphasis upon education and research and development activity. One of the great accomplishments of the Soviet government has been its transformation of a basically illiterate rural population into a literate industrial labor force of considerable quality. Furthermore, it is well known that Soviet education and manpower policies are closely linked to economic objectives:[10]

Science and technology are particularly recognized as the foundation of national strength; and consequently, they receive emphasis on all levels of the educational effort. . . . The quality of Soviet professional training in scientific, engineering, and applied fields today is, on substantive grounds, comparable to that offered in the West . . . in recent years the number of higher education graduates in the sciences and various applied fields—engineering, agriculture, and medicine—has exceeded substantially (by a factor of 2 or 3 to 1) the rate of training such specialists in the United States.

This educational effort provides a solid foundation for a Soviet research and development effort which is comparable to that of the United States in absolute terms, larger as a percentage of GNP, and perhaps more farsighted in terms of distribution between

[10] Nicholas DeWitt, "Education and the Development of Human Resources: Soviet and American Effort," in Joint Economic Committee, *Dimensions of Soviet Economic Power* (Washington, D.C., 1962), pp. 267–268.

basic and applied research. It is not irrelevant to note that new knowledge—technological progress—has a habit of sweeping aside impediments to economic expansion. The important point for our purposes is that future Soviet expansion may well reap a substantial output harvest from past investments in human capital and research and development activity.

3. Planning techniques. Against the tendency of Soviet planning to become less efficient in the face of an increasingly complex economy must be set the likelihood of significant breakthroughs in the techniques and mechanics of central planning. Accelerated interest is evident in the application of advanced mathematical techniques and computers as means to achieve greater balance and coordination in planning. The keynote in Soviet planning today is flexibility and experimentation. It would not be at all surprising if some of these experiments resulted in significant improvements in the planning system.

4. Forced growth. Finally, we must not lose sight of the fact that the ability of the Soviet leadership to mobilize human resources and to exercise wide discretion in determining the composition of output has been a key explanatory factor in past growth. The role of the Soviet government as a mechanism for *forcing* growth is likely to be sustained. Growth accomplishments are partly explainable in terms of economic policy, and there is every reason to suspect that growth-oriented policies will remain the major, if not sole, cornerstone of Soviet planning. In brief, the totalitarian system has advantages in the area of economic growth which cannot be taken lightly.

Future Growth

It is no easy matter to balance the growth-inhibiting and growth-accelerating forces against one another and make an unqualified prediction as to future Soviet growth. Yet there is some empirical evidence to suggest a modest decline in the Soviet Union's growth rate. As a leading student of the Soviet economy has recently indicated:[11]

. . . we can hardly foresee with any accuracy the future growth of the Soviet economy. But it should be difficult for the Russians in the coming years to maintain the six per cent growth rate in output they have realized since Stalin. Still we must assume that they will continue to outpace the U.S.A., at least for some years to come, but most likely the margin by which they do so will tend to diminish.

A modest diminution in Soviet growth, if this indeed proves to be the case, is little cause for complacency in the United States. Needless to say, it would be extremely shortsighted to base either our domestic economic policies or our international political strategy upon the assumption that long-term Soviet growth will decline by any substantial amount. The Soviet economic challenge and its manifold implications are not to be taken lightly.

GENERAL EVALUATION

Our discussion thus far has centered upon central planning and the growth performance which planning has fostered. A more complete evaluation of the Soviet system calls for the consideration of several other accomplishments and shortcomings.

Accomplishments

1. Education. Though circumscribed by Communist doctrine and shaped in terms of government goals, Soviet Russia has made tremendous strides in increasing the quantity and quality of education. Free public education has been a high-priority goal of the Soviet regime from the outset. Much has also been done to encourage cultural pursuits, again within limits imposed by the party.

[11] Abram Bergson, "The Great Economic Race," *Challenge*, March, 1963, p. 6.

2. Economic security. In keeping with socialist tradition, the Soviet Union has developed a quite complete system of social insurance. Medical care is virtually free and disability and sick leave benefits are provided, as are maternity benefits. Rental payments are heavily subsidized and only amount to about 4 or 5 per cent of a worker's income. Retirement pensions are available for industrial workers and are to be extended to collective farmers. Although the size of benefit payments are not overly generous by American standards, they are sufficient in terms of the Soviet standard of living.

Shortcomings

Generally speaking, the major shortcomings of the Soviet system are the offspring of its accomplishments. Two major points merit emphasis.

1. Standard of living. The costs of rapid industrialization and economic growth have been great and borne for the most part by consumers. This is reflected both in the quantity and quality of Soviet consumer goods. Living standards are much lower than in the United States—perhaps only about one-fifth or one-fourth as high.[12]

Soviet city life is similar to life in Western cities fifty years ago. People live in crowded apartments, use public transportation, wear drab clothing, and eat a starchy diet. . . . Soviet rural life compares with still earlier European experience, though the presence of large machinery and trucks makes for noncomparability. The general pattern in both city and country is still "old fashioned," yet elements of modernization run all through it.

Improvements in the Soviet standard of living have been significant in the last decade. But, as far as the consumer is con-

[12] Clair Wilcox, Willis D. Weatherford, Jr., and Holland Hunter, *Economies of the World Today* (New York: Harcourt, Brace & World, Inc., 1962), p. 47.

cerned, the Soviet Union is far from being a society of abundance.

2. Freedom. The decisions which determine the overall economic, political, social, and cultural environment are made by the Soviet dictatorship. Only within governmentally prescribed limits is individual freedom tolerated. Consumers and wage earners are "free" to choose from the goods and jobs planners decide to provide. Artists and writers must conform to, or at least not violate, the party line in their creative efforts.

Viewed in broader perspective, it must be emphasized that the Soviet Union is a dictatorship based ultimately upon coercion, terror, or the effective threat thereof. Though there has been a general relaxation of the tensions which surrounded Stalinist tyranny, the threat of force is omnipresent. Elections are a farce, the press is essentially a propaganda organ of the government, and the role of the secret police in maintaining allegiance and conformity continues to be substantial.[13]

Implications

Of this there is no doubt: The Soviet economic challenge injects an element of urgency to the economizing problem in American capitalism. The goals of sustained economic stability and adequate growth (Parts Two to Four) take on new, critical dimensions in view of rapid Soviet economic expansion. In particular, a prolonged depression would seriously impair our chances of winning the economic war Soviet Russia has imposed upon us. Certainly the question of achieving efficiency in the allocation of resources through the mechanism of the price system becomes increasingly acute (Part Five). American capitalism must continuously appraise the allocative efficiency of the market mechanism and the balance between

[13] For a short study of the history and strategy of communism the reader should consult Andrew Gyorgy, *Communism in Perspective* (Boston: Allyn and Bacon, Inc., 1964).

private and social goods. This obviously entails a detailed reexamination of specific problem areas and existing public policies designed to cope with those problems (Part Six). And clearly the military, political, and economic significance of the less-developed nations of the world calls for a farsightedness in our international trade policies and practices which historically has been highly elusive (Part Seven).

The role of American capitalism in the political, military, and sociocultural affairs of the world can continue to be the dominant one. An awareness of economic principles, problems, and policies can play a central role in preserving that dominance.

SUMMARY

1. The vivid contrast which the Soviet economy provides to American capitalism, the economic challenge it presents to the Western world, and the rapid economic growth achieved in Soviet Russia are important reasons for studying the Soviet economic system.

2. Virtually complete public ownership of property resources and central economic planning are the outstanding institutional features of the Soviet economy.

3. The major goals of the Five- and Seven-year Plans, as determined by the government, have been rapid industrialization and growth and military strength.

4. The basic problem of central planners is to achieve coordination or internal consistency in their plans so as to avoid bottlenecks and the chain reaction of production failures which they cause. The evaluation of preliminary plans by the administrative hierarchy, the assignment of priorities to planned goals, and reserve stocks are used to prevent or alleviate coordination problems in the U.S.S.R.

5. Many agencies check upon the actual execution of the Five-year Plans—the planning hierarchy, the Communist party and its numerous officials, and the secret police. The most important of these agencies is the

Gosbank, which exerts "control by the ruble."

6. In the production process, governmentally determined prices on resources and components and on finished products serve as accounting devices to evaluate the efficiency of production. In consumer goods markets, prices are adjusted through the turnover tax to ration products to consumers, that is, to balance the amount demanded with available supplies.

7. Although the Soviet GNP is only one-half as large as the United States', the Soviet GNP is growing twice as rapidly as ours. A generous natural resource base, great emphasis upon capital formation, the transfer of surplus agricultural labor to industry, the adoption of superior production techniques from the West, and the planning away of cyclical unemployment are factors which have contributed to this high growth rate.

8. A number of factors suggest a future decline in the Soviet growth rate: a diversion of resources from growth-inducing uses,

the growth of replacement investment, a partial closing of the technological gap, a shortage of industrial labor, the stagnation of agriculture, and mounting planning problems attributable to the increasing complexity of the Soviet economy.

9. Other factors suggest the Soviet growth rate is maintainable: large annual GNP increments are now available to meet new demands on resources, past investments in education and research may overcome growth obstacles, new techniques may substantially improve the efficiency of central planning, and the Soviet government will continue to force growth through its allocative decisions.

10. In addition to proving the feasibility of central planning and achieving a high growth rate, the Soviet Union has made significant advances in education and has established a comprehensive social security system. On the other hand, the Soviet standard of living is not enviable by Western standards, and freedom is closely circumscribed by party objectives.

QUESTIONS AND STUDY SUGGESTIONS

1. "So long as a central planning board, as opposed to society as a whole, sets the economic goals, there can be no freedom of occupational or consumer choice." Explain.

2. Compare the sources of insecurity which face an American and a Soviet steelworker.

3. "It has become increasingly difficult for thoughtful men to find meaningful alternatives posed in the traditional choices between socialism and capitalism, planning and the free market, regulation and laissez faire, for they find their actual choices neither simple nor so grand."[14] Explain and evaluate.

4. Compare the institutional framework of the Soviet economy with that of American capitalism. Contrast the manner in which production is motivated in these two economic systems.

5. How does Soviet planning attempt to cope with the Five Fundamental Questions which all economies must face? Discuss the problem of coordination. What mechanisms do Soviet planners use to avoid and correct problems of coordination? Explain: "Soviet planning problems

[14] Robert A. Dahl and Charles E. Lindblom, *Politics, Economics and Welfare* (New York: Harper & Row, Publishers, Incorporated, 1953), p. 1.

mainly arise from the fact that the command economy is rooted in the logic of haste."

6. Evaluate carefully the level of efficiency which has been achieved in Soviet economic planning.

7. Compare the size, composition, and rate of growth of the GNPs of the United States and the Soviet Union. What have been the major sources of Soviet economic expansion? Do you feel that the Soviet Union will be able to sustain its past growth performance? Explain.

8. Carefully contrast the role of the price system in Soviet Russia and the United States. Explain the use of turnover taxes.

9. How is the number of automobiles to be produced determined in American capitalism? In the Soviet Union? How are these decisions implemented in the two economies?

SELECTED REFERENCES

Bergson, Abram: *The Economics of Soviet Planning* (New Haven, Conn.: Yale University Press, 1964).

Bornstein, Morris, and Daniel R. Fusfeld (eds.): *The Soviet Economy* (Homewood, Ill.: Richard D. Irwin, Inc., 1962).

Campbell, Robert W.: *Soviet Economic Power* (Boston: Houghton Mifflin Company, 1960).

Joint Economic Committee: *Dimensions of Soviet Economic Power* (Washington, D.C., 1962).

Nove, Alec: *The Soviet Economy* (New York: Frederick A. Praeger, Inc., 1961).

Richman, Barry M.: *Soviet Management* (Englewood Cliffs, N.J.: Prentice-Hall, Inc., 1965).

Schwartz, Harry: *The Soviet Economy Since Stalin* (Philadelphia: J. B. Lippincott Company, 1965).

Shaffer, Harry G. (ed.): *The Soviet Economy* (New York: Appleton-Century-Crofts, Inc., 1963).

Wellisz, Stanislaw: *The Economies of the Soviet Bloc* (New York: McGraw-Hill Book Company, 1964).